Index to the 1871 Census of Ontario

Y · O · R · K

Bruce S. Elliott
General Editor

Dan Walker
Assistant

David L. Brown
EDP Coordinator

Irena Nosco
Programming

Dorothy Martin
Coordinator
Toronto Branch

Compilers:

Lela Booth
Pat Boultbee
Doris Bourrie
E.R. Brickenden
John W. Campbell
R. Alex Collins
Dorothy Dermody
Peggy Feltmate
Joan Freeman
Elizabeth Hancocks

Louise Hope
Martha Jackson
Marion C. Keffer
Mary H. Knox
Shirley Larkin
Susan MacDonald
Dorothy Martin
Pat McKenzie
Jane McLaren
Jane McNamara
Betty O'Donnell

Carol Ramm
Doreen Ryan
J. Ross Scrimger
D.H. Shuttleworth
Lois Skells
H. Marie Smibert
Fern Stimpson
Jane Thompson
Helen Thompson
Rita Turner

Ontario Genealogical Society
Toronto
1992

Canadian Cataloguing in Publication Data

Main entry under title:

Index to the 1871 census of Ontario : york

ISBN 0-920036-48-1

1. York (Ont. : County)--Census, 1871--Indexes.
2. York (Ont. : County)--Genealogy--Indexes.
3. Toronto Metropolitan Area (Ont.)--Census, 1871--
Indexes. 4. Toronto Metropolitan Area (Ont.)--
Genealogy--Indexes. 5. Registers of births, etc.--
Ontario--York (Regional municipality)--Indexes.
6. Registers of births, etc.--Ontario--Toronto
Metropolitan Area--Indexes. 7. Canada--Census, 1871--
Indexes. I. Elliott, Bruce S.   II. Martin, Dorothy
III. Booth, Lela H., 1908-   . IV. Ontario
Genealogical Society.

FC3095.Y68Z48 1992   929'.371354   C92-090146-8
F1059.Y6I53 1992

This publication is made possible by a grant from the Ontario Heritage
Foundation, an agency of the Ministry of Culture and Communications of the
Province of Ontario.

Cover illustration: Store and residence of John Tingle, lot 35, con. D,
Scarborough Township, from Miles & Co., <u>Illustrated Historical Atlas of the
County of York, Ont.</u> (Toronto, 1878) p. 47.

General Introduction

The original nominal returns of the various nineteenth-century censuses are among the most commonly used and most useful of genealogical sources, providing the name, age, birthplace, religion, ethnic origin, and occupation of every resident at a point in time, in this instance 2 April 1871. It is the only source that comes close to being a comprehensive listing of the population.

The advantages of having an index to the census records of an entire province are many. The existence of an index allows a person engaged in genealogical or biographical research to locate a given individual quickly, even if the place of residence is unknown. It will therefore be of great value to genealogical beginners, who often do not know precisely where their ancestors lived. It will also be of tremendous benefit to descendants of Ontario families resident in the United States and the Canadian West, for whom the place of residence in Ontario of their pioneer ancestors remains a mystery, and the index should prove useful to genealogists in Europe who are attempting to trace elusive families who may have emigrated to Canada in the nineteenth century. Those whose ancestors left Ontario before 1871 will also find it useful for identifying regions of the province in which particular surnames were found, thus suggesting areas from which the ancestor might have come. Because the index includes every head of family and stray individual in the province (unlike land records and indexes to wills and newspapers) it will become a prime source for Ontario one-name studies. Once the comprehensive provincial listing is available it will be possible to identify all families of a given surname in the province and to move on from this starting point to determine whether or not, in the case of unusual surnames, all share a common ancestry. The usefulness of this index extends beyond the field of family history. Social scientists studying internal migration will for the first time have an easy way of tracing the later whereabouts of residents who left specific communities in the 1850s and 1860s.

Why 1871? There are a number of reasons why we selected this year. A major consideration was the fact that the 1871 returns appear to be the most complete and probably the most legible of the Canadian censuses. The returns are generally easier to read than the earlier ones, and in many parts of the province the spelling and handwriting in 1881 were far worse than they had been ten years earlier. Indexing the 1871 returns presented less threat of duplication than would have been the case had another year been selected; most of the indexing that had already been done involved the 1852 and 1861 censuses. 1871 also nicely antedated the massive movement of Ontario population to the Canadian and American West which began in earnest in the late 1870s. Finally, at the time the project was begun the 1881 returns had only recently been opened, but were still subject to some restrictions and the microfilms were not widely available; the 1891 census had not yet been released for purposes of historical research.

This index to the 1871 census of Ontario was undertaken as a project of the Ontario Genealogical Society to mark the organization's twenty-fifth anniversary in 1986. The project began in January 1982 when Bruce Elliott of Ottawa and Laurena Storey of London conceived the idea. Elliott drew up a proposal to OGS Council which was greeted with enthusiasm by the representatives of the Branches and approved by Council on February 13, 1982. Each Branch named a Coordinator to oversee work in its own area and received listings and instructions from Bruce Elliott, who served as Provincial Coordinator. The project was officially inaugurated at the Society's provincial Seminar held in Guelph that May.

Through the kind intercession of Dr. John Clarke an agreement was reached with Machine-Readable Archives of the National Archives of Canada in the autumn of 1982 for computerization of the data extracted by the Society's members from the microfilms of the original census schedules. Work began in the spring of 1983 and the first batch of completed forms was delivered to the Archives in December of that year. By the end of 1985 98.5 per cent of the initial transcription had been completed by more than 400 volunteers and 26 Branch Coordinators, and the inputting of corrections made during double-checking of preliminary printouts against the microfilms, again by Branch volunteers, commenced in February 1986.

This volume is one of thirty in a series which began publication in 1986. When the project has been completed the Society will also make available in microform a single A-Z series for the entire province, containing some 400,000 names. It will eventually be possible for scholars and members of the public to request custom-made printouts and statistical cross-tabulations from the Archives for specialized research projects: families of African origin in the province, percentages of Irish or Scottish Catholics and Protestants in a specific municipality or the province as a whole, lists of photographers in a given region, and so forth. Thus the OGS 25th Anniversary Project will result not only in the production of alphabetical indexes to the population of Ontario just after Confederation but in the creation of a computer-manipulable data base which will be of use to scholars in various disciplines.

This volume indexes the 1871 census of the County of York, excluding the City of Toronto, which will appear in a separate volume. The head of each family recorded in the personal schedules has been listed, with complete data concerning age, sex, birthplace, religion, ethnic origin, and occupation, and a coded reference to the municipality and page number. We have also indexed any individual bearing a surname different from that of the head of family, designating such a person as a "stray", and have included all names recorded in the deaths schedules, which follow the personal schedules on the microfilm.

Many university and public libraries in Canada have copies of the census films, and they may also be borrowed on Interlibrary Loan from the National Archives of Canada in Ottawa by any library possessing a microfilm reader.

Bruce S. Elliott,
Provincial Coordinator
and General Editor.

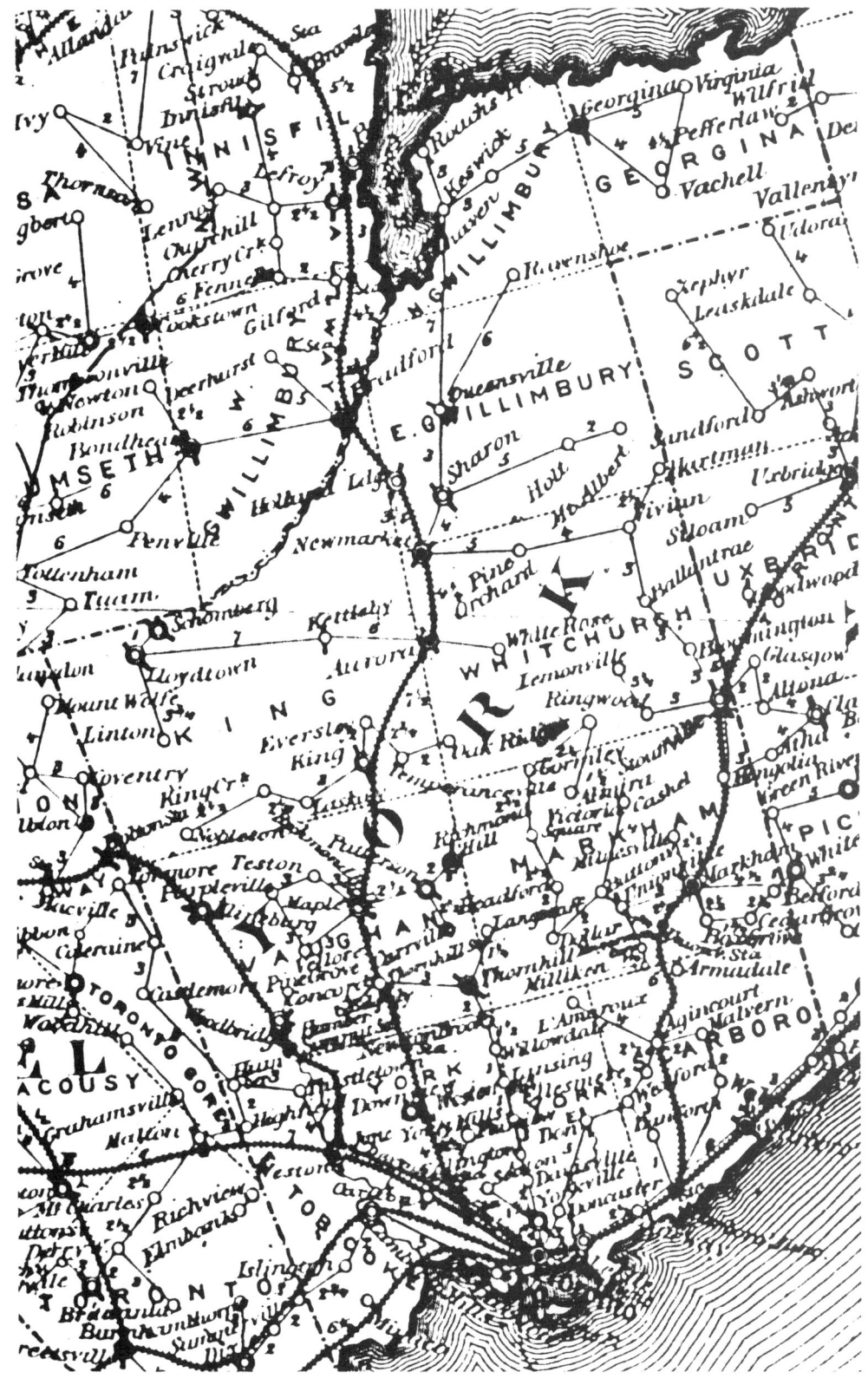

Detail from "New Railway and Postal Map of the Dominion of Canada", Sheet No. 10 in The New Standard Atlas of the Dominion of Canada (Montreal and Toronto: Walker and Miles, 1875), National Archives of Canada, National Map Collection, NMC-80253.

How to Find an Indexed Individual in the Census

    To find an indexed individual in the 1871 census, locate the name of the
municipality and the National Archives of Canada microfilm reel number using the
numerical table below. The first part of the code identifies the Electoral
District (frequently but not always corresponding to county or city), the second
the Sub-District (corresponding to township, town, village, or city ward), the
third the enumerator's division, and the final column the page number. The
names and code numbers of the Districts, Sub-Districts, and Divisions, as well
as the page numbers, appear at the top of each page of the original microfilmed
census. Thus an individual for whom the location reference reads

                    043 B 3 21

was resident in Whitchurch Township, York County (043 B), and can be located on
the 21st page of the 3rd division of Whitchurch, on reel C-9965.

The codes for York County follow.

District	Sub-District	Division	National Archives Microfilm Reel No.
043. YORK NORTH	A. King	1-3	C-9964
		4-6	C-9965
	B. Whitchurch	1-5	C-9965
	C. Aurora village		C-9965
	D. Newmarket village		C-9965
	E. Gwillimbury East	1	C-9965
		2-3	C-9966
	F. Holland Landing		C-9966
	G. Gwillimbury North	1-2	C-9966
	H. Georgina	1-2	C-9966
044. YORK WEST	A. Etobicoke	1-3	C-9966
	B. Vaughan	1	C-9966-67
		2-6	C-9967
	C. York West	1-4	C-9967
045. YORK EAST	A. York East	1-4	C-9968
	B. Yorkville village	1-2	C-9968
	C. Scarborough	1-4	C-9968
	D. Markham	1-6	C-9969

A page number "D" indicates an entry in the Deaths Schedules, microfilmed
immediately following the personal schedules for each division. Some local
libraries still have an old microfilm version of the 1871 census in which only
the personal schedules are included; if this is true of your library, you will
have to obtain the new films from Ottawa to consult the deaths schedules.

Explanation of columns, left to right

<u>Surname</u>   Surnames are entered as they appear in the census. We have attempted
to provide cross-references to more difficult entries, but the degree to which
this has been possible has depended upon the local knowledge of the indexers.
We have assumed that the user of this index will exercise creativity in coming
up with alternate spellings and have not attempted to cross-index spellings the
user should be expected to come up with himself. Thus we assume that someone
looking for McDonnell will also check under MacDonnell and indeed under
McDonald, and that someone looking for an O'Grady will also check Grady and
Johnson Johnstone. On the other hand, it is not so reasonable to expect a
reader to check under Lhulin for Laughlin or King for the French-Canadian name
Roy, so cross-references to these spellings have been included, if the local
indexers have been aware of the proper form of the name.

In some parts of the province native people bearing no surnames were recorded in
the census. These individuals have been listed under the heading "INDIAN".
Native people having surnames have been indexed in the normal way.

<u>Forenames 1 and 2</u>   Forenames or Christian names are recorded as stated in the
census. Thus William George Smith may appear as William, Willm, Wm, William G,
W G, George, George W, etc. Smith may also be entered as Smyth. Do not expect
the 1871 enumerator to have been as fussy about the spelling of names as you
are!

<u>Stray</u>   We have indexed all heads of families and individuals bearing surnames
different from that of the head of family. We have designated the latter
"strays", and they are indicated by a "1" in this column. A "2" in this column
designates an entry in the Deaths Schedules (schedule 2), microfilmed
immediately following the Personal Schedules.

<u>Sex</u>   Women have been designated by a "1" in this column to facilitate computer
retrieval.

<u>Age</u>   Remember that census ages are often approximate at best and may not
correspond to ages recorded in other sources. Ages under one year have been
left blank or indicated "0".

<u>Birthplace</u>   Birthplace is usually a province or country. "O" is Ontario, "Que"
is Quebec.

<u>Religion</u>   Religious denominations were entered in so many ways in the original
returns (we found about two dozen ways of entering Anglicans alone - Church of
England, English Ch., C of E, Episcopalian, Episcopal, etc.) that the Archives
has employed a series of two-letter codes to standardize the references for
computer retrieval. The list of codes is an expanded version of that
recommended by the Social Science Federation of Canada's Working Group on
Historical Census Microdata Usage in "Guidelines for the Transcription of
Historical Census Data for Quantitative Research" (1978). A full alphabetical
explanation of these codes is appended to this Introduction.

<u>Origin</u>   The census enumerator was instructe d to record paternal ethnic origin.
Thus a person whose mother was born in Scotland and father in Ireland was
recorded as Irish. This led to some strange anomalies, such as the Indian
reserve in the Prairie west in which most of the mixed-blood residents were
recorded as Scottish, using the census definition of ethnicity, though all were

legally treaty Indians. Despite some entries to the contrary, "American" was not considered to be an acceptable reply to the question.

<u>Occupation</u>   Occupations have been entered as given in the original enumeration, with some standardization of spelling. "F" indicates a farmer, "Lab" a labourer. Some lengthy occupational designations may be cut off in mid-word if they exceed the space we have allocated for this column.

<u>Muncipality and Page Reference</u>   See the explanation of these columns above: "How to find an indexed individual in the census".

Religion Codes

Because there were so many different ways of writing one religion, the Archives has standardized religion into a two-letter code. Most of these are easy to understand. Thus "CP" is Canada Presbyterian, "CE" is Church of England, "WM" is Wesleyan Methodist, and so on. Some of the more obscure denominations have more difficult codes. The alphabetical list following does not include every long-hand version one will find in the original census schedules, but the major variations are given. We recognize that some of these variants indicate the same denomination, e.g. CE and EP, and even CI, but feeling that there was some value to retaining the original terminology where possible, these have been assigned separate designations.

AA	African Association Baptist	KB	Close Communion Baptist
AD	Adventists	LD	Latter Day Saints
AP	American Presbyterian	LU	Lutheran/Evangelical
AT	Atheist		Lutheran
BA	Baptist	MC	I. Meth. C.
BB	Bible Believer	MD	Mahometan
BC	Bible Christian	ME	Methodist
BE	British Episcopal Methodist	MI	Meth. I.
BR	Brethren	MO	Mormon
CB	Christian Brethren	MN	Mennonite
CC	Christian Conference Baptist	MS	Messiah
CD	Christadelphian	MV	Moravian
CE	Church of England, Anglican	NC	New Connexion Methodist
CI	Church of Ireland	NG	Not Given
CM	Calvinistic Methodist	NP	N. Presbyterian
CN	Christian	OB	[Other Baptist]
CO	Congregationalist	OM	[Other Methodist]
CP	Canada Presbyterian/C. Presb.	OP	[Other Presbyterian]
CS	Church of Scotland/Kirk/	PA	Pagan
	Scotch Presb., etc.	PB	Plymouth Brethren
CX	Church of Christ	PE	Est. Presb.
DE	Deist	PM	Primitive Methodist
DI	Disciple (of Christ)	PR	Protestant
EA	Evangelical Association	PS	Presbyterian
EM	Episcopal Methodist/	PU	Puritan
	Methodist Episcopal	QU	Quaker/Friends
EP	Episcopal(ian)	RB	Reformed Baptist/R. Baptist
EU	Evangelical Union	RC	(Roman) Catholic
EV	Evangelical	RM	R. Methodist
FK	Free Kirk/Free Presb., etc.	RP	Reformed Presb.
FT	Free Thinker (of England)	SD	Seventh Day Adventist
FW	Free Will Baptist/Free	SP	Spiritualist
	Christian	SW	Swedenborgian/New Jerusalem
GB	Regular Baptist/see also RB	TU	Tunker
IF	Infidel	UB	United Brethren
IL	Illegible	UN	Union Baptist
IM	I. Meth. E.	UP	United Presbyterian/
IN	Independent		U. Kirk Presbyterian
IP	Irish Presbyterian	UT	Unitarian
IR	Irvingite/Catholic Apostolic	UV	Universalist
JM	J. Meth. E.	VM	Evangelical Methodist
JU	Jew	WM	Wesleyan Methodist
		WP	W. Presbyterian
		XC	C. C. Baptist
		ZZ	[Strange References]

SURNAME	NAME1	NAME2	STRAY	SEX	AGE	BIRTHPL	RELIGION	ORIGIN	OCCUP	DIST	SUB_DIST	DIV	PAGE
	AGNES		1	1	14	0	CP	SCOTCH		044	C	4	28
	ALEXANDER		1		16	SCOTLAND	CP	SCOTCH		044	C	4	28
	BENNIE		1		20	0	WM	ENGLISH	SERVANT	044	C	1	13
	CHARLES	0			33	0	EM	ENGLISH	MINISTER	044	C	1	21
	JOHN				60	IRELAND	WM	IRISH	F	044	C	1	12
	MARY		1	1	14	IRELAND	RC	IRISH	F LAB	044	C	1	20
	MARY		1	1	13	IRELAND	RC	IRISH	F LAB	044	C	1	20
	THOMAS		1		21	ENGLAND	WM	ENGLISH	F LAB	044	C	1	22
* CUNDY	MARY			1	43	0	WM	ENGLISH	SEAMSTRESS	043	D		8
* NOYLOR	CHARLES		1		22	0	WM	ENGLISH	PRINTER	043	D		33
? BLACK	DORCAS		1	1	19	0	WM	IRISH	SERVANT	044	C	2	20
? HAYSTON	FREDERICK				38	NEW BRUNSWICK	CE	ENGLISH	LABOURER	043	H	2	42
? MCKEOWN	JOHN		1	M	15	0	CP	IRELAND		043	A	5	37
ABBOT	ISAAC				60	IRELAND	CE	IRISH	LAB	043	H	2	3
ABBOT	ISAAC				60	IRELAND	CE	IRISH	LABOURER	043	H	2	3
ABBOT	JAMES		1		50	ENGLAND	PM	ENGLISH	LAB	044	A	3	51
ABBOTT	CHARLES		1			0	CE	ENGLISH		043	B	4	6
ABBOTT	ISAAC				26	ONTARIO	CE	ENGLISH	LABORER	043	G	2	16
ABBOTT	JAMES				67	ENGLAND	WM	ENGLISH	GENTLEMAN	043	C		31
ABBOTT	JAMES				37	IRELAND	UP	IRISH	PEDLER	045	D	1	33
ABBOTT	MARIA		1	1	19	0	CE	ENGLISH	SERVANT	043	B	4	6
ABBS	JAMES				46	ENGLAND	EM	ENGLISH	STONEMASON	043	E	1	51
ABBS	JAMES				71	ENGLAND	WM	ENGLISH	GARDNER	044	C	4	48
ABBS	THOMAS				43	ENGLAND	WM	ENGLISH	F	044	C	4	79
ABBS	WILLIAM		1		74	ENGLAND	EM	ENGLISH	MASON	043	E	1	49
ABBS	WILLIAM				53	ENGLAND	CN	ENGLISH	MASON	043	G	1	3
ABBS	WILLIAM				67	ENGLAND	WM	ENGLISH	GARDNER	044	C	4	41
ABELL	JOHN				49	ENGLAND	CO	ENGLISH	MACHINIST	044	B	5	37
ABRAHAM	ELENOR		1	1	75	IRELAND	CE	IRISH		043	A	2	43
ABRAHAM	ELIJAH				38	0	CE	IRISH	F	045	C	4	43
ABRAHAM	JOSEPH				23	0	WM	IRISH	FARMER	045	D	1	1
ABRAHAM	WILLIAM				58	IRELAND	CE	IRISH	F	045	C	4	44
ABRAHAMS	NANCY		1	1	22	0	CN	ENGLISH	SERVANT	043	E	2	17
ABRAMS	WM				69	ENGLAND	WM	ENGLISH	LAB	044	B	5	62
ACEY	JOHN				55	ENGLAND	WM	ENGLISH	FARMER	045	A	2	15
ACHISON	GEORGE				30	IRELAND	CE	IRISH	FARM LAB	043	E	1	5
ACKROW	JOHN				51	ENGLAND	PM	ENGLISH	F	044	A	3	44
ACTON	ROBERT				39	SCOTLAND	CP	SCOTCH	SAWER	045	C	2	49
ADAIR	HENRY				50	IRELAND	PS	IRISH	LAB	044	C	4	84
ADAIR	JAMES				55	SCOTLAND	CE	SCOTCH	PAPER MAKER	045	A	1	79
ADAIR	JOHN				38	IRELAND	WM	IRISH	CARRIAGE MAKER	045	D	5	27
ADAIR	JOHN	S	2		2	0	WM			045	D	5	D
ADAM	REV	JAMES			46	IRELAND	CP	IRISH	CLERGYMAN	043	A	3	9
ADAMS	CHARLES		1		13	0	PM	ENGLISH		043	H	1	18
ADAMS	CHARLES				26	0	CP	ENGLISH	FARM LABOURER	045	C	4	19
ADAMS	CHARLOT		2		40	ENGLAND	CE			045	B	1	
ADAMS	DAVID	G	1		24	0	CP	IRISH	LAB	045	C	2	25
ADAMS	ELIJAH				51	0	WM	GERMAN	F	045	C	2	16
ADAMS	GEORGE				66	ENGLAND	CE	ENGLISH	LABOURER	045	D	5	33
ADAMS	GEORGE				40	SCOTLAND	CP	SCOTCH	TAYLOR	044	C	4	83
ADAMS	JAMES				63	IRE	CS	IRE	F	044	B	4	48
ADAMS	JANE		1	1	56	SCOTLAND	CP	SCOTCH	F	043	A	6	26
ADAMS	JOHN				24	0	WM	ENGLISH	LAB	045	C	4	15
ADAMS	JOSEPH				31	ENGLAND	BA	ENGLISH	TOLLCOLLECTOR	044	C	4	38
ADAMS	THOMAS				54	ENGLAND	CE	ENGLISH	LAB	045	B	1	13
ADAMS	THOMAS				54	0	BC	GERMAN	F	045	C	2	18
ADAMS	THOMAS		1		18	ENGLAND	CE	ENGLISH		044	C	2	11
ADAMS	WILLIAM		1		38	IRELAND	CE	IRISH	F LAB	044	A	1	34
ADAMSON	WEEDON				40	ENGLAND	CE	ENGLISH	ARCHITECT SURVEYOR P	045	D	5	20
ADDISON	ANN	E	1	1	15	0	EM	ENGISH		043	B	3	58
ADDISON	GEO				34	0	WM	ENGLISH	F	044	B	5	43
ADDISON	JOHN				45	ENGLAND	CO	ENGLISH	F	044	B	6	7
ADDISON	JOHN	E	1		12	0	EM	ENGLISH		043	B	3	58
ADDISON	LEWIS				26	0	WM	GER	LAB	044	B	3	50
ADDISON	MARTHA	JANE	1	1	9	0	EM	ENGLISH		043	B	3	58
ADDISON	ROBERT		1		18	0	EM	ENGLISH		043	B	3	58
ADDISON	THOMAS		1		20	0	EM	ENGLISH	LABOURER	043	B	3	58
ADDISON	WM-	HENRY	1		11	0	EM	ENGLISH		043	B	3	58
AFFLECK	JOHN		1		27	SCOTLAND	CP	ENGLISH	PORTER	045	A	1	70
AGAR	FRANCES		1	1	18	0	WM	ENGLISH	SCHOOL TEACHER	044	C	2	15
AGAR	GEORGE				29	0	PM	ENGLISH	F	044	B	6	42
AGAR	HENRY				62	SCOTLAND	CE	SCOTCH	CARPENTER	043	E	1	30
AGAR	JOHN		1		25	0	WM	ENGLISH	CARPENTER	044	A	2	1
AGAR	RICHARD				56	ENGLAND	PM	ENGLISH	F	044	B	6	20
AGAR	ROBT				45	ENGLAND	PM	ENGLISH	F	044	B	5	74
AGAR	SAMUEL				30	ENG	CE	ENG	F	044	B	2	55
AGAR	WILLIAM				27	0	PM	ENGLISH	F	044	B	6	19
AGER	MARGARET		1		45	IRELAND	WM	IRISH	F	045	A	4	30
AGNEW	WILLIAM				42	0	WM	IRISH	DENTIST	043	A	4	12
AIKEN	EDWARD				33	0	CE	IRISH	SURGEON PHYSICIAN	044	C	3	25
AIKEN	JOHN				71	IRELAND	CE	IRISH	GENTLEMAN	044	C	3	25
AIKINS	JOHN		1		21	ENGLAND	CE	ENGLISH	LAB	045	B	2	4
AIRD	JESSIE		1		19	0	WM	GER	F	044	B	3	21
AIRD	LEVI		1		17	0	WM	GER	F	044	B	3	21
AIRD	MARY	ANN		1	14	0	WM	GER		044	B	3	21
AIRD	WILLIAM				47	SCOTLAND	OP	SCOTCH	F	043	H	2	44
AIRD	WILLIAM				47	SCOTLAND	CS	SCOTCH	FARMER	043	H	2	44
AIRTH	ANN			1	36	SCOTLAND	CS	SCOTCH	HOUSEKEEPER	043	D		26
AITH	ALEXANDER		1		25	SCOTLAND	CP	SCOTCH	FARM LAB	044	C	2	26
AITKEN	ELIZABETH		1	1	19	IRELAND	CP	IRISH	FARM SERVANT	045	C	4	29
AITKEN	WILLIAM				34	SCOT	CS	SCOT	CLERGYMAN	044	B	2	74
AKAM	HENRY				50	GER	CO	GER	F	044	B	3	44
AKIN	ELIZA			1	45	IRELAND	CE	IRISH	MATRON	045	B	1	71
AKIN	JAMES		1		22	IRISH	CP	IRISH		045	D	6	67
AKIN	JOHN		1		23	IRISH	CP	IRISH		045	D	6	67
AKNEY	HERBERT				55	ENGLAND	PM	ENGLISH	FARMER	045	D	3	58
ALAN	RICHARD		1		47	ENGLAND	CE	ENGLISH	ROPE MAKER	044	C	4	45
ALBERT	JOHN				46	GERMANY	CE	GERMAN	GARDNER	044	C	4	37
ALBERT	MARY		1	1	18	ENGLAND	CE	ENGLISH	SERVANT	044	C	3	2
ALBIN	ALBERT				26	IRELAND	CE	IRISH	LAB	045	A	4	32
ALBION	HARRIET		1	1	47	ENGLAND	PM	ENGLISH	SERVANT	045	B	2	31
ALCORN	SAMUEL				63	IRELAND	WM	IRISH		045	B	1	17
ALDEN	EDWIN				62	ENGLAND	CE	ENGLISH	FARMER	043	G	2	25
ALDEN	ELI		1		56	ENGLAND	CE	ENGLISH	FARMER	043	G	2	13
ALDEN	JUNE		1	1	51	ENGLAND	WM	ENGLISH	FARMER	043	G	2	13
ALDERSON	JAS				50	ENG	CE	ENG	F	045	C	1	33

SURNAME	NAME1	NAME2	STRAY	SEX	AGE	BIRTHPL	RELIGION	ORIGIN	OCCUP	DIST	SUB_DIST	DIV	PAGE
ALDERSON	MARY			1	34	IRELAND	RC	IRISH		044	C	3	38
ALEN	ANNE		1	1	15	0	CP	IRISH		045	A	4	12
ALEN	GEORGE				34	0	WM	SCOTTISH	F	043	B	4	28
ALEX	IRA				26	0	WM	GERMAN	LAWYER	043	B	3	36
ALEXANDER	ABRAHAM		1		17	SCOTLAND	BA	SCOTCH	BOOKKEEPER	045	B	2	33
ALEXANDER	ISABELLA			1	29	SCOTLAND	PS	SCOTCH		045	B	1	17
ALEXANDER	JOSEPH				77	0	WM	SCOTCH	LAB	043	E	3	2
ALEXANDER	JOSEPH				37	0	CE	SCOTCH	F	044	A	1	25
ALEXANDER	MARGARET		2	1	30	0	WM			043	D		D
ALEXANDER	ROBERT				37	SCOTLAND	WM	SCOTCH	TEACHER	043	D		28
ALEXANDER	SARAH			1	45	0	CP	SCOTCH		045	D	4	42
ALISON	MARY	ELIZA	2	1	13	ENGLAND	PM			045	A	4	D
ALISON	RICHARD				43	ENGLAND	PM	ENGLISH	F	045	A	4	9
ALLAN	DAVID				28	0	PS	SCOTCH	CARPENTER	044	B	5	9
ALLAN	EDWARD				50	IRELAND	CE	IRISH	F	044	C	1	10
ALLAN	GEORGE				56	SCOTLAND	CE	SCOTCH	LAB	044	A	3	31
ALLAN	GEORGE		1		25	ENGLAND	PM	ENGLISH	LABOURER	045	D	4	51
ALLAN	GEORGE	L			59	IRELAND	CE	IRISH	GAOLER	045	A	1	36
ALLAN	JAMES				45	SCOTLAND	CS	SCOTCH	MACHINIST	043	D		81
ALLAN	JOHN				33	0	CP	SCOTCH	CARPENTER	043	A	4	49
ALLAN	JOSEPH				24	0	CP	SCOTCH	BUTCHER	045	B	2	23
ALLAN	SAMUEL		1		22	ENGLAND	NG	ENGLISH	BUTCHER	045	B	2	30
ALLAN	THOMAS				42	ENGLAND	CE	ENGLISH	LAB	044	C	4	76
ALLCHIN	WILLIAM		1		19	ENGLAND	WM	ENGLISH	SHOEMAKER	045	C	3	30
ALLEN	CHARLES		1		50	IRELAND	CE	IRISH	F LAB	043	B	4	8
ALLEN	DAVID		1		19	0	CE	SCOTCH	F LAB	044	A	3	6
ALLEN	ELISHA				73	U STATES	QU	ENGLISH	F	043	A	6	43
ALLEN	HENRY		1		20	0	WM	ENGLISH	SERVANT	045	A	3	32
ALLEN	HUGH			M	69	IRELAND	PS	IRISH	S TEACHER	043	A	2	20
ALLEN	JAMES		2	M	67	IRELAND	PS			043	A	2	D
ALLEN	JOHN				62	U STATES	QU	ENGLISH		043	A	6	44
ALLEN	JOHN				44	ONTARIO	CE	IRISH	FARMER	043	G	2	22
ALLEN	JOHN				28	0	WM	IRISH	BLACKSMITH	045	B	1	28
ALLEN	JOHN				33	SCOTLAND	PS	SCOTCH	WATCH MAKER	045	D	6	44
ALLEN	JOHN		1		9	0	CP	IRISH		045	A	4	24
ALLEN	JOSEPH		1		3	0	CP	IRISH		045	D	2	42
ALLEN	MARGARET			1	76	IRELAND	CE	IRISH		044	B	6	47
ALLEN	MATHEW				25	IRELAND	CP	IRISH	FARMER	045	D	3	40
ALLEN	OLLIVER				34	IRELAND	PM	IRISH	LAB	045	A	2	21
ALLEN	ROBERT				73	IRELAND	CE	IRISH	LAB	045	A	4	25
ALLEN	THOMAS				33	0	CE	IRISH	LAB	043	C		49
ALLEN	THOMAS				65	IRELAND	CE	IRISH	F	044	A	1	32
ALLEN	THOMAS		1		22	0	CE	IRISH	CARRIAGE MAKER	045	D	3	18
ALLEN	WILLIAM			M	27	US	WM	ENGLAND	PAINTER	043	A	1	51
ALLEN	WILLIAM				27	0	RP	SCOTTISH	F	043	B	5	26
ALLEN	WILLIAM				42	US	PM	GERMAN	F	044	B	6	49
ALLEN	WILLIAM		1		7	0	CP	IRISH		045	D	2	42
ALLEYNE	JOHN	F			54	BARBADOS	CE	ENGLISH	F	043	B	1	33
ALLICE	ELIZA		1	1	14	0	PS	IRISH		043	E	3	12
ALLIS	JOHN		1	M	12	0	WM	ENGLISH		043	A	1	20
ALLISON	ANDREW				36	0	CP	SCOTCH	FARMER	045	D	5	62
ALLISON	ELIZA		1	1	75	0	BA	WELSH		043	E	3	56
ALLISON	JOHN				59	0	CE	ENGLISH	F	045	C	4	6
ALLISON	THOMAS				51	ENGLAND	CE	ENGLISH	LABOURER	045	D	4	8
ALLISTON	JOHN				50	ENG	PM	ENG	MACHINIST	044	B	4	18
ALLSOFF	EDWARD				31	ENGLAND	CE	ENGLISH	WHEELWRIGHT	043	E	1	42
ALLSOPP	JOHN				60	ENGLAND	CE	ENGLISH	LAB	043	A	6	26
ALSTON	JAMES				42	ENGLAND	XC	ENGLISH	BUILDER	045	B	1	55
ALTON	GEORGE				51	ENGLAND	CE	ENGLISH	GARDNER	044	C	4	33
AMBROSE	CAROLINE		1	1	3	0	CE	ENGLISH		045	A	1	23
AMBROSE	ELIZABETH		1	1	30	USA	CE	ENGLISH		045	A	1	23
AMBROSE	HANNAH		1	1	1	0	CE	ENGLISH		045	A	1	23
AMES	ANNA	MARIA	1	1	19	ONTARIO	WM		SERVANT	043	G	2	14
AMOS	JOHN				50	ENGLAND	PM	ENGLISH	GARDNER	044	C	4	69
AMOUS	MARY-A		1	1	19	ENGLAND	CE	ENGLISH	SERVANT	044	C	1	37
AMPTON	HARIOT		1	1	20	ENGLAND	CE	ENGLISH	INMATE	045	B	1	73
ANDERSON	ALEX				47	SCOTLAND	PS	SCOTTISH	F	044	C	1	16
ANDERSON	ALEXANDER				37	IRELAND	WM	IRISH	CARRIAGE MKR	044	C	1	27
ANDERSON	ALLAN		2		21	ONTARIO	CE		M STUDENT	043	G	2	D
ANDERSON	ANDREW				37	0	CP	SCOTCH	F	044	A	2	8
ANDERSON	ARTHUR				38	ONTARIO	CE	ENGLISH	FARMER	043	G	2	17
ANDERSON	BELLA		1	1	18	U STATES	CS	SCOTCH		045	D	5	32
ANDERSON	CHARLOTTE		1	1	74	SCOTLAND	CP	SCOTCH		043	A	3	61
ANDERSON	ELIZABETH				36	SCOTLAND	CS	SCOTCH	CHARWOMAN	043	F		33
ANDERSON	ELIZABETH		1	1	39	SCOTLAND	CS	SCOTCH		043	G	1	57
ANDERSON	ELIZABETH		1	1	63	U STATES	DI	GERMAN		045	D	6	58
ANDERSON	ELIZABETH			1	34	0	CE	ENGLISH		044	C	2	6
ANDERSON	ELIZABETH		1	1	16	IRELAND	CE	IRISH		045	A	4	34
ANDERSON	GEORGE				35	0	RC	IRISH	LAB	044	C	2	50
ANDERSON	ISABELLA		1	1	14	0	WM	IRISH		043	E	2	27
ANDERSON	ISABELLA			1	64	ENGLAND	CE	ENGLISH		044	A	2	46
ANDERSON	JACOB				85	0	CE	SCOTCH	F	043	A	6	28
ANDERSON	JACOB				66	NOVA SCOTIA	CP	SCOTCH	F	044	A	2	8
ANDERSON	JACOB				47	IRELAND	CE	IRISH	GARDNER	044	C	4	63
ANDERSON	JAMES		1		16	0	CN	IRISH	LAB	043	E	2	28
ANDERSON	JAMES				27	ENGLAND	WM	SCOTCH	FARMER	043	G	2	14
ANDERSON	JAMES		1		26	HUDSON BAY	CE	ENGLISH	MERCHANT	043	H	2	7
ANDERSON	JAMES				37	0	CE	SCOTCH	F	043	H	2	41
ANDERSON	JAMES				37	ONTARIO	CE	SCOTCH	FARMER	043	H	2	41
ANDERSON	JAMES		1		26	HUDSON BAY	CE	ENGLISH	MERCHANT	043	H	2	7
ANDERSON	JAMES		1		23	0	CP	SCOTCH	FARMER	045	A	3	35
ANDERSON	JAMES				33	0	FK	SCOTCH	FARMER	045	A	3	35
ANDERSON	JAMES				21	0	WM	IRISH	FARMER	045	D	6	12
ANDERSON	JAMES				50	IRELAND	CE	IRISH	F	044	C	3	3
ANDERSON	JANE		1	1	71	IRELAND	CE	IRISH		045	A	1	30
ANDERSON	JANE		1	1	68	SCOTLAND	CP	SCOTCH		045	A	3	35
ANDERSON	JOHN				45	0	WM	ENGLISH	BLACKSMITH	043	A	4	2
ANDERSON	JOHN				37	ENGLAND	WM	SCOTCH	FARMER	043	G	2	14
ANDERSON	JOHN		1		13	0	BC	ENGLISH		043	H	2	42
ANDERSON	JOHN		1		13	ONTARIO	BC	ENGLISH		043	H	2	42
ANDERSON	JOHN		1		74	SCOTLAND	CP	SCOTCH	FARMER	045	A	3	35
ANDERSON	JOHN				36	SCOTLAND	CP	SCOTCH	FARM SERVANT	045	C	3	21
ANDERSON	JOHN				38	SCOTLAND	CP	SCOTCH	LAB	045	C	4	33
ANDERSON	JOHN				63	CANADA	WM	SCOTCH	FARMER	045	D	6	68
ANDERSON	JOHN		1		14	ONTARIO	CP	SCOTCH		045	D	3	7
ANDERSON	JOHN		1		24	SCOTLAND	CP	SCOTCH	FARM LAB	044	C	2	26

SURNAME	NAME1	NAME2	STRAY	SEX	AGE	BIRTHPL	RELIGION	ORIGIN	OCCUP	DIST	SUB_DIST	DIV	PAGE
ANDERSON	JOHN				34	0	CE	SCOTCH	INN KEEPER	044	C	2	32
ANDERSON	JOHN	F			28	ENGLAND	CE	ENGLISH	COLLAR MAKER	043	C		6
ANDERSON	JOSEPH				71	U STATES	PM	AFRICAN	LAB	045	A	2	23
ANDERSON	LYMAN				27	0	WM	SCOTTISH	F	043	B	5	16
ANDERSON	MARGARET			1	49	RED RIVER	CE	SCOTCH		043	G	2	56
ANDERSON	MARGARET		1	1	30	SCOTLAND	CP	SCOTCH		045	D	3	7
ANDERSON	MARK				45	IRELAND	CE	IRISH	LAB	045	B	1	66
ANDERSON	MARY	JANE			52	IRELAND	BA	IRISH		045	D	6	72
ANDERSON	MILLER				48	SCOTLAND	WM	SCOTCH	CARPENTER	043	C		9
ANDERSON	PETER				58	CANADA	WM	SCOTCH	FARMER	045	D	6	33
ANDERSON	ROBERT		1		25	0	CP	SCOTCH	FARMER	045	A	3	35
ANDERSON	SUSAN			1	69	0	BC	SCOTCH		043	H	2	41
ANDERSON	SUSAN			1	69	ONTARIO	BC	SCOTCH		043	H	2	41
ANDERSON	THOMAS				51	0	PM	SCOTCH	F	043	A	6	39
ANDERSON	THOMAS				44	ENGLAND	PR	ENGLISH	LABORER	043	G	2	41
ANDERSON	THOMAS				29	ENGLAND	SW	ENGLISH	OPTICIAN	045	B	2	21
ANDERSON	THOS	W			61	ONT	CP	SCOTCH	F	044	C	2	6
ANDERSON	WEIR				48	JAMAICA	CE	SCOTCH	COMMISSIONER TRUST &	045	B	2	19
ANDERSON	WILLIAM				39	IRELAND	CN	IRISH	LABOURER	043	B	3	17
ANDERSON	WILLIAM		1		28	0	CP	SCOTCH	F	043	E	1	25
ANDERSON	WILLIAM		1		43	0	BC	SCOTCH	LAB	043	H	2	43
ANDERSON	WILLIAM				43	ONTARIO	BC	SCOTCH	LABOURER	043	H	2	43
ANDERSON	WILLIAM				49	USA	WM	AFRICAN	LABOURER	045	A	1	50
ANDERSON	WILLIAM				35	0	CP	SCOTLAND	FARMER	045	D	2	16
ANDERSON	YORK				30	0	RC	AFRICAN	POTTER	044	C	4	14
ANDREW	BATHGATE				34	SCOTLAND	CS	SCOTCH	TANNER	043	H	1	9
ANDREWS	ABRAM				44	ENGLAND	WM	ENGLISH	SHOEMAKER	043	C		54
ANDREWS	ANDREW				56	ENGLAND	CE	ENGLISH	AUCTIONEER	045	A	2	2
ANDREWS	BENJAMIN				52	ENG	WM	ENG	F	044	B	4	21
ANDREWS	EDWARD				45	ENGLAND	NC	ENGLISH	TAILOR	043	C		43
ANDREWS	EDWARD				23	ENGLAND	CE	ENGLISH	TEAMSTER	043	E	2	44
ANDREWS	GEO	B			23	ONT	WM	ENGLISH	PUMPMAKER	043	D		52
ANDREWS	GEORGE				59	ENGLAND	WM	ENGLISH	FARMER	043	C		19
ANDREWS	HUGH		1		23	ENGLAND	CE	ENGLISH	BUTCHER	043	C		25
ANDREWS	JAMES				42	ENGLAND	WM	ENGLISH	MERCHANT	043	C		10
ANDREWS	JAMES				40	ENGLAND	CE	ENGLISH	BRICK & TILE MAKER	045	C	4	22
ANDREWS	JOSHUA				32	0	NG	ENGLISH	BLACKSMITH	045	B	2	22
ANDREWS	MATHEW				28	ENGLAND	CE	ENGLISH	MERCHANT TAILOR	045	B	1	7
ANDREWS	SARAH			F	49	ENGLAND	EM	ENGLISH	SHOP KEEPER	043	A	1	56
ANDREWS	SUSAN		1	1	54	ENGLAND	WM	ENGLISH		045	B	2	6
ANDREWS	THOMAS				59	ENGLAND	CE	ENGLISH		045	B	1	65
ANDREWS	WILLIAM			M	30	ENGLAND	PS	ENGLISH	F	043	A	1	43
ANDREWS	WILLIAM		1		19	ENGLAND	CE	ENGLISH	LAB	043	B	2	35
ANDREWS	WILLIAM				39	ENGLAND	WM	ENGLISH	LAB	043	C		32
ANDREWS	WILLIAM		1		55	ENGLAND	CE	ENGLISH	LABORER	043	G	2	22
ANDREWS	WILLIAM				24	ENGLAND	CE	ENGLISH	PAINTER	045	A	1	63
ANDREWS	WILLIAM		2		2	ENGLAND	CE		PAINTER	045	A	1	D
ANGST	JACOB		1		22	GERMANY	LU	GERMAN	SERVANT	045	D	5	54
ANGUS	CHARLES				37	SCOTLAND	CP	SCOTCH	F	045	C	3	8
ANGUS	FRANCIS				36	SCOT	CE	SCOT	F	045	C	1	12
ANGUS	GEORGE				36	SCOTLAND	UV	SCOTCH	FARMER	045	D	5	74
ANGUS	MARGARET		1	1	33	SCOTLAND	CP	SCOTCH		045	C	2	53
ANGUS	WILLIAM				31	SCOTLAND	CE	SCOTCH	F	045	C	4	19
ANNIS	ANDREW				48	0	WM	FRENCH	F	045	C	2	22
ANNIS	DAVID				40	0	WM	ENG	F	045	C	1	12
ANNIS	JEREMIAH				49	0	WM	ENG	F	045	C	1	13
ANNIS	MATHEW				55	0	WM	ENGLISH	FARMER	045	A	3	22
ANOS	GEORGE				33	0	PM	ENGLISH	FARMER	045	D	3	40
ANSCOM	JOSEPH		1		16	0	CE	IRISH	SERVANT	045	D	5	14
ANSLEY	THOMAS				35	IRE	VM	IRISH	SCHOOL TEACHER	044	B	1	52
ANTHONY	EDMUND				42	ENGLAND	CE	ENGLISH	LABOURER	045	D	5	16
ANTHONY	JOHN			M	56	IRELAND	CE	IRISH	F	043	A	1	24
ANTHONY	JOHN				38	0	CE	ENGLISH	CARPENTER	045	D	5	27
ANTHONY	ROBERT		1		69	ENGLAND	PM	ENGLISH	LAB	043	B	1	9
ANTHONY	SYDNEY		2		6	0	CE			045	D	5	D
APINE	JAMES				45	ENGLAND	PM	ENGLISH	FARMER	045	A	2	20
APPLEBY	G	H			50	ENGLAND	CE	ENGLISH	MILLER	044	C	1	19
APPLEBY	MOSES				52	ENGLAND	CE	ENGLISH	F	044	A	1	25
APPLETON	CARRIE		1	1	18	0	CE	IRISH	SERVANT	043	C		21
APPLETON	CHARLES				47	ENGLAND	CE	ENGLISH	SAWYER	043	B	3	41
APPLETON	LUKE			M	42	ENGLAND	CE	ENGLISH	CARPENTER	043	A	1	29
APPLETON	MARY		1	F	15	ENGLAND	NG	ENGLAND		043	A	5	34
APPLETON	SIMON				51	ENGLAND	CE	ENGLISH	LAB	043	C		47
APPLETON	TEAVILL	C			48	0	NC	ENGLISH	F & SAWMILLER	043	A	6	18
ARCHER	EMMA		1	1	26	ENGLAND	WM	ENGLISH		045	B	1	49
ARCHER	GEORGE		1		28	ENGLAND	CE	ENGLISH	LABOURER	045	D	3	75
ARCHER	PATRICK				40	IRELAND	RC	IRISH	LAB	045	A	4	28
ARCHER	THOMAS		1		16	0	CE	ENGLISH	SADLER	045	D	1	13
ARCHER	WILLIAM	H	1		32	0	CE	ENGLISH		045	B	1	49
ARCHER	WM				58	SCOTLAND	UP	SCOTCH	F	044	B	5	73
ARCHEY	JOHN				48	ENGLAND	CE	ENGLISH	FARMER	043	G	1	18
ARCHIBALD	BROWNLEE				39	SCOTLAND	CP	SCOTCH	F	044	B	6	2
ARCHIBALD	DAVID			M	57	0	PM	SCOTCH	F	043	A	2	6
ARCHIBALD	JACOB		1		25	0	WM	ENG	LAB	044	B	4	6
ARCHIBALD	JANE		1	1	1	0	LU	GER		044	B	3	19
ARCHIBALD	JESSE				47	0	EM	GER	LAB	044	B	2	71
ARCHIBALD	JOHN			M	59	0	PM	SCOTCH	F	043	A	2	1
ARCHIBALD	JOHN				46	0	OM	SCOTCH	LAB	043	H	2	18
ARCHIBALD	JOHN				46	ONTARIO	NC	SCOTCH	LABOURER	043	H	2	18
ARCHIBALD	LEVI				43	0	PM	SCOTCH	LAB	043	A	6	35
ARCHIBALD	PETER		2		20	ONTARIO	BC		LABOURER	043	H	2	D
ARCHIBALD	PETER		2		20	0	BC		LAB	043	H	2	D
ARCHIBALD	SAMUEL				38	0	PM	ENG	LAB	044	B	4	3
ARCHIBALD	SUSANNAH		1	1	29	0	LU	GER		044	B	3	19
ARCHIBALD	THOMAS				62	NEW BRUNSWICK	WM	ENGLISH	F	043	H	2	33
ARCHIBALD	THOMAS				62	NEW BRUNSWICK	WM	ENGLISH	FARMER	043	H	2	33
ARCHIBALD	WILLIAM		1		5	0	LU	GER		044	B	3	19
ARDEN	WILLIAM				32	ENGLAND	CE	ENGLISH	STEWART	044	C	4	28
ARDILL	GEORGE				76	IRELAND	CE	IRISH	FARMER	043	G	2	29
ARDILL	WILLIAM				45	IRELAND	CE	IRISH		043	G	2	26
ARGNES	MICHL		1		65	ENGLAND	WM	ENGLISH	LAB	044	B	5	5
ARKELE	JOHN				48	ENGLAND	CE	ENGLISH	MILLER	045	A	3	39
ARKSE	JOSEPH				56	ENGLAND	WM	ENGLISH	FARMER	043	G	2	29
ARKSEY	JOHN		1		63	ENGLAND	EM	FRENCH	GENTLEMAN	043	G	1	21
ARKSEY	MARY		2	1	65	ENGLAND	EM			043	G	1	D
ARLEDGE	CHRISTOPHER				42	ENGLAND	DI	ENGLISH	BRICKMAKER	045	B	1	67

SURNAME	NAME1	NAME2	STRAY	SEX	AGE	BIRTHPL	RELIGION	ORIGIN	OCCUP	DIST	SUB_DIST	DIV	PAGE
ARMFIELD	JOSEPH				33	ENGLAND	CE	ENGLISH	R R MASTER	043	C		50
ARMISTEAD	JOHN				67	ENGLAND	WM	ENGLISH	F	044	B	6	10
ARMITAGE	AAMOS		1		80	U STATES	QU	ENGLISH	F	043	A	6	19
ARMITAGE	ELI	J		M	31	0	QU	ENGLAND	F	043	A	5	43
ARMITAGE	ELIAS			M	41	0	QU	ENGLAND	F	043	A	5	32
ARMITAGE	ELIZABETH		2	1	28	0	WM			043	E	3	D
ARMITAGE	ELIZABETH		2	1		0	WM			043	E	3	D
ARMITAGE	ESTER		1	1	33	ENGLAND	CE	ENGLISH		045	B	1	21
ARMITAGE	GEORGE				40	ENGLAND	CE	ENGLISH	MARBLECUTTER	043	E	1	37
ARMITAGE	HANNAH			1	72	NB	PM	GERMAN		043	B	5	15
ARMITAGE	ISAAC				38	0	QU	ENGLISH	F	043	B	4	11
ARMITAGE	ISAAC	WIGGON			45	0	QU	ENGLISH	LAB	043	E	3	38
ARMITAGE	JOHN				49	0	QU	ENGLISH	F	043	B	4	11
ARMITAGE	JOHN				42	0	QU	ENGLISH	LAB	043	E	2	54
ARMITAGE	JOSHUA				45	0	WM	ENGLISH	HOTEL KEEPER	043	E	3	50
ARMITAGE	LEWIS				31	0	QU	ENGLISH	GARDENER	043	B	4	23
ARMITAGE	MARY		2	1	79	U STATES	QU			043	A	6	D
ARMITAGE	SEBE				50	0	QU	ENGLISH	F	043	B	4	7
ARMITAGE	SETH				74	UNITED STATES	QU	ENGLISH	F	043	B	4	1
ARMITAGE	STEPHEN	W			28	0	QU	ENGLISH	FARMER	043	A	4	38
ARMOUR	ALEXANDER				53	SCOT	PS	SCOT	F	044	B	3	3
ARMOUR	FLORA			1	53	0	OP	SCOTCH	FARMER	043	A	3	1
ARMOUR	JAMES		1		10	0	CP	SCOT		044	B	4	53
ARMOUR	JAMES				28	0	CP	SCOTCH	F	044	C	2	31
ARMOUR	JOHN				80	SCOTLAND	CP	SCOTCH	F	044	C	2	29
ARMOUR	JOHN	W	1		17	0	CS	SCOT	SERVANT	044	B	4	32
ARMOUR	WILLIAM		1		20	0	PS	SCOT	SERVANT	044	B	2	66
ARMSDEN	THOS				32	ENG	CE	ENG	LAB	045	C	1	23
ARMSTRONG	ALF		1		21	SCOTLAND	WM	SCOTCH	IRON	044	B	5	41
ARMSTRONG	ANN			1	73	IRELAND	WM	IRISH		044	C	2	43
ARMSTRONG	ARTHUR				36	IRELAND	CE	IRISH	CLERK DIV COURT	043	A	4	3
ARMSTRONG	CHARLES				31	0	CE	IRISH	CARPENTER	043	H	2	11
ARMSTRONG	CHARLES				31	ONTARIO	CE	IRISH	CARPENTER	043	H	2	11
ARMSTRONG	CHATHERINE		1	1	64	IRELAND	ZZ	IRISH		043	E	1	1
ARMSTRONG	CHRISTOPHER		1		29	IRELAND	CE	IRISH	WEAVER	043	B	3	65
ARMSTRONG	EDW				64	ENG	PM	ENG	F	045	C	1	71
ARMSTRONG	EDWARD				62	ENGLAND	CE	ENGLISH	FARMER	045	A	2	32
ARMSTRONG	ELIJAH				36	0	WM	IRISH	F	044	C	2	43
ARMSTRONG	ELIZA			1	65	IRELAND	CE	IRISH		045	B	1	47
ARMSTRONG	ELIZA	A	1	1	28	0	CS	IRISH		045	D	3	28
ARMSTRONG	ELIZABETH		1	1	17	0	WM	SCOTCH		045	C	4	5
ARMSTRONG	EMILY			1	42	0	CS	ENGLISH		045	D	5	4
ARMSTRONG	FRANCIS				57	SCOTLAND	CP	SCOTCH	CARPENTER & FARMER	045	C	4	38
ARMSTRONG	FREDRICK				39	ONTARIO	CN	IRISH	FARMER	043	G	1	28
ARMSTRONG	GEORGE				34	0	WM	IRISH	SAWYER	044	B	6	42
ARMSTRONG	GEORGE				35	ENGLAND	CE	ENGLISH	HOTEL KEEPER	045	A	1	8
ARMSTRONG	HULET		1		20	0	WM	SCOTCH	LAB	045	C	4	5
ARMSTRONG	ISABELLA			1	48	ENGLAND	CO	ENGLISH	MILLINER	045	D	3	78
ARMSTRONG	JAMES				30	0	PM	IRISH	LABOURER	043	B	3	23
ARMSTRONG	JAMES				33	0	CE	IRISH	SHOEMAKER	044	B	6	24
ARMSTRONG	JAMES		1		22	IRELAND	CP	IRISH	SERVANT	044	B	6	53
ARMSTRONG	JAMES				40	IRELAND	CE	IRISH	LAB	044	C	4	87
ARMSTRONG	JOHN			M	29	NS	CP	IRISH	LAB	043	A	1	71
ARMSTRONG	JOHN		1		19	0	CP	SCOTCH	SHOEMAKER	044	A	3	26
ARMSTRONG	JOHN				32	0	CE	SCOTCH	FARMER	045	A	2	34
ARMSTRONG	JOHN		2		1	0	CE			045	A	2	D
ARMSTRONG	JOHN		1		2	0	PM	SCOTCH		045	C	4	6
ARMSTRONG	JOSEPH				33	0	CE	SCOTCH	FARMER	045	A	2	34
ARMSTRONG	JOSEPH				69	ENGLAND	CE	ENGLISH		045	D	3	26
ARMSTRONG	MARGARET		1	1	38	0	CP	SCOTCH		043	A	4	64
ARMSTRONG	MARGARET			1	32	IRELAND	CE	IRISH		045	B	2	31
ARMSTRONG	MARGARET		2	1	2	0	CE			044	C	4	D
ARMSTRONG	MARIAH	H	1	1	21	0	WM	GERMAN		043	B	1	11
ARMSTRONG	MARY			1	72	ENGLAND	WM	ENGLISH		045	B	2	15
ARMSTRONG	MARY			1	63	SCOT	CS	SCOT		045	C	1	61
ARMSTRONG	MARY		1	1	15	0	CP	IRISH		045	C	4	26
ARMSTRONG	MARY		1	1	26	0	PM	SCOTCH		045	C	4	6
ARMSTRONG	NICOLAS				31	NS	CC	ENGLISH	AUCTIONEER	043	A	3	11
ARMSTRONG	PHILIP				61	ENGLAND	WM	ENGLISH	F	044	C	4	78
ARMSTRONG	ROBERT				40	IRELAND	CE	IRISH	SHOEMAKER	043	H	2	6
ARMSTRONG	ROBERT				40	IRELAND	CE	IRISH	SHOEMAKER	043	H	2	6
ARMSTRONG	ROBERT		1		20	0	CE	IRISH	SERVANT	044	B	5	11
ARMSTRONG	ROBERT				31	0	CP	IRISH	FARMER	045	D	3	25
ARMSTRONG	ROBERT				41	ENGLAND	CE	ENGLISH	TINSMITH	045	D	3	70
ARMSTRONG	ROBERT				75	ENGLAND	CE	ENGLISH	FARMER	045	D	6	5
ARMSTRONG	ROBERT		1		4	0	CS	IRISH		045	D	3	28
ARMSTRONG	ROBT				50	IRELAND	PM	IRISH	FARMER	043	B	3	22
ARMSTRONG	SARAH		1	1	17	0	CO	ENGLISH	SERVANT	044	A	3	4
ARMSTRONG	SARAH			1	50	ENGLAND	WM	ENGLISH	F	044	C	1	53
ARMSTRONG	THOMAS			M	44	IRELAND	PS	IRISH	F	043	A	1	75
ARMSTRONG	THOMAS				50	IRELAND	PS	IRISH	LABOURER	043	B	3	21
ARMSTRONG	THOMAS				30	0	CP	SCOTCH	CARPENTER	043	H	1	35
ARMSTRONG	THOMAS				58	IRE	CE	IRE	F	044	B	4	27
ARMSTRONG	THOMAS				34	0	WM	ENGISH	MEDICINE	045	A	3	3
ARMSTRONG	THOMAS				33	0	CE	IRISH	F	045	C	4	4
ARMSTRONG	URSULA		1	1	15	0	CE	ENGLISH	SERVANT	044	A	3	11
ARMSTRONG	WALTER		1		16	0	CP	SCOTCH	F	043	A	3	52
ARMSTRONG	WILLIAM			M	58	US	CN	IRELAND	F	043	A	5	25
ARMSTRONG	WILLIAM		1		15	0	CE	ENGLISH	APPRENTICE	044	B	6	24
ARMSTRONG	WILLIAM		1		21	0	RC	IRISH	COOPER	045	B	2	11
ARMSTRONG	WILLIAM				67	ENGLAND	WM	ENGLISH	F	045	C	3	45
ARMSTRONG	WILLIAM				23	0	PM	SCOTCH	LAB	045	C	4	6
ARMSTRONG	WILLIAM				78	ENGLAND	CE	ENGLISH	FARMER	045	D	5	35
ARMSTRONG	WILLIAM				29	0	CE	ENGLISH	FARMER	045	D	5	59
ARMSTRONG	WILLIAM				28	IRELAND	CE	IRISH	LAB	044	C	3	3
ARMSTRONG	WM				27	NS	PS	IRISH	TEACHER	043	E	3	42
ARMWRIGHT	JOHN				37	IRELAND	RC	IRISH	LAB	045	A	2	33
ARNOLD	ABNER				66	0	CE	ENGLISH	FARMER	045	D	1	2
ARNOLD	GEORGE				39	ENGLAND	CE	ENGLISH	FARMER	043	G	2	6
ARNOLD	GEORGE				50	ENGLAND	PM	ENGLISH	PAINTER	045	A	1	90
ARNOLD	JANE		1	1	17	0	EM	ENGLISH		043	E	2	74
ARNOLD	JOHN				54	0	EP	ENG	F	044	B	2	7
ARNOLD	JOHN		1		23	ENGLAND	FW	ENGLISH	LAB	045	A	2	9
ARNOLD	JOHN	M	1		16	0	PM	SCOT	FARM SERVANT	044	B	4	8
ARNOLD	LEWIS			M	75	U STATES	WM	ENGLISH	FARMER	043	A	1	1
ARNOLD	MATHIAS				24	0	EM	ENG		044	B	3	49

SURNAME	NAME1	NAME2	STRAY	SEX	AGE	BIRTHPL	RELIGION	ORIGIN	OCCUP	DIST	SUB_DIST	DIV	PAGE
ARNOLD	ROBT				64	0	CE	ENGLISH	BREWER	043	C		4
ARNOLD	ROBT	J			44	0	CE	ENGLISH	GENTLEMAN	044	B	1	1
ARNOLD	THOMAS				31	0	PS	IRISH	CLOTHIER	043	E	3	40
ARNOTT	JOHN				50	ENGLAND	UT	ENGLISH	COOPER	043	D		22
ARROWSMITH	SAMUEL		1		25	ENGLAND	WM	ENGLISH	F LAB	044	A	3	18
ARTHUR	ELLEN			1	51	IRELAND	RC	IRISH		045	A	3	14
ARTHUR	GEORGE	A			35	0	PS	IRISH	MERCHANT	044	C	4	58
ARTHUR	ISABELLA		1	1	40	U STATES	CE	ENGLISH	SERVANT	043	A	6	3
ARTHUR	MARGARET		1	1	13	0	CO	ENG		044	B	3	30
ASBURRY	SAMUEL				30	ENGLAND	WM	ENGLISH	BRICK MAKER	045	A	1	26
ASH	ANN		1	F	77	IRELAND	CE	IRISH		043	A	1	54
ASH	BETSIE		1	1	78	ENGLAND	OB	ENGLISH		044	A	2	13
ASH	GEORGE				28	FRANCE	LU	GER	F	044	B	3	11
ASH	GEORGE				56	GER	LU	GER	F	044	B	3	35
ASH	JOHN				30	0	RC	IRISH	TAVERN KEEPER	043	A	4	3
ASH	JOHN				48	IRE	CE	IRE	LAB	044	B	2	62
ASH	JOHN				43	ENGLAND	PM	ENGLISH	FARMER	045	D	3	49
ASH	LIZA	ANN	1	1	12	0	OB	ENGLISH		044	A	2	13
ASH	SAMUEL				53	0	WM	ENGLISH	TAILOR	045	D	3	76
ASHAW	MARGARET		1	1	10	0	EM	AFRICAN		043	E	2	80
ASHBEE	CHARLES				32	ENGLAND	CE	ENGLISH	GARDENER	045	A	1	44
ASHBRIDGE	ISAAC				60	0	WM	ENG	F	045	C	1	32
ASHBRIDGE	JESSE				44	0	WM	ENGLISH	FARMER	045	A	1	15
ASHBRIDGE	LEVI				45	0	CE	ENGLISH	FARMER	045	A	1	15
ASHBRIDGE	SAMUEL		1		49	0	EP	GER	LAB	044	B	3	28
ASHBURN	JOHN				49	0	CE	IRISH	SHOE MAKER	045	D	3	54
ASHBURY	ROBERT				63	IRE	NC	IRE	BLACKSMITH	044	B	3	26
ASHLEE	MATTHEW				45	ENGLAND	CE	ENGLISH	BLACKSMITH	044	C	2	14
ASHLEY	ALBERT				40	ENGLAND	WM	ENGLISH	TAYLOR	045	D	3	1
ASHTON	SAMUEL				52	GERMANY	NC	GERMAN	F	043	B	1	10
ASHTON	SETH				48	0	WM	ENGLISH	GENTLEMAN	043	C		43
ASHWORTH	JONATHAN				27	ENGLAND	WM	ENGLISH	MACHINIST	043	D		9
ASHWORTH	W	H			49	0	CE	ENGLISH	HATER	043	H	2	26
ASHWORTH	W	H			49	ONTARIO	CE	ENGLISH	HATTER	043	H	2	26
ASHWORTH	WM	THOMAS	2			0	WM			043	D		D
ASON	STEPHEN		1		34	IRELAND	WM	IRISH	PLASTERER	043	B	5	21
ASTLE	JOHN				46	ENGLAND	CE	ENGLISH		045	B	1	66
ASTLE	WILLIAM				24	ENGLAND	CE	ENGLISH	LAB	043	E	2	43
ASTLEY	BERTHA		1	1	24	IRELAND	RC	IRISH	SERVANT	045	A	3	1
ASTLY	CHARLES		1		33	ENGLAND	CE	ENGLISH	BOOK KEEPER	043	B	1	34
ATCHISON	SAMUEL				53	IRELAND	OP	IRISH	WEAVER	043	A	3	28
ATHERDON	M		2		1	ENGLAND	WM			044	C	1	D
ATHERLEY	JANE			1	24	ENG	CE	ENG		045	C	1	15
ATHERSDON	JOHN				36	ENGLAND	WM	ENGLISH	LAB	044	C	1	12
ATKIN	ALICE		1	1	56	IRELAND	CE	IRISH		045	B	1	24
ATKIN	THOMAS				41	ENGLAND	EM	ENGLISH	F	043	A	6	34
ATKINS	JOHN			M	59	ENGLAND	CE	ENGLISH	F	043	A	2	37
ATKINSON	ALMA		1	1	16	0	WM	ENGLAND		045	D	2	11
ATKINSON	DAVID				68	ENGLAND	WM	ENGLISH	GENTLEMAN	043	D		53
ATKINSON	DAVID				45	0	WM	ENGLISH	FARMER IRON MOULDER	044	A	1	38
ATKINSON	ELIZABETH		1	1	18	0	WM	ENGLISH		043	D		18
ATKINSON	FRANCES	MARY	1	1	21	ONTARIO	WM	ENGLISH		043	G	2	46
ATKINSON	GEORGE				29	0	PM	ENGLISH	FARM LAB	043	B	1	22
ATKINSON	GEORGE				43	ENGLAND	CE	ENGLISH	F	045	C	2	55
ATKINSON	GEORGE				38	ENGLAND	CE	ENGLISH	F	044	C	2	27
ATKINSON	JACOB				41	0	PM	ENG	CARPENTER	044	B	2	59
ATKINSON	JACOB				42	ENGLAND	CE	ENGLISH	FARMER	045	D	2	62
ATKINSON	JAMES				37	ENGLAND	CE	ENGLISH	SHOEMAKER	043	D		20
ATKINSON	JOHN				63	ENGLAND	PM	ENGLISH	F	043	B	2	22
ATKINSON	JOHN				63	ENGLAND	PM	ENGLISH	F	043	B	2	24
ATKINSON	JOHN				64	ENGLAND	WM	ENGLISH	SHOEMAKER	043	C		29
ATKINSON	JOHN				66	ENGLAND	CE	ENGLISH	F	043	E	2	68
ATKINSON	JOHN				33	0	CE	ENGLISH	F	043	E	3	13
ATKINSON	JOHN				32	0	PM	ENGLISH	F	043	E	3	54
ATKINSON	JOHN				73	ENG	VM	ENG	F	044	B	2	6
ATKINSON	JOHN				28	0	PM	ENGLISH	F	045	C	3	56
ATKINSON	JOHN				40	ENGLAND	CE	ENGLISH	LABOURER	045	D	6	60
ATKINSON	JOSEPH				28	0	PM	ENGLISH	F	043	B	2	26
ATKINSON	JOSEPH				40	ENGLAND	CE	ENGLISH	FARMER	045	A	3	16
ATKINSON	JOSHUA				48	0	EM	ENGLISH	TOLL KEEPER	044	A	2	48
ATKINSON	JUNE		1	1	38	IRELAND	CE	IRISH		043	G	2	46
ATKINSON	LEMINGTON		1		21	0	WM	ENGLISH	WATCHMAKER	043	D		18
ATKINSON	MARGARET		1	1	19	0	LU	ENG	SERVANT	044	B	1	43
ATKINSON	MARY		1	1	17	0	QU	ENGLISH		043	A	1	14
ATKINSON	MARY			1	66	ENGLAND	CE	ENGLISH		045	D	5	15
ATKINSON	ROBERT				50	ENGLAND	PM	ENGLISH	F	043	A	3	31
ATKINSON	ROBERT				61	ENGLAND	PR	ENGLISH	INNKEEPER	043	G	2	51
ATKINSON	ROBERT				33	0	PM	ENGLISH	F	044	A	3	42
ATKINSON	THOMAS				63	ENGLAND	PM	ENGLISH	F	044	A	3	43
ATKINSON	THOS				43	ENGLAND	FW	ENGLISH	AUCTIONEER	043	D		17
ATKINSON	WILLIAM				33	0	PM	ENGLISH	F	043	B	2	26
ATKINSON	WILLIAM				48	ENGLAND	WM	ENGLISH	F	043	E	1	23
ATKINSON	WILLIAM				41	0	WM	ENG	MERCHANT	044	B	2	27
ATKINSON	WILLIAM				34	ENGLAND	CE	ENGLISH	FARMER	045	A	2	21
ATKINSON	WILLIAN		2		1	0	CE	CE		045	C	2	D
ATWELL	ELIJAH				60	ENG	CE	ENG	F	045	C	1	7
ATWELL	LIZA		1	1	19	QUE	CP	IRISH		044	A	2	6
ATWOOD	ADA		1	1	16	ENGLAND	BA	ENGLISH	SERVANT	045	A	1	47
ATWOOD	ELIZA		1	1	19	QUE	WM	IRISH	SERVANT	044	A	3	24
AUBURN	HENRY				42	ENG	CE	ENG	F	045	C	1	73
AUBURN	MARGARET	ANN	1	1	19	0	ZZ	ENGLISH		045	A	1	18
AUGH	JOHN				64	ENGLAND	WM	ENGLISH	MASON	043	F		20
AURBURN	SEPTIMUS		1		44	ENG	CE	ENG		045	C	1	34
AUSTEN	RICHARD		1		15	0	WM	SCOTCH	LAB	044	C	2	47
AUSTIN	ELLEN		1	1	20	IRELAND	WM	IRISH	SERVANT	045	B	1	37
AUSTIN	JAMES				58	IRELAND	WM	IRISH	BANKER	044	C	4	57
AUSTIN	JOHN				68	IRELAND	CE	IRISH	LAB	044	C	4	54
AUSTIN	MARTHA		1	1	28	0	NC	IRISH	SERVANT	043	C		16
AUSTON	THOS				48	IRELAND	WM	IRISH	YEOMAN	044	B	5	29
AVENS	ELIZABETH		1	1	18	ENGLAND	IM	ENGLISH	SERVANT	043	B	4	6
AVISON	JOHN		1		22	ENGLAND	CE	ENGLISH	CARPENTER	045	A	1	62
AWDE	WILLIAM				53	ENGLAND	CE	ENGLISH	BUCHER	044	C	4	48
AWLING	SARAH		1	1	19	0	CP	IRISH		043	A	3	7
AYERAT	WILLIAM				32	ENGLAND	CP	ENGLISH	MERCHANT	045	D	4	42
AYERHART	ELIJAH				44	0	BA	ENGLISH		043	E	3	56
AYERS	ANN			1	53	ENGLAND	WM	ENGLISH		043	E	3	37

SURNAME	NAME1	NAME2	STRAY	SEX	AGE	BIRTHPL	RELIGION	ORIGIN	OCCUP	DIST	SUB_DIST	DIV	PAGE
AYERS	FRANCIS		2		72	ENGLAND	WM		F	043	E	3	D
AYERS	GEORGE				29	ENGLAND	CN	ENGLISH	LABOURER	045	D	4	46
AYERS	WILLIAM				24	ENGLAND	PM	ENGLISH	F	043	B	1	16
AYERST	FRANK				75	ENGLAND	CE	ENGLISH	BAKER	043	F		26
AYLES	ROBERT				63	ENGLAND	BA	ENGLISH	TAILOR	045	D	4	46
AYLWARD	JAMES				70	IRELAND	WM	IRISH	MERCHANT	043	E	1	51
AYLWARD	JOSEPH	L	1		67	IRELAND	WM	IRISH	GENT	043	E	2	50
BABY	CATHERINE			1	55	IRELAND	RC	IRISH		044	C	4	1
BACHE	GEORGE	H			57	ENGLAND	FW	ENGLISH	AGENT	043	D		35
BACKAS	CHARLES	A			33	IRELAND	CE	IRISH	STATIONER	045	B	1	43
BACON	HENRY				54	ENGLAND	CE	ENGLISH	MASON	043	F		20
BACON	JAMES		1		25	ENGLAND	CE	ENGLISH	F LAB	043	F		24
BACON	THOMAS				29	0	CE	ENGLISH	MASON	043	F		22
BADGER	NANCY		1	1	21	ENGLAND	WM	ENGLISH	SERVANT	044	C	2	1
BADGER	THOMAS				44	ENG	EP	ENG	BUTCHER	044	B	3	5
BADGERO	CHARLES				23	0	CN	GERMAN	F	043	B	5	36
BADGERO	ELIZABETH			1	69	US	CN	GERMAN	TAILORESS	043	B	5	12
BADGERO	HENRIETTA		1	1	24	0	LU	GERMAN		045	D	1	38
BADGERO	HENRY				21	0	WM	DUTCH	FARMER	045	D	1	29
BADGERO	JOHN				25	0	WM	DUTCH	FARMER	045	D	1	29
BADGERO	LORENZO				53	US	CN	GERMAN	F	043	B	5	41
BADGERO	MARTINUS		1		53	0	CE	DUTCH	LABORER	045	D	1	31
BADGERO	WILLIAM				37	0	CN	FRENCH	F	043	B	5	13
BADGEROW	ALICE		2	1	2	0	CP			045	C	3	D
BADGEROW	DAVID				77	U STATES	KB	ENGLISH		045	D	5	65
BADGEROW	GEORGE	W			29	ENGLAND	CE	FRENCH	LAWYER	045	A	1	79
BADGEROW	JOSEPH				41	0	KB	ENGLISH	FARMER	045	D	5	65
BADGEROW	LAFAYETTE				37	0	CP	ENGLISH	F	045	C	3	30
BADGEROW	MARTIN				62	US	CP	SCOTCH	F	045	C	3	8
BADGROW	ABRAHAM				30	0	OP	GERMAN	F	043	H	2	29
BADGROW	ABRAHAM				30	ONTARIO	CS	GERMAN	FARMER	043	H	2	29
BADGROW	ELIZABETH		1	1	86	U STATES	CS	ENGLISH		045	D	5	4
BAGEROE	JANE		1	1	23	0	CN	FRENCH	SERVANT	043	A	6	38
BAGG	JANE		1	1	12	SCOT	CS	SCOT		044	B	4	17
BAGG	WILLIAM		1	1	10	SCOT	CS	SCOT		044	B	4	17
BAGNALL	CHAS				27	ENG	CE	ENG	LAB	045	C	1	18
BAGNALL	THOMAS				54	ENGLAND	CP	ENGLISH	LABOURER	045	D	3	64
BAGULEY	FREDERICK				22	0	UP	ENGLISH	F	043	A	6	35
BAGULY	SAMUEL				59	ENGLAND	WM	ENGLISH	LAB	043	C		8
BAILES	GEORGE				43	ENG	WM	ENG	LAB	044	B	2	71
BAILEY	EDWARD				29	SCOT	CP	SCOT	FARM LAB	044	B	1	46
BAILEY	EDWARD				63	ENGLAND	CE	ENGLISH	TAILOR	045	A	2	20
BAILEY	GEORGE				28	ENGLAND	WM	ENGLISH	MILLER	044	A	2	45
BAILEY	GEORGE				45	ENGLAND	CE	ENGLISH	LABOURER	045	D	3	66
BAILEY	GEORGE	SR			55	ENGLAND	PM	ENGLISH	F	044	A	3	14
BAILEY	HENRY	W			58	US	WM	ENGLISH	MERCHANT	045	B	1	41
BAILEY	JAMES				56	ENGLAND	BA	ENGLISH	FARMER	043	G	1	18
BAILEY	JAMES				51	ENGLAND	BC	ENGLISH	CARPENTER	043	H	2	37
BAILEY	JAMES				51	ENGLAND	BC	ENGLISH	CARPENTER	043	H	2	37
BAILEY	JAMES				37	ENGLAND	CE	ENGLISH	LAB	045	B	1	21
BAILEY	MARTIN				39	0	EM	IRISH	F	043	H	2	51
BAILEY	MARTIN				39	ONTARIO	EM	IRISH	FARMER	043	H	2	51
BAILEY	NELSON				30	0	EM	IRISH	F	043	H	2	39
BAILEY	NELSON				30	ONTARIO	EM	IRISH	FARMER	043	H	2	39
BAILEY	REBECCA		1	1	30	IRELAND	WM	IRISH	SALESWOMAN	045	D	1	12
BAILEY	SUSAN			1	52	IRELAND	CP	IRISH		045	B	2	5
BAILEY	THOMAS				60	ENGLAND	CE	ENGLISH	INN KEEPER	044	A	3	8
BAILEY	THOMAS				26	0	PM	ENGLISH	F LAB	044	A	3	8
BAILEY	WILLIAM			M	44	ENGLAND	PM	ENGLISH	F	043	A	2	59
BAILY	GEORGE				48	ENGLAND	CE	ENGLISH		045	B	1	57
BAILY	JOSEPHUS			M	25	ENGLAND	PM	ENGLISH	VETINARY SURGEON	043	A	2	25
BAIN	JAMES				33	ONTARIO	CP	IRISH	FARMER	043	H	2	50
BAIN	JOHN	C			30	SCOTLAND	CP	SCOTCH	SCHOOL TEACHER	045	D	3	17
BAIN	NEIL	K			34	SCOTLAND	PS	SCOTCH	COMM TRAVELLER	045	A	1	32
BAIN	REV JAMES				68	SCOTLAND	PS	SCOTCH	CLERGYMAN	045	C	3	49
BAIN	ROBERT				45	IRELAND	CE	IRISH	LAB	044	C	1	12
BAINE	EDWARD				40	ENGLAND	CE	ENGLISH	LAB	043	E	1	40
BAINE	ELIZABETH		2	1		ONTARIO	CP			043	H	2	D
BAINE	ELIZABETH		2	1		0	CP			043	H	2	D
BAINE	JAMES				33	0	CP	IRISH	F	043	H	2	50
BAIRD	JOHN				45	SCOTLAND	PM	SCOTCH	LAB	044	C	4	88
BAIRD	WILLIAM		1		15	0	WM	ENGLISH	SERVANT	044	C	1	13
BAKE	JOHN				65	IRELAND	WM	IRISH	FARMER	044	C	3	49
BAKER	ABRAHAM				25	0	TU	GERMAN	FARM LAB	043	B	1	26
BAKER	ABRAHAM		2		87	US	TU			045	D	2	D
BAKER	ANNA		1	1	15	0	WM	FRENCH		043	B	3	68
BAKER	BRIDGET		1	1	30	IRELAND	RC	IRISH		044	C	4	74
BAKER	CATHERINE			1	30	IRELAND	RC	IRISH		045	D	2	68
BAKER	CHARLES				46	ENGLAND	EM	ENGLISH	GENT	043	E	2	25
BAKER	CHARLES				62	ENG	CE	ENG	BRICK LAYER	044	B	2	66
BAKER	CHARLES				51	ENGLAND	CE	ENGLISH	FARMER	045	A	1	42
BAKER	CHARLES				36	ENGLAND	CE	ENGLISH		045	B	2	12
BAKER	DAVID				57	0	TU	GERMAN	FARMER	043	B	3	22
BAKER	EDGAR		1	M	7	0	CE	ENGLAND		043	A	5	26
BAKER	EDMUND			M	35	ENGLAND	NR	ENGLAND	WEAVER	043	A	5	32
BAKER	EDWARD				26	0	WM	ENG	SHOEMAKER	044	B	1	59
BAKER	EDWARD				60	ENGLAND	WM	ENGLISH	GARDNER	044	C	4	89
BAKER	ELIAS				24	0	PM	GERMAN	F	043	B	2	16
BAKER	ELIZABETH		1	1	75	0	LU	GER		044	B	1	29
BAKER	ELIZABETH		1	1	8	0	PM	GER		044	B	4	36
BAKER	GEORGE				24	ONTARIO	CN	GERMAN	MERCHANT	043	B	3	50
BAKER	GEORGE				25	ONTARIO	WM	ENGLISH	LABORER	043	G	1	15
BAKER	GEORGE		1		23	ENGLAND	CE	ENGLISH	LAB	045	B	1	45
BAKER	GEORGE				45	0	TU	GERMAN	FARMER	045	D	2	57
BAKER	JACOB				64	0	BA	ENGLISH	FARMER	043	B	3	25
BAKER	JACOB				49	0	TU	GERMAN	CARPENTER	045	D	2	50
BAKER	JESSE				45	0	TU	GER	CARPENTER	044	B	1	44
BAKER	JOEL				48	0	BA	GERMAN	FARMER	043	B	3	20
BAKER	JOHN				40	0	VM	ENGLISH	LABOURER	045	D	5	34
BAKER	JOHN				29	0	TU	GERMAN	FARMER	045	D	2	37
BAKER	JOHN				56	0	TU	GERMAN	FARMER	045	D	2	57
BAKER	JOHN	H			29	ENGLAND	CE	ENGLISH	SEEDSMAN	045	A	2	8
BAKER	JONATHAN				42	0	TU	GERMAN	FARMER	043	B	3	19
BAKER	JONATHAN				40	0	TU	GER	F	044	B	1	44
BAKER	JOSEPHINE	M	1	1	5	0	PM	GERMAN		045	D	4	12
BAKER	JOSEPHUS				31	0	TU	GERMAN	FARMER	045	D	2	60

SURNAME	NAME1	NAME2	STRAY	SEX	AGE	BIRTHPL	RELIGION	ORIGIN	OCCUP	DIST	SUB_DIST	DIV	PAGE
BAKER	MARY			1	45	SCOTLAND	WM	SCOTCH		043	A	1	25
BAKER	MARY		1	1	66	0	TU	GERMAN		043	B	1	25
BAKER	MARY		1	1	16	0	EM	ENGLISH	SERVANT	043	E	2	22
BAKER	MARY		1	1	25	USA	WM	AFRICAN		045	A	1	50
BAKER	MARY	A	1	1	25	0	WM	ENGLISH		045	A	4	10
BAKER	MICHAEL		1		66	0	TU	GERMAN		043	B	1	25
BAKER	MICHAEL				48	IRELAND	WM	GERMAN	F	043	H	1	25
BAKER	MICHAEL				69	US	TU	GERMAN	FARMER	045	D	2	37
BAKER	PETER				37	US	TU	GERMAN	F	043	B	1	25
BAKER	ROSEHANNAH		1	1	14	0	TU	GER	SERVANT	044	B	3	20
BAKER	SAMUEL				47	0	TU	GERMAN	F	043	B	1	16
BAKER	SARAH		1	F	11	0	PS	ENGLISH		043	A	2	30
BAKER	WILLIAM				54	ENGLAND	CE	ENGLISH	F LAB	044	A	1	23
BAKER	WILLIAM				48	GERMANY	LU	GERMAN	FUR DRESSER	045	A	1	10
BALAKESON	JAMES		1		24	ENGLAND	WM	ENGLISH	FARM LAB	044	C	2	38
BALANTINE	MARTHA		1	1	27	0	CP	IRISH		045	C	4	3
BALDRY	FRED'K				28	ENGLAND	KB	ENGLISH	LABOURER	045	D	5	61
BALDWIN	ELIZ			1	50	ENG	CE			044	B	1	25
BALDWIN	GEORGE			M	32	0	CP	ENGLISH	F	043	A	2	24
BALDWIN	HENRY			M	35	0	PM	ENGLISH	MERCHANT	043	A	2	24
BALDWIN	JOSEPH			M	64	ENGLAND	PM	ENGLISH	F	043	A	2	25
BALDWIN	WILLIAM				29	0	CE	ENG	F	044	B	1	26
BALDWIN	WILLIAM	AUGUSTUS			62	0	CE	IRISH	F	044	C	2	1
BALES	JOHN			M	44	0	WM	ENGLISH	F	043	A	1	49
BALES	JOHN				71	ENGLAND	CE	ENGLISH	F	044	C	2	24
BALES	JOSEPH				40	0	WM	ENGLISH	F	044	C	2	33
BALEY	RICHARD		1		19	0	PM	ENGLISH	LAB	045	A	3	12
BALEY	WILLIAM				42	IRELAND	PS	IRISH	LAB	044	C	4	71
BALIEY	JOHN				47	IRELAND	PS	IRISH	OVERSEER OF ROADS	044	C	4	65
BALINTINE	LORETTA	MAY	2	1	4	0				045	C	4	D
BALL	EDWARD				32	ENGLAND	CE	ENGLISH	FARMER	045	A	3	23
BALL	JOHN				44	ENGLAND	WM	ENGLISH	LAB	045	B	1	57
BALL	JOHN				23	ONT	CE	IRISH		045	A	4	2
BALL	MARY			1	55	IRELAND	WM	IRISH		045	D	5	47
BALL	RICHARD		1		37	ENGLAND	CE	ENGLISH	HOSTLER	044	A	3	27
BALL	RICHARD				29	0	EM	ENGLISH	FARMER	045	D	5	40
BALLARD	JAMES				38	ISLE OF WIGHT	QU	ENGLISH	F	043	A	3	13
BALLARD	SILVESTER		1		24	CANADA	PS	IRISH	TANNER	045	D	6	45
BALMER	GEO				52	IRELAND	RC	IRISH	ACCOUNTANT	044	B	5	29
BALWAY	ELIZABETH		1	1	23	0	EM	GERMAN		045	D	1	39
BAMBRIDGE	GEO				67	ENG	WM	ENG		045	C	1	27
BAMBRIDGE	GEORGE		1	M	24	ENGLAND	CE	ENGLISH	SERVANT	043	A	1	49
BAMBRIDGE	GEORGE	YOUL			39	ENGLAND	WM	ENGLISH	BLACKSMITH	045	D	5	2
BAMBRIDGE	L		1	1	32	ENGLAND	CE	ENGLISH	MOULDER	044	B	5	9
BANCOCK	ALFRED				38	ENGLAND	CE	ENGLISH	BUTCHER	045	B	1	65
BANFIELD	JAMES		1		17	ENGLAND	CE	ENGLISH	F LAB	044	A	1	32
BANKS	JOHN				55	ENGLAND	WM	ENGLISH	DRUGGIST	044	C	3	24
BANKS	MICHAEL				34	ENGLAND	PM	ENGLISH	LAB	045	C	3	23
BANKS	SARAH			F	28	0	WM	AFRICA		043	A	5	33
BANN	ANDREW				47	IRELAND	RC	IRISH	FARM LABORER	045	D	1	32
BANNERMAN	ALEXANDER				26	0	WM	SCOTCH	F	043	A	3	44
BANNERMAN	ELIZABETH			1	56	US	PS	IRISH		044	B	3	9
BANNON	PATRICK				30	QUE	RC	IRISH	FARM LAB	044	A	2	40
BARBER	ADA	PERMILLA	2	1	3	ONTARIO	CN			043	G	2	D
BARBER	ALBERT				29	ONTARIO	WM	DUTCH	FARMER	043	G	1	52
BARBER	CHAUNCEY				29	ONTARIO	CN	ENGLISH	FARMER	043	G	2	33
BARBER	EBENESER				28	ENGLAND	WM	ENGLISH	F	045	A	4	17
BARBER	JOSEPH				60	ENGLAND	WM	ENGLISH		044	C	1	57
BARBER	LAWSON				56	U STATES	EP	GERMAN	F	043	A	6	1
BARBOUR	GEORGE				30	US	WM	ENGLISH	LAB	044	B	6	30
BARBOUR	JAMES				42	SCOTLAND	CS	SCOTCH	CURRIER	044	B	6	27
BARCLAY	PETER				53	SCOTLAND	CP	SCOTCH	PRODUCE & COMMISSION	044	C	2	30
BARCLAY	WILLIAM		1		72	ENGLAND	NC	ENGLISH		043	C		25
BARDEN	DAVID	WILLIAM	1		2	0	PM	ENGLISH		045	B	1	63
BARDEN	GEORGE		1		16	0	RC	IRISH	LAB	044	C	2	19
BARDEN	HENRY		1		40	ENGLAND	PM	ENGLISH	BRICK MAKER	045	B	1	63
BARDEN	JOHN	THOMAS	1		4	0	PM	ENGLISH		045	B	1	63
BARDEN	MICHAEL		1		18	0	RC	IRISH	LAB	044	C	2	19
BARDON	MICHAEL				62	IRELAND	RC	IRISH	SHOE MAKER	045	B	2	17
BARGAR	JOSEPH				51	GER	RC	GER	WEAVER	044	B	3	3
BARHEAD	RICHARD			M	45	U STATES	PM	ENGLISH	LAB	043	A	2	29
BARK	CHARLES				55	ENGLAND	PB	ENGLISH	UPHOLSTERER	044	C	4	85
BARKEE	ARCHIBALD				32	SCOTLAND	WM	ENGLISH	MERCHANT	045	D	5	22
BARKER	ANDREW				37	0	PM	ENGLISH	F	044	A	3	4
BARKER	ANN			1	70	ENGLAND	PM	ENGLISH		043	A	4	59
BARKER	DANIEL				54	ENGLAND	WM	ENGLISH	FARMER	045	D	1	27
BARKER	ELIZABETH	ANN	1	1	16	0	WM	SCOTCH		043	H	1	9
BARKER	HENRY				38	ENGLAND	CN	ENGLISH	FARMER	043	G	1	26
BARKER	JAMES	J			37	0	CS	SCOTCH	STORE KEEPER	045	D	3	69
BARKER	JOHN				51	ENGLAND	PM	ENGLISH	LAB	045	A	1	86
BARKER	JOSEPH				23	ENGLAND	CE	ENGLISH	MASON	044	C	3	27
BARKER	MARK	SEN			70	ENGLAND	CE	ENGLISH	FARMER	045	A	2	31
BARKER	RICHARD				41	ENGLAND	CE	ENGLISH	MASON	044	C	3	42
BARKER	ROBERT				49	ENGLAND	CN	ENGLISH	F	043	E	1	40
BARKER	THOMAS		1		12	0	WM	IRISH		043	H	1	9
BARKER	WILLIAM				24	ENGLAND	EM	ENGLISH	FARMER	043	G	2	21
BARKER	WILLIAM		1		14	0	WM	IRISH	TANNER	043	H	1	9
BARKER	WILLIAM	H			45	ENGLAND	CE	ENGLISH	LAB	045	A	1	96
BARKEY	ABRAHAM				40	0	MN	GERMAN	FARMER	043	B	3	73
BARKEY	AMELIA		1	1	19	CANADA	LU	GERMAN		045	D	6	78
BARKEY	CRISTIAN				72	U STATES	MN	GERMAN	FARMER	045	D	6	38
BARKEY	CRISTOPHER				22	CANADA	MN	GERMAN	FARMER	045	D	6	62
BARKEY	HENEREY				65	U STATES	MN	GERMAN	FARMER	045	D	6	63
BARKEY	HENEREY	G			32	CANADA	MN	GERMAN	FARMER	045	D	6	62
BARKEY	JACOB				41	0	CN	GERMAN	F	043	B	2	43
BARKEY	JACOB				30	0	MN	GERMAN	FARMER	043	B	3	72
BARKEY	JOHN				28	0	MN	GERMAN	F	043	B	2	3
BARKEY	JOHN				46	0	CN	GERMAN	CABINET MAKER	043	B	3	4
BARKEY	JOSEPH				31	0	CN	GERMAN	CABINET MAKER	043	B	3	4
BARKEY	PETER	L			27	0	MN	GERMAN	FARMER	045	D	6	17
BARKLEY	JOSEPH				59	CANADA	MN	GERMAN	FARMER	045	D	6	18
BARKS	JAMES				28	ENGLAND	PM	ENGLISH	LAB	044	A	3	50
BARLOW	ROBERT				52	ENG	BA	ENG	SHOP KEEPER	044	B	1	52
BARLOW	WILLIAM				49	QUE	PS	ENGLISH	CARPENTER	044	C	4	91
BARLOW	WILLIAM	H	1		24	ENGLAND	CE	ENGLISH	ENGINEER	043	B	3	32
BARNARD	GEORGE	A			49	0	CE	ENGLAND	MERCHANT	045	D	2	9

SURNAME	NAME1	NAME2	STRAY	SEX	AGE	BIRTHPL	RELIGION	ORIGIN	OCCUP	DIST	SUB_DIST	DIV	PAGE
BARNARD	JAMES	K			40	ENGLAND	CE	ENGLISH	F	043	H	2	15
BARNARD	JAMES	K			40	ENGLAND	CE	ENGLISH	FARMER	043	H	2	15
BARNARD	W	R			33	ENGLAND	CE	ENGLISH	CLERK	043	H	2	4
BARNARD	W	R			35	ENGLAND	CE	ENGLISH	CLERK	043	H	2	4
BARNATH	GEORGE		1		4	0	CP	GERMAN		044	B	6	9
BARNES	CHARLES				50	ENGLAND	CP	ENGLISH	LAB	044	C	2	6
BARNES	CHARLES	G			35	0	WM	ENGLISH	MERCHANT	045	D	5	12
BARNES	ELIJA				71	US	WM	ENGLISH		045	D	3	79
BARNES	JOHN				34	IRE	WM	IRE	MERCHANT	044	B	3	21
BARNES	RICHARD				60	ENGLAND	CO	ENGLISH	CARPENTER	043	B	3	52
BARNET	GANTON				37	ENGLAND	WM	ENGLISH	FARMER	045	D	3	36
BARNET	GRACE			1	39	ENGLAND	WM	ENGLISH		043	B	3	32
BARNETT	GEORGE		1		38	ENGLAND	WM	ENGLISH	F LAB	044	C	1	4
BARNHART	JOHN				76	0	QU	ENGLISH	F	043	E	3	9
BARNS	HEZEKIA				34	ENG	WM	ENG	SADDLER	044	B	2	18
BARNS	ROBERT		1		16	0	NG	ENGLISH	F LAB	043	A	6	54
BARR	ANDREW				48	IRELAND	CE	IRISH	MASON	043	E	2	27
BARR	WILLIAM				52	IRELAND	WM	IRISH	STONE MASON	043	G	1	50
BARRADEL	JOHN			M	35	ENGLAND	NR	ENGLAND	BLACKSMITH	043	A	5	20
BARRADEL	THOMAS			M	45	ENGLAND	WM	ENGLAND	F	043	A	5	20
BARRAGER	GORDON				53	0	EM	GERMAN	LAB	043	H	2	50
BARRAGER	GORDON				53	ONTARIO	EM	GERMAN	LABOURER	043	H	2	50
BARRETT	MARY		1	1	20	INDIA	CE	ENG	HOUSE SERVANT	045	C	1	37
BARRETT	ROBERT	G			48	ENGLAND	CE	ENGLISH	BARRESTER	045	B	2	10
BARRETT	WILLIAM		1		30	IRELAND	WM	IRISH	LAB	045	A	1	67
BARRIE	JOHN	M	2		35	CANADA	DI		YEOMAN	045	D	6	D
BARRIE	MARTHA			1	37	CANADA	DI	ENGLISH		045	D	6	49
BARRISDALE	MARGARET		1	1	75	IRE	PS	IRE		044	B	2	62
BARRON	NANCY			1	74	ENGLAND	PM	ENGLISH		045	A	3	26
BARRY	A	V	1	1	27	0	CE	IRISH	SCHOOL MISTRESS	043	F		19
BARRY	ANN			1	63	SCOT	PS	SCOT		044	B	3	9
BARRY	GANE		1		60	0	CE	ENGLISH	SERVANT	045	A	3	28
BARRY	GARRET				61	IRELAND	RC	IRISH	LABORER	045	D	5	24
BARRY	JAMES				27	IRELAND	RC	IRISH	AGENT	043	D		33
BARRY	JAMES				35	IRELAND	CE	IRISH	DEALER	044	C	4	47
BARRY	JOHN				47	ENGLAND	CE	ENGLISH	F	043	A	3	53
BARRY	JOHN				47	IRELAND	RC	IRISH	LAB	043	D		42
BARRY	MARGARET		1	1	18	0	RC	IRISH	SERVANT	045	D	5	28
BARRY	MICHAEL				50	IRELAND	RC	IRISH	FARMER	045	D	1	25
BARRY	SARAH		1	1	15	0	RC	IRISH	SERVANT	045	D	5	29
BARRY	WILLIAM				41	ENGLAND	CO	ENGLISH	F	043	A	3	56
BARRY	WILLIAM		1		19	0	WM	IRISH	SERVANT	044	C	3	43
BARTHOLOMEW	JOHN				28	0	NG	GERMAN	SAWYER	043	B	3	69
BARTHOLOMEW	PHILLIP				64	0	MN	GERMAN	FARMER	045	D	6	7
BARTLETT	JAMES		1		22	ENGLAND	PM	ENGLISH	WELL DIGGER	043	A	3	47
BARTLETT	WILLIAM	R			67	0	CE	ENGLISH	SUP OF INDIANS	044	C	4	72
BARTON	ANN		2		31	ENGLAND	PM			045	B	1	D
BARTON	FANNY		1	1	6	0	RC	IRISH		044	C	4	6
BARTON	ISAC		1		20	CANADA	BA	SCOTCH		045	D	6	37
BARTON	JOHN				45	ENGLAND	WM	ENGLISH	GARDINER	044	C	3	39
BARTRUM	JAMES		1		28	SCOTLAND	CP	SCOTCH	LAB	045	A	1	100
BARUS	JOSEPH				20	0	CO	GERMAN	MOULDER	044	B	5	39
BARWICK	JOHN				64	RUSSIA	CE	ENGLISH	GENTLEMAN	043	E	1	36
BARWICK	JOSEPH		1		26	ENGLAND	CE	ENGLISH	LAB	044	B	5	5
BASELY	DAVID		1		3	0	PS	ENGLISH		043	E	1	5
BASHLEY	BENJAMIN		1		33	ENGLAND	CE	ENGLISH	LABOURER	045	D	3	45
BASINGTWAIT	WILLIAM				56	ENG	CE	ENG	F	044	B	2	42
BASON	IDA		1	1	3	0	WM	ENGLISH		043	F		19
BASS	MARIAH				45	0	WM	IRISH		044	C	3	54
BASSENDALE	WILLIAM		1		68	ENGLAND	QU	ENGLISH	BLACKSMITH	043	A	6	4
BASSET	ISAAC				52	0	CN	ENGLISH	F LAB	043	B	5	29
BASSET	WILLIAM				27	0	CN	ENGLISH	F	043	B	5	28
BASTEDO	JOSEPH	A			30	0	CE	ENGLISH	MERCHANT	043	D		58
BATEMAN	ARTHUR		1		19	ENG	CE	ENG	SERVANT	044	B	3	5
BATEMAN	ELIZA	ANN	1	1	26	0	CN	ENGLISH	SERVANT	043	D		38
BATEMAN	GEORGE		1		19	0	NC	ENGLISH		043	C		27
BATEMAN	SAMUEL				59	ENGLAND	CE	ENGLISH	LAB	045	A	1	99
BATES	GEORGE				31	ENGLAND	PM	ENGLISH	PAPERMAKER	045	A	1	94
BATES	JONATHAN				43	0	CE	ENGLISH	F	043	B	4	16
BATES	THOMAS				38	IRE	CS	IRE	SHOEMAKER	044	B	4	20
BATHGATE	JAMES				62	SCOTLAND	CS	SCOTCH	F	043	H	1	13
BATT	HENRY	J			31	0	WM	ENGLISH	F	043	E	1	28
BATT	JOHN				60	ENGLAND	WM	ENGLISH	F	043	E	1	28
BATTEY	HENRY		1		23	ENGLAND	PM	ENGLISH	SERVANT	045	A	3	23
BATTICK	WESLEY				31	ENG	WM	ENG	FARM SERVANT	044	B	4	23
BATTY	ADA		1	1	4	ENGLAND	CE	ENGLISH		044	A	2	10
BATTY	ALICE	J	1	1		0	CE	ENGLISH		044	A	2	10
BATTY	RICHARD		1		40	ENGLAND	CE	ENGLISH	F LAB	044	A	2	10
BATTY	THOS				51	ENGLAND	NC	ENGLISH	FARMER	045	A	2	6
BATTY	WILLIAM		1		6	ENGLAND	CE	ENGLISH		044	A	2	10
BAULDRY	ALFRED				34	ENGLAND	PM	ENGLISH	CARPENTER	044	A	3	42
BAVISS	JOHN				56	ENGLAND	CE	ENGLISH	F	043	E	3	13
BAXTER	CHARLES		1		3	0	CO	ENGLISH		044	B	6	7
BAXTER	CHARLES				44	ENGLAND	CE	ENGLISH	FARMER	045	A	1	58
BAXTER	GEO				38	0	CE	ENGLISH	LAB	044	B	5	13
BAXTER	GEORGE				36	SCOT	CP	SCOT	F	045	C	1	12
BAXTER	HANNAH		1	1	12	0	VM	ENG		044	B	3	25
BAXTER	JAS				35	SCOT	WPPES	SCOT	F	045	C	1	14
BAXTER	JOHN		1		20	ENGLAND	CE	ENGLISH		044	C	2	23
BAXTER	MOSELISE		1	1	10	0	VM	ENG		044	B	3	24
BAXTER	SUSANNAH		1	1	7	0	VM	ENG		044	B	3	25
BAYINGTON	WILLIAM				45	ENGLAND	PM	ENGLISH	FARMER	045	D	3	50
BAYLEY	ALBERT		1	M	7	0	PS	IRISH		043	A	2	39
BAYLEY	MARIA	L		1	48	QUEBEC	CE	IRISH	TEACHER	043	D		58
BAYLEY	RICHARD		1		22	ENGLAND	CE	ENGLISH	CARPENTER	045	A	1	96
BAYLEY	SAMUEL		1		21	ENGLAND	CE	ENGLISH	LABOURER	045	A	1	33
BAYLEY	WM		1		40	ENGLAND	CE	ENGLISH	LAB	044	B	5	5
BEADWIN	JOHN		1	M	19	0	CN	ENGLAND	L	043	A	5	18
BEAL	EDWARD				47	0	WM	IRISH	SURGEON	044	C	3	43
BEAL	FRANCES		1	1	20	0	WM	IRISH	SERVANT	044	C	3	44
BEAMISH	ELIZABETH			1	37	IRELAND	WM	IRISH		043	A	4	36
BEAMISH	HENRY				40	0	CE	IRISH	F	044	A	3	44
BEAMISH	JOHN		1		40	0	CE	IRISH	F LAB	044	A	3	54
BEAMISH	WILLIAM				40	IRELAND	CE	IRISH	SHOE MAKER	044	C	3	22
BEAN	AMOS				31	0	CM	ENGLISH	F	044	C	1	40
BEAN	CHAS				46	ENG	PM	ENG	F	045	C	1	63

SURNAME	NAME1	NAME2	STRAY	SEX	AGE	BIRTHPL	RELIGION	ORIGIN	OCCUP	DIST	SUB_DIST	DIV	PAGE
BEAR	JOHN	M			49	ENGLAND	BC	ENGLISH	F	045	C	2	41
BEAR	RICHARD				50	ENGLAND	PM	ENGLISH	F	045	C	3	22
BEAR	SIMON				52	ENGLAND	CE	ENGLISH	F	045	C	3	14
BEAR	WILLIAM				41	ENGLAND	CE	ENGLISH	F	045	C	3	14
BEARD	JONATHAN				49	IRE	CP	IRE	HOTEL KEEPER	045	C	1	21
BEASLEY	GEORGE				27	ENGLAND	WM	ENGLISH	COOPER	045	B	2	11
BEASLEY	SAMUEL				55	0	WM	IRISH	LAB	043	A	3	45
BEASLEY	SAMUEL		1		20	ENGLAND	CE	ENGLISH	COOPER	045	B	2	11
BEASLY	JOHN				28	0	WM	ENGLISH	F	043	A	3	15
BEASTON	JACK		1		25	ENG	CE	ENG	F	044	B	2	45
BEATES	JOHN				76	ENGLAND	CE	ENGLISH	LAB	044	C	4	83
BEATMAN	THOMAS				52	ENGLAND	PM	ENGLISH	FARMER	043	A	4	58
BEATON	ARCHIBALD				40	0	FK	SCOTCH	DENTIST	043	A	3	55
BEATON	CATHARINE		2	1	74	SCOTLAND	CS			043	A	3	D
BEATON	DANIEL		1		21	0	FK	SCOTCH	F LAB	043	A	3	53
BEATON	DONALD				54	SCOTLAND	PS	SCOTCH	F	043	F		7
BEATON	HANNAH		1	1	24	0	PS	IRISH	SERVANT	045	B	2	26
BEATON	JOHN				57	SCOT	CS	SCOT	F	044	B	4	47
BEATSON	THOMAS				60	ENGLAND	SP	ENGLISH	FARMER	043	A	4	48
BEATTEY	GEO				26	ENGLAND	CE	ENGLISH	LAB	044	B	5	5
BEATTIE	JOHN				39	IRELAND	CE	IRISH	MERCHANT	045	B	1	37
BEATTY	JOHN				44	SCOTLAND	PS	SCOTCH	LABORER	045	D	6	71
BEATTY	MARY ?		1	1	8	CANADA	CP	SCOTCH		045	D	6	67
BEATTY	THOMAS		1		22	ONTARIO	CE	ENGLISH	PHYSICIAN	043	H	2	27
BEATTY	THOS				44	IRELAND	WM	IRISH	PHYSICIAN	044	A	2	52
BEATY	ANABELLA		1	1	7	0	CE	IRISH		043	B	4	43
BEATY	FRED		1		2	0	CE	ENGLISH		045	B	1	19
BEATY	JANE		2	1	72	IRELAND	UP			045	D	1	D
BEATY	THOMAS				36	ENGLAND	CE	ENGLISH	FARM LABORER	045	D	1	17
BEATY	WILLIAM				31	0	UP	IRISH	FARMER	045	D	1	42
BEAUCHAMP	JOHN		1		24	ENGLISH	CE	ENGLISH		044	C	3	30
BEAUFORD	CHARLES		1		14	0	WM	FRENCH		043	B	1	41
BEAUFORD	DANIEL		1		22	0	WM	FRENCH	CARVER	043	B	1	41
BEAUMAN	GEORGE				70	GERMAN	LU	GERMANY	CLOCK MAKER	044	B	5	2
BEAUVAIR	JAMES		1		21	0	PM	FRENCH	LAB	044	B	2	63
BEAVER	ALFRED		2		3	ENGLISH	WM			043	D		D
BEAVER	FREDERICK				34	ENGLAND	WM	ENGLISH	MARBLE CUTTER	043	D		50
BEAVER	RACHEL		1	1	8	0	BA	IRISH		043	E	3	56
BEAYNAN	JOHN		1		24	0	WM	ENGLISH	WAGGON MAKER	045	D	3	46
BEAZLEY	THOMAS		1		17	ENGLAND	CE	ENGLISH	SERVANT	045	A	1	38
BECK	JOSEPH				60	ENGLAND	CE	ENGLISH	LAB	045	A	1	102
BECK	THOMAS		1		25	0	WM	ENGLISH	FARM SERVANT	045	A	1	16
BECKET	HANNAH		1	1	73	ENGLAND	CE	ENGLISH		045	A	1	23
BECKET	JOSEPH		1		27	ENGLAND	CE	ENGLISH	HOSTLER	045	D	3	40
BECKET	RICHARD		1		19	ENGLAND	CE	ENGLISH	LABOURER	045	D	5	35
BECKETT	CRAVEN	C			38	ENGLAND	CE	ENGLISH	STORE KEEPER	045	B	1	7
BECKETT	GEORGE		1		24	ENGLAND	CE	ENGLISH	LAB	044	C	2	32
BECKETT	HENRY				32	IRELAND	CE	IRISH	LAB	044	C	4	6
BECKETT	MARGARET		1	1	24	SCOTLAND	CP	SCOTCH		045	B	2	21
BEDFORD	DAVID				43	0	WM	IRISH	JOURNEYMAN	043	E	3	46
BEDFORD	EDWARD		1	M	34	0	RC	ENGLISH	LAB	043	A	2	10
BEDINGFIELD	AMELIA		1	1	31	ENGLAND	CE	ENGLISH		044	A	1	21
BEDINGFIELD	GEORGE				14	0	CE	ENGLISH		044	A	1	16
BEDINGFIELD	JAMES		1		36	ENGLAND	CE	ENGLISH	DROVER	044	A	1	21
BEDLEY	THOMAS		1		30	ENGLAND	CE	ENGLISH	LAB	045	A	1	67
BEEBE	WM	ELLIS			70	U STATES	EM	GERMAN	BLACKSMITH	045	D	5	48
BEECH	WILLIAM				26	ENGLAND	PM	ENGLISH	F LAB	044	A	3	50
BEECHER	ROBT				38	IRELAND	RC	IRISH	LABOURER	045	D	5	25
BEEMISH	CATHERINE		1	1	15	0	WM	ENGLISH	SERVANT	044	C	3	20
BEESLEY	ELSIE	ANN	1	1	23	0	CE	ENGLISH		045	B	1	38
BEESLEY	WILLIAM		1		24	ENGLAND	CE	ENGLISH	BUTCHER	045	B	1	38
BEESTON	FANNY	M	2	1		0	CE			045	D	2	D
BEIRS	JAMES	W			20	IRE	CE	IRE	F	045	C	1	49
BEKERSTAFF	SERAH		1	1	13	CANADA	BA	ENGLISH		045	D	6	64
BELCHER	BENJAMIN				38	0	WM	ENGLISH	BLACKSMITH	044	A	3	1
BELDAM	DAVID				27	ENGLAND	CE	ENGLISH	MILLER	045	C	2	3
BELE	JANE		1	1	13	0	CP	IRISH		045	A	3	11
BELFRY	CHRISTOPHER				52	UNITED STATES	EM	FRENCH	F	043	E	1	22
BELFRY	ORAN				72	0	BA	FRENCH	F	043	E	1	24
BELFRY	PETER				34	0	CN	FRENCH	F	043	E	1	24
BELFRY	WILLIAM				49	ONTARIO	WM	FRENCH	FARMER	043	G	1	35
BELL	ADAM				40	0	PS	SCOTCH	F	045	C	3	34
BELL	AGNESS			1	65	SCOTLAND	PS	SCOTCH		045	B	1	46
BELL	ANDREW		1		11	0	CE	IRISH		045	A	1	56
BELL	ARON				39	ENGLAND	CE	ENGLISH	SAWYER	045	D	4	32
BELL	CARSON			M	67	IRELAND	CP	IRISH	LAB	043	A	2	14
BELL	DONALD				37	SCOTLAND	PS	SCOTCH	LAB	043	F		32
BELL	EDWARD				46	IRELAND	CE	IRISH	F	044	A	2	41
BELL	ELIZABETH			1	66	IRELAND	CE	IRISH		044	A	3	46
BELL	GEORGE				42	SCOT	CS	SCOT	F	044	B	4	38
BELL	GEORGE				37	SCOTLAND	CS	SCOTCH	CARPENTER	045	D	5	28
BELL	GEORGE		1		30	SCOTLAND	CS	SCOTCH	LABOURER	045	D	5	35
BELL	HELEN		1	1	18	NS	CE	SCOTCH		044	A	2	23
BELL	HENDERSON				67	IRELAND	CP	IRISH	WEAVER	045	D	4	41
BELL	HENRY				63	ENG	WM	ENG	LAB	044	B	1	6
BELL	JAMES				42	SCOTLAND	FK	SCOTCH	F	043	A	3	37
BELL	JAMES				20	0	WM	IRISH	BAKER	043	D		17
BELL	JAMES		1		50	IRE	PS	IRE	COOPER	044	B	2	50
BELL	JAMES		1		28	0	EM	SCOT	F	044	B	3	18
BELL	JAMES				34	ENGLAND	PM	ENGLISH	FARMER	045	D	3	58
BELL	JAMES		1		19	SCOTLAND	CS	SCOTCH	LABOURER	045	D	5	35
BELL	JAMES		1		54	SCOTLAND	CP	SCOTCH	LABORER	045	D	2	67
BELL	JAMES				21	0	WM	IRISH	SCHOOL TEACHER	044	C	1	36
BELL	JOHN				65	SCOTLAND	CP	SCOTCH	FARMER	043	A	4	42
BELL	JOHN				24	0	CS	IRISH	F	043	E	2	78
BELL	JOHN				38	ENGLAND	CE	ENGLISH	TEAMSTER	045	A	1	5
BELL	JOHN				41	ENGLAND	CE	ENGAND	FARMER	045	A	3	2
BELL	JOHN				45	ENGLAND	CE	ENGLISH	LAB	045	C	2	9
BELL	JOHN				50	ENGLAND	PM	ENGLISH	WAGGON MAKER	045	D	3	43
BELL	JOHN				30	SCOTLAND	CP	SCOTCH	LABOURER	045	D	4	4
BELL	JOHN		1		33	ENGLAND	CE	ENGLISH		045	D	1	17
BELL	JOHN	E			27	0	EM	ENGLISH	LAB	044	B	6	5
BELL	JOSEPH				37	ENGLAND	CE	ENGLISH	FARM LAB	043	B	2	14
BELL	JOSEPH				63	ENGLAND	WM	ENGLISH	LAB	045	C	2	25
BELL	LETITIA		1	1	17	0	PM	IRISH	SERVANT	044	A	3	43
BELL	MARGARET			1	65	SCOTLAND	CS	SCOTCH		045	D	5	49

SURNAME	NAME1	NAME2	STRAY	SEX	AGE	BIRTHPL	RELIGION	ORIGIN	OCCUP	DIST	SUB_DIST	DIV	PAGE
BELL	MATILDA		2	1	47	IRELAND	CS			043	E	2	D
BELL	MICHAEL	J			42	SCOTLAND	FK	SCOTCH	GENTLEMAN	043	F		15
BELL	MRS ADAM			1	76	SCOTLAND	PS	SCOTCH		045	C	3	34
BELL	ROBERT				53	SCOTLAND	PS	SCOTCH	MERCHANT	045	D	6	68
BELL	ROBERT	J	1		13	O	CE	IRISH		045	A	1	56
BELL	SARAH			1	60	O	CN	FRENCH	WEAVER	043	B	3	35
BELL	SARAH			1	32	ENG	PM	ENG		044	B	1	50
BELL	THOMAS				61	IRELAND	CE	IRISH	TOLL GATE KEEPER	044	A	3	25
BELL	THOMAS				21	O	PM	ENGLISH	LABOURER	045	D	3	32
BELL	THOMAS		1		20	SCOTLAND	CP	SCOTCH		045	D	6	67
BELL	WALTER				43	IRELAND	CE	IRISH	HOTEL KEEPER	043	A	3	25
BELL	WILLIAM				25	IRELAND	CP	IRISH	FARMER	043	A	4	41
BELL	WILLIAM				84	ENGLAND	LU	ENGLISH		043	B	1	17
BELL	WILLIAM		1		9	O	CE	IRISH		045	A	1	56
BELL	WILLIAM				45	ENGLAND	CE	ENGLISH	FARMER	045	A	3	21
BELL	WILLIAM		1		78	ENG	CE	ENG	SHOEMAKER	045	C	1	6
BELL	WILLIAM				62	IRELAND	PS	IRISH	FARMER	045	D	6	36
BELL	WILLIAM	C			36	ENGLAND	WM	ENGLISH	AGENT	045	D	5	9
BELL	WM				50	O	CP	ENG	F	045	C	1	65
BELLAMORE	ANTHONY				56	QUE	RC	FRENCH	F	044	A	1	39
BELLAR	IRA				33	UNITED STATES	CN	GERMAN	PAINTER	043	E	2	38
BEMBRIGE	JOHN		1		25	O	WM	ENGLISH	F LAB	044	A	2	50
BEMON	WILLIAM		1		43	ENGLAND	CE	ENGLISH	SERVANT	045	A	3	15
BEMROSE	FREDRICK				23	O	CE	ENGLISH		044	C	3	63
BENNAN	ELLEN			1	50	IRELAND	RC	IRISH	FARMER	044	A	2	24
BENNET	EMMA		1	1	8	O	BA	SCOTCH		043	B	3	41
BENNET	FRANCES		1	1	32	ONTARIO	WM	GERMAN		043	B	3	50
BENNET	JAMES		1		25	ENGLAND	CE	ENGLISH	SERVANT	045	D	5	64
BENNET	JOHN				25	O	CP	IRE	F	045	C	1	1
BENNET	JOHN	D			37	O	WM	ENGLISH	FARMER	045	D	1	36
BENNET	JOSIAH		1		10	O	UP	ENGLISH		044	B	5	67
BENNET	THOMAS				25	O	PM	GERMAN	LABOURER	045	D	3	48
BENNET	WILLIAM				52	O	PM	DUTCH	F	045	C	3	23
BENNETT	CHARLES				44	POLAND	PM	POLISH	SADLER	045	B	1	51
BENNETT	EDWARD				40	O	CP	IRISH	FARMER	045	D	4	44
BENNETT	ELLEN		1	1	30	IRELAND	WM	IRISH		043	B	3	61
BENNETT	GEORGE				54	O	EM	WELSH	MINISTER	043	E	2	19
BENNETT	GEORGE				69	ENGLAND	CP	ENGLISH	FARMER	045	D	4	44
BENNETT	JACOB				31	O	WM	ENG	F	044	B	1	43
BENNETT	JAMES			M	67	ENGLAND	CE	ENGLAND	F	043	A	5	4
BENNETT	JOHN				30	O	CO	ENG	F	044	B	3	29
BENNETT	JOHN		1		40	O	CE	ENGLISH	HORSE TRAINER	045	A	1	46
BENNETT	MARGARET		1	1	37	IRELAND	RC	IRISH	INMATE	045	B	1	72
BENNETT	MARY		2	1		O	WM			044	B	3	D
BENNETT	PETER				48	ONTARIO	EM	ENGLISH	FARMER	043	G	2	36
BENNETT	RICHARD				28	IRELAND	CE	IRISH	F	044	C	1	46
BENNETT	STEPHEN				75	ENG	CO	ENG	GENT	044	B	3	29
BENNETT	STEPHEN				42	ENG	WM	ENG	F	044	B	3	45
BENNETT	THOS				29	ENGLAND	CE	ENGLISH	MOULDER	044	B	5	18
BENNETT	WILLIAM				30	IRELAND	CE	IRISH	LAB	044	C	1	45
BENNETT	WILLIAM				70	IRELAND	CE	IRISH	F	044	C	1	46
BENNIETT	WILLARD				25	ONTARIO	CN	ENGLISH	FARMER	043	G	1	28
BENNS	PHILIP				48	ENGLAND	CE	ENGLISH	BLACKSMITH	045	A	1	102
BENSON	CHARLES				24	ENGLAND	CE	ENGLISH	MACHINIST	043	D		32
BENSON	DAVID			M	32	O	WM	ENGLISH	FARMER	043	A	1	6
BENSON	EDWARD				69	ENG	CE	ENG	F	044	B	1	41
BENSON	HANNA		2		43	ENGLAND	CE			045	B	1	D
BENSON	WILLIAM		1		14	ENGLAND	CE	ENGLISH	F	045	A	4	33
BENTLEY	JOHN				50	ENGLAND	UT	ENGLISH	PHYSICIAN	043	D		72
BENTLEY	WILLIAM				41	ENGLAND	PM	ENGLISH	SWITCHMAN	043	C		36
BENTLY	THOMAS		1		22	O	CE	ENGLISH	PHYSICIAN	043	H	2	27
BENTLY	WILLIAM				69	ENGLAND	CE	ENGLISH	LAB	043	E	1	35
BENTON	DONALD				47	SCOTLAND	BA	SCOTCH	F	044	B	6	54
BERKETT	JAMES				31	US	BA	AFRICAN	LAB	044	C	4	63
BERMAN	GEORGE		1		23	ENGLAND	CE	ENGLISH	FARM LAB	043	B	1	30
BERNARD	HIRAM				36	O	CE	ENG	F	044	B	2	51
BERNARD	JOHN	G			33	O	CE	ENGLISH	MERCHANT	045	D	2	32
BERNATH	JACOB				28	SWITZERLAND	LU	SWISS	F	044	B	6	39
BERNEY	MARY	ANN	1	1	18	SCOTLAND	PS	SCOTCH		045	D	6	72
BERREY	ROBT		1		45	SCOT	CP	SCOT	LAB	045	C	1	51
BERRIE	ALEX	W			34	SCOTLAND	UP	SCOTCH	TAILOR	043	C		30
BERRY	CALEB		1		20	O	CE	ENGLISH	LAB	043	B	1	34
BERRY	CHARLES		2		1	ONTARIO	CE			043	H	2	D
BERRY	CHARLES		2		1	O	CE			043	H	2	D
BERRY	GEORGE		1		18	ENGLAND	PS	ENGLISH	F LAB	044	C	1	24
BERRY	HENRY				32	ENGLAND	CE	ENGLISH	WAGON MAKER	043	H	2	29
BERRY	HENRY				32	ENGLAND	CE	ENGLISH	WAGON MAKER	043	H	2	29
BERRY	JAMES				50	WEST INDIES	FW	ENGLISH	MERCHANT	045	A	1	38
BERRY	JOHN				44	IRELAND	CE	IRISH	SHOE MAKER	044	C	3	19
BERRY	SARAH		1	1	72	ENGLAND	CE	ENGLISH		043	H	2	11
BERRY	SARAH		1	1	72	ENGLAND	CE	ENGLISH		043	H	2	11
BERRY	WILLIAM		2		72	ENG	PR		BLACKSMITH	045	A	1	D
BERRYMAN	CHARLES				42	ENGLAND	CE	ENGLISH	PHYSICIAN	045	B	1	53
BERRYMAN	FRANCES	EMMELINE	2	1		O	CE			045	B	1	D
BERSTON	CHARLES				27	ENGLAND	CE	ENGLAND	FARMER	045	D	2	22
BERTHON	GEORGE				60	AUSTRIA	RC	FRENCH	ARTIST	045	B	2	25
BERTRAM	HANNAH	ELLA	2	1	5	O	CP			045	C	3	D
BERTRAM	WILLIAM				31	O	CP	SCOTCH	FARM LABOURER	045	C	3	35
BESASSIA	M	J	1	1	17	O	WM	FRENCH	F LAB	044	C	1	10
BESAW	HILDAH		1	1	6	O	CN	ENGLISH		043	B	3	14
BESELEY	SAMUEL		1		75	US	WM	ENGLISH		045	D	3	35
BESEN	SAMUEL		1		15	CANADA	DI	GERMAN		045	D	6	62
BESEW	GEORGE				42	CANADA	DI	FRENCH	COOPER	045	D	6	52
BEST	JAMES				63	ENGLAND	CE	SCOTCH	GARDENER	045	A	1	22
BEST	JAMES				26	ENGLAND	WM	ENGLISH	BRICK MAKER	045	A	1	23
BEST	NICHOLAS				45	ENGLAND	CE	ENGLISH	CARPENTER	044	C	4	14
BESTARD	JOHN				36	ENGLAND	VM	ENGLAND	FARMER	045	D	2	20
BESTARD	ROBERT				38	ENGLAND		ENGLISH	HARNESS MAKER	045	A	4	26
BETHAW	ELIZABETH		1	1	12	O	PM	ENGLISH	SERVANT	045	D	1	49
BETT	GEORGE		1		26	ONT	PM	IRISH	LAB	045	A	4	3
BETTERIDGE	ELIZABETH			1	50	ENGLAND	WM	ENGLISH	F	044	A	3	14
BETTERIDGE	GEORGE				47	O	PM	ENGLISH	FAR	044	A	3	6
BETTERIDGE	GEORGE				25	O	WM	ENGLISH	F LAB	044	A	3	14
BEUMASTER	R	ANTHONY			77	GERMANY	RC	GERMAN	LABOURER	045	D	6	1
BEVAN	GEORGE				55	ONTARIO	RC	FRENCH	FARMER	043	G	2	16
BEWELL	EDWARD				32	ENGLAND	PM	ENGLISH	LAB	043	B	2	21

SURNAME	NAME1	NAME2	STRAY	SEX	AGE	BIRTHPL	RELIGION	ORIGIN	OCCUP	DIST	SUB_DIST	DIV	PAGE
BEWELL	WILLIAM				46	ENGLAND	NC	ENGLISH	F	043	A	6	3
BEXFIELD	THOMAS				40	ENGLAND	PM	ENGLISH	LAB	045	B	1	19
BEYNION	GEORGE				57	IRELAND	WM	IRISH	CLERGYMAN	044	C	3	56
BEYNON	JANE		1	1	38	O	WM	IRISH		045	B	1	27
BEYNON	JOHN			M	46	O	WM	IRISH	F	043	A	1	13
BEYNON	JONATHAN			M	60	IRELAND	WM	IRISH	F	043	A	1	13
BEYNON	LYDIA			F	67	O	WM	IRISH	F	043	A	1	17
BICE	GEORGE				34	U STATES	NC	ENGLISH	PUMPMAKER	043	C		54
BIELBY	JOHN				54	ENGLAND	PM	ENGLISH	F	043	B	5	8
BIELBY	RICHARD				62	ENGLAND	WM	ENGLISH	F	044	B	6	21
BIELBY	WILLIAM				26	ENGLAND	WM	ENGLISH	F	043	B	5	8
BIGCANOE	CHARLES				37	O	WM	CHIPPAWA	F	043	H	2	56
BIGCANOE	CHARLES				37	ONTARIO	WM	CHIPPAWA		043	H	2	56
BIGCANOE	ELISSE		1	1	35	O	WM	CHIPPAWA		043	H	2	56
BIGCANOE	ELISSE		1	1	35	ONTARIO	WM	CHIPPAWA		043	H	2	56
BIGCANOE	EMMA		2	1		ONTARIO	WM			043	H	2	D
BIGCANOE	EMMA		2	1			WM			043	H	2	D
BIGCANOE	PAUL		1		9	O	WM	CHIPPAWA		043	H	2	56
BIGCANOE	THOMAS				43	O	WM	CHIPPAWA	F	043	H	2	56
BIGCANOE	THOMAS				43	ONTARIO	WM	CHIPPAWA	FARMER	043	H	2	56
BIGFORD	FRANCIS		1		30	ENGLAND	CE	ENGLISH	LAB	043	B	2	12
BIGGINS	MARY		1	1	10	O	CE	IRE		044	B	2	21
BIGHAM	ELIZABETH		1	1	5	O	CS	IRISH		043	D		84
BIGHAM	ELIZABETH		1	1	20	O	PM	ENGLISH	SERVANT	044	B	6	42
BIGHAM	JOHN				37	IRELAND	PS	IRISH	F	043	E	3	16
BIGHAM	MARGARET		1	1	8	O	CE	SCOTCH		043	D		75
BIGHAM	MARGARET		1	1	30	IRELAND	CS	IRISH		043	D		84
BIGHAM	MARGARET		1	1	7	O	CS	IRISH		043	D		84
BIGHAM	MARTHA		1	1	37	O	WM	IRISH	SERVANT	043	D		2
BIGHAM	SAML	W			43	O	OB	IRISH	F	044	A	2	13
BIGHAM	SARAH		1	1	9	O	CS	IRISH		043	D		84
BIGHAM	TIMOTHY		1		10	O	CS	IRISH		043	D		84
BIGSAIL	WILLIAM				27	ONTARIO	WM	OJIBWAY INDIAN	HUNTER AND FISHER	043	G	1	60
BILLINGS	CHARLES		1		18	QUE	CE	FRENCH	CARRIAGE MAKER	045	D	5	6
BILLINGSLY	RICHARD				40	O	CE	ENGLISH	LAB	043	H	2	20
BILLINGSLY	RICHARD				40	ONTARIO	CE	ENGLISH	LABOURER	043	H	2	20
BILLINGTON	ANN		1	1	69	O	EM	ENGLISH		045	D	5	47
BILLINSKY	FRANK				36	FRANCE	WM	FRENCH	PLASTERER	044	C	4	83
BIMROSE	FREDRICK		1		23	ENGLAND	NR	ENGLISH	SERVANT	044	C	3	6
BINNS	GEO	M			34	ENGLAND	CO	ENGLISH	PRINTER	043	D		21
BIRBECK	WM				59	ENGLAND	WM	ENGLISH	LAB	044	A	2	34
BIRCH	JAMES				33	O	WM	ENGLISH	LAB	043	B	5	40
BIRCH	JAMES				60	ENGLAND	CE	ENGLISH	LAB	043	H	2	7
BIRCH	JAMES				60	ENGLAND	CE	ENGLISH	LABOURER	043	H	2	7
BIRCHARD	TAMAR		1		70	UNITED STATES	QU	ENGLISH		043	E	1	41
BIRD	EDWARD				27	ENGLAND	CE	ENGLISH	BUTCHER	045	A	1	18
BIRD	GEORGE				38	ENGLAND	CE	ENGLISH	LABOURER	044	C	3	64
BIRD	JAMES				38	ENGLAND	WM	ENGLISH	F	045	C	2	55
BIRDSMITH	FRANCIS			M	34	IRELAND	PR	IRISH	LAB	043	A	1	57
BIRNIE	WILLIAM				42	SCOTLAND	CS	SCOTCH	LABOURER	045	D	5	70
BISHIP	WARNER				30	O	WM	FRENCH	LAB	044	B	4	45
BISHOP	ALFRED				40	ENG	CE	ENG	LAB	044	B	1	63
BISHOP	CHARLES				23	ENGLAND	CE	ENGLISH	LAB	044	C	3	10
BISHOP	HANNAH		1	1	34	O	CE	ENGLISH	SEAMSTRESS	043	D		4
BISHOP	JOHN		1		17	ENGLAND	WM	ENGLISH	FARM LAB	044	C	2	43
BISHOP	LOUISA		1	1	56	ENGLAND	CE	ENGLISH		043	D		4
BISHOP	LUSIA		1		13	O	LU	ENG		044	B	3	18
BISHOP	MARTHA		1	1	15	O	LU	ENG		044	B	3	18
BISHOP	MARY	ANN			54	ENGLAND	WM	ENGLISH		045	B	1	48
BISHOP	PRISCILLA		1	1	11	O	CE	ENGLISH		043	D		4
BISHOP	SAUL		1		22	ENGLAND	CE	ENGLISH	LAB	044	B	5	9
BISHOP	THOMAS		1		64	ENGLAND	CE	ENGLISH	MASON	043	D		3
BISHOP	WARREN				70	U STATES	CS	IRISH?	CLOTH DRESSER	045	D	5	50
BISHOP	WM		1		20	ENGLAND	CE	ENGLISH	MOULDER	044	B	5	9
BISSELL	JOSHUA				38	NS	PM	FRENCH	AGENT	044	B	6	14
BISSET	PETER				53	SCOTLAND	CP	SCOTCH	FARMER	043	G	2	21
BLACK	ALEXANDER				70	SCOTLAND	CS	SCOTCH	LAB	044	B	6	7
BLACK	ALEXR		1		24	O	PS	SCOTCH		044	B	5	45
BLACK	ANGUS				32	O	CS	SCOTCH	LAB	044	B	6	10
BLACK	FANNY		1	1	23	O	CE	IRISH		043	A	6	49
BLACK	IRINY		1		16	O	CE	ENGLISH	F LAB	044	A	3	53
BLACK	ISABELLA		1	1	48	SCOTLAND	CS	SCOTCH		043	B	1	29
BLACK	JACK				28	O	WM	ENGLISH	CLERK	043	D		26
BLACK	JARED				32	O	WM	SCOTCH	F	043	A	6	47
BLACK	JOHN				52	QUE	NG	IRISH	HOTEL KEEPER	043	A	6	49
BLACK	JOHN				46	IRELAND	CE	IRISH	HOTEL KEEPER	044	A	2	45
BLACK	JOHN				55	SCOT	CP	SCOT	ON RAILROAD	044	B	1	27
BLACK	JOHN		1		14	O	UP	SCOTCH		044	B	5	68
BLACK	JOHN				35	SCOTLAND	CS	SCOTCH	LAB	044	B	6	8
BLACK	JOSEPH			M	23	IRELAND	WM	IRISH	LAB	043	A	1	71
BLACK	NEIL		1		15	O	PS	SCOTCH		044	B	5	70
BLACK	ROBERT				45	IRE	CE	IRE	SHOE MAKER	044	B	2	44
BLACK	ROBERT				38	O	WM	IRISH	FARMER	045	D	1	51
BLACK	SAMUEL		1		41	SCOTLAND	CP	SCOTCH	LAB	045	A	2	30
BLACK	WILLIAM				48	ENGLAND	CE	ENGLISH	F	044	A	3	54
BLACK	WILLIAM		1		26	SCOTLAND	PS	SCOTCH	LAB	044	C	4	81
BLACKBIRD	JOHN				60	ONTARIO	WM	OJIBWAY INDIAN	HUNTER AND FISHER	043	G	1	61
BLACKBIRD	JOHN		2		83	ONTARIO	WM		HUNTER AND FISHER	043	G	1	D
BLACKBIRD	PETER				36	ONTARIO	WM	OJIBWAY INDIAN	HUNTER AND FISHER	043	G	1	59
BLACKBIRD	POLLY				75	ONTARIO	WM	OJIBWAY INDIAN		043	G	1	59
BLACKBIRD	SUSAN		2	1	7	ONTARIO	WM			043	G	1	D
BLACKBURN	GEORGE		1		31	ENGLAND	CE	ENGLISH	GENTLEMAN	044	C	4	57
BLACKBURN	JANE			F	45	IRELAND	PS	IRISH		043	A	2	31
BLACKBURN	JOHN	M		M	55	IRELAND	RC	IRELAND	F	043	A	5	21
BLACKBURN	MARGARET		1	1	41	IRELAND	CE	IRISH		044	A	3	23
BLACKBURN	WILLIAM				24	O	CP	IRISH	WHEELWRIGHT	044	A	3	46
BLACKMOORE	JOHN				35	ENG	CE	ENG	LAB	044	B	1	31
BLACKWOOD	THOMAS				36	O	CE	ENGLISH	BOOKKEEPER	045	B	1	36
BLAIN	ANNIE		1	F	25	O	CP	SCOTCH		043	A	2	24
BLAIN	JANE		1	1	14	O	PM	SCOTCH		045	D	4	26
BLAIN	STEWART				44	SCOTLAND	PS	SCOTCH	BLACKSMITH	044	B	5	7
BLAIR	JOHN				21	UNITED STATES	WM	ENGLISH	MANUFACTURER OF MELO	043	B	4	22
BLAISDALE	CHARLES				26	ENG	EP	ENG	MOULDER	044	B	2	7
BLAKE	GEORGE				36	O	CS	IRISH	LAB	044	B	6	7
BLAKE	JOSEPH				33	CANADA	WM	ENGLISH	LABOURER	045	D	6	24
BLAKE	LOUISA			1	56	ENG	CE	IRISH		044	B	1	15

SURNAME	NAME1	NAME2	STRAY	SEX	AGE	BIRTHPL	RELIGION	ORIGIN	OCCUP	DIST	SUB_DIST	DIV	PAGE
BLAKE	MARTHA		1	1	18	0	LU	IRISH	SERVANT	044	B	6	55
BLAKE	MARY			1	65	0	WM	IRISH		044	B	5	32
BLAKE	SAMUEL				35	0	CE	IRISH	BARRESTER	045	B	2	31
BLAKE	THOMAS				60	IRELAND	CP	IRISH	LABORER	045	D	1	9
BLAKELEY	ROBERT		1		60	IRELAND	CS	IRISH	CARPENTER	045	D	5	29
BLAKELY	FRANK		1		25	ENG	CE	ENG	LAB	045	C	1	53
BLAKER	ABSOLEM				60	U STATES	PM	ENGLISH	F	043	A	6	32
BLAKER	CHARLES				29	0	EM	ENGLISH	F	043	A	6	18
BLANCH	JOHN		1		17	0	CE	IRISH		043	B	4	7
BLANCHARD	ALEXANDER				36	QUEBEC	RC	FRENCH	CARPENTER	043	H	2	1
BLANCHARD	ALEXANDER				36	QUEBEC	RC	FRENCH	CARPENTER	043	H	2	1
BLANCHARD	HENRY				24	ENGLAND	CE	ENGLISH	COACH MAN	045	B	2	19
BLANCHARD	JOSEPH				41	QUEBEC	RC	FRENCH	COOPER	043	H	2	14
BLANCHARD	JOSEPH				41	QUEBEC	RC	FRENCH	COOPER	043	H	2	14
BLANCHARD	ROBT				24	0	PM	ENGLISH	AGENT	044	A	2	30
BLAND	THOMAS		1		40	ENGLAND	CE	ENGLISH	LABOURER	045	D	3	40
BLANEY	JOHN				22	IRELAND	RC	IRISH		044	C	3	25
BLEVINS	DAVID				47	IRELAND	CE	IRISH	LAB	043	F		13
BLEWITT	JOHN				55	ENGLAND	LU	ENGLISH	F	044	B	5	28
BLISHER	WILLIAM			M	56	ENGLAND	CE	ENGLISH	HOTEL KEEPER	043	A	1	55
BLISS	JAMES				33	ENGLAND	WM	ENGLISH	WAGGON MAKER	045	D	3	46
BLISS	JOHN	C			61	ENGLAND	BA	ENGLISH	TAILOR	043	E	1	51
BLISSARD	THOMAS				28	0	CN	IPISH	F	043	E	3	11
BLIZARD	JAMES				29	0	CE	ENGLISH	F	043	E	2	49
BLIZARD	OLIVER				60	NB	CE	ENGLISH	F	043	E	2	49
BLOGG	ALBERT		1		10	0	CE	ENGLISH		045	A	2	39
BLOGG	JOHN		1		20	0	CE	ENGLISH		045	A	2	39
BLOGG	KENDRICK		1		18	0	CE	ENGLISH		045	A	2	39
BLOGG	THOMAS		1		18	0	CE	ENGLISH		045	A	2	39
BLOIS	JOHN				23	0	CE	ENGLISH	MILLER	043	D		57
BLOIS	MARY ANN			1	48	ENGLAND	CE	ENGLISH		043	F		11
BLONG	HENRY				30	IRELAND	CE	IRISH	BUTCHER	045	A	1	77
BLOUGH	DAVID		1	M	22	0	LU	SCOTCH	FARMER	043	A	1	41
BLOUGH	GARRETT				48	US	LU	GER	F	044	B	4	30
BLOUGH	JOHN				33	0	LU	GER	F	044	B	4	6
BLOUGH	MARIA		1	1	73	US	LU	ENG		044	B	3	40
BLUE	CATHARIN		1	1	18	0	CP	SCOTCH		045	A	4	25
BLUE	DONALD				55	SCOTLAND	OP	SCOTCH	F	043	A	3	29
BLUE	GRACE		1	1	11	0	CP	SCOTCH		045	A	4	25
BLUNT	WILLIAM		1		28	ENGLAND	CE	ENGLISH	LABOURER	045	D	3	18
BLYTHE	JOHN				49	SCOTLAND	PS	SCOTCH	SAWER	043	E	3	36
BOADWAY	ALEX				28	0	DI	GERMAN	LAWYER	043	B	2	43
BOADWAY	ISABEL			F	42	0	BA	ENGLAND		043	A	5	25
BOAG	ISABELLA		2	1	85	ENGLAND	CS			043	E	2	D
BOAK	EDWARD				37	ONTARIO	WM	IRISH	FARMER	044	C	3	51
BOAKE	FRANCIS				35	0	WM	IRISH	F	043	B	5	1
BOAKE	JOHN	T			31	0	WM	IRISH	F	043	B	5	26
BOAKE	WILLIAM				30	0	CE	ENGLISH	TEAMSTER	044	C	4	24
BOAKS	JESSE				27	ENGLAND	CE	ENGLISH	LAB	043	E	1	47
BOASLEY	LYDIA	A	1	1	7	0	EM	IRISH		043	E	2	80
BOASLEY	MARY	E	1	1	10	0	EM	IRISH		043	E	2	80
BOCHI	WILLIAM				58	ENGLAND	PM	ENGLISH	FARMER	043	G	1	45
BODDY	ISABELLA		1	1	51	IRELAND	CE	IRISH		043	D		40
BODEN	JAMES				40	ENGLAND	CE	ENGLISH	BLACKSMITH	043	B	3	20
BODEWAY	NANCY		1	1	17	CANADA	MN	GERMAN		045	D	6	55
BODFISH	FREDERICK				23	ENGLAND	NC	ENGLISH	F	043	B	4	16
BODFISH	GEORGE				51	ENGLAND	CE	ENGLISH	F	043	A	6	15
BODIE	MOSES				42	ENG	LU	ENG	F	044	B	3	40
BODWAY	ISAC		1		13	CANADA	MN	GERMAN		045	D	6	62
BOEY	DAVID				57	ENGLAND	CS	ENGLISH	F	043	E	2	63
BOEY	JAMES				61	ENGLAND	CS	ENGLISH	F	043	E	2	67
BOGART	CHARLES				27	0	CN	GERMAN	F	043	B	4	21
BOGART	FERDINAND			M	38	0	CN	GERMANY	F	043	A	5	22
BOGART	JOHN	N			48	0	QU	GERMAN	F	043	E	1	18
BOGART	JOSEPH				42	0	WM	GERMAN	CARTER	043	D		35
BOGART	JOSHUA				53	0	CN	GERMAN	F	043	B	4	21
BOGART	LYMAN				37	0	CN	GERMAN	F	043	B	4	20
BOGART	MARTIN	J		M	41	0	CN	GERMANY	F	043	A	5	20
BOGART	MOSES	W			37	0	WM	GERMAN	CLERK	043	D		36
BOGART	PETER			M	37	0	CN	GERMANY	FARMER	043	A	5	19
BOGART	PHILIP				66	0	CN	GERMAN	F	043	B	4	20
BOGGS	MARGARET			1	54	IRELAND	CE	IRISH		045	B	1	30
BOGINGTON	FRANCES		1	1	14	0	CE	ENGLISH		045	A	3	39
BOHLA	HENRY				50	GERMANY	LU	GERMAN	LAB	045	D	4	28
BOID	DANIEL	P	1		16	0	UP	ENG		044	B	4	36
BOID	ELIZABETH		1	1	8	0	UP	ENG		044	B	4	36
BOID	WESLEY		1		11	0	UP	ENG		044	B	4	36
BOLAIN	ROBERT				35	IRELAND	CE	IRISH	F	043	F		18
BOLAN	ANDREW				60	IRELAND	RC	IRISH	F	043	E	3	15
BOLAN	EDWARD				95	IRELAND	RC	IRISH		043	E	3	14
BOLAN	MICHEAL				40	IRELAND	RC	IRISH	F	043	E	3	17
BOLAN	PATRICK				30	IRELAND	RC	IRISH	F	043	E	3	15
BOLAND	CATHARINE		1	1	55	IRELAND	RC	IRISH		043	D		76
BOLAND	THOMAS				30	IRELAND	RC	IRISH	GARDNER	044	C	4	50
BOLDOCK	JOHN				40	ENGLAND	CE	ENGLISH	F LAB	044	A	3	10
BOLER	JOHN				50	ENGLAND	CE	ENGLISH	CONFECTIONER	044	C	4	5
BOLITHO	HENRY				48	ENG	CE	ENG	SHOP KEEPER	044	B	1	47
BOLLAN	DENNIS				45	UNITED STATES	EM	AFRICAN		043	E	3	2
BOLLAN	LAWRANCE				32	IRELAND	CN	IRISH	F	043	E	3	51
BOLSTER	WILLIAM				50	0	CE	IRISH		043	H	1	8
BOLTON	ELISA	ANN	2	1	14	0	PM			043	A	6	D
BOLTON	ISAAC				30	0	BA	ENGLISH	F	044	A	3	11
BOLTON	JAMES				60	ENGLAND	NR	ENGLISH	F	043	A	6	12
BOLTON	JAMES				30	0	BA	ENGLISH	F	044	A	3	12
BOLTON	MARTIN				29	0	WM	ENGLISH	F	043	A	6	12
BOLTON	THOMAS				31	0	BA	ENGLISH	F	044	A	3	11
BOLTON	THOMAS				70	ENGLAND	BA	ENGLISH	F	044	A	3	11
BOLTON	WILLIAM				55	ENG	CE	ENG	F	044	B	4	49
BOLTON	WILLIAM				40	ENGLAND	PS	ENGLISH	BLACK SMITH	045	D	6	50
BOMGASSER	ADAM				36	GERMANY	LU	GERMAN	PEDLER	043	E	1	44
BOMSTOCK	SOVERAN				88	GERMANY	RC	GERMAN	FARMER	045	A	1	10
BOND	ELLEN			1	41	ENGLAND	CE	ENGLISH		043	A	4	46
BOND	GEORGE				56	IRELAND	CE	IRISH	F LAB	044	A	1	30
BOND	HANNAH		1	1	82	NOVA SCOTIA	WM	ENGLISH		044	C	2	8
BOND	JNO	J			41	ENGLAND	CE	ENGLISH	LUMBER AGENT	043	C		42
BOND	JOHN				50	ENGLAND	WM	ENGLISH	DRUGGIST	043	C		26

SURNAME	NAME1	NAME2	STRAY	SEX	AGE	BIRTHPL	RELIGION	ORIGIN	OCCUP	DIST	SUB_DIST	DIV	PAGE
BOND	JOHN				32	ENGLAND	EM	ENGLISH	MILLER	043	D		2
BOND	JOHN	R			27	0	CE	ENGLISH	DRUGGIST	043	A	4	16
BOND	JOSEPH				31	ENGLAND	CE	ENGLISH	LAB	043	C		41
BOND	JOSEPH				41	ENGLAND	CE	ENGLAND	FARMER	045	D	2	15
BOND	LYDIA	R		1	39	ENGLAND	XC	ENGLISH	MILLINERY STORE	043	D		14
BOND	MARY		1	1	20	0	PS	ENG		044	B	3	36
BOND	RICHARD				58	ENGLAND	CE	ENGLISH	F	044	C	4	2
BOND	SARAH		2	1	24	ENGLAND	CE		DOMESTIC SERVANT	044	C	4	D
BOND	THOMAS				54	ENGLAND	CC	ENGLISH	FARMER	045	A	3	40
BOND	WILLIAM				26	ENGLAND	WM	ENGLISH	MILLER	043	B	4	23
BOND	WILLIAM				40	NOVA SCOTIA	CN	ENGLISH	AGENT	043	D		56
BOND	WILLIAM		1		22	0	CO	ENGLISH	BARBER	043	D		69
BONE	BENJAMIN		2			0	NG	ENG		044	B	1	D
BONE	JOHN				40	ENG	WM	ENG	F	044	B	1	56
BONE	THOMAS				56	ENG	PM	ENG	F	044	B	1	65
BONE	WILLIAM				30	ENG	PM	ENG	LAB	044	B	1	51
BONIFACE	HANNAH			1	62	ENGLAND	OB	ENGLISH		044	A	2	47
BONN	MARY		1	1	51	IRELAND	CE	IRISH	SERVANT	044	B	5	2
BONNARD	ROBERT				56	ENGLAND	WM	ENGLISH	MILLER	045	D	1	52
BONNER	CHARLOTTE		2	1	23	ONT	CP			043	A	3	D
BONNER	JAMES				60	SCOTLAND	CP	SCOTCH	F	043	A	3	61
BONNER	MARY		2	1	52	SCOTLAND	CP			043	A	3	D
BONNETS	ROBERT				36	GER	LU	GER	PAINTER	044	B	4	34
BONNITT	WILLIAM		1		50	ENGLAND	CE	ENGLISH	LABORER	043	G	1	16
BOOK	EDWARD				60	IRELAND	WM	IRISH	FARMER	044	C	3	56
BOOL	BERTLE				26	0	WM	IRISH	FARMER	044	C	3	51
BOOL	EDWARD				73	IRELAND	WM	IRISH	CARPENTER	044	C	3	17
BOOL	JOHN	E			39	0	WM	IRISH	FARMER	044	C	3	73
BOOL	JOHN	P			48	0	WM	IRISH	FARMER	044	C	3	69
BOOL	JOSEPH				37	0	WM	IRISH	CARPENTER	044	C	3	17
BOOL	MARGRET		2	1	64	0	WM			044	C	3	D
BOOL	ROBERT				48	IRELAND	WM	IRISH	FARMER	044	C	3	53
BOOL	THOMAS				50	0	WM	IRISH	GARDENER	044	C	3	62
BOOMER	JOHN		1		55	IRELAND	WM	IRISH	LAB	044	C	2	10
BOOMER	SARAH		2		40	0	CE			045	B	1	D
BOOMER	WILLIAM				57	IRELAND	WM	IRISH	LAB	044	C	2	10
BOOTH	ANN		1	1	18	CANADA	WM	ENGLISH	SERVANT	045	D	6	70
BOOTH	CHARLES		1		15	0	BA	ENGLISH		045	C	2	47
BOOTH	CHARLES				50	ENGLAND	CE	ENGLISH	LAB	045	C	2	54
BOOTH	JAMES				43	ENG	CE	ENG	F	044	B	1	41
BOOTH	JOHN				55	ENG	CE	ENG	LAB	045	C	1	19
BOOTH	JOHN		1		20	CANADA	WM	ENGLISH	SERVANT	045	D	6	70
BOOTH	JOSEPH				29	0	WM	ENGLISH	AGENT	045	C	2	30
BOOTH	MARK				50	ENGLAND	CE	ENGLISH	LAB	045	C	2	15
BOOTH	MICHAEL				48	ENGLAND	CE	ENGLISH	MILLER	045	D	1	28
BOOTH	SAMUEL				33	ENGLAND	WM	ENGLISH	BUILDER	045	A	1	62
BOOTH	WILLIAM				35	ENGLAND	PM	ENGLISH	BUTCHER	045	B	1	56
BOOTH	WILLIAM				31	0	CE	ENGLISH	LAB	045	C	2	42
BOOTH	WILLIAM	C			25	ENGLAND	CE	ENGLISH	BUTCHER	045	A	1	46
BOOTHBY	EDWIN				25	0	EM	ENGLISH	BLACKSMITH	045	D	4	43
BOOTHBY	THOMAS				55	ENG	EA	ENG	BLACKSMITH	044	B	2	6
BORDEN	CHARLES			M	42	0	QU	GERMANY	F	043	A	5	29
BORDEN	THOMAS			M	45	0	QU	GERMANY	F	043	A	5	44
BORELAND	JOHN		2		20	IRELAND	RC		GARDNER	044	C	4	D
BORELAND	MICHAEL				22	IRELAND	RC	IRISH	GARDNER	044	C	4	36
BORELAND	THOMAS				50	IRELAND	RP	IRISH	GARDNER	044	C	4	36
BORELAND	WILLIAM				52	IRELAND	CE	IRISH	F	044	C	4	33
BORKA	SUSAN			1	60	US	EM	GER	WEAVER	044	B	4	30
BORMICK	JOSEPH	A			58	ENGLAND	PB	ENGLISH	BUTCHER	045	B	1	8
BORSTWICK	EMMA		1	1	10	0	QU	ENGLISH		043	A	6	11
BOSANKO	ALFRED		1		19	0	CE	ENGLISH	PAINTER	043	C		9
BOSANKO	ALICE		1	1	6	0	CE	ENGLISH		043	C		9
BOSANKO	JOHN		1		32	ENGLAND	CE	ENGLISH	CARPENTER	043	C		8
BOSANKO	RICHARD		1		17	0	CE	ENGLISH		043	C		9
BOSANKO	SAMUEL	A	1		15	0	CE	ENGLISH		043	C		9
BOSLEY	ELIZABETH		1	1	28	0	CE	IRISH	SERVANT	044	B	5	11
BOST	JOHN		1		23	ENGLAND	WM	ENGLISH	LABOURER	045	A	1	39
BOSTON	FRANCIS		1		25	ENGLAND	CE	ENGLISH	FARMER	044	C	3	45
BOSTWICK	GEORGE				60	0	CE	ENGLISH		045	B	1	6
BOSTWICK	JOHN				48	0	NG	ENGLISH	F	043	B	4	39
BOSWELL	JAMES				33	ENGLAND	CP	ENGLISH	LAB	045	C	4	24
BOSWORTH	EDWARD				68	ENGLAND	CE	ENGLISH	F	043	E	3	28
BOSWORTH	EDWARD		1		22	ENGLISH	PM	ENGLISH	LABORER	045	D	2	20
BOSWORTH	MARK				27	0	CE	ENGLISH	F	043	E	3	10
BOSWORTH	SARAH		1	1	64	IRELAND	CE	IRISH		043	A	4	3
BOSWORTH	VINCENT				24	ENGLAND	CN	ENGLISH	F	043	E	1	46
BOTHAM	MOSEY				43	ENGLAND	WM	ENGLISH	TAILOR	043	A	4	19
BOTHAM	THOMAS				61	ENGLAND	PM	ENGLISH	F	044	A	1	38
BOTSFORD	ALBERT		1		30	0	CO	ENGLISH	CLERK	043	D		82
BOTSFORD	JOSEPH				39	0	WM	GERMAN	CABINET MAKER	043	D		24
BOTSFORD	NELSON				34	0	CS	ENGLISH	CARPENTER	043	D		20
BOTSFORD	TIMOTHY				38	0	CO	FRENCH	SADDLER	043	D		12
BOUCHER	THOMAS				40	IRELAND	CE	IRISH	LAB	044	C	4	7
BOUDEVOIN	PETER				54	CANADA	CE	FRENCH	COOPER	045	D	6	49
BOULTBEE	ALFRED				43	ENGLAND	CE	ENGLISH	BARRISTER	043	D		88
BOURCHIER	JAMES	A			74	ENGLAND	CE	ENGLISH		043	H	2	7
BOURCHIER	JAMES	D			76	ENGLAND	CE	ENGLISH		043	H	2	7
BOURKE	WILLIAM				33	IRELAND	RC	IRISH	INNKEEPER	044	C	2	34
BOVAIR	CHARLES			M	53	0	EM	FRENCH	FAR	043	A	1	66
BOVAIR	JOSEPH			M	58	0	EM	FRENCH	F	043	A	2	55
BOVAIR	MARY	J		F	36	0	EM	WELSH	F	043	A	1	40
BOWDEN	EMMA		1	1	10	0	CE	ENGLISH		044	A	3	26
BOWDEN	JOSEPH				48	ENGLAND	WM	ENGLISH	CARPENTER	045	C	3	45
BOWDEN	WM	HENRY			47	ENGLAND	CE	ENGLISH	BAKER	043	D		16
BOWDEN	WM	HENRY			23	ENGLAND	CE	ENGLISH	BAKER	043	D		83
BOWEN	CHAS	C			61	IRE	CE	IRE	YEOMAN	045	C	1	19
BOWER	ELIZABETH		1	1	76	UNITED STATES	EM	SCOTCH		043	E	2	73
BOWERMAN	AMOS				64	0	QU	ENGLISH	F	043	B	4	41
BOWERMAN	AMOS		2		64	0	QU		F	043	B	4	D
BOWERMAN	JAMES				30	0	QU	ENGLISH	TEAMSTER	043	B	4	46
BOWERS	HENRY				45	ENGLAND	WM	ENGLISH	LABOURER	045	D	5	70
BOWERS	JOHN				29	0	CE	ENGLISH	LAB	043	E	1	46
BOWES	ANTHONY				36	0	EM	ENG	F	044	B	1	31
BOWES	ANTHONY		2		80	ENG	WM		GENTLEMAN	044	B	1	D
BOWES	FRANCES				59	IRELAND	CE	IRELAND	LABORER	045	D	2	25
BOWES	GEORGE				35	ENGLAND	WM	ENGLISH	LAB	045	B	2	36

SURNAME	NAME1	NAME2	STRAY	SEX	AGE	BIRTHPL	RELIGION	ORIGIN	OCCUP	DIST	SUB_DIST	DIV	PAGE
BOWES	JAMES				72	SCOTLAND	CP	SCOTCH	F	045	C	3	55
BOWES	MARTHA			1	57	ENG	WM	ENG		044	B	1	6
BOWES	ROBERT				38	SCOTCH	CP	SCOTCH	FARMER	045	D	6	66
BOWES	WILLIAM				51	ENG	EM	ENG	F	044	B	1	36
BOWLAND	DAVID				42	0	WM	AFRICAN	LAB	044	C	4	18
BOWLIN	CATHRINE		1	1	70	0	WM	CHIPPAWA		043	H	2	55
BOWLIN	CATHRINE		1	1	70	ONTARIO	WM	CHIPPAWA		043	H	2	55
BOWLING	GEORGE				45	ENGLAND	PM	ENGLISH	CARTER	045	B	1	20
BOWMAN	ELIZA		1	1	40	0	CP	IRISH		045	D	2	51
BOWMAN	HANNAH		1	1	13	0	UV	SCOTCH		045	D	6	17
BOWMAN	JAMES				35	0	UP	IRISH	F	044	B	1	32
BOWMAN	JAMES				44	0	CE	IRISH	WOOLEN MANUFACTURER	045	D	4	42
BOWMAN	JAMES				66	IRELAND	CP	IRISH	FARMER	045	D	1	17
BOWMAN	JOHN				44	0	CP	IRISH	FARMER MILLER	045	D	4	42
BOWMAN	MARY	JANE	1	1	16	0	CP	IRISH		045	D	2	51
BOWS	MARY		1	1	56	IRELAND	RC	IRISH	SERVANT	044	C	4	48
BOWSEN	HENRY				54	ENGLAND	CE	ENGLISH	FARMER	043	G	2	21
BOWSER	CECILIA			1	64	ENGLAND	WM	ENGLISH		043	H	1	17
BOWSER	CHARLES	HENRY			31	ENGLAND	QU	ENGLISH	F	043	A	6	1
BOWSER	GEORGE		1		40	ENGLAND	CE	ENGLISH	OSTLER	044	C	4	32
BOWSER	MATTHEW		1	M	21	ENGLAND	CE	ENGLAND	SAWYER	043	A	5	6
BOWSER	THOMAS			M	32	0	PR	ENGLISH	FAR	043	A	1	69
BOWSER	WILLIAM				30	ENGLAND	NC	ENGLISH	LAB	043	B	4	1
BOWYE	LACHLIN			M	71	SCOTLAND	PS	SCOTCH	F	043	A	2	15
BOYANTON	JOHN				21	0	CE	ENGLISH	F	044	C	1	36
BOYANTON	JOHN		2		73	ENGLAND	CE		F	044	C	1	D
BOYANTON	THOMAS				27	0	WM	ENGLISH	F	044	C	1	35
BOYCE	ROBERT			M	50	IRELAND	PR	IRISH	LABOURER	043	A	1	26
BOYCE	SARAH	MORRISON		1	47	U STATES	KB	ENGLISH		045	D	5	49
BOYCE	SYLVESTER				50	0	KB	ENGLISH	FARMER	045	D	1	35
BOYD	GEORGE				52	ENGLAND	CE	ENGLISH	MERCHANT	045	B	2	27
BOYD	JAMES		1		40	IRELAND	NR	IRISH	LABOURER	043	A	4	24
BOYD	JAMES				55	IRELAND	CP	IRISH	FARMER	045	D	5	63
BOYD	JOHN				45	IRELAND	CS	IRISH	F	043	H	1	5
BOYD	JOHN				27	0	WM	IRISH	CARPENTER	045	D	5	46
BOYD	JOSEPH				55	IRELAND	CP	IRISH	FARMER	045	A	2	28
BOYD	MALCOLM				64	SCOTLAND	CP	SCOTCH	F	043	A	3	53
BOYD	NEIL				26	0	FK	SCOTCH	F	043	A	3	53
BOYD	RICHARD				45	IRELAND	CE	IRISH	LABORER	043	G	1	16
BOYD	RICHARD				27	ONTARIO	CE	IRISH	INN KEEPER	043	G	2	43
BOYD	ROBERT				52	IRELAND	CE	IRISH	FARMER	045	A	1	59
BOYD	WILLIAM				29	0	CP	IRISH	MERCHANT	045	D	5	59
BOYD	WM		1		24	0	CE	IRE	LAB	045	C	1	32
BOYER	BENJAMIN				32	0	TU	GERMAN	F	043	B	2	3
BOYER	CATHRINE			1	50	0	TU	GERMAN		045	D	6	17
BOYER	JOHN				54	0	TU	GERMAN	F	043	B	2	7
BOYER	SAMUEL		2		4	0	TU		F	043	B	2	D
BOYLE	ANDREW				42	SCOT	PS	SCOT	F	044	B	1	37
BOYLE	DAVID				50	SCOT	PS	SCOT	F	044	B	2	9
BOYLE	MARY			1	58	IRELAND	RC	IRISH		045	D	2	41
BOYLE	MARY		1	1	23	0	CE	IRISH		044	C	4	74
BOYLE	MRS			1	52	ENGLAND	CE	ENGLISH		045	D	4	30
BOYLES	JOHN				76	U STATES	NG	GERMAN	FARMER	045	D	6	66
BOYLES	LENORD	S			41	CANADA	WM	GERMAN	FARMER	045	D	6	66
BOYLES	MARIA			1	50	IRE	RC	IRISH	SERVANT	044	B	2	12
BOYLIN	RATCHEL		1	1	16	0	CE	IRISH	SERVANT	044	C	3	6
BOYNES	CHARLES				32	ENGLAND	CE	ENGLISH	BRICK MAKER	045	B	1	60
BOYNTON	ALINSON				44	0	NC	SCOTCH	PEDDLAR	043	C		5
BOYNTON	FRANCIS				40	ENGLAND	CE	ENGLAND	FARMER	045	D	2	17
BOYNTON	JOHN				37	ENGLAND	PM	ENGLISH	FARMER	045	D	6	5
BOYNTON	PETER				32	0	CE	ENGLISH	FARMER	045	D	2	26
BOYNTON	THOMAS				36	ENGLAND	WM	ENGLISH	FARMER	045	D	1	47
BOYNTON	WILLIAM				21	0	NC	ENGLISH	BLACKSMITH	043	C		51
BOYNTON	WILLIAM				72	ENGLAND	CE	ENGLISH	FARMER	045	D	4	5
BOYNTON	WILLIAM				40	ENGLAND	CE	ENGLISH	FARMER	045	D	2	66
BOYS	ELIZA		2	F	24	0	WM			043	A	2	D
BOYS	ISAIC			M	50	ENGLAND	WM	ENGLISH	F	043	A	2	39
BRACK	JAMES				33	0	PS	SCOTTISH	FARMER	044	C	1	18
BRACKEN	EMMA	J	1	1	11	ONTARIO	CP	ENGLISH		043	G	1	25
BRACKEN	GEORGE				34	0	CE	ENG	F	044	B	2	14
BRACKEN	RACHAEL			1	66	ENG	CE	ENG		044	B	2	14
BRACKIN	JAMES		1		25	0	CE	IRISH	SCHOOL TEACHER	043	B	1	8
BRADBURN	ALEXANDER		1		70	IRELAND	WM	IRISH		045	D	3	55
BRADFIELD	ROBT				37	ENGLAND	CE	ENGLISH	LAB	043	C		57
BRADIE	RACHEL		1	1	8	0	QU	SCOTTISH		043	B	4	38
BRADLEY	ELLEN		1	1	18	0	WM	ENG	SERVANT	044	B	4	32
BRADLEY	JOHN				50	IRELAND	WM	IRISH	COOPER	045	D	1	11
BRADLEY	MINNIE		1	1	2	0	PM	ENGLISH		043	B	1	42
BRADLEY	RODGER				21	ENGLAND	WM	ENGLISH	SERVANT	044	B	6	44
BRADLEY	THOMAS				56	ENGLAND	CE	ENGLISH	F	043	A	3	55
BRADSHAW	ANNIE		1	1	2	0	CE	ENGLISH		043	E	1	45
BRADSHAW	FANNY		1	1	28	ENGLAND	CE	ENGLISH	HOUSEKEEPER	043	E	1	45
BRADSHAW	GEORGE				31	ENGLAND	CE	ENGLISH	BUTCHER	044	C	3	4
BRADSHAW	JOHN				72	ENGLAND	CE	ENGLISH	PEDLAR	043	E	2	48
BRADSHAW	SARAH		1	1	24	0	CO	ENGLISH		043	D		70
BRADWELL	MARY		2	1	7	IRELAND	CE			045	D	6	D
BRADY	ELLEN		1	1	20	0	RC	IRISH		044	C	4	79
BRADY	GEORGE		1		27	0	RC	IRISH	STEWART	044	C	4	78
BRADY	JOHN	CW	1		11	ONTARIO	PS	SCOTCH		043	G	2	40
BRADY	JOSEPH		1		26	IRELAND	RC	IRISH	STEWART	044	C	4	79
BRADY	MARY	JANE	1	1	0	0	RC	IRISH		044	C	4	79
BRAINBRIDGE	SAMUEL				52	ENG	CE	ENG	F	044	B	1	14
BRAITHWAIT	WILLIAM				33	ONTARIO	CE	ENGLISH	LABORER	043	G	2	20
BRAITHWAITE	MARK	M			49	ENGLAND	CO	ENGLISH	STORE KEEPER	045	D	3	1
BRAITHWAITE	WILLIAM				25	0	WM	ENGLISH	SCHOOL TEACHER	045	D	3	10
BRAKEN	ELIZABETH			1	45	IRE	CE	IRE		044	B	2	33
BRAKEY	ISAIAH				47	0	WM	IRISH	FARMER	044	C	3	54
BRAKEY	JAMES				25	0	WM	IRISH	FARMER	044	C	3	33
BRAMMAR	ALFRED				30	0	CN	ENGLISH	F	043	E	1	15
BRAMMAR	CLARISSA			1	46	ONTARIO	EM	ENGLISH		043	G	1	32
BRAMMAR	GEORGE				25	0	CE	ENGLISH	BLACKSMITH	043	E	1	46
BRAMMAR	JOSEPH				62	ENGLAND	CE	ENGLISH	FARMER & SAWYER	043	E	1	15
BRAMMER	EDWARD				26	0	CN	ENGLISH	BLACKSMITH	043	E	2	14
BRAMMER	EDWARD				62	ENGLAND	CE	ENGLISH	BLACKSMITH	043	E	2	37
BRAMMER	GEORGE				63	ENGLAND	CE	ENGLISH	F	043	E	2	12
BRAMMER	JOHN				32	0	CE	ENGLISH	F	043	E	2	57

SURNAME	NAME1	NAME2	STRAY	SEX	AGE	BIRTHPL	RELIGION	ORIGIN	OCCUP	DIST	SUB_DIST	DIV	PAGE
BRAMMER	ROBERT				34	0	WM	ENGLISH	WHEELWRIGHT	043	E	2	33
BRAMPTON	WILLIAM		1		40	ENGLAND	CE	ENGLAND	LABORER	045	D	2	4
BRAND	JAMES		1		35	ENG	CE	ENG	LAB	044	B	2	73
BRANDIGE	JEREMIAH		1		26	0	WM	GER	LAB	044	B	3	43
BRANDON	EDWARD				51	IRELAND	PM	IRISH	FARMER	043	A	4	53
BRANERD	ELI		1		20	0	WM	ENGLISH		043	C		57
BRANNER	WILLIAM				40	IRELAND	RC	IRISH	LABOURER	045	D	3	69
BRANTON	JAMES				45	ENG	EP	ENG	F	044	B	2	1
BRANTON	THOMAS				55	ENGLAND	WM	ENGLISH	LAB	045	B	1	39
BRAUGH	JAMES		1		22	SCOTLAND	CS	SCOTCH	F LAB	044	A	1	14
BREAK	ADAM		2		83	U STATES	MN		FARMER	045	D	5	D
BREAK	DANIEL				40	0	MN	GERMAN	FARMER	045	D	5	37
BREAK	DAVID				39	0	VM	GERMAN	FARMER	045	D	5	36
BREAK	JOSEPH				36	0	MN	GERMAN	FARMER	045	D	5	36
BREAKEY	ANDREW				34	0	WM	IRISH	FARMER	044	C	3	34
BREAKEY	JAMES			M	52	0	CE	IRISH	F	043	A	1	54
BREAKEY	JOSEPH				28	0	WM	IRISH	GENTLEMAN	044	C	3	34
BREAKON	CHRISTOPHER				35	ONTARIO	CE	ENGLISH	FARMER	043	G	1	19
BREARTON	JOHN				60	IRELAND	CE	IRISH	LAB	045	B	1	70
BREATHENE	VIOLETE		1	1	3	0	RC	IRISH		043	H	2	24
BREATHOUR	VIOLETE		1	1	3	ONTARIO	RC	IRISH		043	H	2	24
BRECKON	DAVID				43	0	NC	ENGLISH	F	043	E	1	25
BRECKON	JAMES				29	ONTARIO	CN	ENGLISH	FARMER	043	G	1	43
BRECKON	JAMES				37	0	CE	ENGLAND	CARPENTER	045	D	2	28
BRECKON	JOHN				41	0	CE	ENGLISH	WAGGON MAKER	045	C	4	35
BRECKON	JOSEPH				48	0	CE	ENGLISH	F	043	F		16
BRECKON	WILLIAM		1		11	ONTARIO	WM	ENGLISH		043	G	1	46
BRECKON	WILLIAM				25	ONTARIO	WM	ENGLISH	FARMER	043	G	1	46
BREDEN	JOHN				51	IRELAND	WM	IRISH	CLERGYMAN	045	A	4	31
BREEDON	FREDERICK				36	0	WM	ENGLISH	F	043	A	3	43
BREEDON	HENRY				29	0	WM	ENGLISH	F	043	A	3	43
BREEDON	WILLIAM				50	ENGLAND	WM	ENGLISH	F	043	A	3	19
BREEN	JULIA		1	1	15	0	RC	IRISH	SERVANT	044	C	2	9
BREEN	MARTIN				43	IRELAND	RC	IRISH	LAB	044	C	2	21
BREEN	PATRICK	J			40	IRELAND	RC	IRISH	TAILOR	043	D		27
BREEN	SARAH		2	1	45	IRELAND	RC			044	C	2	D
BREENE	ANNE		2	1	24	IRE	RC			044	B	1	D
BREENE	JOHN				62	IRE	RC	IRISH	F	044	B	1	22
BREIN	THOMAS				50	IRELAND	RC	IRISH	FARMER	045	A	3	12
BREISE	MATTHEW		1		30	IRELAND	RC	IRISH	LAB	045	A	2	21
BRELSFORD	CHARLES				51	U STATES	WM	ENGLISH	GENTLEMAN	043	D		66
BRENIFT	JOHN		1		49	IRELAND	RC	IRISH	COOPER	044	B	6	57
BRENNAN	ELLEN		2	1	23	0	RC		SERVANT	044	C	4	D
BRENNAN	JOHN				33	IRELAND	RC	IRISH	DROVER	044	A	3	42
BRENNAN	JOHN				40	IRELAND	RC	IRISH	BLACKSMITH	044	C	2	34
BRENNAN	LAWRENCE				50	IRELAND	RC	IRISH	FARM SERVANT	045	C	3	48
BRENNAN	MARTIN				76	IRE	RC	IRE	F	044	B	3	46
BRENNAN	MICHAEL				50	IRELAND	RC	IRISH	GARDNER	044	C	4	48
BRENNAN	PATRICK		1		68	IRELAND	WM	IRISH	F	044	C	4	73
BRENT	ELISA			1	52	ENGLAND	WM	ENGLISH		045	B	1	18
BRESNAN	CATHERINE		1	1	11	0	RC	IRISH		043	A	4	4
BRESNAN	WILLIAM		1		10	0	RC	IRISH		043	A	4	4
BRETHEAR	ROBERT				23	0	CE	IRISH	F	043	H	1	20
BRETHOUR	JAMES				29	0	WM	IRISH	F	043	H	1	22
BRETHOUR	JOHN				24	0	CE	IRISH	F	043	H	1	26
BRETHOUR	SAMUEL				52	IRELAND	CE	IRISH	F	043	H	1	26
BRETT	JAMES			M	30	0	EM	ENGLISH	WHEELWRIGHT	043	A	2	48
BRETT	JOHN				63	ENGLAND	EM	ENGLISH	FARMER	045	D	1	3
BREULS	JOHN	A			56	ENGLAND	BA	GERMAN	WAGGON MAKER	045	D	6	40
BREWER	FANNY		1	1	33	0	CN	ENGLISH	SERVANT	043	E	1	15
BREWER	JOHN				33	ENGLAND	WM	ENGLISH	LAB	044	C	2	15
BREWER	JOSEPH		1		61	ENG	WM	ENG	DROVER	045	C	1	54
BREWSTER	SUSANNA		2	1	22	ONTARIO	EM			043	G	1	D
BRIAN	D	MARY	1	1	21	0	RC	IRISH		043	A	3	33
BRIAN	LOUISA	ANN	1	1	19	SCOTLAND	CP	SCOTCH		044	C	2	28
BRIBERGER	BENJAMIN				47	CANADA	MN	GERMAN	FARMER	045	D	6	57
BRICKENDEN	JAMES				35	ENGLAND	CE	ENGLISH	LAB	045	A	1	15
BRICKER	WILLIAM				43	0	CE	ENGLISH	FARMER	045	D	3	30
BRICKERSTAFF	ANN				16	0	WM	IRISH		043	B	3	33
BRICKERSTAFF	JOHN				76	IRELAND	PS	IRISH	SHOEMAKER	043	B	3	58
BRICKNELL	CHARLES				37	ENGLAND	WM	ENGLISH	FARMER	045	D	3	59
BRICKNELL	ISACK				35	ENGLAND	PM	ENGLISH	FARMER	045	D	3	72
BRICKNELL	WILLIAM				44	ENGLAND	PM	ENGLISH	FARMER	045	D	4	4
BRIDAL	JOHN			M	32	ENGLAND	EM	ENGLISH	LAB	043	A	1	50
BRIDAL	JOHN			M	56	ENGLAND	CE	ENGLISH	LAB	043	A	1	51
BRIDGELAND	JAMES	W			54	0	WM	ENGLISH	ENGINEER	044	C	4	71
BRIDGELAND	SAMUEL				52	ENGLAND	CE	ENGLISH	SHOEMAKER	043	B	4	11
BRIDGES	SUSANNA		1	1	29	0	CN	IRISH		045	D	3	66
BRIDGLAND	CLARK	B			56	ENGLAND	WM	ENGLISH	F	044	C	3	7
BRIDGLAND	JAMES				25	0	WM	ENGLISH	F	044	C	3	8
BRIGGS	CALEB				52	0	ZZ	IRISH	F	043	E	2	11
BRIGGS	JANE			1	35	IRELAND	CP	IRISH		045	D	4	41
BRIGGS	JOHN				24	ENG	CE	ENG	LAB	044	B	2	75
BRIGGS	JONATHAN				55	0	UV	ENGLISH	F	043	E	2	11
BRIGGS	JOSEPH		2		7	0				045	D	4	D
BRIGHAM	ROBERT	W			27	ENGLAND	WM	ENGLISH	F LAB	043	A	6	12
BRIGHAM	THOMAS				30	ENGLAND	WM	ENGLISH	F LAB	043	A	6	12
BRIGHT	JOHN				78	QUE	CE	ENGLISH	SHOEMAKER	045	A	1	62
BRIGHT	MARY	L	1	1	12	0	WM	ENGLISH		045	A	1	62
BRIGHT	WILLIAM				45	0	CE	ENGLISH	CARPENTER	045	A	1	63
BRIKENSTAFF	HARIETT		1	1	14	CANADA	WM	GERMAN		045	D	6	61
BRILLINGER	ABRAHM				50	0	TU	GERMAN	F	043	B	2	15
BRILLINGER	ANDW				37	0	PM	GERMAN	CARPENTER	043	B	2	19
BRILLINGER	BENJAMIN				38	0	NG	ENG	F	044	B	1	44
BRILLINGER	DANL				50	0	MN	GERMAN	F	043	B	2	21
BRILLINGER	GEORGE				70	0	TU	GERMAN	F	043	B	1	15
BRILLINGER	GEORGE				55	0	TU	GERMAN	F	043	B	2	16
BRILLINGER	JACOB				31	0	WM	DUTCH	F	044	B	2	15
BRILLINGER	JOHN				60	0	TU	GERMAN	F	043	B	1	15
BRILLINGER	JOHN				78	UNITED STATES	MN	GERMAN	F	043	B	2	29
BRILLINGER	JOHNATHAN				38	0	NG	GERMAN	FARMER	045	D	2	19
BRILLINGER	LEVI				44	0	CE	GERMAN	FARMER	045	D	2	53
BRILLINGER	MARIEA		1	SEX	27	0	PM	GERMAN		043	B	2	18
BRILLINGER	MARTIN				43	0	MN	GERMAN	F	043	B	2	20
BRILLINGER	MARY		1	1	60	0	BA			045	D	2	20
BRILLINGER	PETER				53	0	TU	GERMAN	F	043	B	2	28

SURNAME	NAME1	NAME2	STRAY	SEX	AGE	BIRTHPL	RELIGION	ORIGIN	OCCUP	DIST	SUB_DIST	DIV	PAGE
BRILLINGER	SARAH		1	1	16	O	BA			045	D	2	20
BRILLINGER	WILLIAM		1		32	O	BA			045	D	2	20
BRIMSON	JOHN				46	ENGLAND	WM	ENGLISH	WHEELWRIGHT	043	D		63
BRIMSON	STEPHEN			M	66	ENGLAND	PM	ENGLISH	FARMER	043	A	1	3
BRINE	JOHN				30	IRELAND	CE	IRISH	LABOURER	043	B	3	66
BRINGILER	SERAH		1	1	17	CANADA	WM	GERMAN		045	D	6	61
BRIRLS	HANNAH		1	1	84	ENGLAND	CO	ENGLISH		043	B	3	28
BRISON	ROBERT				47	IRELAND	CE	IRISH	F	044	C	3	12
BRITHAM	WILLIAM	L			40	ENGLAND	WM	ENGLISH	BANK CLARK	045	B	1	71
BRITT	PATRICK		1		60	IRELAND	RC	IRISH	LABOURER	045	A	1	23
BRITT	WILLIAM				60	IRELAND	RC	IRISH	LAB	043	D		37
BRITTAN	C				55	ENG	CE	ENG	SHOE MAKER	045	C	1	49
BRITTIAN	WILLIAM				25	ENGLAND	PM	ENGLISH	LABOURER	045	D	3	17
BRITTON	ANNE		1	1	27	O	RC	ENGLISH		044	C	4	43
BRITTON	EDWARD		1		30	IRELAND	RC	IRISH	BUTCHER	044	C	4	43
BRITTON	FREDERICK		1		4	O	RC	IRISH		044	C	4	43
BRITTON	THOMAS				40	ENGLAND	WM	ENGLISH	LABOURER	045	D	3	38
BROAD	HENRY				40	ENGLAND	WM	ENGLISH	CARPENTER	043	C		42
BROAD	THOMAS				45	ENGLAND	WM	ENGLISH	LAB	043	E	3	34
BROCK	EDWARD				74	US	WM	ENGLISH	GENERAL MERCHANT	045	A	4	7
BROCK	ELIAS				50	O	PM	IRISH	F	045	A	4	8
BROCK	FRANCIS				24	O	WM	ENGLISH	LABOURER	044	C	1	28
BROCK	JANE			1	79	SCOT	PS	SCOT		044	B	2	76
BROCK	MARY			1	60	ONT	PM	SCOTCH		045	A	4	3
BROCK	WILLIAM		1		27	O	WM	IRISH	LAB	043	B	5	43
BROCKVILLE	THOMAS				75	ENGLAND	CE	ENGLISH	BRICKMAKER	045	A	1	16
BRODER	HENRY				69	IRELAND	CE	IRISH		044	C	4	64
BRODERICK	RICHARD				60	IRELAND	RC	IRISH	LABOURER	045	A	1	55
BRODEY	CHARLES				36	SCOTLAND	CP	SCOTCH	F	043	B	2	15
BRODIE			2			O	CP	CP		043	B	3	D
BRODIE	ALEXANDER				41	SCOTLAND	FP	SCOTCH	COOPER	043	C		12
BRODIE	JAMES				42	SCOTLAND	WM	SCOTCH	F	043	A	6	55
BRODIE	JAMES				47	SCOTLAND	CP	SCOTCH	FARMER	043	B	3	36
BRODIE	JESSIE			1	62	SCOTLAND	WM	SCOTCH		043	A	6	21
BRODIE	JESSY		1	1	33	SCOTLAND	PS	SCOTCH		045	B	1	17
BRODIE	JOHN				70	IRELAND	RC	IRISH	LAB	043	E	3	17
BRODIE	JOHN				56	SCOTLAND	PS	SCOTCH	SHOEMAKER	043	E	3	18
BRODIE	JOHN		1		52	SCOTLAND	OP	SCOTCH	BLACKSMITH	043	H	2	37
BRODIE	JOHN		1		52	SCOTLAND	CP	SCOTCH	BLACKSMITH	043	H	2	37
BRODIE	MARY			1	50	ENGLAND	EM	ENGLISH	TAILORESS	043	D		47
BRODIE	THOMAS		1		13	O	CP	SCOTCH		043	D		82
BRODLY	GEORGE				56	ENGLAND	CE	ENGLISH	LAB	044	B	6	10
BRODY	ELIZABETH		1	1	15	O	CE	SCOTCH		043	D		75
BROGAN	HONORA			1	49	IRELAND	RC	IRISH		043	E	1	6
BRONDGEIST	EMELINE		1	1	55	QUEBEC	CE	ENGLISH		045	B	1	53
BROOK	ESTHER		1	1	67	IRELAND	CS	IRISH		043	D		80
BROOK	HENRY		1		24	ENG	WM	ENG	LAB	045	C	1	14
BROOK	RICHARD				47	O	CE	ENGLISH	FARMER	045	A	3	38
BROOK	SAMUEL				83	ENGLAND	QU	ENGLISH	LAB	043	E	1	37
BROOKE	DENNIS				57	O	QU	ENGLISH	F	043	B	4	9
BROOKMIER	WILLIAM				35	O	CE	ENGLISH	F LAB	044	A	2	19
BROOKS	EDW				73	ENG	PM	ENG	GENTLEMAN	045	C	1	52
BROOKS	ELIZABETH			1	74	O	CN	DUTCH	F	045	C	3	41
BROOKS	GEORGE				36	O	CN	ENGLISH	LABOURER	045	D	5	59
BROOKS	HORACE				63	IRELAND	PM	IRISH	LAB	045	A	2	24
BROOKS	JAMES				61	ENGLAND	BA	ENGLISH	BAPTIST MINISTER	044	A	3	7
BROOKS	JAMES	WM	2		22	O	BA		FARMER	044	A	3	D
BROOKS	JAS				31	ONT	PM	ENG	F	045	C	1	52
BROOKS	JEREMIAH				38	O	PM	IRISH	BLACKSMITH	044	A	3	34
BROOKS	JOHN				75	ENGLAND	PM	ENGLISH	F	043	A	3	40
BROOKS	JOHN				45	ENGLAND	CE	ENGLISH	F	043	A	3	50
BROOKS	MARY			1	41	SCOTLAND	CP	SCOTCH		045	C	2	29
BROOKS	NOAH				57	US	WM	AFRICAN	LAB	044	C	4	17
BROOKS	THOMAS				29	O	PM	ENGLISH	F LAB	043	A	3	40
BROOKS	UNREADABLE				48	O	CN	GERMAN	CARPENTER	043	B	3	62
BROOKS	WILLIAM				30	ENGLAND	CE	ENGLISH	SHOEMAKER	043	H	2	14
BROOKS	WILLIAM				30	ENGLAND	CE	ENGLISH	SHOEMAKER	043	H	2	14
BROPHEY	WILLIAM				70	IRELAND	RC	IRISH	LABORER	045	D	1	30
BROTHERS	MARGARET			1	50	IRELAND	QU	IRISH		043	A	6	8
BROTHERS	WILLIAM				41	US	CN	ENGLISH	F	043	B	5	38
BROTHERSTON	WILLIAM				57	SCOTLAND	WM	SCOTCH	BLACKSMITH	045	C	4	36
BROTOW	HENRY	C			34	US	WM	ENG	FINISHER	044	B	2	42
BROUGHTON	ALFRED				23	ENGLAND	CE	ENGLISH	LAB	043	C		23
BROUGHTON	JAMES		1		26	ENGLAND	CE	ENGLISH	SERVANT	043	E	1	12
BROUGHTON	THOMAS				26	ENGLAND	PR	ENGLISH	CARPENTER	045	A	1	4
BROUGHTON	WILLIAM				38	ENGLAND	CE	ENGLISH	F	044	C	4	31
BROUHTON	ELIZA		1	1	21	ENGLAND	CE	ENGLISH	SERVANT	043	E	1	12
BROWN	AGNES	M	1	1	20	O	WM	ENGLISH		045	D	5	32
BROWN	ALEXANDER				43	SCOTLAND	PM	SCOTCH	BAKER	045	B	2	32
BROWN	ALEXANDER				55	IRELAND	FK	IRISH	FARMER	045	D	1	48
BROWN	ALEXANDER				57	ENGLAND	WM	ENGLISH	F	044	C	3	52
BROWN	ALLEN				36	O	WM	ENGLISH	F	043	B	1	10
BROWN	AMELIA			1	62	ENGLAND	WM	ENGLISH		045	A	2	8
BROWN	ANDREW		1		45	GERMANY	RC	GERMAN	LABOURER	045	D	4	16
BROWN	ANDREW	G			24	O	BA	ENGLISH	HOTEL KEEPER	043	B	3	51
BROWN	ANN		1	1	25	IRE	EP	IRE	SERVANT	044	B	3	35
BROWN	ANN		1	1	45	ENGLAND	CE	ENGLISH	INMATE	045	B	1	72
BROWN	ANN		1	1	71	US	WM	ENGLISH		045	D	3	72
BROWN	ANN	E	1	1	16	O	EM	IRE	SERVANT	044	B	4	32
BROWN	CALEB				28	U STATES	NC	IRISH	FARMER	043	A	4	38
BROWN	CHARLES		1		16	O	WM	IRISH	SERVANT	043	A	4	63
BROWN	CHARLES				25	US	CE	ENGLISH	FARMER	045	D	3	42
BROWN	CHARLES				32	US	WM	IRISH	F	044	C	4	62
BROWN	DAVID				34	SCOTLAND	PR	SCOTCH	FARMER	043	G	2	9
BROWN	DAVID				60	SCOTLAND	PS	SCOTCH	F	045	C	3	55
BROWN	DORAH			1	60	US	WM	AFRICAN	WASHER WOMAN	044	C	4	84
BROWN	EDMUND				36	ENGLAND	PM	ENGLISH	BRICKMAKER	045	B	1	58
BROWN	EDWARD		1		17	O	PM	ENGLISH		044	A	3	38
BROWN	EDWARD				45	ENGLAND	PM	ENGLISH	PRINTER	045	B	1	45
BROWN	ELIZA	ANN	2	1	1	O	CN			043	B	3	D
BROWN	EMMA		1	1	9	O	WM	IRISH		045	D	1	9
BROWN	FREDERICK		1		17	O	TU	GER	SERVANT	044	B	3	20
BROWN	GARRETT				52	U STATES	QU	IRISH		043	A	4	16
BROWN	GEDRGE		1		38	ENGLAND	CE	ENGLISH	BUTCHER	045	B	2	1
BROWN	GEORGE		1	M	6	O	CE	ENGLISH		043	A	2	19
BROWN	GEORGE		1	M	35	O	WM	ENGLAND	PHYSICIAN	043	A	5	14

SURNAME	NAME1	NAME2	STRAY	SEX	AGE	BIRTHPL	RELIGION	ORIGIN	OCCUP	DIST	SUB_DIST	DIV	PAGE
BROWN	GEORGE		1	M	32	O	WM	IRELAND	PHYSICIAN	043	A	5	27
BROWN	GEORGE				32	ENGLAND	CN	ENGLISH	FARMER	043	B	3	55
BROWN	GEORGE		1		32	O	CN	GERMAN	CATTLE DEALER	043	B	3	74
BROWN	GEORGE		1		25	O	CE	ENGLISH	HOSTLER	043	D		82
BROWN	GEORGE				59	US	WM	AFRICAN	SAILOR	044	A	1	36
BROWN	GEORGE				51	ENGLAND	PM	ENGLISH	F	044	A	3	38
BROWN	GEORGE				25	O	WM	ENGLISH	CARPENTER	045	C	3	26
BROWN	GEORGE				68	ENGLAND	WM	ENGLISH	FARMER	045	D	4	15
BROWN	HANNAH		1	1	26	SCOTLAND	CP	SCOTCH	TEACHER	045	B	2	12
BROWN	HENNERY				45	IRELAND	CP	IRISH	SHOE MAKER	045	D	6	7
BROWN	HENRY			M	24	O	PR	ENGLISH	SERVANT	043	A	1	3
BROWN	HENRY		1		28	O	WM	ENGLISH		045	B	2	21
BROWN	HENRY				39	ENGLAND	CE	ENGLISH	BUTCHER	045	B	2	24
BROWN	HENRY		2		18	O	CE		F	044	C	4	D
BROWN	HERBERT		2		1	O				045	D	4	D
BROWN	JACOB				32	O	NG	WELSH	BLACKSMITH	043	B	3	56
BROWN	JACOB				27	O	WM	ENGLISH	TEAMSTER	044	B	6	15
BROWN	JAMES				57	O	CN	ENGLISH	FARMER	043	B	3	68
BROWN	JAMES				33	ENGLAND	CE	ENGLISH	CARPENTER	043	C		27
BROWN	JAMES				46	IRELAND	CS	IRISH	TANNER	043	F		15
BROWN	JAMES				34	SCOTLAND	OP	SCOTCH	LAB	043	H	2	32
BROWN	JAMES				34	SCOTLAND	CS	SCOTCH	LABOURER	043	H	2	32
BROWN	JAMES				30	IRE	WM	IRE	LAB	044	B	2	63
BROWN	JAMES				29	O	WM	GER	F	044	B	3	41
BROWN	JAMES				25	O	WM	IRISH	F	044	B	5	32
BROWN	JAMES		1		27	ENGLAND	CE	ENGLISH		045	B	2	25
BROWN	JAMES				56	SCOTLAND	CP	SCOTCH	F	045	C	4	17
BROWN	JAMES				50	IRELAND	RC	IRISH	LABOURER	045	D	3	75
BROWN	JAMES				50	SCOTLAND	WM	SCOTCH	TAILOR	045	D	3	76
BROWN	JAMES				54	IRELAND	CP	IRISH	SHOEMAKER	044	C	4	19
BROWN	JANE			1	59	ENGLAND	PM	ENGLISH		044	B	6	46
BROWN	JANE			1	46	ENGLAND	CE	ENGLISH		044	C	4	7
BROWN	JEREMIAH				82	UNITED STATES	CN	IRISH	FARMER	043	B	3	71
BROWN	JESSEY		1	1	20	QUEBEC	RC	ENGLISH	INMATE	045	B	1	73
BROWN	JOHN				47	ENGLAND	WM	ENGLISH	BLACKSMITH	043	A	4	5
BROWN	JOHN				60	U STATES	NR	IRISH	FARMER	043	A	4	37
BROWN	JOHN				62	ENGLAND	NC	ENGLISH	F	043	A	6	7
BROWN	JOHN				50	ENGLAND	CE	ENGLISH	F	043	A	6	51
BROWN	JOHN		1		71	SCOTLAND	FK	SCOTCH	WATCHMAKER	043	B	3	16
BROWN	JOHN		1		93	ENGLAND	CE	ENGLISH		043	B	3	62
BROWN	JOHN				61	SCOTLAND	CS	SCOTCH	CLERGYMAN	043	D		80
BROWN	JOHN		1		18	ONTARIO	PR	IRISH	LABORER	043	G	2	51
BROWN	JOHN				40	IRELAND	CP	SCOTCH	LAB	043	H	2	12
BROWN	JOHN				40	IRELAND	CS	SCOTCH	LABOURER	043	H	2	12
BROWN	JOHN				80	SCOTLAND	CP	SCOTCH	F	044	A	2	23
BROWN	JOHN				37	ENG	CE	ENG	F	044	B	2	29
BROWN	JOHN				27	ENG	PS	ENG	LAB	044	B	3	50
BROWN	JOHN		1		48	IRELAND	CS	IRISH	LABOURER	044	B	5	2
BROWN	JOHN				29	O	WM	GERMAN	MACHINIST	044	B	5	9
BROWN	JOHN				69	O	CO	IRISH	BLACKSMITH	044	B	5	24
BROWN	JOHN				45	IRELAND	WM	IRISH	F	044	B	5	38
BROWN	JOHN				42	IRELAND	RC	IRISH	FARM SERVANT	045	C	3	41
BROWN	JOHN				50	PRUSSIA	LU	PRUSSIAN	CONTRACTOR	045	D	5	40
BROWN	JOHN				62	SCOTLAND	PS	SCOTCH		045	D	6	57
BROWN	JOHN				23	O	WM	IRISH	WAGGON MAKER	044	C	2	13
BROWN	JOHN				45	IRELAND	CE	IRISH		044	C	3	47
BROWN	JOHN				64	IRELAND	CE	IRISH	MASON	044	C	3	67
BROWN	JOHN				45	US	WM	AFRICAN	LAB	044	C	4	18
BROWN	JOHN	R			53	O	BA	ENGLISH	HOTEL KEEPER	043	B	3	51
BROWN	JOSEPH				72	ENGLAND	RC	ENGLISH	F	044	A	1	8
BROWN	JOSEPH				51	O	VM	GER	F	044	B	3	24
BROWN	JOSEPH				60	ENGLAND	UP	ENGLISH	LABORER	045	D	1	45
BROWN	JOSEPH				32	ENGLAND	CE	ENGLISH	POTTER	044	C	4	13
BROWN	JOSEPHINE		2	1	1	O	WM			044	C	1	D
BROWN	MARGARET		1	1	17	O	WM	GERMAN		043	B	3	56
BROWN	MARGARET		1	1	82	IRELAND	WM	IRISH		045	A	4	31
BROWN	MARK				34	ENGLAND	CE	ENGLISH	F	043	B	4	19
BROWN	MARY		1	1	7	O	WM	ENGLISH		043	B	3	51
BROWN	MARY		1	1	19	O	CE	SCOTCH	DRESS MAKER	043	C		9
BROWN	MARY		1	1	7	O	PS	SCOTCH		045	C	3	37
BROWN	MARY			1	55	SCOTLAND	CP	SCOTCH	WASHER WOMAN	045	C	4	22
BROWN	MARY		1	1	20	CANADA	CN	ENGLISH		045	D	6	52
BROWN	MARY		1	1	19	CANADA	BA	SCOTCH		045	D	6	66
BROWN	MARY			1	73	ENGLAND	CE	ENGLISH		044	C	4	29
BROWN	MARY	ELIZABETH	2	1	11	ENGLAND	CO			044	A	3	D
BROWN	MATILDA		1	1	47	US	UV	GERMAN		045	D	3	41
BROWN	MICHAEL				41	O	VM	GER	F	044	B	3	25
BROWN	NANCY		1	1	73	IRELAND	WM	IRISH		043	F		31
BROWN	O	J	1		27	UNITED STATES	CN	IRISH	TEACHER	043	B	3	50
BROWN	PATRICK				52	IRELAND	RC	IRISH	F	045	C	3	4
BROWN	PERRY		2		62	AM	ME		LAB	044	C	4	D
BROWN	PHILIP				33	ENGLAND	CE	ENGLISH	BUTCHER	045	B	1	10
BROWN	PHILLIP				44	CANADA	BA	IRISH	FARMER	045	D	6	76
BROWN	RACHAEL			F	52	O	CE	GERMAN	F	043	A	1	54
BROWN	RICHARD				49	O	VM	GER	F	044	B	3	25
BROWN	RICHARD				45	IRELAND	CE	IRISH	GENTLEMAN	044	C	4	37
BROWN	ROBERT		1		61	ENGLAND	CE	ENGLISH		045	D	6	51
BROWN	ROSAMIAH		1	1	20	O	CN	GERMAN	SERVANT	043	E	2	73
BROWN	SAMUEL				30	ENGLAND	WM	ENGLISH	FARMER	045	D	4	22
BROWN	SARAH		2	1	91	IRELAND	CE			043	B	3	D
BROWN	SOLOMON				36	ONTARIO	EM	GERMAN	LABORER	043	G	1	29
BROWN	THOMAS				68	U STATES	WM	IRISH	RETIRED	043	A	4	12
BROWN	THOMAS				36	O	CN	IRISH	FARMER	043	B	3	71
BROWN	THOMAS		1		18	SCOTLAND	CN	SCOTCH	FARM LABOURER	043	E	2	56
BROWN	THOMAS				40	ENGLAND	CE	ENGLISH	F	044	A	3	13
BROWN	THOMAS				54	ENGLAND	CO	ENGLISH	LAB	044	A	3	24
BROWN	THOMAS				34	O	WM	ENGLISH	FARMER	045	D	4	15
BROWN	THOMAS		1		24	IRELAND	WM	IRISH	SERVANT	045	D	2	32
BROWN	THOS				43	ENG	CE	ENG	F	045	C	1	59
BROWN	THOS				72	ENG	CE	ENG	GENTLEMAN	045	C	1	59
BROWN	THOS				65	SCOT	CP	SCOT	F	045	C	1	44
BROWN	VIOLET		2	1		O	WM			043	B	3	D
BROWN	W	ROBERT	1		26	O	CE	IRISH	F	044	C	1	5
BROWN	WILLIAM			M	64	IRELAND	CE	IRISH	WEAVER	043	A	1	30
BROWN	WILLIAM			M	32	ENGLAND	CP	ENGLAND	F	043	A	5	37
BROWN	WILLIAM				46	O	CO	ENGLISH	FARMER	043	B	3	67

SURNAME	NAME1	NAME2	STRAY	SEX	AGE	BIRTHPL	RELIGION	ORIGIN	OCCUP	DIST	SUB_DIST	DIV	PAGE
BROWN	WILLIAM		1		15	ONTARIO	CN	IRISH		043	G	1	28
BROWN	WILLIAM				41	IRELAND	CP	IRISH	SAWYER	043	H	1	21
BROWN	WILLIAM				44	IRELAND	CP	SCOTCH	LAB	043	H	2	2
BROWN	WILLIAM				46	IRELAND	CS	SCOTCH	LABOURER	043	H	2	2
BROWN	WILLIAM		2		60	IRELAND	RC		LABOURER	044	A	1	D
BROWN	WILLIAM		1		17	0	CE	ENG	SERVANT	044	B	1	16
BROWN	WILLIAM				80	IRELAND	CE	IRISH	LAB	044	B	6	59
BROWN	WILLIAM		1		32	ENGLAND	WM	ENGLISH		045	A	3	33
BROWN	WILLIAM		1		15	ENGLAND	CE	ENGLISH	BUTCHER	045	B	1	1
BROWN	WILLIAM				51	IRELAND	CE	IRISH	F	044	C	4	1
BROWN	WILLIAM				50	IRELAND	CE	IRISH	GARDNER	044	C	4	9
BROWN	WILLIAM				30	ENGLAND	CE	ENGLISH	POTTER	044	C	4	13
BROWN	WILLSON			M	26	0	CE	IRISH	LABOURER	043	A	1	11
BROWNE	GEORGE				35	ENGLAND	WM	ENGLISH	W MINISTER	043	A	4	7
BROWNE	HENRY				46	IRELAND	PR	IRISH	SCHOOL TEACHER	045	A	1	34
BROWNE	HENRY				33	0	DI	ENGLISH	POTTER	045	A	1	104
BROWNE	ROBERT				35	ENGLAND	CE	ENGLISH	LABOURER	045	A	1	45
BROWNE	WILLIAM				40	USA	RC	AFRICAN	LABOURER	045	A	1	45
BROWNE	WILLIAM				44	ENGLAND	DI	ENGLISH	POTTER	045	A	1	105
BROWNELL	GEORGE				36	ENGLAND	CE	ENGLISH	LAB	044	C	4	11
BROWNING	ELIZA			1	56	ENGLAND	CO	ENGLISH	JEWELLER	045	D	3	79
BROWNING	HENRY				58	ENGLAND	BA	ENGLISH	SHOEMAKER	043	B	3	49
BROWNLEE	JOHN				33	CANADA	CE	IRISH	BLACK SMITH	045	D	6	51
BROWNLEE	JOHN	E	2			CANADA	NG			045	D	6	D
BROWNLEE	THOMAS				61	IRELAND	CE	IRISH	COOPERN	045	D	6	43
BROWNLIE	JANE	P		1	79	SCOT	CP	SCOT		045	C	1	43
BROWNLIE	THOS				48	SCOT	CP	SCOT	F	045	C	1	43
BROWNRIDGE	JOHN				33	0	WM	ENGLISH	DROVER	044	A	2	52
BROWNSBERGER	BENJ				50	0	CN	GERMAN	FARMER	043	B	3	24
BROWNSBERGER	SAMUEL				46	UNITED STATES	MN	GERMANY	FARMER	043	B	3	29
BRUCE	GEORGE				67	SCOTLAND	CP	SCOTCH	FARMER	045	D	4	18
BRUCE	JOHN				36	SCOTLAND	CP	SCOTCH	LABOURER	045	A	1	84
BRUCE	JOHN				63	SCOTLAND	CP	SCOTCH	TEACHER	045	D	4	47
BRUCE	ROBERT				50	SCOTLAND	CP	SCOTCH	MILLER	045	D	4	19
BRUCE	WILLIAM			M	23	0	UP	SCOTCH	MERCHANT	043	A	1	16
BRUELS	JULIUS				46	ENGLAND	EM	ENGLISH	FARMER	045	D	6	10
BRUELS	THOMAS				50	ENGLAND	WM	ENGLISH	FARMER	045	D	6	10
BRUMWELL	AGNESS		2	1		0	UP			045	D	1	D
BRUMWELL	FRANCES			1	60	ENG	WM	WM		045	C	1	4
BRUMWELL	ISAAC				30	ENG	WM	ENG	F	045	C	1	4
BRUMWELL	JACOB				32	ENGLAND	WM	ENGLISH	F	045	C	2	20
BRUMWELL	JOHN				38	ENGLAND	UP	ENGLISH	FARMER	045	D	1	31
BRUMWELL	WILLET				34	ENGLAND	WM	ENGLISH	F	045	C	2	20
BRUNSKILL	HANAH			1	43	ENGLAND	PM	ENGLISH		045	D	4	9
BRUNSKILL	JOHN				22	0	CE	ENGLISH	FARMER	045	D	1	14
BRUSE	ELIZABETH		1	1	25	0	CP	SCOTCH		044	C	3	24
BRYAN	ROBERT				41	IRELAND	CE	IRISH	FARMER	043	A	4	59
BRYAN	THOMAS				38	IRELAND	CE	IRISH	FARMER	043	A	4	57
BRYANS	ANN	J		1	47	IRELAND	WM	IRISH	FARMER	044	A	2	48
BRYANS	JOHN				38	IRELAND	RC	IRISH	F LAB	044	A	1	7
BRYANT	JABEZ				35	ENGLAND	BA	ENGLISH	LABOURER	043	B	3	12
BRYANT	SARAH		2	1		0	CE			043	B	3	D
BRYANT	THOMAS				40	IRELAND	RC	IRISH	LAB	044	C	4	97
BRYCE	ROBERT				35	ENG	CE	ENG	F	044	B	2	48
BRYDEN	ELIZABETH		1	1	30	U S	CX	SCOTCH		045	A	3	10
BRYDEN	OWEN		1		22	0	CX	SCOTCH	CLERK	045	A	3	10
BRYDEN	THOMAS				52	SCOTLAND	CP	SCOTCH	FARMER	043	A	4	32
BRYDON	SAMUEL		1	M	24	0	CE	ENGLAND	SAWYER	043	A	5	6
BRYDON	WILLIAM				20	0	CP	SCOTCH	FARMER	043	A	4	44
BRYSON	ALFRED				25	WALES	WM	ENGLISH	SERVANT	045	B	2	32
BRYSON	JAMES				74	SCOT	UP	SCOT	F	044	B	4	36
BUCHAN	DAVID				64	SCOTLAND	BA	SCOTCH	BURSAR COLLEGE	045	B	2	29
BUCHANAN	JOHN				40	SCOT	PM	SCOT	LAB	045	C	1	62
BUCHANAN	MALCOLM				54	IRELAND	CE	IRISH	LAB	044	B	6	22
BUCHANAN	ROBERT				38	SCOTLAND	PS	SCOTCH	LABORER	043	D		1
BUCHANAN	ROBERT				69	SCOTLAND	CP	SCOTCH	F	045	C	4	45
BUCHANAN	THOMAS		1		22	IRELAND	CP	SCOTCH	SHOEMAKER	044	A	3	26
BUCHANIN	JAMES				40	IRELAND	CE	IRISH	FARMER	044	C	3	68
BUCHER	JOHN		1		27	IRELAND	RC	IRISH	PAINTER	045	D	5	8
BUCK	ALFRED				44	0	WM	IRISH	DROVER	044	C	4	33
BUCK	DAVID	C			35	0	CE	IRISH		043	D		87
BUCK	JAMES		1		20	ENGLAND	CE	ENGLISH	LAB	045	B	2	4
BUCK	ROBERT				48	ENGLAND	WM	ENGLISH	SHOEMAKER	043	F		33
BUCK	SUSAN			F	72	NS	BA	IRELAND		043	A	5	12
BUCKINDALE	JOSIAH				38	0	NG	GERMAN	F LAB	043	B	4	38
BUCKLAND	JOSEPHINE		1	1	3	0	WM	ENGLISH		044	A	2	53
BUCKLE	WILLIAM				41	ENGLAND	WM	ENGLISH	F	043	E	1	29
BUCKLEY	CARRNELEUS				23	ENGLAND	RC	ENGLISH	LAB	043	C		54
BUCKLEY	DAVID				40	ENGLAND	PM	ENGLISH	F	045	C	4	25
BUCKLEY	PATRICK				38	IRELAND	RC	IRISH	LAB	044	C	4	50
BUCKLY	MICHAEL				40	IRELAND	RC	IRISH	LAB	044	C	4	58
BUCKNELL	WILLIAM		1		35	0	CE	ENGLISH		044	C	3	38
BUCKNER	CHARLES				28	ENGLAND	CE	ENGLISH	PLASTERER	045	A	1	66
BUCKWOOD	CHRISTOPHER				30	ENGLAND	CE	ENGLISH	MASON	045	C	3	16
BUDD	WILLIAM				28	ENGLAND	CE	ENGLISH	LAB	045	B	1	15
BUDGE	ALEXANDER				60	SCOTLAND	CO	SCOTCH	BLACKSMITH	043	D		65
BUEGER	THOMAS				56	IRELAND	RC	IRISH	LAB	044	C	4	96
BUGG	JAMES				52	ENGLAND	EP	ENGLISH	F	043	A	6	2
BULGER	ASTATIA		1	1	22	IRELAND	RC	IRISH	SERVANT	044	C	2	42
BULGER	JAMES				68	IRELAND	RC	IRISH	LAB	044	A	3	49
BULGER	MARY		1	1	35	IRELAND	RC	IRISH	SERVANT	045	B	2	9
BULL	BARTHOLEMEW		1		79	IRELAND	WM	IRISH	F	044	C	4	73
BULL	BARTHOLOMEW				40	0	WM	IRISH	F	044	C	4	97
BULL	BARTLEY				50	0	WM	IRISH	F	044	C	1	8
BULL	ELIZABETH		1	1	79	IRELAND	WM	IRISH		044	C	4	73
BULL	JOHN				77	IRELAND	WM	IRISH	F	044	C	4	28
BULL	THOMAS		1		36	0	WM	IRISH	BARRISTER	044	C	4	74
BULL	WILLIAM				50	NEW BRUNSWICK	WM	IRISH	WAGON MAKER	044	C	4	18
BULLEN	GEORGE				20	ENGLISH	CE	ENGLISH	F LAB	044	C	1	29
BULLER	WILLIAM		1		22	ENGLAND	CE	ENGLAND	FARM LABORER	045	D	2	3
BULMER	ISAAC				40	ENGLAND	CE	ENGLISH	BRICK & TILE MANUFAC	045	B	1	10
BUMBER	MARY		1	1	13	0	CN	ENGLISH		043	B	5	13
BUNDEY	PATRICK				65	US	FW	AFRICAN	CARPENTER	045	B	1	26
BUNELL	MARY		1	1	8	UNITED STATES	QU	ENGLISH		043	B	4	47
BUNT	ANN		2	1	39	0	WM			044	B	3	D
BUNT	F	JOHN			69	ENGLAND	WM	ENGLISH	F	044	B	5	67

SURNAME	NAME1	NAME2	STRAY	SEX	AGE	BIRTHPL	RELIGION	ORIGIN	OCCUP	DIST	SUB_DIST	DIV	PAGE
BUNT	FRANCIS		1		22	0	WM	ENG	LAB	044	B	3	46
BUNT	FRANCIS				42	0	WM	ENGLISH	F	044	B	5	66
BUNT	JOHN				39	0	WM	ENGLISH	CARPENTER	044	B	5	39
BUNT	JOSEPH		2		4	0	WM	ENGLISH		044	B	5	D
BUNT	RICHARD				50	0	WM	ENG	F	044	B	3	47
BUNTON	GEORGE				34	ENGLAND	CE	ENGLISH	LAB	045	B	1	43
BUNTON	WILLIAM				32	ENGLAND	WM	ENGLISH	F	045	A	4	17
BURBRIDGE	ROBERT				34	ENGLAND	PM	ENGLISH	STONE MASON	045	C	4	7
BURCH	HARRIET		1	1	17	0	CE	ENGLISH		043	F		2
BURCHARDT	WILLIAM		1		21	ENGLAND	PM	ENGLISH	FARM SERVANT	045	C	3	2
BURD	JOHN		1		16	0	PM	ENGLISH		044	B	6	31
BURD	SARAH		1	1	37	0	PM	GERMAN		044	B	6	31
BURDEKIN	JESSE				35	ENGLAND	WM	ENGLISH	LAB	044	A	3	7
BURDEN	CHARLES		1		56	IRELAND	RC	IRISH	TAILOR	045	B	1	7
BURGES	JOHN				50	ENGLAND	CE	ENGLISH	COOPER	045	D	6	46
BURGESS	ALEXANDER				28	0	CP	SCOTCH	FARMER	044	A	3	1
BURGESS	JAMES				61	0	WM	ENGLISH	F	044	B	6	32
BURGESS	JOHN				35	ENGLAND	CE	ENGLISH	CARPENTER	045	A	2	25
BURGESS	WILLIAM				62	ENGLAND	ZZ	ENGLISH	F	044	A	1	34
BURK	DAVID				68	IRELAND	CE	IRISH	FARMER	045	D	6	65
BURK	EBEN				23	0	CE	IRISH	STORE KEEPER	045	D	3	80
BURK	FANNY			1	32	0	RC	IRISH	DRESS MAKER MILLINER	045	D	5	9
BURK	GEORGE				47	NB	CE	ENGLISH	F	045	C	4	35
BURK	JAMES			M	69	IRELAND	RC	IRISH	LABOURER	043	A	1	3
BURK	JOHN				38	IRELAND	RC	IRISH	LAB	044	C	3	22
BURK	WILLIAM				75	NB	CE	ENGLISH	F	045	C	4	35
BURK	WILLIAM				30	IRELAND	RC	IRISH	LAB	044	C	3	19
BURKE	EDWARD				60	IRELAND	CE	IRISH	FARMER	045	A	2	16
BURKE	ELLEN		1	1	32	IRELAND	RC	IRISH	SERVANT	045	A	3	1
BURKE	JOHN				60	IRELAND	WM	IRISH	FARMER	045	A	2	16
BURKE	URIUS				41	ENGLAND	CE	ENGLISH	SADDLER	043	C		51
BURKE	WILLIAM			M	33	ENGLAND	DI	ENGLISH	WAGGON MAKER	043	A	1	58
BURKELL	WILLIAM				37	ENGLAND	PM	ENGLISH	LAB	044	B	6	35
BURKHOLDER	BARBARA		2	1	23	0	PM			043	B	2	D
BURKHOLDER	CATHRINE		1	1	76	US	MN	GER	INN KEEPER	044	B	3	24
BURKHOLDER	CHRIST				34	0	MN	GERMAN		044	B	5	20
BURKHOLDER	DANIEL				27	0	CN	GERMAN	FARMER	043	B	3	7
BURKHOLDER	DAVID		1		26	0	MN	GERMAN	LAB	043	B	2	5
BURKHOLDER	ELIZA			1	60	0	WM	GERMAN		044	A	2	1
BURKHOLDER	ELIZA		1	1	37	CANADA	MN	GERMAN		045	D	6	22
BURKHOLDER	HENREY		1		25	0	PM	GERMAN	CARPENTER	043	B	2	5
BURKHOLDER	HENRY		1		28	0	LU	GER	CARPENTER	044	B	3	4
BURKHOLDER	HENRY				46	0	MN	GERMAN	F	044	B	5	53
BURKHOLDER	HY		1		21	0	WM	ENGLISH	LAB	044	B	5	70
BURKHOLDER	JACOB				51	0	LU	GERMAN	F	044	B	5	51
BURKHOLDER	JARROTT		1		16	0	EP	GER	F	044	B	3	17
BURKHOLDER	JOHN				32	0	CN	GERMAN	F	043	B	2	43
BURKHOLDER	JOHN		2		77	PEN US	CE		WAGGON MAKER	044	A	2	D
BURKHOLDER	JOHN				41	0	VM	GER	F	044	B	3	24
BURKHOLDER	JOHN				28	CANADA	MN	GERMAN	LABORER	045	D	6	63
BURKHOLDER	JOHN				60	U STATES	MN	GERMAN	FARMER	045	D	6	77
BURKHOLDER	JOHN	G	2		1	0	LU			044	B	3	D
BURKHOLDER	JOSEPH				40	0	EP	GER	F	044	B	3	23
BURKHOLDER	JOSEPH				70	U STATES	MN	GERMAN	FARMER	045	D	6	37
BURKHOLDER	MICHAEL		1		24	0	LU	GER	SCHOOL MASTER	044	B	3	41
BURKHOLDER	MICHL				45	0	MN	GERMAN	F	044	B	5	49
BURKHOLDER	SAMUEL				33	CANADA	MN	GERMAN	FARMER	045	D	6	77
BURKHOLDER	SARAH		1	1	2	0	CN	IRISH		043	B	2	2
BURKHOLDER	SUSAN		1	1	39	0	MN	GERMAN		045	C	2	39
BURKHOLDER	ULRICK				65	0	MN	GERMAN	LABOURER	045	D	5	69
BURKHOLDER	WILLIAM				48	0	EP	GER	F	044	B	3	31
BURKITT	HENRY		1	M	25	0	PR	ENGLISH	F	043	A	1	59
BURLING	CHARLES	H	1		13	0	CS	SCOTCH	FARMER	043	A	4	43
BURLING	CHARLES	H	1		14	0	CE	ENGLISH		043	A	6	45
BURLING	HENRY				27	0	CE	ENGLISH	LABOURER	043	A	4	26
BURLING	JAMES			M	34	0	CE	ENGLAND	L	043	A	5	12
BURLING	MARY		1	1	9	0	CS	SCOTCH		043	A	4	43
BURLING	RICHARD			M	26	0	WM	ENGLAND	BLACKSMITH	043	A	5	14
BURLING	SARAH		1	1	12	0	CS	SCOTCH		043	A	4	43
BURLING	WILLIAM		1		7	0	CS	SCOTCH		043	A	4	43
BURN	ANN			1	55	IRELAND	WM	IRISH		043	D		61
BURN	JAMES		2		54	IRELAND	WM		ACCOUNTANT	043	D		D
BURN	MARY			1	77	ENGLAND	CE	ENGLISH		043	D		28
BURN	ROBT	H	1		22	SCOTLAND	CP	SCOTCH	F	044	A	1	20
BURNDAGE	ELIZABETH			1	45	0	PM	GERMAN		044	B	5	35
BURNET	JOSEPH				39	SCOTLAND	CP	SCOTCH	MILLER	043	A	6	21
BURNETT	DANIEL				22	0	CN	ENGLISH	FARMER	043	B	3	74
BURNETT	JOHN				50	SCOTLAND	UP	SCOTCH	LAB	043	A	6	60
BURNIE	CHARLES				42	IRELAND	RC	IRISH	F	043	H	1	16
BURNIE	CHARLES	J			43	ENGLAND	CE	ENGLISH	LABORER	043	H	D	67
BURNIE	JAMES				51	IRELAND	RC	IRISH	F	043	H	1	3
BURNIE	JAMES				49	IRELAND	RC	IRISH	F	043	H	1	8
BURNIE	WILLIAM				45	IRELAND	RC	IRISH	F	043	H	1	4
BURNS	ANDREW		2	M	27	0	PS			043	A	2	D
BURNS	ANN		1	1	45	SCOTLAND	CP	SCOTCH	INMATE	045	B	1	72
BURNS	DAVID				28	IRE	WM	IRISH	F	044	B	1	41
BURNS	ELIZABETH		1	1	18	0	CE	IRISH	INMATE	045	B	1	73
BURNS	ELIZABETH		1	1	25	IRELAND	RC	IRISH	SERVANT	045	D	1	3
BURNS	ISABELLA		2	1		0	NG			045	C	2	D
BURNS	JAMES			M	58	SCOTLAND	PS	SCOTCH	F	043	A	2	48
BURNS	JAMES		1		12	0	RC	IRISH		045	D	1	26
BURNS	JAMES	H			24	IRELAND	WM	IRISH	POTTER	044	C	2	18
BURNS	JANE		1	1	35	IRELAND	RC	IRISH	SERVANT	043	F		15
BURNS	JOHN			M	33	0	PS	SCOTCH	F	043	A	2	36
BURNS	JOHN			M	55	IRELAND	RC	IRELAND	FARMER	043	A	5	8
BURNS	JOHN		1		38	IRELAND	RC	IRISH	TAILOR	043	C		28
BURNS	JOHN		1		72	IRE	WM	IRISH	LAB	044	B	1	7
BURNS	JOHN		2		61	IRELAND	WM		POTTER	044	C	2	D
BURNS	MARGARET		1	1	15	US	RC	IRISH		045	C	2	34
BURNS	MARGARET			1	54	SCOTLAND	PS	SCOTCH		045	C	3	9
BURNS	MARTIN				28	IRELAND	RC	IRISH	SADDLER	044	A	2	39
BURNS	MARTIN				46	IRELAND	RC	IRISH	LAB	045	C	2	13
BURNS	MARY		1	1	14	0	RC	IRISH		043	A	3	52
BURNS	MARY		1	1	5	0	ME	IRISH		044	B	1	13
BURNS	MARY		1	1	18	US	RC	IRISH		045	C	2	34
BURNS	MATTHEW		1		38	IRELAND	RC	IRISH	F LAB	044	A	2	37

SURNAME	NAME1	NAME2	STRAY	SEX	AGE	BIRTHPL	RELIGION	ORIGIN	OCCUP	DIST	SUB_DIST	DIV	PAGE
BURNS	NICOLAS				70	IRELAND	RC	IRISH	F	044	C	1	25
BURNS	PATRICK				35	IRELAND	RC	IRISH	F LAB	043	A	3	56
BURNS	ROSE		1	1	58	IRELAND	RC	IRISH		044	A	3	22
BURNS	SAMUEL				30	IRELAND	WM	IRISH	POTTER	045	D	6	27
BURNS	WALTER		1		40	IRELAND	RC	IRISH	SERVANT	043	C		19
BURNS	WILLIAM		1		11	0	CP	SCOTCH		045	C	3	31
BURNS	WILLIAM				70	IRELAND	RC	IRISH	F	044	C	4	10
BURNS	WILLIAM		2		75	0	CE		CARPENTER	044	C	4	D
BURNS	WM		1		6	0	CE	ENG		045	C	1	19
BURNSIDE	REBECCA		1	1	70	IRELAND	WM	IRISH		043	B	5	8
BURNSTONE	JOHN		1		29	ENGLAND	CE	ENGLISH	SALESMAN	044	C	3	15
BURR	HESTER		1	1	68	IRELAND	CE	IRISH		044	C	3	20
BURR	JOHN				39	0	EM	GERMAN	FARMER	045	D	2	53
BURR	WILLIAM					0	EM	GERMAN	FARMER	045	D	2	42
BURRELL	EMELY		1	1	29	0	CE	ENGLISH	SERVANT	045	D	2	7
BURRELL	GEO				26	ENGLAND	WM	ENGLISH	MOULDER	044	B	5	16
BURRIDGE	ALFRED				41	ENGLAND	BA	ENGLISH	LABORER	043	G	1	14
BURRIDGE	ROBERT				29	ENGLAND	CE	ENGLISH	GARDENER	043	G	1	9
BURRIGER	CHARITY	A	1	1	18	ONTARIO	CE	IRISH		043	G	1	46
BURRIGER	MALCOLM		1		22	ONTARIO	CE	GERMAN	FARMER	043	G	1	46
BURRIGER	WILLIAM		1	1		ONTARIO	CE	GERMAN		043	G	1	46
BURROWS	FREDERICK			M	54	IRELAND	CE	IRISH	F	043	A	2	54
BURROWS	GEORGE			M	45	IRELAND	PS	IRISH	CABINET MAKER	043	A	1	31
BURROWS	GEORGE				35	IRELAND	CE	IRISH	FARMER	043	G	2	3
BURROWS	JAMES				45	ENGLAND	CE	ENGLISH	FARMER	045	D	5	62
BURROWS	JOHN			M	27	0	EM	IRISH	FAR	043	A	1	67
BURROWS	JOHN				43	IRELAND	CE	IRISH	FARMER	043	G	2	2
BURROWS	MARTHA				40	IRELAND	CE	IRISH		043	G	2	2
BURT	JOHN				39	ENGLAND	BA	ENGLISH	BOOKKEEPER	044	C	4	6
BURTON	ANN		1	1	36	0	OB	ENGLISH		044	A	2	10
BURTON	ARTHUR		1		2	CANADA	WM	ENGLISH		045	D	6	51
BURTON	CHRISTP		1		26	ENGLAND	OB	ENGLISH	F	044	A	2	10
BURTON	EDGAR		1			0	OB	ENGLISH		044	A	2	10
BURTON	EDWARD				52	ENGLAND	DI	ENGLISH	MILLER	045	C	2	3
BURTON	ELIZABETH			1	74	ENGLAND	WM	ENGLISH		045	D	1	5
BURTON	FRANKLAND		1		5	CANADA	WM	ENGLISH		045	D	6	51
BURTON	HENRY				65	SCOTLAND	UP	SCOTCH	F	044	B	5	74
BURTON	HENRY				36	ENGLAND	CE	ENGLISH	FARM LABOURER	045	C	3	11
BURTON	INGOL				52	US	CE	ENG		045	C	1	45
BURTON	JAMES				60	SCOTLAND	CP	SCOTCH	FARMER	043	A	4	57
BURTON	JOHN				38	0	CP	SCOTCH	F	044	A	3	45
BURTON	MARY		1	1	31	CANADA	WM	ENGLISH		045	D	6	51
BURTON	SUSANAH		2	1		0	PM			043	A	4	D
BURTON	THOMAS				36	ENGLAND	PM	ENGLISH	WHEELWRIGHT	043	A	4	51
BURTON	VIOLET			1	65	SCOTLAND	CP	SCOTCH		043	A	4	50
BURTON	WILLIAM				63	ENGLAND	WM	ENGLISH	COOPER	045	C	3	11
BURTON	WILLIAM				37	CANADA	PS	ENGLISH	INN KEEPER	045	D	6	42
BURTON	WM				42	0	CP	SCOTCH	F	044	B	5	63
BUSBY	JOHN				39	IRE	CE	ENG	SHOE MAKER	044	B	2	15
BUSBY	WILLIAM		1		28	IRELAND	CE	IRISH		044	B	6	26
BUSECH	THEADORE				21	CANADA	LU	GERMAN	SADLER	045	D	6	77
BUSH	BRANTWOOD				48	ENGLAND	CE	ENGLISH	GENTLEMAN	045	A	1	29
BUSH	MELON		1		21	0	EP	ENG	SERVANT	044	B	3	48
BUSHBY	JAMES		2		38	IRELAND	CE		HOTELKEEPER	043	A	3	D
BUSHBY	JOHN				51	ENGLAND	CE	ENGLISH	F	045	C	3	27
BUSHBY	MARY			1	39	ENGLAND	CE	SCOTCH		043	A	3	28
BUSNESS	DAVID		1		26	SCOTLAND	CS	SCOTCH	BAKER	043	D		17
BUTCHER	CHAS				32	0	NC	ENGLISH	MERCHANT	043	C		26
BUTLER	JAMES				42	ENGLAND	CE	ENGLISH	LAB	043	D		40
BUTLER	JESSE			M	26	ENGLAND	CE	ENGLISH	LAB	043	A	1	61
BUTLER	JOSEPH			M	49	ENGLAND	CE	ENGLAND	FARMER	043	A	5	28
BUTLER	MARY			1	77	IRELAND	RC	IRISH		045	B	2	32
BUTLER	RICHARD			M	53	US	CE	IRISH	FAR	043	A	1	58
BUTLER	STEPHEN		1		35	ENGLAND	CE	ENGLISH	FARM LABOURER	045	C	4	29
BUTLER	WILLIAM				50	SCOTLAND	CP	SCOTCH	MAIL CONTRACTOR	044	C	4	45
BUTLIN	GEORGE		1		15	ENGLAND	CE	ENGLISH	SERVANT	043	A	6	53
BUTTERICK	CHARLES				30	ENGLAND	FW	ENGLISH	ARCHITECT	045	A	1	68
BUTTERY	JOHN		1		16	0	CE	ENGLISH		044	B	5	48
BUTTERY	THOMAS				46	ENG	CE	ENG	HOTEL KEEPER	044	B	1	27
BUTTLER	MARTIN		1		55	IRELAND	CE	IRISH	LAB	044	B	5	11
BUTTON	FRANCIS				37	0	WM	ENGLISH	AUCTIONEER	045	D	3	47
BUTTON	FRANCIS				76	US	WM	ENGLISH	FARMER	045	D	3	47
BUTTON	GEORGE		1		13	CANADA	NG			045	D	6	32
BUTTON	JOHN				52	0	WM	GERMAN	FARMER	045	D	3	55
BUTTON	JOHN				37	ENGLAND	WM	ENGLISH	FARMER	045	D	1	35
BUTTON	JOSEPH				30	ENGLAND	WM	ENGLISH	F	044	A	3	37
BUTTON	NEWBERY				45	0	CE	ENGLISH	FARMER	045	D	6	12
BUTTON	PHOEBE		1	1	21	0	WM	ENGLISH		045	D	3	46
BUTTON	WILLIAM	M			53	0	WM	FRENCH	FARMER	045	D	5	69
BWRTON	RICHARD				33	ENGLAND	CE	ENGLISH	BUTCHER	044	C	2	22
BYE	WILLIAM				55	ENGLAND	PM	ENGLISH	PEDLER	045	D	1	44
BYER	DAVID				51	CANADA	TU	GERMAN	FARMER	045	D	6	22
BYER	JOHN				51	CANADA	TU	GERMAN	FARMER	045	D	6	21
BYERS	JOHN		1		22	ENG	CE	ENG	LAB	044	B	2	59
BYRESS	JAMES		1		84	USA	BC	GERMAN		043	H	2	18
BYRESS	JOSHUA				35	0	CP	GERMAN	LAB	043	H	2	19
BYRNE	ALEXANDER				34	SCOTLAND	CP	SCOTCH	STONECUTTER	043	D		69
BYSOM	MRS	JOS		1	47	ENGLAND	WM	ENGLISH	MERCHANT TAILOR	045	D	5	12
BYWATER	RICHARD				64	ENGLAND	WM	ENGLISH	MERCHANT	044	B	6	9
CADDEN	ANDREW				40	SCOTLAND	CS	IRISH	LAB	043	B	1	31
CADDEN	SAMUEL				50	SCOTLAND	CS	IRISH	LAB	043	B	1	31
CADIEUX	CLARA		1	1	22	0	RC	FRENCH	SERVANT	044	A	2	47
CADIEUX	JOSEPH				50	QUE	RC	FRENCH	COOPER	044	A	2	47
CADIEUX	JOSEPH		1		20	0	RC	FRENCH	COOPER	044	A	2	47
CAFREY	MARGARET			1	60	IRELAND	RC	IRISH		043	F		25
CAHILL	EDWARD				50	IRELAND	RC	IRISH	FARMER	045	A	1	23
CAIN	CHRISTIAN		1	1	74	U STATES	MN	GERMAN	SERVANT	045	D	6	7
CAIN	JOHN			M	65	IRELAND	RC	IRISH	F	043	A	2	50
CAIN	JOHN	B		M	40	IRELAND	RC	IRISH	BLACKSMITH	043	A	2	46
CAIN	MICHAEL			M	38	IRELAND	RC	IRISH	F	043	A	1	44
CAIN	MICHAEL			M	43	0	RC	IRISH	F	043	A	2	50
CAIN	MICHAEL				34	IRELAND	RC	IRISH	R R STATION AGENT	043	D		6
CAIN	PATRICK				30	IRELAND	RC	IRISH	F	043	H	2	52
CAIN	PATRICK				30	IRELAND	RC	IRELAND	FARMER	043	H	2	52
CAIN	ROGER				50	IRELAND	RC	IRISH	TINSMITH	043	A	4	1
CAIN	SAMUEL		1	M	9	0	EM	IRISH		043	A	1	46

SURNAME	NAME1	NAME2	STRAY	SEX	AGE	BIRTHPL	RELIGION	ORIGIN	OCCUP	DIST	SUB_DIST	DIV	PAGE
CAIN	THOMAS			M	59	IRELAND	EM	IRISH	F	043	A	2	9
CAIN	WILLIAM			M	27	0	RC	IRELAND	F	043	A	5	8
CAIN	WINNIFRED		1	1	68	IRELAND	RC	IRISH		043	D		36
CAINE	WILLIAM				41	IRELAND	WM	IRISH	MILLWRIGHT	044	B	6	42
CAINS	GEORGE				24	SCOTLAND	PS	SCOTTISH	F LAB	044	C	1	56
CAIRNS	ADAM				32	0	FK	SCOTCH	F	043	A	3	34
CAIRNS	ADAM				69	SCOTLAND	FK	SCOTCH	F	043	A	3	35
CAIRNS	DUNCAN				37	0	NG	SCOTCH	F	043	A	3	36
CAIRNS	JAMES				63	SCOTLAND	CS	SCOTCH	F	043	A	3	30
CAIRNS	JAMES				27	0	FK	SCOTCH	F LAB	043	A	3	32
CAIRNS	JOHN				70	SCOTLAND	FK	SCOTCH	F	043	A	3	35
CAIRNS	MARY			1	82	SCOTLAND	FK	SCOTCH		043	A	3	55
CAIRNS	MARY		2	1	15	0	WM			044	B	6	D
CAIRNS	THOMAS				36	IRELAND	RC	IRISH	GARDENER	044	A	1	4
CAIRNS	THOMAS				35	0	CS	SCOT	F	044	B	4	31
CAIRNS	WILLIAM			M	52	SCOTLAND	PS	SCOTCH	LAB	043	A	1	42
CAKE	JAMES				33	0	CN	GERMAN	F	043	E	2	49
CALBART	JOHN				32	0	CE	ENGLISH	LABOURER	044	C	3	36
CALDER	ALEXANDER				32	SCOTLAND	CP	SCOTCH	F	044	A	2	30
CALDER	DONALD				34	SCOTLAND	CS	SCOTCH	FARMER	043	G	1	57
CALDER	MARY		1	1	19	SCOT	CE	SCOT		045	C	1	12
CALDWELL	ELIZABETH			1	37	0	CE	IRISH		043	E	2	35
CALDWELL	GEORGE	C			45	SCOTLAND	CP	SCOTCH	VETERINARY SURGEON	045	D	5	13
CALDWELL	JAMES	B			62	IRELAND	CO	IRISH	PRINTER	043	D		70
CALDWELL	THOMAS				40	0	WM	ENGLISH	FARM LABOURER	045	C	3	27
CALFORD	BRIGEET		1	1	14	IRELAND	RC	IRISH		045	D	3	62
CALFORD	ELLEN		1	1	16	0	RC	IRISH		045	D	3	76
CALFORD	JAMES		1		8	0	RC	IRISH		045	D	3	62
CALHOUN	JOHN				59	IRE	WM	IRE	F	044	B	4	33
CALHOURD	JAMES				46	IRELAND	WM	IRISH	F	044	C	1	41
CALLAGHAN	FRANK		2		2	0	RC			045	D	5	D
CALLAGHAN	HUGH				21	0	RC	IRISH	LAB	044	C	4	3
CALLAGHAN	JOHN				62	IRELAND	RC	IRISH	F	044	C	4	2
CALLAGHAN	PATRICK				36	IRELAND	RC	IRISH	SHOEMAKER	045	D	5	22
CALLANDER	PETER		1		52	0	WM	IRISH		045	A	1	16
CALLAWAY	WILLIAM				29	ENGLAND	CE	ENGLISH	LAB	043	H	2	43
CALLAWAY	WILLIAM		2			0	CE			043	H	2	D
CALLENDER	ABRAHAM				45	0	PM	ENG	F	045	C	1	33
CALLENDER	HENRY				47	0	CE	IRISH	FARMER	045	A	1	8
CALLENDER	JOHN				45	0	CP	IRISH	F	045	C	3	11
CALLENDER	WILLIAM				55	0	PS	ENGLISH	LAB	045	C	2	50
CALLIGAN	JOHN				84	IRELAND	WM	IRISH	LABOURER	045	D	5	19
CALLOWAY	WILLIAM				29	ENGLAND	CE	ENGLISH	LABOURER	043	H	2	43
CALLOWAY	WILLIAM		2	1		ONTARIO	CE			043	H	2	D
CALVERLY	ISABELLA		1	1	28	0	BA	ENGLISH		044	C	4	89
CALVERT	JAMES				30	ENG	PM	ENG	MILLER	044	B	2	4
CALVERT	JOHN				25	0	WM	ENGLISH	CONDUCTOR	045	B	1	29
CALVERT	JONATHAN				39	SCOTLAND	CP	SCOTCH	BLACKSMITH	045	D	4	1
CALVERT	MARY		1	1	16	IRELAND	CP	IRISH	SERVANT	045	D	1	12
CALVERT	WILFRED				33	ENGLAND	CE	ENGLISH	BUTCHER	045	D	3	80
CALVERT	WILLIAM				31	SCOTLAND	CP	SCOTCH	FARMER	045	D	4	1
CALVET	ELIZABETH			1	67	SCOTLAND	PS	SCOTCH		045	D	6	63
CALWELL	THOMAS				30	SCOTLAND	CS	SCOTCH	MOULDER	045	D	3	74
CAMBLE	ANDREW				51	SCOTLAND	RP	SCOTCH	WEAVER	044	C	3	13
CAMBRIDGE	JAMES		1		16	ENGLAND	CE	ENGLISH	SERVANT	045	A	1	21
CAMERON	ALEXANDER				43	0	CS	SCOT	F	044	B	4	28
CAMERON	ALLEN		1	M	18	0	RC	IRISH	LABOURER	043	A	1	32
CAMERON	ANGUS				34	0	CS	SCOT	F	044	B	4	47
CAMERON	ANGUS				32	0	CS	SCOTCH	F	044	B	6	59
CAMERON	ARCHIBALD			M	79	SCOTLAND	PS	SCOTCH	LAB	043	A	2	1
CAMERON	ARCHIBALD				44	0	PS	SCOT	F	044	B	3	37
CAMERON	ARCHIBALD				32	0	CS	SCOTCH	CARPENTER	044	B	6	12
CAMERON	COLIN		1		30	SCOTLAND	CS	SCOTCH	BLACKSMITH	045	D	3	78
CAMERON	DONALD				29	0	CS	SCOTCH	F	044	B	6	13
CAMERON	ELIZA		1	1	22	SCOTLAND	UP	SCOTCH		045	D	1	30
CAMERON	ELIZABETH		1	1	38	0	TU	GER		044	B	4	42
CAMERON	GEORGE				48	CANADA	PS	SCOTCH	CARPENTER	045	D	6	52
CAMERON	HELEN				63	SCOTLAND	CP	SCOTCH		043	G	2	21
CAMERON	JAMES				72	SCOTLAND	PS	SCOTCH	FARMER	043	G	2	40
CAMERON	JOHN			M	39	0	PM	SCOTCH	LAB	043	A	2	4
CAMERON	JOHN				27	0	OP	SCOTCH	LAB	043	H	2	54
CAMERON	JOHN				27	ONTARIO	CS	SCOTCH	LABOURER	043	H	2	54
CAMERON	KENNETH				61	SCOTLAND	OP	SCOTCH	F	043	H	2	39
CAMERON	KENNETH				61	SCOTLAND	CS	SCOTCH	FARMER	043	H	2	39
CAMERON	MARGRETT		2	1	11	CANADA	NG			045	D	6	D
CAMERON	MRS			1	70	SCOT	UP	SCOT		044	B	4	42
CAMERON	NIEL		1		13	0	CS	SCOTCH		044	B	6	10
CAMERON	ROBT	JR			39	SCOTLAND	UP	SCOTCH	F	044	B	5	75
CAMERON	SOPHIE		1	1	22	CANADA	DI	GERMAN		045	D	6	75
CAMERON	WILLIAM				64	SCOT	CS	SCOT	F	044	B	4	52
CAMERON	WM	JOHN	1	M	31	SCOTLAND	DI	SCOTCH	COTTON WEAVER	043	A	2	4
CAMPBELL	ALEXANDER				50	N B	CE	SCOTCH	LAB	043	A	6	62
CAMPBELL	ARCHIBALD			M	41	SCOTLAND	PS	SCOTCH	F	043	A	2	3
CAMPBELL	ARCHIBALD				38	SCOTLAND	WM	SCOTCH	TINSMITH	043	D		84
CAMPBELL	CAROLINE		1	1	74	QUE	CE	GERMAN		044	A	1	17
CAMPBELL	CASSIN				30	0	ME	SCOTCH	SCHOOL TEACHER	043	B	3	31
CAMPBELL	COLIN		1	M	35	SCOTLAND	CP	SCOTCH	LAB	043	A	2	24
CAMPBELL	COLIN				23	U STATES	CE	SCOTCH	LAB	043	A	6	60
CAMPBELL	DAVID			M	65	SCOTLAND	CP	SCOTCH	F	043	A	2	11
CAMPBELL	DOUGALL		1		21	0	WM	SCOT	SERVANT	044	B	3	7
CAMPBELL	DUNCAN				42	SCOTLAND	BA	SCOTCH	F	043	A	3	30
CAMPBELL	DUNCAN		1		23	SCOTLAND	CP	SCOTCH	LAB	045	C	2	53
CAMPBELL	FLORA		1	1	29	SCOTLAND	CS	SCOTCH		043	G	1	57
CAMPBELL	GEORGE		1		15	0	UP	SCOTCH		045	D	1	38
CAMPBELL	HENRETTA		2	1	1	0				045	D	4	D
CAMPBELL	HENRY	M			36	SCOTLAND	CP	SCOTCH	TEACHER	045	C	3	38
CAMPBELL	HUGH				55	SCOTLAND	BA	SCOTTISH	BLACKSMITH	043	B	5	6
CAMPBELL	HUGH				79	SCOTLAND	NC	SCOTCH	GENTLEMAN	043	C		17
CAMPBELL	HUGH				39	NS	CP	SCOTCH	WATCH MAKER	045	D	4	37
CAMPBELL	ISABELLA			1	70	SCOTLAND	WM	SCOTLAND	SCHOOL TEACHER	045	D	2	28
CAMPBELL	JAMES		1		31	SCOTLAND	CP	SCOTCH	FARM SERVANT	045	C	3	50
CAMPBELL	JAMES				50	SCOTLAND	CO	SCOTCH	SHOEMAKER	045	D	5	15
CAMPBELL	JOHN				50	SCOTLAND	UP	SCOTCH	F	043	A	6	34
CAMPBELL	JOHN		1		26	0	CE	SCOTCH	FARM LAB	043	B	1	12
CAMPBELL	JOHN				53	SCOTLAND	FK	SCOTCH	ROPEMAKER	043	C		30
CAMPBELL	JOHN				43	SCOT	LU	SCOT	F	044	B	3	4

SURNAME	NAME1	NAME2	STRAY	SEX	AGE	BIRTHPL	RELIGION	ORIGIN	OCCUP	DIST	SUB_DIST	DIV	PAGE
CAMPBELL	JOHN		1		22	SCOTLAND	CP	SCOTCH		044	B	6	19
CAMPBELL	JOHN		2		58	ENG	EP			045	A	1	D
CAMPBELL	JOHN	N			28	0	BA	SCOTCH	MERCHANT	043	A	4	17
CAMPBELL	LUDLOW		1		40	ST JOHN NB	CE	SCOT	SERVANT	044	B	3	7
CAMPBELL	MARGARET		1	1	48	IRELAND	CO	SCOTCH		045	A	1	76
CAMPBELL	MARY		1	1	19	IRELAND	CE	ENGLISH		044	B	5	57
CAMPBELL	MARY			1	48	N BRUNSWICK	WM	ENGLISH		045	A	2	6
CAMPBELL	MARY			1	50	IRELAND	RC	IRISH		045	A	3	28
CAMPBELL	NEIL				28	0	EV	SCOT	LAB	044	B	1	43
CAMPBELL	NEIL				30	0	WM	SCOTCH	FARM LABORER	045	D	1	22
CAMPBELL	RICHARD				32	IRELAND	CP	IRISH	LAB	044	C	4	34
CAMPBELL	ROBERT				52	IRELAND	CS	IRISH	LAB	044	B	6	47
CAMPBELL	SAMUEL				57	IRELAND	CS	IRISH	LAB	044	B	6	14
CAMPBELL	WILLIAM			M	34	0	CE	IRISH	LABOURER	043	A	1	2
CAMPBELL	WILLIAM				50	IRELAND	WM	ENGLISH	F	044	C	4	35
CAMPBELL	WM		1		22	SCOTLAND	PS	SCOTCH	CARPENTER	044	B	5	20
CAMPION	JOB	L			71	IRELAND	CS	IRISH	SOLICITOR	043	D		47
CAMPLIN	CHARLES				54	ENGLAND	CE	ENGLISH	LABOURER	045	A	1	27
CAMPS	WILLIAM				46	ENGLAND	CE	ENGLISH	LAB	045	C	2	6
CANADA	DONALS		1		18	0	WM	IRISH	SERVANT	045	D	6	13
CANADA	JOHN				46	IRELAND	RC	IRISH	FARMER	044	C	3	33
CANDOW	DAVID				34	NEWFOUNDLAND	CS	SCOTCH	MERCHANT	043	E	2	69
CANE	CATHERINE		1	1	15	0	CP	ENGLISH	SERVANT	045	D	2	2
CANE	ELISA		1	1	20	0	PM	ENGLISH	SERVANT	045	D	2	20
CANE	JOHN				84	IRELAND	RC	IRISH	LAB	043	D		44
CANE	MARTIN				40	IRELAND	CE	IRISH	SAWYER	044	A	2	42
CANE	MILES				60	IRELAND	RC	IRISH	LAB	043	E	1	7
CANE	WILLIAM				48	UNITED STATES	NC	IRISH	LUMBERMAN	043	E	2	46
CANIMOR	GERSIN	W			28	0	WM	ENGLISH	F	045	A	4	34
CANINGTON	WILLIAM				37	ENGLAND	CE	ENGLISH	LABOURER	045	D	3	71
CANNING	HUGH				27	0	CS	IRISH	FARMER	045	D	3	39
CANNING	JOHN				50	IRELAND	CS	IRISH	FARMER	045	D	3	34
CANNING	MATTHEW				45	US	PM	IRISH	F	044	A	2	30
CANNON	MICHAEL			M	60	IRELAND	RC	IRISH	FARMER	043	A	1	22
CANTWELL	MARY		2	1	51	0	CE		HOUSEKEEPER	044	B	1	D
CAPNER	JOSEPH				68	ENGLAND	CE	ENGLISH	F	044	B	6	4
CARD	ALEXANDER				70	NOVA SCOTIA	WM	SCOTCH	F	044	A	3	19
CARD	ALEXANDER	JR			27	0	WM	SCOTCH	F	044	A	3	19
CARD	DAVID				63	0	WM	FRENCH	COOPER	045	C	2	20
CARD	JAS		1		24	0	CE	ENGLISH		044	B	5	59
CARD	L	JOHN			27	NS	WM	ENGLISH	CARP & JOINER	043	A	3	8
CARD	ST GEORGE				24	0	WM	SCOTCH	F	044	A	3	19
CARD	WOODBARY				74	NB	WM	IRISH		044	C	3	38
CARD	WOODBURY				31	ENGLAND	WM	ENGLISH	F	044	C	1	50
CAREY	JOHN		1		19	0	WM	IRISH		044	B	2	3
CAREY	JOSEPH				25	FRANCE	CE	FRENCH	LAB	044	C	4	15
CARGIN	JOHN		1		45	0	PS	IRISH	LAB	044	B	5	40
CARL	JOHN				36	IRELAND	RC	IRISH	F LAB	043	B	4	42
CARL	MICHAEL				50	IRELAND	RC	IRISH	F LAB	043	B	1	36
CARLAW	CHESTER		1		6	0	CP	ENGLISH		045	C	2	18
CARLEY	ABRAM			M	33	0	EM	IRISH	SCHOOL TEACHER	043	A	2	43
CARLEY	BENJAMIN			M	56	U STATES	WM	IRISH	F	043	A	2	49
CARLEY	CHARLES		2	M	30	0	WM			043	A	2	D
CARLEY	PETER			M	54	U STATES	EM	IRISH	F	043	A	2	49
CARLEY	WILLIAM				75	U STATES	FW	ENGLISH		043	A	3	50
CARLIE	SARAH			1	21	0	CE	IRE	SERVANT	044	B	2	58
CARLING	ANDREW				23	0	CP	IRISH	LAB	043	H	1	27
CARLISLE	ORR				45	IRELAND	CP	IRISH	F	043	B	1	19
CARLISLE	WILLIAM				64	IRELAND	CP	IRISH	F	043	B	1	19
CARLTON	CHARLES				22	0	WM	ENGLISH	MERCHANT	045	D	5	32
CARLYLE	THOMAS				38	SCOTLAND	OP	SCOTCH	FIREMAN IN RAILWAY	044	C	3	65
CARLYON	JOHN				57	ENGLAND	WM	ENGLISH	RETIRED	043	A	4	9
CARMAN	ALFRED				32	0	WM	ENG	WHEELWRIGHT	044	B	1	10
CARMAN	GEORGE		1		21	0	WM	ENG	WHEELWRIGHT	044	B	1	49
CARMICHAEL	JAMES	REV		M	42	0	CS	SCOTCH	MINISTER	043	A	2	38
CARMICHAEL	REV	JAS	1		36	SCOTLAND	CS	SCOTCH	CLERGYMAN	045	D	5	23
CARNAGAHAN	B				38	0	CP	IRE	F	045	C	1	12
CARNAGHAN	JAMES				27	0	PS	ENGLISH	F	045	C	3	38
CARNAHAN	MARY			1	62	IRELAND	CP	IRISH	F	043	B	4	25
CARNE	DANIEL			M	27	IRELAND	RC	IRISH	LAB	043	A	1	71
CARNEGIE	DAVID				55	SCOT	PS	SCOT	F	044	B	2	69
CARNEY	ELIZABET			1	68	IRELAND	RC	IRISH		044	C	3	49
CARNEY	THOMAS				32	IRELAND	RC	IRISH	FARMER	044	C	3	62
CAROLINE	ALICE			1	24	ENGLAND	PM	ENGLISH	DRESS MAKER	044	A	3	43
CAROLINE	JOHN				45	IRELAND	RC	IRISH	GARDNER	044	C	4	91
CARPENTER	DEXTER				33	UNITED STATES	BA	ENGLISH	COM TRAVELLER	043	E	2	13
CARPENTER	WILLIAM				38	ENGLAND	CE	ENGLISH	SHOEMAKER	045	D	4	5
CARR	ANN		1	F	17	0	NG	ENGLISH		043	A	2	16
CARR	CARLTON				59	0	WM	ENGLISH	LAB	045	C	2	14
CARR	EDWARD				50	IRELAND	RC	IRISH	WEAVER	045	D	3	62
CARR	GEORGE				25	IRELAND	RC	IRISH	LAB	044	C	1	9
CARR	JAMES		1		16	0	CO	ENGLISH	CABINET MAKER	043	D		86
CARR	JOHN		1		12	0	WM	ENGLISH	F LAB	043	A	3	19
CARR	JOHN				25	ENGLAND	PM	ENGLISH	F LAB	044	A	3	8
CARR	JOHN	THOMAS			25	ENGLAND	WM	ENGLISH	FARMER	045	D	3	25
CARR	JOSEPH		1		18	0	WM	ENGLISH	F LAB	043	A	3	19
CARR	MARGARET		2	1	36	IRELAND	RC		SERVANT	045	C	3	D
CARR	MARTHA		2	1	36	0	CP			045	D	3	D
CARR	MARY AN		1	1	35	ENG	WM	ENG	HOUSEKEEPER	044	B	4	38
CARR	MATHEW				40	ENG	CE	ENG	F	044	B	1	40
CARR	ROBERT		1		18	0	CE	ENGLISH	MILLER	044	A	3	27
CARR	THOMAS				39	ENGLAND	WM	ENGLISH	MERCHANT	045	D	1	8
CARR	WILLIAM		1		14	0	CE	ENGLISH		043	A	3	48
CARR	WILLIAM				34	ENGLAND	WM	ENGLISH	LAB	044	A	3	37
CARRENS	MARY		1	1	65	IRELAND	RC	IRISH		044	C	3	38
CARRICK	JOHN		1		27	SCOT	BA	SCOT	LAB	044	B	2	61
CARRINGTOW	ROBERT		1		38	ENGLAND	CE	ENGLISH	GENTLEMAN	044	C	4	57
CARROL	CATHERINE		1	1	30	IRELAND	RC	IRISH	SERVANT	044	C	2	20
CARROL	DANIEL		1		2	0	RC	IRISH		044	C	4	42
CARROL	JOHN		1		35	0	WM	IRE	LAB	044	B	3	15
CARROLL	ALICE			1	60	IRELAND	RC	IRISH		044	A	2	42
CARROLL	ANNE		1	1	40	IRELAND	RC	IRISH		044	C	4	60
CARROLL	FANNY		1	1	36	IRELAND	CE	IRISH	SERVANT	045	A	1	34
CARROLL	PATRICK				26	IRELAND	RC	IRISH	LAB	045	C	2	2
CARRUTHERS	ELISA		1	1	36	SCOTLAND	CP	SCOTCH	SERVANT	045	B	2	20
CARRUTHERS	FRANCIS	H G	1		17	0	CE	ENGLISH		044	A	2	40

SURNAME	NAME1	NAME2	STRAY	SEX	AGE	BIRTHPL	RELIGION	ORIGIN	OCCUP	DIST	SUB_DIST	DIV	PAGE
CARRUTHERS	GEORGE				29	0	WM	ENGLISH	F	044	C	3	9
CARRUTHERS	ISAAC				25	0	WM	ENGLISH	F	044	A	3	18
CARRUTHERS	JAMES				57	ENGLAND	CE	ENGLISH	F	044	A	3	29
CARRUTHERS	JAMES				30	0	WM	ENGLISH	F	044	C	3	8
CARRY	JOHN				47	IRELAND	CE	IRISH	CLERGYMAN	043	F		15
CARRY	SAMUEL			M	41	ENGLAND	PM	ENGLISH	LABOURER	043	A	1	28
CARRY	WILLIAM		2	M	16	0	PM			043	A	1	D
CARSCADDEN	JAMES			M	54	QUE	WM	IRISH	FARMER	043	A	1	12
CARSON	ANDREW				23	0	PM	IRE	F	044	B	4	37
CARSON	JOHN				40	IRELAND	CE	IRISH	BAKER FARMER	044	C	4	23
CARSON	MARY		2	1	11	0	NG			045	A	3	D
CARSON	MARY	A		1	45	IRELAND	RC	IRISH		045	A	1	24
CARSON	ROBERT			M	52	0	PM	IRISH	WEAVER	043	A	2	27
CARSON	THOMAS				30	CANADA	PM	IRISH	LABORER	045	D	6	74
CARSON	WALLAS				36	IRELAND	CP	IRISH	HOTEL KEEPER	045	A	3	5
CARSWELL	JAMES				45	ENGLAND	CE	ENGLISH	FARMER	045	D	2	30
CARTER	ALEX		1		23	SCOTLAND	CP	SCOTCH	F LAB	044	A	3	16
CARTER	GEORGE		1		35	ENGLAND	CE	ENGLISH	BRICK MAKER	045	A	1	26
CARTER	JOHN			M	78	ENGLAND	PM	ENGLISH	LAB	043	A	1	31
CARTER	JOHN				50	ENGLAND	WM	ENGLISH	BUTCHER	045	D	3	45
CARTER	ROBERT				37	ENGLAND	BC	ENGLISH	F	045	C	2	42
CARTER	WILLIAM			M	36	0	CE	IRELAND	F	043	A	5	42
CARTER	WILLIAM				53	IRELAND	WM	IRISH	F	043	E	3	28
CARTER	WILLIAM				26	ENGLAND	WM	ENGLISH	LAB	045	C	2	5
CARTER	WILLIAM		1		30	ENGLAND	CE	ENGLISH	PAINTER	045	D	5	8
CARTEY	MARY		1	1	50	IRELAND	RC	IRISH	SERVANT	043	A	6	14
CARTHEW	ARTHUR				70	ENGLAND	CE	ENGLISH	GENTLEMAN	043	B	4	31
CARTHWRIGHT	GEORGE				31	ENGLAND	PM	ENGLISH	FARMER	045	D	1	49
CARTNEY	JOHN		1		19	ONTARIO	WM	IRISH	SERVANT	044	C	3	52
CARTWRIGHT	GEORGE				39	ENGLAND	CO	ENGLISH	LAB	043	D		19
CARTWRIGHT	JOSEPH				28	ENGLAND	CE	ENGLISH	CARPENTER	045	A	1	73
CARVER	EDWIN		1	M	14	0	CE	ENGLISH		043	A	1	7
CARVER	FRANCES		1	1	18	0	PM	ENGLISH	SERVANT	043	E	2	6
CARVER	FREDERICK		1		18	0	WM	ENGLISH	FARM LAB	043	B	1	26
CARVER	FREDERICK	S	1		18	0	NC	ENGLISH	LAB	043	B	1	2
CARVER	JAMES		1		30	ENGLAND	CE	ENGLISH	LABOURER	045	D	4	11
CARVER	ROBERT				40	ENGLAND	PM	ENGLISH	F	043	B	1	14
CARY			2		0	0	CE			044	C	4	D
CARY	JAMES				75	0	WM	IRISH	LABOURER	045	D	3	25
CASE	CHARLES				23	0	CN	ENGLISH	F	043	B	5	31
CASE	CHAS				49	ENGLAND	CE	ENGLISH	CARPENTER	043	C		19
CASE	EDWARD				55	ENGLAND	CE	ENGLISH	LAB	043	B	1	3
CASE	HENRY			M	29	0	CE	ENGLISH	FARMER	043	A	1	24
CASE	WILLIAM		1		30	0	QU	ENGLISH	F	043	B	5	43
CASELEY	WILLIAM				29	ENGLAND	WM	ENGLISH	F	045	A	4	34
CASELY	CLEMENT				51	ENGLAND	WM	ENGLISH	FARMER	045	D	4	32
CASELY	JOHN				24	ENGLAND	WM	ENGLISH	FARMER	045	D	2	34
CASELY	THOMAS				27	ENG	WM	ENG	F	044	B	1	54
CASEY	DONALD				52	IRE	RC	IRISH	LAB	044	B	1	10
CASEY	MAURICE				60	IRELAND	RC	IRISH	LABORER	045	D	1	4
CASEY	PATRICK		1		23	0	RC	IRELAND	SERVANT	045	D	2	23
CASH	DAVID				55	ENGLAND	CO	ENGLISH	PUMP & FANNING MILLS	045	D	5	2
CASSELLS	RICHARDSON				38	ENGLAND	CE	ENGLISH	CATTLE DEALER	045	B	1	26
CASSERLY	JAMES				60	IRELAND	RC	IRISH	FARMER	043	A	4	56
CASSERLY	PATRICK				65	IRELAND	RC	IRISH	FARMER	043	A	4	66
CASSIDY	JOHN				72	IRELAND	CE	IRISH	COOPER	043	A	4	46
CASSIDY	THOMAS				41	U STATES	CE	IRISH	MANUFACTURER	043	A	4	55
CASSIDY	WILLIAM				54	IRELAND	CE	IRISH	TURNKEY	045	A	1	71
CASTATOR	ESTHER		1	1	17	0	WM	GERMAN	SERVANT	044	B	5	9
CASTATOR	ESTHER		1	1	21	0	CO	ENGLISH		044	B	5	24
CASTATOR	GEORGE				36	0	LU	GER	F	044	B	3	26
CASTATOR	HENRY				45	0	LU	GER	F	044	B	3	27
CASTELLI	MARK				47	ENG	EM	ENG	BLACKSMITH	044	B	1	49
CASTER	LEYNORD				48	CANADA	CN	GERMAN	FARMER	045	D	6	75
CASTLE	ALLEN				42	0	PM	ENGLISH	F	044	A	3	3
CASTLE	FREDERICK		1		8	0	CE	ENGLISH		045	A	1	26
CASTLE	JANE		1	1	17	0	CE	ENGLISH		045	A	1	26
CASTLE	JOHN		1		11	0	CE	ENGLISH		045	A	1	26
CASTLE	JOSEPH		1		15	0	CE	ENGLISH	BRICK MAKER	045	A	1	26
CATCHER	CHAS				44	SCOTLAND	FK	SCOTCH	CARPENTER	043	C		35
CATCHER	JOHN		1		32	SCOTLAND	UP	SCOTCH	LAB	043	C		45
CATE	ADAM				32	0	NG	SCOTCH	F	043	A	6	50
CATHERWOOD	BRIDGET			1	52	IRELAND	RC	IRISH		044	C	3	71
CATHERWOOD	JOHN		1		18	ONTARIO	CE	IRISH	SERVANT	044	C	3	50
CATHERWOOD	MARY		1	1	18	ONTARIO	CE	IRISH		044	C	3	50
CATTLE	JOHN				44	ENG	CE	ENG	F	045	C	1	4
CATTLE	ROBERT				41	ENGLAND	CE	ENGLISH	FARMER	043	G	1	41
CATTLE	THOS		2		77	ENGLAND	CE	ENGLISH	F	045	C	1	D
CAULDER	WILLIAM			M	52	SCOTLAND	PS	SCOTCH	LAB	043	A	1	60
CAUSEBROOK	JOSEPH		1		33	ENGLAND	CE	ENGLISH	LAB	045	C	4	45
CAVAN	MCMAN		1		22	0	CE	IRISH	SERVANT	045	A	3	15
CAVANA	ANNE		1	1	22	0	WM	IRISH	SERVANT	044	B	6	58
CAVANA	ISABELLA		1	1	15	0	CE	IRISH	SERVANT	044	B	6	15
CAVANA	THOMAS				54	IRELAND	CE	IRISH	SHOEMAKER	044	B	6	25
CAVANAH	MICHEL				31	IRELAND	RC	IRISH	LAB	045	C	2	36
CAVANAH	RICHARD				60	IRELAND	RC	IRISH	GARDENER	045	A	1	85
CAVE	EDWARD				30	0	CE	ENGLISH	CARPENTER	044	A	3	28
CAVE	GEO	L			32	0	CE	ENGLISH	LAB	044	A	3	42
CAVE	WILLIAM				63	ENGLAND	CE	ENGLISH	CARPENTER	044	A	3	23
CAVILL	WILLIAM				38	ENGLAND	CE	ENGLISH	FARMER	043	G	2	42
CAVNEUGH	JAMES				53	IRELAND	RC	IRISH	F	044	C	3	7
CAWTHRA	JOSEPH				48	0	CE	ENGLISH	BANKER	043	D		85
CAYLEY	JOHN				55	ENGLAND	CE	ENGLISH	CLERK	045	A	1	6
CAZENBY	ROBERT		1		21	ENGLAND	WM	ENGLISH	CARPENTER	043	D		62
CHADWICK	FANNY		1	1	19	0	MN	IRISH	SERVANT	045	D	2	46
CHADWICK	GEORGE				49	ENGLAND	PM	ENGLISH	F	044	A	2	9
CHADWICK	JAMES				54	ENGLAND	CE	ENGLISH	FARMER	045	A	3	27
CHAFFY	JOHN				45	IRELAND	RC	IRISH	LABORER	045	D	2	31
CHALENON	HENRY				31	ENG	WM	ENG	MERCHANT	044	B	4	21
CHALFIELD	FANNY		1	1	25	0	CO	ENGLISH		044	B	6	4
CHAMBERLAIN	JOHN				59	ENGLAND	FK	ENGLISH	F	043	A	3	39
CHAMBERLAIN	WILLIAM				71	ENG	CE	ENG	CONVEYANCER	045	C	1	4
CHAMBERS	JOSEPH				30	ENGLAND	CE	ENGLISH	INN KEEPER	045	B	1	9
CHAMPAIGN	CHARLES				81	QUEBEC	RC	FRENCH	LAB	045	C	3	43
CHAMPION	GEORGE		1		6	0	WM	ENGLISH		043	A	3	56
CHAMPION	WALTER		1		7	0	WM	ENGLISH		043	A	3	56

SURNAME	NAME1	NAME2	STRAY	SEX	AGE	BIRTHPL	RELIGION	ORIGIN	OCCUP	DIST	SUB_DIST	DIV	PAGE
CHANCY	JOHN				50	IRELAND	RC	IRISH	LAB	044	C	3	5
CHANT	CHRISTOPHER				36	ENGLAND	WM	ENGLISH	CABINET MAKER	045	D	3	43
CHANTLER	MARY	ANN		1	45	U STATES	CN	ENGLISH		043	D		78
CHAPELL	FRANCIS				27	0	EM	FRENCH	LAB	043	E	2	40
CHAPELLE	LEWIS	L			34	0	RC	FRENCH	F	043	H	1	2
CHAPLIN	WILLIAM				33	SCOTLAND	CP	SCOTCH	F	044	C	2	37
CHAPMAN	ALFRED		1		40	ENGLAND	CE	ENGLISH	CARPENTER	045	A	1	34
CHAPMAN	ALFRED	W	1		17	ENGLAND	CE	ENGLISH		045	A	1	34
CHAPMAN	CHARLES				35	ENGLAND	WM	ENGLISH	MUSICAL INSTRUMENTS	045	D	3	70
CHAPMAN	CHAS				49	ENGLAND	CE	ENGLISH	LAB	043	E	2	36
CHAPMAN	DILWORTH		1		65	US	QU	IRISH	LAB	043	B	5	34
CHAPMAN	ELIZA		1	1	16	ENGLAND	CE	ENGLISH		045	A	1	34
CHAPMAN	EMMA		1		5	ENGLAND	CE	ENGLISH		043	F		17
CHAPMAN	GEORGE				53	ENGLAND	CO	ENGLISH	FARMER	045	D	1	2
CHAPMAN	HARRIETT		1	1	37	ENGLAND	CE	ENGLISH		045	A	1	34
CHAPMAN	HENRY				70	ENGLAND	CE	ENGLISH	BREWER	043	F		10
CHAPMAN	IDA		1	1	15	0	WM	ENGLISH		045	D	3	45
CHAPMAN	ISAAC				48	0	WM	ENG	F	044	B	1	8
CHAPMAN	JAMES				50	0	WM	ENG	F	044	B	1	8
CHAPMAN	JAMES				38	0	CE	ENGLISH	F	045	C	4	14
CHAPMAN	JESSE				36	0	WM	ENGLISH	F	045	C	3	43
CHAPMAN	JOHN				30	0	CP	ENGLISH	F	044	A	2	38
CHAPMAN	JOHN				66	0	NR	ENG	F	044	B	1	17
CHAPMAN	JOHN				77	ENGLAND	FW	ENGLISH	FARMER	045	A	1	55
CHAPMAN	JOHN				43	0	WM	ENGLISH	F	045	C	2	26
CHAPMAN	JOHN				30	0	WM	ENGLISH	F	045	C	4	14
CHAPMAN	JOSEPH			M	24	0	CE	ENGLISH	STATION MASTER	043	A	1	55
CHAPMAN	JOSHUA				43	ENGLAND	CE	ENGLISH	BRICKMAKER	043	E	2	36
CHAPMAN	MARGARET		1	1	48	0	WM	GERMAN		043	B	4	11
CHAPMAN	NATHAN				59	0	PM	ENGLISH	F	045	C	4	1
CHAPMAN	ORRIN		1		18	0	WM	ENGLISH	F LAB	043	B	4	11
CHAPMAN	PARISH				42	ENGLAND	WM	ENGLISH	F	044	A	1	13
CHAPMAN	PHOEBE		1	1	19	0	WM	ENGLISH	SERVANT	043	E	1	32
CHAPMAN	ROBERT				67	ENGLAND	BA	ENGLISH	F	044	A	3	4
CHAPMAN	ROBERT	F			33	ENGLAND	CE	ENGLAND	LABORER	045	D	2	9
CHAPMAN	SARAH		1	1	11	ENGLAND	DI	ENGLISH		045	A	1	105
CHAPMAN	SEITH				56	0	OP	ENGLISH	F	043	H	2	34
CHAPMAN	SEITH				56	ONTARIO	CS	ENGLISH	FARMER	043	H	2	34
CHAPMAN	THOMAS		1		49	ENGLAND	DI	ENGLISH	LAB	045	A	1	105
CHAPMAN	WILLIAM				42	0	CP	ENGLISH	F	045	C	2	24
CHAPPEL	ELISHA			M	59	US	CN	ENGLAND	F	043	A	5	22
CHAPPEL	JOHN				49	ENGLAND	PM	ENGLISH	FARMER	045	D	2	43
CHAPPELL	EDWARD				32	0	QU	ENGLISH	F	043	A	6	28
CHAPPELL	LOMIS				28	0	QU	ENGLISH	F	043	A	6	28
CHAPPELL	ORLIN				60	U STATES	QU	ENGLISH	F	043	A	6	28
CHAPPELL	STERLIN				56	U STATES	CN		F	043	A	6	24
CHARBONEAU	MARY	J		1	79	QUE	RC	FRENCH		044	A	2	31
CHARLES	GEORGE				36	ONTARIO	WM	OJIBWAY INDIAN	HUNTER AND FISHER	043	G	1	60
CHARLES	JACOB				63	ONTARIO	WM	OJIBWAY INDIAN	HUNTER AND FISHER	043	G	1	58
CHARLES	JAMES				48	IRELAND	QU	ENGLISH	WHEELWRIGHT	043	A	6	3
CHARLES	JAMES				38	0	WM	CHIPPAWA	F	043	H	2	57
CHARLES	JAMES				38	ONTARIO	WM	CHIPPAWA		043	H	2	57
CHARLES	JOHN		2			ONTARIO	WM			043	G	1	D
CHARLES	LOUISA		2	1		ONTARIO	WM			043	G	1	D
CHARLES	SARAH	M		1	53	0	CE	ENGLISH		044	C	4	62
CHARLES	THOMAS				30	ONTARIO	WM	CHIPPAWA	FARMER	043	H	2	55
CHARLES	THOMS				30	0	WM	CHIPPAWA	F	043	H	2	55
CHARLES	WILLIAM		1	M	21	ENGLAND	PM	ENGLISH	LAB	043	A	1	42
CHARLES	WILLIAM				26	ONTARIO	WM	INDIAN	LABORER	043	G	1	17
CHARLETON	THOMAS				54	ENGLAND	CE	ENGLISH	BLACKSMITH & FARMER	044	C	4	31
CHARLTON	GEORGE				28	0	EM	ENG	F	044	B	1	45
CHARLTON	JOHN				64	ENG	CE	ENG	F	044	B	1	21
CHARLTON	MARGARET		1	1	18	0	CE	IRISH		045	A	1	38
CHARLTON	THOMAS				31	0	EM	ENG	F	044	B	1	21
CHARLTON	THOMAS		1		16	0	CE	IRISH	BRICKMAKER	045	A	1	38
CHARPONTER	ANTHONY				66	QUEBEC	RC	FRENCH	FARMER	043	H	2	29
CHARPONTIER	ADOLPHUS				57	QUEBEC	RC	FRENCH	LAB	043	H	2	19
CHARPONTIER	ADOLPHUS				57	QUEBEC	RC	FRENCH	LABOURER	043	H	2	19
CHARPONTIER	ANTHONY				66	QUEBEC	RC	FRENCH	F	043	H	2	29
CHARPONTIER	EDWARD				27	0	RC	FRENCH	F	043	H	2	22
CHARPONTIER	EDWARD				27	ONTARIO	RC	FRENCH	FARMER	043	H	2	22
CHARPONTIER	JOHN	B			29	QUEBEC	RC	FRENCH	LAB	043	H	2	18
CHARPONTIER	JOHN	B			29	QUEBEC	RC	FRENCH	F	043	H	2	18
CHATMAN	PATRICK				49	IRELAND	RC	IRISH	LAWYER	044	C	3	35
CHATTERLEY	WILLIAM				41	ENGLAND	WM	ENGLISH	FARM LABORER	045	D	1	16
CHECKELEY	WILLIAM				47	IRELAND	CE	IRISH	CLERGYMAN	044	C	3	30
CHECKLEY	EMILY		1	1	16	ENGLAND	CE	ENGLISH	SERVANT	044	C	3	33
CHECKLY	ALFRED		1		20	ENGLAND	NG	ENGLISH	BUTCHER	045	B	2	30
CHEEDLE	BENJAMIN		1		54	ENGLAND	CE	ENGLISH	BLACKSMITH	044	A	2	46
CHEESBORO	HILTON				60	ENGLAND	WM	ENGLISH	MINISTER	045	A	2	1
CHEESEMAN	ABNER				70	US	WM	GERMAN	LABOURER	045	D	3	57
CHEESWRIGHT	REB				75	ENGLAND	WM	ENGLISH	MERCHANT	045	C	2	3
CHEFFIN	W	D			36	ENGLAND	CE	ENGLISH	HOSTLER	044	B	5	4
CHELEW	CATHERINE		1	1	19	0	WM	ENG	SERVANT	045	C	1	13
CHELEW	JOHN				32	ENGLAND	PM	ENGLISH	F	045	C	4	32
CHENEY	WILLIAM				37	ENGLAND	PM	ENGLISH	LAB	045	A	3	36
CHERREY	WILLIAM				65	IRELAND	UP	IRISH	FARMER	045	D	1	43
CHERRY	ABNER				38	ENGLAND	WM	ENGLISH	HOTEL KEEPER	044	C	1	19
CHERRY	JAMES				49	IRELAND	FK	IRISH	F	043	A	3	36
CHERRY	JOHN				58	IRELAND	LU	IRISH	F	044	B	6	46
CHERRY	JOSEPH				27	ENG	EM	ENG	F	044	B	2	6
CHERRY	JOSEPH				23	ENGLAND	WM	ENGLISH	PAINTER	045	D	4	45
CHERRY	MARY		1	1	71	ENGLAND	CE	ENGLISH		045	B	1	69
CHERRY	ROBERT		1		17	0	PM	ENGLISH		043	E	2	68
CHERRY	SAMUEL				62	IRELAND	CP	IRISH	F	043	A	3	53
CHERRY	WM	JAMES	1		8	0	CN	IRISH		043	B	3	68
CHERY	JOSEPH		1		43	IRELAND	PS	IRISH	SHOEMAKER	043	B	3	24
CHESHIRE	RICHARD			M	35	ENGLAND	CE	ENGLAND	SHOEMAKER	043	A	5	14
CHESTER	ELIZABETH		1	1	81	ENG	WM	ENG		045	C	1	48
CHESTER	GEORGE				49	0	CE	ENG	STOREKEEPER	045	C	1	22
CHESTER	HENRY				28	0	WM	ENG	F	045	C	1	49
CHESTER	ISAAC		2		87	ENGLAND	WM		MASON	045	C	1	D
CHESTER	ISAAC				53	ENG	WM	ENG	F	045	C	1	63
CHESTER	MATTHEW		1		40	0	CE	ENGLISH	WHEELRIGHT	045	A	1	13
CHEW	ELIZABETH			1	39	0	CE	ENGLISH		044	C	3	64
CHEW	WILLIAM				30	0	CE	ENGLISH	FARMER	044	C	3	64

SURNAME	NAME1	NAME2	STRAY	SEX	AGE	BIRTHPL	RELIGION	ORIGIN	OCCUP	DIST	SUB_DIST	DIV	PAGE
CHEWETT	ALEXANDER				39	O	CE	ENGLISH	GENTLEMAN	044	C	4	8
CHICK	JAMES		1		20	ENGLAND	WM	ENGLISH	LAB	045	B	1	31
CHIDLEY	HENRY				58	ENGLAND	WM	ENGLISH		045	B	1	49
CHIDLEY	JOHN				30	ENGLAND	WM	ENGLISH	SALESMAN	045	B	1	50
CHILDS	WILLIAM				49	ENGLAND	PM	ENGLISH	WAGON MAKER	043	A	3	12
CHIN	CHARLES		2			O	CE			043	B	3	D
CHIN	FREDERICK				28	ENGLISH	CE	ENGLISH	FARMER	043	B	3	67
CHIPPERFIELD	GEORGE	M			61	ENGLAND	WM	ENGLISH	F	043	H	2	51
CHIPPERFIELD	GEORGE	M			61	ENGLAND	WM	ENGLISH	FARMER	043	H	2	51
CHIPPERFIELD	JOHN		1		71	ENGLAND	CE	ENGLISH	FARMER	043	G	1	51
CHIREPACE	ALBERT		1		18	O	WM	FRENCH	F LAB	044	C	1	10
CHISHOLM	EMMA		1	1	19	O	WM	ENGLISH		044	C	4	32
CHISHOLM	GEORGE				57	SCOTLAND	CP	SCOTCH	CLERK	045	A	1	53
CHISHOLM	KEZIA		1	1	10	O	PM	ENGLISH		044	A	3	36
CHOLWITT	JOHN		1		9	O	WM	ENGLISH		045	B	1	9
CHOLWITT	MARY	JANE	1	1	6	O	WM	ENGLISH		045	B	1	9
CHOLWITT	RACHEL		1	1	8	O	WM	ENGLISH		045	B	1	9
CHOLWITT	WILLIAM	HENRY	1		1	O	WM	ENGLISH		045	B	1	9
CHOWER	HENRY				45	ENGLAND	CE	ENGLISH	F LAB	043	B	4	24
CHRISLEY	ESTER		1		16	O	CE	ENGLISH		043	A	4	45
CHRISTIAN	ANNIE			1	37	IRE	RC	IRE	HOTEL KEEPER	044	B	2	34
CHRISTIE	WILLIAM				42	O	WM	IRISH	F	045	C	4	9
CHRITTENDON	ROSILLIA		2	1			BC			043	H	2	D
CHRYSLER	ELIZABETH		1	1	25	O	NC	IRISH	SERVANT	043	E	1	16
CHURCH	ANNE			1	50	ENGLAND	CE	ENGLISH	INNKEEPER	044	C	4	43
CHURCH	ELLENOR		1	1	23	O	CE	ENGLISH		044	C	4	43
CHURCHELL	OLIVE	J	1	1	18	O	CO	GERMAN	SERVANT	044	A	3	37
CHURCHILL	SYLVESTOR				49	ENGLAND	PM	ENGLISH	LAB	044	B	5	33
CHURCHILL	WM				28	O	WM	ENG		045	C	1	12
CHURNSIDE	JOHN				70	SCOTLAND	CS	SCOTCH	F	043	H	1	9
CHURNSIDE	REBECCA			1	50	O	CS	GERMAN		043	H	1	9
CHUTER	ELIZA		1	1	24	ENGLAND	CE	ENGLISH		045	B	1	54
CLANCY	JOHN		1		30	IRELAND	RC	IRISH	SERVANT	044	B	6	44
CLANCY	LAWRENCE				45	IRE	RC	IRE	LAB	045	C	1	56
CLANCY	PATRICK				60	IRELAND	RC	IRISH	STONE BREAKER	043	F		31
CLARE	HENRY				33	ENGLAND	RC	ENGLISH	LAB	043	C		13
CLARE	MARY	ANN	1	1	17	QUEBEC	RC	IRISH		045	B	2	32
CLAREY	EDMUND				65	IRE	RC	IRISH	LAB	044	B	2	5
CLAREY	MARGARET		1	1	36	SCOT	CP	SCOTCH		044	B	1	7
CLARK	AARON				34	O	WM	ENGLISH	F	043	B	1	26
CLARK	ADAM		2			O	NG			045	C	2	D
CLARK	ADAM				50	SCOTLAND	CP	SCOTCH	FARMER	045	D	4	18
CLARK	ADAM				52	SCOTLAND	CP	SCOT	GENTLEMAN	045	A	4	27
CLARK	ALEXANDER		1		22	SCOTLAND	CP	SCOTCH	SERVANT	045	A	3	32
CLARK	ALISTER	M			38	B INDIA	CE	SCOTCH	BARISTER	045	B	1	69
CLARK	ASINETH		2	1	2	O	NG			045	A	3	D
CLARK	DAVID				49	SCOTLAND	CS	SCOTCH	FARMER	043	G	1	31
CLARK	EDWARD				32	O	WM	ENGLISH	F	043	B	1	20
CLARK	ELIZABETH		1		50	O	LU	GERMAN		045	D	3	41
CLARK	FRANCIS				30	O	WM	ENGLISH	FARMER	045	A	3	25
CLARK	FREDERICK		1		13	O	CE	ENGLAND	SERVANT	045	D	2	26
CLARK	GEORGE				64	SCOTLAND	CP	SCOTCH	SHOEMAKER	044	C	2	8
CLARK	GEORGE	W			70	ENGLAND	WM	ENGLISH		045	B	1	49
CLARK	HENRY				29	ENGLAND	CE	ENGLISH	COOPER	043	H	2	16
CLARK	HENRY				29	ENGLAND	CE	ENGLISH	COOPER	043	H	2	16
CLARK	HENRY				33	O	WM	IRELAND	SADLER	045	D	2	10
CLARK	HUGH				43	SCOTLAND	CP	SCOTCH	F	045	C	4	13
CLARK	JAMES			M	59	IRELAND	WM	IRELAND	F	043	A	5	35
CLARK	JAMES				68	IRE	WM	IRISH	PAINTER	044	B	1	30
CLARK	JAMES				40	O	CP	IRISH	F	045	C	2	45
CLARK	JAMES				54	ENGLAND	WM	ENGLISH	FARMER	045	D	1	22
CLARK	JAMES				29	ENGLAND	WM	ENGLISH	FARM LABORER	045	D	1	37
CLARK	JAMES				30	IRELAND	WM	IRISH	SCHOOL TEACHER	044	C	3	65
CLARK	JOHN				62	ENGLAND	CE	ENGLISH	F LAB	043	B	4	12
CLARK	JOHN				56	SCOTLAND	CS	SCOTCH	F	044	A	1	6
CLARK	JOHN				25	SCOT	PS	SCOT	MACHINIST	044	B	2	17
CLARK	JOHN		1		19	SCOTLAND	CP	SCOTCH	COOPER	045	B	2	11
CLARK	JOSEPH				32	ENGLAND	CE	ENGLISH	MUSIC TEACHER	045	D	4	9
CLARK	LEWIS				28	O	WM	SCOTCH	SCHOOL TEACHER	044	B	1	11
CLARK	MARY		1	1	24	IRELAND	CP	IRISH		045	A	2	18
CLARK	MATHEW				43	IRE	RC	IRE	LAB	044	B	2	42
CLARK	MATTHEW		1		26	IRELAND	CP	IRISH	LAB	045	A	2	18
CLARK	MELINDA		1	1	61	US	CP	SCOT	HOUSEKEEPER	044	B	1	38
CLARK	PHILIP	JAMES			27	IRELAND	WM	IRISH	SCHOOL TEACHER	044	C	4	77
CLARK	ROBERT				48	SCOT	CS	SCOT	BLACKSMITH	044	B	2	7
CLARK	ROBERT				32	O	WM	ENGLISH	FARMER	045	A	3	40
CLARK	ROBERT				52	IRELAND	WM	IRISH	FARMER POSTMASTER	044	C	3	56
CLARK	SARAH		1	1	63	IRELAND	CP	ENGLISH		043	B	2	10
CLARK	SARAH		2	1	66	ENGLAND	CE			045	C	2	D
CLARK	SARAH	J	1	1	24	IRELAND	WM	IRISH		044	C	4	77
CLARK	SILAS				65	O	CN	ENGLISH	F	043	E	1	21
CLARK	SINCLAIR		1		18	O	LU	WELSH	FARMER	045	D	3	43
CLARK	THOMAS				25	IRELAND	CE	IRISH	F	043	E	3	27
CLARK	THOMAS				47	ENGLAND	CE	ENGLISH	LABOURER	045	A	1	83
CLARK	WILLIAM		1		60	ENGLAND	WM	ENGLISH	LAB	045	A	3	34
CLARK	WILLIAM				64	ENGLAND	CE	ENGLISH	TEACHER	045	C	2	10
CLARK	WILLIAM				47	SCOTLAND	CP	SCOTCH	F	045	C	3	34
CLARK	WILLIAM				76	SCOTLAND	CP	SCOTCH	F	045	C	4	7
CLARK	WILLIAM				45	O	WM	IRISH	F	044	C	3	6
CLARKE	A	B			35	O	CO	SCOTCH	SCHOOL TEACHER	044	B	5	52
CLARKE	ANN		1	1	45	O	WM	GERMAN		045	A	3	4
CLARKE	CHARLES		1	1	15	O	WM	ENGLISH	PRINTER	043	D		33
CLARKE	ELISEBETH		1	1	67	U STATES	QU	ENGLISH		043	A	6	6
CLARKE	ELVIRA		1	1	25	IRELAND	CE	IRISH	F SERVANT	044	C	1	1
CLARKE	GEORGE				55	ENGLAND	CE	ENGLISH	BAKER	044	A	3	56
CLARKE	HENRY		1		30	ENGLAND	CE	ENGLISH	LABOURER	045	D	5	53
CLARKE	HIRAM				45	O	BA	SCOTCH	LAB	044	B	6	45
CLARKE	J DICKINSON				34	O	WM	IRISH	F	044	C	1	10
CLARKE	JAMES	P			62	SCOTLAND	NG	SCOTCH	PROFESSOR OF MUSIC	045	B	2	28
CLARKE	JANE				59	ENGLAND	CE	ENGLISH		044	B	5	77
CLARKE	JOHN				33	IRELAND	CE	IRISH	F	043	H	1	32
CLARKE	JOHN				26	O	WM	ENGLISH	FARMER	045	D	2	68
CLARKE	JOHN	H			32	O	WM	IRISH	F	044	C	2	16
CLARKE	THOMAS		1		21	IRELAND	CE	DENMARK	CLERK	043	A	4	25
CLARKE	THOMAS		1		73	IRELAND	CE	IRISH	F LAB	044	A	1	31
CLARKE	THOMAS				62	ENGLAND	WM	ENGLISH	FARMER	045	A	3	4

SURNAME	NAME1	NAME2	STRAY	SEX	AGE	BIRTHPL	RELIGION	ORIGIN	OCCUP	DIST	SUB_DIST	DIV	PAGE
CLARKE	THOMAS				40	ENGLAND	PM	ENGLISH	FARM LABOURER	045	C	4	31
CLARKE	WASHINGTON		1		26	0	CE	IRISH	LAB	045	A	3	6
CLARKE	WILLIAM				46	ENGLAND	WM	ENGLISH	LAB	043	C		15
CLARKSON	FRANCIS		1		23	0	CX	ENGLISH	CLERK	045	A	3	10
CLARKSON	GEORGE				28	ENGLAND	WM	ENGLISH	F	044	A	2	25
CLARKSON	JOHN				52	ENGLAND	CE	ENGLISH	LAB	043	A	6	17
CLARKSON	JOHN				30	ENGLAND	PM	ENGLISH	F	044	B	5	74
CLARKSON	MARY ANN			1	61	0	WM	GERMAN	FARMER	045	D	4	3
CLARKSON	ROBT				28	ENGLAND	WM	ENGLISH	FARMER	043	B	3	35
CLARY	JAMES				30	IRE	RC	IRISH	LAB	044	B	1	8
CLARY	MARY		1	1	24	0	RC	IRE		044	B	2	37
CLAUS	DENIS				40	Q	RC	FRENCH	LAB	043	A	6	65
CLAXTON	THOMAS				48	ENGLAND	WM	ENGLISH	COOPER	045	D	1	9
CLAY	SARAH			1	66	ENGLAND	WM	ENGLISH		045	D	1	9
CLAYBURG	JANE			1	27	0	ZZ	WELSH	SEAMSTRESS	043	E	2	39
CLAYTON	CHARLES				25	ENGLAND	CE	ENGLISH	GARDENER	044	A	2	44
CLAYTON	GEORGE	H			50	ENGLAND	CE	ENGLISH	PAINTER	045	B	1	43
CLAYTON	JOSEPH				45	U STATES	QU	ENGLISH	F	044	B	5	17
CLAYTON	JOSEPH				38	ENGLAND	PM	ENGLISH	F	044	B	6	20
CLAYTON	JOSHUA				41	U STATES	QU	ENGLISH	FARMER	043	A	4	54
CLAYTON	LYDIA	ANN	1	1	40	UNITED STATES	QU	ENGLISH		043	E	2	3
CLAYTON	SUSAN		1	1	16	0	PM	ENGLISH	SERVANT	044	A	3	54
CLEARY	WILLIAM				50	IRELAND	RC	IRISH	LABORER	043	G	1	44
CLEAVER	SARAH		1	1	22	ENGLAND	CN	ENGLISH		043	B	3	72
CLEGG	JOHN				27	ENGLAND	CE	ENGLISH	F	045	A	4	4
CLELAND	JAMES		1		28	IRELAND	CE	IRISH	LAB	043	H	1	28
CLELAND	SAMUEL			M	32	IRELAND	PS	IRISH	SHOEMAKER	043	A	2	24
CLELAND	THOMAS		1		19	0	WM	IRISH		045	B	1	8
CLELLAND	ROBERT				54	SCOTLAND	PS	SCOTCH	F	043	E	1	33
CLEMENT	DAVID				50	0	WM	ENGLISH	LABORER	045	D	2	38
CLEMENT	WILLIAM			M	32	SCOTLAND	UP	SCOTCH	F	043	A	2	54
CLEMENTS	JOHN				25	ENGLAND	CE	ENGLISH	FARMER	045	D	1	34
CLENDENAN	HIRAM				30	CANADA	CN	IRISH	LABORER	045	D	6	38
CLENDENAN	MOSES				51	CANADA	WM	IRISH	FARMER	045	D	6	33
CLENDENAN	RANSON				32	CANADA	WM	IRISH	FARMER	045	D	6	39
CLENDENAN	WILLIAM				42	CANADA	WM	IRISH		045	D	6	30
CLENDENING	ALBERT		1		17	0	WM	GERMAN		043	B	3	36
CLENDENNAN	JAMES				39	CANADA	MN	IRISH	FARMER	045	D	6	29
CLENDENNEN	ADAM				60	CANADA	WM	IRISH	FARMER	045	D	6	32
CLENDENNING	GEO				28	0	MN	GERMAN	F	043	B	2	29
CLENDENNING	MARION		1	F	32	0	PM	GERMAN		043	A	1	14
CLENDENNING	WILLIAM				28	0	VM	GERMAN	LABOURER	045	D	3	68
CLENDINEN	DERIUS				23	CANADA	CO	IRISH	FARMER	045	D	6	56
CLENDINING	AARON		1		5	0	WM			045	D	5	25
CLENDINING	JACOB				58	CANADA	BA	IRISH	LABOURER	045	D	6	31
CLENDINING	JANE		1	1	10	0	WM			045	D	5	25
CLENDINING	RACHAEL		1	1	40	0	WM	ENGLISH		045	D	5	25
CLENNAN	SARAH		1	1	66	IRELAND	PS	IRISH		044	C	4	71
CLENNING	THOMAS		1		19	0	WM	IRISH	CARPENTER	045	B	2	14
CLERKIN	PHILLIP				32	ENGLAND	CE	ENGLISH	FARMER	045	D	6	23
CLERONEY	ELIZABETH		1	1	59	SCOTLAND	WM	SCOTCH		045	B	2	7
CLERRY	WILLIAM				39	CANADIAN	WM	IRISH	FARMER	045	D	6	23
CLEVER	ELIZABETH		1	1	20	0	CN	ENGLISH	SERVANT	043	E	2	56
CLEWES	JOHN				38	ENGLAND	CE	ENGLISH	TINSMITH	045	B	2	2
CLIFFORD	ANDREW				37	0	PS	ENGLISH	STOREKEEPER	043	B	3	63
CLIFFORD	JAMES				62	ENGLAND	CE	ENGLISH	FARMER	045	D	2	36
CLIFFORD	JOHN				55	ENGLAND	CE	ENGLISH	F	044	C	4	97
CLIFFORD	SAMUEL				62	ENGLAND	CE	ENGLISH	LAB	045	A	1	105
CLIFT	JOHN	W			54	ENGLAND	WM	ENGLISH	BLACKSMITH	043	C		40
CLIFT	SAMUEL				42	ENGLAND	CE	ENGLISH	BLACKSMITH	043	B	2	19
CLIFTON	JANE			1	23	0	CP	SCOTCH		044	B	6	41
CLIFTON	JARVIS	H			26	ENGLAND	CE	ENGLISH	MERCHANT	045	D	2	8
CLIMIE	JOHN	M			37	0	CO	SCOTCH	MILLER & FARMER	044	A	2	44
CLINIC	ALEX		1		20	0	CO	SCOTCH	MERCHT	044	B	5	5
CLINK	THOMAS				44	ENGLAND	CE	ENGLISH	CARPENTER	045	B	1	59
CLISSOLD	SAMUEL				32	ENGLAND	PM	ENGLISH	COOPER	043	H	1	24
CLISSOLD	THOMAS				66	ENGLAND	PM	ENGLISH	WEAVER	043	B	2	33
CLODD	WILLIAM				34	0	CP	ENGLISH	LAB	045	C	2	53
CLOFFY	MARY		1	1	10	0	CE	IRISH		043	D		15
CLOSE	FRED		1		22	0	UP	IRISH	PAINTER	043	C		15
CLOSSEN	LENORA		1	1	17	0	EM	ENGLISH		045	D	5	48
CLOSSON	LORENZO	D			41	USA	CE	ENG	PHYSICIAN	045	C	1	22
CLOSSON	STEPHEN				53	US	WM	SCOTCH	F	045	C	2	16
CLUBINE	DANIEL	W			27	0	PR	GERMAN	LAWYER	043	B	1	18
CLUBINE	EZRA			M	43	0	WM	FRENCH	F	043	A	1	36
CLUBINE	ISRAEL				51	0	BA	GERMAN	F	043	B	2	14
CLUBINE	JOHN				21	0	EM	GERMAN	F	043	B	2	16
CLUBINE	JOHN				60	0	IM	GERMAN	F	043	B	4	5
CLUBINE	WARD				34	US	CE	GERMAN	SAWYER	043	B	5	39
CLUBINE	WILLIAM	H			27	0	EM	IRE	F	044	B	4	32
CLUNE	ALEX R		1		19	SCOTLAND	FK	SCOTCH	MILLER	044	B	5	2
CLUNEY	THOMAS		1		22	0	PM	IRISH	LAB	043	B	2	13
CLUNIE	JOHN		1		42	SCOTLAND	CS	SCOTCH	BARTENDER	043	D		66
CLUSTON	J	C	1		37	0	PS	ENGLISH	PAINTER	043	F		32
COADY	FREDERICK		1		13	0	CN	IRISH		043	B	5	15
COATES	THOMAS				23	0	CE	ENGLISH	F	043	B	1	10
COATES	THOMAS				56	0	WM	ENGLISH	F	043	B	4	15
COATES	THOMAS				36	ENGLAND	CE	ENGLISH	F	045	C	4	4
COATES	WESLEY				57	WEST INDIES	EM	AFRICAN	LAB	044	C	2	48
COATS	JAMES				46	0	CE	ENGLISH	F	043	B	4	27
COATS	JOHN				42	ENGLAND	WM	ENGLISH	F	045	A	4	12
COBB	ANN		2	1	1	0	PM			044	C	2	D
COBB	CHARLES				45	ENGLAND	WM	ENGLISH	F	044	A	2	8
COBB	GEORGE				58	ENGLAND	CE	ENGLISH	FARMER	045	A	2	11
COBB	GEORGE				22	ENGLAND	PM	ENGLISH	LAB	044	C	2	11
COBBIN	FREDERICK				31	ENGLAND	WM	ENGLISH	LABORER	045	D	2	8
COBER	CATHERINE			1	33	0	MN	GER		044	B	1	24
COBER	GEORGE				45	0	TU	GER	F	044	B	1	42
COBER	PETER				71	0	TU	GER	RETIRED MERCHANT	045	B	1	42
COBURN	MINNIE		1	1	65	SCOTLAND	UP	SCOTCH		045	D	1	34
COCHERAN	JOHN				47	SCOTLAND	CS	SCOTCH	TINSMITH	044	B	6	11
COCHRAN	WILLIAM				40	SCOTLAND	CP	SCOTCH	PAINTER	043	A	4	23
COCHRANE	WM		1		23	IRELAND	CE	IRISH	F SERVANT	044	C	1	1
COCKALINE	MATTHEW		1		69	ENGLAND	CE	ENGLISH	MILLWRIGHT	045	A	1	90
COCKBURN	JOSEPH				39	SCOTLAND	OP	SCOTCH	F	043	H	2	38
COCKBURN	JOSEPH				39	SCOTLAND	CS	SCOTCH	FARMER	043	H	2	38

SURNAME	NAME1	NAME2	STRAY	SEX	AGE	BIRTHPL	RELIGION	ORIGIN	OCCUP	DIST	SUB_DIST	DIV	PAGE
COCKBURN	PETER				60	SCOTLAND	PS	SCOTCH	LAB	044	B	5	45
COCKBURN	WM				48	SCOT	CP	SCOT	F	045	C	1	36
COCKEREL	JOHN				50	ENGLAND	CE	ENGLISH	LABOURER	045	D	3	63
COCKERILL	WILLIAM				32	ENGLAND	CE	ENGLISH	F	043	A	6	54
COCKLINE	ROBERT				75	ENGLAND	WM	ENGLISH	F	043	E	3	37
COCKLUM	PETER				60	SCOT	PS	SCOT	LUMBERMAN	044	B	3	49
CODD	JAMES				44	ENGLAND	OB?	ENGLISH	LAB	045	A	4	15
CODE	MARGARET		1	1	16	O	WM	IRISH		045	D	5	42
CODLIN	MARY			1	57	ENGLAND	CE	ENGLISH	F	044	A	3	53
CODLIN	MATTHEW				32	O	CE	ENGLISH	F	044	A	3	53
CODLIN	THOS				27	O	CE	ENGLISH	F	044	A	3	53
CODNEY	THOMAS				32	IRELAND	RC	IRISH	FARM LABOURER	045	B	1	3
CODY	AARON				73	U STATES	CN	IRISH	F	043	A	3	16
CODY	ALLAN				48	O	WM	IRISH	CARPENTER	044	B	5	13
CODY	ALLEN				40	O	QU	WELSH	F	043	E	1	32
CODY	BENJAMIN				49	O	QU	WELSH	FARMER & WHEELWRIGHT	043	E	1	19
CODY	STEPHEN				78	O	QU	WELSH	F	043	E	1	32
COE	MARK				55	ENGLAND	CE	ENGLISH	F	044	C	4	3
COGSWELL	MASON				51	NS	WM	ENG	WHEELWRIGHT	044	B	1	49
COGSWELL	SARAH	C	1	1	19	O	CE	ENGLISH	DRESS MAKER	045	D	1	14
COHEN	AGNES		1	1	38	ENGLAND	CE	ENGLISH	INMATE	045	B	1	72
COIN	THOMAS				50	IRELAND	RC	IRISH	LABORER	043	D		71
COLBERT	DAVID				54	IRELAND	CP	IRISH	WEAVER	045	D	3	54
COLBERT	FRANCIS		1		20	IRELAND	CP	IRISH	SADLER	045	D	1	13
COLBORNE	DINAH		1	1	21	QUE	CE	ENGLISH		044	C	2	14
COLBORNE	ELLEN			1	55	IRELAND	RC	IRISH	PEDDLING	043	A	3	16
COLDER	JOHN		1		20	SCOTCH	CP	SCOTCH	CLERK	043	D		55
COLDREY	THOMAS				48	ENGLAND	RC	ENGLISH	GARDENER	045	A	1	20
COLDWELL	MORGAN				34	IRELAND	CE	IRISH	BARRISTER	043	F		31
COLE	AMOS				28	ENGLAND	WM	ENGLISH	FARMER	045	D	5	60
COLE	BENJAMIN				70	US	WM	AFRICAN	LAB	044	C	4	86
COLE	FREDERICK		1		23	ENGLAND	CE	ENGLISH	WATCH MAKER	045	A	1	96
COLE	JOHN				45	ENGLAND	EM	ENGLISH	F	043	E	2	52
COLE	MARY		2	1	71	ENGLAND	EM			043	E	3	D
COLE	ROBERT				33	ENGLAND	PM	ENGLISH	FARMER	045	D	4	50
COLE	SAMUEL				42	ENGLAND	EM	ENGLISH	F	043	E	2	75
COLE	SAMUEL				53	NB	WM	ENGLISH	LABOURER	045	D	5	70
COLE	WARREN	P			34	USA	WM	ENGLISH	TINSMITH	043	H	2	6
COLE	WARREN	W			34	UNITED STATES	WM	ENGLISH	TINSMITH	043	H	2	6
COLE	WILLIAM				36	O	EM	ENGLISH	F	043	E	3	12
COLE	WILLIAM				48	ENGLAND	CE	ENGLISH	COMMERCIAL TRAVELER	045	B	1	70
COLEHOUN	JOHN				30	IRELAND	CP	IRISH	LAB	044	A	3	3
COLEMAN	ANN		1	1	28	ENGLAND	CE	ENGLISH		045	D	2	64
COLEMAN	DENIS				46	IRELAND	RC	IRISH	FARMER	045	D	2	35
COLEMAN	GEORGE		1		12	ENG	CE	ENG		044	B	2	52
COLEMAN	GEORGE		1		16	O	PS	ENGLISH	F LAB	044	C	1	24
COLEMAN	HENRY		1		37	ENG	CE	ENG	LAB	044	B	2	52
COLEMAN	JAMES				28	ENGLAND	WM	ENGLISH	FARM LABOURER	045	C	4	27
COLEMAN	JOHN				32	O	EM	ENG	FARM LAB	044	B	1	47
COLEMAN	JOHN		1		30	ENGLAND	CE	ENGLISH	FARMER	045	D	2	64
COLEMAN	JOHN				62	ENGLAND	WM	ENGLISH	F	044	C	1	8
COLEMAN	JOHN				32	O	WM	ENGLISH	F	045	A	4	9
COLEMAN	THOMAS	W			29	O	EM	ENGLISH	WAGGON MAKER	044	C	2	14
COLEMAN	WILLIAM				46	ENG	EM	ENG	F	044	B	1	49
COLES	WILLIAM				37	ENGLAND	CE	ENGLISH	BAKER	045	B	2	1
COLFER	ANN		1	1	16	O	RC	IRISH		045	D	2	34
COLFORD	CATHARINE		1	1	17	O	RC	IRISH	SERVANT	045	D	5	2
COLGROVE	JOHN	H			44	ENG	CE	ENG	WHEELWRIGHT	045	C	1	27
COLIN	THOMAS				44	ENGLAND	CE	ENGLISH	F	043	E	2	48
COLLARD	GEORGE				36	U STATES	WM	ENGLISH	F & CARPENTER	043	B	1	18
COLLARD	JOSEPH				34	O	WM	IRISH	DROVER	044	C	4	42
COLLENS	JOSEPH		1		17	GERMANY	CE	ENGLISH		045	A	3	4
COLLETON	PATRICK		2		50	IRELAND	RC			044	C	3	D
COLLETT	CHARLES		1	M	30	ENGLAND	CE	ENGLISH	BLACKSMITH	043	A	1	11
COLLETT	JOHN		2			O	CE			045	A	1	D
COLLETT	JOHN	WM			33	ENGLAND	CE	ENGLISH	LAB	045	A	1	14
COLLEY	JOHN				35	ENGLAND	CE	ENGLISH	INNKEEPER	044	C	4	24
COLLIGHAN	JANET		1	1	51	SCOTLAND	RC	SCOTCH		043	C		18
COLLING	WILLIAM				42	IRELAND	EV	IRISH	FARMER	045	D	6	53
COLLINGTON	DANIEL		1		4	CANADA	CN	GERMAN		045	D	6	25
COLLINGWOOD	CHARLES				42	ENGLAND	PM	ENGLISH	LAB	045	A	4	2
COLLINS		MRS R		1	42	ENGLAND	PM	ENGLISH	F	045	C	3	43
COLLINS	BEN		1	M	20	O	PR	IRISH	LAB	043	A	1	74
COLLINS	BRIDGET		1	1	50	IRELAND	RC	IRISH		044	A	1	31
COLLINS	CATHERINE		1	1	13	O	RC	IRISH	SERVANT	044	C	1	24
COLLINS	ELIZABETH		1	1	9	O	WM	SCOTCH		045	A	2	29
COLLINS	ELLEN		1	F	60	IRELAND	RC	IRISH		043	A	1	61
COLLINS	EMILY		1	1	12	O	CE	ENGLISH	SERVANT	045	A	3	26
COLLINS	EMMA			F	12	O	PS	IRISH		043	A	1	28
COLLINS	GEORGE				55	ENGLAND	WM	ENGLISH	LABOURER	045	A	1	83
COLLINS	HANNAH		1	1	43	ENGLAND	CE	ENGLISH	SERVANT	044	C	3	28
COLLINS	HENRY	G	1		28	ENGLAND	CE	ENGLISH	MUSIC TEACHER	045	D	5	12
COLLINS	J	W			55	O	CN	WELSH	TOWNSHIP CLERK	043	B	4	20
COLLINS	JAMES		1		15	O	CE	ENGLISH		044	A	1	21
COLLINS	JANE		1	1	20	O	WM	ENGLISH	SERVANT	043	E	1	3
COLLINS	JOHN				50	IRELAND	RC	IRISH	F	043	A	3	27
COLLINS	JOHN				60	IRELAND	PM	IRISH	F	043	B	2	38
COLLINS	JOHN		1		25	O	WM	IRISH	SERVANT	043	E	1	3
COLLINS	JOHN				58	O	CN	ENGLISH	CARPENTER	043	E	2	1
COLLINS	JOHN				69	IRELAND	RC	IRISH	LAB	044	B	1	5
COLLINS	JOHN				44	ENGLAND	BC	ENGLISH	BLACKSMITH	045	C	2	5
COLLINS	JOHN	A			33	ENGLAND	CE	ENGLISH	CABINET MAKER	043	A	4	17
COLLINS	JOSEPH				62	ENGLAND	CE	ENGLISH	F	045	C	2	38
COLLINS	JOSHUA				49	IRELAND	CS	IRISH	PHYSICIAN	043	D		54
COLLINS	LUCINDA			1	58	O	QU	ENGLISH		043	D		65
COLLINS	MARY			1	90	IRE	RC	IRE		044	B	2	23
COLLINS	PATRICK				50	IRELAND	RC	IRISH	F	044	C	1	25
COLLINS	PETER		1		11	ENGLAND	WM	SCOTCH		045	A	2	29
COLLINS	RICHARD				50	ENGLAND	EP	ENGLISH	WELL DIGGER	045	C	3	4
COLLINS	SARAH		1	1	14	ENGLAND	WM	SCOTCH		045	A	2	29
COLLINS	THOMAS				40	IRELAND	RC	IRISH	LAB	044	C	4	96
COLLINS	WILLIAM				48	IRELAND	WM	IRISH	FARMER	043	G	1	11
COLLINS	WILLIAM				30	ENGLAND	WM	ENGLISH	F	045	C	2	3
COLLINS	WILLIAM		1		50	ENGLAND	CE	ENGLISH	LAB	045	C	2	22
COLLITON	ELLEN		1	1	15	O	RC	IRISH	SERVANT	044	C	2	21
COLLITON	JANE			1	44	US	RC	IRISH		044	C	3	36

SURNAME	NAME1	NAME2	STRAY	SEX	AGE	BIRTHPL	RELIGION	ORIGIN	OCCUP	DIST	SUB_DIST	DIV	PAGE
COLLOME	HENRY			M	32	E	PR	ENGLISH	HOTEL KEEPER	043	A	1	3
COLLS	JOHN				39	ENGLAND	CE	ENGLISH	FOUNDRY	045	B	1	23
COLMAN	N	G	1		28	ENGLAND	CE	ENGLISH	SADDLER	044	C	3	4
COLMEMAN	CLARA	MAY	2	1	0	0	EM			044	C	2	D
COLPITTS	CHARLES	H	2			0	NG			044	B	2	D
COLPITTS	THOMAS				27	ENG	EP	ENG	LAB	044	B	2	6
COLSON	JAMES				26	0	FK	ENGLISH	FARMER	045	A	3	29
COLSON	JOHN				64	ENGLAND	FK	ENGLISH	FARMER	045	A	3	29
COLTER	JAMES				49	IRELAND	WM	IRISH	MILLWRIGHT	044	C	3	74
COLTER	MARTHA		1	1	56	IRELAND	WM	IRISH		045	B	1	4
COLTHAM	EDWARD				55	ENGLAND	WM	ENGLISH	F	043	B	1	23
COLTMAN	GEORGE				46	ENGLAND	CE	ENGLISH	F	043	B	4	38
COLVIN	EMMA		1	1	20	ENGLAND	WM	ENGLISH		045	D	5	30
COLWELL	WILLIAM				50	ENGLAND	WM	ENGLISH	LUMBER MERCHANT	044	C	4	62
COMA	CAROLINE			1	68	ENGLAND	CE	ENGLISH		043	E	2	65
COMER	WILLIAM				36	ONTARIO	CN	ENGLISH	FARMER	043	G	1	43
COMERFORD	WILLIAM				45	IRELAND	CE	IRISH	SCHOOL TEACHER	044	B	6	27
COMISKEY	MICHAEL				50	IRELAND	RC	IRISH	LAB	045	C	2	1
CONAGHAN	JAMES				59	SCOTLAND	PS	SCOTTISH	F	044	C	1	31
CONBOY	JAMES				30	IRELAND	WM	IRISH	LAB	044	C	4	93
CONDRACK	MARY		1	1	60	IRELAND	RC	IRISH		043	B	4	13
CONDUIT	FRANK		1		25	ENG	EP	ENG	LAB	044	B	2	7
CONGDON	JAMES				34	ENGLAND	WM	ENGLISH	F	044	A	2	7
CONGER	ALANSON	P			42	US	PM	UNKNOWN	FOREMAN	044	B	2	35
CONLIGHTY	JAMES				32	IRELAND	RC	IRISH	LAB	044	C	4	80
CONLON	WILLIAM				51	IRELAND	RC	IRISH	FARMER	045	A	3	19
CONN	SOLOMON			M	28	0	FK	IRELAND	F	043	A	5	34
CONNELL	JAMES				48	IRELAND	WM	IRISH	LABORER	043	G	1	15
CONNELL	JOHANN				66	IRELAND	RC	IRISH		045	C	2	2
CONNELL	MICHAEL				37	IRELAND	RC	IRISH	FARMER	045	A	1	86
CONNELL	PATRICK				41	IRELAND	CN	IRISH	FARMER	043	G	1	24
CONNELL	WILLIAM				24	ONTARIO	CP	IRISH	LABOURER	043	G	1	10
CONNELY	WILLIAM				55	IRELAND	RC	IRISH	FARMER	045	D	6	74
CONNER	CONRAD				87	UNITED STATES	CN	GERMAN	FARMER	043	B	3	56
CONNER	JACOB				30	0	WM	GERMAN	LABOURER	043	B	3	47
CONNER	JACOB				30	0	CN	GERMAN	LAB	043	B	5	17
CONNER	JAMES				42	0	WM	IRISH	FARMER	043	B	3	39
CONNER	JOHN				52	0	WM	GERMAN	FARMER	043	B	3	57
CONNER	RACHEL		1	1	14	0	CN	GERMAN		043	B	3	72
CONNER	SOPHINA		1	1	21	0	CN	GERMAN		043	B	3	19
CONNERS	DENNIS				50	IRELAND	RC	IRISH	LABOURER	045	A	1	80
CONNISKY	WILLIAM				25	IRELAND	CE	IRISH	DOCTOR MEDCINE	045	D	5	14
CONNLLY	MARY		1	1	40	IRELAND	WM	IRISH	SERVANT	044	C	3	41
CONNOR	CATHERINE		2	1	55	IRELAND	RC			043	A	6	D
CONNOR	CORNELIUS				60	IRELAND	RC	IRISH	F	043	A	3	20
CONNOR	DAVID				50	IRELAND	RC	IRISH	F	044	C	4	2
CONNOR	ELMIRA		1	1	11	0	CE	IRISH		045	D	2	49
CONNOR	JOHN	0?			25	0	RC	IRISH	F	043	A	3	20
CONNOR	ROBERT				56	IRELAND	WM	IRISH	GEN INSURANCE AGENT	043	C		42
CONNOR	ROBERT		2		23	CANADA	WM		MERCHANTS CLERK	043	C		D
CONNOR	TMOS				33	0	CE	IRISH	MOULDER	043	C		18
CONNOR	WILLIAM			M	50	IRELAND	RC	IRISH	SHOEMAKER	043	A	1	4
CONNORS	ANN		1		46	IRELAND	CE	IRISH		043	D		82
CONNORS	JAMES				51	IRELAND	RC	IRISH	F LAB	043	A	6	14
CONOLLY	FRANCIS				55	IRELAND	RC	IRISH	LABORER	043	G	1	51
CONOVER	WILLIAM			M	44	US	PR	GERMANY	F	043	A	5	6
CONRON	JAMES				46	IRELAND	CE	IRISH	BUTCHER	044	C	3	72
CONRON	WILLIAM				51	IRELAND	CE	IRISH		044	C	4	64
CONROY	JOHN				36	IRELAND	CE	IRISH	F	043	A	3	48
CONRY	THOMAS				57	IRELAND	RC	IRISH	F	043	H	2	23
CONRY	THOMAS				57	IRELAND	RC	IRISH	FARMER	043	H	2	23
CONSTABLE	GEORGE		1		19	0	PS	SCOT	LAB	044	B	2	58
CONSTABLE	WILLIAM				60	ENG	PM	ENG	F	044	B	3	13
CONWAY	ROBERT				50	ENGLAND	CE	ENGLISH	F	044	C	1	1
COODY	BRIDGET		1	1	20	IRELAND	RC	IRISH	SERVANT	044	C	2	54
COODY	THOMAS				53	IRELAND	RC	IRISH	LAB	044	C	2	3
COOK	ADALINE		1	1	17	0	CN	GERMAN		045	D	4	46
COOK	ALFRED		2			0	PM			043	B	2	D
COOK	AMOS				30	ENGLAND	CE	ENGLISH	LAB	044	B	5	38
COOK	BENJAMIN				36	0	CE	ENGLISH	F	043	H	1	29
COOK	CHARLES				25	0	BA	ENGLISH	F	045	C	2	47
COOK	CORNELIUS				37	0	PM	IRISH	LAB	043	H	1	27
COOK	EBENEZER		2		78	US	BP		F	043	B	2	D
COOK	ELISABETH		1	F	34	ENGLAND	PR	IRISH	HOUSEKEEPER	043	A	1	54
COOK	ELIZABETH		1	1	9	0	WM	IRISH		045	A	4	30
COOK	FANNY		1	1	60	IRELAND	RC	IRISH		044	C	4	53
COOK	FRANCIS				31	ENG	CE	ENG	LAB	044	B	2	26
COOK	FREDRIC	R	1		3	U STATES	NG	DUTCH		043	A	6	31
COOK	GEORGE		1		50	ENGLAND	CE	ENGLISH	FARM LABOURER	043	E	2	48
COOK	GEORGE				36	0	CE	ENG	CARPENTER	044	B	2	39
COOK	GEORGE				40	ENGLAND	CE	ENGLISH	BRICK MAKER	045	A	1	25
COOK	GEORGE				28	0	BA	ENGLISH	F	045	C	2	46
COOK	GEORGE				40	ENGLAND	PM	ENGLISH	FARMER	045	D	3	16
COOK	HANNAH		2	1	34	0	CE			044	A	1	D
COOK	HENERY				49	0	CN	ENGLISH	F	043	B	5	16
COOK	HENREY				30	0	WM	GERMAN	LAB	043	B	2	34
COOK	JABEZ			M	52	ENGLAND	WM	ENGLISH	FARMER	043	A	1	23
COOK	JAMES				35	IRELAND	CE	IRISH	HOTEL KEEPER	045	A	2	9
COOK	JAMES				66	ENGLAND	CE	ENGLISH	WATCHMAN ON RAILWAY	044	C	4	62
COOK	JANE		1	1	62	ENGLAND	CE	ENGLISH		044	A	1	6
COOK	JOHN		1	M	73	ENGLAND	EM	ENGLISH		043	A	1	57
COOK	JOHN		2	M	45	IRELAND	PR		WEAVER	043	A	1	D
COOK	JOHN				35	0	NG	GERMAN	FARMER	043	B	3	8
COOK	JOHN				54	ENGLAND	WM	ENGLISH	CLERK DIVISION COURT	043	D		64
COOK	JOHN				29	0	WM	ENGLISH	F	044	A	2	21
COOK	JOHN				41	0	CE	GERMAN	LABOURER	045	D	3	24
COOK	JOHN	W			61	ENG	WM	ENG	CABINET MAKER	044	B	1	8
COOK	JONAS				48	0	NG	GERMAN	FARMER	043	B	3	10
COOK	JOSEPH				52	0	PS	ENGLISH	F	043	E	1	58
COOK	JOSEPH		1		44	0	NG	GERMAN	CARDER	045	D	4	42
COOK	MARGARET				73	0	WM	GERMAN		043	B	3	9
COOK	MARGARET		1	1	1	0	CE	SCOTCH	F	045	C	4	20
COOK	MARY			1	74	UNITED STATES	BA	GERMAN		043	B	2	1
COOK	MARY			1	39	ENGLAND	PM			045	D	4	4
COOK	MARY		1	1	16	0	CE	ENGLISH	SERVANT	045	D	6	12
COOK	MATILDA			1	27	ENGLAND	CE	ENGLISH		045	D	1	18

SURNAME	NAME1	NAME2	STRAY	SEX	AGE	BIRTHPL	RELIGION	ORIGIN	OCCUP	DIST	SUB_DIST	DIV	PAGE
COOK	NANCY			1	44	0	QU	ENGLISH		043	E	1	34
COOK	PHILIP				39	0	BA	GERMAN	F	043	B	2	1
COOK	ROBERT			M	42	ENGLAND	ME	ENGLAND	F	043	A	5	26
COOK	ROBERT				52	IRELAND	WM	IRISH	F	043	B	2	38
COOK	ROBERT		2		12	0	CP			043	B	2	D
COOK	ROBERT				52	IRELAND	WM	IRISH	CARPENTER	043	D		65
COOK	ROBERT		1		15	0	CE	ENGLISH	SERVANT	045	D	2	62
COOK	SARAH		1	1	16	ENGLAND	CE	ENGLISH	SERVANT	044	A	3	8
COOK	STEPHEN				40	ENGLAND	CE	ENGLISH	FARM LABOURER	045	A	1	2
COOK	STEPHENSON				46	ENGLAND	PM	ENGLISH	F	045	C	4	19
COOK	THOMAS				22	0	PM	IRISH	LAB	043	B	2	28
COOK	THOMAS				66	IRELAND	CP	IRISH	F	043	B	2	39
COOK	THOMAS				40	ENGLAND	CE	ENGLAND	GENTLEMAN	045	D	2	5
COOK	THOS				60	0	NG	GERMAN	F	043	B	2	43
COOK	WILLIAM			M	45	ENGLAND	EM	ENGLISH	F	043	A	2	51
COOK	WILLIAM				42	0	WM	IRISH	FARMER	043	B	3	8
COOK	WILLIAM				59	ENGLAND	CN	ENGLISH	COOPER	043	D		2
COOK	WILLIAM				45	ENGLAND	CE	ENGLISH	CARPENTER	045	D	4	7
COOKE	ELLEN		1	1	21	0	CE	ENG	HOUSEKEEPER	044	B	1	24
COOKE	JAMES		1		23	IRELAND	CE	IRISH	FARM LABOURER	043	B	3	7
COOKE	JANE			1	71	ENG	CE	ENG	HOTEL KEEPER	044	B	1	16
COOKE	SUSANNAH		2	1	59	ENG		WM			044	B	1	D
COOKE	THOMAS				55	ENG	CE	ENG	F	044	B	1	22
COOKE	THOMAS				70	ENG	PM	ENG	MERCHANT MILLER	044	B	1	55
COOKE	WILLIAM				66	ENG	CE	ENG	F	044	B	1	57
COOL	JOHN		1		12	0	CN	ENGLISH		043	B	3	16
COOL	LONIE		1	1	15	0	CN	ENGLISH		043	B	3	16
COOMBS	GEORGE				30	ENG	PM	ENG	TEAMSTER	044	B	1	52
COOMBS	JAMES				35	ENG	PM	ENG	F LAB	044	B	1	55
COOMBS	JOHN				61	ENG	PM	ENG	LAB	044	B	1	54
COOMBS	MARY		1	1	19	0	NC	ENGLISH		043	C		53
COOMBS	WILLIAM		1		13	0	NC	ENGLISH		043	C		53
COOMER	EDWARD				38	0	CE	ENGLISH	F	043	H	2	33
COOMER	JOHN				71	ENGLAND	EM	ENGLISH	FARMER	043	G	1	42
COOMER	SAMUEL				26	ONTARIO	PR	ENGLISH	FARMER	043	G	2	34
COOMIE	EDWARD				38	ONTARIO	CE	ENGLISH	FARMER	043	H	2	33
COOMS	PRUDENCE		1	1	22	0	WM	IRISH	INMATE	045	B	1	72
COONEY	JAMES		1		24	IRELAND	RC	IRISH	FARM LABOURER	043	B	3	27
COONEY	PATRICK				60	IRELAND	RC	IRISH	LABORER	045	D	6	35
COONEY	PETER				40	IRELAND	RC	IRISH	LAB	045	A	2	13
COOP	JOHN				39	ENGLISH	CE	ENGLISH	FARMER	044	C	3	50
COOPER	ANN			1	65	ENGLAND	CE	ENGLISH		045	D	4	40
COOPER	CHARLES				29	0	CE	ENG	F	044	B	1	24
COOPER	ELISABETH			1	64	ENGLAND	CE	ENGLISH	F	045	A	4	13
COOPER	ELIZABETH		1	1	37	0	PM	IRISH	SERVANT	044	A	3	14
COOPER	ELIZABETH		1	1	72	SCOTLAND	CP	SCOTCH		044	C	4	65
COOPER	FRANCIS		1	1	20	0	WM	ENGLISH	SERVANT	043	E	3	32
COOPER	GEORGE				56	ENGLAND	CE	ENGLISH	LAB	043	A	3	20
COOPER	GEORGE				26	ENGLAND	CE	ENGLISH	F	043	B	2	30
COOPER	GEORGE		1		25	0	LU	SCOT		044	B	3	14
COOPER	GEORGE				30	ENGLAND	CE	ENGLISH	GARDENER	045	A	1	41
COOPER	GEORGE				74	ENGLAND	WM	ENGLISH	F	044	C	4	75
COOPER	H	C			64	ENGLAND	CE	ENGLISH	CLERGYMAN	044	A	2	54
COOPER	HEFETZ		1	1	60	ENGLAND	WM	ENGLISH		044	C	4	75
COOPER	HUGH				23	0	WM	ENGLISH	BLACKSMITH	043	E	3	46
COOPER	HUGH				52	IRELAND	OP	SCOTCH	MERCHANT	043	H	2	37
COOPER	HUGH				52	IRELAND	CS	SCOTCH	MERCHANT	043	H	2	37
COOPER	ISABELLA		1	1	37	SCOTLAND	CP	SCOTCH		045	A	4	23
COOPER	JAMES				29	ENGLAND	CE	ENGLISH	FARMER	043	A	4	69
COOPER	JAMES		1		41	IRELAND	CP	IRISH	MILLER	045	A	4	23
COOPER	JOHN				33	0	LU	IRE	F	044	B	3	4
COOPER	JOHN				29	0	PS	SCOTCH	WATCH MAKER	044	B	5	27
COOPER	JOHN				33	UNITED STATES	CE	ENGLISH	WAGGON MAKER	044	C	2	35
COOPER	JOSEPH				24	0	CE	ENGLISH	FARMER	043	A	4	33
COOPER	ROBERT				21	ENGLAND	NC	ENGLISH	F	043	E	2	81
COOPER	ROBERT		1		18	SCOTLAND	CE	SCOTCH	LAB	043	F		12
COOPER	ROBERT				45	ENGLAND	CE	ENGLISH	LAB	045	B	1	32
COOPER	SAMUEL				40	IRELAND	OP	SCOTCH	F	043	H	2	47
COOPER	SAMUEL				40	IRELAND	CS	SCOTCH	FARMER	043	H	2	47
COOPER	SARAH		1	1	18	0	EM	ENGLISH		043	D		23
COOPER	SERA		1	1	84	ENGLAND	PM	ENGLAND		045	D	6	2
COOPER	THOMAS	H	1		24	ENGLAND	EM	ENGLISH	TEACHER	043	G	2	25
COOPER	WILLIAM				25	ENGLAND	PM	ENGLISH	F L	043	B	4	36
COOPER	WILLIAM				57	ENG	CE	ENG	PAINTER	044	B	2	28
COOPERTHWAITE	W		1		51	ENG	CE	ENG	F	044	B	1	17
COOPERTHWAITE	WM		1		80	ENG	CE	ENG		044	B	1	17
COPE	JOHN				66	ENGLAND		ENGLISH	LABOURER	044	C	1	29
COPELAND	JAMES				40	IRE	WM	IRISH	WOOLEN MANUFACTURER	044	B	2	4
COPELAND	MAGGIE		2	1	4	0				045	D	4	D
COPELAND	PETER				47	ENGLAND	PM	ENGLISH	FARMER	045	D	4	53
COPELAND	RICHARD		1		25	ENGLAND	CC	ENGLISH		045	A	3	40
COPELAND	RICHARD		1		36	0	PM	ENGLISH		044	C	2	45
COPELAND	VIDARINE		2	1	2	0				045	D	4	D
COPPIN	JESSIE		2	1	0	0	WM			044	C	2	D
COPPIN	NICHOLAS				40	ENGLAND	WM	ENGLISH	MILLER	044	C	2	32
COPSON	HENRY				67	ENGLAND	CO	ENGLISH	F	043	A	6	16
CORBETT	THOMAS			M	38	0	DI	IRISH	LAB	043	A	1	74
CORBIT	MALISHA		1		19	0	RC	IRISH	F	043	F		17
CORBWIRE	ELI				52	0	RC	FRENCH	SHOEMAKER	043	F		26
CORCORAN	CATHARINE		1	1	19	0	RC	IRISH	DRESSMAKER	045	D	5	16
CORCORAN	JOHN				29	IRELAND	RC	IRISH	LABORER	045	D	5	36
CORCORAN	LAVINA		1	1	20	IRELAND	RC	IRISH	SERVANT	045	D	5	16
CORCORAN	MICHAEL				26	IRELAND	RC	IRISH	LABOURER	045	D	5	36
CORCORAN	MICHAEL				55	IRELAND	RC	IRISH	LAB	044	C	4	95
CORKRIN	PATRIK		1	1	18	0	CP	IRISH	LAB	045	C	2	39
CORKUT	DAVID				46	ENGLAND	BA	ENGLISH	LABORER	045	D	6	72
CORNEL	HIRAM				18	0	WM	ENG	F	045	C	1	1
CORNEL	JORDAN				33	0	WM	ENG	F	045	C	1	2
CORNELIUS	ALFRED		1			0	CE	ENGLISH		045	A	1	60
CORNELIUS	FREDERICK		1		3	ENGLAND	CE	ENGLISH		045	A	1	60
CORNELIUS	WM				70	ENGLAND	WM	ENGLISH	FARMER	045	D	5	59
CORNELL	ABRAM				67	U STATES	CO	FRENCH	BLACKSMITH	043	D		11
CORNELL	CHAS				54	0	CE	ENG	F	045	C	1	20
CORNELL	JAS				28	0	WM	SCOT	CARPENTER	045	C	1	18
CORNELL	RUSSELL				26	0	CE	ENG	F	045	C	1	25
CORNELL	SUSAN	EMILY	1	1	16	0	WM	ENGLISH		045	D	5	72

SURNAME	NAME1	NAME2	STRAY	SEX	AGE	BIRTHPL	RELIGION	ORIGIN	OCCUP	DIST	SUB_DIST	DIV	PAGE
CORNER	HENRY				34	0	CE	SCOTCH	F	043	H	1	36
CORNER	JOHN				38	ENGLAND	CE	SCOTCH	F	043	H	1	37
CORNER	RACHEL		1	1	50	0	CE	ENGLISH		043	H	1	36
CORNER	WILLIAM				41	ENGLAND	CE	SCOTCH	SAWYER	043	H	1	36
CORNISH	CHRISTINA		1	1	14	0	RC	AFRICAN		045	A	2	8
CORNISH	FRANCIS				50	ENGLAND	CE	ENGLISH	F	044	A	1	20
CORNWALLIS	TIMOTHY				21	0	WM	ENGLISH	F LAB	044	C	1	55
CORSCADDEN	ANN			F	57	QUE	WM	IRISH		043	A	1	15
CORSON	HENRY	R			46	0	WM	GERMAN	PUBLISHER NEWS P	045	D	5	20
CORTNEY	ANN		1	1	40	IRELAND	CE	IRISH		044	C	3	62
CORY	ALBERT		1		16	0	CN	IRISH	LABOURER	043	B	3	34
COSBURN	RICHARD	C			36	ENGLAND	CE	ENGLISH	GARDENER	045	A	1	94
COSFORD	THOMAS				74	ENGLAND	WM	ENGLISH	F	043	B	4	4
COSFORD	THOMAS	W			39	0	NC	ENGLISH	F	043	A	6	1
COSGROVE	BERNARD				61	IRELAND	RC	IRISH	FARMER	045	D	2	37
COSGROVE	JAMES		1		32	IRELAND	RC	IRISH	LAB	043	H	1	26
COSGROVE	JOHN		1		20	0	RC	IRISH	SERVANT	045	D	6	16
COSTELLO	CATHERINE		1	1	55	IRELAND	RC	IRISH		045	D	3	50
COSTLOW	WILLIAM				40	IRELAND	RC	IRISH	LAB	044	C	4	55
COTES	ELIZABETH			1	24	SCOT	WP	SCOT		045	C	1	14
COTES	MARGARET		1	1	1	0	WP	SCOTCH		045	C	1	17
COTTER	ALEXANDER				80	IRELAND	CE	IRISH	WEAVER	045	D	3	8
COTTER	THOMAS		1		19	ENGLAND	RC	ENGLISH	LABOURER	045	D	3	42
COTTERILL	SAMUEL				50	ENGLAND	CE	ENGLISH	LAB	045	B	1	25
COTTINGHAM	JOHN				37	ENG	PM	CE	LAB	044	B	3	45
COTTOR	MICHAEL		2		26	IRELAND	RC		SHOE-MAKER	043	A	6	D
COUCH	WILLIAM				54	ENGLAND	CE	ENGLISH	CARPENTER	045	D	1	42
COULSON	JAMES				26	0	FK	ENGLISH	LAB	045	A	2	30
COULTER	ABERT	J WELLINGTON	2	M		0	PS			043	A	2	D
COULTER	ADAM		1		18	0	CP	SCOTCH	SERVANT	044	B	6	57
COULTER	ANDREW				46	0	PM	IRISH	F	044	A	2	31
COULTER	ANN		2	1	43	IRELAND	CE			045	A	1	D
COULTER	CHARLES				31	ENGLAND	CE	ENGLISH	F	043	A	6	3
COULTER	ELIZABETH		1	1	25	0	CE	ENGLISH	SERVANT	044	B	6	58
COULTER	FANNY			1	59	IRELAND	CE	IRISH		044	A	1	31
COULTER	HENRY				43	0	PM	IRISH	F	044	A	2	23
COULTER	JAMES				26	IRELAND	CE	IRISH	F	044	A	1	39
COULTER	JAMES				54	SCOTLAND	CS	SCOTCH	F	044	B	6	34
COULTER	JOHN			M	24	0	PS	IRISH	F	043	A	2	3
COULTER	JOHN			M	24	IRELAND	FK	IRELAND	WEAVER	043	A	5	12
COULTER	JOHN				50	0	PM	IRISH	F	044	A	2	36
COULTER	JOHN				52	IRELAND	CP	IRELAND	TAILOR	045	D	2	12
COULTER	JOHN				37	IRELAND	PM	IRISH	SHOEMAKER	044	C	2	22
COULTER	LIBBIE		1	1	21	0	NC	IRISH	DOMESTIC	043	C		5
COULTER	LILLY		2	1		0	PM			044	A	2	D
COULTER	MARY		1	1	92	IRELAND	BA	IRISH		044	A	3	24
COULTER	ROBERT				49	IRELAND	PM	IRISH	F	044	A	2	13
COULTER	ROBERT				46	IRELAND	CE	IRISH	GARDENER	045	A	1	67
COULTER	SARAH		1	1	22	IRELAND	CE	IRISH		044	B	5	30
COULTER	WILLIAM			M	56	IRELAND	PS	IRISH	F	043	A	2	16
COULTER	WILLIAM				60	IRELAND	CP	IRISH	FARMER	043	A	4	53
COULTER	WILLIAM				32	0	PM	IRISH	F	044	A	2	35
COUPE	SAMUEL				52	ENGLAND	CE	ENGLISH	BUTCHER	045	D	5	31
COUPLAND	HENRY				34	0	WM	ENGLISH	AGENT	044	B	6	24
COUPLAND	ROBERT	W			27	SCOTLAND	PS	SCOTCH	SAFE MAKER	045	A	1	69
COUPLAND	THOMAS				64	ENGLAND	WM	ENGLISH	F	044	B	6	53
COUPLAND	WILLIAM				45	ENG	PM	ENG	F	044	B	2	32
COURTNEY	ISREAL				30	IRELAND	PS	IRISH	MILL RIGHT	045	D	6	15
COURTNEY	MARGRET		2	1	21	0	PS			045	D	6	D
COURTS	JAMES		1		30	ENGLAND	CE	ENGLISH	LAB	045	B	2	4
COUSINS	JOHN				49	ENG	WM	ENG	F	044	B	4	23
COVERDALE	WILLIAM				49	ENGLAND	EM	ENGLISH	FARMER	043	G	2	39
COWAN	ANN			1	33	0	WM	IRISH	SPINSTER	044	B	4	45
COWAN	ARTHUR		1		55	IRELAND	WM	IRISH	MILL LAB	044	C	1	11
COWAN	SUSAN		1	1	59	IRELAND	WM	IRISH		044	B	6	28
COWARD	JOHN				60	ENGLAND	CE	ENGLISH	F	044	C	1	51
COWDRY	JAMES		1		20	ENGLAND	CE	ENGLISH	LAB	045	A	2	39
COWEN	CHARLES			M	45	IRELAND	CP	IRISH	MILLER	043	A	2	5
COWIESON	JAMES				42	SCOTLAND	CS	SCOTCH	F	043	E	2	63
COWIESON	JOHN				34	SCOTLAND	CN	SCOTCH	F	043	E	2	56
COWIESON	JOHN				76	SCOTLAND	CS	SCOTCH	F	043	E	2	57
COWLING	DAVID				49	ENGLAND	WM	ENGLISH	FARMER	043	A	4	30
COWLING	J	M	1	1	2	0	CP	SCOTCH		043	A	4	49
COWLING	WILLIAM				50	ENGLAND	PM	ENGLISH	FARMER MILKMAN	045	A	1	72
COWLING	WILLIAM				25	0	WM	ENGLISH	DAIRYMAN	045	A	1	86
COX	FRANCES		1	1	18	ENGLAND	CE	IRISH		044	C	4	58
COX	JOHANNAH			F	42	IRELAND	WM	IRELAND		043	A	5	30
COX	JOHN				45	IRELAND	CP	IRISH	FARMER	045	D	3	21
COX	JOSEPH				40	IRELAND	UP	IRISH	GENTLEMAN	045	D	1	35
COX	MARY JANE		2	F	16	0	WM			043	A	5	D
COX	ROBERT		1		22	ENGLAND	WM	IRISH	SERVANT	044	C	4	58
COX	WILLIAM				75	IRELAND	UP	IRISH	FARMER	045	D	1	34
COX	WILLIAM	W			35	ENG	WM	ENG	BUTCHER	044	B	2	13
COXHEAD	JOHN				60	ENGLAND	PM	ENGLISH	FARMER	045	D	4	4
COXWORTH	JAMES				25	0	CE	ENGLISH	FARMER	045	D	5	55
COXWORTH	JOHN				59	ENGLAND	CE	ENGLISH	F	045	C	2	40
COXWORTH	JOHN		1		9	0	FK	IRISH		045	D	1	49
COXWORTH	WILLIAM				34	0	CE	ENGLISH	FARMER	045	D	5	64
COYLE	FANNY		1	1	21	0	RC	IRISH	INMATE	045	B	1	72
COYLE	THOMAS				31	US	RC	IRE	BLACKSMITH	044	B	2	34
COYNE	JAMES		1		25	IRELAND	RC	IRISH	F LAB	044	A	1	13
COYNE	MARGARET		1	1	20	IRELAND	CE	IRISH	SERVANT	045	B	2	8
CRABBE	JOSEPH				45	ENGLAND	WM	ENGLISH	ROPEMAKER	043	C		29
CRABTREE	ROBERT				51	ENGLAND	CE	ENGLISH	BLACKSMITH	045	A	2	25
CRADDOCK	ANTHONY				28	0	WM	ENG	F	044	B	2	23
CRADDOCK	JOHN				32	0	PM	ENG	F	044	B	2	66
CRADDOCK	WILLIAM				53	0	WM	ENG	F	044	B	4	8
CRAIG	ANN	JANE	1	1	32	0	WM	GERMAN		044	A	2	11
CRAIG	ELDRED		1	1	14	0	CE	IRISH		045	A	1	77
CRAIG	HENRIETTA		1	1	12	0	WM	IRISH		044	A	2	11
CRAIG	JOHN		1		24	0	CE	IRISH	COOPER	044	B	5	30
CRAIG	MARY			1	71	IRELAND	CP	IRISH		045	D	2	37
CRAIG	ROBERT		1		22	SCOTLAND	PS	SCOTCH	FARM SERVANT	045	C	3	23
CRAIG	ROBERT				36		CE	IRELAND	BRICK LAYER	045	D	2	15
CRAIG	WILLIAM				47	IRELAND	CE	IRISH	TANNER	043	G	2	16
CRAIG	WILLIAM				40	SCOTLAND	CS	SCOTCH	F LABOURER	045	D	3	54

SURNAME	NAME1	NAME2	STRAY	SEX	AGE	BIRTHPL	RELIGION	ORIGIN	OCCUP	DIST	SUB_DIST	DIV	PAGE
CRAIG	WM				38	IRELAND	CE	SCOTCH	MACHINIST	044	B	5	24
CRAIGE	JOHN				61	IRELAND	CE	IRISH	COOPER	045	A	3	14
CRAIGIE	ALEXANDER				29	SCOTLAND	CP	IRISH	LAB	045	C	4	26
CRAIGIE	JAMES				46	ORKNEY ISLAND	CP	SCOTCH	FARMER	045	D	5	56
CRAIK	JANE		1		61	SCOT	PS	SCOT		044	B	2	51
CRAIK	PETER				24	0	PS	SCOT	BLACKSMITH	044	B	2	51
CRAKE	THOMAS				55	ENGLAND	CE	ENGLISH	F	043	B	1	30
CRAM	ELIZABETH		1	1	20	0	CE	SCOTCH		043	C		31
CRAM	HENRY	A	1		24	0	CE	SCOTCH	LAB	043	C		31
CRAMP	DAVID				39	ENGLAND	PM	ENGLISH	PAPERMAKER	045	A	1	88
CRAN	PETER				39	SCOTLAND	CP	SCOTCH	F	043	E	1	53
CRANDALL	DAVID				30	US	CP	GERMAN	F	045	C	2	24
CRANDALL	WILLIAM				67	US	CP	GERMAN	F	045	C	2	24
CRANE	THOMAS		1		17	ENGLAND	CE	ENGLISH	LAB	045	C	4	42
CRANEY	THOMAS				27	0	RC	IRISH	MACHINIST	043	A	4	24
CRANG	JAMES				28	ENGLAND	CE	ENGLISH	BRICKLAYER	045	B	1	24
CRANLEY	ELLEN			1	30	IRELAND	RC	IRISH		043	E	1	49
CRANLEY	KENNEDY				79	IRELAND	RC	IRISH	F	043	E	1	49
CRANNEY	THOMAS				27	0	RC	IRE	FOUNDRY MAN	044	B	4	7
CRANSTON	CHARLES				30	SCOTLAND	CP	SCOTCH	F	045	C	3	46
CRANSTON	WILLIAM				40	SCOTLAND	OP	SCOTCH	MERCHANT	043	A	3	12
CRANSTON	WILLIAM		1		25	0	CP	SCOTCH	SAWYER	045	C	3	29
CRANSWICK	JOHN				33	ENGLAND	CE	ENGLISH	FARMER	045	D	3	81
CRANSWICK	MATTHEW				39	ENGLAND	PM	ENGLISH	F	044	A	3	48
CRATES	JAMES		1		19	ENGLAND	WM	ENGLISH	MILLER	045	D	1	26
CRAULEY	MICHAEL				34	IRELAND	RC	IRISH	F	043	E	2	57
CRAVEN	CELINA		1	1	20	ENGLAND	CE	ENGLISH		045	C	2	30
CRAVEN	CRANSIE				51	ENG	CE	ENG	TEACHER	045	C	1	5
CRAVEN	JOSHUAH				38	ENGLAND	NC	ENGLISH	LAB	043	E	2	43
CRAWFORD	ALEX				32	0	CP	SCOTCH	FARMER	043	A	4	50
CRAWFORD	ALEXANDER				40	SCOTLAND	OP	SCOTCH	F	043	H	2	43
CRAWFORD	ALEXANDER				40	SCOTLAND	CS	SCOTCH	FARMER	043	H	2	43
CRAWFORD	ANDREW				39	SCOTLAND	CP	SCOTCH	TAILOR	043	A	4	22
CRAWFORD	BARBER	H			41	0	QU	SCOTCH	CARPENTER	043	D		55
CRAWFORD	FRANK		1		14	ONT	WM	IRISH		044	C	3	69
CRAWFORD	FREDERICK				52	IRE	RC	IRE	PENSIONER	044	B	2	44
CRAWFORD	JOHN				60	IRELAND	PS	IRISH	TAILOR	044	B	5	40
CRAWFORD	JOHN				47	SCOTLAND	CP	SCOTCH	F	045	C	3	56
CRAWFORD	MARGARET			1	52	US	WM	ENGLISH		045	A	4	34
CRAWFORD	MARY		1	1	38	SCOTLAND	CS	SCOTCH		043	A	4	19
CRAWFORD	THOMAS		1		50	SCOTLAND	PS	SCOTCH	OSTLER	044	C	4	48
CRAWFORD	WILLIAM				45	IRELAND	CE	IRISH	TURNKEY	045	A	1	36
CRAWFORD	WILLIAM				44	SCOTLAND	CP	SCOTCH	F	045	C	3	1
CRAWLEY	JOHN		1		84	ENGLAND	CE	ENGLISH		044	C	1	37
CRAYMER	MARY		1	1	14	0	WM	GERMAN		045	D	3	45
CREALOCK	JOHN				56	ENGLAND	WM	ENGLISH	DROVER	044	C	4	46
CREASER	JAMES				52	ENGLAND	CE	ENGLISH	F	043	A	6	24
CREASOR	CHARLES				43	ENG	CE	ENG	F	044	B	2	54
CREEDON	CATHERINE		2	F	21	0	RC			043	A	5	D
CREEDON	JOHN		1	M	25	0	RC	IRELAND	F	043	A	5	23
CREIGHTON	ROBT				56	SCOTLAND	UP	SCOTCH	F	044	B	5	58
CREMORD	JAMES				50	ENGLAND	WM	ENGLISH		045	C	2	28
CREW	GEORGE				60	ENGLAND	CE	ENGLISH	MILLWRIGHT	045	D	5	33
CREW	HAYSEN		2		5	N BRUNSWICK	CE			045	D	5	D
CREW	JAMES	BAILEY	2		21	PE ISLAND	CE		IRON FINISHER	045	D	5	D
CREW	MARY		2	1	46	NOVA SCOTIA	CE			045	D	5	D
CREW	MARY	JANE		1	45	0	CE	SCOT		045	C	1	31
CREW	REBECCA		2	1	16	0	CE			045	C	1	D
CRINS	JOSEPH		1		26	IRELAND	WM	ENGLISH	STUDENT	043	D		83
CRINTON	JANE	B	1	1	7	0	PR	SCOTCH		045	A	1	34
CRITON	ANN		1		40	IRELAND	PM	IRISH		045	A	1	93
CRITTENDEN	AMOS				75	UNITED STATES	CN	ENGLISH	FARMER	043	G	1	27
CRITTENDEN	FRANKLIN				33	ONTARIO	PR	ENGLISH	FARMER	043	G	2	49
CRITTENDEN	JAMES				47	ONTARIO	QU	ENGLISH	FARMER	043	G	1	26
CRITTENDEN	LEVI				70	UNITED STATES	BC	ENGLISH	FARMER	043	H	2	46
CRITTENDEN	LYMAN				63	ONTARIO	CE	ENGLISH	FARMER	043	G	1	7
CRITTENDEN	MARTIN				24	ONTARIO	BC	ENGLISH	LABOURER	043	H	2	37
CRITTENDEN	ORIN				53	ONTARIO	WM	ENGLISH	FARMER	043	G	2	46
CRITTENDON	LEVI				70	USA	BC	ENGLISH	F	043	H	2	46
CRITTENDON	MARTIN				24	0	BC	ENGLISH	LAB	043	H	2	37
CRITTENDON	ROSILLIA		2	1		ONTARIO	BC			043	H	2	D
CRITTERDON	BENJAMIN		1		16	0	CE	ENGLISH		045	D	2	34
CROCKART	ROBERT				50	SCOTLAND	CP	SCOTCH	F	043	B	1	6
CROCKER	JOHN		1		75	ENGLAND	CE	ENGLISH	LABORER	043	D		83
CROCKER	THOMAS		1		22	0	BA	ENGLISH	TINSMITH	043	C		24
CROFT	HENRY	H			51	ENGLAND	CE	ENGLISH	TEACHER	045	B	2	8
CROFT	ROBERT				63	ENGLAND	PM	ENGLISH	F	044	B	6	43
CROFT	ROBERT	J			27	0	WM	ENGLISH	FARMER	045	D	3	19
CROFT	STEPHEN		2		8	0	CE			045	B	2	D
CROFT	THOMAS		1		25	ENGLAND	CE	ENGLISH	LAB	043	B	1	25
CROFTON	GEORGE		1		40	IRELAND	CE	ENGLISH		044	C	3	30
CROFTS	CHARLES	H			37	ENGLAND	CE	ENGLISH	TEACHER	043	G	1	56
CROMBY	SUSAN			1	35	ONTARIO	WM	IRISH		044	C	3	52
CROMEY	ANN		2	1	47	IRE	RC			044	B	4	D
CRONAN	RICHARD				63	IRELAND	RC	IRISH	F	043	A	3	17
CRONBERRY	FRANCIS				45	IRELAND	CE	IRISH	F	043	H	1	4
CRONBERRY	RICHARD	JR			26	IRELAND	CE	IRISH	F	043	H	1	3
CRONE	JOEL				59	0	CN	IRISH	F	043	E	3	37
CRONE	JOHN				39	0	CN	ENGLISH	BUILDER	043	D		25
CRONE	WILLIAM				30	US	PM	ENGLISH	CARPENTER	045	B	2	13
CRONIN	PATRICK				27	IRE	RC	IRE	LAB	044	B	2	67
CROOKE	JANE		1	1	18	ONT	WM	SCOTCH		044	C	2	32
CROOKENDEN	JOHN				28	ENGLAND	CE	ENGLISH	CARPENTER	045	B	1	46
CROOKER	MARK	T	1		25	0	WM	GERMAN	CLERK	044	B	6	1
CROOKS	ISAAC				51	ENGLAND	NC	ENGLISH	COOPER	043	D		27
CROOKS	WILLIAM				40	ENGLAND	WM	ENGLISH	F LAB	044	C	1	36
CROOKSHANK	MARGARETH		1	1	50	SCOTLAND	PS	SCOTCH		044	C	4	84
CROPEN							NG			043	A	3	54
CROPPER	HERBERT		1		16	0	CE	ENGLISH	F	044	C	4	29
CROSBY	ANDREW				58	0	WM	SCOTCH	FARMER	045	D	3	63
CROSBY	CHANEY				71	US	WM	SCOTCH	FARMER	045	D	3	62
CROSBY	DAVID		1		26	SCOTLAND	CS	SCOTCH	FARM LABOURER	043	E	2	34
CROSBY	EVA	D	2	1		0	CP			044	B	6	D
CROSBY	GEORGE				36	ENG	EM	ENG	LAB	044	B	1	34
CROSBY	H	P			44	0	WM	SCOTCH	MERCHANT MILLER FARM	045	D	3	3
CROSBY	ISAAC				28	ENGLAND	WM	ENGLAND	MERCHANT	045	D	2	12

SURNAME	NAME1	NAME2	STRAY	SEX	AGE	BIRTHPL	RELIGION	ORIGIN	OCCUP	DIST	SUB_DIST	DIV	PAGE
CROSBY	JAMES				80	U STATES	WM	IRISH		045	D	5	44
CROSBY	JOHN	W	1		72	US	CP	GERMAN	GENTLEMAN	045	D	4	24
CROSBY	LYMAN				52	O	WM	IRISH	NURSERY MAN	045	D	5	44
CROSBY	PARKER				55	ENGLAND	WM	ENGLAND	FARMER	045	D	2	14
CROSBY	PERRY				26	O	WM	IRISH	CHEESEMAKING	045	D	5	30
CROSBY	WILLIAM	D			34	O	WM	SCOTCH	FARMER	045	D	3	63
CROSIER	CHRISTOPHER				40	IRELAND	CE	IRISH	FARMER	045	D	6	48
CROSLEY	MARSHAL				40	O	CP	SCOTCH	MERCHANT	044	B	6	25
CROSS	ALICE		1	1	9	O	OB	ENGLISH		044	A	2	13
CROSS	HARRIETT		1	1	25	ENGLAND	XC	ENGLISH		045	B	1	52
CROSS	LEVI		1		28	ENGLAND	XC	ENGLISH		045	B	1	52
CROSS	MICHAEL				60	ENGLAND	CE	ENGLISH	FARMER	045	D	1	46
CROSS	ORLANDO		1		8	O	NC	ENGLISH		043	E	2	38
CROSS	SKELTON				48	ENGLAND	CE	ENGLISH	PHYSICIAN	043	D		53
CROSS	THOMAS				26	O	CE	ENGLISH	FARMER	045	D	1	38
CROSS	THOMAS				51	IRELAND	CE	IRISH	F	044	C	2	16
CROSS	WILLIAM			M	49	ENGLAND	PR	ENGLISH	FARMER	043	A	1	23
CROSSAN	MARGARET		2	F	33	O	LU			043	A	2	D
CROSSEN	JOHN				65	O	PM	GERMAN	F	043	A	3	54
CROSSEN	JOHN				45	SCOTLAND	PS	SCOTCH	LABOURER	045	D	6	15
CROSSLEY	JAMES	W		M	28	O	EM	IRISH	F	043	A	2	53
CROSSLEY	PEARSON			M	59	O	EM	ENGLISH	F	043	A	1	59
CROSSLEY	WILLIAM				38	O	WM	GERMAN	CARPENTER	043	A	4	9
CROSSON	ELIZABETH			1	70	US	LU	GER		044	B	4	46
CROSSON	ISAIC			M	49	O	LU	GERMANY	LAB	043	A	2	32
CROSSON	JOSEPH				46	O	WM	GERMAN	F	044	C	1	43
CROSSON	MAGGIE		1		20	O	WM	IRISH	LAB	044	C	1	48
CROSSON	MARGARET		1	1	20	O	EM	ENG	SERVANT	044	B	4	52
CROSSON	SAMUEL		1		60	O	LU	GER	CARPENTER	044	B	4	25
CROSSON	WILLIAM		1		12	CANADA	MN	SCOTCH		045	D	6	55
CROSSON	WILLIAM				56	O	WM	GERMAN	F	044	C	1	51
CROTOE	CHARLES				50	O	RC	FRENCH	LAB	043	H	2	18
CROTOE	CHARLES		1		50	ONTARIO	RC	FRENCH	LABOURER	043	H	2	18
CROTOE	JOHN				46	O	RC	FRENCH	LAB	043	H	2	17
CROTTY	MICHAEL				60	IRELAND	RC	IRISH	TAILOR	044	B	6	13
CROUCH	JAMES		1		51	ENGLAND	CE	ENGLISH	F LAB	044	A	2	8
CROUDER	GORDON				35	O	WM	GERMAN	LAB	043	H	2	36
CROUDER	GORDON				35	ONTARIO	WM	GERMAN	LABOURER	043	H	2	36
CROUDER	JACOB				46	O	WM	GERMAN	LAB	043	H	2	42
CROUDER	JACOB				46	ONTARIO	WM	GERMAN	LABOURER	043	H	2	42
CROUTCH	FRANCIS				39	ENGLAND	PM	ENGLISH	F	043	E	2	71
CROW	ROBERT				35	SCOTLAND	CP	SCOTCH	BLACKSMITH	045	C	4	25
CROWDER	JEREMIAH				28	ONTARIO	PR	FRENCH	FARMER	043	G	2	37
CROWN	DAVID				49	ENGLAND	WM	ENGLISH	BOOT MAKER	045	B	2	9
CROWN	EDWARD				52	ENGLAND	WM	ENGLISH	TOLL G KEEPER	045	B	1	13
CROWN	WILLIAM			M	75	ENGLAND	PM	ENGLISH	SHOEMAKER	043	A	2	30
CROWN	WILLIAM				50	ENGLAND	PM	ENGLISH	CONTRACTOR	045	B	2	12
CROYN	JAMES				50	IRELAND	RC	IRISH	LABOURER	043	A	4	71
CROZIER	ELIZABETH		1	1	17	O	CE	ENG		045	C	1	59
CROZIER	MARTIN				55	ENG	CE	ENG	LAB	045	C	1	8
CRUCK	MEADE				46	IRELAND	WM	IRISH	CARPENTER	044	A	2	50
CRUICKSHANKS	JAMES				40	SCOTLAND	RP	SCOTCH	WAGGON MAKER	044	C	3	14
CRUIKSHANK	LOUIS				73	SCOTLAND	RC	SCOTCH	LAB	044	A	3	31
CRUIKSHANKS	ROBERT				33	SCOTLAND	PB	SCOTCH	BOOKKEEPER	045	B	1	38
CRUMPTON	ARTHUR				56	ENGLAND	FW	ENGLISH		045	B	1	40
CRUST	JOSEPH				37	ENGLAND	PM	ENGLISH	FARM LABOURER	045	C	3	19
CRUTCH	GEORGE		1		40	ENGLAND	CE	ENGLISH	F	045	B	1	9
CRUTHERS	WILLIAM				60	ENGLAND	CE	ENGLISH	FARMER	045	D	4	38
CRUTOE	JOHN				46	ONTARIO	RC	FRENCH	LABOURER	043	H	2	17
CRYDERMAN	ELIZABETH		1	1	20	O	EM	GERMAN	SERVANT	043	E	2	55
CRYDERMAN	JOHNSON				36	ONTARIO	PR	GERMAN	FARMER	043	G	2	9
CRYDERMAN	SARAH		1	1	17	O	CE	ENGLISH	SERVANT	043	E	1	45
CRYDERMAN	SILAS				41	O	PM	GERMAN	F	043	E	2	73
CRYDERMAN	VALENTINE				42	ONTARIO	EM	GERMAN	FARMER	043	G	2	11
CRYER	GEORGE		1		20	O	CE	ENGLISH	SERVANT	045	A	3	28
CUDDEO	NELSON				29	Q	RC	FRENCH	LAB	043	A	6	64
CUDDY	MARY		1	1	34	IRELAND	RC	IRISH		045	A	2	22
CUDMORE	EDWIN				27	O	CE	ENGLISH	FARMER	045	A	2	19
CUDMORE	GEORGE				33	ENGLAND	PM	ENGLISH	PAPERMAKER	045	A	1	104
CUDMORE	GEORGE				67	ENGLAND	CE	ENGLISH	FARMER	045	A	2	19
CUDMORE	JOHN				31	ENGLAND	DI	ENGLISH	FARMER	045	A	1	105
CULHAM	JOHN				60	ENGLAND	WM	ENGLISH	F	044	A	2	33
CULHAM	TRUMAN				27	O	WM	ENGLISH	F	044	A	1	3
CULHAM	TURPIN				67	ENGLAND	PM	ENGLISH	GENTLEMAN	044	B	6	30
CULHAM	TURPIN	JR			32	O	WM	ENGLISH	F	044	B	6	30
CULL	MARGARET			F	47	IRELAND	RC	IRISH		043	A	2	50
CULLETON	JOHANAH			1	56	IRELAND	RC	IRISH	SEXTON	044	C	4	66
CULLEY	FRANK		1		25	ENGLAND	CE	ENGLISH	F LAB	044	C	1	20
CULLIGAN	CHARLES				25	O	CE	IRISH	CLOTH FINISHER	044	C	3	67
CULLNAN	MARGARET			1	50	IRELAND	RC	IRISH		044	A	1	25
CULVER	HARMAN		1		17	US	PM	UNKNOWN		044	B	2	35
CULVERWELL	ROBERT				60	ENGLAND	CE	ENGLISH	F	043	E	1	2
CULVERWELL	ROBERT				39	ENGLAND	CE	ENGLISH	F	043	E	2	8
CUMINGS	WILLIAM				50	ENGLAND	PM	ENGLISH	LAB	045	B	1	21
CUMMER	SAMUEL				32	O	EM	GERMAN	FARMER	045	D	1	47
CUMMER	SAMUEL				55	O	WM	GERMAN	F	045	A	4	35
CUMMER	W	W			36	O	WM	GERMAN	MERCHANT	044	C	1	27
CUMMIN	JACOB				70	O	EM	GERMAN	TINSMITH	044	C	1	21
CUMMING	JOHN				37	O	CP	SCOTCH	CARRIAGE MAKER	045	D	6	8
CUMMINGS	DANIEL				70	SCOT	CS	SCOT	LAB	044	B	4	41
CUMMINGS	JAMES				40	IRELAND	RC	IRISH	LABOURER	045	D	5	16
CUMMINGS	THOMAS				60	SCOTLAND	CP	SCOTCH	TAILOR	045	D	5	3
CUMMINGS	THOMAS				48	ENGLAND	PM	ENGLISH	GARDNER	044	C	4	88
CUMMINGS	THOMAS	R		M	35	IRELAND	CE	IRELAND	TEACHER	043	A	5	14
CUMMINS	JAMES				42	IRELAND	CP	IRISH	CARPENTER	044	A	2	6
CUMMINS	RICHARD				30	IRELAND	RC	IRISH	LAB	045	B	1	44
CUMMOR	DAVID				68	O	EM	GERMAN	CARPENTER	044	C	1	57
CUNDELL	FREDERICK		1		19	ENGLAND	CE	ENGLISH	BUTCHER	045	B	1	1
CUNIO	ANDREW				32	ITALY	RC	ITALIAN	BARBER	043	D		15
CUNNINGHAM	ANDREW				31	IRELAND	RC	IRISH	LAB	043	D		36
CUNNINGHAM	ANDREW				32	IRELAND	EM	IRISH	BLACKSMITH	043	E	2	21
CUNNINGHAM	DAVID		1		24	SCOTLAND	CP	SCOTCH	F	044	A	1	20
CUNNINGHAM	GEORGE				31	O	CP	IRISH	F	043	B	1	29
CUNNINGHAM	JANE		2	1	73	IRELAND	PS			043	E	2	D
CUNNINGHAM	JOHN				30	ONTARIO	WM	IRISH	FARMER	043	G	1	46
CUNNINGHAM	MARY			1	60	IRELAND	CS	IRISH		044	B	6	9

SURNAME	NAME1	NAME2	STRAY	SEX	AGE	BIRTHPL	RELIGION	ORIGIN	OCCUP	DIST	SUB_DIST	DIV	PAGE
CUNNINGHAM	ROBERT				30	IRE	CS	IRE	FARM SERVANT	044	B	4	37
CUNNINGHAM	ROBERT		1		46	SCOTLAND	CP	SCOTCH	FARMER	045	D	3	21
CUNNINGHAM	SARAH			1	72	IRELAND	WM	IRISH		043	B	1	30
CUNNINGHAM	THOMAS				25	O	CN	IRISH	F	043	E	1	27
CUNNINGHAM	WILLIAM				32	IRE	CS	IRE	F	044	B	4	12
CUNNINGHAM	WM		1		50	SCOTLAND	CS	SCOTCH		045	A	4	18
CUNNINHAM	JAMES				45	IRELAND	WM	IRISH	F	043	E	2	29
CUNYHAN	MARY		1	1	37	ENGLAND	CE	ENGLISH		044	C	3	18
CUNYHAN	WILLIAM		1		17	ONT	CE	ENGLISH		044	C		
CURBY	THOMAS		1		32	IRELAND	NG	IRISH	F LAB	044	C	1	1
CURLY	JULIA			1	53	IRELAND	RC	IRISH		044	C	3	11
CURN	THOMAS				23	O	RC	IRE	LAB	044	B	4	8
CURRAH	MAGARY			1	66	ENGLAND	CE	ENGLISH	F	045	C	3	5
CURRAN	JOHN				34	IRELAND	RC	IRISH	LABOURER	043	A	4	14
CURRAN	JOHN				60	IRELAND	RC	IRISH	LABOURER	044	C	3	66
CURRAN	JOHN				40	SCOTLAND	RC	IRISH	LAB	044	C	4	59
CURRAN	PATRICK				34	IRELAND	RC	IRISH	SHOEMAKER	043	A	4	6
CURRAN	THOMAS				50	IRE	RC	IRE	F	044	B	2	67
CURREEN	BRIDGET		2	1	50	IRELAND	RC			043	E	3	D
CURREEN	WILLIAM		1		48	IRELAND	RC	IRISH	F	043	E	3	15
CURRIE	ARCHIBALD				27	O	UP	SCOTCH	FARMER	045	D	1	27
CURRIE	HANNAH		1	1	13	O	CP	SCOTCH		045	D	2	2
CURRIE	JANE		1	1	50	SCOT	CP	SCOT	SERVANT	044	B	1	27
CURRIE	MATHEW		1		11	O	CP	SCOTCH	FARM LABORER	045	D	2	2
CURRIE	THOMAS				29	ENGLAND	WM	ENGLISH	FARM LABOURER	045	C	4	12
CURRIE	WALTER				33	SCOTLAND	CP	SCOTCH	LAB	044	C	4	11
CURRIL	MARY	A		1	47	O	WM	SCOTCH		043	B	2	10
CURRIN	CHARLES				60	IRELAND	RC	IRISH	LAB	044	C	4	51
CURRON	PHILIP				71	IRELAND	RC	IRISH	LAB	044	C	4	44
CURRY	ANN			1	63	IRELAND	RC	IRISH		044	A	2	51
CURRY	ELISHA				48	O	CE	ENGLISH	BUTCHER	043	D		39
CURRY	HANNAH			1	74	UNITED STATES	QU	WELSH		043	E	1	4
CURRY	ISAAC		1		7	O	CE	IRISH		045	B	1	60
CURRY	JESSIE		1	1	35	SCOT	CE	SCOT	SERVANT	044	B	2	9
CURRY	JOHN				43	ENGLAND	NC	ENGLISH	F	043	E	2	8
CURRY	PATRICK		1		32	IRELAND	RC	IRISH	F LAB	044	A	2	12
CURRY	WILLIAM				50	IRELAND	CE	IRISH	LAB	045	A	3	14
CURSON	ROBERT				43	ENGLAND	CE	ENGLISH	GATE AND IRON MANUF	045	A	1	48
CURTAIN	WALLIS		1		28	O	CE	ENGLISH	BLACKSMITH	043	B	4	37
CURTIN	JAMES		1		70	IRELAND	RC	IRISH	LAB	044	C	4	42
CURTIN	MARY		1	1	65	IRELAND	RC	IRISH		044	C	4	42
CURTIS	CORNELIUS				39	ENGLAND	CE	ENGLISH	LABOURER	045	A	1	51
CURTIS	ISAAC			M	29	O	EM	GERMAN	LAB	043	A	2	51
CURTIS	JOHN				41	ENGLAND	CE	ENGLISH	F	043	H	2	28
CURTIS	JOHN				41	ENGLAND	CE	ENGLISH	FARMER	043	H	2	28
CURTIS	JOHN				60	IRELAND	RC	IRISH	LAB	045	A	2	3
CURTIS	MARY	A	1	1	34	ENGLAND	WM	ENGLISH		043	C		45
CURTIS	ROBERT				41	ENGLAND	WM	ENGLISH	STORE KEEPER	045	D	6	64
CURTIS	WILLIAM			M	52	ENGLAND	DI	ENGLISH	F	043	A	1	64
CURTIS	WM				39	ENG	CE	ENG	STONE CUTTER	045	C	1	46
CURTISS	JOHN			M	65	ENGLAND	CN	ENGLAND	F	043	A	5	17
CURTISS	JOHN	JUNIOR		M	24	O	CN	ENGLAND	F	043	A	5	18
CURTON	GEORGE				24	O	CN	ENGLISH	LAB	043	E	3	32
CUSIA	SAMUEL		1		24	IRELAND	RC	IRISH	LAB	045	A	2	39
CUSTEAD	ALICE			1	35	O	WM	IRISH		044	A	2	10
CUSTEAD	CATHARINE	E	1	1	8	O	WM	ENGLISH		044	A	2	11
CUSTEAD	DANIEL				75	US	OB	IRISH	F	044	A	2	10
CUTHBERTSON	SAMUEL				45	IRELAND	NC	IRISH	MERCHANT	043	E	1	52
CUTTERLEY	CHARLES		1		28	ENGLAND	CE	ENGLISH	LAB	044	C	3	31
CUTTERLEY	JOHN		1		30	ENGLAND	CE	ENGLISH	LAB	044	C	3	31
CUTTING	CORNELIUS	C			52	ENG	WM	ENG	CORDWAINER	045	C	1	68
CUTTING	ELISEBETH		1	1	15	O	PM	ENGLISH		043	A	6	28
CUTTING	JULIA	A	1	1	50	O	PM	SCOTCH		043	A	6	28
CUTTING	MATHEW				52	O	PM	ENGLISH	F	043	A	6	41
CUTTLE	GEORGE				29	ENGLAND	BA	ENGLISH	MANAGER WOOLEN FACTO	043	H	2	9
CUTTLE	GEORGE				29	ENGLAND	BA	ENGLISH	MANAGER WOOLLEN FACT	043	H	2	9
CUTTONG	JOHN				35	O	WM	ENGLISH	LAB	043	A	6	27
CUYLER	ANNAH		2	1	85	UNITED STATES	CN			043	E	3	D
CUYLER	MARGERT	JANE	2	1	11	O	CN			043	E	3	D
CUYLER	OSCAR	R	1		13	O	BA	ENGLISH		043	E	3	21
CUYLER	THOMPSON				44	O	CN	GERMAN	F	043	E	3	57
D'EVELYN	JOHN				35	O	CE	IRISH	PHYSICIAN	044	B	5	11
DACK	AGNES			1	42	IRELAND	WM	IRISH	BOARDINGHOUSE KEEPER	045	D	5	6
DACKER	WM				49	O	WM	ENGLISH	F	044	B	5	34
DAFOE	ALBERT				38	ONTARIO	EM	FRENCH	WHEELWRIGHT	043	G	2	51
DAFOE	ELVA		1	1	23	O	CN	FRENCH		043	E	2	64
DAFOE	HARRIETT		1	1	18	ONTARIO	CN	IRISH		043	G	1	5
DAFOE	JOHN	N			37	O	WM	ENGLISH	F	043	H	2	48
DAFOE	JOHN	N			37	ONTARIO	OM	ENGLISH	FARMER	043	H	2	48
DAFOE	WILLIAM				75	O	EM	FRENCH	CARPENTER	043	E	3	13
DAILY	JAMES				38	NEWFOUNDLAND	RC	IRISH	SHOEMAKER	043	B	3	66
DAILY	WM		1		19	O	CO	GERMAN	MACHINIST	044	B	5	37
DAIN	SARAH			1	50	ENGLAND	WM	ENGLISH	BUTCHER	045	B	1	1
DALE	JOHN				42	O	WM	ENGLISH	FARMER	043	A	4	47
DALE	JOHN				85	IRE	CS	IRISH		044	B	4	45
DALE	SOPHIA		1	1	19	ENGLAND	WM	ENGLISH	SERVANT	043	A	4	5
DALE	THOMAS		1		28	O	WM	IRISH	SERVANT	043	A	4	56
DALES	DAVID			M	41	ENGLAND	CE	ENGLAND	F	043	A	5	24
DALES	THOS	J			30	O	WM	ENGLISH	MELODION MAKER	043	D		4
DALES	WILLIAM	S		M	73	ENGLAND	CE	ENGLAND	F	043	A	5	25
DALLAMORE	MARY			1	66	ENGLAND	CE	ENGLISH		045	A	2	23
DALLIMORE	EDWARD				44	ENGLAND	PM	ENGLISH	LAB	045	A	2	27
DALLYN	JOHN				29	ENGLAND	CE	ENGLISH	LAB	043	F		1
DALSON	S	D			23	ENGLAND	CE	ENGLISH	MOULDER	044	B	5	1
DALTON	CATHRINE		1	1	32	IRELAND	RC	IRISH	INMATE	045	B	1	72
DALTON	JONATHAN				39	ENG	PS	ENG	F	044	B	2	52
DALTON	MICHAEL				40	IRELAND	RC	IRISH	LAB	043	F		23
DALTON	RICHARD				38	IRELAND	RC	IRISH	LAB	043	F		12
DALTON	RICHARD				51	ENGLAND	WM	ENGLISH	F	043	H	2	31
DALTON	RICHARD				51	ENGLAND	WM	ENGLISH	FARMER	043	H	2	31
DALTON	ROBERT				50	O	CE	ENGLISH	CLERK OF CROWN	044	C	4	90
DALY	CHARLES	T			70	IRELAND	RC	IRISH	F	043	A	6	24
DALY	MICHAL		1	M	70	IRELAND	RC	IRELAND		043	A	5	8
DALY	WILLIAM		1		22	IRELAND	RC	IRISH	GARDNER	044	C	4	10
DALZIEL	JAMES				31	O	CP	SCOTCH	F	044	B	6	41
DALZIEL	JOHN				33	O	CS	SCOTCH	F	044	B	6	29

SURNAME	NAME1	NAME2	STRAY	SEX	AGE	BIRTHPL	RELIGION	ORIGIN	OCCUP	DIST	SUB_DIST	DIV	PAGE
DALZIEL	JOHN		2		69	SCOTLAND	CP		YEDMAN	044	B	6	D
DALZIEL	JOHN	WILLIAM	2		0		CS		YEOMAN	044	B	6	D
DALZIEL	MARY			1	55	SCOTLAND	CP	SCOTCH		044	B	6	9
DALZIEL	WILLIAM		2		23	0	CP		CLERK	044	B	6	D
DAMEREAU	CHARLES				42	ENGLAND	CE	ENGLISH	WOOD ENGRAVER	045	B	2	17
DAMP	JOHN				45	ENGLAND	CE	ENGLISH	BUILDER	044	C	4	76
DAN	ELEN		1	1	55	IRELAND	RC	IRISH		043	A	2	57
DANBROOK	CHAS				44	0	NC	ENGLISH	LAB	043	C		13
DANBROOK	DAVID				42	ENGLAND	WM	ENGLISH	F	043	C		3
DANBROOK	HENRY				42	ENGLAND	WM	ENGLISH	SHOEMAKER	043	C		41
DANBROUGH	ANN			1	48	ENGLAND	CE	ENGLISH		045	A	1	13
DANBY	HENRY				30	ENG	CE	ENG	BUTCHER	045	C	1	55
DANBY	JAMES				28	0	EM	GERMAN	F	044	C	1	6
DANBY	JOHN				60	ENGLAND	EM	ENGLISH	F	044	C	1	7
DANCE	RICHARD				40	QUE	CE	ENGLAND	LABORER	045	D	2	54
DANCEY	JOHN				51	IRELAND	CE	IRISH	SAWYER	044	A	2	42
DANCEY	JOHN				37	0	WM	IRE	CARPENTER	044	B	2	21
DANCEY	P--IDGE				84	IRE	CE	IRE	PENSIONER	044	B	2	26
DANEY	JOHN		1		50	ENGLAND	CE	ENGLISH	LABOURER	045	D	3	67
DANIELS	DENNIS				42	ENGLAND	PM	ENGLISH	F	045	B	2	30
DANIELS	FRANCIS				70	ENGLAND	CE	ENGLISH	GARDNER	045	B	2	9
DANIELS	FRANCIS				28	0	PM	ENGLISH	GARDNER	045	B	1	39
DANIELS	JAMES				46	ENG	PM	ENG	LAB	044	B	2	25
DANIELS	JAMES				50	0	CS	IRISH	FARMER	045	D	3	48
DANIELS	JOHN				39	ENGLAND	PM	ENGLISH	CONSTABLE	045	B	1	36
DANIELS	JOHN				56	0	CP	SCOTCH	FARMER	045	D	3	28
DANIELS	MARY		1	1	28	0	WM	ENGLISH	SERVANT	045	B	2	31
DANIELS	WILLIAM				23	0	PM	ENGLISH	CARPENTER	045	B	1	23
DARBY	GEORGE				37	ENGLAND	CE	ENGLISH	BOOKKEEPER	044	C	3	47
DARBY	JOHN				66	ENGLAND	PR	ENGLISH	TOLL BARR	045	A	1	72
DARBY	MARY		1	1	26	0	WM	IRISH	SERVANT	045	B	2	26
DARCY	GEORGE		1		20	0	RC	IRISH	COOPER	044	B	6	58
DARK	JOHN	C			18	ENGLAND	CE	FRENCH	LIGHT HOUSE KEEPER	043	G	1	1
DARK	M				38	ENG	WM	ENG	LAB	045	C	1	23
DARLEY	DENNIS		1		38	IRELAND	RC	IRISH	LAB	043	D		30
DARLING	JANE			1	42	SCOTLAND	UP	SCOTCH		045	D	1	20
DARLING	ROBERT		1		15	0	CE	IRELAND	FARM LABORER	045	D	2	3
DARNEY	WILLIAM		1		20	ENGLAND	CE	ENGLISH	SERVANT	045	A	3	27
DARRAH	MARGARET		1	1	21	0	EM	ENGLISH	SERVANT	043	E	2	22
DART	JAMES				32	ENGLAND	CE	ENGLISH	LAB	045	A	1	87
DART	JOHN				38	ENGLAND	PM	ENGLISH	FARMER	045	A	1	95
DART	WILLIAM				70	ENGLAND	CE	ENGLISH	FARMER	045	A	1	101
DASSEPT	HENRY				28	U STATES	RC	FRENCH	LAB	043	A	6	64
DAVEY	HENRY				49	ENGLAND	PM	ENGLISH	CARPENTER	045	A	1	92
DAVEY	THOMAS				73	ENGLAND	CE	ENGLISH	GARDENER	045	A	1	28
DAVEY	WILLIAM				40	ENGLAND	CE	ENGLISH	SHOEMAKER	045	A	1	29
DAVICK	GEO				37	ENGLAND	CE	ENGLISH	BAKER	044	B	5	42
DAVID	HENRY		1	M	57	ENGLAND	CE	ENGLISH	BRICKLAYER	043	A	1	21
DAVID	SLONE				38	0	RP	SCOTCH	CARPENTER	044	C	3	74
DAVIDSON	ANN			1	56	ENGLAND	WM	ENGLISH		045	A	2	4
DAVIDSON	BENJAMIN				66	ENG	PS	ENG	MILL WRIGHT	044	B	2	18
DAVIDSON	GEORGE		1		44	SCOTLAND	BA	SCOTTISH	F LAB	044	C	1	21
DAVIDSON	GEORGE		1		28	SCOTLAND	CP	SCOTCH	FARM LAB	044	C	2	34
DAVIDSON	HUGH				56	SCOTLAND	CP	SCOTCH	F	045	A	4	28
DAVIDSON	JANET		2	1	66	SCOTLAND	CP			045	A	4	D
DAVIDSON	JOHN			M	52	SCOTLAND	PS	SCOTCH	F	043	A	1	10
DAVIDSON	JOHN				42	IRELAND	CS	IRISH	SADDLER	043	D		67
DAVIDSON	JOHN				66	SCOT	RC	SCOT	PENSIONER	044	B	2	56
DAVIDSON	JOHN				31	ENGLAND	NG	ENGLISH	ACCOUNTANT	045	B	2	9
DAVIDSON	JOSEPH		1		21	ONTARIO	PS	SCOTCH	FARMER	043	G	2	39
DAVIDSON	M			1	63	SCOT	CP	SCOT		045	C	1	43
DAVIDSON	ROBT				29	0	CP	SCOT	F	045	C	1	43
DAVIDSON	THOMAS				27	0	PS	SCOTCH	F	045	C	3	13
DAVIDSON	THOMAS				51	SCOTLAND	CP	SCOTCH	STEWART	044	C	4	36
DAVIDSON	THOS				70	SCOT	CS	SCOT	GENTLEMAN	045	C	1	42
DAVIDSON	WILLIAM				55	SCOTLAND	CP	IRISH	F	045	C	3	33
DAVIS	ALEX	JOHN			28	ENGLAND	WM	ENGLISH	POTTER	044	C	2	12
DAVIS	ALFRED				38	0	WM	IRISH	F	043	A	3	39
DAVIS	ALFRED				37	ENGLAND	WM	ENGLISH	POTTER	044	C	2	11
DAVIS	ANDREW			M	47	0	EM	ENGLISH	F	043	A	2	47
DAVIS	CALVIN				51	0	QU	ENGLISH	F	043	A	6	47
DAVIS	CLARISSA		1	1	20	0	BA	SCOTCH		043	B	3	41
DAVIS	CLAYTON				44	0	NG	ENGLISH	BLACKSMITH	043	A	6	27
DAVIS	DAVID				27	0	CN	GERMAN	LABOURER	043	B	3	34
DAVIS	EDWARD				40	US	FW	AFRICAN	CARPENTER	045	B	1	32
DAVIS	EDWARD		1		22	0	CE	ENGLISH	SERVANT	044	C	4	48
DAVIS	ELIZABETA		1	1	68	QUE	SP	SCOTCH		045	A	1	64
DAVIS	ELLA		1	1	13	0	PS	FRENCH		045	C	2	35
DAVIS	FREDK	H			30	ENGLAND	PM	ENGLISH	DEALER	044	C	2	18
DAVIS	GEORGE		2		61	CANADA	WM		F	043	C		D
DAVIS	GEORGE				38	0	PS	IRISH	F	043	E	3	53
DAVIS	GEORGE				32	ENGLAND	WM	ENGLISH	LABOURER	045	A	1	71
DAVIS	ISAAC				28	0	CE	FRENCH	LAB	045	C	2	41
DAVIS	JAMES		1		25	ENGLAND	CO	ENGLISH	CLERGYMAN	043	D		70
DAVIS	JAMES	B			40	IRELAND	CE	IRISH	BARRESTER	045	B	2	15
DAVIS	JAMES	M			59	0	UV		AGENT	045	D	2	15
DAVIS	JEFFERSON		1		22	0	BA	SCOTCH	LABOURER	043	B	3	41
DAVIS	JNO		1		22	ENGLAND	WM	ENGLISH	LAB	045	A	2	11
DAVIS	JOHN		1	M	21	ENGLAND	PB	ENGLAND	L	043	A	5	20
DAVIS	JOHN				52	0	CN	GERMAN	FARMER	043	B	3	70
DAVIS	JOHN				58	ENGLAND	WM	ENGLISH	POTTER	045	A	2	9
DAVIS	JOHN				35	0	BC	ENGLISH	SAW MILL HAND	045	D	5	54
DAVIS	JOHN	C			37	ONTARIO	CS	ENGLISH	HOTEL KEEPER	043	G	1	17
DAVIS	JOHN	P			44	US	PM	WELSH	JOINER	043	B	2	42
DAVIS	JOSEPH				53	0	QU	WELSH	FARMER	043	B	3	56
DAVIS	JOSEPH				32	0	WM	ENGLISH	FARMER	045	A	2	11
DAVIS	LYDIA			1	60	U STATES	WM	ENGLISH		043	C		55
DAVIS	MARGARET		1	1	68	US	WM	IRISH		045	A	4	23
DAVIS	MARGRET		1	1	22	0	WM	IRISH	SERVANT	045	D	6	13
DAVIS	MARK		1		67	IRELAND	WM	IRISH	F	043	B	4	3
DAVIS	MARTHA		1	1	17	0	BA	SCOTCH		043	B	3	41
DAVIS	MARY			1	60	0	QU	IRISH		043	D		31
DAVIS	MARY		1	1	16	QUE	WM	SCOT		044	B	2	16
DAVIS	MELENA			F	14	0	EM	ENGLISH		043	A	1	53
DAVIS	MITTON				29	0	NC	GERMAN	FARMER	043	A	4	69
DAVIS	PETER		1		50	0	QU	ENGLISH	CLERK	043	D		18

SURNAME	NAME1	NAME2	STRAY	SEX	AGE	BIRTHPL	RELIGION	ORIGIN	OCCUP	DIST	SUB_DIST	DIV	PAGE
DAVIS	ROBERT		1	M	22	ENGLAND	PB	ENGLAND	L	043	A	5	20
DAVIS	ROBERT		1		35	ENG	CE	ENG	LAB	044	B	2	72
DAVIS	RUTH			1	70	U STATES	QU	SCOTCH		043	A	6	26
DAVIS	SAMUEL				71	U STATES	QU	ENGLISH		043	A	4	23
DAVIS	SAMUEL				46	0	CN	GERMAN	FARMER	043	B	3	31
DAVIS	SAMUEL				90	U STATES	CN	ENGLISH	FARMER	045	D	6	47
DAVIS	SILAS				35	0	QU	ENGLISH	F	043	A	6	26
DAVIS	THOMAS				32	0	QU	ENGLISH	F	043	A	6	26
DAVIS	THOMAS				28	0	WM	ENGLISH	F	043	A	6	47
DAVIS	THOMAS				30	0	PM	ENGLISH	FARMER	044	A	2	21
DAVIS	THOMAS				44	IRELAND	RC	IRISH	F	044	B	6	32
DAVIS	THOMAS				30	0	EM	AFRICAN	LABOURER	045	A	1	50
DAVIS	WILLIAM				30	ENGLAND	CE	ENGLISH	LAB	043	B	2	35
DAVIS	WILLIAM		1		10	0	BA	SCOTCH		043	B	3	41
DAVIS	WM	G			24	0	CE	IRISH	MERCHANT	043	D		16
DAVISON	GEORGE	M			55	ENGLAND	CE	ENGLISH	FARMER	045	D	3	13
DAVISON	JOHN				62	IRELAND	CE	IRISH	HOTEL KEEPER	043	D		14
DAVISON	JOHN		1		29	0	CE	ENGLISH	MERCHANT	043	D		83
DAVISON	MARY		1	1	17	SCOTLAND	PM	SCOTCH	DRESS MAKER	044	C	2	4
DAVISON	OWEN				42	NS	WM	IRISH	F	045	A	4	22
DAVISS	JOSHUA				68	0	QU	ENGLISH	F	043	E	2	3
DAVISS	ROBERT				43	0	QU	ENGLISH	F	043	E	2	3
DAVITT	WILLIAM			M	38	IRELAND	CE	IRELAND	F	043	A	5	41
DAVY	CATHRINE		1	1	14	ENGLAND	CE	ENGLISH		045	B	1	31
DAVY	ELIZABETH		1	1	24	ENGLAND	BA	ENGLISH	SERVANT	043	B	3	25
DAVY	PATRICK				23	IRELAND	RC	IRISH	INNKEEPER	044	C	4	48
DAWES	DAVID	B	1		7	0	CE	ENGLISH		045	A	1	10
DAWKIN	WILLIAM		1		22	ENGLAND	CE	ENGLISH	LAB	045	B	2	2
DAWSON	ALICE		1	1	27	WALES	CE	WELSH	SERVANT	045	B	2	36
DAWSON	DENNIS				45	ENGLAND	CE	ENGLISH	F	044	A	3	41
DAWSON	GEORGE				44	ENGLAND	CE	ENGLISH	CARPENTER	043	E	1	33
DAWSON	MARGARET		1	1	15	0	WM	ENGLISH		045	D	4	54
DAWSON	MARK				28	0	PM	ENGLISH	F	044	A	2	17
DAWSON	MARY			1	66	ENGLAND	PM	ENGLISH		044	A	2	17
DAWSON	MARY			1	53	ENGLAND	CE	ENGLISH	STORE KEEPER	045	B	1	2
DAWSON	MARY			1	59	ENGLAND	WM	ENGLISH		045	B	1	50
DAWSON	WILLIAM				40	0	CE	ENGLISH	F	043	E	1	34
DAWSON	WILLIAM		1		54	ENGLAND	WM	ENGLISH	BUTCHER	045	B	2	28
DAY	B	W			36	ENGLAND	CO	ENGLISH	CLERGYMAN	043	B	3	60
DAY	GEORGE				26	ENGLAND	CE	ENGLISH	BLACKSMITH	044	C	4	6
DAY	JANE		1	1	25	QUE	WM	SCOTCH	SEAMSTRESS	043	D		19
DAY	TIMOTHY				68	ENGLAND	CE	ENGLISH	F LAB	044	A	2	3
DAYKES	WILLIAM		1		22	ENGLAND	PM	ENGLISH	BRICK LAYER	045	B	1	19
DAZAIELL	JAMES				54	SCOT	PS	SCOT	F	044	B	3	26
DAZELL	JOHN				36	0	IN	SCOT	GENT	044	B	3	19
DEACOFF	GEORGE				35	NOVA SCOTIA	WM	SCOTCH	F	044	C	4	29
DEACON	WILLIAM				38	U STATES	CE	IRISH	FARMER	043	A	4	61
DEACON	WILLIAM	H	1		23	ENGLAND	CE	ENGLISH	MERCHANT	045	D	2	8
DEADMAN	HANNAH		1	1	24	ENGLAND	PM	ENGLAND	SERVANT	045	D	2	9
DEADMAN	JOHN				43	ENG	PM	ENG	F	044	B	2	53
DEAGAN	EDWARD				59	IRE	RC	IRISH	LAB	044	B	1	40
DEAN	ISABEA		1	1	22	0	WM	IRISH		045	A	4	20
DEAN	JAMES				31	IRELAND	WM	IRISH	BOOTMAKER	045	B	2	10
DEAN	JAMES				45	IRELAND	CE	IRISH	LABORER	045	D	1	9
DEAN	JAMES				43	IRELAND	PM	IRISH	F	044	C	2	24
DEAN	JOHN				30	0	WM	IRISH	HOTEL KEEPER	043	F		18
DEAN	JOHN				35	IRELAND	RC	IRISH	LAB	045	B	1	61
DEAN	JOHN				50	ENGLAND	EM	ENGLISH	FARMER	044	C	1	16
DEAN	JOHN	B			18	0	CE	ENGLISH	LAB	045	A	1	65
DEAN	MARGRET		1	1	17	0	CE	IRISH		045	A	3	34
DEAN	MATHEW				43	ENG	CE	ENG	F	044	B	1	19
DEAN	THOMAS				55	ENGLAND	CE	ENGLISH	DROVER	044	C	4	43
DEAN	WILLIAM				49	IRELAND	RELIGION	IRISH	F	043	H	1	15
DEAN	WILLIAM		1		18	0	EM	ENGLISH		044	C	2	14
DEANE	SAMUEL				45	ENG	WM	ENG	GARDENER	044	B	2	20
DEARLING	JOHN				33	0	IF	ENGLISH	SPINNER	043	E	3	41
DEARLING	WM				32	0	RC	ENGLISH	PAINTER	044	B	5	3
DEATH	ABEL	B			51	ENGLAND	WM	ENGLISH	F	044	A	1	21
DEATH	WILLIAM	T			28	0	WM	ENGLISH	F	044	A	2	23
DEAVITT	JOHN				75	IRELAND	CE	IRISH	RETIRED	043	A	4	36
DECOURSIER	EMMA			1	41	ENGLAND	CE	ENGLISH		044	A	2	49
DEDANCOURT	ANTHONY				62	FRANCE	RC	FRENCH	LAB	043	H	2	12
DEDUNCOURT	ANTHONY				62	FRANCE	RC	FRENCH		043	H	2	12
DEEBLE	WILLIAM				45	ENGLAND	PS	ENGLISH	SHOE MAKER	045	A	1	64
DEEGAN	JOHN				40	IRELAND	RC	IRISH	F	044	C	4	54
DEER	JAMES		1		19	SCOTLAND	PS	SCOTCH	LAB	045	C	2	47
DEFRIES	ANN			1	40	IRELAND	RC	IRISH		045	A	1	50
DEFRIES	ISABELLA			1	55	0	CE	SCOTCH		045	A	1	73
DEFRIES	RICHARD				39	0	CE	ENGLISH	GARDENER	045	A	1	72
DEFRIES	ROBERT		2		65	ENGLAND	CE		GENT	045	A	1	D
DEFROSS	HENRY		1		36	ENGLAND	CP	ENGLAND	FARM LABORER	045	D	2	1
DEGEER	JOHN				47	0	CN	FRENCH	FARMER	043	B	3	43
DEGEER	PETER				47	0	CD	GERMAN	F	043	E	2	18
DEGEERE	JAMES				67	CANADA	BA	ENGLISH	FARMER	045	D	6	64
DELA ROSE	GEORGE		1		22	ENGLAND	CE	ENGLISH	F	044	C	4	97
DELAHA	JOSEPH		1		16	0	WM	FRENCH		045	D	4	2
DELAHAY	MARY			1	34	ENGLAND	PM	ENGLISH		045	D	2	50
DELAMORE	EMILY		1	1	40	IRELAND	CE	IRISH	GOVERNESS	044	C	2	47
DELANCY	ROBT				60	IRELAND	CE	IRISH	WEAVER	044	B	5	37
DELANEY	CATHERINE			1	70	IRELAND	RC	IRISH		043	A	6	53
DELCHUNTY	MICHAEL				50	IRELAND	RC	IRISH	SHOEMAKER	045	B	1	28
DELL	DANIEL		1		20	ENGLAND	CE	ENGLISH	LABORER	043	G	1	55
DELONE	ABRAHM				36	0	PM	FRENCH	CARPENTER	043	B	2	21
DELONE	MARGARET		2	1	29	0	PM			043	B	2	D
DELONG	SUSAN			1	38	0	WM	UNKNOWN		044	A	2	1
DELONY	MICHAEL				60	IRELAND	RC	IRISH	LAB	044	C	4	28
DELRY	JOHN				36	IRELAND	RC	IRISH	LAB	044	C	4	22
DELWORTH	CORNELIUS				49	ENGLAND	BA	ENGLISH	BASKET MAKER	044	C	4	81
DEMERY	WILLIAM		1		18	0	WM	ENGLISH	FARM LAB	044	A	2	29
DEMPSEY	CATHERINE		2	1	32	0	RC			044	A	3	D
DEMPSEY	MARY	ELLEN	1	1	1	0	RC	IRISH		044	A	3	48
DEMPSEY	WILLIAM	JAMES	1		6	0	RC	IRISH		044	A	3	48
DEMPSTER	HUGH				30	SCOTLAND	CE	SCOTCH	F	044	A	2	4
DEMPSTER	THOMAS				30	0	CE	SCOTCH	BUTCHER	044	A	1	37
DENBY	GEORGE				50	ENGLAND	PM	ENGLISH	FARMER	045	A	2	17
DENBY	HENRY				25	ENGLAND	PM	ENGLISH	FARMER	045	A	2	17

SURNAME	NAME1	NAME2	STRAY	SEX	AGE	BIRTHPL	RELIGION	ORIGIN	OCCUP	DIST	SUB_DIST	DIV	PAGE
DENISON	CHARLES				38	O	CE	ENGLISH	F	044	C	3	13
DENISON	EDWIN	PERINS			30	O	CE	ENGLISH	GENTLEMAN	044	C	3	75
DENISON	GEORGE				35	ONT	CE	ENGLISH	FARMER	044	C	3	18
DENISON	THOMAS				50	ENGLAND	WM	ENGLISH	FARMER	045	D	4	21
DENNE	ROBERT				40	ENGLAND	CE	ENGLISH	F	043	B	5	5
DENNIS	ARTHUR				35	ENGLAND	CE	ENGLISH	LABOURER	045	D	3	16
DENNIS	DANIEL				36	O	RC	IRISH	F	043	A	3	41
DENNIS	ELIZABETH		1	F	17	O	CS	IRISH		043	A	2	38
DENNIS	GEORGE				39	ENGLAND	CE	ENGLISH	FARM SERVANT	045	C	3	27
DENNIS	HENERY				48	O	WM	ENGLISH	FARMER MILLER	044	C	3	35
DENNIS	JOHN				43	ENGLAND	RC	ENGLISH	MACHINIST	043	D		73
DENNIS	JOHN				47	O	CE	ENGLISH	GENTLEMAN	044	C	3	31
DENNIS	JOHN	STOUGHTON			50	O	CE	ENGLISH	SURVEYOR GENERAL	044	C	3	74
DENNIS	JOSEPH		1	M	13	O	PS	IRISH		043	A	2	39
DENNIS	LEVI				56	O	QU	ENGLISH	FARMER	043	A	4	27
DENNIS	MARGRET		1	1	82	O	WM	SCOTCH		044	C	3	60
DENNIS	ROBERT		1	M	14	O	CE	GERMAN		043	A	1	49
DENNIS	WALTER		1		24	ENGLAND	WM	ENGLISH	FARM LAB	044	C	2	5
DENNIS	WILLIAM				46	AT SEA	RC	IRISH	F	043	A	3	41
DENNIS	WILLIAM				63	ENGLAND	WM	ENGLISH	TANNER	043	F		1
DENNIS	WILLIAM				44	ENGLAND	PM	ENGLISH	BUTCHER	045	B	2	27
DENNISON	ELIZABETH		2	1	46	O	WM			045	D	4	D
DENNISON	HENRY	T			22	O	CE	ENGLISH	ACCOUNTANT	043	D		27
DENOON	GEORGE				43	SCOTLAND	PS	SCOTCH	DROVER	044	A	1	17
DENT	HENRY		1		24	ENGLAND	CE	ENGLISH	BRICK MAKER	045	B	1	63
DENT	THOMAS				52	NEW BRUNSWICK	CE	ENGLISH	LAB	043	H	2	12
DENT	THOMAS				52	NEW BRUNSWICK	CE	ENGLISH	LABOURER	043	H	2	12
DENTON	BROWN	A			43	ENG	CE	ENG	F	044	B	2	32
DENTON	FRANCIS				69	ENGLAND	WM	ENGLISH	F	044	B	5	63
DENTON	JAMESON			M	51	ENGLAND	BA	ENGLAND	CARPENTER	043	A	5	41
DENTON	JOHN				30	ENGLAND	CE	ENGLISH	LAB	043	C		38
DENTON	MARY		1	1	31	O	CE	ENGLISH	SERVANT	043	C		28
DENTON	MAT				32	ENGLAND	PM	ENGLISH	F	044	B	5	65
DENTON	WILLIAM		1		4	O	CE	ENGLISH		043	C		29
DENTON	WILLIAM				40	ENG	PM	ENGLISH	F	044	B	2	58
DENTZ	HENRY				48	NEW BRUNSWICK	PR	DUTCH	FARMER	043	G	2	15
DEREHAM	RICHARD				45	IRELAND	CE	IRELAND	SHOE MAKER	045	D	2	11
DERMITY	MATHEW				60	IRELAND	RC	IRISH	FARMER	043	G	2	11
DERRACH	ARCHIBALD			M	36	SCOTLAND	PS	SCOTCH	LAB	043	A	2	21
DERRY	WM				38	IRE	CE	IRE	F	045	C	1	52
DESMOND	JOHN			M	56	IRELAND	RC	IRISH	PEDLAR	043	A	5	7
DESMOND	MARY		1	1	22	IRELAND	RC	IRISH	SERVANT	045	B	2	27
DEVANEY	MARY		1	1	46	IRELAND	RC	IRISH		044	C	2	38
DEVANY	MARY			1	90	IRELAND	RC	IRISH		044	C	4	55
DEVANY	PAT				35	IRELAND	RC	IRISH	LAB	043	F		26
DEVENISH	TIMOTHY				58	O	CE	ENG	F	045	C	1	64
DEVENS	ALMIRA		1	1	12	O	CE	ENGLISH		044	A	1	38
DEVEREUX	MARGARET		1	1	23	IRELAND	RC	IRISH	COOK	044	A	2	40
DEVERILL	WILLIAM				26	O	OB	ENGLISH	MERCHANT	043	E	1	50
DEVINE	ISAAC				36	O	PS	SCOTTISH	BLACKSMITH	044	C	1	45
DEVINE	J	C			62	O	PS	SCOTTISH	F	044	C	1	45
DEVINE	MARY			1	62	O	RC	ENGLISH	F	045	C	3	24
DEVINE	VINCENT				45	ENGLAND	CE	ENGLISH	BUTCHER	043	E	1	16
DEVINS	JAMES				66	O	WM	ENGLISH	F	044	B	5	76
DEVINS	JOHN				49	O	WM	GER	F	044	B	3	42
DEVINS	PETER				33	O	NG	GERMAN	F	044	B	6	19
DEVINS	WILLIAM				26	O	EA	GERMAN	F	044	B	6	19
DEVIO	SHEDRICK				35	O	CE	FRENCH	CARPENTER	045	A	3	41
DEVITT	JAMES				25	IRELAND	WM	IRISH	F	043	E	2	26
DEVITT	ROBERT				34	IRELAND	WM	IRISH	F	043	E	2	26
DEVLIN	HUGH				52	IRE	WM	IRISH	F	044	B	1	58
DEVLIN	WILLIAM				56	SCOT	WM	IRE	F	044	B	2	65
DEVONS	J	R			28	O	WM	SCOTTISH	CARPENTER	044	C	1	38
DEW	JOHN				26	O	WM	ENGLISH	F	044	C	2	2
DEW	WILLIAM				38	ENGLAND	CS	ENGLISH	MASON	043	D		60
DEW	WILLIAM		1		20	ENGLAND	XC	ENGLISH		045	B	1	52
DEW	WILLIAM		1		19	ENGLAND	WM	ENGLISH	MACHINIST	044	C	2	3
DEWAN	JULIA			1	43	IRELAND	RC	IRISH		044	C	4	56
DEWBERRY	WILLIAM				25	ENG	WM	ENG	F	044	C	1	28
DEWER	CHRISTINA		1	1	31	SCOTLAND	CP	SCOTCH		045	B	1	62
DEWER	HENRY		1		2	O	CP	SCOTCH		045	B	1	62
DEWSBERRY	JAMES		2			O	WM			044	C	1	D
DEWSBURRY	THOMAS				28	ENGLAND	CE	ENGLISH	GENERAL JOBBER	045	A	4	33
DEWSBURY	ANN			1	66	ENGLAND	WM	ENGLISH		043	B	4	48
DEWSBURY	THOMAS				64	ENGLAND	PM	ENGLISH	F	045	A	4	32
DEWSON	THOMAS	HENRY	1			O	CE	ENGLISH		043	F		28
DEYSMAN	JAMES				32	O	WM	SCOT		044	B	4	47
DIBB	GEORGE				48	ENG	CE	ENG	F	044	B	2	30
DIBB	THOMAS				50	ENG	CE	ENG	F	044	B	1	15
DIBBLER	ELLEN		1	F	80	NEW BRUNSWICK	CE	SCOTCH		043	A	1	50
DICEMAN	ADAM				31	O	PM	GER	F	044	B	4	35
DICEMAN	ANN			1	56	O	WM	GER	F	044	B	4	27
DICEMAN	HENRY				36	O	PM	GER	F	044	B	4	26
DICK	AGNES			1	40	SCOTLAND	CP	SCOTCH		043	A	4	41
DICK	JAMES				62	SCOT	PS	SCOT	CLERGYMAN	044	B	2	8
DICK	ROBERT				36	O	CP	SCOTCH	F	044	B	6	56
DICKEN	THOS	H	1		21	ENGLAND	CE	ENGLISH	F LAB	044	A	3	52
DICKENSON	CHARLES				27	SCOTLAND	CE	SCOTCH	FARIER	043	B	3	54
DICKENSON	GEORGE		1		25	ENG	EM	ENG	FARM LAB	044	B	1	31
DICKINS	JOHN		1		25	ENGLAND	CE	ENGLISH	LAB	044	C	2	54
DICKINSON	JAMES				49	O	CE	ENGLISH	LAB	043	F		18
DICKINSON	JANE			F	65	ENGLAND	WM	ENGLISH		043	A	2	37
DICKOUT	HENRY				44	O	WM	GER	F	044	B	3	14
DICKOUT	PETER				36	O	EM	GER	LAB	044	B	3	15
DICKOUT	WILLIAM				73	USA	WM	GER	F	044	B	3	14
DICKSON	ALEX				42	UNITED STATES	CS	SCOTCH	F	043	F		16
DICKSON	ALICE		1	1	11	O	PM	ENGLISH		044	B	6	43
DICKSON	ANDREW				69	SCOTLAND	PS	SCOTCH	F	043	E	1	31
DICKSON	ANN			1	80	IRELAND	CP	IRISH		045	A	4	23
DICKSON	ANNE		1	1	24	ENG	CE	ENG	SERVANT	044	B	2	64
DICKSON	DAVID				40	SCOTLAND	PS	SCOTCH	BLACKSMITH	045	C	3	42
DICKSON	ELIZABETH		1	1	55	SCOTLAND	PS	SCOTCH		045	D	6	15
DICKSON	JAMES		2		60	U STATES	CE		CARPENTER	045	D	5	D
DICKSON	JOHN		1		17	ENG	CE	ENG	LAB	044	B	2	64
DICKSON	MARY		1		14	O	PS	SCOTCH		045	D	6	15
DICKSON	ROBERT			M	48	NS	RC	IRELAND	MASON	043	A	5	23

SURNAME	NAME1	NAME2	STRAY	SEX	AGE	BIRTHPL	RELIGION	ORIGIN	OCCUP	DIST	SUB_DIST	DIV	PAGE
DICKSON	ROBERT				32	0	CP	SCOTCH	MILLER	045	D	6	7
DICKSON	ROBT		1		24	0	PM	ENGLISH	LAB	044	B	5	65
DICKSON	THOMAS		1		20	0	CP	ENGLISH	FARM LABOURER	045	C	4	41
DIELINSKIE	JACOB				31	POLAND	LU	GERMAN	DRUGGIST	044	B	6	1
DIGBY			2			0	WM			043	B	3	D
DIGBY	GEORGE				30	IRELAND	WM	IRISH	SADDLE HARNESS MAKER	045	D	5	11
DIGBY	HENRY				26	0	WM	IRISH	PAINTER	043	B	3	67
DIGGINS	ANN		1	1	16	0	RC	IRISH	SERVANT	045	D	1	13
DIKE	CORNELEUS				31	ENGLAND	PM	ENGLISH	F	043	B	5	21
DILLER	JOHN				36	US	MN	GERMAN	F	045	C	2	40
DILLON	EDWARD				45	IRELAND	CE	IRISH	GARDENER	045	A	1	34
DILLON	LUKE		1		21	0	RC	IRISH	CARPENTER	044	C	4	40
DILLON	MINNIE		1	1	18	0	WM	IRISH	INMATE	045	B	1	72
DILLON	PATRICK		1		19	0	RC	IRISH	ROPE MAKER	044	C	4	40
DILMAN	ELISHA				46	0	CN	GERMAN	F	043	B	4	45
DILMON	JOHN		1		22	0	CN	GERMAN	F	043	B	5	36
DIMMA	JAMES				51	SCOTLAND	CS	SCOTCH	FARMER	045	D	5	62
DIMMA	THOS				61	SCOTLAND	RP	SCOTCH	CARPENTER	043	C		2
DINGLE	JOHN				57	0	WM	ENGLISH	DROVER	044	C	2	22
DINGLE	JOSEPH	E	2		17	UNITED STATES	WM			044	C	2	D
DINIS	WILLIAM		1		78	ENG	CE	ENG	LAB	044	B	2	52
DINNISON	THOMAS				50	ENGLAND	WM	ENGLISH	FARMER	045	D	4	33
DISMAN	CORNELAS				55	IRELAND	RC	IRISH	LAB	043	A	6	32
DIX	JOHN				30	ENGLAND	WM	ENGLISH	F	045	C	4	5
DIX	JOHN				58	ENGLAND	PM	ENGLISH	F	045	C	4	46
DIX	MATTHEW				33	ENGLAND	WM	ENGLISH	F	044	B	5	49
DIXON	EDWARD				60	ENGLAND	PM	ENGLISH	FARMER	045	D	3	29
DIXON	ELLEN			1	42	IRELAND	CE	IRISH		044	A	2	32
DIXON	FLORENCE	I	1	1	14	0	CP	IRE		045	C	1	4
DIXON	FRANCIS		2		10	ONTARIO	EM			043	G	1	D
DIXON	GEORGE				40	ENGLAND	CN	ENGLISH	FARMER	043	B	3	35
DIXON	HENERY		1		30	ENGLAND	WM	ENGLISH	WOOLEN CARDER	044	C	3	15
DIXON	HENRY				35	SCOT	CP	SCOT	BLACKSMITH	045	C	1	28
DIXON	HIRAM				31	0	CP	IRISH	ENGINEER	045	C	4	18
DIXON	ISAAC				32	IRELAND	EM	IRISH	FARMER	045	A	2	6
DIXON	JAMES				55	ENGLAND	CE	ENGLISH	LAB	043	D		19
DIXON	JAMES	B			21	ENGLAND	CE	ENGLISH	F	044	A	2	27
DIXON	JOHN				38	ENGLAND	EM	ENGLISH	F	043	E	3	14
DIXON	JOHN				61	ENGLAND	BA	ENGLISH	F	044	A	3	15
DIXON	JOHN	JR			30	0	BA	ENGLISH	F MANAGER	044	A	3	16
DIXON	RICH	P			32	ENGLAND	OB	ENGLISH	F	044	A	2	27
DIXON	RICHARD				59	ENGLAND	CE	ENGLISH	F	044	A	2	27
DIXON	ROBERT		1		30	0	QU	IRISH	SERVANT	043	E	3	33
DIXON	ROBERT				40	ENGLAND	CP	ENGLISH	F	045	C	2	18
DIXON	SICILEY		1	1	33	ENGLAND	CE	ENGLISH		045	A	4	5
DIXON	WM				40	IRELAND	CE	IRISH	LAB	044	B	5	54
DIXON	WM				28	IRE	CE	IRE	F	045	C	1	33
DIXSON	BARBARA		1	1	26	0	CE	ENGLISH		044	C	3	30
DIXSON	ROGER				31	ENGLAND	CE	ENGLISH	F	044	C	1	14
DOAK	GEORGE		1		21	0	CE	IRISH	FARM LAB	044	C	2	5
DOAK	JOHN				57	IRELAND	CE	IRISH	TEAMSTER	045	D	1	16
DOAN	ABRAHAM				69	UNITED STATES	ZZ	ENGLISH	F	043	E	2	22
DOAN	ANN		2	1	52	IRELAND	CE			043	D		D
DOAN	AUSTIN	T			37	0	QU	ENGLISH	DENTIST	043	E	1	45
DOAN	CHARLES				61	0	NC	GERMANY	GENTLEMAN	043	C		16
DOAN	DAVID				33	0	NC	IRISH	MERCHANT	043	C		43
DOAN	DAVID				50	0	QU	ENGLISH	F	043	E	2	12
DOAN	EDWARD				30	0	EM	ENGLISH	STONE CARVER	043	D		66
DOAN	ELIAS				66	UNITED STATES	CN	ENGLISH	F	043	E	2	19
DOAN	EZRA	H			36	0	NC	ENGLISH	F	043	E	1	48
DOAN	GEORGE				30	0	ZZ	ENGLISH	F	043	E	1	43
DOAN	HENRY				37	0	CN	ENGLISH	FARM LABOURER	043	E	2	23
DOAN	HEZEKIAH				43	0	CN	DUTCH	F	043	A	6	48
DOAN	IRA				61	0	ZZ	ENGLISH	F	043	E	1	48
DOAN	JAMES	H			26	0	NC	ENGLISH	F	043	E	1	24
DOAN	JAMES	J			28	0	WM	ENGLISH	F	043	E	2	19
DOAN	JOSEPH				37	0	WM	ENGLISH	F	043	A	6	52
DOAN	JUDAH				54	0	WM	ENGLISH	F	043	E	1	53
DOAN	KATIE		1	1	15	IRELAND	NC	IRISH		043	C		54
DOAN	MAHLON				32	0	NC	ENGLISH	F	043	E	2	33
DOAN	MATHIAS				37	0	EM	ENGLISH	F	043	E	2	31
DOAN	OLIVER				63	U STATES	EM	ENGLISH	LAB	043	D		50
DOAN	ROBERT	W			30	0	NC	ENGLISH	SCHOOL TEACHER	043	C		48
DOAN	SENICA				52	0	QU	GERMAN	F	043	A	6	8
DOAN	TIMOTHY				35	0	CN	ENGLISH	F	043	A	6	52
DOAN	WAIT	ANN		1	54	UNITED STATES	ZZ	IRISH		043	E	2	35
DOAN	WILLIAM				29	0	QU	GERMAN	F	043	A	6	9
DOBLE	LUKE				23	0	CE	IRISH	BLACKSMITH	043	H	1	17
DOBSON	JAMES				60	IRELAND	WM	IRISH	POSTMASTER	045	B	1	6
DOBSON	JOHN		M		42	ENGLAND	WM	ENGLISH	F	043	A	2	14
DOBSON	THOMAS	J			50	IRELAND	CE	IRELAND	FARMER	045	D	2	5
DOBSON	WILLIAM	E			30	0	WM	IRISH	TRADER	045	B	1	48
DOCHERTY	CATHERINE		1	1	17	IRELAND	CE	IRISH	SERVANT	044	C	2	44
DODD	ANNIE		1	1	81	ENGLAND	WM	ENGLISH		045	C	3	44
DODD	FREDERICK				29	ENGLAND	BA	ENGLISH	LEATHER MAKER	045	B	2	19
DODD	JAMES		M		56	ENGLAND	CE	ENGLISH	FARMER	043	A	1	26
DODD	MARY		1	1	17	0	CE	UNKNOWN	SERVANT	044	B	3	11
DODD	ROBERT				37	ENG	CE	ENG	F	045	C	1	6
DODDS	ELIZABETH		1	1	25	0	PM	ENGLISH		044	B	6	30
DODDS	GLADSTONE	JOHN			32	ENGLAND	WM	SCOTCH	STATION MASTER	044	C	4	17
DODDS	RACHEL		1	1	15	0	CE	ENG	SERVANT	044	B	3	8
DODDS	WILLIAM				29	0	CN	ENGLISH	WHEELWRIGHT	043	E	2	39
DODENEAD	DAVID				32	ENGLAND	BA	ENGLISH	LEATHER CLOTH MAKER	045	B	1	11
DODGE	ANSON	GP			37	UNITED STATES	CE	ENGLISH	LUMBERMERCHANT	043	G	1	57
DODGE	ARTHUR				43	0	CE	ENGLISH	F	043	H	1	41
DODINGTON	EDWARD		1		30	ENGLAND	CE	ENGLISH	CABINET MAKER	045	B	1	9
DODINGTON	SARAH		1	1	31	ENGLAND	CE	ENGLISH		045	B	1	9
DOER	SOPHIA		2	1		0	NG			044	B	2	D
DOERR	ROBERT	F			57	GER	LU	GER	SAWYER	044	B	2	21
DOES	WILLIAM				36	ENGLAND	BA	ENGLISH	F	043	A	6	5
DOHENY	CATHARINE			1	30	IRELAND	RC	IRISH	CHAR WOMAN	045	D	5	30
DOHENY	EDWARD				36	IRELAND	RC	IRISH	LABOURER	045	D	5	51
DOHERTY	ELIZA		1	1	23	0	WM	IRISH		045	D	3	62
DOHERTY	JOHN				80	IRELAND	RC	IRISH	F	043	H	1	17
DOHERTY	JOHN				50	IRELAND	CS	IRISH	DOCTOR OF MED	045	D	5	34
DOHERTY	JOSEPH				42	0	CN	IRISH	F	043	E	3	6

SURNAME	NAME1	NAME2	STRAY	SEX	AGE	BIRTHPL	RELIGION	ORIGIN	OCCUP	DIST	SUB_DIST	DIV	PAGE
DOHERTY	MARGRET			1	55	IRELAND	CE	IRISH		043	F		29
DOHERTY	PHILLIP		1		22	ONTARIO	CE	IRISH	LABORER	043	G	1	4
DOHERTY	THOMAS		1		19	ONTARIO	CE	IRISH	LABORER	043	G	1	4
DOIDGE	ARTHUR				23	0	CE	ENGLISH	POTTER	045	A	1	104
DOIGE	GEORGE				50	ENGLAND	CE	ENGLISH	F	044	C	4	4
DOLAN	JOHN				32	IRELAND	RC	IRISH	MILLER	043	F		5
DOLAN	THOMAS				33	IRELAND	RC	BLACKSMITH		043	B	4	33
DOLERY	ISAAC				36	0	RP	ENGLISH	CARPENTER	044	C	3	1
DOLMAGE	TOBIAS				36	IRE	WM	GER	SHOE MAKER	044	B	2	14
DOLTON	CATHRINE		1		80	IRELAND	RC	IRISH		043	A	6	57
DONAHOE	JOHN				67	IRE	RC	IRE	LAB	045	C	1	36
DONALDSON	ALEX		1		26	SCOT	CP	SCOT	LAB	045	C	1	57
DONALDSON	M	JANE	2	1	7	0	WM			045	D	5	D
DONALDSON	WILLIAM				30	0	WM	IRISH	LABOURER	045	D	5	42
DONALLY	MARY		1	1	28	IRELAND	RC	IRISH	SERVANT	045	B	2	29
DONAVAN	PATRICK				35	IRELAND	RC	IRISH	RAILWAY LABORER	044	A	1	32
DONAWAY	STEPHEN				44	IRELAND	NG	IRISH	FARMER	043	B	3	20
DONELLY	BRIDGET		1	F	60	IRELAND	RC	IRELAND		043	A	5	23
DONELLY	MARGARET		1	1	23	0	RC	IRISH	SERVANT	045	B	2	21
DONELLY	MARY		1		26	IRELAND	RC	IRISH		045	B	1	43
DONER	DAVID				66	US	TU	GERMAN	FARMER	045	D	4	17
DONER	EMANUEL				61	0	TU	GERMAN	FARMER	045	D	2	39
DONER	JACOB				52	0	CE	GERMAN	CARPENTER	045	D	2	59
DONER	JOHN				28	0	TU	GERMAN	FARMER	045	D	4	16
DONER	JOHN				70	US	TU	GERMAN	GENTLEMAN	045	D	4	18
DONER	PETER				50	0	TU	GERMAN	FARMER	045	D	2	58
DONER	SUSANNAH		1	1	18	0	CP	GERMAN	SERVANT	045	D	2	69
DONER	SYLVANUS				25	0	WM	GERMAN	LABORER	045	D	2	39
DONERY	ELIZABETH		1	1	19	0	CE	ENGLISH		043	D		74
DONGUN	OWEN				39	US	RC	IRISH	LAB	045	C	2	34
DONNALLY	EDWIN				43	IRE	RC	IRE	LAB	045	C	1	6
DONNALLY	JOHN				70	IRE	RC	IRE	F	045	C	1	38
DONNATT?	RUTH			1	47	0	EM	ENGLISH	SHOPKEEPER	045	D	5	42
DONNELL	JAMES				78	IRELAND	CE	IRISH	F	043	H	1	5
DONNELL	MARGARET		1	1	65	IRELAND	CE	IRISH		043	H	1	5
DONNELL	THOMAS				61	IRELAND	CE	IRISH	F	043	H	1	5
DONNELLEY	JAMES				42	IRELAND	RC	IRISH	LAB	043	C		35
DONNELLY	ELLEN			1	38	IRELAND	RC	IRISH		044	A	1	15
DONNELLY	JOHN				45	IELAND	RC	IRISH	F	045	C	2	26
DONNELY	MARY		1	1	25	IRELAND	RC	IRISH	SERVANT	044	A	1	4
DONOHOE	ANN		1	1	23	IRELAND	RC	IRISH	SERVANT	045	B	2	29
DONOHOE	MICHAEL				30	IRE	RC	IRE	LAB	045	C	1	39
DONOHUE	JAMES				38	0	WM	IRISH	F	044	B	6	11
DOODS	JOHN				57	IRELAND	PM	SCOTCH	FARMER	043	A	4	48
DOOKS	HENRY				29	ENG	PM	ENG	F LAB	044	B	1	54
DOOKS	THOMAS				34	ENG	PM	ENG	F	044	B	1	53
DOOLAN	MARY		1	1	23	0	RC	IRISH	SERVANT	045	B	2	33
DOOLING	JAMES				78	IRELAND	RC	IRISH	LAB	044	C	2	9
DOORTY	ELLEN			1	44	IRELAND	RC	IRISH		045	C	2	11
DORAN	MARY		1	1	30	IRELAND	RC	IRISH	SERVANT	045	A	1	88
DORHERTY	ALEX				34	SCOT	CP	SCOT	F	045	C	1	52
DORITHY	LEWIS				65	USA	BA	AFRICAN	LABOURER	045	A	1	40
DORLEY	RACHEL			1	43	0	BA	GERMAN	CHARWOMAN	043	B	2	45
DORSEY	JANE		1	1	23	0	WM	ENGLISH	SERVANT	044	C	3	20
DOSSER	MOSES		1		42	ENGLAND	CE	ENGLISH	BLACKSMITH	044	A	2	16
DOTY	WILLIAM				22	0	CE	ENGLISH	LAB	043	H	1	14
DOUGELL	THOMAS				43	CANADA	PS	IRISH	PHOTOGRAPHER	045	D	6	42
DOUGHERTY	ISAIH				38	IRELAND	PM	IRISH	F	043	B	5	21
DOUGHERTY	JAMES		1		7	0	CP	FRENCH		045	C	2	42
DOUGHERTY	JOHN				48	IRELAND	CN	IRISH	FARMER	043	B	3	38
DOUGHERTY	JOHN	E	1		10	0	CP	IRISH		045	C	2	41
DOUGHERTY	MARY	JANE	1	1	5	0	CP	IRISH	F RETIRED	045	C	2	42
DOUGHERTY	SAML				74	IRELAND	CN	IRISH	F RETIRED	043	B	2	41
DOUGHERTY	SAMUEL				30	IRELAND	CN	IRISH	FARMER	043	B	3	34
DOUGLAS	ARCHIBALD		1		19	UNITED STATES	WM	IRISH	SERVANT	043	E	3	9
DOUGLAS	CHARLES	J			33	SCOTLAND	CE	SCOTCH	F	043	B	1	29
DOUGLAS	DONALD				38	SCOTLAND	CP	SCOTCH	FARMER	045	D	3	14
DOUGLAS	HECTOR				67	IRELAND	CP	IRISH	WEAVER	045	C	4	24
DOUGLAS	JOHN				50	SCOTLAND	CP	SCOTCH	TAILOR	045	B	1	29
DOUGLAS	MARTHA		1	1	12	0	QU	SCOTCH		043	E	1	21
DOUGLAS	MARY		1	1	20	SCOTLAND	RC	IRISH	SERVANT	045	B	2	20
DOUGLAS	RODGER				45	ENGLAND	CE	ENGLISH	BRICK & TILE MANUFAC	045	B	1	11
DOUGLAS	SAMUEL				58	SCOTLAND	PS	SCOTCH	F	043	E	3	6
DOUGLAS	SARAH		1	1	17	0	WM	ENGLISH		045	B	2	11
DOUGLAS	THOMAS				44	ENGLAND	CE	ENGLISH	LAB	043	C		44
DOUGLAS	THOMAS				31	SCOTLAND	CP	SCOTCH	F	044	C	4	14
DOUGLAS	WILLIAM				37	0	PM	IRISH	WHEELWRIGHT	045	A	2	7
DOUGLASS	ALEX		1		40	SCOT	CP	SCOT	F	045	C	1	29
DOUTHWAIT	ELISABETH		1	1	17	0	WM	ENGLAND	SERVANT	045	D	2	3
DOUTHWAITE	GEORGE				67	ENGLAND	WM	ENGLISH	LAB	043	D		19
DOVE	ELIJAH			M	36	ENGLAND	PR	ENGLISH	F	043	A	1	45
DOVE	MATHEW			M	84	ENGLAND	CE	ENGLISH	F	043	A	1	29
DOVE	THEOFFULES		1		11	0	WM	ENGLISH		043	A	6	35
DOVE	WILLIAM			M	34	ENGLAND	ME	ENGLAND	F	043	A	5	34
DOW	ANN	JANE	1	1	20	0	PS	SCOTTISH	SERVANT	044	C	1	38
DOW	JOHN				48	SCOTLAND	PS	SCOTTISH	F LAB	044	C	1	35
DOWD	THOMAS				52	IRELAND	RC	IRISH	BUTCHER	043	F		17
DOWDING	JEMIMA		1	1	17	0	CE	ENGLISH		044	C	4	1
DOWEL	EDWARD				33	ENGLAND	CE	ENGLISH	LAB	043	F		32
DOWLER	ANN		1	1	30	IRELAND	CE	IRISH		044	A	3	27
DOWLING	HUGH				34	0	WM	IRISH	WEAVER	043	E	2	69
DOWNES	ROBERT				30	IRELAND	WM	IRISH	LABOURER	045	D	5	67
DOWNEY	ANNA		1	1	17	ENGLAND	CE	ENGLISH		045	D	5	8
DOWNEY	EVAN				44	ENGLAND	CO	ENGLISH	LABOURER	045	D	5	31
DOWNING	MARSHALL		1		24	IRELAND	CP	IRISH	FARM LABOURER	045	C	3	13
DOWNS	CATHERINE		1	1	22	0	RC	IRISH	SERVANT	044	B	6	58
DOWNS	JEREMIAH		1		20	0	PM	IRISH	BROOM MANUFACTURER	045	B	1	11
DOWNS	JOHN		1		20	0	RC	IRISH	COOPER	044	B	6	58
DOWNS	MICHAEL				62	IRELAND	RC	IRISH	LAB	044	B	6	33
DOWNS	WATSON				49	ENGLAND	CE	ENGLISH	TAILOR	043	B	5	37
DOWSON	CLIFTON				26	ENGLAND	PM	ENGLISH	BRICK LAYER	045	B	1	45
DOWSON	RICHARD				35	ENGLAND	PM	ENGLISH	BRICKLAYER	045	B	1	48
DOWZER	WILLIAM				40	IRELAND	PM	IRISH	F	043	A	3	58
DOYLE	ELLEN		1	1	17	0	RC	SCOT	SERVANT	044	B	3	47
DOYLE	JAMES				50	0	RC	IRISH	FARMER	043	A	4	46
DOYLE	JAMES		1		11	0	RC	IRISH		043	H	2	30

SURNAME	NAME1	NAME2	STRAY	SEX	AGE	BIRTHPL	RELIGION	ORIGIN	OCCUP	DIST	SUB_DIST	DIV	PAGE
DOYLE	JAMES		1		11	ONTARIO	RC	IRISH		043	H	2	30
DOYLE	JAMES				68	IRELAND	RC	IRISH	F	044	A	3	48
DOYLE	JAMES				60	IRELAND	RC	IRISH	LAB	044	C	4	8
DOYLE	JANE			1	65	IRELAND	RC	IRISH		043	A	4	3
DOYLE	JOHN		1		18	0	CE	IRISH	SERVANT	043	A	4	34
DOYLE	JOHN				69	IRELAND	RC	IRISH	F	043	H	1	1
DOYLE	JOHN		1		9	0	RC	IRISH		043	H	2	30
DOYLE	JOHN		1		9	ONTARIO	RC	IRISH		043	H	2	30
DOYLE	JOHN				41	0	RC	IRISH	F	044	A	3	48
DOYLE	MICHAEL				55	IRELAND	RC	IRISH	F	043	E	3	1
DOYLE	PATRICK				27	0	RC	IRISH	F	043	A	4	1
DOYLE	PETER				36	0	RC	IRISH	FARMER	043	A	4	66
DOYLE	ROSANNA			1	47	IRE	RC	IRE		044	B	2	50
DOYLE	THOMAS				39	0	RC	IRISH	INNKEEPER	044	B	6	40
DOYLE	WM				36	QUE	CE	IRISH	LAB	044	B	5	47
DRACOCK	SARAH	E	1	1	15	0	WM	ENGLISH		045	B	1	14
DRAKE	JOHN				53	ENGLAND	CE	ENGLISH	FARMER	045	D	1	29
DRAKE	SUSAN		2	1		0	CE			045	D	1	D
DRAKE	WILLIAM				61	US	FW	AFRICAN	CARPENTER	045	B	1	32
DRAPER	DAVID				39	ONTARIO	CE	ENGLISH	FARMER	043	G	1	14
DRAPER	DAVID				29	ONTARIO	CE	ENGLISH	FARMER	043	G	1	52
DRAPER	EBENEZER				51	0	EM	ENGLISH	CARPENTER	043	E	1	23
DRAPER	ELIZA		1	1	30	0	BA	GERMAN		043	B	3	20
DRAPER	ENOS	I			26	0	EM	ENGLISH	F	043	E	1	12
DRAPER	HENRY				53	ONTARIO	EM	ENGLISH	F	043	G	1	28
DRAPER	JACOB				42	0	CE	ENGLISH	F	043	H	2	24
DRAPER	JACOB				42	ONTARIO	CE	ENGLISH	FARMER	043	H	2	24
DRAPER	JOEL				56	ONTARIO	CE	ENGLISH	FARMER	043	G	1	26
DRAPER	LUTHER				52	ONTARIO	CN	IRISH	FARMER	043	G	1	29
DRAPER	LUTHER				78	UNITED STATES	CN	IRISH	FARMER	043	G	1	52
DRAPER	MARTHA		1	1	14	ONTARIO	CE	ENGLISH		043	G	1	21
DRAPER	MARY			1	84	UNITED STATES	EM	ENGLISH		043	G	1	14
DRAPER	REUBEN				63	0	CN	ENGLISH	F	043	E	2	63
DRAPER	RICHARD	P			54	ONTARIO	EM	ENGLISH	FARMER	043	G	1	20
DRAPER	SAMUEL				30	ONTARIO	CE	ENGLISH	FARMER	043	G	2	51
DRAPER	WILLIAM	H			70	ENGLAND	CE	ENGLISH	CHIEF JUSTICE A	045	B	2	33
DREDGE	THOMAS				75	ENGLAND	BA	ENGLISH	GARDNER	044	C	3	27
DRENNON	JANE		1	1	49	QUEBEC	WM	SCOTCH	SUB MATRON	045	B	1	71
DRESSER	ANNA		1	1	6	US	BA	ENGLISH		043	B	2	45
DRESSER	WILLIAM				42	ENGLAND	CE	ENGLISH	LABOURER	045	D	4	21
DRETERLO	WILLIAM				46	GERMANY	LU	GERMAN	WATCHMAKER	043	D		18
DREW	CHARLES				26	ENGLAND	CE	ENGLISH	LAB	045	C	2	8
DRINEY	ELISABETH			1	48	IRELAND	CE	IRISH	LAB	045	A	4	22
DRISCOLL	EMILA			1	31	0	CE	ENGLISH		045	B	1	50
DRISCOLL	PRISCILLA		1	1	30	0	JU	GERMAN		044	C	4	66
DRIVER	GEORGE		1		21	0	CE	ENGLISH	PRINTER	043	D		33
DRIVER	GEORGE				51	ENGLAND	CE	ENGLISH	CORDWAINER	043	E	2	13
DROTHCOTT	EMANUEL		1		27	ENGLAND	CS	ENGLISH	AGENT	044	B	6	24
DROWLEY	JOHN				55	ENGLISH	CE	ENGLISH	LABOURER	044	C	3	45
DRUMMOND	ALEXANDER				44	SCOTLAND	CP	SCOTCH	LAB	045	C	4	42
DRUMMOND	DANIEL				71	SCOTLAND	CS	SCOTCH	F	043	A	3	40
DRUMMOND	DAVID				49	SCOTLAND	CS	SCOTCH	LAB	043	E	2	46
DRUMMOND	JANETT			1	40	0	CS	SCOT		044	B	4	24
DRURIE	JAMES				63	ENG	CE	ENG	F	044	B	2	73
DRURRY	HARRIET		1	1	40	0	NC	IRISH	SERVANT	043	E	2	22
DRURY	ELLEN		1	1	14	0	CE	ENGLISH		043	D		30
DRURY	GEORGE				36	ENG	EP	ENG	LAB	044	B	3	25
DRURY	HANNAH		1	1	18	0	CE	ENGLISH	SERVANT	043	D		15
DRURY	HANNAH		1	1	18	0	CE	ENGLISH		043	D		87
DRURY	JOHN				31	ENGLAND	CE	ENGLISH	BLACKSMITH	045	D	2	46
DRURY	JOSHUA		1		24	ENGLAND	CE	ENGLISH	F LAB	043	B	4	6
DRURY	THOMAS				11	0	WM	ENGLISH		043	B	5	1
DRYSDALE	DAVID				58	SCOTLAND	WM	SCOTCH	MILL WRIGHT	044	B	5	17
DUCAN	GEORGE				32	0	CP	IRISH	F	045	A	4	12
DUCK	JEREMIAH				32	0	PM	ENGLISH	LAB	044	B	5	60
DUCK	JONATHAN				70	ENGLAND	PM	ENGLISH	TAILOR	044	A	3	39
DUCK	PETER		1		20	0	PM	ENGLISH	LAB	044	B	5	60
DUCLANT	MICHAEL				29	ONTARIO	RC	FRENCH	LABORER	043	G	2	43
DUCLAW	SUSAN		1	1	22	0	RC	FRENCH	SERVANT	043	E	3	14
DUDLEY	WALTER				58	ENGLAND	CE	ENGLISH	R R STATION AGENT	043	D		34
DUDSON	WILLIAM		1	M	21	ENGLAND	WM	ENGLISH	CARPENTER	043	A	2	50
DUDY	HENRY				36	0	RC	IRISH	FARMER	045	A	1	100
DUESBERREY	JOHN				24	ENGLAND	PM	ENGLISH	F	045	A	4	14
DUFF	ALEXANDER				39	SCOTLAND	CS	SCOTCH	BLACKSMITH	045	D	5	59
DUFF	ELIZABETH		1	1	19	0	WM	SCOTCH	SERVANT	044	C	2	44
DUFF	ELLEN		1	1	15	0	WM	SCOTCH	SERVANT	044	C	2	44
DUFF	JAMES				30	IRELAND	RC	IRISH	BRICKLAYER	044	C	4	9
DUFF	JOS				42	SCOT	CP	SCOT	F	045	C	1	51
DUFF	SAMUEL		1		19	0	CP	SCOTCH		045	A	3	25
DUFF	SAMUEL		1		18	0	CP	SCOTCH	SERVANT	045	A	3	35
DUFF	WM				54	SCOT	CE	SCOT	BLACKSMITH	045	C	1	28
DUFFIELD	HENRY				33	0	CE	ENGLISH	FARMER	045	D	5	41
DUFFIELD	THOMAS				29	0	WM	ENGLISH	FARMER	045	D	3	36
DUFFUS	GEO				55	SCOTLAND	PS	SCOTCH	PATTERN MAKER	044	B	5	22
DUFFY	JOHN				45	IRELAND	WM	IRISH	F	044	C	1	50
DUFFY	ROBERT				59	IRELAND	EM	IRISH	GENTLEMAN	044	C	3	36
DUGGAN	JAMES				32	IRELAND	RC	IRISH	TAVERN KEEPER	043	A	4	4
DUGGAN	JAMES				35	IRELAND	RC	IRISH	GARDNER	044	C	4	49
DUGGAN	PATRICK				59	IRELAND	RC	IRISH	FARMER	043	A	4	60
DULMAGE	ELIZABETH		1	1	29	0	WM	GERMAN		043	E	3	59
DULMAGE	SARAH	JANE	1	1	13	0	WM	GERMAN		043	E	3	59
DUMBLETON	JAMES				50	ENGLAND	QU	ENGLISH	LAB	043	A	6	12
DUMOND	SIMON	P			51	0	WM	DUTCH	F	045	C	3	13
DUMREEL	WM	HENRY	1		30	ENG	CE	ENG		045	C	1	61
DUNARL	NICHOLAS				26	FRANCE	LU	FRENCH	F	044	B	3	51
DUNBAR	RICHARD				39	0	CE	SCOTCH	GROCER	045	A	1	34
DUNCALF	WILLIAM			M	75	ENGLAND	CE	ENGLISH	F	043	A	1	44
DUNCALF	WILLIAM			M	33	ENG	EM	ENGLISH	LAB	043	A	1	74
DUNCAN	ALEXANDER				43	SCOTLAND	UP	SCOTCH	FARMER	045	D	1	34
DUNCAN	ALEXR				50	SCOTLAND	CP	SCOTCH	BLACKSMITH	045	D	4	17
DUNCAN	ALLEN	G	1		25	0	CE	SCOTCH	F	044	A	2	35
DUNCAN	DAVID				33	0	WM	IRISH	FARMER	045	A	3	36
DUNCAN	ELIZABETH			1	45	IRELAND	WM	IRISH	F	044	C	1	49
DUNCAN	FRANCIS				37	SCOTLAND	CP	SCOTCH	MINISTER	045	D	3	33
DUNCAN	HANNAH		1	1	12	0	KB	SCOTCH		045	A	3	23
DUNCAN	HENRY				37	ENGLAND	PM	IRISH	FARMER	045	A	3	36

SURNAME	NAME1	NAME2	STRAY	SEX	AGE	BIRTHPL	RELIGION	ORIGIN	OCCUP	DIST	SUB_DIST	DIV	PAGE
DUNCAN	J	JAMES			25	0	PM	IRISH	F	044	C	1	52
DUNCAN	JAMES				45	SCOTLAND	CP	SCOTCH	F	045	C	3	20
DUNCAN	JAMES				67	IRELAND	WM	IRISH	F	044	C	1	48
DUNCAN	JAMES				35	0	WM	IRISH	F	044	C	1	48
DUNCAN	JOHN				65	SCOT	CP	SCOT	STATION MASTER	044	B	1	25
DUNCAN	JOHN				65	IRELAND	WM	IRISH	F	045	C	2	35
DUNCAN	JOHN				30	0	PM	IRISH	BUTCHER	045	C	3	55
DUNCAN	JOHN				29	0	WM	IRISH	FARMER	045	D	1	22
DUNCAN	JOSEPH		2		30	0	PM		F	044	C	1	D
DUNCAN	MARY	JANE		1	24	0	CE	ENGLISH		044	C	3	23
DUNCAN	PETER				51	SCOTLAND	CP	SCOTCH	FARMER	045	D	3	15
DUNCAN	RICHARD				46	IRELAND	WM	IRISH	LAB	044	C	2	18
DUNCAN	ROBT		1		40	SCOT	CP	SCOT	LAB	045	C	1	51
DUNCAN	SARAH			1	29	0	PM	IRISH	F	044	C	1	52
DUNCAN	THOMAS				32	IRELAND	CE	IRISH	LAB	045	A	2	13
DUNCAN	WILLIAM				63	SCOTLAND	CS	SCOTTISH	BLACKSMITH	044	C	1	9
DUNCAN	WILLIAM				70	IRELAND	CE	IRISH	F	044	C	1	20
DUNCAN	WM	A			31	0	WM	IRISH	F	044	C	1	42
DUNCOMB	JOHN				62	ENGLAND	CE	ENGLAND	DOCTOR	045	D	2	3
DUNDASS	MARY		1	1	27	SCOTLAND	PS	SCOTCH	SERVANT	045	B	2	27
DUNDERDALE	JOSEPH		1		23	ENGLAND	CE	ENGLISH	FARM LAB	044	C	2	8
DUNHAM	ANNIE		1	1	65	UNITED STATES	ZZ	ENGLISH		043	E	2	85
DUNHAM	EPHRAM				47	0	CN	ENGLISH	CARPENTER	043	E	2	58
DUNHAM	HIRAM				56	ONTARIO	CE	SCOTCH	F	043	B	1	4
DUNHAM	JOSEPH	E	1		3	0	NC	IRISH		043	A	4	38
DUNHAM	MARTHA		1	1	4	0	NC	IRISH		043	A	4	38
DUNHAM	MARTHA		2		17	0	CN			043	E	2	D
DUNHAM	MARY	A	1	1	1	0	NC	IRISH		043	A	4	38
DUNHAM	RACHEL		1	1	23	0	NC	IRISH		043	A	4	38
DUNHAM	REID				38	0	CN	ENGLISH	F	043	E	2	16
DUNHAM	THOS	G			71	NB	CN	ENGLISH	GENT	043	E	2	63
DUNKIN	JOHN		1		26	SCOTLAND	CP	SCOTCH	FARM LABOURER	045	C	4	10
DUNKINS	AMELIA	E	2	1	15	0	PM			044	A	2	D
DUNKINS	MARY			1	56	US	PM	AFRICAN		044	A	2	11
DUNKINS	SARAH		2	1	30	0	PM			044	A	2	D
DUNLOP	MRS		2	1	75	IRELAND	CS			044	B	6	D
DUNLOP	THOMAS		1		25	0	CE	IRISH	F	044	B	6	38
DUNN	ALEXANDER				38	0	CP	IRISH	FARMER	045	D	3	30
DUNN	DAVID		1		18	0	CE	ENGLISH	BLACKSMITH	045	D	3	2
DUNN	ELIZABETH			1	56	IRELAND	CP	IRISH		045	D	2	42
DUNN	HENRY				27	0	WM	ENGLISH	CARPENTER	044	B	5	27
DUNN	HENRY		1		38	ENGLAND	CE	ENGLISH	HOSTLER	045	C	3	38
DUNN	JOHN				42	0	PS	IRISH	F	043	E	3	52
DUNN	JOHN				50	ENGLAND	CE	ENGLISH	F	044	A	2	36
DUNN	JOHN				55	ENGLAND	CE	ENGLISH	BRICK MAKER	045	B	2	35
DUNN	JOHN				57	ENG	CE	ENG	DRAINING	045	C	1	46
DUNN	JOHN	J	1		18	0	WM	ENGLISH	CLOTHIER	045	D	3	4
DUNN	JUSTUS				58	USA	EM	IRISH	FRUIT DEALER	045	A	1	60
DUNN	LEVI				43	ENG	PM	ENG	F	045	C	1	51
DUNN	REUBEN				70	ENGLAND	WM	ENGLISH	F	044	A	1	32
DUNN	ROBERT				30	ENGLAND	CE	ENGLISH	F	044	A	1	41
DUNN	SAMUEL	G			29	0	WM	ENGLISH	F	045	A	4	9
DUNN	SARAH		1	F	5	0	CE	ENGLAND		043	A	5	28
DUNN	WILLIAM				31	0	WM	ENGLISH	BUCHER	044	C	4	48
DUNNE	WILLIAM				47	ENGLAND	CE	ENGLISH	F	043	E	1	7
DUNNET	HENRY		1		24	SCOTLAND	CP	SCOTCH	F	045	A	4	5
DUNNETT	JAMES				52	ENGLAND	WM	ENGLISH	COOPER	045	D	1	24
DUNNING	ANNIE		1	1	46	GIBRALTER	CE	ENGLISH		045	B	2	30
DUNNING	CHARLES				40	ENGLAND	CE	ENGLISH	BUTCHER	045	B	2	30
DUNNING	JOHN			M	54	ENGLAND	RC	ENGLAND	F	043	A	5	10
DUNNING	MARTHA		1	1	24	0	QU	SCOTCH		043	A	2	55
DUNNING	WILLIAM			M	43	ENGLAND	EP	ENGLISH	CLERK	043	A	2	26
DUNNINGTON	ELINOR			1	55	0	WM	DUTCH		043	B	1	2
DUNSLING	ELISABETH		1	1	23	0	WM	ENGLISH		045	A	4	10
DUNSMORE	GILBERT		1		13	0	WM	GERMAN		045	D	2	13
DUNTON	CHARLOTTE		2	1	18	IRE	WM			044	B	2	D
DUNTON	JAMES				42	ENG	WM	ENG	F	044	B	2	64
DUNTON	JANE			1	74	ENGLAND	PM	ENGLISH		045	B	1	19
DUPUIS	LUCY		1	1	30	QUEBEC	RC	FRENCH		045	B	1	74
DURHAM	ARON		1		59	ENGLAND	CE	ENGLISH	LAB	045	B	1	14
DURHAM	JAMES				40	0	NG	DUTCH	LUMBERMAN	043	A	6	59
DUROSE	WILLIAM				85		CE	ENGLISH	GENTLEMAN	045	D	4	6
DUTCHBURN	HENRY				50	ENGLAND	CE	ENGLISH	SHOEMAKER	044	A	3	12
DUTCHER	ELENOR		1	1	47	0	NG	GERMAN		043	A	2	53
DUTTON	WILLIAM		1		55	U STATES	CE	AFRICAN	LAB	045	A	2	16
DWYER	MARY		1	1	70	IRELAND	RC	IRISH		043	D		41
DWYER	PATRICK		1		2	0	RC	IRISH		043	D		37
DYER	LEVI				33	ENGLAND	PM	ENGLISH	LAB	044	A	3	38
DYER	MARTHA		1	1	70	ENG	WM	ENG		044	B	3	15
DYER	MARY	H	1	1	36	0	WM	ENG		044	B	3	15
DYER	RICHARD	J			39	ENGLAND	WM	ENGLISH	CARPENTER	043	D		28
DYKES	MATHEW				31	SCOTLAND	CP	SCOTCH	LAB	045	C	2	44
EAD	JOHN				24	CANADA	WM	ENGLISH	MASON	045	D	6	36
EAD	JOSEPH				56	ENGLAND	WM	ENGLISH	MASON	045	D	6	36
EADE	ANN		2	1	24	ENGLAND	WM			043	C		D
EADE	JAMES				51	ENGLAND	WM	ENGLISH	F	043	C		3
EADE	STEPHEN				26	ENGLAND	WM	ENGLISH	SAILOR	043	C		30
EADES	GEORGE				73	ENG	BA	ENG	F	045	C	1	4
EAGAN	ELIZA		1	1	19	0	CO	ENGLISH		044	B	6	52
EAGAN	JOHN				40	0	CE	IRE	F	045	C	1	57
EAGAN	RICHARD				53	IRELAND	CS	IRISH	F	044	B	6	52
EAGLE	JOHN				50	ENGLAND	CE	ENGLISH	HOTELL KEEPER	044	C	3	30
EAGLE	THOMAS				54	ENGLAND	CE	ENGLISH	GENTLEMAN	044	C	3	18
EAKIN	DAVID				38	0	CP	IRISH	FARMER	045	D	4	35
EAKIN	GEORGE				40	0	CS	IRISH	STORE KEEPER	045	D	3	61
EAKIN	JNO	P			37	0	CP	IRISH	MECHANIC	043	C		36
EAKIN	NANCY	B	1	1	13	0	CP	IRISH		045	D	1	18
EAKIN	SAMUEL				75	IRELAND	CP	IRISH	FARMER	045	D	3	1
EAKIN	WILLIAM				42	0	CS	IRISH	CARRIAGE MAKER	045	D	3	18
EALES	MARY			1	40	U STATES	CN	GERMAN	SEAMSTRESS	043	D		51
EALES	WILLIAM		1		61	ENGLAND	WM	ENGLISH	F LAB	043	A	6	48
EARHART	DELIA			1	45	ONTARIO	CN	GERMAN		043	G	1	22
EARHART	MARGARET		1	1	70	UNITED STATES	WM	GERMAN	HOUSEKEEPER	043	F		1
EARL	GEORGE				28	0	WM	ENGLISH	CARPENTER	043	H	2	29
EARL	GEORGE				28	ONTARIO	WM	ENGLISH	CARPENTER	043	H	2	29
EARL	JOSEPH				50	IRELAND	CE	IRISH	LABOURER	043	G	1	42

SURNAME	NAME1	NAME2	STRAY	SEX	AGE	BIRTHPL	RELIGION	ORIGIN	OCCUP	DIST	SUB_DIST	DIV	PAGE
EARLE	GEORGE				60	UNITED STATES	EM	ENGLISH	FARMER	043	G	2	54
EARLE	JAMES				35	ONTARIO	PR	ENGLISH	FARMER	043	G	2	25
EARLE	MARY	ANN	1	1	12	ONTARIO	CE	ENGLISH	SERVANT	043	G	2	25
EARLES	ERWIN				56	IRELAND	CE	IRISH	LAB	044	B	5	23
EARLES	ROBT				27	IRELAND	CE	IRISH	COOPER	044	B	5	35
EARLES	WILLIAM				38	ONTARIO	PR	ENGLISH	MACHINE CONTRACTOR	043	G	2	21
EARLS	ISABELLA		1	1	14	O	CE	ENGLISH		044	A	2	7
EARLS	ISABELLA		1	1	22	O	PM	IRISH	SERVANT	045	C	4	22
EARNEST	GEORGE		1		13	O	CE	ENGLISH	LAB	043	B	1	34
EAST	MATHEW				34	ENGLAND	WM	ENGLISH	AGENT	044	B	6	28
EASTBROOK	HANNAH		1	1	73	ENGLAND	WM	ENGLISH		043	C		33
EASTERBY	WILLIAM		1	M	70	ENGLAND	CE	ENGLISH		043	A	2	44
EASTICK	DANIEL				51	ENGLAND	CE	ENGLISH	SHOEMAKER	045	A	3	40
EASTMAN	JONATHAN				63	Q	BA	ENGLISH	F	043	A	6	9
EASTWOOD	ALFRED				23	O	CE	ENGLISH	DRUGGIST	043	A	4	5
EASTWOOD	ANTHONY				58	ENGLAND	CE	ENGLISH	MERCHANT	043	A	4	4
EASTWOOD	JAMES				50	ENGLAND	CE	ENGLISH	F	044	A	1	10
EATON	JOHN		1		8	SCOTLAND	CP	SCOTCH		045	C	2	29
EATON	MARGARET		1	1	2	O	CP	SCOTCH		045	C	2	29
EBEY	JOHN		1		11	O	CP	IRISH		045	D	4	52
EBEY	THOMAS		1		13	O	CP	IRISH		045	D	4	52
EBOY	JOHN				25	NS	CN	IRISH	SAWYER	043	B	5	22
EBY	HENERY				42	CANADA	CN	GERMAN	FARMER	045	D	6	28
EBY	MIKEL				73	U STATES	MN	GERMAN		045	D	6	29
EBY	PETER				22	O	CN	IRISH	LABOURER	045	D	6	3
EBY	WELLINGTON		2		3	O	NG			045	D	6	D
ECCLESTON	JOHN				27	ENGLAND	CO	ENGLISH	BLACKSMITH	044	A	3	28
ECHARDT	WM	PHILLIP			36	O	WM	ENGLISH	MERCHANT	043	E	3	47
ECHARETT	MALCOM	ED	2			O	CO			045	D	3	D
ECK	DANIEL				69	U STATES	WM	GERMAN	TANNER	043	A	4	7
ECKARDT	ABRAHAM				70	O	VM	GERMAN	FARMER	045	D	3	39
ECKARDT	CHARLOTTE		1	1	56	O	LU	IRISH		045	D	3	61
ECKARDT	EDWARD				28	O	CO	GERMAN	FARMER	045	D	3	19
ECKARDT	GEORGE				33	O	NG	ENGLISH	FARMER	043	B	3	35
ECKARDT	ISABELLA			1	63	ENGLAND	VM	ENGLISH		045	D	3	12
ECKARDT	JACOB				40	O	DM	GERMAN	FARMER	045	D	3	37
ECKARDT	JAMES				33	O	LU	GERMAN	FARMER	045	D	3	60
ECKARDT	JARUM				40	O	LU	GERMAN	FARMER	045	D	3	40
ECKARDT	JOHN				27	O	VM	ENGLISH	FARMER	045	D	3	12
ECKARDT	PHILIP				67	O	CO	GERMAN		045	D	3	19
ECKARDT	SALEM				46	O	LU	GERMAN	AUCTIONEER	045	D	3	1
ECKARDT	THOMAS				34	O	WM	GERMAN	MERCHANT	043	B	3	62
ECKARDT	THOS	P			38	O	CO	GERMAN	PHYSICIAN	045	D	3	3
ECKARDT	WILLIAM				47	O	LU	GERMAN	FARMER	045	D	3	8
ECKAROT	EUPHY		1	1	22	O	CE	IRISH		045	D	3	61
ECKART	FREDERICK				61	O	WM	GERMAN	FARMER	045	D	4	54
ECKHARDT	GEORGE				38	O	WM	GERMAN	F	045	C	3	25
EDEN	CHARLES				44	ENGLAND	CE	ENGLISH	BLACKSMITH	045	A	3	9
EDEY	JANE			1	49	IRELAND	CE	IRISH		044	B	1	4
EDGAR	ISABLE		1	1	16	ENGLAND	CP	SCOTCH		045	B	1	29
EDGAR	JAMES				46	O	PM	IRE	PREACHER	045	C	1	64
EDMISON	ISABELLA		2	F	89	SCOTLAND	PS	ENGLISH		043	A	5	D
EDMOND	EMILY		1	1	31	O	CE	ENGLISH		043	D		64
EDMOND	FREDERICK	B	1		5	O	CE	ENGLISH		043	D		64
EDMOND	W	K	1		32	O	CE	ENGLISH	COMM TRAVELER	043	D		64
EDMONDSON	SAMUEL				75	NB	CE	IRISH	MASON	045	D	3	5
EDMONSON	JAMES		2		25	ENGLAND	CE		PHYSICIAN	043	D		D
EDMONSON	JANE			1	40	O	CE	IRISH		043	D		29
EDMONSTON	JAMES			M	76	IRELAND	NC	IRISH	YEOMAN	043	A	1	21
EDMUND	CHARLES		2		1	ENGLAND	NG			045	D	6	D
EDNY	JAMES		1		33	ENGLAND	PM	ENGLISH	LAB	043	B	5	43
EDWARD	GEORGE				78	ENGLAND	CE	ENGLISH		043	B	4	7
EDWARDS	DANIEL				31	ENGLAND	UV	ENGLISH	LABOURER	045	D	5	70
EDWARDS	ELIJAH				28	ONTARIO	EM	ENGLISH	FARMER	043	G	2	12
EDWARDS	FRANCIS				82	IRELAND	CE	IRISH	FARMER	043	G	2	45
EDWARDS	GEO		1		40	O	PS	ENGLISH	LAB	044	B	5	40
EDWARDS	GEORGE				58	ENGLAND	WM	WELSH	LABOURER	043	A	4	6
EDWARDS	GEORGE				46	ENGLAND	WM	ENGLISH	F	044	C	2	54
EDWARDS	JAMES				50	ENGLAND	QU	ENGLISH	F	043	A	6	34
EDWARDS	JAMES	G			67	U STATES	QU	GERMAN	FARMER	043	A	4	32
EDWARDS	JOEL			M	32	O	BA	GERMANY	F	043	A	5	31
EDWARDS	JOHN				26	O	EM	ENGLISH	LAB	043	A	6	33
EDWARDS	JOHN				32	ENG	CE	ENG	BOOK KEEPER	044	B	4	16
EDWARDS	LETITIA		1	1	50	IRELAND	CS	IRISH		045	D	5	19
EDWARDS	MARY			1	68	ENGLAND	WM	ENGLISH		043	A	6	25
EDWARDS	MEREAB			1	42	O	PM	ENGLISH		043	A	6	38
EDWARDS	SARAH		1	1	32	ENGLAND	CD	ENGLISH	NURSE	045	A	1	1
EDWARDS	WILLIAM			M	30	O	CE	GERMANY	F	043	A	5	45
EDWARDS	WILLIAM				45	ENGLAND	NC	ENGLISH	LAB	043	C		36
EDWARDS	WILLIAM	W			36	ENGLAND	WM	ENGLISH	PAINTER	044	C	2	3
EDWARDS	WM		1		21	SCOT	CP	SCOT	LAB	045	C	1	58
EDWORTHY	HENRY				35	ENGLAND	WM	ENGLISH	GARDNER	044	C	4	67
EDWORTHY	JAMES		1		21	ENGLAND	WM	ENGLISH	SERVANT	044	C	4	54
EGAN	ANN		1	1	20	O	RC	IRISH	SERVANT	044	A	3	18
EGAN	JOHNSTON			M	56	IRELAND	PS	IRISH	F	043	A	2	1
EGAN	SAMUEL			M	59	IRELAND	PS	IRISH	F	043	A	2	17
EGAR	JOHN				45	O	TU	GERMAN	MILLER & CLOTH MAN	045	D	2	51
EGO	ANDREW				39	SCOTLAND	CS	SCOTCH	F	043	H	2	25
EGO	ANDREW				39	SCOTLAND	CS	SCOTCH	FARMER	043	H	2	25
EGO	ANGUS				45	SCOTLAND	CS	SCOTCH	F	043	H	2	25
EGO	ANGUS				45	SCOTLAND	CS	SCOTCH	FARMER	043	H	2	25
ELDEN	MARY		1	1	47	IRELAND	CE	IRISH		043	D		41
ELDER	ALEX				23	O	WP	SCOTCH	CLK	044	B	5	5
ELDER	JAMES				35	CANADA	CP	SCOTCH	MILLER	044	B	6	5
ELDER	MARY	ANN		1	47	O	CS	SCOTCH		043	D		57
ELGIE	THOMAS				56	ENGLAND	CE	ENGLISH	FARMER	045	A	2	16
ELIOT	ROBART				67	ENGLAND	CE	ENGLISH		044	C	3	32
ELIOTT	EDWARD				24	O	PM	ENGLISH	FARMER	045	A	3	23
ELIOTT	JAMES				44	ENGLAND	EM	ENGLISH	F	043	A	6	25
ELKINGTON	GEORGE				63	ENGLAND	CE	ENGLISH	GARDENER	045	A	1	77
ELLA	GEORGE				48	ENGLAND	PM	ENGLISH	F	044	A	3	32
ELLAR	WILLIAM			M	56	ENGLAND	PR	ENGLISH	LAB	043	A	1	46
ELLARLY	JOSEPH				46	ENGLAND	PM	ENGLISH	FARMER	045	D	4	4
ELLERBY	DAVID				72	ENGLAND	CE	ENGLISH	F	043	F		24
ELLERBY	JAMES				43	ENGLAND	CE	ENGLISH	TAILOR	044	A	2	16
ELLERBY	JAMES				26	O	PM	ENGLISH	SADDLER	044	B	5	28

SURNAME	NAME1	NAME2	STRAY	SEX	AGE	BIRTHPL	RELIGION	ORIGIN	OCCUP	DIST	SUB_DIST	DIV	PAGE
ELLERBY	JONATHAN				47	ENGLAND	PM	ENGLISH	F	044	B	5	58
ELLERBY	WILLIAM				70	ENGLAND	WM	ENGLISH	GENTLEMAN	044	C	3	43
ELLERBY	WM				29	0	PM	ENGLISH	F	044	B	5	50
ELLICE	MAXWELL		1		16	ONTARIO	WM	IRISH	SERVANT	044	C	3	49
ELLIOT	ARCHIBALD				46	0	CP	SCOTCH	CARPENTER	045	C	3	29
ELLIOT	FRED				28	0	WM	ENGLISH	WAGON MAKER	044	B	5	29
ELLIOT	GEO				31	0	CO	ENGLISH	F	044	B	5	48
ELLIOT	GEORGE				50	ONTARIO	BA	ENGLISH	CARPENTER	043	G	2	41
ELLIOT	HUGH				52	0	CP	SCOTCH	F	045	C	3	29
ELLIOT	JAMES		1		31	0	WM	IRISH	FARMER	045	D	3	56
ELLIOT	JOHN				50	0	WM	CHIPPAWA	F	043	H	2	56
ELLIOT	JOHN				50	ONTARIO	WM	CHIPPAWA	FARMER	043	H	2	56
ELLIOT	JOHN				29	0	CO	ENGLISH	F	044	B	5	48
ELLIOT	JOHN				40	0	PS	ENGLISH	MERCHANT	045	C	2	4
ELLIOT	JOHN				52	IRELAND	RC	IRISH	LABORER	045	D	1	6
ELLIOT	LEVI				24	0	WM	ENGLISH	BLACKSMITH	044	B	5	27
ELLIOT	MARYANN		1	1	31	0	WM	IRISH		045	D	3	56
ELLIOT	MRS JAMES			1	87	0	CP	SCOTCH		045	C	3	29
ELLIOT	SARAH			1	51	IRELAND	EM	IRISH		045	D	5	49
ELLIOT	SOPHIA		1	1	9	0	WM	CHIPPAWA		043	H	2	56
ELLIOT	THOMAS				74	ENGLAND	CP	ENGLISH	F	045	C	2	4
ELLIOT	WILLIAM				25	ENGLAND	CE	ENGLISH	F	043	B	2	10
ELLIOTT	DAVID		2		53	SCOTLAND	PS		LABRORER	043	A	6	D
ELLIOTT	DAVID		1		22	0	WM	ENGLISH		045	A	3	41
ELLIOTT	ELLEN		1	1	20	IRELAND	CE	IRISH		044	C	4	81
ELLIOTT	FREDERICK		1		18	ENG	CO	ENG	SERVANT	044	B	3	22
ELLIOTT	GEO	B	1		26	0	WM	ENGLISH	TEACHER	044	A	2	53
ELLIOTT	GEORGE				33	ENG	CE	ENG	LAB	045	C	1	28
ELLIOTT	JAMES			M	41	0	WM	IRISH	FARMER	043	A	1	21
ELLIOTT	JAMES				66	ENGLAND	CE	ENGLISH	FARMER	045	A	3	35
ELLIOTT	JANE		1	1	59	ENGLAND	WM	ENGLISH		045	A	3	41
ELLIOTT	JANET		1	1	85	USA	CP	SCOTCH		045	C	4	17
ELLIOTT	JOHN				38	ENGLAND	WM	ENGLISH	MILLER	043	A	6	20
ELLIOTT	JOHN				38	ENGLAND	CE	ENGLISH	F	043	B	5	32
ELLIOTT	JOHN				56	ENGLAND	CE	ENGLISH	BLACKSMITH	044	B	5	42
ELLIOTT	JOHN				63	0	CP	SCOTCH	F	045	C	4	18
ELLIOTT	JOHN				34	0	WM	IRISH	FARMER	044	C	3	55
ELLIOTT	JOHN	F			45	0	WM	IRISH	CARPENTER	045	B	1	27
ELLIOTT	JOSEPH				81	ENGLAND	WM	ENGLISH	MERCHANT	043	C		45
ELLIOTT	MARY				59	0	CO	ENGLISH		044	B	5	48
ELLIOTT	MARY			1	63	IRELAND	WM	IRISH	FARMER	045	D	2	40
ELLIOTT	MATILDA			1	60	IRELAND	CE	IRISH		043	B	3	8
ELLIOTT	ROBERT		1		8	0	WM	IRISH		045	D	3	56
ELLIOTT	ROBERT	J	1		22	0	NC	ENGLISH	MINISTER	043	E	2	7
ELLIOTT	SOPHIA			1	47	0	PS	ENGLISH		043	A	6	62
ELLIOTT	SUSANAH			1	63	0	PM	ENGLISH		045	A	1	106
ELLIOTT	THOMAS			M	56	SCOTLAND	PS	SCOTCH	LAB	043	A	1	60
ELLIOTT	WILLIAM				47	ENGLAND	EM	ENGLISH	F	043	A	6	29
ELLIOTT	WM				56	IRE	CE	IRE	F	045	C	1	38
ELLIS	A		1		65	UNITED STATES	EP	ENGLISH	CARRIAGE BUILDER	043	E	2	24
ELLIS	ABRAM				28	0	WM	ENGLISH	MILLER	044	A	2	45
ELLIS	CHARLOTTE		1	1	19	0	WM	ENGLISH	SERVANT	044	A	2	18
ELLIS	ELIZABETH		1	1	14	CANADA	CE	IRISH		045	D	6	20
ELLIS	GEORGE				27	0	CE	FRENCH	LAB	045	C	2	14
ELLIS	GEORGE				26	0	VM	ENGLISH	FARMER	045	D	3	39
ELLIS	GEORGE	P			49	0	WM	GERMAN	F	045	C	2	32
ELLIS	HENRIETTE		1	1	21	0	CE	ENGLISH		043	A	4	4
ELLIS	ISABELLA		1	1	40	0	WM	ENGLISH	F	045	C	2	37
ELLIS	JAMES		1		55	0	BC	GERMAN		045	C	2	48
ELLIS	JOHN				65	ENGLAND	CE	ENGLISH	MARINER	043	G	1	8
ELLIS	JOHN				42	0	LU	ENGLISH	F	044	B	6	52
ELLIS	JOHN				62	ENGLAND	WM	ENGLISH		045	B	2	8
ELLIS	JOHN				46	0	CE	FRENCH	LAB	045	C	2	13
ELLIS	JOHN				75	ENGLAND	CE	ENGLISH	F	044	C	4	3
ELLIS	LOUISA	J	1	1	23	0	CE	ENGLISH	SCHOOL TEACHER	044	A	3	9
ELLIS	MARTHA		1	1	5	CANADA	WM	ENGLISH		045	D	6	61
ELLIS	MARTHA	A	1	1	3	0	CE	FRENCH		045	B	1	38
ELLIS	MARY		1	1	31	0	CE	FRENCH	SERVANT	045	B	1	38
ELLIS	MARY		1	1	14	0	WM	IRISH		045	C	2	30
ELLIS	PETER		1	1	23	0	PM	DUTCH	FARM SERVANT	045	C	3	40
ELLIS	ROBERT				37	ENGLAND	CE	ENGLISH	SAILOR	043	G	1	8
ELLIS	THOMAS		1		60	IRELAND	CE	IRISH	F LAB	044	A	1	26
ELLIS	THOMAS				43	0	WM	GERMAN	LAB	045	C	2	50
ELLIS	THOMAS		1		7	CANADA	WM	ENGLISH		045	D	6	61
ELLIS	THOS	H	1		19	0	CE	ENGLISH	CLERK	043	A	4	4
ELLIS	WILLIAM				40	0	CE	ENGLISH	F	044	B	6	45
ELLIS	WILLIAM				43	ENGLAND	CE	ENGLISH	GARDNER	044	C	4	9
ELLISON	JOSEPH		1		11	ONTARIO	WM	ENGLISH	SERVANT	043	G	2	12
ELLISTON	MANUEL				31	ENGLAND	CE	ENGLISH	WEAVER	043	E	3	8
ELLSTON	BENJAMIN				55	ENGLAND	CE	ENGLISH	PEDDLAR	043	C		8
ELLSTON	JOHN				25	ENG	CE	ENG	CROCKERY PEDDLER	044	B	1	9
ELMER	THOMAS				42	ENGLAND	CE	ENGLISH	F & B'SMITH	043	A	3	61
ELMER	WILLIAM				52	ENGLAND	ZZ	ENGLISH	F	043	E	2	81
ELMORE	MARY		1	1	40	IRELAND	CE	IRISH	SERVANT	044	C	4	97
ELRINGTON	JOHN				33	ENGLAND	CE	ENGLISH	F	044	B	6	18
ELSE	ROBERT				67	ENGLAND	PM	ENGLISH	F	043	E	2	72
ELSIE	LAVINIA			1	35	ENGLAND	CE	ENGLISH		044	C	3	26
ELSTON	HENRY				73	0	EM	GERMAN	GENTLEMAN	045	D	1	42
ELSTON	JOSEPH				43	0	EM	GERMAN	FARMER	045	D	1	42
ELSTONE	JOHN				45	ENGLAND	CN	ENGLISH	PAPERMAKER	045	A	1	104
ELSY	SOPHIRE		1	1	16	0	WM	ENGLISH	SERVANT	044	C	3	20
ELVES	JAMES				64	ENGLAND	RC	ENGLISH	F	043	H	1	2
ELVES	JOHN				25	0	RC	ENGLISH	F	043	H	1	2
ELVIDGE	CHARLES				42	0	CO	ENGLISH	IRONFOUNDER	043	D		10
ELVIDGE	EDMOND				56	ENGLAND	CS	ENGLISH	MILLWRIGHT	043	D		59
ELVIDGE	GEORGE				35	QUEBEC	WM	ENGLISH	MILLWRIGHT	043	D		61
ELVIDGE	JOSEPH				58	ENGLAND	CS	ENGLISH	MILLWRIGHT	043	D		11
ELVIDGE	WILLIAM				45	QUEBEC	WM	ENGLISH	MILLWRIGHT	043	D		61
ELVIESS	JOSEPH				33	ENGLAND	WM	ENGLISH	F	043	A	3	17
ELWOOD	CELINA		1	1	20	0	WM	ENGLISH		043	A	3	49
ELWOOD	MARK		1		21	ENGLAND	WM	ENGLISH	LAB	043	A	3	49
ELWOOD	ROBERT		1		19	IRELAND	CP	IRISH	FARM SERVANT	045	C	5	2
ELWOOD	THOMAS		1		4	0	QU	SCOTTISH		043	B	5	4
EMBODEN	PETER				56	GERMANY	LU	GERMAN	TAILOR	044	C	2	51
EMBROW	STEPHEN				28	ENGLAND	PB	ENGLISH	BRICK MAKER	045	B	1	54
EMERSON	FRANCIS				34	ENGLAND	PM	ENGLISH	LABOURER	045	D	3	31

SURNAME	NAME1	NAME2	STRAY	SEX	AGE	BIRTHPL	RELIGION	ORIGIN	OCCUP	DIST	SUB_DIST	DIV	PAGE
EMERSON	MARGARET		1	1	40	O	PM	IRISH	DRESS MAKER	045	C	4	6
EMERSON	THOMAS				27	ENGLAND	IM	ENGLISH	FARMER	045	D	3	33
EMERSON	WILLIAM		1		15	O	WM	ENGLISH	SERVANT	045	D	5	69
EMERY	J	R			33	O	BA	ENGLISH	MERCHANT	043	B	1	18
EMERY	ROBERT				72	O	BA	ENGLISH	CARRIAGE BUILDER	045	A	2	4
EMERY	THOMAS				38	O	BA	ENGLISH	TINSMITH	045	A	2	4
EMES	AARON				44	ONTARIO	RC	IRISH	FARMER	043	G	1	34
EMES	ANNA		2	1	79	ONTARIO	CN			043	G	2	D
EMES	CALVIN				60	ONTARIO	CN	IRISH	FARMER	043	G	1	37
EMES	HENRY				53	O	CN	ENGLISH	F	043	H	1	16
EMES	MOSES				45	ONTARIO	EM	ENGLISH	LABORER	043	G	2	38
EMES	SILAS				25	O	CN	ENGLISH	F	043	H	1	4
EMES	THOMAS	G			36	ONTARIO	CE	ENGLISH		043	G	2	27
EMPRINGHAM	WM				55	ENG	CE	ENG	F	045	C	1	68
EMPRYNGHAM	GEORGE				33	ENGLAND	CE	ENGLISH	FARMER	045	A	2	29
ENDERSTICE	JOSEPH				66	ENG	CE	ENG	F	044	B	4	21
ENEVER	THOMAS		1		15	ENGLAND	CE	ENGLISH	GARDENER	045	D	3	67
ENGLISH	ALBERT		1		10	O	CE	IRISH		043	D		22
ENGLISH	JOHN				24	O	OP	ENGLISH	MILLER	043	A	3	24
ENGLISH	MARY			1	60	IRELAND	RC	IRISH		044	A	1	5
ENGLISH	MARY	ANN	1	1	16	O	TU	ENGLAND	SERVANT	045	D	2	17
ENGLISH	ROBERT		1		14	O	CE	IRISH		043	D		22
ENGLISH	SARAH	CATHARINE	1	1	12	O	CE	IRISH		043	D		22
ENGLISH	WILLIAM				33	O	CE	IRISH	FARMER	045	A	1	5
ENGLISH	WM		1		18	O	CE	IRISH	TINSMITH	043	D		22
ENGST	ANNEY		1	1	37	GERMANY	NG	GERMAN	SERVANT	045	D	6	63
ENOVY	GEORGE				41	ENG	CE	ENG	ENGINEER	044	B	2	40
ENRIGHT	THOMAS				35	IRELAND	RC	IRISH	LAB	044	C	1	20
ENRIGHT	WILLIAM				35	IRELAND	RC	IRISH	LAB	044	C	1	20
ENSMINGER	ADAM				25	US	PM	DUTCH	FARM SERVANT	045	C	3	52
ENSMIZLER	JOHN				32	US	PM	GERMANY	LAB	045	A	3	35
ENTWISTLE	JOHN		1		27	ENGLAND	PM	ENGLISH	PAINTER	045	A	1	63
ENTWISTLE	RACHEL		1	1	60	ENGLAND	PM	ENGLISH		045	A	1	63
ENTWISTLE	THOMAS		1		24	ENGLAND	PM	ENGLISH	PAINTER	045	A	1	63
E0F2F022800015230	DC30670001000	B	92	03	800	00004NIXDORF-60055	BA	ENGLISH	SERVANT	044	C	4	22
E0F2F022800015230	DC30680001000	B	92	03	800	00006NIXDORF-60055	CE	GERMAN		045	D	2	47
ERICKSON	JOHN		1		23	NORWAY	LU	NORWEGIAN	LAB	044	B	1	60
ERVING	RICHARD				30	SCOT	PS	SCOT	LAB	044	B	2	57
ESK	SARAH		1	1	24	O	IM	ENGLISH		045	D	3	33
ESPY	JOSEPH				55	IRE	PS	IRE	F	044	B	2	68
ESQUABE	BENJAMIN		1		23	ONTARIO	WM	OJIBWAY INDIAN	HUNTER AND FISHER	043	G	1	59
ESQUABE	ELIZABETH		1	1		ONTARIO	WM	OJIBWAY INDIAN		043	G	1	59
ESQUABE	JAMES				46	ONTARIO	WM	OJIBWAY INDIAN	HUNTER AND FISHER	043	G	1	61
ESQUABE	JANE		1	1	46	ONTARIO	WM	OJIBWAY INDIAN		043	G	1	59
ESQUABE	JOHN		2		2	ONTARIO	WM			043	G	1	D
ESQUABE	JOSEPH				40	ONTARIO	WM	OJIBWAY INDIAN	HUNTER AND FISHER	043	G	1	58
ESQUABE	MARY	A	1	1	18	ONTARIO	WM	OJIBWAY INDIAN		043	G	1	59
ESTEN	JOHN				60	BERMUDA	CE	ENGLISH	F	043	B	4	42
ETHERINGTON	ANNE		2	1		O	WM			045	A	2	D
ETHERINGTON	HENRY				28	ENGLAND	WM	ENGLISH	LAB	045	A	2	15
ETHYBRIDGE	EDWD		1		28	ENGLAND	CE	ENGLISH	SERVANT	045	D	5	61
EVANS	B	H	1		48	ENGLAND	CE	ENGLISH	CONVEYENCER	043	H	2	6
EVANS	BETSEY			1	48	O	CS	SCOTCH	F	043	E	2	4
EVANS	CHARLES		1		19	O	CE	WELSH	F	043	H	1	2
EVANS	CHARLES				50	ENGLAND	CE	ENGLISH	FARM LAB	044	A	2	33
EVANS	DAVID				52	UNITED STATES	CS	IRISH	F	043	E	2	59
EVANS	DAVID				32	O	NC	IRISH	F	043	E	2	81
EVANS	ELIZA		1	1	45	ENGLAND	CE	ENGLISH	FARM SERVANT	045	C	4	10
EVANS	ELMIRA		1	F	30	O	WM	ENGLAND		043	A	5	16
EVANS	EMILY	JANE		1	49	O	CN	IRISH		043	E	2	15
EVANS	EPHRAIM				67	ENGLAND	WM	ENGLISH	WM MINISTER	045	B	1	42
EVANS	GEORGE				55	ENGLAND	CE	ENGLISH	F	043	H	2	22
EVANS	GEORGE				55	ENGLAND	CE	ENGLISH	FARMER	043	H	2	22
EVANS	GEORGE				55	ENGLAND	PM	ENGLISH	F	045	C	4	39
EVANS	GEORGE		1		25	O	CP	IRISH	SERVANT	045	D	2	57
EVANS	HANNAH		1	1	15	O	CE	WELSH		043	H	1	2
EVANS	ISABELLA		1	1	57	UNITED STATES	CE	IRISH		043	G	1	16
EVANS	JAMES				71	IRELAND	CE	IRISH	F	043	E	2	4
EVANS	JAMES	B			68	IRELAND	CE	IRISH	FARMER	043	F		1
EVANS	JANE		1	1	64	IRELAND	CE	IRISH		043	E	2	36
EVANS	JOHN	T		M	33	ENGLAND	QU	ENGLAND	CARPENTER	043	A	5	30
EVANS	MAHALA		1	1	58	ONTARIO	CN	ENGLISH		043	G	1	27
EVANS	MARGARET		1	1	33	IRELAND	CP	IRISH	SERVANT	045	B	1	61
EVANS	MARY		1	1	65	IRE	CE	IRE		045	C	1	38
EVANS	R	H	1		48	ENGLAND	CE	ENGLISH	CONVEYENCER	043	H	2	6
EVANS	ROBERT				22	O	PM	ENGLISH	F	045	C	4	39
EVANS	ROBERT		1		35	ENGLAND	CE	ENGLISH	SERVANT	045	D	6	6
EVANS	SILAS				30	ONTARIO	CE	IRISH	FARMER	043	G	1	5
EVANS	THOMAS				24	O	CS	IRISH	F	043	E	2	79
EVANS	THOMAS		1		20	O	CE	WELSH	F	043	H	1	2
EVANS	WILLIAM		1	M	64	ENGLAND	CE	ENGLAND	L	043	A	5	29
EVANS	WILLIAM				35	ENGLAND	CE	ENGLISH	F LAB	043	B	4	32
EVANS	WILLIAM				61	O	CE	IRISH	F	043	E	2	55
EVANS	WILLIAM				62	WALES	CP	WELSH	CARPENTER	043	G	2	48
EVANS	WILLIAM	J			40	ENGLAND	WM	ENGLISH	BRICK MAKER	043	D		87
EVENS	DUNCAN		1		26	WALES	RC	WELSH	LABOURER	045	A	1	38
EVENS	ELIZA		1	1	19	O	WM	IRISH		043	B	3	7
EVENS	JOHN	H	1		21	ENGLAND	WM	ENGLISH	LAB	045	A	4	34
EVENS	WILLIAM				55	ENGLAND	CE	ENGLISH	F	043	B	4	38
EVENSON	WM		1		25	IRE	CE	IRE	F	045	C	1	20
EVEREST	GEORGE	J			35	ENGLAND	CE	ENGLISH	STUDENT	043	H	2	27
EVEREST	GEORGE	J	1		35	ENGLAND	CE	ENGLISH	STUDENT	043	H	2	27
EVEREST	THOS				46	ENG	WM	ENG	HORSEMAN	045	C	1	73
EVERET	HENRY				60	ENG	PM	ENG	LAB	044	B	2	67
EVERINGSHAM	JOHN				56	ENGLAND	CN	ENGLISH	FARMER	043	G	1	22
EVERLIGH	WILLIAM				30	ENGLAND	PM	ENGLISH	LAB	044	C	4	61
EVERSET	JOHN				32	ENGLAND	PM	ENGLISH	FARM SERVANT	045	C	3	7
EVES	ALEX				31	O	EM	IRISH	F	043	E	2	56
EVES	ELIZABETH		1	1	8	O	QU	ENGLISH		043	B	4	46
EVES	NEAMIAH				69	O	EM	IRISH	F	043	E	2	55
EVES	SARAH			1	76	UNITED STATES	QU	IRISH		043	E	1	41
EVIS	BENJAMIN				38	ONTARIO	EM		FARMER	043	G	2	23
EVITT	MARGARET		1	1	20	O	CE	IRISH	SERVANT	044	B	6	27
EVY	ELIAS				26	O	CN	GERMAN	FARM LABOURER	043	B	3	68
EWART	JAMES		1	M	26	SCOTLAND	CP	SCOTCH	LAB	043	A	2	11
EWING	ARTHUR		1		22	ENGLAND	CE	ENGLISH	GARDNER	044	C	4	67

SURNAME	NAME1	NAME2	STRAY	SEX	AGE	BIRTHPL	RELIGION	ORIGIN	OCCUP	DIST	SUB_DIST	DIV	PAGE
EWING	ELIE		1		72	U STATES	NC	SCOTCH		043	A	6	2
EXTER	JAMES				30	ENGLAND	CE	ENGLISH	LAB	044	C	2	48
EYER	ABRAHAM				38	O	MN	GERMAN	AGRICULTURE IMPLEMEN	045	D	2	45
EYER	DAVID				35	O	TU	GERMAN	FARMER	045	D	4	5
EYER	DAVID				74	US	MN	GERMAN		045	D	2	39
EYER	DAVID				43	O	WM	GERMAN	SHINGLE & STOVE MAKE	045	D	2	44
EYER	EDEN		2			O	MN			045	D	2	D
EYER	JACOB				28	O	MN	GERMAN	FARMER	045	D	2	45
EZARD	ANNIE		1	1	15	O	LU	ENG	SERVANT	044	B	3	41
EZARD	GEO				28	ENGLAND	UP	ENGLISH	F	044	B	5	74
EZARD	JOHN			M	45	ENGLAND	NG	ENGLISH	F	043	A	2	21
FAARIOR	JOSEPH				67	US	WM	SCOTCH	FARMER	045	D	3	23
FAIN	JOHN		1		25	ENGLAND	CE	ENGLISH	F LAB	044	C	1	9
FAIR	GEORGE				35	IRELAND	PM	IRISH	FARMER	043	B	3	42
FAIRBAIRN	ELIZABETH		2	1	66	SCOTLAND	PS			043	E	3	D
FAIRBAIRN	JOHN				59	ENGLAND	PR	ENGLISH	FARMER	043	G	2	30
FAIRBAIRN	RELIEF		1	1	24	ONTARIO	PR	ENGLISH		043	G	2	24
FAIRBANKES	HANNAH		2	1	75	IRELAND	RC			045	A	4	D
FAIRBANKES	JAMES				73	IRELAND	RC	IRISH	F	045	A	4	25
FAIRBURN	ARCH		1		26	SCOTLAND	CS	SCOTCH	COOPER	044	B	6	57
FAIRBURN	ELIZABETH		1	1	77	ENGLAND	CP	ENGLISH		043	H	1	1
FAIRBURN	JAMES				36	ONTARIO	CN	ENGLISH	FARMER	043	G	1	32
FAIRBURN	JOHN				34	ONTARIO	CN	ENGLISH	FARMER	043	G	1	2
FAIRBURN	SAMUEL				28	ONTARIO	EM	ENGLISH	FARMER	043	G	1	14
FAIRCHILD	JOHN		1		37	O	WM	GERMAN	SERVANT	045	D	2	46
FAIRFIELD	ARCHIBALD				54	O	QU	GERMAN	SAWYER	043	H	1	20
FAIRLES	THOMAS				44	ENGLAND	WM	ENGLISH	FARMER	043	B	3	40
FAIRLESS	ELIZABETH			1	72	O	WM	ENGLISH		045	D	3	24
FAIRLESS	JAMES				47	ENGLAND	WM	ENGLISH	STORE KEEPER	045	D	3	23
FALBY	JOHANNA			1	60	IRELAND	RC	IRISH	LAB	044	C	2	21
FALBY	PATK				40	IRELAND	RC	IRISH	LAB	044	C	2	21
FANCHER	GEORGE	T			47	US	WM	FRENCH	DROVER	044	C	4	70
FANN	MARGARET			1	71	IRELAND	CE	IRISH		045	A	1	102
FANNAH	GEO				36	ENGLAND	CE	ENGLISH	LAB	044	B	5	39
FANNING	BERNARD				54	IRELAND	RC	IRISH	SHOEMAKER	043	A	4	5
FAR	JOSEPH				25	ENGLAND	WM	ENGLISH	FARMER	044	C	3	1
FARDLE	JOHN		1		32	O	WM	ENGLISH	LAB	044	B	5	38
FARDY	GEORGE				28	O	RC	FRENCH	WEAVER	043	E	3	43
FARELL	PATRICK		1		35	IRELAND	RC	IRISH	LAB	043	H	2	50
FARELL	PATRICK			1	35	IRELAND	RC	IRISH	LABOURER	043	H	2	50
FARIND	JAMES		1		25	ENGLAND	CE	ENGLISH	STAGE DRIVER	044	A	3	27
FARLEY	HUGH				50	IRELAND	CX	IRISH	LABOURER	045	D	6	27
FARLEY	JAMES				43	ENGLAND	WM	ENGLISH	GARDNER	044	C	4	77
FARLEY	MATHEW		1		15	O	MN	IRISH	FARM LAB	043	B	2	2
FARLEY	SARAH		1	1	28	O	PM	IRISH	SERVANT	045	B	1	69
FARLEY	SARAH	ANN	1	1	22	O	PM	IRISH	SERVANT	045	B	1	69
FARMER	THOMAS				42	ENGLAND	TU	ENGLISH	FARMER	045	D	4	18
FARNE	ANNIE		1	1	13	O	RC	IRISH		045	A	1	30
FARNE	JAMES				28	IRELAND	RC	IRISH	LABOURER	045	A	1	32
FARNELL	HENRY	WILLIAM			26	ENGLAND	CE	SCOTCH	F	044	A	3	23
FARNHAM	JAMES				49	ENGLAND	CE	ENGLISH	F	043	E	1	29
FARQHUASON	ELIZA		1	1	38	SCOTLAND	PS	SCOTCH	SERVANT	045	A	1	6
FARQUHAR	MARGARET		1	1	63	SCOTLAND	CS	SCOTCH		043	E	2	59
FARR	ALBERT				23	O	CE	ENGLISH	BUTCHER	044	C	2	11
FARR	ELISHA				55	ENGLAND	WM	ENGLISH	F	044	B	5	70
FARR	JAMES				24	O	CE	ENGLISH	F	044	A	3	34
FARR	JAMES		1		21	O	PM	ENGLISH	LAB	044	B	5	58
FARR	JAMES				46	O	WM	ENGLISH	FARMER	045	D	1	1
FARR	JOHN				62	IRELAND	CE	IRISH	LAB	043	H	2	16
FARR	JOHN				62	IRELAND	CE	IRISH	LABOURER	043	H	2	16
FARR	JOHN		1		33	O	WM	ENGLISH	LAB	044	B	5	9
FARR	JOSEPH				22	O	WM	ENG	F	044	C	1	28
FARR	MARY				67	O	WM	ENGLISH		044	B	5	51
FARR	THOMAS				49	O	PM	ENGLISH	F	044	A	3	45
FARR	THOMAS				31	O	CE	ENGLISH	F	044	B	1	3
FARR	WILLIAM				55	ENGLAND	WM	ENGLISH	F	044	C	4	34
FARR	WM				40	O	WM	ENGLISH	F	044	B	5	52
FARR	WM				30	O	WM	ENGLISH	F	044	B	5	72
FARR	WM	THOS	2		18	O	WM		F	044	B	5	D
FARREL	JAMES		1		18	O	RC	IRISH	HOSTLER	044	C	2	9
FARREL	MICHAEL				55	IRELAND	RC	IRISH	LAB	044	C	2	7
FARRELL	DANIEL				40	IRELAND	RC	IRISH	MACHINIST	044	C	4	61
FARRELL	ELLEN		1	1	13	O	RC	IRISH	SERVANT	043	H	1	12
FARRELL	GEORGE				39	IRE	CE	IRE	BLACKSMITH	044	B	2	36
FARRELL	JOHN				60	IRELAND	RC	IRISH	FARMER	045	A	2	23
FARRELL	MARTIN				50	IRELAND	RC	IRISH	LABOURER	045	A	1	81
FARROW	JOHN		1		34	ENGLAND	WM	ENGLISH	MOULDER	044	B	5	66
FARROW	WILLIAM				59	ENGLAND	WM	ENGLISH	FRUIT MERCHANT	045	B	1	1
FARTHING	JAMES				60	ENGLAND	CE	ENGLISH	LABOURER	043	A	4	39
FAULKENER	SAMUEL		1		58	IRELAND	CE	IRISH		045	A	1	30
FAULKNER	EDWARD				45	IRELAND	RC	IRISH	F	044	A	1	7
FAULKNER	FRANCIS				85	IRELAND	RC	IRISH	F	044	A	1	10
FAWCETT	EDWARD				32	O	WM	ENGLISH	F	045	C	3	48
FAWCETT	FANNY			1	63	ENGLAND	WM	ENGLISH	F	045	C	3	43
FAWCETT	ISAAC	C			32	O	WM	ENGLISH	F	045	C	3	41
FAWCETT	WILLIAM				70	ENGLAND	WM	ENGLISH	F	045	C	3	44
FAWCETT	WILLIAM	A			47	ENGLAND	WM	ENGLISH	F	045	C	3	44
FEAD	WILLIAM				25	O	CO	SCOTCH	DRUGGIST	043	B	3	55
FEARNEY	MARGARET		1	1	20	NB	WM	ENGLISH	SERVANT	045	D	1	8
FEATHERBRIDGE	HENERY				30	ENGLAND	CE	ENGLISH	LAB	045	C	2	51
FEATHERSTONE	HANNAH			1	35	ENGLAND	CE	ENGLISH		045	D	1	10
FEATHERSTONE	THOMAS		1	M	24	ENGLAND	CE	ENGLAND	SAWYER	043	A	5	6
FEE	ANN			1	41	IRELAND	RC	IRISH		043	B	3	15
FEITZ	FRED				22	US	CE	GERMAN	LAB	045	B	1	23
FELIZ	VICTOR		1		32	U STATES	WM	FRENCH	MOULDER	044	B	5	20
FENBY	GEORGE				46	ENGLAND	CE	ENGLISH	F	043	E	2	80
FENBY	JAMES				45	ENGLAND	WM	ENGLISH	F	045	A	4	23
FENEY	THOMAS				34	IRELAND	RC	IRISH	LAB	045	A	1	86
FENLAYSON	JOHN		2		25	O	PS		SERVANT	044	C	4	D
FENNELL	LOT				58	ENGLAND	WM	ENGLISH	CARPENTER	045	D	5	18
FENNEY	JOHN				71	ENGLAND	CE	ENGLISH	BRICKMAKER	044	A	3	18
FENTON	EDWARD		1		22	O	PM	ENGLISH	LABOURER	045	D	4	7
FENTON	RICHARDSON				35	O	CN	GERMAN	F	043	E	2	56
FENTON	SAMUEL				43	U STATES	DI	ENGLISH	FARMER	045	D	6	50
FENTON	THOMAS		1		17	ONTARIO	PR	ENGLISH	SERVANT	043	G	2	56
FENTON	WHITNEY				38	O	CN	GERMAN	F	043	E	2	53

SURNAME	NAME1	NAME2	STRAY	SEX	AGE	BIRTHPL	RELIGION	ORIGIN	OCCUP	DIST	SUB_DIST	DIV	PAGE
FENWICK	BARBRA	A		1	47	0	CP	GERMAN		045	D	4	35
FENWICK	BENJAMIN		1		22	0	LU	SCOTCH	STORE CLERK	045	D	3	45
FENWICK	GEORGE	G			25	0	CP	GERMAN	FARMER	045	D	4	36
FENWICK	J	W			29	0	CP	SCOTCH	STORE KEEPER	045	D	3	1
FENWICK	JOHN				48	ENG	LU	ENG	F	044	B	3	17
FENWICK	WILLIAM		1		29	0	CE	ENGLISH	FARMER	045	D	4	35
FERGUSON	ARCHD				31	SCOTLAND	PS	SCOTCH	CARPENTER	044	B	5	55
FERGUSON	DAVID				39	SCOTLAND	UP	SCOTCH	MILLER	044	B	5	56
FERGUSON	HUGH				62	IRELAND	CE	IRISH	LAB	044	B	5	7
FERGUSON	JAMES				54	SCOTLAND	CS	SCOTCH	MILL RIGHT	045	D	3	18
FERGUSON	JAMES		1		55	0	CP	SCOTCH	BLACKSMITH	044	C	2	30
FERGUSON	JOHN			M	52	U STATES	PS	SCOTCH	F	043	A	1	37
FERGUSON	JOHN				56	0	CN	SCOTCH	F	043	E	2	73
FERGUSON	JOHN				66	SCOTLAND	CP	SCOTCH	F	045	C	4	17
FERGUSON	MARK			M	37	0	CP	SCOTCH	FARMER	043	A	1	32
FERGUSON	MRS	D		1	43	0	CP	DUTCH	F	045	C	3	28
FERGUSON	THOMAS			M	50	0	PS	SCOTCH	F	043	A	1	40
FERGUSON	THOMAS				50	SCOTLAND	CP	SCOTCH	LABOURER	045	D	3	25
FERGUSON	WILLIAM				58	SCOTLAND	CP	SCOTCH	PUMPMAKER	045	C	3	12
FERIN	SAMUEL			M	34	IRELAND	ME	IRISH	LAB	043	A	1	72
FERNETT	JOSEPH			M	30	0	EM	FRENCH	F	043	A	1	41
FERRETT	WILLIAM				65	ENGLAND	WM	ENGLISH	CARPENTER	045	B	1	34
FERRIER	JOHN	C			49	ENGLAND	WM	SCOTCH	BAKER	044	A	2	2
FERRINGTON	SAML				35	0	EM	ENGLISH	F	043	E	2	81
FERRIS	EDWARD				20	ONTARIO	RC	IRISH	LABORER	043	G	1	8
FERRIS	EDWARD		2		61	IRELAND	RC		WEAVER	043	G	1	D
FERRIS	ISABELLA			1	73	IRELAND	CP	IRISH		045	D	4	25
FERRIS	MARY	A		1	40	IRELAND	PM	IRISH		043	B	2	39
FERRIS	ROBERT		1		43	IRELAND	CE	IRISH	FARMER	045	D	2	4
FETHERSON	JOHN			M	48	ENGLAND	WM	ENGLISH	FARMER	043	A	1	6
FEUTON	JOHN				46	0	CN	ENGLISH	F	043	E	2	30
FIDEL	JAMES	A	1		11	0	CE	IRISH		043	E	2	5
FIDEL	MATILDA			1	32	0	CE	IRISH		043	E	2	5
FIDELL	JOSEPH				42	ENGLAND	NC	ENGLISH	FARMER	043	G	1	22
FIDGET	MARGARET		1	1	12	0	WM	IRISH		045	D	5	70
FIDLE	JANE			1	71	ENGLAND	NC	ENGLISH		043	E	1	51
FIDLE	THOMAS		1		25	ENGLAND	WM	ENGLISH	SCHOOL TEACHER	043	E	2	75
FIEHL	JOHN				45	GERMANY	CP	GERMAN	BASKET MAKER	045	A	2	15
FIELD	JOHN				31	ENGLAND	CE	ENGLISH	MERCHANT	043	C		56
FIELD	RICHARD			M	40	ENGLAND	PR	ENGLISH	F	043	A	1	30
FIERHELLER	JOHN				44	0	LU	GERMAN	BLACKSMITH	043	B	5	6
FIERHELLER	WILLIAM				50	0	LU	GERMAN	FARMER	045	D	1	38
FIKE	CHARLES		1		21	0	PM	GERMAN	LAB	043	B	5	28
FIKE	JACOB		1		11	0	PM	GERMAN		043	B		
FIKE	JANE		1	1	14	0	PM	GERMAN		043	B		
FIKE	MARGARET		1	1	16	0	PM	GERMAN		043	B		
FILE	RICHARD				30	ENGLAND	WM	ENGLISH	FARMER	045	A	2	29
FILSTEAD	GEORGE				48	ENGLAND	CE	ENGLISH	FARMER	045	A	1	18
FINAN	MICHAEL				45	IRELAND	RC	IRISH	WATCHMAN G W R	044	A	1	34
FINCH	ANN	JANE	1	1	34	0	BA	ENGLISH		044	A	3	7
FINCH	JOHN	D			66	ENGLAND	CE	ENGLISH		044	C	2	18
FINCH	JOHN	DAY			32	0	CE	ENGLISH	F	045	A	4	32
FINDLAY	AGNES			1	21	SCOT	PS	SCOT		044	B	2	54
FINDLAY	JAS				72	SCOT	CP	SCOT	F	045	C	1	44
FINDLAY	THOMAS		2		32	SCOT	PS	SCOT	F	044	B	2	D
FINDLEY	ANDREW		1		40	IRE	CP	IRE		045	C	1	66
FINEN	AND	P			37	IRELAND	RC	IRISH	CATHOLIC PRIEST	045	D	1	11
FINES	JOSEPH				44	ENGLAND	WM	ENGLISH	LAB	043	B	2	24
FINES	RACHEL				55	0	CE	ENGLISH		043	H	1	2
FINKLER	THOMAS				39	ENGLAND	WM	ENGLISH	BUTCHER	045	D	6	40
FINLAY	SAMUEL				28	0	PS	IRE	COOPER	044	B	2	45
FINLAYSON	ALEXANDER				27	SCOTLAND	CP	SCOTCH	COMMERCIAL TRAVELER	045	B	1	41
FINLAYSON	JAMES				53	SCOTLAND	CP	SCOTCH	LAB	044	C	4	62
FINLEY	MOSES		1		75	IRELAND	RP	IRISH		044	C	3	65
FINLY	BARNARD				55	IRELAND	RC	IRISH	F	043	B	1	37
FINN	MARGRET		1	1	22	QUE	RC	IRISH	SERVANT	045	A	1	9
FINN ?	RACHEL		1	1	22	0	NC	ENGLISH	SERVANT	045	D	5	62
FINNIE	PETER				35	SCOTLAND	CP	SCOTLAND	FARMER	045	D	2	16
FINUCAN	THOMAS				64	IRELAND	RC	IRISH	FARMER	045	A	1	16
FISH	CHARLES				50	ENGLAND	WM	ENGLISH	WESLEYAN MINISTER	045	D	2	28
FISHBURN	JEREMIAH				48	US	LU	GER	MINISTER	044	B	1	54
FISHER	BERNHARD				42	GER	RC	GER	CURRIER	044	B	2	49
FISHER	CHARLES				42	GERMANY	NG	GERMAN	SHOE MAKER	043	B	3	52
FISHER	DAVID				30	SCOTLAND	CP	SCOTCH	JOINER	045	C	4	36
FISHER	EDWIN	C JR			23	0	CE	ENGLISH	MILLER & FARMER	044	A	2	44
FISHER	JAMES				70	ENGLAND	WM	ENGLISH	F	045	C	3	47
FISHER	JOHN				33	QUEBEC	CE	ENGLISH	SHOEMAKER	043	B	3	52
FISHER	JOHN		1		30	SCOTLAND	WM	SCOTCH	CARPENTER	045	A	2	5
FISHER	JOSEPH				33	0	EM	GER	F	044	B	1	26
FISHER	MARGARET			1	56	SCOTLAND	CP	SCOTCH	WASHERWOMAN	045	C	4	36
FISHER	MARY		1	1	23	SCOTLAND	CP	SCOTCH	SEAMSTRESS	043	D		79
FISHER	MICHAEL				58	0	LU	GER	F	044	B	1	26
FISHER	RICHARD			M	49	ENGLAND	CE	ENGLAND	F	043	A	5	4
FISHER	SUSAN		1	1	78	ENGLAND	WM	ENGLISH		043	C		42
FISHER	WILLIAM			M	40	SCOTLAND	PS	SCOTCH	CORSET MANUFACTURER	043	A	1	35
FISHER	WILLIAM				39	ENG	ME	ENG	FARM LAB	044	B	1	12
FISHER	WILLIAM				61	ENGLAND	CE	ENGLISH	F	045	C	2	38
FISHERSEN	E	C			54	ENGLAND	CE	ENGLISH	F	044	A	2	7
FISKEN	JOHN				52	SCOTLAND	CP	SCOTCH	COMMISSION MERCHANT	044	C	2	19
FITCH	GEORGE				21	ENGLAND	PM	ENGLISH	FARM SERVANT	045	A	1	72
FITCHET	BETHIA		1	1	23	0	WM	IRISH		045	C	2	42
FITCHET	MARY		1	1	20	0	MN	SCOTCH		043	B	2	3
FITKEN	ROBERT		2		33	ENGLAND	CE			043	H	2	D
FITKEN	ROBERT		2		33	ENGLAND	CE			043	H	2	D
FITKIN	THOMAS				57	ENGLAND	CE	ENGLISH	SADDLER	043	H	2	28
FITKIN	THOMAS				57	ENGLAND	CE	ENGLISH	SADDLER	043	H	2	28
FITSPATRICK	JOHN		1		19	IRELAND	RC	IRISH		045	A	3	20
FITZGERALD	EDWARD				50	IRELAND	RC	IRISH	FARM LAB	044	A	2	27
FITZGERALD	GARRET				27	IRELAND	RC	IRISH	LABOURER	045	D	5	41
FITZGERALD	MARGT		1	1	14	0	RC	IRISH		044	B	5	45
FITZGERALD	MARIA		1	1	87	ENGLAND	IM	ENGLISH		043	B	4	10
FITZGERALD	MARY		1	1	15	0	RC	IRE	SERVANT	044	B	3	48
FITZGERALD	MICHAEL				45	IRELAND	RC	IRISH	COOPER	044	B	5	1
FITZGERALD	MICHAEL				50	IRELAND	RC	IRISH	LAB	044	C	4	35
FITZGERRALD	ANN	M	2	1	1	0	RC			045	A	1	D
FITZGERRALD	DANIEL				68	IRELAND	RC	IRISH	FARMER	045	A	1	99

SURNAME	NAME1	NAME2	STRAY	SEX	AGE	BIRTHPL	RELIGION	ORIGIN	OCCUP	DIST	SUB_DIST	DIV	PAGE
FITZGERRALD	LEWIS				35	USA	RC	IRISH	FARMER	045	A	1	95
FITZGERRALD	MICHAEL				30	O	RC	IRISH	FARMER	045	A	1	7
FITZGERRALD	MORRIS				68	IRELAND	RC	IRISH	LAB	045	A	1	7
FITZGIBBON	JOHN				52	IRELAND	RC	IRISH	LAB	044	A	2	50
FITZGIBBON	JOHN				50	IRE		IRE	F	045	C	1	51
FITZGIBBON	MARY		1	1	26	IRELAND	PS	IRISH	SERVANT	045	C	3	8
FITZGIBBONS	MICHAEL				74	IRELAND	RC	IRISH	WEAVER	043	F		21
FITZHUE	SAMUEL				50	USA	ME	AFRICAN	LAB	045	A	1	86
FITZPATRICK	DUNCAN				36	O	PM	IRISH	MERCHANT	045	C	4	24
FITZPATRICK	EDWARD				42	O	RC	IRISH	SHOEMAKER	044	C	2	49
FITZPATRICK	ELIZABETH		2	1	104	IRELAND	PS			045	A	1	D
FITZPATRICK	GEORGE				32	O	PM	IRISH	FARMER	045	A	2	35
FITZPATRICK	MARK		1		32	O	RC	IRISH	FARM LAB	044	C	2	52
FITZPATRICK	MARY		1	1	70	IRELAND	WM	IRISH		045	D	1	33
FITZPATRICK	MICHAEL		1		40	IRELAND	RC	IRISH	BLACKSMITH	045	D	5	29
FITZPATRICK	RICHARD				35	O	PM	IRISH	PHOTOGRAPHER	045	C	4	24
FITZPATRICK	WILLIAM				50	IRELAND	RC	IRISH	LAB	044	A	3	29
FITZSIMMONS	PATRICK		1		60	IRE	CE	IRISH	LAB	044	B	1	15
FITZSIMMONS	WILLIAM				27	QUEBEC	RC	IRISH	F	043	H	1	12
FLAHERTY	TIM				40	IRE	RC	IRISH	LAB	044	B	1	29
FLAHORTY	ELIZA		1	1	28	IRELAND	RC	IRISH	INMATE	045	B	1	72
FLANAGAN	PETER		1		21	O	RC	IRISH	SERVANT	045	B	1	37
FLANNIGAN	JOHN			M	26	O	RC	IRELAND	F	043	A	5	23
FLANNIGAN	JOHN		1		40	IRELAND	RC	IRISH	SERVANT	045	B	2	21
FLANNIGAN	PATRICK				60	IRELAND	RC	IRISH	F	044	A	1	24
FLANNIGAN	PETER			M	24	O	RC	IRELAND	INNKEEPER	043	A	5	12
FLANNIGAN	WILLIAM			M	30	O	RC	IRELAND	F	043	A	5	23
FLAVELL	HINREY				36	IRELAND	PM	IRISH	F	045	A	4	14
FLAY	JANE		1	1	19	O	EM	ENGLISH		043	A	2	55
FLAY	WALTER				50	ENGLAND	WM	ENGLISH	CARPENTER	043	E	3	25
FLEMING	ANDREW				73	SCOTLAND	CP	SCOTCH		045	C	2	29
FLEMING	BEARCE				26	IRELAND	RC	IRISH	BRICK MAKER	045	B	1	11
FLEMING	ELIZABETH			1	34	IRELAND	CP	IRISH	F	045	C	2	29
FLEMING	JAMES				33	O	PS	SCOTCH	CARPENTER	045	C	3	10
FLEMING	JOHN				65	SCOTLAND	CS	SCOTCH	F	044	B	5	76
FLEMING	JOHN	JAMES	1		12	O	CP	IRISH		044	C	2	15
FLEMING	MARY	E	1	1	5	O	CP	SCOTCH		045	C	3	10
FLEMING	MARY	I	1	1	18	IRELAND	WM	IRISH	SERVANT	043	A	4	22
FLEMING	PATRICK				69	IRELAND	RC	IRISH	LAB	045	B	1	11
FLEMING	ROBERT				60	SCOT	CP	SCOT	WEAVER	045	B	1	21
FLEMING	WILLIAM				30	O	CS	SCOTCH	SCHOOL TEACHER	045	D	5	51
FLEMMING	JAMES		1		68	SCOT	PS	SCOT	ORDERLY	044	B	4	1
FLEMMING	RICHARD		1		46	IRELAND	CP	IRISH	SERVANT	045	B	2	33
FLEMMING	THOMAS				84	SCOTLAND	CS	SCOTCH	GENT	043	E	2	62
FLETCHER	ALFRED		1		15	O	CE	IRISH		045	C	2	27
FLETCHER	ANN		1	1	30	SCOTLAND	PS	SCOTCH	SERVANT	045	B	2	34
FLETCHER	D	H			37	SCOTLAND	CP	SCOTCH	CLERGYMAN	045	C	4	17
FLETCHER	EDWD				33	O	WM	IRISH	F	044	B	5	65
FLETCHER	HENRY		1		46	ENGLAND	CE	ENGLAND	SERVANT	045	D	2	4
FLETCHER	JANE		1	1	25	ENGLAND	CE	ENGLISH	INMATE	045	B	1	73
FLETCHER	JOHN				59	O	CN	ENGLISH	F	043	E	2	57
FLETCHER	JOHN				56	QUE	CE	IRISH	CLERGYMAN	045	C	2	1
FLETCHER	JOHN	W			30	O	CO	SCOTCH	BARRISTER	045	A	1	76
FLETCHER	JOSEPH		1		20	ENGLAND	CE	ENGLISH	LABOURER	043	G	1	9
FLETCHER	PIERCE				35	O	PM	IRISH	F	044	B	5	65
FLETCHER	RHODA		1	1	13	O	WM	ENGLISH		043	B	5	1
FLETCHER	ROBERT		1		20	O	CE	IRISH		045	C	2	27
FLETCHER	SAMANTHA			1	55	UNITED STATES	CN	SCOTCH		043	E	3	40
FLETCHER	SARAH		1	1	25	IRELAND	CE	IRISH		045	C	2	27
FLETCHER	THOMAS		1		23	O	CE	IRISH		045	C	2	27
FLEURY	ALEXANDER				47	O	WM	FRENCH	MACHINIST	045	D	5	16
FLEURY	JAMES		2	M	1	O	WM			043	A	1	D
FLEURY	JAMES	HY	2	M	15	O	WM			043	A	1	D
FLEURY	JOHN			M	52	O	WM	IRISH	FARMER	043	A	1	8
FLEURY	JOSEPH				39	O	WM	FRENCH	MANUFACTURER	043	C		40
FLEURY	MARY			F	74	QUE	WM	GERMAN		043	A	1	6
FLEURY	OBEDIAH			M	26	O	WM	FRENCH	LABOURER	043	A	1	2
FLEURY	SARAH		1	1	16	O	WM	FRENCH		043	A	1	11
FLEURY	WILLIAM			M	27	O	WM	FRENCH	F	043	A	1	28
FLINNERY	ROBERT				59	IRELAND	CE	IRISH	TAILOR	044	C	3	54
FLINT	GEORGE				48	ENGLAND	PM	ENGLISH	CABINET MAKER	043	B	3	61
FLINT	MATHEW				65	ENGLAND	CE	ENGLISH	FARMER	045	D	6	58
FLINTOFF	HENRY			M	35	ENGLAND	WM	ENGLISH	F	043	A	2	43
FLONGHNAN	MARY			1	74	IREL	RC	IRISH		043	D		43
FLOOD	RICHARD				37	ONTARIO	CE	ENGLISH	MERCHANT	043	G	1	54
FLOOK	ALL		1		12	US	WM	ENGLISH		045	A	4	34
FLORENCE	WILLIAM		1		1	O	PS	SCOTCH		045	C	3	36
FLUMERFELT	ANN			1	81	O	WM	ENGLISH		045	D	5	4
FLUMMERFITT	CYNTHIA			1	44	O	WM	ENGLISH		045	D	3	77
FLUMMERFITT	WILLIAM				53	O	WM	ENGLISH		045	D	3	77
FLYN	MICHAEL		1		42	IRELAND	RC	IRISH	FARM SERVANT	045	A	1	13
FLYNN	CORNELIUS		1		15	O	RC	IRISH	F LAB	044	A	1	19
FLYNN	DANIEL				28	IRELAND	WM	IRISH	SCHOOL TEACHER	043	A	4	9
FLYNN	DANIEL				70	IRELAND	RC	IRISH	SHOEMAKER	044	C	1	29
FLYNN	EUGENIA		1	1	19	IRELAND	RC	FRENCH	SERVANT	044	C	4	74
FLYNN	JAMES				50	O	RC	IRISH	SHOEMAKER	045	A	4	17
FLYNN	MARY			1	47	IRELAND	RC	IRISH		045	A	1	33
FLYNN	ROBERT				34	IRELAND	CE	IRISH	SHOE MAKER	044	C	3	17
FOCKLER	ALFRED				30	O	QU	ENGLISH	F	043	E	2	3
FOCKLER	GEORGE		1		21	O	MM	GERMAN	APPRENTICE	045	D	6	13
FOCKLER	LUDWICK				55	CANADA	CN	GERMAN	FARMER	045	D	6	46
FOGAL	AMOS				45	O	QU	GERMAN	LAB	043	B	5	30
FOGAL	CLARINDA				75	US	QU			043	B	5	30
FOGARTY	PATRICK				25	O	RC	IRISH	GARDENER	045	A	1	39
FOGEL	HENERY				37	O	QU	GERMAN	F	043	B	5	26
FOGG	JOHN				37	ENGLAND	CE	ENGLISH	BAKER	045	D	3	77
FOGG	WRIGHT				46	ENGLAND	EM	ENGLISH	CORDWAINER	043	E	2	24
FOGLE	NORRIS				43	O	QU	GER	SAWYER	044	B	3	29
FOLEY	FRANCIS				77	ENG	WM	ENG	PENSIONER	045	C	1	67
FOLEY	HANNAH		1	1	6	O	WM	IRISH		044	C	4	38
FOLEY	JOHN		1		6	O	WM	IRISH		044	C	4	38
FOLEY	JOHN				60	IRELAND	RC	IRISH	LAB	044	C	4	39
FOLEY	PATRICK	G			44	IRELAND	RC	IRISH	CABINET MAKER	045	A	1	51
FOLEY	SARAH		1	1	26	ENGLAND	WM	ENGLISH		044	C	4	38
FOLEY	THOMAS				38	IRE	RC	IRE	F	044	B	3	17
FOLEY	WM	F	1		19	O	WM	ENGLISH	SERVANT	043	D		74

SURNAME	NAME1	NAME2	STRAY	SEX	AGE	BIRTHPL	RELIGION	ORIGIN	OCCUP	DIST	SUB_DIST	DIV	PAGE
FOLKEARD	JOHN		1		25	ENGLAND	CE	ENGLISH	FARM SERVANT	043	E	1	18
FOLLIETT	GILBERT			M	58	ENGLAND	UP	ENGLISH	F	043	A	1	14
FOLLIOT	HENRY			M	30	0	PS	ENGLISH	BLACKSMITH	043	A	1	11
FOLLIOTT	THOMAS			M	59	ENGLAND	UP	ENGLISH	FARMER	043	A	1	15
FONBONE	ALFRED				26	ENGLAND	WM	ENGLISH	LAB	044	C	4	76
FONSHAW	EDWARD				37	ENG	CE	ENG	LAB	044	B	3	8
FOOKLER	ABE				46	0	BA	GERMAN	FARMER	043	B	3	11
FOOKLER	GEORGE				39	0	NG	GERMAN	LABOURER	043	B	3	12
FOOKLER	JACOB				30	0	CN	GERMAN	FARMER	043	B	3	38
FOOKLER	JOHN				58	0	BA	GERMAN	FARMER	043	B	3	4
FOOKLER	JOHN				60	0	CN	GERMAN	FARMER	043	B	3	74
FOOKLER	SAMUEL				48	0	NG	GERMAN	FARMER	043	B	3	1
FOOT	ABRAHAM				64	ENGLAND	CE	ENGLISH	FARMER	045	D	1	47
FOOT	CHAS	JAS			26	ENG	CE	ENG	BUTCHER	045	C	1	72
FOOT	JOHN				41	ENGLAND	PM	ENGLISH	LAB	043	H	2	9
FOOT	JOHN				41	ENGLAND	WM	ENGLISH	LABOURER	043	H	2	9
FOOT	NELSON				26	0	CE	ENGLISH	LAB	043	B	5	28
FOOT	SAMUEL				65	ENGLAND	CE	ENGLISH	F	043	B	5	3
FOOT	THOMAS				41	ENGLAND	PM	ENGLISH	F	043	B	2	19
FOOT	WALTER				60	ENGLAND	CE	ENGLISH	F	043	B	5	4
FOOTE	WM				55	NEWFOUNDLAND	BA		F	044	A	3	2
FORAN	JOHN				33	IRELAND	RC	IRISH	FARM LABORER	045	D	1	15
FORBES	ABRAM				38	0	WM	ENGLISH	FARMER	044	C	1	24
FORBES	ELIZABETH			1	28	QUE	CE	ENGLISH		044	A	2	40
FORBES	HUGH				30	SCOTLAND	CP	SCOTCH	GARDNER	045	B	1	62
FORBES	JANE			1	50	IRELAND	PS	IRISH		044	B	5	46
FORBES	NELSON		1		16	0	CP	SCOTCH	SERVANT	044	B	1	3
FORBES	WILLIAM		1		24	SCOTLAND	CP	SCOTCH	TEAMSTER	044	C	2	35
FORBES	WM		1		15	0	PS	IRISH	BLACKSMITH	044	B	5	7
FORD	AGNES			1	40	IRELAND	RC	IRISH		045	C	2	12
FORD	GEORGE	C			45	ENGLAND	CE	ENGLISH	BRICKLAYER	045	B	1	18
FORD	JOHN				50	ENGLAND	CE	ENGLISH	LAB	043	H	2	26
FORD	JOHN				50	ENGLAND	CE	ENGLISH	LABOURER	043	H	2	26
FORD	SAM'L				52	IRELAND	CS	IRISH	TANNER	043	F		30
FORD	SAMUEL				61	ENGLAND	CE	ENGLISH	LAB	044	A	3	7
FORD	THOMAS				48	ENGLAND	WM	ENGLISH	FARMER	043	G	1	6
FORD	THOMAS				58	ENGLAND	CE	ENGLISH	SHOE MAKER	045	B	1	21
FORD	WILLIAM				33	ENGLAND	PM	ENGLISH	FARMER	045	D	4	5
FORDY	BRIDGET		2	F	42	IRELAND	RC			043	A	2	D
FORDY	DAVID			M	41	IRELAND	RC	IRISH	TANNER	043	A	2	47
FOREMAN	HARRIET		1	1	19	ENGLAND	CE	ENGLISH	SERVANT	043	C		30
FOREMAN	WILLIAM		1		15	ENGLAND	CE	ENGLISH		044	C	4	74
FORESITH	CHARLES				38	SCOTLAND	EM	SCOTCH		044	C	3	38
FORESYTH	JEREMIAH				33	ONTARIO	EM	ENGLISH	CARPENTER	043	B	3	50
FORFAR	ARCHIBALD				61	0	CP	SCOTCH	F	045	C	4	26
FORFAR	DAVID				45	0	CP	SCOTCH	CARPENTER	045	C	4	28
FORFAR	JOSEPH				30	0	CP	SCOTCH	F	045	C	4	31
FORFAR	THOMAS				35	0	CP	IRISH	F	045	C	4	26
FORFAR	WILLIAM				33	0	CP	SCOTCH	F	045	C	4	21
FORFAR	WILLIAM				53	0	CP	SCOTCH	F	045	C	4	23
FORHAN	MICHAEL				63	IRELAND	RC	IRISH	LAB	043	F		13
FORREST	JENNUTHA			1	60	SCOTLAND	PS	SCOTCH		043	E	3	45
FORREST	ROBERT	W			30	SCOTLAND	PS	SCOTCH	PHYSICIAN	043	E	3	45
FORRESTER	EDWARD				42	IRELAND	RC	IRISH	LAB	043	D		4
FORRESTER	JOHN				51	0	CE	ENGLISH	F	043	B	1	32
FORRESTER	THOMAS				63	SCOTLAND	CP	SCOTCH	F	044	B	6	35
FORSITH	EDWIN		1		14	CANADA	NG	GERMAN		045	D	6	66
FORSTER	ALEX				25	0	BA	ENGLISH	F	044	A	3	16
FORSTER	ANTHONY				26	0	WM	ENGLISH	FARMER	045	D	5	38
FORSTER	BYRON				23	0	WM	ENGLISH	FARMER	045	D	5	73
FORSTER	ELIZABETH			1	64	ENGLAND	CE	ENGLISH		045	D	5	18
FORSTER	GEORGE		2		21	0	CE		WOOD TURNER	045	D	5	D
FORSTER	JAMES	HERBERT	2		2	0	WM			045	D	5	D
FORSTER	JOHN				64	ENGLAND	BA	ENGLISH	F	044	A	3	16
FORSTER	JOHN				37	ENGLAND	CE	ENGLISH	WOOD TURNER	045	D	5	18
FORSTER	JOHN		2		62	ENGLAND	CE		ENGINEER	045	D	5	D
FORSTER	THOMAS				29	0	WM	ENGLISH	WOOD TURNER	045	D	5	29
FORSTER	THOMAS	WALTER	2			0	WM			045	D	5	D
FORSTER	WILLIAM				57	IRELAND	CE	IRISH	FARMER	045	A	1	99
FORSTER	WILLIAM	R C	1		18	0	CE	ENGLISH	F LAB	044	A	3	11
FORSYTH	DONALD		1		26	SCOTLAND	CP	SCOTCH	LAB	045	C	4	4
FORSYTH	EMMA			1	50	0	PM	ENGLISH		043	B	4	16
FORSYTH	JOHN				35	SCOTLAND	CP	SCOTCH	CLERK POST OFFICE	044	C	2	19
FORSYTH	MARGARET			1	52	0	CP	SCOTCH	HOTEL KEEPER	043	D		82
FORSYTH	SAMUEL				29	0	EM	ENGLISH	F	043	A	1	19
FORSYTH	WALLIS				29	0	CE	SCOTTISH	F	043	B	4	27
FORSYTHE	ANDREW				45	IRELAND	CP	IRISH	F	044	C	2	28
FORSYTHE	JOSEPH				50	IRELAND	PS	IRISH	LAB	045	A	3	7
FORTH	GEORGE				27	ENGLAND	PM	ENGLISH	F LAB	043	B	4	31
FORTH	MARY		1	1	70	ENGLAND	CE	ENGLISH		043	B	4	31
FORTH	RICHARD		1		18	0	CE	ENGLISH	SERVANT	043	B	4	31
FORTH	WILLIAM		1		21	ENGLAND	WM	ENGLISH	MARBLE CUTTER	043	B	5	32
FORTIER	CHARLES				44	0	CE	FRENCH	LAB	043	E	2	44
FORTINER	JOHN		1	M	12	0	PR	GERMAN		043	A	1	29
FORWARD	CHARLES		1		45	USA	NONE	ENGLISH	LUMBER MEASURER	043	H	2	27
FORWARD	CHARLES		1		45	UNITED STATES	NR	ENGLISH	LUMBER MEASURER	043	H	2	27
FOSSET	MARY		1	1	28	0	RC	ENGLISH		044	A	1	34
FOSTER	BERNARD		1		16	0	CE	ENGLISH	F LAB	044	A	3	15
FOSTER	CAROLINE			1	47	0	WM	IRE		044	B	3	16
FOSTER	ELISABETH		1	1	71	UNITED STATES	PS	IRISH		043	E	2	16
FOSTER	EMANUEL				40	0	PM	ENGLISH	F	044	B	5	61
FOSTER	GEORGE				21	ENGLAND	CE	ENGLISH	LABOURER	043	A	4	60
FOSTER	GEORGE				33	0	WM	ENGLISH	F	043	B	5	34
FOSTER	GEORGE		2		1	0	WM			043	B	5	D
FOSTER	GEORGE				50	ENGLAND	CN	ENGLISH	FARM LABOURER	043	E	1	10
FOSTER	GEORGE				36	0	CN	ENGLISH	F	043	E	2	15
FOSTER	GEORGE		2		74	ENGLAND	CN		F	043	E	2	D
FOSTER	GEORGE				86	ENGLAND	CE	ENGLISH	FARMER	045	D	2	61
FOSTER	GEORGE				42	0	CE	ENGLISH	FARMER	045	D	2	61
FOSTER	GOLDSMITH		1		56	0	CN	ENGLISH	CARPENTER	043	E	1	31
FOSTER	HENERY	V			50	0	PM	ENGLISH	GENTLEMAN	044	C	3	25
FOSTER	JAMES				37	ENGLAND	CE	ENGLISH	STEWART	044	C	4	74
FOSTER	JOHN		1		60	IRELAND	CE	IRISH	OSTLER	044	B	6	27
FOSTER	JOHN				25	0	WM	ENGLISH	BLACKSMITH	045	D	5	13
FOSTER	MAURICE			M	38	ENGLAND	CE	ENGLISH	MASON	043	A	5	3
FOSTER	OSWALD				24	0	WM	ENGLISH	CLERK	045	B	2	35

SURNAME	NAME1	NAME2	STRAY	SEX	AGE	BIRTHPL	RELIGION	ORIGIN	OCCUP	DIST	SUB_DIST	DIV	PAGE
FOSTER	OSWALD				62	ENGLAND	QU	ENGLISH	F	044	C	1	26
FOSTER	THOMAS				24	ENGLAND	CE	ENGLISH	BUTCHER	043	A	4	25
FOSTER	THOMAS				27	ENGLAND	CE	ENGLISH	FARMER	043	A	4	70
FOSTER	THOS		1		24	ENGLAND	NC	ENGLISH		043	C		16
FOSTER	WILLIAM				48	ENGLAND	PM	ENGLISH	F	043	B	2	22
FOSTER	WILLIAM				88	ENGLAND	PM	ENGLISH	F	043	B	2	23
FOSTER	WILLIAM				71	ENGLAND	CE	ENGLISH	F	043	B	5	34
FOSTER	WILLIAM				25	0	CE	ENGLISH	F	043	E	1	9
FOSTER	WILLIAM				67	IRELAND	CP	IRISH	FARMER	045	A	3	11
FOSTER	WILLIAM				41	QUEBEC	CE	IRISH	F	045	C	4	29
FOSTER	WILLIAM				57	ENGLAND	WM	ENGLISH	FARMER	045	D	5	73
FOUCAR	JOHN	P			57	GERMANY	NC	GERMAN	TINSMITH	043	A	4	25
FOUNTAIN	DAVID		1		20	ENGLAND	CE	ENGLISH	LABOURER	043	G	1	9
FOUNTAIN	JOSEPH				41	0	CE	FRENCH	F	043	E	1	12
FOUNTAIN	LEWIS				41	ONTARIO	PR	FRENCH	FARMER	043	G	2	1
FOURTH	THOMAS				50	ENGLAND	CE	ENGLISH	F LAB AND SERVANT	043	B	4	35
FOWLER	ALEXANDER				65	IRELAND	PS	IRISH	BLACKSMITH	043	E	3	16
FOWLER	BENJAMINE				28	ENGLAND	WM	ENGLISH	FARMER	045	D	3	54
FOWLER	ENOCK				50	ENGLAND	PM	ENGLISH	F	045	C	3	16
FOWLER	GEORGE		1		55	IRELAND	RC	IRISH	FARM LAB	044	C	2	31
FOWLER	JOHN		1		60	ENGLAND	CE	ENGLISH	LABOURER	043	A	3	3
FOWLER	SETH		2		56	ENGLAND	PM		LAB	045	C	3	D
FOX	FRANCIS				47	ENGLAND	CE	ENGLISH	LAB	045	B	1	34
FOX	GEORGE				32	ENGLAND	CE	ENGLISH	CARPENTER	043	C		47
FOX	GODFREY				51	GERMANY	LU	GERMAN	COOPER	043	D		22
FOX	JOHN		2		81	ENG	WM		COMTRAVELLER	044	B	2	D
FOX	LOUISA		1	1	17	0	MN	GERMAN	SERVANT	044	C	1	36
FOX	MARY			1	70	IRELAND	RC	IRISH		043	E	3	50
FOX	PATRICK				35	IRELAND	RC	IRISH	F	043	E	3	52
FOX	STEPHEN				50	0	WM	ENGLISH	FARMER	044	C	3	32
FOX	THOMAS				57	ENGLAND	CE	ENGLISH	BRICKMAKER	045	A	1	27
FOX	WILLIAM			M	45	ENGLAND	CE	ENGLAND	F	043	A	5	25
FOX	WM				49	0	WM	IRISH	CARPENTER	044	B	5	8
FOX	WM				30	0	WM	ENGLISH	LAB	044	B	5	31
FOXWELL	ALBERT				30	ENGLAND	CE	ENGLISH	F	044	C	4	97
FOYSTON	CARLIN				45	ENGLAND	CE	ENGLISH	F	044	A	3	22
FRAIN	PATRICK		1		72	IRELAND	RC	IRISH	LABOURER	043	A	4	13
FRAME	JOHN				63	SCOTLAND	CP	SCOTCH	F	045	C	4	43
FRANCEY	WILLIAM				48	IRELAND	CP	IRISH	MERCHANT & HOTELKEEP	045	D	2	66
FRANCIS	ANN		1	1	30	0	BA	GERMAN		043	B	3	25
FRANCIS	JOHN				50	ENGLAND	WM	ENGLISH	F	045	A	4	33
FRANCIS	PATTY	L	1	1	43	ENGLAND	CE	ENGLISH		043	H	2	46
FRANCIS	PATTY	L	1	1	43	ENGLAND	CE	ENGLISH		043	H	2	46
FRANCIS	THOMAS				58	ENGLAND	CE	ENGLISH	CARPENTER	045	A	1	91
FRANCIS	WALTER				46	ENGLAND	CE	ENGLISH	F	044	C	2	39
FRANCIS	WILLIAM		1		20	0	CE	IRISH		045	A	1	9
FRANK	EARNEST				46	PRUSSIA	LU	PRUSSIAN	CABINET MAKER	045	A	1	41
FRANK	HENRY				43	0	WM	ENG	BLACKSMITH	044	B	3	38
FRANK	JOHN				72	US	PS	ENG	GENT	044	B	3	38
FRANK	PETER				48	0	WM	ENG	F	044	B	3	39
FRANK	RICHARD				33	0	EM	IRISH	F	043	E	1	15
FRANKLAND	GARRETT	F			36	ENGLAND	CE	ENGLISH	CATTLE DEALER	045	A	1	83
FRANKS	MATILDA		1	1	22	0	WM	ENGLISH		044	B	5	37
FRANSISCO	JEREMIAH				35	US	RC	IRISH	CARPENTER	045	C	2	11
FRASER	ALEXANDER				33	0	WM	SCOTLAND	F	043	A	5	39
FRASER	CHARLOTTE		1	1	15	0	CN	SCOTCH	SERVANT	043	E	1	16
FRASER	GEORGE	T	1	M	3	0	FK	SCOTLAND		043	A	5	39
FRASER	JOHN				69	SCOTLAND	WM	SCOTCH	SCHOOL TEACHER	045	B	1	47
FRASER	JOHN				50	IRELAND	CE	IRISH	F LAB	044	C	1	56
FRASER	MARY			1	34	ON SEA	RC	IRISH	DRESS MAKER	044	B	6	55
FRASER	ROBERT		1		30	SCOTLAND	CP	SCOTCH	LAB	045	A	2	34
FRASIER	CHARLOTTE		1	1	42	ENGLAND	CE	ENGLISH		045	B	2	7
FRAZER	A	B	1	1	61	SCOTLAND	CP	SCOTCH		045	D	3	17
FRAZER	ALEX		1		30	SCOT	CE	SCOT	LAB	045	C	1	32
FRAZER	ANNE		1	1	29	SCOTLAND	CP	SCOTCH		045	D	3	17
FRAZER	HARRIET		1	1	25	0	WM	GERMAN		044	B	5	73
FRAZER	WILLIAM				70	0	WM	AFRICAN	LAB	043	B	2	38
FRAZIER	WILLIAM				49	SCOTLAND	CP	SCOTCH	FARM LABORER	045	D	1	18
FREEK	JAMES				52	ENG	WM	ENG	BRICK MAKER	044	B	2	26
FREEL	JAMES	G			60	U STATES	CE	IRISH	DOCT OF MED	045	D	5	6
FREELAND	ANDREW		1		12	0	BA	SCOTCH		045	B	2	29
FREELAND	EDWARD	B	1		10	0	BA	SCOTCH		045	B	2	29
FREELAND	MARGARET		1	1	37	SCOTLAND	BA	SCOTCH		045	B	2	29
FREEMAN	ELIZABETH		1	1	25	0	CE	ENGLISH		043	D		88
FREEMAN	HENRY				40	ENG	WM	ENG	MILLER	045	C	1	15
FREEMAN	JOSEPH				40	0	ME	SCOTCH	FARMER	045	D	6	17
FREEMAN	JOSEPH				60	ENGLAND	CE	ENGLISH	LAB	044	C	4	72
FREER	JAMES				35	ENGLAND	CE	ENGLISH	LAB	045	B	1	27
FREESE	PHILIP				37	ONTARIO	PR	DUTCH	LABORER	043	G	2	29
FRENCH	AGNES		1	1	71	SCOTLAND	CS	SCOTCH		045	D	3	18
FRENCH	ANN	C	1	1	11	0	WM	SCOTCH		045	A	4	29
FRENCH	CHRISTIAN		1	F	12	0	CE	ENGLISH		043	A	2	29
FRENCH	ISAAC				31	0	CO	IRELAND	GROCER	045	D	2	6
FRENCH	JAMES				43	SCOTLAND	CS	SCOTCH	FARMER	045	D	3	59
FRENCH	RICHARD				63	IRELAND	CO	IRISH	FARMER	045	D	1	31
FRENCH	THOMAS		1		60	ENGLAND	CE	ENGLISH	LAB	045	A	3	25
FREUD	JOHN		1		24	0	CE	ENGLISH	LAB	044	B	5	22
FRIEL	SILVESTER	LOYD			30	U STATES	CO	GERMAN	MEDICAL DOCTOR	045	D	6	76
FRISBY	THOMAS				49	ENGLAND	CE	ENGLISH	FARMER	045	D	4	21
FRISLY	JOHN				22	0	CM	ENGLISH	FARMER	045	D	4	1
FRISLY	WILLIAM				33	0	CE	ENGLISH	FARMER	045	D	4	6
FRITZ	MICHAEL				40	0	MN	GERMAN	FARMER	045	D	5	38
FROST	DAVID				43	ENGLAND	WM	ENGLISH	LAB	044	C	1	54
FROST	MARY-ANN		1	1	11	0	PS	IRISH	F LAB	044	C	1	47
FRUG	ALICE		1	1	30	IRELAND	CE	IRISH		043	C		41
FRUMP	WILLIAM				35	ENGLAND	WM	GERMAN	FARMER	045	D	6	28
FRY	CHARLES				63	ENGLAND	CE	ENGLISH	F	043	A	3	18
FRY	GEORGE				40	IRELAND	CE	ENGLISH	MERCHANT	043	G	2	16
FRY	JANE	ANNE	1	F	34	IRELAND	CE	IRISH		043	A	1	1
FRY	JOHN				32	0	CE	ENGLISH	F	043	A	3	21
FRY	STEPHEN				31	0	CE	IRISH	STATION MASTER	043	C		50
FRY	WILLIAM		1		36	IRELAND	CE	IRISH	CLERK DIVISION COURT	043	H	2	15
FRY	WILLIAM		1		36	IRELAND	CE	IRISH	CLERK	043	H	2	15
FRYATH	HENRY				47	ENGLAND	WM	ENGLISH	LAB	043	C		38
FRYATT	HENRY				69	ENGLAND	EM	ENGLISH	GENTLEMAN	043	D		26
FUGE	THOMAS		1		50	ENGLAND	CE	ENGLISH		045	D	5	8

SURNAME	NAME1	NAME2	STRAY	SEX	AGE	BIRTHPL	RELIGION	ORIGIN	OCCUP	DIST	SUB_DIST	DIV	PAGE
FULES	THOMAS				53	ENGLAND	WM	ENGLISH	F	043	E	3	23
FULLARTON	JOHN				25	ENG	CE	ENG	LAB	044	B	2	20
FULLER	GEORGE				26	ENGLAND	CE	ENGLISH	LABOURER	045	A	1	49
FULLER	JAMES				48	ENGLAND	PM	ENGLISH	F	043	A	3	59
FULLER	JOHN				36	ENGLAND	CE	ENGLISH	HOTEL KEEPER	043	E	2	23
FULLER	JOHN				29	ENGLAND	CE	ENGLISH	BRICKMAKER	045	A	1	43
FULLER	RICHARD		1		25	ENGLAND	CE	ENGLISH	CARPENTER	045	A	1	65
FULLER	SARAH			1	72	SPAIN	CE	ENGLISH		045	A	1	43
FULLJAMES	MARY			1	50	US	CE	ENGLISH		045	B	1	38
FULTON	CATHARINE			1	42	IRELAND	CE	IRISH		044	A	1	11
FULTON	CHARLES				28	IRELAND	CE	IRISH	F LAB	044	A	1	4
FULTON	GEORGE		1		30	O	PR	IRISH	F LAB	044	A	1	2
FULTON	THOMAS		1		18	O	RC	IRISH	F LAB	044	A	1	6
FULTON	WILLIAM				23	O	CE	ENG	FARM LAB	044	B	1	37
FUNSLAIN	ELIZABETH		1	1	48	IRELAND	CE	IRISH	DRESSMAKER	045	A	1	43
FURHELLER	JOHN				65	O	LU	GERMANY	FARMER	045	D	2	43
FURHELLER	MICHAEL		1		60	O	CE	GERMAN	F	043	H	1	9
FURHELLER	WILLIAM				34	O	LU	GERMAN	FARMER	045	D	4	1
FURNEVAL	FREDK		1		16	ENGLAND	CE	ENGLISH	F LAB	044	A	2	18
FURZE	EDWARD				34	ENGLAND	CE	ENGLISH	F	043	H	2	54
FURZE	EDWARD				34	ENGLAND	CE	ENGLISH	FARMER	043	H	2	54
FYDDEL	AUSTON				23	ENGLAND	WM	ENGLISH	FARMER	043	G	1	40
FYFE	ARCHIBALD		1		64	SCOTLAND	CS	SCOTCH	ASST POSTMASTER	043	D		22
GABY	FREDERICK				45	ENG	WM	ENG	F	044	B	2	45
GADDES	RICHARD	S			53	ENGLAND	CE	ENGLISH	F	044	A	3	10
GAFFNEY	CATHARINE			1	47	IRELAND	RC	IRISH		044	B	6	34
GAGER	DIANA			1	52	ONTARIO	PR	ENGLISH		043	G	2	51
GAINER	BARNEY		1		18	O	WM	IRISH	F	044	C	2	31
GAINER	MARGARET		1	1	13	O	RC	IRISH		044	C	2	34
GAINES	ALBERT				51	U STATES	EM	AFRICAN	FARMER	045	A	2	14
GAINS	THOMAS				49	IRELAND	WM	IRISH	TAILOR	043	D		52
GALAGER	ROBERT				36	IRELAND	RC	IRISH	F LAB	043	B	4	24
GALBRAITH	DANIEL				75	IRELAND	CP	IRISH	F	045	C	4	31
GALBREATH	JAMES				48	SCOTLAND	CP	SCOTCH	F	045	C	4	2
GALBREATH	ROBERT				72	IRELAND	CP	IRISH	F	045	C	4	30
GALE	JOHN		1	M	15	O	CE	ENGLISH	SERVANT	043	A	1	5
GALE	JOHN				70	ENGLAND	EM	ENGLISH		044	C	1	3
GALE	LOUIE		2	1		O	NG			044	B	2	D
GALE	WILLIAM	J			29	O	CE	ENG	CARPENTER	044	B	2	31
GALL	THOMAS				28	SCOTLAND	CP	SCOTCH	F	044	A	3	47
GALLAGHER	WM				58	IRELAND	RC	IRISH	LAB	043	D		38
GALLANNOUGH	ARCHIBALD				57	O	WM	IRISH	MERCHANT	045	D	1	12
GALLOW	WILLIAM				64	SCOTLAND	CS	SCOTCH	GARDENER	045	A	1	77
GALLOWAY	ANN			1	75	IRE	CE	IRE		045	C	1	7
GALLOWAY	IGNATIUS				55	IRE	CE	IRE	F	045	C	1	7
GALLOWAY	JAS				50	IRELAND	EM	IRISH	F	043	E	2	39
GALLOWAY	JOHN				55	ENGLAND	WM	ENGLISH	FARMER	045	D	1	46
GALLOWAY	WM				48	IRE	CE	IRE	F	045	C	1	13
GALOWAY	JOANNA		1	1	24	IRELAND	CP	IRISH		045	D	3	29
GALT	SAMUEL		1		70	IRE	CS	IRE	LAB	045	C	1	58
GALVIN	JEROME				28	ENGLAND	RC	ENGLISH	MOULDER	044	B	5	23
GAMBEL	JOHN				66	U STATES	WM	IRISH	FARMER	045	D	6	73
GAMBLE	GEORGE				48	O	CE	IRISH	FARMER	043	A	4	34
GAMBLE	I	W			71	O	CE	IRISH	GENTLEMAN	044	B	5	36
GAMBLE	MOSES				65	U S	CP	IRISH	FARMER	045	D	4	28
GAMBLE	W	K			39	O	CE	IRISH	F	043	B	4	6
GAMBLE	WILLIAM		1	M	21	O	PR	SCOTCH	LABOURER	043	A	1	26
GAMBLE	WILLIAM		1		35	O	WM	IRISH	SHOE MAKER	045	D	2	28
GAMBLE	WILLIAM		2		70	O	CP		FARMER	045	D	2	D
GANER	ELLEN		1	1	15	O	RC	IRISH	SERVANT	044	C	2	34
GANER	JOSEPH		1		14	O	RC	IRISH	SERVANT	045	D	1	11
GANGE	SAMUEL				34	QUE	CE	ENGLISH	LAB	044	C	4	65
GANON	ANNE		1	1	5	O	PM	IRISH		045	A	4	8
GANTON	MARIA			1	50	ENGLAND	CE	ENGLISH		045	D	3	46
GANTOW	MARY			1	58	ENGLAND	WM	ENGLISH		045	D	1	39
GARBILL	ROBT		1		45	ENG	CE	ENG	LAB	045	C	1	62
GARBUTT	ELIZABETH		1	1	7	O	WM	ENGLISH		044	A	3	8
GARBUTT	FRANCIS				36	O	CN	ENGLISH	F	043	A	6	7
GARBUTT	GEO				42	O	BA	ENGLISH	F	044	A	3	3
GARBUTT	GEORGE		1		9	O	WM	ENGLISH		044	A	3	8
GARBUTT	JOHN		1		10	O	WM	ENGLISH		044	A	3	8
GARBUTT	ROBERT				40	O	WM	ENGLISH	F	044	A	1	3
GARD	JOHN		1		24	ENGLAND	CE	ENGLISH	BRICK MAKER	045	A	1	27
GARDEN	GEORGE	L		M	42	NEW BRUNSWICK	CE	SCOTCH	MERCHANT	043	A	1	50
GARDHOUSE	JAMES	M	2		1	O	BA			044	A	3	D
GARDHOUSE	JOHN				87	ENGLAND	PM	ENGLISH		044	A	3	50
GARDINER	EMMA		1	1	21	ENGLAND	CE	ENGLISH		043	E	1	13
GARDINER	GEORGE				37	ENGLAND	WM	ENGLISH	LABOURER	045	D	5	76
GARDINER	LUCINDA			1	48	US	CE	IRISH		045	D	1	3
GARDINER	SARAH		2	1		O	WM			045	D	5	D
GARDNER	ANN		1	1	50	IRELAND	CE	IRISH		045	A	4	7
GARDNER	JAMES				54	ENGLAND	CE	ENGLISH	F LAB	044	A	2	13
GARDNER	JOHN				35	ENG	EM	ENG	F	044	B	3	13
GARDNER	THOMAS				39	ENGLAND	WM	ENGLISH	MOULDER	043	D		41
GARFIELD	SARAH		2	1	73	QUE	CP			045	A	2	D
GARNET	SAMUEL		1		22	IRELAND	CE	IRISH		044	B	6	4
GARNETT	WILLIAM				51	ENGLAND	WM	ENGLISH	STORE KEEPER	045	D	3	60
GARNISH	RICHARD				35	ENGLAND	WM	ENGLAND	LABORER	045	D	2	18
GAROW	HENRY			M	50	O	EM	FRENCH	F	043	A	1	45
GARRET	HENRY		1		18	O	WM	ENGLISH	LAB	043	B	5	3
GARRICK	JAMES				50	SCOTLAND	CS	SCOTCH	MERCHANT	043	E	2	22
GARROD	ROBERT				61	ENGLAND	CE	ENGLISH	LABOURER	045	D	4	22
GARROW	GEORGE			M	42	O	EM	FRENCH	F	043	A	1	53
GARTON	JAMES				27	ENG	EP	ENG	F	044	B	3	17
GARTON	JOHN				66	ENG	WM	ENG	AGENT	044	B	1	10
GARTSHORE	JOHN	G	1		21	O	BA	SCOTCH	CLERK	044	C	2	54
GARVIN	CONNOR				60	IRELAND	RC	IRISH	LABORER	045	D	1	5
GARVIN	MATHEW				36	IRELAND	WM	IRISH	MACHINIST	043	C		54
GARVIS	JAMES			M	45	ENGLAND	PM	ENGLISH	LAB	043	A	2	20
GARVIS	SAMUEL			M	36	ENGLAND	PM	ENGLISH	F	043	A	2	5
GASCOYNE	JOHN		1		21	ENGLAND	WM	ENGLISH	BUTCHER	043	D		59
GASS	SAMUEL				33	IRELAND	CP	SCOTCH	FARM SERVANT	045	C	3	3
GASTON	THOMAS				32	ENGLAND	CP	ENGLISH	WIRE WORKER	045	B	1	34
GATES	CHARLES				53	O	CE	IRISH	HOTEL KEEPER	045	A	1	46
GATES	ISABELLA		1	1	15	O	CE	ENG		045	C	1	26
GATES	JONATHAN				43	O	CE	ENGLISH	INNKEEPER	045	C	3	11

SURNAME	NAME1	NAME2	STRAY	SEX	AGE	BIRTHPL	RELIGION	ORIGIN	OCCUP	DIST	SUB_DIST	DIV	PAGE
GATES	M	J	1		20	0	CE	ENG	F	045	C	1	26
GATES	NEILSON				53	0	CS	ENG		045	C	1	26
GAUBY	JOHN				34	0	WM	IRISH	FARMER	045	D	4	2
GAVAN	PATRICK			M	46	IRELAND	RC	IRISH	LAB	043	A	1	61
GAY	ALFRED		1	M	18	0	CE	ENGLISH	LABOURER	043	A	1	31
GAY	MARIA		1	1	21	0	CE	IRISH	SERVANT	045	A	3	6
GEDDIS	SARAH	JANE	1	1	14	0	WM	SCOTCH		044	C	3	7
GEE	GEORGE				53	ENGLAND	WM	ENGLISH	CATTLE DEALER	045	B	1	20
GEE	JOSEPH				35	ENG	PS	ENG	F	044	B	2	29
GEE	REV	DANIEL E			31	CANADA	WM	ENGLISH	MINISTER	045	D	6	47
GEE	SAMUEL		1		22	U STATES	CE	ENGLISH	IRON MOULDER	045	D	5	10
GEER	WILLIAM				46	ENGLAND	NC	ENGLISH	F	043	A	6	17
GEGG	JOSEPH		1		29	ENGLAND	CE	ENGLISH	FARM LAB	044	C	2	26
GELLATY	PETER			M	45	SCOTLAND	CP	SCOTCH	FAR	043	A	1	67
GEMMEL	AMELIA		1	1	28	0	CE	ENGLISH		044	A	2	5
GENGILL	GEORGE				60	ENG	CE	ENG	LAB	044	B	1	15
GENGILL	JONAS				42	ENG	CE	ENG	CARPENTER	044	B	1	15
GENTLE	WILLIAM				62	0	WM	SCOTCH	GENTLEMAN	044	C	3	60
GENTLEMAN	MARY			1	60	IRE	RC	IRISH		044	B	1	10
GENTZ	WILLIAM		1		19	ONTARIO	PR	DUTCH	FARM LABORER	043	G	2	29
GEORGE	CANES				28	0	WM	ENGLISH	F	044	C	3	31
GEORGE	HENERY				32	IRELAND	RP	IRISH	LABOURER	044	C	3	57
GEORGE	RICHARD		1		25	ENGLAND	CE	ENGLISH	LABOURER	045	D	3	75
GEORGE	WILLIAM		1		5	0	CE	ENGLISH		045	C	3	39
GERMAIN	ALEXANDER				50	0	CE	FRENCH	F	043	A	6	18
GERMAIN	ANN			1	80	IRELAND	CE	IRISH		043	A	6	18
GERMAIN	JOHN		2		47	0	CE		FARMER	043	A	6	D
GERMAN	HENRY				73	ENGLAND	WM	ENGLISH	BLACKSMITH	045	D	5	12
GERMAN	ROBERT		1		30	ENGLAND	WM	ENGLISH	LABOURER	045	D	3	65
GERNETT	VICTOR		1		22	QUEBEC	RC	FRENCH	LUMBERMAN	043	G	1	49
GEROW	HENERY				45	PRINCE EDWARD	CN	FRENCH	LAB	043	A	6	37
GERRY	JAMES				53	ENGLAND	WM	ENGLISH	STORE KEEPER	045	B	1	3
GERRY	RICHARD		2		80	ENGLAND	WM		F	045	B	1	D
GETCH	WM				25	ENGLAND	CE	ENGLISH	FITTER	044	B	5	26
GIBB	ALEXANDER				84	SCOTLAND	CP	SCOTCH		044	C	2	39
GIBB	ALEXANDER				42	0	CP	SCOTCH	F	044	C	2	40
GIBB	JAMES				37	0	CP	SCOTCH	F	044	C	2	38
GIBB	JOHN		1		19	0	CP	SCOTCH	FARM LAB	044	C	2	39
GIBBERT	ELISHA				27	CANADA	DI	ENGLISH	MASON	045	D	6	53
GIBBONEY	HUGH				56	IRELAND	CE	IRISH	F	043	E	3	30
GIBBONEY	JAMES				42	IRELAND	WM	IRISH	F	043	E	3	28
GIBBONEY	JAMES				74	IRELAND	CE	IRISH	GENT	043	E	3	29
GIBBONEY	THOMAS				33	IRELAND	PS	IRISH	F	043	E	3	31
GIBBONS	JAMES				62	IRELAND	WM	IRISH	F	043	A	6	42
GIBBONS	PATRICK				63	IRELAND	RC	IRISH	F	043	A	6	23
GIBBS	ABRAHAM		1		28	0	EM	IRISH	SERVANT	044	B	1	63
GIBBS	HENERY				35	ENGLAND	CE	ENGLISH	LABOURER	044	C	3	41
GIBBS	JOHN				36	PEI	WM	IRISH	F	044	B	1	25
GIBBS	ROSEANNA		1	1	23	ENGLAND	WM	ENGLISH		045	B	1	56
GIBBS	SUSANNA		1	1	43	IRELAND	CE	IRISH		044	A	1	35
GIBBS	THOMAS		1		70	ENGLAND	WM	ENGLISH	BRICKMAKER	045	B	2	17
GIBNER	OTTO				35	GER	LU	GER	F	044	B	2	53
GIBNEY	JOHNSTON				47	IRELAND	PS	IRISH	IRON FOUNDER	045	D	6	41
GIBSON				1	61	US	BA	SCOTTISH	FARMER	044	C	1	20
GIBSON	ELISA		1	1	26	IRELAND	WM	IRISH	SERVANT	045	B	2	36
GIBSON	ELIZABETH			1	42	0	CE	ENGLISH		043	H	2	15
GIBSON	ELIZABETH			1	42	ONTARIO	CE	ENGLISH		043	H	2	15
GIBSON	FULLARTON				45	SCOT	CS	SCOT	F	044	B	2	60
GIBSON	GEORGE	F			36	0	OP	SCOTCH	F	045	C	4	3
GIBSON	JANE			F	28	IRELAND	CE	IRISH	SEAMSTRESS	043	A	1	56
GIBSON	JOHN				27	SCOTLAND	CS	SCOTCH	BLACKSMITH	043	D		78
GIBSON	JOHN				40	IRELAND	CE	IRISH	LABOURER MILKMAN	045	A	1	52
GIBSON	JOHN				50	SCOTLAND	CS	SCOTCH	FARMER	045	D	3	17
GIBSON	JOHN		1		21	0	WM	IRISH	STUDENT	044	C	3	73
GIBSON	JOHN	L			29	0	PM	ENGLISH	F	043	E	2	77
GIBSON	JOSEPH				38	IRELAND	CP	IRISH	MERCHANT	045	B	2	5
GIBSON	MARION		1	1	75	SCOTLAND	CS	SCOTCH		045	D	3	21
GIBSON	PETER				34	0	BA	SCOTTISH	SURVEYOR	044	C	1	21
GIBSON	THOMAS				33	0	CS	SCOTCH	WAGGON MAKER	045	D	3	25
GIES	NICHOLAS				49	GERMANY	RC	GERMAN	MASON	043	A	6	8
GIGHAN	OLIVER				24	0	RC	FRENCH	MOULDER	043	C		18
GIGHAN	ROBT	L	2		1	CANADA	RC			043	C		D
GILBERT	ANDREW				35	0	PM	ENGLISH	LAB	043	B	2	30
GILBERT	GEORGE				40	ENGLAND	CE	ENGLISH	F	044	C	2	26
GILBERT	JAMES		1		23	ENGLAND	WM	ENGLISH	LAB	044	C	4	75
GILBERT	JANE			1	60	IRELAND	CE	IRISH		044	C	3	62
GILBERT	JOHN				48	ENGLAND	CE	ENGLISH	LAB	043	F		28
GILBERT	SAMUEL				41	0	PM	ENGLISH	PLASTERER	043	B	2	41
GILBERT	THOMAS				27	0	WM	IRISH	F	044	C	4	22
GILBIE	ANDREW				60	ENGLAND	NC	ENGLISH	CARPENTER TF	043	F		2
GILCHRIST	DAVID				19	IRELAND	CE	IRISH	F	044	A	2	14
GILCHRIST	DONALD				40	SCOT	CS	SCOT	F	045	C	1	30
GILCHRIST	JOSEPH				68	SCOTLAND	NG	SCOTCH	WEAVER	043	B	1	2
GILCRISTSON	MARY		1	1	26	IRELAND	PS	IRISH	SERVANT	045	A	1	2
GILDER	GEORGE		1		47	0	WM	IRISH	FARM LAB	044	C	2	36
GILDING	GEORGE				46	ENGLAND	WM	ENGLISH	BRICKLAYER	045	A	1	82
GILES	ANN			1	52	ENGLAND	CE	ENGLISH		044	A	1	36
GILES	ELIZABETH	ANN		1	59	ENGLAND	NC	ENGLISH		043	E	2	11
GILES	HENERY				32	ENGLAND	CE	ENGLISH	MASON	044	C	3	70
GILES	THOS	H			28	0	CE	ENGLISH	F	044	A	1	22
GILES	WILLIAM				56	ENGLAND	CE	ENGLISH	SHOEMAKER	045	D	2	64
GILES	WM				36	ENG	WM	ENG	F	045	C	1	62
GILL	JANE		2	1	1	0	NR			045	C	1	D
GILL	JOHN				65	ENGLAND	CN	ENGLISH	F LAB	043	B	4	10
GILL	JOHN		1		20	ENGLAND	CE	ENGLISH	SERVANT	043	E	1	2
GILL	JOHN				48	ENGLAND	CE	ENGLISH	CEMETERY/CARETAKER	043	E	1	5
GILL	JOHN				63	ENGLAND	WM	ENGLISH	F	044	A	2	2
GILL	JOHN		1		22	ENGLAND	WM	ENGLISH	SAILOR	045	A	1	64
GILL	ROBERT				33	IRELAND	CE	SCOTCH	WAGGON MAKER	043	H	2	17
GILL	THOMAS				40	ENGLAND	CE	ENGLISH	F	043	E	1	19
GILL	WM				30	ENG	NR	ENG	LAB	045	C	1	68
GILLCHRIST	ALEX	ARCH	2			0	CP			045	C	1	D
GILLCHRIST	ROBT				48	SCOT	CP	SCOT	F	045	C	1	59
GILLES	ANN		1	1	58	SCOT	PS	SCOT		044	B	3	34
GILLES	MALCHOLM		1		60	SCOT	PS	SCOT	F	044	B	3	34
GILLES	MALCHOLM		1		12	0	PS	SCOT		044	B	3	34

SURNAME	NAME1	NAME2	STRAY	SEX	AGE	BIRTHPL	RELIGION	ORIGIN	OCCUP	DIST	SUB_DIST	DIV	PAGE
GILLESPIE	JAMES		1		25	O	WM	IRISH	BLACKSMITH	045	B	2	5
GILLESPIE	SAMUEL				70	IRELAND	CP	IRISH	LAB	045	B	2	23
GILLET	ALVA	J			55	US	WM	FRENCH	CARPENTER	045	C	2	22
GILLET	J	L			35	O	EM	GERMAN	COOPER	043	E	2	81
GILLHAM	HENRY			M	38	ENGLAND	CE	ENGLISH	F	043	A	2	54
GILLHAN	GEORGE			M	41	ENGLAND	CE	ENGLISH	F	043	A	2	41
GILLIES	ARCHIBALD			M	48	SCOTLAND	PS	SCOTCH	F	043	A	2	33
GILLIES	JOHN			M	61	SCOTLAND	CP	SCOTCH	FARMER	043	A	1	33
GILLIGAN	JAS				63	IRE	RC	IRE	F	045	C	1	39
GILLION	AGNESS			1	26	O	PS	IRISH		043	E	3	17
GILLION	EDWARD		1		5	O	CE	ENGLISH		043	B	2	11
GILLION	ELIZABETH		1	1	29	O	CE	ENGLISH		043	B	2	11
GILLION	GEORGE		1		7	O	CE	ENGLISH		043	B	2	11
GILLION	JONATHAN				67	ENGLAND	CN	ENGLISH	F	043	E	3	5
GILLION	THOMAS				29	O	CN	ENGLISH	F	043	E	3	5
GILLION	WILLIAM	JOHN	1		2	O	CE	ENGLISH		043	B	2	11
GILLIS	ALEXANDER		1		15	O	CP	SCOT	SERVANT	044	B	1	53
GILLIS	JOHN				32	SCOT	CP	SCOT	F	044	B	1	64
GILLYATT	GEORGE	P	1		70	ENGLAND	WM	ENGLISH	CLERK	043	D		51
GILLYATT	MARY	ANN	1	1	57	ENGLAND	WM	ENGLISH		043	D		51
GILMORE	ROBERT			M	37	O	PS	IRISH	FAR	043	A	1	58
GILMOUR	ALFRED				35	ENGLAND	WM	ENGLISH	LABOURER	045	D	6	20
GILMOUR	BRIDGET		1	1	45	IRELAND	RC	IRISH		044	C	4	58
GILMOUR	GILBERT				29	ENGLAND	PS	ENGLISH	INN KEEPER	044	B	5	40
GILMOUR	JAMES		1		47	O	CS	IRISH	STORE KEEPER	045	D	1	43
GILROY	JAMES				46	O	QU	ENGLISH	F	043	B	4	30
GILROY	JANE		1	1	17	O	PS	SCOTTISH	F SERVANT	044	C	1	19
GILROY	WILLIAM				40	O	CP	ENGLISH	F	043	B	4	39
GINN	THOMAS				54	IRE	CE	IRE	F	044	B	4	14
GITLAR	ALFRED		1		23	ENGLAND	CP	ENGLISH	LAB	045	C	4	28
GITLAR	JOSEPH		1		27	ENGLAND	CP	ENGLISH	LAB	045	C	4	28
GITMAN	RICHARD				40	ENGLAND	CE	ENGLISH		044	C	3	32
GLADSTONE	MORGAN				50	ENG	CE	ENG	F	045	C	1	14
GLANCEY	MATTHEW		1	M	65	IRELAND	RC	IRELAND	F	043	A	5	13
GLANCEY	MICHAEL				64	IRELAND	RC	IRISH	LAB	044	C	2	12
GLANCIE	THOMAS			M	51	IRELAND	RC	IRISH	LABOURER	043	A	1	28
GLANSEY	JAMES				35	IRELAND	RC	IRISH	ROAD OVERSEER	045	D	2	30
GLASS	DANIEL				35	QUE	CE	IRISH	F	044	B	2	32
GLASS	HUGH				67	IRE	CE	IRE	F	044	B	2	56
GLASSFORD	PETER				64	SCOTLAND	CP	SCOTCH	MINISTER	044	B	5	64
GLEASON	ALMANA		1		53	U STATES	WM	ENGLISH		043	A	6	19
GLEASON	JOHN				44	O	PS	ENGLISH	F	043	E	1	52
GLEASON	JOHN				45	IRE	RC	IRISH	LAB	044	B	1	65
GLEASON	MICHAEL		1		60	IRELAND	RC	IRISH	SERVANT	045	A	3	30
GLEASON	PATRICK				27	IRELAND	RC	IRISH	LABOURER	043	A	4	13
GLEASON	PATRICK				50	IRELAND	RC	IRISH	LAB	044	C	2	53
GLEESON	DANIEL		2			O	RC			045	D	5	D
GLEESON	EDWARD		1			ENGLAND	CE	ENGLISH	SERVANT	044	C	4	9
GLEESON	JOHN				42	IRELAND	RC	IRISH	LABOURER	045	D	5	31
GLEESON	MARGARET		1	1	19	IRELAND	RC	IRISH	SERVANT	045	D	1	19
GLEESON	MORTY				40	IRELAND	RC	IRISH	FARMER	045	D	3	72
GLEESON	WILLIAM				75	IRELAND	RC	IRISH		045	D	3	53
GLEN	JOHN				71	SCOTLAND	CS	SCOTCH	WEAVER	045	D	5	41
GLEN	JOHN		1		1	US	WM	AFRICAN		044	C	4	10
GLEN	ROBERT				32	SCOTLAND	WM	ENGLISH	F	045	A	4	19
GLEN	WILLIAM				48	SCOTLAND	PS	SCOTCH	LABOURER	045	A	1	47
GLENDENING	ANDREW				38	O	CE	SCOTCH	FARM LABOURER	045	D	3	17
GLENDENING	ANNE		1	1	19	ENGLAND	CE	ENGLISH	INMATE	045	B	1	72
GLENDENNING	JOHN		1		38	O	WM	GERMAN	LABOURER	045	D	5	42
GLENDENNING	MARY		1	1	75	IRELAND	CE	IRISH		043	A	4	18
GLENDINING	ARCHIBALD				66	SCOTLAND	CP	SCOTCH	F	045	C	4	33
GLENDINING	THOMAS				34	O	OP	SCOTCH	F	045	C	4	2
GLENDINNING	FRANCIS				36	O	CP	SCOTCH	F	045	C	4	34
GLENDINNING	GEORGE		1		16	O	PM	IRISH		045	D	4	5
GLENHOLM	HENRY				63	IRELAND	CE	IRISH	F	043	F		27
GLENN	GEORGE				27	O	CS	SCOTCH	LABOURER	045	D	3	54
GLENN	THOMAS				42	IRELAND	CE	IRISH	LAB	043	C		52
GLOSSY	ROSE		1	1	50	IRELAND	RC	IRISH	SERVANT	045	B	1	56
GLOVER	EDWARD				27	ENG	CE	ENG	LAB	044	B	2	55
GLOVER	GEORGE				33	ONTARIO	PR	ENGLISH	FARMER	043	G	2	42
GLOVER	JOSEPH				33	O	PM	ENGLISH	MERCHANT	043	E	2	70
GLOVER	JOSHUA				60	US	XC	AFRICAN	F LAB	044	A	2	48
GLOVER	THOMAS				26	ONTARIO	PR	ENGLISH	FARMER	043	G	2	41
GLOVER	THOMAS				60	ENGLAND	PR	ENGLISH	FARMER	043	G	2	44
GLOVER	THOMAS				52	ENG	CE	ENG	MASON	044	B	2	23
GLOVER	WILLIAM				58	ENGLAND	PM	ENGLISH	F	043	E	2	69
GNASSICK	CHARLES		1		25	SCOTLAND	CP	SCOTCH	RAILROAD ENGINEER	045	D	5	10
GODARD	JAMES				21	ENG	WM	ENG	SHOEMAKER	044	B	4	11
GODDARD	GEORGE		1		37	ENGLAND	CE	ENGLISH	FARMER	043	G	1	51
GODFREY	DAVID				21	O	CE	FRENCH	F	043	H	1	37
GODFREY	EDWARD				54	ENGLAND	WM	ENGLISH	SADDLER	043	A	3	15
GODFREY	GEORGE		1		16	ENGLAND	WM	ENGLISH	LABOURER	043	B	3	46
GODFREY	HENRY				36	O	CE	FRENCH	F	043	H	1	38
GODFREY	LEONARD				30	O	CE	FRENCH	F	043	H	1	38
GODFREY	LEWIS				25	O	CP	FRENCH	LAB	043	H	1	37
GODFREY	LEWIS				30	ENGLAND	BA	ENGLISH	COMMERCIAL TRAVELER	045	B	2	6
GODFREY	MARYANN		1	1	53	O	WM	ENGLISH		043	B	5	2
GODFRY	BARBARA		1	1	76	ENGLAND	PM	ENGLISH		045	D	3	66
GODFRY	DAVID		1		60	ONTARIO	CE	FRENCH	HOOP MAKER	043	G	1	17
GODSON	JOHN				63	ENGLAND	CE	ENGLISH	F	043	A	3	33
GODSON	THOMAS				28	O	WM	ENGLISH	F LAB	043	A	3	33
GODWIN	JOHN		1		21	O	CE	ENGLISH	BUTCHER	045	B	1	2
GODWIN	SARAH		1	1	27	ENGLAND	CE	ENGLISH	DRESS MAKER	045	B	1	2
GODWIN	THOMAS				27	ENGLAND	CE	ENGLISH	BUTCHER	045	B	2	21
GODWIN	WILLIAM				75	ENGLAND	CE	ENGLISH		044	C	2	29
GOFFIN	REBECCA		1	1	35	ENGLAND	BA	ENGLISH		043	G	1	19
GOGIN	ANNE		1	1	40	IRELAND	RC	IRISH	FARMER	043	G	1	28
GOHN	CHRISTOPHER				40	O	LU	GERMAN	FARMER	045	D	1	37
GOHN	GEORGE				30	O	LU	GERMAN	FARMER	045	D	1	37
GOHN	WILLIAM				49	O	LU	GERMAN	FARMER	045	D	1	29
GOLD	JOHN				40	ENGLAND	NR	ENGLISH	CARPENTER	045	D	6	77
GOLDEN	JONATHAN				27	O	WM	ENGLISH	FARMER	043	A	3	53
GOLDING	JOHN				38	ONTARIO	WM	IRISH	FARMER	044	C	3	51
GOLDSMITH	ALFRED				26	ENGLAND	CE	ENGLISH	MERCHANT	044	C	4	85
GOLDSMITH	SOPHIA		1	1	60	QUE	JU	GERMAN		044	C	4	66
GOLDTHORP	HANNAH		1	1	21	O	CE	ENGLISH	SERVANT	044	C	2	37

SURNAME	NAME1	NAME2	STRAY	SEX	AGE	BIRTHPL	RELIGION	ORIGIN	OCCUP	DIST	SUB_DIST	DIV	PAGE
GOLDTHORPE	BENJAMIN				39	0	CE	ENGLISH	F	044	A	1	26
GOLDTHORPE	HANNA		1	1	22	0	CE	ENGLISH	INMATE	045	B	1	73
GOLLINGER	CHRISTOPHER				68	0	WM	GERMAN	LAB	043	E	2	48
GOLLINGER	NELSON				27	0	CN	DUTCH	F	043	E	2	80
GOLLINGER	REUBEN				30	0	WM	DUTCH	WHEELWRIGHT	043	E	1	50
GOLLOWAY	WILLIAM				31	ENGLAND	WP	ENGLISH	F	043	B	1	33
GONBUR	ELIZA		1		30	0	RC	ENGLISH		043	H	2	21
GOOCH	ROBERT				36	ENGLAND	CE	ENGLISH	INSURANCE AGENT	044	C	4	79
GOOD	CHARLES			M	56	ENGLAND	NR	ENGLAND	F	043	A	5	37
GOOD	GEORGE				39	ENGLAND	CE			045	B	1	44
GOOD	JOHN				33	ENG	RC	ENG	LAB	044	B	2	12
GOOD	JOHN		1		18	0	CO		LAB	044	B	5	24
GOODCHILD	CHARLEY				36	ENGLAND	CE	ENGLISH	BUCHER	044	C	4	82
GOODDALE	ROBT				65	SCOTLAND	UP	SCOTCH	F	044	B	5	75
GOODE	FRANCIS		1		10	ONTARIO	CE	ENGLISH		043	G	1	41
GOODE	SEPTUS		2		78	ENGLAND	CE			043	G	1	D
GOODENOUGH	JOHN				68	ENGLAND	CE	ENGLISH	F	045	C	4	12
GOODERHAM	ALFRED				35	0	CE	ENGLISH	MILLER	044	B	5	10
GOODERHAM	THOMAS				40	ENGLAND	CC	ENGLISH	FARMER	045	A	3	20
GOODERHAM	WILLIAM				28	0	CP	ENGLISH	F	045	C	4	39
GOODFELLOW	AGNESS		1	1	23	0	CP	SCOTCH	INMATE	045	B	1	73
GOODGER	CHARLES				41	ENGLAND	CE	ENGLISH	LAB	043	H	2	3
GOODGER	CHARLES				41	ENGLAND	CE	ENGLISH	LABOURER	043	H	2	3
GOODMAN	HENRY		1		21	ENGLAND	CE	ENGLISH	F LAB	044	A	1	17
GOODRIDGE	ELIZABETH		1	1	16	0	WM	IRISH		044	C	2	13
GOODRIDGE	FRANCIS				44	IRELAND	CE	ENGLISH	LABOURER	044	C	3	57
GOODSON	DAVID		1		25	ENGLAND	BA	ENGLISH	LABORER	043	G	1	15
GOODWIN	ARTHUR				44	IRELAND	CE	IRISH	F	043	E	3	4
GOODWIN	HERBERT				29	ENGLAND	CE	ENGLISH	F	043	A	6	13
GOODWIN	JOHN		1		42	ENGLAND	CE	ENGLISH	LAB	043	D		17
GOODYEAR	ROBERT				35	ENG	EP	ENG	F	044	B	2	1
GOOFELOW	SARAH			F	55	0	CP	SCOTCH		043	A	2	29
GORDEN	ELIXANDER				38	SCOTLAND	CP	SCOTCH	SECTION BOSS ON RAIL	044	C	3	37
GORDEN	JOHN				40	SCOTLAND	CP	SCOTCH		044	C	3	37
GORDI	WILLIAM				50	ENGLAND	CE	ENGLISH	LAB	043	B	1	38
GORDINIER	JAMES	B			27	ONTARIO	EM	GERMAN	BLACKSMITH	043	G	1	23
GORDMEER	JOHN	W			48	0	PM	GERMAN	MAIL CARRIER	043	E	2	70
GORDON	ALEXANDER				35	IRE	WM	IRE	LAB	044	B	2	71
GORDON	ALEXANDER	J	1	1	14	0	WM	SCOTTISH		044	C	1	3
GORDON	ANDREW			M	33	0	WM	SCOTCH	F	043	A	2	40
GORDON	ANNE		1	1	18	0	CE	SCOTCH	SERVANT	045	A	2	34
GORDON	CHARLES		1		20	0	WM	IRISH		045	D	2	58
GORDON	ENOS		1	M	19	0	FK	SCOTLAND		043	A	5	22
GORDON	GEORGE				64	ENGLAND	CE	ENGLISH		045	B	1	65
GORDON	GEORGE	A	1		0	0	WM	SCOTTISH		044	C	1	3
GORDON	HENRY				26	0	EM	ENG	F	044	B	4	30
GORDON	ISAAC			M	43	0	WM	SCOTLAND	F	043	A	5	15
GORDON	ISAAC				70	US	EM	SCOT	F	044	B	4	30
GORDON	JAMES			M	51	0	PM	SCOTCH	F	043	A	2	23
GORDON	JOHN				58	SCOTLAND	NR	SCOTCH	F	043	A	6	2
GORDON	JOHN		1		16	U STATES	WM	IRISH	LAB	043	B	1	19
GORDON	JOHN	WM			45	SCOT	CE	SCOT	TOLLKEEPER	045	C	1	35
GORDON	JOSEPH				79	IRE	PS	IRISH	F	044	B	2	73
GORDON	MAY-JANE		1	1	17	0	WM	SCOTTISH		044	C	1	3
GORDON	ROBERT			M	32	IRELAND	PS	IRISH	LAB	043	A	1	55
GORDON	ROBERT				54	0	WM	SCOTCH	F	044	B	1	2
GORDON	THOMAS				50	IRE	PS	IRISH	LAB	044	B	2	72
GORDON	WILLIAM		1		30	ENGLAND	CE	SCOTCH	SERVANT	043	A	6	63
GORDON	WILLIAM	J	1		12	0	WM	SCOTTISH		044	C	1	3
GORE	JAMES				56	IRELAND	RC	IRISH	F LAB	044	A	1	18
GORHAM	CHARLES				53	0	CS	ENGLISH	GENTLEMAN	043	D		53
GORHAM	NELSON				59	ONT	CE	ENGLISH	MANUFACTURER	043	D		54
GORMAN	JOHN				56	IRE	RC	IRE	LAB	045	C	1	48
GORMAN	JOHN				41	IRELAND	RC	IRISH	FARMER	045	D	2	41
GORMAN	MARY	A	1	1	14	0	RC	IRISH	INMATE	045	B	1	72
GORMAN	WILLIAM				33	IRELAND	RC	IRISH	F	044	C	2	2
GORMLEY	JAMES		1		72	IRELAND	RC	IRISH		043	B	1	2
GORMLEY	JAMES				54	IRELAND	CP	IRISH	FARMER	045	D	4	26
GORMLEY	JOHN				39	IRELAND	NG	IRISH	FARMER	045	D	3	12
GORMLEY	PATRICK				37	IRELAND	RC	IRISH	BLACKSMITH	045	D	2	64
GORWILL	SUSANNA		1	1	22	ENGLAND	WM	ENGLISH		045	C	3	45
GOSLINE	PETER				47	US	CP	FRENCH	LAB	045	C	2	19
GOSLING	JAMES			M	27	ENGLAND	CE	ENGLISH	LAB	043	A	2	52
GOSMAN	MURRY				35	NOVA SCOTIA	WM	ENGLISH	LABOURER	045	A	1	49
GOUBUR	ELIZA			1	30	ONTARIO	RC	ENGLISH		043	H	2	21
GOUGH	ALEXANDER				49	0	CP	SCOTCH	MASTER COOPER	044	B	6	57
GOUGH	BRIDGET			1	56	IRELAND	RC	IRISH		044	C	3	32
GOUGH	THOMAS		1		19	0	RC	IRISH	SERVANT	044	C	3	31
GOUGH	WILLIAM				28	IRELAND	CE	IRISH	LAB	043	H	1	27
GOULD	ALBERT				42	0	WM	IRISH	SAWER & CARDER	043	E	3	46
GOULD	CHARLES				26	0	PM	ENGLISH	LABOURER	045	D	6	13
GOULD	DAVID				32	0	CS	ENGLISH	INNKEEPER	044	B	6	17
GOULD	HUGH				30	IRELAND	CP	IRISH	LABOURER	043	A	4	60
GOULD	JAMES				32	IRELAND	CP	IRISH	FARMER	043	A	4	60
GOULD	JAMES				39	IRELAND	PS	IRISH	MASON	044	B	5	43
GOULD	JOHN				64	IRELAND	CP	IRISH	FARMER	043	A	4	59
GOULD	JOHN			M	43	0	FK	IRELAND	F	043	A	5	40
GOULD	JOHN				65	ENGLAND	BA	ENGLISH	LABOURER	043	B	3	3
GOULD	SAMUEL				51	0	WM	ENGLISH	F LAB	043	A	6	20
GOULD	THOMAS				46	IRELAND	FK	IRISH	HOTELKEEPER	043	A	3	23
GOULDING	EDWARD				30	0	RC	IRISH	F	044	C	1	34
GOULDING	JOHN		1		23	0	WM	IRISH	LAB	044	C	1	48
GOULDING	MICHAEL				59	IRELAND	RC	IRISH	F	044	C	1	32
GOULDING	WILLIAM				45	0	WM	IRISH	F	045	A	4	29
GOULETT	DENNIS		1		22	QUE	CE	FRENCH	WAY MASTER	045	A	1	9
GOUNT	MARY		1	1	9	0	WM	ENGLISH		043	B	4	4
GOURLAY	CONSTANCE		1	1	9	SCOTLAND	CP	SCOTCH		045	B	1	48
GOURLAY	REBECCA		1	1	35	MALTA	CP	ENGLISH	PRIVATE GOVERNESS	045	B	1	48
GOVE	REBECCA			1	50	ENGLAND	CE	ENGLISH		045	B	2	7
GOWDY	WILLIAM				75	IRELAND	WM	IRISH	LAB	044	C	4	86
GOWER	AGNES		1	F	19	0	WM	ENGLAND		043	A	5	16
GOWER	AMELIA		1	1	18	0	WM	GERMAN	SERVANT	043	D		14
GOWER	BENJAMIN				22	0	BA	GERMAN	LAB	043	B	2	26
GOWER	GEORGE				51	ENGLAND	CE	ENGLISH	COOPER	043	B	3	71
GOWER	MARY		1	1	21	0	WM	ENG	SERVANT	044	B	2	11
GOWER	NORMAN		1		15	0	QU	GERMAN	F LAB AND SERVANT	043	B	4	42

SURNAME	NAME1	NAME2	STRAY	SEX	AGE	BIRTHPL	RELIGION	ORIGIN	OCCUP	DIST	SUB_DIST	DIV	PAGE
GOWER	PHILIP				60	UNITED STATES	CE	GERMAN	F	043	B	2	27
GOWER	RICHARD				63	UNITED STATES	CN	GERMAN	LAB	043	B	2	32
GOWER	ROBERT		1		15	0	QU	ENGLISH	F	043	A	6	11
GOWER	SARAH		1	1	22	0	WM	GERMAN	SERVANT	045	D	2	33
GOWER	WM				25	0	CP	ENG	BLACKSMITH	045	C	1	68
GOWLAND	MAT				59	ENGLAND	WM	ENGLISH	F	044	B	5	58
GRACE	JANE		1	1	14	0	EM	ENGLISH		043	A	6	33
GRACE	JOHN	J	1		18	0	EM	ENGLISH	LAB	043	A	6	33
GRACE	THOMAS		1		12	0	EM	ENGLISH		043	A	6	33
GRACE	WILLIAM	H	1		16	0	EM	ENGLISH	LAB	043	A	6	33
GRACEY	ALEXANDER				57	IRELAND	RC	IRISH	F	044	A	3	47
GRACEY	HANS				38	0	CE	IRISH	F	044	A	2	33
GRACEY	JAMES				60	IRELAND	PM	IRISH	F	044	A	2	15
GRACEY	JAMES	BOOTH			55	0	CE	IRISH	F	044	A	3	5
GRACEY	JOHN				57	IRELAND	PM	IRISH	F	044	A	2	24
GRACEY	JOSEPH				48	0	PM	IRISH	F	044	A	2	17
GRACY	JOHN			M	63	IRELAND	PS	IRISH	WEAVER	043	A	2	10
GRACY	NORRA		1	1	18	0	RC	IRISH	SCHOOL TEACHER	044	C	3	23
GRAFTON	CHARLES				31	IRELAND	RC	IRISH	LAB	044	C	4	57
GRAFTON	CHARLES				60	IRELAND	RC	IRISH	LAB	044	C	4	57
GRAFTON	FRANCES		1	1	77	IRELAND	WM	IRISH		045	A	2	17
GRAGE	WILLIAM				29	0	WM	ENGLISH	LAB	043	E	3	12
GRAHAM	ADAM				72	0	CP	SCOTCH	GARDENER	043	B	1	1
GRAHAM	ALEXANDER				30	SCOTLAND	WM	SCOTCH	WEAVER	043	A	4	35
GRAHAM	ALEXANDER		1		30	0	CP	SCOTCH	BOOK KEEPER	045	C	3	57
GRAHAM	ALFRED				30	0	WM	SCOTCH	F	043	B	1	1
GRAHAM	ALLEN				45	ENGLAND	CE	ENGLISH	F	043	E	3	32
GRAHAM	ANDREW		2		66	0	CN		FARMER	043	B	3	D
GRAHAM	ANDREW				39	IRELAND	CP	IRISH	F	043	H	1	25
GRAHAM	ANDREW				30	IRE	CE	IRE	LAB	045	C	1	40
GRAHAM	ANDREW				54	SCOTLAND	CS	SCOTCH	FARMER	045	D	3	15
GRAHAM	ANDREW		1		24	0	WM	IRISH	F	044	C	2	31
GRAHAM	ANN			1	66	0	CE	SCOTCH		043	D		53
GRAHAM	ANTHONY				34	ONTARIO	RC	ENGLISH	FARMER	043	G	2	22
GRAHAM	ANTHONY				34	ENGLAND	RC	ENGLISH	BLACKSMITH	045	D	5	53
GRAHAM	CHARLES				34	SCOTLAND	WM	SCOTCH	BLACKSMITH	043	A	3	11
GRAHAM	CHARLES		1		32	0	ZZ	IRISH	DENTIST	043	E	2	85
GRAHAM	DAVID				43	ONTARIO	CN	SCOTCH	FARMER	043	G	2	1
GRAHAM	DELILAH			1	59	UNITED STATES	CN	GERMAN		043	B	3	72
GRAHAM	DONALD				63	SCOTLAND	CP	SCOTCH	FARMER	043	A	4	28
GRAHAM	ELIZA			1	26	IRELAND	RC	IRISH		044	C	2	49
GRAHAM	ELIZABETH		1	1	14	0	CN	IRISH		043	B	3	20
GRAHAM	ELIZABETH		1	1	72	UNITED STATES	CS	GERMAN		043	D		13
GRAHAM	ELIZABETH		1	1	3	0	ZZ	IRISH		043	E	1	45
GRAHAM	FRANCES		1	F	22	0	WM	IRELAND		043	A	5	5
GRAHAM	GEO	L			40	0	CP	SCOTCH	TAVERN KEEPER	043	C		35
GRAHAM	GEO	W			45	N BRUNSWICK	WM	IRISH	CARPENTER	043	C		21
GRAHAM	GEORGE				58	ENGLAND	CE	ENGLISH	FARMER	045	D	3	78
GRAHAM	HENRY				25	ENGLAND	RC	ENGLISH	F & TRAPPER	043	A	6	22
GRAHAM	HENRY				29	0	CN	GERMAN	FARM LABOURER	043	B	3	70
GRAHAM	JAMES		1	M	45	IRELAND	PR	IRISH	LAB	043	A	1	74
GRAHAM	JAMES				36	SCOTLAND	WM	SCOTCH	WEAVER	043	A	4	22
GRAHAM	JAMES				30	IRELAND	RC	IRISH	LAB	044	C	2	48
GRAHAM	JANE		1	1	28	IRELAND	TU	IRISH	SERVANT	043	B	2	4
GRAHAM	JANE			1	55	IRE	WM	IRE	WASHER WOMAN	044	B	4	38
GRAHAM	JEREMIAH				64	UNITED STATES	CN	IRISH	F	043	E	1	46
GRAHAM	JOHN				42	SCOTLAND	CS	SCOTCH	WEAVER	043	A	4	10
GRAHAM	JOHN				45	0	WM	SCOTTISH	F	043	B	4	37
GRAHAM	JOHN				35	IRELAND	PM	IRISH	SADDLER	043	E	1	39
GRAHAM	JOHN				60	UNITED STATES	PS	IRISH	JOINER	043	E	2	14
GRAHAM	JOHN				60	IRELAND	WM	IRISH	F	043	E	3	1
GRAHAM	JOHN				37	IRELAND	RP	IRISH	F	043	H	1	25
GRAHAM	JOHN				32	0	WM	ENG	F	044	B	2	63
GRAHAM	JOHN		1		50	IRE	RC	IRE	LAB	044	B	3	42
GRAHAM	JOHN		1		45	IRELAND	CE	IRISH	LAB	044	C	1	46
GRAHAM	JOHN	D			25	0	ZZ	IRISH	MUSICIAN	043	E	1	54
GRAHAM	JOSEPH				26	0	WM	ENG	F	044	B	1	65
GRAHAM	JOSEPH				31	0	CE	ENGLISH	FARMER	045	D	3	53
GRAHAM	JOSEPH				78	ENGLAND	CE	ENGLISH	FARMER	045	D	6	6
GRAHAM	JULIA		2	1	40	CANADA	CE			043	C		D
GRAHAM	MARTHA		1	1	58	IRELAND	NG	IRISH		044	B	5	53
GRAHAM	MARY			1	65	ENGLAND	CE	ENGLISH		044	C	4	32
GRAHAM	NEHEMIAH		1		45	IRELAND	CE	IRISH	SERVANT	043	A	4	29
GRAHAM	OWEN				80	IRELAND	RC	IRISH	LAB	044	C	2	53
GRAHAM	PETER				43	0	WM	SCOTTISH	F	043	B	4	26
GRAHAM	RICHARD				61	0	CN	GERMAN	FARMER	043	B	3	45
GRAHAM	RICHARD				60	IRELAND	CE	SCOTCH	F	043	H	1	10
GRAHAM	RICHD		1		81	IRELAND	CN	IRISH	GENT	043	E	2	54
GRAHAM	SARAH			1	64	ENGLAND	CE	ENGLISH		044	B	6	41
GRAHAM	THOMAS				53	ENGLAND	PM	ENGLISH	F	044	A	3	14
GRAHAM	WILLIAM				63	0	ZZ	IRISH	F	043	E	1	45
GRAHAM	WILLIAM				42	0	CN	IRISH	CARPENTER	043	E	1	49
GRAHAM	WILLIAM				60	IRELAND	CE	IRISH	F	043	H	1	38
GRAHAM	WILLIAM				67	ENG	CE	ENG	F	044	B	1	56
GRAHAME	HUGH	B			47	IRELAND	RC	IRISH	FARMER	043	A	4	62
GRAHAME	JAMES				33	0	PS	SCOTCH	F	044	B	5	45
GRAHAME	JANE		1	1	33	IRELAND	CE	IRISH	SERVANT	044	C	2	34
GRAHAME	THOMAS				34	0	PS	SCOT	GENT	044	B	3	48
GRAINGER	EDMUND				45	ENGLAND	WM	ENGLISH	BUTCHER	045	B	1	6
GRAINGER	FREDERIC			M	32	0	CE	ENGLISH	LAB	043	A	1	48
GRAINGER	JOHN			M	65	ENGLAND	CE	ENGLISH	LAB	043	A	1	48
GRAINGER	JOHN		1		30	ENGLAND	CE	ENGLISH	BUTCHER	043	E	1	17
GRAINGER	JOSEPH				48	ENG	VM	ENG	TAILOR	044	B	2	5
GRAINGER	OLIVER				28	0	WM	ENGLISH	GARDENER	044	C	2	21
GRAINGER	THOMAS				42	ENGLAND	WM	ENGLISH	F	045	A	2	24
GRAINGER	WILLIAM			M	38	ENGLAND	CE	ENGLISH	LAB	043	A	1	48
GRAINGER	WILLIAM				48	ENGLAND	WM	ENGLISH	BUTCHER	045	B	1	14
GRAM	CATHERINE			1	65	0	EM	GERMAN		044	C	1	6
GRAM	JOHN				35	0	EM	GERMAN	CARRIAGE MAKER	044	C	1	7
GRAMAN	JOHN				31	IRELAND	RC	IRISH	F	045	A	4	21
GRAME	WILLIAM				64	NS	WM	ENGLISH	LAB	045	A	4	19
GRANGER	CHARLOTTE		1	1	27	0	EM	GERMAN		043	E	2	32
GRANGER	EMMA		1	1	17	QUEBEC	PM	IRISH		043	B	1	28
GRANGER	GEORGE		1		21	0	PM	ENG	FARM SERVANT	044	B	4	47
GRANGER	HENRY				34	0	CE	IRISH	F LAB	043	B	4	15
GRANGER	JOHN		1		22	ENGLAND	CE	ENGLISH	SERVANT	043	C		24

SURNAME	NAME1	NAME2	STRAY	SEX	AGE	BIRTHPL	RELIGION	ORIGIN	OCCUP	DIST	SUB_DIST	DIV	PAGE
GRANGER	JOHN				59	ENGLAND	WM	ENGLISH	GARDNER	044	C	4	53
GRANGER	JOHN	EDWARD	1			0	EM	GERMAN		043	E	2	32
GRANGER	JOSEPH		1		9	0	EM	GERMAN		043	E	2	32
GRANGER	WILLIAM				32	0	CE	GERMAN	LAB	043	E	2	42
GRANGER	WILLIAM				40	ENGLAND	CE	ENGLISH	FARMER	045	D	4	13
GRANT	CHARLES		1			SCOTLAND	RC		FARM SERVANT	045	C	3	50
GRANT	EMANUEL				40	ENGLAND	CN	ENGLISH	F	043	E	1	30
GRANT	GEORGE				39	0	CP	SCOTLAND	FARMER	045	D	2	30
GRANT	JAMES				37	SCOTLAND	CP	SCOTCH	FARMER	045	A	2	29
GRANT	JAMES		1		26	SCOTLAND	CP	SCOTCH	FARM LABOURER	045	C	4	31
GRANT	JAMES				51	SCOTLAND	PS	SCOTCH	WATCH MAKER	045	D	6	42
GRANT	JESSE				40	ENG	WM	ENG	GROCER	044	B	2	16
GRANT	JOHN		1	M	45	SCOTLAND	PS	SCOTCH	LAB	043	A	2	39
GRANT	JOHN		1		40	0	RC	SCOTCH	F LAB	044	A	1	14
GRANT	JOHN				50	SCOTLAND	PS	SCOTCH	FARMER	045	D	6	28
GRANT	MACEY		1	1	19	0	PM	SCOTCH	SERVANT	044	A	3	52
GRAVES	EMMA		1	1	19	US	CE	ENGLISH		044	C	4	57
GRAY	ABRAHAM		1	M	25	US	BA	ENGLISH	MILL WRIGHT	043	A	5	7
GRAY	ALEXANDER				64	SCOTLAND	OP	SCOTCH	FARMER	045	A	3	22
GRAY	ALLEN				68	ENGLAND	WM	ENGLISH	GENTLEMAN	044	C	3	18
GRAY	DAVID				42	SCOTLAND	CP	SCOTCH	BLACKSMITH	045	A	4	30
GRAY	EDWARD				34	IRELAND	WM	IRISH	FARMER	043	B	3	45
GRAY	ELIZABETH		1	1	15	0	PM	IRISH		043	B	5	24
GRAY	JAMES				34	IRELAND	PM	IRISH	FARMER	043	B	3	16
GRAY	JAMES				31	IRELAND	CE	IRISH	F	043	B	5	13
GRAY	JAMES				46	ENGLAND	CE	ENGLISH	LAB	043	F		2
GRAY	JOHN				45	ENGLAND	WM	ENGLISH	F LAB	043	B	5	32
GRAY	JOHN				44	SCOT	PS	SCOT	MILLWRIGHT	044	B	2	36
GRAY	JOHN		1		18	0	WM	ENG	LAB	044	B	3	43
GRAY	JOHN				47	ENGLAND	BA	ENGLISH	MERCHANT	045	B	2	23
GRAY	JOHN				59	IRELAND	CE	IRISH	NURSERY MAN	044	C	4	38
GRAY	JOHN	JR			34	0	CE	IRISH	NURSERYMAN	044	C	4	59
GRAY	JOSEPH		1		11	0	PM	ENG	LAB	044	B	3	14
GRAY	JOSEPH				29	0	CP	SCOTCH	FARMER	045	A	3	33
GRAY	JOSEPH		1		17	0	WM	IRISH	F	044	C	1	33
GRAY	MARY		1	1	17	0	PM	IRISH		043	B	5	24
GRAY	MARY		1	1	57	0	WM	DUTCH		043	H	1	32
GRAY	MARY		2	1	72	ENGLAND	WM			045	A	1	D
GRAY	RICHARD				71	ENGLAND	PM	ENGLISH	LAB	043	F		21
GRAY	ROBERT				41	IRELAND	PM	IRISH	F	043	B	5	17
GRAY	ROBERT				37	ENGLAND	PM	ENGLISH	F	045	C	3	8
GRAY	ROBINSON				27	0	CE	ENGLISH	FARM LABOURER	045	D	3	12
GRAY	SAMUEL		1		58	ENGLAND	WM	ENGLISH		043	H	1	32
GRAY	THOMAS				34	ENGLAND	CE	ENGLISH	TEAMSTER	043	F		14
GRAY	THOMAS				29	0	WM	SCOTCH	FARMER	045	A	3	25
GRAY	WILLIAM				61	IRELAND	PS	IRISH	LABOURER	043	B	3	21
GRAY	WILLIAM				91	IRELAND	CP	IRISH		043	B	5	24
GRAY	WILLIAM				47	ENGLAND	WM	ENGLISH	BUTCHER	045	A	1	94
GRAY	WILLIAM				68	SCOTLAND	FK	SCOTCH	FARMER	045	A	3	27
GRAY	WILLIAM				39	SCOTLAND	CP	SCOTCH	BLACKSMITH	044	C	2	30
GRAY	WILLIAM				54	ENGLAND	CE	ENGLISH	LAB	044	C	3	5
GRAY	WM		1		14	0	LU	GER	F	044	B	4	25
GREAVES	JOHN				62	ENG	CE	ENG	LAB	044	B	1	40
GREEN	BARNABAS				38	ENGLAND	CE	ENGLISH	LABORER	045	D	1	8
GREEN	BEATRICE		1	1	11	ONTARIO	WM	IRISH		043	H	2	40
GREEN	BETRICE		1	1	11	0	WM	IRISH		043	H	2	40
GREEN	ELISEBETH			1	73	ENGLAND	CE	ENGLISH		043	A	6	25
GREEN	ELIZA		1	1	65	IRELAND	CE	IRISH		043	A	4	5
GREEN	GEORGE	W			31	ENGLAND	PM	ENGLISH	FARM LABOURER	043	E	2	40
GREEN	HENRY		1		55	ENGLAND	CE	ENGLISH	HOSTLER	043	C		29
GREEN	HENRY				29	IRELAND	PS	IRISH	GARDNER	044	C	4	68
GREEN	JAMES				50	ENGLAND	CE	ENGLISH	F	045	C	2	14
GREEN	JAMES				56	SCOTLAND	PS	SCOTCH	F	045	C	3	52
GREEN	JAMES				36	SCOTLAND	CP	SCOTCH	LAB	044	C	2	53
GREEN	JAMES	J N			64	ENGLAND	PM	ENGLISH	CARPENTER	045	A	1	105
GREEN	JOHN			M	37	0	CN	GERMAN	WELL DIGGER	043	A	5	14
GREEN	JOHN				66	UNITED STATES	CE	AFRICAN	LAB	043	E	2	82
GREEN	JOSEPH				43	US	WM	ENGLISH	STATION MASTER	044	C	4	75
GREEN	MARIA		1	1	27	IRELAND	WM	IRISH	INMATE	045	B	1	72
GREEN	SUSANNAH			F	47	0	WM	GERMAN		043	A	5	14
GREEN	WILLIAM				36	ENGLAND	WM	ENGLISH	BRICK MAKER	045	B	1	54
GREEN	WILLIAM				23	0	PS	SCOTCH	F	045	C	3	52
GREENBERRY	ROBERT				36	CANADA	PM	ENGLISH	PEDLAR	045	D	6	49
GREENBERRY	WILLIAM				28	ENGLAND	DI	ENGLISH	LAB	043	B	2	38
GREENE	WILLIAM				50	ENGLAND	CE	ENGLISH	LAB	045	B	1	34
GREENEWAY	MARY	JANE	1	1	5	0	PS	IRISH		045	D	6	12
GREENFIELD	JAMES				39	IRELAND	WM	IRISH	FARMER	043	B	3	8
GREENFIELD	MARY		1	1	25	IRELAND	RC	IRISH	SERVANT	045	B	2	34
GREENSIDES	JOHN				34	0	PM	ENGLISH	BRICK MAKER	045	B	1	64
GREENSIDES	WILLIAM				32	0	PM	ENGLISH	BRICK MAKER	045	B	1	63
GREENWOOD	ANTHONY				40	QUEBEC	RC	FRENCH	LAB	043	H	1	41
GREENWOOD	CATHARINE			1	39	IRELAND	CE	IRISH	HOTEL KEEPER	045	A	1	19
GREENWOOD	JOHN				83	ENGLAND	CE	ENGLISH	F	043	E	2	24
GREENWOOD	JOHN				50	ENGLAND	CN	ENGLISH	F	043	E	2	51
GREENWOOD	JOHN				22	0	EM	ENGLISH	F	043	E	2	52
GREENWOOD	WILLIAM				59	ENG	CE	ENG	F	044	B	2	55
GREENWOOD	WM				49	ENGLAND	CE	ENGLISH	F	043	E	2	72
GREER	MICHAEL				29	IRELAND	CE	IRISH	MILLER	043	H	1	35
GREGG	ALEX		1		26	SCOTLAND	PS	SCOTCH	LAB	045	C	2	32
GREGG	JAMES				29	0	WM	SCOTLAND	IRON MOULDER	045	D	2	10
GREGG	ROBERT				33	SCOTLAND	CS	SCOTCH	F	043	E	2	59
GREGORY	ANDREW				36	IRELAND	PM	IRISH	F	044	A	3	52
GREGORY	DANIEL				32	ENGLAND	CE	ENGLISH	MANAGER OF SAWMILL	043	F		23
GREGORY	GEORGE		1		22	ENGLAND	PM	ENGLISH	FARM LABOURER	045	C	4	41
GREGORY	JOHN				57	ENGLAND	FW	ENGLISH	GARDNER	045	D	6	22
GREGORY	MARY	ELIZABETH	1	1	6	0	WM	IRISH		044	C	2	14
GREGORY	THOMAS				69	ENGLAND	CE	ENGLISH	MILLER	043	B	1	6
GREGORY	WM				29	ENGLAND	CE	ENGLISH	PAINTER	044	B	5	42
GREGORY	WM				29	IRELAND	CE	ENGLISH	PAINTER	044	B	5	43
GREGORY	WM		1		24	ENG	WM	ENG	SERVANT	045	C	1	13
GREIG	JAMES		1	M	14	0	PS	SCOTCH		043	A	2	13
GREIGIE	EDWARD		1		20	ENGLAND	CE	ENGLISH	LAB	045	C	2	24
GREY	ALBERT		1		32	0	WM	WELSH	LABOURER	043	A	4	39
GREY	CAROLINE		1	1	24	0	WM	WELSH		043	A	4	39
GREY	ELIZABETH		1	1	7	0	WM	WELSH		043	A	4	39
GREY	JAMES				45	0	CP	SCOTCH	FARMER	045	A	3	22

SURNAME	NAME1	NAME2	STRAY	SEX	AGE	BIRTHPL	RELIGION	ORIGIN	OCCUP	DIST	SUB_DIST	DIV	PAGE
GREY	JOHN				25	0	CE	ENGLISH	LAB	044	B	5	5
GREY	JOHN				71	SCOTLAND	CP	SCOTCH	FARMER	045	A	3	21
GREY	MARGARET		1	1	21	0	CE	ENGLISH	SERVANT	045	D	2	7
GREY	RACHEL		1	1	23	0	WM	WELSH		043	A	4	39
GREY	ROBERT				45	0	CP	SCOTCH	CARPENTER	045	A	3	18
GREY	ROBERT		1		23	0	CE	ENGLISH	LABORER	045	D	2	7
GREY	ROBERT	0			26	0	WM	IRELAND	SCHOOL TEACHER	045	D	2	28
GREY	SARAH		1	1	40	IRELAND	RC	IRISH		043	E	1	6
GREY	THOMAS			M	32	0	UP	SCOTCH	MERCHANT	043	A	2	45
GREY	WILLIAM				60	ENGLAND	CE	ENGLISH	LAB	044	B	5	13
GREY	WILLIAM				45	0	WM	GERMAN	LABOURER	045	D	4	39
GREY	WM				30	0	CE	ENGLISH	LAB	044	B	5	17
GREY	WM				34	0	CE	ENGLISH	LAB	044	B	5	22
GRICE	BENJAMIN				27	ENGLAND	WM	ENGLISH	COOPER	045	D	1	10
GRICE	GEORGE				51	ENGLAND	CE	ENGLISH	F	043	A	6	16
GRICE	JOSEPH				61	ENGLAND	WM	ENGLISH	CARPENTER	045	D	1	10
GRICE	WILLIAM				33	0	CE	ENGLISH	F	043	A	6	42
GRIDALL	EDWARD				30	ENGLAND	CE	ENGLISH	PUMPMAKER	043	E	3	21
GRIEVE	SOPHIA			1	43	SAXONY	CE	GERMAN		043	D		30
GRIEVE	WALTER		2		57	SCOTLAND	CS		FARMER	043	D		D
GRIFFIN	ANNA		1	1	21	IRELAND	RC	IRISH	SERVANT	045	B	2	17
GRIFFIN	EDWARD		1		50	ENGLAND	CE	ENGLISH	LAB	045	A	3	34
GRIFFIN	HUBBARD		1		18	ENGLAND	QU	ENGLISH	F	043	E	2	4
GRIFFIN	JOHN				46	IRELAND	RC	IRISH	F	043	H	1	12
GRIFFIN	MICHAEL				55	IRELAND	RC	IRISH	TAILOR	044	C	4	41
GRIFFIN	WILLIAM		1		34	U STATES	CE	ENGLISH	BAR KEEPER	043	D		69
GRIFFITH	ABRAHAM				33	0	CE	ENGLISH	FARMER	044	C	3	70
GRIFFITH	ANNE		1	1	14	IRELAND	CP	IRISH	SERVANT	044	C	2	24
GRIFFITH	CHRISTOPHER				52	IRELAND	CE	IRISH	F	043	H	2	8
GRIFFITH	CHRISTOPHER				52	IRELAND	CE	IRISH	FARMER	043	H	2	8
GRIFFITH	HUGH		1		19	0	CE	IRISH	FARM LAB	044	C	2	35
GRIFFITH	JAMES				30	0	CE	IRISH	FARMER	044	C	3	73
GRIFFITH	JOSEPH				69	IRELAND	CE	IRISH	FARMER	044	C	3	68
GRIFFITH	MARTHA			1	45	IRELAND	CE	IRISH	F	044	C	1	49
GRIFFITH	ROBERT	E			60	IRELAND	CE	ENGLISH	CLERK	045	A	1	73
GRIFFITH	THOMAS				74	IRELAND	CE	IRISH	FARMER	044	C	3	68
GRIFFITH	THOMAS				29	0	CE	IRISH	FARMER	044	C	3	71
GRIFFITH	WILLIAM				56	IRELAND	CE	IRISH	LAB	044	C	2	30
GRILLS	CHARLES				41	ENGLAND	CE	ENGLISH	MISSIONARY TEACHER	043	H	2	58
GRILLS	CHARLES				41	ENGLAND	CE	ENGLISH	TEACHER	043	H	2	58
GRIMASON	ROBERT				50	IRELAND	CP	IRISH	LAB	045	B	1	43
GRIMETT	RICHARD				32	ENGLAND	CE	ENGLISH	FARMER	045	A	3	14
GRIMSBY	HENRY				45	ENGLAND	CE	ENGLISH	LAB	044	C	4	78
GRIMSHAW	J	JOSEPH			27	ENGLAND	PM	ENGLISH	F	043	B	1	12
GRIMSHAW	WILLIAM				25	0	WM	ENGLISH	F	043	B	1	12
GRISE	FRANCIS				25	0	CE	ENGLISH	F LAB	043	B	4	43
GRIST	JAMES		1		23	ENG	WM	ENG	BLACKSMITH	044	B	2	3
GROGAN	BARNEY				36	IRELAND	RC	IRISH	LAB	044	C	4	93
GROGAN	JAMES				50	IRELAND	RC	IRISH	F	044	C	4	94
GROGAN	JOHN				37	IRELAND	CE	IRISH	BOOT AND SHOEMAKER	045	A	1	45
GROGAN	ROBERT				35	IRELAND	CE	IRISH	F	043	H	1	8
GROLTON	MARY		1	1	40	IRELAND	RC	IRISH	SERVANT	043	D		2
GROLTON	RICHARD		1		21	0	RC	IRISH	CARPENTER	043	D		2
GROOVE	DAVID		2			0	NG		F LAB	045	D	6	D
GROOVE	JOHN		1		18	0	MN	GERMAN	F LAB	043	B	5	16
GROSE	JOHN				34	ENGLAND	NG	ENGLISH	F	043	B	5	7
GROSE	WILLIAM				43	ENGLAND	CN	ENGLISH	F	043	E	3	4
GROSKURTH	AUGUST				43	GERMANY	LU	GERMAN	CABINET MAKER	044	B	6	55
GROUT	ROXCY		1	1	72	U STATES	DI	IRISH		043	A	6	46
GROVE	ABRAHAM				43	0	MN	GERMAN	FARMER	045	D	6	14
GROVE	ABRAHAM	S			35	0	MN	GERMAN	FARMER	045	D	6	6
GROVE	JACOB				30	0	MN	GERMAN	SHINGLE MAKER	043	B	5	23
GROVE	JACOB				35	0	MN	GERMAN	FARMER	045	D	6	6
GROVE	JOSEPH				24	CANADA	MN	GERMAN	FARMER	045	D	6	39
GROVER	F	CHARLES	1		16	0	CO	ENGLISH	CLERK	043	D		11
GROVES	HENRY				37	ENGLAND	CN	ENGLISH	CARPENTER	043	G	1	45
GROVES	JOSEPH		1		37	ENGLAND	CE	ENGLISH	SERVANT	045	B	2	20
GROVES	MATTIE		1	1	20	0	MN	GERMAN		045	D	4	49
GROW	SOLOMON		1		22	ENGLAND	CE	ENGLISH	LAB	043	B	1	26
GRUBBE	JESSIE			1	40	SCOTLAND	CE	SCOTCH		044	A	3	55
GRUBBE	WILLIAM				60	SCOTLAND	CP	SCOTCH	F	044	A	3	17
GRUNGH	MARY		1	1	24	ENGLAND	CE	ENGLISH	SERVT	044	B	5	59
GUARDHOUSE	JAMES				37	ENGLAND	BA	ENGLISH	F	044	A	3	52
GUARDHOUSE	THOMAS				44	ENGLAND	PM	ENGLISH	WAGON MAKER	044	A	3	50
GUERUES	WM				23	ENGLAND	PM	ENGLISH	LAB	044	B	5	55
GUILLIAT	WILLIAM				42	ENGLAND	CP	ENGLISH	F	044	A	3	55
GUILROY	JOHN		1		19	0	EM	SCOTCH		045	A	3	9
GUINET	MICHAEL				24	Q	RC	FRENCH	LAB	043	A	6	64
GUNDY	CHRISTIANNA			1	35	SCOTLAND	CP	SCOTCH	TEACHER	045	B	2	12
GUNDY	SAMUEL				38	IRELAND	NC	IRISH	MINISTER	043	C		7
GUNN	DANIEL				46	SCOT	CS	SCOT	F	044	B	4	16
GUNN	GEORGE				31	ENGLAND	CE	ENGLISH	LAB	045	C	2	52
GUNN	HENRY				30	ENGLAND	CE	ENGLISH	LABOURER	045	D	5	44
GUNSTEAD	JOSEPH				39	IRELAND	CE	IRISH	F	043	B	1	31
GUNTHER	EDMUND				40	GERMANY	PS	GERMAN	JEWELLER	044	C	4	69
GUSSTON	JOHN				45	ENGLAND	EM	ENGLISH	LAB	043	D		23
GUTHREY	THOMAS				42	IRELAND	RC	IRISH	LAB	043	B	5	15
GUTHRIE	JOHN				75	IRELAND	RC	IRISH	F	043	E	3	1
GUTHRIE	PATRICK				37	IRELAND	RC	IRISH	F LAB	043	B	4	31
GUTHRIE	RICHARD				37	IRELAND	CE	IRISH	GARDNER	044	C	4	36
GUTHRIE	WILLIAM				43	SCOTLAND	UP	SCOTCH	FARMER	043	B	3	3
GUY	CHARLES				61	ENGLAND	FW	ENGLISH	LAB	045	B	1	35
GUYNAN	CHARLES				38	IRELAND	RC	IRISH	F	043	F		24
GWYNNE	WILLIAM				64	IRELAND	CE	IRISH	DOCTOR & F	044	C	4	78
HAACKE	GEORGE				62	0	LU	GERMAN		045	D	3	11
HAACKE	WILLIAM				31	0	PM	GERMAN	FARMER	045	D	4	53
HABGOOD	JOHN				40	ENGLAND	CE	ENGLISH	SHOEMAKER	043	H	2	5
HABGOOD	JOHN				40	ENGLAND	CE	ENGLISH	SHOEMAKER	043	H	2	5
HACKERT	MICHEL				40	IRELAND	RC	IRISH	LAB	045	A	4	28
HACKET	HENRY		1		12	0	CE	IRISH		045	B	1	15
HACKET	WILLIAM			M	51	IRELAND	PS	IRISH	F	043	A	2	56
HACKETT	JAMES				42	0	CS	SCOTCH	PHYSICIAN	043	D		51
HACKETT	JOHN			M	33	IRELAND	PS	IRISH	SAWYER	043	A	1	68
HACKETT	JOHN				44	IRELAND	CE	IRISH	LAB	045	B	1	22
HACKETT	MARIA	C	1	1	26	QUEBEC	CE	IRISH	TEACHER	043	D		58
HACKING	JOHN				45	0	WM	ENGLISH	F	043	B	4	37

SURNAME	NAME1	NAME2	STRAY	SEX	AGE	BIRTHPL	RELIGION	ORIGIN	OCCUP	DIST	SUB_DIST	DIV	PAGE
HACKING	JOHN		1		12	O	WM	ENGLISH		045	D	4	2
HADDEN	JOHN		1		19	SCOTLAND	CP	SCOTCH	FARM LABOURER	045	C	4	37
HADDEN	WILLIAM				66	IRELAND	RC	IRISH	F LAB	044	A	2	5
HADLEY	JAMES		1		26	O	CP	FRENCH	LAB	045	C	2	42
HADLEY	MARGARET		1	1	1	O	PS	FRENCH		045	C	2	42
HADLEY	MARTHA		1	1	22	O	PS	FRENCH		045	C	2	42
HADWEN	JOHN				45	ENG	WM	ENG	F	044	B	4	12
HAFFY	BARNEY				35	O	RC	IRE	PAINTER	044	B	2	43
HAFFY	JAMES				34	O	RC	IRE	FINISHER	044	B	2	44
HAGAN	JOHN				60	IRELAND	RC	IRISH	LABOURER	045	D	5	39
HAGARTY	JOHN				31	IRELAND	CP	IRISH	F	045	C	3	33
HAGEN	MARY		1	1	19	O	RC	IRISH	SERVANT	044	B	1	10
HAGEN	THOMAS				50	IRELAND	CE	IRISH	LAB	045	C	2	50
HAGERMAN	BENJ				24	O	WM	ENGLISH	FARMER	045	D	5	69
HAGERMAN	EMELINE	A		1	48	ENGLAND	WM	ENGLISH	SEAMSTRESS	045	D	3	25
HAGERMAN	GEORGE		1		23	O	WM	GERMAN	LABOURER	045	D	4	45
HAGERMAN	JOHN				33	O	WM	GERMAN	FARMER	045	D	3	13
HAGERMAN	LESLIE		1		20	O	WM	SCOTCH		045	D	3	23
HAGERMAN	NICHOLAS				44	O	WM	GERMAN	FARMER	045	D	3	22
HAGERMAN	SINCLAIR				39	O	WM	GERMAN	FARMER	045	D	3	14
HAGIN	JAMES		1		62	IRELAND	CE	IRISH	LAB	044	B	5	21
HAGUE	RICHARD				27	IRELAND	WM	IRISH	FARM LABOURER	045	C	3	15
HAIGH	GEORGE			M	39	ENGLAND	PS	ENGLISH	MINISTER	043	A	2	30
HAIGH	GEORGE				26	O	WM	ENGLISH	CLOTHIER	043	E	3	48
HAIGHT	ARNOLD				54	O	QU	GERMAN	F	043	B	4	30
HAIGHT	JOHN				27	O	QU	ENGLISH	F	043	B	4	43
HAINES	CLINESAR				29	O	QU	ENGLISH	YEOMAN	043	E	2	35
HAINES	EDWIN		1		14	O	CN	DUTCH		043	E	1	21
HAINES	ELIZA		1	1	19	ENGLAND	WM	ENGLISH	SERVANT	043	D		86
HAINES	GEORGE				42	ENGLAND	WM	ENGLISH	LAB	043	E	1	34
HAINES	GEORGE				81	UNITED STATES	EM	IRISH	FARMER	043	G	2	19
HAINES	ISRAEL				56	O	QU	ENGLISH	F	043	E	1	40
HAINES	LEVI		1		12	O	CN	GERMAN		043	B	4	20
HAINES	MARY		1	1	15	ENGLAND	WM	ENGLISH	SERVANT	043	D		86
HAINES	RUTH		1	1	38	ENGLAND	WM	ENGLISH	SERVANT	043	E	1	17
HAINES	SAMUEL				87	UNITED STATES	QU	ENGLISH	F	043	E	1	41
HAINES	SIMPSON				37	ENGLAND	EM	ENGLISH	FARMER	043	G	2	30
HAINON	JOHN	A	1		11	O	CN	ENGLISH		043	E	1	8
HAINS	JOHN				46	ENGLAND	CE	ENGLISH	F LAB	043	B	4	40
HAIR	JOHN		1		11	CANADA	MN	GERMAN		045	D	6	18
HAKE	WILLIAM				47	ENGLAND	CE	ENGLISH	LABORER	045	D	6	48
HAKNEY	JAMES					ENG	WM	ENG	F	044	B	2	29
HALBE	JAMES		1		64	ONTARIO	WM	IRISH	SHINGLE MAKER	044	C	3	49
HALBERT	EDWARD				31	ENGLAND	CE	ENGLISH	LAB	045	C	4	2
HALDER	MARY			1	59	ONTARIO	WM	ENGLISH		043	B	3	50
HALE	JOHN				67	O	WM	ENGLISH	CARPENTER	044	A	3	29
HALE	JOHN				33	O	PM	ENGLISH	LAB	044	A	3	54
HALES	JOHN				44	ENGLAND	CE	ENGLISH	BRICKMAKER	043	H	1	10
HALES	ROBERT		1	M	31	O	PM	ENGLAND	F	043	A	5	18
HALEY	JOSEPH				45	O	CE	ENGLISH	FARMER	044	C	3	46
HALEY	JOSEPH	DR			79	US	CE	ENGLISH		044	C	3	40
HALEY	THOMAS				23	O	CE	GERMAN	FARMER	044	C	3	59
HALEY	THOMAS				52	O	CE	GERMAN	FARMER	044	C	3	59
HALEY	WILLIAM	R			39	O	CE	ENGLISH	FARMER	044	C	3	40
HALL	A	CATHARINE	2	1	12	ONT	CP			043	A	3	D
HALL	ALEXANDER				44	ENGLAND	PM	ENGLISH	FARMER	043	A	4	63
HALL	AMBROSE			M	41	ENGLAND	CE	ENGLISH	MACHINIST	043	A	1	9
HALL	CATHERINE			1	50	SCOTLAND	CP	SCOTCH	F	045	C	3	41
HALL	CHARLES		1		17	O	CE	GER	APPRENTICE	044	B	2	10
HALL	EDWARD		1		24	ENGLAND	CE	ENGLISH	FARM LAB	044	C	2	39
HALL	EMILY		1	1	24	O	WM	IRISH	INMATE	045	B	1	72
HALL	HAMILTON				60	US	CP	SCOTCH	HOTEL KEEPER	045	D	3	81
HALL	JAMES		1		78	ENG	CE	ENG	LAB	044	B	4	15
HALL	JAMES				34	ENGLAND	PM	ENGLISH	SPINNER	044	B	5	22
HALL	JAMES				34	ENGLAND	CE	ENGLISH	LAB	044	C	2	37
HALL	JAMES		1		22	O	CE	SCOTCH	FARMER	044	C	3	45
HALL	JAMES	B			45	ENGLAND	CE	ENGLISH	F	043	A	3	47
HALL	JOHN				60	ENGLAND	CE	ENGLISH	RAILWAY EMPLOYEE	044	A	1	30
HALL	JOHN				23	O	WM	ENGLAND	IRON MOULDER	045	D	2	13
HALL	JOHN				28	ENGLAND	WM	ENGLISH	BLACKSMITH	044	C	3	10
HALL	JOSEPH				30	ENGLAND	PM	ENGLISH	WAGGON MAKER	045	D	2	50
HALL	JOSIAH				33	IRELAND	PM	IRISH	BRICK LAYER	045	C	3	46
HALL	R	G			56	ENGLAND	CE	ENGLISH	F	043	H	2	46
HALL	R	G			56	ENGLAND	CE	ENGLISH	FARMER	043	H	2	46
HALL	RACHEL		2	1	67	ENGLAND	WM			045	C	1	D
HALL	RICHARD		1		60	ENGLAND	WM	ENGLISH	CARPENTER	045	A	3	36
HALL	RICHARD				68	ENGLAND	CE	ENGLISH	LAB	044	C	2	25
HALL	RICHARD				36	ENGLAND	WM	ENGLISH	LAB	044	C	2	46
HALL	ROBERT				59	ENGLAND	CE	ENGLISH	LAB	044	B	5	13
HALL	SAMUEL				41	ENG	EM	ENG	F	044	B	1	46
HALL	THOMAS				66	ENGLAND	CE	ENGLISH	FARMER	043	A	4	60
HALL	THOMAS				27	ENGLAND	CE	ENGLISH	LAB	044	C	2	10
HALL	THOMAS	H			37	O	CP	ENGLISH	F	045	C	2	44
HALL	WILLIAM				52	SCOTLAND	CP	SCOTCH	F	043	A	3	48
HALL	WILLIAM			M	50	IRELAND	WM	IRELAND	L	043	A	5	40
HALL	WILLIAM				32	ENGLAND	CE	ENGLISH	PAINTER	043	D		8
HALL	WILLIAM				30	ENGLAND	WM	ENGLISH	FARM LABORER	045	D	1	21
HALL	WM				68	ENG	WM	ENG	F	045	C	1	22
HALLAM	JEREMIAH		1		21	O	PM	ENGLISH	FARM LAB	044	A	2	32
HALLAM	THOMAS				28	ENGLAND	CE	ENGLISH	LABOURER	045	A	1	71
HALLAT	JOSEPH				43	ENGLAND	PM	ENGLISH	HIDE DEALER	045	A	1	97
HALLER	THOMAS				45	O	EM	ENGLISH	LABOURER	045	D	6	12
HALLIDAY	WILLIAM				75	ENGLAND	CE	ENGLISH	F	043	E	3	7
HALLIGHAN	WILLIAM				66	IRELAND	RC	IRISH	F	044	A	3	46
HALLSTOCK	ELLIS	H	1		19	ONTARIO	CN	ENGLISH	FARMER	043	G	1	27
HALLSTOCK	JOHN				57	ENGLAND	EM	ENGLISH	FARMER	043	G	1	31
HALLSTOCK	JOHN		1		13	ONTARIO	WM	ENGLISH		043	G	1	37
HAM	CHARLES				24	ENGLAND	CE	ENGLISH	BLACK SMITH	045	D	6	20
HAMBLETON	CHARLES			M	76	US	QU	ENGLISH	FARMER	043	A	5	1
HAMBLY	CATHARINE		2	1	34	ONTARIO	WM			043	A	3	D
HAMBLY	CHARLES				62	N SCOTIA	PM	ENGLISH	FARMER	043	A	3	3
HAMBLY	CHARLES				36	O	WM	ENGLISH	MERCHANT	043	A	3	10
HAMBLY	EDWIN				31	O	WM	IRISH	F	043	A	3	42
HAMBLY	GEORGE				65	NS	WM	ENGLISH	FARMER	043	A	3	3
HAMBLY	GEORGE				38	O	PM	ENGLISH	GLOVE MAKERS	043	A	3	7
HAMBLY	O	JOHN			62	N SCOTIA	WM	ENGLISH	F	043	A	3	38

SURNAME	NAME1	NAME2	STRAY	SEX	AGE	BIRTHPL	RELIGION	ORIGIN	OCCUP	DIST	SUB_DIST	DIV	PAGE
HAMBLY	S	WILLIAM			36	O	WM	ENGLISH		043	A	3	2
HAMBLY	THOMAS				33	O	WM	IRISH	F	043	A	3	40
HAMEL	ELIZABETH			1	36	ENGLAND	CE	ENGLISH		044	C	4	73
HAMELTON	ABRAHAM				53	CANADA	WM	IRISH	FARMER	045	D	6	59
HAMELTON	ANNEY			1	56	CANADA	WM	IRISH		045	D	6	62
HAMELTON	ANTHONY				31	CANADA	BA	IRISH	FARMER	045	D	6	54
HAMELTON	ELIAS				34	CANADA	BA	IRISH	FARMER	045	D	6	55
HAMELTON	HIRAM				43	CANADA	WM	IRISH	FARMER	045	D	6	60
HAMELTON	JAMES				63	CANADA	BA	IRISH	FARMER	045	D	6	54
HAMELTON	JAMES				36	CANADA	WM	IRISH	FARMER	045	D	6	59
HAMILTON	ANDREW				68	IRELAND	CO	IRISH	MERCHANT	045	B	2	15
HAMILTON	CATHARINE			1	78	IRELAND	CE	IRISH		045	B	1	44
HAMILTON	ELISABETH		1	1	28	O	PM	IRISH	SERVANT	045	B	2	32
HAMILTON	GAVIN				36	SCOTLAND	UP	SCOTCH	CARPENTER	044	B	5	71
HAMILTON	GEORGE				31	SCOTLAND	WM	SCOTCH	MILLER	043	D		4
HAMILTON	GEORGE				70	IRELAND	PS	IRISH	FARMER	043	G	2	14
HAMILTON	GEORGE				65	IRELAND	CE	IRISH	F	043	H	1	33
HAMILTON	HELLEN		1	1	86	SCOT	CP	SCOT		045	C	1	44
HAMILTON	ISABELLA		1	1	83	IRELAND	PS	IRISH		044	B	5	54
HAMILTON	JAMES				46	NEW BRUNSWICK	CP	IRISH	FARMER	043	G	2	56
HAMILTON	JAMES		1		28	IRELAND	WM	IRISH	F LAB	044	A	3	2
HAMILTON	JAMES				48	SCOT	CP	SCOT	COOPER	044	B	2	50
HAMILTON	JAMES				60	IRELAND	PS	IRISH	BRICKMAKER	045	A	1	68
HAMILTON	JANE		1	1	28	IRELAND	WM	IRISH		044	C	4	86
HAMILTON	JESSIE		1	1	57	ENGLAND	WM	ENGLISH		043	D		85
HAMILTON	JOHN				56	SCOT	CP	SCOT	COOPER	044	B	2	49
HAMILTON	JOHN				53	O	WM	IRISH	F	044	B	4	11
HAMILTON	JOHN				35	O	CE	SCOTCH	HORTICULTURIST	045	A	1	85
HAMILTON	RICHARD				39	SCOTLAND	UP	SCOTCH	F	043	A	6	63
HAMILTON	ROBERT		1		76	SCOTLAND	OP	SCOTCH	SUPERANUATED TEACHER	043	H	2	41
HAMILTON	ROBERT		1		76	SCOTLAND	CS	SCOTCH	SUPERANNUATED TEACHE	043	H	2	41
HAMILTON	ROBERT				82	SCOTLAND	CP	SCOTCH	F	045	C	4	19
HAMILTON	WILLIAM				65	US	CN	IRISH	WEAVER	044	B	6	11
HAMILTON	WILLIAM		1		3	O	CD	IRISH		045	A	2	19
HAMILTON	WILLIAM				47	ENGLAND	PM	ENGLISH	F	044	C	1	53
HAMLIN	JAMES		1		17	O	WM	FRENCH	F	045	C	2	30
HAMMEL	NORAH			1	44	NB	WM	SCOTCH		043	C		44
HAMMELL	FRANCIS				46	GERMANY	CE	GERMAN	LAB	045	B	1	20
HAMMOND	BENJAMIN		1		22	O	CE	IRISH	F	045	C	2	48
HAMMOND	DAVID				24	IRELAND	CE	IRISH	LAB	045	C	2	46
HAMMOND	ELLEN			1	50	IRELAND	CE	IRISH		045	C	2	54
HAMPTON	JAMES				36	ENGLAND	PS	ENGLISH	LAB	044	C	4	85
HAMSHAW	WILLIAM				60	ENGLAND	CE	ENGLISH	SHOEMAKER	043	H	2	5
HAMSHAW	WILLIAM				60	ENGLAND	CE	ENGLISH	SHOEMAKER	043	H	2	5
HANAH	CALVERLY		1	1	26	O	CE	ENGLISH		044	C	4	59
HANCOCK	MARY		1	1	38	ENGLAND	CE	ENGLISH		044	A	3	55
HANCOCK	SUSAN			1	69	GERMANY	PM	GERMAN		043	A	3	20
HAND	EDWARD				46	IRELAND	RC	IRISH	GARDNER	044	C	4	94
HAND	JOHN				70	IRELAND	CE	IRISH	BAKER	043	B	3	60
HAND	JOHN				40	IRELAND	WM	IRISH	SHOEMAKER	045	D	3	38
HAND	WILLIAM				58	IRELAND	WM	IRISH	HARNESS MAKER	045	B	2	3
HANDCOCK	HERBERT				35	ENGLAND	SW	ENGLISH	CLERK	045	B	2	18
HANDS	GEORGE		1		25	O	CE	ENGLISH		043	C		28
HANDS	RICHARD		1		37	ENGLAND	CE	ENGLISH	BUTCHER	045	A	1	66
HANDSON	JOHN		1		15	IRELAND	CE	IRISH	PAINTER	044	B	5	12
HANDSON	LIONEL		1		13	IRELAND	CE	IRISH	CLK	044	B	5	11
HANDY	WILLIAM	J			28	O	RC	IRISH	BOOT MAKER	045	B	2	2
HANDY	WINIFRED		2		78	IRELAND	RC			045	B	2	D
HANES	RICHARD				62	ENGLAND	WM	ENGLISH		045	D	6	51
HANEY	JAMES				25	O	CE	IRISH	F	044	C	2	31
HANLAN	HENRY		1		30	IRELAND	RC	IRISH		043	G	2	21
HANLEY	JOHN		1		55	IRELAND	RC	IRISH	LAB	044	B	5	26
HANLEY	MATTHEW				67	IRELAND	RC	IRISH	FARMER	043	A	4	58
HANLEY	PATRICK				58	IRELAND	RC	IRISH	FARMER	043	A	4	59
HANLEY	THOS				34	ENGLAND	CE	ENGLISH	LAB	043	A	4	1
HANLIN	JOHN				56	IRELAND	RC	IRISH	FARMER	043	A	4	44
HANLON	JAMES				37	IRELAND	RC	IRISH	LAB	043	D		43
HANMER	CLARK				43	UNITED STATES	WM	ENGLISH	HOTEL KEEPER	043	D		1
HANNA	MOSES				57	IRELAND	CP	IRISH	TOLL GATE KEEPER	044	C	2	14
HANNAH	JAMES				72	IRELAND	CE	IRISH		043	B	1	35
HANNAH	RICHARD		1		20	QUEBEC	CE	ENGLISH	BLACKSMITH	045	C	3	32
HANNAH	ROBERT				29	IRELAND	CN	IRISH	TEAMSTER	043	B	3	15
HANNAH	WILLIAM				32	IRELAND	CE	IRISH	SAWYER	043	B	1	34
HANNER	WM				53	ENGLAND	WM	ENGLISH	SHOEMAKER	044	B	5	12
HANNIEL	JOHN				51	O	WM	IRISH	TEAMSTER	043	E	3	48
HANNRAET	JAMES				53	ENGLAND	BA	ENGLISH	F	043	E	3	5
HANNY	JOHN	M			50	IRE	WM	IRE	F	044	B	4	30
HANREHAN	PATRICK				34	IRELAND	NG	IRISH	HORSE DEALER	043	B	3	58
HANSON	JAMES		1		31	ENG	CO	ENGLISH	CLERK	044	B	2	72
HANSTOCK	ROBERT				49	ENGLAND	CE	ENGLISH	F	043	B	1	12
HANTLEY	CHARLES				47	ENGLAND	WM	ENGLISH	GARDNER	044	C	4	38
HANTLEY	GEORGE				22	ENGLAND	WM	ENGLISH	GARDNER	044	C	4	38
HARAH	GEORGE				37	ENGLAND	CE	ENGLISH	F	044	A	2	24
HARDICK	ALFRED		1		18	ENGLAND	WM	ENGLISH	CABINET MAKER	043	D		8
HARDICK	LIZGAR		1		19	O	CE	ENGLISH	LAB	044	B	5	20
HARDIE	ANDW				28	O	WM	SCOTCH	F	044	B	5	33
HARDIE	JAS	GEO			60	SCOTLAND	PS	SCOTCH	F	044	B	5	33
HARDIE	LYDIA		1	1	21	O	CO	SCOTCH		044	B	5	14
HARDIMAN	JOHN				60	IRELAND	RC	IRISH	LAB	043	B	4	7
HARDIMAN	MARY		1		22	IRELAND	RC	IRISH	SERVANT	043	D		85
HARDING	AMELIA			1	65	ENGLAND	WM	ENGLISH		045	A	4	10
HARDING	DAVID				48	ENGLAND	WM	ENGLISH	F	043	E	1	27
HARDING	MARY			1	47	O	WM	ENGLISH		045	D	5	28
HARDING	THOMAS				56	ENGLAND	PM	ENGLISH	F	045	C	3	25
HARDING	TIMOTHY				68	IRELAND	RC	IRISH	F	043	H	2	21
HARDING	TIMOTHY				68	IRELAND	RC	IRISH	FARMER	043	H	2	21
HARDING	WILLIAM				70	ENGLAND	CE	ENGLISH	LAB	043	F		25
HARDING	WILLIAM				58	ENGLAND	CE	ENGLISH	FARMER	045	D	3	51
HARDING	WILLIAM				45	ENGLAND	WM	ENGLAND	FARMER	045	D	2	3
HARDING	WILLIAM				79	IRELAND	BA	IRISH	GENTLEMAN	044	C	4	44
HARDWICK	JEREMIAH				59	ENGLAND	CE	ENGLISH	F	043	A	6	45
HARDWICK	JOHN				40	O	CE	ENG	F	044	C	1	51
HARDWICK	MARY ANN		1	1	16	O	PM	ENGLISH	SERVANT	044	A	3	26
HARDY	BRIDGET			1	47	IRELAND	RC	IRISH		043	D		71
HARDY	DAVID		1		25	O	WM	ENGLAND	LABORER	045	D	2	5
HARDY	DIANA		1	1	18	O	OP	ENGLISH		045	C	4	3

SURNAME	NAME1	NAME2	STRAY	SEX	AGE	BIRTHPL	RELIGION	ORIGIN	OCCUP	DIST	SUB_DIST	DIV	PAGE
HARDY	HANNAH		1	1	16	0	OP	ENGLISH		045	C	4	4
HARDY	MARMADUKE				62	ENGLAND	WM	ENGLISH	LABORER	045	D	2	68
HARDY	MARTIN		1		45	IRELAND	CS	IRISH	LABOURER	045	D	4	26
HARDY	ROBERT		1		20	0	WM	ENGLAND	SERVANT	045	D	2	14
HARDY	THOMAS		1		50	ENGLAND	CE	ENGLISH	F LAB	044	A	3	4
HARE	BENJAMIN				55	UNITED STATES	MN	GERMAN	FARMER	043	B	3	59
HARE	GEORGE		1	M	11	0	CP	SCOTCH		043	A	1	67
HARE	GEORGE		1		60	IRELAND	CE	IRISH		045	C	1	13
HARE	JOSHUA				50	USA	WM	ENGLAND	LABOURER	045	A	1	101
HARE	SAMUEL		1		30	CANADA	MN	GERMAN		045	D	6	58
HARGRAVE	JOHN				35	ENGLAND	WM	ENGLISH	LABOURER	043	A	4	20
HARGRAVE	JOSEPH				50	ENGLAND	FW	ENGLISH	SHOEMAKER	045	A	2	7
HARGRAVES	WILLIAM				70	ENGLAND	CE	ENGLISH	SHOEMAKER	045	A	1	80
HARKER	JAS				46	ENGLAND	WM	ENGLISH	BAKER	044	B	5	42
HARKETT	HENRY		1		12	0	CE	ENGLISH	SERVANT	045	B	2	1
HARKINGS	PETER		1		20	0	VM	ENG	LAB	044	B	3	25
HARKINS	SARAH			1	75	IRELAND	RC	IRISH		044	A	3	40
HARLAND	MARGARET		1	1	6	0	PM	ENGLISH		043	E	2	75
HARLEY	SUSANA		1	1	52	IRELAND	CE	IRISH		045	C	4	46
HARMAN	EMMANUEL			M	38	0	EM	GERMAN	LAB	043	A	1	69
HARMAN	GEORGE			M	35	0	WM	GERMAN	F	043	A	1	9
HARMAN	HENRY				40	0	NC	DUTCH	LAB	043	C		38
HARMAN	ISAAC				44	0	WM	GERMAN	MERCHANT	043	E	3	22
HARMAN	JAMES			M	29	0	WM	GERMAN	F	043	A	1	19
HARMAN	JAMES			M	67	0	CE	GERMAN	LAB	043	A	1	68
HARMAN	JANE			F	33	0	EM	GERMAN		043	A	1	70
HARMAN	JOHN				50	0	WM	GERMAN	LAB	043	B	1	36
HARMAN	JOSEPH			M	65	0	WM	GERMAN	LABOURER	043	A	1	18
HARMAN	MICHEAL				36	IRELAND	RC	IRISH	LABOURER	045	A	1	54
HARMAN	SAMUEL		1		25	0	WM	GERMAN	FIREMAN	043	B	3	28
HARMAN	THOMAS			M	31	0	PR	GERMAN	FARMER	043	A	1	67
HARMAN	TIMMOTHY			M	32	0	PR	GERMAN	LAB	043	A	1	68
HARMAN	WESLEY		1	M	5	0	EM	ENGLISH		043	A	1	18
HARMAN	WILLIAM			M	72	0	WM	GERMAN	FARMER	043	A	1	21
HARMAN	WILLIAM			M	50	0	PR	GERMAN	FARMER	043	A	1	29
HARMEN	CHARLES				66	0	PM	DUTCH	F	043	A	6	32
HARNIMA	MARIA		1	1	13	ENGLAND	CE	ENGLISH		045	B	1	41
HARNS	SARAH		2	1	26	ONTARIO	RC		SERVANT	043	H	2	D
HAROLD	NELSON				36	0	CE	ENGLISH	F	043	E	2	6
HAROLD	WILLIAM				43	0	EP	ENGLISH	F	043	A	6	21
HARPER	GEORGE			M	40	ENGLAND	CE	ENGLISH	LABOURER	043	A	1	2
HARPER	HENRY	W			25	0	UP	ENGLISH	FARMER	045	D	1	34
HARPER	JAMES				45	SCOTLAND	CP	SCOTCH	FARMER	045	D	3	29
HARPER	JANE			1	60	IRELAND	WM	IRISH		043	A	6	35
HARPER	JOHN				30	IRELAND	CP	IRISH	BAKER	044	C	4	43
HARPER	MARY		2	1	63	SCOTLAND	UP			045	D	1	D
HARPER	MARY-ANN		1	1	13	0	PS	IRISH	F LAB	044	C	1	15
HARPER	RICHARD		1		20	0	CP	ENGLISH	F LAB	043	B	4	36
HARPER	THOMAS				55	ENGLAND	RC	ENGLISH	F	044	C	1	26
HARPER	WILLIAM				33	IRELAND	WM	IRISH	F	043	A	6	35
HARRAL	ROBT		1		45	ENGLAND	WM	ENGLISH	LAB	044	B	5	66
HARRILL	JAMES				40	0	CE	IRISH	FARMER	043	B	3	71
HARRINGTON	CHRISTOPHER				35	0	EM	GERMAN	PUMPMAKER	043	E	2	70
HARRINGTON	GAMALIEL				31	0	PM	GERMAN	FARMER	045	D	3	49
HARRINGTON	JAMES				40	CANADA	CE	ENGLISH	FARMER	045	D	6	32
HARRINGTON	JEFFERN				63	0	WM	FRENCH	F	045	C	2	28
HARRINGTON	JOHN		1		5	0	EM	IRISH		043	E	2	55
HARRINGTON	JOHN				42	ENGLAND	CE	ENGLISH	BRICKMAKER	045	B	1	58
HARRINGTON	LUCINDA		1	1	16	US	CP	SCOTCH		045	C	3	8
HARRINGTON	MARY		1	1	11	UNITED STATES	EM	GERMAN		043	E	3	12
HARRINGTON	MRS	S		1	58	0	PM	DUTCH	F	045	C	3	40
HARRINGTON	NELLIE			1	62	IRELAND	RC	IRISH		044	C	4	11
HARRINGTON	ROBERT				40	0	WM	IRISH	BUILDER	045	C	3	15
HARRINGTON	WILLIAM		1		50	ENGLAND	CE	ENGLISH	SERVANT	045	D	3	76
HARRIS	AARON				51	ENGLAND	CE	ENGLISH	F	044	A	1	35
HARRIS	ALBERT		1		9	0	WM	SCOTCH		045	B	2	3
HARRIS	ANDREW				34	0	CP	IRISH	LAB	044	C	2	29
HARRIS	BARBARA			1	29	0	CE	SCOTCH	DRESSMAKER	043	D		20
HARRIS	ELISA		1	1	45	IRELAND	CP	IRISH	SERVANT	045	B	2	33
HARRIS	ELISHA				33	0	CP	IRISH	TAVERN KEEPER	045	D	4	9
HARRIS	F	JANE	1	1	21	0	WM	GERMAN	F	044	C	1	33
HARRIS	FREDRICK				36	ENGLAND	CS	ENGLISH	CARPENTER	044	B	6	9
HARRIS	GEORGE				35	ENGLAND	CE	ENGLISH	PAINTER	045	B	2	18
HARRIS	HENRY				40	ENGLAND	NC	ENGLISH	JOINER	043	C		22
HARRIS	HENRY		1		14	0	PM	IRISH		045	A	2	23
HARRIS	HUMPHRY				35	IRELAND	DI	IRISH	MACHINIST	045	B	1	29
HARRIS	ISAAC		1		24	0	CE	IRISH	HORSE TRAINER	044	C	4	32
HARRIS	JAMES				29	0	CP	IRISH	HOTELKEEPER	044	B	1	64
HARRIS	JANE		1	1	66	ENGLAND	CE	ENGLISH		045	A	1	54
HARRIS	JOHN				41	ENG	WM	ENG	CARPENTER	044	B	2	28
HARRIS	JOHN				73	ENG	WM	ENG		044	B	4	32
HARRIS	JOHN		1		24	ENGLAND	CE	ENGLISH	BAKER	045	D	3	77
HARRIS	JOSEPH				35	0	NC	SCOTCH	MOALDER	043	C		10
HARRIS	MATHEW				38	IRELAND	RC	IRISH	LABOURER	044	C	3	66
HARRIS	PARMINAS				60	ENGLAND	CE	ENGLISH	SHOEMAKER	044	A	1	35
HARRIS	PATRICK				32	IRELAND	RC	IRISH	FARMER	044	C	3	50
HARRIS	PATRICK				66	IRELAND	RC	IRISH		044	C	3	50
HARRIS	RICHARD				73	ENGLAND	WM	ENGLISH	F	045	A	4	16
HARRIS	ROBERT				23	ENGLAND	CE	ENGLISH	F	044	A	3	46
HARRIS	ROBERT		1		60	ENGLAND	CE	ENGLISH	GENTLEMAN	045	A	1	54
HARRIS	ROBERT				24	ENGLAND	WM	ENGLISH	F	045	A	4	6
HARRIS	SAMUEL				47	ENGLAND	CE	ENGLISH	LAB	043	C		45
HARRIS	SAMUEL		2		2	0	CE			044	A	1	D
HARRIS	WALTER		1		31	ENGLAND	PM	ENGLISH		044	A	3	38
HARRIS	WILLIAM				32	ENGLAND	CE	ENGLISH	CARRIAGE BLDR	043	C		51
HARRIS	WILLIAM				49	ENGLAND	FW	ENGLISH	MILLER	045	A	3	28
HARRISON	ANNIE		1	1	12	0	PM	ENGLISH		045	D	2	50
HARRISON	CHARLES		1			ENGLAND	CE	ENGLISH	SERVANT	045	A	3	26
HARRISON	CHRISTOPHER				45	0	CE	ENGLISH	FARMER	045	A	3	6
HARRISON	CHRISTOPHER				55	0	EM	ENGLISH	FARMER	045	A	3	9
HARRISON	CHRISTOPHER				41	0	CE	ENGLISH	FARMER	045	A	3	20
HARRISON	EDGAR				35	ENGLAND	RELIGION	ENGLISH	TAILOR	043	A	4	35
HARRISON	ELIZABETH		1	1	84	NOVA SCOTIA	CE	ENGLISH		043	G	1	31
HARRISON	ELIZABETH			1	79	NB	CE	SCOTCH		045	A	3	19
HARRISON	EMMA		2	1	36	0	CE			043	E	1	D
HARRISON	EMMA		2	1		0	CE			043	E	1	D

SURNAME	NAME1	NAME2	STRAY	SEX	AGE	BIRTHPL	RELIGION	ORIGIN	OCCUP	DIST	SUB_DIST	DIV	PAGE
HARRISON	GEORGE				60	0	CE	ENGLISH	GENTLEMAN	043	C		23
HARRISON	GEORGE				30	0	RC	IRISH	LAB	044	C	1	11
HARRISON	HENRY				45	ENGLAND	EM	ENGLISH	MERCHANT	043	D		61
HARRISON	HENRY		1		23	ENGLAND	WM	ENGLISH	F LAB	044	C	1	4
HARRISON	ISAAC				35	ENGLAND	WM	ENGLISH	F	044	C	1	4
HARRISON	JAMES				25	0	CE	IRISH	BLACKSMITH	043	H	1	34
HARRISON	JOHN				52	IRELAND	CE	IRISH	F	044	A	1	23
HARRISON	JOHN				54	ENG	EM	ENG	LAB	044	B	3	36
HARRISON	JOHN				39	ENGLAND	PM	ENGLISH	F	044	B	6	16
HARRISON	JOHN				58	ENGLAND	WM	ENGLISH	F	044	C	4	33
HARRISON	JOSEPH		1		16	0	NG	ENGLISH		045	B	2	22
HARRISON	LUKE				28	ENG	PM	ENG	LAB	044	B	3	31
HARRISON	MARTHA		1		60	ENGLAND	PM	ENGLISH		044	A	3	42
HARRISON	NELSON				36	0	CE	ENGLISH	LAB	043	E	1	36
HARRISON	RICHARD	REV			29	0	EP	IRE	CLERGYMAN	044	B	3	46
HARRISON	THOMAS				70	ENGLAND	CE	ENGLISH	F	043	E	3	58
HARRISON	THOMAS				41	ENGLAND	RC	ENGLISH	LAB	044	A	3	40
HARRISON	WILLIAM				63	ONTARIO	PR	ENGLISH	LABORER	043	G	2	52
HARRISON	WILLIAM				28	ENGLAND	CE	ENGLISH	F	044	A	3	55
HARRISON	WILLIAM				37	ENG	WM	ENG	SADDLER	044	B	2	16
HARRISON	WILLIAM		1		20	ENGLAND	WM	ENGLISH	POTTER	045	A	2	10
HARRISON	WILLIAM				51	0	CE	ENGLISH	FARMER	045	A	3	24
HARSHAW	JAMES		1		52	IRELAND	RP	IRISH	CARPENTER	043	B	5	18
HART	ARON				46	NEW BRUNSWICK	CE	ENGLISH	LAB	043	H	2	34
HART	ARON				46	NEW BRUNSWICK	CE	ENGLISH	LABOURER	043	H	2	34
HART	CHARLES				49	NEW BRUNSWICK	BC	ENGLISH	F	043	H	2	47
HART	CHARLES				49	NEW BRUNSWICK	BC	ENGLISH	FARMER	043	H	2	47
HART	DAVID				65	ENG	PM	ENG	F	044	B	2	76
HART	GEORGE				28	0	WM	ENGLISH	CARPENTER	043	E	1	4
HART	GEORGE				55	ENGLAND	CE	ENGLISH	CARPENTER	043	E	1	6
HART	JAMES				58	IRELAND	RC	IRISH	LABORER	043	D		76
HART	JAMES		1		42	IRE	CS	IRISH	FARM SERVANT	044	B	4	39
HART	JOHN				57	ENGLAND	CE	ENGLAND		045	D	2	11
HART	JOSEPH				77	NEW BRUNSWICK	CE	ENGLISH	F	043	H	2	36
HART	JOSEPH				77	NEW BRUNSWICK	CE	ENGLISH	FARMER	043	H	2	36
HART	MARIA			1	40	IRELAND	CP	IRISH		045	B	1	45
HART	MARY			1	35	0	PM	ENGLISH	MERCHANT	044	B	6	33
HART	NANCY		1	1	13	0	CN	ENGLISH	SERVANT	043	E	2	63
HART	SAMUEL				40	IRE	PS	IRE	SHOEMAKER	044	B	3	40
HART	STEPHEN				24	0	BC	ENGLISH	LAB	043	H	2	53
HART	STEPHEN				24	ONTARIO	BC	ENGLISH	LABOURER	043	H	2	53
HART	WILLIAM		1		25	0	NR	ENGLISH	SERVANT	043	A	4	45
HART	WILLIAM				36	IRELAND	CS	IRISH	F	044	B	6	54
HART	WILLIAM		1		12	0	CP	IRISH		044	C	2	15
HARTLEY	ELIZA		1	1	22	0	CO	IRISH		044	B	5	37
HARTLEY	JAMES				47	ENGLAND	PR	ENGLISH	CARPENTER	043	G	2	20
HARTLEY	JONATHAN		1		18	ENGLAND	WM	ENGLISH	F LAB	044	A	1	27
HARTLY	GEORGE				68	ENGLAND	CE	ENGLISH	LAB	044	B	6	31
HARTMAN	ANN		1	1	61	IRELAND	RC	IRISH		045	D	1	31
HARTMAN	HENRY		1		18	0	WM	GERMAN		043	B	4	4
HARTMAN	ISAAC				29	0	UP	GERMAN	MERCHANT	043	C		41
HARTMAN	MARY	ANN	1	1	49	0	WM	ENGLISH		043	B	4	4
HARTMAN	SARAH			1	44	0	WM	GERMAN	F	043	B	1	14
HARTMAN	WM				55	0	CO	GERMAN	F	044	B	5	59
HARTNEY	JOHN			M	48	0	PM	IRISH	F	043	A	1	14
HARTNEY	MARY		1	1	5	0	WM	ENGLISH		045	D	4	3
HARTON	JAMES				60	IRELAND	CP	IRISH	THONG MAKER	044	C	2	3
HARTOP	SAMUEL	BREG			31	0	WM	ENGLISH	MERCHANT	043	E	3	41
HARTRY	JOHN				37	0	CE	IRISH	TANNER	043	D		79
HARVEY	ARTHUR				37	ENGLAND	CE	ENGLISH	MANAGER INSURANCE CO	045	B	2	9
HARVEY	BARBARIA			1	50	0	CE	ENGLISH		044	C	3	64
HARVEY	JARVIS		1		17	0	WM	ENGLISH	SERVANT	045	D	2	68
HARVEY	MICHAEL				37	IRE	RC	IRISH	F	044	B	4	40
HARVEY	SAMUEL		1		30	ENGLAND	PM	ENGLISH	FARM LABOURER	045	C	4	40
HARVEY	WILFORD		1		12	0	WM	ENGLISH		045	D	4	23
HARVIE	JAMES				55	IRELAND	RC	IRISH	F LAB	043	B	4	42
HARVY	ROBERT				64	ENGLAND	WM	ENGLISH	LAB	045	B	1	13
HARVY	WILLIAM				82	ENGLAND	CE	IRISH		045	A	3	12
HARWOOD	WILLIAM				40	ENGLAND	CE	ENGLISH	CARPENTER	044	C	4	23
HASELIP	THOMAS				57	IRELAND	WM	IRISH	F LAB	043	A	6	19
HASEY	MARY		1	1	16	IRELAND	RC	IRISH	SERVANT	044	C	4	67
HASIE	HANNAH		1	1	46	0	BA	GERMAN		043	B	3	18
HASKETT	DAVID				40	IRELAND	RC	IRISH	LABORER	043	D		77
HASKETT	DAVID				70	IRELAND	RC	IRISH	LABORER	043	D		78
HASKETT	GEORGE				31	IRELAND	RC	IRISH	LABORER	043	D		76
HASKETT	MARY			1	48	IRELAND	RC	IRISH		043	D		24
HASKETT	MICHAEL				41	IRELAND	RC	IRISH	LABORER	043	D		77
HASKEW	REV	J B			49	ENGLAND	CE	ENGLISH	CLERK IN HOLY ORDERS	045	D	5	27
HASLEM	RICHD				41	IRELAND	CE	IRISH	LAB	044	B	5	30
HASSEY	MARGARET		1	1	23	IRELAND	RC	IRISH	SERVANT	045	B	2	33
HASTING	WILLIAM				43	0	CP	ENGLISH	F	045	C	3	19
HASTINGS	ADAM				41	IRELAND	CP	SCOTCH	STOREKEEPER	043	B	2	39
HASTINGS	ADAM		2			0	CP			043	B	2	D
HASTINGS	ALEX		1		50	0	WM	ENG		045	C	1	57
HASTINGS	ANNE		1	1	40	IRELAND	WM	IRISH		043	G	1	56
HASTINGS	ELLEN		1	1	19	ENGLAND	WM	ENGLISH		045	B	2	10
HASTINGS	JAMES				56	IRELAND	CP	IRISH	F	043	B	2	6
HASTINGS	JOHN				63	IRELAND	WM	IRISH	F	043	B	2	44
HASTINGS	RICHARD				26	0	WM	ENGLISH	FARMER	043	A	4	65
HASTINGS	RICHARD				59	ENGLAND	WM	ENGLISH	CLARK	045	B	1	60
HASTINGS	THOMAS				62	0	CE	ENGLISH	AXEMAKER	045	A	1	22
HASTINGS	THOMAS				47	0	PM	IRISH	FARMER	045	D	4	50
HASTINGS	WILLIAM		1		45	IRELAND	WM	IRISH	LABORER	043	G	1	56
HASTY	JAMES		1	M	19	ENGLAND	CE	ENGLISH	LAB	043	A	1	49
HATT	ROLAND				28	ENGLAND	CE	ENGLISH		043	H	2	27
HAW	MARTHA			1	74	ENG	WM	ENG		045	C	1	68
HAWKE	JOHN				33	ENGLAND	WM	ENGLISH	DAIRY MAN	045	A	1	81
HAWKINS	GEORGE	W			28	ENGLAND	CE	ENGLISH	LAB	045	B	1	48
HAWKINS	JAMES				51	NEW BRUNSWICK	WM	ENGLISH	FARMER	045	D	6	26
HAWKINS	ROGER	T			40	NB	KB	ENGLISH	FARMER	045	D	5	68
HAWKINS	WILLIAM				30	ENGLAND	CE	ENGLISH	LAB	044	C	4	30
HAWLY	HANNAH	E	1	1		ENGLAND	CE	ENGLISH		045	D	3	69
HAWLY	MARY		1	1	26	ENGLAND	CE	ENGLISH		045	D	3	69
HAWLY	WILLIAM		1		29	ENGLAND	CE	ENGLISH	LABOURER	045	D	3	69
HAWLY	WILLIAM		1		1	ENGLAND	CE	ENGLISH		045	D	3	69
HAWMAN	ELLEN			1	26	ON SEA	PM	IRISH	WIDOWER	043	A	3	13

SURNAME	NAME1	NAME2	STRAY	SEX	AGE	BIRTHPL	RELIGION	ORIGIN	OCCUP	DIST	SUB_DIST	DIV	PAGE
HAWMAN	JACOB		2		32	O	PM		FARMER	043	A	3	D
HAWMAN	MICHAEL				47	O	PM	GERMAN	F	043	A	3	13
HAWMAN	WILLIAM				23	O	PM	GERMAN	F	043	A	3	32
HAWTIN	GEORGE				30	ENGLAND	WM	ENGLISH	F	043	B	4	11
HAYCOCK	WILLIAM				63	ENGLAND	WM	ENGLISH	CONFECTIONER	045	B	2	7
HAYCOTT	ROBERT		1		21	ENGLAND	CE	ENGLISH	F LAB	044	C	1	19
HAYCREW	FRED		1		17	O	CE	ENGLISH		044	B	5	45
HAYDAN	JAMES				41	O	RC	IRISH	INNKEEPER	044	B	6	24
HAYDEN	BARBARA			1	59	IRELAND	CE	IRISH		044	C	4	88
HAYDEN	EDWD				31	ENGLAND	WM	ENGLISH	BLACKSMITH	044	B	5	15
HAYDEN	FRANCIS				40	O	RC	IRISH	INNKEEPER	044	C	4	19
HAYDON	JAMES		1		32	IRELAND	RC	IRISH	LABOURER	045	D	3	26
HAYES	HUGH				70	IRELAND	PS	IRISH	LAB	044	C	1	13
HAYLOCK	JOSEPH				60	ENGLAND	PM	ENGLISH	LAB	044	B	5	38
HAYNES	CHARLES	U	1		16	O	CN	ENGLISH	SERVANT	043	A	6	7
HAYNES	MIKEL		1		17	CANADA	RC	IRISH		045	D	6	78
HAYS	JOSIAH				46	ENGLAND	CE	ENGLISH	BLACKSMITH	043	H	2	11
HAYS	JOSIAH				46	ENGLAND	CE	ENGLISH	BLACKSMITH	043	H	2	11
HAYS	LUKE		1		35	O	RC	IRISH	COOPER	044	B	6	58
HAYS	MARY ANN			1	66	O	WM	ENGLISH		043	B	5	39
HAYS	MATTHEW		1		16	IRELAND	RC	IRISH	SERVANT	045	A	1	46
HAYS	ROBERT				25	IRELAND	PM	IRISH	LABOURER	045	D	3	30
HAYSTEAD	CHARLOTTE			1	78	ENGLAND	CE	ENGLISH		044	B	5	13
HAYSTEAD	FREDERICK		1		16	O	PM	ENG		044	B	3	33
HAYSTEAD	FREDERICK				42	O	EP	ENG	LAB	044	B	3	52
HAYSTEAD	MAGT		1	1	34	O	PS	IRISH		044	B	5	40
HAYSTEAD	THOMAS				48	ENGLAND	CE	ENGLISH	F	044	C	1	54
HAYWARD	JEMIMA		1	1	29	ONTARIO	CP	DUTCH		043	G	2	50
HAYWARD	JOHN	HENRY	1		7	ONTARIO	CP	DUTCH		043	G	2	50
HAYWOOD	JAMES				57	ENGLAND	CE	ENGLISH	FARMER	045	A	1	98
HAYWOOD	JANE		1	1	19	ENGLAND	CE	ENGLISH	SERVANT	045	A	1	102
HAZARD	WILLIAM				38	IRELAND	CE	IRISH	LAB	043	C		20
HAZELTON	JOSEPH				44	IRELAND	WM	IRISH	HACK MAN	045	B	1	14
HAZELWOOD	JOHN		1	M	50	ENGLAND	NG	ENGLISH	F	043	A	2	36
HAZELWOOD	WILLIAM		1		17	ENGLAND	WM	ENGLISH		045	B	1	69
HAZLETON	ALMIRA		1	1	21	O	CE	ENGLISH	HOUSE MAID	043	H	2	46
HAZLETON	ELMIRA		1	1	21	ONTARIO	CE	ENGLISH	HOUSEMAID	043	H	2	46
HAZLETON	FREDRICK		1		38	NEW BRUNSWICK	CE	ENGLISH	LAB	043	H	2	42
HAZLETON	HANNAH		1	1	33	O	BC	SCOTCH		043	H	2	42
HAZLETON	JOHN				28	O	CE	ENGLISH	LAB	043	H	2	42
HEACOCK	AMOS			M	66	O	CN	WELSH	F	043	A	2	16
HEACOCK	DELILAH		1		55	O	QU	ENGLISH		043	A	6	40
HEACOCK	EDWARD			M	36	O	QU	ENGLISH	BLACKSMITH	043	A	2	16
HEACOCK	GEVE				62	O	QU	ENGLISH	LAB	043	B	4	5
HEACOCK	JARED				32	O	QU	ENGLISH	F LAB	043	B	4	4
HEACOCK	LINVILLE				28	O	QU	WELSH	F LAB	043	B	4	33
HEACOCK	SETH				48	O	QU	ENGLISH	F	043	A	6	39
HEACOCK	WILFRED				23	O	NG	ENGLISH	F	043	A	6	40
HEAFEY	HANNAH			1	58	IRELAND	RC	IRISH		043	H	1	9
HEAL	MARGRETT		2	1	16	O	PM			045	C	1	D
HEAL	ROBERT				62	ENGLAND	CE	ENGLISH	F	043	B	4	3
HEAL	SAMUEL				34	ENGLAND	WM	ENGLISH	FARMER	043	B	3	56
HEAL	WILLIAM		2		6	O	PM			045	C	1	D
HEAL	WM				43	ENG	PM	ENG	F	045	C	1	36
HEALEY	ELLEN			1	50	IRELAND	RC	IRISH	TAILORESS	043	A	4	14
HEALEY	JOHN				45	IRELAND	RC	IRISH	LAB	044	C	2	20
HEARNS	FRANCES		1	1	19	PRINCE EDWARD	EM	FRENCH		043	A	6	37
HEARNS	MARY		1	1	2	O	EM	IRISH		043	A	6	37
HEART	HENRY				51	O	WM	ENGLISH	FARM LABORER	045	D	1	49
HEASLIP	BENJAMIN				47	IRELAND	CE	IRISH	F	043	A	6	53
HEATH	JOHN				44	ENGLAND	CE	ENGLISH	BOOT MAKER	045	B	2	2
HEATH	WILLIAM				60	ENGLAND	WM	ENGLISH	FARMER	045	A	3	1
HEATH	WILLIAM		1		30	O	PM	ENGLISH	LABORER	045	D	2	20
HEBBETH	H	WILLIAM			59	ENGLAND	CE	ENGLISH	FARMER	045	A	1	75
HEBER	CHARLES				37	GERMANY	RC	GERMAN	FARMER & MILKMAN	045	A	1	78
HECTOR	MARY			1	60	IRE	RC	IRE		044	B	2	77
HEDGES	MARTHA		1	1	26	ENG	WM	ENG		044	B	1	6
HEENAN	MICHAEL		1		20	IRELAND	RC	IRISH	SERVANT	045	D	1	8
HEENAN	PATRICK		1		24	IRE	RC	IRISH	SERVANT	044	B	1	23
HEIGHTON	JANE			1	59	ENGLAND	WM	ENGLISH		045	B	1	9
HEISE	CHRISTAIN				53	O	TU	GERMAN	FARMER	045	D	2	63
HEISE	CHRISTOPHER				42	O	TU	GERMAN	FARMER	045	D	2	48
HEISE	DANIEL				30	O	TU	GERMAN	STOREKEEPER	045	D	2	49
HEISE	DANIEL	B			26	O	TU	GERMAN	F	043	B	1	33
HEISE	ELISABETH		2	1	79	US	TU			045	D	2	D
HEISE	JACOB				40	O	TU	GERMAN	FARMER	045	D	2	17
HEISE	JACOB				75	US	TU	GERMAN	FARMER	045	D	2	28
HEISE	JOHN				33	O	TU	GERMAN	FARMER	045	D	2	16
HEISE	JOHN				82	US	TU	GERMAN		045	D	2	63
HEISE	PETER				40	O	EM	GERMAN	FARMER	045	D	2	60
HEISE	SAMUEL		1		21	O	TU	GERMAN	SERVANT	045	D	2	61
HEISEY	CHRISTOPHER				56	CANADA	CN	GERMAN	FARMER	045	D	6	25
HELLER	JOHN		1		11	O	PS	SCOTCH	SERVANT	043	A	6	58
HELLEWELL	FRANK				31	O	CE	IRISH	MILLER	045	A	3	2
HELLIWEL	WILLIAM	P			39	O	CE	ENGLISH	FARMER	045	A	1	92
HELLIWELL	HARRIET		1	1	28	O	CE	ENGLISH		045	C	2	56
HELLIWELL	MARGARET		1	1	30	O	CE	ENGLISH		045	C	2	56
HELLIWELL	WILLIAM				59	ENGLAND	CE	ENGLISH	MILLER	045	C	2	5
HELMER	SUSAN			1	42	ENGLAND	CE	ENGLISH	SEAMSTRESS	043	E	2	36
HELMKEY	ANN			1	45	O	CN	FRENCH		043	B	3	43
HELMKEY	EMILY			1	24	ENGLAND	CN	ENGLISH		043	B	3	44
HELMKEY	GEORGE		2		39	O	CN		FARMER	043	B	3	D
HELMKEY	GEORGE		2			O	CN			043	B	3	D
HELMKEY	HANNAH			1	66	O	EM	GERMAN		045	D	2	22
HELMKEY	ISAIAH		1		32	O	CN	GERMAN	LABOURER	043	B	3	47
HELMKEY	ISAIH		1		34	O	WM	GERMAN	LAB	043	B	5	10
HELMKEY	JOHN				42	O	WM	GERMAN	FARMER	043	B	3	47
HELMKEY	JOHN				46	O	WM	GERMAN	FARMER	045	D	2	22
HEMINGWAY	FOSTER				32	O	WM	GERMAN	FARMER	045	D	3	46
HEMINGWAY	GEORGE		1		25	O	WM	GERMAN	FARMER	045	D	1	37
HEMINGWAY	MOSES				62	O	WM	SCOTCH	FARMER	045	D	3	14
HEMINGWAY	PAULINE		1	1	21	O	WM	GERMAN		045	D	1	37
HEMON	TERESA		1	1	20	GERMANY	PS	GERMAN	SERVANT	044	C	4	69
HEMPHILL	JOSEPH				77	IRELAND	CS	IRISH	F	044	B	6	47
HEMPSHALL	ELIZABETH		1	1	24	O	WM	ENGLISH	SERVANT	043	E	1	51
HENAN	EDWARD				74	IRELAND	RC	IRISH	LABOURER	044	C	3	42

SURNAME	NAME1	NAME2	STRAY	SEX	AGE	BIRTHPL	RELIGION	ORIGIN	OCCUP	DIST	SUB_DIST	DIV	PAGE
HENDERSBY	JOHN				39	ENG	CE	ENG	F	044	B	2	75
HENDERSON	ANDREW				42	SCOTLAND	CP	SCOTCH	MERCHANT	043	D		16
HENDERSON	ANDREW				42	SCOTLAND	CP	SCOTCH	BOOK SELLER	043	D		86
HENDERSON	ANDREW				33	IRELAND	CE	IRISH	TAPE WEAVER	043	H	1	22
HENDERSON	ANDW				44	0	BA	IRISH	F	043	B	2	45
HENDERSON	CATHARINE		2	1	81	IRELAND	CE			044	A	2	D
HENDERSON	DAVID				26	US	WM	AFRICAN	LAB	043	B	5	2
HENDERSON	ELMS				30	0	CE	ENGLISH	BARRESTER	045	B	2	31
HENDERSON	GEORGE				44	0	CE	IRISH	LAB	044	B	6	36
HENDERSON	JAMES				53	SCOTLAND	WM	SCOTCH	FARMER	043	A	4	37
HENDERSON	JAMES				35	SCOTLAND	CP	SCOTCH	F	044	B	6	3
HENDERSON	JAMES				55	IRELAND	CE	IRISH	SHOEMAKER	045	D	5	73
HENDERSON	JAMES		2		30	0	CE		BUTCHER	045	D	5	D
HENDERSON	JOSEPH	L			25	0	CE	IRISH	F	043	E	2	50
HENDERSON	MARY		1	1	71	IRELAND	CE	IRISH		044	A	2	15
HENDERSON	MARY	A	1	1	24	0	CE	IRISH	INMATE	045	B	1	72
HENDERSON	NEIL		1		18	0	OP	ENGLISH	FARMER	043	A	3	1
HENDERSON	SARAH			1	50	IRELAND	CS	IRISH		045	D	5	13
HENDERSON	WILLIAM				30	SCOTLAND	CP	SCOTCH		045	B	2	13
HENDRICK	ANGELINA			1	44	0	EM	GERMAN		045	D	1	38
HENDRICK	JOHN				36	0	CN	GERMAN	FARMER	045	D	4	45
HENDRICK	MILES				32	IRELAND	RC	IRISH	LAB	044	C	4	56
HENDRICK	SAMUEL				65	0	MN	GERMAN	FARMER	045	D	4	45
HENDRIE	JOHN				28	SCOTLAND	RP	SCOTCH	AGENT FOR RAILWAY	044	C	4	5
HENDRIE	WILLIAM		1		25	SCOTLAND	CP	SCOTCH	FARM LAB	044	C	2	38
HENDRY	ELIZABETH		1	1	81	SCOTLAND	CS	SCOTCH		043	E	2	21
HENDRY	GEORGE				72	SCOTLAND	CP	SCOTCH	F	044	A	1	29
HENDRY	JAMES				39	QUE	CP	SCOTCH	F	044	A	1	30
HENDRY	THOMAS				38	SCOTLAND	CN	SCOTCH	FOUNDER SMITH	043	D		81
HENESEY	DENNIS				50	IRELAND	RC	IRISH	F	043	B	1	35
HENESEY	MICHAEL				70	IRELAND	RC	IRISH	F	043	B	1	35
HENESSY	JAMES				45	IRE	RC	IRE	GARDINER	044	B	2	23
HENLY	WILLIAM				39	ENGLAND	CE	ENGLISH	BUTCHER	045	D	5	48
HENNESSY	CAROLINE			F	68	IRELAND	RC	IRISH		043	A	1	7
HENNESY	ELISA			1	36	ENGLAND	CE	ENGLISH		045	B	2	7
HENNESY	JOHN				45	IRELAND	RC	IRISH	LAB	043	B	2	32
HENNESY	PATRICK				35	IRELAND	CP	IRISH	LABOURER	045	D	6	4
HENRICK	GEORGE				27	0	WM	GERMAN	LABOURER	045	D	4	7
HENRICK	JACOB				33	0	WM	GERMAN	FARMER	045	D	2	51
HENRICK	JOHN				40	0	LU	GERMAN	FARMER	045	D	2	27
HENRICKS	ROSINA		1	1	24	0	VM	GERMAN		045	D	3	39
HENRY	ALEXANDER		1	M	9	0	FK	SCOTLAND		043	A	5	33
HENRY	BARNES		1		8	0	PM	ENGLISH		044	B	6	30
HENRY	CHARLES				38	IRELAND	PS	IRISH	F	043	E	3	11
HENRY	ELIZABETH			1	70	IRE	CS	IRE	WEAVER	044	B	4	10
HENRY	JAMES				39	SCOTLAND	NC	SCOTCH	F	043	E	2	31
HENRY	JAMES				28	0	CE	ENG	F	044	B	2	64
HENRY	JAMES		1		14	0	CP	SCOTCH		044	B	6	2
HENRY	JAMES	R			70	SCOTLAND	CP	SCOTCH		045	B	1	18
HENRY	JESSE				49	0	CE	IRE	F	045	C	1	65
HENRY	JOHN		2		72	IRE	CE		F	044	B	2	D
HENRY	JOHN				66	SCOTLAND	CP	SCOTCH	FARMER	045	A	3	30
HENRY	ROBERT		1		6	0	FK	SCOTLAND		043	A	5	33
HENRY	ROBERT		1		16	0	PM	ENG	FARM SERVANT	044	B	1	44
HENRY	THOMAS			M	40	IRELAND	PS	IRISH	MERCHANT	043	A	2	47
HENRY	WILLIAM			M	32	IRELAND	PR	IRISH	LUMBER	043	A	1	74
HENRY	WILLIAM				44	IRELAND	CE	IRISH	FARMER	043	A	4	62
HENRY	WILLIAM		1		10	0	WM	GERMAN		043	B	1	20
HENRY	WILLIAM				46	SCOTLAND	OP	SCOTCH	F	043	H	2	32
HENRY	WILLIAM				46	SCOTLAND	CS	SCOTCH	FARMER	043	H	2	32
HENRY	WILLIAM				67	SCOTLAND	CP	SCOTCH	FARMER	045	D	4	19
HENSEY	MARY		1	1	55	IRELAND	RC	IRISH		045	B	1	21
HENSON	DAVID			M	60	ENGLAND	WM	ENGLISH	F	043	A	2	17
HEPSON	WILLIAM				49	ENGLAND	CE	ENGLISH	SHOE MAKER	045	D	3	80
HERBERT	JAMES		1	M	35	ENGLAND	PR	ENGLISH	LAB	043	A	1	74
HERBUT	ANDW				50	ENGLAND	WM	ENGLISH	PAINTER	044	B	5	23
HERD	ROBERT		1		21	SCOTLAND	PS	SCOTCH	LAB	045	C	2	32
HERD	WILLIAM				40	0	WM	ENGLISH	F	044	C	1	8
HERINGTON	JOHN				81	IRELAND	WM	IRELAND		045	D	2	22
HERON	AGNESS			1	55	IRELAND	UP	IRISH	SHOPKEEPER	045	D	1	38
HERON	ANDREW				70	0	PS	SCOTCH	LAND AGENT	045	B	1	69
HERON	CAROLINE		1	1	19	0	WM	ENGLISH		045	C	2	16
HERON	CHARLOTTE			1	26	0	WM	ENG		045	C	1	66
HERON	GEORGE				26	0	WM	ENG	F	045	C	1	4
HERON	HANNAH		1	1	16	0	WM	ENGLISH		045	C	2	16
HERON	JANE			1	52	0	CP	ENG		045	C	1	4
HERON	JOHN				73	0	CP	SCOT	F	045	C	1	57
HERON	JOHN				54	ENG	BA	ENG	BRICKLAYER	045	C	1	66
HERON	SAMUEL		2		34	0	PM		BRICKLAYER	045	C	1	D
HERON	WILLIAM				65	0	WM	SCOT	F	045	C	1	3
HERRICK	ADAM				35	0	LU	GERMANY	FARMER	045	D	2	25
HERRICK	DAVID				53	0	EM	ENGLISH	CARPENTER	045	D	5	49
HERRICK	ESTHER		1	1	16	0	CO	ENGLISH		045	D	5	5
HERRINGTON	JANE		1	1	40	0	CN	ENGLISH		045	D	5	59
HERRINGTON	JOHN				26	0	WM	ENGLISH	HOTEL KEEPER	043	E	3	24
HERTZ	EDWARD				40	ENGLAND	CE	ENGLISH	FARM LABOURER	043	B	1	7
HESIE	ABRAHAM				27	0	CN	GERMAN	FARMER	045	D	4	46
HESIE	ENEAS				28	0	CN	GERMAN	FARMER	045	D	4	53
HESIE	SAMUEL		1		20	0	TU	GERMAN	LABOURER	045	D	4	5
HESK	GEORGE				42	ENGLAND	PM	ENGLISH	FARM LABOURER	045	C	3	32
HESLIP	MARGARET		1	1	19	0	WM	ENG	SERVANT	044	B	1	66
HESLOP	GIDEON				62	SCOT	CP	SCOT	F	044	B	2	53
HESLOP	JAMES				38	ENGLAND	CE	ENGLISH	FARMER	045	D	1	39
HESLOP	JAMES				74	ENGLAND	WM	ENGLISH	F	044	C	2	41
HESLOP	THOMAS				45	ENGLAND	CE	ENGLISH	FARMER	044	C	1	17
HESS	JOHN	D			29	US	MN	GERMAN	LABOURER	045	D	4	45
HETH	THOMAS				27	ENGLAND	CE	ENGLISH	LABOURER	045	D	6	30
HETHRINGTON	GEORGE				44	ENGLAND	CE	ENGLISH	FARMER	045	A	1	14
HETT	ROLAND		1		28	ENGLAND	CE	ENGLISH		043	H	2	27
HEVENER	FANY		1	1	19	0	IM	GERMAN		045	D	3	33
HEWARD	JOHN	0			50	0	CE	ENGLISH		045	B	2	28
HEWARD	VIOLET		2	1			CE			045	B	2	D
HEWETT	ELISA		1	1	22	IRELAND	WM	IRISH	SERVANT	045	B	2	17
HEWISON	ANN	E		1	47	0	WM	ENGLISH		045	D	2	10
HEWIT	ROBERT				37	IRELAND	CE	IRISH	F	043	E	1	54
HEWITT	CATHARINE			1	65	IRELAND	CE	IRISH		045	A	1	49

SURNAME	NAME1	NAME2	STRAY	SEX	AGE	BIRTHPL	RELIGION	ORIGIN	OCCUP	DIST	SUB_DIST	DIV	PAGE
HEWITT	ELEANOR			1	64	0	CE	IRISH		043	D		65
HEWITT	ELIZABETH			1	55	IRELAND	CP	IRISH	F	045	C	2	14
HEWITT	JAMES				30	0	CE	IRISH	CARPENTER	045	A	1	70
HEWITT	JAMES				22	0	CE	IRISH	LAB	045	A	1	93
HEWITT	JAMES				53	IRELAND	CE	IRISH	FARMER	045	A	2	27
HEWITT	ROBERT				40	IRELAND	CE	IRISH	LAB	043	B	1	28
HEWITT	ROBERT				35	0	CE	ENGLISH	HOTEL KEEPER	043	D		68
HEWITT	ROBERT				52	ENGLAND	WM	ENGLISH	MACHINIST	045	D	5	17
HEWITT	WILLIAM				41	ENGLAND	CE	ENGLISH	STORE KEEPER	045	B	1	5
HEWITT	WILLIAM				52	ENGLAND	CE	IRISH	LAB	044	C	4	16
HEWS	HEWS		1	1	51	ENGLAND	WM	ENGLISH		044	C	3	31
HEY	KING				38	SCOTLAND	PS	SCOTCH	LABORER	045	D	6	71
HEYNS	MATHEW		1		19	CANADA	WM	GERMAN		045	D	6	40
HEYS	MARY	ANN	2	1	57	ENGLAND	CO	ENGLISH		044	C	2	D
HEYS	RICHARD				59	ENGLAND	CO	ENGLISH	GARDENER	044	C	2	18
HEZELL	GEORGE		1		24	ENGLAND	CE	ENGLISH	BLACKSMITH	044	C	2	34
HICKEY	ANNE			1	50	IRELAND	RC	IRISH		044	C	4	53
HICKEY	JAMES				46	0	WM	ENGLISH	STATION AGENT	044	C	3	67
HICKEY	JAMES	C	2		0	0	WM			044	C	3	D
HICKEY	JOHN	J			25	IRELAND	RC	IRISH	F	044	A	2	39
HICKEY	MARY		1	1	15	0	RC	IRISH		045	C	2	1
HICKEY	PATRICK				45	IRELAND	RC	IRISH	LAB	045	C	2	35
HICKEY	ROBERT		1		20	IRELAND	RC	IRISH	F LAB	043	F		24
HICKMAN	JOHN		1		20	0	PM	ENGLISH	FARM LABOURER	045	D	3	6
HICKS	ANNIE		1	1	19	0	WM	IRISH	SERVANT	045	B	2	37
HICKS	HENRY	M			36	0	WM	ENGLISH	STUDENT	045	B	2	16
HICKS	JOHN				38	ENGLAND	NC	ENGLISH	F	043	E	2	29
HICKS	WILLIAM				45	ENGLAND	CE	ENGLISH	MILLER	044	B	5	1
HIDE	WILLIAM		1		20	ENGLAND	CE	ENGLISH	HOSTLER	043	B	3	54
HIGGINS	CHARLES		1		12	0	CE	IRISH		045	C	2	54
HIGGINS	JOHN	A			34	0	CE	IRISH	F	045	C	2	38
HIGGINS	SARAH		1	1	27	0	WM	ENGLISH		044	A	1	3
HIGGINS	WILLIAM				73	QUE	CE	ENGLISH	HIGH BAILIFF	045	A	1	30
HIGGS	HENRY				70	ENGLAND	CE	ENGLISH	LAB	043	E	2	6
HIGGS	JOHN				41	IRELAND	CE	IRISH	LAB	044	B	5	34
HIGH	WILLIAM				48	ENG	WM	ENG	SHOEMAKER	044	B	1	63
HIGHAM	WILLIAM				33	ENGLAND	CE	ENGLISH	LABOURER	045	D	5	7
HIGHFIELD	HENRY				37	ENGLAND	CO	ENGLISH	PEDLAR	043	B	3	64
HIGHLAND	MARY			1	80	IRELAND	RC	IRISH		043	E	1	6
HIGINS	CHARLES		1		39	ENGLAND	CE	ENGLISH	LAB	045	A	3	36
HIGINS	MARY		1	1	26	SCOTLAND	CE	SCOTCH		045	A	3	36
HIGMAN	WILLIAM		1		33	ENGLAND	CE	ENGLISH	SERVANT	045	B	2	34
HILANA	EDWARD				38	IRELAND	RC	IRISH	F LAB	043	B	4	21
HILBORN	ABIGAIL		1	1	55	NEW BRUNSWICK	EM	ENGLISH		043	E	1	4
HILBORN	PETER			M	35	0	CN	SCOTLAND	F	043	A	5	11
HILBORN	SETH				37	0	CN	IRISH	F	043	A	6	45
HILBORN	WILLIAM	S			27	ONT	CN	GERMAN	PUMPMAKER	043	D		52
HILBOURN	SARAH			F	63	0	CN	IRELAND		043	A	5	20
HILBURN	JESSE				65	0	CN	IRISH	F	043	A	6	46
HILL	ALBERT	ARTHUR	1		9	0	WM	GERMAN		043	D		46
HILL	ALEXANDER				73	IRELAND	WM	IRISH	FARMER	043	B	3	42
HILL	ALEXANDER		1		27	IRELAND	CP	IRISH	F LAB	043	B	4	13
HILL	ALEXANDER				64	SCOTLAND	PS	SCOTCH	GARDNER	044	C	4	46
HILL	AMOS	H	1		14	0	WM	GERMAN		043	D		46
HILL	CHARLES				26	FRANCE	CE	FRENCH	FARMER	043	B	3	3
HILL	CHARLES	ALEXANDER	1		20	0	WM	GERMAN	LABORER	043	D		46
HILL	EDWARD				47	ENGLAND	CE	ENGLISH	GARDENER	045	A	1	81
HILL	ELIZ	JANE	2	1	3	0	CE			043	B	3	D
HILL	ELIZABETH		1	1	46	0	WM	ENGLISH	SERVANT	045	D	3	58
HILL	ELIZABETH		1	1	40	IRELAND	WM	IRISH	F LAB	044	C	1	31
HILL	EMILY		1	1	8	0	WM	ENGLISH		045	D	3	58
HILL	ESTHER		1	1	18	0	WM	ENGLISH	SERVANT	043	D		85
HILL	FRANCES		1	1	50	ENGLAND	CE	ENGLISH		044	C	4	5
HILL	GEORGE				30	0	PM	ENGLISH	CARPENTER	043	A	3	14
HILL	GEORGE		1		35	IRELAND	CE	IRISH	COOPER	044	B	6	58
HILL	GEORGE		1		18	CANADA	MN	GERMAN		045	D	6	58
HILL	GEORGE		1		70	0	CE	IRISH	SERVANT	044	C	3	17
HILL	GEORGEE		1		8	0	CN	ENGLISH		043	B	4	29
HILL	HANNAH			1	57	0	CN	IRISH		043	B	3	37
HILL	HARRIET	LOUISA	1	1	6	0	WM	GERMAN		043	D		46
HILL	HENRY	HARRINGTON	1		10	0	WM	GERMAN		043	D		46
HILL	HONOR			1	45	IRELAND	RC	IRISH		044	C	3	60
HILL	JAMES				66	IRELAND	WM	IRISH	WEAVER	043	B	2	41
HILL	JANE			1	56	IRELAND	RP	IRISH		044	C	3	65
HILL	JERAMIAH				51	ENGLAND	CP	ENGLISH	F	043	B	4	19
HILL	JOHN				60	IRELAND	PM	IRISH	MERCHANT	043	B	3	9
HILL	JOHN				30	0	CE	IRISH	GENTLEMAN	043	B	3	10
HILL	JOHN	F			43	0	WM	IRISH	F	044	A	2	34
HILL	MARGARET	ANN	1	1	22	0	WM	GERMAN		043	D		46
HILL	MINNIE		1	1	1	0	WM	GERMAN		043	D		47
HILL	MOSES				26	0	WM	IRISH		043	B	3	43
HILL	MOSES				47	0	CP	ENGLISH	F	043	H	2	10
HILL	MOSES				47	ONTARIO	CS	ENGLISH	FARMER	043	H	2	10
HILL	RACHEL		1	1	33	0	CN	ENGLISH		043	B	4	29
HILL	ROBERT				38	SCOTLAND	OP	SCOTCH	MACHINIST	043	A	3	17
HILL	ROBERT				37	0	WM	IRISH	CARPENTER	043	B	3	24
HILL	ROBERT		2		89	IRELAND	CP		F	044	C	4	D
HILL	SAMUEL		1		52	ENGLAND	CE	ENGLISH	F	044	C	4	5
HILL	SARAH		1	1	12	0	CE	IRISH	F LAB	044	C	1	20
HILL	SILAS				40	ENGLAND	CE	ENGLISH	F	045	A	4	4
HILL	SUSAN			1	55	0	WM	ENGLISH		043	E	1	13
HILL	THOMAS			M	43	ENGLAND	WM	ENGLAND	F	043	A	5	4
HILL	THOMAS		1		63	0	WM	GERMAN	HOSTLER	043	D		46
HILL	THOMAS		1		19	0	WM	ENGLISH	LABORER	045	D	3	58
HILL	THOMAS				60	IRELAND	WM	IRISH	SHOE MAKER	044	C	1	31
HILL	THOMAS		1		30	SCOTLAND	RP	SCOTCH		044	C	3	31
HILL	THOMAS	JOHN	2		6	0	CE			043	B	3	D
HILL	WILLIAM				55	IRELAND	CN	IRISH	FARMER	043	B	3	37
HILL	WILLIAM				36	0	WM	IRISH	FARMER	043	B	3	46
HILL	WILLIAM				27	0	NC	ENGLISH		043	E	1	13
HILL	WILLIAM				41	0	CE	IRISH	COOPER	044	C	3	27
HILL	WILLIAM	JOHN	1		16	0	WM	GERMAN	LAB	043	D		46
HILL	WILLIAM	JOHN	1		4	0	WM	GERMAN		043	D		47
HILL (REV)	GEO	S J			50	EAST INDIES	CE	ENGLISH	MINISTER	045	D	4	28
HILLARD	THOMAS				62	ENGLAND	CE	ENGLISH	F	044	C	1	34
HILLARY	ELLEN			1	60	IRELAND	CE	IRISH		043	C		37

SURNAME	NAME1	NAME2	STRAY	SEX	AGE	BIRTHPL	RELIGION	ORIGIN	OCCUP	DIST	SUB_DIST	DIV	PAGE
HILLARY	ROBERT				39	IRELAND	CE	FRENCH	PHYSICIAN	043	C		40
HILLER	WILLIAM		1		26	ENGLAND	CE	GERMAN		044	C	4	62
HILLERY	MICHAEL				29	IRELAND	CE	IRISH	PHYSICIAN	045	D	6	77
HILLIAR	UNDERILL				39	ENG	WM	ENG	BLACKSMITH	044	B	2	42
HILLIARD	ELIZABETH		1	1	21	ENGLAND	PM	ENGLISH		044	B	5	36
HILLIS	JOHN				58	IRELAND	PS	IRISH	F	043	E	3	11
HILLS	ANNE		1	1	26	0	CE	IRISH	COOK	044	C	4	5
HILLS	CHARLES		1		30	ENGLAND	CE	ENGLISH	GROOM	044	C	4	5
HILLYARD	ALFRED				50	0	NC	ENGLISH	LAB	043	C		16
HILSON	GEO				70	SCOTLAND	UP	SCOTCH	F	044	B	5	73
HILTON	ABRAHAM				44	ENGLAND	WM	ENGLISH	F	044	A	3	21
HILTON	JOHN				56	ENGLAND	CE	ENGLISH	LAB	044	C	2	50
HILTS	FREDRICK		1		85	UNITED STATES	PM	GERMAN		043	B	2	28
HILTS	GODFREY				41	0	TU	GERMAN	FARMER	045	D	2	55
HILTS	HUGH				36	0	TU	GERMAN	LABORER	045	D	2	52
HILTS	JAMES				24	0	VM	ENGLISH	LABOURER	045	D	5	66
HILTS	JANE			1	61	ENGLAND	CE	ENGLISH		045	D	2	66
HILTS	JILES				29	0	WM	GERMAN	LAB	045	C	2	48
HILTS	JOHN				75	US	TU	US		045	D	2	55
HILTS	JOHN				42	0	TU	GERMAN	FARMER	045	D	2	56
HILTS	LASH	ELISHA			31	0	CP	GERM	F	045	C	1	1
HILTS	MARY	A	1	1	19	0	TU	GERMAN	SERVANT	043	B	1	26
HILTS	MARY	ANN	1	1	18	0	CP	GERMAN	SERVANT	043	H	2	50
HILTS	MARY ANN		1	1	18	ONTARIO	CP	GERMAN	SERVANT	043	H	2	50
HILYER	ANN		1	1	45	0	WM	FRENCH		043	A	6	49
HILYER	ELI				45	0	WM	ENGLISH	LABOURER	045	D	5	67
HILYER	MARIAH		1	1	71	0	WM	FRENCH		043	A	6	49
HILYER	ZENAS		2		82	U STATES			FARMER	043	A	6	D
HINCHEY	JAMES				38	IRELAND	RC	IRISH	CARPENTER	044	B	5	3
HINCKS	WILLIAM				78	IRELAND	UT	IRISH	PROFESSOR	045	B	1	18
HINDLE	GREENWOOD				41	ENGLAND	CE	ENGLISH	F	044	A	2	40
HINSON	FLORA			F	80	SCOTLAND	PS	SCOTCH		043	A	2	44
HIRCLIFF	THOMAS				47	ENGLAND	CE	ENGLISH	FARMER	043	G	2	53
HIRSCH	ALMIRA			F	48	0	CE	IRELAND		043	A	5	7
HIRSOPP	JOHN				61	ENGLAND	CE	ENGLISH	GENTLEMAN	043	C		44
HIRST	THOMAS				66	ENGLAND	CE	ENGLISH	BUTCHER	043	D		50
HIRST	THOMAS				36	ENGLAND	PM	ENGLISH	TILE MAKER	045	B	1	61
HIRTIS	ASA				35	ENGLAND	CE	ENGLISH	HOTEL KEEPER	043	B	1	8
HISLOP	JOHN				62	SCOT	PS	SCOT	F	044	B	2	57
HISSON	HENRY				28	0	BA	AFRICAN	LAB	043	E	2	79
HISSON	ROBERT				52	0	WM	AFRICAN	LAB	044	C	4	17
HISSON	WILLIAM				56	UNITED STATES	EM	AFRICAN	LAB	043	E	2	82
HITCH	JOHN				28	ENGLAND	OB	ENGLISH	BRICK MAKER	045	B	1	64
HITCHCOOK	JAMES				56	ENGLAND	PM	ENGLISH	MASON	045	D	4	23
HITCHNGS	WILLIAM	H			46	ENG	CE	ENGLISH	FARM SERVANT	044	B	4	11
HITTS	WILLIAM				28	0	TU	GERMAN	LABOURER	045	D	4	17
HOAG	AGNES		1	1	16	0	CE	IRELAND	SERVANT	045	D	2	27
HOAG	FRED	C	1		11	US	WM	ENGLISH		043	D		72
HOARE	CHRISTOPHER				34	0	MN	GERMAN	FARMER	045	D	4	19
HOBBS	ELLEN		2	1	33	0	CE			044	B	1	D
HOBBS	EMILY		1	1	35	AUSTRALIA	CE	ENGLISH		044	C	4	57
HOBBS	GEORGE		1		37	IRELAND	CE	IRISH	GOVERNMENT CLERK	044	C	4	57
HOBBS	JAMES				43	ENGLAND	WM	ENGLISH	MILLER	043	E	3	19
HOBBS	JAMES				37	ENGLAND	CE	ENGLISH	BREWER	043	F		29
HOBBS	JAMES				47	ENG	CE	ENG	MILLER	044	B	1	55
HOBBS	MAUDE		1	1	6	NEW ZEALAND	CE	IRISH		044	C	4	57
HOBBS	PERCY		1			0	CE	IRISH		044	C	4	57
HOBDEN	JAMES	W			25	ENGLAND	CE	ENGLISH	CARPENTER	045	A	1	49
HOCKELEY	WILLIAM		1		11	ENGLAND	PM	ENGLISH		045	A	4	1
HODGE	JAMES				43	ENGLAND	CO	ENGLISH	TINSMITH	043	D		17
HODGE	JOHN				55	IRELAND	EM	IRISH	BLACKSMITH	043	D		10
HODGE	JOHN				33	ENGLAND	DI	ENGLISH	TINSMITH	043	D		17
HODGE	P	THOMAS			49	ENGLAND	CE	ENGLISH	MINISTER	045	A	3	5
HODGIN	MICHAEL				24	IRELAND	RC	IRISH	LAB	043	D		6
HODGIN	SOLOMON		1		18	0	WM	ENGLISH	LABOURER	045	D	4	27
HODGINS	JAMES				34	0	CE	ENGLISH	FARMER	045	D	2	34
HODGINS	JOHN				30	IRELAND	RC	IRISH	F LAB	043	A	6	15
HODGINS	JOHN				63	IRELAND	RC	IRISH	FARMER	043	G	1	19
HODGINS	JOHN	G			49	IRELAND	CE	IRISH	DEP SUPT EDUCATION	045	B	2	36
HODGINS	MICHAEL				53	IRELAND	RC	IRISH	F	043	A	6	57
HODGINS	MICHAEL				27	IRELAND	RC	IRISH	FARMER	043	G	1	20
HODGINS	PATRIC				52	IRELAND	RC	IRISH	F	043	A	6	14
HODGINS	ROSA		2	1		0	RC			043	A	6	D
HODGSON	HANNAH		1	1	12	0	PM	ENGLISH		044	A	3	3
HODGSON	JAMES				59	ENGLAND	WM	ENGLISH	TEACHER	044	C	3	48
HODGSON	THOMAS				41	ENGLAND	CE	ENGLISH	F	044	A	1	16
HODGSON	THOMAS				35	CANADA	WM	ENGLISH	FARMER	045	D	6	69
HODGSON	WILLIAM				27	0	CE	ENGLISH	CARPENTER	045	A	1	73
HOFFER	SAMUEL				30	0	CE	GERMAN	PHOTOGRAPHER	043	B	3	66
HOFFMAN	ESTHER			1	49	0	WM	GERMAN		043	A	3	44
HOGABOOM	JOHN	C			69	0	CE	ENGLISH	GENTLEMAN	043	D		74
HOGAN	JOHN			M	36	0	CE	IRISH	HOTEL KEEPER	043	A	1	48
HOGAN	MARY		1	1	27	0	CE	IRISH	SERVANT	044	B	1	16
HOGAN	PATRICK				43	IRELAND	RC	IRISH	LAB	043	B	4	2
HOGAR	JOHN				38	U STATES	BA	ENGLISH	LAB	043	A	6	59
HOGART	SARAH		1	1	23	0	CP	IRISH	MUSIC TEACHER	045	C	2	24
HOGART	SUSAN		1	1	19	0	CP	IRISH	SCHOOL TEACHER	045	C	2	24
HOGARTH	HENRY				60	ENG	WM	ENG	POSTMASTER	045	C	1	42
HOGG	ANDREW				70	IRELAND	CE	IRISH	LAB	043	F		8
HOGG	ANNE		1	1	16	0	CE	IRISH	SERVANT	044	C	3	28
HOGG	EDWARD				40	IRE	PS	IRE	LAB	044	B	2	67
HOGG	ELIZABETH			1	21	0	CP	SCOTCH		045	A	3	17
HOGG	GEORGE				40	ENGLAND	PM	ENGLISH	F	043	B	5	8
HOGG	JOHN				75	SCOTLAND	CP	SCOTCH	FARMER	045	A	3	38
HOGG	JOHN				40	SCOTLAND	CP	SCOTCH	MERCHANT	045	A	3	39
HOGG	JOHN		2		44	0	PS		MERCHANT	045	A	3	D
HOGG	MARGARET		1	1	9	0	BA	ENGLISH		045	A	2	4
HOGG	MARY		2	1	42	ENGLAND	PS			045	A	3	D
HOGG	PHILLIP				30	IRELAND	CE	IRISH	F	043	A	6	54
HOGG	ROBERT				57	IRELAND	CE	IRISH	F	043	E	1	25
HOGG	ROBERT				35	0	CP	SCOTCH	FARMER	045	A	3	39
HOGG	THOMAS				41	SCOTLAND	CS	SCOTCH	LAB	044	C	2	29
HOGG	THOMAS				68	IRELAND	CE	IRISH	LAB	044	C	3	12
HOGG	WILLIAM				42	0	CP	SCOTCH	MILLER	045	A	3	9
HOGGARD	CHRIST		1		14	ENGLAND	CE	ENGLISH		044	B	5	69
HOGGARD	GEORGE				38	ENGLAND	CE	ENGLISH	HOTEL KEEPER	043	D		66

SURNAME	NAME1	NAME2	STRAY	SEX	AGE	BIRTHPL	RELIGION	ORIGIN	OCCUP	DIST	SUB_DIST	DIV	PAGE
HOILES	WILLIAM				41	ENG	CE	ENG	F	044	B	4	15
HOLBORN	GEORGE				67	ENGLAND	PM	ENGLISH	GENT	043	E	2	20
HOLBORN	GEORGE				37	O	NC	ENGLISH	F	043	E	2	32
HOLBORN	JOHN				35	O	PM	ENGLISH	F	043	E	2	67
HOLDEN	ISAAC				43	ENGLAND	PM	ENGLISH	BUTCHER	043	A	3	8
HOLDEN	JANE		1	1	62	IRELAND	WM	IRISH		043	B	3	63
HOLDEN	JOHN				42	CANADA	DI	IRISH	FARMER	045	D	6	76
HOLDEN	WILLIAM				47	IRELAND	BA	IRISH	FARMER	045	D	6	54
HOLDEN	WILLIAM				38	ENGLAND	PM	ENGLISH	GARNER	044	C	4	92
HOLDENBY	GEORGE			M	63	ENGLAND	CE	ENGLAND	L	043	A	5	8
HOLDENBY	WILLIAM			M	66	ENGLAND	CE	ENGLAND	F	043	A	5	33
HOLDICH	ANNA			1	54	O	WM	GERMAN		045	D	1	37
HOLDON	SINCLAIR				68	IRELAND	WM	IRISH	DRUGGIST	045	D	5	9
HOLDSWORTH	JOHN				46	ENGLAND	CE	ENGLISH	SHOEMAKER	045	D	1	13
HOLLADAY	CHARLES		1		19	O	CE	ENGLISH	PAINTER	043	E	1	17
HOLLAND	EDWARD				26	O	RC	IRISH	BUTCHER	045	A	1	48
HOLLAND	JOHN		1		67	ENG	CE	ENG	RETIRED	044	B	1	27
HOLLAND	JOHN		1		18	IRELAND	RC	IRISH	COOPER	045	B	2	11
HOLLAND	JOSEPH		1		22	IRELAND	RC	IRISH		045	A	1	88
HOLLAND	MARY				50	IRELAND	RC	IRISH	WASHER WOMAN	045	B	1	33
HOLLAND	ROBERT				28	O	EP	ENG	F	044	B	2	7
HOLLAND	SAMUEL			M	25	L CANADA	WM	IRISH	SCHOOL TEACHER	043	A	2	14
HOLLAND	TERRANCE				55	IRELAND	RC	IRISH	BUTCHER	045	A	1	26
HOLLAND	TERRANCE				28	IRELAND	RC	IRISH	BUTCHER	045	A	1	43
HOLLERAN	CATHERINE			1	46	IRELAND	RC	IRISH		043	D		55
HOLLERAN	HANNAH			1	35	IRELAND	RC	IRISH		043	D		49
HOLLIDAY	MARY			1	33	ENGLAND	WM	SCOTCH		043	C		25
HOLLINGSHEAD	AMIS				62	O	QU	ENGLISH	F	043	A	6	43
HOLLINGSHEAD	AMOS		1		40	O	CO	ENGLISH	DENTIST	043	D		59
HOLLINGSHEAD	ANNA		1	1	17	O	EM	GERMAN	SERVANT	043	D		7
HOLLINGSHEAD	BENJAMIN				32	O	WM	ENGLISH	F	043	A	6	41
HOLLINGSHEAD	CATHARINE		1	1	11	O	WM	GERMAN		043	D		47
HOLLINGSHEAD	CHARLES				31	O	EM	ENG	F	044	B	1	18
HOLLINGSHEAD	EDWARD	GEORGE	1		14	O	CO	ENGLISH	CLERK	043	D		59
HOLLINGSHEAD	ELI				38	O	QU	ENGLISH	F	043	B	4	23
HOLLINGSHEAD	ISAAC				36	O	WM	ENGLISH	BLACKSMITH	043	A	6	44
HOLLINGSHEAD	JACOB				43	O	QU	ENGLISH	BLACKSMITH	043	A	4	19
HOLLINGSHEAD	JOEL			M	45	O	EM	ENGLISH	LAB	043	A	2	45
HOLLINGSHEAD	JOHN	ELI	1		15	O	WM	GERMAN		043	D		47
HOLLINGSHEAD	MARY		1	1	33	O	WM	GERMAN		043	D		47
HOLLINGSHEAD	SAML				39	O	EM	GERMAN	LAB	043	E	2	32
HOLLINGSHEAD	SAMUEL			M	62	O	WM	ENGLISH	F	043	A	2	23
HOLLINGSHEAD	SETH				46	O	WM	GERMAN	BLACKSMITH	043	D		49
HOLLINGSHEAD	SUSAN			1	70	UNITED STATES	EM	GERMAN		043	E	2	32
HOLLINGSHEAD	WILLIAM				39	O	WM	ENGLISH	F	043	B	5	3
HOLLINGSHEAD	WILLIAM				30	O	NG	GERMAN	F	044	B	6	46
HOLLINGSHED	GEO				32	ONT	OP	ENGLISH	FARMER	043	A	3	1
HOLLINGSHED	JOSEPH				25	O	EP	ENGLISH	FARMER	043	A	3	1
HOLLINGSHED	ROBERT				30	O	WM	ENGLISH	CARP & JOINER	043	A	3	2
HOLLINGSWORTH	ELI				50	US	WM	ENGLISH	LAB	044	C	4	76
HOLLYMAN	EDWARD				66	ENGLAND	CE	ENGLISH	CARPENTER	044	C	4	85
HOLMAN	EDWARD				37	ENGLAND	CE	ENGLISH	BLACKSMITH	043	C		37
HOLMAN	JOHN	E	1		20	O	CE	ENGLISH		045	A	4	8
HOLMBY	JOHN		1		61	ENGLAND	CE	ENGLISH	F LAB	043	B	4	35
HOLMES	FRANCES		1		45	ENGLAND	CE	ENGLISH	LABOURER	043	H	2	47
HOLMES	FRANCIS		1		45	ENGLAND	CE	ENGLISH	LAB	043	H	2	47
HOLMES	JAMES				35	ENGLAND	CM	ENGLISH	FARMER	045	D	4	1
HOLMES	JOHN				23	IRELAND	WM	IRISH	CLARK	045	B	1	61
HOLMES	JOHN		1		35	ENGLAND	PM	ENGLISH	GARDNER	045	B	1	62
HOLMES	JOHN				36	O	CP	SCOT	BLACKSMITH	045	C	1	54
HOLMES	JOHN				62	SCOTLAND	CP	SCOTCH	BLACKSMITH	045	C	4	23
HOLMES	MARTHA		1	1	76	O	UP	IRISH		045	D	1	33
HOLMES	RICHARD				54	IRELAND	RELIGION	IRISH	LAB	045	B	1	68
HOLMES	THOMAS				48	IRELAND	CE	IRISH	INN KEEPER	044	A	3	26
HOLMES	WILLIAM		1		16	O	CE		F	044	B	6	4
HOLMES	WILLIAM				61	IRELAND	RC	IRISH	WEAVER	045	D	6	8
HOLMES	WILLIAM				59	ENGLAND	BA	ENGLISH	F	045	A	4	34
HOLSTON	ELIZA		1	1	24	ENGLAND	CE	ENGLISH		044	C	4	48
HOLSWORTH	WILLIAM				38	ENGLAND	CE	ENGLISH	PEDLAR	045	C	2	25
HOLT	JOHN				45	O	CE	ENGLISH	LAB	043	F		31
HOLT	MIRON	E	1		17	USA	WM	IRE		045	C	1	14
HOLT	SARAH		2	1		O				043	F		D
HOLT	THOMAS				38	ENGLAND	PM	ENGLISH	LAB	043	A	6	41
HOLTON	WILLIAM				22	ENGLAND	IN	ENGLISH	BRICK MAKER	045	B	2	7
HOMAN	CHARLES		1		28	ENG	EM	ENG	FARM LAB	044	B	1	47
HOMELY	RICHARD				41	ENGLAND	CP	ENGLISH	FARMER	045	A	3	25
HOMER	EDWARD		1			O	CP	SCOTCH		045	C	3	30
HOMER	GEORGE				21	ENGLAND	NC	ENGLISH	LAB	043	F		23
HOMLEY	HENRY				35	ENGLAND	PM	ENGLISH	LAB	043	B	2	15
HONISHON	MATTHEW				66	IRELAND	RC	IRISH	LAB	043	D		30
HONSBERGER	ELI		1		14	O	MN	GERMAN		045	D	2	58
HONSBERGER	GEORGE		1		15	O	MN	GERMAN		045	D	2	58
HONSBERGER	MICHAEL		1		12	O	MN	GERMAN		045	D	2	58
HOOD	ANDREW				28	O	CP	SCOTCH	F	045	C	4	43
HOOD	ANDREW				42	US	WM		PHOTOGRAPHER	045	D	2	4
HOOD	CHARLES				41	QUE	PS	SCOTCH	ENGINEER	045	A	1	44
HOOD	FREDERICK				40	WALES	BA	ENGLISH	GREDER	044	C	4	87
HOOD	GEORGE		1		25	ENGLAND	PM	ENGLISH	SERVANT	045	D	6	6
HOOD	JAMES				44	IRELAND	CP	IRISH	F	043	B	5	24
HOOD	JAMES		1		45	IRE	PS	IRE	LAB	044	B	2	74
HOOD	JAMES		1		24	O	WM	ENGLISH	FARM LAB	044	C	2	17
HOOD	JOHN				40	GERMANY	LU	GERMAN	WEAVER	045	D	4	39
HOOD	REBECCA			1	68	IRELAND	PS	IRISH		044	A	1	14
HOOD	WILLIAM				65	SCOTLAND	OP	SCOTCH	F	045	C	4	1
HOOD	WILLIAM				43	SCOTLAND	CS	SCOTCH	FARMER	045	D	3	21
HOODLESS	CHARLES				41	ENGLAND	CE	ENGLISH	LAB	045	C	2	30
HOOK	CATHARINE			1	41	IRELAND	RC	IRISH		043	B	3	54
HOOPER	EDWARD				60	ENGLAND	CE	ENGLISH	CHEMIST & DRUGGIST	044	C	4	66
HOOPER	GEORGE				27	O	CE	ENGLISH	F	043	B	1	21
HOOPER	HENRY				54	ENGLAND	CE	ENGLISH	F	043	B	2	36
HOOPER	SAMUEL		1		15	O	WM	ENG	SERVANT	044	B	1	22
HOOPER	SUSANN	MARGARET		1	35	IRELAND	CE	IRISH		045	A	1	71
HOOVER	A	MARGARET	2	1	80	U STATES	WM			043	A	3	D
HOOVER	ABRAHAM				50	O	MN	GERMAN		043	B	2	15
HOOVER	ABRAHAM				49	O	WM	GERMAN	F	044	C	1	34
HOOVER	ABRAM				23	O	WM	ENGLISH	F	044	C	1	46

SURNAME	NAME1	NAME2	STRAY	SEX	AGE	BIRTHPL	RELIGION	ORIGIN	OCCUP	DIST	SUB_DIST	DIV	PAGE
HOOVER	CHRISTIAN				44	0	TU	GERMAN	F	045	D	2	59
HOOVER	CHRISTOPHER				56	0	TU	GERMAN	F	043	B	1	17
HOOVER	CHRISTOPHER				41	CANADA	MN	GERMAN	FARMER	045	D	6	22
HOOVER	CRISTIEN				36	0	MN	GERMAN	FARMER	045	D	6	4
HOOVER	DANIEL				45	CANADA	NG	GERMAN	FARMER	045	D	6	69
HOOVER	DAVID		1		20	0	MN	GERMAN		045	D	5	41
HOOVER	ELIJAH				30	ONTARIO	WM	GERMAN	FARMER	043	G	2	28
HOOVER	EMELINE		1	1	10	CANADA	WM	DUTCH		045	D	6	27
HOOVER	HENRY			M	63	0	WM	GERMAN	LAB	043	A	2	6
HOOVER	HENRYETTA		1	1	5	CANADA	WM	GERMAN		045	D	6	28
HOOVER	ISAAC				25	0	MN	GERMAN	F	043	B	2	20
HOOVER	J	R			27	0	WM	GERMAN	MILLER	045	D	3	3
HOOVER	JACOB				46	CANADA	MN	GERMAN	FARMER	045	D	6	57
HOOVER	JACOB				25	0	WM	GERMAN	F	044	C	1	35
HOOVER	JAMES		1	M	40	0	WM	GERMAN	FAR	043	A	1	68
HOOVER	JOHN				47	0	MN	GERMAN	F	043	B	2	3
HOOVER	JOHN				31	ONTARIO	CN	DUTCH	FARMER	043	G	1	48
HOOVER	JOHN				60	CANADA	MN	GERMAN	FARMER	045	D	6	19
HOOVER	JOHN				49	0	TU	GERMAN	FARMER	045	D	2	59
HOOVER	JOHN				81	US	TU	GERMAN		045	D	2	59
HOOVER	JOHN	B			36	CANADA	MN	GERMAN	FARMER	045	D	6	38
HOOVER	JOSEPH				30	0	WM	GERMAN	LAB	043	B	5	27
HOOVER	LUCY			1	50	0	EM	GERMAN		043	E	2	14
HOOVER	MARY		1	1	81	0	MN	GERMAN		045	D	6	17
HOOVER	MICHAEL			M	30	0	NG	IRISH	F	043	A	2	56
HOOVER	SAMUEL				33	0	MN	GERMAN	FARMER	045	D	6	7
HOOVER	SAMUEL				28	CANADA	MN	GERMAN	FARMER	045	D	6	20
HOOVER	SAMUEL		2		74	U STATES	MN		FARMER	045	D	6	D
HOPCROFT	JOHN				45	ENGLAND	CD	ENGLISH	SHOEMAKER	045	A	2	19
HOPE	ALFRED		1		26	ENGLAND	WM	ENGLISH		043	C		45
HOPE	ANDREW				48	ENGLAND	WM	ENGLISH	LABOURER	043	A	4	7
HOPE	DANIEL				36	ENGLAND	PM	ENGLISH	FARM LABOURER	045	C	3	20
HOPE	EDWARD				39	ENGLAND	WM	ENGLISH	BAKER	045	B	2	3
HOPE	GEORGE				30	0	NR	ENGLISH	FARMER	043	A	4	69
HOPE	JAMES				46	ENGLAND	CE	ENGLISH	FARM LABOURER	045	C	4	8
HOPE	JOHN				42	ENGLAND	CE	ENGLISH	FARMER	045	D	6	19
HOPE	JOSEPH		2		1	0	PS			045	D	6	D
HOPE	THOMAS		1		34	ENGLAND	CE	ENGLISH	LABOURER	045	D	3	45
HOPE	THOMAS	JEFFERSON	2		12	0	PM			045	C	3	D
HOPKINGS	JAMES	E			35	ENGLAND	CE	ENGLISH	F	044	C	2	45
HOPKINS	ANNIE		1	1	35	IRELAND	RC	IRISH	SERVANT	045	C	3	41
HOPKINS	CHARLES	D	1		16	0	CO	ENGLISH		045	D	3	77
HOPKINS	DAVID				50	IRE	CE	IRE	STORE KEEPER	044	B	2	22
HOPKINS	JAMES				44	IRELAND	WM	IRISH	F	043	E	3	9
HOPKINS	JOHN				42	IRELAND	WM	IRISH	F	043	E	3	11
HOPKINS	JOHN				69	IRELAND	WM	IRISH	GENT	043	E	3	26
HOPKINS	LAURA		1	1	21	0	BA	IRISH		045	B	2	22
HOPKINS	LOUIS		1		11	CANADA	WM	ENGLISH		045	D	6	26
HOPKINS	ROSINA		1	1	9	CANADA	WM	ENGLISH		045	D	6	26
HOPPER	DAVID				59	ENGLAND	PM	ENGLISH	FARMER	045	D	4	10
HOPPER	GEORGE				40	IRELAND	RC	IRISH	F	043	B	5	1
HOPPER	GEORGE		1		27	ENGLAND	CE	ENGLISH	BUTCHER	045	A	1	83
HOPPER	HENRY				31	0	PM	ENGLISH	FARMER	045	D	4	31
HOPPER	HENRY				38	ENGLAND	WM	ENGLISH	LABORER	045	D	1	50
HOPPER	JOHN				44	IRELAND	RC	IRISH	LAB	043	B	5	40
HOPPER	JOHN		2		20	0	WM		F LAB	043	B	5	D
HOPPER	JOHN		2			0	WM			043	B	5	D
HOPPER	ROBERT				48	ENG	WM	ENG	BUTCHER	044	B	2	27
HOPPER	ROBERT				27	0	PM	ENGLISH	FARMER	045	D	4	10
HOPPER	THOMAS				24	0	WM	ENGLISH	FARM LABORER	045	D	1	49
HOPPER	WILLIAM				37	IRELAND	RC	IRISH	LABORER	045	D	1	24
HOPS	THOMAS				50	ENGLAND	CE	ENGLISH	FARMER	044	A	2	21
HORAN	PATRICK				32	IRISH	RC	IRISH	INNKEEPER	043	E	2	12
HORD	JAMES				26	0	WM	ENG	F	044	B	1	51
HOREN	MICHAEL				34	IRE	RC	IRISH	LAB	044	B	1	13
HORGAN	ELIZABETH		1	1	77	IRELAND	RC	IRISH		044	C	4	87
HORNBROOK	HENRY				43	0	CE	ENGLAND	CARPENTER	044	B	5	11
HORNE	MARGARET			1	70	IRE	CE	IRE		044	B	1	17
HORNE	SARAH		1	1	21	ENGLAND	CE	ENGLISH	SERVANT	043	E	1	32
HORNER	BENJ				50	IRELAND	CE	IRISH	WEAVER	044	B	5	25
HORNER	DANIEL				71	US	TU	GERMAN	FARMER	045	D	2	19
HORNER	DANIEL				47	0	IL	GERMANY	FARMER	045	D	2	23
HORNER	DANIEL	F			35	0	TU	GERMAN	FARMER	045	D	4	16
HORNER	EDWARD				47	ENGLAND	CE	ENGLISH	LAB	044	B	6	58
HORNER	EMANUEL				33	0	CN	GERMAN	CARPENTER	045	D	6	8
HORNER	JACOB				48	0	EM	GERMAN	FARMER	045	D	2	19
HORNER	JACOB				44	0	TU	GERMAN	F & CIDER MAKER	045	D	2	61
HORNER	JOHN				40	0	TV	GERMANY	LABORER	045	D	2	23
HORNER	JOHN		1		11	0	CE	GERMAN		045	D	2	47
HORNER	MATHEW				33	ENGLAND	CE	ENGLISH	F	043	E	1	34
HORNER	NORMAN		1		4	0	CE	GERMAN		045	D	2	47
HORNER	REUBEN		1		9	0	CE	GERMAN		045	D	2	47
HORNER	SAMUEL				39	0	TU	GERMAN	FARMER	045	D	2	62
HORNER	SARAH			1	48	ENGLAND	WM	ENGLISH	SCHOOL TEACHER	045	B	1	30
HORNER	SUSANNAH		1	1	11	0	TU	GER		044	B	3	22
HORNER	WILLIAM				66	ENGLAND	CE	ENGLISH	F	043	E	1	35
HORNING	HENRY				31	0	CE	ENGLISH	LAB	043	H	1	31
HORNLEY	WILLIAM	H	2		1	0	PM			043	B	2	D
HORSELEY	HENERY				50	ENGLAND	WM	ENGLISH	F	044	C	3	15
HORSEY	SAMUEL				63	ENGLAND	WM	ENGLISH	F	045	C	4	11
HORSFALL	HENERY		1		26	ENGLAND	CE	ENGLISH	WEAVER	044	C	3	15
HORSLEY	HENRY		2			0	PM			043	B	1	D
HORSLEY	RICHARD				42	ENGLAND	CE	ENGLISH	F	043	B	1	40
HORSLEY	RICHD				38	0	PM	ENGLISH	F	044	B	5	80
HORTHOP	DORCAS		1	1	13	0	WM	ENGLISH		043	B	4	41
HORTHOP	ELIZABETH		1		7	0	WM	ENGLISH		043	B	4	41
HORTON	JOHN		1		17	ENGLAND	CE	ENGLISH	BLACKSMITH'S APPRENT	043	B	3	7
HORTON	WILLIAM				61	ENGLAND	PM	ENGLISH	CARPENTER	044	A	3	32
HORTOP	JOHN				27	0	WM	ENGLISH	MILLER	044	C	1	13
HOSE	RICHARD				28	ENGLAND	CE	ENGLISH	MILLER	044	B	6	15
HOSETTER	JOHN				40	0	CE	ENGLISH	DOCTOR M D	045	D	2	32
HOSHEL	BENJAMIN				61	0	PM	DUTCH	WEAVER CARPENTER	045	C	1	25
HOSHEL	GEORGE				46	0	WM	GERMAN	FARMER	045	D	1	28
HOSHOM	LYDIA		1	1	20	0	WM	ENGLISH	SERVANT	045	B	2	1
HOSLEY	CAROLINE		1	F	9	0	CE	ENGLISH		043	A	1	7
HOSTLER	WILLIAM				84	ENGLAND	CE	ENGLISH	FARMER	045	D	4	12

SURNAME	NAME1	NAME2	STRAY	SEX	AGE	BIRTHPL	RELIGION	ORIGIN	OCCUP	DIST	SUB_DIST	DIV	PAGE
HOUCK	EDWARD				43	QUEBEC	CP	GERMAN	FARMER	045	D	4	37
HOUGH	ANDREW				35	O	PS	ENGLISH	CARPENTER	045	C	3	46
HOUGH	ANNA	MATILDA	1	1	24	O	WM	ENGLISH	TEACHER	044	C	3	27
HOUGH	HENRY				40	O	PM	ENG	WAGGONMAKER BLACKSMI	045	C	1	71
HOUGH	JAS				77	USA	PM	ENG	F	045	C	1	68
HOUGH	WM				47	O	WM	ENG	F	045	C	1	56
HOURIGAN	DANIEL	W			34	IRELAND	RC	IRISH	SHOEMAKER	043	A	4	16
HOUSE	GEORGE				39	ENGLAND	BA	ENGLISH	F	043	B	2	13
HOUSTON	JOHN		1		31	ENGLAND	WM	ENGLISH	LAB	044	C	1	19
HOVENDAN	RICHARD				32	IRELAND	CE	IRISH	PAINTER	045	B	2	14
HOVER	ABRAHAM				43	O	MN	GERMAN	FARMER	045	D	4	48
HOVER	CHRIS				73	U STATES	MN	GERMAN	FARMER	045	D	6	16
HOVER	DANIEL				38	O	MN	GERMAN	FARMER	045	D	4	48
HOVER	FRANCY			1	69	US	MN	GERMAN		045	D	4	48
HOWARD	BROOK				53	O	CN	ENGLISH	F	043	E	1	8
HOWARD	CHARLES	H			68	ENGLAND	CE	ENGLISH	F	043	H	2	20
HOWARD	CHARLES	H			68	ENGLAND	CE	ENGLISH	FARMER	043	H	2	20
HOWARD	CHAS				42	ENGLAND	CE	ENGLISH	F	044	A	1	37
HOWARD	JAMES				35	UNITED STATES	PR	ENGLISH	LABORER	043	G	2	43
HOWARD	JOHN				45	ENGLAND	CE	ENGLISH	LABORER	044	A	2	46
HOWARD	JOHN				67	ENGLAND	CE	ENGLISH	ARCHITECT PL	044	C	4	5
HOWARD	MARGARET			1	60	IRELAND	RC	IRISH		043	D		55
HOWARD	MARY			1	64	IRELAND	RC	IRISH		043	D		55
HOWARD	MICHAEL				32	IRELAND	RC	IRISH	SADDLER	043	D		50
HOWARD	NICHOLAS				50	US	WM	AFRICAN	LAB	044	A	1	35
HOWARD	PATRICK				28	IRELAND	RC	IRISH	CARPENTER	043	E	3	43
HOWARD	STEPHEN				47	O	CN	ENGLISH	F	043	E	1	15
HOWARD	THOMAS				30	O	NG	ENGLISH	FARMER	043	B	3	47
HOWARTH	THOMAS				60	ENGLAND	CE	ENGLISH	MERCHANT	044	C	4	43
HOWELL	JOHN				75	ENGLAND	CO	ENGLISH	POST MASTER	044	B	5	34
HOWELL	RICHARD		1		18	O	PM	ENGLISH	BLACKSMITH	044	A	3	39
HOWES	JOHN		1		23	O	NG	ENG	SERVANT	044	B	1	23
HOWIE	CATHARINE		1	1	29	ONTARIO	PR	ENGLISH		043	G	2	27
HOWIE	IZELLA		1	1	4	ONTARIO	PR	ENGLISH		043	G	2	27
HOWIE	JOHN		1		24	ONTARIO	CE	IRISH	LABORER	043	G	1	4
HOWLAND	HENRY		1		40	NB	ZZ	ENGLISH	MERCHANT	044	B	6	58
HOWLAND	MATILDA		2	1	37	O	CE			044	C	4	D
HOWLETT	MARY	B	1	1	12	ENGLAND	CS	ENGLISH		043	E	2	68
HOWLETT	THOMAS				46	ENGLAND	CE	ENGLISH	F	043	E	2	72
HOY	WILLIAM				55	IRELAND	CE	IRISH	SHOEMAKER	044	A	2	3
HUBBARD	JANE		1	1	14	O	RC	GERMAN		043	H	2	24
HUBBARD	JANE		1	1	14	ONTARIO	RC	GERMAN		043	H	2	24
HUBURTUS	WILLIAM				33	O	CE	ENGLISH	MERCHANT	045	B	2	34
HUCHEN	WILLIAM				49	SCOTLAND	PS	SCOTCH	LABORER	045	D	6	70
HUDGENS	DEBORAH			F	58	O	CN	ENGLAND		043	A	5	22
HUDGIN	AMOS				66	NEW BRUNSWICK	QU	DUTCH	TEAMSTER	043	E	1	5
HUDLEY	THOMAS				26	O	PM	ENGLISH	LAB	043	H	1	23
HUDSON	JOHN				32	QUE	WM	ENGLISH	COOPER	044	A	2	50
HUDSON	THOMAS				35	QUE	CE	ENGLISH	CARPENTER	044	A	2	49
HUDSON	TIFFIN		1		10	O	BA	ENGLISH	F LAB	044	A	3	8
HUDSON	WILLIAM		2			O	CE			044	A	2	D
HUFF	PETER				53	O	WM	GERMAN	COOPER	043	E	3	46
HUFF	WILLIAM	JOHN			24	O	WM	GERMAN	COOPER	043	E	3	46
HUFFMAN	WM	C			30	O	WM	DUTCH	DROVER	044	A	2	50
HUGELL	JAMES				46	ENGLAND	CE	ENGLISH	F	044	C	3	9
HUGHES	AARON				49	O	NG	IRISH	CARPENTER	043	A	6	37
HUGHES	CHRISTOPHER			M	74	IRELAND	CE	ENGLAND	F	043	A	5	42
HUGHES	ELWOOD				50	ONT	WM	ENGLISH	INSURANCE AGENT	043	D		52
HUGHES	GEO	L			40	O	EM	ENGLISH	HARNESS MAKER	043	A	4	18
HUGHES	GEORGE				63	U STATES	QU	ENGLISH	MERCHANT	043	A	4	25
HUGHES	HENRY		1		16	ENGLAND	CE	ENGLISH	LAB	044	A	1	34
HUGHES	JAMES	H			27	O	CP	SCOTCH	GRAM S TEACHER	045	D	5	5
HUGHES	JESSE				30	ENGLAND	WM	ENGLISH	MASON	043	D		45
HUGHES	JOB				61	O	ZZ	ENGLISH	F	043	E	2	37
HUGHES	JOEL				79	U STATES	QU	ENGLISH	F & S MILLER	043	A	6	22
HUGHES	JOHN				50	IRELAND	RC	IRISH	F	043	E	1	35
HUGHES	JOHN				50	IRELAND	CE	IRISH	F	044	A	1	37
HUGHES	JOHN	S			47	O	WM	ENGLISH	CABINET MAKER	043	A	4	21
HUGHES	JOHN	W			37	O	QU	ENGLISH	MERCHANT	043	D		59
HUGHES	JOSEPH	G			27	O	NR	ENGLISH	FARMER	043	A	4	28
HUGHES	MARK			M	55	O	QU	ENGLAND	CARPENTER	043	A	5	45
HUGHES	ROBERT		1		20	O	PM	ENGLISH	F LAB	044	A	3	45
HUGHES	SARAH		2	1	74	U STATES	QU			043	A	6	D
HUGHES	SUSAN			1	36	ENGLAND	CE	ENGLISH		045	B	2	13
HUGHES	THOMAS		1		16	O	CE	IRISH	F LAB	044	C	1	46
HUGHES	WILLIAM			M	43	O	CN	IRELAND	F	043	A	5	43
HUGHEY	JAMES			M	80	O	PS	IRISH		043	A	1	7
HUGHEY	JOHN			M	52	O	PS	IRISH	FARMER	043	A	1	7
HUGHEY	JOSEPH		1		75	IRELAND	CS	IRISH		043	B	1	31
HUGHEY	JOSEPH				28	O	WM	IRISH	LAB	043	B	2	35
HUGHS	FRANCES			1	35	O	WM	IRISH	SCHOOL TEACHER	044	B	1	9
HUGHSON	JAMES				37	O	WM	ENGLISH	CARPENTER	044	C	1	53
HUGILL	JOHN				70	ENG	WM	ENG	RETIRED	044	B	1	11
HUGO	THOMAS		1		20	O	CE	ENG	TEAMSTER	044	B	2	50
HULBERT	MARY		1	1	19	O	CN	ENGLISH	SERVANT	043	B	4	20
HULLBERT	JOHN		1		28	ENG	CE	ENG	LAB	045	C	1	32
HULSE	HENRY				30	ENGLAND	CE	ENGLISH	HOTEL KEEPER	043	A	4	16
HULSE	LETITIA			1	38	IRELAND	CE	IRISH		043	A	4	26
HULSE	MARY			1	69	ENGLAND	CE	ENGLISH		043	A	4	3
HULSE	MATTHEW				42	ENGLAND	CE	ENGLISH	FARMER	043	A	4	47
HULSE	WILLIAM				27	O	CE	ENGLISH	BLACKSMITH	043	A	4	25
HUMBERSON	THOMAS				60	O	CE	ENGLISH	POTTER	045	A	4	31
HUMBERSTONE	L	T			24	O	PS	ENGLISH	POTTER	044	C	1	28
HUME	JOHN	F			36	SCOT	PS	SCOT	F	045	C	1	67
HUMPHEY	JAMES	D			27	O	CE	ENG	STATION MASTER	044	B	2	72
HUMPHREY	HENRY				40	O	CE	IRISH	F	045	C	3	5
HUMPHREY	JAS				42	O	CE	IRE	F	045	C	1	15
HUMPHREY	JOS	SR			72	IRE	CE	IRE	F	045	C	1	9
HUMPHREY	WILLIAM				47	IRELAND	CE	IRISH	F	045	C	2	33
HUMPHREYS	ANN		1	1	13	O	CE	IRISH	SERVANT	044	C	3	75
HUMPHREYS	FREDERICK		1		11	O	WM	ENGLISH		045	D	3	7
HUMPHREYS	JOHN		1		13	ONTARIO	WM	ENGLISH		045	D	3	7
HUMPHREYS	MARGARET			1	61	IRELAND	CE	IRISH		044	C	3	13
HUMPHREYS	ROBT		1		18	US	WM	ENGLISH	FARM LABOURER	045	D	3	7
HUMPHY	WILLIAM				54	IRELAND	CE	IRISH	LAB	044	C	3	11
HUNNEY	JAMES		1	M	11	O	CE	ENGLAND		043	A	5	26

SURNAME	NAME1	NAME2	STRAY	SEX	AGE	BIRTHPL	RELIGION	ORIGIN	OCCUP	DIST	SUB_DIST	DIV	PAGE
HUNT	AMBROSE			M	37	0	EM	IRISH	CLERGYMAN	043	A	2	44
HUNT	BENJAMIN				23	ENGLAND	CE	ENGLISH	SECTION MASTER	043	C		36
HUNT	EDWARD				53	0	CN	ENGLISH	FARM LABOURER	043	E	2	42
HUNT	FRANCIS		1		25	ENG	EP	ENG	LAB	044	B	2	7
HUNT	GEORGE		1		22	ENG	CE	ENG		045	C	1	44
HUNT	HENRY			M	40	ENGLAND	PR	ENGLISH	LAB	043	A	1	73
HUNT	JOHN				51	ENGLAND	WM	ENGLISH	MINISTER	043	C		19
HUNT	JOSEPH		1	M	77	ENG	WM	ENG		043	A	1	66
HUNT	JOSEPH			M	41	ENGLAND	EM	ENGLISH	LAB	043	A	1	70
HUNT	JOSEPH		1		84	ENGLAND	WM	ENGLISH		043	B	4	28
HUNT	JOSEPH	J			54	ENGLAND	WM	ENGLISH	SHOEMAKER	043	C		46
HUNT	MARY	J	1	1	26	0	WM	IRISH	SERVANT	045	B	2	26
HUNT	ROBERT				34	0	WM	ENGLISH	CARDER	045	A	1	65
HUNT	THOMAS				41	ENGLAND	CE	ENGLISH	LABOURER	045	D	4	7
HUNT	WALTER				34	0	PM	ENGLISH	CARPENTER	045	D	2	64
HUNT	WILLIAM				40	0	CE	ENGLISH	LAB	043	E	2	36
HUNT	WILLIAM	JOHN			20	0	CN	ENGLISH	LAB	043	E	2	40
HUNTER	ALEX				55	US	CE	AFRICAN	LABORER	044	A	2	53
HUNTER	ALEXANDER				50	0	WM	IRISH	CARPENTER	045	A	3	40
HUNTER	ALEXANDER	J	1		3	0	CS	SCOTCH		045	A	1	91
HUNTER	ALLEN			M	23	0	WM	IRELAND	F	043	A	5	40
HUNTER	ANN		1		59	ENGLAND	WM	ENGLISH		045	D	4	27
HUNTER	CHRISTINA		1	1	14	0	CE	ENGLISH	SERVANT	044	C	2	9
HUNTER	DAN				70	IRELAND	CP	IRISH	F	043	B	2	41
HUNTER	DAVID				40	0	WM	IRISH	FARMER	045	A	3	38
HUNTER	DAVID				40	0	WM	IRISH	FARMER	045	A	3	41
HUNTER	EDWARD				48	0	WM	IRISH	MILLER	045	A	3	41
HUNTER	EDWIN				51	ENGLAND	CE	ENGLISH	F	043	E	1	17
HUNTER	ELIZABETH		1	1	15	ENGLAND	PM	ENGLISH	LAB	045	C	3	23
HUNTER	GEORGE				32	IRE	WM	IRISH	LAB	044	B	1	7
HUNTER	GEORGE	WATSON			29	SCOT	CN	SCOTCH	CARPENTER	043	D		28
HUNTER	HANNAH		1		83	GERMANY	CE	GERMAN		045	D	3	2
HUNTER	ISABELLA		1	1	23	SCOTLAND	CP	SCOTCH	SERVANT	044	A	1	17
HUNTER	JAMES				63	IRELAND	CP	IRISH	FARMER	043	A	4	30
HUNTER	JAMES				51	ENGLAND	CE	SCOTCH	MEDICAL DOCTOR	043	B	2	11
HUNTER	JAMES	JR	2			IRELAND	WM		CARPENTER	045	A	3	D
HUNTER	JAMES	SEN	2		86	IRELAND	WM		TAILOR	045	A	3	D
HUNTER	JAS				30	0	PS	IRISH	CARPENTER	044	B	5	19
HUNTER	JEANNIE		1	1	35	0	CS	SCOTCH		045	A	1	91
HUNTER	JOHN				62	IRELAND	WM	IRISH	SHOEMAKER	043	E	3	45
HUNTER	JOHN				62	ENGLAND	WM	ENGLISH	FARMER	045	D	3	56
HUNTER	JOHN				78	IRELAND	WM	IRISH	F	045	A	4	13
HUNTER	JOHN	G	2		1	0	PB		IRISH		045	A	1	D
HUNTER	JOSEPH				49	IRELAND	WM	IRISH	F	043	A	3	34
HUNTER	LUCY		1	56	U STATES	PS	ENGLISH		045	D	6	28
HUNTER	MAGGIE		1	1	22	0	WM	SCOTCH	SERVANT	044	C	2	9
HUNTER	MARGARET		1	1	68	SCOTLAND	CP	SCOTCH		045	D	3	30
HUNTER	RACHEL		1	1	63	IRELAND	WM	IRISH		043	B	1	5
HUNTER	RICHARD				38	SCOTLAND	CP	SCOTLAND	FARMER	045	A	2	33
HUNTER	ROBERT				60	IRELAND	CP	IRISH	FARMER	043	A	4	31
HUNTER	ROBERT				53	SCOTLAND	FK	SCOTCH	BLACKSMITH	043	C		31
HUNTER	ROBERT				44	QUE	WM	IRISH	MERCHANT	043	E	3	55
HUNTER	ROBERT		1		16	0	WM	SCOTCH	SERVANT	044	C	2	9
HUNTER	THOMAS				30	0	CE	ENGLISH	INN KEEPER	043	B	3	6
HUNTER	THOMAS				21	ENG	PS	ENG	CLERK	044	B	2	18
HUNTER	THOMAS		1		74	SCOTLAND	CP	SCOTCH		045	D	3	30
HUNTER	THOMAS				36	ENGLAND	CE	ENGLISH	LABOURER	045	D	5	53
HUNTER	WILLIAM				33	0	CP	IRISH	F	043	B	2	42
HUNTER	WILLIAM				61	ENGLAND	WM	IRISH	FARMER	045	A	1	20
HUNTER	WM				25	IRELAND	CE	IRISH	LAB	044	B	5	55
HUNTLEY	ALFRED		2			ONTARIO	PR			043	G	2	D
HUNTLEY	AUSTIN				76	UNITED STATES	EM	ENGLISH	FARMER	043	G	2	36
HUNTLEY	ELIZABETH			1	50	0	EM	ENGLISH		043	E	2	23
HUNTLEY	JAS	G			22	0	EM	ENGLISH	LAB	043	E	2	33
HUNTLEY	JOHN			M	45	0	RC	IRISH	F	043	A	2	58
HUNTLEY	JOSEPH		1		32	ONTARIO	CP	ENGLISH	FARMER	043	G	1	5
HUNTLEY	JOSEPH				31	ONTARIO	PR	ENGLISH	FARMER	043	G	2	35
HUNTLEY	LUCY		2	1	60	UNITED STATES	EM			043	G	2	D
HUNTLEY	MARGARET			1	46	IRELAND	RC	IRISH		043	G	1	24
HUNTLEY	NELSON				47	ONTARIO	PR	ENGLISH	FARMER	043	G	2	36
HUNTLEY	THOMAS				50	ONTARIO	EM	ENGLISH	FARMER	043	G	2	37
HUNTLY	THEODORE				68	0	QU	ENGLISH	F	043	E	1	20
HURLEY	DENNIS		1		30	IRELAND	RC	IRISH	LAB	043	D		5
HURLEY	JAMES				60	IRELAND	RC	IRISH	LAB	043	E	1	6
HURLEY	MICHAL			M	52	IRELAND	RC	IRISH	F	043	A	5	8
HURLEY	NANCY		1	1	50	IRELAND	RC	IRISH		044	B	5	65
HURLEY	PATRICK		1		80	IRELAND	RC	IRISH		043	D		5
HURLEY	WILLIAM		1		23	0	NG	IRISH	LAB	043	D		11
HURST	ABSALOM				83	ENGLAND	CE	ENGLISH	WEAVER	043	H	1	2
HURST	HENRY				25	IRE	PM	IRE	FINISHER	044	B	2	37
HURST	SAMUEL				39	ENGLAND	PM	ENGLISH	F LAB	044	A	2	14
HUSBAND	ELLEN		2	1	31	0	WM			045	D	1	D
HUSBAND	GEORGE				34	0	WM	IRISH	DENTIST	045	D	1	1
HUSON	CATHERINE		2	1	72	UNITED STATES	PM			044	A	3	D
HUSON	CHARLES				49	0	PM	ENGLISH	F	044	A	3	19
HUSON	JOSEPH				70	NOVA SCOTIA	PM	ENGLISH		044	A	3	22
HUSON	JOSEPH	JR			34	0	PM	ENGLISH	F	044	A	3	21
HUSON	PAFFORD				42	ENG	PM	ENG	LAB	045	C	1	52
HUSSEY	JAMES				45	IRELAND	CE	IRISH	LAB	043	B	5	20
HUSSEY	MARIA		1	1	25	ENGLAND	IN	ENGLISH	SERVANT	043	E	1	12
HUSTON	MARGARET		1	1	16	0	CO	IRE		044	B	3	30
HUSTON	PHILLIP				44	IRE	RC	IRE	FINISHER	044	B	2	41
HUSTON	SARAH			1	74	IRELAND	CP	IRISH		045	C	2	25
HUSTON	WILLIAM				40	IRELAND	CE	IRISH	LAB	043	E	1	39
HUTCHCROFT	GEORGE	B			48	ENGLAND	CE	ENGLISH	CARRIAGE MAKER	043	D		59
HUTCHESON	WILLIAM				38	ENGLAND	CE	ENGLAND		045	D	2	2
HUTCHINS	JOHN	WALKER			25	ONTARIO	CE	ENGLISH	SCHOOL TEACHER	043	G	2	32
HUTCHINSON	DAVID				52	ENGLAND	CE	ENGLISH		045	B	2	7
HUTCHINSON	HARRY		1		16	0	PR	SCOTCH	SERVANT	045	A	1	45
HUTCHINSON	J		1		14	0	PS	IRISH	F LAB	044	C	1	47
HUTCHINSON	JACOB				38	ENGLAND	PM	ENGLISH	F	043	B	5	36
HUTCHINSON	JAMES			M	61	0	BA	ENGLISH	YEOMAN	043	A	1	D
HUTCHINSON	JAMES		1		19	ENGLAND	CE	ENGLISH		043	E	2	4
HUTCHINSON	JAMES				35	SCOTLAND	CS	SCOTCH	WEAVER	043	E	2	12
HUTCHINSON	JOHN			M	63	U STATES	WM	ENGLISH	F	043	A	1	20
HUTCHINSON	JOHN				30	ENG	EP	ENG	F	044	B	3	31

SURNAME	NAME1	NAME2	STRAY	SEX	AGE	BIRTHPL	RELIGION	ORIGIN	OCCUP	DIST	SUB_DIST	DIV	PAGE
HUTCHINSON	JOHN				49	ENG	EP	ENG	F	044	B	3	31
HUTCHINSON	JOHN				23	O	WM	ENGLISH	FARMER	045	A	3	32
HUTCHINSON	JOHN				41	O	CE	ENGLISH	LAB	045	B	1	32
HUTCHINSON	JOHN				78	ENGLAND	PM	ENGLISH	GENTEMAN	045	C	3	12
HUTCHINSON	JOHN		1		25	O	LU	ENGLISH		045	D	1	38
HUTCHINSON	MARTIN			M	35	O	PR	ENGLISH	F	043	A	1	41
HUTCHINSON	MARY		1	1	66	ENGLAND	PM	ENGLISH		045	C	3	43
HUTCHINSON	MATHEW				45	O	CE	ENGLISH	CARRIAGE MAKER	043	B	2	8
HUTCHINSON	SAMUEL				29	ONTARIO	CN	ENGLISH	FARMER	043	G	1	43
HUTCHINSON	THOMAS				37	O	WM	ENGLISH	LAB	044	C	1	43
HUTCHINSON	WILLIAM				44	ENGLAND	CP	ENGLISH	F	045	C	3	2
HUTCHISON	ELISABETH		1	1	62	ENGLAND	CE	ENGLAND	HOUSE KEEPER	045	D	2	4
HUTCHISON	JOHN		1		11	CANADA	WM	SCOTCH		045	D	6	29
HUTT	JAMES				43	ENGLAND	PM	ENGLISH	LAB	043	A	6	30
HUTT	JOHN		1		19	ENGLAND	CE	ENGLISH	BRICK MAKER	045	B	1	63
HUTT	WILLIAM				48	ENGLAND	PM	ENGLISH	F	043	A	6	29
HUTT	WILLIAM				25	ENGLAND	PM	ENGLISH	F	043	C		19
HUTTING	SARAH		1	1	47	ENGLAND	PM	ENGLISH		043	A	6	28
HUTTON	JESSE		1	1	59	ENGLAND	PM	ENGLISH	F	045	A	4	15
HUTTON	WILLIAM				67	US	WM	ENGLISH	LAB	044	A	1	35
HUTTY	EDWARD		1		26	ENGLAND	WM	ENGLISH	F LAB	044	C	1	13
HUTTY	JOSEPH		1		72	ENGLAND	WM	ENGLISH	F	044	A	3	3
HUXTABLE	EDWARD				70	ENGLAND	CE	ENGLISH	F	045	C	2	24
HYLAND	JOHN		1		50	IRELAND	RC	IRISH	ASHER	045	D	3	63
HYLE	ANN JANE		1	1	21	O	CE	ENG	SERVANT	044	B	3	6
HYLE	JAMES				50	IRE	PS	IRE	LAB	044	B	3	37
IANSON	JOHN				80	ENGLAND	WM	ENGLISH	GENT	043	E	3	48
IANSON	THOMAS				41	ENGLAND	BA	ENGLISH	F	043	E	3	30
IANSON	WILLIAM				75	ENGLAND	CE	ENGLISH	F	044	B	1	3
IANSON	WILLIAM		2		34	O	CE		F	044	B	1	D
IDE	JOHN	C			28	ENGLAND	CE	ENGLISH	F	044	A	2	27
IDE	THOMAS	H			36	ENGLAND	CE	ENGLISH	CARPENTER	044	A	2	1
IDE	WILLIS	A			68	ENGLAND	CE	ENGLISH	BLACKSMITH	044	A	2	4
ILIFF	THOMAS			M	40	ENG	CE	ENGLISH	LAB	043	A	1	71
ILLIGITIMATE			2			O	NG			045	C	3	D
INEE?	THOMAS	H			43	IRELAND	CE	IRISH	BARRESTER	045	B	2	36
INFANT			2	M		O	NG			043	A	5	D
INFANT	STILL BORN		2	M		O	NG			043	A	5	D
INFANT	STILL BORN		2	M		O	NG			043	A	5	D
INGHAM	JOSHUA				38	ENGLAND	UT	ENGLISH	CATTLE DEALER	045	A	1	91
INGLESON	JOHN				65	ENGLAND	WM	ENGLISH	FARMER	045	A	1	14
INGRAIM	ELIZABETH		1	1	30	ENGLAND	BA	ENGLISH		044	C	2	10
INGRAM	JOHN				54	ENG	CE	ENG	F	044	B	2	55
INMAN	CHARLES				26	O	PM	ENGLISH	LAB	043	E	2	70
INNIS	LESLIE				43	SCOTLAND	CP	SCOTCH	CARPENTER	043	B	2	29
INSON	CHARLES				33	O	WM	ENGLISH	F	043	E	3	44
INWOOD	WILLIAM		1		21	ENGLAND	RC	ENGLISH		045	C	1	8
IONSON	WILLIAM				36	O	PM	ENGLISH	F	045	C	4	40
IREDALE	WILLIAM				41	ENGLAND	PM	ENGLISH	PAINTER	045	B	1	28
IRELAND	ALFRED			M	30	ENGLAND		ENGLISH	F	043	A	2	7
IRELAND	ELEN		1	1	10	O	WM	ENGLISH		043	A	2	6
IRELAND	GEORGE			M	57	ENGLAND	PM	ENGLISH	F	043	A	2	18
IRELAND	JAMES		1	M	50	ENGLAND	PM	ENGLISH	F	043	A	2	17
IRELAND	JOHN		1	M	64	ENGLAND	CE	ENGLISH	F	043	A	1	29
IRELAND	JOHN			M	54	SCOTLAND	CP	SCOTCH	F	043	A	2	26
IRELAND	JOHN	THOMAS	2	M	11	O	PM			043	A	2	D
IRELAND	SAMUEL				48	ENGLAND	WM	ENGLISH	F	043	B	4	17
IRELAND	WILLIAM				51	ENGLAND	CE	ENGLISH	CARPENTER	043	C		32
IRESON	JOSEPH				44	ENGLAND	CE	ENGLISH	HOTEL KEEPER	045	D	5	58
IRESON	JOSEPH		2		6	O	CE			045	D	5	D
IRONFIELD	THOMAS				40	ENGLAND	CO	ENGLISH	GARDENER	045	A	1	84
IRONS	GEORGE				60	US	CE	AFRICAN	SHOEMAKER	043	A	3	23
IRONSIDES	CHRISTIAN			1	55	SCOTLAND	CP	SCOTTISH		043	B	4	19
IRONSIDES	JOHN				23	O	CP	SCOTTISH	F	043	B	4	19
IRONSON	CHARLES				27	ENGLAND	CP	ENGLISH	BLACKSMITH	043	H	1	37
IRSH	JAMES				69	ENG	CE	ENG	LAB	045	C	1	35
IRVIN	JOHN		1		15	O	CP	SCOTCH	F	044	B	5	61
IRVIN	JOHN				29	IRE	CE	IRE	LAB	045	C	1	38
IRVINE	ALEXANDER		1		19	O	CE	SCOTCH	BUTCHER	044	C	3	45
IRVINE	JAMES		1		40	IRELAND	CE	IRISH	SERVANT	044	C	6	23
IRVINE	JAMES				40	O	CE	IRISH	MASON	044	C	3	65
IRVINE	MARY		1	1	14	O	PM	IRISH	SERVANT	044	A	3	52
IRVINE	RUTLEDGE		1		19	O	WM	IRISH	F LAB	044	C	1	31
IRVINE	SARAH		1	1	27	IRE	PS	IRE	SERVANT	044	B	3	41
IRVINE	WILLIAM				71	SCOTLAND	CP	SCOTCH	SCHOOL TEACHER	044	B	6	4
IRVINE	WILLIAM				46	IRELAND	CE	SCOTCH	BLACKSMITH	044	C	3	23
IRVING	WILLIAM		1		24	O	CP	SCOTCH	SCHOOL TEACHER	045	C	3	30
IRWIN	ANDREW				23	IRE	PS	IRE	BOOT SHOEMAKER	044	B	3	9
IRWIN	CHAS				40	O	NC	ENGLISH	MILLER	043	C		14
IRWIN	ELIZABETH		1	1	23	IRELAND	WM	IRISH		044	C	4	64
IRWIN	ESTHER			1	55	ENGLAND	PM	ENGLISH		045	D	3	42
IRWIN	GEORGE				45	O	PM	ENGLISH	FARM LABOURER	045	C	3	54
IRWIN	ISAIAH				65	IRELAND	CS	IRISH	LAB	043	F		13
IRWIN	JAMES		2		6	O	CN			043	B	5	D
IRWIN	JAMES				50	IRE	PS	IRE	LAB	044	B	2	71
IRWIN	JAMES				54	IRELAND	WM	IRISH	LABOURER	044	C	1	27
IRWIN	JARED				32	O	QU	IRISH	F	043	B	4	12
IRWIN	JARED				67	U STATES	QU	IRISH	GENTLEMAN	043	D		40
IRWIN	JOHN				45	O	CN	IRISH	F	043	B	5	18
IRWIN	JOHN				25	ENGLAND	PM	ENGLISH	FARMER	045	D	3	41
IRWIN	JOHN				69	IRELAND	WM	IRISH	LABORER	045	D	1	24
IRWIN	JOSEPH				38	O	NG	IRISH	FARMER	043	B	3	11
IRWIN	MARSHALL				27	O	CM	WELSH	F	043	C		17
IRWIN	NATHAN				64	IRELAND	CP	IRISH	F	043	A	3	29
IRWIN	ROBERT				58	NOVA SCOTIA	PS	IRISH	FARMER	043	B	2	38
IRWIN	ROBERT				64	IRE	CS	IRE	F	044	B	4	37
IRWIN	ROBT	P			66	U STATES	NC	WELSH	GENTLEMAN	043	C		53
IRWIN	SAMUEL				44	O	WM	IRISH	F	043	B	5	34
IRWIN	SAMUEL	P			37	O	NC	ENGLISH	MILLER	043	C		14
IRWIN	SARAH	ELIZABETH	2		4	O	CN			043	B	5	D
IRWIN	SARAH	H	2	1		CANADA	NC			043	C		D
IRWIN	WILLIAM				33	IRELAND	WM	IRISH	WESLEYAN MINISTER	043	E	3	42
IRWIN	WILLIAM				32	ENGLAND	PM	ENGLISH	FARMER	045	D	3	6
IRWIN	WM	ROBERT	2		1	O	WM			043	E	3	D
ISMAN	REBECCA		1	1	26	O	WM	ENGLISH	SERVANT	045	D	5	70
ISMAN	STELLA		1	1	1	O	WM	ENGLISH		045	D	5	70

SURNAME	NAME1	NAME2	STRAY	SEX	AGE	BIRTHPL	RELIGION	ORIGIN	OCCUP	DIST	SUB_DIST	DIV	PAGE
ISSLARD	RICHARD				42	ENGLAND	EM	ENGLISH	LAB	044	C	1	40
IVANSON	JOHN				42	ENGLAND	CE	ENGLISH	F	043	A	6	66
IZAREL	GEORGE				47	ENGLAND	PM	ENGLISH	LAB	044	B	6	20
JABBITT	THOMAS				46	0	WM	ENGLISH	SHOEMAKER	045	D	3	64
JACK	MARY	ANN	1	1	41	IRELAND	WM	IRISH	WATCHMAKER	043	D		69
JACKES	CATHERINE			1	63	SCOTLAND	CE	ENGLISH		044	C	2	9
JACKES	JOSEPH				39	0	CE	ENGLISH	LAWYER	045	A	1	33
JACKES	WILLIAM				43	0	QU	ENGLISH	FARMER	045	A	2	2
JACKMAN	BULAH	ANN	2	1	6	0	BA			043	B	3	D
JACKMAN	JOHN				39	ENGLAND	BA	ENGLISH	FARM LABOURER	043	B	3	28
JACKMAN	WILLIAM				31	ENGLAND	BA	ENGLISH	LABOURER	043	B	3	26
JACKSON	ANN			1	40	0	WM	ENGLISH		045	A	2	1
JACKSON	ANN		2	1	74	ENGLAND	EM			044	C	1	D
JACKSON	CATHERINE			1	60	0	EM	ENGLISH	F	044	C	1	13
JACKSON	CHRISTOPHER	P			69	0	EM	IRISH	SHOEMAKER	043	D		13
JACKSON	DAVID		1		19	SCOT	CP	SCOT	LAB	045	C	1	44
JACKSON	EDWARD		1		14	0	CE	ENGLISH		045	A	3	14
JACKSON	EDWARD				53	ENGLAND	CE	ENGLISH	LAB	045	B	1	33
JACKSON	ELIZA	J	1	1	28	0	WM	IRISH		045	A	4	30
JACKSON	ELIZABETH			1	37	ENG	EM	ENG		044	B	1	23
JACKSON	ERASTUS				40	0	WM	IRISH	PUBLISHER	043	D		33
JACKSON	FRANCIS				49	ENGLAND	FT	ENGLISH	FARMER	043	A	4	50
JACKSON	FRANCIS				66	IRELAND	WM	IRISH	GENTLEMAN	044	C	3	43
JACKSON	GEORGE				65	ENGLAND	CE	ENGLISH	FARMER	045	A	3	25
JACKSON	GEORGE		1		76	ENGLAND	EM	ENGLISH	F	044	C	1	2
JACKSON	GEORGE		1		68	IRELAND	WM	IRISH		044	C	3	53
JACKSON	GEORGE				36	0	WM	IRISH	FARMER	044	C	3	71
JACKSON	HENRY				46	ENGLAND	CE	ENGLISH	F	044	A	2	43
JACKSON	HENRY				68	USA	WM	AFRICAN	LAB	045	C	1	22
JACKSON	JOHN		1		21	0	WM	ENGLISH	LAB	044	B	5	53
JACKSON	JOHN		1		60	ENG	CE	ENG	LAB	045	C	1	35
JACKSON	JOHN	F			32	0	EM	IRISH	PRINTER & GROCER	043	D		7
JACKSON	MARGARET		1	1	19	0	CS	SCOTCH		045	D	3	32
JACKSON	MARY			1	40	U STATES	WM	AFRICAN	WASHERWOMAN	043	A	4	8
JACKSON	MARY		2	1	60	US	WM			045	C	1	D
JACKSON	MARY		2	1	52	IRELAND	CP		FARMER'S WIFE	045	C	3	D
JACKSON	MICHAEL				30	IRELAND	CE	IRISH	LUMBERMAN	043	B	5	19
JACKSON	NATHAN				41	ENGLAND	CE	ENGLISH	MASON	045	C	3	55
JACKSON	PETER		1		0	0	CE	ENGLISH		045	A	3	14
JACKSON	RICHARD				50	ENGLAND	BA	ENGLISH	ENGINEER	043	G	1	12
JACKSON	SARAH		1	1	16	0	CP	SCOTCH		045	C	4	27
JACKSON	THOMAS				63	IRELAND	WM	IRISH	F	043	H	1	13
JACKSON	THOMAS				43	ENG	CE	ENG	F	044	B	1	61
JACKSON	THOMAS		1		25	ENGLAND	CE	ENGLISH	FARM LABOURER	045	C	4	28
JACKSON	THOMAS		1		35	ENGLAND	CP	ENGLISH	SERVANT	045	D	6	6
JACKSON	THOMAS				37	ONT	WM	IRISH	F	044	C	1	15
JACKSON	THOMPSON				21	0	CE	ENG	F	045	C	1	14
JACKSON	THOS				37	ENGLAND	CE	ENGLISH	F	044	A	1	27
JACKSON	TIMOTHY				33	ENGLAND	PM	ENGLISH	PEDLAR	045	D	3	33
JACKSON	WILLIAM				25	0	WM	IRISH	BLACKSMITH	045	D	5	15
JACKSON	WILLIAM				78	IRELAND	WM	IRISH	FARMER	044	C	3	66
JACKSON	WILLIAM				40	0	WM	IRISH	FARMER	044	C	3	69
JACKSON	WM				36	0	EM	ENGLISH	F	044	C	1	2
JACOBS	WILLIAM				65	UNITED STATES	WM	ENGLISH	LABORER	043	G	1	57
JACQUES	EDMUND	R			36	0	CP	ENGLISH	SCHOOL TEACHER	045	C	3	10
JACQUES	THOMAS				69	ENGLAND	CP	ENGLISH	F	045	C	3	4
JAGGER	ALLEN		1		23	ENGLAND	WM	ENGLISH	SERVANT	043	E	3	55
JAKEMAN	JOHN	J	1		36	ENGLAND	ME	ENGLISH	FARM SERVANT	045	A	1	82
JAKEMAN	RICHARD				32	ENGLAND	PM	ENGLISH	BLACKSMITH	043	B	2	6
JAKEMAN	WILLIAM	J	2		5	0	PM			043	B	2	D
JAKEMAY	AARON				62	ENGLAND	WM	ENGLISH	TINSMITH	043	F		30
JAMES	BENJAMIN				44	ENGLAND	CE	ENGLISH	F	043	H	1	14
JAMES	DAVID				27	0	WM	IRISH	FARMER	045	D	1	19
JAMES	ELI				59	0	QU	ENGLISH	LAB	043	B	4	8
JAMES	GEORGE	D			57	ENGLAND	CE	ENGLISH	BROKER	045	B	1	42
JAMES	ISABELLE			1	89	NS	CE	IRISH		044	C	1	11
JAMES	JANE		1	1	32	ENGLAND	CE	ENGLISH		045	D	6	39
JAMES	JOHN		1		60	IRELAND	CE	IRISH	VETERINARY SURGEON	045	A	1	9
JAMES	JOSEPH				58	IRELAND	WM	IRISH	F	044	C	1	10
JAMES	MERCEY		1	1	20	CANADA	WM	GERMAN	SCHOOL TEACHER	045	D	6	40
JAMES	ROBERT		2		94	IRELAND	CE		F	044	C	1	D
JAMES	WILLIAM				69	ENGLAND	CE	ENGLISH	LABOURER	045	D	6	31
JAMES	WILLIAM				69	IRELAND	WM	IRISH	F	044	C	1	15
JAMES	WILSON				62	ENGLAND	WM	ENGLISH	F	044	B	6	2
JAMESALT	JAMES				26	ENGLAND	CE	ENGLISH	LAB	044	B	5	34
JAMESON	ANDREW				50	IRE	CS	IRISH	F	044	B	4	48
JAMESON	JOHN				27	IRE	WM	IRISH	F	044	B	4	43
JAMIESON	JAMES				50	ENGLAND	CE	SCOTCH		044	A	3	55
JAMIESON	JOHN				35	0	BA	SCOTCH	FARMER	043	B	3	27
JAMIESON	SAMUEL				55	IRELAND	CE	IRISH	LAB	044	C	1	47
JAMIESON	WILLIAM				75	SCOTLAND	PS	SCOTCH	GENTLEMAN	045	A	1	5
JAMISON	FRANK		1		23	IRELAND	WM	IRISH	LAB	045	B	2	5
JAMISON	JAMES				38	U STATES	CE	IRISH	LAB	043	A	6	60
JARDINE	JEAN			1	61	SCOTLAND	CS	SCOTCH		045	A	1	91
JARDINE	JOHN		2		68	SCOTLAND	PB			045	A	1	D
JARRETT	SAMUEL		1		47	ENGLAND	CE	ENGLISH	SPECULATOR	043	A	6	13
JARRETT	SUSANNAH		2	1	53	ENG	WM			044	B	1	D
JARROTT	CHARLES		1		23	0	WM	ENG	SCHOOL TEACHER	044	B	1	9
JARROTT	EDWARD				22	ENG	CO	ENG	F	044	B	3	47
JARROTT	JAMES				18	0	VM	ENG	F	044	B	3	21
JARROTT	MARMADUKE				55	ENG	EP	ENG	F	044	B	3	31
JARROTT	MARY			1	25	0	WM	ENG	CHAR WOMAN	044	B	1	49
JARROTT	THOMAS				47	ENG	EP	ENG	F	044	B	3	32
JARVIN	RICHARD				55	QUE	RC	FR	LAB	045	C	1	37
JARVIS	EDGAR				36	0	CE	ENGLISH	BROKER	045	B	2	20
JARVIS	JOHN				43	ENGLAND	CE	ENGLISH	LABOURER	045	D	5	63
JARVIS	WILLIAM	F			23	0	WM	ENGLISH	F	043	H	2	52
JARVIS	WILLIAM	F			23	ONTARIO	WM	ENGLISH	FARMER	043	H	2	52
JAVIS	MARY			1	68	ENGLAND	CE	ENGLISH		045	D	5	63
JEFFERSON	ANNA	BELL	1	1	5	UNITED STATES	CN	ENGLISH		043	E	2	7
JEFFERSON	JAMES			M	28	ENGLAND	PR	ENGLISH	HARNESS MAKER	043	A	1	50
JEFFERSON	JANE			1	64	ENG	CE	ENG		044	B	2	30
JEFFERSON	WILLIAM		1		7	0	CN	ENGLISH		043	E	2	7
JEFFRAY	JOHN				58	0	WM	ENGLISH	F	044	B	5	73
JEFFRAY	RICHD		1		19	0	PS	ENGLISH	CARPENTER	044	B	5	9
JEFFRAY	RICHD				53	ENGLAND	WM	ENGLISH	F	044	B	5	76

SURNAME	NAME1	NAME2	STRAY	SEX	AGE	BIRTHPL	RELIGION	ORIGIN	OCCUP	DIST	SUB_DIST	DIV	PAGE
JEFFRAY	RICHD	W			33	O	UP	ENGLISH	F	044	B	5	67
JEFFRAY	WILLIAM			M	67	O	PS	SCOTCH	F	043	A	2	34
JEFFRAY	WM				33	O	CO	ENGLISH	F	044	B	5	62
JEFFREY	JOHN				32	O	UP	SCOT	F	044	B	4	29
JEFFREY	JOHN				64	SCOTLAND	CP	SCOTCH	F	044	B	6	51
JEFFREY	WILLIAM				68	SCOTLAND	CP	SCOTCH	F	044	B	6	51
JEFFREY	WILLIAM				50	SCOTLAND	PS	SCOTTISH	F LAB	044	C	1	40
JEFFRY	DAVID				71	SCOT	CP	SCOT	F	044	B	4	52
JEMISON	GEORGE	S	1		17	US	WM	IRISH	APPRENTICE	045	B	1	4
JENKINS	BENJAMIN				47	O	CP	SCOTCH	FARMER	045	D	4	24
JENKINS	HANNAH	P H		1	44	O	PS	SCOT	DRESS MAKER	044	B	2	46
JENKINS	HENRY				53	UNITED STATES	WM	AFRICAN	LAB	044	A	3	1
JENKINS	JAMES			M	58	US	PS	SCOTCH	F	043	A	2	32
JENKINS	JANE		1	1	58	IRELAND	CP	IRISH	SERVANT	044	A	2	2
JENKINS	MARY		1	1	60	IRELAND	WM	IRISH		045	D	3	43
JENKINS	PHILIP	H			25	ENGLAND	CE	ENGLISH	SADLER	045	A	1	34
JENKINS	THOMAS		1		16	IRISH	RP	IRISH	SERVANT	044	C	3	17
JENNER	EDWARD				23	ENGLAND	CE	ENGLISH		045	B	2	27
JENNING	ROBINSON				38	ENGLAND	WM	ENGLISH	F	043	E	3	22
JENNING	SAMUEL				37	IRELAND	CE	IRISH	SHOEMAKER	043	E	3	47
JENNINGS	DAVID				25	O	CE	IRISH	SHOE MAKER	045	D	4	37
JENNINGS	DAVID				60	ENGLAND	WM	ENGLISH	MINISTER	044	C	3	47
JENNINGS	HENRY				58	ENGLAND	PM	ENGLISH	FARMER	045	D	4	4
JENNINGS	HENRY				60	ENGLAND	PM	ENGLISH	FARMER	045	D	4	51
JENNINGS	HENRY				32	ENGLAND	CE	ENGLISH	GARDENER	044	C	2	19
JENNINGS	JOHN				28	O	CE	ENGLISH	FARMER	043	A	4	62
JENNINGS	ROBERT				30	O	CE	ENGLISH	LABOURER	043	A	4	61
JENNINGS	THOMAS				33	O	CE	ENGLISH	FARMER	043	A	4	34
JENNISON	RUEBEN	R			37	ENGLAND	WM	ENGLISH	SCHOOL TEACHER	043	E	2	3
JENSEN	DUDSON			M	64	ENGLAND	WM	ENGLISH	F	043	A	2	49
JEPHSON	WM		1		13	IRE	CE	IRE		045	C	1	20
JERMAN	FRANCIS		2		8	O	CO			043	B	3	D
JERMAN	JOHN				49	ENGLAND	CO	ENGLISH	BLACKSMITH	043	B	3	60
JEROME	CHAUNCEY		1		20	O	QU	IRISH	LAB	043	F		18
JESSOPP	DUDLEY	F			39	ENGLAND	CE	ENGLISH	F	044	C	2	52
JEWEL	ARTHUR		1		23	ONTARIO	PR	IRISH	LABORER	043	G	2	40
JEWEL	CLARISSA		2		17	ONTARIO	EM			043	G	2	D
JEWEL	GEORGE				33	ONTARIO	PR	IRISH	LABORER	043	G	2	38
JEWEL	HENRY				39	ONTARIO	PR	IRISH	FARMER	043	G	2	37
JEWEL	LEWIS				27	ONTARIO	CN	IRISH	LABORER	043	G	1	15
JEWEL	NELSON				29	ONTARIO	PR	IRISH	FARMER	043	G	2	40
JEWEL	WILLIAM				59	ONTARIO	EM	IRISH	FARMER	043	G	2	38
JEWELL	SAMUEL	A			64	U STATES	NC	IRISH	BLACKSMITH	043	C		5
JEWITT	GIBSON				52	ENG	EM	ENG	F	044	B	4	51
JOBBET	JAMES		1		22	US	EM	ENGLISH	SHOE MAKER	045	D	2	7
JOBBITT	ELIZABETH			1	71	O	CP	SCOTCH	F	045	C	2	7
JOBSON	JOSEPH				57	ENGLAND	WM	ENGLISH	F	044	A	2	11
JOHNS	ELIZA		1	1	59	ENGLAND	WM	ENGLISH		045	D	3	1
JOHNS	FRANCIS		1	M	26	O	PR	ENGLISH	BARKEEPER	043	A	1	3
JOHNSON					63	O	WM	ENGLISH	FARMER	044	C	1	22
JOHNSON	ADA		1	1	25	O	CE	IRISH		045	B	1	24
JOHNSON	ALFRED				49	O	WM	IRISH	FARMER	043	B	3	33
JOHNSON	ANDREW		1		19	O	CS	IRISH	LABOURER	045	D	5	46
JOHNSON	ANN		1	F	15	SCOTLAND	CN	SCOTCH		043	A	5	2
JOHNSON	ANN		1	1	65	IRELAND	RC	IRISH		045	D	5	31
JOHNSON	ARTHUR		1	M	40	IRELAND	FK	IRELAND	L	043	A	5	35
JOHNSON	CATHARINE			1	29	O	WM	IRISH		045	A	4	19
JOHNSON	CHARLES		1		19	O	CE	IRISH	APPRENTICE	043	D		41
JOHNSON	CHARLES				32	O	CE	IRISH	F	043	H	1	24
JOHNSON	DAVID				60	SCOTLAND	UP	SCOTCH	F	044	B	5	50
JOHNSON	DAVID				54	SCOTLAND	WM	SCOTCH	SHOEMAKER	045	D	3	4
JOHNSON	DELIA			1	41	O	CE	IRISH		044	C	2	53
JOHNSON	EDWARD				32	O	WM	IRISH	F	045	A	4	13
JOHNSON	ELIJAH				32	O	CN	ENGLISH	F	043	E	2	17
JOHNSON	EZRA				41	O	CN	GERMAN	FARMER	043	B	3	69
JOHNSON	GEORGE				37	O	CP	SCOTCH	MERCHANT	043	H	1	35
JOHNSON	HENERY				65	US	RC	IRISH	LABOURER	044	C	3	68
JOHNSON	HENRY		1		28	O	CN	GERMAN	FACTORY LABOURER	043	B	3	33
JOHNSON	HENRY				49	CANADA	BA	SCOTCH	FARMER	045	D	6	36
JOHNSON	HENRY				33	O	WM	ENGLISH	F	045	A	4	19
JOHNSON	HIRAM				27	O	FW	GERMAN	BOOKKEEPER	043	D		29
JOHNSON	HUGH		1		27	O	CS	IRISH	LABOURER	045	D	5	41
JOHNSON	ISAAC				70	O	CN	ENGLISH	WEAVER	043	E	3	3
JOHNSON	JABEZ				51	O	CN	WELSH	F	043	B	4	46
JOHNSON	JACOB				60	O	CN	ENGLISH	REVEREND	043	B	3	14
JOHNSON	JACOB				35	USA	EM	SIX NATION	F	043	H	2	58
JOHNSON	JACOB				35	UNITED STATES	EM	SIX NATIONS	FARMER	043	H	2	58
JOHNSON	JACOB	H			32	O	CN	GERMAN	BUILDER	043	D		61
JOHNSON	JAMES				64	SCOTLAND	PS	SCOTCH	FARMER	043	B	3	64
JOHNSON	JAMES				50	IRELAND	CP	IRISH	F	044	C	2	40
JOHNSON	JAMES				50	IRELAND	CE	IRISH	LAB	044	C	4	80
JOHNSON	JAMES				32	ENGLAND	WM	ENGLISH	BLACKSMITH	045	A	4	28
JOHNSON	JOHN			M	51	ENGLAND	PM	ENGLISH	F	043	A	2	32
JOHNSON	JOHN			M	47	ENGLAND	CE	ENGLAND	F	043	A	5	31
JOHNSON	JOHN		1		16	ONTARIO	WM	OJIBWAY INDIAN	HUNTER AND FISHER	043	G	1	58
JOHNSON	JOHN				33	ONTARIO	WM	OJIBWAY INDIAN	HUNTER AND FISHER	043	G	1	59
JOHNSON	JOHN				48	NOVA SCOTIA	WM	IRISH	F	043	H	1	28
JOHNSON	JOHN		1		16	O	WM	IRISH	WOOLEN PICKER	044	C	3	15
JOHNSON	JOHN				38	O	WM	IRISH	F	045	A	4	20
JOHNSON	JOHN	C			42	IRELAND	BA	SCOTCH	MINISTER	043	A	4	18
JOHNSON	JOSEPH				42	ENGLAND	WM	ENGLISH	FARMER	043	B	3	46
JOHNSON	JOSEPH				49	O	WM	SCOTCH	SPORTSMAN	043	F		9
JOHNSON	JOSEPH		1		18	ONTARIO	WM	OJIBWAY INDIAN		043	G	1	59
JOHNSON	JOSEPH				61	O	CE	ENGLISH	F	044	C	1	42
JOHNSON	MARGARET		1	1	19	SCOTLAND	PS	SCOTTISH	SERVANT	044	C	1	30
JOHNSON	MARTIN				44	O	EM	GERMAN	FARMER	043	B	3	67
JOHNSON	MARY			F	40	ENGLAND	DI	ENGLISH		043	A	1	51
JOHNSON	MARY		1	1	3	ONTARIO	RC	ENGLISH		043	H	2	19
JOHNSON	MARY	ANN	1	1	25	ENGLAND	EM	ENGLISH	SERVANT	043	G	2	20
JOHNSON	MARY	L	1	1	3	O	RC	ENGLISH		043	H	2	19
JOHNSON	NANCY		1	1	50	ONTARIO	WM	OJIBWAY INDIAN		043	G	1	59
JOHNSON	NEIL				42	SCOTLAND	CP	SCOTCH	MERCHANT	045	B	1	56
JOHNSON	NELSON				27	O	CN	ENGLISH	CABINETMAKER	043	D		62
JOHNSON	ROBART				49	IRELAND	CE	IRISH	POST MASTER	044	C	3	24
JOHNSON	ROBT				50	O	CN	IRISH	BLACKSMITH	043	B	3	39
JOHNSON	ROBT				61	SCOTLAND	UP	SCOTCH	F	044	B	5	50

SURNAME	NAME1	NAME2	STRAY	SEX	AGE	BIRTHPL	RELIGION	ORIGIN	OCCUP	DIST	SUB_DIST	DIV	PAGE
JOHNSON	SAMUEL				60	O	CN	ENGLISH	F	043	E	2	2
JOHNSON	SAMUEL				26	O	PS	IRISH	F	043	E	3	27
JOHNSON	SILAS				58	O	WM	IRISH	F	045	A	4	18
JOHNSON	SUSAN		1	1	54	O	CN	FRENCH		043	B	3	35
JOHNSON	THOMAS		1		30	ENGLAND	CE	ENGLISH	BAKER	045	D	3	77
JOHNSON	VINCENT				76	UNITED STATES	CN	ENGLISH	FARMER	043	B	3	7
JOHNSON	WILLIAM				55	O	CN	IRISH	FARMER	043	B	3	31
JOHNSON	WILLIAM				45	O	NC	SCOTCH	CLOTHIER	043	H	1	34
JOHNSON	WILLIAM				71	SCOTLAND	CS	SCOTCH	FARMER	045	D	5	74
JOHNSON	WILLIAM				23	O	WM	SCOTCH	LABOURER	045	D	5	76
JOHNSON	WILLIAM				54	ENGLAND	CE	ENGLISH	CLERGYMAN	044	C	3	72
JOHNSON	WILLIAM				36	O	WM	IRISH	F	045	A	4	13
JOHNSTON	ALEXANDER				20	O	RC	AFRICAN	FARMER	045	A	2	24
JOHNSTON	ANDREW				43	IRELAND	CP	IRISH	LAB	045	C	2	7
JOHNSTON	ANDREW				27	O	CP	SCOTCH	PEDLAR	045	C	3	33
JOHNSTON	BENJAMIN				62	O	WM	IRISH	F	044	A	2	6
JOHNSTON	DANIEL				57	IRELAND	WM	ENGLISH	F	045	C	3	18
JOHNSTON	DAVID			M	48	SCOTLAND	CP	SCOTCH	INSURANCE AGENT	043	A	2	47
JOHNSTON	DAVID				40	O	PS	SCOTCH	F	045	C	3	52
JOHNSTON	DAVID				23	O	CS	SCOTCH	SADLER	045	D	3	71
JOHNSTON	ELIZABETH		1	1	56	IRELAND	CE	IRISH	DRESS MAKER	045	D	1	14
JOHNSTON	GEORGE				50	IRELAND	CE	IRISH	F	043	A	3	47
JOHNSTON	GEORGE		1		13	O	RC		FARM SERVANT	045	C	3	41
JOHNSTON	HENRY				60	UNITED STATES	RC	AFRICAN	LAB	044	C	2	49
JOHNSTON	HOPE				23	O	CP	SCOTCH	FARM LABOURER	045	C	4	12
JOHNSTON	ISABELLA			1	50	SCOTLAND	CP	SCOTCH		045	C	3	53
JOHNSTON	JAMES				60	ENG	CE	ENG	F	044	B	2	69
JOHNSTON	JAMES		1		18	ON THE OCEAN	NG	ENGLISH	BUTCHER	045	B	2	30
JOHNSTON	JAMES				52	ENGLAND	CE	ENGLISH	FARMER	045	D	2	34
JOHNSTON	JANE		1	1	22	O	CN	WELSH		043	B	3	22
JOHNSTON	JOHN				56	IRELAND	CE	IRISH	F	043	E	2	52
JOHNSTON	JOHN				29	O	CP	SCOTCH	MERCHANT	043	H	1	34
JOHNSTON	JOHN				48	IRELAND	CE	ENGLISH	F LAB	044	A	1	7
JOHNSTON	JOHN		1		17	ENGLAND	CE	ENGLISH	SERVANT	045	D	1	14
JOHNSTON	JOHN	M			36	SCOTLAND	CP	SCOTCH	BREWER	043	D		6
JOHNSTON	JOSEPH				28	IRELAND	CE	IRISH	LAB	045	B	1	19
JOHNSTON	LANATT	W			30	UNITED STATES	CP	ENGLISH	AGENT AGRICULTURAL	044	C	2	4
JOHNSTON	MARGARET			1	38	IRELAND	WM	IRISH	SEAMSTRESS	045	D	1	4
JOHNSTON	MARY		1	1	6	O	WM	IRISH		044	B	1	5
JOHNSTON	MARY			1	50	IRELAND	WM	IRISH		045	A	2	13
JOHNSTON	MARY		1	1	72	IRELAND	WM	IRISH		045	B	1	8
JOHNSTON	MARY		1	1		O	CP			045	C	3	1
JOHNSTON	RICH		1		60	ENG	CE	ENG	LAB	045	C	1	41
JOHNSTON	RICHARD				41	O	CP	IRISH	MERCHANT	044	A	3	18
JOHNSTON	RICHARD		1		21	IRELAND	CE	IRISH		045	A	1	94
JOHNSTON	ROBERT		2		80	SCOTLAND	CP		MERCHANT	043	H	1	D
JOHNSTON	ROBERT				36	IRELAND	CE	IRISH	F	044	A	2	44
JOHNSTON	ROBERT				59	IRELAND	PM	SCOTCH	F	045	C	3	28
JOHNSTON	ROBERT				43	O	CP	SCOTCH	F	045	C	3	32
JOHNSTON	ROBERT				60	IRELAND	WM	IRISH	FARMER	045	D	3	49
JOHNSTON	SAMUEL				65	IRELAND	CN	IRISH	WEAVER	043	B	3	16
JOHNSTON	SAMUEL				30	O	CN	IRISH	FARMER	043	B	3	16
JOHNSTON	SARAH		1	1	41	IRELAND	CP	IRISH		043	A	6	20
JOHNSTON	THOMAS		1		17	ENG	PM	ENG	LAB	044	B	1	51
JOHNSTON	THOMAS		1		74	IRELAND	WM	IRISH		045	B	1	8
JOHNSTON	THOMAS		1		23	ENGLAND	CE	ENGLISH	FARM LAB	045	D	1	14
JOHNSTON	VINCENT				47	O	CS	IRISH	FARMER	045	D	1	43
JOHNSTON	WILLIAM				43	IRELAND	RC	IRISH	COOPER	043	E	2	78
JOHNSTON	WILLIAM				51	SCOTLAND	CS	SCOTCH	LABOURER	045	A	1	75
JOHNSTON	WILLIAM				52	IRELAND	CE	IRISH	LAB	045	A	1	87
JOHNSTON	WILLIAM				46	O	PS	SCOTCH	INN KEEPER	045	C	3	38
JOHNSTONE	BENJAMIN				68	SCOTLAND	CP	SCOTCH	F	045	C	4	16
JOHNSTONE	JAMES				60	IRELAND	CE	IRISH		045	B	2	13
JOHNSTONE	RACHEL		1	1	30	IRELAND	WM	IRELAND	SERVANT	045	D	2	5
JOICE	JOHN				61	ENGLAND	CE	ENGLISH	FARMER	045	D	3	2
JOICE	MARY			1	50	IRELAND	RC	IRISH		043	B	2	7
JOLLY	NATHANIEL				28	SCOTLAND	CP	SCOTCH	CABINETMAKER	043	D		75
JONES	ABINA		1	1	25	O	PM		SERVANT	045	C	3	54
JONES	AMBROSE				44	ENGLAND	WM	ENGLISH	COMMERCIAL TRAVELER	045	B	1	17
JONES	ANDREW				24	O	PM	ENG	MASON	045	C	1	21
JONES	BENJAMIN				48	O	WM	IRISH	WATCH MAKER	045	A	2	8
JONES	BERTA		1	1	14	O	CN	WELSH		043	B	3	34
JONES	BURLY?		1		32	O	CE	ENGLISH	BARRESTER	045	B	2	31
JONES	DAVID		1		17	O	WM	ENGLISH	WEAVER	045	D	5	28
JONES	ELIAS	A			54	US	WM	WELCH	TRAINER OF HORSES	044	C	4	33
JONES	GEORGE		1		21	O	ME	IRISH	SERVANT	044	B	2	9
JONES	GEORGE		1		15	ENGLAND	PM	ENGLISH		044	C	4	24
JONES	HENRY		1	M	24	ENGLAND	CE	ENGLISH	BLACKSMITH	043	A	1	8
JONES	HENRY				24	ENGLAND	CE	ENGLISH	BRICK MAKER	045	A	1	25
JONES	HUGH				59	ENGLAND	CE	ENGLISH	F	043	H	2	52
JONES	HUGH				59	ENGLAND	CE	ENGLISH		043	H	2	52
JONES	JAMES				58	O	NR	SCOT	F	045	C	1	53
JONES	JAMES				85	USA	BA	ENG	GENTLEMAN	045	C	1	55
JONES	JOAB				51	ENG	PM	ENG	F	045	C	1	42
JONES	JOHN				27	O	CE	ENGLISH	F	043	H	2	52
JONES	JOHN				27	ONTARIO	CE	ENGLISH	FARMER	043	H	2	52
JONES	JOHN		1		34	ENG	BA	ENG	SAWYER	044	B	1	52
JONES	JOHN				28	ENGLAND	CE	ENGLISH	GARDENER	045	A	1	33
JONES	JOHN		1		16	O	CE	ENGLISH		045	D	3	51
JONES	JOSEPH				61	ENGLAND	CE	ENGLISH	FARMER	045	A	1	80
JONES	JUDITH			1	72	ENGLAND	CE	ENGLISH		045	D	6	46
JONES	LEVI				40	O	WM	ENGLISH	BELL FOUNDER	045	D	5	5
JONES	M				50	UNITED STATES	WM	ENGLISH	FARMER	043	B	3	74
JONES	MARY		1	1	14	O	PS	SCOTCH		045	D	2	51
JONES	MARY			1	61	O	CE	ENGLISH		044	C	3	28
JONES	NORMAN				70	UNITED STATES	CN	WELSH	FARMER	043	B	3	33
JONES	ROBT	JN			50	O	WM	IRISH	FARMER	045	A	2	22
JONES	SARAH		1	1	22	O	PS	GERMAN		043	B	3	40
JONES	THOMAS				26	O	CE	ENGLISH	F	043	H	2	52
JONES	THOMAS				26	ONTARIO	CE	ENGLISH	FARMER	043	H	2	52
JONES	THOMAS				36	IRELAND	CP	IRISH	SERVANT	045	A	3	11
JONES	THOMAS				58	IRELAND	CP	IRISH	SERVANT	045	A	3	17
JONES	WILLIAM				36	ENG	CE	ENG	LAB	044	B	2	66
JONES	WILLIAM				26	O	PM	ENGLISH	LAB	045	C	3	17
JONES	WILLIAM				56	IRELAND	WM	IRISH	F	044	C	2	27
JONES	WILLIAM	A	2		2	O	CE		GARDENER	045	A	1	D

SURNAME	NAME1	NAME2	STRAY	SEX	AGE	BIRTHPL	RELIGION	ORIGIN	OCCUP	DIST	SUB_DIST	DIV	PAGE
JONES	WILLIAM	J	1		3	0	PM			045	C	3	54
JONES	WM		1		30	ENGLAND	CE	ENGLISH	PHOTOGRAPHER	043	D		66
JONES	WM	JOHN	1		15	0	WM	ENGLISH		045	D	5	28
JONSON	JAS				72	ENG	CE	ENG	F	045	C	1	69
JONSTON	THOMAS				44	ENGLAND	CE	ENGLISH	LAB	043	C		9
JORDAN	JAMES				30	ENGLAND	WM	ENGLISH	BLACKSMITH	044	C	1	30
JORDAN	PATRICK				58	IRELAND	RC	IRISH	F LAB	044	A	1	2
JORDAN	RICHARD				52	ENGLAND	WM	ENGLAND	LABORER	045	D	2	9
JORDAN	SAMUEL				34	IRELAND	CP	IRISH	LAB	043	B	5	20
JORDAN	THOMAS		1		41	ENGLAND	CE	ENGLISH	F LAB	043	A	3	24
JORDAN	THOMAS				30	0	WM	IRISH	LAB	043	B	5	34
JORDAN	TIMOTHY				60	IRELAND	RC	IRISH	CARPENTER	044	C	4	96
JORDAN	WILLIAM		1		13	0	PS	ENGLISH		043	A	1	35
JORDEN	WILLIAM				44	SCOTLAND	CP	SCOTCH	CARPENTER	045	D	6	72
JORDISON	JOHN		1		20	ENG	WM	ENG	LAB	044	B	4	2
JORDON	LUKE				52	IRELAND	RC	IRISH	F	043	B	5	35
JORDON	MARGARET		2	1	12	0	WM			045	D	2	D
JORY	URUIS				26	0	BA	ENGLISH	TINSMITH	043	C		24
JOYCE	PATRICK				46	IRELAND	RC	IRISH	PIPER	043	E	3	2
JOYCE	REDMAN		1		25	IRE	RC	IRE	COOPER	044	B	2	50
JOYCE	WILLIAM				31	ENGLAND	WM	ENGLISH		044	C	3	64
JUDD	REUBEN				48	0	QU	GERMAN	CARPENTER	043	A	6	38
JUDE	BENJAMIN		1		25	ENGLAND	PM	ENGLISH	BRICK MAKER	045	B	1	65
JULIAN	THOMAS				41	ENG	PM	ENG	F	044	B	3	6
JULIAN	WM				40	ENGLAND	EM	ENGLISH	F	044	C	1	3
JULION	JOHN				30	ENG	PM	ENG	F	044	B	4	24
JULION	WILLIAM				66	ENG	PM	ENG	RETIRED	044	B	4	24
JURY	JANE		1	1	70	ENGLAND	EM	ENGLISH		044	C	1	7
JUSTICE	CHARLES				63	ENGLAND	CE	ENGLISH	SURGEON	045	D	3	7
JUSTIN	WILLIAM				33	ENGLAND	CE	ENGLISH	FARMER	045	A	1	97
KAAKE	ADAM				30	0	WM	GERMAN	F	043	A	3	30
KAAKE	ADAM				71	UNITED STATES	WM	GERMAN	F LAB	044	A	3	18
KAAKE	AGNES			1	42	0	CE	UNKNOWN		044	A	3	25
KAAKE	CHARLES				63	GERMANY	WM	GERMAN	F	043	A	3	37
KAAKE	JAMES				30	0	CE	GERMAN	F	043	A	3	14
KAILTEN	FAITH	A	1	1	11	ENGLAND	CE	ENGLISH	NURSE	043	E	2	24
KAISER	BENJ				62	0	LU	GERMAN	F	044	B	5	46
KAISER	BENJAMIN				39	0	LU	GERMAN	F	044	B	6	32
KAISER	DANIEL				65	US	LU	GERMAN	F	044	B	6	32
KAISER	JOHN	P	1		10	0	CP	UNKNOWN	SERVANT	044	B	6	4
KAISER	MICHAEL				29	0	LU	GERMAN	F	044	B	5	46
KAISOR	ABRAM				40	0	WM	GERMAN	F	044	C	1	42
KAISOR	ANNIE				45	ENGLAND	CE	ENGLISH	F	044	C	1	41
KAISOR	JACOB				42	0	WM	GERMAN	F	044	C	1	37
KAISOR	JACOB				48	0	EM	GERMAN	WHEELWRIGHT	044	C	1	39
KAISOR	JACOB	LOU			75	U STATES	MN	GERMAN	F	044	C	1	38
KAISOR	JESSIE				30	0	EM	GERMAN	F	044	C	1	37
KAISOR	JOHN				38	0	MN	GERMAN	F	044	C	1	39
KALE	WILLIAM	H			43	ENGLAND	CE	ENGLISH	F	044	C	4	8
KANE	BRIDGET		1	1	86	IRE	RC	ENG		044	B	1	40
KANE	JAMES			M	55	IRELAND	OP	IRELAND	L	043	A	5	30
KANE	PATRICK				40	IRELAND	RC	IRELAND	FARM LABORER	045	D	2	2
KATON	THOMAS		1		71	ENG	CE	ENG	F	044	B	4	33
KAVANAGH	JAMES				40	0	NC	IRISH	BUTCHER	043	E	1	50
KAVANAGH	JOHN	H			36	0	QU	IRISH	CARPENTER	043	E	2	84
KAVANAGH	MATTHEW				44	IRELAND	RC	IRISH	STONE MASON	043	A	4	28
KAVANAGH	PATRICK				39	IRELAND	RC	IRISH	LAB	044	C	3	16
KAVANAUGH	MATTHEW			M	44	IRELAND	RC	IRELAND	MASON	043	A	5	41
KAY	FRANCES				41	ONTARIO	CE	ENGLISH	FARMER	043	H	2	50
KAY	FRANCIS				41	0	CE	ENGLISH	F	043	H	2	50
KAY	GEORGE				32	0	CE	ENGLISH	F	043	H	2	49
KAY	GEORGE				32	ONTARIO	CE	ENGLISH	FARMER	043	H	2	49
KAY	JANE		1	1	24	0	CP	SCOTCH		045	C	4	22
KAY	JOHN		1		32	SCOTLAND	RC	SCOTCH	CARPENTER	043	C		55
KAY	JOSEPH				28	0	CE	ENGLISH	F	043	H	1	40
KAY	JOSEPH				67	ENGLAND	CE	ENGLISH	F	043	H	2	28
KAY	JOSEPH				25	0	CE	ENGLISH	F	043	H	2	47
KAY	JOSEPH				67	ENGLAND	CE	ENGLISH	FARMER	043	H	2	28
KAY	JOSEPH				25	ONTARIO	CE	ENGLISH	FARMER	043	H	2	47
KAY	RICHARD				37	ONTARIO	CE	ENGLISH	FARMER	043	H	2	50
KAY	THOMAS		1		17	0	CP	SCOTCH	FARM LABOURER	045	C	4	22
KAYLOR	JACOB				34	0	PM	GER	CARPENTER	044	B	1	39
KAYLOR	JOHN				77	US	LU	GER	CARPENTER	044	B	1	39
KAYS	ELIZA		1	1	14	IRELAND	CE	IRISH		043	G	2	44
KAYS	JOHN				32	IRELAND	CE	IRISH	HOTEL KEEPER	043	F		21
KAYS	SARAH		1	1	17	IRELAND	CE	IRISH		043	G	2	44
KEALL	ANNE	E	1	1	23	ENG	CE	ENG		045	C	1	67
KEALL	CHAS		1		6	ENG	CE	ENG		045	C	1	68
KEALL	FRANCIS				55	ENG	WM	ENG	LAB	044	B	2	27
KEALL	MARY ANN		1	1	27	ENG	CE	ENG		045	C	1	68
KEALL	WILLIAM				30	ENGLAND	CE	ENGLISH	FARM LABOURER	045	C	4	11
KEAN	PATRICK	J			48	IRELAND	RC	IRISH	PRIEST	043	D		47
KEAR	GEORGE				23	0	WM	ENGLISH	F	043	E	3	49
KEARLEY	HARRY				36	ENGLAND	CE	ENGLISH	LABOURER	045	A	1	49
KEARNS	PATRICK				42	0	RC	IRISH	CARPENTER	044	C	4	50
KEAT	THOMAS				33	ENGLAND	CS	ENGLISH	FARMER	045	D	3	59
KEATH	MARY		1	1	17	0	RC	IRISH	SERVANT	044	A	3	27
KEATING	THOMAS				69	IRELAND	RC	IRISH	LABORER	043	G	2	17
KEAY	JOSEPH		1		10	0	FW	ENGLISH		045	A	1	55
KEAY	SARAH		1	1	8	0	FW	ENGLISH		045	A	1	55
KEDGER	SOREL				48	QUEBEC	RC	FRENCH	COOPER	043	H	2	8
KEDGER	SOREL				48	QUEBEC	RC	FRENCH	COOPER	043	H	2	8
KEEFLER	MATHIAS				45	NOVA SCOTIA	CE	GERMAN	BOOKKEEPER	045	B	1	60
KEEKIE	DAVID				44	0	BA	SCOTCH	MILLWRIGHT	043	H	1	12
KEEL	THOMAS				56	ENGLAND	PM	ENGLISH	FARMER	043	B	3	13
KEELE	WILLIAM	C			73	ENGLAND	IR	ENGLISH	F	044	C	4	30
KEELER	ORSON				64	US	WM	GERMAN	F	045	C	2	19
KEELER	STEPHEN		1		32	ENGLAND	CE	ENGLISH	F	045	C	2	5
KEELER	WILLIAM				49	ENGLAND	WM	ENGLISH	FARMER	043	G	2	47
KEELER	WILLIAM				36	ENGLAND	CE	ENGLISH	HOTEL KEEPER	045	C	2	10
KEELEY	JAMES				67	IRELAND	CE	IRISH	LAB	043	E	2	42
KEENA	ROBERT				39	IRELAND	RC	IRISH	F	044	C	4	72
KEES	ROBERT				60	GUERNSEY	CS	IRISH	SCHOOL TEACHER	044	B	4	40
KEETCH	NELSON				55	NEW BRUNSWICK	PR	ENGLISH	FARMER	043	G	2	8
KEETCH	WM				29	ENGLAND	WM	ENGLISH	MERCHANT	043	D		17
KEFFER	ALBERT		2		20	0	CE		STUDENT	044	B	1	D

SURNAME	NAME1	NAME2	STRAY	SEX	AGE	BIRTHPL	RELIGION	ORIGIN	OCCUP	DIST	SUB_DIST	DIV	PAGE
KEFFER	ANNE			1	52	O	LU	GER		044	B	1	61
KEFFER	ANTHONY				39	O	LU	GER	F	044	B	1	50
KEFFER	FREDERICK				32	O	LU	GER	F	044	B	1	55
KEFFER	GEORGE				34	O	CE	GER	AGENT	044	B	1	34
KEFFER	GEORGE				32	O	LU	GER	F	044	B	1	48
KEFFER	HENRY				36	O	LU	GER	F	044	B	1	61
KEFFER	JACOB				34	O	LU	GER	F	044	B	1	49
KEFFER	JACOB					O	CO	GERMAN	CARPENTER	044	B	5	72
KEFFER	JOHN				39	O	LU	GER	LAB	044	B	1	60
KEFFER	JOSEPH				46	O	CE	GER	F	044	B	1	50
KEFFER	MICHAEL				37	O	CE	GER	BLACK SMITH	044	B	1	33
KEFFER	MICHAEL				73	US	CE	GER	MECHANIC	044	B	1	62
KEFFER	PETER				70	US	LU	GER	F	044	B	1	61
KEFFER	VALENTINE				65	US	CE	GER	F	044	B	1	33
KEFFER	WILLIAM				60	O	CE	GER	F	044	B	1	28
KEIF	ELSIE			1	54	ONTARIO	PR	DUTCH		043	G	2	22
KEIF	MARGARET		1	1	20	ONTARIO	CP	SCOTCH		043	G	2	21
KEIFF	GEORGE		1		18	ONTARIO	CE	DUTCH	SERVANT	043	G	2	39
KEITH	PHIPPS		1		16	O	RC	SCOT		044	B	2	34
KEITH	WILLIAM				53	IRELAND	CE	IRISH	LAB	043	E	1	37
KEIZER	ELIZABETH		1	1	25	O	VM	ENG		044	B	3	21
KEIZER	EMELINE		1	1		O	VM	GER		044	B	3	21
KEIZER	GEORGE				30	O	WM	GERMANY	F	043	C		20
KELBY	FRANCIS				38	IRELAND	CE	ENGLISH	BUTCHER	043	C		46
KELLAM	GEORGE				23	O	PM	ENGLISH	F	044	A	3	45
KELLAM	GEORGE				61	ENGLAND	WM	ENGLISH	F	044	B	6	18
KELLAM	ISAAC				30	O	PM	ENGLISH	TOLL GATE KEEPER	044	A	3	32
KELLAM	JOHN				64	ENGLAND	PM	ENGLISH	F	044	A	3	44
KELLAM	RACHEL	ANN	2	1	17	O	PM			044	A	3	D
KELLAM	RACHEL	JANE	2	1	1	O	PM			044	A	3	D
KELLAM	ROBERT				31	O	WM	ENGLISH	F	044	B	6	18
KELLAR	ADELINE		1	1	5	O	CN	SCOTTISH		043	B	4	21
KELLAR	ALFRED				23	ENGLAND	WM	ENGLISH	LAB	043	E	3	58
KELLAR	JOHN		1		32	GERMANY	CE	GERMAN	HOSLER	045	D	3	81
KELLER	ARTHUR		1			O	CE	ENGLISH		043	E	1	34
KELLER	HENRY				30	GERMANY	LU	GERMAN	LAB	043	E	2	42
KELLER	JAMES				36	FRANCE	CE	FRENCH	LAB	045	C	2	8
KELLER	JAMES				45	O	WM	IRISH	STORE KEEPER	045	D	3	61
KELLER	JANNET		1	1	8	O	WM	ENGLISH		043	F		8
KELLER	SARAH		1	1	15	O	CE	ENGLISH	SERVANT	043	E	1	34
KELLET	JANE			1	55	IRELAND	CE	IRISH		043	B	5	22
KELLETT	JANE		1	1	58	IRELAND	CE	ENGLISH		045	C	4	35
KELLEY	JOHN		1		48	IRELAND	CE	IRISH	SHOEMAKER	043	B	3	64
KELLEY	JOHN				45	IRELAND	UP	IRISH	LABORER	045	D	1	44
KELLEY	MICHAEL		1		65	IRE	RC	IRE	LAB	044	B	3	45
KELLEY	MICHAEL				30	IRELAND	RC	IRISH	FARM LABORER	045	D	1	16
KELLINGTON	ELIZABETH			1	63	ENGLAND	PM	ENGLISH		043	E	2	55
KELLINGTON	ROBERT				29	ONTARIO	EM	ENGLISH	FARMER	043	G	2	12
KELLOUGH	ARCH				24	O	WM	IRISH	LAB	043	F		32
KELLS	JOHN				42	IRELAND	CE	IRISH	LAB	043	F		19
KELLY	ALAIN		1		16	O	PS	FRENCH		045	D	2	32
KELLY	ANNIE		1	1	12	O	PS	SCOTCH		045	A	1	21
KELLY	ARCHIBALD			M	75	SCOTLAND	PS	SCOTCH	F	043	A	2	20
KELLY	DANIEL				43	IRELAND	QU	IRISH	F	043	E	1	17
KELLY	DAVID		1		14	O	CN	IRISH		043	B	5	14
KELLY	HECTOR			M	35	O	PS	SCOTCH	CARPENTER	043	A	2	39
KELLY	JAMES				42	IRELAND	RC	IRISH	TAILOR	043	D		35
KELLY	JANE		1	1	12	O	WM	ENGLISH		044	A	3	35
KELLY	JOHN		1		34	IRELAND	RC	IRISH	LABORER	043	D		54
KELLY	JOHN				40	IRELAND	RC	IRISH	LAB	043	H	2	22
KELLY	JOHN				40	IRELAND	RC	IRISH	LABOURER	043	H	2	22
KELLY	JOHN				50	IRELAND	RC	IRISH	F	044	A	1	6
KELLY	JOSEPH		1		19	IRELAND	CE	IRISH	LABORER	043	G	1	56
KELLY	MARGARETH		1	1	30	ENGLAND	RC	ENGLISH	SERVANT	044	C	4	97
KELLY	MARGARETH		1	1	0	O	RC	IRISH		044	C	4	97
KELLY	MARY	ANNE	1	1	5	O	RC	IRISH		044	C	4	97
KELLY	MATTHEW				66	IRELAND	RC	IRISH	F	044	A	1	26
KELLY	MICHAEL				13	O	RC	IRISH		043	E	1	6
KELLY	MICHAEL				55	IRELAND	CE	IRISH	LAB	044	B	5	6
KELLY	MINNIE		1	1	9	O	CE	IRISH		043	F		4
KELLY	PATRICK		1	M	22	O	RC	IRELAND	SAWYER	043	A	5	6
KELLY	PATRICK			M	39	IRELAND	RC	IRELAND	L	043	A	5	21
KELLY	PATRICK				47	IRELAND	RC	IRELAND	BRICK LAYER	045	D	2	14
KELLY	PATRICK				68	IRELAND	RC	IRISH	LAB	044	C	4	51
KELLY	PATRICK		1		19	IRELAND	RC	IRISH	LAB	044	C	4	52
KELLY	STEPHEN				37	IRELAND	CP	IRISH	CARPENTER	045	A	3	15
KELLY	THOMAS				27	IRE	RC	IRE	CARPENTER	044	B	2	38
KELLY	WILLIAM		1		14	ONTARIO	WM	IRISH		043	G	1	36
KELLY	WILLIAM				33	IRELAND	RC	IRISH	DROVER	045	A	1	7
KELLY	WILLIAM				60	IRELAND	RC	IRISH	MATCH DEALER	045	A	1	52
KELLY	WILLIAM				58	IRELAND	RC	IRISH	FARMER	045	D	3	62
KELMAN	JAMES	HODGINS			36	SCOTLAND	RC	SCOTCH	CHEMIST & DRUGGIST	043	D		15
KELSHER	HENRY		1		19	ENGLAND	WM	ENGLISH	LABOURER	045	D	3	65
KEMP	ALEXANDER		1		44	SCOTLAND	PS	SCOTCH	FARM SERVANT	045	A	1	32
KEMP	FRANCES		1	1	18	SCOTLAND	RP	SCOTCH		044	C	3	45
KEMP	GEORGE				44	ENGLAND	CP	ENGLISH	BUTCHER	043	H	2	10
KEMP	GEORGE				44	ENGLAND	CS	ENGLISH	BUTCHER	043	H	2	10
KEMP	JOHN				33	ENGLAND	CE	ENGLISH	HOTEL KEEPER	044	C	3	44
KEMP	PRESTON		1		23	ENG	CE	ENG	LAB	044	B	1	21
KEMPSHELL	ALFORD				30	O	CE	ENGLISH	CLERK	044	C	3	41
KEMPSHELL	MICHEL				69	ENGLAND	CE	ENGLISH	BLACKSMITH	044	C	3	46
KENDAL	ALFRED		1		21	ENG	WM	ENG	F SERVANT	044	B	1	51
KENDAL	HIRAM		1		23	O	WM	AFRICAN	TEAMSTER	044	C	4	2
KENDALE	JOHN				42	ENGLAND	BA	ENGLISH	MILLER	045	A	3	5
KENDRIC	BRIDGET			1	47	IRE	RC	IRISH		044	B	2	12
KENDRICK	JANE		1	1	50	IRELAND	CE	ENGLISH		045	A	1	65
KENDRICK	JOHN				19	IRE	RC	IRISH	LAB	044	B	2	13
KENDRICK	REBEKAH	J	1	1	9	O	CE	ENGLISH		045	A	1	65
KENDRICK	WILLIAM	J	1		14	USA	CE	ENGLISH		045	A	1	65
KENEDAY	ALEXANDER			M	27	IRELAND	PS	IRISH	BLACKSMITH	043	A	1	59
KENEDY	GEORGE				46	IRELAND	CE	IRISH	LAB	043	B	1	35
KENEDY	SARAH			1	45	IRELAND	RC	IRISH		043	B	1	21
KENIDA	JAMES		1		24	IRELAND	PM	IRISH	F	045	A	4	13
KENIECE	ADAM				37	ONTARIO	WM	OJIBWAY INDIAN	HUNTER AND FISHER	043	G	1	61
KENNEDY	ANGUS		1		15	O	XC	SCOTCH		043	A	4	52
KENNEDY	ANN			1	48	IRELAND	CE	IRISH		045	D	5	21

SURNAME	NAME1	NAME2	STRAY	SEX	AGE	BIRTHPL	RELIGION	ORIGIN	OCCUP	DIST	SUB_DIST	DIV	PAGE
KENNEDY	CATHERINE		1	1	9	0	XC	SCOTCH		043	A	4	52
KENNEDY	DANIEL				46	0	WM	IRISH	F & SAWMILLER	043	A	6	31
KENNEDY	DAVID				27	SCOTLAND	CP	SCOTCH	TAILOR	045	D	4	18
KENNEDY	DONALD				88	SCOTLAND	CC	SCOTCH	WEAVER	043	A	3	51
KENNEDY	DONALD		1		19	0	XC	SCOTCH	FARMER	043	A	4	52
KENNEDY	DUNCAN				51	SCOTLAND	CC	SCOTCH	F	043	A	3	50
KENNEDY	DUNCAN		1		35	SCOT	CP	SCOT	SERVANT	044	B	1	18
KENNEDY	ELIZABETH		1	1	4	0	CP	SCOTCH		045	C	4	26
KENNEDY	ELIZABETH	M	1	1	8	0	PS	SCOTCH		045	C	3	8
KENNEDY	EVELYN		1	1	60	0	WM	IRISH		043	D		73
KENNEDY	GEORGE				57	IRELAND	CE	IRISH	F	044	C	3	15
KENNEDY	HANNAH		1	1	23	0	NC	IRISH		043	C		7
KENNEDY	HECTOR				42	0	FK	SCOTCH	F	043	A	3	50
KENNEDY	HENRY				27	0	CP	IRISH	F	045	C	4	30
KENNEDY	JAMES				40	UNITED STATES	WM	SCOTCH	SCHOOL TEACHER	043	E	1	30
KENNEDY	JAMES				63	IRELAND	RC	IRISH	LABOURER	045	A	1	57
KENNEDY	JAMES				55	0	CP	IRISH	F	045	C	4	26
KENNEDY	JOHN				40	SCOTLAND	CP	SCOTCH	TAILOR	043	D		14
KENNEDY	JOHN				42	SCOTLAND	CP	SCOTCH	AGENT	043	D		87
KENNEDY	JUNE		1	1	48	IRE	CE	IRE		045	C	1	7
KENNEDY	MARGARET			1	50	SCOTLAND	CP	SCOTCH	F	045	C	4	13
KENNEDY	MARGARET				90	IRELAND	RC	IRISH		044	C	2	38
KENNEDY	MARGARETH		1	1	50	IRELAND	RC	IRISH		044	C	4	55
KENNEDY	MARY		1	1	13	0	XC	SCOTCH		043	A	4	52
KENNEDY	MARY		1	1	66	N B	CS	FRENCH		045	D	3	27
KENNEDY	MARY	A	1	1	46	ENGLAND	CE	ENGLISH		045	D	6	40
KENNEDY	MICHAEL				25	IRELAND	RC	IRISH	FARMER	045	D	3	9
KENNEDY	MICHAEL				40	IRELAND	RC	IRISH	LAB	044	C	4	92
KENNEDY	PETER		1		17	0	XC	SCOTCH	HARNESS MAKER	043	A	4	52
KENNEDY	ROBERT				54	IRELAND	RC	IRISH	F	043	A	3	16
KENNEDY	SAMUEL				27	0	CP	IRISH	F	045	C	4	26
KENNEDY	SIMON				36	0	CP	ENGLISH	FARMER	045	D	3	27
KENNEDY	SUSAN		1	1	7	0	XC	SCOTCH		043	A	4	52
KENNEDY	SUSAN		1	1	22	0	CS	IRISH		044	B	6	56
KENNEDY	THOMAS				57	0	CP	IRISH	F	045	C	4	17
KENNEDY	THOMAS		1		21	IRELAND	RC	ENGLISH	LAB	044	C	2	37
KENNEY	MICHAEL				50	IRELAND	RC	IRISH	LAB	044	C	4	70
KENNEY	PATRICK				49	IRELAND	RC	IRISH	RAILWAY LABORER	044	A	1	31
KENNEY	PETER				28	IRELAND	RC	IRISH	F	043	E	3	19
KENNY	MARGRET		1	1	15	0	WM	GERMAN	SERVANT	043	C		22
KENRICK	SUSAN				69	ENGLAND	CE	ENGLISH		045	B	1	16
KENT	DOWER	J			37	ENGLAND	CE	ENGLISH	LAB	043	D		27
KENT	JOHN				58	ENGLAND	CE	ENGLISH	MERCHANT CLERK	045	D	6	47
KENT	P	FELIX			56	ENGLAND	RC	ENGLISH	MERCHANT	044	C	3	48
KERBERSON	THOMAS				32	ENGLAND	WM	ENGLISH	LAB	043	C		55
KERBY	JOHN		1		23	CANADA	CE	ENGLISH	FARMER	045	D	6	39
KERBY	MRS			1	72	ENGLAND	PM	ENGLISH		045	D	4	10
KERNEY	CALEB				60	0	WM	ENGLISH	F	044	B	6	59
KERNIGHAN	JAMES				38	IRELAND	CP	IRISH	LAB	043	B	1	15
KERNS	ANN			1	50	IRELAND	RC	IRISH		043	H	2	13
KERNS	ANN			1	50	IRELAND	RC	IRISH		043	H	2	13
KERNS	SARAH		2	1	26	0	RC		SERVANT	043	H	2	D
KERR	ANN	JANE	1	1	9	0	CP	ENGLISH		043	D		19
KERR	ATKINSON				40	0	BA	IRISH	ENGINEER	043	C		52
KERR	DAVID		1		10	0	CP	IRISH		045	B	2	4
KERR	ELIZABETH				60	IRELAND	CE	IRISH		044	C	3	59
KERR	EMELINE		1	1	6	0	CP	ENGLISH		043	D		19
KERR	HARRIET		1	1	60	ENGLAND	CE	ENGLISH		044	A	2	53
KERR	ISABELLA		1	1	36	SCOTLAND	CP	SCOTCH		043	D		19
KERR	ISABELLA		2	1	36	SCOTLAND	CP			043	D		D
KERR	JAMES			M	62	IRELAND	PR	IRISH	FAR	043	A	1	66
KERR	JAMES		1		17	0	CP	SCOTCH	CABINETMAKER	043	D		19
KERR	JAMES		1		19	0	CO	ENGLISH	CABINET MAKER	043	D		86
KERR	JAMES		1		11	0	CP	IRISH		045	B	2	4
KERR	JAMES				02	0	WM	ENGLISH		044	C		
KERR	JOHN			M	38	IRELAND	PR	IRISH	LAB	043	A	1	69
KERR	JOHN		1		56	IRELAND	CE	IRISH	LAB	043	F		18
KERR	LETITIA		1	1	22	IRELAND	CP	IRISH		045	B	2	4
KERR	MARGARET		1	1	13	0	CP	IRISH		045	B	2	4
KERR	MARGRIT		1	1	9	0	CE	IRISH		043	F		18
KERR	REBECCA		1	1	27	0	WM	ENGLISH		044	C	3	19
KERR	WILLIAM			M	29	0	EM	IRISH	FAR	043	A	1	66
KERR	WILLIAM		2	M		0	NG			043	A	1	D
KERR	WILLIAM		1		42	QUE	CP	ENGLISH	LAB	043	D		18
KERRISON	JOHN	D			27	ENGLAND	CE	ENGLISH	PIANOIST	045	A	1	8
KERSEY	WILLIAM				71	ENGLAND	CE	ENGLISH	F	044	B	6	23
KERSTEMAN	WILLIAM				53	ENGLAND	CE	ENGLISH		045	B	2	28
KERSWELL	CHARLES				29	ENG	CE	ENG	F	044	B	2	60
KERSWELL	DANIEL				39	ENG	CE	ENG	F	044	B	2	55
KERSY	JAMES		1		48	NORWAY	LU	NORWEGIAN	WHEELWRIGHT	045	A	2	7
KESNAR	EDGAR		1		13	0	QU	GERMAN		043	B	4	39
KESSIOK	SAMUEL		1		19	IRELAND	CS	IRISH	FARMER	043	G	1	57
KESTER	GEORGE				54	0	CN	GERMAN	CORDWAINER	043	E	2	14
KESTER	JOHN				40	CANADA	WM	ENGLISH	FARMER	045	D	6	78
KETCH	JOHN				44	NEW BRUNSWICK	BC	ENGLISH	LAB	043	H	2	17
KETCH	JOHN				44	NEW BRUNSWICK	BC	ENGLISH	LABOURER	043	H	2	17
KETCH	SARAH		1	1	14	0	BA	GERMAN		043	H	2	54
KETCH	SARAH		1	1	14	ONTARIO	BA	GERMAN		043	H	2	54
KEW	THOMAS		1		62	ENGLAND	CE	ENGLISH	SHOEMAKER	044	A	3	26
KEY	ANGELINE		1	1	16	0	CP	ENGLISH		045	C	2	24
KEY	HENERY				46	ENGLAND	CP	ENGLISH	LAB	045	C	2	13
KEYES	THOMAS		1		15	US	CI	IRISH		044	B	1	32
KEYS	HENRY				40	IRELAND	CE	IRISH	TEAMSTER	044	B	5	31
KEYS	JOHN		1		27	IRE	LU	IRISH	FARM LAB	044	B	1	33
KEYS	THOMAS				42	IRE	EP	IRE	F	044	B	3	44
KIDD	ELIZABETH		1	1	73	ENGLAND	PM	ENGLISH		044	A	3	44
KIELY	GEORGE				41	0	RC	IRISH		045	B	1	74
KIGHTLEY	JAMES				75	ENGLAND	CE	ENGLISH	LAB	045	A	3	14
KIGHTLEY	JOHN				52	ENGLAND	CE	ENGLISH	FARMER	045	A	3	19
KILBECK	JAMES				48	IRELAND	CE	IRISH	CARPENTER	044	C	3	13
KILEY	ELIZABETH		2	1	40	SCOTLAND	PS		DRESSMAKER	045	A	3	D
KILEY	JOHN				25	ONTARIO	WM	IRISH	LABORER	043	G	1	25
KILLOPS	WILLIAM				35	IRE	PS	IRE	F	044	B	2	69
KILLOUGH	JOHN				45	IRELAND	CS	IRISH	LAB	043	F		24
KILLOUGH	WILLIAM				25	0	PM	IRISH	FARM LABOURER	043	E	1	9
KILWEE	ANN			1	40	IRELAND	RC	IRISH	WASHERWOMAN	045	D	5	30

SURNAME	NAME1	NAME2	STRAY	SEX	AGE	BIRTHPL	RELIGION	ORIGIN	OCCUP	DIST	SUB_DIST	DIV	PAGE
KILWEE	REDMUND		1		42	IRELAND	RC	IRISH	MOULDER	045	D	5	32
KIMSON	BETTY		1	1	71	IRELAND	WM	IRISH	SERVANT	045	B	1	41
KINERNEY	DENNIS		1		27	IRELAND	RC	IRISH	COACHMAN	044	C	2	47
KING	CHRISTINA			1	31	O	WM	ENGLISH		044	B	5	52
KING	ELLEN		1	1	44	IRELAND	CE	IRISH	SERVANT	043	D		68
KING	GORDON				31	SCOTLAND	CS	SCOTCH	BLACKSMITH	044	B	6	23
KING	HERBERT		1		28	ENGLAND	CE	ENGLISH	GENTLEMAN	045	D	5	11
KING	HONORA			1	64	IRELAND	RC	IRISH		043	D		48
KING	JOEL				50	O	EM	ENGLISH	F	043	E	2	53
KING	JOHN				23	O	OM	GERMAN	F	043	E	2	45
KING	JOHN				22	O	CE	ENGLISH	BRICKMAKER	045	A	1	27
KING	JOSEPH				45	ENGLAND	CE	ENGLISH	MOULDER	044	B	5	15
KING	LEVI				47	USA	WM	ENGLISH	LAB	043	H	2	32
KING	LEVI				47	UNITED STATES	WM	ENGLISH	LABOURER	043	H	2	32
KING	MARGARET	E	1	1	24	ENGLAND	CE	ENGLISH		045	D	5	11
KING	ROBERT	JR			35	O	UP	SCOTCH	F	044	B	5	75
KING	ROBT	JR			39	SCOTLAND	UP	SCOTCH	F	044	B	5	75
KING	ROBT	SR			70	SCOTLAND	CO	SCOTCH	F	044	B	5	75
KING	SAMUEL				50	ENGLAND	CE	ENGLISH	F	043	E	2	73
KING	THOMAS		1		16	O	RC	IRISH	FARM SERVANT	043	E	1	6
KING	WILLIAM				31	ENGLAND	WM	ENGLISH	FARMER	045	D	6	75
KINGDOM	JAMES				44	ENGLAND	CE	ENGLISH	F LAB	044	A	2	43
KINGSBERRY	DAVID				35	IRELAND	PS	IRISH	F	044	A	1	11
KINGSTONE	JOHNATHAN				38	IRELAND	CE	ENGLISH	LAB	045	A	2	25
KINGSWOOD	ABRAHAM		1		25	ENGLAND	CE	ENGLISH	LABOURER	045	A	1	26
KINKADE	ELIZABETH			1	47	ENGLAND	CE	SCOTCH		043	B	3	10
KINNEE	JAMES				30	O	WM	GER	SHINGLE MAKER	044	B	4	4
KINNEE	JOEL				80	US	WM	GER	RETIRED MERCH	044	B	4	4
KINNEE	MOSES				50	O	WM	GER	LAB	044	B	4	21
KINNEE	ROBERT				27	O	PM	GER	F	044	B	4	3
KINNEY	BRIDGET		2	1	35	IRELAND	RC		LAB	043	E	3	D
KINNEY	JAMES				47	IRELAND	RC	IRISH	LAB	043	E	3	17
KINSEL	SARAH		1	1	28	IRELAND	RC	IRISH	SERVANT	045	B	2	33
KINSLAY	THOMAS				40	IRELAND	RC	IRISH	LAB	044	C	4	76
KINSLEY	JAMES			M	33	O	CE	ENGLAND		043	A	5	33
KION	JOHN			M	45	IRELAND	WM	IRELAND	BLACKSMITH	043	A	5	36
KIRBY	ELIZABETH			1	49	ENG	WM	ENG		044	B	2	75
KIRBY	ELIZABETH		2	1	50	ENGLAND	WM			045	D	1	D
KIRBY	JOHN	H	1		70	ENGLAND	CE	ENGLISH	GENTLEMAN	045	D	1	14
KIRBY	MARY			1	56	ENGLAND	WM	ENGLISH		044	A	2	50
KIRBY	NATHANIEL				65	ENG	CE	ENG	GENTLEMAN	044	B	1	18
KIRBY	WILLIAM				40	ENG	PM	ENG	F	044	B	4	8
KIRBY	WILLIAM				62	ENGLAND	WM	ENGLISH	FARMER	045	D	1	3
KIRBYSON	RICHARD			M	40	ENGLAND	PS	ENGLISH	F	043	A	2	7
KIRK	AGNES	J	2	1	50	SCOTLAND	CO			043	D		D
KIRK	ALLAN			M	41	ENGLAND	PM	ENGLISH	F	043	A	1	47
KIRK	ELLEN		1		23	O	UP	SCOTCH	SERVANT	043	A	6	48
KIRK	ELLENER		1	1	1	O	UP	SCOTCH		043	A	6	48
KIRK	MARIA		1		21	ENGLAND	EM	ENGLISH		044	C	2	32
KIRK	MARK				44	ENGLAND	PM	ENGLISH	LAB	044	A	3	13
KIRK	MARY		1	1	19	ENGLAND	PM	ENGLISH	SERVANT	045	A	2	36
KIRK	ROBERT				38	ENGLAND	PM	ENGLISH	MOLSTER	045	B	1	51
KIRK	THOMAS				57	SCOTLAND	CO	SCOTCH	BLACKSMITH	043	D		74
KIRK	WILLIAM				39	ENGLAND	PM	ENGLISH	F	045	A	4	16
KIRK	WILLIAM				44	ENGLAND	ME	ENGLISH	HOTELKEEPER	045	A	4	32
KIRK	WILLIAM	C	2		26	SCOTLAND	UP		STATION MASTER	043	A	6	D
KIRK	WM	B			41	QUE	PM	ENG	GARDNER	045	C	1	42
KIRKLAND	ALEXANDER				26	IRE	PS	IRE	MOULDER	044	B	2	24
KIRKLAND	CHARLES				39	IRE	PS	IRE	F	044	B	2	57
KIRKLAND	JAMES				25	IRE	PS	IRE	F	044	B	2	58
KIRKLAND	WILLIAM				44	IRELAND	CE	IRISH	SHOEMAKER	043	H	1	19
KIRKLIND	SARAH			1	40	IRELAND	CP	SCOTCH		044	A	2	47
KIRKPATRICK	ANDREW				36	IRELAND	WM	IRISH	SADDLE & HARNESS MAK	045	B	1	4
KIRKPATRICK	CHAS	D	2		1	O	CE		SADLER	045	D	1	D
KIRKPATRICK	JOSEPH				31	IRELAND	CE	IRISH	SADLER	045	D	1	13
KIRKPATRICK	MARY			1	63	ENGLAND	CS	SCOTCH		043	D		72
KIRKPATRICK	SOPHIA			1	21	IRELAND	CE	IRISH	LAB	045	B	2	5
KIRKPATRICK	WILLIAM				41	IRELAND	CE	IRISH	SADLER	045	D	1	12
KIRKTON	JAMES				36	SCOTLAND	CP	SCOTCH	F	043	B	2	2
KIRKY	JOSEPH				30	QUE	RC	IRISH	LAB	044	C	4	96
KIRTIS	ELLEN		1		44	US	CE	ENGLISH	HOUSEMAID	044	C	3	30
KIRTON	JOB		1	M	50	ENGLAND	CE	ENGLAND	L	043	A	5	4
KIRTON	JOHN				31	ENGLAND	EM	ENGLISH	LABOURER	045	D	5	37
KIRTON	RICHARD				48	ENGLAND	CN	ENGLISH	F	043	A	6	22
KISE	GEORGE		1		32	GERMANY	RC	GERMAN	WHEEL WRIGHT	043	C		42
KISER	BRIDGET		1	1	26	IRELAND	RC	IRISH		043	D		48
KISER	HELENA		1	1	8	IRELAND	RC	IRISH		043	D		48
KISER	LOVINA		1	1	19	O	WM	GERMAN		043	A	1	21
KISSOCK	DAVID		1		16	O	CS	SCOTCH	APPRENTICE	045	D	3	18
KITCHING	FRED	J	1		23	ENGLAND	CE	ENGLISH	CLERK	043	F		16
KITELEY	JAMES				30	O	QU	ENGLISH	F	043	E	3	33
KITELEY	JAS	WESLY			29	O	CN	GERMANY	CLOTHIER	043	B	2	41
KITELY	WILLIAM				52	O	CN	ENGLISH	F	043	E	1	41
KITSON	THOMAS			M	42	O	CP	ENGLISH	SAWYER	043	A	1	25
KITTO	ANN		1	1	22	O	WM	IRISH	SERVANT	045	B	2	27
KITTRIDGE	JOSEPH				30	ENGLAND	CE	ENGLISH	LABOURER	044	C	3	66
KIZER	JOHN				41	O	MN	GER	F	044	B	3	43
KLINCK	JAMES				27	O	WM	GERMAN	FARMER	045	D	4	24
KLINCK	JOHN				33	O	PR	ENGLISH	F	043	B	1	16
KLINE	ELENAOR		2	1	19	O	WM		MILLINER	043	A	4	D
KLINE	JOHN				50	O	BA	GERMAN	CARPENTER	043	B	2	7
KLINE	JOSEPHINE		1	1	17	O	CP	GERMAN		043	A	4	23
KLINE	PETER				39	GER	WM	GER	CARPENTER	044	B	2	17
KLINE	SARAH	I	1	1	15	O	CP	GERMAN		043	A	4	23
KLINE	WM	H	1		18	O	CP	GERMAN	PAINTER	043	A	4	23
KLINK	JOSEPH				33	O	BA	ENGLISH	FARMER	045	D	2	38
KLINK	MARY			1	52	O	TU	GERMAN		045	D	2	50
KLINK	WILLIAM				64	O	WM	GERMAN	FARMER	045	D	2	38
KNAGGS	GEORGE				55	ENGLAND	CN	ENGLISH	BUTCHER	044	A	2	18
KNAGGS	WILLIAM				57	ENGLAND	DI	ENGLISH	F	044	A	2	16
KNEESHAW	THOMAS				46	ENGLAND	EM	ENGLISH	BLACKSMITH	043	A	6	33
KNIGHT	EBENEZER		1	M	19	ENGLAND	PR	ENGLISH	BLACKSMITH	043	A	1	59
KNIGHT	GEORGE		1		29	ENGLAND	CE	ENGLISH	BRICK MAKER	045	A	1	26
KNIGHT	HENRY		1		22	ENGLAND	WM	ENGLISH	LAB	045	C	4	5
KNIGHT	JOHN	C			42	ENGLAND	CE	ENGLISH	BUTCHER	045	A	1	12
KNIGHT	MACLEAN				65	ENGLAND	CE	ENGLISH	F	043	E	2	34

SURNAME	NAME1	NAME2	STRAY	SEX	AGE	BIRTHPL	RELIGION	ORIGIN	OCCUP	DIST	SUB_DIST	DIV	PAGE
KNIGHT	MARY	LOUISA	2	1		0	CE			045	A	1	D
KNIGHT	RICHARD				65	ENGLAND	WM	ENGLISH	F	043	B	1	22
KNIGHT	SARAH			1	64	NOVA SCOTIA	CN	ENGLISH		043	E	2	3
KNIGHT	THOMAS				59	ENGLAND	WM	ENGLISH	F	045	C	3	45
KNIGHT	WILLIAM				52	ENGLAND	CN	ENGLISH	LUMBERMAN	043	E	2	41
KNIGHT	WILLIAM				21	0	PM	ENG	WAGON MAKER	044	B	4	19
KNIGHTS	ZACKARIAH				37	ENG	CE	ENG	L	045	C	1	26
KNILL	FLORENCE	F	2	1	2	0	CN			043	B	3	D
KNILL	RICHARD				40	IRELAND	CE	IRISH	TAVERN KEEPER	043	B	3	54
KNISELEY	DANIEL		1		34	0	BA	GERMAN	FACTORY LABOURER	043	B	3	33
KNOTT	ARTHUR				28	ENGLAND	OB	ENGLISH	BRICK LAYER	045	B	1	46
KNOTT	GEORGE		2		27	ENGLAND	CE		LABOURER	043	A	4	D
KNOWLES	GEORGE				39	ENGLAND	NC	ENGLISH	LAB	043	C		33
KNOWLES	RICHARD				29	0	DI	FRENCH	F	045	C	2	23
KNOWLES	THOMAS		1		79	IRE	CE	IRE	FARMER	044	B		
KNOWLIN	JANE		1	1	20	IRELAND	CE	IRISH	SERVANT	045	B	2	26
KNOWLYS	CULLING	E			41	ENGLAND	CE	ENGLISH	SURGEON	045	B	1	42
KNOX	CUNNINGHAM				39	IRELAND	OP	IRISH	F	043	A	3	31
KNOX	HUGH				42	IRELAND	OP	IRISH	F & B SMITH	043	A	3	31
KNOX	JANE	SARAH	2	1		ONT				043	A	3	D
KNOX	JOHN				55	IRELAND	WM	IRISH	MILLER	045	C	2	8
KOCH	DAVID				18	CANADA	WM	IRISH	FARMER	045	D	6	60
KOCH	ELIZABETH			1	49	CANADA	MN	GERMAN		045	D	6	25
KOSTER	NICHOLAS				47	GERMANY	RC	GERMAN	SAWYER	043	B	5	22
KRIBS	MARGARET			1	27	0	WM	IRISH		043	B	3	55
KULEY	MAURICE				71	IRELAND	RC	IRISH	BOOKKEEPER	045	B	1	44
KURTS	MARY ANNE				22	0	WM	GER		044	B	2	27
KURTZ	JOHN				68	US	PM	GERMAN	F	044	B	6	31
KURTZ	JOSHUA	W			24	0	CE	GERMAN	F	044	C	2	52
KYLE	WILLIAM		1		23	0	WM	IRISH	F LAB	044	A	3	37
KYLES	EDLEY				54	US	WM	IRISH	CARPENTER	044	B	1	66
LA CHAPELLE	EDWARD				40	ONTARIO	RC	FRENCH	LABOURER	043	G	2	6
LA CHAPELLE	LEWIS				55	ONTARIO	RC	FRENCH	FARMER	043	G	2	6
LA CHAPELLE	LEWIS		1		16	ONTARIO	RC	FRENCH	LABORER	043	G	2	45
LA ROSE	DANIEL				59	0	WM	FRENCH	F	044	A	2	37
LA RUSH	ANTHONY				40	0	WM	FRENCH	F	044	A	2	35
LACEY	MARK		1		55	ENGLAND	WM	ENGLISH	F LAB	044	A	3	55
LACKAY	SARAH		1	1		IRELAND	P	IRISH		044	C	4	44
LACKEY	ELLEN		1	1	17	0	CE	IRELAND	SERVANT	045	D	2	26
LACKEY	JANE		1	1	14	0	RC	IRELAND	SERVANT	045	D	2	24
LACKIE	DAVID				31	0	WM	SCOTCH	F	044	C	2	43
LACKIE	EDWARD				50	IRELAND	RC	SCOTCH	FARMER	045	D	2	52
LACKIE	THOMAS				37	0	WM	SCOTCH	FARMER	045	D	2	24
LACKIE	THOMAS				67	UNITED STATES	WM	SCOTCH	F	044	C	2	44
LACOCH	JAMES				50	IRELAND	CE	IRISH	LAB	044	C	3	21
LACON	JOSEPH				52	ENGLAND	CE	ENGLISH	SHOEMAKER	044	A	1	36
LAFFERTY	WM	D			37	0	WM	IRISH	F	044	A	1	25
LAHEY	JOHN				60	IRELAND	RC	IRISH	F	043	E	3	18
LAHMER	JACOB				44	0	MN	GER	F	044	B	3	12
LAIRD	ALEXANDER				39	SCOT	PS	SCOT	MOULDER	044	B	2	39
LAIRD	HUGH				64	SCOTLAND	KB	SCOTCH	FARMER	045	A	3	23
LAIRD	THOMAS		1	M	17	0	PR	GERMANY	L	043	A	5	7
LAKE	JOHN				53	0	DI	ENGLISH	F	045	C	2	15
LAKE	WILLIAM				66	ENGLAND	CE	ENGLISH	FARMER	043	H	2	37
LAKE	WILLIAM	W			66	ENGLAND	CE	ENGLISH	F	043	H	2	37
LAKEY	MARY		1	1	26	IRELAND	CE	IRISH	SERVANT	044	C	2	48
LALONE	BERNARD		1		28	0	CE	IRE	LAB	045	C	1	32
LAMB	LAUGHLAN				60	IRELAND	RC	IRISH	F	044	A	2	38
LAMB	MATHIAS		1		17	0	CE	ENGLISH		045	B	2	3
LAMB	SAMUEL		1		26	ENGLAND	CE	ENGLISH	LABOURER	045	D	3	75
LAMB	THOMAS				45	IRELAND	CE	IRISH	PEDLER	045	D	1	14
LAMBER	JOSEPH		1		26	SCOT	CP	SCOT	LAB	045	C	1	44
LAMBERT	GEORGE		1		54	ENGLAND	WM	ENGLISH	SERVANT	045	A	3	3
LAMBERT	GEORGE				35	ENGLAND	CE	ENGLISH	FARMER	045	A	3	32
LAMBIE	ANDREW				48	0	QU	SCOTCH	F	043	B	2	36
LAMBIE	JAS				34	SCOT	CP	SCOT	F	044	C	1	33
LAMERIEUX	CHRISTOPHER				60	CANADA	PM	FRENCH	F	045	C	4	1
LAMON	TAYLOR				50	AFRICA	CE	AFRICAN	LAB	043	E	3	3
LAMOND	MURDOCK				63	SCOTLAND	CS	SCOTCH	SHOEMAKER	045	D	3	38
LAMOND	WILLIAM				37	SCOTLAND	VM	SCOTCH	STORE KEEPER	045	D	3	23
LAMOUREAUX	JOSHUA				58	0	WM	IRISH	BLACKSMITH	045	D	3	28
LANAGHAM	BRIDGET		1	1	18	0	RC	IRISH	SERVANT	044	A	3	4
LANDER	MARGT		1	1	12	0	CE	IRISH		044	B	5	20
LANDER	SUSANA			1	50	0	WM	IRISH		045	B	1	15
LANDER	THOMAS				23	ENGLAND	SW	ENGLISH	OPTICIAN	045	A	1	3
LANDON	GEO				22	0	WM	IRISH	LAB	044	B	5	32
LANE	CYRUS				64	0	WM	ENGLISH		045	D	3	27
LANE	ELIZABETH		1	1	74	ENGLAND	WM	ENGLISH		045	B	1	25
LANE	ELLEN		2	1	2	0	WM			045	D	3	D
LANE	JAMES		1	M	18	ENGLAND	WM	ENGLISH	LAB	043	A	2	35
LANE	JAMES				36	0	WM	IRISH	SHOP KEEPER	044	B	1	4
LANE	JOHN				26	0	CE	IRISH	COOPER	043	F		4
LANE	JOHN				52	IRELAND	WM	IRISH	COOPER	045	D	1	9
LANE	MARY JANE		2	1	15	0	CE			044	B	1	D
LANE	SUSAN		1	1	22	ONTARIO	PM	IRISH	SERVANT	045	A	3	36
LANE	THOMAS				66	IRELAND	CE	IRISH	COOPER	043	F		3
LANE	THOMAS				26	0	WM	IRISH	F	044	B	1	22
LANE	THOMAS				42	IRELAND	CE	IRISH	TEAMSTER	045	D	1	14
LANE	WILLIAM				24	0	CE	IRISH	COOPER	043	F		3
LANE	WILLIAM				68	IRE	WM	ENGLISH	GENTLEMAN	044	B	1	22
LANE	WILLIAM				67	ENGLAND	CP	ENGLISH	GARDNER	045	B	1	63
LANE	WILLIAM	J			52	IRELAND	CE	IRISH	LAB	044	B	1	5
LANE	WILMOT	L	2		4	0	WM			045	D	3	D
LANG	HENRIETTA		1	1	15	0	NC	SCOTCH		043	C		18
LANG	ISABELLA		1	1	48	SCOTLAND	NC	SCOTCH		043	C		18
LANG	JAMES				32	QUE	PS	SCOT	CARPENTER	044	B	2	26
LANGDON	JAMES				33	ENGLAND	CE	ENGLISH	FARM LAB	044	A	2	40
LANGFORD	WM				60	IRELAND	WM	IRISH	F	044	A	1	19
LANGLEY	BENJAMIN				36	0	FW	IRISH	CLERK	045	A	1	75
LANGLEY	JULIA	A	2	1	31	0	BP			045	A	1	D
LANGRILL	FRANCIS				39	0	PM	IRISH	DROVER	044	C	2	13
LANGRILL	WILLIAM				66	IRELAND	PM	IRISH	DROVER	044	C	2	13
LANGSTAFF	ISABELLA			1	50	IRELAND	NG	IRISH		044	C	3	26
LANGSTAFF	JAMES				46	0	PS	ENG	DOCTOR	044	B	2	45
LANGSTAFF	JOHN				48	0	CE	ENGLISH	MANUFACTURER	045	D	1	19
LANGSTAFF	LEWIS			M	48	0	CE	ENGLISH	M D	043	A	1	59

SURNAME	NAME1	NAME2	STRAY	SEX	AGE	BIRTHPL	RELIGION	ORIGIN	OCCUP	DIST	SUB_DIST	DIV	PAGE
LANGSTAFF	NOLTON				27	0	WM	ENGLISH	BRAKEMAN ON RAIL	044	C	3	37
LANGSTAFF	THOMAS				65	ENGLAND	WM	ENGLISH	PUMP MAKER	044	C	3	18
LANGTON	JULEY	ANN		F	49	0	PR	GERMAN	FARMER	043	A	1	26
LANIGAN	THOMAS				48	IRELAND	RC	IRISH	F	044	C	4	90
LANKIM	ROBT		1		17	0	WM	ENG		045	C	1	28
LANKIN	BENJ				32	0	LU	IRISH	CARPENTER	044	B	5	46
LANKIN	CHARLES		1	M	25	ENGLAND	CE	ENGLISH	MECHANIC	043	A	2	34
LANKIN	JAS		1		22	0	WM	ENGLISH	BLACKSMITH	044	B	5	9
LANKIN	JOHN		2	M	41	0	CE		F	043	A	5	D
LANKIN	JOSEPH				47	0	WM	IRE	F	044	B	3	30
LANKIN	ROBERT				37	0	CN	IRISH	CARPENTER	043	E	2	61
LANKTREE	HENERY				33	0	WM	IRISH	F	045	C	2	27
LAPOINT	STEPHEN				65	QUE	RC	FRENCH	LAB	045	A	1	93
LAPP	DAVID				40	0	CP	GERMAN	MERCHANT	045	D	5	53
LAPP	JOSEPH				36	0	CP	GERMAN	FARMER	045	D	5	54
LAPP	PETER				51	0	CP	GERMAN	FARMER	045	D	5	61
LAPP	RACHAEL		1	1	10	0	CP	GERMAN		045	D	5	53
LAPPIN	PATRICK				50	IRELAND	RC	IRISH	F	044	C	4	94
LAPSLEY	WILLIAM				34	0	CE	IRISH	PHYSICIAN	045	C	3	38
LAREN	ALEXANDER				29	SCOTLAND	CP	SCOTCH	F	043	H	1	40
LARKIN	CHARLES				46	IRELAND	RC	IRISH	LAB	043	F		6
LARKIN	JOHN				37	ONTARIO	WM	ENGLISH	FARMER	043	G	1	14
LARKIN	JOSEPH			M	63	ENGLAND	CE	ENGLAND	F	043	A	5	35
LARKINS	JOHN				38	IRELAND	RC	IRISH	LAB	045	B	2	22
LARMOTH	JOHN				55	SCOTLAND	CP	SCOTCH	LAB	044	C	4	31
LAROC	MICHEAL				31	0	BA	FRENCH	F	043	E	3	21
LARONE	CANE				60	0	RC	FRENCH	LAB	043	H	2	57
LARONE	CANE				60	ONTARIO	RC	FRENCH	LABOURER	043	H	2	57
LARUSH	JOHN				38	0	WM	FRENCH	WELL DIGGER	044	A	2	33
LARWAY	THOMAS				67	ENGLAND	CP	ENGLISH	F	045	C	3	30
LARWAY	WILLIAM				30	ENGLAND	CP	ENGLISH	F	045	C	4	16
LASCELLES	RICHARD				39	ENGLAND	WM	ENGLISH	LAB	045	A	4	11
LASCELS	GEORGE				66	ENGLAND	CE	ENGLISH	LAB	044	C	2	35
LASHFORD	JACKSON				26	0	CE	ENGLISH	LABOURER	043	B	3	22
LASHINER	FRANCIS		1		30	PRUSSIA	RC	PRUSSIAN	LAB	045	A	2	37
LATAMORE	REBECCA			1	68	IRELAND	WM	IRISH		044	C	1	51
LATER	ASHER			M	51	ENGLAND	CE	ENGLISH	FARM LABOURER	043	A	1	52
LATHAM	ALEX		1		15	0	CE	ENG		045	C	1	58
LATHAM	ALEXANDER		1		40	IRELAND	RP	IRISH	ENGINEER	043	B	5	18
LATHAM	ISAAC				52	IRE	CP	IRE	F	045	C	1	65
LATHAM	JAMES				50	IRELAND	CE	IRISH	LABOURER	045	A	1	61
LATHAM	JOHN				35	IRELAND	PR	IRISH	FARMER	043	G	2	32
LATHAM	PETER				32	ENGLAND	PM	ENGLISH	GARDENER	045	A	1	2
LATHAM	ROBERT		1		6	ONTARIO	CE	SCOTCH		043	G	1	53
LATIMER	EDWARD				66	SCOTLAND	OP	SCOTCH	F	043	H	2	35
LATIMER	EDWARD				66	SCOTLAND	CS	SCOTCH	FARMER	043	H	2	35
LATIMER	ROBERT				40	IRELAND	UP	IRISH	FARM LABORER	045	D	1	32
LATTER	JOSEPH		1		22	ENGLAND	PM	ENGLISH	SCHOOL TEACHER	043	B	3	9
LATTIA	SARAH		2	1		0	EM			044	C	1	D
LAUDER	CATHERIN		1	1	18	0	RC	IRISH	LAB	044	C	1	54
LAUDER	JAMES				50	IRELAND	WM	IRISH	LAB	044	C	1	52
LAUDER	JAMES		1		16	0	RC	IRISH	LAB	044	C	1	54
LAUDER	JAMIE		1		15	0	RC	IRISH	LAB	044	C	1	54
LAUDER	JOHN				59	SCOTLAND	PS	SCOTCH	TAILOR	045	C	3	51
LAUDER	JOHN				48	SCOTLAND	CP	SCOTCH		044	C	2	23
LAUDER	THOMAS				45	SCOTLAND	CP	SCOTCH	F	045	C	3	51
LAUGHLIN	SYLVESTER				60	IRELAND	RC	IRISH	LAB	044	C	2	51
LAUR	MARY		1	1	22	0	OM	SCOTCH	SERVANT	045	D	3	80
LAUR	NANCY	JANE		1	40	0	VM	IRISH		045	D	3	12
LAURIE	JEMIMA		1	1	16	SCOTLAND	CP	SCOTCH	SERVANT	045	B	2	37
LAUTON	CHARLES		2		1	0	PM			045	D	3	D
LAUTON	DAVID				26	0	WM	ENGLISH	LABOURER	045	D	4	14
LAUTON	WILLIAM				34	ENGLAND	PM	ENGLISH		045	D	3	31
LAVENDER	JOHN				40	IRELAND	MV	IRISH	FARMER	045	D	6	65
LAVENDER	ROBERT		1		16	IRELAND	CE	IRISH		045	D	6	37
LAVIGNOUR	THOMAS				41	QUE	RC	FRENCH	CARPENTER	045	A	1	69
LAVIOLETT	JOSEPH				38	0	RC	FRENCH	F	043	H	1	3
LAVIOLETTE	CHARLES				48	QUEBEC	RC	FRENCH	F	043	H	1	6
LAVIOLETTE	MATILDA		1	1	65	IRELAND	RC	IRISH		043	H	2	31
LAVIOLETTE	PETER				49	QUEBEC	RC	FRENCH	F	043	H	1	7
LAVOLETTE	MATILDA			1	65	IRELAND	RC	IRISH		043	H	2	31
LAW	ABRAHAM				64	US	WM	SCOT	TANNER	044	B	2	17
LAW	BENJAMIN				24	0	CN	GERMAN	FARMER	043	B	3	72
LAW	DAVID				56	UNITED STATES	CN	ENGLISH	FARMER	043	B	3	62
LAW	EDWIN				37	0	CN	ENGLISH	FARMER	045	D	5	28
LAW	ISAAC				53	UNITED STATES	NG	GERMAN	FARMER	043	B	3	49
LAW	JAMES				25	0	CN	ENGLISH	CARPENTER	045	C	3	40
LAW	JOHN				55	ENGLAND	CE	ENGLISH	F	045	C	3	10
LAW	LEVY				30	CANADA	CN	ENGLISH	STORE KEEPER	045	D	6	52
LAW	MARY			1	82	ENGLAND	CE	ENGLISH		045	C	3	6
LAW	ROBERT	E			39	0	WM		DRUGGIST	045	D	2	21
LAW	THOMAS				45	0	CN	ENGLISH	F	045	C	3	5
LAW	WILLIAM				77	ENGLAND	WM	ENGLISH	TEACHER	043	G	1	56
LAWLOR	ELLEN			1	40	IRELAND	RC	IRISH		044	A	2	53
LAWOBY	EMMA		1	1	17	US	CE	ENGLISH	SERVANT	045	B	2	32
LAWRANCE	ROBERT				40	ENGLAND	PM	ENGLISH	LAB	045	B	2	16
LAWRANCE	STEPHEN				27	ENGLAND	PM	ENGLISH	GARDNER	045	B	2	35
LAWRENCE	A	P			65	NEW BRUNSWICK	UV	ENGLISH	GENTLEMAN	043	G	1	3
LAWRENCE	ELIZABETH			1	78	U STATES	WM	ENGLISH		045	A	2	3
LAWRENCE	FRANKLIN				19	0	WM	ENGLISH	FARMER	045	A	2	1
LAWRENCE	GEORGE	H			51	U STATES	WM	ENGLISH	AGENT	043	A	6	6
LAWRENCE	GRACE			1	42	IRELAND	CE	IRISH		045	D	1	21
LAWRENCE	JAMES				56	ENGLAND	CE	ENGLISH	FARMER	043	A	4	46
LAWRENCE	JAMES				38	ENGLAND	PM	ENGLISH	GARDNER	045	B	1	57
LAWRENCE	JAMES	M			42	0	WM	ENG	CLERK DIV COURT	044	B	2	18
LAWRENCE	JOHN				55	0	WM	ENGLISH	INSURANCE AGENT	045	B	1	40
LAWRENCE	MARIA		1	1	18	0	CE	ENGLISH	TEACHER	045	A	3	33
LAWRENCE	PETER				52	0	WM	ENGLISH	FARMER	044	C	1	22
LAWRENCE	ROBERT				57	ENGLAND	PM	ENGLISH	FARMER	045	A	2	18
LAWRENCE	WILLIAM				66	ENGLAND	PM	ENGLISH	GARDNER	045	B	1	57
LAWRIE	DAVID				39	SCOT	CS	SCOT	F	044	B	4	41
LAWRIE	GAVIN				34	0	UP	SCOTCH	F	044	B	5	66
LAWRIE	JAMES				50	SCOTLAND	PS	SCOTCH	F	045	C	2	31
LAWRIE	JAMES				22	0	PS	SCOTCH	F	045	C	2	32
LAWRIE	JOHN				68	SCOTLAND	UP	SCOTCH	F	044	B	5	66
LAWS	JAMES		1		24	SCOTLAND	CP	SCOTCH	MANUFACTURER	045	D	4	42

SURNAME	NAME1	NAME2	STRAY	SEX	AGE	BIRTHPL	RELIGION	ORIGIN	OCCUP	DIST	SUB_DIST	DIV	PAGE
LAWSON	ALFRED				35	ENGLAND	CE	ENGLISH	F	043	B	1	27
LAWSON	DAVID		1		32	SCOTLAND	CP	SCOTCH	LAB	045	C	2	53
LAWSON	ELISABETH			1	43	ENGLAND	WM	ENGLISH		045	B	2	14
LAWSON	GEORGE				31	ENGLAND	WM	ENGLISH	FARMER	045	D	4	23
LAWSON	JAMES		1		26	SCOTLAND	CP	SCOTCH	LAB	043	H	1	28
LAWSON	JAMES				31	0	PS	ENGLISH	F	044	C	1	34
LAWSON	LOIS		1	1	37	0	PM	SCOTCH	DRESS MAKER	045	C	4	6
LAWSON	THOMAS			M	50	SCOTLAND	PS	SCOTCH		043	A	2	39
LAWSON	THOMAS				62	ENGLAND	PS	ENGLISH	FARMER	044	C	1	23
LAWSON	WILLIAM				22	0	CE	ENGLISH	F	043	A	6	13
LAWSON	WILLIAM				53	ENGLAND	WM	ENGLISH	FARMER	045	D	4	3
LAYTON	JOHN			M	44	ENGLAND	PM	ENGLISH	F	043	A	1	21
LEA	GEORGE				49	IRELAND	CE	IRISH	FORK KEEPER	045	A	3	2
LEA	JOHN				48	0	CE	ENGLISH	FARMER	045	A	2	20
LEA	REUBEN				52	E	CE	ENGLAND	SHOE MAKER	045	D	2	6
LEA	RICHARD				50	ENGLAND	CE	ENGLISH	FARMER	045	A	2	11
LEA	WILLIAM				56	ENGLAND	CE	ENGLISH	FARMER	045	A	2	38
LEACE	HENRY				25	ENG	WM	ENG	FARM LAB	044	B	4	13
LEACE	JOHN		1		29	ENG	PM	ENG	LAB	044	B	4	14
LEACH	ELLEN			1	52	ENGLAND	CE	ENGLISH		044	C	3	47
LEACH	HENRY				39	IRE	EM	IRE		044	B	4	33
LEACH	MARY			1	50	SCOTLAND	CP	SCOTCH	MERCHANT	045	A	3	11
LEACH	RUTH		1	1	42	0	PM	ENGLISH		043	A	6	12
LEACY	NANCY		1	1	60	IRELAND	RC	IRISH		043	D		37
LEADER	E	GEORGE	2			0	NG			045	A	3	D
LEADER	FREDRICK				32	0	CE	ENGLISH	LAB	045	A	3	12
LEADLAY	ALLSON				64	ENGLAND	WM	ENGLISH	FARMER	045	A	3	30
LEADLAY	JOHN				35	0	WM	ENGLISH	FARMER	045	A	3	29
LEAF	GEORGE				42	ENG	VM	ENG	F	044	B	2	6
LEAF	WILLIAM				43	ENGLAND	CE	ENGLISH	FARMER	043	A	4	67
LEAN	THOS	C			26	ENGLAND	CO	ENGLISH	SCHOOL TEACHER	044	C	2	44
LEAPER	WILLIAM				49	ENGLAND	WM	ENGLISH	LABOURER	045	D	5	14
LEARDY	WILLIAM				62	0	QU	ENGLISH	F	043	A	3	19
LEARY	JOHN				37	IRELAND	WM	IRISH	F	043	B	1	18
LEARY	PATRICK				40	IRELAND	RC	IRISH	POTASH BOILER	045	A	3	7
LEARY	ROBERT				35	0	DI	IRELAND	CARPENTER & FARMER	045	D	2	58
LEARY	WILLIAM				28	0	WM	IRISH	DEALER IN SEWING MAC	043	B	1	18
LEASK	JAMES				67	SCOTLAND	CP	SCOTCH	ALE MERCHANT	045	B	1	16
LEATHERLAND	SAMUEL		1		23	ENGLAND	WM	ENGLISH	CABINETMAKER	043	A	4	21
LEATHERS	EDWARD				28	ENGLAND	PM	ENGLISH	FARMER	045	D	4	1
LEATHERS	EDWARD				50	ENGLAND	CE	ENGLISH	FARMER	045	D	6	42
LEATHERS	FREDERICK				26	ENGLAND	CE	ENGLISH	LABOURER	045	D	6	27
LEATHERS	HENERY		1		10	0	WM	ENGLISH		045	D	6	12
LEATHUS	EMILY		1	1	14	ENGLAND	CE	ENGLISH		045	D	6	37
LEAVENS	ZILLAH			1	43	0	EM	GERMAN		045	D	5	49
LEAVER	GEORGE				43	ENGLAND	CE	ENGLISH	FARMER	044	C	3	58
LEAVER	SARAH		1	1	80	ENGLAND	EM	ENGLISH		044	C	3	69
LEBBON	CHARLES		1		21	0	CE	IRISH	LAB	045	A	3	34
LEDGERWOOD	JOHN				33	0	CP	IRE	F	044	B	1	18
LEDLOW	ELIZABETH		2	1	89	ENGLAND	BA			045	D	6	D
LEDLOW	ROBERT				41	ENGLAND	BA	ENGLISH	FARMER	045	D	6	36
LEE	ALEXANDER				47	IRELAND	PM	IRISH	FARMER	045	D	6	5
LEE	ALLICE			1	72	US	CE			044	C	3	16
LEE	CHRISTOPHER	W			31	0	CE	ENGLISH	MERCHANT	043	D		56
LEE	ESTHER			1	54	IRELAND	CE	IRISH		043	B	3	2
LEE	FRANCIS				62	US	WM	ENGLISH	F LAB	043	B	5	5
LEE	HANNAH			1	56	ENGLAND	PM	ENGLISH		045	D	2	50
LEE	JOSEPH				48	ENGLAND	CE	ENGLISH	WATCH & CLOCK MAKER	043	A	4	4
LEE	MARY		2	1	88	IRELAND	PS			045	C	2	D
LEE	MARYANN		1	1	12	0	CN	ENGLISH		045	D	3	11
LEE	MICHAEL				52	ENGLAND	CE	ENGLISH	FARMER	043	G	1	47
LEE	PRISCILLA				79	NOVA SCOTIA	WM	ENGLISH		044	C	2	36
LEE	SARAH			1	55	IRELAND	DI	IRISH	MATRON	045	A	1	35
LEE	THOMAS				40	IRELAND	WM	IRISH	FARMER	045	D	6	61
LEEDS	ANN		1	1	7	ONT	RC	ENG		045	C	1	26
LEEDS	MARY		1	1	35	IRE	RC	IRE		045	C	1	26
LEEDS	WILLIAM				64	SCOTLAND	CP	SCOTCH	SHOEMAKER	045	C	4	36
LEEK	DANIEL				70	US	EM	GERMAN	FARMER	045	D	2	42
LEEK	DAVID				73	US	EM	GERMAN	FARMER	045	D	1	40
LEEK	JONAH				45	0	EM	GERMAN	FARMER	045	D	1	39
LEEK	MARY		1	1	71	ENGLAND	WM	ENGLISH		045	B	1	28
LEEK	WATSON				34	0	EM	ONTARIO	FARMER	045	D	2	25
LEEK	WILBER				40	0	EM	GERMAN	FARM LABORER	045	D	1	41
LEEK	WILLIAM				37	0	WM	GERMAN	MERCHANT	043	E	3	41
LEES	CHRISTINA		1	1	65	SCOTLAND	CE	SCOTCH		045	A	2	38
LEGGE	GEORGE				26	0	CE	ENG	F	044	B	2	52
LEGGE	GILBERT			M	24	0	CE	ENGLISH	FARMER	043	A	1	5
LEGGE	HANNAH			1	48	IRE	CE	ENG		044	B	2	31
LEGGE	HENRY			M	34	ENGLAND	CE	ENGLISH	F	043	A	1	17
LEGGE	HERBERT				32	ENGLAND	CE	ENGLISH	F	043	B	1	7
LEGGE	JAMES			M	37	0	CE	ENGLISH	F	043	A	1	5
LEGGE	THOMAS				36	ENGLAND	CE	ENGLISH	F	043	B	1	8
LEGGET	SAMUEL				46	ENGLAND	CE	ENGLISH	BLACKSMITH	045	D	1	38
LEGGET	THOMAS		1		40	ENG	PM	ENG	BLACKSMITH	044	B	4	14
LEHMAN	CHRISTIAN				63	UNITED STATES	CN	GERMAN	FARMER	043	B	3	70
LEHMAN	DANIEL				40	0	MN	GERMAN	FARMER	045	D	4	45
LEHMAN	JOHN				46	0	CN	GERMAN	HORSEMAN	045	D	3	37
LEHMAN	JONAS		1		16	0	MN	GERMAN		045	D	6	14
LEHMAN	LUDWIG				28	0	CN	GERMAN	MERCHANT	043	B	3	1
LEHMAN	MARY			1	46	0	MN	GERMAN		045	D	4	49
LEHMAN	SAMUEL				34	0	CN	GERMAN	FARMER	043	B	3	32
LEIGH	JOHN			M	47	ENGLAND	DI	ENGLISH	CARPENTER	043	A	1	44
LEISLIE	MINNIE		1	1	31	0	CE	ENGLISH		044	A	2	33
LEITH	JAMES				50	SCOTLAND	CP	SCOTCH	F	043	H	2	46
LEITH	JAMES				50	SCOTLAND	CP	SCOTCH	FARMER	043	H	2	46
LEKER	CHARLES				26	ENGLAND	CE	ENGLISH	CONDUCTOR	045	B	1	41
LELEVRE	CHARLES		1		22	ENGLAND	CE	ENGLISH	C ENGINEER	045	D	5	8
LELLIOT	WILLIAM				35	0	CE	ENGLISH	MASON	045	D	1	14
LEMON	CATHARINE			F	68	0	WM	IRELAND		043	A	5	27
LEMON	ELIZABETH		1	1	22	0	CN	SCOTCH		043	B	3	14
LEMON	EMANUEL				26	0	BA	GERMAN	CARPENTER	043	B	3	28
LEMON	GEORGE				47	0	PM	GERMAN	F	043	B	2	12
LEMON	GEORGE				30	0	PS	GERMAN	STOREKEEPER	043	B	3	64
LEMON	GEORGE				26	0	CE	ENGLISH	HOTEL KEEPER	043	C		28
LEMON	HENRY				36	ENGLAND	CE	ENGLISH	FARMER	045	D	1	7
LEMON	HIRAM			M	33	0	WM	ENGLAND	F	043	A	5	15

SURNAME	NAME1	NAME2	STRAY	SEX	AGE	BIRTHPL	RELIGION	ORIGIN	OCCUP	DIST	SUB_DIST	DIV	PAGE
LEMON	JACOB				61	ONTARIO	BA	SCOTCH	FARMER	043	B	3	1
LEMON	JAMES				29	O	BA	SCOTCH	F	043	B	2	9
LEMON	JENNETT		1	1	19	O	CP	SCOTCH	DRESS MAKER	045	B	1	19
LEMON	JOHN				35	ENGLAND	WM	ENGLISH	COOPER	044	B	5	6
LEMON	JONATHAN				38	O	CN	GERMAN	FARMER	043	B	3	27
LEMON	JOSEPH				65	O	TU	GERMAN	FARMER	043	B	3	27
LEMON	JOSHUA				60	O	BA	GERMAN	CARPENTER	043	B	3	24
LEMON	MARY		1	1	22	O	CP	SCOTCH	DRESS MAKER	045	B	1	19
LEMON	SIMEON			M	31	O	WM	IRELAND	F	043	A	5	27
LEMON	WALTER				31	O	CE	ENGLISH	HOTEL KEEPER	043	C		42
LEMON	WILLIAM				23	O	CN	WELSH	F	043	B	2	7
LEMON	WILLIAM				41	ENGLAND	WM	ENGLISH	LAB	045	C	2	1
LENEHAN	JOHN		1		16	IRELAND	RC	IRISH	F LAB	044	A	3	23
LENEHAN	MICHAEL				52	IRELAND	RC	IRISH	PEDLAR	044	A	3	23
LENNEY	WILLIAM				59	IRELAND	CE	IRISH	MERCHANT	043	B	3	61
LENNOX	EDWARD	FRANCIS	1		23	O	CE	IRE		045	C	1	7
LENNOX	ELIZA		1	1	22	O	CE	IRISH		045	C	2	5
LENNOX	JAMES				21	O	CE	IRISH	SADDLER	045	C	2	22
LENNOX	JOHN				48	IRE	CE	IRE	F	045	C	1	7
LENNOX	RICHARD				30	IRELAND	CP	IRISH	HOTEL KEEPER	045	B	2	4
LENNOX	ROBERT				57	IRELAND	CE	IRISH	LAB	045	A	1	67
LENNOX	WILLIAM				32	IRELAND	RP	IRISH	FARMER	044	C	3	32
LENON	EDWARD				38	IRELAND	RC	IRISH	F	045	C	2	7
LENOX	JOSEPH				30	O	WM	IRISH	F	044	C	1	30
LEONARD	ABRAHAM				43	ENGLAND	CE	ENGLISH	MILLER	045	D	1	26
LEONARD	JULIA			1	50	IRELAND	RC	IRISH		043	C		52
LEONARD	OWEN		1		40	IRELAND	RC	IRISH	COOPER	044	B	6	57
LEONARD	SIDNEY				32	ENGLAND	BA	ENGLISH	MERCHANT	043	A	4	22
LEONARD	STEPHEN				34	ENGLAND	XC	ENGLISH	FARMER	043	A	4	35
LEPARD	ABRAM				63	O	EM	GERMAN	F	043	E	3	8
LEPARD	ADAM				53	UNITED STATES	WM	GERMAN	LAB	043	E	2	28
LEPARD	ARTHUR				20	O	CN	IRISH	F	043	E	3	7
LEPARD	BENJAMIN				53	O	NC	GERMAN	F	043	E	2	7
LEPARD	CHARLES				36	O	NC	DUTCH	F	043	E	1	14
LEPARD	DANIEL				25	O	CN	GERMAN	AGENT	043	E	2	84
LEPARD	DANIEL	MOORE			27	O	WM	GERMAN	F	043	E	3	26
LEPARD	EVAN				29	O	EM	GERMAN	LAB	043	E	2	74
LEPARD	HENRY				29	O	EM	GERMAN	F	043	E	2	59
LEPARD	JACOB				52	O	ZZ	GERMAN	F	043	E	2	9
LEPARD	JOHN	C			65	O	CN	GERMAN	F	043	E	3	8
LEPARD	PHEBE			1	59	O	EM	ENGLISH		043	E	2	25
LEPARD	SILAS				41	O	CN	GERMAN	F	043	E	2	66
LEPARD	WILLIAM				61	O	ZZ	GERMAN	F	043	E	2	1
LEPARD	WILLIAM				45	O	QU	GERMAN	F	043	E	3	10
LEPARD	WILLIAM	C			40	O	EM	GERMAN	LAB	043	E	2	10
LEPPARD	ELIZABETH	A	2	1		ONTARIO	EM			043	G	1	D
LEPPARD	LEONARD				40	GERMANY	WM	GERMAN	CARPENTER	043	E	3	24
LEPPARD	MANUEL				36	O	CN	GERMAN	F	043	E	3	7
LEPPARD	WILLIAM		1		21	O	PM	GERMAN	LAB	043	E	2	72
LEPPER	JAS				46	IRE	CE	IRE		045	C	1	26
LEPPER	MATTHEW				51	IRELAND	CE	IRISH	MERCHANT	043	C		14
LEPPER	PAUL		1		15	O	CE	IRISH		043	C		56
LEPPINGTON	ROBERT				39	ENGLAND	WM	ENGLISH	FARMER	044	C	1	17
LESHMAN	ABRAHEM				46	O	MN	GERMAN	FARMER	045	D	6	5
LESLIE	ALEXANDER				45	SCOTLAND	WM	SCOTCH	COMMERCIAL TRAVELER	045	B	2	6
LESLIE	CHARLES		1		36	ENGLAND	CE	ENGLISH	SERVANT	045	B	2	21
LESLIE	EMMA		1	1	14	O	EP	ENG		044	B	3	46
LESLIE	GEORGE				65	SCOTLAND	PS	SCOTCH	NURSERY MAN	045	A	1	20
LESLIE	JOSEPH				47	IRELAND	CE	IRISH	CORDWAINER	045	C	2	11
LESSLIE	JAMES				68	SCOTLAND	BA	SCOTCH	F	044	C	2	54
LETENDRESS	FRANK				26	Q	RC	FRENCH	LAB	043	A	6	65
LEVER	HENRY				54	ENGLAND	CE	ENGLISH	FARMER	045	D	4	12
LEVER	JAMES				32	O	CE	ENGLISH	FARMER	045	D	4	12
LEVER	WILLIAM	H	1		7	O	WM	ENGLISH		045	D	4	4
LEVI	SNIDER				32	O	CO	GERMAN	GENTLEMAN	044	B	5	26
LEVITT	MELEANDER		1	1	5	O	VM	GER		044	B	3	25
LEVITT	SUSANNAH			1	37	O	EM	GERMAN	F	044	C	1	2
LEVITT	THOMAS		1		30	O	VM	GER	LAB	044	B	3	24
LEVITT	WILLIAM				53	IRE	EP	IRE	LAB	044	B	3	32
LEWIN	JAMES	D			27	WEST INDIES	CE	ENGLISH	STUDENT AT LAW	045	B	1	14
LEWIS	A	MARY		1	45	O	EP	ENGLISH		043	A	3	1
LEWIS	ANN		2	1	75	UNITED STATES	QU			043	B	4	D
LEWIS	ANNA		1	1	75	UNITED STATES	QU	GERMAN		043	B	4	42
LEWIS	BARBARA		2	1	58	O	TU	GERMAN		045	D	4	D
LEWIS	BENJAMIN		1		20	O	WM	GERMAN		043	C		21
LEWIS	DAVID				27	O	TU	GERMAN	FARMER	045	D	4	16
LEWIS	DAVID				31	O	PM	WELSH	SAWYER	045	D	4	17
LEWIS	EDWARD				33	ENGLAND	WM	ENGLISH	GARDNER	044	C	4	64
LEWIS	ELYOS				42	O	QU	ENGLISH	F	043	B	4	12
LEWIS	F	CATHARINE	2	1		ONTARIO	CE	ENGLISH	GARDNER	043	A	3	D
LEWIS	GEORGE				57	ENGLAND	CE	ENGLISH	GARDNER	044	C	4	64
LEWIS	IL	STRONG			46	US	RC	IRE	FOREMAN	044	B	2	34
LEWIS	JANE		1	1	42	IRELAND	PS	IRISH	SERVANT	045	B	1	4
LEWIS	JOHN				33	O	PM	IRISH	HOUSE JOINER	043	A	3	8
LEWIS	JOHN		1		28	ENGLAND	CE	ENGLAND	FARM LABORER	045	D	2	1
LEWIS	JOHN	EBER			53	U STATES	EM	GERMAN	YEOMAN	043	D		49
LEWIS	LEMUEL				28	O	EM	ENGLISH	F	043	E	2	67
LEWIS	LEONARD				39	O	WM	ENGLISH	F	043	E	2	65
LEWIS	LEWIS				24	ENGLAND	WM	ENGLISH	F	045	C	2	27
LEWIS	REID				36	O	WM	ENGLISH	F	043	E	2	60
LEWIS	RICHARD				32	O	PM	WELSH	FARMER	045	D	4	26
LEWIS	RICHARD				25	O	PM	WELSH	FARMER	045	D	4	44
LEWIS	THOMAS				67	WALES	PM	WELSH	FARMER	045	D	4	17
LEWIS	THOMAS	A			46	O	QU	ENGLISH	F	043	E	1	18
LEWIS	WILLIAM				35	ENGLAND	CE	ENGLISH	PLUMBER	045	A	1	72
LEWTHWAITE	ROBERT		1		21	O	NR	ENGLISH	SERVANT	043	A	4	28
LEWTY	WILLIAM				39	ENGLAND	WM	ENGLISH	CARDER	044	C	3	14
LEY	GEORGE				60	O	WM	ENGLISH	F	045	C	4	4
LEYMAN	DAVID	B			33	CANADA	MN	GERMAN	FARMER	045	D	6	34
LEYMAN	SAMUEL				32	CANADA	MN	GERMAN	FARMER	045	D	6	64
LEYS	ELIZABETH		1	1	65	SCOTLAND	CP	SCOTCH		045	D	3	69
LIEUFRINIA	LOUIS		1		12	QUE	CE	FRENCH		044	B	1	33
LILLICO	ALEXANDER		1		66	ENGLAND	CP	SCOTCH	FARM SERVANT	045	C	3	54
LILLICO	ALEXANDER		1		17	O	CS	SCOTCH		045	D	3	32
LILLIES	GEORGE				45	ENGLAND	CE	ENGLISH	LAB	043	E	1	39
LILLIOT	WILLIAM				60	ENGLAND	CE	ENGLISH	MASON	045	D	1	5

SURNAME	NAME1	NAME2	STRAY	SEX	AGE	BIRTHPL	RELIGION	ORIGIN	OCCUP	DIST	SUB_DIST	DIV	PAGE
LILLY	JOHN	C			55	ENGLAND	WM	ENGLISH	ACCOUNTANT	045	B	2	6
LINDNEAR	WILLIAM		1		10	0	LU	GERMAN		044	C	4	93
LINDNER	JOHN				53	GERMANY	CE	GERMAN	WEAVER	044	C	4	17
LINDSAY	ALFRED		1		25	0	CE	ENGLISH	BARRESTER	045	B	2	31
LINDSAY	JOHN				26	0	CP	IRISH	LAB	043	B	5	35
LINDSAY	JOHN				70	IRELAND	WM	IRISH	GENTLEMAN	045	A	4	30
LINDSAY	THOMAS		1		21	SCOT	PS	SCOT	FINISHER	044	B	2	7
LINE	HENRY				33	0	WM	GERMAN	F	043	B	4	26
LINE	HENRY		2		62	0	LU		YEOMAN	044	B	3	D
LINE	JACOB				30	0	LU	GER	F	044	B	3	7
LINE	JOHN		1		18	ENG	PM	ENG	F	044	B	2	5
LINE	JOHN				30	0	LU	GER	F	044	B	3	7
LINE	JOHN				39	0	WM	GER	F	044	B	3	7
LINE	JOHN	H	1		17	0	TU	GER	F	044	B	3	22
LINE	MARGARET			1	52	0	WM	SCOTTISH		043	B	4	26
LINE	SAMUEL				25	0	LU	GER	F	044	B	3	13
LINE	WILLIAM				55	0	LU	GER	F	044	B	3	5
LINFOOT	MARY			1	75	ENGLAND	CE	ENGLAND		045	D	2	28
LINK	GEORGE				29	0	WM	ENGLISH	LAB	043	E	3	44
LINK	JOHN				25	0	NC	ENGLISH	LAB	043	E	1	23
LINKLATER	THOMAS				55	SCOTLAND	CP	SCOTCH	SHOEMAKER	045	D	4	47
LINN	JANE		1	1	68	IRELAND	CE	IRISH		045	C	2	55
LINSTEAD	BENJAMIN				24	0	CN	IRISH	F	043	E	2	28
LINSTEAD	JOSEPH				25	0	CE	IRISH	F	043	E	2	27
LINSTEAD	MARTHA		1		64	IRELAND	WM	IRISH		043	E	2	27
LINSTEAD	WILLIAM				30	0	CE	ENGLISH	LAB	043	E	2	44
LINTON	HENRY				44	ENGLAND	CE	ENGLISH	LAB	044	C	4	91
LINTON	JOHN				29	0	PM	ENGLISH	MERCHANT	044	A	3	38
LINTON	JOHN	THOMAS	2			0	PM			044	A	3	D
LINTON	WILSON				55	ENGLAND	CE	ENGLISH	F	044	A	3	40
LINTOW	WILLIAM				32	ENGLAND	CE	ENGLISH	SPICE MGF	043	C		1
LIPPARD	CHRISTOPHER				26	ONTARIO	EM	GERMAN	LABORER	043	G	1	21
LISTER	FREDERICK				50	ENGLAND	BA	ENGLISH	F	043	B	2	1
LISTER	ROBERT				40	ENGLAND	PM	ENGLISH	LAB	044	B	6	36
LISTER	THOMAS				51	ENGLAND	CE	ENGLISH	F	044	A	3	17
LISTON	JAMES				66	SCOTLAND	DI	SCOTCH	MERCHANT	045	A	1	37
LITHGOW	ALEX	P			36	IRELAND	CP	IRISH	MILLWRIGHT	044	A	3	2
LITTLE	DAVID				57	0	CP	SCOT	F	045	C	1	46
LITTLE	FRANCIS				39	SCOTLAND	CP	SCOTCH	AUCTIONEER	045	C	3	26
LITTLE	HENRY				23	ONTARIO	CE	ENGLISH	FARMER	043	G	1	19
LITTLE	JENNET	E	1	1	33	0	WM	SCOTCH		043	B	3	51
LITTLE	JOHN				43	SCOTLAND	BA	SCOTCH	TAILOR	043	F		19
LITTLE	JOHN				52	IRE	WM	IRE	LAB	044	B	2	2
LITTLE	JOHN				34	ENG	EP	ENG	F	044	B	2	4
LITTLE	JOHN				30	IRE	CO	IRE	F	044	B	3	30
LITTLE	JOHN				41	SCOTLAND	CP	SCOTCH	F	045	C	2	29
LITTLE	JOHN				34	IRELAND	RP	IRISH	HOTELL KEEPER	044	C	3	17
LITTLE	JOHN				31	IRELAND	CE	IRISH	F	045	A	4	5
LITTLE	JOSEPH				73	IRE	CO	IRE	GENT	044	B	3	30
LITTLE	LOUISA		1	1	1	ONTARIO	EM	IRISH		043	G	1	53
LITTLE	MARY	A	1	1	24	ONTARIO	EM	IRISH		043	G	1	53
LITTLE	ROBERT				31	0	EM	ENGLISH	LAB	043	E	2	53
LITTLE	SAMUEL				55	IRELAND	CE	IRISH	LAB	045	C	2	1
LITTLE	THOMAS				41	SCOTLAND	CP	SCOTCH	CARPENTER	045	C	4	25
LITTLE	WILLIAM				38	QUE	CN	ENGLISH	LAB	043	E	3	10
LITTLE	WILLIAM				58	SCOTLAND	CP	SCOTCH	PEDLAR	045	C	3	39
LITTLEFIELD	WILLIAM				38	ENGLAND	CE	ENGLISH	HOTEL KEEPER	045	A	2	10
LITTLEJOHN	SAMUEL				42	0	WM	SCOTCH	FARMER	044	C	3	54
LITTLEJOHN	WILLIAM		1		54	ENGLAND	CE	IRISH	SERVANT	044	C	3	20
LIVINGSTON	HUGH				36	IRELAND	PS	IRISH	LAB	043	E	1	36
LIVINGSTON	JAMES				56	IRELAND	CP	IRISH	F	043	B	1	1
LIVINGSTON	JOSEPH		1		11	0	CE	IRISH		045	A	3	19
LIVINGSTON	MARY		1	1	18	0	CE	ENGLISH	SERVANT	045	D	5	12
LIVINGSTON	ROBERT				25	0	CE	IRISH	BLACKSMITH	043	B	4	37
LIVINGSTON	SARAH		1	1	14	0	PS	IRISH		043	A	1	24
LIVINGSTON	WILLIAM				27	IRELAND	CE	IRELAND	SHOEMAKER	044	A	3	28
LIVINGSTON	WILLIAM		1		16	0	WM	IRISH		045	C	2	27
LIVINGSTON	WILLIAM		1		13	0	CP	IRISH		045	C	2	35
LIVINGSTONE	JAMES					SCOTLAND	WM	SCOTCH	MERCHANT	044	B	6	1
LIVINGSTONE	MARYAN			1	70	IRE	WM	IRISH		044	B	4	49
LIVINGSTONE	SARAH			1	88	IRE	CE	IRE		044	B	2	24
LIVOCK	JOHN				50	ENGLAND	CE	ENGLISH	GARDENER	044	C	2	46
LLOYD	ALICE		1	1	19	0	QU	GERMAN	MILLINER	043	D		86
LLOYD	BENJAMIN			M	29	0	EM	WELSH	MERCHANT	043	A	1	51
LLOYD	CHARLES				33	0	WM	ENGLISH	F	043	A	6	44
LLOYD	CHARLES				26	0	WM	WELSH	F	043	B	1	41
LLOYD	CHARLOTTE			1	38	0	WM	ENGLISH		043	A	6	42
LLOYD	DAVID				29	0	WM	WELSH	SCHOOL TEACHER	043	D		59
LLOYD	DAVID		1		50	UNITED STATES	CN	ENGLISH	FARM SERVANT	043	E	1	18
LLOYD	ELI				46	0	QU	ENGLISH	F	043	A	6	10
LLOYD	ELIHU				44	0	NR	ENGLISH	LAB	043	A	6	10
LLOYD	ELISEBETH		1	1	27	0	QU	ENGLISH	DRESSMAKER	043	A	6	47
LLOYD	ELLIS				44	0	WM	ENGLISH	F	043	A	6	40
LLOYD	GEORGE				48	0	WM	WELSH	CARPENTER	043	B	2	35
LLOYD	HARRIET		1	1	22	0	CN	ENGLISH		043	E		
LLOYD	HARRY				37	0	CE	ENGLISH	TANNER	043	F		4
LLOYD	JAMES			M	35	0	EM	GERMAN	F	043	A	1	64
LLOYD	JAMES		1		20	0	WM	ENGLISH	SERVANT	043	A	6	47
LLOYD	JAMES				70	U STATES	NG		LAB	043	B	1	25
LLOYD	JANE		1	1	26	0	QU	ENGLISH	SERVANT	043	B	4	1
LLOYD	JANE		1	1	17	0	QU	GERMAN	MILLINER	043	D		86
LLOYD	JARED				44	0	WM	ENGLISH	F	043	B	1	39
LLOYD	JOEL				49	0	NC	WELSH	FARMER	043	A	4	39
LLOYD	JOHN			M	59	0	PS	GERMAN	F	043	A	1	75
LLOYD	JOHN	R			31	0	WM	ENGLISH	F	043	A	6	24
LLOYD	JOSEPH				61	U STATES	WM	WELSH	FARMER	043	A	4	65
LLOYD	MARTHA		1	1	15	0	CN	WELSH	SERVANT	043	A	6	7
LLOYD	NELSON				29	0	WM	WELSH	SCHOOL TEACHER	043	A	4	65
LLOYD	OWEN		2		68	ENGLAND	CE		DRUGGIST	043	F		D
LLOYD	ROLPH				26	0	WM	WELSH	MEDICAL DOCTOR	043	B	3	53
LLOYD	SETH		1	M	34	0	QU	ENGLAND	CARPENTER	043	A	5	26
LLOYD	SILAS			M	45	0	QU	WELSH	SAWYER	043	A	5	17
LLOYD	SUSAN		1		58	0	WM	GERMAN		043	B	4	40
LLOYD	THOMAS				73	0	WM	ENGLISH	F	043	A	6	44
LLOYD	THOMAS				43	0	WM	ENGLISH	F	043	B	1	25
LLOYD	THOMAS	H			23	0	EM	SCOTCH	VETERINARY SURGEON	043	D		83

SURNAME	NAME1	NAME2	STRAY	SEX	AGE	BIRTHPL	RELIGION	ORIGIN	OCCUP	DIST	SUB_DIST	DIV	PAGE
LLOYD	WALKER				44	0	WM	GERMAN	F	043	B	2	30
LLOYD	WILLIAM			M	39	0	PS	GERMAN	F	043	A	1	35
LLOYD	WILLIAM				41	0	WM	WELSH		043	A	4	38
LLOYD	WILLIAM			M	70	US	QU	WELSH	F	043	A	5	18
LLOYD	WILLIAM				77	UNITED STATES	QU	WELSH	F	043	B	4	3
LLOYD	WILLIAM				23	0	WM	ENGLISH	F	043	B	4	47
LLOYD	WILLIAM	G			46	0	WM	GERMAN	F	043	B	1	11
LOAN	MARY		1	1	19	0	CE	IRISH		045	A	1	11
LOAN	SARAH		1	1	24	IRELAND	CE	IRISH		045	A	1	11
LOBB	MARY		1	1	78	ENGLAND	CE	ENGLISH		045	C	2	6
LOCHRIE	ELIZABETH		1	1	24	SCOTLAND	CP	IRISH		044	C	4	40
LOCHRIE	JAMES				22	SCOTLAND	CP	IRISH	ROPE MAKER	044	C	4	40
LOCHRIE	JESSIE		1	1	45	SCOTLAND	CP	SCOTCH		044	C	4	40
LOCHRIE	JESSIE		1	1	19	SCOTLAND	CP	IRISH		044	C	4	40
LOCK	LEWIS				33	ENG	LU	ENG	F	044	B	1	32
LOCKARD	CHARLES	H			30	0	WM	SCOTCH	CLERK	043	D		73
LOCKE	JOHN				59	IRELAND	CE	IRISH	STOREKEEPER	045	B	1	50
LOCKE	JOSEPH	REV			27	IRELAND	WM	IRISH	MINISTER	044	B	6	15
LOCKHART	DAVID		1		55	SCOTLAND	CS	SCOTCH	MERCHANT	043	E	2	22
LOCKHART	JOHN				49	IRE	CP	IRISH	WHEELWRIGHT	044	B	1	35
LOCKHEART	DAVID		2			0	CP			044	B	1	D
LOCKING	THOMAS				58	ENGLAND	WM	ENGLISH	F	044	C	1	26
LOCKINTON	EDWARD		1		26	0	CE	IRISH	LAB	044	C	3	31
LOCKWOOD	AMELIA		1	1	25	ENGLAND	CE	ENGLISH	MILINER & DRESSMAKER	045	B	1	4
LOCKWOOD	HELEN		1	1	28	0	CE	IRISH		045	A	2	10
LOCKWOOD	MARTHA		1	1		0	CP	SCOTCH	SERVANT	044	B	6	38
LOCKYER	RICHARD				54	ENGLAND	CE	ENGLISH		045	C	3	27
LODGE	JAMES		1		23	ENGLAND	CE	ENGLISH	LAB	044	C	2	21
LODGE	ROBERT				48	ENGLAND	CE	ENGLISH	F &	043	A	4	2
LOFT	ANN	JANE		1	37	0	WM	ENGLISH	STOREKEEPER	044	C	2	11
LOFTUS	JOHN				42	ENG	CE	ENG	FARM LAB	044	B	1	14
LOGAN	EDWARD				71	IRELAND	PM	IRISH	F	043	B	2	22
LOGAN	ELIZABETH		1		45	IRELAND	PR	IRISH	GARDENER	045	A	1	45
LOGAN	GEORGE				30	0	CE	SCOTCH	GENTLEMAN	043	C		21
LOGAN	JAMES		1		20	SCOTLAND	RP	SCOTCH		044	C	3	45
LOGAN	JOHN		2		70	SCOTLAND	PR		GARDENER	045	A	1	D
LOMEX	ISAAC				49	ENGLAND	CE	ENGLISH	BLACKSMITH	044	C	4	86
LOMON	GEORGE				47	GERMAN	MN	GERMAN	LABORER	045	D	6	74
LONEY	JOHN		1		40	IRELAND	CE	IRISH	F LAB	044	A	1	33
LONG	EDWARD		1	M	32	ENGLAND	NG	ENGLISH	LAB	043	A	2	59
LONG	EDWARD				39	ENGLAND	WM	ENGLISH	WEAVER	044	A	3	55
LONG	ELIZABETH		1	1	12	UNITED STATES	CE	ENGLISH		043	G	1	51
LONG	ELIZABETH	VICTORIA	2	1	1	0	CE			045	A	4	D
LONG	FRED'K				42	ENGLAND	NC	ENGLISH	MECHANIC	043	C		31
LONG	GEORGE		1		47	ENGLAND	CE	ENGLISH		045	D	1	21
LONG	GEORGE				24	ONT	CE	IRISH		045	A	4	3
LONG	GODFERY				32	ENGLAND	CE	ENGLISH	GENTLEMAN	045	A	1	32
LONG	HANORAH			1	50	IRELAND	RC	IRISH		044	A	3	39
LONG	JAMES				24	0	WM	ENGLISH	F	044	C	3	3
LONG	JAMES		2		62	IRELAND	CE		F	045	A	4	D
LONG	JOHN				33	0	RC	IRISH	F	044	B	5	70
LONG	JOHN				30	ONT	CE	IRISH	F	045	A	4	3
LONG	JOSHUA				78	ENGLAND	WM	ENGLISH		045	B	2	6
LONG	MARGARET			1	45	IRE	EM	IRISH	WASHERWOMAN	044	B	1	24
LONG	RICHARD				65	IRELAND	WM	IRISH	F	043	E	2	18
LONG	ROBINSON				35	0	WM	IRISH	F	043	E	2	18
LONG	SERAH			1	68	CANADA	BA	IRISH		045	D	6	76
LONG	WILLIAM				34	0	NG	ENGLISH	HORSE DEALER	045	A	4	26
LONGBOTTOM	ANN		1	1	54	ENGLAND	CE	ENGLISH		043	A	4	26
LONGBOTTOM	CHARLES	B	1		12	0	CE	ENGLISH		043	A	4	26
LONGDO	FRANCIS				54	USA	RC	FRENCH	CARPENTER	043	H	1	7
LONGDO	FRANCIS				75	QUEBEC	RC	FRENCH	CARPENTER	043	H	1	16
LONGDO	MARY		1		42	0	RC	FRENCH		043	H	2	24
LONGDO	MARY		1		42	ONTARIO	RC	FRENCH		043	H	2	24
LONGDO	STEPHEN				48	USA	RC	FRENCH	F	043	H	1	42
LONGFIELD	ALFRED				34	0	EM	DUTCH	F	043	E	1	14
LONGHIRST	WILLIAM				37	0	CE	ENGLISH	LAB	043	E	3	20
LONGHOUSE	GEO				49	0	LU	GERMAN	F	044	B	5	62
LONGHOUSE	HENRY				35	0	LU	GER	AGENT	044	B	2	44
LONGHURST	ANN		1	1	15	0	CE	ENGLISH		044	B	6	24
LONSDALE	WILLIAM			M	32	ENGLAND	PR	ENGLISH	WAGGON MAKER	043	A	1	16
LONSGEWAY	LOUIS				40	0	WM	FRENCH	LAB	044	A	3	10
LOONEY	JACOB		1		27	GER	LU	GER	LAB	044	B	1	63
LOOVITT	ESTHER		1	1	6	0	MN	GER		044	B	3	42
LORD	HENRY		1		50	ENGLAND	CE	ENGLISH	BUTCHER	044	A	2	4
LOTEN	JAKE				42	ENGLAND	CE	ENGLISH	LABOURER	044	C	3	49
LOTT	MARYANN		1	1	27	0	WM	IRISH	SERVANT	044	C	3	28
LOTT	WILLIAM				26	0	WM	IRISH	CARPENTER	044	C	3	27
LOTT	WILLIAM				59	IRELAND	WM	IRISH	GROCER	044	C	3	27
LOTTON	MARY	ANN		1	55	ENGLAND	CE	ENGLISH		045	D	5	54
LOUDON	FREDERICK	W			30	ENGLAND	CE	ENGLISH	BOOKKEEPER	045	A	1	25
LOUGHRAN	HENRY			M	69	IRELAND	RC	IRELAND	L	043	A	5	41
LOVE	AARON			M	27	0	EM	IRISH	F	043	A	1	46
LOVE	CATHARINE		1	F	25	IRELAND	WM	IRISH		043	A	2	15
LOVE	CHRISTENA		1	F	9	0		IRISH		043	A	2	7
LOVE	DAVID			M	61	0	WM	IRISH	F	043	A	2	7
LOVE	JOHN			M	70	U STATES	WM	IRISH	F	043	A	1	11
LOVE	JOHN				32	IRELAND	WM	IRISH	SHOEMAKER	044	A	3	26
LOVE	MATHEW				59	0	EM	IRISH	F & LUMBER MERCHANT	043	B	1	40
LOVEL	ISAAC			M	45	0	CE	IRISH	FARMER	043	A	1	25
LOVELACE	ROBERT				45	0	PM	ENGLISH	F	045	C	4	30
LOVELESS	EDWARD		1		32	ENGLAND	WM	ENGLISH		045	C	1	14
LOVELESS	WM				29	0	CP	ENG	F	045	C	1	62
LOVETT	MARGARET		1	1	16	0	WM	IRISH	SERVANT	044	C	1	46
LOVETT	SARAH		1	1	20	0	CE	IRISH	SERVANT	044	C	1	44
LOW	DAVID				29	SCOTLAND	CP	SCOTCH	FARM LABOURER	045	C	4	15
LOWE	FRANCIS				46	ENGLAND	CE	ENGLISH	LAB	043	E	1	43
LOWE	JAMES				47	SCOTLAND	CP	SCOTTISH	F AND CARDER	043	B	4	22
LOWE	MARGARET			1	58	US	CE	ENGLISH		045	B	1	36
LOWE	MARY		1	1	50	IRELAND	WM	IRISH		043	E	1	10
LOWE	WILLIAM				29	ENGLAND	CE	ENGLISH	BRASS FINISHER	043	F		22
LOWELL	JOHN				50	ENGLAND	CE	ENGLISH	F	044	A	1	12
LOWNSBROUGH	THOMAS				59	ENGLAND	CE	ENGLISH	SHOEMAKER	045	D	4	28
LOWREY	JAMES		1		54	IRELAND	CS	IRISH	SCHOOL TEACHER	044	B	6	32
LOWRY	EDWARD				48	IRELAND	CP	IRISH	LABORER	044	A	2	21
LOWRY	JOHN				70	IRELAND	CP	IRISH	FARMER	045	D	3	49

SURNAME	NAME1	NAME2	STRAY	SEX	AGE	BIRTHPL	RELIGION	ORIGIN	OCCUP	DIST	SUB_DIST	DIV	PAGE
LOWST	GEORGE	WILLIS			29	ONT	CE	ENGLISH	BARRISTER ETC	043	D		43
LOXTON	ELIJAH				30	ENGLAND	CE	ENGLISH	BLACKSMITH	044	C	4	83
LOYD	ANDREW	C			54	CANADA	PS	SCOTCH	MEDICAL PROFFERN	045	D	6	53
LOYD	JANE		1	1	40	ENGLAND	WM	ENGLISH	SERVANT	045	B	1	72
LOYD	JOHN				51	IRELAND	CE	ENGLISH	FARMER	045	A	3	24
LUBBOCK	JOHN				36	ENGLAND	WM	ENGLISH	FARMER	045	D	1	30
LUBBOCK	RICHARD				62	ENGLAND	WM	ENGLISH	FARMER	045	D	1	30
LUBICK	RICHARD				24	ENGLAND	CE	ENGLAND	FARM MANAGER	045	D	2	27
LUCA	FRISLY			1	68	ENGLAND	WM	ENGLISH		045	D	4	1
LUCAS	HENRY		1		24	ENGLAND	CE	ENGLAND	CLERK	045	D	2	8
LUCE	ELLEN		1	1	20	0	PM	ENG	SERVANT	044	B	3	13
LUCK	WILLIAM				37	0	WM	ENGLISH	WHEELWRIGHT	043	F		22
LUDDILY	ALFARD		1		15	0	WM	ENGLISH		044	C	3	38
LUDFORD	CALV				40	QUE	WM	ENG	SADDLER	044	B	1	9
LUDFORD	THOMAS				65	ENG	WM	ENG	LAB	044	B	1	6
LUDFORD	WILLIAM				40	QUE	WM	ENG	LAB	044	B	2	47
LUFF	JOSEPH				43	ENGLAND	CE	ENGLISH	PENSIONER	044	C	4	87
LUKE	JOHN				57	ENGLAND	CE	ENGLISH	MILLER	045	A	3	34
LUKE	SILAS				28	0	BC	ENGLISH	F	043	H	1	30
LUKE	WALLACE				48	ENG	CE	ENG	CARPENTER	045	C	1	25
LUKER	ALFRED				31	ENGLAND	CE	ENGLISH	LAB	045	B	1	49
LUKES	CAROLL	E	1	1	2	0	WM	IRISH		043	E	3	42
LUKES	FANNEY		1	1	31	IRELAND	WM	IRISH		043	E	3	42
LUKES	JOHN			M	66	ENGLAND	WM	ENGLAND	MILLER	043	A	5	12
LUKES	WILLIAM				43	ENGLAND	WM	ENGLISH	MILLER	043	D		1
LUKES	WILLIAM		1		12	0	WM	IRISH		043	E	3	42
LUMLEY	GEORGE				26	ENGLAND	BA	ENGLISH	HOUSE PAINTER	045	D	5	4
LUNAN	ROBERT				22	SCOT	CS	SCOT	F	044	B	4	17
LUNAU	HENRY				42	0	OM	GERMAN	FARMER	045	D	3	42
LUNAU	JOHN				70	0	IM	GERMAN	FARMER	045	D	3	33
LUNAU	JONATHAN				34	0	IM	GERMAN	FARMER	045	D	3	34
LUNAU	JOSEPH				30	0	IM	GERMAN	FARMER	045	D	3	31
LUNAU	SILAS				28	0	IM	GERMAN	FARMER	045	D	3	33
LUNAU	WILLIAM				40	0	MC	GERMAN	FARMER	045	D	3	56
LUND	JOSEPH				49	ENG	PM	ENG	CARRIAGE MAKER	044	B	4	13
LUND	RICHARD		1		94	ENG	PM	ENG		044	B	1	50
LUND	THOMAS		1		30	ENGLAND	CE	ENGLISH	FARM LAB	044	C	2	34
LUND	WILLIAM				61	ENG	PM	ENG	F	044	B	2	5
LUNDEY	JOSEPH				66	IRELAND	WM	IRISH	FARMER	045	D	1	47
LUNDY	AMOS				25	0	NC	ENGLISH	F	043	E	2	37
LUNDY	CHARLES		1		7	0	WM	ENGLISH		043	B	5	42
LUNDY	CHARLES				31	0	WM	ENGLISH	F	043	E	1	3
LUNDY	CHAS	H	2			0	WM			043	C		D
LUNDY	DANIEL				31	0	QU	GERMAN	F	043	B	5	31
LUNDY	EBENEZER				68	0	QU	GERMAN	F	043	B	5	38
LUNDY	EDWARD				38	0	QU	GERMAN	F	043	B	5	4
LUNDY	GEORGE				24	0	WM	ENGLISH	LAB	043	B	5	42
LUNDY	HANNAH			1	50	0	QU	ENGLISH		043	B	4	47
LUNDY	HORACE	D			35	0	WM	IRISH	CARPENTER	043	C		5
LUNDY	ISRAIL				32	0	ZZ	WELSH	MILLER	043	E	1	1
LUNDY	JACOB				62	0	ZZ	WELSH	F	043	E	1	16
LUNDY	JOHN				61	0	QU	GERMAN	F	043	B	5	31
LUNDY	JOHN	WILSON	2		3	0	ZZ			043	E	1	D
LUNDY	JOSEPH				45	0	CE	IRISH	LABOURER	043	A	4	69
LUNDY	JOSEPH	A	1		10	0	CN	WELSH		043	E	2	50
LUNDY	JUDAH				58	0	NC	ENGLISH	F	043	E	2	34
LUNDY	MORDICA				27	0	QU	ENGLISH	F	043	B	4	33
LUNDY	OLIVER				36	0	CN	WELSH	F	043	E	1	16
LUNDY	RACHAEL		1	1	5	0	WM	ENGLISH		043	B	5	42
LUNDY	REUBEN				64	0	ZZ	WELSH	FARMER & MILLER	043	E	1	1
LUNDY	REUBEN	H	1		7	0	CN	WELSH		043	E	2	50
LUNDY	S	SAMUEL			49	0	QU	ENGLISH	CARPENTER AND WHEELW	043	B	4	46
LUNDY	SARAH			1	54	0	QU	ENGLISH		043	B	4	47
LUNDY	SHADDRACK				51	0	WM	ENGLISH	F	043	B	4	28
LUNDY	SILAS				42	0	NC	ENGLISH	F	043	C		20
LUNDY	SYLVESTER				30	0	WM	ENGLISH	TEACHER	043	C		20
LUNDY	WILLIAM				34	0	CP	IRISH	FARMER	045	D	4	12
LUNNEY	GEORGE				28	IRELAND	CE	IRISH	GARDENER	045	A	1	1
LUNNIS	WILLIAM				55	ENGLAND	CE	ENGLISH	BUTCHER	045	B	1	19
LUNNIS	WILLIAM		1		19	ENGLAND	CE	ENGLISH	CATTLE DEALER	045	B	1	74
LUSCOMB	AARON				35	0	WM	ENGLISH	LABOURER	045	D	5	25
LUSH	JOHN				36	ENGLAND	CE	ENGLISH	WELL DIGGER	045	C	4	3
LUSTIE	PETER				30	GERMANY	WM	GERMAN	LABORER	045	D	6	56
LUVET	MARY		1	1	27	IRELAND	WM	IRISH		045	A	4	21
LUXTON	WILLIAM				35	ENG	PM	ENG	LAB	044	B	4	15
LY MON	FRANCES		1	1	9	0	CO	ENGLISH		043	D		23
LY MON	JANES		1	1	5	0	CO	ENGLISH		043	D		23
LY MON	MARY		1	1	34	ENGLAND	CO	ENGLISH		043	D		23
LYALL	WILLIAM				63	SCOTLAND	CE	SCOTCH	F	043	H	2	20
LYALL	WILLIAM				63	SCOTLAND	CE	SCOTCH	FARMER	043	H	2	20
LYE	LETITIA		1	1	65	ENGLAND	CE	ENGLISH		045	B	2	25
LYLE	MARY		1	1	58	ENGLAND	PM	ENGLISH		045	B	2	8
LYLE	WILLIAM		1		75	ENGLAND	PM	ENGLISH	MINISTER	045	B	2	8
LYMBURNER	MATHEW		2		79	NB	PS		F	044	B	2	D
LYMBURNER	ROBERT				33	0	WM	SCOT	F	044	B	2	1
LYNCH	CATHERINE		1	1	26	IRELAND	RC	IRISH	SERVANT	045	C	3	38
LYNCH	MICHAEL				73	IRELAND	RC	IRISH	F	044	B	6	33
LYNE	SAMUEL				56	0	LU	GER	GENTLEMAN	044	B	1	62
LYNEMBIE	MOSES				65	ENGLAND	WM	ENGLISH	F	043	E	2	28
LYNN	ADELINE		1	1	18	0	CE	ENGLISH		045	D	4	13
LYNN	CATHERINE		1	1	19	0	CE	ENGLISH		045	D	4	13
LYNN	CHARLES		1		20	ENGLAND	PM	ENGLISH	LABOURER	045	A	1	79
LYNN	DANIEL				34	ENGLAND	BA	ENGLISH	LAB	043	B	5	6
LYNN	DAVID				55	ENGLAND	CE	ENGLISH	FARMER	045	A	2	13
LYNN	ELLENOR		1	1	23	0	CE	ENGLISH		045	D	4	13
LYNN	JAMES				46	IRELAND	CP	IRISH	E TEACHER	043	A	3	28
LYNN	JOSEPH				45	IRELAND	FK	IRISH	POSTMAN & STOREKEEPE	043	A	3	28
LYNN	RACHEL		1	1	21	0	CE	ENGLISH		045	D	4	13
LYNN	SARAH		1	1	12	0	NC	IRISH		043	E	2	22
LYNN	THOMAS				24	0	CE	ENGLISH	FARMER	045	A	2	14
LYNN	WILLIAM				35	IRELAND	CP	IRISH	FARMER	043	A	4	34
LYNN	WILLIAM				32	0	CE	IRE	HOTEL KEEPER	044	B	4	6
LYNN	WILLIAM		1		17	0	CE	ENGLISH		045	D	4	13
LYON	CHARLES				30	0	PR	SCOTCH	LAB	043	B	1	21
LYONS	ANN		1	1	65	0	CN	FRENCH		043	B	5	36
LYONS	BARNABAS				66	0	WM	IRISH	F	044	B	1	41

SURNAME	NAME1	NAME2	STRAY	SEX	AGE	BIRTHPL	RELIGION	ORIGIN	OCCUP	DIST	SUB_DIST	DIV	PAGE
LYONS	BENJAMIN				32	0	PM	ENG	CARPENTER	044	B	2	22
LYONS	CATHARINE		1	1	34	0	RC	IRISH		043	H	2	31
LYONS	DANIEL		1		25	0	RC	IRISH	F	043	H	2	31
LYONS	DAVID				47	0	CN	ENGLISH	F	043	B	5	36
LYONS	FRANCIS		1		21	0	RC	IRISH	F	043	H	2	31
LYONS	FRANCIS				21	ONTARIO	RC	IRISH	FARMER	043	H	2	31
LYONS	FRANK		1	M	50	ENGLAND	CE	ENGLISH	LAB	043	A	1	49
LYONS	FREDERICK		2			0	WM	WM		044	B	1	D
LYONS	HARVEY		2			0	WM	WM		044	B	1	D
LYONS	HUGH		1		23	0	RC	IRISH	F	043	H	2	31
LYONS	JAMES				36	ENGLAND	CE	ENGLISH	F	043	H	2	30
LYONS	JAMES				46	IRELAND	RC	IRISH	F	043	H	2	48
LYONS	JAMES				36	ENGLAND	CE	ENGLISH	FARMER	043	H	2	30
LYONS	JAMES				46	IRELAND	RC	IRISH	FARMER	043	H	2	48
LYONS	JOHANAH		1	1	43	IRELAND	RC	IRISH		044	C	4	79
LYONS	JOHN				60	0	TU	GER	LAB	044	B	1	42
LYONS	JOHN				39	IRE	WM	IRISH	SAWYER	044	B	1	64
LYONS	THOMAS		1		20	0	CE	ENGLISH	F LAB	044	A	1	13
LYONS	THOMAS				36	ENGLAND	CE	ENGLISH	LABOURER	045	D	4	13
LYONS	WILLIAM		1		18	0	WM	ENGLISH	F LAB	044	A	2	18
MABEE	JESSE				60	NOVA SCOTIA	WM	ENGLISH	BLACKSMITH	044	A	3	35
MABEY	JOHN				64	ENGLAND	BC	ENGLISH	STONE MASON	045	D	5	48
MABLEY	ALBERT			M	26	ENGLAND	BA	ENGLISH	STORE KEEPER	043	A	1	3
MABLEY	CHARLES				47	ENG	WM	ENG	SHOEMAKER	045	C	1	16
MABLEY	JOHN				58	ENGLAND	CE	ENGLISH	F	043	A	6	16
MACALISTER	MARGARET		1	1	40	SCOTLAND	CP	SCOTCH	SERVANT	045	C	4	37
MACALLUM	DANIEL				44	SCOTLAND	CO	SCOTCH	MINISTER	045	D	3	3
MACDONALD	CATHERINE			1	50	IRELAND	RC	IRISH		044	C	4	80
MACDONALD	EDWARD				60	IRELAND	RC	IRISH		044	C	1	29
MACDONALD	HUGH		1		40	SCOTLAND	CE	SCOTCH	CLERK	043	D		82
MACDONALD	PETER				35	NS	PS	SCOTCH	MEDICAL STUDENT	045	B	2	1
MACDONALD	WILLIAM		1		26	0	RC	IRISH		045	A	1	29
MACFADDEN	MARTHA		1	1	27	0	PM	SCOTCH		043	A	3	10
MACFADDEN	NANCY		1	1	60	NS	PM	SCOTCH		043	A	3	10
MACFARLANE	MICHAEL				60	IRELAND	RC	IRISH	LAB	044	C	1	9
MACGREGOR	H		1		12	0	WM	ENGLISH	SERVANT	044	C	1	13
MACHALL	PHOEBE		2	1		CANADA	WM			043	C		D
MACHALL	WILLIAM		2			CANADA	WM			043	C		D
MACHAR	CHARLES				42	ENGLAND	CE	ENGLISH	BLACKSMITH	043	G	2	45
MACHELL	EMMA			1	54	ENGLAND	CE	ENGLISH	LADY	043	C		24
MACHELL	HENRY				43	0	WM	ENGLISH	GENTLEMAN	043	C		39
MACHELL	SAMUEL			M	48	0	PR	ENGLISH	F	043	A	1	52
MACHERT	JOHN				55	SCOTLAND	CP	SCOTCH	F	045	A	4	25
MACINTOSH	ELIZABETH		1	1	80	SCOTLAND	CS	SCOTCH		044	B	6	56
MACKAY	MARGARET				40	IRELAND	RC	IRISH	WASHERWOMAN	044	B	6	13
MACKEY	ALEXDR		1		37	SCOTLAND	CE	SCOTCH	F	043	B	2	8
MACKEY	EVE			1	59	0	TU	GERMAN		043	B	1	34
MACKEY	MARY	ANN	1	1	22	0	CE	GERMAN		043	B	2	8
MACKEY	WILLIAM		2		67	IRELAND	CE		F	043	B	1	D
MACKINSEY	ALEXANDER				70	IRELAND	WM	IRISH		044	C	3	49
MACKINTOSH	JAMES		1		35	SCOTLAND	PS	SCOTCH	SERVANT	043	A	6	2
MACKLEIN	ALFRED		1		16	US	BA	IRISH		043	B	2	45
MACKLEM	JOHN				72	UNITED STATES	CN	IRISH	F	043	B	2	2
MACKLEM	PHILIP				48	0	CN	IRISH	F	043	B	2	2
MACKLEM	WILLIAM				57	0	CN	IRISH	F	043	B	5	27
MACKLIM	CATHERINE		2	1	22	0	CS		IRISH	DRESS MAKER	045	D	3	D
MACKLIM	JANE		1	1	23	IRELAND	CS	IRISH	DRESS MAKER	045	D	3	49
MACKLIM	WILLIAM		1		70	IRELAND	CS	IRISH	FARMER	045	D	3	28
MACKLIN	JAMES				30	0	CP	IRISH	F	045	C	4	3
MACKLIN	MARSHAL				32	0	CP	IRISH	F	045	C	3	33
MACKLIN	MARSHALL				71	IRELAND	CP	SCOTCH	F	045	C	3	26
MACKLIN	MARY	ANN	2	1	25	0	CP			045	C	4	D
MACKLIN	PHILLIP				38	0	BA	IRISH	MILLER	045	D	6	15
MACKLIN	ROBERT				26	0	CP	IRISH	F	045	C	3	15
MACKNAROW	MICHAEL				55	IRELAND	RC	IRISH	LAB	045	A	1	103
MACKNESS	BRANSOM		1		26	ENGLAND	WM	ENGLISH		045	B	1	50
MACLEAN	ANNE			1	60	ENG	CE	ENG		045	C	1	10
MACLEAN	DONALD				34	0	CE	SCOT	STOREKEEPER	045	C	1	10
MACLEOD	NORMAN	F		M	49	IRELAND	CE	SCOTTISH	FARMER	043	A	1	1
MACPHERSON	DAVID	L			52	SCOTLAND	CE	SCOTCH	GENTLEMAN	045	B	2	37
MACY	WILLIAM				32	ENGLAND	CE	ENGLISH	SHOEMAKER	045	B	1	31
MADAN	JANE		1	1	70	IRELAND	RC	IRISH		044	C	4	96
MADDEN	A	MARY	1	1	24	IRELAND	CP	IRISH		043	A	3	9
MADDEN	AMBROSE				45	IRE	RC	IRISH	TRACK MAN NOR RRY	044	B	1	47
MADDEN	GEORGE				40	IRELAND	CE	IRISH	YEOMAN	045	A	1	57
MADDEN	MATTHEW				40	IRELAND	RC	IRISH	LAB	043	D		36
MADDEN	PATRICK				42	IRELAND	RC	IRISH	BLACKSMITH	045	B	1	33
MADDEN	RICHARD				60	IRELAND	RC	IRISH	F	044	A	2	38
MADDEN	THOMAS				49	IRELAND	RC	IRISH	LAB	043	C		56
MADDILL	EMMA		1	1	3	0	RC	ENGLISH		044	C	2	25
MADER	ANNIE		1	1	14	0	CE	GERMAN		043	D		30
MADER	JULIUS		1		8	0	CE	GERMAN		043	D		30
MADER	LYDIA		1	1	11	0	CE	GERMAN		043	D		30
MADER	WILLIAM		1		17	0	LU	GERMAN	APPRENTICE	043	D		18
MADGET	JOHN				55	ENGLAND	CE	ENGLISH	LAB	044	A	3	30
MADGET	ROBT				30	ENGLAND	WM	ENGLISH	F	044	A	2	35
MADIL	JAS		1		17	0	PM	ENGLISH	LAB	044	B	5	36
MADILL	BENJAMIN				54	U STATES	AD	IRISH	F	043	A	6	22
MADILL	BENJAMIN				24	CANADA	BA	IRISH	FARMER	045	D	6	73
MADILL	EBENEZER				52	IRELAND	BA	IRISH	FARMER	045	D	6	73
MADILL	SAMUEL				38	IRELAND	WM	IRISH	F	044	A	3	6
MAEGRA	BRIDGET		1	1	72	IRELAND	RC	IRISH		043	H	2	46
MAGEE	JOHN				45	IRELAND	CE	IRISH	LABOURER	045	A	1	58
MAGEE	JOHN				55	IRE	CP	IRE	LAB	045	C	1	39
MAGET	HARRY		1		24	ENGLAND	WM	IRISH	SERVANT	044	C	3	49
MAGHAR	THOMAS				49	IRELAND	RC	IRISH	FARMER	045	A	2	24
MAGINN	JAS				38	0	PM	IRE	F	045	C	1	62
MAGINS	THOMAS				40	IRELAND	RC	IRISH	LAB	043	D		42
MAGLADERY	SAMUEL				58	IRELAND	CE	IRISH	LAB	044	C	2	5
MAGNER	EDMUND		1		70	IRELAND	RC	IRISH	F	044	C	1	25
MAGNER	POLLY		1	1	12	0	RC	IRISH	SERVANT	044	C	1	24
MAGNISON	GEORGE		1		38	ENG	PS	ENG	SERVANT	044	B	3	12
MAGOR	IDE		1	1	2	CANADA	WM	ENGLISH		045	D	6	70
MAGRATH	THOMAS		1		26	IRELAND	RC	IRISH	FARM SERVANT	045	A	1	47
MAGUFFIN	DAVID			M	48	IRELAND	PS	IRISH	FARMER	043	A	1	26
MAGUIRE	ANN			1	52	IRELAND	CE	IRISH		044	C	3	38

SURNAME	NAME1	NAME2	STRAY	SEX	AGE	BIRTHPL	RELIGION	ORIGIN	OCCUP	DIST	SUB_DIST	DIV	PAGE
MAGUIRE	CATHARINE			1	60	IRELAND	PS	IRISH		045	A	1	44
MAGUIRE	CHARLES				33	0	WM	IRISH	LABOURER	045	D	5	37
MAGUIRE	CONSTANTINE				73	IRELAND	CE	IRISH	MASON	044	C	4	18
MAGUIRE	DAVID				44	IRELAND	EM	IRISH	SHOE MAKER	044	C	3	37
MAGUIRE	GRACE	D		1	49	0	CE	GERMAN		043	E	2	34
MAGUIRE	HUGH		2		60	IRELAND	CE		LABORER	045	A	1	D
MAGUIRE	JOHN		1		40	IRELAND	RC	IRISH	LAB	045	A	1	17
MAGUIRE	WILLIAM				40	IRELAND	RC	IRISH	FARMER	045	A	3	33
MAHAFFY	JOHN	DR			58	IRELAND	EP	IRISH	MEDICAL DR	043	A	3	15
MAHAN	HARRIET		1	1	14	0	NR	IRISH		043	A	6	1
MAHAN	MILTON		1		12	0	NR	IRISH		043	A	6	1
MAHAN	PATRICK				64	IRELAND	RC	IRISH	LAB	044	C	3	11
MAHAN	SUSANNAH		1	1	38	0	NR	SCOTCH	HOUSEKEEPER	043	A	6	1
MAHAN	WILLIAM				44	IRELAND	PS	IRISH	FARMER	043	B	3	13
MAHER	PIERCE				29	0	WM	IRISH	CABINET MAKER	043	A	4	3
MAHON	ANDREW				41	IRELAND	WM	IRISH	LAB	043	B	2	31
MAHON	BRINE		1		53	IRELAND	RC	IRISH	SERVANT	044	C	3	20
MAHONEY	CATHERINE			1	48	IRELAND	RC	IRISH		043	G	1	23
MAHONEY	DENNIS		1		40	IRE	RC	IRE	LAB	044	B	2	72
MAHONEY	ELLEN		1	1	19	0	RC	IRISH	SERVANT	043	E	1	48
MAHONEY	FRANCESS			F	40	IRELAND	RC	IRISH	TOAL KEEPER	043	A	1	23
MAHONEY	JAMES				54	IRELAND	RC	IRISH	LAB	043	D		48
MAHONEY	JAMES				32	IRE	RC	IRISH	LAB	044	B	2	13
MAHONEY	WILLIAM				36	IRELAND	RC	IRISH	F	043	E	2	33
MAHONY	JOHANNA		2	1	2	0	RC			045	C	1	D
MAIDLOW	EDWARD		1		20	ENGLAND	WM	ENGLISH	LAB	045	A	2	11
MAINES	SAMUEL				39	IRELAND	PS	ENGLISH	F	043	E	3	54
MAINPRIZE	DAVID		1		3	0	CO	ENG		044	B	3	47
MAINPRIZE	GEO				36	ENGLAND	WM	ENGLISH	F	044	B	5	38
MAINPRIZE	WM				64	ENGLAND	QU	ENGLISH	F	043	E	3	35
MAIR	JACOB				33	0	CE	GERMAN	LAB	043	A	3	47
MAIR	WILLIAM			M	53	SCOTLAND	UP	SCOTCH	FARMER	043	A	1	19
MAIRS	ALEXANDER		1		35	0	CE	ENGLISH	BARRISTER	045	D	3	81
MAJOR	ANDREW				31	0	PM	GER	SAW MILLER	044	B	2	22
MAJOR	JOHN				45	ENGLAND	CE	ENGLISH	MERCHANT	045	D	4	36
MAJOR	MAGGIE		1	1	10	0	WM	IRISH		045	D	5	9
MAJOR	MARY	EDNA	1	1	13	0	WM	IRISH		045	D	5	9
MALCOLM	ARCHIBALD				34	0	PS	SCOTCH	F	045	C	3	9
MALCOLM	JOHN				51	SCOTLAND	RC	SCOTCH	F	044	C	2	2
MALCOLM	LETITICIA			1	40	0	PS	SCOTCH	F	045	C	3	36
MALCOLM	THOMAS				43	SCOTLAND	PS	SCOTCH	LAB	045	C	3	9
MALIBY	PETER				48	ENGLAND	CE	ENGLISH	BLACKSMITH	044	C	3	44
MALLINSON	JOHN		1		23	ENGLAND	WM	ENGLISH	BRICK MAKER	045	B	1	73
MALLON	CHARLES		1		29	IRELAND	CS	IRISH		044	B	6	53
MALLON	JOHN				33	IRELAND	RC	IRISH	BUCHER	044	C	4	47
MALLORY	JOHN				28	0	CE	GERMAN	LAB	043	H	1	18
MALLOY	GEO				31	IRELAND	RC	IRISH	LAB	044	B	5	43
MALLOY	JOHN				30	IRE	RC	IRISH	SAWYER	044	B	2	19
MALLOY	MARY		1	1	45	IRELAND	RC	IRISH	SERVANT	043	D		54
MALLOY	WILLIAM				47	0	ZZ	IRISH	BAILIFF	043	E	2	8
MALONE	ANDREW				33	IRELAND	RC	IRISH	CHEESE MAKER	045	D	5	21
MALONE	JAMES				80	IRELAND	RC	IRISH	F	043	B	4	8
MALONE	PETER				36	IRELAND	RC	IRISH	IRON MOULDER	045	D	5	21
MALONE	SHARLOT				8	0	CE	ENGLISH		045	B	1	58
MALONEY	TIMOTHY				32	IRELAND	RC	IRISH	F LAB	044	A	1	40
MALORY	ROBERT				41	ENGLAND	CE	ENGLISH	F	043	B	4	34
MALOUNEY	MICHAEL		1		50	IRE	RC	IRISH	LAB	044	B	1	7
MALOWNEY	THO				58	IRELAND	RC	IRISH	FARMER	043	A	4	68
MALOY	ALEXANDER				26	0	PS	SCOT	F	044	B	4	29
MALOY	ANN		2	1	22	0	CS			044	B	4	D
MALOY	ARCHIBALD				66	SCOT	CS	SCOT	F	044	B	4	17
MALOY	DANIEL				31	0	CS	SCOT	F	044	B	4	34
MALOY	JAMES				24	0	CS	SCOT	F	044	B	4	28
MALOY	JOHN				68	SCOT	CS	SCOT	F	044	B	4	17
MALOY	MALCOME				61	0	CS	SCOT	F	044	B	4	26
MALOY	NEIL				33	0	CS	SCOT	F	044	B	4	29
MALOY	NEIL				73	SCOT	CS	SCOT	GENT	044	B	4	34
MALOY	NEIL	A			28	0	CS	SCOT	F	044	B	4	29
MALPASS	WILLIAM	F			40	ENGLAND	WM	ENGLISH	FARMER	045	D	4	23
MALTBY	WILLIAM				40	ENGLAND	PM	ENGLISH	F	044	B	6	40
MALTES	ELIZA		1	1	21	CANADA	CN	ENGLISH		045	D	6	29
MANEY	STEPHEN		1		40	IRELAND	RC	IRISH	LAB	043	D		5
MANIVAN	EDWARD				38	IRELAND	RC	ENGLISH	LAB	044	C	2	25
MANN	ALFRED				35	ONTARIO	WM	SCOTCH	FARMER	043	G	1	35
MANN	CALEB				29	ONTARIO	CN	ENGLISH	FARMER	043	G	1	31
MANN	CALEB				50	ONTARIO	PR	ENGLISH	FARMER	043	G	2	28
MANN	DARIUS				47	ONTARIO	CN	ENGLISH	FARMER	043	G	2	54
MANN	EDWARD	JAMES	2		13	0	RC		FARM SERVANT	045	C	3	D
MANN	ELISHA				32	ONTARIO	CN	SCOTCH	FARMER	043	G	1	6
MANN	JOHN				36	IRELAND	RC	IRISH	LAB	045	C	3	1
MANN	JOHN	R			29	0	PM	ENGLISH	SCHOOL TEACHER	043	B	3	60
MANN	MARY		2	1		0	RC			045	C	3	D
MANN	RICHARD				67	ONTARIO	CN	ENGLISH	FARMER	043	G	1	5
MANN	SILAS				40	ONTARIO	CN	ENGLISH	FARMER	043	G	1	4
MANN	STEPHEN				55	ONTARIO	CN	SCOTCH	FARMER	043	G	1	30
MANN	WILLIAM				28	ONTARIO	CN	ENGLISH	FARMER	043	G	1	5
MANNERS	JOHN				46	0	PS	DUTCH	WAGGON MAKER	043	E	3	19
MANNING	GEORGE				34	ENGLAND	WM	ENGLISH	F	043	A	6	31
MANNING	JAMES				39	ENG	EM	ENG	F	044	B	1	62
MANNING	JOHN				42	ENGLAND	WM	ENGLISH	BLACKSMITH	043	A	6	9
MANNING	ROBERT				29	ENGLAND	WM	ENGLISH	F	043	C		56
MANNING	ROSE		2	1		0	WM			043	A	6	D
MANSFIELD	JOS				40	IRE	CE	IRE	PEDDLAR	045	C	1	8
MANSON	MARGERY		1	F	14	0	PM	ENGLISH		043	A	2	59
MANTON	JOHN				65	IRE	RC	IRISH	F	044	B	2	9
MANTON	MARIA	B	1	1	30	ENGLAND	CO	ENGLISH	SERVANT	044	B	6	26
MAPES	ABNER				41	0	WM	ENGLISH	F	043	B	2	11
MAPES	CYRUS				40	0	EM	ENGLISH	CARPENTER	045	D	5	52
MAPES	JAMES				51	0	UV	GERMAN	COOPER	045	D	5	40
MAPES	JESSE				43	0	EM	DUTCH	FARM LABOURER	043	E	1	43
MAPES	JOHN				60	0	WM	GERMAN	HOTEL KEEPER	045	D	5	40
MAQUIN	D	CHARLES			64	0	WM	ENGLISH	FARMER	045	A	3	28
MAR	EDWARD				50	IRELAND	RC	IRISH	LABOURER	044	C	3	36
MARCH	ALFRED				21	0	PM	IRISH	SCHOOL TEACHER	043	B	1	42
MARCH	CHARLES				28	0	PM	IRISH	LAB	043	B	2	17
MARCH	DAVID				66	UNITED STATES	PM	IRISH	CARPENTER	043	B	2	17

SURNAME	NAME1	NAME2	STRAY	SEX	AGE	BIRTHPL	RELIGION	ORIGIN	OCCUP	DIST	SUB_DIST	DIV	PAGE
MARCH	JOHN				33	O	PM	IRISH	F	043	B	2	17
MARE	JAMES				71	IRELAND	RC	IRISH	LAB	044	C	3	24
MARGERSON	WILLIAM				69	ENGLAND	OM	ENGLISH	GARNER	044	C	4	88
MARGHRUM	CHRISTOPHER			M	37	ENGLAND	WM	ENGLISH	LABOURER	043	A	1	21
MARGRA	BRIDGET		1	1	72	IRELAND	RC	IRISH		043	H	2	46
MARK	ELSPET		1	1	60	SCOT	CE	SCOT		045	C	1	28
MARK	ISAAC				45	ENGLAND	EM	ENGLISH	CABINET MAKER	043	B	3	53
MARKS	SAMUEL				56	ENGLAND	WM	ENGLISH	F	043	E	1	13
MARKS	WILLIAM				69	IRELAND	CE	IRISH	FARMER	043	A	4	31
MARKS	WILLIAM				41	IRELAND	CE	IRISH	FARMER	043	A	4	42
MARMION	MAY		1	1	20	IRELAND	CE	IRISH	GOVERNESS	044	C	2	1
MARONEY	BRIDGET		1	1	24	IRELAND	RC	IRISH	SERVANT	043	D		36
MARONEY	JOS		1		24	IRELAND	WM	IRISH	CARPENTER	044	B	5	20
MARQUIS	FLORA		1	1	50	SCOTLAND	BA	SCOTTISH	SERVANT	044	C	1	21
MARQUIS	JANNET			1	65	SCOTLAND	BA	SCOTCH		045	A	3	2
MARR	FRED	LEWIS	1		5	O	WM	GERMAN		045	D	5	76
MARR	HENRY				28	O	WM	IRISH	FARMER	045	D	5	42
MARR	JOSEPH				71	US	WM	ENGLISH		045	D	3	66
MARR	RUFUS		1		15	O	CP	IRISH		043	B	2	6
MARR	WILLIAM				37	O	WM	ENGLISH	BOARDING HOUSE K	045	D	3	75
MARR	WILLIAM				56	O	WM	IRISH	LABOURER	045	D	5	73
MARRIS	JAMES		1		60	ENGLAND	CE	ENGLISH	GARDENER	043	D		88
MARRITT	ISAAC				42	ENGLAND	EM	ENGLISH	FARMER	043	G	1	10
MARRITT	JOHN				37	ENGLAND	WM	ENGLISH	CARPENTER	043	C		2
MARRON	THOMAS				50	IRELAND	RC	IRISH	F LAB	043	B	1	3
MARSDEN	JOHN	W			50	ENGLAND	WM	ENGLISH	MERCHANT MILLER	043	D		88
MARSH	ALEXANDER				41	O	CP	ENGLAND	FARMER	045	D	2	1
MARSH	ANNE		1	1	6	O	CE	ENGLISH		043	C		23
MARSH	JAMES			M	39	O	PS	ENGLISH	F	043	A	2	33
MARSH	ROBERT				47	O	CP	ENGLAND	FARMER	045	D	2	1
MARSH	VICTORIA		1	1	9	O	CE	ENGLISH		043	C		23
MARSHALL	CHRISTOPHER		2	M	81	ENGLAND	WM			043	A	2	D
MARSHALL	DAVID				57	SCOTLAND	CP	SCOTCH	F	045	C	4	41
MARSHALL	ELIZA			F	63	ENGLAND	WM	ENGLISH		043	A	2	37
MARSHALL	ELIZABETH		1	1	2	O	CE	IRISH		044	C	4	51
MARSHALL	ESTHER		1	1	27	IRELAND	CE	IRISH		044	C	4	51
MARSHALL	HAMILTON		1		32	QUE	CE	IRISH	LAB	044	C	4	51
MARSHALL	HAMILTON		1			O	CE	IRISH		044	C	4	51
MARSHALL	JAMES				41	O	RC	IRE	F	044	B	3	47
MARSHALL	JAMES				43	IRELAND	CE	IRISH	INNKEEPER	044	C	4	21
MARSHALL	JOHN				44	ENGLAND	CE	ENGLISH	LIVERY KEEPER	045	D	3	71
MARSHALL	JOHN				27	O	CE	IRISH	F	044	C	4	16
MARSHALL	JOHN				46	IRELAND	CE	IRISH	CARPENTER	044	C	4	52
MARSHALL	JOSEPH		1		29	ENGLAND	CE	ENGLISH	GARDENER	045	A	1	32
MARSHALL	MARY	JANE	1	1	4	O	CE	IRISH		044	C	4	51
MARSHALL	ROBERT				76	IRELAND	CE	IRISH	F	044	C	4	13
MARSHALL	ROBERT		1		6	O	CE	IRISH		044	C	4	51
MARSHALL	THOMAS				37	ENGLAND	CE	ENGLISH	F	043	B	1	28
MARSHALL	WILLIAM				70	ENGLAND	CE	ENGLISH	F	044	A	1	28
MARSHALL	WILLIAM	T			28	ENGLAND	WM	ENGLISH	CARPENTER	045	B	1	28
MARSHALL	WM		2		21	SCOTLAND	PS		LAB	044	B	5	D
MARSHALL	WM	L			45	ENGLAND	CE	ENGLISH	FARMER	043	G	1	14
MARTIN	ARTHUR				65	IRE	CP	IRE	F	045	C	1	58
MARTIN	BARBARA		1	1	14	O	CE	SCOTLAND		045	D	2	17
MARTIN	CLAUS		2		87	GERMANY	CO		FARMER	045	D	6	D
MARTIN	DANIEL				40	ENGLAND	WM	ENGLISH	LABOURER	045	D	4	23
MARTIN	DANIEL				30	IRELAND	CE	IRISH	F	044	C	1	33
MARTIN	DONALD		1		13	O	PS	SCOTCH		045	D	2	34
MARTIN	DUGALD				60	SCOTLAND	CP	SCOTCH	F	044	C	2	28
MARTIN	EDWARD				26	O	WM	ENGLISH	CARPENTER	045	D	1	13
MARTIN	ELIZABETH		1	1	24	IRELAND	CE	IRISH		043	H	1	35
MARTIN	GEORGE				40	ENGLAND	CE	ENGLISH	BRICK MAKER	045	B	1	53
MARTIN	GEORGE				41	ENGLAND	CE	ENGLISH	FARMER	045	D	4	4
MARTIN	HENRY				30	ENGLAND	CE	ENGLISH	F	043	E	1	23
MARTIN	HUGH				32	IRELAND	OP	IRISH	WEAVER	043	G	2	32
MARTIN	JAMES				50	ENGLAND	BA	ENGLISH	FARMER	043	B	3	26
MARTIN	JAMES				53	IRELAND	UP	IRISH	BLACKSMITH	043	C		49
MARTIN	JAMES		2			CANADA	CE			043	C		D
MARTIN	JESSE				39	ENG	CE	ENG	BLACKSMITH	044	B	2	40
MARTIN	JOHN				57	ENG	WM	ENG	CARPENTER	044	B	1	66
MARTIN	JOHN				77	SCOT	PS	SCOT	F	045	C	1	71
MARTIN	JOHN				45	ENGLAND	CE	ENGLISH	FARMER	045	D	2	68
MARTIN	JOHN		1		11	O	PS	SCOTCH		045	D	2	34
MARTIN	JOSEPH		1		45	ENGLAND	CE	ENGLISH		045	A	1	28
MARTIN	PHILLIP				53	ENGLAND	CE	ENGLISH	LABORER	043	D		57
MARTIN	RACHEL		1	1	14	IRELAND	CE	IRISH		044	C	2	36
MARTIN	REBECCA		1	1	15	O	CP	IRISH		045	D	3	30
MARTIN	ROBT				30	O	CS	SCOT	F	045	C	1	50
MARTIN	SAMUEL				49	IRELAND	CE	IRISH	FARMER	045	A	2	32
MARTIN	SAMUEL				40	O	CP	IRISH	FARMER	045	A	2	34
MARTIN	SAMUEL		1		28	IRELAND	CE	IRISH	SERVANT	044	C	3	2
MARTIN	THOMAS				27	IRELAND	CE	IRISH	BLACKSMITH	043	C		37
MARTIN	THOMAS				71	ENG	CE	ENG	LAB	044	B	2	20
MARTIN	THOMAS				59	ENGLAND	PM	ENGLISH	FARMER	045	D	1	42
MARTIN	THOMAS		1		21	ENGLAND	CE	ENGLISH	SERVANT	045	D	2	67
MARTIN	THOMAS	M			32	ENGLAND	SW	ENGLISH	ARTIST	045	A	1	4
MARTIN	WILLIAM				54	SCOTLAND	CP	SCOTCH	F	044	A	1	26
MARTIN	WILLIAM				40	IRELAND	WM	IRISH	SHOEMAKER	044	A	3	28
MARTIN	WILLIAM				34	O	CE	IRISH	DEALER	045	A	1	12
MARTIN	WRIGHT				27	O	PM	IRISH	F	043	H	1	31
MARTINDALE	MATTHEW				41	ENGLAND	CE	ENGLISH	SHOE MAKER	043	G	1	2
MARTINS	JOHN		1		25	SCOTLAND	CS	SCOTCH	LAB	043	D		30
MARTINS	MARGARET		1	1	17	O	CS	IRISH		043	D		30
MARTINSON	JOHN				50	O	CE	FRENCH	F	043	E	1	30
MARTSON	MARY			1	76	ENGLAND	PM	ENGLISH		045	D	2	41
MARWOOD	WILLIAM		1		16	ENGLAND	WM	ENGLISH	SERVANT	043	E	3	35
MARWOOD	WILLIAM				42	O	WM	ENG	F	044	B	4	6
MARZOLF	JACOB				32	O	VM	FRENCH	MINISTER	045	D	3	50
MASEY	RICHARD				37	ENGLAND	WM	ENGLISH	CARPENTER	045	D	2	48
MASHINTER	GEO		1		18	O	PM	ENGLISH	LAB	044	B	5	60
MASHINTER	RICHARD				45	ENGLAND	PM	ENGLISH	LAB	044	A	3	31
MASKITER	JOHN				55	ENGLAND	WM	ENGLISH	GENTLEMAN	044	C	3	25
MASON	CHARLES				30	ENGLAND	CE	ENGLISH	F	044	A	2	7
MASON	CHARLES		1		20	ENGLAND	CE	ENGLISH	LAB	044	C	2	34
MASON	DAVID				25	O	CE	ENGLISH	F	045	C	4	46
MASON	EDWARD				40	IRELAND	RC	IRISH	LABOURER	044	C	3	39

SURNAME	NAME1	NAME2	STRAY	SEX	AGE	BIRTHPL	RELIGION	ORIGIN	OCCUP	DIST	SUB_DIST	DIV	PAGE
MASON	ELIZA		2	1		0				045	C	4	D
MASON	FRANCES			1	66	ENGLAND	CE	ENGLISH	F	045	C	4	9
MASON	FRANCIS				28	0	CE	ENGLISH	F	045	C	4	9
MASON	HENRY				45	ENGLAND	CE	ENGLISH	F	045	C	4	10
MASON	JOHN				43	ENGLAND	PM	ENGLISH	F	044	B	5	57
MASON	LOUISA			1	9	0	CE	ENG		044	B	2	46
MASON	LYDIA		1	1	20	ENGLAND	WM	ENGLISH		044	B	5	36
MASON	MARGRET		1	1	20	0	WM	ENGLISH	SERVANT	045	D	6	4
MASON	ROBERT		1		47	ENGLAND	WM	ENGLISH	FARM LABOURER	043	B	3	47
MASON	THOMAS				36	USA	CE	ENGLISH	F	045	C	4	37
MASON	THOMAS				33	IRELAND	CE	IRISH	FARMER	044	C	3	34
MASON	WILLARD				53	ONTARIO	CN	ENGLISH	FARMER	043	G	1	30
MASON	WILLIAM				26	ENGLAND	WM	ENGLISH	FARMER	043	B	3	51
MASON	WILLIAM				24	0	PM	ENG	FARM SERVANT	044	B	4	10
MASON	WILLIAM				32	0	CE	ENGLISH	F	045	C	4	10
MASON	WILLIAM				60	ENGLAND	WM	ENGLISH	FARMER	045	D	4	33
MASON	WM				45	ENGLAND	WM	ENGLISH	BRICK MAKER	044	B	5	31
MASON	WM	RUNDLE	1		23	0	WM	ENGLISH	TEACHER	043	D		28
MASSINGHAM	JAMES				27	ENG	WM	ENG	F	044	B	2	31
MASTERMAN	GEORGE			M	49	ENGLAND	WM	ENGLISH	F	043	A	1	17
MASTERMAN	GEORGE		1		20	ENGLAND	WM	ENGLISH	BUTCHER	043	D		14
MASTERMAN	J			1	66	ENG	WM	ENG		045	C	1	19
MASTERMAN	JOHN		1		22	ENGLAND	CE	ENGLISH	F LAB	043	B	1	24
MATHER	ADAM	E			35	SCOTLAND	CP	SCOTCH	F	044	A	2	33
MATHER	JOHN	MORRISON			39	ENGLAND	CE	ENGLISH	LAB	045	B	1	47
MATHER	WILLIAM				72	SCOTLAND	CP	SCOTCH	LAB	044	A	2	1
MATHERS	DAVID				39	SCOTLAND	CP	SCOTCH	HOTEL KEEPER	045	A	1	101
MATHERS	JAMES				38	ENGLAND	WM	ENGLISH	MASON	044	A	2	51
MATHESON	ANNE			1	45	0	WM	SCOT		044	B	1	38
MATHESON	HARPER			M	28	0	LU	IRISH	F	043	A	1	14
MATHESON	JOSEPH				60	IRE	EM	IRE	F	044	B	3	11
MATHESON	MARIA		1	1	5	0	WM	SCOT		044	B	1	59
MATHESON	WILLIAM				60	SCOT	CP	SCOT	F	044	B	1	60
MATHESON	WILLIAM				33	0	CP	SCOT	F	044	B	4	52
MATHEWS	ALEXANDER				50	IRELAND	CP	IRISH	LAB	045	B	2	22
MATHEWS	ANES	C			60	QUE	WM	ENG	F	044	B	4	34
MATHEWS	JOHN				41	ENGLAND	CE	ENGLISH	F	044	C	4	51
MATHEWS	NICHOLAS				56	ENGLAND	CE	ENGLISH	F LABOURER	045	D	3	57
MATHEWS	ROBT				41	IRELAND	WM	IRISH	CARPENTER	044	B	5	15
MATHEWSON	SARAH		1	1	18	ENGLAND	WM	ENGLISH		044	B	5	41
MATHEWSON	SUSANNAH		1	1	50	0	LU	GER		044	B	3	45
MATHISON	JAMES			M	46	0	EM	IRISH	F	043	A	2	44
MATHISON	PETER			M	39	SCOTLAND	PS	SCOTCH	TAILOR	043	A	2	30
MATHY	WILLIAM				44	SCOT	PS	SCOT	PAINTER	044	B	2	39
MATICE	JOHN		2		71	ENGLAND	EM			044	C	3	D
MATICE	REBECCA			1	64	ENGLAND	EM	ENGLISH		044	C	3	26
MATIER	ELIZABETH		1	1	69	ONTARIO	PR	FRENCH		043	G	2	9
MATT	CANDES		1	1	69	QUEBES	RC	FRENCH		043	H	2	7
MATT	JOSEPH				30	0	RC	FRENCH	F	043	H	2	36
MATT	JOSEPH				30	ONTARIO	RC	FRENCH	FARMER	043	H	2	36
MATT	THEODORE				46	ONTARIO	RC	FRENCH	FARMER	043	G	2	5
MATTHEW	ROBERT		1		13	0	CE	IRISH	F AB	044	A	3	16
MATTHEW	WILLIAM				45	SCOTLAND	CP	SCOTCH	SODA WATER MAKER	044	A	3	29
MATTHEW	WILLIAM				37	SCOTLAND	PS	SCOTCH	FARMER	045	A	1	2
MATTHEWS	ALEX		1		20	0	PS	SCOTCH	MACHINIST	044	B	5	37
MATTHEWS	HENRY				25	ENGLAND	WM	ENGLISH	LAB	044	B	5	79
MATTHEWS	RANDAL		1		32	0	CH	IRISH	AGENT	045	D	5	31
MATTHEWSON	JAMES				54	SCOTLAND	CP	SCOTCH	CONTRACTOR	043	B	1	6
MATTICK	MARY		1	1	15	ENG	EP	ENG		044	B	3	4
MATTOCKS	FREDERICK				46	ENG	CE	ENG	LAB	044	B	1	30
MAUGER	NICHOLAS				33	0	LU	GER	FARM LAB	044	B	1	46
MAUGER	SAMUEL				30	0	PM	GER	SAWYER	044	B	1	52
MAW	JAMES				63	ENGLAND	CE	ENGLISH	F	043	A	3	58
MAW	JOHN				54	ENGLAND	PM	ENGLISH	F	044	A	3	33
MAW	JOSEPH				38	0	CE	ENGLISH	F	043	A	3	57
MAW	NEWTON				37	0	FK	ENGLISH	F	043	A	3	57
MAXWELL	ISABEL			1	54	ENGLAND	DI	ENGLISH		045	D	6	51
MAXWELL	BERNARD		1		42	IRELAND	CP	IRISH	LAB	044	A	2	4
MAXWELL	GEORGE		1		19	0	CP	SCOTCH	LABORER	045	D	3	41
MAXWELL	ISAAC				69	ENGLAND	CE	ENGLISH	F	044	A	3	36
MAXWELL	ISAAC				35	0	PM	ENGLISH	F	044	A	3	36
MAXWELL	ISAAC		2			0	CE			044	A	3	D
MAXWELL	JAMES				56	SCOTLAND	PS	SCOTCH	MILLER	045	C	2	37
MAXWELL	JAMES				26	IRELAND	PS	IRISH	FARM LABOURER	045	C	3	35
MAXWELL	JAMES				26	0	CE	ENGLISH	CARPENTER	045	D	5	33
MAXWELL	JANE		1	1	15	0	CS	IRISH		045	A	4	13
MAXWELL	JOHN		1		40	IRELAND	CE	IRISH	SERVANT	043	A	4	41
MAXWELL	JOHN				38	0	CE	ENGLISH	F	044	A	3	15
MAXWELL	JOHN				55	ENG	CE	ENG	F	044	B	1	20
MAXWELL	MARGARET		1	1	17	0	CP	SCOTCH		045	D	3	41
MAXWELL	MATILDA		1	1	19	US	WM	ENGLISH		045	A	4	7
MAXWELL	PHILIP				59	ENGLAND	CE	ENGLISH	LAB	044	A	2	41
MAXWELL	SUSAN			1	52	US	WM	AFRICAN		045	D	2	41
MAY	A	B	1	1	27	SCOT	CP	ENG		045	C	1	32
MAY	EPHRIAM				56	0	QU	IRISH	F	043	B	4	46
MAY	ISAAC				50	ONTARIO	CE	IRISH	MASTER MARINER	043	G	1	55
MAY	MARY		1	1	30	IRELAND	RC	IRISH	SERVANT	043	D		72
MAY	NELSON				30	0	QU	IRISH	CARPENTER	043	B	4	47
MAY	P	SAMUEL			42	ENGLAND	CE	ENGLISH	PHYSICAN	045	A	3	1
MAY	SERAH	ANN	1	1	14	CANADA	CO	ENGLISH		045	D	6	77
MAYBERRY	ANNA		1	1	23	QUEBEC	CE	IRISH	SERVANT	045	B	2	8
MAYHEW	JOSHUA				28	0	CP	FRENCH	F	043	H	1	31
MAYLON	MARTIN				52	IRELAND	RC	IRISH	LABORER	043	D		54
MAYNAN	JOHN				56	ENGLAND	CE	ENGLISH	INN KEEPER	044	B	5	4
MAYNARD	ALFRED				48	ENGLAND	CE	ENGLISH	F	044	B	5	69
MAYNARD	GEORGE				55	ENGLAND	CE	ENGLISH	MINISTER	044	C	4	79
MAYS	DAVID				36	ENGLAND	WM	ENGLISH	MILLER	043	D		24
MAYS	ELIZABETH			1	56	ENGLAND	PM	ENGLISH		043	D		33
MAYWEATHER	JAMES			M	30	SCOTLAND	NR	SCOTLAND	F	043	A	5	30
MAYWETTERS	THOMAS			M	33	0	CE	ENGLISH	LAB	043	A	1	71
MC DONALD	COLAN		1		22	0	UP	SCOT	LAB	044	B	4	42
MC FADYEN	JOHN				63	0	UP	SCOT	F	044	B	4	41
MC GARR	PHILLIP				28	U STATES	RC	IRISH	LAB	043	D		38
MCAFEE	MARY			1	57	IRELAND	CP	IRISH		043	A	4	54
MCAFFRAY	JANE			1	46	IRE	WM	IRE		044	B	2	59
MCALL	ROBERT				29	SCOTLAND	CS	SCOTCH	SHOEMAKER	045	D	3	26

SURNAME	NAME1	NAME2	STRAY	SEX	AGE	BIRTHPL	RELIGION	ORIGIN	OCCUP	DIST	SUB_DIST	DIV	PAGE
MCANDEE			1		40	IRELAND	WM	IRISH	LAB	044	C	1	10
MCARTHUR	ANNIE		1	1	18	0	CS	SCOTCH		043	D		59
MCARTHUR	ARTHUR				70	SCOTLAND	FK	SCOTCH	F	043	A	3	45
MCARTHUR	CATHARINE			1	43	0	WM	SCOTCH	F	043	A	6	43
MCARTHUR	CHAS				37	SCOTLAND	CS	SCOTCH	MARBLE DEALER	043	E	2	84
MCARTHUR	DUNCAN		2		26	0	PS		F	044	B	3	D
MCARTHUR	HUGH				60	SCOT	PS	SCOT	F	044	B	3	51
MCARTHUR	JOHN				64	SCOT	PS	SCOT	F	044	B	3	36
MCAULEY	JOHN		1		14	0	WM	GERMAN		045	D	2	40
MCAULEY	WALTER		1		20	0	WM	SCOTCH	SERVANT	044	B	6	19
MCAVODY	MARGARET		1	1	24	0	XC	IRISH	SERVANT	045	B	1	37
MCAVOY	DANIEL				41	ENGLAND	RC	ENGLISH	COOPER	043	B	3	54
MCBAIN	JOSEPH		2		4	0	CE			045	D	5	D
MCBEAN	ELISA		1	1	15	SCOTLAND	CP	SCOTCH	SERVANT	045	B	2	31
MCBEATH	JAS	T			51	SCOT	PS	SCOT	POSTMASTERSTOREKEEPE	045	C	1	71
MCBENNON	MARGRET		1	1	60	IRELAND	OP	SCOTCH		043	H	2	47
MCBETH	ANDREW				38	SCOT	PS	SCOT	CARRIAGE MAKER	044	B	2	28
MCBRIDE	CHARLES				39	0	WM	IRISH	INN KEEPER	044	C	2	8
MCBRIDE	DAVID				45	0	WM	IRISH	GENTLEMAN	045	A	4	31
MCBRIDE	ISAAC			M	34	0	WM	GERMAN	F	043	A	1	52
MCBRIDE	JOHN				47	0	WM	IRISH	F	044	B	1	20
MCBRIDE	JOHN				44	IRE	RC	IRE	F	044	B	2	61
MCBRIDE	LOUIS		1		5	0	CE	IRISH		044	C	2	34
MCBRIDE	NICHOLAS				63	IRELAND	RC	IRISH		044	A	2	51
MCBRIDE	PATRICK	J			29	IRELAND	RC	IRISH	DROVER	044	A	2	25
MCBRIDE	PETER				30	IRELAND	RC	IRISH	LAB	044	C	2	43
MCBRIDE	ROBERT	J			25	0	EM	IRISH	F	045	A	4	27
MCBRIDE	SAMUEL				35	0	WM	IRISH	F	043	C		7
MCBRIDE	WALLIS				34	0		IRISH	F	045	A	4	27
MCBRIDE	WILLIAM			M	50	IRELAND	RC	IRISH	LAB	043	A	1	56
MCBRIDE	WILLIAM				70	IRE	CS	IRISH	F	044	B	4	42
MCBRIDE	WILLIAM				59	IRELAND	CP	IRISH	FARMER	045	A	1	54
MCBRIEN	JAMES				30	0	CE	IRISH	CONTRACTOR	045	D	5	12
MCBURNY	ANNE			1	63	IRELAND	CP	IRISH		045	B	1	27
MCCABE	JAMES		1		70	IRELAND	RC	IRISH		043	A	4	28
MCCABE	JAMES		1	M	70	IRELAND	RC	IRELAND		043	A	5	41
MCCABE	JAMES				26	IRE	RC	IRE	LAB	044	B	4	16
MCCABE	MATHEW		1		28	SCOTLAND	RP	SCOTCH		044	C	3	45
MCCABE	PATRICK			M	63	IRELAND	RC	IRISH	F	043	A	2	57
MCCABE	ROBERT		1		30	SCOTLAND	RP	SCOTCH		044	C	3	45
MCCAFFERY	FRANCIS		1		85	IRELAND	RC	IRISH		044	A	1	10
MCCAFFRAY	JOHN				7	0	RC	GER		044	B	2	48
MCCAFFRAY	JOHN				34	IRELAND	RC	IRISH	MERCHANT	045	D	5	40
MCCAFFREY	CHARLES				45	IRELAND	RC	IRISH	F	044	C	2	42
MCCAFFREY	ELLEN		1	1	28	0	RC	IRISH		045	C	3	25
MCCAFFREY	JAMES				61	IRELAND	RC	IRISH	F	045	C	2	1
MCCAFFREY	PETER		1		29	IRELAND	RC	IRISH	FARM LABOURER	045	C	3	25
MCCAGNA	JOHN				39	IRELAND	CP	IRISH	FARMER	045	D	2	40
MCCAGUE	JOHN				23	0	RC	IRISH	WAGGON MAKER	044	B	5	57
MCCALISTER	JAMES				71	SCOTLAND	FK	SCOTCH	FARMER	043	A	3	57
MCCALISTER	THOMAS				65	SCOTLAND	ZZ	SCOTCH	F	044	B	6	19
MCCALL	MARY		1	1	22	SCOTLAND	WM	SCOTCH		043	A	3	58
MCCALLMON	JOHN		1		25	IRELAND	PS	IRISH	PRESBYTERIAN MINISTE	043	E	3	39
MCCALLUM	ALEXANDER			M	25	0	FK	SCOTLAND	F	043	A	5	10
MCCALLUM	ARCH'D			M	31	0	PS	SCOTCH	F	043	A	2	39
MCCALLUM	ARCHIBALD			M	60	SCOTLAND	PS	SCOTCH	F	043	A	2	36
MCCALLUM	BRUCE		1		19	0	CO	SCOTCH	BLACKSMITH	045	D	5	6
MCCALLUM	DANIEL			M	26	0	QU	SCOTLAND	F	043	A	5	11
MCCALLUM	DONALD			M	55	SCOTLAND	FK	SCOTLAND	F	043	A	5	38
MCCALLUM	DOUGALD				57	SCOTLAND	CS	SCOTCH	FARMER	043	A	4	50
MCCALLUM	DUNCAN			M	65	SCOTLAND	PS	SCOTCH	F	043	A	2	51
MCCALLUM	DUNCAN				51	SCOTLAND	PS	SCOTCH	CLK D COURT	044	B	5	48
MCCALLUM	GEORGE				54	SCOTLAND	PS	SCOTCH	TAILOR	045	D	6	41
MCCALLUM	JAMES			M	63	SCOTLAND	PS	SCOTCH	F	043	A	2	38
MCCALLUM	JAMES				41	QUE	CE	SCOTCH	ENGINEER	043	A	6	61
MCCALLUM	JAMES				49	QUEBEC	CE	SCOTCH	SURVEYOR	043	H	1	9
MCCALLUM	JAMES				78	QUE	WM	SCOTCH	BREWER	044	B	1	11
MCCALLUM	JAMES	H			40	IRELAND	CE	IRISH	MINISTER	043	C		30
MCCALLUM	JOHN			M	71	SCOTLAND	PS	SCOTCH	F	043	A	2	51
MCCALLUM	JOHN				63	SCOTLAND	FK	SCOTCH	F	043	A	3	38
MCCALLUM	JOHN		1	M	20	0	FK	SCOTLAND	L	043	A	5	10
MCCALLUM	JOHN				42	SCOTLAND	CS	SCOTCH	WHEELWRIGHT	044	B	6	58
MCCALUM	ARCHIBALD			M	50	SCOTLAND	PS	SCOTCH	F	043	A	2	32
MCCALUM	DONALD			M	87	SCOTLAND	CS	SCOTCH		043	A	2	36
MCCALUM	DUNCAN			M	57	SCOTLAND	PS	SCOTCH	F	043	A	2	9
MCCALUM	JOHN			M	64	SCOTLAND	PS	SCOTCH	F	043	A	2	42
MCCALUM	MALCOLM		1	M	25	0	PS	SCOTCH	PORTER	043	A	2	19
MCCALUM	MARY		1	F	20	0	PS	SCOTCH		043	A	2	9
MCCALUM	PETER			M	62	SCOTLAND	PS	SCOTCH	F	043	A	2	8
MCCALUM	PETER			M	48	SCOTLAND	PS	SCOTCH	F	043	A	2	35
MCCAM	JAMES				35	IRELAND	RC	IRISH	LAB	044	C	1	5
MCCAMES	CAROLINE			1	55	US	CS	IRE	WASHER WOMAN	044	B	4	38
MCCANN	ANTHONY				68	SCOTLAND	PS	IRISH	TOLL KEEPER	044	C	4	77
MCCANN	CORNELIUS				26	0	RC	IRISH	LAB	043	A	6	46
MCCANN	DANIEL				28	ENGLAND	WM	ENGLISH	LAB	043	H	2	16
MCCANN	DANIEL				28	ENGLAND	WM	ENGLISH	LABOURER	043	H	2	16
MCCANN	FRANCIS				70	IRELAND	RC	IRISH	LAB	045	A	2	13
MCCANN	FRANCIS				33	IRELAND	RC	IRISH	LAB	044	C	2	23
MCCANN	JAMES				59	ENGLAND	WM	ENGLISH	SHOEMAKER	043	H	2	14
MCCANN	JAMES				59	ENGLAND	WM	ENGLISH	SHOEMAKER	043	H	2	14
MCCANN	JAMES		1		14	0	RC	IRISH	FARM LAB	044	C	2	2
MCCANN	JAMES				40	IRELAND	RC	IRISH	LAB	044	C	2	51
MCCANN	JOHN				50	IRELAND	RC	IRISH	LAB	045	A	2	12
MCCANN	LAWRENCE				43	IRELAND	RC	IRISH	LAB	044	C	2	12
MCCANN	PATRIC				60	IRELAND	RC	IRISH	LAB	043	A	6	52
MCCANN	PATRICK				40	IRELAND	RC	IRISH	LAB	044	C	2	10
MCCANNA	JAMES			M	46	IRELAND	RC	IRISH	SHOE MAKER	043	A	2	3
MCCARDLE	ELLISON		2	1		ONTARIO	RC			043	H	2	D
MCCARDLE	ELLISON		2			0	RC			043	H	2	D
MCCARDLE	JAMES				40	IRELAND	RC	IRISH	MERCHANT	043	H	2	10
MCCARTER	JOHN		1		28	SCOTLAND	OP	SCOTCH	LAB	043	A	3	15
MCCARTHUR	MARY		1	1	30	SCOT	CP	SCOT	SERVANT	044	B	4	53
MCCARTHY	CHARLES				34	QUE	WM	IRISH	FARMER	045	D	5	73
MCCARTNEY	HENRY				60	IRELAND	RC	IRISH	SHOEMAKER	044	A	1	8
MCCARTNEY	JAMES				45	IRELAND	RC	IRISH	F LAB	044	A	1	11
MCCARTNEY	JOHN				27	IRELAND	CE	IRISH	LAB	043	A	3	58

SURNAME	NAME1	NAME2	STRAY	SEX	AGE	BIRTHPL	RELIGION	ORIGIN	OCCUP	DIST	SUB_DIST	DIV	PAGE
MCCARTNEY	ROBERT				38	IRE	CS	IRISH	BOOKKEEPER	044	B	4	45
MCCARTY	ALFRED				39	ONTARIO	PR	IRISH	FARMER	043	G	2	33
MCCARTY	CHARLES				46	IRELAND	WM	IRISH	SHOEMAKER	043	E	3	23
MCCARTY	DENNIS				63	IRELAND	RC	IRISH	LAB	044	C	2	50
MCCARTY	HARRIET		1	1	30	0	WM	ENGLISH		043	E	3	51
MCCARTY	IAACE				41	UNITED STATES	WM	AFRICAN	LAB	043	E	3	4
MCCARTY	JEROME				58	0	CE	IRISH	F	043	E	3	52
MCCARTY	JOHANNA		1	1	23	IRELAND	RC	IRISH		044	A	2	24
MCCARTY	JOHN			M	52	IRELAND	RC	IRELAND	F	043	A	5	8
MCCARTY	JOHN				30	0	CE	IRISH	F	043	E	2	4
MCCARTY	JOHN				37	SCOTLAND	CP	SCOTCH	BUTCHER	045	A	2	38
MCCARTY	JOHN				50	IRELAND	RC	IRISH	CONTRACTOR	044	C	2	51
MCCARTY	JOSEPH				34	0	WM	AFRICAN	LAB	043	E	3	3
MCCARTY	MARY		1	1	50	IRELAND	RC	IRISH	SERVANT	043	E	1	4
MCCARTY	WILLIAM				32	0	CE	IRISH	WATCH MAKER	043	C		27
MCCASKILL	JANE		1	1	64	SCOTLAND	CP	SCOTCH		044	C	2	1
MCCASLIN	THOMAS				46	IRELAND	CE	IRISH	F LAB	044	A	2	41
MCCAUDIA	INFANT		1	1		0	CN	SCOTCH		043	E	2	21
MCCAUDIA	MARIAH		1	1	20	0	CN	SCOTCH		043	E	2	21
MCCAUGE	ALEX				65	IRELAND	RC	IRISH	F	044	C	1	25
MCCAUGE	DUNCAN				57	IRELAND	RC	IRISH	ROAD OVERSEER	044	C	1	30
MCCAUL	DAVID			M	39	IRELAND	PS	IRISH	CARPENTER	043	A	1	10
MCCAUL	JOHN				48	IRELAND	CP	IRISH	FARMER	043	A	4	58
MCCAUL	JOHN				36	SCOTLAND	CS	SCOTCH	FARMER	045	D	5	44
MCCAUL	MARGARET		1	1	57	IRELAND	WM	IRISH	SERVANT	045	B	2	36
MCCAULEY	ELIZABETH		1	F	11	0	CS	SCOTCH		043	A	2	36
MCCAULEY	JANE		1	1	20	0	DI	SCOTCH	SERVANT	043	A	4	27
MCCAULEY	MARY			1	69	IRELAND	CO	IRISH		044	B	5	53
MCCAULEY	MARY	ANN	1	1	17	0	CE	SCOTCH	SERVANT	045	D	1	21
MCCAULEY	SARAH		1	1	20	SCOTLAND	CP	SCOTCH	SERVANT	044	B	6	38
MCCAULEY	WM		2		81	IRELAND	CO		WEAVER	044	B	5	D
MCCAULLY	HENRY				55	IRELAND	WM	IRISH	F	043	E	3	22
MCCAULY	THOMAS				54	SCOTLAND	OM	SCOTCH	FARMER	045	D	3	52
MCCAULY	WILLIAM				25	0	CP	SCOTCH	F LABOURER	045	D	3	53
MCCAUSLAND	ROBERT				49	IRELAND	WM	IRISH	SCHOOL TEACHER	045	B	1	41
MCCAUSLAND	THOMAS				35	0	CE	GERMAN	PHYSICIAN	045	D	3	69
MCCHEWING	ANNE		1	1	64	IRELAND	CE	IRISH		044	C	4	8
MCCHYLINCHIE	ROBERT			M	28	0	CE	IRISH	SAWYER	043	A	1	73
MCCLAN	THOMAS				40	IRELAND	CE	IRISH	CLERK IN CUSTOMS	044	C	4	97
MCCLAREN	ALEXANDER		1	M	14	0	PM	SCOTCH		043	A	2	46
MCCLEAN	MARGARET				78	IRELAND	PS	IRISH	F	044	C	1	47
MCCLEAR	ELISABETH		1	1	15	IRELAND	WM	IRISH		045	A	4	31
MCCLEARY	HESSEY		1	1	25	IRELAND	BA	IRISH	STRAW M	043	A	4	18
MCCLEARY	MATILDA		1	1	27	IRELAND	CS	IRISH	SALES WOMAN	043	A	4	18
MCCLELAN	ROBT REV				46	IRELAND	BA	IRISH	CLERGYMAN	045	D	4	44
MCCLELAND	WILLIAM			M	30	QUE	CP	IRISH	LAB	043	A	2	5
MCCLENNY	SAMUEL		1		40	IRELAND	RP	IRISH	LAB	043	B	5	18
MCCLIMATE	MARY			1	70	SCOTLAND	CP	SCOTCH		045	A	3	35
MCCLINCHY	JAMES				30	0	CE	IRISH	MILLER	044	A	2	45
MCCLINSHY	JOHN			M	35	0	CE	IRELAND	SAWYER AGENT	043	A	5	6
MCCLINTOCK	JAMES				31	0	WM	IRISH	INNKEEPER	043	E	2	37
MCCLOSKY	I	MARY		1	43	IRELAND	OP	IRISH		043	A	3	12
MCCLUNG	ELIZABETH		1	1	15	0	EM	IRISH		043	A	2	44
MCCLURE	ANDREW			M	28	0	PS	IRISH	F	043	A	2	58
MCCLURE	ANDW				57	IRELAND	PS	IRISH	F	044	B	5	54
MCCLURE	DAVID				47	IRELAND	PM	IRISH	F	043	A	6	58
MCCLURE	HANNAH		1	1	47	0	CE	ENG		045	C	1	34
MCCLURE	JAMES				51	IRELAND	CE	IRISH	MERCHANT	043	F		19
MCCLURE	JAS	H			26	0	PS	IRISH	SADDLER	044	B	5	16
MCCLURE	JOHNSTON				35	0	WM	IRISH	F	044	B	4	49
MCCLURE	JOSEPH				44	0	PM	SCOT	F	045	C	1	31
MCCLURE	MARY	ANN	1	1	38	0	CE	IRE	SEAMSTRESS	044	B	4	10
MCCLURE	SARAH		1	1	14	0	EM	ENG		044	B	4	52
MCCLURE	WILLIAM		1		3	0	CS	SCOT		044	B	4	42
MCCLUSHY	JAS				38	0	CE	IRISH	LAB	044	B	5	8
MCCLUSKEY	JOHN				68	IRELAND	CE	IRISH	CARPENTER	044	B	5	24
MCCLUSKY	MAT				60	IRELAND	CE	IRISH	LAB	044	B	5	16
MCCLYNCHIE	ROBERT		2	M		0	NG			043	A	1	D
MCCOLL	BULEY		1	1	4	0	BA	ENGLISH		043	B	3	25
MCCOLL	MARGETIM		1	1	6	0	BA	ENGLISH		043	B	3	25
MCCOLLAUGH	GEO				61	IRE	CE	IRE	YEOMAN FARMER	045	C	1	39
MCCOLLUM	D		1		22	0	PS	SCOTTISH	SCHOOL TEACHER	044	C	1	48
MCCOLUM	ISABLA			1	58	SCOT	CS	SCOT		044	B	4	31
MCCOMB	GEORGE				23	0	CE	IRISH	SAWYER	043	F		9
MCCOMB	JAMES				26	0	CP	IRISH	SAWYER	043	F		8
MCCOMB	JANE			1	56	IRELAND	CP	IRISH		044	A	2	35
MCCONACHIE	FRACIS				30	IRELAND	CE	IRISH	SHOE MAKER	045	D	2	7
MCCONIKIE	ANDREW				70	SCOTLAND	PS	SCOTCH	FARMER	045	D	6	17
MCCONNEL	F	A W	2			0	WM			045	D	1	D
MCCONNEL	GEORGE				29	0	NC	IRISH	ENGINEER	043	C		28
MCCONNEL	JOHN				28	0	WM	IRISH	MEDICAL DR	045	D	1	7
MCCONNELL	ANN		1	1	30	IRELAND	CS	IRISH	SERVANT	045	D	5	20
MCCONNELL	JOHN				59	IRELAND	WM	IRELAND	FARMER	045	D	2	18
MCCONNELL	JOSEPH		2		28	0	WM		FARMER	045	D	2	D
MCCONVEY	JOHN		1		30	IRELAND	RC	IRISH	LAB	045	B	1	14
MCCONVEY	PATRICK				26	IRELAND	RC	IRISH	BUTCHER	045	B	1	54
MCCONVEY	PATRICK				26	IRELAND	RC	IRISH	DROVER	044	C	4	45
MCCORDICK	ROBERT				39	IRELAND	WM	IRISH	MAIL CONTRACTOR	043	G	1	10
MCCORDLE	JAMES				40	IRELAND	RC	IRISH	MERCHANT	043	H	2	10
MCCORMACK	DANIEL				73	IRELAND	CE	IRISH	TAILOR	043	B	4	12
MCCORMACK	JAMES				40	SCOTLAND	PS	SCOTTISH	F LAB	044	C	1	55
MCCORMACK	JANE		1	1	30	0	CP	IRISH	SERVANT	045	B	2	37
MCCORMACK	JOHN				67	0	CE	IRISH	FARMER	045	A	2	18
MCCORMACK	JOHN		2		30	0	CE		FARMER	045	A	2	D
MCCORMACK	JOSEPH				55	IRE	CP	IRISH	LAB	044	B	1	57
MCCORMACK	LYDIA			1	59	IRELAND	WM	IRISH		045	A	2	18
MCCORMACK	ROBERT				52	US	RP	IRISH	LUMBERMAN	043	B	5	18
MCCORMIC	JOHN				45	IRELAND	RC	IRISH	LAB	044	C	3	29
MCCORMICK	MARY	ANN	1	1	14	0	RC	IRISH	SERVANT	044	C	2	39
MCCORMICK	PATRICK				51	IRELAND	RC	IRISH	BLACKSMITH	044	C	2	41
MCCOUGH		MICHEAL			34	IRELAND	RC	IRISH	LAB	045	A	1	98
MCCOWAN	JAMES				29	0	CS	SCOTCH	FARMER	045	D	1	27
MCCOWAN	JAS				57	SCOT	CS	SCOT	F	045	C	1	61
MCCOWAN	ROBERT				25	0	PS	SCOTCH	F	045	C	3	52
MCCOWAN	ROBT				57	SCOT	CS	SCOT	F	045	C	1	29
MCCOWAN	WILLIAM					SCOTLAND	PS	SCOTCH	F	045	C	3	56

SURNAME	NAME1	NAME2	STRAY	SEX	AGE	BIRTHPL	RELIGION	ORIGIN	OCCUP	DIST	SUB_DIST	DIV	PAGE
MCCOY	BRIDGET			1	60	IRELAND	RC	IRISH		044	C	2	40
MCCOY	CHARLES		1		25	0	CE	SCOTCH	FARM LAB	044	C	2	52
MCCOY	JAMES			M	58	IRELAND	WM	IRISH	F	043	A	1	22
MCCOY	JAMES				28	0	EP	SCOT	F	044	B	3	31
MCCOY	JOHN		1		32	IRELAND	RC	IRISH	F	044	C	2	40
MCCRACKEN	A	J			46	0	CO	SCOTCH	CARRIAGE MAKER	043	D		60
MCCRACKEN	LOUISA		2	1	7	0	CO			043	D		D
MCCREA	JOHN				55	SCOTLAND	CP	SCOTCH	LAB	044	C	2	7
MCCREA	JOHN				59	IRELAND	CE	IRISH	LAB	044	C	2	25
MCCREA	WILLIAM		1		24	0	CE	IRISH	LAB	044	C	2	19
MCCREARY	EDWARD				47	IRELAND	CE	IRISH	FARM LAB	044	A	2	52
MCCREERY	JANE		1	1	25	IRELAND	CE	IRISH	COOK	045	A	1	1
MCCREERY	WILLIAM		1		28	IRELAND	CE	IRISH	FARM SERVANT	045	A	1	1
MCCREIGHT	ANDREW				44	IRELAND	CP	IRISH	F	045	C	2	39
MCCREIGHT	JOHN				56	IRELAND	CP	IRISH	F	045	C	2	45
MCCUBBAN	ELIZABETH			1	60	SCOT	PM	SCOT	WASHERWOMAN	044	B	4	35
MCCUDDEN	CATHARINE			1	75	IRELAND	RC	IRISH		043	G	2	3
MCCUDDEN	JOHN				27	IRELAND	RC	IRISH	LABOURER	043	G	2	2
MCCUE	GEORGE				43	ONTARIO	WM	OJIBWAY INDIAN	HUNTER AND FISHER	043	G	1	58
MCCULLIGHAN	CATHERINE		1	1	37	IRELAND	CE	IRISH		044	A	3	20
MCCULLOCH	DAVID		1		26	SCOTLAND	CP	SCOTCH	BLACKSMITH	045	A	4	30
MCCULLOUGH	EPHRAIM				47	IRELAND	FK	IRISH	MARINER	043	G	1	39
MCCULLOUGH	HUGH				46	IRELAND	CP	IRISH	FARMER	045	A	2	15
MCCULLOUGH	REV	WM			56	IRELAND	WM	SCOTCH	WES M MINISTER	045	D	5	29
MCCURDY	DANIEL				54	IRELAND	RC	IRISH		044	A	1	18
MCCUTCHEON	DAVID				65	IRELAND	CP	IRISH	F	044	B	6	50
MCCUTCHEON	ELIZA		1	1	12	IRELAND	CS	IRISH		044	B	6	15
MCCUTCHEON	HUGH				60	IRE	CP	IRISH	F	044	B	4	49
MCCUTCHEON	JAMES				66	IRELAND	CP	IRISH	F	044	B	6	50
MCCUTCHEON	PATRICK				63	IRELAND	CP	IRISH	F	044	B	6	50
MCCUTCHEON	SAMUEL				54	IRELAND	RC	IRISH	F	043	A	3	42
MCDEAVITT	WILLIAM				49	IRELAND	CP	IRISH	FARMER	043	A	4	30
MCDERMOT	JOHN				60	SCOTLAND	CP	SCOTCH	LABOURER	045	D	3	16
MCDIARMID	DUNCAN				36	0	CP	SCOTCH	PHYSICIAN	045	C	3	35
MCDOEL	ROBERT				29	IRELAND	OM	IRISH	LABORER	045	D	6	67
MCDONALD	ADAM				34	SCOTLAND	CP	SCOTCH	SCHOOL TEACHER	045	A	2	8
MCDONALD	ALEX		1		26	0	RC	SCOTCH	F	044	B	6	50
MCDONALD	ALEX		1		34	SCOT	CP	SCOT		045	C	1	11
MCDONALD	ALICE		1	1	30	0	RC	IRISH		044	C	4	79
MCDONALD	ANGUS				41	0	PS	SCOTCH	LAB	044	A	3	34
MCDONALD	ANNE		1	1	12	0	RC	IRISH		044	C	4	45
MCDONALD	ANNIE		1	1	6	0	CE	ENGLISH		043	D		33
MCDONALD	ANTHONY				40	IRELAND	RC	IRISH	TAILOR	045	D	5	24
MCDONALD	ARCHIBALD		1		15	SCOTLAND	WM	SCOTCH		043	A	3	58
MCDONALD	ARCHIBALD				63	SCOT	PS	SCOT	GENT	044	B	3	51
MCDONALD	BENJAMIN				42	SCOTLAND	CP	SCOTCH	FARMER	045	D	4	11
MCDONALD	CATHERINE			F	30	SCOTLAND	CP	SCOTCH		043	A	1	30
MCDONALD	CATHERINE		1	1	18	SCOTLAND	WM	SCOTCH		043	A	3	58
MCDONALD	DANIEL			M	53	SCOTLAND	CP	SCOTCH	FARMER	043	A	1	30
MCDONALD	DANIEL				30	0	PS	SCOT	F	044	B	3	38
MCDONALD	DELIAH		1	1	6	0	CP	SCOT		045	C	1	32
MCDONALD	DONALD				34	0	CS	SCOTCH	F	043	H	2	23
MCDONALD	DONALD				34	ONTARIO	CS	SCOTCH	FARMER	043	H	2	23
MCDONALD	DUNCAN		1		14	0	WM	SCOTCH	F	044	B	5	52
MCDONALD	EDWARD				48	IRELAND	WM	IRISH	F	044	C	3	52
MCDONALD	ELLEN		1	1	17	0	LU	SCOT		044	B	1	60
MCDONALD	GEORGE			M	55	SCOTLAND	FK	SCOTLAND	F	043	A	5	39
MCDONALD	GEORGE				22	UNITED STATES	CE	SCOTCH	F	043	E	3	27
MCDONALD	GEORGE				53	0	EM	SCOT	CARPENTER	044	B	3	18
MCDONALD	HUGH		1		24	SCOTLAND	WM	SCOTCH	LAB	044	B	5	63
MCDONALD	HUGH				39	SCOTLAND	CP	SCOTCH	F	045	C	4	44
MCDONALD	JAMES				34	0	WM	SCOT	F	044	B	1	59
MCDONALD	JAMES		1		22	0	PS	SCOT	F	044	B	3	37
MCDONALD	JAMES		1		21	ENG	CE	ENG	SERVANT	044	B	4	1
MCDONALD	JAMES		1		17	0	RC	IRISH	FARM LAB	044	C	2	42
MCDONALD	JAMES				28	0	CE	IRISH	GENTLEMAN	044	C	4	61
MCDONALD	JAMES				45	IRELAND	RC	IRISH	F	045	A	4	24
MCDONALD	JANET		1	1	29	SCOTLAND	FW	SCOTCH		045	A	3	37
MCDONALD	JNO				47	SCOTLAND	WM	SCOTCH	BLACKSMITH	043	C		23
MCDONALD	JOHN		2	M	65	SCOTLAND	CP		LAB	043	A	1	D
MCDONALD	JOHN		1		13	0	WM	SCOTCH		043	A	3	58
MCDONALD	JOHN		1		17	SCOTLAND	NG	SCOTTISH	LAB	043	B	5	27
MCDONALD	JOHN		1		8	0	CE	ENGLISH		043	D		33
MCDONALD	JOHN				42	SCOTLAND	CS	SCOTCH	HOTEL KEEPER	043	H	2	27
MCDONALD	JOHN				42	SCOTLAND	CS	SCOTCH	HOTEL KEEPER	043	H	2	27
MCDONALD	JOHN				33	0	PS	SCOT	CARPENTER	044	B	3	8
MCDONALD	JOHN				38	0	PS	SCOT	MERCHANT	044	B	3	38
MCDONALD	JOHN		1		40	IRELAND	RC	IRISH		045	A	2	32
MCDONALD	JOHN		1		8	0	PM	SCOTCH		045	C	1	32
MCDONALD	JOHN				60	SCOTLAND	CP	SCOTCH	SHIP CAPTAIN	045	D	4	27
MCDONALD	JOHN				47	SCOTLAND	WM	SCOTLAND	FARM LABORER	045	D	2	12
MCDONALD	JOHN		1		19	RED RIVER	RC	IRISH	LAB	044	C	4	45
MCDONALD	JOHN				50	IRELAND	RC	IRISH	LAB	044	C	4	56
MCDONALD	JOHN				45	SCOTLAND	WM	SCOTCH	MERCHANT	044	C	4	67
MCDONALD	JOSEPH		1		4	0	PM	SCOTCH		045	C	1	32
MCDONALD	MURDOCK				58	SCOTLAND	CP	SCOTCH	LABOURER	043	A	4	67
MCDONALD	NEIL				77	SCOTLAND	CP	SCOTCH	F	043	H	2	11
MCDONALD	NEIL				77	SCOTLAND	CS	SCOTCH	FARMER	043	H	2	11
MCDONALD	PETER		1		21	0	RC	IRISH	FARM LAB	044	C	2	42
MCDONALD	RODERICK				45	SCOTLAND	CP	SCOTCH	RAILWAY EMP	044	A	1	39
MCDONALD	SAMUEL				32	0	PS	SCOT	CARRIAGE FACTORY	044	B	3	39
MCDONALD	SARAH		1	1	25	IRELAND	RC	IRISH	SERVANT	045	D	1	11
MCDONALD	SIMON				52	0	CE	SCOTCH	CABINET MAKER	044	C	2	22
MCDONALD	THOMAS				57	IRELAND	RC	IRISH	FARMER	045	A	1	30
MCDONALD	THOMAS				43	SCOTLAND	CP	SCOTCH	SCHOOL TEACHER	045	C	4	43
MCDONALD	WILLIAM		1		35	0	VM	GERMAN	PUMP MAKER	045	D	3	39
MCDONALD	WILLIAM		1		35	SCOTLAND	CS	SCOTCH	CARPENTER	045	D	5	6
MCDONNALD	ELISEBETH		1	1	62	0	NG	SCOTCH	SERVANT	043	A	6	47
MCDONNEL	JAMES				24	SCOTLAND	UP	SCOTCH	CARPENTER	043	C		55
MCDONNEL	JOHN		1		40	IRELAND	PS	IRISH	TANNER	045	D	6	45
MCDONOUGH	JAMES				37	IRELAND	RC	IRISH	F	044	B	6	43
MCDONOUGH	JOHN				34	IRELAND	RC	IRISH	WHEELWRIGHT	044	B	6	59
MCDONOUGH	LUKE				40	IRELAND	RC	IRISH	LAB	044	A	1	31
MCDONOUGH	LUKE		2		2	0	RC			044	A	1	D
MCDOUGAL	BELLA		1	1	22	IRELAND	RC	IRISH	SERVANT	045	B	2	29
MCDOUGAL	DONALD		1		13	USA	OP	SCOTCH		043	H	2	46

SURNAME	NAME1	NAME2	STRAY	SEX	AGE	BIRTHPL	RELIGION	ORIGIN	OCCUP	DIST	SUB_DIST	DIV	PAGE
MCDOUGAL	DONALD		1		13	UNITED STATES	CP	SCOTCH		043	H	2	46
MCDOUGAL	ELLEN		1	1	15	0	PS	SCOTCH	SERVANT	045	B	2	34
MCDOUGAL	JANE		1	1	21	0	CE	SCOTCH	SCHOOL TEACHER	044	C	4	86
MCDOUGAL	ROBART				60	SCOTLAND	CP	SCOTCH	MILLER	044	C	3	24
MCDOUGALD	CHRISTY		1	1	27	0	CS	SCOTCH		043	A	3	41
MCDOUGALD	JAMES				36	SCOTLAND	CP	SCOTCH	FARMER	043	A	4	54
MCDOUGALL	DAVID				57	ENG	CP	SCOTCH	MERCHANT MILLER	044	B	1	11
MCDOUGALL	JOHN				38	SCOT	WM	SCOT	F	044	B	1	45
MCDOUGALL	JOHN				43	SCOTLAND	UP	SCOTCH	TINSMITH	045	D	1	12
MCDOUGALL	WILLIAM				60	SCOT	WM	SCOT	F	044	B	3	3
MCDOUGLE	JAMES		1		16	CANADA	DI	ENGLISH		045	D	6	49
MCDOWD	MARGARET		1	1	30	0	RC	IRISH	SERVANT	045	B	2	21
MCDOWEL	MARY		1	1	25	0	CE	ENG		045	C	1	25
MCDOWELL	ADAM				23	0	WM	IRISH	HARNESS MAKER	045	D	3	5
MCDOWELL	GEORGE				32	IRELAND	CP	IRISH	LAB	043	C		44
MCDOWELL	GEORGE		1		23	0	WM	IRISH	FARMER	045	D	3	5
MCDOWELL	WILLIAM				30	0	CE	IRISH	INN KEEPER	044	A	1	33
MCDUFFE	ROSE			F	79	SCOTLAND	CS	SCOTCH		043	A	2	11
MCEACHREN	DONALD		1	M	45	SCOTLAND	PS	SCOTCH	LAB	043	A	2	44
MCEACHRIN	HENRY				75	SCOT	CS	SCOT		044	B	4	5
MCECHRIN	HUGH				30	SCOT	CS	SCOT		044	B	4	26
MCELROY	HENRY				58	IRE	RC	IRISH	SHOP KEEPER	044	B	1	22
MCELVEEN	JAMES				43	IRELAND	CS	IRISH	FARMER	043	G	1	38
MCENERY	ELLEN		2	1	54	IRELAND	RC		F	045	C	3	D
MCENERY	ROBERT		2		65	IRELAND	RC		F	045	C	3	D
MCENERY	ROBERT				18	0	RC	IRISH	F	045	C	3	7
MCEWAN	WILLIAM				32	0	CP	IRISH	FARMER	043	A	4	64
MCFADDEN	CHRISTINA		1	1	23	SCOTLAND	CP	SCOTCH	SERVANT	044	C	2	1
MCFADDEN	JAMES				50	IRELAND	WM	IRISH	LABOURER	045	A	1	37
MCFADEN	JANE		1	1	6	0	CE	IRISH		043	B	3	15
MCFALL	ANDREW				32	0	CS	IRISH	ACCOUNTANT	044	B	6	15
MCFALL	WILLIAM				39	0	PS	IRISH	F	043	A	3	37
MCFALL	WILLIAM				64	IRELAND	CP	IRISH	F	043	A	3	40
MCFALLY	WILLIAM				30	IRE	EP	IRE	F	044	B	3	27
MCFARLAND	MARY		1	1	58	IRELAND	WM	IRISH		045	B	2	3
MCFARLAND	PETER		1		17	SCOTLAND	RC	IRISH	F LAB	044	A	3	47
MCFARLANE	ALEX				71	SCOTLAND	BA	SCOTCH	F	044	A	1	13
MCFARLANE	ARTHUR				62	IRELAND	CP	IRISH	F	043	B	5	25
MCFARLANE	DONALD				54	SCOTLAND	WM	SCOTCH	F	044	A	1	13
MCFARLANE	GEO				45	SCOTLAND	PS	SCOTCH	LAB	044	B	5	24
MCFARLANE	JAMES				55	IRELAND	WP	IRISH	F	044	B	5	56
MCFARLANE	JOSEPH		1		20	0	RC	IRISH		045	B	2	23
MCFARLANE	MICH		1		28	SCOT	CS	SCOT		045	C	1	29
MCFARLANE	OLIVE		2	1		0	BA			044	A	1	D
MCFARLENE	ALLEN				25	0	PS	SCOTCH	MILLER	045	D	6	15
MCFARLING	FRANCIS				36	IRELAND	CE	IRISH	HOTEL KEEPER	044	C	3	1
MCFARLING	JOHN		1		10	ONTARIO	WM	IRISH		044	C	3	49
MCFARLING	WILLIAM				59	IRELAND	PS	IRISH	F	043	E	3	30
MCFAYDEN	CHRISTINA		1	1	20	0	CP	SCOTLAND		045	D	2	28
MCFAYDEN	DONALD				67	SCOTLAND	OP	IRISH	F	043	A	3	19
MCFERSON	HUGH				50	SCOTLAND	CP	SCOTCH	WAGGON MAKER	045	D	6	9
MCGACHIE	MALCOLM		1		28	SCOT	PS	SCOT	SERVANT	044	B	2	9
MCGAFFIN	JAMES				42	IRELAND	WM	IRISH	MERCHANT	043	C		29
MCGANN	ELIZABETH			1	44	0	QU	ENGLISH		043	E	1	37
MCGANN	ELIZABETH		1	1	11	0	QU	ENGLISH		043	E	1	37
MCGANN	JOHN		1		13	0	QU	ENGLISH		043	E	1	37
MCGANN	MARY		1	1	25	IRELAND	RC	IRISH		045	D	2	35
MCGAREY	WM				44	ENGLAND	RC	ENGLISH	LAB	044	B	5	21
MCGARITY	FRANCIS				45	IRELAND	RC	IRISH	TAILOR	043	A	4	21
MCGARR	EDWARD				35	0	RC	IRISH	FARM LAB	043	B	1	12
MCGARR	MARGARET		1	1	20	0	WM	IRISH	SERVANT	044	B	6	25
MCGARR	PHILLIP		2		3	0	RC			043	D		D
MCGARRY	ELIZABETH			F	25	IRELAND	FK	IRELAND		043	A	5	15
MCGARY	JAMES		1		64	0	CP	IRISH		045	C	4	16
MCGEACHY	DUNCAN				26	SCOTLAND	UP	SCOTCH	BLACKSMITH	044	B	5	58
MCGEARY	MICHAEL				30	IRELAND	RC	IRISH	F LAB	043	A	3	42
MCGEE	J		1		34	IRELAND	WM	IRISH	PAINTER	043	C		5
MCGEE	JAMES			M	50	IRELAND	WM	IRISH	LUMBER MERCHANT	043	A	1	56
MCGEE	JAMES		1		21	IRELAND	CE	IRISH	LAB	044	C	4	16
MCGEE	JOHN				36	SCOTLAND	CP	SCOTCH	TEAMSTER	043	D		10
MCGEE	JOHN				67	IRE	RC	IRE	LAB	044	B	2	26
MCGEE	MARGARET		2	1	3	0	NG			043	D		D
MCGEE	MARGARET		1	1	29	IRELAND	CE	IRISH	SERVANT	044	C	4	22
MCGEE	WILLIAM			M	45	IRELAND	CE	IRISH	ENGINEER	043	A	1	72
MCGEE	WILLIAM				74	IRELAND	WM	IRISH	FARMER	044	C	3	55
MCGERN	JANE		1	1	31	SCOTLAND	CP	SCOTCH	SERVANT	045	B	2	20
MCGILL	ARCHIBALD			M	60	SCOTLAND	FK	SCOTCH	F	043	A	5	3
MCGILL	DUNCAN			M	59	SCOTLAND	PS	SCOTCH	LAB	043	A	1	53
MCGILL	MARGARET		1	1	11	0	PS	SCOTCH		045	A	1	5
MCGILL	MARGARET		2	1	44	0	PR			045	A	1	D
MCGILL	MARY			F	70	SCOTLAND	PS	SCOTCH		043	A	2	9
MCGILL	WILLIAM				30	0	CE	SCOTCH	FARMER	045	A	1	56
MCGILLAN	JOHN				55	IRELAND	RC	IRISH	F	044	A	1	14
MCGILLIVRAY	DONALD				63	0	UP	SCOTCH	F	044	B	5	68
MCGILLIVRAY	NEIL				41	SCOTLAND	PS	SCOTCH	CARPENTER	044	B	5	19
MCGILLIVRAY	NEIL				69	SCOTLAND	UP	SCOTCH	F	044	B	5	69
MCGILVARY	ALEX	R			27	SCOTLAND	FK	SCOTCH	MERCHANT	043	C		47
MCGILVARY	ARCHIBALD			M	66	SCOTLAND	PS	SCOTCH	F	043	A	2	12
MCGILVERY	DONALD		1		3	0	CE	SCOTCH		043	B	1	29
MCGILVERY	DONALD				35	SCOTLAND	RP	SCOTCH	FARMER	044	C	3	1
MCGILVERY	JOHN		1		12	0	CE	SCOTCH		043	B	1	29
MCGILVERY	JOHN				30	0	CS	SCOT	F	044	B	4	50
MCGILVERY	LAUCHLIN				65	SCOT	CS	SCOT	F	044	B	4	50
MCGILVRAY	JOHN				78	SCOTLAND	CP	SCOTCH	F	044	B	6	37
MCGILVRAY	NIEL				69	SCOTLAND	CP	SCOTCH	F	044	B	6	19
MCGILVRY	MARY	ANNE	1	1	21	SCOTLAND	PS	SCOTCH	SERVANT	044	C	4	58
MCGINNIS	ANGUS		1		25	0	PS	SCOT	F	044	B	2	75
MCGINNIS	JAMES				64	IRELAND	UP	IRISH	F	043	A	6	46
MCGINNIS	JOHN		1	M	18	0	NG	IRISH	LAB	043	A	2	3
MCGINNISS	JAMES				32	IRELAND	CE	IRISH	MERCHANT	043	A	4	16
MCGINTY	ELIZABETH			1	44	0	CE	FRENCH		043	F		12
MCGLASHAN	JAMES				22	0	CP	SCOTCH	F	044	C	2	35
MCGLASHAW	ANN			1	62	SCOTLAND	CP	SCOTCH	F	044	C	2	29
MCGLASHEN	ANDREW				35	ENGLAND	CP	SCOTCH	FARMER	045	A	3	15
MCGLOUGHAN	HUGH				60	SCOTLAND	FW	SCOTCH	FARMER	043	A	4	29
MCGLOUGHLIN	WM				44	0	BA	IRISH	STORE KEEPER	045	D	6	3

SURNAME	NAME1	NAME2	STRAY	SEX	AGE	BIRTHPL	RELIGION	ORIGIN	OCCUP	DIST	SUB_DIST	DIV	PAGE
MCGOUGH	JOHN				29	O	RC	IRISH	FARMER	045	A	1	80
MCGOVERN	DANIEL				50	IRELAND	RC	IRISH	F	044	A	3	47
MCGOVERN	JOHN				30	O	RC	IRISH	LAB	043	A	3	49
MCGOVERN	MARGARET		1	1	20	O	RC	IRISH	SERVANT	044	A	3	49
MCGOVERN	THOMAS			M	52	IRELAND	RC	IRISH	F	043	A	2	57
MCGOWAN	AGNES		1	1	11	O	CE	SCOTCH		044	B	6	41
MCGOWAN	JAMES		1		19	O	RC	IRE	LAB	044	B	3	47
MCGOWAN	JAMES	R			61	ENGLAND	CE	ENGLISH	H M PENSIONER	043	G	1	18
MCGOWAN	JAS		1		50	IRELAND	CE	IRELAND	TAILOR	044	B	5	20
MCGOWEN	ELIZABETH		1	1	16	O	WM	IRISH	SERVANT	044	A	2	6
MCGRATH	JOHN				43	IRELAND	RC	IRISH	F LAB	044	A	1	24
MCGRATH	MARY		1	1	42	IRELAND	RC	IRISH	WASHER WOMAN	045	A	1	69
MCGRATH	THOMAS				42	IRELAND	RC	IRISH	LAB	043	B	5	4
MCGRAW	JAMES		1		26	IRE	RC	IRE	LAB	044	B	2	63
MCGRAW	PATRICK				60	IRELAND	RC	IRISH	LAB	044	C	3	32
MCGREGOR	ARCHIBALD				32	SCOTLAND	CP	SCOTCH	ROPE MANUFACTURER	044	C	4	40
MCGREGOR	JAMES				27	SCOTLAND	PS	SCOTCH	GARDENER	045	A	1	22
MCGREGOR	MARYANN			1	36	IRELAND	CE	IRISH		044	C	4	40
MCGREGOR	PATRICK				55	SCOTLAND	WM	SCOTCH	BARRISTER	044	C	4	81
MCGRISKEN	MARY		2	1	30	IRELAND	RC			045	C	1	D
MCGRISKEN	PAT				35	IRE	RC	IRE	LAB	045	C	1	16
MCGRUER	CATHERINE		1	1	23	O	CP	SCOTCH		044	C	2	8
MCGUANE	NANCY			1	47	IRELAND	RP	IRISH		044	C	3	62
MCGUIGGAN	RICHARD				63	IRELAND	RC	IRISH	PEDLER	043	F		30
MCGUIN	ELLEN		1	1	65	IRELAND	WM	IRISH		044	B	5	38
MCGUINESS	WILLIAM				60	IRELAND	CE	IRISH	LAB	045	C	4	38
MCGUIRE	BERNARD		2		77	IRELAND	RC		FARMER	043	A	3	D
MCGUIRE	FRANCIS				33	IRELAND	RC	IRISH	LAB	044	A	3	22
MCGUIRE	JOHN				40	IRELAND	RC	IRISH	F LAB	044	A	1	41
MCGUIRE	MARY			1	58	IRELAND	RC	IRISH	F	043	A	3	49
MCGUIRE	MARY JANE		2	1		O	RC			044	A	1	D
MCGUIRE	THOMAS				76	IRELAND	RC	IRISH	F	044	A	1	27
MCGUIRE	WM				48	O	PS	SCOTCH	COOPER	044	B	5	6
MCHALE	JOHN				33	IRELAND	RC	IRISH	F	043	F		25
MCHARROW	JAMES				32	SCOTLAND	CP	SCOTCH	CARPENTER	045	A	1	61
MCHENERY	ISAC		1		21	CANADA	WM	GERMAN	SERVANT	045	D	6	31
MCHENERY	THOMAS				35	IRELAND	WM	IRISH	LAB	043	B	5	12
MCHENRY	JOHN				43	UNITED STATES	EM	SCOTCH	SAWYER	043	B	3	58
MCILLMURRAY		CAPR WILLIAM			68	IRELAND	PS	SCOTCH	F	045	C	3	41
MCILLMURRAY	WILLIAM				60	IRELAND	CP	IRISH	F	045	C	3	42
MCILROY	MATHEW				67	IRE	RC	IRE	LAB	044	B	2	43
MCINARTING	JOHN		1		24	O	RC	IRISH	F LAB	044	A	1	10
MCINEEN	ALEXANDER				39	SCOTLAND	PS	SCOTLAND	FARM LABORER	045	D	2	32
MCINNIS	DONALD				60	SCOTLAND	UP	SCOTCH	LAB	044	B	5	55
MCINNIS	JAMES		1	M	28	IRELAND	PR	IRISH	LAB	043	A	1	74
MCINTOSH	ALEXANDER				47	SCOTLAND	FK	SCOTCH	LAB	044	B	6	25
MCINTOSH	CHARLES		1		25	O	CP	SCOTCH	F	045	C	2	4
MCINTOSH	JAMES				47	SCOTLAND	PS	SCOTLAND	BAKER	045	D	2	29
MCINTOSH	MARY		1	1	64	US	CS	SCOTCH		043	F		31
MCINTYRE	DUNCAN				44	SCOT	CS	SCOT	FARM SERVANT	044	B	4	24
MCINTYRE	HUGH				35	IRELAND	WM	IRISH	COOPER	044	A	2	48
MCKAHANIE	MALCOLM				31	SCOTLAND	CS	SCOTCH	BUTCHER	044	B	6	8
MCKANE	MARGARET			1	56	SCOT	CS	SCOT		045	C	1	24
MCKAY	DANIEL		1		21	SCOTLAND	PS	SCOTCH	LAB	044	C	4	75
MCKAY	DAVID				42	SCOTLAND	RP	SCOTCH	SWITCH MAN	044	C	3	42
MCKAY	DONALD			M	35	SCOTLAND	PS	SCOTCH	TEACHER	043	A	1	47
MCKAY	DONALD		1		35	SCOTLAND	PS	SCOTCH	FARM SERVANT	043	E	1	19
MCKAY	DONALD				27	SCOTLAND	CS	SCOTCH	LABOURER	045	D	3	39
MCKAY	EDWARD				48	SCOTLAND	CC	SCOTCH	F	043	A	3	59
MCKAY	ELLEN		1	1	9	O	CE	ENGLISH		044	B	5	77
MCKAY	GEORGE				34	SCOTLAND	PM	SCOTCH	BLACKSMITH	043	B	3	9
MCKAY	HANNAH		1	1	11	O	CE	SCOTCH		045	D	3	54
MCKAY	HENRY		1		7	O	CE	SCOTCH		045	D	3	54
MCKAY	JAMES				55	IRELAND	VM	IRISH	TURNER	045	D	3	52
MCKAY	JAS	A			47	IRELAND	CE	SCOTCH	PHYSICIAN	044	B	5	59
MCKAY	JESSIE		1	1	20	SCOTLAND	PS	SCOTCH	SERVANT	044	C	4	58
MCKAY	JOHN		1		60	SCOTLAND	FK	SCOTCH		043	C		31
MCKAY	JOHN				63	SCOT	PS	SCOT	BOOK AGENT	044	B	2	73
MCKAY	JOS		1		22	SCOTLAND	PS	SCOTCH	MILLMAN	044	B	5	20
MCKAY	MARY			1	65	O	WM	FRENCH		043	B	1	25
MCKAY	MARY		1	1	33	O	CP	SCOTCH		045	B	1	28
MCKAY	NANCY			1	48	USA	WM	AFRICAN	LABOURER	045	A	1	57
MCKAY	ROBERT				47	SCOTLAND	CE	SCOTCH	INNKEEPER	044	B	6	26
MCKAY	ROSEY		1	1	81	SCOTLAND	BA	SCOTCH		043	A	3	61
MCKAY	SAMUEL				37	SCOT	PS	SCOT	LAB	044	B	2	74
MCKAY	SOPHIA		1	1	30	IRELAND	RC	IRISH		044	C	2	52
MCKAY	WILLIAM		1		3	O	BA	SCOTCH		043	E	1	51
MCKAY	WILLIAM				40	SCOTLAND	CP	SCOTCH	TRADER	045	B	1	28
MCKAY	WILLIAM				32	SCOTLAND	CP	SCOTCH	LABOURER	045	D	5	36
MCKAY	WILLIAM		1		13	O	EM	ENGLISH		045	D	2	44
MCKECHREN	ALLAN				70	SCOT	CS	SCOT	F & SAWYER	044	B	4	31
MCKEE	ALEXANDER				78	IRELAND	CS	IRISH	FARMER	043	A	4	49
MCKEE	ALEXDR				24	O	PM	IRISH	SCHOOLTEACHER	043	B	2	31
MCKEE	CATHARINE		1	1	13	O	WM	IRISH		045	B	1	37
MCKEE	MARGARET			1	27	SCOTLAND	PB	SCOTCH	BOARDING HOUSE KEEPE	045	B	1	52
MCKEE	MARTIN				31	O	PS	IRISH	MERCHANT	045	A	1	21
MCKELLAR	ALEXANDER			M	35	SCOTLAND	PS	IRISH	F	043	A	1	65
MCKELLAR	JAMES			M	86	SCOTLAND	PS	SCOTCH		043	A	1	65
MCKELLAR	PETER			M	50	SCOTLAND	PS	SCOTCH	F	043	A	1	65
MCKELVEY	JAMES				37	IRELAND	OP	IRISH	F	043	H	2	32
MCKELVEY	JAMES				37	IRELAND	CS	IRISH	FARMER	043	H	2	32
MCKELVEY	ROBT				32	IRELAND	WM	IRISH	CARPENTER	044	B	1	6
MCKENNA	EDWARD				46	IRELAND	RC	IRISH	TAILOR	044	C	4	41
MCKENNAN	JOHM				41	SCOTLAND	CS	SCOTCH	LABOURER	043	B	3	5
MCKENNE	JOHN				50	IRELAND	CE	IRISH	ENGINE DRIVER	045	A	1	53
MCKENNEL	KATE		1	1	17	SCOTLAND	CS	SCOTCH		045	D	3	80
MCKENNEY	PATRICK				24	IRELAND	RC	IRISH	FARMER	043	B	3	42
MCKENNEY	SAMUEL				50	O	RC	IRISH	LAB	043	E	3	51
MCKENNEY	THOMAS				42	IRELAND	CE	IRISH	DEP GOV GEN	045	A	1	35
MCKENNY	JOHN				26	O	CE	IRISH	PAINTER	044	A	1	12
MCKENSIE	EDWARD				38	O	WM	SCOTCH	FARMER	045	D	2	68
MCKENSIE	JAMES				27	SCOTLAND	CE	SCOTCH	FARMER	045	D	2	33
MCKENZIE	ALEXANDER				55	IRELAND	PM	SCOTCH	F	045	C	3	4
MCKENZIE	ANDREW		1		23	SCOTLAND	CS	SCOTCH	BLACKSMITH	043	E	2	21
MCKENZIE	CELISTA		1	1	20	CANADA	MN	GERMAN		045	D	6	38
MCKENZIE	ELIZA		1	F	17	O	WM	SCOTLAND		043	A	5	44

SURNAME	NAME1	NAME2	STRAY	SEX	AGE	BIRTHPL	RELIGION	ORIGIN	OCCUP	DIST	SUB_DIST	DIV	PAGE
MCKENZIE	ELIZABETH		1	1	25	SCOTLAND	PS	SCOTCH	SERVANT	044	C	4	67
MCKENZIE	FRANCIS				25	0	WM	IRISH	F	043	B	1	28
MCKENZIE	FRANK		1		5	ONTARIO	CE	ENGLISH		043	G	2	56
MCKENZIE	HENRY			M	47	ENGLAND	WM	ENGLISH	LABOURER	043	A	1	1
MCKENZIE	JOHN				52	IRELAND	RC	IRISH	F	043	A	3	17
MCKENZIE	JOHN				69	SCOTLAND	CS	SCOTCH		043	F		9
MCKENZIE	JOHN		1		23	SCOTLAND	CS	SCOTCH	GARDENER	045	A	1	29
MCKENZIE	JOHN	JR			34	0	CS	SCOTCH	LABOURER	045	D	4	36
MCKENZIE	JOHN	SR			60	ENGLAND	CP	SCOTCH	CARPENTER	045	D	4	36
MCKENZIE	MARTHA			1	40	0	CE	GERMAN		045	D	4	34
MCKENZIE	MARY	M	1	1	14	0	QU	ENGLISH		043	E	2	11
MCKENZIE	MURDOCH			M	51	SCOTLAND	UP	SCOTCH	SHOEMAKER	043	A	1	4
MCKENZIE	PETER				27	SCOTLAND	CE	ENGLISH	FARM SERVANT	045	C	4	35
MCKENZIE	PHILIP			M	44	ENGLAND	CE	ENGLISH	CARPENTER	043	A	1	8
MCKENZIE	RODERICK				27	SCOTLAND	CS	SCOTCH	BUTCHER	043	A	4	70
MCKENZIE	THOMAS		1		10	0	CE	ENGLISH		044	C	3	28
MCKENZIE	THOMAS	MARTIN	1		12	ONTARIO	CE	ENGLISH	SERVANT	043	G	2	56
MCKENZIE	WILLIAM				27	0	PS	SCOTCH	LAB	043	F		11
MCKENZIE	WILLIAM				52	SCOT	PS	SCOT	TOLLKEEPER	044	B	3	49
MCKEOUGH	MICHEAL		1		55	IRELAND	RC	IRISH	LAB	045	A	1	8
MCKEOWN	JOHN		1		18	0	FK	SCOTCH		043	A	3	51
MCKERR	JOHN				50	SCOTLAND	CP	SCOTTISH	FARMER	045	A	2	1
MCKERSON	JOANNE		1	1	23	SCOTLAND	CE	SCOTLAND		045	D	2	17
MCKEWAN	MATHEW				35	IRELAND	CE	IRISH	LAB	043	B	5	19
MCKEWAN	SAMUEL				35	IRELAND	CP	IRISH	LAB	043	B	5	23
MCKEWAN	SAMUEL		1		70	IRELAND	RP	IRISH		043	B	5	23
MCKEWEN	JOHN				50	IRE	RC	IRE	LAB	045	C	1	24
MCKEWEN	MARY	A	1	1	62	IRELAND	CP	IRISH		044	A	2	6
MCKEWON	FARQUER		1		3	0	CP	SCOTCH		044	B	6	55
MCKEWON	JOHN				43	IRELAND	RP	IRISH	HOTEL KEEPER	043	E	3	40
MCKEWON	MAUD		2	1		0	RP			043	E	3	D
MCKEY	WILLIAM				43	IRELAND	PS	SCOTCH	GARDENER	045	A	1	48
MCKIBBON	ADAM				45	IRELAND	CE	IRISH	F	044	B	5	44
MCKINEL	FLORENCE		1	1	2	CANADA	CO	ENGLISH		045	D	6	46
MCKINEL	JULIA		1	1	6	CANADA	CO	ENGLISH		045	D	6	46
MCKINEL	WILLIAM		1		4	CANADA	CO	ENGLISH		045	D	6	46
MCKINELL	JULIE		1	1	36	ENGLAND	CO	ENGLISH		045	D	6	46
MCKINLEY	WILLIAM				72	IRELAND	CE	IRISH	WEAVER	043	A	3	31
MCKINLY	JOHN				45	IRELAND	CE	IRISH	FARMER	043	A	4	52
MCKINLY	JOHN				63	IRELAND	CE	IRISH	FARMER	043	A	4	53
MCKINLY	WILLIAM				28	0	PM	IRISH	FARMER	043	A	4	54
MCKINNELE	ELIZABETH		1	1	29	SCOTLAND	CS	SCOTCH	SERVANT	045	D	5	16
MCKINNON	ALEX				61	0	PS	IRISH	LAB	044	B	5	44
MCKINNON	ALLEN				37	0	CP	SCOT	F	044	B	1	41
MCKINNON	ANGUS				60	SCOTLAND	CS	SCOTCH	FARMER	045	D	4	38
MCKINNON	ANN	U	1	32		0	XC	ENGLISH		043	A	4	33
MCKINNON	ARCHIBALD		2		49	SCOTLAND	CS		CARPENTER	044	B	6	D
MCKINNON	ARCHIBALD				74	SCOTLAND	CS	SCOTCH	FARMER	045	D	3	35
MCKINNON	DONALD		1		18	0	PS	SCOT	SERVANT	044	B	3	48
MCKINNON	DONALD				58	SCOTLAND	CP	SCOTCH	F	044	B	6	4
MCKINNON	DOUGALL				31	PE ISLAND	CS	SCOTCH	FARMER	045	D	5	26
MCKINNON	DUNCAN				55	SCOTLAND	CS	SCOTCH	F	044	B	6	7
MCKINNON	FLORA		1	1	19	PEI	WM	SCOT		044	B	3	39
MCKINNON	HUGH				33	0	WM	SCOTCH	SCHOOL TEACHER	043	A	4	33
MCKINNON	ISABELLA		1	1	27	0	CS	SCOTCH	TEACHER	045	D	5	12
MCKINNON	JANNET		1	1	8	0	CP	SCOTCH		044	B	6	19
MCKINNON	JOHN				47	0	PS	IRE	F	044	B	3	41
MCKINNON	JOHN				29	0	PS	SCOT	F	044	B	3	50
MCKINNON	JOHN				50	0	CS	SCOT	FARM LAB	044	B	4	44
MCKINNON	JOHN		1		13	0	CP	SCOTCH		044	B	6	19
MCKINNON	LACHLIN			M	68	SCOTLAND	PS	SCOTCH	F	043	A	2	41
MCKINNON	MARGRET		1	1	37	SCOTLAND	CS	SCOTCH		043	H	2	47
MCKINNON	MARY		1	1		0	XC	SCOTCH		043	A	4	33
MCKINNON	NANCY		2	1	35	0	PS		F	044	B	3	D
MCKINNON	NEIL				30	0	CS	SCOT	F	044	B	4	28
MCKINNON	NEIL				23	0	CS	SCOTCH	CARPENTER	045	D	3	43
MCKINNON	NIEL		1		27	0	CS	SCOTCH	DEALER IN CATTLE	044	B	6	24
MCKINNON	SARAH		1	1	12	0	CE	SCOTCH		044	B	5	45
MCKINNON	SARAH		1	1	10	0	CP	SCOTCH		044	B	6	19
MCKINSIE	JOHN				38	SCOTLAND	PS	SCOTCH	BLACKSMITH	045	D	2	49
MCKINZIE	ELIZABETH		1	1	20	SCOTLAND	CP	SCOTCH	SERVANT	043	B	1	17
MCKONEKY	JAMES				26	SCOTLAND	PS	SCOTCH	FARMER	045	D	6	70
MCKOWEN	BRIDGET			1	60	IRELAND	RC	IRISH		044	A	1	12
MCKUEN	JOHN				34	IRELAND	PS	IRISH	LABOURER	043	B	3	18
MCLAHILL	ALEX		1		32	SCOTCH	WM	SCOTCH	IRON	044	B	5	41
MCLAREN	ALEXANDER				50	SCOTLAND	OP	SCOTCH	TAILOR	043	A	3	11
MCLAREN	ALEXANDER				65	SCOTLAND	CS	SCOTCH	GARDINER	043	G	1	54
MCLAREN	ELLEN		1	1	10	0	CN	SCOTTISH		043	B	5	36
MCLAREN	JOHN		1		17	US	CP	SCOTCH	F LAB	044	A	1	36
MCLAREN	PETER				55	SCOTLAND	WM	SCOTCH	STORE KEEPER	044	C	4	84
MCLAREN	SUSANNA		1	1		0	CP	SCOTCH		044	A	1	36
MCLAUCHLIN	JAMES				60	IRE	RC	IRE	LAB	044	B	4	34
MCLAUCHLIN	PHILLIP				39	IRELAND	WM	IRISH	BLACKSMITH	043	C		51
MCLAUGHLEN	MARTIN				32	IRELAND	RC	IRISH	LAB	043	H	2	3
MCLAUGHLIN	ALEXANDER				29	IRE	CE	IRE	LAB	044	B	2	21
MCLAUGHLIN	CORNELIUS				30	IRELAND	RC	IRISH	MILLER	043	E	1	1
MCLAUGHLIN	JOHN				41	IRELAND	RC	IRISH	F	045	C	3	24
MCLAUGHLIN	JOHN		1		17	IRELAND	RC	IRISH	F LAB	045	C	4	3
MCLAUGHLIN	MARTIN				32	IRELAND	RC	IRISH	LABOURER	043	H	2	3
MCLAUGHLIN	THOMAS		1		23	0	WM	IRISH	F LAB	044	A	2	6
MCLEALAN	JAMES		1		29	SCOTLAND	CP	SCOTCH	SERVANT	043	H	2	8
MCLEAN	ALEXANDER				64	SCOT	CS	SCOT	F	044	B	4	16
MCLEAN	ALEXANDER				36	0	CP	SCOTCH	FARMER	045	D	3	13
MCLEAN	ALLAN				24	SCOTLAND	PS	SCOTCH	SCHOOL TEACHER	045	D	2	54
MCLEAN	ALLEN				26	SCOT	CS	SCOT	STONE MASON	044	B	4	50
MCLEAN	ALLEN				50	US	CE	IRISH	FARMER	045	D	3	52
MCLEAN	ARCHIBALD				40	0	CS	SCOT	BLACKSMITH	044	B	4	47
MCLEAN	ARCHIBALD				28	SCOTLAND	CP	SCOTCH	FARMER	045	D	2	69
MCLEAN	DANIEL			M	37	SCOTLAND	PS	SCOTCH	LAB	043	A	1	57
MCLEAN	DUGALD				45	SCOTLAND	CP	SCOTCH	F	044	C	2	44
MCLEAN	DUNCAN		1		28	0	BA	SCOTCH	SERVANT	044	B	6	56
MCLEAN	DUNCAN				48	0	PS	SCOTCH	FARMER	045	D	2	46
MCLEAN	FLORA		1	1	60	SCOTLAND	CP	SCOTCH		045	D	3	6
MCLEAN	HUGH		1		16	UNITED STATES	CN	SCOTCH	FARM SERVANT	043	E	1	30
MCLEAN	JAMES		1		10	0	UP	SCOT		044	B	4	36
MCLEAN	JAMES		1		68	SCOTLAND	CP	SCOTCH		045	D	3	6

SURNAME	NAME1	NAME2	STRAY	SEX	AGE	BIRTHPL	RELIGION	ORIGIN	OCCUP	DIST	SUB_DIST	DIV	PAGE
MCLEAN	JESSIE		1	1	27	SCOT	PS	SCOT		044	B	3	26
MCLEAN	JOHN				53	SCOTLAND	CP	SCOTCH	SHOEMAKER	043	A	3	20
MCLEAN	JOHN		1		10	ONTARIO	CE	ENGLISH		043	G	2	42
MCLEAN	JOHN				75	SCOT	PS	SCOT	F	044	B	3	36
MCLEAN	JOHN				33	O	CE	IRISH	FARMER	045	D	5	61
MCLEAN	MARGARET		1	1	8	ONTARIO	CE	ENGLISH		043	G	2	42
MCLEAN	MARY		1	1	30	IRELAND	CE	IRISH		043	A	3	55
MCLEAN	NEIL		1		13	O	CS	SCOT		044	B	4	34
MCLEAN	PRESTON				40	US	CE	IRISH	FARMER	045	D	3	48
MCLEAN	RICHARD		1		5	ONTARIO	CE	ENGLISH		043	G	2	42
MCLEAN	ROBERT		1		19	SCOTLAND	CP	SCOTLAND	FARM LABORER	045	D	2	2
MCLEAN	RODERICK				40	SCOT	PS	SCOT	LAB	044	B	3	52
MCLEAREN	CAROLINE		1	1	27	O	CE	SCOTCH		043	D		83
MCLEES	PENELOPE			1	42	IRELAND	OP	IRISH		043	H	2	40
MCLEES	PENELOPE			1	42	IRELAND	CS	IRISH		043	H	2	40
MCLELLAN	JOHN				63	SCOTLAND	CP	SCOTCH	F	044	A	3	6
MCLELLAND	JAMES				38	NS	WM	IRISH	TEACHER UC COLLEGE	045	B	1	59
MCLELLAND	MARTHA		1	1	55	IRELAND	CE	IRISH		045	A	1	8
MCLELLAND	RACHEL			1	56	IRELAND	CP	IRISH		045	B	1	9
MCLENNAN	CATHERINE		1	1	15	O	CE	ENGLISH		044	B	6	23
MCLENNAN	LUCINDA		1	1	50	IRE	CE	IRE		045	C	1	7
MCLEOD	CLARIBEL		1	1	2	O	QU	SCOTCH		043	E	1	21
MCLEOD	DAVID				48	ONTARIO	CE	SCOTTISH	GARDENER	043	B	4	3
MCLEOD	DONALD				52	SCOTLAND	EV	SCOTLAND	BOOK AGENT	045	D	2	29
MCLEOD	IDA		1	1	6	O	QU	SCOTCH		043	E	1	21
MCLEOD	ROBERT				34	O	NR	SCOTCH	F	043	A	6	1
MCLEOLAN	JAMES				29	SCOTLAND	CS	SCOTCH	SERVANT	043	H	2	8
MCLERTY	DAVID				49	IRELAND	CE	IRISH	F	044	C	1	36
MCLEVIN	DONALD				59	SCOTLAND	CP	SCOTCH	F	045	C	3	31
MCLEVIN	ISABELLA				58	SCOTLAND	CP	SCOTCH	F	045	C	3	32
MCLOUD	DANIEL	MORDICA	1		16	O	EP	SCOTCH		043	A	6	1
MCLOUD	IDA	LOUISA	1	1	19	O	EP	SCOTCH		043	A	6	1
MCLOUGHLIN	RICHARD				28	IRELAND	RC	IRISH	TINSMITH	043	D		67
MCLURE	WILLIAM				33	O	PM	IRISH	CABINET MAKER	043	A	3	25
MCLUSKY	MARY		1	1	19	O	FK	IRISH		043	A	3	36
MCMACKON	ROBT				73	IRELAND	CS	IRISH	COOPER	045	D	5	34
MCMACKON	THOMAS				40	IRELAND	CS	IRISH	FARMER	045	D	5	65
MCMAHON	BRIDGET		1	1	21	IRELAND	RC	IRISH		045	D	4	6
MCMAHON	FRANCIS				57	IRELAND	RC	IRISH	F	044	A	3	36
MCMAHON	MARGARET			1	64	IRELAND	CE	IRISH		043	B	1	24
MCMAHON	MARY	A	1	1	24	IRELAND	RC	IRISH	SERVANT	045	D	2	32
MCMAHON	PATRICK				62	IRELAND	RC	IRISH	LABOURER	045	A	1	80
MCMAHON	PATRICK				55	IRELAND	RC	IRISH	LABORER	045	D	1	6
MCMAHON	WALTER		1		18	O	CE	IRE	LAB	044	B	2	67
MCMAIN	CARSON				52	O	WM	IRISH	F	043	A	6	13
MCMANN	MICKLE				38	IRELAND	RC	IRISH		044	C	3	48
MCMANUS	MARGARET		1	1	13	O	RC	IRISH		045	A	2	19
MCMASTER	ANGUS		1		54	SCOTLAND	PS	SCOTCH	LAB	044	B	5	9
MCMASTER	CHARLES		2			IRISH	CP			043	D		D
MCMASTER	DONALD				34	O	CP	IRISH	GLOVE MAKER	044	A	3	31
MCMASTER	JAMES				54	IRELAND	CP	IRISH	LAB	044	C	2	49
MCMASTER	WILLIAM				35	IRELAND	CP	IRISH	MERCHANT	043	D		67
MCMASTER	WILLIAM				60	IRELAND	BA	IRISH	G BANKER	044	C	4	69
MCMAUGHN	FANNY			1	60	IRELAND	CE	IRISH		045	A	3	12
MCMICHAEL	DANIEL				28	IRELAND	CS	IRISH	TANNER	045	D	3	67
MCMICKEN	DANIEL				50	IRELAND	CE	IRISH	LABOURER	045	D	5	32
MCMIEL	HUGH	J			28	O	CE	SCOTCH	F	044	A	1	25
MCMILLAN	ALEX			M	50	O	PS	SCOTCH	MERCHANT	043	A	2	7
MCMILLAN	ARCHIBALD				69	SCOTLAND	CS	SCOTCH	F	043	E	2	26
MCMILLAN	DOUGAL			M	66	SCOTLAND	PS	SCOTCH	F	043	A	2	9
MCMILLAN	DUNCAN				28	O	PS	SCOT	F	044	B	2	65
MCMILLAN	DUNCAN				50	SCOT	PS	SCOT	LAB	044	B	3	21
MCMILLAN	JAMES				30	O	CP	SCOTCH	F	044	A	3	36
MCMILLAN	JOSEPH		1		21	O	CO	IRISH	LABOURER	043	B	3	53
MCMILLAN	LUCY		1	1	19	US	PS		GENERAL SERVANT	045	C	4	12
MCMILLAN	WILLIAM				45	UNITED STATES	CN	SCOTCH	COOPER	043	E	1	38
MCMILLAN	WILLIAM				33	IRELAND	CS	SCOTCH	BLACKSMITH	045	D	3	28
MCMILLEN	AGNES	A	1	1	24	U STATES	WM	ENGLISH		043	D		89
MCMILLEN	WILLIAM		1		24	O	WM	ENGLISH	PRINTER	043	D		88
MCMILLIN	DUNCAN		1		26	SCOTLAND	RP	SCOTCH	LABOURER	044	C	3	70
MCMILLIN	ELLEN		1	1	22	IRELAND	RP	IRISH	SERVANT	044	C	3	17
MCMILLIN	JOHN				38	SCOTLAND	QU	SCOTTISH	F	043	B	4	41
MCMINN	ALEX				34	IRELAND	CP	SCOTCH	DROVER	043	A	4	14
MCMORAN	ELIZABETH		1	1	19	O	CP	IRISH		044	C	2	39
MCMORRIS	AGNES		1	1	82	IRELAND	CO	IRISH		045	D	5	6
MCMULLAN	WILLIAM		1		35	IRELAND	CP	IRISH	LAB	043	B	5	20
MCMULLEN	ALEXANDER				29	IRELAND	RC	IRISH	LAB	045	B	1	21
MCMULLEN	CATHERINE		1	1	19	IRELAND	RC	IRISH	SERVANT	043	A	4	21
MCMULLEN	GEORGE				30	IRELAND	CE	IRISH	F	043	B	5	16
MCMULLEN	HENERY				45	IRELAND	OP	IRISH	F	043	B	5	23
MCMULLEN	JOHN				62	IRE	WM	IRE	F	044	B	4	46
MCMULLEN	JOSEPH				34	IRELAND	WM	IRISH	F	043	B	5	25
MCMULLEN	JOSEPH		2		85	IRELAND	WM		FARMER	045	D	6	D
MCMULLEN	SAMUEL				31	IRELAND	PM	IRISH	F	043	B	5	24
MCMULLEN	THOMAS				64	IRELAND	WM	IRISH	WM MINISTER	045	B	1	47
MCMULLEN	WILLIAM		1		41	O	WM	IRISH	STORE KEEPER	045	B	1	2
MCMULLEN	WILLIAM				50	IRELAND	DI	IRISH	FARMER	045	D	6	59
MCMULLIN	JANE		1	1	40	IRELAND	PS	IRISH	SERVANT	043	E	2	67
MCMURCHEE	CHARLES				56	SCOT	CS	SCOT	F	044	B	4	24
MCMURCHEY	DONALD				38	SCOTLAND	PS	SCOTCH	FARMER	045	D	6	44
MCMURCHIE	ARCH'D				45	O	CS	SCOT	F	044	B	4	46
MCMURCHIE	DOUGAL				33	O	CS	SCOT	F	044	B	4	45
MCMURCHIE	JAMES				70	SCOT	CP	SCOT	F	044	B	4	53
MCMURCHY	ALEXANDER				38	SCOT	EM	SCOT	F	044	B	3	18
MCMURCHY	ARCH'D			M	54	SCOTLAND	PS	SCOTCH	F	043	A	2	53
MCMURCHY	DOUGAL			M	57	SCOTLAND	PS	SCOTCH	F	043	A	2	8
MCMURCHY	NEIL		1	M	77	SCOTLAND	CS	SCOTCH	F	043	A	2	11
MCMURCHY	NEIL			M	50	SCOTLAND	CP	SCOTCH	F	043	A	2	11
MCMURCHY	THOMAS		1	M	4	O	PS	SCOTCH		043	A	2	6
MCMURCHY	THOMAS			M	59	SCOTLAND	CP	SCOTCH	F	043	A	2	11
MCMURRY	JAMES		2			O	UP			043	A	6	D
MCMURRY	WILLIAM				38	SCOTLAND	UP	SCOTCH	LAB	043	A	6	64
MCNAB	JOHN				40	SCOTLAND	CP	SCOTCH	BLACKSMITH	045	C	3	12
MCNAB	JOHN				46	O	CP	SCOTCH	BARRISTER	044	C	2	52
MCNAIR	FLORA		1	1	20	O	CE	SCOTCH		044	B	5	45
MCNAIR	JAMES			M	62	SCOTLAND	PS	SCOTCH	WEAVER	043	A	2	21

SURNAME	NAME1	NAME2	STRAY	SEX	AGE	BIRTHPL	RELIGION	ORIGIN	OCCUP	DIST	SUB_DIST	DIV	PAGE
MCNAIR	JAMES				42	SCOT	PS	SCOT	F	044	B	2	57
MCNAIR	MATHEW				38	SCOT	PS	SCOT	JOINER	044	B	2	28
MCNAIR	WILLIAM			M	47	SCOTLAND	CP	SCOTCH	F	043	A	2	42
MCNALLY	JOHN	E			42	0	WM	IRISH	MERCHANT	043	C		6
MCNALLY	LUCY	C	2	1	38	0	NG			043	C		D
MCNALLY	THOMAS				28	IRE	CO	IRE	F	044	B	3	43
MCNAMARA	BRIDGET		1	1	50	IRELAND	RC	IRISH		043	D		55
MCNAMARA	ELLEN		1	1	65	IRELAND	RC	IRISH		045	B	1	49
MCNAMARA	JOHN				39	IRELAND	CE	IRISH	GARDNER	044	C	4	71
MCNAMARA	MALACHI				61	IRELAND	RC	IRISH	LAB	044	C	4	53
MCNAMARA	MARY			1	46	IRELAND	RC	IRISH		043	D		56
MCNAMARA	PATRICK		1		28	IRELAND	CE	IRISH	GARDNER	044	C	4	72
MCNAMARA	THOMAS				67	IRELAND	RC	IRISH	LABOURER	043	H	2	30
MCNAMARA	THOMAS	JR			30	USA	RC	IRISH	F	043	H	2	30
MCNAMARA	THOMAS	JR			30	UNITED STATES	RC	IRISH	FARMER	043	H	2	30
MCNAMARA	THOMAS	SR			67	IRELAND	RC	IRISH	LAB	043	H	2	30
MCNAMARAH	JAMES		1		19	0	RC	IRISH	SERVANT	045	A	1	76
MCNARNEY	JOHNSON				40	SCOTLAND	CS	SCOTCH	LABOURER	045	D	5	43
MCNAUGHTON	ALEXANDER				28	QUE	OP	SCOTCH	MERCHANT	043	A	3	7
MCNAUGHTON	NANCY			F	42	SCOTLAND	PS	SCOTCH		043	A	2	19
MCNAUGHTON	PETER				72	SCOT	CS	SCOT	GENT	044	B	4	3
MCNAY	DAVID				34	ENG	PS	SCOT	SHOEMAKER	044	B	3	9
MCNEELY	JOSEPH				70	IRELAND	WM	IRISH	FARMER	045	D	5	68
MCNEIL	ARTHUR				70	IRE	PS	IRE	GENT	044	B	3	34
MCNEIL	FLORA		1	1	13	0	CS	SCOT		044	B	4	50
MCNEIL	KATE		1	1	30	SCOTLAND	RC	SCOTCH	SERVANT	044	C	2	47
MCNEIL	WILLIAM				47	IRELAND	CS	IRISH	FARMER	043	G	1	50
MCNEILL	JOHN				27	SCOTLAND	PS	SCOTCH	SAWYER	043	B	3	28
MCNERNAY	ANNE		1	1	9	0	MN	SCOTCH		045	D	5	1
MCNERNY	MICHAEL				76	IRELAND	RC	IRISH	HAWKER	045	D	1	5
MCNERRY	JOHN		1		20	0	RC	IRISH	SERVANT	045	B	2	15
MCNERTNEY	BERNAN				56	IRELAND	RC	IRISH	LABORER	043	D		53
MCNICOL	JAMES		1		29	SCOTLAND	PS	SCOTCH	BUCHER	044	C	4	48
MCNORTNEY	JAMES			M	36	IRELAND	RC	IRISH	FARMER	043	A	1	27
MCPHAIL	ARCHIBALD		1		12	SCOTLAND	CP	SCOTCH		044	C	4	11
MCPHAIL	BARBARA		1	1	10	SCOTLAND	CP	SCOTCH		044	C	4	11
MCPHAIL	DUNCAN				36	U STATES	WM	SCOTCH	LAB	043	B	1	35
MCPHAIL	MARY	JANE	1	1	6	SCOTLAND	CP	SCOTCH		044	C	4	11
MCPHERSON	ALEX				48	0	WM	SCOTCH	MERCHANT	044	A	2	54
MCPHERSON	ALEXANDER				42	SCOTLAND	RC	SCOTCH	F	043	H	1	42
MCPHERSON	ALEXANDER				37	QUE	CP	SCOTCH	FARMER	045	A	3	22
MCPHERSON	ALEXANDER				48	NS	CS	SCOTCH	FARMER	045	D	3	27
MCPHERSON	ALEXANDER				84	SCOTLAND	CS	SCOTCH	FARMER	045	D	3	27
MCPHERSON	ANGUS				70	SCOTLAND	RC	SCOTCH		043	G	2	26
MCPHERSON	ELIZABETH		1	1	18	0	OP	SCOTCH		045	C	4	1
MCPHERSON	JOHN				26	0	CN	SCOTCH	AGENT	043	D		18
MCPHERSON	JOHN				40	SCOTLAND	RC	SCOTCH	FARMER	043	G	2	26
MCPHERSON	JOHN		1		57	SCOTLAND	CP	SCOTCH	SHOEMAKER	044	A	3	26
MCPHERSON	MARY		2	1	74	SCOTLAND	CP			044	C	2	D
MCPHERSON	THOS		1		21	0	UP	SCOTCH	WAGGON MAKER	044	B	5	57
MCPHERSON	TIMOTHY				53	0	CP	SCOT	F	044	B	1	38
MCPHERSON	WILLIAM		1		27	0	CN	SCOTCH	SERVANT	043	E	1	8
MCQAUDE	JAMES				23	0	RC	IRISH	LAB	044	C	4	73
MCQUADE	EDWARD		1		18	0	RC	IRISH	LAB	044	C	4	72
MCQUAID	PETER		1		20	IRELAND	LU	IRISH	F LAB	044	C	1	18
MCQUARRIE	ALEXANDER		1		24	0	PS	SCOT	LAB	044	B	3	48
MCQUARRIE	ARCHIBALD				52	US	CS	SCOT	F	044	B	4	2
MCQUARRIE	JACOB	B	2		1	0	NG			044	B	4	D
MCQUARRIE	JOHN				46	US	WM	SCOT	F	044	B	1	59
MCQUAY	ANDREW				30	0	CP	IRISH	FARMER	045	D	3	41
MCQUAY	ELIZABETH		1	1	30	0	CP	IRISH		045	D	3	30
MCQUAY	JAMES		1		3	0	CP	IRISH		045	D	3	30
MCQUAY	SARAH			1	72	IRELAND	CP	IRISH		045	D	3	42
MCQUAY	THOMAS		1		5	0	CP	IRISH		045	D	3	30
MCQUE	MICHAEL				50	IRE	RC	IRE	LAB	044	B	2	77
MCQUE	PATRICK		1		55	IRE	RC	IRE	HOSTLER	044	B	2	34
MCQUILLAN	EDWD				60	IRELAND	RC	IRISH	F	043	B	2	40
MCQUILLAN	JOHN		1		17	0	CE	ENGLISH		045	A	2	19
MCQUILLAN	MICHAEL				58	IRELAND	RC	IRISH	LAB	045	A	2	21
MCQUILLAN	PATK				65	IRELAND	RC	IRISH	F	043	B	2	40
MCQUIRE	BRIDGET			1	30	IRELAND	RC	IRISH		044	C	4	16
MCRAE	DONALD		1		22	SCOTLAND	CS	SCOTCH	TAILOR	045	D	5	12
MCREEL	MARY			1	55	IRELAND	WM	IRISH		045	D	1	33
MCRITCHIE	JAMES		1		49	SCOTLAND	PM	SCOTCH		044	B	6	21
MCROBERTS	WM				57	SCOTLAND	CE	SCOTCH	GENTLEMAN	045	D	5	47
MCSHANE	EDWARD				29	0	PS	IRISH	FARM LABOURER	043	E	2	40
MCSHANNICK	ARCHIBALD			M	31	0	PS	SCOTCH	F	043	A	2	15
MCSHANNOC	ARCHIBALD				71	SCOTLAND	CS	SCOTCH	RETIRED	043	A	3	27
MCSHERRY	ANN			1	52	IRELAND	RC	IRISH	F	043	A	3	52
MCSHERRY	JAMES				65	IRELAND	RC	IRISH	LAB	045	A	2	12
MCTAGGART	ALEX			M	40	SCOTLAND	PS	SCOTCH	F	043	A	2	19
MCTAGGART	JAMES				40	SCOTLAND	OP	SCOTCH	FARMER	043	A	3	2
MCTAGGERT	ARCHY		1		20	SCOTLAND	CP	SCOTCH		044	B	6	2
MCTAGGERT	JOHN				62	SCOTLAND	BA	SCOTCH	TAILOR	044	B	6	23
MCTIGE	JOHN				30	IRELAND	RC	IRISH	LAB	043	E	1	2
MCVICAR	ELIZABETH		1	1	32	0	CS	ENG	SERVANT	044	B	4	30
MCVITTEY	GEORGE				34	0	CE	IRISH	BANK OFFICER	045	B	2	32
MCWADE	ANN			1	45	0	CE	IRISH		044	B	6	38
MCWAIN	WILLIAM				36	0	CN	SCOTCH	F	043	E	3	5
MCWATERS	SAMUEL				32	IRELAND	CP	IRISH	FARMER	043	A	4	37
MCWHIRTER	HUGH		1		9	0	WM	IRISH		043	E	3	29
MCWHIRTER	ISABELLA		1	1	23	0	CE	IRISH	SERVANT	043	E	1	1
MCWHIRTER	ISABELLA		1	1	22	0	WM	IRISH		043	E	3	29
MCWHIRTER	JAMES		1		17	0	WM	IRISH		043	E	3	29
MCWHIRTER	JOHN		1		14	0	WM	IRISH		043	E	3	29
MCWHIRTER	THOMAS		1		19	0	WM	IRISH	F	043	E	3	29
MCWILLIAM	MARY		1	1	80	0	CP	IRISH		043	A	4	41
MCWILLIAM	SAMUEL		1		35	0	CP	IRISH	SERVANT	043	A	4	41
MCWILLIAMS	HIRAM				57	0	PS	DUTCH	LAB	043	A	6	32
MCWILLIAMS	JAMES				42	IRE	RC	IRISH	F	044	A	2	56
MEAD	DAVID				26	ENGLAND	WM	ENGLISH	SERVANT	045	A	3	35
MEARNS	ALEXANDER				26	SCOTLAND	CP	SCOTCH	GARDENER	044	C	2	50
MECKS	WILLIAM				28	0	WM	FRENCH	BLACKSMITH	043	C		35
MEDCALF	IANSON		1		66	ENG	EM	ENG	SERVANT	044	B	1	45
MEDCALF	ROBERT				62	ENG	WM	ENG	F	044	B	2	43
MEDD	CATHERINE			1	48	IRELAND	CE	IRISH	DRESS MAKER	045	D	1	14

SURNAME	NAME1	NAME2	STRAY	SEX	AGE	BIRTHPL	RELIGION	ORIGIN	OCCUP	DIST	SUB_DIST	DIV	PAGE
MEDD	JAMES				42	ENGLAND	WM	ENGLISH	LABORER	045	D	6	73
MEDDOCK	DAVID		1		19	O	PS	IRISH	LAB	044	C	4	84
MEDDOWS	JOHN				31	ENG	CE	ENG	LAB	045	C	1	64
MEDFORTH	CHAS				34	ENGLAND	PM	ENGLISH	IRON FINISHER	044	B	5	21
MEDFORTH	WILLIAM				62	ENGLAND	PM	ENGLISH	MILLWRIGHT	045	A	1	79
MEDLEY	GEORGE				40	ENGLAND	PM	ENGLISH	WELL DIGGER	043	B	4	15
MEED	JAMES				55	ENGLAND	BA	ENGLISH	LABOURER	045	D	6	18
MEEDS	HARRIET		1	1	71	USA	EM	AFRICAN		045	A	1	50
MEEHAN	CHARLES				60	IRELAND	RC	IRISH	GARDNER	044	C	4	10
MEEK	WILLIAM				31	O	WM	ENGLISH	AGENT	045	D	1	10
MEEKS	ROBERT		1		23	O	CE	ENGLISH		043	C		28
MEGAN	PATRICK				45	IRELAND	RC	IRISH	LAB	043	B	5	2
MEGANN	EDWARD				37	O	CP	IRISH	FARM LABOURER	045	C	3	39
MEGANS	PETER				40	IRELAND	RC	IRISH	F	043	E	3	16
MEGILL	HUGH				34	O	WM	IRISH	WAGGON MAKER	045	D	5	11
MEGILL	WILLIAM				35	O	CE	IRISH	F	043	A	6	25
MEHAN	OWEN				50	IRE	RC	IRE	F	044	B	3	50
MEHARG	ARCHIBALD		1		59	SCOTLAND	CP	IRISH	FARM SERVANT	045	C	4	29
MELISTONE	MATTEW		1		40	ENGLAND	CE	ENGLISH	FARM LABOURER	045	D	3	52
MELLISH	FRANK				55	ENG	EM	ENG	F	044	B	1	40
MELLISH	SARAH		2	1	2	O	PM			044	B	4	D
MELLISH	WILLIAM				28	O	PM	ENG	F	044	B	4	10
MELLON	JANE	A			13	O	RC	IRISH		045	A	4	13
MELLOW	WILLIAM	H			35	ENGLAND	PM	ENGLISH	LABOURER	045	D	4	27
MELON	JOHN				45	IRELAND	RC	IRISH	LAB	045	A	4	21
MELVILLE	ROBERT		1		78	SCOT	PS	SCOT	F	044	B	3	26
MENAGH			2	1		O	UP			043	A	6	D
MENAGH	WILLIAM				40	IRELAND	UP	IRISH	LAB	043	A	6	59
MENDELSON	MARK		1		45	PRUSSIA	RC	PRUSSIAN	PHRENOLOGIST	043	C		29
MENTO	JOHN				43	SCOTLAND	BA	SCOTCH	FARMER	043	B	3	2
MERCER	ANN			1	78	NB	CE			044	A	2	22
MERCER	JAMES				50	ENGLAND	CE	ENGLISH	LAB	044	C	2	50
MERCER	SAMUEL	A			40	O	OB	IRISH	F	044	A	2	9
MERCER	SENECA	K			44	O	WM	IRISH	F	044	A	2	19
MERCER	THOMAS				78	NS	CE	IRISH	FARMER	045	A	3	13
MEREDITH	MARGARET		1	1	21	ENGLAND	CE		SERVANT	043	D		87
MEREDITH	WILLIAM	H			44	ENGLAND	WM	ENGLISH	TEACHER	045	A	1	95
MEREWEATHER	JOHN				33	O	CE	ENGLISH	CARPENTER	043	E	1	49
MERGAN	WILLIAM				55	PRUSIA	RC	PRUSIAN	LABOURER	045	D	4	37
MERREDITH	MAGGIE		1	1	18	ENGLAND	BA	ENGLISH	SERVANT	045	A	1	47
MERRIDON	JAMES				22	ENG	CE	ENG	LAB	044	B	2	67
MERRYWEATHER	HENRY				33	O	CN	ENGLISH	SAWYER	043	A	6	62
MERTENS	CLAUSE	DERICK			41	GERMANY	CO	GERMAN	FARMER	045	D	6	57
MERTENS	E	MERTENS	2			O	CN	GERMAN		043	B	3	D
MERTINS	JOHN	GEORGE			38	GERMANY	CO	GERMAN	FARMER	045	D	6	57
MERTON	FREDERICK				35	GERMAN	CO	GERMAN	MAIL CARRIER	043	B	3	53
MESER	JOHN				39	GERMAN	MN	GERMAN	WEAVER	045	D	6	11
MESITER	JAMES		1		45	ENGLAND	CE	ENGLISH	CARPENTER	045	A	1	19
MESLER	JUDSON				26	O	BA	ENGLISH	CARPENTER	045	D	5	16
MESSILER	ISAAC				34	O	EP	GER	LAB	044	B	3	42
METCALF	LOUISA		1	1	50	ENGLAND	CE	ENGLISH		045	B	2	26
METCALFE	JAMES				48	ENGLAND	WM	ENGLISH		045	B	1	70
METHEREL	JOHN				55	ENGLAND	CE	ENGLISH	LABORER	043	G	2	15
METYS	ALEXANDER		1		24	ENGLAND	WM	ENGLISH	LAB	045	A	1	64
MEYER	DAVID				25	GERMANY	MN	GERMAN	CARPENTER	045	D	3	65
MEYER	EDWARD				28	SWITZERLAND	MN	SWISS	LABOURER	045	D	4	47
MICHAEL	WALLACE				37	ENGLAND	CE	ENGLISH	LABOURER	045	D	4	7
MICHEL	JAS		1		31	SCOT	CS	SCOT		045	C	1	29
MICHELL	JOHN				79	SCOTLAND	PS	SCOTCH		043	B	3	67
MICKS	JAMES				24	O	WM	GERMAN	BLACKSMITH	043	B	5	42
MICKS	JOHN				41	O	PM	IRISH	LAB	044	B	6	46
MIDDLEBROOK	GEO				42	O	CE	ENGLISH	F	044	A	2	24
MIDDLETON	ALFRED		1		27	ENGLAND	CE	ENGLISH	LAB	045	A	4	15
MIDDLETON	EDWARD		1		17	ENGLAND	CE	ENGLAND	SERVANT	045	D	2	9
MIDDLETON	EDWARD				50	ENGLAND	CE	ENGLISH	FARMER	045	D	2	44
MIDDLETON	JAMES		1		84	ENGLAND	PM	ENGLISH		043	E	2	68
MIDDLETON	JOHN				26	O	PM	ENGLISH	LAB	043	A	3	51
MIDDLETON	STEPHEN				28	ENGLAND	WM	ENGLISH	CARPENTER	045	B	1	55
MIDDLETON	THOMAS				36	IRELAND	CE	IRISH	LABOURER	043	A	4	43
MIDDLETON	WILLIAM		1		25	ENGLAND	CE	ENGLISH	FARM LAB	044	C	2	48
MIDGLEY	THOS				29	ENG	WM	ENG	F	045	C	1	62
MIDLETON	ELIZABETH		2	1	70	ENGLAND	EM			044	B	6	D
MIGHTON	SAMUEL				51	IRELAND	NR	IRISH	CARDER	044	B	6	5
MILES	ALFRED				41	ENGLAND	CE	ENGLISH	GARDNER	044	C	4	88
MILES	JAMES				50	ENGLAND	CE	ENGLISH	LAB	045	A	4	26
MILES	JOSEPH				34	ENGLAND	CE	ENGLISH	LAWYER	043	B	2	34
MILES	RICHARD	A			38	ENGLAND	RC	ENGLISH	FARMER	045	D	5	41
MILLAN	MARGARET		1	1	24	SCOTLAND	RC	IRISH	SERVANT	045	B	2	33
MILLAR	JAMES				50	O	WM	SCOTCH	F	043	E	1	10
MILLARD	EMMA		1	1	34	O	CP	SCOTCH		045	D	2	8
MILLARD	JOHN	J			46	O	CN	ENGLISH	F	043	E	1	31
MILLARD	JOHN	S			29	O	CO	WELSH	CABINET MAKER	043	D		85
MILLARD	JOSEPH				54	O	CO	WELSH	CABINET MAKER	043	D		70
MILLARD	MARTHA			1	53	ENGLAND	CE	ENGLISH	F	043	E	1	31
MILLARD	ROBERT				35	O	IN	ENGLISH	F	043	B	4	13
MILLARD	THOMAS				25	O	CE	ENGLISH	F	043	E	1	30
MILLBURN	GEORGE		1		11	O	CE	IRE		044	B	2	46
MILLER	ABRAHAM				26	O	CN	GERMAN	FARMER	045	D	4	46
MILLER	ABRAHAM		1		12	CANADA	CE	ENGLISH		045	D	6	39
MILLER	ALFRED				56	CANADA	BA	SCOTCH	CARPENTER	045	D	6	34
MILLER	ANDREW				59	SCOTLAND	CP	SCOTCH	FARMER	043	A	4	48
MILLER	ANDREW				30	CANADA	BA	GERMAN	LABORER	045	D	6	36
MILLER	ANDREW				32	O	UP	GERMAN	FARMER	045	D	1	18
MILLER	ANNEY		1	1	8	O	RC	GERMAN		045	D	6	1
MILLER	ANTHONY				51	O	WM	IRISH	F	043	E	3	48
MILLER	BETSY		1	1	38	O	WM	GERMAN	SERVANT	044	B	1	2
MILLER	BRIDGET		1	1	51	IRELAND	CE	ENGLISH		045	A	4	26
MILLER	CATHARINE		1	1	70	U STATES	TU	GERMAN		043	B	1	17
MILLER	CATHARINE		1	1	32	O	CE	ENGLISH		045	A	1	21
MILLER	CHARLES		1		20	ONTARIO	WM	SCOTCH	FARMER	043	G	1	46
MILLER	CHARLOTTE			1	50	ENGLAND	PM	ENGLISH		043	B	1	41
MILLER	CHARLOTTE		1	1	25	US	WM	IRISH	MUSIC TEACHER	045	D	3	71
MILLER	CHRISTINE	A	1	1	8	O	WM	GERMAN		045	D	5	43
MILLER	CRAWFORD				24	ENG	BA	ENG	CURRIER	044	B	2	48
MILLER	DANIEL				39	CANADA	BA	SCOTCH	FARMER	045	D	6	35
MILLER	DAVID				28	IRELAND	CP	IRISH	F	043	E	1	27

SURNAME	NAME1	NAME2	STRAY	SEX	AGE	BIRTHPL	RELIGION	ORIGIN	OCCUP	DIST	SUB_DIST	DIV	PAGE
MILLER	DOROTHY		1	1	82	FRANCE	LU	GERMAN	F	044	B	6	49
MILLER	EDWARD				72	IRE	CS	IRE	F	044	B	4	37
MILLER	ELIJAH				39	O	BA	GERMAN	INN KEEPER	043	B	3	15
MILLER	GEORGE				41	O	EM	ENGLISH	MINISTER	043	E	2	21
MILLER	GEORGE		1		28	SCOTLAND	CS	SCOTCH	LAB	045	A	2	6
MILLER	GEORGE				73	SCOTCH	CP	SCOTCH	FARMER	045	D	6	67
MILLER	HENRY				39	O	CP	IRISH	AGENT	044	B	2	18
MILLER	HENRY		1		19	ENGLAND	CE	ENGLISH	LAB	045	B	2	4
MILLER	HENRY				73	O	UP	US	GENTLEMAN	045	D	1	18
MILLER	HYRAM				35	CANADA	BA	SCOTCH	FARMER	045	D	6	37
MILLER	JACOB				58	CANADA	BA	SCOTCH	FARMER	045	D	6	73
MILLER	JACOB	M			50	CANADA	BA	SCOTCH	FARMER	045	D	6	70
MILLER	JAMES				77	SCOTLAND	UP	GERMAN	GENTLEMAN	043	C		25
MILLER	JAMES				41	SCOTLAND	CP	SCOTCH	F	045	C	4	44
MILLER	JAMES				36	QUEBEC	CS	SCOTCH	LABOURER	045	D	3	34
MILLER	JAMES		1		33	ENGLAND	CE	ENGLAND	BLACKSMITH	045	D	2	5
MILLER	JAMES				75	ONT	WM	GERMANY	F	045	A	4	5
MILLER	JOHN				39	SCOTLAND	WM	SCOTTISH	F	043	B	5	2
MILLER	JOHN				34	SCOTLAND	CP	SCOTCH	MOULDER	043	D		5
MILLER	JOHN				32	IRELAND	CP	IRISH	FARMER	043	G	1	21
MILLER	JOHN		1		25	SCOTLAND	CP	SCOTCH	FARM SERVANT	045	C	3	55
MILLER	JOHN				40	CANADA	MN	SCOTCH	LABORER	045	D	6	39
MILLER	JOHN				29	CANADA	PS	SCOTCH	FARMER	045	D	6	71
MILLER	JOHN				40	O	CE	ENGLISH	FARM LABORER	045	D	1	17
MILLER	JOHN		1			ENGLAND	CE	ENGLISH	FARM LABORER	045	D	1	49
MILLER	JONAS				45	O	MN	GERMAN	FARMER	045	D	4	49
MILLER	JULIUS	L			23	O	PM	GERMAN	LABOURER	043	B	3	13
MILLER	LAWRY		1	1	49	CANADA	NG	GERMAN		045	D	6	66
MILLER	LEVI				43	USA	NR	GERMAN	FOREMAN	043	H	2	16
MILLER	LEVI				43	UNITED STATES	NR	GERMAN	FOREMAN	043	H	2	16
MILLER	LUTTON				62	CANADA	FW	ENGLISH	FARMER	045	D	6	30
MILLER	MARTHA	A	1	1	1	O	CE	ENGLISH		043	B	1	35
MILLER	MARTIN				23	CANADA	NG	SCOTCH	LABORER	045	D	6	63
MILLER	MARY		1	1	45	ENGLAND	CE	ENGLISH		043	B	1	35
MILLER	MARY	L	1	1	24	ENGLAND	BA	ENGLISH	SERVANT	045	B	2	29
MILLER	PETER	R			29	O	CO	GERMAN	STORE KEEPER	045	D	3	72
MILLER	PHILLIP				38	CANADA	BA	IRISH	FARMER	045	D	6	76
MILLER	ROBERT				37	SCOTLAND	PS	SCOTCH	SAWYER	043	B	3	46
MILLER	ROBERT				36	UNITED STATES	CN	ENGLISH	MANUFACTURER	043	B	4	10
MILLER	SAMUEL				47	O	BA	GERMAN	FARMER	045	D	4	46
MILLER	SARAH		1	1	76	IRELAND	PS	IRISH		044	B	5	41
MILLER	SIMON				44	O	CP	ENGLISH	F	045	C	4	3
MILLER	THOMAS		1		25	O	WM	ENGLISH	STORE CLERK	045	D	3	71
MILLER	WALTER		1		18	U STATES	QU	DUTCH	SERVANT	043	A	6	27
MILLER	WALTER				65	SCOTLAND	CP	SCOTCH	FARMER	045	D	4	41
MILLER	WALTER				36	CANADA	BA	SCOTCH	FARMER	045	D	6	66
MILLER	WILLIAM				33	O	WM	IRISH	TRAIDER	043	A	6	56
MILLER	WILLIAM				36	O	PM	GERMAN	FARM LAB	043	B	1	11
MILLER	WILLIAM				60	IRELAND	PS	SCOTCH	F	043	E	2	47
MILLER	WILLIAM		1		10	O	CS	SCOT		044	B	4	46
MILLER	WILLIAM				53	SCOTLAND	CP	SCOTCH	SHOEMAKER	045	A	3	4
MILLER	WILLIAM				42	SCOTLAND	PP	SCOTCH	SHIP WRIGHT	044	C	3	8
MILLER	WILLIAM	J			63	CANADA	NG	SCOTCH	FARMER	045	D	6	69
MILLET	LEWIS				51	O	QU	FRENCH	LAB	045	C	2	41
MILLIGAN	JAMES				60	IRELAND	FK	IRISH	F	043	A	3	14
MILLIKEN	BENJAMINE				30	O	WM	ENGLISH	FARMER	045	D	3	26
MILLIKEN	HENRY				27	O	WM	SCOTCH	MILLER	045	D	3	27
MILLIKEN	JOHN		1		62	O	ME	IRISH		045	C	4	12
MILLIKEN	NORMAN				65	O	WM	SCOTCH	FARMER	045	D	3	25
MILLIKEN	ROBERT				70	US	WM	GERMAN		045	D	3	60
MILLIKEN	WILLIAM				36	O	WM	SCOTCH	FARMER	045	D	3	23
MILLOY	JOSEPH				45	IRELAND	NR	IRISH	AXE MAKER	045	D	5	39
MILLS	CHARLES				45	ENGLAND	CE	ENGLISH	F	044	A	2	31
MILLS	DAVID	S	1		0	O	BA	IRISH		044	C	4	70
MILLS	GEORGE		1		24	SCOTLAND	CP	SCOTCH	TINSMITH	045	D	3	20
MILLS	HENRY				39	ENGLAND	CE	ENGLISH	MACHINIST	045	D	5	18
MILLS	JAMES		1		52	USA	WM	AFRICAN	LABOURER	045	A	1	60
MILLS	JAMES	HG	1		11	O	BA	IRISH		044	C	4	69
MILLS	JOHN		1		16	O	UP	IRISH	LAB	044	B	5	75
MILLS	JOHN				45	ENGLAND	CE	ENGLISH	FARMER	045	A	1	78
MILLS	JONATHAN				42	ENGLAND	WM	ENGLISH	COOPER	044	A	2	49
MILLS	MARTHA		2	1	88	IRELAND	CP			043	A	3	D
MILLS	MARY	J	1	1	35	US	BA	IRISH		044	C	4	69
MILLS	MONTRAVILLE	W	1		38	US	BA	IRISH	GENTLEMAN	044	C	4	69
MILLS	MONTRAVILLE	W	1		7	O	BA	IRISH		044	C	4	70
MILLS	ROBERT				83	IRELAND	CE	IRISH	LAB	044	C	4	85
MILLS	ROSANNE		1	1	6	O	WM	ENGLISH		045	D	5	73
MILLS	SAMUEL		1		26	ENGLAND	WM	ENGLISH	LABOURER	045	D	4	2
MILLS	SARAH			1	66	IRELAND	WM	IRISH		044	C	3	26
MILLS	SEPTIMUS				34	ENGLAND	CE	ENGLISH	F	043	E	1	21
MILLS	THOMAS		1		33	SCOTLAND	EM	SCOTCH		043	G	2	19
MILLS	THOMAS		2		32	O	WM		COOPER	044	A	2	D
MILLS	THOMAS				56	IRELAND	CE	IRISH	TAILOR	044	B	6	25
MILLS	THOMAS	C	1		8	O	BA	IRISH		044	C	4	70
MILLS	THOS	G			21	O	CE	IRISH	TAILOR	044	B	5	3
MILLS	WILLIAM	MCMASTER	1		10	O	BA	IRISH		044	C	4	69
MILLYARD	JAMES				52	ENG	WM	ENG	COOPER	044	B	1	7
MILNE	ALEX	J			31	O	NC	SCOTCH	F	043	E	2	20
MILNE	ALEXANDER				37	O	PM	SCOTCH	CLOTH MANUFACTOR	045	A	2	36
MILNE	ALEXANDER				95	SCOTLAND	CD	SCOTCH	F	045	A	2	36
MILNE	DAVID A				31	O	CP	SCOTCH	GENTLEMAN	045	C	2	49
MILNE	ELIZABETH		2	1	31	O	CP			045	D	4	D
MILNE	ELIZABETH	C	1	1	85	UNITED STATES	EM	SCOTCH		043	E	2	20
MILNE	JAMES				43	O	WM	SCOTCH	LAB	043	E	1	10
MILNE	JOHN				42	SCOTLAND	CP	SCOTCH	STORE KEEPER	045	C	3	28
MILNE	PETER				58	O	EM	SCOTCH	F	043	E	1	48
MILNE	PETER				55	SCOTLAND	CS	SCOTCH	F	044	B	6	17
MILNE	PETER				30	O	PM	SCOTCH	FARMER	045	A	2	22
MILNE	PETER				60	U STATES	UV	SCOTCH	FARMER	045	D	6	17
MILNE	THOMAS	A			41	O	CS	SCOTCH	FARMER MILLER	045	D	3	79
MILNE	WILLIAM				34	SCOTLAND	CP	SCOTCH	GENTLEMAN	045	D	4	19
MILNE	WILLIAM	A			33	O	CP	SCOTCH	F	045	C	2	53
MILNER	CLARA		1	F	13	ENGLAND	CP	ENGLISH		043	A	2	27
MILNER	JOHN				36	ENGLAND	PM	ENGLISH	F	043	B	4	2
MILNER	JOHN				67	ENGLAND	PM	ENGLISH	F	043	B	4	3
MILNOR	RHODA		1	1	9	O	WM	ENGLISH		045	A	2	6

SURNAME	NAME1	NAME2	STRAY	SEX	AGE	BIRTHPL	RELIGION	ORIGIN	OCCUP	DIST	SUB_DIST	DIV	PAGE
MILROY			2			0	CP			045	D	5	D
MILROY	ELIZABETH		1	1	31	0	CE	GERMAN		045	D	5	74
MILROY	JAMES				49	SCOTLAND	CP	SCOTCH	FARMER	045	D	5	57
MILROY	JOHN				34	0	CP	SCOTCH	FARMER	045	D	5	55
MILROY	PATRICK				50	IRE	RC	IRE		045	C	1	27
MILROY	ROBERT		1		10	0	CE	GERMAN		045	D	5	74
MINDICK	JOEL			M	22	ENGLAND	CE	ENGLISH	F	043	A	1	9
MINER	SAMUEL				70	US	CE	AFRICAN		044	A	1	37
MINNET	EPHRAIM		1		20	0	CE	FRENCH	TEAMSTER	043	F		8
MINOGUE	SARAH			1	50	IRELAND	RC	IRISH		043	D		25
MINS	CIDNEY		1		14	CANADA	CO	ENGLISH		045	D	6	46
MINS	FRANCIS		1		16	CANADA	CO	ENGLISH		045	D	6	46
MINS	JAMES				48	IRELAND	CE	ENGLISH	SADLER	045	D	6	43
MINSHAW	HARRY				48	0	WM	GERMAN	F	044	C	1	12
MINTERN	HENRY				56	0	CN	ENGLISH	CARPENTER	043	B	4	23
MINTHAES	WILLIAM		1		45	U STATES	*QU	GERMAN	CARPENTER	043	D		84
MINTUN	PHEPE		1	1	11	0	QU	ENGLISH		043	B	5	5
MITCHEL		CATHARINE	1	1	40	IRELAND	WM	IRISH	SERVANT	045	A	2	30
MITCHEL	ALEX				26	0	CN	SCOTCH	LAB	043	E	2	46
MITCHEL	ALEXANER				41	SCOTLAND	CP	SCOTCH	F	043	A	3	29
MITCHEL	BETSY		1	1	19	0	CS	SCOT	SERVANT	044	B	4	17
MITCHEL	HENRY		1		7	0	CE	0		045	D	1	3
MITCHEL	JOHN			M	66	SCOTLAND	PS	SCOTCH	F	043	A	2	7
MITCHEL	LOUISA		1	1	9	0	CE	IRISH		045	D	1	2
MITCHEL	MARGARET		1	1	28	0	CE	IRISH		045	D	1	2
MITCHEL	MARY		1	1	7	ONTARIO	CP	SCOTCH		043	G	2	47
MITCHEL	MARY	JANE	1	1	49	IRELAND	WM	IRISH		045	D	4	5
MITCHEL	ROBERT			M	48	SCOTLAND	CP	SCOTCH	LABOURER	043	A	1	32
MITCHEL	SARAH		1	1	21	ENGLAND	CE	ENGLISH	INMATE	045	B	1	72
MITCHEL	WALTER				40	ENGLAND	CE	ENGLISH		044	C	3	66
MITCHEL	WILLIAM				47	0	OP	SCOTCH	LABOURER	043	A	3	4
MITCHEL	WILLIAM				48	IRELAND	PS	IRISH	BRICK MAKER	045	D	6	11
MITCHELL	ANDREW				58	SCOT	WM	SCOT	GENT	044	B	3	41
MITCHELL	ANNIE		1	1	16	0	WM	ENG	SERVANT	045	C	1	62
MITCHELL	BARTLETT				30	ONTARIO	CN	ENGLISH	LABORER	043	G	1	4
MITCHELL	CHARLES				50	ENG	CE	ENG	LAB	044	B	4	16
MITCHELL	CONIGAN				36	0	CN	IRISH	BRICKLAYER	043	B	3	5
MITCHELL	D				80	USA	BC	ENGLISH	LAB	043	H	2	43
MITCHELL	DAVID				56	SCOTLAND	CP	SCOTCH	FARMER	043	A	4	49
MITCHELL	DAVID		1		17	0	CE	ENGLISH		043	C		39
MITCHELL	DAVID				38	SCOTLAND	EM	SCOTCH	CARPENTER	043	D		75
MITCHELL	DRCURS				80	UNITED STATES	BC	ENGLISH	LABOURER	043	H	2	43
MITCHELL	GEORGE		1		55	ATLANTIC	CE	ENGLISH	LAB	043	B	5	3
MITCHELL	GRACE			1	76	SCOTLAND	CP	SCOTCH		044	B	6	35
MITCHELL	HUGH			M	35	SCOTLAND	PS	SCOTCH	FARMER	043	A	2	26
MITCHELL	JAMES				55	SCOTLAND	CP	SCOTCH	F	044	B	6	37
MITCHELL	JAMES				58	IRELAND	WM	IRISH	FARMER	045	A	2	2
MITCHELL	JAMES		1		87	IRELAND	CP	IRISH		045	D	3	29
MITCHELL	JANNET			1	45	SCOTLAND	CS	SCOTCH		044	B	6	12
MITCHELL	JOHN				37	SCOTLAND	WM	SCOTCH	CARPENTER	043	D		73
MITCHELL	JOHN				36	ENGLAND	PM	ENGLISH	FARMER	043	G	1	49
MITCHELL	JOHN				31	0	WM	IRISH	CARPENTER	044	B	5	15
MITCHELL	JOHN		1		27	SCOTLAND	CP	SCOTCH	FARM LABOURER	045	C	3	34
MITCHELL	JOSEPH				50	SCOTLAND	ME	SCOTCH	PAINTER	045	A	1	13
MITCHELL	MARGARET		1	1	8	0	CE	ENGLISH		044	B	6	23
MITCHELL	MATILDA		1	1	16	0	CE	ENGLISH		043	C		39
MITCHELL	NATHAN				41	0	BC	ENGLISH	F	043	H	2	51
MITCHELL	NATHAN				41	ONTARIO	BC	ENGLISH	FARMER	043	H	2	51
MITCHELL	NELSON				57	ONTARIO	CN	SCOTCH	FARMER	043	G	1	13
MITCHELL	ROBERT				36	SCOTLAND	CP	SCOTCH	F	044	B	6	35
MITCHELL	THOMAS				49	ENGLAND	CE	ENGLISH	FARMER	045	A	1	36
MITCHELL	WALTER		1		21	0	CE	ENGLISH		043	C		39
MITCHELL	WILLIAM		1		5	0	CE	ENGLISH		044	B	6	23
MITCHELL	WILLIAM				51	SCOTLAND	CS	SCOTCH	F	044	B	6	37
MITCHELL	WILLIAM	J			57	IRELAND	CP	IRISH	F	045	C	3	26
MITCHIL	CHARLES				61	ENGLAND	CE	ENGLISH		044	C	3	47
MOAT	JAMES	HUTTY			28	ENGLAND	WM	ENGLISH	F	044	A	3	3
MOAT	JOSEPH				44	ENGLAND	WM	ENGLISH	MILK SELLER	045	B	1	66
MOCLEAN	COL	ALLAN	2		88	QUEBEC	CE			045	C	1	D
MOFFAT	ALEXANDER				33	SCOTLAND	EM	SCOTCH	COOPER	043	E	1	5
MOFFAT	GEORGE				50	SCOTLAND	CP	SCOTCH	F	045	C	3	47
MOFFAT	JOSEPH	G			40	ENGLAND	CE	ENGLISH	LABORER	045	D	2	63
MOFFATT	ALEX				38	0	CE	ENG	HOTELKEEPER	045	C	1	58
MOFFATT	CHARLES				28	0	WM	ENGLISH	BUTCHER	045	B	2	16
MOFFATT	MARY		1	1	20	IRELAND	RC	IRISH		043	D		66
MOFFATT	ROBERT				60	ENGLAND	PR	ENGLISH	BRICKMAKER	045	A	1	16
MOFFITT	JAMES		1		28	IRELAND	WM	IRISH	CARPENTER	045	B	1	27
MOFFITT	WILLIAM		1		22	IRELAND	WM	IRISH	CARPENTER	045	B	1	27
MOGAR	LILLIAN		2	1		0	BA			043	A	6	D
MOGG	JOHN		1		62	ENGLAND	CE	ENGLISH	LAB	043	F		2
MOHANY	JEREMIAH				65	IRE	RC	IRE	F	045	C	1	10
MOHUN	JAMES				49	ENGLAND	CE	ENGLISH	TAILOR	044	A	3	26
MOLES	EDMUND				46	ENGLAND	CE	ENGLISH	F	043	B	5	33
MOLES	HENRY				45	ENGLAND	CE	ENGLISH	PEDLER	043	B	4	48
MOLSON	JOHN				50	ENGLAND	RP	ENGLISH	GENTLEMAN	044	C	3	24
MOMKINS	THOMAS		1		20	ENGLAND	CE	ENGLISH	LAB	045	B	2	4
MONAGAN	MARY		1	1	14	0	RC	IRISH	SERVANT	044	C	3	73
MONAGHAN	JOHN				25	IRELAND	RC	IRISH	LAB	044	C	3	21
MONCK	CHARLES		1		21	ENGLAND	CE	ENGLISH	FARM LABOURER	045	C	3	57
MONDEBANK	HIRAM				36	US	WM	GERMAN	F	044	C	4	79
MONEY	CHARLES		1		7	0	CS	ENGLISH		045	D	5	48
MONEY	EMMA		1	1	5	0	CS	ENGLISH		045	D	5	48
MONIGHAN	MARY		1	1	27	IRELAND	RC	IRISH	SERVANT	044	C	3	73
MONKMAN	GEORGE		1		20	0	PM	ENGLISH	F LAB	044	A	3	41
MONKMAN	GEORGE				61	ENGLAND	CE	ENGLISH	GENTLEMAN	045	D	1	5
MONKMAN	GEORGE				36	0	CE	ENGLISH	FARMER	045	D	2	24
MONKMAN	JANE			1	50	0	WM	ENGLISH		043	D		51
MONKMAN	WILLIAM				44	ENGLAND	CE	ENGLISH	F	044	C	2	26
MONRO	ALEXANDER		2		33	IRELAND	CE		CUSTOM HOUSE OFFICER	045	B	1	D
MONRO	CATHRINE				58	IRELAND	WM	IRISH		045	B	1	70
MONROE	JOHN				35	SCOTLAND	PS	SCOTCH	FARMER	043	G	2	4
MONTEATH	ROBERT				56	SCOTLAND	CP	SCOTCH	C PRESBYTERIAN MINIS	044	C	2	30
MONTGOMERY	ALEX R				35	0	WM	ENGLISH	BLACKSMITH	044	A	2	45
MONTGOMERY	GEORGE				39	IRELAND	CE	IRISH	LABORER	043	G	1	17
MONTGOMERY	JANE			1	57	ENGLAND	PM	ENGLISH		045	A	1	79
MONTGOMERY	JOHN				84	NEW BRUNSWICK	EM	SCOTCH		043	G	1	1

SURNAME	NAME1	NAME2	STRAY	SEX	AGE	BIRTHPL	RELIGION	ORIGIN	OCCUP	DIST	SUB_DIST	DIV	PAGE
MONTGOMERY	JOHN				40	0	CP	SCOTCH	BLACKSMITH	045	B	1	26
MONTGOMERY	JOSEPH			M	52	IRELAND	CE	IRISH	F	043	A	1	62
MONTGOMERY	ROBERT		1		45	SCOTLAND	CP	SCOTCH	F LAB	044	A	3	6
MONTGOMERY	ROBERT				46	IRELAND	PM	IRISH	LAB	045	A	1	89
MONTGOMERY	THOS				79	IRELAND	CE	IRISH	F	044	A	2	12
MONTGOMERY	WILLIAM		1		23	ONTARIO	FK	IRISH	MARINER	043	G	1	39
MOODIE	GEORGE		1		31	ENG	WM	ENG	F & DROVER	044	B	4	38
MOODIE	JANE		1	1	36	0	RC	IRISH	SERVANT	043	D		70
MOODY	ALEXANDER				40	SCOT	PS	SCOT	CARPENTER	044	B	2	36
MOODY	ISAAC				46	ENGLAND	CE	ENGLISH	CARPENTER	045	B	2	19
MOODY	JAMES				65	ENGLAND	PM	ENGLISH	F	044	B	6	21
MOODY	JOHN				56	ENGLAND	BA	ENGLISH	F	044	A	3	49
MOODY	JOHN				27	0	BA	ENGLISH	F	044	A	3	50
MOODY	LEUKE				30	0	WM	SCOTCH	F	043	A	6	56
MOODY	MARY		1	1	21	0	PM	ENGLISH	SERVANT	044	A	3	49
MOODY	ROBERT				29	0	BA	ENGLISH	F	044	A	3	50
MOODY	THOS				25	0	PM	ENGLISH	F	044	A	3	54
MOON	HENERY				27	0	CE	ENGLISH	F	045	C	2	17
MOON	JOSEPH				57	ENG	CE	ENG	HOTELKEEPER	045	C	1	2
MOON	THOMAS				30	IRE	WM	IRISH	SCHOOL TEACHER	044	B	4	43
MOON	THOMAS				55	ENGLAND	PM	ENGLISH	F	045	A	4	4
MOONEY	JOHN		1		18	0	PS	IRISH	FARM LAB	043	B	1	2
MOORBY	SAMUEL				42	ENGLAND	CE	ENGLISH	MERCHANT	045	D	2	64
MOORE	ABRAHAM			1	33	CANADA	CN	GERMAN		045	D	6	29
MOORE	ALVINA		1	1	19	0	WM	IRISH	SERVANT	045	D	5	72
MOORE	ANDREW		1		30	IRELAND	CP	IRISH	LAB	045	A	2	31
MOORE	ARCHIBALD				24	IRELAND	CP	IRISH	LAB	044	C	4	20
MOORE	CALVIN				33	0	CN	DUTCH	FARM SERVANT	043	E	1	29
MOORE	CAROLINE		1	1	4	0	WM	ENGLISH		043	D		67
MOORE	CAROLINE	S	1	1	15	0	WM	ENGLISH		044	C	2	2
MOORE	CHARLES		1		13	0	PS	IRISH	SERVANT	044	B	3	7
MOORE	DAVID				36	0	WM	IRISH	CARPENTER	043	H	1	17
MOORE	EDWARD		1		21	ENGLAND	CP	ENGLISH	FARM LAB	044	C	2	17
MOORE	ELEANOR			1	73	IRELAND	CE	IRISH		045	A	2	10
MOORE	ELIZA		1	1	45	IRELAND	WM	IRISH	SERVANT	045	B	1	71
MOORE	GEO	F			33	0	NC	IRISH	MERCHANT	043	C		10
MOORE	GEORGE	C			37	0	WM	IRISH	F	045	B	1	36
MOORE	GEORGE	Y			54	0	WM	SCOTCH	F	043	E	2	31
MOORE	HIRAM	JP			58	ONTARIO	CE	ENGLISH	LUMBERMAN	043	G	1	16
MOORE	JAMES				52	IRELAND	WM	IRISH	F	044	A	1	17
MOORE	JAMES		1		27	SCOTLAND	CP	SCOTCH	FARM LAB	044	C	2	33
MOORE	JOHN				36	0	CN	DUTCH	LAB	043	E	1	11
MOORE	JOHN				47	0	WM	SCOTCH	F	043	E	2	30
MOORE	JOHN				65	IRELAND	CE	IRISH	F	044	A	2	35
MOORE	JOHN				49	IRELAND	CP	IRISH	NO LABOURER	044	B	6	49
MOORE	JOHN		1		26	0	DI	ENGLISH		045	A	1	105
MOORE	MARIA		1	1	14	0	LU	GERMAN		045	D	1	39
MOORE	MARIAH		1	1	21	0	WM	IRISH		043	B	3	33
MOORE	MARY	JANE	2	1	28	0	CN			043	E	1	D
MOORE	MATILDA		1	1	65	CANADA	WM	IRISH		045	D	6	34
MOORE	MINNIE		1	1	17	0	WM	IRISH		044	B	1	5
MOORE	PATRICK				40	0	PS	IRE	WEAVER	044	B	3	10
MOORE	PETER	M			34	ONTARIO	CE	GERMAN	CARPENTER	043	G	1	54
MOORE	ROBERT				52	0	WM	ENGLISH	SAWYER	043	E	1	26
MOORE	ROBERT				43	IRELAND	CS	IRISH	LAB & F	043	F		18
MOORE	ROBERT				42	0	WM	IRISH	F	044	C	2	38
MOORE	SAMUEL				64	0	CN	DUTCH	F	043	E	1	11
MOORE	THOMAS				46	0	QU	IRISH	F	043	E	1	32
MOORE	THOMAS				62	IRELAND	CE	IRISH	F	044	A	1	37
MOORE	THOMAS	S			31	0	CE	IRISH	COOPER & BRICKLAYER	043	F		2
MOORE	WILLIAM				36	ONTARIO	CE	ENGLISH	CARPENTER	043	G	1	40
MOORE	WILLIAM	A			44	0	BA	IRISH	F	044	C	2	39
MOORING	ISAAC		1		16	0	CP	ENGLISH		045	C	2	18
MOORING	JAMES		1		12	0	CP	ENGLISH		045	C	2	18
MOORING	RICHARD				54	ENGLAND	CP	ENGLISH	F	045	C	2	18
MOORING	SARAH		1	1	18	0	CP	ENGLISH		045	C	2	18
MORAN	JAMES				58	IRELAND	CE	IRISH	SHOEMAKER	043	H	2	6
MORAN	JAMES				58	IRELAND	CE	IRISH	SHOEMAKER	043	H	2	6
MORAN	SIMON				50	IRELAND	RC	IRISH	LABOURER	045	D	3	53
MORAN	WILLIAM		1		13	US	RC	IRE		044	B	2	34
MORDEN	EMILINE		1	1	22	0	WM	ENGLISH	SERVANT	044	B	6	22
MORDEN	J	R			47	0	WM	SCOTCH	TAILOR	044	B	5	23
MORDEN	JACOB				64	0	EM	ENG	F	044	B	2	3
MORDEN	JAMES				37	ONTARIO	OB	IRISH	CARPENTER	043	G	1	45
MORE	HEZEKIAH				23	0	EM	IRISH	CARPENTER	045	D	5	50
MORE	MARY	JANE	1	1	2	0	CN	ENGLISH		045	D	5	59
MORE	PATRICK				60	IRELAND	RC	IRISH	LABO	044	C	3	29
MORE	SAMUEL				34	ENGLAND	BA	ENGLISH	LABOURER	043	B	3	48
MORE	WILLIAM		1		18	0	WM	IRISH	SERVANT	045	D	5	43
MOREAN	LAVINIA		1	1	31	0	CE	IRISH		044	A	2	35
MORELL	ALFRED		1		22	ONTARIO	WM	ENGLISH	LABORER	043	G	1	4
MORGAN	EDWARD				34	WEST INDIES	CE	WELSH	LAWYER	043	D		66
MORGAN	ELIZA	JANE	1	1	18	0	CE	IRISH		045	B	1	47
MORGAN	GEORGE				35	0	CP	IRISH	F	045	C	4	45
MORGAN	HUMPHRY		1		23	ENGLAND	CE	ENGLISH	CARPENTER	045	D	6	40
MORGAN	JAMES				45	IRELAND	CE	IRISH	F	045	C	3	45
MORGAN	JOHN				57	IRELAND	WM	IRISH	F	045	C	4	45
MORGAN	JOHN				47	0	CP	SCOTCH	FARMER	045	D	1	1
MORGAN	JOHN				48	IRELAND	CE	IRISH	F	044	C	2	34
MORGAN	RICHARD		1		13	0	CE	IRISH		044	A	2	35
MORGAN	SAM		1		26	0	WM	ENGLISH	F	044	B	5	52
MORGAN	SARAH	M		1	54	IRELAND	CE	IRISH		044	A	1	37
MORGAN	THOMAS				40	SCOTLAND	CS	SCOTCH	BLACKSMITH	045	D	3	78
MORGAN	WILLIAM		1		17	ENGLAND	CO	ENGLISH	F LAB	044	A	3	20
MORGAN	WILLIAM				42	0	CP	SCOTCH	F	044	B	1	3
MORIATY	JOHN				30	IRELAND	RC	IRISH	F	044	C	1	11
MORISON	EDWARD				45	0	PS	SCOT	LAB	044	B	2	64
MORLEY	CHARLES				40	ENGLAND	PM	ENGLISH	F	044	A	2	25
MORLEY	JOHN		1		18	QUEBEC	PR	ENGLISH	FARM LABORER	043	G	2	19
MORLEY	JOHN				73	ENGLAND	RC	ENGLISH	BRICKMAKER	045	A	1	9
MORLEY	ROBERT		1		43	ENGLAND	CE	ENGLISH	BOOT AND SHOEMAKER	045	A	1	64
MORLEY	WALTER				36	ENGLAND	CE	ENGLISH	BRICKMAKER	045	A	1	9
MORLEY	WILLIAM				41	ENGLAND	PM	ENGLISH	FARM LAB	043	B	1	13
MORLOCK	ROSA		1	1	22	0	CE	ENGLISH		043	D		85
MORLY	ROBERT		1	M	11	0	PS	SCOTCH		043	A	2	39
MORLY	THOMAS				37	ENGLAND	WM	ENGLISH	SHOEMAKER	045	D	3	43

SURNAME	NAME1	NAME2	STRAY	SEX	AGE	BIRTHPL	RELIGION	ORIGIN	OCCUP	DIST	SUB_DIST	DIV	PAGE
MORNING	ARTHUR				28	ENGLAND	CE	ENGLISH	LAB	045	A	2	2
MORRAIN	ANN			1	42	IRELAND	WM	IRISH	SEAMSTRESS	043	E	2	39
MORRAIN	JAMES		1		16	0	EM	IRISH		043	E	2	38
MORRIS	ANN			1	60	SCOTLAND	CS	SCOTCH		043	H	1	11
MORRIS	EVAN				34	WALES	WM	WELSH	CARPENTER	043	E	3	6
MORRIS	JOHN				35	ENGLAND	EM	ENGLISH	BUTCHER	043	D		58
MORRIS	LORINDA		1	1	17	0	MN	GERMAN		045	C	2	43
MORRIS	RICHARD				62	WALES	NC	WELSH	HARNESS MAKER	043	E	2	33
MORRIS	SAM'L				41	ENGLAND	CE	ENGLISH	LAB	043	F		28
MORRIS	WILLIAM			M	30	0	EM	GERMAN	TEAMSTER	043	A	1	69
MORRISH	JOHN				49	ENGLAND	DI	ENGLISH	F	045	C	2	21
MORRISON	ADAM				39	QUE	CE	SCOT	TEACHER	044	B	3	6
MORRISON	ANNIE		1	1	13	0	CE	IRISH		044	A	2	42
MORRISON	B	F			48	UNITED STATES	CN	SCOTCH	F	043	E	1	38
MORRISON	EDWARD		1		17	0	WM	ENGLISH	LABOURER	045	D	4	12
MORRISON	G	W			33	0	WM	ENGLISH	BLACKSMITH	043	C		25
MORRISON	GEORGE				42	SCOTLAND	UP	SCOTCH	FARM LABORER	045	D	1	15
MORRISON	JAMES				53	IRELAND	CP	IRISH	FARMER	045	A	2	28
MORRISON	JAMES				63	0	WM	SCOTCH	LABORER	045	D	1	51
MORRISON	JAMES				53	SCOTLAND	PS	SCOTCH	JUDGE OF QUEEN'S BEN	044	C	4	66
MORRISON	JAMES	H	2			0	UP			045	D	1	D
MORRISON	JANE		1	1	8	0	CE	IRISH		044	A	2	42
MORRISON	JOHN				37	SCOT	CS	SCOT	F	045	C	1	29
MORRISON	LEWIS		1		61	SCOTLAND	PS	SCOTCH	FARM LABOURER	045	C	3	9
MORRISON	MARY		1	1	10	0	CE	IRISH		044	A	2	42
MORRISON	PETER				23	0	CP	SCOTCH	LAB	043	E	2	47
MORRISON	PETER				36	NS	CS	SCOT	LAB	044	B	4	14
MORRISON	SAMUEL				58	0	EM	SCOTCH	EPISCOPAL MINISTER	045	D	2	25
MORRISON	SARAH		1	1	35	0	CE	DUTCH		044	A	2	42
MORRISON	THOMAS		1		70	IRELAND	RC	IRISH	LAB	044	A	3	27
MORRISS	BENNETT		2		28	0	NG			043	E	2	D
MORRISS	JOHN				64	UNITED STATES	ZZ	WELSH	TINSMITH	043	E	2	38
MORROW	ANDREW				70	IRE	CS	IRISH		044	B	4	45
MORROW	ARCH'D				35	0	WM	IRISH	F	044	B	4	48
MORROW	GEORGE	L	2		0	0	CE			044	C	2	D
MORROW	MARTHA		1	1	74	0	OB	IRISH		044	A	2	8
MORROW	MARTHA		2	1	29	0	WM			044	B	4	D
MORROW	RICHARD				60	IRELAND	CE	IRISH	FARM MANAGER	044	C	2	47
MORROW	WILLIAM				37	IRELAND	NC	IRISH	LABORER	043	G	1	39
MORROW	WILLIAM		1		42	0	OB	IRISH	F	044	A	2	8
MORSE	ELIZABETH			1	64	ENGLAND	PM	ENGLISH		045	A	1	88
MORTIMER	ANN	MARIA	1	1	10	ENGLAND	CE	ENGLISH		043	D		17
MORTIMER	PHILIP				43	SCOTLAND	CE	ENGLISH	CABINET MAKER	045	A	1	42
MORTIMER	WM				64	ENGLAND	NC	ENGLISH	LAB	043	C		18
MORTLEY	JOHN				37	0	CE	ENGLAND	CARPENTER	045	D	2	13
MORTLEY	SUSANNAH			1	39	0	TU	ENGLISH		045	D	2	66
MORTON	ANDREW			M	69	SCOTLAND	PS	SCOTCH	WEAVER	043	A	1	38
MORTON	DARIUS				50	0	CN	ENGLISH	HOTEL KEEPER	043	H	1	6
MORTON	EDWARD				65	0	CE	ENGLISH	F	043	E	1	47
MORTON	FRANCIS				42	ONTARIO	CN	ENGLISH	FARMER	043	G	1	6
MORTON	FRANCIS	J			27	ONTARIO	CN	ENGLISH	FARMER	043	G	1	30
MORTON	FRIEND				52	UNITED STATES	CE	ENGLISH	FARMER	043	G	2	31
MORTON	IRA		1		24	ONTARIO	PR	SCOTCH	LABORER	043	G	2	27
MORTON	JAMES		1		27	ONTARIO	CN	ENGLISH	FARMER	043	G	1	29
MORTON	JEREMIAH				35	0	CP	ENGLISH	F	043	B	2	31
MORTON	JOHN				29	ONTARIO	PR	SCOTCH	FARMER	043	G	2	26
MORTON	JOHN				56	UNITED STATES	CN	ENGLISH	FARMER	043	G	2	32
MORTON	LAVINA		2	1	39	ONTARIO	CN			043	G	1	D
MORTON	MARGARET		1	1	26	0	CS	SCOTCH	DRESSMAKER	043	D		69
MORTON	MARGARET		1	1	27	0	CS	SCOTCH	MILLINER	043	D		86
MORTON	MARY			1	64	0	CS	ENGLISH		043	A	1	1
MORTON	MARY		1	1	20	0	CP	ENGLISH		043	H	1	2
MORTON	RACHEL		1	1	23	ENGLAND	CE	ENGLISH	SERVANT	044	A	3	24
MORTON	REBECCA		1	1	95	ONTARIO	CN	IRISH		043	G	1	38
MORTON	RELIEF		1	1	78	USA	BC	ENGLISH		043	H	2	47
MORTON	RICHARD				51	0	CN	IRISH	F	043	H	1	14
MORTON	ROBERT			M	52	IRELAND	WM	IRISH	FARMER	043	A	1	20
MORTON	RUSSEL				47	USA	OP	SCOTCH	F	043	H	2	43
MORTON	RUSSELL				47	UNITED STATES	CS	SCOTCH	FARMER	043	H	2	43
MORTON	SAMUEL		1		83	USA	BC	ENGLISH		043	H	2	47
MORTON	SAMUEL		1		83	UNITED STATES	BC	ENGLISH		043	H	2	47
MORTON	SAVILLE				28	0	CE	ENGLISH	F	043	E	1	53
MORTON	SHEPPARD				39	ONTARIO	CN	ENGLISH	FARMER	043	G	1	56
MORTON	SIMEON				35	0	CN	ENGLISH	FARMER	043	B	3	49
MORTON	TIMOTHY				24	ONTARIO	WM	ENGLISH	LABORER	043	G	1	57
MORTON	WILLIAM				48	IRELAND	CE	IRISH	FARMER	045	A	2	19
MORTSON	JOSEPH				33	0	PM	ENGLISH	FARMER	045	D	2	68
MORTSON	MATHEW				37	0	PM	ENG	F	044	B	2	51
MORTSON	THOMAS				40	0	PM	ENGLISH	FARMER	045	D	2	20
MOSBY	CATHERINE		1	1	7	0	CE	ENGLISH		045	A	3	27
MOSGROVE	MARY		2	1	21	0	WM		SPINSTER	045	A	1	D
MOSGROVE	RICHARD				57	IRELAND	WM	IRISH	LABOURER	045	A	1	50
MOSHER	JOHN		1		82	0	PS	IRISH	CARPENTER	043	E	3	51
MOSHER	JOHN				44	0	CP	SCOTCH	TEAMSTER	045	C	2	14
MOSHOR	ARCH	J			43	NS	PS	IRISH	CARPENTER	043	F		6
MOSIER	ALONZO				29	0	CE	GERMAN	TEAMSTER	043	D		32
MOSIER	CHARLES		1		17	US	CP	SCOT	FARM LAB	044	B	1	27
MOSIER	HENRY				45	0	CE	ENGLISH	FARMER & LUMBERMAN	043	E	1	47
MOSIER	JOHN				42	0	CE	GERMAN	CARPENTER	043	D		34
MOSIER	MINERVA		1	1	13	0	EM	ENG		044	B	1	29
MOSIER	THOMAS				84	0	CE	ENGLISH	BAKER	043	D		75
MOSLEY	JAMES				53	0	CE	ENGLISH	F	043	C		38
MOSS	DAVID				30	IRELAND	RP	IRISH	F	043	B	5	23
MOSSINGTON	ALBERT				28	0	CE	ENGLISH	F	043	H	2	4
MOSSINGTON	ALBERT				28	ONTARIO	CE	ENGLISH	FARMER	043	H	2	4
MOSSINGTON	ELIZABETH	G		1	52	0	CE	ENGLISH		043	H	2	9
MOSSINGTON	ELIZABETH	G		1	52	ONTARIO	CE	ENGLISH		043	H	2	9
MOSSINGTON	MOSES				68	ENGLAND	CE	ENGLISH	FARMER	043	G	2	39
MOTSAS	STERENSARA		1	1	59	GERMANY	RC	GERMAN	SERVANT	045	A	1	78
MOTT	CANDES		1	1	69	QUEBEC	RC	FRENCH		043	H	2	7
MOTTON	WILLIAM				40	ENGLAND	WM	ENGLISH	FARMER	045	D	3	10
MOTTS	ELIZABETH		1	1	63	0	PM	IRISH	HOUSE SERVANT	043	B	5	7
MOTTS	LOUISA		1		14	0	PM	GERMAN		043	B	5	7
MOULDEN	BILL		1		30	U STATES	CE	IRISH	MOULDER	044	B	5	20
MOULDS	JOHN				53	ENGLAND	CP	ENGLISH	FARMER	043	G	2	44
MOULDS	WILLIAM				43	ENGLAND	CE	ENGLISH	FARMER	043	G	2	44

SURNAME	NAME1	NAME2	STRAY	SEX	AGE	BIRTHPL	RELIGION	ORIGIN	OCCUP	DIST	SUB_DIST	DIV	PAGE
MOUNSEY	THOS				56	SCOTLAND	PS	SCOTCH	F	044	B	5	55
MOUNT	JOHN		1	M	11	0	CE	ENGLAND		043	A	5	4
MOUNT	LOUIS				37	U STATES	CN	IRISH	F	043	A	6	43
MOUNTAIN	ANN		1	1	78	ENGLAND	PM	ENGLISH		045	B	1	42
MOUNTFORD	WM		1		28	ENGLAND	CE	ENGLISH	IRON FINISHER	044	B	5	20
MOWAT	JOHN				49	SCOTLAND	CP	SCOTCH	CARPENTER	045	B	1	30
MOWAT	THOMAS				46	SCOTLAND	PS	SCOTCH	LABOURER	043	B	3	65
MOWDER	HENRY				49	0	QU	GERMAN	F	043	B	4	46
MOWDER	JOSEPH				84	UNITED STATES	WM	GERMAN	F	043	B	4	17
MOWDER	JOSEPH				40	0	QU	GERMAN	F	043	B	4	45
MOWDER	WILLIAM				45	0	QU	GERMAN	F	043	B	4	17
MOYLAN	HANNAH		1	1	70	IRELAND	RC	ENGLISH		044	C	2	25
MOYLAN	JAMES		2		71	IRELAND	RC		LAB	044	C	2	D
MOYLAN	PATRICK				30	IRE	RC	IRE	BLACKSMITH	044	B	2	24
MOYLE	JAMES				70	IRELAND	CP	IRISH	TAILOR	045	C	4	25
MOYNIHAN	DENNIS				39	IRELAND	RC	IRISH	LAB	044	C	2	46
MOYNIHAN	HANNAH		1	1	20	IRELAND	RC	IRISH		044	C	2	2
MOYNIHAN	HANNAH		1	1	20	IRELAND	RC	IRISH	SERVANT	044	C	2	20
MOYNIHAN	JOHN				28	IRELAND	RC	IRISH	LAB	044	C	2	2
MUIR	AGNES		1	1	29	0	PS	SCOTCH	SERVANT	045	C	3	54
MUIR	ARCH				80	SCOT	CS	SCOT	F	045	C	1	28
MUIR	ARCH				26	0	CP	SCOT	F	045	C	1	11
MUIR	DOUGLAS		1		16	SCOTLAND	CS	SCOTCH	FARMER	045	D	3	16
MUIR	JAMES		1		29	QUE	CE	SCOTCH	LAWYER	045	A	1	80
MUIR	JOHN		1		5	0	PS	SCOTCH		045	C	3	54
MUIR	JOHN		1		38	SCOTLAND	PS	SCOTCH	SERVANT	045	C	3	54
MUIR	JOHN				49	SCOTLAND	CP	SCOTCH	FARM MANAGER	044	C	2	5
MUIR	MARY		1	1	11	0	CS	SCOTCH		045	D	3	16
MUIR	WILLIAM				64	SCOTLAND	CP	SCOTCH	MERCHANT	045	C	2	4
MUIRHEAD	JAMES				48	SCOTLAND	CP	SCOTCH	FARMER	045	A	3	37
MUIRHEAD	NORMAN		1		11	0	WM	ENGLISH		045	D	3	26
MUIRHEAD	WILLIAM		2		5	0	CP			045	A	3	D
MULBERRY	JOHN				65	IRELAND	CS	IRISH	LAB	043	E	2	79
MULBURY	JAMES				22	NS	WM	IRISH	LAB	043	B	4	48
MULBY	ROBERT		1		28	IRELAND	CE	IRISH	MACHINIST	045	D	5	31
MULDOWNEY	JAMES				40	IRELAND	RC	IRISH		045	B	1	58
MULEACHY	MICHAEL				30	IRELAND	RC	IRISH	MOULDER	043	D		37
MULHALL	WILLIAM				67	IRELAND	RC	IRISH	F	045	C	2	36
MULHOLLAND	DAVID				60	0	WM	IRISH	F	045	A	4	10
MULHOLLAND	JOHN				37	IRE	PS	IRE	COOPER	044	B	2	50
MULHOLLAND	THOMAS				54	0	WM	IRISH	F	044	C	2	41
MULHOLLAND	WILLIAM				62	ONT	WM	IRISH	F	045	A	4	6
MULLANEY	MARY ANN			1	42	0	DI	IRISH		044	C	2	5
MULLEN	ALEXANDER				49	IRELAND	CP	IRISH	F	044	B	6	53
MULLEY	WILLIAM				30	ENGLAND	WM	ENGLISH	STONE CUTTER	045	A	1	21
MULLIGAN	MARTHA			1	40	IRELAND	CE	IRISH		043	A	6	65
MULLINS	JOHN		1		62	IRELAND	CE	IRISH	LAB	044	C	4	28
MULONEY	JAMES				69	IRELAND	RC	IRISH	LAB	044	C	4	34
MULONEY	PATRICK				48	IRELAND	RC	IRISH	LAB	044	C	4	49
MULONEY	TIMOTHY				66	IRELAND	RC	IRISH	LAB	044	C	4	34
MULVEY	FRANCIS				45	IRELAND	RC	IRELAND	LAB	043	C		48
MUMFORD	JOSEPH				44	ENGLAND	CE	ENGLISH	BUTCHER	044	C	3	1
MUNDEY	JOSEPH				38	ENGLAND	WM	ENGLISH	BLACKSMITH	045	D	1	6
MUNDEY	SARAH	A	2	1	6	0	WM			045	D	1	D
MUNDLE	WILLIAM				40	SCOTLAND	CE	SCOTCH	LAB	043	B	1	4
MUNDY	THOMAS				32	ENGLAND	PM	ENGLISH	TEAMSTER	044	C	4	24
MUNN	CHARLES				31	ENGLAND	CE	IRISH		044	C	3	40
MUNN	JAMES				25	QUEBEC	WM	SCOTCH	WATCH MAKER	045	B	1	1
MUNNS	JOHN				23	0	WM	IRISH	STORE KEEPER	045	D	3	80
MUNNS	WILLIAM				63	IRELAND	WM	IRISH	F	043	A	6	56
MUNRO	DONALD				72	SCOTLAND	OP	SCOTCH	F	043	H	2	44
MUNRO	DONALD		1		72	SCOTLAND	CS	SCOTCH	FARMER	043	H	2	44
MUNRO	JOHN		1		29	0	WM	ENGLISH	F	045	C	2	32
MUNRO	ROBERT				57	SCOTLAND	CP	SCOTCH	SHOEMAKER	045	A	4	29
MUNRO	WILLIAM				37	SCOTLAND	CP	SCOTCH		045	B	1	15
MUNROE	CATHARINE			F	61	SCOTLAND	PS	SCOTCH		043	A	2	35
MUNROE	MARGARET		1	1	60	SCOTLAND	CP	SCOTCH		045	C	1	43
MUNROE	WILLIAM	L			44	0	WM	ENGLISH	FARMER	045	D	2	44
MUNSHAW	NATHAN				26	0	WM	GERMAN	FARM LABORER	045	D	1	19
MUNSHAW	NICLAS				48	0	WM	ENGLISH	F	045	A	4	11
MUNSHAW	REBECCA			1	67	0	WM	GERMAN	FARMER	045	D	1	19
MUNSHAW	THOMAS				40	0	WM	GER	F	044	B	2	2
MUNSHAW	WILLIAM				44	0	WM	GERMAN	F	044	B	1	3
MUNSHAW	WILLIAM				32	0	PS	GER	BLACKSMITH	044	B	2	2
MUNSIE	WILLIAM				36	SCOTLAND	CP	SCOTCH	MERCHANT	043	A	3	7
MURDOCH	JAMES				60	SCOTLAND	CP	SCOTCH	FARM LABOURER	045	C	3	57
MURDOCK	JAMES				52	SCOTLAND	CP	SCOTCH	LAB	045	C	2	15
MURDY	JOSEPH				77	IRELAND	CE	IRISH	LAB	044	C	3	12
MUREHEAD	ALEXANDER				84	SCOTLAND	CP	SCOTCH	FARMER	045	A	3	32
MURISON	WILLIAM				45	SCOTLAND	CP	SCOTCH	F	045	C	2	39
MURONEY	JOHN				60	IRELAND	RC	IRISH	F	044	C	4	4
MURONEY	JOHN				63	IRELAND	RC	IRISH	GARDNER	044	C	4	37
MURPHEY	ANNA		1	1	26	IRELAND	RC	IRISH	SERVANT	045	B	2	30
MURPHY	ALEXANDER				35	IRELAND	CE	IRISH	ACCOUNTANT	045	B	1	4
MURPHY	BRIDGET		1	1	40	IRELAND	RC	IRISH	SERVANT	044	A	1	40
MURPHY	CATHERINE		1	1	18	0	CE	IRISH		044	C	3	43
MURPHY	DANIEL				40	IRELAND	RC	IRISH	F	043	B	1	4
MURPHY	DANIEL				60	IRELAND	RC	IRISH	F	043	B	2	12
MURPHY	ED	T			34	IRELAND	RC	IRISH	CONTRACTOR	043	D		26
MURPHY	EDWARD				49	IRE	RC	IRE	F	044	B	4	4
MURPHY	ELIZABETH		1	1	70	IRE	RC	IRE		044	B	3	18
MURPHY	ELLEN			1	35	IRELAND	RC	IRISH		044	C	4	16
MURPHY	HUGH				56	IRELAND	RC	IRISH	F	043	H	1	13
MURPHY	JAMES				63	IRE	RC	IRE	LAB	044	B	3	10
MURPHY	JOHN				38	IRELAND	RC	IRISH	LAB	043	F		4
MURPHY	JOHN				28	0	RC	ENGLISH	BEAMSMAN	043	F		5
MURPHY	JOHN				39	IRE	RC	IRE	LAB	044	B	3	12
MURPHY	JOHN				18	USA	RC	IRISH		045	A	1	50
MURPHY	JOHN				34	IRE	RC	IRE	STATION MASTER	045	C	1	49
MURPHY	JOSEPH		1		19	0	RC	IRISH	LAB	043	F		5
MURPHY	MARY		1	1	55	IRELAND	RC	IRISH		045	A	1	50
MURPHY	MICHAEL			M	46	IRELAND	RC	IRISH	CARPENTER	043	A	2	14
MURPHY	MICHAEL		1		12	0	CP	IRISH		044	A	1	30
MURPHY	PATRICK				50	IRELAND	RC	IRISH	F	043	B	2	37
MURPHY	PATRICK				50	IRELAND	RC	IRISH	LABORER	044	A	2	39
MURPHY	PATRICK				58	IRELAND	RC	IRISH	LABORER	045	D	2	35

SURNAME	NAME1	NAME2	STRAY	SEX	AGE	BIRTHPL	RELIGION	ORIGIN	OCCUP	DIST	SUB_DIST	DIV	PAGE
MURPHY	RICHARD				58	IRELAND	RC	IRISH	F	043	A	3	26
MURPHY	RICHARD				48	IRELAND	RC	IRISH	LAB	044	A	3	38
MURPHY	THOMAS				50	IRELAND	RC	IRISH	LAB	043	E	1	4
MURPHY	THOMAS		1		20	0	RC	IRISH	TEAMSTER	043	F		23
MURPHY	THOMAS				75	IRELAND	RC	IRISH	F	043	H	2	39
MURPHY	THOMAS				75	IRELAND	RC	IRISH	FARMER	043	H	2	39
MURPHY	WILLIAM				52	0	PM	IRISH		045	A	4	16
MURRAY	ANNE		1	1	18	ENGLAND	RC	IRISH		045	A	2	8
MURRAY	CATHARINE			1	65	SCOTLAND	CE	SCOTCH		044	A	1	40
MURRAY	DAVID				51	US	LU	GER	F	044	B	4	25
MURRAY	ELIZABETH		1	1	92	SCOTLAND	CP	SCOTCH		043	A	4	29
MURRAY	ELLEN		2	1	64	IRELAND	RC			045	A	2	D
MURRAY	ELLEN			1	60	ENGLAND	CE	ENGLISH		045	B	2	26
MURRAY	GIDEON				55	SCOTLAND	CP	SCOTCH	F	044	C	2	35
MURRAY	ISAAC				48	US	LU	GER	F	044	B	4	33
MURRAY	JAMES				71	IRELAND	RC	IRISH	FARMER	045	A	2	18
MURRAY	JAMES				63	IRELAND	RC	IRISH	LAB	044	C	2	18
MURRAY	JANE		1	1	65	SCOTLAND	CS	SCOTCH		043	A	3	27
MURRAY	JOHN		1		99	SCOTLAND	CP	SCOTCH		043	A	4	29
MURRAY	JOHN		1		30	SCOTLAND	PS	SCOTCH	SERVANT	044	C	4	69
MURRAY	JOSEPH			M	34	0	PS	SCOTCH	F	043	A	2	15
MURRAY	MARY		1	1	26	0	CS	SCOTCH		043	A	3	27
MURRAY	MERSAH			1	60	IRE	WM	IRE		044	B	3	12
MURRAY	ROBERT		1		23	QUE	WM	ENGLISH	LABOURER	043	A	3	4
MURRAY	ROBERT				40	SCOTLAND	CS	SCOTCH	WHEELWRIGHT	043	D		32
MURRAY	WILLIAM		1		40	IRELAND	CE	IRISH	LAB	044	C	4	78
MURRELL	JOHN				24	0	WM	ENGLISH	FARMER	045	D	1	43
MURRY	FRANK		1	M	13	0	CP	SCOTCH		043	A	2	24
MURRY	JOHN				39	SCOTLAND	CP	SCOTCH		045	A	4	20
MURTON	ALFRED		1		14	0	WM	ENGLISH	APPRENTICE	044	A	2	51
MURTON	JOSEPH				32	ENGLAND	CE	ENGLISH	F	045	C	2	12
MURTON	THOMAS				70	ENGLAND	WM	ENGLISH	LAB	044	C	1	9
MUSK	JOHN		1		24	ENGLAND	CE	ENGLISH	BRICK MAKER	045	A	1	26
MUSSELMAN			2			0	BA			043	B	3	D
MUSSELMAN	CHRISTIAN				31	0	LU	GER	F	044	B	3	34
MUSSELMAN	DAVID				41	0	BA	GERMAN	FARMER	043	B	3	5
MUSSELMAN	ELIZA		1	1	15	0	MN	GERMAN	SERVANT	045	D	5	42
MUSSELMAN	JACOB				33	0	WM	GERMAN	LABOURER	043	B	3	41
MUSSELMAN	MIKE				33	0	CN	GERMAN	FARMER	043	B	3	1
MUSSELMAN	PETER				67	0	MN	GER	F	044	B	3	34
MUSSELMAN	SAMUEL				40	0	CE	GERMAN	DENTIST	045	D	5	7
MUSSELMAN	W	H			21	ONTARIO	BA	GERMAN	LABOURER	043	B	3	4
MUSSELMAN	WILLIAM				70	UNITED STATES	CN	GERMAN	FARMER	043	B	3	2
MUSSELMAN	WILLIAM				35	0	CN	GERMAN	TEAMSTER	043	B	5	19
MUSSLEMAN	ANDREW				25	0	BA	GERMAN	F	043	B	2	14
MUSSON	EDWARD				64	ENGLAND	CE	ENGLISH	F	044	A	2	5
MUSSON	EDWARD	JR			34	0	CE	ENGLISH	STORE KEEPER FARMER	044	C	3	44
MUSSON	THOS				39	0	CE	ENGLISH	BOOKEEPER	044	A	2	12
MUSTARD	ALEXANDER				61	CANADA	PS	SCOTCH	FARMER	045	D	6	71
MUSTARD	JAMES				57	0	CP	SCOTCH	FARMER	045	D	4	40
MUSTARD	JAMES				32	CANADA	CP	SCOTCH	FARMER	045	D	6	32
MUSTARD	JOHN				59	0	CP	SCOTCH	FARMER	045	D	4	24
MUSTARD	PETER				64	CANADA	PS	SCOTCH	FARMER	045	D	6	31
MUSTARD	WILLIAM				59	0	CP	SCOTCH	FARMER	045	D	4	25
MUTART	HORATIO				41	QUEBEC	BC	GERMAN	F	043	H	2	40
MUTART	HORATIS				41	QUEBEC	BC	GERMAN	FARMER	043	H	2	40
MYER	LUCINDA		1	1	15	CANADA	MN	GERMAN		045	D	6	39
MYERS	ALFRED		2			ONTARIO	CE			043	H	2	D
MYERS	ALFRED		2			0	CE			043	H	2	D
MYERS	HENRY				41	GERMANY	MN	GERMAN	LAB	043	B	2	17
MYERS	ROBERT				28	0	CE	ENGLISH	F	045	A	4	15
MYERS	WILLIAM				36	ENG	CE	ENG	HARNESS MAKER	044	B	2	10
MYRES	ULRICK				42	SWITZERLAND	CE	DUTCH	LAB	043	H	2	9
MYRES	ULRICK				42	SWITZERLAND	CE	DUTCH	LABOURER	043	H	2	9
NAIDAS	DAVID				30	ENGLAND	WM	ENGLISH	ENGINE DRIVER	044	C	3	39
NAIRN	MRS		1	1	54	IRELAND	RC	IRISH		044	B	6	55
NAISMITH	JOHN				36	SCOTLAND	RP	SCOTCH	FARMER	044	C	3	70
NANTON	EDWARD				47	ENGLAND	CE	ENGLISH	BROKER	045	A	1	47
NAOND	JANET		1	1	12	SCOTLAND	CP	SCOTCH		045	D	2	57
NASH	EUGENE			M	31	US	NG	ENGLISH	MILLER	043	A	2	24
NASH	JAMES				58	ENGLAND	BA	ENGLISH	LAB	043	B	2	18
NASH	JOHN				57	ENGLAND	FW	ENGLISH	PHYSICIAN	043	D		13
NASH	JOHN				28	0	WM	GERMAN	BOILER MAKER	044	B	5	4
NASH	ROBERT		1		21	0	CP	ENGLISH	FARM SERVANT	045	C	3	33
NASH	ROBERT				54	NS	RC	ENGLISH	F	045	A	4	1
NASH	WILLIAM				60	NS	RC	IRISH	F	045	C	3	15
NASON	WILLIAM				51	ENGLAND	WM	ENGLISH	MERCHANT	044	C	3	13
NATRESS	WILLIAM		1		19	0	WM	ENGLISH	SCHOOL TEACHER	044	B	6	33
NATTRASS	JOHN				31	0	UP	ENGLISH	SCHOOL TEACHER	044	B	5	57
NATTRESS	ISAAC				35	0	PM	ENGLISH	F	044	B	5	77
NAUGHTON	JOHN				27	IRE	RC	IRE	STORE KEEPER	044	B	2	47
NAYLON	JOHN				33	IRELAND	RC	IRISH	AGENT	043	D		4
NAYLON	PATRICK				70	IRELAND	RC	IRISH	LAB	043	D		40
NEAL	GEORGE				74	ENGLAND	CE	ENGLISH	LAB	045	C	2	19
NEAL	JOHN				45	ENGLAND	CN	ENGLAND	LAB	043	B	5	14
NEAL	WILLIAM				40	0	WM	ENGLISH	CARPENTER	043	B	4	2
NEBLETT	CHARLES	T	1		9	USA	ME	ENGLISH		045	A	1	46
NEEDHAM	EDWD		1		55	ENGLAND	CE	ENGLISH	FARM LAB	044	A	2	52
NEEDMAN	RICHARD				68	ENG	CE	ENG	SECT FOREMAN GTR	045	C	1	45
NEIGHSWNDER	DAVID				59	U STATES	MN	GERMAN	FARMER	045	D	6	63
NEIL	CHARLES		1		40	ENGLAND	CE	ENGLISH	SERVANT	045	B	2	2
NEIL	CHARLES		1		50	ENGLAND	WM	ENGLISH	SERVANT	044	C	1	19
NEIL	JAMES				38	IRELAND	CP	IRISH	FARMER	045	D	6	2
NEIL	MATILDA		1	1	22	0	CE	ENGLISH		045	B	1	20
NEILL	ELVIRA			1	60	IRELAND	CE	IRISH	LABOURER	044	C	1	29
NEILL	O	MICHAEL			56	IRELAND	RC	IRISH	F	043	A	3	33
NEILSON	ALEX		1		25	0	CS	SCOT		045	C	1	28
NEILSON	ALEX				65	SCOT	CP	SCOT	F	045	C	1	3
NEILSON	ELLEN		1	1	40	SCOT	CS	SCOT		045	C	1	28
NEILSON	JOHN				51	SCOT	CP	SCOT	F	045	C	1	3
NEILSON	ROBERT				28	0	CP	SCOT	F	045	C	1	3
NEILSON	ROBT		1		22	0	CS	SCOT		045	C	1	28
NEILSON	SAMUEL				36	IRELAND	CE	IRISH	FARM LABOURER	045	C	3	11
NEISWANDER	JOSEPH		1		14	CANADA	MN	GERMAN		045	D	6	64
NELLIS	THOMAS				60	IRELAND	RC	IRISH	FARMER	043	B	4	13
NELSON	CATHERINE			1	40	IRELAND	RC	IRISH	SERVANT	045	A	3	34

SURNAME	NAME1	NAME2	STRAY	SEX	AGE	BIRTHPL	RELIGION	ORIGIN	OCCUP	DIST	SUB_DIST	DIV	PAGE
NELSON	CLAYTON		1	M	32	0	QU	DUTCH	L	043	A	2	55
NELSON	EMANUEL				38	ENGLAND	PM	ENGLISH	F	043	E	2	26
NELSON	HENRY				37	ENGLAND	PM	ENGLISH	F	043	E	2	68
NELSON	HENRY		1		44	ENG	CE	ENG	LAB	044	B	2	47
NELSON	JAMES				42	ENGLAND	CE	ENGLISH	F	043	E	2	65
NELSON	JEREMIAH				34	ENGLAND	WM	ENGLISH	FARMER	045	A	2	7
NELSON	JOHN				42	SCOTLAND	OP	SCOTCH	F	043	H	2	45
NELSON	JOHN				42	SCOTLAND	CS	SCOTCH	FARMER	043	H	2	45
NELSON	JOHN				54	ENG	WM	ENG	F	044	B	4	2
NELSON	MARY	A		1	51	0	BA	GERMAN		043	B	3	41
NELSON	THOMAS				50	IRELAND	RC	IRISH	F	043	A	6	48
NELSON	WILLIAM				26	0	CN	IRISH	FARM LABOURER	043	B	3	68
NELSON	WILLIAM				38	IRELAND	WM	IRISH	PAINTER & GLAZIER	045	B	1	49
NESBET	HUGH				29	IRISH	CE	IRISH	LABOURER	044	C	3	43
NESBIT	GEORGE				44	IRELAND	PS	IRISH	FARMER	043	B	3	40
NESBIT	JAMES				35	IRELAND	PM	IRISH	LABOURER	043	B	3	33
NESBIT	ROBERT		1		30	IRELAND	BA	IRISH	FARMER	043	B	3	48
NESBIT	SAMUEL		1		26	IRELAND	BA	IRISH	FARMER	043	B	3	48
NESBITT	ANN		1	1	70	IRELAND	BA	IRISH		043	B	3	59
NESBITT	WILLIAM		1		17	0	PM	IRISH	CARPENTER	043	B	2	22
NESBITT	WILLIAM		1		35	IRELAND	CN	IRISH	FARM LABOURER	043	B	3	71
NESS	JAMES				35	SCOT	PS	SCOT	CARPENTER	044	B	2	38
NESS	JOHN				42	ENG	PM	ENG	F LAB	044	B	1	51
NESS	MARSHALL		1		22	ENG	CE	ENG	SERVANT	044	B	3	11
NEVILLE	HENRY				65	ENGLAND	CE	ENGLISH	MILLER	045	D	4	43
NEVIN	THOMAS		1		19	CANADA	PS	ENGLISH	LABORER	045	D	6	70
NEWALL	HOMER				56	SCOTLAND	PS	SCOTCH	SHOEMAKER	045	C	3	30
NEWBERRY	JAMES				68	HALIFAX	PM	ENGLISH	GARDNER	044	C	4	87
NEWBERRY	JOHN		2		39	ENGLAND	CE		FARMER	045	D	2	D
NEWBERRY	ROBERT				26	ENGLAND	CE	ENGLISH	PHOTOGRAPHER	043	C		25
NEWBERY	GEORGE				32	ENGLAND	CE	ENGLISH	FARMER	045	D	2	33
NEWBERY	MARY			1	65	ENGLAND	CE	ENGLISH	FARMER	045	D	2	33
NEWBURN	JOHN				57	IRELAND	CE	IRISH	FARMER	043	G	2	50
NEWBURN	RICHARD				72	ENGLAND	CE	ENGLISH	F	044	A	1	25
NEWBURN	THOMAS				40	IRELAND	CE	IRISH	BLACKSMITH	043	H	2	5
NEWBURN	THOMAS				40	IRELAND	CE	IRISH	BLACKSMITH	043	H	2	5
NEWBURN	WILLIAM				24	ONTARIO	PR	IRISH	FARMER	043	G	2	53
NEWELL	CHARLES	A	1		51	UNITED STATES	OP	FRENCH	LUMBER INSPECTOR	043	D		1
NEWELL	LOUISA		1	1	48	ENGLAND	CE	ENGLISH		043	D		1
NEWLOVE	JOHN				48	ENGLAND	WM	ENGLISH	F	044	A	2	36
NEWLOVE	JOSEPH		1		70	ENGLAND	EM	ENGLAND		045	D	2	15
NEWLOVE	MARGARET		1	1	65	ENGLAND	EM	ENGLAND		045	D	2	15
NEWLOVE	WILLIAM				23	0	WM	ENGLISH	F	044	A	2	15
NEWLOVE	WILLIAM				39	ENGLAND	WM	ENGLISH	LABORER	045	D	1	37
NEWLOVE	WM				73	ENGLAND	WM	ENGLISH		044	A	2	54
NEWMAN	CHARLES				34	SAXONY	LU	GERMAN	F	043	B	1	28
NEWMAN	CLIFFORD		1		4	0	CE	IRISH		044	A	2	42
NEWMAN	DAVID		1		12	0	CE	IRISH		044	A	2	42
NEWMAN	THOMAS				73	IRELAND	CE	IRISH		044	A	2	37
NEWMAN	THOMAS				30	ENGLAND	CE	ENGLISH	LAB	044	B	6	6
NEWMAN	WILLIAM				50	ENGLAND	CE	ENGLISH	TAVERN KEEPER	045	A	1	76
NEWTON	GEORGE				40	ENGLAND	CE	ENGLISH	LAB	043	H	1	34
NEWTON	JAMES				42	SCOT	PS	SCOT	F	044	B	2	47
NEWTON	JAMES				64	SCOT	PS	SCOT	CARPENTER	044	B	2	48
NEWTON	JOHN				48	ENGLAND	CE	ENGLISH	F	043	A	6	15
NEWTON	JOSEPH		1		11	0	NG	ENGLISH	SERVANT	043	A	6	4
NEWTON	MARY		1	1	19	0	NG	ENGLISH	SERVANT	043	A	6	4
NEWTON	R	TAYLOR	2		50	QUEBEC	CS			044	B	6	D
NEWTON	SAMUEL				35	0	PM	IRISH	F	043	B	2	24
NICHLESON	ANDREW				45	IRELAND	CE	IRISH	COOPER	045	D	3	9
NICHOL	JOHN				61	ENGLAND	PM	ENGLISH	F	044	A	3	35
NICHOL	JOHN				30	0	PM	ENGLISH	DROVER	044	A	3	43
NICHOL	ROBERT				42	SCOTLAND	CP	SCOTCH	TAILOR	043	H	2	15
NICHOL	ROBERT				42	SCOTLAND	CS	SCOTCH	TAILOR	043	H	2	15
NICHOL	WILLIAM		1		35	0	VM	GER		044	B	3	22
NICHOLL	JAMES				40	ENGLAND	WM	ENGLISH	BRICK MAKER	043	C		8
NICHOLLS	JAS				70	ENG	PM	ENGLISH	F	044	B	5	61
NICHOLLS	LUCY			1	35	ENGLAND	CE	ENGLAND		045	D	2	4
NICHOLS	ALBERT	EDWARD	2		4	0	PM			043	E	2	D
NICHOLS	EMA		1	1	23	US	SW	ENGLISH		045	B	2	18
NICHOLS	GEORGE				47	0	WM	ENGLISH	FARMER	045	D	4	2
NICHOLS	JAMES				67	ENGLAND	CO	ENGLISH	FARMER	043	B	3	62
NICHOLS	JAMES				35	ENGLAND	PM	ENGLISH	F	043	E	2	6
NICHOLS	JOHN				55	ENGLAND	PM	ENGLISH	F	043	E	2	75
NICHOLS	JOSEPH				45	ENGLAND	CE	ENGLISH	CARPENTER	045	B	2	37
NICHOLS	JOSEPH				71	ENGLAND	CE	ENGLISH	CARPENTER	045	B	1	22
NICHOLS	ROBERT				25	0	PM	ENGLISH	F	043	E	2	74
NICHOLS	SAMUEL		1		25	0	NG	UNKNOWN		044	B	3	52
NICHOLS	VALENTINE		1		36	0	LU	GER	LAB	044	B	3	1
NICHOLS	WILLIAM				73	ENGLAND	WM	ENGLISH	FARMER	045	D	3	45
NICHOLSON	FRANCIS				21	0	CE	ENGLISH	GARDENER	045	A	1	30
NICHOLSON	GEORGE				33	IRELAND	CE	IRISH	COOPER	045	D	5	24
NICHOLSON	JAMES		1		22	SCOTLAND	CS	SCOTCH	LABOURER	045	D	5	2
NICHOLSON	JOHN				28	0	CE	ENGLISH	GARDENER	045	A	1	31
NICHOLSON	JOHN				89	ENGLAND	CE	ENGLISH	F	045	A	4	7
NICHOLSON	WILLIAM				24	0	CE	ENGLISH	GARDENER	045	A	1	30
NICKLE	WILLIAM			M	36	IRELAND	PS	IRISH	F	043	A	1	24
NICKOL	GEORGE		1	M	78	IRELAND	PS	IRISH	YEOMAN	043	A	1	45
NICOL	GEORGE	B			28	0	CE	ENG	BARRISTER	044	B	2	8
NICOL	HENRY		1		31	ENGLAND	CE	ENGLISH	LAB	045	A	2	1
NICOL	ISABELLA			1	60	SCOTLAND	CS	SCOTCH		043	A	6	3
NICOL	JAMES				63	SCOTLAND	WM	SCOTCH	F	045	A	4	29
NICOL	JOHN				45	0	WM	ENGLISH	FOUNDRY MAN	045	D	5	30
NICOL	PETER				57	SCOTLAND	CE	SCOTCH	F	043	A	6	3
NICOL	WILLIAM				54	SCOTLAND	CP	SCOTCH	F	045	A	4	3
NIDDLE	MARIAN		1	1	19	0	CP	SCOTCH		043	A	4	14
NIGH	ELIAS				39	0	MN	GERMAN	FARMER	045	D	2	58
NIGH	JOHN				43	0	MN	GERMAN	FARMER	045	D	2	62
NIGH	JONATHAN	SR			57	0	CP	GERMAN	FARMER	045	D	4	46
NIGH	WILLIAM				50	0	MN	GERMAN	FARMER	045	D	2	62
NIGHSWANDER	ELIZAB		2	1	13	0	MN			045	D	5	D
NIGHSWANDER	SAMUEL				25	0	CN	GERMAN	MILLER	045	D	5	75
NIGHT	WILLIAM				27	ENGLAND	WM	ENGLISH	LABOURER	045	D	4	15
NIGHTENGALE	THOMAS				42	ENGLAND	CE	ENGLISH	BRICK & TILE MANUFAC	045	B	1	73
NIGHTINGALE	BRIDGET			1	40	IRE	RC	IRISH		044	B	2	12
NIGHTINGALE	HENRY		2		50	ENGLAND	CE	ENGLISH	BUTCHER	044	C	2	D

SURNAME	NAME1	NAME2	STRAY	SEX	AGE	BIRTHPL	RELIGION	ORIGIN	OCCUP	DIST	SUB_DIST	DIV	PAGE
NIGHTINGALE	JANE		1	1	57	ENGLAND	CE	ENGLISH		044	C	2	10
NIGHTINGALE	MARY		1	1	27	ENGLAND	CE	ENGLISH		044	C	2	10
NIMMO	JOHN		1		18	O	CP	SCOTCH	LAB	045	C	4	30
NIMMO	ROBERT		1		19	O	CP	SCOTCH		045	C	4	33
NISBET	JAMES				45	SCOTLAND	CS	SCOTCH	LAB	043	F		27
NIVEN	D	P	1		30	O	CP	SCOTCH	CLERGYMAN	043	H	2	11
NIVEN	D	P	1		30	ONTARIO	CS	SCOTCH	CLERGYMAN	043	H	2	11
NIXON	CHARLES				53	ENGLAND	PM	ENGLISH	LAB	043	A	6	33
NIXON	CHARLES				27	O	PM	ENG	F	044	B	4	8
NIXON	ELISA		1	1	38	O	CE	IRISH	SERVANT	045	B	2	16
NIXON	ELISABETH		1	1	17	O	PM	IRISH		045	B	2	14
NIXON	ELIZABETH		1	1	16	ENGLAND	PM	ENGLISH	SERVANT	044	B	6	53
NIXON	HENREY				39	ENGLAND	EM	ENGLISH	F	045	A	4	27
NIXON	JAMES				72	IRELAND	CE	IRISH	F	044	B	6	44
NIXON	JOHN				45	O	CP	IRISH	DROVER	043	A	4	14
NIXON	JOHN		1		23	ENG	CE	ENG	SERVANT	044	B	2	11
NIXON	WILLIAM				59	ENG	PM	ENG	F	044	B	4	9
NOBLE	ADAM				38	IRELAND	CE	IRISH	MOLSTER	045	B	1	51
NOBLE	AMBROSE				76	U STATES	FW	SCOTCH	FARMER	045	D	6	28
NOBLE	ARTHUR				24	O	PS	IRISH	MERCHANT & F	044	B	1	58
NOBLE	C	T			40	O	CE	ENGLISH	PHYSICIAN	043	H	2	8
NOBLE	C	T			40	ONTARIO	CE	ENGLISH	PHYSICIAN	043	H	2	8
NOBLE	GEORGE				29	SCOTLAND	CP	SCOTCH	STORE KEEPER	045	B	1	2
NOBLE	GEORGE	F	2			O	WM	ENGLISH		045	D	3	D
NOBLE	HEROD				65	ENGLAND	CE	ENGLISH	TOLLKEEPER	044	C	4	60
NOBLE	HIRAM				42	O	CP	ENGLISH	DOCTOR	045	D	2	65
NOBLE	JESSE				44	O	WM	SCOTCH	FARMER	045	D	3	37
NOBLE	JESSE				50	ENGLAND	CE	ENGLISH	CARPENTER	044	C	3	16
NOBLE	JOHN		1		30	IRE	PS	IRE	F	044	B	2	64
NOBLE	JOHN		1		20	IRELAND	CE	IRISH	L	044	C	4	5
NOBLE	JOHN	L			34	O	CE	ENGLISH	F	044	A	1	22
NOBLE	NANCY			1	45	IRELAND	CE	IRISH		045	A	1	106
NOLAN	ANN		1	1	55	IRELAND	RC	IRISH		043	D		2
NOLAN	BRIDGET		1	1	23	IRELAND	RC	IRISH		043	D		2
NOLAN	FRANCIS				32	IRELAND	RC	IRISH	F	043	H	2	21
NOLAN	FRANCIS				32	IRELAND	RC	IRISH	FARMER	043	H	2	21
NOLAN	JAMES		1		61	IRELAND	RC	IRISH	MERCHANT	043	D		2
NOLAN	MICHAEL				62	IRELAND	RC	IRISH	STOREKEEPER	044	C	4	44
NOLAN	THOMAS				24	IRELAND	RC	IRISH	BLACKSMITH	045	D	5	39
NOLEN	JAMES		1		24	IRELAND	RC	IRISH	LABOURER	045	A	1	26
NOLLER	JAMES				37	ENGLAND	CP	ENGLISH	COOPER	043	D		79
NORMAN	ANNIE	E	2	F		O	PR			043	A	1	D
NORMAN	CHARLES			M	28	O	PR	ENGLISH	FARMER	043	A	1	31
NORMAN	EDWARD			M	65	ENGLAND	BA	ENGLAND	F	043	A	5	31
NORMAN	ELIZABETH			F	77	ENGLAND	BA	ENGLAND	F	043	A	5	34
NORMAN	GEORGE			M	34	O	BA	ENGLISH	F	043	A	1	40
NORMAN	HUGH			M	62	ENGLAND	BA	ENGLAND	F	043	A	5	31
NORMAN	JAMES		2	M		O	BA			043	A	5	D
NORMAN	ROBERT			M	54	ENGLAND	BA	ENGLISH	F	043	A	1	33
NORMAN	WILLIAM				55	ENGLAND	WM	ENGLISH	F	043	B	1	5
NORRIS	CHARLES				38	ENGLAND	PM	ENGLISH	F	043	A	3	46
NORRIS	FREDERICK		1		32	O	CE	ENGLISH	CARPENTER	045	C	2	4
NORRIS	GREY				24	O	WM	IRE	BLACKSMITH	044	B	3	21
NORRIS	MARGARET		1	1	35	ENGLISH	PS	ENGLISH	SERVANT	045	D	2	33
NORRIS	WILLIAM				45	ENGLAND	WM	ENGLISH	MUSIC DEALER	045	A	2	4
NORRIS	WILLIAM				35	ENGLAND	CE	ENGLISH	FARMER	045	D	3	28
NORRIS	WILLIAM	H			54	ENGLAND	CE	ENGLISH	FARMER	045	A	2	33
NORTH	ALFRED	G	1		38	ENGLAND	WM	ENGLISH	STOKER	045	C	4	5
NORTH	ANDREW				39	ENGLAND	CE	ENGLISH	F	043	B	1	20
NORTH	HARRIET		1	1	19	ENGLAND	BA	ENGLISH	SERVANT	044	C	2	1
NORTHCOTE	CHARLES				24	O	CE	ENGLISH	F	044	A	1	9
NORTHEY	HENRY				34	ENGLAND	NC	ENGLISH	LAB	043	C		17
NORTHGRAVES	JOHN			M	59	ENGLAND	CE	ENGLAND	F	043	A	5	4
NORTHGREAVES	WILLIAM				40	ENG	CE	ENG	F	044	B	1	57
NORTHY	JOHN		1		15	O	QU	ENGLISH		043	A	3	19
NORTHY	MARTHA		1	1	45	U STATES	QU	ENGLISH		043	A	3	19
NORTON	CHARLES		1		16	ENGLAND	CE	ENGLISH	CARPENTER	043	D		33
NORTON	GEORGE				24	ENGLAND	CE	ENGLISH	CARPENTER	043	D		6
NORTON	JOHN				32	IRELAND	RC	IRISH	LAB	045	A	4	6
NORTON	MARTIN				67	IRELAND	RC	IRISH	LAB	045	A	1	16
NORTON	PATRICK				36	IRELAND	RC	IRISH	BRICKMAKER	045	A	1	28
NOSE	GEORGE				60	SCOTLAND	CP	SCOTCH	SHOEMAKER	045	D	6	3
NOTTAGE	HENRY				28	ENGLAND	CE	ENGLISH	F	044	C	4	51
NOTTAGE	THOMAS		1		23	ENGLAND	CO	ENGLISH		044	C	2	2
NOTTER	JANE			1	60	IRE	CE	IRISH		044	B	1	13
NOX	ROBERT		1		25	SCOTLAND	CP	SCOTCH	LAB	045	A	4	21
NUFFERS	HENRY				41	SWITZERLAND	BA	SWISS	F	043	E	3	57
NUGENT	ROBERT				25	O	NC	GERMAN	LAB	043	E	2	44
NUGENT	SAML				57	O	CE	IRISH	EDGE TOOL MAKER	043	E	2	82
NUNN	JESSE			1	37	O	PM	ENGLISH	F	043	A	3	46
NURSLER	CHRISTIAN				38	GERMANY	LU	GERMAN	SADDLER	044	B	6	26
NUTT	JANE	EVA	2		6	CANADA	CE			045	D	6	D
NUTT	THOMAS				35	ENGLAND	CE	ENGLISH	LABORER	045	D	6	72
NYE	JOHN				52	ENGLAND	CE	ENGLISH	LAB	044	B	5	18
NYE	SARAH		1		72	ENGLAND	CE	ENGLISH	LAB	044	B	5	5
NYE	THOS				52	ENGLAND	CE	ENGLISH	LAB	044	B	5	18
O'BRIAN	DANIEL			M	38	O	PS	IRISH	BLACKSMITH	043	A	2	34
O'BRIAN	JAMES			M	32	O	NG	SCOTCH	CARPENTER	043	A	2	23
O'BRIAN	PATRICK				45	IRELAND	RC	IRISH	LAB	044	C	4	60
O'BRIEN	BERNARD		1		12	O	RC	IRISH		047	D		44
O'BRIEN	BERNARD		1		12	O	RC	IRISH		047	D		44
O'BRIEN	CATHARINE		1	1	1	O	RC	IRISH		047	D		44
O'BRIEN	CATHARINE		1	1	1	O	RC	IRISH		047	D		44
O'BRIEN	CATHERINE		1	1	26	O	CP	IRISH		045	D	4	8
O'BRIEN	CHRISTOPHER				70	IRELAND	RC	IRISH	F	044	A	3	49
O'BRIEN	ELISA		1	1	4	O	RC	IRISH		043	A	3	33
O'BRIEN	ELLEN		1	1	7	O	RC	IRISH		043	A	3	33
O'BRIEN	HUGH			M	31	O	PS	IRISH	F	043	A	2	31
O'BRIEN	JAMES				66	O	RC	IRISH	F	044	A	1	9
O'BRIEN	JANE			1	38	QUE	RC	IRISH		043	A	3	32
O'BRIEN	JOHN		1		21	O	RC	IRISH	LAB	047	D		44
O'BRIEN	JOHN		1		21	O	RC	IRISH	LAB	047	D		44
O'BRIEN	MARGARET		1	1	40	IRELAND	RC	IRISH		047	D		44
O'BRIEN	MARGARET		1	1	40	IRELAND	RC	IRISH		047	D		44
O'BRIEN	MARIAN		1	1	21	O	RC	IRISH	SERVANT	045	D	2	33
O'BRIEN	MARY		1	1	68	IRELAND	RC	IRISH		043	D		48

SURNAME	NAME1	NAME2	STRAY	SEX	AGE	BIRTHPL	RELIGION	ORIGIN	OCCUP	DIST	SUB_DIST	DIV	PAGE
O'BRIEN	MARY		1	1	27	O	RC	IRISH		043	D		48
O'BRIEN	MARY	ANN	1	1	16	O	RC	IRISH		047	D		44
O'BRIEN	MARY	ANN	1	1	16	O	RC	IRISH		047	D		44
O'BRIEN	MATTHEW				68	IRELAND	RC	IRISH	LAB	044	C	2	49
O'BRIEN	MICHAEL				60	IRELAND	RC	IRISH	LAB	044	C	2	50
O'BRIEN	NATHANIEL				65	NS	PS	IRISH	F	043	E	3	50
O'BRIEN	PATRICK		1		59	IRELAND	RC	IRISH	LAB	043	D		44
O'BRIEN	PETER				64	IRELAND	RC	IRISH	F LAB	043	A	3	58
O'BRIEN	ROBERT				35	O	RP	IRISH	F	043	E	3	49
O'BRIEN	THOMAS		1		25	O	RC	IRISH	LAB	043	D		48
O'BRIEN	THOMAS		1		9	O	RC	IRISH		047	D		44
O'BRIEN	THOMAS		1		9	O	RC	IRISH		047	D		44
O'BRION	EDWARD				63	IRELAND	RC	IRISH	FARMER	045	A	1	12
O'CONNELL	DANIEL				68	IRELAND	RC	IRISH	CARPENTER	044	C	4	39
O'CONNER	SARAH			1	50	O	CE	ENGLISH		045	B	2	11
O'CONNOR	BRIDGET			F	65	IRELAND	RC	IRISH		043	A	2	12
O'CONNOR	JOHN				40	IRELAND	RC	IRISH	F	044	A	1	9
O'CONNOR	MICHAEL				67	IRE	RC	IRISH	F	044	B	1	42
O'CONNOR	THOMAS				34	IRELAND	RC	IRISH	STOREKEEPER	044	C	4	46
O'DONNELL	ELLEN		1	1	22	O	RC	ENGLISH	SERVANT	044	A	3	53
O'DONNELL	JAMES				43	IRELAND	RC	IRISH	F	044	A	1	6
O'DONNELL	JAMES				52	IRELAND	RC	IRISH	LAB	044	A	3	40
O'DONNELL	MICHAEL				41	IRELAND	RC	IRISH	F	044	A	1	14
O'DONNELL	WILLIAM		1		26	IRELAND	RC	IRISH	F LAB	044	A	1	16
O'FLAHERTY	WINAFRAD		1	1	25	IRELAND	RC	IRISH	SERVANT	045	C	3	4
O'HALLERAN	MARY		1	1	23	O	RC	IRISH		043	D		26
O'HARA	THOMAS				42	IRELAND	RC	IRISH	ASHER	045	D	3	62
O'HARA	W	COL			70	IRELAND	CE	IRISH	GENTLEMAN	044	C	4	60
O'HARE	MARTIN			M	56	IRELAND	RC	IRISH	F	043	A	1	24
O'HERN	JOHN				65	IRE	RC	IRE	LAB	044	B	2	48
O'HERRON	CATHARINE		1	1	60	IRELAND	RC	IRISH		045	A	1	48
O'KEEFE	MARY				61	IRELAND	RC	IRISH	SHOPKEEPER	043	F		19
O'NEIL	JAMES		1		4	O	CE	IRISH		045	B	1	76
O'NEIL	JOHN				32	IRELAND	RC	IRISH	F	043	A	3	32
O'NEIL	JOHN		1		23	O	RC	IRISH	TELEGRAPH OP	043	A	3	33
O'NEIL	JOHN				52	IRELAND	RC	IRISH	LAB	043	E	1	3
O'NEIL	JOHN				36	IRELAND	RC	IRISH	LAB	043	H	1	15
O'NEIL	MARGARET		1	1	19	ENGLAND	WM	IRISH	INMATE	045	B	1	72
O'NEIL	MORRIS				49	IRELAND	RC	IRISH	F LAB	044	A	2	43
O'NEIL	PATRICK				58	IRELAND	RC	IRISH	F & STONE MASON	043	A	3	34
O'NEIL	PATRICK				65	IRELAND	RC	IRISH	LAB	045	B	1	22
O'NEILL	PATRICK				43	IRELAND	CE	ENGLISH	LAB	045	B	1	35
O'REILLY	MARY		1	1	50	IRELAND	RC	IRISH		045	B	1	49
O'SULLIVAN	DANIEL				63	IRELAND	RC	IRISH	FARMER	045	A	1	7
OBERLIN	NICHOLAS				71	FRANCE	LU	GERMAN	F	044	B	6	48
OBRIAN	DAN'L		1		21	O	RC	IRISH	LAB	043	F		27
OBRIAN	MICHAEL				51	IRELAND	RC	IRELAND	FARMER	045	D	2	18
OBRIEN	CATHARINE		1	1	23	O	RC	IRISH	SERVANT	043	F		27
OBRIEN	DENNIS	COR			57	IRE	CE	IRE	F	044	B	2	20
OBRIEN	EDWARD				37	ENGLAND	BA	ENGLISH	LAB	045	A	3	10
OBRIEN	JAMES				34	CANADA	WM	IRISH	CABINET MAKER	045	D	6	45
OBRIEN	MARGARET		2	1	3	O	RC			043	D		D
OBRIEN	MARY			1	40	IRELAND	RC	IRISH		045	A	3	8
OBRINE	MARGRIT			1	46	IRELAND	RC	IRISH		044	C	3	23
OBRINE	MARTHA		1	1	19	O	RC	IRISH	SERVANT	044	B	6	24
OCONNELL	JAMES				48	IRELAND	RC	IRISH	LAB	045	A	2	37
OCONNOR	HUGH				50	IRELAND	RC	IRISH	F	044	A	1	5
OCONNOR	JOHN		1		33	IRELAND	RC	IRISH	SERVANT	044	C	3	17
OCONNOR	PATRICK				65	IRE	RC	IRE	F	044	B	4	25
ODELL	CHAS				32	ENG	CE	ENG	LAB	045	C	1	23
ODLIN	WILLIAM		1		28	ENGLAND	CE	ENGLISH	OSTLER	043	E	2	37
OGDEN	MARY		2	1	42	ENGLAND	MO			045	A	4	D
OGDEN	THOMAS				36	ENGLAND	WM	ENGLISH	WEAVER	045	A	4	1
OGILVIE	HUGH				27	ONTARIO	CN	SCOTCH	FARMER	043	G	1	34
OGILVIE	CLARRISA		1	1	70	UNITED STATES	CN	GERMAN		043	E	2	3
OGLESBY	WILLIAM		1		25	ENGLAND	CE	ENGLISH	LABOURER	045	D	3	75
OGRADY	THOMAS				30	IRELAND	RC	IRELAND	TAILOR	045	D	2	12
OHARA	BART		1		20	O	RC	IRISH	COOPER	044	B	6	58
OHARA	MICHAL				38	IRELAND	RC	IRISH	LAB	044	C	3	5
OLDHAM	WILLIAM				40	ENGLAND	PM	ENGLISH	F	043	B	5	8
OLDON	JOHN				30	ENGLAND	WM	ENGLISH	BRICK MAKER	043	C		9
OLIVER	GEORGE				67	ENGLAND	CE	ENGLISH	F	043	B	4	33
OLIVER	JANE		1	1	24	IRELAND	PS	IRISH	SERVANT	044	C	4	66
OLIVER	JOSHUA				27	O	QU	ENGLISH	F	043	B	4	41
OLIVER	JOSHUA				50	ENG	WM	ENG	F	044	B	1	59
OLIVER	THOMAS				29	O	CE	ENGLISH	F	043	B	5	37
OLIVER	THOMAS				45	IRELAND	CE	IRISH	CARPENTER	044	A	1	30
OLIVER	WILLIAM				56	SCOTLAND	PS	SCOTCH	F	045	C	2	35
OLIVER	WILLIAM	C			38	O	FP	IRISH	CARRIAGE MAKER	043	C		12
OLNER	RICHARD	K			67	ENGLAND	WM	ENGLISH	SILVERSMITH	045	A	1	62
OLSON	MARTIN		1		15	NORWAY	LU	NORWEGIAN	LAB	044	B	1	60
OMEN	DAVID				38	SCOTLAND	CP	SCOTCH	CARTER	044	C	4	64
ONEAL	MARY		1	1	20	IRELAND	RC	IRISH	SERVANT	044	C	3	30
ONEIDY	SARAH		1	1	20	O	RC	IRISH		043	D		86
ONEIL	HUGH				66	IRE	RC	IRE	WEAVER	044	B	3	10
ORAM	JOHN	W	1		23	ENGLAND	CE	ENGLISH	TIN SMITH	045	B	1	21
OREILLY	HARVEY		1		18	IRELAND	ME	IRISH	SERVANT	045	A	1	88
ORILEY	MICHAEL				42	IRELAND	RC	IRISH	FARMER	045	A	3	30
ORMAND	WM		1		26	O	MN	SCOTCH	F	044	B	5	53
ORMEROD	ISABELLA		2	1	70	ENGLAND	CE		FARMER'S WIFE	045	C	3	D
ORMEROD	THOMAS				45	ENGLAND	CE	ENGLISH	F	045	C	3	4
ORR	ALLAN				36	IRELAND	CE	IRISH	CARPENTER	044	C	4	84
ORR	ARCHIBALD				25	IRELAND	CE	IRISH	MERCHANT	043	D		16
ORR	JAMES				73	IRELAND	CE	IRISH	F	044	B	6	12
ORR	JAMES		1		12	O	WM	IRISH		044	B	6	48
ORR	JAMES		1		22	IRELAND	PS	IRISH	F LAB	044	C	1	47
ORR	JOSEPH		1		14	QUE	WM	ENGLISH		043	A	3	43
ORR	JOSEPH				70	IRELAND	CE	IRISH	WEAVER	044	B	5	43
ORR	ROBERT		1		45	O	CE	IRISH	COOPER	044	B	6	58
ORTH	JONATHAN				53	O	OB	GERMAN	F	044	A	2	11
ORTON	WILLIAM				36	O	BA	ENGLISH	F	043	B	2	8
OSBORN	EDWARD				63	ENGLAND	CE	ENGLISH	GARDENER	045	A	1	28
OSBORNE	SYDNEY				25	O	WM	ENGLISH	LAB	045	C	4	33
OSBOURNE	FRANCIS		1		24	O	WM	ENGLISH	COOPER	045	B	2	11
OSBURN	CHARLES		1		19	ENGLAND	CE	ENGLISH	BLACKSMITH	045	D	3	78
OSLER	HENRY	B			55	ENGLAND	CE	ENGLISH	CLERGYMAN	043	A	4	11

SURNAME	NAME1	NAME2	STRAY	SEX	AGE	BIRTHPL	RELIGION	ORIGIN	OCCUP	DIST	SUB_DIST	DIV	PAGE
OSLER	WILLIAM				31	ENGLAND	CE	ENGLISH	F	043	B	4	5
OSMAN	CONRAD				36	0	CN	ENGLISH	F	043	E	2	49
OSTER	ANNE		2	1		0	NG			044	B	1	D
OSTER	EDWARD		1		3	0	WM	GER		044	B	3	17
OSTER	JAMES				27	0	LU	GER	F	044	B	1	48
OSTER	JANE	A		1	52	IRE	CE	IRISH		044	B	2	56
OSTER	JOHN				33	0	LU	ONTARIO	FARM LABORER	045	D	2	27
OSTER	MARY		1	1	14	0	WM	GER		044	B	3	17
OSTER	MICHAEL				54	0	LU	GER	F	044	B	1	32
OSTER	SAMANTHA		1	1	32	0	WM	IRE		044	B	3	16
OSTER	SAMUEL				52	0	LU	GER	F	044	B	1	27
OSTER	SAMUEL		1		35	0	PM	GER		044	B	3	28
OSTER	THOMAS		1		5	0	WM	GER		044	B	3	17
OSTER	WILLIAM		1		10	0	WM	GER		044	B	3	17
OSTERLEG	CHARLETT		1	1	12	CANADA	CE	DUTCH		045	D	6	45
OSTERLEG	ELMER		1	1	3	CANADA	CE	DUTCH		045	D	6	45
OSTERLEG	JOSEPH		1		14	CANADA	CE	DUTCH		045	D	6	45
OSTERLEG	JULIUS		1		9	CANADA	CE	DUTCH		045	D	6	45
OSTERLEG	WILLIAM		1		6	CANADA	CE	DUTCH		045	D	6	45
OSULLAVAN	ANN			1	42	IRELAND	RC	IRISH	HOTEL KEEPER	045	A	3	31
OSWOLD	JOSLING		1		52	ENGLAND	CE	ENGLISH	BRICKMAKER	044	C	4	5
OUDERKIRK	PETER		1		32	0	UP	DUTCH	MACHINIST	043	A	6	62
OUGH	ELISABETH		1	1	11	0	CN	ENGLISH	SERVANT	043	E	3	8
OUGH	JOHN		1		17	0	CN	ENGLISH	SERVANT	043	E	3	8
OUGH	THOMAS				37	ENGLAND	CE	ENGLISH	F	043	E	1	9
OUGH	THOMAS				34	ENGLAND	WM	ENGLISH	LABORER	043	G	1	52
OUGH	WILLIAM				33	ENGLAND	WM	ENGLISH	TINSMITH	043	C		34
OUTHWAITE	JOSEPH				63	ENGLAND	WM	ENGLISH	LAB	044	C	3	29
OUTHWEST	EDWARD		1		25	ENGLAND	CP	ENGLISH	TIN SMITH	045	B	1	27
OUTHWEST	MARYANNE		1	1	20	0	CP	IRISH		045	B	1	27
OUTHWEST	ROBERT		1			0	CP	ENGLISH		045	B	1	28
OUTHWEST	WILLIAM	S	1		1	0	CP	ENGLISH		045	B	1	27
OUTHWETT	ROBERT		2			0	PS			045	B	1	D
OUTRAM	JOHN	HENRY			21	0	WM	ENGLISH	BAKER	043	D		46
OWEN	CATHARINE			1	50	IRELAND	RC	IRISH		043	D		41
OWENS	JAMES			M	55	IRELAND	WM	IRISH	LABOURER	043	A	1	18
OWENS	JAMES				26	IRELAND	RC	IRISH	MOULDER	043	D		41
OWENS	WILLIAM		1		37	IRELAND	OP	IRISH	LAB	043	A	3	26
OXONDALE	JOHN				36	ENGLAND	CE	ENGLISH	F	043	B	2	14
OXTABY	CHRISTOPHER				40	0	PS	ENGLISH	BLACKSMITH	043	E	2	34
PACKER	WILLIAM				36	ENGLAND	NC	ENGLISH	CARPENTER	043	C		39
PADDEN	GEORGE				44	ENGLAND	WM	ENGLISH	LAB	044	C	3	25
PADDON	THOMAS				30	ENGLAND	CE	ENGLISH	CABINET MAKER	045	A	1	60
PADGET	WILLIAM				45	ENGLAND	CE	ENGLISH	FARMER	045	D	4	29
PAGAN	WILLIAM				38	SCOTLAND	CO	SCOTCH	F	043	B	2	26
PAGE	AMELIA		1	1	30	0	BA	SCOTCH		043	B	3	41
PAGE	ELLEN		1	1	20	ENGLAND	CE	ENGLISH	SERVANT	044	C	3	6
PAGE	JAMES			M	68	IRELAND	WM	IRISH	F	043	A	2	15
PAGE	JOHN				43	0	EM	ENG	F	044	B	1	36
PAGE	THOMAS				45	0	DI	ENG	F	044	B	1	45
PAGET	ELLEN	C	1	1	28	ENGLAND	EP	ENGLISH		043	A	6	21
PAGETER	JAMES				70	ENGLAND	NC	ENGLISH	F	043	C		55
PAGGENT	FANNY		1	1	19	0	EM	IRISH		044	C	1	37
PAGGENT	JONATHAN		1		21	0	EM	IRISH		044	C	1	37
PAGGENT	WILLIAM		1		21	0	EM	IRISH	F	044	C	1	37
PAIGE	FREDERICK				52	ENGLAND	CE	ENGLAND	FARMER	045	D	2	17
PAIGEON	RAIMEY			M	54	0	WM	FRENCH	F	043	A	1	10
PAINE	THOMAS				73	ENGLAND	CE	ENGLISH	FARMER	045	D	3	16
PAISLEY	ANN		1	1	25	ENGLAND	CE	ENGLISH	SERVANT	044	C	2	6
PAISLEY	HECTOR		1		15	0	WM	SCOTCH	FARM LAB	044	C	2	44
PAISLEY	JAMES				35	0	CN	IRISH	F	043	B	5	11
PAISLEY	JOHN				46	IRELAND	BA	IRISH	HOTEL KEEPER	043	E	3	1
PAISLEY	MARY ANN			1	62	IRELAND	WM	IRISH		043	B	3	33
PAISLEY	SAMUEL				27	0	CN	IRISH	F	043	B	5	15
PAISLEY	THOMAS				40	US	BA	IRISH	F	043	B	5	13
PAISLEY	THOMAS				38	ENGLAND	CE	SCOTCH	WEAVER	044	C	2	7
PAISLEY	WILLIAM				35	0	CN	IRISH	F	043	B	5	12
PALIN	JOHN	H			43	ENGLAND	WM	ENGLISH	GARDNER	045	B	1	67
PALIN	SARAH		2		84	ENGLAND	WM			045	B	1	D
PALINATIRE	ALLEN		1		26	0	EM	GERMAN	F	043	E	2	81
PALMER	CHARLES				23	0	DI	FRENCH	TEACHER	045	C	2	8
PALMER	FREDERICK		2			0	CE			045	D	3	D
PALMER	GEORGE		1		6	0	PM	ENGLISH		045	A	2	23
PALMER	HENRY				45	ENGLAND	CE	ENGLISH	DANCING MASTER	045	B	2	24
PALMER	J	S			55	0	CS	IRE	F	045	C	1	47
PALMER	JAMES				73	0	PM	IRE	F	045	C	1	41
PALMER	JAMES	C			40	0	WM	ENG	F	045	C	1	56
PALMER	JOHN				63	ENG	CE	ENG	F	044	B	2	46
PALMER	JOHN				33	0	CE	ENGLISH	STAGE AND MAIL CARRI	045	D	3	76
PALMER	MUSONE				50	IRELAND	CE	IRISH	F	045	C	2	21
PALMER	PETER		1		14	0	PM	ENGLISH		045	A	2	23
PALMER	RICHARD				64	ENGLAND	WM	ENGLISH	FARMER	043	A	4	65
PALMER	SARAH		1	1	26	0	PM	ENGLISH		045	A	2	23
PALMER	THOMAS				41	ENGLAND	CE	ENGLISH	F	045	C	4	41
PALMER	WILLIAM				36	0	WM	ENGLISH	FARMER	043	A	4	66
PANBARTH	JOHN		1		47	ENGLAND	CE	ENGLISH	WATCH MAKER	043	G	1	35
PANE	ALEXANDER				40	0	CE	IRISH	FARMER	045	D	4	50
PAPE	JAMES				27	0	RC	ENGLISH	GARDENER	045	A	1	31
PAPE	JOSEPH				56	ENGLAND	RC	ENGLISH	GARDENER	045	A	1	39
PARCE	THOMAS				51	ENGLAND	FW	ENGLISH	SHOEMAKER	045	D	6	21
PARK	ALFRED				54	0	CN	ENGLISH	F	043	E	2	84
PARK	HENRY				37	0	CE	ENGLISH	F	043	H	2	41
PARK	HENRY				37	ONTARIO	CE	ENGLISH	FARMER	043	H	2	41
PARK	ISABELLA		2	1	2	ONTARIO	CE			043	H	2	D
PARK	ISABELLA		2	1	2	0	CE			043	H	2	D
PARK	JAMES				64	ENGLAND	WM	ENGLISH	JOINER	045	D	3	75
PARK	JAMES	F	1		16	0	CE	IRISH		044	C	3	40
PARK	JOSEPH				26	0	CE	ENGLISH	SASH & W BLIND MAKER	045	D	5	9
PARK	MILES				47	ENGLAND	CE	ENGLISH	F	043	H	2	53
PARK	MILES				47	ENGLAND	CE	ENGLISH	FARMER	043	H	2	53
PARK	RICHARD		1		32	ENGLAND	CE	ENGLISH	TANNER	043	D		20
PARK	SAMUEL				69	ENGLAND	CE	ENGLISH	F	043	H	2	54
PARK	SAMUEL				69	ENGLAND	CE	ENGLISH	FARMER	043	H	2	54
PARK	WILLIAM	S			42	ENGLAND	CO	ENGLISH	CARPENTER	045	D	5	8
PARKE	JAMES				67	ENGLAND	PM	ENGLISH	BUTCHER	044	A	3	43
PARKER	A	ROBERT	2			ONT				043	A	3	D

SURNAME	NAME1	NAME2	STRAY	SEX	AGE	BIRTHPL	RELIGION	ORIGIN	OCCUP	DIST	SUB_DIST	DIV	PAGE
PARKER	CHARLES				40	ENGLAND	CE	ENGLISH	L	044	C	4	9
PARKER	HENRY	A	1		15	ENGLAND	WM	ENGLISH	BUTCHER	045	B	1	6
PARKER	JAMES				71	ENGLAND	CE	ENGLISH	LABOURER	043	B	3	33
PARKER	JOHN				45	ENGLAND	EM	ENGLISH	CARPENTER	044	C	3	31
PARKER	JOHN				43	SCOTLAND	PM	ENGLISH	STORE KEEPER	044	C	4	82
PARKER	KING				66	ENGLAND	CE	ENGLISH	F	045	C	2	47
PARKER	MARGARET			1	58	O	QU	ENGLISH		045	B	1	4
PARKER	MARY		1	1	80	ENGLAND	BA	ENGLISH		043	E	3	47
PARKER	THOMAS				24	O	WM	IRISH	LAB	043	A	3	58
PARKER	THOMAS				50	ENGLAND	CE	ENGLISH	BUTCHER	045	C	2	10
PARKHILL	WILLIAM			M	32	IRELAND	PR	IRISH	FOREMAN LUMBER YARD	043	A	1	50
PARKIN	GEORGE				38	ENGLAND	CP	ENGLISH	F	045	C	4	30
PARKINS	JOHN				54	ENG	LU	ENG	F	044	B	4	10
PARKINSON	ANN		1		28	O	WM	ENGLISH		045	C	2	33
PARKINSON	CATHARINE		2	1	3	O	NG			045	C	2	D
PARKINSON	GEORGE				36	ENGLAND	WM	ENGLISH	F	045	C	2	31
PARKINSON	MARY	ELLEN	1	1	2	O	WM	ENGLISH		045	C	2	33
PARKINSON	THOMAS		1		35	ENGLAND	WM	ENGLISH	LAB	045	C	2	33
PARKINSON	WILLIAM		1		4	O	WM	ENGLISH		045	C	2	33
PARKS	ALVA				41	O	CN	GERMAN	CARPENTER	043	E	3	24
PARKS	JOHN				32	ONTARIO	EM	GERMAN	CARPENTER	043	G	1	12
PARKS	MATHEW				28	IRELAND	CN	IRISH	CARRIAGE MAKER	043	E	2	18
PARQUTER	THOMAS				35	ENGLAND	CE	ENGLISH	F	043	B	4	2
PARROTT	JOSEPH				44	ENGLAND	WM	ENGLISH	LAB	044	C	2	28
PARRY	ROBERT				40	ENGLAND	CE	ENGLISH	DEALER	045	A	1	75
PARRY	WILLIAM	E			30	ENGLAND	CE	ENGLISH	DEALER	045	A	1	74
PARSONS	ALICE				50	IRELAND	CE	IRISH	CHARWOMAN	043	F		17
PARSONS	ELIZABETH			1	56	ENGLAND	CE	ENGLISH		045	D	5	66
PARSONS	ELLA		2	1		O				044	C	3	D
PARSONS	HENRY				33	ENGLAND	WM	ENGLISH	LAB	044	B	5	26
PARSONS	HENRY				58	IRELAND	WM	IRISH	PLASTERER	045	B	1	44
PARSONS	JOHN		1		5	O	CE	ENGLISH		045	C	3	16
PARSONS	JOSEPH				28	O	WM	ENGLISH	F	044	C	3	3
PARSONS	MATHEW				54	ENGLAND	WM	ENGLISH	GENTLEMAN	044	C	3	2
PARSONS	SUSANNA			1	79	ENGLAND	CE	ENGLISH	FARMER	045	D	1	15
PARSONS	WILLIAM				26	ONT	WM	ENGLISH	F	044	C	3	2
PARSONS	WILLIAM	M			68	IRELAND	CE	IRISH	LAB	043	F		21
PARTON	JOSEPH		1		61	ENGLAND	CE	ENGLISH	LABORER	043	G	1	17
PARTRIDGE	GEORGE		1		21	ENGLAND	WM	ENGLISH	BUTCHER	043	D		80
PASCO	MARY	A	1	1	27	O	CE	ENGLISH		045	A	1	73
PASK	STEPHEN				38	ENGLAND	CE	ENGLISH	F	043	H	2	30
PASK	STEPHEN				28	ENGLAND	CE	ENGLISH	FARMER	043	H	2	30
PATCHELL	EDWARD				49	NEW BRUNSWICK	CP	IRISH	LABORER	043	G	1	25
PATCHELL	ROBERT	C			54	IRELAND	WM	IRISH	GARDENER	043	G	1	17
PATCHELL	WILLIAM				25	ONTARIO	CN	IRISH	SAWYER	043	G	1	2
PATER	THOMSON				31	O	PM	ENGLISH	F	044	B	5	60
PATERMAN	DANIEL			M	29	O	PS	GERMAN	CARPENTER	043	A	2	29
PATERSON	ANDREW			1	73	SCOTLAND	CP	SCOTCH	F	045	C	4	13
PATERSON	ANDREW				33	O	CP	SCOTCH	F MANAGER	045	C	4	13
PATERSON	ANNIE		1	1	24	O	CP	SCOTCH	SEAMSTRESS	045	A	2	5
PATERSON	JOHN				41	O	CP	SCOTCH	F	045	C	4	27
PATERSON	JOHN				43	O	CP	SCOTCH	F	045	C	4	32
PATERSON	SARAH			1	75	SCOTLAND	CP	SCOTCH	F	045	C	4	27
PATERSON	THOMAS				32	O	CP	SCOTCH	F	045	C	4	28
PATERSON	WILLIAM		2		75	SCOTLAND	CP		F	045	C	4	D
PATRICK	GEORGE				21	O	EM	ENGLISH	F	043	A	6	42
PATTENDEN	RICHARD				45	ENGLAND	PM	ENGLISH	F	043	B	1	33
PATTERSON	ADAM				64	IRELAND	CP	SCOTCH	F	044	A	2	20
PATTERSON	AGNES			1	48	SCOTLAND	KB	SCOTCH		045	A	3	7
PATTERSON	ANDREW		1		26	SCOTLAND	PS	SCOTTISH	F SERVANT	044	C	1	19
PATTERSON	ANNA		1	1	19	O	WM	IRE		044	B	3	16
PATTERSON	BENJAMIN		1		63	IRELAND	PS	IRISH	LABOURER	045	A	1	23
PATTERSON	CATHARINE		2	F	23	O	PS			043	A	2	D
PATTERSON	ELISABETH		1	1	37	ENGLAND	CE	ENGLISH	SERVANT	045	B	2	29
PATTERSON	ELIZABETH		1	1	66	ENGLAND	CE	ENGLISH		044	A	3	37
PATTERSON	HENRY	J			73	O	CN	SCOTCH	CARPENTER	043	B	3	2
PATTERSON	HIRAM				70	O	CN	IRISH	CARPENTER	043	B	5	14
PATTERSON	ISABELLA		1	1	26	ONTARIO	PR	SCOTCH		043	G	2	27
PATTERSON	ISABELLA		1	1	15	O	CP	SCOTCH	SERVANT	044	B	6	56
PATTERSON	ISABELLA		1	1	40	IRELAND	PR	IRISH	HOUSEKEEPER	045	A	1	45
PATTERSON	JAMES			M	53	SCOTLAND	PS	SCOTCH	L	043	A	2	56
PATTERSON	JAMES				44	ENGLAND	CE	ENGLISH	LAB	045	C	2	37
PATTERSON	JAMES		1		29	IRELAND	PS	IRISH	F LAB	044	C	1	15
PATTERSON	JAMES	M			56	O	CN	SCOTCH	AUCTIONEER	043	B	3	28
PATTERSON	JANET			1	61	SCOT	CS	SCOT		045	C	1	48
PATTERSON	JOHN				36	O	CP	SCOTCH	FARMER	045	D	3	6
PATTERSON	JULIA		1	1	22	O	WM	SCOTCH		043	C		42
PATTERSON	LAURA		1	1		O	WM	GER		044	B	3	17
PATTERSON	MARY		2	1		O	CN			043	B	3	D
PATTERSON	MARY JANE			1	29	ONTARIO	CN	GERMAN		043	B	3	50
PATTERSON	PETER				45	US	PS	IRE	MANUFACTURER	044	B	2	37
PATTERSON	PETER				63	SCOT	CE	SCOT	GENTLEMAN	045	C	1	37
PATTERSON	SAMUEL		2		33	O	CN		PHOTOGRAPHER	043	B	3	D
PATTERSON	SAMUEL		1		32	IRELAND	CE	IRISH	HOSTLER	043	D		82
PATTERSON	SILAS		1		20	O	CN	SCOTCH	TELEGRAPH OPERATOR	043	B	3	54
PATTERSON	THERAN				33	O	CN	SCOTCH	CARPENTER	043	B	3	66
PATTERSON	THOMAS				48	O	CS	SCOTCH	FARMER	045	D	3	32
PATTERSON	WILLIAM				45	US	WM	UNKNOWN	F	044	B	2	54
PATTERSON	WILLIAM				55	SCOTLAND	CP	SCOTCH	F	044	B	6	30
PATTERSON	WILLIAM		1		34	O	CP	SCOTCH	LAB	045	A	2	30
PATTERSON	WILLIAM		1		45	IRELAND	CP	IRISH	DROVER	045	B	2	4
PATTERSON	WILLIAM				28	O	CS	SCOT	F	045	C	1	48
PATTERSON	WILLIAM		1		25	O	BA	IRISH	MILLER	044	C	2	32
PATTON	ALEXANDER			M	37	IRELAND	WM	IRISH	BUTCHER	043	A	1	34
PATTON	CHARLES				50	O	EM	ENGLISH	CARPENTER	045	D	5	47
PATTON	DANIEL				50	IRELAND	RC	IRISH	FARMER	043	A	4	67
PATTON	DONALD			M	50	SCOTLAND	WM	SCOTCH	L	043	A	2	56
PATTON	GEORGE				35	O	CP	SCOTCH	F	045	C	4	15
PATTON	JANET		1	1	22	SCOTLAND	PS	SCOTLAND	SERVANT	045	D	2	23
PATTON	JOSEPH				36	O	WM	IRISH	BUTCHER	045	D	3	65
PATTON	LOUESIA		2	F		O	WM			043	A	1	D
PATTON	WILLIAM		1	M	45	SCOTLAND	UP	SCOTLAND	L	043	A	5	39
PATTON	WILLIAM				27	O	PS	SCOTCH	F	045	C	3	16
PAUL	ELIZABETH		1	1	6	O	WM	ENG		045	C	1	41
PAUL	FRED				35	GERMANY	WM	GERMAN	MOULDER	044	B	5	41
PAUL	HENRY				58	ENGLAND	CE	ENGLISH	F	044	B	6	17

SURNAME	NAME1	NAME2	STRAY	SEX	AGE	BIRTHPL	RELIGION	ORIGIN	OCCUP	DIST	SUB_DIST	DIV	PAGE
PAUL	HENRY		1		13	O	WM	ENG		045	C	1	41
PAUL	JOHN		1		11	O	NG	SCOTCH		045	C	4	22
PAUL	LYDIA	R	1	1	73	NB	CS	SCOTCH		045	D	5	44
PAUL	MARTHA		1	1	60	ENGLAND	CE	ENGLISH		044	B	6	35
PAUL	MARY		1	1	10	ONT	WM	ENG		045	C	1	41
PAUL	REMBLER				38	QUE	SP	ENGLISH	VETERINARIAN SURGEON	045	A	1	63
PAULE	JOHN				69	SCOTLAND	CP	SCOTCH	CONVEYANCER	044	C	3	40
PAXMAN	JOHN			M	53	ENGLAND	CE	ENGLAND		043	A	5	30
PAXTON	JOHN			M	26	O	RC	ENGLISH	F	043	A	5	7
PAXTON	JOHN				35	O	CE	ENGLISH		043	E	2	7
PAXTON	JOHN				36	SCOTLAND	CP	SCOTCH	FARM SERVANT	045	C	3	7
PAXTON	PETER			M	41	SCOTLAND	CP	SCOTCH	FARMER	043	A	1	33
PAYNE	JAMES				58	U STATES	WM	AFRICAN	LAB	045	A	2	22
PAYNE	JANE		1	1	30	IRELAND	WM	IRISH	WATCHMAKER	043	D		69
PAYNE	JOHN				48	ENGLAND	CO	ENGLISH	F	043	A	3	47
PAYNE	THOS		1		31	IRELAND	CO	IRISH	TIN SMITH	044	B	5	24
PAYNE	WILLIAM		1		19	ENGLAND	CE	ENGLISH	SERVANT	045	A	3	36
PAYSON	CHARLES		2			ONTARIO	CE			043	G	1	D
PAYSON	EPHRIAM				74	NOVA SCOTIA	WM	ENGLISH	FARMER	043	G	1	37
PAYSON	RUFUS				42	ONTARIO	CE	ENGLISH	FARMER	043	G	1	37
PEACH	GEORGE		2		51	ENGLAND	PM		FARMER	045	D	4	D
PEACH	ISABELLA			1	46	ENGLAND	PM	ENGLISH		045	D	4	10
PEACH	JAMES		1		20	ENGLAND	CE	ENGLISH	LAB	044	C	4	98
PEACH	THOMAS				79	ENGLAND	PM	ENGLISH	FARMER	045	D	6	3
PEACOCK	CHARLOTTE		1	1	19	O	CP	ENGLISH		045	D	5	53
PEACOCK	FREDK		1		13	O	CE	ENGLISH		044	A	2	52
PEACOCK	HUGH			M	35	IRELAND	PS	IRISH	CARPENTER	043	A	2	13
PEACOCK	JAMES				40	O	PM	ENGLISH	F	044	A	2	16
PEACOCK	JOHN				48	ENGLAND	PM	ENGLISH	F	044	A	3	9
PEACOCK	THOMAS			M	53	IRELAND	PS	IRISH	LAB	043	A	2	12
PEACOCK	THOMAS				44	ENGLAND	WM	ENGLISH	MASON	043	B	5	11
PEACOCK	THOMAS				72	ENGLAND	PM	ENGLISH	LAB	044	A	3	12
PEACOCK	THOMAS		1		17	O	WM	ENGLISH	CLERK	045	B	1	2
PEARCE	CHAS				38	ENG	WM	ENG	F	045	C	1	33
PEARCE	WILLIAM	J			38	O	ME	ENG	OVERSEER	044	B	4	14
PEARCY	JOHN				58	IRE	CP	ENG	TOLLKEEPER	045	C	1	41
PEARCY	MARY		2	1	33	IRELAND	CS			044	B	6	D
PEARCY	WILLIAM				28	O	CS	IRISH	BLACKSMITH	044	B	6	60
PEARS	LEONARD				44	ENGLAND	WM	ENGLISH	BRICK MANUFACTURER	045	B	1	60
PEARSE	ELIZABETH			1	54	ENGLAND	BC	ENGLISH		045	C	2	47
PEARSE	ELIZABETH		1	1	12	O	TU	ENGLISH		045	D	4	5
PEARSE	GEORGE		2		53	ENGLAND	BC			045	C	2	D
PEARSE	JAMES				24	O	BC	ENGLISH	F	045	C	2	48
PEARSE	JOHN				62	ENGLAND	BC	ENGLISH	F	045	C	2	31
PEARSON	ALEXANDER		1		23	QUEBEC	NG	SCOTCH	FARM SERVANT	043	B	3	33
PEARSON	BEN	F			31	O	NC	ENGLISH	PHYSICIAN	043	E	2	39
PEARSON	BENJAMIN				57	ONTARIO	NC	ENGLISH	MILL WRIGHT	043	C		2
PEARSON	EDW	C			29	O	CP	ENGLISH	F	044	A	2	29
PEARSON	EDWARD				63	ENGLAND	WM	ENGLISH	GENTLEMAN	044	C	3	19
PEARSON	FANNEY			1	46	CANADA	BA	ENGLISH		045	D	6	64
PEARSON	FRANCIS				52	ENGLAND	CE	ENGLISH		045	B	1	10
PEARSON	FREDERICK		1		17	O	WM	IRISH		043	D		40
PEARSON	GEO				55	ENGLAND	PM	ENGLISH	F	044	B	5	79
PEARSON	GEORGE				47	O	QU	ENGLISH	F	043	B	4	2
PEARSON	GEORGE				37	ENGLAND	PM	ENGLISH	F	044	A	2	26
PEARSON	GEORGE				33	O	PM	ENGLISH	F	045	C	3	53
PEARSON	GEORGE	L		M	47	O	QU	ENGLAND	F	043	A	5	42
PEARSON	HANNAH		1	1	40	ENG	WM	ENG		045	C	1	22
PEARSON	HORATIO				36	O	PM	ENGLISH	F	044	A	2	32
PEARSON	JAMES				38	SCOTLAND	CS	SCOTCH	MINISTER	043	D		6
PEARSON	JAMES				54	ENG	WM	ENG	F	044	B	1	18
PEARSON	JAMES				34	O	WM	ENGLISH	F	044	C	1	2
PEARSON	JAMES	J			42	O	WM	ENGLISH	REGISTRAR	043	D		71
PEARSON	JANE			1	52	ENGLAND	NC	ENGLISH		043	F		4
PEARSON	JOHN				60	ENGLAND	WM	ENGLISH	F	044	C	1	3
PEARSON	JOHN	J	1		9	O	RC	ENGLISH		044	C	2	40
PEARSON	LAMBERT	B			42	O	EP	ENGLISH	F	043	A	6	2
PEARSON	MARY			1	38	O	WM	ENGLISH		043	C		43
PEARSON	NATHANIEL				69	O	QU	ENGLISH	GENTLEMAN	043	C		7
PEARSON	PETER				64	O	EM	ENGLISH	F	043	B	4	9
PEARSON	PHOEBE		1	1	9	O	ME	ENGLISH		045	C	4	12
PEARSON	REBECCA		1	1	7	O	ME	ENGLISH		045	C	4	12
PEARSON	RICHARD				27	O	NC	ENGLISH	DENTIST	043	D		71
PEARSON	ROBERT				34	O	QU	ENGLISH	F	043	B	4	10
PEARSON	SAMUEL		1		76	U STATES	QU	IRISH	GENTLEMAN	043	D		60
PEARSON	SARAH	JANE	2	1	1	O	PM			044	A	2	D
PEARSON	THOMAS				50	ENGLAND	CE	ENGLISH	LABOURER	045	A	1	52
PEARSON	THOMAS				32	O	WM	ENGLISH	F	044	C	1	44
PEARSON	WILLIAM				40	ONTARIO	CN	ENGLISH	FARMER	043	G	2	18
PEARSON	WILLIAM				45	ENGLAND	CE	ENGLISH	FARM LABORER	045	D	1	27
PEARSON	WILLIAM				50	ENGLAND	CE	ENGLISH	FARM LAB	044	C	2	27
PEAS	CATHARINE			1	73	O	WM	ENGLISH		045	A	4	34
PEASE	EDWARD				46	O	EM	ENGLISH	TANNER	043	C		22
PEASE	GEORGE	S	1		24	US	LU	SCOTCH	FARM LABORER	045	D	1	37
PECK	GEORGE				32	ENGLAND	PM	ENGLISH	F	043	B	1	9
PECK	JOHN				37	SCOTLAND	CP	SCOTCH	GARDNER	045	B	2	18
PECK	NORTHRUP		1		38	US	WM	ENG	DENTIST	044	B	2	11
PECK	SUSAN			1	40	U STATES	CE	SCOTCH		043	D		83
PECKHAM	STEPHEN				59	U STATES	QU	ENGLISH	LUMBERMAN	043	D		34
PEDLAR	JOHN				50	ENGLAND	PM	ENGLISH	LAB	045	A	2	26
PEEKNESS	THOMAS		1		20	O	PS	SCOT	LAB	044	B	3	50
PEEL	EARNEST				32	ENGLAND	CE	ENGLISH	GENTLEMAN	043	C		19
PEELER	JOSEPH				58	O	CE	FRENCH	F	044	A	1	27
PEELER	WILLIAM				30	O	WM	FRENCH	F	044	A	1	37
PEER	ANN				59	ENGLAND	WM	ENGLISH		043	B	3	59
PEERS	THOMAS				50	ENGLISH	CE	ENGLISH	CARPENTER	044	C	3	16
PEGG	CHAS		1		24	IRELAND	CE	SCOTCH	MACHINIST	044	B	5	24
PEGG	ELISHA				41	O	WM	WELSH	F	043	E	2	47
PEGG	JAMES		1		22	ENG	CE	ENG	FARM LAB	044	B	1	24
PEGG	JOHN				49	O	BA	WELSH	F	043	E	2	83
PEGG	JOSEPH				72	UNITED STATES	CN	ENGLISH	F	043	E	2	4
PEGG	JOSEPH				47	O	WM	WELSH	F	043	E	3	50
PEGG	NATHAN			M	26	O	PR	WELSH	F	043	A	1	47
PEGG	SAMUEL				32	O	PM	WELSH	F	043	E	3	54
PEGG	VALURIA		1	1	20	O	CE	SCOTCH		043	E	2	36
PEGG	WILLIAM				46	O	CN	WELSH	F	043	E	3	11

SURNAME	NAME1	NAME2	STRAY	SEX	AGE	BIRTHPL	RELIGION	ORIGIN	OCCUP	DIST	SUB_DIST	DIV	PAGE
PEIRCE	THOMAS				35	ENGLAND	CE	ENGLISH	FARMER	045	A	3	15
PELL	GEORGE	HENRY	2		0	0	CE			044	C	2	D
PELL	WILLIAM				33	ENGLAND	CE	ENG	LAB	043	D		42
PELL	WILLIAM				29	ENGLAND	CE	ENGLISH	LAB	044	C	2	13
PENDAR	BRIDGET		1	1	18	0	RC	IRISH	SERVANT	044	B	6	25
PENDER	JAMES			M	39	0	RC	IRISH	LAB	043	A	2	4
PENDER	LETETIA		1	1	14	0	CS	IRISH	SERVANT	045	D	1	27
PENDERGRAST	JAMES		1		30	IRELAND	RC	IRISH	AUCTIONEER	044	C	3	15
PENDRICT	RICHARD		1		40	ENGLAND	CE	ENGLISH	LAB	045	B	1	21
PENNOCK	AMBROSE				43	0	CO	GERMAN	TEAMSTER	045	D	4	27
PENNOCK	MARGARA		1	1	20	0	CE	GERMAN		045	D	3	7
PENNOCK	MARTHA		2	1		0				045	D	4	D
PENNOOK	ELIJAH				34	0	CN	ENGLISH	FARMER	043	B	3	48
PENNY	WILLIAM				36	ENG	WM	ENG	CARPENTER	044	B	2	7
PENOCK	JOSEPH				46	0	WM	ENGLISH	CARPENTER	045	A	3	13
PENROSE	ALMA	U	1	1	16	0	CP	ENGLISH	SERVANT	045	D	2	2
PENROSE	EMELY		1	1	26	CANADA	WM	IRISH		045	D	6	30
PENROSE	GEORGE				47	0	QU	IRISH	F	043	B	5	25
PENROSE	JOSEPH				74	US	QU	ENGLISH	F	043	B	5	30
PENTRISS	BENJAMIN				30	ENGLAND	PM	ENGLISH	PAPER MAKER	045	A	1	79
PEOPLE	JAMES		1		39	USA	CE	ENGLISH	LAB	045	A	1	19
PEPKIN	MARY			1	63	US	WM	AFRICAN		044	C	4	92
PEPPER	ROBERT				37	ENGLAND	CE	ENGLISH	LABOURER	045	D	3	19
PERAULT			2			ONTARIO	NG			043	G	2	D
PERAULT	FRANKLIN				27	ONTARIO	RC	FRENCH	FARMER	043	G	2	5
PERAULT	JACOB				55	0	WM	FRENCH	LAB	043	E	2	76
PERAULT	PAUL				32	QUEBEC	RC	FRENCH	FARMER	043	G	2	5
PERAULT	PETER				34	QUEBEC	RC	FRENCH	FARMER	043	G	2	5
PERCELL	PATRICK				47	IRELAND	RC	IRISH	LABOURER	044	C	1	26
PERCY	JOHN		1		40	IRELAND	RC	IRISH	FARM LABOURER	043	E	2	17
PERCY	MATHEW				66	ENG	UT	ENG	F	045	C	1	65
PERCY	SILVANUS		1		27	0	CN	ENGLISH		045	D	3	79
PERCY	SOPHIA		1	1	22	0	CO	ENGLISH		045	D	3	79
PERCY	WILLIAM				35	0	CN	ENGLISH	CLERGYMAN	043	D	3	38
PERDUE	HENRY				46	IRELAND	CE	IRISH	F	043	A	3	20
PEREGRINE	DAVID				57	ENGLAND	OM	ENGLISH	MECHANIC	043	E	2	58
PEREGRINE	JAMES				49	0	EM	WELSH	F	043	E	2	59
PEREGRINE	R	T			27	0	OM	ENGLISH	F	043	E	2	58
PERKIN	JOHN				45	0	CE	ENGLISH	LAB	045	A	1	12
PERKIN	JOHN				45	0	WM	ENGLISH	FARMER	045	D	4	34
PERKINS	ALEXANDER				30	0	WM	IRISH	LAB	043	E	1	22
PERKINS	JAMES				63	ENGLAND	WM	ENGLISH	F	043	H	1	26
PERKINS	SARAH		1	1	63	ENGLAND	PM	IRISH		045	D	3	31
PERKINS	THOMAS				52	ENGLAND	CE	ENGLISH	LAB	045	B	2	5
PERKINS	THOMAS		1		23	ENGLAND	PM	ENGLISH	BLACKSMITH	045	C	4	7
PERKINS	THOMAS		1		24	ENGLAND	PM	IRISH		045	D	3	31
PERKINS	TOM				42	ENGLAND	CE	ENGLISH	COMM TRAVELLER	045	A	1	68
PERKISS	JOHN				26	ENGLAND	PM	ENGLISH	LAB	045	B	1	63
PERKS	ENOCH				25	ENGLAND	CE	ENGLISH		044	C	3	40
PERRAULT	ANDREW				22	ONTARIO	RC	FRENCH	FARMER	043	G	2	4
PERREY	MARY		1	1	32	IRE	RC	ENG		044	B	1	10
PERREY	ROBERT		1		39	ENG	PS	SCOTCH	MUSICIAN	044	B	1	10
PERRY	DAVID				37	0	EM	ENGLISH	MINISTER	043	E	2	20
PERRY	HENRY				46	IRELAND	CE	IRISH	FARMER	043	A	4	69
PERRY	JOHN			M	45	IRELAND	CE	IRELAND	F	043	A	5	39
PERRY	NANCY			1	46	IRE	CE	IRE		045	C	1	7
PERRY	RICHARD			M	73	IRELAND	CE	IRELAND	F	043	A	5	39
PERRY	S	ROBERT			36	0	EP	IRISH	SCHOOL TEACHER	043	A	3	12
PERRY	THOMAS				37	0	EP	IRISH	SAWMILLER	043	A	3	26
PERRY	WILLIAM				31	0	CE	IRISH	F	043	A	3	27
PERRY	WILLIAM				27	0	WM	IRISH	BLACKSMITH	043	B	1	21
PERRY	WILLIAM		1		23	ENGLAND	CE	WELSH	LABOURER	045	A	1	26
PERRY	WILLIAM				40	IRELAND	CE	IRISH	HOTEL KEEPER	045	D	3	40
PERRY	WM				55	SCOT	CS	SCOT	LAB	045	C	1	58
PESLY	ROBART		1		66	SCOTLAND	RP	SCOTCH		044	C	3	43
PETCH	ISAAC				49	0	WM	ENGLISH	F	043	B	4	25
PETCH	JOHN				45	0	WM	ENGLISH	F	043	B	4	24
PETCH	ROBERT				66	ENGLAND	PM	ENGLISH	GENTLEMAN	045	C	3	2
PETCH	ROBERT	JR			33	0	PM	ENGLISH	F	045	C	3	1
PETERBAUGH	HENRY			M	41	0	CP	GERMAN	F	043	A	2	27
PETERBAUGH	PETER			M	68	U STATES	NG	GERMAN	GENTLEMAN	043	A	2	28
PETERMAN	GEORGE		1		83	US	LU	GER	INVALID	044	B	1	33
PETERMAN	GEORGE				39	0	PM	GER	F	044	B	4	36
PETERMAN	HENRY				52	0	WM	GER	F	044	B	4	37
PETERMAN	MICHAEL				55	0	PM	GER	JOBBER	044	B	4	35
PETERMAN	SAMUEL				47	0	WM	IRE	F	044	B	4	11
PETERMAN	SAMUEL				25	0	WM	GER	MERCHANT	044	B	4	44
PETERS	CHARLES				54	IRELAND	CE	IRISH	F	044	A	3	12
PETERS	ELISABETH		1	1	21	0	LU	GERMAN		045	B	2	16
PETERS	HENERY				48	IRELAND	CE	IRISH	F	045	C	2	42
PETERS	HENERY		1	1	23	0	CE	IRISH	F	045	C	2	47
PETERS	HUGH				34	0	WM	ENGLISH	F	043	H	1	32
PETERS	JOHN				64	IRELAND	CE	IRISH	F	045	C	2	48
PETERS	THO'S		1		20	QUE	WM	ENGLISH	BARBER	043	D		15
PETERS	WILLIAM		1		21	0	CS	IRISH	LABOURER	045	D	5	6
PETERSON	JANE			1	68	AMERICA	CE	AFRICAN		044	C	4	15
PETERSON	NELSON				37	0	CN	ENGLISH	LAB	043	B	5	28
PETERSON	PHILIP				75	GERMANY	LU	GERMAN	FARMER	045	D	4	52
PETERSON	THOMAS				49	IRELAND	RC	IRISH	MERCHANT	043	D		3
PETHYBRIDGE	WILLIAM		1		22	ENGLAND	CE	ENGLISH	FARM LAB	044	C	2	48
PETTET	JOHN				78	ENGLAND	CE	ENGLISH	FARMER	043	B	3	22
PETTET	WILLIAM				63	IRELAND	CE	IRISH	FARMER	043	B	3	18
PETTIT	JOHN		1		40	ENGLAND	CE	ENGLISH	LABOURER	045	A	1	38
PETTY	JAMES		1		20	ENGLAND	CE	ENGLISH	LAB	043	E	3	7
PEW	JOSEPH				28	WALES	CE	WELSH	LAB	043	D		45
PEW	ROBERT		1		18	CANADA	MN	GERMAN		045	D	6	75
PEWS	CHARLES				57	IRELAND	PS	IRISH	FARMER	043	B	3	7
PEWS	ROBERT				67	IRELAND	PM	IRISH	FARMER	043	B	3	10
PEXTON	ELIZABETH			1	72	ENGLAND	CE	ENGLISH		045	D	1	6
PHAIR	JASON				36	IRELAND	WM	IRISH	F	044	C	4	1
PHAIR	JOHN				39	IRELAND	CE	IRISH	SAWYER	044	B	6	36
PHELON	NICHOLES				60	IRELAND	RC	IRISH	F	045	C	3	21
PHEONIX	SILAS				42	0	PM	IRISH	F	045	C	3	24
PHERRELL	ADNA				54	0	CE	ENG	F	045	C	1	31
PHERRELL	RUSSELL				24	0	CE	ENG	F	045	C	1	31
PHERRILL	DAVID				45	0	CS	ENG	F	045	C	1	30

SURNAME	NAME1	NAME2	STRAY	SEX	AGE	BIRTHPL	RELIGION	ORIGIN	OCCUP	DIST	SUB_DIST	DIV	PAGE
PHERRILL	WM				32	0	CE	ENG	F	045	C	1	61
PHIBBS	ELIZA		1	1	23	IRELAND	CE	ENGLISH	SERVANT	044	C	4	68
PHIFER	ELIZABETH		1	1	27	0	CX	GER		044	B	2	44
PHILBRICK	CORNELIUS				48	ENGLAND	CE	ENGLISH	DOCTOR	045	B	2	27
PHILIPS	ANNIE			F	75	U STATES	QU	ENGLISH		043	A	1	14
PHILIPS	ELLENOR	A	1	F	13	0	CE	ENGLISH		043	A	1	1
PHILIPS	GEORGE				54	0	EM	GERMAN	FARMER	045	D	1	40
PHILIPS	JACOB				76	0	WM	DUTCH		044	A	2	38
PHILIPS	JAMES				33	0	WM	IRISH	F	043	B	2	10
PHILIPS	JAMES				60	ENGLAND	CE	ENGLISH	LAB	045	C	4	24
PHILIPS	JAMES	N			24	QUE	WM	IRISH	FARM LABORER	045	D	1	19
PHILIPS	JOHN				45	IRELAND	WM	IRISH	F	043	B	2	12
PHILIPS	JOHN	D			56	0	QU	ENGLISH	CARPENTER	043	A	6	4
PHILIPS	LYDIA		1	1	18	0	WM	ENGLISH	SERVANT	043	B	4	40
PHILIPS	PHILIP		M		21	0	CE	GERMAN	FARMER	043	A	1	3
PHILIPS	RICHARD				35	IRELAND	CP	IRISH	GROSER	044	C	4	66
PHILIPS	SAMUEL	E			81	U STATES	QU	ENGLISH	GENTLEMAN	043	A	6	4
PHILIPS	SOLOMON				38	0	CE	GERMAN	SAWYER	044	C	4	11
PHILIPS	WILLIAM			M	50	U STATES	WM	ENGLISH	LABOURER	043	A	1	14
PHILIPS	WILLIAM				36	0	WM	IRISH	F	043	B	2	38
PHILIPS	WILLIAM		2		2	0	WM			043	B	2	D
PHILLIPS	ALEX	R			35	SCOTLAND	FK	SCOTCH	BLACKSMITH	043	C		50
PHILLIPS	ASA				45	0	QU	ENGLISH	F	043	E	1	32
PHILLIPS	CHRISTINA		1	1	10	0	WM	GERMAN		044	B	6	7
PHILLIPS	DAVID				27	0	QU	ENGLISH	CH? LABOURER?	043	A	4	26
PHILLIPS	DAVID	S			40	0	QU	ENGLISH	CHEESE MANUFACTURER	043	A	6	5
PHILLIPS	EDWARD		1		19	ENG	CE	ENG	LAB	045	C	1	44
PHILLIPS	EDWD				75	0	CE		F	044	B	5	32
PHILLIPS	FRANCES		1	1	13	UNITED STATES	NC	GERMAN		043	E	2	7
PHILLIPS	GEORGE				53	ENGLAND	CE	ENGLISH	LABORER	045	D	2	68
PHILLIPS	HARRIET		1	1	22	0	PM	ENGLISH		044	B	5	36
PHILLIPS	HENRY				47	0	EM	GERMANY	FARMER	045	D	2	15
PHILLIPS	HENRY				34	0	WM	IRISH	LABOURER	044	C	3	59
PHILLIPS	ISAAC	S			55	0	QU	ENGLISH	FARMER	043	A	4	27
PHILLIPS	JAS	B			29	0	EM	SCOTCH	F	043	E	2	70
PHILLIPS	JOEL				52	0	QU	ENGLISH	FARMER	043	A	4	26
PHILLIPS	JOHN				42	IRELAND	EP	IRISH	CORDWAINER	043	A	3	6
PHILLIPS	JOHN				54	0	EM	SCOTCH	F	043	E	2	71
PHILLIPS	JOHN		1		25	0	CE	GERMAN	F LAB	044	A	3	6
PHILLIPS	JOHN				43	0	PM	IRISH	F	044	B	5	73
PHILLIPS	JOSEPH				37	0	WM	SPANISH	MERCHANT	043	C		27
PHILLIPS	MARY		1	1	77	0	PM	GERMAN		043	E	2	70
PHILLIPS	MARY		1	1	82	UNITED STATES	WM	ENGLISH		044	A	3	24
PHILLIPS	MARY	A	2	1		0	QU			043	E	1	D
PHILLIPS	NICHOLAS				63	ENGLAND	QU	ENGLISH	PUMP MAKER	043	H	1	19
PHILLIPS	OLIVER	S			47	0	QU	ENGLISH	CHEESE MANUFACTURER	043	A	6	5
PHILLIPS	OWEN				70	UNITED STATES	QU	WELSH	F	043	E	1	33
PHILLIPS	PETER				42	0	EM	GERMANY	PUMP MAKER	045	D	2	13
PHILLIPS	RICHD		1		15	0	UP	SCOTCH	LAB	044	B	5	73
PHILLIPS	SARAH		1	1	19	0	WM	IRISH	SERVANT	044	B	5	11
PHILLIPS	SARAH		1	1	19	0	CE	ENGLISH		044	B	6	46
PHILLIPS	THOMAS				32	0	EM	SCOTCH	CORDWAINER	043	E	2	69
PHILLIPS	THOMAS				45	0	WM	IRE	F	044	B	4	28
PHILLIPS	WEALTHY		1		79	UNITED STATES	EM	GERMAN		043	E	2	7
PHILLIPS	WILLIAM		1		20	0	PM	IRISH	F	043	B	5	24
PHILLIPS	WILLIAM				27	0	PM	ENGLISH	PUMP MAKER	043	H	1	18
PHILLIPS	WM	B			52	ONTARIO	WM	ENGLISH	FARMER	043	G	1	2
PHILP	ROBERT		1		23	SCOTLAND	UP	SCOTH	FARM LABORER	045	D	1	46
PHILPOT	JAMES				48	ENGLAND	CE	ENGLISH	TRADER	045	B	1	46
PHOENIX	JAMES				58	0	PM	IRISH	F	045	C	3	22
PICHARD	WM		1		23	ENG	PM	ENG	LAB	045	C	1	57
PICKERING	ANDREW		1		32	IRELAND	PM	IRISH	LABOURER	045	D	4	20
PICKERING	ELISABETH			1	53	IRELAND	WM	IRISH		045	A	4	5
PICKERING	FRANK		1		19	0	PM	IRISH	CARPENTER	045	B	2	14
PICKERING	ISAAC				34	ENGLAND	CE	ENGLISH	F	044	C	4	95
PICKERING	RICHARD				24	0	WM	ENGLISH	PAINTER	045	B	1	24
PICKERING	ROBERT		1		17	ENG	CE	ENG	LAB	045	C	1	41
PICKERING	ROBERT		1		25	ENGLAND	WM	ENGLISH	SERVANT	044	C	4	54
PICKERING	THOMAS		1		27	ENG	CE	ENG	SERVANT	044	B	2	11
PICKLES	HENRY		1		25	ENGLAND	PM	ENGLISH	F LAB	044	A	3	49
PICKMAN	JOHN		1		25	ENGLAND	CE	ENGLISH	FARM SERVANT	045	A	1	90
PIDGEON	WILLIAM				32	ENG	CE	ENGLISH	LAB	045	A	3	11
PIERCE	ANNE		1	1	20	0	CE	ENGLISH		044	C	2	9
PIERCE	HENRY	S K M	1		17	0	CE	ENGLISH		044	A	2	22
PIERCE	JOSEPH				41	ENGLAND	WM	ENGLISH	SHOEMAKER	045	D	5	18
PIERCE	JOSEPH		2			ENGLAND	WM			045	D	5	D
PIERCE	WILLIAM				45	ENGLAND	CE	ENGLISH	PLASTERER	045	A	1	36
PIERSON	ALLITSON				33	0	PM	ENGLISH	CABINET MAKER	045	B	1	46
PIGGOTT	JAMES				60	ENGLAND	CE	ENGLISH	TOLL KEEPER	045	B	1	67
PIGGOTT	JOHN		1		17	0	RC	IRE	LAB	044	B	3	47
PIKE	DANIEL				32	CANADA	MN	GERMAN	FARMER	045	D	6	55
PIKE	FRANCIS				67	U STATES	MN	GERMAN	FARMER	045	D	6	55
PIKE	JOHN				40	0	MN	GERMAN	FARMER	045	D	5	71
PIKE	PETER				44	CANADA	MN	GERMAN	FARMER	045	D	6	32
PILFER	THOMAS				34	0	PS	GERMAN	LAB	043	E	3	36
PILKEY	DAVID		2		20	0	PM		F	045	C	4	D
PILKEY	GEORGE				49	0	PM	FRENCH	F	045	C	4	40
PILKINGTON	JAMES				39	0	CE	ENGLISH	FARM MANAGER	043	B	1	42
PILLOW	WILLIAM		1		8	0	WM	ENGLISH		043	B	4	41
PILMAN	ELIZABETH		1	1	25	DUTCH	CE	DUTCH	SERVANT	044	C	3	72
PIM	THOMAS	H	1		32	IRELAND	QU	IRISH		043	H	2	6
PINCHIN	ROBERT				30	ENGLAND	PM	ENGLISH	F	044	A	1	42
PINDAR	RICHARD				55	ENGLAND	CE	ENGLISH	INNKEEPER	043	E	2	15
PINDAR	WILLIAM				45	ENGLAND	CE	ENGLISH	F	043	E	2	5
PINDER	ADAM				46	ENGLAND	PM	ENGLISH	F	044	C	2	45
PINGE	MRS WILLIAM			1	35	0	CE	GERMAN		045	D	4	30
PINGLE	CAROLINE			1	56	0	WM	GERMAN		045	D	3	18
PINGLE	GEORGE				60	0	CE	DANISH	FARMER	045	D	4	14
PINGLE	GEORGE				35	0	CE	GERMAN	FARMER	045	D	4	33
PINGLE	HENRY				58	0	LU	GERMAN	FARMER	045	D	4	29
PINGLE	HENRY	H		1	55	US	CE	GERMAN	FARMER	045	D	4	31
PINGLE	JACOB				53	0	LU	GERMAN	FARMER	045	D	4	53
PINGLE	JOHN				66	0	CE	ENGLISH	FARMER	045	D	4	32
PINKERTON	JAMES				29	ONTARIO	CP	IRISH	FARMER	043	A	4	33
PINKERTON	JAMES				42	0	NR	IRISH	FARMER	043	A	4	68
PINKERTON	JOHN				26	0	CP	IRISH	FARMER	043	A	4	33

SURNAME	NAME1	NAME2	STRAY	SEX	AGE	BIRTHPL	RELIGION	ORIGIN	OCCUP	DIST	SUB_DIST	DIV	PAGE
PINKERTON	JOHN				48	IRELAND	CE	IRISH	FARMER	043	A	4	40
PINKERTON	SAMUEL				60	IRELAND	CE	IRISH	FARMER	043	A	4	68
PINKERTON	WILLIAM				27	0	CP	IRISH	FARMER	043	A	4	33
PINKERTON	WILLIAM				27	0	WM	IRISH	FARMER	043	A	4	68
PINNEY	TIBA				67	UNITED STATES	PS	ENGLISH	WOOLCARDER	043	E	1	37
PIPER	CATHRINE		1		37	CANADA	WM	GERMAN		045	D	6	31
PIPER	ISAAC				23	0	MN	GERMAN	FARMER	045	D	6	16
PIPER	JAMES				40	ENGLAND	CE	ENGLISH	LAB	045	A	4	28
PIPHER	ABRAHAM		2		29	0	CX		F	044	B	2	D
PIPHER	ABRAHAM				25	0	MN	GERMAN		045	D	6	16
PIPHER	CATHARINE			1	63	0	BA	GERMAN		043	B	3	18
PIPHER	CHRISTINA		1	1	45	0	BA	GERMAN		043	B	3	20
PIPHER	GEORGE				45	0	BA	GERMAN	FARMER	043	B	3	19
PIPHER	GEORGE				43	0	CN	GERMAN	F	043	B	5	36
PIPHER	JOSEPH				39	0	WM	GERMAN	FARMER	045	D	4	51
PIPHER	LEA			1	45	0	MN	GERMAN		045	D	6	16
PIPHER	MARGARET		2	1		0	NG			044	B	2	D
PIPHER	MARY		1	1	7	0	MN	GERMAN		045	D	6	14
PIPHER	MATILDA		1	1	12	CANADA	MN	GERMAN		045	D	6	45
PIPHER	SUSANNA		1	1	16	0	PM	GERMAN		043	B	5	20
PIPHER	WILLIAM		1		76	UNITED STATES	TU	GERMAN		043	B	3	18
PITT	ELIZA		1	F	26	0	EM	ENGLISH		043	A	1	60
PITT	ELIZA		2	F		0	NG			043	A	1	D
PITT	WILLIAM		2	M	26	0	EM		LAB	043	A	1	D
PIVITT	FLETCHER				45	ENG	BA	ENG	LAB	045	C	1	47
PLATT	ANNIE		1	1	42	0	CE	IRISH		044	A	2	33
PLAXTON	ANTHONY				49	ENGLAND	PM	ENGLISH	F	043	A	3	59
PLAYFAIR	JOHN	S			44	SCOTLAND	PS	SCOTCH	MERCHANT	045	B	2	34
PLAYTER	AARON				71	0	CE	ENGLISH	STORE KEEPER	043	B	1	2
PLAYTER	CATH			1	31	0	WM	ENGLISH		044	B	5	49
PLAYTER	CHARLES				24	0	QU	ENGLISH	F	043	B	4	44
PLAYTER	CHARLES				40	0	EP	ENG	F	044	B	2	3
PLAYTER	EDWARD				35	0	CE	ENGLISH	PHYSICIAN	043	D		59
PLAYTER	GEORGE				66	US	QU	ENGLISH	F	043	B	5	33
PLAYTER	JAMES				38	0	WM	ENGLISH	MACHINIST	043	C		46
PLAYTER	JOHN				36	0	WM	ENGLISH	F	043	B	4	18
PLAYTER	NELSON				29	0	CE	ENG	F	044	B	2	46
PLAYTER	PHOEBE	ELMA	1	1	23	0	QU	ENGLISH	HOUSEKEEPER	043	D		51
PLAYTER	PIVILERTON	M			39	0	*QU	ENG	AGENT	043	D		84
PLAYTER	PRICILLA			1	58	0	WM	ENGLISH		043	C		33
PLAYTER	RICHARD	E			58	0	CE	ENGLISH	FARMER	045	A	1	84
PLAYTER	ROBERT				41	0	CE	ENGLISH	FARMER	045	A	1	91
PLAYTER	T	H			30	0	WM	ENGLISH	F	044	B	5	49
PLAYTER	THOMAS				60	0	WM	ENGLISH	F	044	B	5	49
PLAYTER	WATSON				58	0	QU	ENGLISH	F	043	B	4	44
PLAYTER	WATSON				25	0	QU	ENGLISH	F	043	B	5	27
PLAYTER	WM	WALTER	1		28	0	WM	ENGLISH	GENTLEMAN	043	D		51
PLAYTON	ANN		1	1	18	0	PM	ENGLISH		044	B	5	79
PLEUX	ANTHONY				24	0	RC	FRENCH	LAB	043	H	2	22
PLEUX	ANTHONY		1		24	ONTARIO	RC	FRENCH	LABOURER	043	H	2	22
PLOUGHMAN	BENJAMIN				37	ENGLAND	WM	ENGLISH	MOLDER	044	C	3	10
PLOUGHMAN	GEORGE				50	ENG	CE	ENG	F	044	B	2	41
PLOWMAN	WILLIAM				50	ENGLAND	CE	ENGLISH	TANNER	045	B	1	73
PLOWRIGHT	ISAAC				57	ENGLAND	CE	ENGLISH	LAB	044	A	3	24
PLOWRIGHT	SAMUEL				40	ENGLAND	CE	ENGLISH	F	044	A	2	32
PLUMMERAGE	JAS		1		60	ENGLISH	CE	ENGLISH	LAB	044	B	5	55
PLUNKETT	ROBERT				32	IRELAND	CE	IRISH	F	044	C	1	57
PLUNKETT	ROBERT				74	IRELAND	CE	IRISH	F	044	C	4	60
POFF	SARAH		1	1	21	0	WM	SCOTCH	SERVANT	044	C	2	48
POGUE	THOMAS				27	0	CP	IRELAND	COOPER	045	D	2	5
POGUE	WILLIAM				33	IRELAND	CP	SCOTLAND	COOPER	045	D	2	29
POINTEN	JAMES				29	0	PM	ENGLISH	LAB	043	B	2	4
POINTON	HENRY				64	ENGLAND	PM	ENGLISH	PEDLAR	043	B	1	32
POINTON	HENRY				41	ENGLAND	WM	ENGLAND	FARMER	045	D	2	3
POLLACK	ALEXANDER		1		21	SCOTLAND	CP	SCOTCH	FARMER	045	D	2	63
POLLACK	WILLIAM				66	N SCO	CP	IRISH	BOOKEEPER	045	D	2	6
POLLARD	JOHN		1		18	ENGLAND	PM	ENGLISH	F LAB	043	B	5	8
POLLARD	JOHN				38	IRELAND	WM	IRISH	F	044	C	1	1
POLLARD	MARIAH		1	1	81	UNITED STATES	CN	ENGLISH		043	B	3	2
POLLARD	WILLIAM				56	ENGLAND	PM	ENGLISH	F	043	B	5	7
POLLING	MATHEW		1		16	0	NC	ENGLISH	LAB	043	E	2	7
POLLOCK	DUNCAN	JAMES			28	0	CP	SCOTCH	PHYSICIAN	045	C	3	50
POLLOCK	JAMES	E			60	NOVA SCOTIA	CP	SCOTCH	FARMER	043	G	1	25
POLLOCK	JAMES	E	2			ONTARIO	CP			043	G	1	D
POLLOCK	MATILDA		1	1	26	0	WM	SCOTLAND	DRESS MAKER	045	D	2	8
POLLOCK	WILLIAM				25	ONTARIO	CP	SCOTCH	FARMER	043	G	1	26
POLLY	MARTHA		1	1	20	ENGLAND	BA	ENGLISH		045	D	4	48
POLSON	JOHN				52	SCOTLAND	CP	SCOTCH	F	044	A	1	20
POOL	ANN		1	1	40	SCOTLAND	CS	SCOTCH	FARMER	045	D	3	51
POOL	JOHN		1	1	35	ENGLAND	CO	ENGLISH	FOREMAN	044	B	5	22
POPE	JAMES				24	0	CE	ENGLISH	STORE KEEPER	044	C	4	65
POPPLEWELL	SAMUEL				41	ENGLAND	CE	ENGLISH	WEAVER	045	A	2	34
PORRIT	THOMAS				63	ENGLAND	CE	ENGLISH	BLACKSMITH	043	B	1	23
PORRIT	THOMAS				27	0	WM	ENGLISH	GENERAL AGENT	043	B	1	23
PORT	JAMES				48	ONTARIO	EM	CHIPPAWA	FARMER	043	H	2	58
PORT	JAMES				48	0	WM	CHIPPAWA	F	043	H	2	58
PORT	JOHN		1		16	ENGLAND	CE	ENGLISH	SERVANT	045	B	2	27
PORT	WILLIAM				67	0	EM	CHIPPAWA	F	043	H	2	58
PORT	WILLIAM				67	ONTARIO	EM	CHIPPAWA	FARMER	043	H	2	58
PORTER	BETSY	ANN	2	1	74	IRELAND	CE			045	A	2	D
PORTER	CAROLINE			F	41	ENGLAND	PM	ENGLISH	FARMER	043	A	1	27
PORTER	DELILA		1	1	49	0	CE	FRENCH	SERVANT	043	E	2	67
PORTER	JOHN		1		72	ENGLAND	CE	ENGLISH	GENT	043	E	2	8
PORTER	JOHN				61	ENGLAND	WM	ENGLISH	F	044	B	5	63
PORTER	JOHN				73	0	WM	IRISH	FARMER	044	C	3	19
PORTER	MATTHEW				39	ENGLAND	WM	ENGLISH	TAILOR	043	E	3	44
PORTER	RICHARD		1		18	ENGLAND	WM	ENGLISH	BAKER	043	D		17
PORTER	ROBERT				55	ENGLAND	PM	ENGLISH	LAB	045	B	1	53
PORTER	SARAH		1	1	80	IRELAND	CE	IRISH		043	G	2	16
PORTER	THOMAS			M	68	ENGLAND	WM	ENGLISH	F	043	A	2	37
PORTER	WALTER		1		2	0	CE	ENGLISH		045	B	1	19
PORTER	WILLIAM				37	0	WM	ENGLISH	FARMER	043	A	4	63
PORTWINE	FRANCIS				54	GERM	CE	GERM	FISHERMAN	045	C	1	12
POSSON	WILLIAM			M	39	ENGLAND	PR	ENGLISH	F	043	A	1	54
POST	ANN		1		55	IRELAND	RC	IRISH		045	B	1	49
POTTAGE	EDWARD			M	65	ENGLAND	CE	ENGLAND	F	043	A	5	28

SURNAME	NAME1	NAME2	STRAY	SEX	AGE	BIRTHPL	RELIGION	ORIGIN	OCCUP	DIST	SUB_DIST	DIV	PAGE
POTTAGE	FRANCIS		2	M	23	0	CE		F	043	A	5	D
POTTAGE	JOHN			M	39	ENGLAND	CE	ENGLAND	F	043	A	5	27
POTTER	DANIEL				37	0	WM	GERMAN	PLASTERER	043	B	3	21
POTTER	GERMAN				37	0	WM	ENGLISH	F	045	C	2	1
POTTER	OLIVER		1		31	ENGLAND	ME	ENGLISH	FARM LABOURER	045	C	4	27
POTTS	JOHN		1	M	40	IRELAND	CE	IRISH	LAB	043	A	2	54
POTTS	MARY		1	1	11	0	PR	IRISH	SERVANT	045	A	1	34
POULTER	JOHN				51	ENGLAND	CE	ENGLISH	INNKEEPER	044	C	4	82
POULTON	RICHARD		1	M	26	ENGLAND	CE	ENGLAND	L	043	A	5	25
POWEL	MARTHA		1	1	71	US	QU	GERMAN		043	B	5	33
POWELL	CHARLES				33	ENGLAND	CE	ENGLISH	PUMP MKR	044	C	1	29
POWELL	EDITH			1	38	0	EM	IRISH	TAILORESS	043	D		8
POWELL	GEORGE				48	ENGLAND	CE	ENGLISH	F	043	B	2	33
POWELL	ISAAC			M	35	0	QU	ENGLAND	F	043	A	5	45
POWELL	JOSEPH				50	IRELAND	CE	IRISH	F	045	C	3	5
POWELL	MARIAH		1	1	40	IRELAND	CE	IRISH		043	B	3	16
POWELL	REUBEN				60	0	QU	ENGLISH	F	043	E	1	20
POWELL	SUSAN			1	54	ENGLAND	WM	ENGLISH		044	C	2	42
POWELL	THOMAS		1		28	ENGLAND	FW	ENGLISH	SERVANT	045	A	3	28
POWELL	WILLIAM				56	ENG	CE	ENG	F	044	B	2	24
POWER	CATHARINE		1	1	18	0	RC	IRISH	SCHOOL TEACHER	043	D		4
POWER	JAMES				50	IRELAND	RC	IRISH	LAB	044	C	4	7
POWER	PATRICK				32	IRELAND	RC	IRISH	F	044	A	2	35
POWERS	CATHRINE			1	26	0	MN	IRISH		045	D	6	11
POWERS	JAMES				38	IRELAND	RC	IRISH	FARMER	044	C	3	60
POWERS	JOHN		1		5	0	MN	IRISH		045	D	6	11
POWERS	MARY		1	1	38	IRELAND	RC	IRISH	SERVANT	045	D	5	59
POWERS	MICHAEL				39	0	RC	IRE	F	044	B	3	10
POWERS	RICHARD				26	0	RC	IRE	LAB	044	B	3	10
POWERS	THOMAS		1		70	IRE	RC	IRE	HELPER	044	B	4	4
POWLEY	HENRY				29	0	FK	ENGLISH	F	043	A	3	49
POWLEY	JOSEPH				23	0	WM	ENGLISH	F	043	A	3	49
POYNTON	WILLIAM				60	ENGLAND	NC	ENGLISH	PEDLAR	043	B	4	1
PRATT	JOSEPH	L			39	ENGLAND	CE	ENGLISH	F	044	C	1	8
PRAYLING	WILLIAM				56	ENGLAND	CE	ENGLISH	BLACKSMITH	044	C	1	22
PREBBLE	MARY	A	1	1	19	0	WM	ENGLISH		043	B	1	18
PREMMER	WILLIAM				43	ENGLAND	PS	ENGLISH	FARM LABOURER	045	C	3	49
PRENTICE	AARON				46	0	EV	GER	F	044	B	1	38
PRENTISS	OLIVER				40	0	CE	SCOTCH	WAGON MAKER	044	A	3	43
PRENTISS	WM	HERBERT	2			0	CE			044	A	3	D
PRESCOTT	JABEZ				50	ENG	CP	ENG	MILLER	044	B	1	13
PRESS	CYNTHIA	MARIA	1	1	20	US	CP	IRISH		045	C	3	2
PRESS	GEORGE		1		22	0	CN	GERMAN	F LAB	043	B	5	13
PRESS	JAMES				40	0	VM	GERMAN	TEAMSTER	045	D	3	2
PRESS	SARAH	JANE	1	1	18	0	NC	ENGLISH		043	C		13
PRESS	WILLIAM	S	1		13	0	NC	ENGLISH		043	C		13
PREST	ALBERT		1		10	0	WM	ENGLISH		043	D		38
PREST	ELIZABETH		1	1	24	0	WM	ENGLISH		043	D		38
PREST	ROBERT				42	ENGLAND	WM	ENGLISH	SHOEMAKER	043	D		68
PRESTLY	ROBERT				56	IRELAND	CE	IRISH	F	044	C	4	12
PRESTON	ANN			1	53	IRELAND	WM	IRISH		045	D	1	3
PRESTON	JAMES				36	IRE	EM	IRISH	LAB	044	B	1	33
PRESTON	JONATHAN				45	ENGLAND	BA	ENGLISH	GARDENER	045	A	1	82
PRESTON	WILLIAM				48	ENGLAND	CE	ENGLISH	F	043	B	5	37
PRETTY	HENRY				49	ENGLAND	CE	ENGLISH	MILLER	045	A	3	7
PRETTY	HEZEKIAH				23	0	PM	ENGLISH	STOREKEEPER	043	B	2	18
PRETTY	JOSEPH				68	ENGLAND	PM	ENGLISH	F	043	B	2	18
PREW	ANTHONY		1		24	0	RC	FRENCH	LAB	043	H	1	16
PREW	DAVID		1		18	0	RC	FRENCH	LAB	043	H	1	16
PREW	EDWARD		1		22	0	RC	FRENCH	LAB	043	H	1	16
PREW	JOSEPH		1		26	0	RC	FRENCH	LAB	043	H	1	16
PREW	MARY		1	1	20	0	RC	FRENCH		043	H	1	16
PRICE	ELISA		1	1	40	ENGLAND	CE	ENGLISH	SERVANT	045	B	2	37
PRICE	EVANS				27	ENGLAND	WM	ENGLISH	LAB	045	A	3	37
PRICE	HENRY	C		M	49	ENGLAND	CE	ENGLISH	INN KEEPER	043	A	2	46
PRICE	MARY			1	56	ENGLAND	CE	ENGLISH		044	C	4	3
PRICE	ROBERT				41	IRELAND	CE	IRISH	TEACHER	043	G	1	1
PRICE	SARAH			1	51	US	CE	ENGLISH		045	B	2	17
PRICE	STEPHEN				37	ENGLAND	CE	ENGLISH	PEDLER	045	A	1	101
PRICHARD	HENRY				24	US	PS	ENG	FINISHER	044	B	2	23
PRICKET	ANNIE		1	1	15	0	WM	IRISH	SERVANT	044	C	3	58
PRICKET	WILLIAM		1		18	US	WM	IRISH	SERVANT	044	C	3	58
PRIDDLE	STEPHEN				57	ENGLAND	CO	ENGLISH	FARM LABOURER	045	D	3	9
PRIEDUCK	WILLIAM				41	ENGLAND	CE	ENGLISH	CLERGYMAN	044	C	3	28
PRIGIEON	THOMAS				35	ENGLAND	CE	ENGLISH	LAB	045	A	1	98
PRIMDY	HENRY				33	UNITED STATES	WM	ENGLISH	CARDER & SPINNER	043	E	3	47
PRINCE	ABIAH				42	ENGLAND	CE	ENGLISH	LAB	043	H	1	11
PRINCE	ABRAHAM				50	ENGLAND	CE	ENGLISH	LAB	043	H	2	25
PRINCE	ABRAHAM				50	ENGLAND	CE	ENGLISH	LABOURER	043	H	2	25
PRINDEL	PHILLIP				44	ONTARIO	PR	SCOTCH	FARMER	043	G	2	19
PRINDLE	DARIUS				27	ONTARIO	PR	SCOTCH	FARMER	043	G	2	45
PRINDLE	SIMON				23	ONTARIO	PR	SCOTCH	FARMER	043	G	2	9
PRINGELE	ANDREW				70	U STATES	MN	GERMAN	FERMER	045	D	6	60
PRINGLE	CHARLES		1		10	0	WM	ENGLISH		043	H	2	33
PRINGLE	CHARLES		1		10	ONTARIO	WM	ENGLISH		043	H	2	33
PRINGLE	EDWARD			M	27	0	PS	IRISH	SAWYER	043	A	1	72
PRINGLE	ELLEN		1	1	4	0	WM	ENGLISH		043	H	2	33
PRINGLE	ELLEN		1	1	4	ONTARIO	WM	ENGLISH		043	H	2	33
PRINGLE	GEORGE			M	58	IRELAND	WM	IRISH	F	043	A	2	1
PRINGLE	GEORGE				22	0	CE	IRISH	F	043	A	3	16
PRINGLE	GEORGE				30	0	WM	SCOTCH	WAGGON MAKER	045	D	5	5
PRINGLE	GEORGE				28	IRELAND	CP	IRISH	BLACKSMITH	044	C	2	22
PRINGLE	JAMES		1		30	0	UP	SCOTCH	WATCH MAKER	043	C		27
PRINGLE	JAMES				67	SCOTLAND	CS	SCOTCH	WAGGONMAKER	045	D	5	8
PRINGLE	JOHN				45	0	CE	IRISH	F	043	A	3	16
PRINGLE	LUCY		1	1	11	ONTARIO	EM	SCOTCH		043	G	1	28
PRINGLE	MARY			1	22	0	PM	IRISH	DRESSMAKER	043	A	3	12
PRINGLE	ROBT				34	0	WM	SCOTCH	WAGGON MAKER	045	D	5	3
PRIOR	DANIEL				42	ENGLAND	PM	ENGLISH	POSTMASTER	043	B	3	23
PRISKET	HANNAH			1	50	ENGLAND	WM	ENGLISH		044	C	3	21
PRITCHARD	JOHN				45	ENGLAND	WM	ENGLISH	BREWER	045	B	1	51
PROCTER	ISAAC			M	56	0	CN	ENGLAND	F	043	A	5	18
PROCTOR	FRANCES		1	1	50	ENGLAND	CE	ENGLISH		045	A	1	73
PROCTOR	GERSHAM			M	54	0	QU	ENGLAND	F	043	A	5	26
PROCTOR	HARRISON				46	0	QU	ENGLISH	F	043	E	1	19
PROCTOR	JOHN			M	55	IRELAND	WM	IRELAND	F	043	A	5	37

SURNAME	NAME1	NAME2	STRAY	SEX	AGE	BIRTHPL	RELIGION	ORIGIN	OCCUP	DIST	SUB_DIST	DIV	PAGE
PROCTOR	MARGARET		2	1	9	0	CE			045	D	2	D
PROCTOR	RICHARD		1		19	ENGLAND	CE	ENGLISH	PAINTER	043	A	1	73
PROCTOR	SAMUEL				40	0	WM	ENGLISH	CARPENTER	043	E	1	42
PROCTOR	SAMUEL		1		90	0	CE	ENGLISH		045	A	2	32
PROCTOR	SIMON				35	0	CE	IRELAND	HOTEL KEEPER	045	D	2	7
PROCTOR	WILLIAM				57	IRELAND	WM	IRISH	FARMER	043	A	4	15
PROCTOR	WILLIAM	H	1	M	29	0	QU	ENGLAND	FARMER	043	A	5	26
PROSSER	ASA	W			25	UNITED STATES	WM	ENGLISH	LAB	043	E	3	27
PROSSER	DANIEL				25	ONTARIO	CN	IRISH	MERCHANT	043	G	2	50
PROSSER	ELIJAH				39	ONTARIO	CN	IRISH	FARMER	043	G	2	52
PROSSER	GEORGE				47	ONTARIO	CN	ENGLISH	FARMER	043	G	1	44
PROSSER	ISAAC				26	ONTARIO	WM	IRISH	FARMER	043	G	2	35
PROSSER	JOHN				45	ONTARIO	CN	IRISH	FARMER	043	G	1	24
PROSSER	JOHN	H	1		9	ONTARIO	EM	IRISH		043	G	1	28
PROSSER	LORETTA	C	2	1	3	ONTARIO	CN			043	G	1	D
PROSSER	MARY		1	1	10	ONTARIO	CN	IRISH		043	G	1	28
PROSSER	NELSON				33	ONTARIO	CN	DUTCH	FARMER	043	G	1	40
PROSSER	PETER				50	ONTARIO	CN	IRISH	FARMER	043	G	2	35
PROSSER	ROBERT		2			ONTARIO	CN			043	G	1	D
PROSSER	SOLOMON				38	ONTARIO	CN	IRISH	BLACKSMITH	043	G	1	8
PROUD	JAMES				60	ENGLAND	CE	ENGLISH	F	043	B	4	16
PROUD	RUTH		1	1	73	ENGLAND	CP	SCOTCH		045	C	4	32
PROUT	GEORGE				24	0	BC	ENGLISH		043	H	2	48
PROUT	GEORGE				24	ONTARIO	BC	ENGLISH		043	H	2	48
PROVAN	THOMAS				49	SCOTLAND	WM	SCOTCH	LABOURER	043	A	4	9
PROVO	ANDREW				23	0	WM	FRENCH	BARBER	043	C		6
PRYNE	JACOB				50	0	CN	GERMAN	F	043	B	5	12
PUICE	WM		1		51	ENGLAND	CE	ENGLISH	HOSTLER	044	B	5	30
PULFORD	GEORGE				50	ENGLAND	CE	ENGLISH	MILLER	043	F		6
PULLIN	FRANCIS		1	1	33	QUE	CE	FRENCH		045	A	3	2
PULLIN	LAPORTE		1	1	60	QUE	CE	FRENCH		045	A	3	2
PULLIN	MINNIE		1	1	20	QUE	CE	FRENCH		045	A	3	2
PURCELL	JAMES				44	IRELAND	RC	IRISH	TAILOR	043	D		64
PURCHASE	GEORGE	E			21	USA	CE	ENGLISH	PAPERMAKER	045	A	1	103
PURCHES	HENRY				58	ENGLAND	CE	ENGLISH	LAB	045	A	1	92
PURDIE	WILLIAM				60	SCOTLAND	PS	SCOTCH	F	045	C	3	36
PURDY	BETHENA			1	58	0	CN	ENGLISH	WEAVER	043	E	3	21
PURDY	FANNY		1	1	35	IRELAND	WM	IRISH	SERVANT	045	D	3	74
PURDY	HANNAH			1	48	0	CN	WELSH		043	E	2	6
PURDY	ISABELLA		1	1	63	IRELAND	CP	IRISH		045	D	5	10
PURDY	JOHN				52	ONTARIO	CN	WELSH	FARMER	043	G	1	2
PURDY	ROSINA			1	70	0	CS	ENG		045	C	1	24
PURKISS	JENNIE		2	1		0	WM			045	D	1	D
PURKISS	JOSIAH				46	0	WM	ENGLISH	MERCHANT	045	D	1	11
PURSE	WILLIAM				57	IRELAND	CP	IRISH	LAB	045	B	1	36
PURSELL	THOMAS				51	SCOTLAND	CP	SCOTCH	F	045	C	4	32
PURTLE	JOHN				37	IRELAND	RC	IRISH	F	044	C	4	15
PURVIS	JAMES				58	SCOTLAND	PS	SCOTCH	F	045	C	3	40
PURVIS	WM		1		21	0	CE	ENGLISH	CLK	044	B	5	30
PUTERBAUGH	ISAAC				23	0	WM	GER	F	044	B	3	15
PUTERBAUGH	ISAAC	SR			68	USA	WM	GER	GENT	044	B	3	15
PUTERBAUGH	JACOB				43	0	WM	GER	F	044	B	3	34
PUTERBAUGH	JOSEPH				38	0	LU	GER	F	044	B	1	50
PYBUS	DORIS		2	1	2	0	CE			043	D		D
PYBUS	EDWIN	J			24	ENGLAND	CE	ENGLISH	SADDLER	043	D		50
PYFER	HANNAH		1	1	17	0	WM	GERMAN		045	D	5	4
PYMAN	JOHN		1		76	ENGLAND	CE	ENGLISH	SHOEMAKER	043	E	1	42
PYNE	MARY	ANN		1	28	0	CS	IRISH		044	B	6	27
PYPHER	ELIZABETH		1	1	14	0	MN	GERMAN		043	B	3	18
PYPHER	JOHN				65	0	CN	GERMAN	FARMER	043	B	3	10
PYPHER	JOSEPH				24	0	CN	GERMAN	FARMER	043	B	3	11
PYPHER	SILVESTER		1		10	0	MN	GERMAN		043	B	3	18
QINLAN	OWEN			M	40	IRELAND	RC	IRISH	LAB	043	A	1	55
QUAID	ROBERT		1		53	ENGLAND	CE	ENGLISH	SERVANT	045	B	2	29
QUAIL	ROBERT		2		67	IRELAND	CE		SOLDIER	044	A	2	D
QUANCE	GEORGE		1		88	GERMANY	TU	GERMAN		045	D	3	11
QUANTZ	ALBERT				28	0	WM	GERMAN	FARMER	045	D	1	23
QUANTZ	ALFRED				33	0	WM	GERMAN	CARPENTER	045	D	1	51
QUANTZ	DANIEL				41	0	LU	GERMAN	FARMER	045	D	1	39
QUANTZ	FREDERICK				58	0	WM	GERMAN	FARMER	045	D	2	43
QUANTZ	GEORGE				59	0	LU	ENGLISH	FARMER	045	D	1	23
QUANTZ	GEORGE	B			45	0	CN	GERMAN	F	043	B	5	11
QUANTZ	HENRY				56	0	WM	GERMAN	FARMER	045	D	1	23
QUANTZ	ISACK				22	0	CN	GERMAN	CHEESE MAKER	045	D	3	78
QUANTZ	JACOB		1		20	0	WM	GER	F	044	B	3	15
QUANTZE	JOHN				48	0	CN	GERMAN	CARPENTER	045	D	3	10
QUANTZE	PHILIP				40	0	CN	GERMAN	CARPENTER	045	D	3	10
QUARY	JOHN				25	0	PM	ENGLISH	WAGGON MAKER	043	C		21
QUERY	MARY			1	60	ENGLAND	PM	ENGLISH		045	D	4	8
QUEWE	JOHN				36	QUEBEC	RC	SCOTCH	LUMBERMAN	043	G	1	49
QUIBELL	JOHN				36	ENGLAND	WM	ENGLISH	MERCHANT	043	E	3	7
QUIGLEY	MARY	ANN		1	45	IRELAND	RC	IRISH		043	E	3	15
QUIGLY	JAMES		1		25	ENGLAND	PS	IRISH	LAB	044	C	4	84
QUIGLY	JOHN				60	IRELAND	RC	IRISH	F	043	B	1	3
QUIGLY	JOHN				22	0	RC	IRISH	F	043	B	1	4
QUILED	SHARLOTT			1	65	ENGLAND	WM	ENGLISH		044	C	3	41
QUINLAVIN	JAMES				60	IRELAND	RC	IRISH	F	043	E	2	51
QUINN	ANN			1	42	IRELAND	RC	IRISH	SERVANT	045	A	3	35
QUINN	JOHN				30	IRELAND	CE	IRISH	LAB	044	C	4	52
QUINN	NEIL				60	IRELAND	RC	IRISH	TANNER	043	F		27
QUINN	PATRICK				55	IRELAND	RC	IRISH	LABOURER	045	A	1	38
QUINN	ROBERT				27	IRELAND	CE	IRISH	STATION AGENT	043	F		9
QUINN	ROBT	A	2			0	CE			043	F		D
QUINN	THOMAS				36	IRELAND	RC	IRISH	F	044	A	3	22
QUINN	THOMAS				46	IRELAND	RC	IRISH	LAB	045	C	2	12
QUINTON	BENJAMIN				62	SCOTLAND	CP	SCOTCH	LAB	044	C	4	20
QUIRK	JOHANNA		1	1	35	IRELAND	RC	IRISH	SERVANT	043	D		5
QUIRK	MARGARET		1	1	25	IRELAND	RC	IRISH	SERVANT	043	D		72
QUIRY	GEORGE		2		61	ENGLAND	PM		MASON	045	D	4	D
RACISH	MARY		1	F	17	U STATES	EM	ENGLISH		043	A	1	18
RACKERT	CHARLES			M	38	GERMANY	LU	GERMAN	LAB	043	A	2	14
RACKHAM	ROBERT				62	ENGLAND	PM	ENGLISH	FARMER	045	A	1	101
RADDICK	WILLIAM				64	SCOTLAND	NG	SCOTCH	WHEELWRIGHT	043	B	3	61
RAE	ALEXANDER		1		30	0	OP	SCOTCH	SCHOOL TEACHER	043	H	2	45
RAE	ALEXANDER				30	ONTARIO	CS	SCOTCH	SCHOOL TEACHER	043	H	2	45
RAE	ALLEN		1		19	SCOTLAND	CS	SCOTCH		045	D	3	60

SURNAME	NAME1	NAME2	STRAY	SEX	AGE	BIRTHPL	RELIGION	ORIGIN	OCCUP	DIST	SUB_DIST	DIV	PAGE
RAE	ELIZABETH			1	70	SCOTLAND	OP	SCOTCH		043	H	2	29
RAE	ELIZABETH		1	1	70	SCOTLAND	CS	SCOTCH		043	H	2	29
RAE	JAMES				30	0	PS	SCOTCH	FARMER	043	B	3	51
RAE	JANE		1	1	23	SCOTLAND	CS	SCOTCH	SERVANT	045	D	3	60
RAE	JOHN				68	SCOTLAND	CP	SCOTCH	WEAVER	043	H	1	39
RAE	MATTHEW				35	0	WM	SCOTCH	FARMER	043	B	3	72
RAE	MICHAEL				50	SCOTLAND	OP	SCOTCH	LAB	043	H	2	38
RAE	MICHAEL				50	SCOTLAND	CS	SCOTCH	LABOURER	043	H	2	38
RAE	ROBERT		1		28	SCOTLAND	CS	SCOTCH	F LABOURER	045	D	3	60
RAE	WALTER				37	0	CP	SCOTCH	F	043	H	1	40
RAEMAND	WILLIAM		1		25	0	LU	GER	LAB	044	B	3	4
RAFFERTY	FRANCES		1	M	89	IRELAND	RC	IRISH	RETIRED	043	A	1	32
RAFFERTY	JAMES			M	26	0	RC	IRISH	F	043	A	1	32
RAHAM	WILLIAM				24	0	WM	ENGLISH	LAB	043	F		21
RAHM	CHARLES				37	ENGLAND	WM	ENGLISH	CARPENTER	043	B	1	40
RAILTON	BILTON				42	ENGLAND	PR	ENGLISH	FARMER	043	G	2	27
RAILTON	DAVID				43	ENGLAND	CE	ENGLISH	FARMER	043	G	2	18
RAILTON	ISABELLA		1		1	ONTARIO	EM	ENGLISH		043	G	1	11
RAINEY	ELIZA		1	1	30	IRELAND	WM	IRISH		044	B	5	53
RAITH	THOMAS				38	PEI	EM	ENG	BLACKSMITH	044	B	3	6
RALL	JOHN				65	IRELAND	CE	IRISH	INN KEEPER	044	B	5	11
RALPH	SAMUEL				55	IRELAND	RC	IRISH	LAB	043	D		30
RAMAGE	THOMAS				44	SCOTLAND	CP	SCOTCH	F	044	A	2	25
RAMER	A	JOHN			39	0	MN	GERMAN	FARMER	045	D	5	1
RAMER	ABRAHAM				57	0	MN	GERMAN	FARMER	045	D	5	42
RAMER	CHRISTIAN		1		73	GERMANY	TU	GERMAN		045	D	2	56
RAMER	JACOB				23	0	CN	GERMAN	F	043	B	5	14
RAMER	JACOB				42	0	MN	GERMAN	FARMER	045	D	5	55
RAMER	JESSIE		2			0	CN			043	B	5	D
RAMER	JOHN				41	0	MN	GERMAN	LABOURER	045	D	5	26
RAMER	JOHN	N			35	0	VM	GERMAN	CHEESE MAKER	045	D	5	51
RAMER	PETER				71	U STATES	MN	GERMAN	FARMER	045	D	5	1
RAMER	SIMON				29	0	MN	GERMAN	FARMER	045	D	5	1
RAMSAY	ARCHIBALD				36	SCOTLAND	CP	SCOTCH	FARM LABOURER	045	C	4	42
RAMSAY	EDWIN		1		9	0	CE	IRISH		044	A	3	38
RAMSAY	FRANK	D	1		24	0	CP	SCOTCH	MERCHANT	043	A	4	22
RAMSAY	HANNAH		1	1	41	0	CE	GERMAN	SERVANT	044	A	3	37
RAMSAY	JOHN		2		1	ONTARIO	CS			043	H	2	D
RAMSAY	JOHN		2		1	0	OP			043	H	2	D
RAMSAY	MARIA		1	1	12	0	CE	ENG		044	B	1	62
RAMSAY	MARY		1	1	31	ENGLAND	WM	ENGLISH		043	A	4	7
RAMSAY	MARY		1	1	9	0	CE	IRISH		043	A	4	46
RAMSAY	MICHAEL		1		16	0	CE	IRISH	F LAB	044	A	3	38
RAMSAY	ROBERT				36	ENGLAND	NR		WHEELWRIGHT	043	A	4	7
RAMSAY	SEPTIMUS	F			65	ENGLAND	CE	ENGLISH	CLERGYMAN	043	D		72
RAMSAY	THOMAS		1		19	0	CE	ENG	F	044	B	1	62
RAMSAY	WILLIAM				27	SCOTLAND	CS	SCOTCH	BUILDER	043	H	2	11
RAMSAY	WILLIAM				60	SCOTLAND	PM	SCOTCH	LAB	044	C	2	4
RAMSAY	WILLIAM				36	SCOTLAND	CP	SCOTCH	WHOLESALE GROCER	044	C	2	20
RAMSDEN	DAVID		1	M	71	ENGLAND	CE	ENGLAND	F	043	A	5	22
RAMSDEN	GEORGE		1	M	17	0	CE	ENGLAND	F	043	A	5	22
RAMSDEN	JOHN				52	0	WM	ENGLISH	MILLER	043	E	3	22
RAMSDEN	THOMAS			M	60	ENGLAND	CE	ENGLAND	F	043	A	5	19
RAMSDEN	WILLIAM			M	30	0	CE	ENGLAND	F	043	A	5	19
RAMSEY	DUGALD				42	SCOTLAND	CP	SCOTCH	FARMER	045	D	2	56
RAMSEY	ELIZABETH		1	1	19	SCOTLAND	CS	SCOTCH		045	D	3	27
RAMSEY	GEO				31	ENGLAND	WM	ENGLISH	WAGON MAKER	044	B	5	25
RAMSEY	ROBERT		1		63	IRELAND	OP	IRISH		043	A	3	13
RAMSEY	WILLIAM				27	SCOTLAND	CP	SCOTCH	BUILDER	043	H	2	11
RAMSEY	WM		1		13	0	PS	SCOTCH		044	B	5	63
RAMSY	JOHN	B			41	0	CE	IRISH	F	043	A	6	45
RANDALL	ALFRED				27	0	WM	ENGLISH	F	043	B	5	42
RANDALL	COMBY				58	0	QU	ENGLISH	F	043	B	4	45
RANDALL	EDWARD				63	0	NG	ENGLISH	SAWYER	043	B	5	41
RANDALL	GEORGE				33	0	QU	GERMAN	LAB	043	B	5	29
RANDALL	JOHN				58	0	QU	ENGLISH	F	043	B	4	31
RANDALL	JOHN				27	0	QU	GERMAN	F	043	B	5	31
RANDALL	JONATHAN				60	0	CE	GERMAN	F	043	B	5	17
RANDALL	JOSEPH				49	0	EM	ENGLISH	FARMER	043	B	3	38
RANDS	GEORGE		2			0	CE			045	D	2	D
RANDS	JAMES		1		19	0	WM	GERMAN	LABOURER	045	D	4	3
RANDS	WILLIAM				61	ENGLAND	CE	ENGLISH	LABOURER	045	D	3	24
RANDS	WILLIAM				23	0	CE	ENGLISH	LABORER	045	D	2	47
RANIE	ELIZABETH		1	1	30	0	CE	IRISH		043	B	3	8
RANK	ELIZABETH		1	F	16	0	CE	ENGLISH		043	A	1	30
RANK	GEORGE				30	0	FW	ENGLISH	LAB	043	B	1	13
RANKIN	ELIZA			1	43	0	WM	IRISH		045	D	5	10
RANKIN	MARGRET			1	53	IRE	EP	IRE		044	B	3	26
RANKIN	MARY			1	70	IRISH	CS	SCOTCH		043	B	1	5
RANKIN	THOMAS				25	SCOTLAND	EM	SCOTTISH	LAB	044	C	1	40
RANNIE	WILLIAM				23	SCOTLAND	CS	SCOTCH	S TEACHER	043	E	2	57
RANSOM	ABRAHAM		1		85	ENGLAND	CE	ENGLISH	PENSIONER	045	B	1	4
RANSOM	ANN			1	69	ENGLAND	WM	ENGLISH		043	C		6
RANSOM	JOHN			M	45	ENGLAND	EM	ENGLISH	LAB	043	A	2	48
RANSOM	JOHN		1	M	15	0	CE	ENGLAND	SAWYER	043	A	5	6
RANSOM	THOMAS				27	0	NC	ENGLISH	GENTLEMAN	043	C		48
RANSOM	URSULE		1	1	87	ENGLAND	CE	ENGLISH		045	B	1	4
RAPPLE	MATHEW				61	IRELAND	CE	IRISH	GARDNER	044	C	4	77
RAPSAN	WILLIAM		1		65	0	PM	ENGLISH	FARM LABOURER	043	E	3	54
RATCLIFF	DAVID				33	ENGLAND	BA	ENGLISH	F	043	B	2	2
RATCLIFF	HENRY				40	ENGLAND	BA	ENGLISH	FARMER	045	D	4	48
RATCLIFF	JOSEPH				35	ENGLAND	BA	ENGLISH	FARMER	045	D	4	43
RATCLIFF	THOMAS				50	ENGLAND	WM	ENGLISH	COOPER	043	F		3
RATCLIFF	THOMAS				27	ENGLAND	BA	ENGLISH	SAWYER	045	D	4	48
RATCLIFF	WM				70	ENGLAND	BA	ENGLISH	FARMER	045	D	4	48
RATHMELL	GEORGE		1		20	0	PM	ENGLISH	FARM LABOURER	043	E	2	67
RATHNELL	HANNAH		1	1	17	0	EM	ENGLISH		043	E	3	12
RATTAN	JAMES				60	ENGLAND	CE	ENGLISH		043	G	1	26
RATTERY	JAMES		1		15	SCOTLAND	PS	SCOTCH		045	D	6	34
RATTLE	FREDERICK		1		2	0	WM	ENGLISH		045	C	2	13
RATTLE	JAMES		1		7	0	DI	ENGLISH		045	C	2	3
RATTLE	SAMUEL		1		5	0	WM	ENGLISH		045	C	2	13
RAWLINGS	ANN			F	54	ENGLAND	EM	ENGLISH		043	A	2	52
RAWSON	ISABELLA		1	1	9	0	CP	ENGLISH		045	C	3	46
RAY	CHARLOTT		1	1	33	IRELAND	CE	IRISH	INMATE	045	B	1	72
RAY	MARY	ANN	1	1	2	0	PM	ENGLISH		044	B	6	46

SURNAME	NAME1	NAME2	STRAY	SEX	AGE	BIRTHPL	RELIGION	ORIGIN	OCCUP	DIST	SUB_DIST	DIV	PAGE
RAYMAN	WILLIAM				52	ENGLAND	WM	ENGLISH	GARDNER	045	B	1	46
RAYMER	DANIEL				37	0	PM	GERMAN	F	043	H	1	21
RAYMER	DANIEL		2		68	U STATES	MN		FARMER	045	D	5	D
RAYMER	JONAS				45	0	MN	GERMAN	FARMER	045	D	3	67
RAYMER	JOSEPH				38	0	MN	GERMAN	FARMER	045	D	3	51
RAYMER	LEVI				28	0	MN	GERMAN	FARM LAB	043	B	2	3
RAYMER	MARGARET		1	1	20	0	CN	GERMAN	SERVANT	045	D	3	68
RAYMER	PETER				25	0	VM	GERMAN	FARMER	045	D	3	50
RAYMER	WILLIAM				68	ENGLAND	PM	ENGLISH	LAB	045	A	4	18
RAYMN	CHRISTIAN		1		12	0	WM	GERMAN		045	D	5	27
RAYMN	LUDWICK		1		17	0	WM	GERMAN	SERVANT	045	D	5	27
RAYMN	PHILIP		1		14	0	WM	GERMAN		045	D	5	27
RAYMN	WILLIAM		1		10	0	WM	GERMAN		045	D	5	27
RAYMOND	MICHL				69	U STATES	LU	GERMAN	F	044	B	5	63
RAYMOND	ROBERT				44	0	WM	GER	HOTEL KEEPER	044	B	2	10
RAYMOND	THOMPSON				48	NB	CE	ENG	GENTLEMAN	044	B	1	19
REA	JAMES				63	IRELAND	CP	IRISH	FARMER	043	A	4	56
READ	ISABELLA				35	SCOTLAND	CP	SCOTCH	FARMER	045	D	2	63
READ	ISAC				60	US	CE	IRISH	LABOURER	044	C	3	63
READ	WILLIAM				68	U STATES	WM	SCOTCH	FARMER	045	D	6	29
READE	HARRISON				29	0	WM	IRISH	SCH TEACHER	044	C	1	22
READHEAD	ANN			1	59	ENGLAND	PM	ENGLISH	HATMAKER	043	B	5	21
READHEAD	ROBERT				56	ENGLAND	PM	ENGLISH	F	043	B	5	21
READING	GEORGE				44	ENGLAND	CE	ENGLISH	GARDENER	045	A	1	21
READMAN	JOHN				38	0	PM	ENGLISH	LAB	044	B	6	35
READMAN	JOSEPH				34	0	UP	ENG	F	044	B	4	36
READMAN	MICHLE				73	IRELAND	RC	IRISH		044	C	3	61
READMAN	THOMAS				59	ENGLAND	CO	ENGLISH	F	044	B	6	51
READWIN	GEORGE	K			38	ENGLAND	RC	ENGLISH	MELODIAN MAKER	045	B	1	59
REAMAN	ANNE			1	80	US	TU	GER		044	B	1	36
REAMAN	DANIEL				43	0	EM	GER	F	044	B	1	35
REAMAN	DAVID				28	0	EV	GER	F	044	B	1	42
REAMAN	JACOB				42	0	RC	GERMAN	SAWYER	043	B	5	19
REAMAN	JOEL				58	0	WM	GERMAN	F	044	B	5	52
REAMAN	JOHN				26	0	LU	GERMAN	F	044	B	5	73
REAMAN	LYONA		2	1		0	NG			045	D	6	D
REAMAN	NICHOLAS				32	0	PM	GER	F	044	B	1	51
REAMAN	THOMAS		2			0	EM			044	B	1	D
REAMEN	JOHN				20	0	CN	GERMAN	FARMER	045	D	6	13
REAMEN	SAMUEL				44	0	MN	GERMAN	BLACKSMITH	045	D	6	13
REAR	GEORGE				63	ENGLAND	WM	ENGLISH	F	043	E	3	43
REAR	JOHN				23	ENGLAND	WM	ENGLISH	CARPENTER	043	E	3	47
REAR	THOMAS				50	ENGLAND	WM	ENGLISH	F	043	E	3	41
REASOR	ABBE		1		16	0	PM	ENGLISH		043	E	2	55
REDDIT	MARY	ELIZABETH		1	6	0	CE	ENGLISH		043	H	1	10
REDDIT	ROBERT			M	40	ENGLAND	PS	ENGLISH	WAGGON MAKER	043	A	1	39
REDDIT	WILLIAM				36	ENGLAND	CE	ENGLISH	MASON	043	H	1	10
REDDIT	WILLIAM				40	0	WM	IRE	MASON	044	B	2	46
REDDITT	BENJAMIN				29	0	CE	ENG	CARPENTER	044	B	2	12
REDDITT	JOHN		1	M	18	0	CE	ENGLAND	CLERK	043	A	1	51
REDDITT	MARY		2	1		0	NG			044	B	2	D
REDFORD	HENRY	B			32	ENGLAND	CE	ENGLISH		044	C	2	21
REDFORD	JOSEPH				43	ENGLAND	CE	ENGLISH	BAILIFF	045	A	1	69
REDMAN	PATRICK				26	ONT	RC	IRISH	BRAKES MAN	044	C	3	61
REDMOND	CHRISTINA		1	F	19	0	PS	SCOTCH		043	A	2	17
REDON	HELLEN			1	45	SCOTLAND	CS	SCOTCH	SEAMSTRESS	043	A	4	16
REDPATH	ISABELLA			1	43	SCOTLAND	FK	SCOTCH		043	F		14
REDPATH	JANE		1	1	14	0	CP	SCOT	ADOPTED	044	B	1	48
REDWOOD	KESIAH			1	75	ENGLAND	WM	ENGLISH		045	D	3	25
REECH	JOSEPH				31	ENG	WM	ENG	LAB	044	B	2	14
REED	ALEY MAY		1	1	6	CANADA	WM	ENGLISH		045	D	6	64
REED	ANN		1	1		0	CE	IRISH		044	C	2	13
REED	ESEEY		1		8	CANADA	WM	ENGLISH		045	D	6	64
REED	HANNAH			1	48	0	CE	ENGLISH	SEAMSTRESS	045	D	3	2
REED	JAMES				57	ENGLAND	BA	ENGLISH	FARMER	043	G	2	40
REED	JAMES				40	CANADA	BA	SCOTCH	FARMER	045	D	6	33
REED	JOHN				40	ENGLAND	WM	ENGLISH	FARMER	045	A	3	3
REED	MARGRET		1	1	28	CANADA	WM	ENGLISH		045	D	6	64
REED	MICHAEL				35	ENGLAND	CE	ENGLISH	BLACKSMITH	043	B	3	68
REED	ROBERT				61	SCOTLAND	CP	SCOTCH	FARMER	045	D	3	22
REED	THURZA		1	1	18	ENGLAND	CE	ENGLISH		045	D	3	77
REEDE	WILLIAM		1		25	SCOT	CP	SCOTCH	SERVANT	044	B	1	24
REESOR	ABRAHAM				28	0	WM	GERMAN	FARMER	045	D	5	60
REESOR	ANDREW				27	0	WM	GERMAN	FARMER	045	D	5	52
REESOR	BENJAMIN				34	0	MN	GERMAN	FARMER	045	D	5	57
REESOR	CHRISTIAN				38	0	MN	GERMAN	F	045	C	2	39
REESOR	CHRISTIAN				65	U STATES	CE	GERMAN	FARMER	045	D	5	72
REESOR	DAVID				26	0	CE	GERMAN	FARMER	045	D	5	75
REESOR	ELIZA		2	1		0	MN			045	D	5	D
REESOR	ELIZABETH			1	76	U STATES	MN	GERMAN		045	D	5	1
REESOR	FRED K				23	0	WM	GERMAN	SCHOOL TEACHER	045	D	5	37
REESOR	HENRY	B			25	0	WM	GERMAN	FARMER	045	D	5	73
REESOR	HON	DAVID			48	0	WM	GERMAN	DOMINION SENATOR	045	D	5	76
REESOR	JACOB				28	0	WM	GERMAN	FARMER	045	D	3	79
REESOR	JESSE				30	0	MN	GERMAN	FARMER	045	D	5	38
REESOR	JOHN				52	0	CE	GERMAN	FARMER MERCHANT MILL	045	D	5	26
REESOR	JOHN				51	0	MN	GERMAN	FARMER	045	D	5	60
REESOR	JOHN	L			59	CANADA	MN	GERMAN	FARMER	045	D	6	30
REESOR	JOSEPH				50	0	VM	GERMAN	FARMER	045	D	5	35
REESOR	JOSEPHUS				37	0	WM	GERMAN	FARMER	045	D	3	78
REESOR	JOSEPHUS				50	0	WM	GERMAN	FARMER	045	D	5	41
REESOR	NICOLAS		1		21	0	WM	GERMAN	FARMER	045	D	5	72
REESOR	NOAH				39	0	WM	GERMAN	F	045	C	2	43
REESOR	PETER				30	0	WM	GERMAN	F	045	C	2	47
REESOR	PETER				62	0	WM	GERMAN	RETIRED FARMER	045	D	5	52
REESOR	ROBERT				28	0	CE	GERMAN	FARMER	045	D	5	74
REESOR	SAMUEL				53	0	MN	GERMAN	MERCHANT MILLER	045	D	5	52
REESOR	SAMUEL	G			40	0	MN	GERMAN	FARMER	045	D	5	37
REESOR	SIMEON				42	0	MN	GERMAN	F	045	C	2	44
REEVELEY	THOMAS				31	ENGLAND	PM	ENGLISH	F	045	A	4	9
REEVES	EDWARD				60	ENGLAND	CE	ENGLISH	F	044	A	1	19
REEVES	JOHN				60	IRELAND	CE	IRISH	BAKER	043	C		48
REGAN	MARY			1	77	IRELAND	RC	IRISH		043	E	1	5
REGAN	PETER				53	IRELAND	RC	IRISH	F	043	B	2	8
REHMAN	JOHN				41	0	CN	GERMAN	ENGINEER	043	B	3	25
REHMAN	JOHN				60	UNITED STATES	MN	GERMAN	FARMER	043	B	3	17

SURNAME	NAME1	NAME2	STRAY	SEX	AGE	BIRTHPL	RELIGION	ORIGIN	OCCUP	DIST	SUB_DIST	DIV	PAGE
REID	ANN			1	62	ENGLAND	WM	ENGLISH		045	D	4	8
REID	ANN		1	1	32	O	CE	IRISH	SERVANT	044	C	2	32
REID	CHARLES				38	ENGLAND	WM	ENGLISH	F	043	B	5	10
REID	DAVID				40	O	EM	SCOTCH	MARBLER DEALER	043	D		53
REID	ELLEN	H		1	57	O	ZZ	ENGLISH	SEAMSTRESS	043	E	2	37
REID	GEORGE			M	39	O	WM	SCOTLAND	F	043	A	5	16
REID	GEORGE				45	ENGLAND	WM	ENGLISH	LABORER	043	D		37
REID	HANNAH			1	40	IRELAND	WM	IRISH		043	E	3	25
REID	JAMES				42	SCOTLAND	CS	SCOTCH	PHOTOGRAPHER	043	D		72
REID	JANE		1	1	85	IRELAND	CS	IRISH		043	A	4	49
REID	JAS				37	SCOTLAND	PS	SCOTCH	WEAVER	044	B	5	19
REID	JESSIE		2	1	33	SCOTLAND	CS			043	D		D
REID	JOHN		2			O	PM			043	B	5	D
REID	JOHN		1		24	ENGLAND	PR	ENGLISH	FARMER	043	G	2	28
REID	JOHN				25	O	CE	IRISH	SAWYER	044	B	2	64
REID	JOHN		1		4	O	CE	ENGLISH		045	A	1	100
REID	JOHN	N			37	IRELAND	WM	IRISH	MEDICAL DR	045	D	1	8
REID	JOSEPH				35	ENGLAND	CE	ENGLISH	BRICK MAKER	045	A	1	51
REID	MARGARET		1	1	77	IRELAND	CE	IRISH		043	E	2	55
REID	MARGARET			1	40	IRE	CE	IRE		044	B	2	63
REID	MARGARET			1	35	US	RC	IRISH		045	D	2	41
REID	MARY			1	59	O	CE	ENGLISH		043	D		64
REID	NELSON				45	O	EM	SCOTCH	MARBLE ZEALER	043	D		62
REID	ROBERT				72	ENGLAND	CE	ENGLISH		045	A	1	101
REID	ROSS				66	IRELAND	CE	IRISH	BRICKMAKER	045	A	1	3
REID	THEODORE				39	O	WM	SCOT	BRICK MAKER	044	B	2	15
REID	THOMAS		1		30	ENGLAND	CE	ENGLISH	LAB	043	E	3	28
REID	WILLIAM				28	O	PM	ENGLISH	F	043	B	5	10
REID	WILLIAM				48	IRELAND	PS	IRISH	F	043	E	3	17
REID	WILLIAM				30	ENGLAND	WM	ENGLISH	F	043	E	3	19
REID	WILLSON				59	O	CE	SCOTCH	F	043	E	2	48
REIDER	ALICE		1		3	O	CE	ENGLISH		043	B	4	31
REIDER	ELIZA		1	1	30	ENGLAND	CE	ENGLISH	SERVANT	043	B	4	31
REIFSNIDER	E		1	1	18	U STATES	QU	GERMAN		043	C		41
REILLY	BERNARD				47	IRELAND	RC	IRISH	LABOURER	043	A	4	57
REILLY	GEORGE				46	US	RC	IRISH	FARMER	045	A	3	33
REILLY	O	JOHN			60	IRELAND	RC	IRISH	F	043	A	3	24
REILLY	WILLIAM				22	O	CE	IRISH	F	043	A	6	58
REMAN	AGNES		1	1	18	US	CN	GERMAN		045	D	4	44
REMER	DAVID				41	CANADIAN	MN	GERMAN	FARMER	045	D	6	23
REMER	PETER				53	U STATES	MN	GERMAN	FARMER	045	D	6	14
REMMAND	THOS				55	ENGLAND	CE	ENGLISH	LAB	044	A	2	5
RENDOLDS	JOHN				50		O	IRISH	LAB	043	E	3	56
RENNEY	CATHERINE		1	1		INDIA	CE	INDIA		044	C	4	9
RENNIE	SIMPSON				31	O	CP	SCOTCH	F	045	C	4	4
RENNIE	WILLIAM				35	O	CP	SCOTCH	AGENT	045	A	2	5
RENOLDS	JOHN				33	O	WM	IRISH	F	044	C	1	33
RENTON	JOSEPH				24	O	WM	ENGLISH	FARMER	043	A	4	63
RENTON	THOMAS				37	SCOTLAND	CP	SCOTCH	BLACKSMITH	045	A	1	10
RESSLEY	HENRY				51	ENGLAND	CE	ENGLISH	STORE KEEPER	045	B	1	12
RESTON	CATHERINE	R	2	1		O	BP			045	A	1	D
REVELY	GEORGE				56	ENGLAND	WM	ENGLISH	F	045	A	4	18
REVES	ELIZABETH			1	30	CANADA	WM	ENGLISH		045	D	6	47
REYMER	CATHARINE		1	1	52	CANADA	MN	GERMAN		045	D	6	26
REYMER	CHRISTIAN				45	CANADA	MN	GERMAN	FARMER TANNER	045	D	6	26
REYMER	JOHN				23	CANADA	CO	GERMAN		045	D	6	56
REYMER	JOHN				61	U STATES	MN	GERMAN	FARMER	045	D	2	2
REYMER	PHILIP				27	CANADA	MN	GERMAN	FARMER	045	D	6	55
REYNOLDS	ALEX		2			O	CE			043	F		D
REYNOLDS	ALLIS			1	67	IRELAND	CE	IRISH		043	F		2
REYNOLDS	AMELIA		2	1	27	O	CE			043	F		D
REYNOLDS	EDWARD				46	IRELAND	CE	IRISH	F	043	B	5	26
REYNOLDS	JIM		1		26	ENGLAND	CE	ENGLISH	MILLER	044	B	5	5
REYNOLDS	JOHN				27	ENGLAND	EM	ENGLISH	F	043	A	6	18
REYNOLDS	KATE		1	1	27	IRELAND	RC	IRISH	SERVANT	044	C	2	19
REYNOLDS	MARY		1	1	72	IRELAND	CE	IRISH		043	A	4	3
REYNOLDS	MARY	ANN		1	42	ENGLAND	WM	ENGLISH		045	D	5	60
REYNOLDS	ROBERT				53	ENGLAND	CE	ENGLISH	FARMER	043	A	4	55
REYNOLDS	THOMAS			M	40	IRELAND	RC	IRELAND	L	043	A	5	31
REYNOLDS	WILLIAM				38	ENGLAND	CE	ENGLISH	BLACKSMITH	043	B	3	73
REYNOLDS	WM				55	ENGLAND	PM	ENGLISH	F	043	B	4	14
REYNOLDS	WM				26	O	PM	ENGLISH	FARMER	043	B	4	15
RHINEHART	JACOB				54	UNITED STATES	EM	GERMAN	SHOEMAKER	043	D		10
RHINESS	JAMES				33	O	PM	GERMAN	LAB	043	E	2	43
RHODES	DENNIS				55	US	WM	AFRICAN	LAB	044	C	4	10
RHYDNARD	PHILLIP				66	IRELAND	CE	IRISH	F	043	H	1	23
RHYNDNESS	SARAH			1	28	ENGLAND	PM	ENGLISH		043	H	2	49
RHYNDRESS	ELISHA				29	ONTARIO	EM	GERMAN	FARMER	043	G	1	28
RHYNDRESS	GEORGE	F	1		8	O	PM	GERMAN		043	H	2	49
RHYNDRESS	SARAH		1	1	28	ENGLAND	PM	ENGLISH		043	H	2	49
RHYNER	JOHN				50	ENGLAND	CE	ENGLISH	F	043	E	2	79
RIBGE	THOMAS		1		40	ENGLAND	CE	ENGLISH		045	A	4	10
RICE	ANN		1	1	35	IRELAND	RC	IRISH	HOUSEKEEPER	045	A	1	47
RICE	EDWD		1		76	IRELAND	CE	IRISH		045	D	5	10
RICE	GEORGE				34	ENGLAND	CE	ENGLISH	PAPER MAKER	045	A	1	97
RICE	GEORGE	H	1		14	ENGLAND	CE	ENGLISH		043	E	1	2
RICE	GILBERT				39	O	WM	DUTCH	F	044	A	1	1
RICE	JOHN			M	28	ENGLAND	CE	ENGLAND	F	043	A	5	3
RICE	JOHN				44	ENGLAND	PM	ENGLISH	F	043	B	5	9
RICH	SAMUEL		1		23	O	PS	IRISH	FARM SERVANT	045	C	3	50
RICHARD	HENRY				62	US	BA	AFRICAN	GARDNER	044	C	4	89
RICHARD'N	WILLIAM		1		12	ENGLAND	CE	ENGLISH		043	A	3	3
RICHARDS	HENRY				59	ENG	CE	ENG	TOLL COLLECTOR	044	B	1	15
RICHARDS	HUGH				49	IRELAND	CE	IRISH	CARPENTER	043	H	1	3
RICHARDS	JESSE				39	O	WM	GER	F	044	B	4	22
RICHARDS	JOHN				68	O	WM	GER	F	044	B	4	11
RICHARDS	PETER				38	ENGLAND	CE	ENGLISH	BRICKLAYER	045	D	5	66
RICHARDS	RICHARD				70	US	BA	AFRICAN	JEE MERCHANT	044	C	4	63
RICHARDS	VIOLA		2	1	3	O	CE			044	B	1	D
RICHARDSON	ADAM				25	O	PM	ENGLISH	F	045	C	4	39
RICHARDSON	ANN		2	1		O	NG			045	C	2	D
RICHARDSON	BEN			M	45	ENGLAND	NC	ENGLISH	F	043	A	1	64
RICHARDSON	C	L			23	O	WM	ENGLISH	HARNESS MAKER	045	B	2	2
RICHARDSON	CHARLES				24	O	WM	ENGLISH	F	043	B	1	21
RICHARDSON	DAVID				65	O	WM	ENGLISH	F	043	B	1	24
RICHARDSON	ELIZA			1	35	IRELAND	RC	IRISH		045	B	1	53

SURNAME	NAME1	NAME2	STRAY	SEX	AGE	BIRTHPL	RELIGION	ORIGIN	OCCUP	DIST	SUB_DIST	DIV	PAGE
RICHARDSON	ELIZABETH		2	1	28	O	WM			043	B	1	D
RICHARDSON	ELIZABETH			1	54	ENGLAND	WM	ENGLISH		044	B	1	4
RICHARDSON	ELIZABETH			1	64	ENG	PM	ENG	SEAMSTRESS & WASHER	044	B	4	9
RICHARDSON	GEO				29	O	WM	ENGLISH	F	044	B	5	71
RICHARDSON	GEO		2			O	WM			044	B	5	D
RICHARDSON	GEORGE				33	O	WM	ENGLISH	LUMBERMAN	043	B	5	42
RICHARDSON	GEORGE				80	ENGLAND	PM	ENGLISH	F	045	C	4	39
RICHARDSON	HENRY				34	O	EM	ENGLISH	CARPENTER	043	D		29
RICHARDSON	JAMES				52	ENGLAND	CE	ENGLISH	MACHINIST	045	A	1	74
RICHARDSON	JAMES				33	O	WM	IRE	F	045	C	1	2
RICHARDSON	JESSE				42	ENGLAND	PM	ENGLISH	BLACKSMITH	045	C	4	6
RICHARDSON	JOHN				30	O	WM	ENGLISH	F	043	B	4	47
RICHARDSON	JOHN				24	O	WM	IRE	F	045	C	1	8
RICHARDSON	JOHN				30	O	CE	IRISH	F	045	C	2	4
RICHARDSON	JOHN				85	IRELAND	WM	IRISH	RETIRED	045	C	2	4
RICHARDSON	JOHN	C			28	O	WM	ENGLISH	F	043	B	1	27
RICHARDSON	JOSEPH		1		10	O	BC	IRISH		043	H	2	40
RICHARDSON	JOSEPH		1		10	ONTARIO	BC	IRISH		043	H	2	40
RICHARDSON	LEEDS				25	O	WM	ENG	SADDLER	044	B	3	9
RICHARDSON	LEVI				36	O	WM	ENGLISH	F	043	B	1	23
RICHARDSON	LUCY			1	35	O	WM	ENGLISH		045	D	1	3
RICHARDSON	MARY			1	65	ENGLAND	CE	ENGLISH		043	D		29
RICHARDSON	ROBT		1		41	ENGLAND	CE	ENGLISH	OSTLER	043	E	2	24
RICHARDSON	ROBT				28	O	PM	ENG	F	045	C	1	43
RICHARDSON	SAMUEL		1		28	IRELAND	CE	IRISH	ASSIST ENGINEER	045	D	5	8
RICHARDSON	THOMAS				62	ENGLAND	PM	ENGLISH	F	044	B	6	34
RICHARDSON	THOMAS				60	ENGLAND	CE	ENGLISH	FARMER	045	D	3	13
RICHARDSON	THOS				42	O	WM	ENGLISH	F	044	B	5	53
RICHARDSON	THOS				84	ENGLAND	WM	ENGLISH	F	044	B	5	71
RICHARDSON	WM				30	O	WM	ENGLISH	TEAMSTER	043	C		54
RICHARDSON	WM				67	ENGLAND	NC	ENGLISH		043	F		4
RICHARDSON	WM				62	ENGLAND	CE	ENGLISH	F	044	B	5	51
RICHARDSON	WM	NORTH	2		83	ENGLAND	CE		CONVEYANCER	043	D		D
RICHEN	JOHN		1		42	SWITZERLAND	LU	GERMAN	F	043	B	1	28
RICHESON	CHARLOTT		1	1	17	NEW BRUNS	PM	ENGLISH		043	A	6	40
RICHEY	SAMUEL		1		21	O	WM	IRISH		045	A	4	30
RICHIE	HARRIET		1	1	50	IRELAND	WM	IRISH	SERVANT	045	B	2	30
RICHIE	WILLIAM	REV			71	SCOTLAND	CE	SCOTCH	MINISTER	043	G	2	39
RICHMOND	EDWIN		1		23	ENGLAND	CE	ENGLISH	GARDENER	045	A	1	2
RICKER	FREDERICK		1		22	ENGLAND	CE	ENGLISH	FARM LAB	044	C	2	39
RIDDEL	ELIZABETH		1	1	29	ONTARIO	CP	SCOTCH	SCHOOL TEACHER	043	G	2	35
RIDDELL	ANDW				31	O	UP	SCOTCH	F	044	B	5	72
RIDDELL	ARCHIBALD		1		56	SCOTLAND	OP	SCOTCH	F	043	H	2	45
RIDDELL	ARCHIBALD				56	SCOTLAND	CS	SCOTCH	FARMER	043	H	2	45
RIDDELL	ELIZABETH			1	61	SCOTLAND	UP	SCOTCH		044	B	5	72
RIDDELL	JOHN				64	SCOTLAND	OP	SCOTCH	F	043	H	2	38
RIDDELL	JOHN				64	SCOTLAND	CS	SCOTCH	FARMER	043	H	2	38
RIDDELL	MARGARET		1	1	1	O	CS	ENGLISH		043	H	2	22
RIDDELL	MARGRET		1	1	1	ONTARIO	CS	ENGLISH		043	H	2	22
RIDDELL	MARTHA		2	1	26	ONTARIO	CS			043	H	2	D
RIDDELL	MARTHA		2	1	26	O	OP			043	H	2	D
RIDDELL	ROBERT				63	SCOTLAND	OP	SCOTCH	F	043	H	2	34
RIDDELL	ROBERT				30	O	OP	SCOTCH	F	043	H	2	47
RIDDELL	ROBERT				63	SCOTLAND	CS	SCOTCH	FARMER	043	H	2	34
RIDDELL	ROBERT				30	ONTARIO	CS	SCOTCH	FARMER	043	H	2	47
RIDDLE	GEORGE				64	IRELAND	CS	IRISH	LABORER	045	D	5	24
RIDDLE	HUGH			M	53	IRELAND	CP	IRISH	F	043	A	2	13
RIDDLE	ISAAC				50	IRE	CS	IRE	F	044	B	2	61
RIDDLE	ISABELLA			1	60	SCOTLAND	CS	SCOTCH		045	D	5	75
RIDDLE	JAMES				28	O	WM	IRELAND	FARMER	045	D	5	74
RIDDLE	JOHN		1		18	ENGLAND	CE	ENGLISH	LAB	043	B	2	34
RIDDLE	JOHN		1		31	SCOT	CP	SCOT	CARPENTER	044	B	1	27
RIDDLE	LOUISA		1	1	40	IRELAND	CS	IRISH		045	D	5	31
RIDDLE	ROBERT		1		22	O	PS	IRE	LAB	044	B	2	63
RIDDLE	SERAH		1	1	18	O	CE	ENGLISH	SERVANT?	045	D	6	12
RIDER	HENRY				50	O	CE	GERMAN	F	044	B	6	33
RIDER	SAMUEL				41	O	CE	GERMAN	CARPENTER	044	B	6	8
RIDLEY	CHRISTINA		1	4	4	O	RC	IRISH		043	D		3
RIDLEY	EDWARD		1		48	IRELAND	RC	IRISH	LABORER	043	D		2
RIDLEY	EDWARD	JOHN	1		11	O	RC	IRISH		043	D		2
RIDLEY	ELLEN		1	1	30	QUE	RC	ENGLISH		043	D		2
RIDLEY	ELLEN	E	1	1	6	O	RC	IRISH		043	D		3
RIDLEY	MARY		1	1	10	O	RC	IRISH		043	D		33
RIDLEY	MARY	OLIVE	1	1	9	O	RC	IRISH		043	D		2
RIDLEY	THOMAS	GEORGE	1		7	O	RC	IRISH		043	D		3
RIED	JOHN				24	IRELAND	RC	IRISH	LABOURER	044	C	3	42
RIED	JOSEPH		2		0	IRELAND	RC			044	C	3	D
RIELLY	GEORGE				39	O	CE	IRISH	F	043	A	6	57
RIESBOROUGH	MATTW				28	ENGLAND	PM	ENGLISH	F	043	E	3	19
RIFFIDDEN	JOHN		1		5	US	PS	IRE		044	B	2	37
RIGLER	THOMAS				46	ENGLAND	CP	ENGLISH	FARMER	043	G	1	20
RIGLEY	ROBERT				36	O	WM	WELSH	F	043	B	4	23
RIGNEY	HANNAH		1	1	45	IRELAND	CE	IRISH	TEACHER	045	B	2	9
RILE	MARGARET		1	1	49	O	CE	IRE	SERVANT	044	B	3	12
RILEY	CHRISTOPHER				66	IRELAND	CE	IRISH	FARMER	045	B	3	22
RILEY	ELIZABETH		1	1	45	SCOTLAND	CP	SCOTCH	SERVANT	045	D	1	14
RILEY	JAMES				40	IRELAND	CE	IRISH	F	043	F		7
RILEY	JAMES				36	IRELAND	RC	IRISH	F	045	A	4	21
RILEY	JOHN		1		29	ENGLAND	WM	ENGLISH	MACHINIST	044	B	5	9
RILEY	JOHN				44	IRELAND	RC	IRISH	LABORER	045	D	2	47
RILEY	PATTICK				60	IRELAND	RC	IRISH	LAB	045	C	2	1
RILEY	WILLIAM			M	42	SCOTLAND	WM	SCOTLAND	TAILOR	043	A	5	13
RILEY	WM				45	IRELAND	CE	IRISH	F	044	C	1	46
RILLFOIL	JOHANNA		1	1	65	IRE	RC	IRE		044	B	2	48
RINDER	THOMAS		1		26	IRELAND	CP	SCOTCH	FARM LABOURER	045	C	4	13
RINE	JOHN				50	IRELAND	RC	IRISH	LAB	044	C	3	9
RING	BARTHOLEMEW		1		39	IRELAND	RC	IRISH	LAB	044	C	4	75
RINUS	ESAW				48	ONTARIO	PR	DUTCH	LABORER	043	G	2	14
RISBROUGH	WILLIAM				30	CANADA	WM	ENGLISH	F	045	A	4	1
RISEBROUGH	ROBERT				44	ENGLAND	WM	ENGLISH	F	045	A	4	10
RISHAN	GABRIEL		1		30	ENGLAND	CE	ENGLISH	TAILOR	044	B	5	30
RITCHIE	DAVID				37	IRELAND	PS	IRISH	HOTEL KEEPER	043	E	2	24
RITCHIE	JAMES	H	2		4	O	PS			043	E	2	D
RITCHIE	WILLIAM				40	IRELAND	CO	IRISH	FARMER	044	C	3	70
RITT	M				29	GERMANY	RC	GERMAN	BLACKSMITH	043	A	3	10
RITTER	RACHEL			1	53	O	LU	GERMANY		045	D	2	25

SURNAME	NAME1	NAME2	STRAY	SEX	AGE	BIRTHPL	RELIGION	ORIGIN	OCCUP	DIST	SUB_DIST	DIV	PAGE
RITTER	WILLIAM		1		22	0	LU	GERMAN	SERVANT	045	D	2	24
RIVERS	WILLIAM				72	ENGLAND	CE	ENGLISH	FURRIER	045	A	1	56
RIVERS	WILLIAM		2		2	0	CE			045	A	1	D
RIVETT	ROBERT			M	49	ENGLAND	PR	ENGLISH	BEE KEEPER	043	A	1	60
RIVIS	RICHARD		1		35	ENGLAND	WM	ENGLISH	FARM LABOURER	045	D	3	15
ROACH	MARY ANN		1	1	22	0	CP	IRISH		043	H	1	35
ROACH	WILLIAM				65	IRELAND	RC	IRISH	LABOURER	045	A	1	85
ROACH	WILLIAM				32	IRELAND	RC	IRISH	LAB	045	C	2	42
ROACHE	PETER				27	IRE	RC	IRISH	EXPRESS DELIVERER	044	B	1	11
ROADHOUSE	SAMUEL				46	0	WM	ENGLISH	CABINET MAKER	043	D		7
ROBARG	EXAVY				44	QUE	RC	FRENCH	F	045	C	1	6
ROBB	DAVID			M	29	IRELAND	RC	IRISH	F	043	A	2	10
ROBB	JOHN		1		7	0	WM	SCOTCH		045	D	3	55
ROBB	ROBERT				34	IRELAND	CS	IRISH	F	044	B	6	53
ROBB	WILLIAM			M	52	IRELAND	PS	IRISH	F	043	A	2	18
ROBB	WILLIAM				63	SCOTLAND	CS	SCOTCH	FARMER	045	D	5	56
ROBBINS	JANE		2	1	77	ENG	WM			044	B	3	D
ROBBY	JOHN		1		27	ENGLAND	CE	ENGLISH	F LAB	044	C	1	50
ROBERTS	ANNA	E	1	1	8	0	CP	ENGLISH		045	D	2	37
ROBERTS	CELIA			1	47	ENGLAND	WM	ENGLISH		045	C	2	9
ROBERTS	CELINA		1	1	20	0	CE	ENGLISH		045	A	2	39
ROBERTS	CHARLOTT	M	1	1	32	0	QU	IRISH		043	F		18
ROBERTS	G	F	1		8	0	QU	IRISH		043	F		18
ROBERTS	JANE			1	45	NS	CE	IRISH	LAB	045	A	4	18
ROBERTS	JOHN		1		45	FRANCE	CN	FRENCH	PAINTER	045	D	6	13
ROBERTS	RICHARD				41	IRELAND	CE	IRISH	F	045	C	4	46
ROBERTS	SAMUEL				43	0	CP	IRISH	F	044	A	3	54
ROBERTS	WILLIAM				49	IRELAND	WM	IRISH	F MANAGER	045	C	4	46
ROBERTSHAW	ALBERT				22	0	BA	ENGLISH	LAB	043	E	2	84
ROBERTSON	AGNES		1	1	5	0	CP	SCOTCH		045	C	3	30
ROBERTSON	ALEXANDER		1		27	0	CP	SCOTCH	SAWYER	045	C	3	29
ROBERTSON	BARBRA			1	65	US	NG	GERMAN		045	D	4	5
ROBERTSON	CHARLES				55	SCOTLAND	PS	SCOTCH	MERCHANT	043	E	1	45
ROBERTSON	ISABELLA		1	F	22	SCOTLAND	CP	SCOTCH		043	A	1	67
ROBERTSON	JAMES				45	ONTARIO	CP	SCOTCH	FARMER	043	G	1	32
ROBERTSON	JAMES	C			43	SCOTLAND	CE	SCOTCH	CLERK	043	D		54
ROBERTSON	JANE			1	55	IRELAND	CE	IRISH		045	C	2	55
ROBERTSON	JOHN				45	ENGLAND	WM	ENGLISH	F	044	C	1	56
ROBERTSON	MATHEW				24	ONTARIO	CE	SCOTCH	LABOURER	043	H	2	36
ROBERTSON	MATTHEW				24	0	CE	SCOTCH	LAB	043	H	2	36
ROBERTSON	ROBERT				42	SCOTLAND	FW	SCOTCH	SAWYER	045	A	1	71
ROBERTSON	THOMAS				40	SCOTLAND	CP	SCOTCH	WHEELWRIGHT	043	A	4	22
ROBERTSON	THOMAS				50	SCOTLAND	CP	SCOTCH	F	044	C	4	15
ROBERTSON	WILLIAM	J			30	0	XC	SCOTCH	BANK CLARK	045	B	1	38
ROBINET	JAMES		1		81	US	OB	ENGLISH		044	A	2	10
ROBINS	ALMON				50	UNITED STATES	WM	FRENCH	LAB	043	B	2	24
ROBINS	THOMAS				42	0	PM	ENGLISH	F	045	C	3	42
ROBINSON	ALEX				51	IRELAND	CP	IRISH	F	044	A	2	20
ROBINSON	ALFRED				40	ENGLAND	CE	ENGLISH	DENTIST	043	C		17
ROBINSON	ANDREW				50	0	CO	IRISH	FARMER	045	D	5	2
ROBINSON	ANDRINA		1	1	14	QUE	PM	IRISH	SERVANT	045	A	1	4
ROBINSON	CHARLES				34	0	CE	ENGLISH	LAB	045	C	2	2
ROBINSON	CHRISTOPHER				46	ENGLAND	PM	ENGLAND	FARMER	045	D	6	1
ROBINSON	COLLINGWOOD				25	ENG	EM	ENG	F	044	B	2	33
ROBINSON	DAVID				30	0	CP	SCOTCH	F	043	H	1	40
ROBINSON	DAVID				75	0	WM	IRISH	F	044	B	6	22
ROBINSON	ELENOR		1	1	88	IRELAND	WM	IRISH		045	A	4	11
ROBINSON	ELIZ			1	15	0	EM	ENG		044	B	1	34
ROBINSON	ELIZABETH		2	1		0	NG			044	B	2	D
ROBINSON	ELIZEAR				45	0	WM	IRE	F	044	B	3	48
ROBINSON	GEORGE				45	ENGLAND	OB	ENGLISH	F	044	A	2	28
ROBINSON	GEORGE				40	0	WM	IRISH	F	044	B	6	22
ROBINSON	GEORGE				41	ENGLAND	WM	ENGLISH	BUTCHER	045	B	1	62
ROBINSON	GEORGE				53	ENGLAND	LU	ENGLISH	CARPENTER	045	D	4	30
ROBINSON	GEORGE				46	ENGLAND	CO	ENGLISH	F	044	C	1	19
ROBINSON	HANNAH	E	2	1		0	EM			043	E	2	D
ROBINSON	HARIOT		1	1	25	0	CE	ENGLISH	INMATE	045	B	1	73
ROBINSON	HENEREY				45	ENGLAND	WM	ENGLISH	FARMER	045	D	6	68
ROBINSON	HENRY				42	ENGLAND	CE	ENGLISH	DENTIST	043	A	4	17
ROBINSON	HENRY				32	0	WM	IRISH	F LAB	043	B	4	35
ROBINSON	HENRY				22	0	NC	ENGLISH	LAB	043	E	1	14
ROBINSON	HENRY				27	ENG	CE	ENG	F	044	B	2	68
ROBINSON	HENRY				21	0	CE	IRISH	FARMER	045	D	3	65
ROBINSON	ISAAC				61	ENGLAND	WM	ENGLISH	F	044	C	2	24
ROBINSON	ISABELLA		1	1	21	0	CP	IRISH	FARM SERVANT	045	C	4	21
ROBINSON	JAMES				58	IRELAND	WM	IRISH	FARMER	043	A	3	6
ROBINSON	JAMES				45	0	NG	ENGLISH	LAB	043	B	4	27
ROBINSON	JAMES				37	0	WM	IRISH	LAB	044	B	6	15
ROBINSON	JAMES		1		60	SCOTLAND	CS	SCOTCH		044	B	6	15
ROBINSON	JAMES				37	0	CS	IRISH	TANNER	045	D	3	64
ROBINSON	JOHN				33	0	WM	IRISH	F	043	A	3	18
ROBINSON	JOHN				50	ENGLAND	QU	ENGLISH	F	043	A	6	11
ROBINSON	JOHN				37	0	PM	ENGLISH	LAB	043	B	2	23
ROBINSON	JOHN				29	0	EM	ENGLISH	F	043	E	2	13
ROBINSON	JOHN				24	0	PM	IRISH	CARPENTER	045	B	2	14
ROBINSON	JOHN				67	0	CE	IRISH	FARMER	045	D	3	65
ROBINSON	JOHN				71	ENGLAND	CE	ENGLISH	FARMER	045	D	4	31
ROBINSON	JOHN				58	ENGLAND	WM	ENGLISH	F	044	C	2	15
ROBINSON	JOHN				57	ENGLAND	NG	ENGLISH	DROVER	044	C	2	25
ROBINSON	JOHN	C			62	ENGLAND	WM	ENGLISH	GARDENER	043	B	4	21
ROBINSON	JOSEPH			M	35	ENGLAND	PR	ENGLISH	F	043	A	1	29
ROBINSON	JOSEPH				39	0	WM	GERMAN	F	043	B	1	39
ROBINSON	JOSEPH				46	ENGLAND	EM	ENGLISH	F	044	C	2	32
ROBINSON	KATE		1	1	24	0	WM	ENGLISH	SERVT	044	B	5	10
ROBINSON	MALCOLM		2		13	0	CO		FARMER	045	D	5	D
ROBINSON	MARGARET		1	1	71	SCOTLAND	PS	SCOTCH		043	E	3	3
ROBINSON	MARGARET	J		F	40	0	CN	GERMANY	F	043	A	5	9
ROBINSON	MARIA		1	1	28	ENG	PM	ENG	SERVANT	044	B	3	7
ROBINSON	MARION		1	1	30	ONTARIO	CE	ENGLISH	TEACHER	043	G	1	16
ROBINSON	MARK				42	ENG	CE	ENG	F	044	B	3	6
ROBINSON	MARTIN				37	ENGLAND	WM	ENGLISH	SHOEMAKER	043	D		23
ROBINSON	MATHEW				62	ENGLAND	CE	ENGLISH	LAB	043	B	4	33
ROBINSON	NIXON?				45	ENGLAND	CE	ENGLISH	HOTEL KEEPER	045	B	2	1
ROBINSON	REUBEN				72	ENGLAND	WM	ENGLISH	SHOEMAKER	043	D		26
ROBINSON	ROBERT				41	ENGLAND	WM	ENGLISH	SHOEMAKER	043	A	4	10
ROBINSON	ROBERT				55	0	PM	ENGLISH	FARM LAB	043	B	1	17

SURNAME	NAME1	NAME2	STRAY	SEX	AGE	BIRTHPL	RELIGION	ORIGIN	OCCUP	DIST	SUB_DIST	DIV	PAGE
ROBINSON	ROBERT				55	ENGLAND	CE	ENGLISH	F	043	B	4	18
ROBINSON	ROBERT				22	0	CE	ENGLISH	CARRIAGE MAKER	044	A	2	46
ROBINSON	ROBERT				47	ENGLAND	PM	ENGLAND	FARMER	045	D	2	13
ROBINSON	ROBT				36	SCOTLAND	UP	SCOTCH	CARPENTER	043	C		52
ROBINSON	SAMUEL				38	ENGLAND	CE	ENGLISH	LAB	043	D		49
ROBINSON	SAMUEL				36	ENG	PM	ENG	FARM LAB	044	B	4	24
ROBINSON	SILAS				31	0	PM	IRISH	LAB	043	B	5	35
ROBINSON	THOMAS				25	0	WM	GERMAN	F	043	B	1	39
ROBINSON	THOS				29	ENGLAND	WM	ENGLISH	LAB	044	B	5	51
ROBINSON	WILLIAM				27	0	WM	IRISH	F	043	A	3	19
ROBINSON	WILLIAM		1		33	0	EP	IRISH	MACHINIST	043	A	6	62
ROBINSON	WILLIAM				47	0	WM	SCOTCH	CARPENTER	043	B	1	38
ROBINSON	WILLIAM				36	ENGLAND	CN	ENGLISH	F	043	B	4	26
ROBINSON	WILLIAM				40	ENGLAND	PM	ENGLISH	F	043	E	3	34
ROBINSON	WILLIAM				34	0	WM	IRISH	F	044	B	6	28
ROBINSON	WILLIAM				40	IRELAND	CE	IRISH	LAB	045	A	1	19
ROBINSON	WILLIAM		1		26	0	PM	IRISH	CARPENTER	045	B	2	14
ROBINSON	WILLIAM				31	ONT	CE	ENG	L	045	C	1	27
ROBINSON	WILLIAM				34	0	CE	IRISH	FARMER	045	D	5	2
ROBINSON	WILLIAM				60	IRELAND	WM	IRISH	FARMER	045	D	5	25
ROBINSON	WILLIAM		1		78	ENGLAND	EM	ENGLISH	F	044	C	2	32
ROBINSON	WILLIAM	S			37	ENGLAND	SW	ENGLISH	CHEMIST & DRUGGIST	045	B	1	5
ROBINSON	WILLM		1		40	ENGLAND	CE	ENGLISH	LAB	043	B	2	17
ROBLIN	JAMES	A			25	0	WM	SCOTCH	TELEGRAPH OPERATOR	045	B	1	29
ROBLIN	WILLIAM	G	2				WM			045	B	1	D
ROBSON	FLORA			1	60	SCOTLAND	FW	SCOTCH		045	D	3	74
ROBSON	GEORGE				44	ENGLAND	EM	ENGLISH	FARMER	045	A	3	20
ROBSON	HENRY				32	ENGLAND	WM	ENGLISH	SHOE MAKER	045	D	3	44
ROBSON	JOHN				32	SCOTLAND	CS	SCOTCH	MILLRIGHT	045	D	3	71
ROBSON	JOSEPH				33	ENGLAND	CE	ENGLISH	FARMER	043	B	3	32
ROBSON	NICHOLAS				64	ENGLAND	CO	ENGLISH	BIBLE AGENT	045	D	3	7
ROBSON	ROBINA		1	1	17	0	OB	ENGLISH		044	A	2	10
ROBSON	WILLIAM				40	ENG	CE	ENG	F	044	B	2	61
ROBSON	WILLIAM				24	0	CO	ENG	F	044	B	3	43
ROCHFORD	ANDW		1		23	0	WM	ENGLISH	IRON FINISHER	044	B	5	20
ROCHFORT	EDWARD				40	IRELAND	RC	IRISH	LAB	045	A	2	17
ROCK	JOHN				48	CANADIAN	MN	GERMAN	FARMER	045	D	6	23
RODDEN	WILLIAM				46	IRELAND	WM	IRISH	MANUFACTURER	045	B	2	26
RODGERS	AGNES			F	58	SCOTLAND	UP	SCOTCH		043	A	1	11
RODGERS	ALEXANDER				55	IRELAND	PM	IRISH	F	045	A	4	13
RODGERS	JAMES			M	36	0	DI	WELSH	F	043	A	1	42
RODGERS	JOHN				33	0	PS	ENGLISH	F	044	C	1	50
RODGERS	JOSIAH	B			64	0	WM	ENGLISH	F	043	C		57
RODGERS	JULIUS			M	23	0	PR	WELSH	F	043	A	1	47
RODGERS	MARY			1	55	IRELAND	RC	IRISH	F LAB	044	C	1	50
RODGERS	OLIVE		2	1	11	CANADA	WM			043	C		D
RODGERS	TIMOTHY			M	61	0	QU	IRISH	F	043	A	1	38
RODWELL	WILLIAM				53	ENGLAND	WM	ENGLISH	LAB	044	A	3	30
ROE	ALFRED				31	0	CE	IRISH	MERCHANT MANUFACTURE	044	B	5	11
ROE	GEORGE			M	60	ENGLAND	CE	ENGLAND	F	043	A	5	10
ROE	HATTIE		1	1	6	0	CO	ENGLISH		045	D	3	9
ROE	JAMES				30	0	WM	IRISH	FARMER	043	A	4	71
ROE	PHILLIS			1	47	QUE	CE	IRISH		044	B	5	10
ROE	WILLIAM				75	0	CE	ENGLISH	MERCHANT &POSTMASTER	043	D		21
ROE	WILLIAM		1		61	IRELAND	CE	IRISH	LABORER	043	G	1	30
ROFS	JOHN				36	PEI	CP	SCOTCH	TEACHER	044	A	2	53
ROGAN	EDWARD		1		40	IRELAND	RC	IRISH	LAB	044	B	6	51
ROGARS	HENERY				35	0	BA	IRISH	FARMER	044	C	3	33
ROGERS	ALBERT		1	1		ENGLAND	BA	ENGLISH		043	B	2	1
ROGERS	ALLEN				53	0	CN	ENGLISH	F	043	E	2	9
ROGERS	ALLEN				21	0	CN	ENGLISH	F	043	E	2	39
ROGERS	ASA				40	0	QU	ENGLISH	PUMPMAKER	043	B	4	8
ROGERS	BETSEY		1	1	34	ENGLAND	BA	ENGLISH		043	B	2	1
ROGERS	CATHERINE		1	1	26	0	CP	IRELAND	SERVANT	045	D	2	1
ROGERS	DAVID			M	41	0	QU	GERMANY	F	043	A	5	10
ROGERS	DAVID				47	0	QU	GERMAN	F	043	A	6	19
ROGERS	EDITH		1	1	51	0	QU	ENGLISH		043	E	1	32
ROGERS	GEORGE		1	1	4	ENGLAND	BA	ENGLISH		043	B	2	1
ROGERS	JAMES		1		20	IRELAND	CP	IRISH	SERVANT	045	A	3	15
ROGERS	JAMES				42	0	CE	IRISH	RAILWAY CONDUCTOR	045	B	1	29
ROGERS	JOHN				50	ENGLAND	QU	ENGLISH	F	043	A	6	11
ROGERS	JOHN	G			64	ENGLAND	WM	ENGLISH	SADDLER	044	A	2	51
ROGERS	LEVI				29	0	CH	IRISH	F	043	A	6	9
ROGERS	LEVI				57	0	QU	ENGLISH	F	043	E	1	17
ROGERS	MARY			1	61	U STATES	QU	FRENCH		043	A	6	7
ROGERS	PETER				37	0	FK	ENGLISH	F LAB	043	A	3	46
ROGERS	RACHAEL		1	1	51	0	CE	ENGLISH		045	A	1	11
ROGERS	RICHARD				44	ENGLAND	WM	ENGLISH	F	043	A	6	52
ROGERS	SAMUEL		1		34	ENGLAND	BA	ENGLISH	LAB	043	B	2	1
ROGERS	SARAH			1	61	0	QU	ENGLISH		043	B	4	9
ROGERS	THOMAS				36	ENGLAND	CE	ENGLISH	BRICKMAKER	044	C	4	20
ROGERS	THOMAS	E			33	N BRUNSWICK	WM	ENGLISH	COMMERCIAL TRAVELLER	044	C	4	7
ROGERS	WINRO	A			27	0	QU	ENGLISH		043	E	2	11
ROGERSON	ROBERT				43	ENGLAND	CE	ENGLISH	F	045	C	2	51
ROGERSON	THOMAS		1		20	0	QU	ENGLISH	F	043	B	4	40
ROGERSON	WM				77	IRELAND	CE	IRISH	PENSIONER	044	B	5	15
ROINSON	CATHARINE		1	1		0	CN	GERMAN		043	B	3	31
ROINSON	ELIZABETH		1	1	20	0	CN	GERMAN		043	B	3	31
ROLAND	MARTIN				53	USA	CE	ENGLISH	HORN FARRIER	043	H	1	19
ROLING	BENJAMIN			M	36	0	BA	ENGLISH	PEDLAR	043	A	2	29
ROLLANDS	WILLIAM		1		17	0	CE	IRISH	SHOEMAKER	045	B	2	17
ROLLER	ELIZABETH		1	1	19	0	CP	SCOTCH	SERVANT	044	B	6	57
ROLLIN	DORAH		2		4	0	WM			043	B	2	D
ROLLIN	ELI				34	0	WM	ENGLISH	LAB	043	B	2	10
ROLLIN	FRANCIS		2			0	WM			043	B	2	D
ROLLING	BENJAMIN		2	M	74	US	BA		LAB	043	A	5	D
ROLLING	JAMES				35	0	PM	ENGLISH	CARPENTER	043	B	5	33
ROLLING	WILLIAM			M	28	0	NR	AFRICA	L	043	A	5	36
ROLLISON	WILLIAM				36	ENGLAND	CE	ENGLISH	LAB	045	C	2	53
ROLLS	CHARLES				60	ENGLAND	CE	ENGLISH	PHYSICIAN	044	C	4	40
ROLLS	GEORGE				30	0	WM	ENGLISH	F	044	C	3	12
ROLPH	WILLIAM				69	ENGLAND	CE	ENGLISH	F	045	C	2	17
ROLSTON	JAMES		1		64	IRELAND	CP	IRISH	FARM LAB	044	A	2	30
ROLSTON	JOHN		1		55	IRELAND	CE	IRISH	F LAB	044	A	1	25
ROMLEY	LEWIS		1		25	ENGLAND	CE	ENGLISH	PAINTER	045	A	1	36
RONAN	THOMAS				35	IRELAND	NG	IRISH	LAB	043	A	6	36

SURNAME	NAME1	NAME2	STRAY	SEX	AGE	BIRTHPL	RELIGION	ORIGIN	OCCUP	DIST	SUB_DIST	DIV	PAGE
ROOKE	JOHN				45	IRELAND	RC	IRISH	LAB	044	C	4	55
ROOKE	WILLIAM	H			43	IRELAND	WM	IRISH	MARINER	045	A	1	52
ROOME	ELIZABETH		1	1	21	ENGLAND	CE	ENGLISH	INMATE	045	B	1	73
ROONEY	JOSHUA		1		25	O	CE	IRISH		045	A	1	27
ROPER	HERBERT		1		17	ENGLAND	WM	ENGLISH	SERVANT	044	C	3	14
ROPER	JOHN	A			40	O	CE	ENGLISH	HOTEL KEEPER	043	D		83
ROPER	JOSEPH				35	ONTARIO	PR	ENGLISH	FARMER	043	G	2	54
ROPER	PERCIVAL		2			O	NG			043	D		D
ROPER	THOMAS				64	ENGLAND	CE	ENGLISH	TAILOR	043	D		35
ROSBOROUGH	MARGARET			1	60	IRELAND	CE	IRISH		045	D	3	24
ROSE	ALBERT				34	O	CN	IRISH	CARPENTER	043	E	3	31
ROSE	ALEXANDER			M	28	JAMAICA WEST INDIES	PS	SCOTCH	SAWYER	043	A	1	73
ROSE	ALONZO				24	O	BA	ENGLISH	F	043	B	5	30
ROSE	EDWARD				33	ONTARIO	PR	IRISH	FARMER	043	G	2	33
ROSE	ELIJAH		1		20	O	BA	ENGLISH	F LAB	043	B	5	30
ROSE	GEORGE				44	O	WM	SCOTTISH	TEACHER	043	B	4	35
ROSE	HENRY	P			54	O	BC	ENGLISH	F	043	H	2	49
ROSE	HENRY	P			56	ONTARIO	BC	ENGLISH	FARMER	043	H	2	49
ROSE	ISAAC				62	O	CN	IRISH	F	043	E	3	31
ROSE	ISAAC	P			40	O	CN	ENGLISH	F	043	E	2	65
ROSE	JACOB				23	O	PM	ENGLISH	F	043	B	5	6
ROSE	JANE	I	1	1	11	ONTARIO	CN	IRISH		043	G	1	49
ROSE	JOHN		1		9	ONTARIO	CN	IRISH		043	G	1	49
ROSE	LUCY		1	1	32	O	WM	ENGLISH		045	B	1	42
ROSE	MARY			1	54	O	BA	IRISH		043	E	3	32
ROSE	OLIVER				37	ONTARIO	EM	GERMAN	PUMP MAKER	043	G	1	23
ROSE	ROBERT				36	ONTARIO	CN	IRISH	FARMER	043	G	1	41
ROSE	ROBERT	R			29	O	CN	ENGLISH	F	043	E	2	28
ROSE	ROSELIN		1	1	15	O	CP	SCOTCH		043	H	1	1
ROSE	SARAH		1	1	16	O	BA	ENGLISH		043	B	5	30
ROSE	WESLEY				15	ONTARIO	CN	IRISH		043	G	1	49
ROSE	WILLIAM			M	66	SCOTLAND	PS	SCOTCH	F	043	A	2	17
ROSE	WILLIAM		1		13	ONTARIO	CN	IRISH		043	G	1	49
ROSE	WILLIAM				49	ONTARIO	EM	IRISH	LABORER	043	G	2	29
ROSE	WILLIAM		1		22	ENGLAND	CE	ENGLISH	FARM LABOURER	045	C	4	46
ROSS	ALEXANDER				55	SCOTLAND	CP	SCOTCH	GATE KEEPER	045	A	1	62
ROSS	AUGUSTA	E		1	39	O	CE	IRISH		044	C	4	74
ROSS	CATHERINE		1	1	16	O	WM	SCOTCH		045	A	3	16
ROSS	CHARLES		1		31	O	CP	SCOTCH	BARKEEPER	043	D		82
ROSS	CRAWFORD				40	SCOT	CP	SCOT	LAB	044	B	1	43
ROSS	D	S			62	SCOTLAND	CS	SCOTCH		043	F		12
ROSS	DAVID				48	SCOT	CS	SCOT	BLACK SMITH	044	B	4	20
ROSS	GEORGE				45	SCOTLAND	PS	SCOTTISH	LABOURER	044	C	1	24
ROSS	HENRY			M	29	O	PS	SCOTCH	SAW MILLER	043	A	2	39
ROSS	JACOB	PHILIP			46	O	CP	IRISH	F	044	C	2	17
ROSS	JAMES			M	26	O	PR	SCOTCH	SCHOOL TEACHER	043	A	1	35
ROSS	JAMES				48	O	CP	SCOTCH	MERCHANT	043	A	4	22
ROSS	JAMES				50	ENGLAND	CE	ENGLISH	WEAVER	045	A	2	36
ROSS	JAMES				55	SCOTLAND	CP	SCOTCH	CARPENTER	045	B	2	17
ROSS	JAMES		2		59	IRELAND	RC		LABORER	045	D	6	D
ROSS	JOHN			M	25	O	DI	SCOTCH	BLACKSMITH	043	A	1	59
ROSS	JOHN			M	60	O	DI	SCOTCH	F	043	A	1	62
ROSS	JOHN		2		23	SCOTLAND	WM		BLACKSMITH	045	A	1	D
ROSS	JOHN				38	SCOTLAND	PS	SCOTCH	F	045	C	3	37
ROSS	JOHN	HON	2		53	IRELAND	CE		BARRISTER	044	C	4	D
ROSS	JOHN	M			72	SCOTLAND	PS	SCOTCH	GARDENER	045	A	1	72
ROSS	MALCOLM				23	ENGLAND	CE	ENGLISH	SHOEMAKER	044	C	4	86
ROSS	MARY		2	1	86	SCOTLAND	CP			044	B	6	D
ROSS	MARY			1	56	IRELAND	RC	IRISH	FARMER	045	D	6	30
ROSS	PHILIP			M	32	O	PR	SCOTCH	LAB	043	A	1	73
ROSS	ROBERT			M	74	O	CS	SCOTCH	F	043	A	2	38
ROSS	SARAH	JANE	1	1	26	ONTARIO	NG			043	G	2	28
ROSS	SIMON				38	SCOTLAND	RC	SCOTTISH	FARMER	045	A	1	98
ROSS	THOMAS			M	33	O	PS	SCOTCH	F	043	A	1	63
ROSS	WILLIAM		1		20	O	CP	SCOTCH	F LAB	044	A	3	46
ROSS	WILLIAM	G			39	SCOTLAND	CP	SCOTCH	COMMERCIAL TRAVELER	045	B	1	16
ROSSIN	JANE			1	29	O	PM	ENGLISH		045	D	2	62
ROSSITER	JAS	FELL			26	ENG	CE	ENG	PLASTERER	045	C	1	44
ROUNDTREE	DAVID				25	O	CE	ENGLISH	BUTCHER	044	C	3	45
ROUNDTREE	DAVID				51	ENGLAND	BA	ENGLISH	F	044	C	4	21
ROUNDTREE	HANNAH		1	1	15	O	WM	ENGLISH		044	C	3	27
ROUNDTREE	JAMES				24	ENGLAND	WM	ENGLISH	F	044	C	1	55
ROUNDTREE	REBECCA			1	54	ENGLAND	CE	ENGLISH	F	044	C	1	53
ROUTLEDGE	HARRISON				68	ENGLAND	WM	ENGLISH		045	B	2	7
ROUTLIFFE	JOHN				44	ENGLAND	CE	ENGLISH	LAB	045	A	2	23
ROW	EDWD		1		11	O	CO	GERMAN		044	B	5	59
ROW	JOSEPH				39	IRELAND	WM	IRISH	SHOE MAKER	044	B	5	18
ROWAN	PETER				59	O	ZZ	IRISH	BLACKSMITH	043	E	1	43
ROWAN	RICHARD				35	O	CN	GERMAN	F	043	E	3	25
ROWBOTHAM	JOHN		1		18	O	WM	ENGLISH	CARRIAGE MAKER	045	D	3	18
ROWE	BENNETT				35	ENGLAND	WM	ENGLISH	SAWYER	043	G	1	52
ROWE	JAMES				33	ENGLAND	WM	ENGLISH	LAB	044	B	6	14
ROWE	JONAS			M	37	US	DI	GERMAN	MERCHANT	043	A	1	51
ROWE	MATHEW		1		22	ENGLAND	CE	ENGLISH	LABOURER	045	D	3	63
ROWE	THOMAS				60	ENGLAND	CE	ENGLISH	TAILOR	043	D		71
ROWE	THOMAS				38	ENGLAND	WM	ENGLISH	LAB	044	B	5	12
ROWE	WILLIAM			M	42	ENGLAND	CE	ENGLISH	INN KEEPER	043	A	2	31
ROWELL	AMOS				70	ENGLAND	WM	ENGLISH	LAB	044	C	4	75
ROWELL	JAMES		1		25	O	CO	ENGLISH	F LAB	044	A	3	4
ROWEN	D	R			24	UNITED STATES	NC	GERMAN	INNKEEPER	043	E	2	38
ROWEN	THOMAS				80	IRELAND	RC	IRISH	LAB	043	D		48
ROWILL	WILLIAM				46	ENGLAND	CE	ENGLISH	BUILDER	045	B	1	3
ROWLAND	FRANCIS		1		25	ENG	CE	ENG	LAB	045	C	1	73
ROWLAND	WILLIAM				40	WALES	WM	WELSH	F	043	E	1	44
ROWLING	JOHN				64	ENGLAND	PM	ENGLISH	F	043	E	3	33
ROWLSON	WM		1		45	ENG	CE	ENG	LAB	045	C	1	32
ROWNTREE	JOHN				28	ENGLAND	BA	ENGLISH	BUTCHER	044	B	5	50
ROWNTREE	JOSEPH				53	ENGLAND	PM	ENGLISH	MILLER	044	A	3	19
ROWSON	JOHN				36	ENGLAND	CE	ENGLISH	LAB	045	C	2	49
ROYCE	ALAN		1		35	ENGLAND	WM	ENGLISH	F	044	C	4	75
ROYCE	FANNY		1	1	13	ENGLAND	RC	ENGLISH		044	C	4	48
ROYCE	GEORGE		1		6	O	WM	ENGLISH		044	C	4	75
ROYCE	GILBERT		1		1	O	WM	ENGLISH		044	C	4	75
ROYCE	HENRY		1		3	O	WM	ENGLISH		044	C	4	75
ROYCE	HENRY	W			60	ENGLAND	CE	ENGLISH	TOLL KEEPER	044	C	4	20
ROYCE	SARAH		1	1	32	O	WM	ENGLISH		044	C	4	75

SURNAME	NAME1	NAME2	STRAY	SEX	AGE	BIRTHPL	RELIGION	ORIGIN	OCCUP	DIST	SUB_DIST	DIV	PAGE
ROYSTON	CHRISTOPHER		1		31	ENGLAND	WM	ENGLISH	SERVANT	043	E	1	55
ROYSTON	JOHN				25	ENGLAND	WM	ENGLISH	F	043	E	1	9
RUDD	AMBROSE				42	ENGLAND	CE	ENGLISH	GARDENER	045	A	1	36
RUDD	NATHANIEL				46	ENGLAND	CE	ENGLISH	GARDENER	045	A	1	32
RUDKIN	WILLIAM				40	ENGLAND	WM	ENGLISH	FARM LABOURER	045	D	3	6
RUEBOTTOM	JOSEPH				39	ENGLAND	CE	ENGLISH	HOTELKEEPER	045	D	5	8
RUIGHAM	DANIEL		1		9	O	CS	SCOT		044	B	4	42
RUMBLE	FRANCIS		1		22	O	VM	ENGLISH	SERVANT	045	D	2	20
RUMBLE	GEORGE				32	O	PM	ENG	F	044	B	2	2
RUMBLE	JAMES				28	ENG	WM	ENG	F	044	B	1	56
RUMBLE	JOSEPH		1		28	O	PM	ENG	MILLER	044	B	2	4
RUMBLE	MARY	JANE	2	1	22	O	PM			044	B	2	D
RUMBLE	ROBERT				30	ENG	WM	ENG	HOTEL KEEPER	044	B	4	1
RUMBLE	THOMAS				36	ENG	PM	ENG	F	044	B	2	70
RUMBLE	WILLIAM				60	ENG	PM	ENG	F	044	B	2	70
RUMMERFIELD	JOHN				71	O	LU	GERMAN		043	B	1	28
RUMSEY	GEORGE	J			31	O	CE	ENGLISH	MERCHANT	043	D		65
RUNDLE	JOHN				43	ENGLAND	WM	ENGLISH	F	044	A	1	38
RUNDLE	LETTY		2	1	14	O	WM			045	A	2	D
RUNDLE	RICHARD				45	ENGLAND	WM	ENGLISH	FARMER	045	A	2	8
RUNDLE	WILLIAM		2			O	WM			045	A	2	D
RUNDLE	WILLIAM				57	ENGLAND	WM	ENGLISH	FARMER	045	D	3	63
RUPERT	ADAM				64	O	WM	GER	GENT	044	B	3	9
RUPERT	ADAM	J		M	27	O	WM	GERMAN	F	043	A	2	6
RUPERT	ALANSON	SCOTT	2			O	NG			044	B	2	D
RUPERT	J	P			39	O	WM	GER	MERCHANT	044	B	4	1
RUPERT	JOHN	M			41	O	WM	GER	AGENT	044	B	2	38
RUPERT	JOHN	WM			34	O	WM	GER	CABINET MAKER	044	B	3	9
RUPERT	OLIVER				35	O	WM	GER	PHYSICIAN	044	B	4	7
RUPERT	PETER				32	O	WM	GER	F	044	B	1	53
RUPERT	PETER				62	O	EM	GER	F	044	B	1	53
RUPERT	ROLPH		2			O	NG			044	B	4	D
RUPERT	THOMAS				25	O	WM	GER	F	044	B	1	53
RUSH	BENJAMIN				46	O	NG	ENGLISH	F	043	A	6	30
RUSH	MARY	M		1	68	O	QU	DUTCH		043	A	6	30
RUSH	PETER				65	O	PM	ENGLISH	FARMER	043	B	3	44
RUSH	RICHARD	Y			32	O	WM	ENGLISH	F	043	A	6	1
RUSK	JOSEPH		1		21	ENGLAND	CE	ENGLISH	LAB	044	A	1	34
RUSNELL	PETER				41	O	BA	FRENCH	FARMER	043	B	3	59
RUSSEL	ELLEN		1	1	22	O	WM	ENGLISH		044	B	5	14
RUSSEL	GEORGE				34	O	NC	ENGLISH	LAB	043	C		15
RUSSEL	JAMES				61	SCOTLAND	CP	SCOTCH	F	045	C	2	29
RUSSEL	JANE			1	47	SCOTLAND	CP	SCOTCH		045	A	2	22
RUSSEL	SAMUEL		2			O	CE		BRICKMAKER	045	A	1	D
RUSSEL	WILLIAM				26	IRELAND	CE	IRISH	BRICKMAKER	045	A	1	28
RUSSEL	WILLIAM				57	SCOTLAND	CP	SCOTISH	PAPERMAKER	045	A	2	25
RUSSELL	FRANK				32	ENGLAND	CE	ENGLISH	BUTCHER	043	D		13
RUSSELL	GEO		1		41	ENGLAND	CE	ENGLISH	LAB	044	B	5	59
RUSSELL	GEORGE				50	ENGLAND	CE	ENGLISH	LABOURER	045	A	1	49
RUSSELL	HENRY				28	O	WM	ENGLISH	INNKEEPER	044	C	4	32
RUSSELL	J	M			24	O	CE	IRISH	IRON FINISHER	044	B	5	16
RUSSELL	JAMES				26	IRELAND	CE	IRISH	BRICKMAKER	045	A	1	50
RUSSELL	JAMES				27	O	CP	SCOTCH		045	B	1	20
RUSSELL	JAMES				67	ENGLAND	CE	ENGLISH		045	B	1	46
RUSSELL	JAMES				34	O	UP	SCOTCH	FARMER	045	D	1	22
RUSSELL	JOHN				30	IRELAND	CE	IRISH	BRICKMAKER	045	A	1	37
RUSSELL	JOSEPH				63	IRELAND	CE	IRISH	BRICKMAKER	045	A	1	38
RUSSELL	MARY		1		68	IRELAND	WM	IRISH		044	B	5	5
RUSSELL	MARY	EMILY	2	1		O	PM			044	A	3	D
RUSSELL	SIMEON				30	ENGLAND	NC	ENGLISH	LAB	043	C		16
RUSSELL	STEPHEN	A	1		23	U STATES	CE	ENGLISH	CLERK	043	D		54
RUSSELL	THOMAS				30	O	PM	ENGLISH	F	044	A	3	51
RUSSELL	THOMAS				32	IRELAND	CP	IRELAND	LABORER	045	D	2	11
RUSSELL	WILLIAM				68	SCOTLAND	UP	SCOTCH	FARMER	045	D	1	22
RUSSELL	WILLIAM				47	ENGLAND	WM	ENGLISH	BAKER	044	C	4	43
RUSSLE	JAMES		1		21	O	NG	IRISH	F LAB	043	B	4	45
RUSSLE	MERCY		1	1	1	O	WM	ENGLISH		043	B	4	22
RUTHERFORD	JAMES				50	IRE	WM	IRE	F	044	B	2	30
RUTHERFORD	JOHN			M	63	SCOTLAND	DI	SCOTCH	COTTON WEAVER	043	A	2	4
RUTHERFORD	R	C			27	U STATES	PM	IRISH	F	044	B	5	68
RUTLEDGE	ALEXANDER				25	IRELAND	WM	IRISH	F	043	E	3	28
RUTLEDGE	ELISHA				50	ENG	PM	ENG	F	044	B	2	76
RUTLEDGE	GEORGE				50	ENGLAND	WM	ENGLISH	F	044	C	1	29
RUTLEDGE	MARVIN				30	IRELAND	WM	IRISH	F	043	E	3	28
RUTLEDGE	THOMAS		1		21	IRELAND	WM	IRISH	LAB	044	C	4	75
RUTLEDGE	WILLIAM				64	IRELAND	WM	IRISH	F	043	E	3	27
RUTLEDGE	WILLIAM				26	ENGLAND	PM	ENGLISH	F	043	E	3	53
RUTLIDGE	PETER			M	27	ENGLAND	CE	ENGLISH	BLACKSMITH	043	A	1	8
RUTSAY	GEORGE			M	63	ENGLAND	CE	ENGLISH	F	043	A	1	46
RUTSEY	JAMES				27	O	RC	ENGLISH	SADDLER	043	C		8
RYAN	CATHERINE		1	1	25	IRELAND	RC	IRISH	HOUSEKEEPER	043	E	1	44
RYAN	CORNELIUS				61	IRELAND	RC	IRISH	SHOEMAKER	044	B	6	14
RYAN	DANIEL				29	O	RC	IRISH	FARMER	045	A	2	19
RYAN	DANIEL				60	IRELAND	RC	IRISH	LABOURER	045	D	5	42
RYAN	EDWARD			M	42	IRELAND	RC	IRISH	TRACKMAN	043	A	1	53
RYAN	EDWARD				50	IRELAND	RC	IRISH	LABOURER	045	D	3	36
RYAN	JAMES			M	60	IRELAND	RC	IRELAND	F	043	A	5	23
RYAN	JAMES				30	IRELAND	RC	IRISH	LAB	045	A	1	17
RYAN	JAMES				61	IRELAND	RC	IRISH	LABORER	045	D	1	26
RYAN	JOHN		1		39	IRELAND	RC	IRISH	LABORER	043	D		84
RYAN	JOHN		1		54	IRELAND	RC	IRISH	CARPENTER	043	E	1	30
RYAN	JOHN				60	IRELAND	RC	IRISH	LABOURER	045	A	1	31
RYAN	JOHN		1		9	US	RC	IRISH		045	D	3	53
RYAN	JOHN				64	IRELAND	RC	IRISH	F	044	C	4	93
RYAN	MAGGIE	EMMA	1	1	18	UNITED STATES	WM	IRISH	SERVANT	044	A	3	11
RYAN	MARGARET			1	50	IRE	RC	IRE		045	C	1	40
RYAN	MARTIN				37	IRELAND	RC	IRISH	LABOURER	045	D	5	47
RYAN	MARY		1	1	30	IRELAND	RC	IRISH	SERVANT	043	H	1	34
RYAN	MARY		1	1	48	IRELAND	RC	IRISH		044	B	1	5
RYAN	MATTHEW				34	IRELAND	RC	IRISH	F	043	H	1	32
RYAN	MICHAEL		2		50	IRE	RC		LAB	044	B	1	D
RYAN	MICHAEL		1		20	IRELAND	PS	IRISH	FARM LABOURER	045	C	3	37
RYAN	PATRICK				37	IRELAND	RC	IRISH	LAB	043	H	1	39
RYAN	PATRICK		1		45	IRELAND	RC	IRISH	LABOURER	045	A	1	72
RYAN	RICH				32	O	CP	ENG	FIREMAN GTR	045	C	1	54
RYAN	TIMOTHY		1		24	O	RC	IRISH	SERVANT	045	D	2	51

SURNAME	NAME1	NAME2	STRAY	SEX	AGE	BIRTHPL	RELIGION	ORIGIN	OCCUP	DIST	SUB_DIST	DIV	PAGE
RYAN	WILLIAM				29	IRELAND	RC	IRISH	FURNACE MAN	045	A	1	43
RYAN	WILLIAM				33	IRELAND	RC	IRISH	LABOURER	045	D	5	33
RYDE	DANIEL				43	ENGLAND	CE	ENGLISH	COOPER	045	B	1	12
RYDE	EDWARD		1		16	ENGLAND	CE	ENGLISH	COOPER	045	B	2	11
RYDER	HENRY				40	ENGLAND	CE	ENGLISH	CARPENTER	045	B	1	62
RYNAS	MILLAN				50	0	NG	ENG	LAB	044	B	4	6
RYNDHARD	PHILLIP				27	IRELAND	CE	IRISH	F	043	H	1	18
RYNDNESS	SARAH	A	2	1	1	ONTARIO	PM			043	H	2	D
RYNDNESS	SARAH	A	2	1	1	0	PM			043	H	2	D
RYNESS	JAMES		1		84	UNITED STATES	BC			043	H	2	18
RYNESS	JOSHUA				35	ONTARIO	CS	GERMAN	LABOURER	043	H	2	19
RYNUS	JOHN				40	ONTARIO	PR	DUTCH	FARMER	043	G	2	49
SACELBY	THOMAS		1		54	ENGLAND	CE	ENGLISH	HOSTLER	044	C	2	32
SACKS	CHRISTIAN		1		14	0	CE	ENGLISH		043	E	1	9
SACKS	GEORGE		1		12	0	CE	ENGLISH		043	E	1	9
SACKS	HELEN		1	1	15	0	CE	ENGLISH		043	E	1	9
SACKS	SUSAN		1	1	20	0	BA	ENGLISH		043	E	1	9
SADLER	WILLIAM		1		26	ENGLAND	CE	ENGLISH		045	B	1	13
SAGAL	MARGARET			F	58	0	PR	IRISH	RETIRED	043	A	1	48
SAGE	GEORGE				29	0	CE	ENGLISH	FARM LABOURER	043	B	3	64
SAGE	JAMES				20	0	CE	ENGLISH	LAB	045	A	3	22
SALES	ADALINE		1	1	19	0	BA	ENGLISH		043	B	3	75
SALES	DANIEL		1		18	0	CN		FARM LABOURER	043	B	3	2
SALES	ELIJAH		1		21	0	CN	UNKNOWN	FARM SERVANT	043	B	3	33
SALES	SARAH		1	1	52	0	CN	UNKNOWN		043	B	3	33
SALSBERRY	CORNELIUS				44	USA	NR	GERMAN	LAB	043	H	2	13
SALSBERRY	CORNELIUS				44	UNITED STATES	NR	GERMAN	LABOURER	043	H	2	13
SALTER	JOHN				44	ENGLAND	CE	ENGLISH	F	043	E	1	22
SAMPLY	SAMUEL		2			IRELAND	CE		BREAKSMAN	045	A	1	D
SAMPSON	JAMES				70	ENGLAND	CP	ENGLISH	FARMER	045	A	3	34
SAMPSON	JOHN				29	0	IM	ENGLISH	F	043	B	4	20
SAMPSON	JOHN		1		29		NG			043	F		23
SAMSON	EMMA		1	1	11	ENGLAND	CO	ENGLISH	SERVANT	044	A	3	37
SANDERS	ANDREW				70	0	WM	ENGLISH	GENTLEMAN	044	C	3	6
SANDERS	ELIZABETH		2	1		0	WM			044	C	3	D
SANDERS	GEO		1		50	SCOTLAND	PS	SCOTCH	BLACKSMITH	044	B	5	5
SANDERS	GEORGE				32	0	CN	ENGLISH	LABOURER	043	B	3	34
SANDERS	HENERY				22	0	WM	DUTCH	F	044	C	3	6
SANDERS	HENRY		2		24	ENGLAND	CE		LAB	043	E	3	D
SANDERS	JOHN		1		20	ENGLAND	CO	GERMAN	LABOURER	043	B	3	53
SANDERS	JOSEPH		2		76	ENGLAND	CE		CARPENTER	043	B	3	D
SANDERS	MARY		2	1	46	IRELAND	RP			044	C	3	D
SANDERS	NANCY			1	69	UNITED STATES	CN	GERMAN		043	B	3	24
SANDERS	THOMAS				55	ENGLAND	CE	ENGLISH	LAB	043	E	3	45
SANDERS	WILLIAM				25	ENGLAND	WM	ENGLISH	STOREKEEPER	045	D	6	40
SANDERS	WILLIAM				26	0	NG	ENGLISH	BLACKSMITH	044	C	3	6
SANDERSON	CHAS				52	ENG	NR	ENG	BLACKSMITH	045	C	1	70
SANDERSON	DAVID				35	0	WM	ENGLISH	TOLL KEEPER	044	B	5	35
SANDERSON	DIANNAH		1	1	89	ENGLAND	CE	ENGLISH		045	D	3	53
SANDERSON	EDWARD				44	ENGLAND	WM	ENGLISH	FARMER	045	D	2	67
SANDERSON	ELIZABETH		1	1	18	0	WM	ENGLISH	SERVANT	044	A	3	20
SANDERSON	ELIZABETH		1	1	67	ENGLAND	WM	ENGLISH		045	D	1	52
SANDERSON	HANAH		1	1	19	0	WM	IRISH	SERVANT	044	C	3	73
SANDERSON	HENRY				55	EN	WM	ENGLAND	VET SURGEON	045	D	2	10
SANDERSON	JOHN				48	ENGLAND	CE	ENGLAND	FARMER	045	D	6	2
SANDERSON	JOHN				36	0	WM	ENGLISH	CARPENTER	045	D	1	50
SANDERSON	LETITIE				2	0	NG			045	D	6	D
SANDERSON	MARY	ANN	1	1	16	0	PM	ENGLISH	SERVANT	044	A	3	45
SANDERSON	RICKINON				33	ENGLAND	CE	ENGLISH	F	043	E	2	58
SANDERSON	SAMUEL				57	ENG	EP	ENG	LAB	044	B	2	5
SANDERSON	THOMAS				41	ENGLAND	WM	ENGLISH	FARMER	045	D	5	57
SANDFORD	EDWARD				39	0	RC	FRENCH	F	044	A	1	28
SANDFORD	MARTIN				37	0	RC	ENGLISH	F	044	A	1	12
SANDON	THOMAS				44	ENGLAND	CE	SCOTCH	FARMER	045	A	3	19
SANDOR	JOHN	C	1		25	QUEBEC	WM	ENGLISH	CHEMIST	045	B	2	1
SANDWICH	JOSEPH				37	0	CN	ENGLISH	LABOURER	045	D	6	13
SANFORD	ELIZABETH		1	1	36	0	CE	NOT KNOWN	INMATE	045	B	1	72
SANGSTER	EMMA	C	2		4	0	CP			045	B	1	D
SANGSTER	JOHN				40	ENGLAND	CP	ENGLISH	PROFESSOR	045	B	1	39
SANGSTER	WILLIAM				60	SCOTLAND	CP	SCOTCH	CARRIAGE MAKER	044	A	3	23
SANGSTER	WILLIAM				26	NOVA SCOTIA	PM	SCOTCH	FARM MANAGER	044	C	2	48
SANSOM	ALFRED				35	ENGLAND	CO	ENGLISH	STONEMASON	044	A	3	41
SANTON	JOHN				56	ENGLAND	CE	ENGLISH	FARMER	045	A	3	3
SANVIDGE	JOHN				58	ENG	PM	ENG	GARDENER	044	B	2	24
SANVIDGE	JOHN				23	ENG	WM	ENG	LAB	044	B	2	24
SANVIDGE	WILLIAM				29	ENG	WM	ENG	LAB	044	B	2	26
SARGENT	WALTER	J			25	ENGLAND	CO	ENGLISH	SHOEMAKER	045	A	1	36
SARJUNT	ELIZABETH		1	1	40	BARBADOS	CE	ENGLISH	SERVANT	044	C	3	28
SARLES	INDIANA		1	1	10	0	WM	GERMAN		045	D	5	40
SARNBERGER	GEORG	W			31	0	CN	GERMAN	MACHINIST	045	D	3	10
SAUER	ELIZABETH		1	1	78	GERMANY	CE	GERMAN		044	C	4	17
SAUL	SARAH		1	1	63	ENGLAND	CE	ENGLISH	BOARDER	043	C		32
SAUNDERS	ALFRED		1		15	ENGLAND	WM	ENGLISH	SERVANT	045	B	1	43
SAUNDERS	EMMA		1	1	27	ENGLAND	WM	ENGLISH	SERVANT	045	B	2	37
SAUNDERS	JOHN				28	ENGLAND	CE	ENGLISH	WHITESMITH	043	G	1	9
SAUNDERS	JOSEPH				89	ENGLAND	CE	ENGLISH	F	044	A	2	17
SAUNDERS	WILLIAM				57	ENGLAND	CE	ENGLISH	BOAT BUILDER	045	A	1	66
SAUNDERS	WILLIAM				48	ENGLAND	XC	ENGLISH	POTTER	045	B	1	52
SAVAGE	GEORGE				73	ENGLAND	CE	ENGLISH	FARMER	045	D	2	64
SAVAGE	JOHN				25	0	CE	ENGLISH	F	043	B	2	28
SAVAGE	PETER				26	SCOT	PS	SCOT	MACHINIST	044	B	2	16
SAVAGE	SYLVESTER				46	SCOT	PS	SCOT	MACHINIST	044	B	2	35
SAVERN	JOHN				49	0	WM	ENGLISH	F	045	C	2	51
SAVILL	GEORGE		1		27	ENGLAND	CE	ENGLISH	LABOURER	045	D	3	80
SAWDON	CHARLES		1		16	ENGLAND	CE	ENGLISH	SERVANT	045	D	1	8
SAWDON	MARY			1	43					044	B		
SAWDON	THOMAS				28	0	PM	ENGLISH	F	043	B	5	8
SAWDON	WILLIAM				59	ENGLAND	CE	ENGLISH	F	043	E	2	20
SAXTON	JOHN	B			46	ENGLAND	CO	ENGLISH	WATCH MAKER	043	D		15
SAXTON	JOHN	B			46	ENGLAND	CO	ENGLISH	TEAMSTER	043	D		86
SAZE	JOHN				26	0	BA		FARMER	045	B	3	6
SCADDING	WILLIAM				33	0	CE	ENGLISH	BANK CLERK	045	B	1	37
SCALES	CHARLES				33	ENGLAND	CE	ENGLISH	BRICKMAKER	044	C	4	5
SCALES	EDWARD				26	ENGLAND	CE	ENGLISH	BRICKMAKER	044	C	4	7
SCANLIN	PATRICK				35	IRELAND	EM	IRISH	LAB	043	E	2	27
SCANLON	CONNER		1		67	IRELAND	RC	IRISH	LAB	045	A	1	9

SURNAME	NAME1	NAME2	STRAY	SEX	AGE	BIRTHPL	RELIGION	ORIGIN	OCCUP	DIST	SUB_DIST	DIV	PAGE
SCANLON	PATRICK		1		18	IRELAND	RC	IRISH	FARM SERVANT	043	H	1	3
SCANLON	WILLIAM	M	1		4	O	PE	SCOTCH		043	F		7
SCARLETT	EDWARD	C			52	O	CE	ENGLISH	F	044	A	2	41
SCARLETT	RACHEL		1	1	30	IRISH	WM	IRISH	SERVANT	043	D		17
SCHACKLETON	MARY			1	53	ENGLAND	CP	ENGLISH	HOTEL KEEPER	045	C	2	3
SCHAINERHORN	THOMAS				24	O	EM	DUTCH	LAB	043	E	1	26
SCHLAGER	CHRISTIAN				59	GERMANY	LU	GERMAN	CARPENTER	044	B	6	26
SCHLANKTER	JACOB				30	GERMANY	LU	GERMAN	FARMER	043	B	3	23
SCHLANKTER	JOSEPH				53	GERMANY	CN	GERMAN	LABOURER	043	B	3	31
SCHLUTER	EDWARD				58	GERMANY	LU	GERMAN	PROFESSOR OF LANGUAG	044	C	4	93
SCHMIDT	LOUIS		2		7	O	PR	GERMAN		045	A	1	D
SCHOLES	JAMES				70	IRELAND	CP	IRISH	F	045	C	2	35
SCHOLFIELD	WILLIAM				34	O	CE	ENGLISH	PHYSICIAN	043	A	4	4
SCHUNK	WILLIAM		1		11	O	CE	GERMAN		044	C	4	21
SCOBLE	THOS	C			30	ENGLAND	CE	ENGLISH	CIVIL ENGINEER	044	A	2	39
SCOLLAY	ROBERT				38	O	EA	SCOTCH	PUMP MAKER CARPENTER	043	B	3	62
SCOTT	ADAM				38	ENGLAND	CS	SCOTCH	SCHOOL TEACHER	045	D	5	16
SCOTT	AGNESS		1	1	78	SCOTLAND	CP	SCOTCH		043	A	1	45
SCOTT	ALEXANDER				37	SCOT	PS	SCOT	PRINTER	044	B	2	8
SCOTT	ANDREW				57	IRE	CS	SCOT	LAB	044	B	4	43
SCOTT	CATHERINE			1	39	O	RC	IRISH	WASHERWOMAN	043	A	4	27
SCOTT	CHRISTOPHER				78	IRELAND	CP	IRISH	WEAVER	043	A	6	20
SCOTT	FRANCES		1	1	4	IRE	WM	IRISH		044	B	4	49
SCOTT	FRANCIS				36	O	PS	SCOTCH	F	045	C	3	52
SCOTT	GEO				43	SCOTLAND	CO	SCOTCH	BLACKSMITH	044	B	5	16
SCOTT	GEORGE				66	SCOTLAND	CO	SCOTCH	CARPENTER	044	A	1	39
SCOTT	GEORGE				40	SCOTLAND	CO	SCOTCH	STORE KEEPER	045	B	1	5
SCOTT	GEORGE	W			22	O	CP	SCOTCH	F	045	C	2	28
SCOTT	HARRIET		1	1	5	O	CE	ENGLISH		045	D	1	47
SCOTT	ISAAC				50	UNITED STATES	WM	ENGLISH	F	043	B	2	23
SCOTT	ISABELLA		1	1		O	WM	IRISH	SERVANT	044	B	6	1
SCOTT	ISABELLA		1	1	90	SCOTLAND	CP	SCOTCH		045	B	2	17
SCOTT	JAMES				27	O	WM	ENGLISH	F	043	B	2	25
SCOTT	JAMES				60	ENGLAND	PM	ENGLISH	F	043	B	2	25
SCOTT	JAMES				45	IRELAND	CS	IRISH	CARPENTER	043	G	1	12
SCOTT	JAMES				27	O	PM	ENG	F	044	B	4	18
SCOTT	JANE			1	47	IRELAND	CP	SCOTCH		044	A	2	26
SCOTT	JOHN		1		23	IRELAND	CO	IRISH	LABOURER	043	B	3	53
SCOTT	JOHN				28	SCOTLAND	CP	SCOTCH	BUCHER	044	C	4	47
SCOTT	L	HENRY			26	ENGLAND	CE	ENGLISH	SCHOOL TEACHER	044	C	1	30
SCOTT	LOUISA		1	1	15	O	CO	ENGLISH		045	D	5	8
SCOTT	MARGARET		1	1	22	O	WM	IRISH	SERVANT	045	C	2	33
SCOTT	MRS GEORGE			1	66	SCOTLAND	PS	SCOTCH		045	C	3	50
SCOTT	ROBERT		1		28	ENGLAND	CE	ENGLISH	F	045	C	2	38
SCOTT	ROBERT				44	O	UP	ENGLISH	FARMER	045	D	1	44
SCOTT	ROBERT				50	IRELAND	WM	IRISH	FARMER	044	C	1	16
SCOTT	SAMUEL				41	O	WM	IRISH	F	043	H	1	21
SCOTT	SETH				43	ENGLAND	CE	ENGLISH	PHYSICIAN	043	E	3	33
SCOTT	STANLEY				32	O	CN	SCOTCH	PHYSICIAN	043	D		13
SCOTT	THOMAS			M	59	SCOTLAND	CP	SCOTCH	F	043	A	1	36
SCOTT	THOMAS				31	O	PM	ENGLISH	F	043	B	2	25
SCOTT	THOMAS		1		14	O	CE	ENGLISH	FARM LABOURER	043	E	2	48
SCOTT	WALTER			M	47	SCOTLAND	PS	SCOTCH	F	043	A	1	19
SCOTT	WILLIAM				32	O	PM	ENGLISH	F	043	B	1	32
SCOTT	WILLIAM				52	ENGLAND	PM	ENGLISH	LAB	043	B	2	33
SCOTT	WILLIAM				20	SCOTLAND	WM	SCOTCH	LABOURER	043	B	3	51
SCOTT	WILLIAM				30	ENGLAND	CE	ENGLISH	LAB	043	C		34
SCOTT	WILLIAM		1		19	O	CE	ENGLISH	FARM LABOURER	043	E	2	48
SCOTT	WILLIAM				62	ENG	BA	ENG	F	044	B	4	33
SCOTT	WILLIAM	R			58	SCOTLAND	CP	SCOTCH	F	044	A	1	31
SCOVELL	GEORGE				36	ENGLAND	CE	ENGLISH	F	044	C	2	17
SCRACE	GEORGE				29	O	PM	ENGLISH	F	045	A	4	15
SCRACE	WILLIAM				34	O	PM	ENGLISH	F	045	A	4	15
SCRIVENER	JAMES				31	ENGLAND	CE	ENGLISH	F	044	C	2	25
SCRIVENS	DANIEL				50	ENG	CE	ENG	LAB	045	C	1	57
SCRIVER	ANTOINE		1		3	O	CE	FR		045	C	1	38
SCRIVER	JOSE		1	1	8	O	CE	FR		045	C	1	38
SCRIVER	PHEBA		1	1	11	O	CE	FR		045	C	1	38
SCRIVER	WH		1		14	O	CE	FR		045	C	1	38
SCULLY	ANN			1	50	IRELAND	RC	IRISH		043	B	4	10
SCULLY	LAWRINCE				25	IRELAND	RC	IRISH	SHOEMAKER	043	B	4	10
SCULLY	MITCHAEL				30	QUE	RC	IRISH	F LAB	043	B	4	20
SCULLY	ROBERT		1		17	O	RC	IRISH	SADDLER	043	D		19
SEAGER	EDMUND				59	ENG	CE	ENG	GENTLEMAN	044	B	1	19
SEAGER	EDWARD				61	ENG	RC	ENG	F	044	B	1	39
SEAGER	JOHN	E	2			O	EM			043	B	1	D
SEAGER	WILLIAM				34	O	CE	ENGLISH	F	043	B	1	9
SEAGLE	HENRY		2	M	70	O	PR		F	043	A	1	D
SEAGRAM	FREDERICK				58	ENGLAND	CE	ENGLISH	GENERAL AGENT	045	A	1	3
SEAGRIFF	PATRICK				30	O	RC	IRISH	CATTLE DEALER	045	A	1	77
SEARL	GEORGE		1		24	ENGLAND	PM	ENGLISH	BRICK MAKER	045	B	1	65
SEARLE	EUGENIE		1	1	34	O	CP	SCOTCH		045	D	2	6
SEARLE	FREDERICK	H	1		12	O	CP	ENGLISH		045	D	2	6
SEARLE	STEPHEN	S	1		10	O	CP	ENGLISH		045	D	2	6
SEARS	SARAH			1	51	ENGLAND	CE	ENGLISH		045	A	1	22
SECOR	ALEXANDER	M			51	O	WM	GERMAN	F	045	C	3	44
SECOR	DAVID	THOMAS			34	O	CE	ENG	F	045	C	1	21
SECOR	GEORGE	R			35	O	WM	ENG	AGENT	045	C	1	37
SECOR	ISAAC				46	O	WM	ENG	F	045	C	1	24
SECOR	ISAAC		1		18	O	WM	FRENCH	LAB	045	C	1	16
SECOR	ISAAC	T			50	O	CP	ENG	F	045	C	1	46
SECOR	JOS	M			43	O	CE	ENG	F	045	C	1	55
SECOR	JOSEPH				80	O	CE	ENG	F	045	C	1	22
SECOR	LEWIS	W			49	O	WM	GERMAN	F	045	C	3	6
SECOR	MARK		1		15	O	WM	FRENCH		045	C	1	16
SECOR	WILLIAM				20	O	WM	FRENCH	LAB	045	C	2	16
SECORD	STEPHEN				44	ONTARIO	RC	FRENCH	LABORER	043	G	2	42
SEDMAN	THOMAS				49	ENGLAND	CE	ENGLAND	WAGON MAKER	045	D	2	7
SEDORE	ABRAHAM		1		35	ONTARIO	WM	SCOTCH	FARMER	043	G	1	49
SEDORE	ANDREW				23	ONTARIO	PR	ENGLISH	LABORER	043	G	2	55
SEDORE	GEORGE				53	ONTARIO	PR	GERMAN	SHINGLE MAKER	043	G	2	5
SEDORE	HIRAM				45	O	CN	DUTCH	FARMER	043	G	1	42
SEDORE	ISAAC				61	O	EM	GERMAN	F	043	E	2	65
SEDORE	ISAAC				24	ONTARIO	WM	GERMAN	FARMER	043	G	1	47
SEDORE	JEREMIAH				50	ONTARIO	EM	FRENCH	FARMER	043	G	1	21
SEDORE	JOHN				60	ONTARIO	EM	DUTCH	FARMER	043	G	1	48

SURNAME	NAME1	NAME2	STRAY	SEX	AGE	BIRTHPL	RELIGION	ORIGIN	OCCUP	DIST	SUB_DIST	DIV	PAGE
SEDORE	JOSIAH				27	ONTARIO	EM	GERMAN	FARMER	043	G	2	39
SEDORE	MILES				35	ONTARIO	EM	GERMAN	FARMER	043	G	2	4
SEDORE	ORIN				34	O	WM	FRENCH	F	043	E	2	28
SEDORE	ORIN		2		1	ONTARIO	NG			043	G	2	D
SEDORE	THOMAS				37	O	CN	GERMAN	F	043	E	2	64
SEED	DAVID				35	ENG	CE	ENG	F	044	B	4	40
SEGAR	EDWARD				27	O	RC	ENG	F	044	B	1	10
SEGAR	HENRY				74	US	CE	ENGLISH	LABORER	045	D	1	31
SEGNON	HENRY				25	ENGLAND	CE	ENGLISH	BOILER MAKER	044	B	5	27
SEIDLER	C	H			52	PRUSSIA	CE	GERMAN	F	043	H	2	45
SEIDLER	C	H			52	PRUSSIA	CE	GERMAN	FARMER	043	H	2	45
SELBY	JOHN		1		27	ENGLAND	CE	ENGLISH	CLERK	043	D		82
SELBY	SARAH			1	46	O	CE	SCOTCH		043	D		75
SELBY	WILLIAM				24	SCOTLAND	WM	SCOTCH	CLERK	043	D		28
SELBY	WILLIAM				55	O	CE	IRISH	FARMER	043	E	1	45
SELLARS	CHARLES				48	ENGLAND	CE	ENGLISH	STOREKEEPER	044	C	4	64
SELLARS	DANIEL				29	NOVA SCOTIA	CE	IRISH	INNKEEPER	044	C	4	53
SELLARS	JOEL		1	M	68	ENGLAND	CE	ENGLAND		043	A	5	44
SELLARS	JOHN	J			37	NS	CP	SCOTCH	F	045	A	4	20
SELLARS	JOSEPH			M	33	ENGLAND	CE	ENGLAND	F	043	A	5	35
SELLER	WILLIAM				38	ENGLAND	CE	ENGLISH	F LAB	043	B	4	28
SELLERS	ROBERT				62	O	CE	ENGLISH	F	045	C	3	19
SELLERS	THOMAS				47	ENGLAND	PM	ENGLISH	FARMER	045	D	1	45
SENIOR	BENJAMIN				22	ENGLAND	WM	ENGLISH	BRICK MAKER	043	D		31
SERIVIER	WILLIAM				48	ONTARIO	EM	ENGLISH	FARMER	043	G	1	37
SERVEL	MATHEW				47	ENGLAND	CE	ENGLISH	LAB	045	A	4	23
SERVIE	WALTER		1		16	O	WM	IRISH	FARM LAB	043	B	1	23
SERVIE	WILLIAM		1		14	O	WM	IRISH	FARM LAB	043	B	1	24
SERVISS	CHARLES				39	QUE	WM	GERMAN	F LAB	043	B	4	24
SEVERN	WILLIAM				26	O	WM	ENGLISH	CLARK	045	B	1	69
SEVERS	JAS	W			32	ENGLAND	WM	ENGLISH	LAWYER	043	C		43
SEVILLE	SUSAN		1	1	27	ENGLAND	CE	ENGLISH		044	C	4	68
SEVIRE	JOHN	E			21	CANADA	WM	ENGLISH	LABORER	045	D	6	56
SEWELL	SAMUEL				74	USA	BA	AFRICAN	FARMER	045	A	1	40
SEXMITH	GEO				49	IRELAND	WM	IRISH	MERCHANT	043	B	3	23
SEXON	JEREMIAH				50	IRE	RC	IRE	LAB	045	C	1	9
SEXSMITH	SAMUEL				50	IRELAND	CE	IRISH	COOPER	043	F		22
SEXTON	ALEXANDER				36	O	CN	SCOTCH	LABOURER	043	B	3	39
SEXTON	THOMAS		1		18	IRELAND	CE	IRISH	LABORER	043	G	1	30
SEYMORE	WILLIAM				30	SCOTLAND	CE	SCOTCH	F	045	A	4	33
SEYMOUR	ANDREW				30	SCOTLAND	CP	SCOTCH	FARMER	043	A	4	41
SEYMOUR	WILLIAM			M	70	SCOTLAND	FK	SCOTLAND	WEAVER	043	A	5	15
SHADLOCK	GEORGE				38	ENGLAND	PM	ENGLISH	FARMER	045	D	3	55
SHAES	PATRICK				50	IRELAND	RC	IRISH	F LAB	044	A	2	4
SHAFFER	DANIEL				26	O	MN	GERMAN	F	043	B	2	17
SHAND	JOHN				38	SCOTLAND	CP	SCOTCH	SHOEMAKER	045	B	1	31
SHAND	WILLIAM		1		50	SCOTLAND	PS	SCOTCH	SERVANT	044	C	4	66
SHANK	WM		1		26	ENGLAND	PM	ENGLISH	LAB	044	B	5	36
SHANKEL	GODFRY				28	GERMANY	CO	GERMAN	HARNESS MAKER	043	B	3	52
SHANKLIN	REV ROBERT				48	IRE	CE	IRISH	MINISTER	044	B	1	64
SHANKS	ANN		1	1	1	O	WM	ENGLISH		044	B	5	70
SHANKS	JOHN				35	O	PS	ENGLISH	F	043	A	6	47
SHANKS	MARTIN				43	ENG	PM	ENG	F	044	B	4	12
SHANKS	PETER				55	ENGLAND	CE	SCOTCH	CARPENTER	043	A	4	12
SHANKS	THOMAS		1		1	SCOTLAND	CP	SCOTCH	FARM LABOURER	045	C	4	44
SHANLS	THOMAS			M	33	QUE	RC	FRANCE	BLACKSMITH	043	A	1	39
SHANLY	FRANCIS				50	IRELAND	CE	IRISH	ENGINEER	044	C	4	68
SHANNON	JAMES			M	40	IRELAND	RC	IRISH	LAB	043	A	1	61
SHANON	CATHERINE		1	1	18	O	CE	IRISH		043	A	2	47
SHARP	CATHERINE		1	1	30	IRELAND	RC	IRISH		044	C	4	35
SHARP	GEORGE				50	ENGLAND	WM	ENGLISH	FARMER	045	D	4	49
SHARP	GEORGE		1		45	IRELAND	CE	IRISH	MASON	044	C	4	35
SHARP	HENRY				32	ENGLAND	WM	ENGLISH	FARMER	043	B	3	35
SHARP	JOHN				69	IRELAND	CE	IRISH	RETIRED	043	A	6	53
SHARP	JOHN		1		26	ENGLAND	NG	ENGLISH	FARM LABOURER	045	C	4	35
SHARP	WILLIAM				51	O	EM	AFRICAN	LAB	043	E	2	79
SHARP	WILLIAM		1		19	O	PM	ENG	LAB	044	B	2	30
SHARPE	FRANCIS		1		19	SCOTLAND	CP	SCOTCH	F	044	C	4	15
SHARPE	GEORGE				42	ENGLAND	EP	ENGLISH	MILLER	043	A	3	24
SHARPE	INGHAM				42	O	CE	IRISH	MERCHANT	043	D		83
SHARPE	ISAAC		1		30	O	WM	GERMAN	CLERK	043	D		68
SHARPE	JOHN	A			25	O	CE	IRISH	F	043	A	6	52
SHARPE	THERESA		1	1	20	O	WM	ENGLISH		043	D		68
SHARPE	WILLIAM				45	O	CE	IRISH	F	043	A	6	49
SHARPMAN	MATHEW		1		40	ENGLAND	PM	ENGLISH	LAB	043	B	4	1
SHAUGHNESSY	ELLEN		1	1	13	O	RC	IRISH	SERVANT	045	B	1	43
SHAVER	CATHERINE		1	1	17	O	LU	GER		044	B	3	6
SHAVER	CHARLES				42	O	WM	GERMAN	F	044	A	2	19
SHAVER	CHRISTIENE		1	1	30	GER	LU	GER		044	B	3	14
SHAVER	ESTHER		2	1	56	O	WM			044	A	2	D
SHAVER	GEORGE				67	O	WM	GERMAN		044	A	2	19
SHAVER	JAMES				21	O	LU	FRENCH	F	044	B	5	14
SHAVER	JOSEPH				29	O	WM	GERMAN	LABOURER	045	D	3	57
SHAVER	NICHS				24	O	LU	GERMAN	LAB	044	B	5	45
SHAVER	PETER				61	O	WM	GERMAN	F	044	A	2	9
SHAW	ANDREW				48	SCOTLAND	CP	SCOTCH	TOLLGATE KEEPER	044	A	3	16
SHAW	ARCHIBALD				45	SCOTLAND	PS	SCOTTISH	F LAB	044	C	1	39
SHAW	CATHERINE		1	1	15	O	FK	SCOTCH		043	A	3	51
SHAW	CHAS				49	SCOTLAND	CO	SCOTCH	TIN SMITH	044	B	5	24
SHAW	ELIZA		1	1	18	O	CO	ENGLISH	SERVANT	044	A	3	18
SHAW	ELIZABETH		1	1	22	O	CE	NOT KNOWN		043	A	1	45
SHAW	FREDERICK				46	ENGLAND	NC	ENGLISH	F	043	H	2	35
SHAW	FREDRICK				46	ENGLAND	NC	ENGLISH	FARMER	043	H	2	35
SHAW	GEORGE				21	O	EM	IRISH	LAB	043	E	2	80
SHAW	HENRY	A	1		46	ENGLAND	CE	ENGLISH	ACCOUNTANT	043	D		67
SHAW	JAMES				32	SCOT	PS	SCOT	MOULDER	044	B	2	35
SHAW	JOHN		1		29	O	CE	ENGLISH	WATCH MAKER	044	B	5	27
SHAW	JOHN				40	QUEBEC	WM	IRISH	W MINISTER	044	C	3	41
SHAW	MARY			1	75	IRELAND	CE	IRISH		044	A	2	48
SHAW	MARY			1	34	O	WM	ENGLISH		045	D	6	46
SHAW	NAOMI		1	1	20	O	WM	ENGLISH	SERVT	044	B	5	10
SHAW	NELSON				22	O	EM	IRISH	LAB	043	E	2	80
SHAW	RICHARD	JAMES	1		11	ONTARIO	CE	ENGLISH		043	G	2	46
SHAW	ROBERT				53	IRELAND	PM	IRISH	STOREKEEPER	045	B	1	8
SHAW	SOPHIA		2		77	NEW BRUNSWICK	WM			045	B	1	D
SHAW	THOMAS				40	IRELAND	EM	IRISH	LABORER	043	D		79

SURNAME	NAME1	NAME2	STRAY	SEX	AGE	BIRTHPL	RELIGION	ORIGIN	OCCUP	DIST	SUB_DIST	DIV	PAGE
SHAW	THOMAS				34	CANADA	CO	ENGLISH	PRINTER	045	D	6	43
SHAW	THOMAS	R			58	0	QU	ENGLISH	FARMER	043	A	4	34
SHAW	WILLIAM				55	0	CP	ENGLISH	CABINET MAKER	043	A	4	1
SHAW	WILLIAM				33	0	WM	IRISH	MERCHANT	044	C	4	58
SHAW	WILLIAM	JOHN	1		15	0	CP	SCOTCH	F LAB	044	A	3	1
SHAW	WILLIAM	SWAIN	1		13	ONTARIO	CE	ENGLISH		043	G	2	46
SHAW	WM	ROBERT			24	0	WM	ENGLISH	COOPER	043	E	3	8
SHEA	CORNELIUS				43	IRELAND	RC	IRISH	LAB	043	A	3	22
SHEA	JOHN				88	IRELAND	RC	IRISH	SOLDIER	045	A	1	93
SHEA	JOHN				50	IRELAND	RC	IRISH	LAB	044	C	4	39
SHEAN	PATRICK				44	IRELAND	RC	IRISH	F LAB	044	A	1	16
SHEANS	FRANCIS			M	35	NEWFOUNDLAND	ME	ENGLAND	SAWYER	043	A	5	6
SHEAR	ZELLE?		1	1	10	0	MN	GERMAN		045	D	6	7
SHEARD	CHARLES				29	ENGLAND	CE	ENGLISH	LABOURER	045	A	1	25
SHEARDON	GEORGE				30	ENGLAND	PM	ENGLISH	F	043	A	3	41
SHEARDOWN	HARRIET		1	1	8	0	WM	ENGLISH		043	A	3	45
SHEARDOWN	HENRY		1		13	0	WM	ENGLISH		043	A	3	45
SHEARDOWN	JOHN				31	0	WM	ENGLISH	F	043	A	3	45
SHEARDOWN	SAMUEL				29	0	PM	ENGLISH	FARMER	043	A	3	3
SHEARDOWN	SAMUEL				58	ENGLAND	WM	ENGLISH	F	043	A	3	40
SHEARDOWN	WILLIAM				34	0	WM	ENGLISH	F	043	A	3	15
SHEDGWICK	ELIZABETH			1	50	ENGLAND	CE	ENGLISH	GARDENER	045	A	1	28
SHEDRACK	DAVID				30	FRANCE	CE	FRENCH	CARPENTER	045	A	2	36
SHEEN	JOHN				27	IRELAND	RC	IRISH	LAB	045	B	1	11
SHEFFER	GEORGE				33	0	TU	GERMAN	F	043	B	1	19
SHEFFER	MARY			1	58	0	TU	GERMAN		043	B	1	26
SHEFFIELD	ELI		1		25	0	WM	GERMAN	FARM LABOURER	043	B	3	58
SHEFFIELD	ELI				55	CANADA	CO	ENGLISH	FARMER	045	D	6	60
SHEFFIELD	GORDON				29	CANADA	WM	ENGLISH	FARMER	045	D	6	61
SHEFFIELD	THOMAS				60	0	WM	ENGLISH	LAB	043	E	1	26
SHELDON	THOMAS		1		20	0	WM	IRISH	F	044	B	6	48
SHELL	COLIN				33	0	WM	GERMAN	FARMER	045	D	4	22
SHELL	ISRAEL		1		21	0	PM	GERMAN	LAB	043	B	2	26
SHELL	JACOB				24		WM	GERMAN	COOPER	043	E	3	47
SHELL	JONATHAN				58	0	EM	GER	F	044	B	1	56
SHELL	LEVI				36	0	NC	GERMAN	F	043	B	1	19
SHELL	MINNA		1	1	11	0	PM	GERMAN	LAB	043	B	2	26
SHELL	PAUL				66	0	WM	GERMAN	FARMER	045	D	4	24
SHELL	PHILIP				36	0	NG	GERMAN	F	043	B	1	14
SHELL	STEPHEN				27	0	CN	GERMAN	LAB	043	E	3	57
SHELL	WILLIAM				36	0	WM	GERMAN	FARMER	045	D	2	40
SHELLEY	JOHN		1		30	IRELAND	RC	IRISH	BLACKSMITH	045	D	5	39
SHELVEY	THOMAS				39	ENGLAND	EM	ENGLISH	TANNER	043	C		1
SHENEE	JOHN		1		35	IRELAND	WM	IRISH	LAB	045	B	2	4
SHENEY	MARGARET		1	1	18	0	RC	IRELAND	DRESS MAKER	045	D	2	10
SHEPARD	EDWIN				25	0	EM	GERMAN	F	044	C	1	2
SHEPARD	JAMES				36	0	EP	GER	SAWYER	044	B	2	3
SHEPARD	JOHN				32	0	WM	IRISH	F	044	C	1	4
SHEPARD	JOSEPH				56	0	CE	GERMAN	MERCHANT	044	C	1	14
SHEPARD	JOSEPH				48	0	PM	ENGLISH	F	045	A	4	14
SHEPARD	MICHAEL				62	0	EM	GERMAN	F	044	C	1	14
SHEPHERD	CHAS		1		45	ENGLAND	CE	ENGLISH	MERCHANTS CLERK	043	C		28
SHEPHERD	JAMES	L			23	0	WM	ENGLISH	SADDLER	045	D	6	7
SHEPHERD	JOHN				34	ENGLAND	PM	ENGLISH	FARMER	045	A	3	37
SHEPHERD	JOHN				52	ENGLAND	WM	ENGLISH	BRICK MANUFACTURER	045	B	1	68
SHEPHERD	JOHN				30	ENGLAND	WM	ENGLISH	GARDENER	044	C	2	48
SHEPHERD	PETER				60	SCOTLAND	CP	SCOTCH	LAB	044	A	1	33
SHEPHERD	THOMAS				66	0	CE	ENGLISH	MILLER	045	A	3	17
SHEPHERD	WILLIAM				26	0	WM	ENGLISH	BRICK MAKER	045	B	1	69
SHEPPARD	CHARLES				40	ENG	PM	ENG	F	044	B	1	41
SHEPPARD	DAVID				39	ENGLAND	PM	ENGLISH	FARMER	045	A	2	35
SHEPPARD	DEBORAH			1	38	IRELAND	CE	IRISH		043	H	2	14
SHEPPARD	DEBORAH			1	38	IRELAND	RELIGION	IRISH		043	H	2	14
SHEPPARD	EDWARD				62	IRELAND	EM	IRISH	FARMER	043	G	2	9
SHEPPARD	EDWARD				51	ENG	WM	ENG	F	044	B	2	19
SHEPPARD	ELLIS				37	ONTARIO	EM	IRISH	FARMER	043	G	2	19
SHEPPARD	GEORGE				32	0	CE	ENGLISH	F	045	C	4	34
SHEPPARD	IBRAD				40	ONTARIO	EM	ENGLISH	FARMER	043	G	2	10
SHEPPARD	JARAIL				33	IRELAND	WM	IRISH	FARMER	043	G	1	38
SHEPPARD	JOHN				32	ENGLAND	CE	ENGLISH	F	043	E	2	61
SHEPPARD	JOHN				46	ENGLAND	CE	ENGLISH	HOTEL KEEPER & CARPE	043	F		28
SHEPPARD	JOHN		1		18	ENGLAND	CE	ENGLISH		045	C	2	38
SHEPPARD	JOHN				55	ENGLAND	CE	ENGLISH	F	044	C	2	33
SHEPPARD	JOSEPH				48	ENGLAND	CE	IRISH	HOTEL KEEPER	043	H	2	5
SHEPPARD	MARY		1	1	26	0	CE	ENGLISH		044	C	4	60
SHEPPARD	MATHEW		1		20	ENGLAND	CE	ENGLISH	OSTLER	044	C	4	53
SHEPPARD	NICHOLUS				57	ENGLAND	WM	ENGLISH	MILLER	045	A	2	2
SHEPPARD	OLIVER	B			23	ONTARIO	CE	IRISH	TEACHER	043	G	1	41
SHEPPARD	PAUL				72	ENGLAND	CE	ENGLISH	F	045	C	4	35
SHEPPARD	RICHARD				48	IRELAND	WM	IRISH	FARMER	043	G	1	35
SHEPPARD	RICHARD				67	IRELAND	CE	IRISH	FARMER	043	G	2	52
SHEPPARD	RICHARD				28	0	WM	IRISH	F	043	H	2	40
SHEPPARD	RICHARD				28	ONTARIO	WM	IRISH	FARMER	043	H	2	40
SHEPPARD	RICHARD	A			27	ONTARIO	CE	IRISH	FARMER	043	G	1	4
SHEPPARD	ROGER				30	0	CE	ENGLISH	LAB	043	E	1	13
SHEPPARD	RUTH		2	1	53	ENGLAND	WM			045	A	2	D
SHEPPARD	SUSAN		1	1	50	0	CE	ENGLISH		043	H	2	9
SHEPPARD	SUSAN		1	1	50	ONTARIO	CE	ENGLISH		043	H	2	9
SHEPPARD	SUSANNAH			1	77	IRELAND	CE	IRISH		043	G	2	20
SHEPPARD	THOMAS				35	ENGLAND	CE	ENGLISH	CABINET MAKER	043	F		14
SHEPPARD	W	H W			43	ENGLAND	WM	ENGLISH	MERCHANT	043	D		62
SHEPPARD	WILLIAM				58	ENGLAND	CE	ENGLISH	FARMER & TAILOR	043	E	1	50
SHEPPARD	WILLIAM				49	ENGLAND	CE	ENGLISH	FARMER	043	G	1	33
SHEPPARD	WILLIAM				29	IRELAND	WM	IRISH	FARMER	043	G	1	40
SHEPPERD	CHARLOTTE			1	64	ENGLAND	PM	ENGLISH		045	B	2	16
SHEPPERD	JOHN				45	ENGLAND	WM	ENGLISH	F	043	B	5	1
SHEPPERD	JOSEPH				48	IRELAND	CE	IRISH	HOTEL KEEPER	043	H	2	5
SHEPPERD	MAY		1	1	25	0	WM	IRISH		044	B	1	22
SHERBACK	CHRISTOPHER				39	NORWAY	LU	NORWEGIAN	LAB	044	B	1	60
SHERICK	DANIEL				29	0	MN	GERMAN	FARMER	045	D	4	18
SHERIDAN	HANNAH		1	1	24	0	RC	IRISH	SERVANT	044	B	1	9
SHERIDAN	LAWRA				30	IRELAND	RC	IRISH	LAB	045	C	2	54
SHERIDAN	MARY		1	1	23	IRELAND	RC	IRISH	SERVANT	045	D	1	9
SHERMAN	JAMES		1		28	0	PS		CARPENTER	043	A	6	64
SHERMAN	PHILANA		1	1	4	0	WM	ENGLISH		043	E	2	62
SHERWOOD	BARTLETT				25	0	CN	ENGLISH	F	043	H	1	32

SURNAME	NAME1	NAME2	STRAY	SEX	AGE	BIRTHPL	RELIGION	ORIGIN	OCCUP	DIST	SUB_DIST	DIV	PAGE
SHERWOOD	EZRA				54	0	CN	ENGLISH	F	043	H	1	39
SHERWOOD	JOHN				45	ENGLAND	PM	ENGLISH	F	045	A	4	1
SHERWOOD	JUSTICE				23	0	CP	ENGLISH	F	043	H	1	33
SHERWOOD	NELSON				32	0	OP	ENGLISH	F	043	H	2	40
SHIELDS	CHARLES		1		17	SCOTLAND	CP	SCOTCH	F	044	C	4	28
SHIELDS	JAMES				49	IRELAND	WM	SCOTCH	MERCHANT	043	E	3	45
SHIELDS	JOHN		1		25	ENGLAND	WM	ENGLISH		045	A	1	16
SHIELDS	PATRICK				74	IRELAND	RC	IRISH	LAB	045	A	2	12
SHIELDS	WILLIAM				34	0	CE	ENGLISH	HARNESS MAKER	043	C		24
SHIELES	JOHN				29	0	RP	IRISH	COOPER	044	C	3	23
SHILLARS	JOHN				60	ENGLAND	CE	ENGLISH	GARDNER	044	C	4	90
SHILLING	THOMAS				63	ONTARIO	WM	OJIBWAY INDIAN	HUNTER AND FISHER	043	G	1	58
SHILSON	JOHN			M	60	ENGLAND	EM	ENGLISH	FARMER	043	A	1	18
SHILSON	MATTHEW			M	51	ENGLAND	WM	ENGLAND	F	043	A	5	43
SHILSON	ROBERT	M			61	ENGLAND	WM	ENGLISH	COOPER	043	A	4	13
SHINE	FREDERICK		1		20	ENG	EP	ENG	LAB	044	B	3	4
SHINE	MARY			1	60	IRELAND	RC	IRISH		043	A	6	7
SHIPMAN	ROBERT		1		36	ENGLAND	CE	ENGLISH	CONFECTIONER	044	C	4	5
SHIRE	JACOB				47	QUEBEC	WM	ENGLISH	F	043	H	1	20
SHIRELEY	WILLIAM		1		18	0	CP	ENGLISH	FARM LABOURER	045	C	3	19
SHIRK	JOSEPH				42	0	MN	GERMAN	FARMER	045	D	4	11
SHIRLEY	HENRY				32	ENG	CE	ENG	LAB	045	C	1	14
SHITTLEWORTH	JAMES				48	ENGLAND	EM	ENGLISH	CARRAGE MAKER	044	C	3	46
SHMIDT	JULIUS				38	PRUSSIA	LU	PRUSSIAN	PROFESSOR MUSIC	045	A	1	29
SHOLDICE	THOMAS				24	IRELAND	RC	IRISH	F	043	F		26
SHORT	JOHN		1		35	ENGLAND	CE	ENGLISH	LABOURER	045	D	3	26
SHORT	JOSEPH				60	IRELAND	CE	IRISH	PAIL MAKER	045	D	1	20
SHORT	THOMAS				33	ENGLAND	WM	ENGLISH	FARM LABORER	045	D	1	28
SHOULTS	GEORGE	H			30	0	CN	GERMAN	WAGGON MAKER	045	D	3	11
SHOULTS	H	J			62	0	CN	GERMAN	FARMER	045	D	3	11
SHRINGLE	BETSEY		1	1	21	ENGLAND	PS	ENGLISH	SERVANT	045	D	6	71
SHROPSHIRE	CHARLES			M	56	ENGLAND	CE	ENGLISH	CARPENTER	043	A	5	1
SHROPSHIRE	CHARLES				31	0	CE	ENGLISH	CARPENTER	043	A	6	37
SHROPSHIRE	JAMES				36	0	CE	ENGLISH	CARPENTER	043	A	4	36
SHULTS	ANNA		2	1		0	EM			045	D	3	D
SHUNK	ABRAHAM				29	0	LU	GERMAN	HOTEL KEEPER	043	A	4	25
SHUNK	GEORGE				53	0	LU	GER	LAB	044	B	2	74
SHUNK	SAMUEL				40	0	VM	GERMAN	FARMER	045	D	5	58
SHUNK	SIMON				56	0	WM	GER	GENT	044	B	3	18
SHUNK	SUSANNAH			1	50	US	LU	GER	F	044	B	3	15
SHUNK	WILLIAM				32	0	WM	GER	F	044	B	3	4
SHURP	EALENOR			1	77	IRELAND	WM	IRISH		044	B	6	43
SHURWOOD	NELSON				32	ONTARIO	CS	ENGLISH	FARMER	043	H	2	40
SHUTER	DAVID				39	0	CP	IRISH	F	044	C	2	40
SHUTER	JAMES				46	0	WM	IRISH	SHOP KEEPER	044	B	1	6
SHUTER	JANE		1	1	45	IRELAND	CE	IRISH	HOUSEKEEPER	044	A	1	37
SHUTT	WILLIAM				48	ENGLAND	CE	ENGLISH	CIVIL ENGINEER	045	A	1	102
SHUTTLEWORK	ROBT		1		40	ENGLAND	NG	ENGLISH	SERVANT	043	B	4	6
SHUTTLEWORTH	EDMUND				38	0	WM	ENGLISH	F	043	E	3	38
SHUTTLEWORTH	JAMES		2		10	0	EM			044	C	3	D
SHUTTLEWORTH	JOHN				68	ENGLAND	WM	ENGLISH	F	043	E	3	50
SHUTTLEWORTH	JOHN				44	ENGLAND	EM	ENGLISH	CARPENTER	044	C	3	38
SHUTTLEWORTH	JOSEPH				26	0	WM	ENGLISH	F	043	E	3	39
SHUTTLEWORTH	ROBERT				52	ENGLAND	WM	ENGLISH	F	043	E	3	51
SHUTTLEWORTH	SAMUEL				59	ENGLAND	PS	ENGLISH	F	043	E	3	39
SHWARTS	JOHN				31	ENGLAND	PM	ENGLISH	FARMER	045	A	3	32
SIBBALD	THOMAS				60	ENGLAND	CE	SCOTCH	RN	043	H	2	27
SIBBALD	THOMAS				60	ENGLAND	CE	SCOTCH	RN	043	H	2	27
SIBBALD	WILLIAM				57	SCOTLAND	CE	SCOTCH	F	043	H	2	4
SIBBALD	WILLIAM				57	SCOTLAND	CE	SCOTCH	FARMER	043	H	2	4
SIBLEY	JOHN				59	ENGLAND	WM	ENGLISH	F & BLACKSMITH	043	A	6	21
SIBLEY	ROBERT				24	ENGLAND	CN	ENGLISH	BLACKSMITH	043	E	3	21
SIDDALL	HENRY				42	ENGLAND	CE	ENGLISH	WAGON MAKER	044	A	2	1
SIGSWORTH	JAMES				62	ENGLAND	CE	ENGLISH	SHOEMAKER	045	C	2	56
SILBAN	GEO	WM	2		1	ENGLAND	CE			043	C		D
SILBAN	THOMAS				37	ENGLAND	CE	ENGLISH	LAB	043	C		17
SILBURN	CHARLES	H	1			ENGLAND	CP	ENGLISH	FARM SERVANT	045	C	3	56
SILBY	WILLIAM				28	0	WM	CHIPPAWA	F	043	H	2	57
SILBY	WILLIAM				28	ONTARIO	WM	CHIPPAWA	FARMER	043	H	2	57
SILICO	JAMES		1		13	0	CP	SCOTCH		045	C	4	27
SILVER	JAMES				51	0	CN	SCOTCH	GENTLEMAN	043	E	1	52
SILVER	MYRON				26	ONTARIO	EM	SCOTCH	BLACKSMITH	043	G	2	51
SILVERSIDE	CHARLES				29	CANADA	WM	ENGLISH	LABORER	045	D	6	38
SILVERTHORN	GORDON				51	0	WM	ENGLISH	F	044	A	2	22
SILVERTHORN	NEWMAN				40	0	UV	ENGLISH	F	044	A	1	4
SILVERTHORNE	FRANCIS				56	0	WM	ENGLISH	F	044	A	1	1
SILVESTER	GEORGE				44	ENGLAND	CE	ENGLISH	MERCHANT	043	B	3	25
SIMMONDS	RICHARD		1		12	0	CE	ENGLISH		045	D	5	16
SIMMONS	ARTHUR	N			34	ENGLAND	CO	ENGLISH	PRINTER	045	A	1	96
SIMMONS	ELIZABETH		1	1	12	ENGLAND	CE	ENGLISH		043	D		56
SIMON	ROBERT				28	UNITED STATES	PS	IRISH	F	043	E	3	11
SIMONDS	JAMES				28	ENGLAND	CE	ENGLISH	BRICKMAKER	045	A	1	19
SIMPKINS	JOHN		1		21	ENG	EM	ENG	FARM LAB	044	B	1	31
SIMPSON	AGNES		1	1	11	ENGLAND	WM	ENGLISH		043	D		6
SIMPSON	ALEXANDRA			1	50	SCOTLAND	CP	SCOTCH		043	D		54
SIMPSON	ANN		1	1	58	U STATES	CP	IRISH		043	A	3	40
SIMPSON	ARCHIBALD				60	IRELAND	OP	IRISH	F	043	A	3	25
SIMPSON	CHARLES				34	ENGLAND	CE	ENGLISH	DRUGGIST	043	D		68
SIMPSON	DAVID		1		82	ENGLAND	WM	ENGLISH		044	C	2	16
SIMPSON	FRANK		1		71	ENGLAND	WM	ENGLISH	LAB	044	C	1	37
SIMPSON	GEORGE		1		30	ENGLAND	WM	ENGLISH	LAB	043	D		6
SIMPSON	HENRY		1		59	ENGLAND	WM	ENGLISH	BREWER	043	D		6
SIMPSON	HENRY		1		17	ENGLAND	WM	ENGLISH	LAB	043	D		6
SIMPSON	JAMES				40	IRELAND	OP	IRISH	CARP & JOINER	043	A	3	25
SIMPSON	JAMES		1		87	QUE	CE	ENG	F	044	B	2	24
SIMPSON	JOHN				28	0	CE	ENGLISH	F LAB	043	A	6	13
SIMPSON	JOHN	W	1		29	ENGLAND	CE	ENGLISH	SCHOOL TEACHER	043	E	2	7
SIMPSON	LAVINIA		1	1	36	ENGLAND	WM	ENGLISH		043	D		6
SIMPSON	LEVI				48	ONT	WM	ENGLISH	COOPER	043	D		45
SIMPSON	MARGARETH		1	1	32	IRELAND	PS	IRISH	SERVANT	044	C	4	66
SIMPSON	MARMADUKE				41	ENGLAND	CE	ENGLISH	LABOURER	045	D	4	31
SIMPSON	MARY	BESSIE	1	1	13	ENGLAND	WM	ENGLISH		043	D		6
SIMPSON	MINNIE		1	1	18	0	WM	SCOTCH	DRESS MAKER	045	D	2	26
SIMPSON	ROBERT				36	SCOTLAND	CO	SCOTCH	MERCHANT	043	D		80
SIMPSON	ROBERT		1		38	RUSSIA	CE	ENGLISH	GENTLEMAN	043	E	1	36
SIMPSON	ROBERT				65	IRELAND	CE	IRISH	LAB	044	C	3	10

SURNAME	NAME1	NAME2	STRAY	SEX	AGE	BIRTHPL	RELIGION	ORIGIN	OCCUP	DIST	SUB_DIST	DIV	PAGE
SIMPSON	SARAH			1	50	IRELAND	PM	IRISH		043	B	5	16
SIMPSON	THEODORE				32	ENGLAND	WM	ENGLISH	BAKER	043	D		15
SIMPSON	THOMAS		1	M	17	O	EM	IRISH	F	043	A	2	55
SIMPSON	THOMAS				35	O	CE	ENGLISH	F	043	A	6	24
SIMPSON	THOMAS				48	ENGLAND	CE	ENGLISH	INNKEEPER	044	B	6	24
SIMPSON	WILLIAM			M	40	IRELAND	PS	IRISH	F	043	A	2	20
SIMPSON	WILLIAM				64	ENGLAND	CE	SCOTCH	F	043	A	6	12
SIMPSON	WILLIAM				33	IRELAND	CE	IRISH	FARMER	043	B	3	15
SIMPSON	WILLIAM				39	ENGLAND	CE	ENGLISH	COOPER	044	C	3	71
SIMS	JOHN				45	ENG	WM	ENG	BLACKSMITH	044	B	2	22
SIMSON	GEORGE				43	ENG	CE	ENG	JACK OF ALL TRADES	044	B	1	12
SIMSON	READMAN				27	ENGLAND	CE	ENGLISH	F	043	B	4	6
SINCLAIR	CHARLES				27	O	CP	SCOTCH		043	H	1	1
SINCLAIR	DAVID				63	O	RC	IRISH	LAB	045	C	2	9
SINCLAIR	JOHN				34	SCOTLAND	BA	SCOTCH	LABORER	045	D	6	34
SINCLAIR	PETER				38	SCOTLAND	CN	SCOTCH	STONE MASON	043	E	3	42
SINCLAIR	PETER				55	SCOT	UP	SCOTS	SHOEMAKER	044	B	4	39
SINCLAIR	WILLIAM				61	ENGLAND	CE	ENGLISH	BLACKSMITH	044	A	3	51
SINCLAIR	WILLIAM		1		25	SCOTLAND	CP	SCOTCH	FARM SERVANT	045	C	3	51
SINGLETON	WILLIAM		1		23	ENGLAND	PM	ENGLISH	LAB	043	A	3	47
SINNAMON	JAMES				64	IRELAND	CE	IRISH	LAB	045	C	3	26
SINNETT	THOMAS				45	IRELAND	WM	IRISH	FARMER	043	G	2	31
SISCOE	ISACC				53	US	WM	AFRICAN	FARMER	045	D	2	36
SISILY	JOSEPH		1		15	O	CE	ENGLISH		045	C	3	37
SISLEY	BOW				45	ENG	CE	ENG	MASON	045	C	1	64
SISLEY	EDITH		2	1		O	CP			045	D	2	D
SISLEY	JENNET			1	46	O	WM	SCOTCH		045	C	2	16
SISLEY	JOSHUA				48	O	CP	SCOTCH	FARMER	045	D	2	8
SISSELY	SUSAN			1	67	O	BA	GERMAN		045	D	6	16
SIVERS	ROBERT				50	ENGLAND	CE	ENGLAND	SHOE MAKER	045	D	2	5
SIZE	ANTHONY				66	O	CE	GERMAN	TAVERNKEEPER	045	D	3	7
SIZE	DOHERETHY			1	48	O	LU	GER		044	B	3	34
SIZE	JACOB				64	US	WM	GERMAN	BLACKSMITH	045	D	3	5
SIZE	JAMES				48	O	LU	GERMAN	CARPENTER	045	D	3	8
SIZE	JOHN				69	US	CN	GERMAN	SHOE MAKER	045	D	3	6
SIZE	PETER				54	O	LU	GER	F	044	B	3	33
SIZE	WILLIAM				35	O	WM	GERMAN	FARM LABOURER	045	D	3	7
SKEELE	ANDREW	L			51	US	CX	ENG	WATCH MAKER	044	B	2	46
SKELTON	JOHN				33	ENGLAND	PM	ENGLISH	F	045	C	4	5
SKELTON	JOHN	SR			61	IRE	CP	IRE		045	C	1	8
SKELTON	RICHARD				38	ENGLAND	BA	ENGLISH	BOOT & SHOEMAKER	045	C	4	11
SKELTON	THOS				55	O	CE	ENG	YEOMAN	045	C	1	24
SKERRY	TIMOTHY				55	IRELAND	CE	IRISH	LAB	045	B	1	22
SKILLOW	EDMUND		1		30	ENGLAND	CE	IRISH	SERVANT	044	C	4	58
SKINNER	GEORGE				44	ENGLAND	NC	SCOTCH	GROCER	043	A	4	15
SKINNER	JOSEPH				70	O	WM	SCOTTISH	F	043	B	5	4
SKIRROW	JAMES				40	O	BA	ENGLISH	MERCHANT	044	C	4	89
SKULLY	ROBERT			M	60	IRELAND	RC	IRISH	LABOURER	043	A	1	24
SLACK	EDWARD				28	ENGLAND	CE	ENGLISH	LAB	045	B	1	32
SLACK	ELIZABETH			1	50	IRELAND	FW	IRISH	WASHER WOMAN	045	B	1	29
SLACK	MARY ANN			1	37	O	PS	ENG		045	C	1	71
SLADE	ANN		1	1	55	ENGLAND	CE	ENGLISH		045	D	2	25
SLANEY	WILLIAM				54	IRE	RC	IRE	F	044	B	2	68
SLATER	JONATHAN				31	O	UP	GERMAN	FARMER	045	D	1	45
SLATTERY	LAURENCE				50	IRELAND	RC	IRISH	FARMER	043	A	4	68
SLATTERY	MICHAEL				30	IRELAND	RC	IRISH	INNKEEPER	044	C	4	35
SLAVEN	MICHEL				32	IRELAND	RC	IRISH	FARMER	044	C	3	49
SLAVEN	PATRICK				38	IRELAND	RC	IRISH	FARMER	044	C	3	51
SLAVIN	JOHN		1		48	IRE	RC	IRE	LAB	044	B	2	73
SLAVIN	SARAH			1	57	IRELAND	RC	IRISH		044	C	4	29
SLEGMANN	JOHN				32	O	WM	FRENCH	LAB	044	B	5	6
SLEMEN	RICHARD		2		79	ENGLAND	BC		FARMER	045	A	1	D
SLEMIN	WM				41	IRE	CE	IRE	LAB	045	C	1	44
SLIGHT	HENRY		1		23	ENGLAND	WM	ENGLISH	DRUGGIST	043	D		72
SLINKER	MARTIN				35	GERMANY	LU	GERMAN	PAPERMAKER	045	A	2	26
SLOAN	HUGH				60	IRELAND	CP	IRISH	FARMER	043	A	4	42
SLOAN	JAMES				38	IRELAND	CE	IRISH	FARMER	043	A	4	40
SLOAN	WM				32	O	WM	IRISH	LAB	044	B	5	41
SLOANE	JANE			1	64	IRELAND	PE	IRISH		043	F		6
SLONE	DAVID								SEE DAVID	044	C	3	74
SLORREN	MATHEW				40	IRELAND	RC	IRISH	LAB	044	C	4	52
SLOSS	JAMES				28	IRELAND	CS	IRISH	F	045	A	4	6
SLY	WILLIAM	HENRY	1			O	WM	IRISH		043	E	2	82
SMAIL	THOMAS		1		24	ENGLAND	NG	ENGLISH	LABOURER	045	D	6	63
SMALL	CHARLES	C			38	O	CE	IRISH	FARMER	045	A	1	13
SMALLEY	HENRY				36	ONTARIO	PR		FARMER	043	G	2	53
SMALLEY	RUTH		1	1	20	O	CN	ENGLISH	SERVANT	043	A	6	54
SMALLEY	WILLIAM				25	ONTARIO	CE	ENGLISH	FARMER	043	G	1	17
SMALLWOOD	HENRY		1		12	ONTARIO	PR	ENGLISH		043	G	2	24
SMALLWOOD	MARGARET		1	1	43	IRELAND	XC	IRISH	SERVANT	045	B	1	39
SMALLWOOD	ROBERT		1		11	ONTARIO	PR	ENGLISH		043	G	2	24
SMALLWOOD	SUSANNAH			1	40	ENGLAND	CE	ENGLISH		043	G	2	10
SMALLY	MARY		1	1	60	ENGLAND	CE	ENGLISH		043	H	2	5
SMALLY	MARY		1	1	60	ENGLAND	CE	ENGLISH		043	H	2	5
SMALLY	SOPHIA		1	1	28	O	CE	SCOTCH		043	H	2	5
SMARDON	SOPHIA			1	40	ENGLAND	WM	ENGLISH	BOOT & SHOE BUSINESS	045	D	5	14
SMARDON	WILLIAM		2		51	ENGLAND	WM		BOOT & SHOE MAKER	045	D	5	D
SMART	ALEXANDER				66	SCOTLAND	CP	SCOTCH	F	043	A	3	58
SMART	GEORGE		1		50	O	CP	ENGLISH	SERVANT	044	B	6	56
SMART	HENRY				28	O	CN	ENGLISH	MILLER	043	E	2	19
SMART	JOHN				38	O	CP	SCOTCH	F	043	A	3	51
SMELLIE	DAVID				38	O	CP	SCOT	F	044	B	1	27
SMELSER	ISAAC			M	50	O	CS	GERMAN	F	043	A	2	2
SMELSER	LORENA		1	1	18	O	CP	GERMAN	SCHOOL TEACHER	044	C	2	17
SMELSOR	DANIEL			M	47	O	EM	GERMAN	F	043	A	2	42
SMELSOR	HENRY			M	42	O	PS	GERMAN	AUCTIONEER	043	A	2	28
SMELSOR	ISABELLA		1	1	13	O	NG	SCOTCH		043	A	2	51
SMELSOR	JOHN			M	32	O	CE	GERMAN	F	043	A	2	28
SMELSOR	JOSEPH			M	35	O	CE	GERMAN	F	043	A	2	28
SMELSOR	MARY		1	F	73	U STATES	LU	GERMAN		043	A	2	28
SMILEY	ANDREW				60	IRELAND	WM	IRISH	BRICKMAKER	045	B	2	17
SMILSER	HENRIETTA		1	1	16	O	PS	GER		044	B	3	8
SMISON	JOHN		1		20	O	CE	ENGLISH	FARM LAB	044	A	2	39
SMITH			2			O				044	A	3	D
SMITH	ABRAHAM				40	O	MN	GER	F	044	B	3	19
SMITH	ALFRED		2			SCOTCH	WM			043	D		D

SURNAME	NAME1	NAME2	STRAY	SEX	AGE	BIRTHPL	RELIGION	ORIGIN	OCCUP	DIST	SUB_DIST	DIV	PAGE
SMITH	ALFRED				45	ENGLAND	BA	ENGLISH	GROOM	044	C	4	70
SMITH	ANDREW		1		19	O	WM	ENGLISH	PRINTER	043	D		21
SMITH	ANDREW				60	O	LU	GERMAN	FARMER	045	D	4	50
SMITH	ANDREW	A			45	O	WM	SCOTCH	CLERGYMAN	043	D		63
SMITH	ANN		1	1	55	ENGLAND	PM	ENGLISH		043	B	3	55
SMITH	ANN			1	40	ENGLAND	CO	ENGLISH	SCHOOL TEACHER	045	D	5	34
SMITH	ANTHONY				54	ENGLAND	PM	ENGLISH	F	043	E	2	68
SMITH	BETSY		1	1	22	ENGLAND	CE	ENGLISH		045	B	1	7
SMITH	CHARLES				38	QUEBEC	EM	ENGLISH	CARPENTER	043	D		63
SMITH	CHARLESS		1		21	ENGLAND	PS	ENGLISH	LABORER	045	D	6	71
SMITH	CHARLOTTE		1	1	24	SCOTLAND	CE	SCOTCH		044	C	4	62
SMITH	CHARLOTTE	M	2	1	1	O	LU			045	D	1	D
SMITH	CHRISTOPHER				66	ENGLAND	WM	ENGLISH	F	043	B	1	27
SMITH	DAVID				56	IRELAND	UP	IRISH	LAB	043	C		15
SMITH	DAVID		1		17	O	EM	ENGLISH	FARM SERVANT	043	E	1	24
SMITH	DAVID				67	US	MN	GER	F	044	B	3	2
SMITH	DAVID				35	O	MN	GER	CARPENTER	044	B	3	42
SMITH	EBENEZER				49	ENGLAND	WM	ENGLISH	F	044	C	1	44
SMITH	EDWARD				52	ENGLAND	EM	ENGLISH	F	043	E	2	76
SMITH	EDWARD				43	ENGLAND	CE	ENGLISH	LABOURER	045	D	5	7
SMITH	EDWARD				36	ENGLAND	CE	ENGLISH	TAILOR	045	D	5	45
SMITH	EDWARD				55	ENGLAND	CE	ENGLISH	FARMER	045	D	2	56
SMITH	EDWARD				53	ENGLAND	CE	ENGLISH	TAILOR	044	C	3	16
SMITH	EDWARD		1		20	ENGLAND	CE	ENGLISH	CONFECTIONER	044	C	4	5
SMITH	EDWD	J			33	O	WM	ENGLISH	GRAIN DEALER	045	D	5	22
SMITH	ELIJAH		1		18	US	EM	GERMAN	SCHOOL TEACHER	045	D	2	42
SMITH	ELIZA		1	1	29	O	PM	ENGLISH		044	B	5	64
SMITH	ELIZA			1	63	ENGLAND	WM	ENGLISH	DRESS MAKER	045	D	6	40
SMITH	ELIZABETH			1	72	ENGLAND	WM	ENGLISH		043	A	4	6
SMITH	ELIZABETH		1	1	26	O	CP	SCOTCH	SERVANT	043	D		69
SMITH	ELIZABETH		1	1	7	ONTARIO	WM	ENGLISH		043	G	1	25
SMITH	ELIZABETH		1	1	31	US	CE	IRISH	SERVANT	044	C	4	9
SMITH	EMMA		1	1	47	ENGLAND	WM	ENGLISH		043	G	1	25
SMITH	EMMA		1	1	22	O	EM	SCOTCH	SERVANT	044	C	2	4
SMITH	EMMA			1	46	ENGLAND	CE	ENGLISH		045	A	4	32
SMITH	F	J DIGNAN			32	O	CE	ENGLISH	BARRISTER	045	D	5	4
SMITH	FANNY		1	1	39	IRELAND	WM	IRISH	SERVANT	045	B	1	71
SMITH	FRANCES	M	1	1	10	ONTARIO	CN	ENGLISH		043	G	1	44
SMITH	FRANCIS				48	O	WM	GERMAN	F	043	B	2	5
SMITH	FRANCIS				33	O	LU	GERMAN	FARM LABORER	045	D	1	51
SMITH	FRANK		1		13	ENGLAND	CE	ENGLISH		044	C	2	54
SMITH	FREDERICK				40	ENGLAND	CE	ENGLISH	LAB	043	B	1	36
SMITH	FREDERICK				28	ENGLAND	BA	ENGLISH	CARPENTER	045	B	2	7
SMITH	GEORGE				31	O	WM	ENGLISH	CLERK	043	D		75
SMITH	GEORGE				25	O	PM	ENGLISH	FARM LABOURER	043	E	2	60
SMITH	GEORGE				48	ENG	PS	ENG	F	044	B	2	65
SMITH	GEORGE				23	O	WM	IRISH	LAB	045	A	3	2
SMITH	GEORGE				53	ENGLAND	PM	ENGLISH	FARMER	045	D	4	51
SMITH	GEORGE		1		46	ENGLAND	CE	ENGLISH	LAB	044	C	4	32
SMITH	GEORGE	P			46	ENGLAND	WM	ENGLISH	MERCHANTTAILOR	043	E	1	44
SMITH	GODLIP		1		36	GERMANY	LU	GERMAN	FARM LABORER	045	D	1	23
SMITH	GUSTAVE		1		25	GERMANY	LU	GERMAN		044	B	6	26
SMITH	HANNAH		1	1	19	O	FW	ENGLISH		045	A	1	75
SMITH	HARRIETT		1	1	24	ENGLAND	ME	ENGLISH	SERVANT	045	A	1	7
SMITH	HARRY		1		23	ENGLAND	CE	ENGLISH	LABOURER	045	D	3	75
SMITH	HENRY				47	ENGLAND	CE	ENGLISH	BUTCHER	045	B	1	63
SMITH	HURN				39	ENGLAND	CN	ENGLISH	F	043	E	2	41
SMITH	ISABELL			1	55	O	CN	ENGLISH		043	E	2	61
SMITH	JACOB				53	US	MN	GER	GENTLEMAN	044	B	1	60
SMITH	JAMES			M	28	SCOTLAND	PS	SCOTCH	F	043	A	1	23
SMITH	JAMES				67	ENGLAND	CO	ENGLISH	FARMER	043	B	3	28
SMITH	JAMES		1		8	O	EM	ENGLISH		043	E	1	14
SMITH	JAMES				44	O	WM	GER	LAB	044	B	3	39
SMITH	JAMES				32	O	CE	ENGLISH	MERCHANT	045	A	1	11
SMITH	JAMES		1			CANADA	CE	IRISH	SERVANT	045	A	3	1
SMITH	JAMES		1		12	O	CP	SCOTCH		045	A	3	39
SMITH	JAMES				40	SCOTLAND	PS	SCOTCH	CARPENTER	045	B	1	37
SMITH	JAMES				59	IRELAND	CE	IRISH	F	045	C	3	45
SMITH	JAMES	H			35	O	BA	ENGLISH	F	044	A	3	8
SMITH	JAMES	REVD			37	ENGLAND	PM	ENGLISH	MINISTER	045	D	4	11
SMITH	JANET		1	1	14	US	WM	ENGLISH		044	A	2	48
SMITH	JOHN		2		72	ENGLAND	WM			043	A	4	D
SMITH	JOHN			M	26	O	WM	ENGLAND	WHEELWRIGHT	043	A	5	13
SMITH	JOHN				35	O	WM	ENGLISH	F	043	B	1	9
SMITH	JOHN				29	O	BA	ENGLISH	FARMER	043	B	3	29
SMITH	JOHN				58	ENGLAND	WM	ENGLISH	MUSICIAN	043	D		3
SMITH	JOHN				26	O	QU	ENGLISH	CLERK	043	D		12
SMITH	JOHN				31	O	WM	ENGLISH	F	043	E	2	30
SMITH	JOHN				42	IRELAND	EM	IRISH	F	043	E	2	76
SMITH	JOHN				28	US	XC	AFRICAN	LAB	044	A	2	48
SMITH	JOHN				32	O	WM	IRISH	COOPER	044	B	2	18
SMITH	JOHN		1		17	O	WM	GER	F	044	B	3	14
SMITH	JOHN				32	O	MN	GER	F	044	B	3	41
SMITH	JOHN		1		23	O	WM	GERMAN	LAB	044	B	5	14
SMITH	JOHN				24	O	PS	ENGLISH	F	044	B	5	67
SMITH	JOHN				50	IRELAND	RC	IRISH	GARDENER	045	A	1	94
SMITH	JOHN				68	ENGLAND	PM	ENGLISH	FARMER	045	A	2	23
SMITH	JOHN				29	ENGLAND	FW	ENGLISH	BRICK LAYER	045	B	1	16
SMITH	JOHN				42	ENG	CE	ENG	LAB	045	C	1	23
SMITH	JOHN				23	O	WM	ENGLISH	FARMER	045	D	3	26
SMITH	JOHN				50	O	WM	GERMAN	FARMER	045	D	3	29
SMITH	JOHN				50	ENGLAND	PM	ENGLISH	FARMER	045	D	3	32
SMITH	JOHN		1		22	O	PM	ENGLISH	LABOURER	045	D	4	18
SMITH	JOHN		1		26	O	WM	IRISH	PAINTER	045	D	5	10
SMITH	JOHN				60	ENGLAND	WM	ENGLISH	FARMER	045	D	6	36
SMITH	JOHN				32	IRELAND	CE	IRISH	LABORER	045	D	6	45
SMITH	JOSEPH		1	M	35	O	PR	ENGLISH	LAB	043	A	1	74
SMITH	JOSEPH				46	ENGLAND	CE	ENGLISH	F	044	A	1	17
SMITH	JOSEPH				63	O	BA	ENGLISH	F	044	A	3	8
SMITH	JOSEPH				21	O	WM	GER	F	044	B	3	21
SMITH	JOSEPH				48	O	CO	GERMAN	F	044	B	6	23
SMITH	JOSEPH				49	ENGLAND	CE	ENGLISH	STONE CUTTER	045	D	4	30
SMITH	JOSEPH				41	ENGLAND	CE	ENGLISH	F	044	C	1	8
SMITH	JOSEPH				35	O	BA	ENGLISH	DROVER	044	C	3	70
SMITH	LARRATT	WILLIAM			50	ENGLAND	CE	ENGLISH	BARRISTER AT LAW	045	A	1	1
SMITH	LAWRENCE				36	PRUSSIA	LU	PRUSSIAN	FARMER	045	D	2	35

SURNAME	NAME1	NAME2	STRAY	SEX	AGE	BIRTHPL	RELIGION	ORIGIN	OCCUP	DIST	SUB_DIST	DIV	PAGE
SMITH	LILLY		1	F	7	0	CE	IRISH		043	A	1	49
SMITH	LOUISA	R	1	1	45	0	WM	ENGLISH	HOUSEKEEPER	043	D		35
SMITH	MALCOLM		1	M	30	SCOTLAND	FK	SCOTLAND	TEACHER	043	A	5	10
SMITH	MARGARET		1	1	75	SCOT	CP	SCOT		044	B	1	18
SMITH	MARTHA		1	1	13	0	CE	IRISH		043	B	1	42
SMITH	MARTHA	E	1	1	16	ENGLAND	CP	ENGLISH	SERVANT	044	A	3	55
SMITH	MARTIN				61	US	FT	DUTCH	F	044	B	6	1
SMITH	MARY			1	62	ENGLAND	CE	ENGLISH		043	F		12
SMITH	MARY		1	1	57	SCOTLAND	CP	SCOTCH	HOUSEKEEPER	044	A	2	28
SMITH	MARY		1	1	84	NOVA SCOTIA	WM	ENGLISH		044	A	3	35
SMITH	MARY		1	1	18	0	WM	ENGLISH	SERVT	044	B	5	10
SMITH	MARY			1	59	ENGLAND	PM	ENGLISH	DRESSMAKER	045	D	3	33
SMITH	MARY		1	1	19	0	CE	IRISH		044	C	4	89
SMITH	MARY	J	1	1	28	0	CE	ENGLISH		045	A	1	106
SMITH	MATTHEW				31	0	BA	ENGLISH	F	044	A	3	9
SMITH	MATTHEW				36	NS	CE	ENGLISH	CARPENTER	045	D	5	32
SMITH	OLIVER	G			53	ENGLAND	WM	ENGLISH	F CARPENTER	043	A	6	38
SMITH	PETER		1		15	ENG	EP	ENG		044	B	3	27
SMITH	PETER				38	GERMANY	RC	GERMAN	FARMER	045	A	3	24
SMITH	REBECCA		1	1	16	0	W	GERMAN	SERVANT	044	B	6	1
SMITH	RICHARD				31	0	PM	ENGLISH	F	044	A	3	15
SMITH	RICHARD				32	0	CE	ENGLISH	HOTEL KEEPER	045	A	1	9
SMITH	RICHARD	T	1		12	0	CE	ENGLISH		044	C	4	2
SMITH	RICHD		1		35	IRELAND	CE	IRISH	LAB	043	B	2	34
SMITH	ROBERT				34	0	WM	ENGLISH	F	043	B	1	41
SMITH	ROBERT				64	0	WM	ENGLISH	F	043	E	2	62
SMITH	ROBERT				47	ENGLAND	PM	ENGLISH	F	043	E	2	66
SMITH	ROBERT		1		78	ENG	CE	ENG		044	B	1	16
SMITH	ROBERT				39	ENGLAND	CE	ENGLISH	CONDUCTOR ON STREET	045	B	1	20
SMITH	ROBERT				60	ENGLAND	RC	ENGLISH	GARDNER	044	C	4	10
SMITH	ROBERT	H			53	0	CE	ENGLISH	MERCHANT	043	D		69
SMITH	ROBERT	JAMES			63	ENGLAND	CE	ENGLISH		045	B	1	38
SMITH	SAML				70	U STATES	MN	GERMAN	F	044	B	5	14
SMITH	SAMUEL				49	ENGLAND	CE	ENGLISH	LAB	044	A	3	25
SMITH	SAMUEL				38	0	MN	GER	F	044	B	3	20
SMITH	SAMUEL				61	0	CE	SCOTCH	F	044	C	3	11
SMITH	SAMUL				28	IRELAND	RP	IRISH	SHOEMAKER	044	C	3	41
SMITH	SARAH		1	1	17	0	WM	GER		044	B	3	15
SMITH	STEVEN				38	ENGLAND	CE	ENGLISH	LAB	044	C	3	4
SMITH	THOMAS				26	0	CN	ENGLISH	F	043	E	2	61
SMITH	THOMAS				25	0	EM	ENGLISH	F	043	E	3	12
SMITH	THOMAS		1		19	0	CE	ENGLISH	FARM LAB	044	A	2	24
SMITH	THOMAS				59	ENGLAND	CE	ENGLISH	F	044	A	2	52
SMITH	THOMAS				47	IRELAND	RC	IRISH	F	044	B	6	39
SMITH	THOMAS				69	ENGLAND	CE	ENGLISH	FARMER	045	A	1	13
SMITH	THOMAS				49	ENGLAND	FW	ENGLISH	SHOEMAKER	045	A	1	88
SMITH	THOMAS				25	0	PM	ENGLISH	SHOEMAKER	045	A	1	88
SMITH	THOMAS				56	ENGLAND	CO	ENGLISH	POST MASTER	045	D	2	25
SMITH	THOMAS				47	0	CE	SCOTTISH	LAB	044	C	1	47
SMITH	THOMAS				58	ENGLAND	CE	ENGLISH	LABOURER	044	C	3	47
SMITH	THOS	C	1		6	0	EM	ENGLISH		043	E	2	33
SMITH	VINCENT				37	UNITED STATES	WM	AFRICAN	LAB	044	C	2	46
SMITH	W	G			48	IRELAND	WM	IRISH	HOUSE PAINTER	043	B	3	6
SMITH	WALTER		1		15	ENGLAND	WM	ENGLISH	FARMER	043	G	1	35
SMITH	WILKINSON		1		29	ENGLAND	EM	ENGLISH	WOOLCARDER	044	C	1	8
SMITH	WILLIAM				48	ENGLAND	CE	ENGLISH	LABOURER	043	A	4	10
SMITH	WILLIAM				37	0	WM	ENGLISH	F	043	B	1	24
SMITH	WILLIAM				60	ENGLAND	CE	ENGLISH	F	043	B	2	28
SMITH	WILLIAM				35	SCOTLAND	CP	SCOTCH	MACHINIST	043	C		7
SMITH	WILLIAM				33	0	CS	ENGLISH	F	043	E	2	17
SMITH	WILLIAM				54	IRELAND	CE	IRISH	FARMER	043	G	1	45
SMITH	WILLIAM				68	ENGLAND	PM	ENGLISH	F	044	A	3	15
SMITH	WILLIAM				29	ENGLAND	PM	ENGLISH	BLACKSMITH	044	A	3	39
SMITH	WILLIAM				28	ENG	PS	ENG	SAWYER	044	B	3	28
SMITH	WILLIAM				45	ENG	NG	ENG	LAB	044	B	4	3
SMITH	WILLIAM				37	0	CE	ENGLISH	FARMER	045	A	1	55
SMITH	WILLIAM				62	ENGLAND	WM	ENGLISH	LAB	045	A	2	20
SMITH	WILLIAM				44	0	WM	ENGLISH	FARMER	045	A	3	18
SMITH	WILLIAM		1		30	ENGLAND	WM	ENGLISH	LAB	045	B	2	5
SMITH	WILLIAM				51	SCOTLAND	CS	SCOTCH	FARMER	045	D	1	31
SMITH	WILLIAM				51	ENGLAND	CE	ENGLISH	FARMER	045	D	1	48
SMITH	WILLIAM				38	0	CE	ENGLISH	BUTCHER	044	C	4	44
SMITH	WILLIAM	A			26	ENGLAND	WM	ENGLISH	GARDENER	044	A	1	18
SMITH	WILLIAM	H			53	ENGLAND	CE	ENGLISH	MERCHANT	044	C	3	14
SMITH	WILLIAM	JOHN			18	0	WM	IRISH	TIN SMITH	043	B	3	6
SMITH	WILLIAM	M			33	0	BA	ENGLISH	F	044	A	3	11
SMITH	WM				44	SCOTLAND	CO	IRISH	MINISTER	044	B	5	41
SMITH	WM				25	0	CP	IRE	F	045	C	1	37
SMITH	WM	JOHN			26	0	CP	SCOTCH	MARBLE CUTTER	045	D	6	10
SMITHERS	CHARLES				65	ENGLAND	WM	ENGLISH	LAB	044	B	6	29
SMITHERS	ELIZABETH		1	1	10	US	CE	ENGLISH		045	A	3	4
SMITHERS	WILLIAM		1		14	0	BA	IRISH		044	C	2	33
SMITHSON	WILLIAM				39	ENGLAND	CE	ENGLISH	FARMER	044	C	3	72
SMOKIN	GEORGE				32	ENGLAND	PM	ENGLISH	F	043	B	5	9
SMYTH	HENRY				44	IRELAND	CE	IRISH	PORTER	043	D		27
SMYTH	WILLIAM				43	IRELAND	RC	IRISH	F	044	B	6	39
SNAKE	JAMES				59	ONTARIO	WM	OJIBWAY INDIAN	HUNTER AND FISHER	043	G	1	59
SNAKE	JOSEPH				83	ONTARIO	WM	OJIBWAY INDIAN	HUNTER AND FISHER	043	G	1	59
SNAKE	NOAH				40	0	WM	CHIPPAWA	F	043	H	2	56
SNAKE	NOAH				40	ONTARIO	WM	CHIPPAWA	FARMER	043	H	2	56
SNAKE	WILLIAM				25	ONTARIO	WM	OJIBWAY INDIAN	HUNTER AND FISHER	043	G	1	60
SNEAD	ROBERT				46	ENGLAND	PM	ENGLISH	F	044	A	3	5
SNELL	BENJAMIN				38	ENGLAND	PM	ENGLISH	F	044	B	6	39
SNELL	JOHN				62	GERMANY	RC	GERMAN	FARMER	045	D	5	53
SNELL	PETER		1		15	0	RC	GERMAN		045	C	2	47
SNELL	ROBERT		1		30	ENGLAND	CE	ENGLISH	SERVANT	045	D	5	64
SNIDER	ABRAHAM		1		61	0	MN	GERMAN	GENTLEMAN	045	D	4	20
SNIDER	ABRAM				25	0	WM	GERMAN	F	044	C	1	36
SNIDER	CHARLES				48	0	WM	GERMAN	FARMER	043	A	3	5
SNIDER	DANIEL				29	0	LU	GER	F	044	B	3	2
SNIDER	EDWIN				48	0	CE	GERMAN	FARMER	045	A	2	5
SNIDER	EDWY	W			37	0	WM	GERMAN	F	044	C	2	4
SNIDER	ELIAS				56	0	WM	GERMAN	F	044	C	2	5
SNIDER	ELIZABETH		1	1	20	0	WM	SCOTCH		044	C	2	44
SNIDER	ELIZABETH	MINA		1	6	0	LU	GER		044	B	3	6
SNIDER	ELLEN		1	1	27	IRE	EM	IRISH	HOUSEKEEPER	044	B	1	26

SURNAME	NAME1	NAME2	STRAY	SEX	AGE	BIRTHPL	RELIGION	ORIGIN	OCCUP	DIST	SUB_DIST	DIV	PAGE
SNIDER	FANNY			1	50	ENGLAND	WM	ENGLISH	F	045	A	2	5
SNIDER	FRANCIS				69	US	LU	GER		044	B	3	1
SNIDER	GEORGE				48	O	WM	ENGLISH	CARPENTER	043	B	2	34
SNIDER	HARRY				63	O	MN	GERMAN	F	044	C	1	35
SNIDER	HENRY				29	O	EM	GER	F	044	B	3	1
SNIDER	ISAAC				46	O	WM	GERMAN	FARMER	043	A	3	4
SNIDER	ISAAC		1		20	O	LU	GER	F	044	B	3	18
SNIDER	JACOB		1		16	O	LU	GER	F	044	B	3	18
SNIDER	JACOB				41	O	MN	GER	F	044	B	3	51
SNIDER	JACOB				81	NEW BRUNSWICK	WM	GERMAN		045	A	2	5
SNIDER	JACOB				33	ONT	EM	GERMAN	F	044	C	1	1
SNIDER	JOHN				39	O	LU	GER	F	044	B	1	43
SNIDER	JOHN				49	O	LU	GER	F	044	B	3	11
SNIDER	JOHN		1		24	O	LU	GER	F	044	B	3	18
SNIDER	JOHN				31	O	TU	GER	F	044	B	3	22
SNIDER	JOSEPH				37	O	WM	GERMAN	F	043	B	1	10
SNIDER	JOSEPH				35	O	TU	GER	F	044	B	3	22
SNIDER	MARTIN				50	O	WM	GERMAN	FARMER	043	A	3	5
SNIDER	MARY		1	1	8	O	PM	GER	F	044	B	3	33
SNIDER	MATILDA		1	1	3	O	EM	IRISH		044	B		
SNIDER	NICHOLAS				37	O	LU	GER	F	044	B	3	28
SNIDER	NICHOLAS		2		32	O	LU		F	044	B	3	D
SNIDER	SAMUEL				55	O	MN	GERMAN	F	043	B	2	27
SNIDER	SAMUEL				26	O	LU	GER	F	044	B	3	2
SNIDER	SAMUEL				60	O	TU	GER	F	044	B	3	22
SNIDER	SUSAN		2	1	4	O	LU			044	B	3	D
SNIDER	WALTER			M	25	O	WM	GERMAN	F	043	A	2	2
SNIDER	WILLIAM		1		23	O	W	GERMAN	ASSESSOR	044	B	6	1
SNODDEN	JOHN				35	O	WM	ENGLISH	F	043	H	1	33
SNODDEN	JOSEPH				39	O	WM	ENGLISH	F	043	H	1	24
SNOWBALL	JOHN				50	ENGLAND	WM	ENGLISH	BRICK MAKER	045	D	3	44
SNOWDON	ROBT				41	ENGLAND	PM	ENGLISH	TAILOR	043	C		4
SNOWDON	WILLIAM				54	ENG	CE	ENG	BOARDING HOUSE KEEPE	044	B	2	34
SNOWTON	MARY		1	1	15	CANADA	FW	ENGLISH		045	D	6	30
SNUDDON	WALTER		1		15	CANADA	WM	IRISH		045	D	6	59
SODDEN	THOMAS		1		18	O	CE	ENGLISH	F LAB	043	A	6	26
SOMERS	BERNARD				58	IRELAND	CE	IRISH	GARDENER	045	A	1	85
SOMERS	FRANCIS				40	IRE	CP	IRE	LAB	045	C	1	70
SOMERS	JOHN				31	IRELAND	PR	IRISH	FARMER	045	A	1	86
SOMERSET	ELLENOR			1	60	IRELAND	CE	IRISH		043	A	4	26
SOMERSETT	CHARLOTTE		1	1	25	O	WM	WELSH		043	A	4	36
SOMERSETT	LENA	A	1	1	2	O	WM	WELSH		043	A	4	36
SOMERVILLE	COLIN	C			42	SCOTLAND	FK	SCOTCH	MERCHANT	043	F		15
SOMERVILLE	JAMES				42	SCOTLAND	CS	SCOTCH	F	043	A	3	26
SOMERVILLE	JAS				60	SCOTLAND	CP	SCOTCH	F	044	B	5	61
SOMERVILLE	ROBT				29	O	UP	SCOTCH	F	044	B	5	68
SORLEY	JAMES	B			44	SCOTLAND	CE	SCOTCH	MERCHANT	045	B	1	17
SORREL	THOMAS				65	ENGLAND	RC	ENGLISH	LAB	043	D		44
SORREL	THOMAS				31	ENGLAND	PM	ENGLISH	LABOURER	045	D	3	65
SOTHERGILL	THOMAS				57	IRELAND	CE	IRISH	PHYSICIAN	045	A	1	91
SOULES	DANIEL				53	O	CE	IRISH	F	043	E	2	60
SOULES	GEORGE				30	O	WM	GER	BAKER	044	B	2	27
SOULES	HANNAH		1		70	IRELAND	CN	IRISH		043	E	2	13
SOULES	HARRIET		1	1	40	O	WM	ENGLISH		043	E	2	19
SOULES	JOHN				52	O	CN	ENGLISH	LUMBER DEALER	043	E	2	21
SOULES	JOHN	W			41	O	CN	ENGLISH	F	043	E	2	16
SOULES	LYDIA		1	1	45	O	EM	ENGLISH	MILLENER	043	E	1	23
SOULES	MATILDA		1	1	8	O	WM	ENGLISH		043	E	2	19
SOULES	PETER				44	O	WM	ENGLISH	F	043	E	2	62
SOUTER	JAMES				52	SCOTLAND	CS	SCOTCH	WATCHMAN G W R	044	A	1	11
SOUTH	GEORGE				57	ENG	CE	ENG	F	045	C	1	55
SOUTHARD	JOHN	S	1		16	O	CN	SCOTCH		043	D		24
SOUTHARD	MARY	E	1	1	26	O	CN	SCOTCH	SEAMSTRESS	043	D		24
SOUTHARD	RACHAEL	E	1	1	29	O	CN	SCOTCH	SEAMSTRESS	043	D		24
SOUTHERN	THOMAS		1		21	ENGLAND	CE	ENGLISH	SERVANT	044	B	1	2
SOUTHWELL	JAMES				39	ENGLISH	CE	ENGLISH	F LAB	044	A	2	3
SPADONE	ANTONIO				64?	ITALY	RC	ITALIAN	GARDENER	045	A	1	94
SPALDING	ALEXANDER				50	SCOT	PS	SCOT	CARPENTER	044	B	2	40
SPANG	ANTHONY				30	GERMANY	PM	GERMAN	FARMER	045	D	4	44
SPARKHALL	CUBITT				50	ENGLAND	CE	ENGLISH	FARMER	045	A	1	71
SPARKHALL	WILLIAM				28	O	DI	ENGLISH	GARDENER	045	A	1	77
SPARKS	ELIZABETH			1	77	IRELAND		IRISH		044	C	3	21
SPARKS	JAMES				65	SCOTLAND	CE	ENGLISH	MARINER	045	A	1	35
SPARLING	JOHN				60	ENG	EP	ENG	F	044	B	3	45
SPARROW	THOMAS		1		74	ENGLAND	WM	ENGLISH	WEAVER	043	D		24
SPAULDING	WILLIAM				40	ENGLAND	CE	ENGLISH	F	045	C	4	42
SPEAD	HENRY				50	SCOTLAND	CE	SCOTCH	GENTLEMAN	044	C		62
SPEARS	ADAM				57	SCOTLAND	CP	SCOTCH	FARMER	045	A	2	10
SPECK	CHARLES				40	O	CN	ENGLISH	F	043	E	2	71
SPEIGHT	HENRY				31	O	CE	ENGLISH	CARRIAGE PAINTER	045	D	5	14
SPEIGHT	JAMES				40	O	WM	ENGLISH	WAGGON MAKER	045	D	3	74
SPEIGHT	THOMAS				69	ENGLAND	WM	ENGLISH	WAGGON MAKER	045	D	3	74
SPEIGHT	THOMAS				37	O	WM	ENGLISH	BLACKSMITH	045	D	5	13
SPEIGHT	WILLIAM				29	O	WM	ENGLISH	MACHINIST	045	D	3	68
SPEIGHT	WM				37	ENGLAND	EM	ENGLISH	BOOTMAKER	044	C	1	8
SPENCE	JAMES		1		30	IRELAND	WM	IRISH	LABORER	045	D	6	48
SPENCE	JOHN		1		71	ENGLAND	WM	ENGLISH	STONE MASON	044	C	1	32
SPENCE	JONATHON				40	O	WM	ENGLISH	F	043	B	4	1
SPENCE	SAMUEL				36	US	CP	ENGLISH	LAB	045	C	2	43
SPENCE	WILLIAM				25	O	CE	ENGLISH	MERCHANT	043	D		68
SPENCER	ANNIE	M	1	1	28	O	CS	ENGLISH		043	D		27
SPENCER	ELI				42	ENGLAND	RC	ENGLISH	TAILOR	043	D		31
SPENCER	GEORGE		1		40	ENGLAND	CE	ENGLISH	SERVANT	045	D	2	57
SPENCER	JOHN				44	ENGLAND	CE	ENGLISH	TIN SMITH	044	C	4	93
SPENCER	JOSEPH				40	ENGLAND	WM	ENGLISH	BLACKSMITH	043	B	5	35
SPENSLEY	JOHN		2	M		O	CE	ENGLISH		043	A	1	D
SPENSLEY	SIMON			M	46	ENGLAND	CE	ENGLISH	FARMER	043	A	1	5
SPICER	HENRY				40	ENGLAND	CE	ENGLISH	F	044	A	2	9
SPIKER	JACOB		2		79	U STATES	LU		CARPENTER	043	A	4	D
SPIKER	JACOB		2		76	O	LU		CARPENTER	044	B	5	D
SPIKER	LUCINDA		1		50	O	LU	GERMAN		044	B	5	28
SPIKER	MARY		1	1	64	O	BA	ENGLISH		043	A	3	22
SPINDLOE	JAMES				31	ENGLAND	CE	ENGLISH	MILLER	044	A	2	45
SPINK	JAMES	J		M	35	O	WM	ENGLISH	FARMER	043	A	5	1
SPINK	JOHN			M	65	ENGLAND	CN	ENGLISH	F	043	A	5	2
SPOFFARD	ALFRED				27	O	PM	ENGLISH	FARMER	045	D	4	40

SURNAME	NAME1	NAME2	STRAY	SEX	AGE	BIRTHPL	RELIGION	ORIGIN	OCCUP	DIST	SUB_DIST	DIV	PAGE
SPOFFARD	ARTHUR				23	0	CP	ENGLISH	FARMER	045	D	4	43
SPOFFARD	CHARLES				39	ENGLAND	PM	ENGLISH	FARMER	045	D	4	26
SPOFFARD	WILLIAM				38	ENGLAND	PM	ENGLISH	MILLER	045	D	4	41
SPOFFARD	WILLIAM				62	ENGLAND	CP	ENGLISH	FARMER	045	D	4	43
SPOONER	ASA		1		20	ONTARIO	CN	ENGLISH	FARMER	043	G	1	43
SPOONER	JAMES				27	0	CN	ENGLISH	F	043	A	6	54
SPOONER	MARGARET		1	1	55	UNITED STATES	CN	ENGLISH		043	E	2	56
SPOONER	MARGARET		1	1	16	ONTARIO	CN	GERMAN	SERVANT	043	G	2	29
SPOONER	SYBILL			1	33	ONTARIO	CN	GERMAN		043	G	2	34
SPRAGGE	MINNIE	M	1	1	11	0	CP	ENGLAND		045	D	2	2
SPRAGUE	DAVID				59	ONTARIO	CE	ENGLISH	GENTLEMAN	043	G	1	21
SPRAGUE	DAVID				27	ONTARIO	CN	ENGLISH	FARMER	043	G	1	28
SPRATT	CHARLES				60	ENGLAND	CE	ENGLISH	F	043	B	4	13
SPRAY	GEORGE		1		30	ENGLAND	CP	ENGLISH	BLACKSMITH	045	C	4	25
SPRIGGS	ALEXANDER				47	USA	CE	AFRICAN	LAB	045	A	1	89
SPRING	ALBERT				55	0	CN	GERMAN	FARMER	043	B	3	26
SPRING	ELIZABETH		2	1	2	0	CN			043	B	3	D
SPRING	IDA		2	1	0	0	WM			045	D	3	D
SPRING	JACOB				42	0	CN	GERMANY	LABOURER	043	B	3	29
SPRING	JOSEPH				47	0	BC	DUTCH	LAB	045	C	3	17
SPRING	KINEIN				30	0	ME	GERMAN	HOTEL KEEPER	044	B	1	13
SPRING	PETER				50	0	CN	GERMAN	LABOURER	043	B	3	45
SPRING	PETER				58	0	PM	ENGLISH	F	045	C	3	17
SPRING	WILLIAM				33	0	WM	GERMAN	HOTEL KEEPER	045	D	3	20
SPRING RICE	EDWARD				42	IRELAND	CE	IRISH	PROFESSOR OF LANGUAG	044	C	3	30
SPRINGLE	JOSEPH				50	ENGLAND	CE	ENGLISH	LABOURER	045	D	3	69
SPROULE	JANE		1	1	26	0	CE	IRISH		043	A	4	34
SPROULE	MATILDA		1	1	28	0	CE	IRISH		043	A	4	34
SPROULE	PRUDENCE		1	1	40	IRELAND	WM	IRISH		043	A	3	10
SPROULE	WILLIAM	I			58	IRELAND	WM	IRISH	FARMER	043	A	4	27
SPROXON	GEORGE				67	ENGLAND	CE	ENGLISH	F	043	B	1	26
SPROXON	JOSEPH				29	0	CE	ENGLISH	F	043	B	1	27
SPRY	FRANCIS	P			45	UNITED STATES	CE	ENGLISH	LAB	043	D		7
SQUAIR	ALEXR				29	0	CS	SCOTCH	MILLER	045	D	5	52
SQUIRE	JOHN				27	ENGLAND	CE	ENGLISH	LAB	045	A	3	10
SQUIRE	JOHN		2		75	ENGLAND	CE		LAB	045	A	3	D
SQUIRE	WILLIAM		1		24	ENGLAND	CE	ENGLISH	CARPENTER	043	A	4	39
SQUIRES	AARON				36	0	PM	ENGLISH	LAND AGENT	043	D		31
SQUIRES	GEORGE		1		20	ENG	CE	ENG	LAB	045	C	1	12
SQUIRES	JAMES				50	ENGLAND	CE	ENGLISH	GARDENER	045	A	1	41
SRIGLEY	ELIZA	FRANCES	2	1	1	0	EM			043	D		D
SRIGLEY	ENOCH				58	0	CN	WELSH	CARPENTER	043	E	1	4
SRIGLEY	GEORGE	J			27	0	EM	GERMAN	CARPENTER	043	D		9
SRIGLEY	JESSE			M	63	0	CE	ENGLAND	F	043	A	5	26
SRIGLEY	JOEL			M	33	0	CE	WELSH	F	043	A	5	24
SRIGLEY	MARY		1	1	26	0	CP	ENGLISH	SEAMSTRESS	043	D		34
SRIGLEY	NELSON				35	0	CE	WELSH	PHYSICIAN	043	A	4	15
SRIGLEY	RICHARD				52	0	CO	ENGLISH	PUMP MAKER	043	D		31
SRUSS	THOMAS				29	ENGLAND	BA	ENGLISH	BASKET MAKER	044	C	4	85
ST GEORGE	HENRY	Q			50	ENGLAND	RC	FRENCH	F & WINE MERCHANT	043	B	1	42
ST GERMAIN	A	H			44	0	CE	ENGLISH	PUBLISHING BUS	044	C	1	23
ST JOHN	PHILLIP				38	0	CP	IRISH	F	043	H	1	3
STAFFORD	CHARLES	E			29	ENGLAND	PM	ENGLISH	PM MINISTER	045	B	1	45
STAFFORD	JAMES				58	ENGLAND	CE	ENGLISH	BRICKLAYER	045	A	2	22
STAINTON	RICHARD				52	ENGLAND	WM	ENGLISH	F	045	C	2	25
STAKELY	JACOB				39	0	MN	GERMAN	F	043	B	2	18
STAKLEY	CHRISTIAN				42	0	MN	GERMAN	F	043	B	2	4
STAKLEY	DANIEL				50	0	TU	GERMAN	F	043	B	2	4
STAKLEY	JOHN				45	0	MN	GERMAN	F	043	B	2	5
STAKLEY	JOHN		2		19	0	TU		CLERK	043	B	2	D
STAKLEY	SAML				47	0	TU	GERMAN	F	043	B	2	20
STALEY			2			0	CN			043	B	3	D
STALEY	BALTUS				80	UNITED STATES	BA	GERMAN	LABOURER	043	B	3	41
STALEY	HYRAM				34	0	PS	GERMAN	SHINGLE MAKER	043	B	3	40
STALEY	JACOB				23	0	CN	GERMAN	LABOURER	043	B	3	44
STALEY	JACOB				21	0	WM	GERMAN	LAB	043	B	5	10
STALEY	JOHN				35	0	CN	GERMAN	LABOURER	043	B	3	46
STALEY	PHILIP				69	UNITED STATES	WM	GERMAN		043	E	3	9
STAMM	LOUISA		1	1	16	0	LU	IRISH		045	D	3	61
STAMP	AAMOS				42	ENGLISH	CE	ENGLISH	BOARDING HOUSEKEEPER	043	A	6	61
STAMP	JOSEPH				23	0	WM	GERMAN	FINISHER	044	B	5	12
STANBROUGH	GEORGE				29	UNITED STATES	CN	GERMAN	GENERAL MANAGER	043	E	3	10
STANDERS	ELIZABETH		1	1	55	IRELAND	CE	SCOTCH		045	A	1	104
STANDRING	JOHN				43	ENGLAND	CE	ENGLISH	WEAVER	043	B	4	39
STANION	WILLIAM		1		35	ENGLAND	CP	ENGLISH	F	045	C	2	18
STANLEY	ELIZA		1	1	19	0	CS	ENGLISH	SERVANT	043	D		11
STANTON	ROBT	J			25	ENGLAND	CE	ENGLISH	FARMER	045	D	1	7
STAPLE	MARY		1	1	9	0	CO	ENGLISH		044	C	1	50
STAPLETON	JOSEPH		1		16	0	EM	GERMAN		044	C	1	5
STAPLETON	ROBERT				50	ENGLAND	CN	ENGLISH	FARMER	043	B	3	74
STARK	ALEXANDER		1		22	0	CP	SCOTCH	FARM LAB	044	C	2	39
STARK	CHARLES				37	SCOTLAND	PS	SCOTCH	FARMER	045	D	6	34
STARK	JOHN				63	IRELAND	WM	IRISH	F	043	H	1	30
STARK	JOHN		1		21	0	CP	SCOTCH		045	C	2	30
STARK	JOHN				45	SCOTLAND	CP	SCOTCH	F	045	C	2	48
STARK	RENEL				63	US	WM	SCOTCH	LABOURER	045	D	3	35
STARR	CHARLES				35	0	QU	ENGLISH	F	043	B	4	44
STARR	CHARLES				39	ENGLAND	WM	ENGLISH	TOLLKEEPER	044	C	3	64
STARR	FRANCIS				48	0	QU	ENGLISH	F	043	B	4	33
STARR	JAMES				46	0	QU	ENGLISH	F	043	B	4	44
STARR	MORDICA				74	US	QU	ENGLISH	F	043	B	4	44
STARR	PIERSON				50	0	WM	GERMAN	F	043	B	1	35
STARR	SARAH		2	1	70	0	QU			043	B	4	D
STARRAT	C	THOMAS			54	IRELAND	OP	IRISH	HOTEL KEEPER	043	A	3	10
STARTUP	JOHN		1		25	ENGLAND	CE	ENGLISH	SERVANT	043	A	4	33
STATTON	ROBERT				52	ENGLAND	CE	ENGLISH	F	043	H	2	37
STATTON	ROBERT				52	ENGLAND	CE	ENGLISH	FARMER	043	H	2	37
STATTON	WILLIAM				24	ENGLAND	CE	ENGLISH	BLACKSMITH	043	H	2	37
STATTON	WILLIAM				24	ENGLAND	CE	ENGLISH	BLACKSMITH	043	H	2	37
STATTS	WM	HENRY			30	0	WM	GERMAN	LAB	043	E	3	43
STAYLE	ALBERT				27	US	FW	GERMAN		045	C	2	44
STEAD	JOHN				45	IRELAND	WM	IRISH	LAB	044	C	4	29
STEAD	WILLIAM		1		16	0	CE	IRISH	LAB	044	C	2	51
STEADMAN	MICHAEL				47	IRELAND	CE	IRISH	LAB	045	A	1	11
STECKLEY	FANNY		1	1	21	0	PM	GERMAN		045	D	4	12
STECKLEY	NANCY			1	61	0	TU	GERMAN		045	D	4	16

SURNAME	NAME1	NAME2	STRAY	SEX	AGE	BIRTHPL	RELIGION	ORIGIN	OCCUP	DIST	SUB_DIST	DIV	PAGE
STECKLEY	RUBEN				24	O	PM	GERMAN	FARMER	045	D	4	21
STECKLY	DAVID		1		25	O	PM	ENGLISH	LABORER	045	D	2	65
STECKLY	ELIZABETH		1	1	18	O	PM	ENGLISH	SERVANT	045	D	2	65
STECKLY	FANNY		1	1	21	O	PM	ENGLISH	SERVANT	045	D	2	65
STECKLY	LYDIA		1	1	22	O	PM	ENGLISH	SERVANT	045	D	2	65
STECKLY	SARAH		1	1	19	O	PM	ENGLISH	SERVANT	045	D	2	65
STEEL	DANIEL				67	ENGLAND	CE	ENGLISH	F	043	B	1	28
STEEL	JOHN				59	ENGLAND	PM	ENGLISH	LAB	043	B	1	42
STEEL	JOHN				24	O	WM	ENGLISH	WOOD WORKER	045	D	5	14
STEEL	MARK				50	ENGLAND	WM	ENGLISH	F	043	B	1	41
STEEL	MARY		1	1	22	SCOTLAND	CP	SCOTCH		044	B	6	51
STEEL	PETER				40	ENGLAND	WM	ENGLISH	CARPENTER	043	B	1	27
STEEL	WILLIAM		1		15	O	CS	IRISH		043	A	4	49
STEELE	DANIEL				61	ENGLAND	PM	ENGLISH	F	044	B	5	69
STEELE	JOHN				61	IRELAND	RC	IRISH	LAB	045	C	2	39
STEELES	JAMES				30	O	PM	ENGLISH	F	044	B	6	47
STEELES	THOMAS				65	ENGLAND	CE	ENGLISH	HOTEL KEEPER	044	B	1	1
STEEPER	DAVID				51	ENGLAND	WM	ENGLISH	FARMER	045	D	5	66
STEERS	RICHARD				48	ENGLAND	CE	ENGLISH	F	045	C	4	15
STEGMAN	MARY		1	1	55	O	CE	ENGLISH		044	B	5	10
STEM	JOHN		2		77	U S	LU			045	D	3	D
STEMUTT	THOMAS				41	ENGLAND	PM	ENGLISH	MERCHANT	045	B	2	15
STENAFE	HOMER		1		22	O	CE	SCOTTISH	LAB	044	C	1	44
STENAK	JACOB		1		19	O	WM	GERMAN	CARPENTER	044	B	5	37
STENNET	JOHN		1		20	CANADA	PS	ENGLISH	LABORER	045	D	6	70
STENNETT	ELIZABETH			1	76	ENGLAND	CE	ENGLISH		043	G	1	54
STENNETT	HENRY				70	ENGLAND	CE	ENGLISH	POSTMASTER	043	G	1	2
STENNETT	MARTHA		2	1	69	ENGLAND	CE			043	G	1	D
STENNETT	RALPH	M			32	ONTARIO	CE	ENGLISH	FARMER	043	G	1	18
STENNETT	WILLIAM				65	ENGLAND	CO	ENGLISH	LABORER	045	D	6	45
STENNITT	MARY		2	1	38	ENGLAND	CE			045	B	2	D
STENSON	WILLIAM				80	IRELAND	CE	IRISH	FARMER	043	A	4	29
STEPHENOFF	WILLIAM		1		30	ENGLAND	CE	GERMAN	LABOURER	045	D	5	73
STEPHENS	ALBERT				33	O	CE	WELSH	F	043	B	4	18
STEPHENS	ALFRED				55	U STATES	QU	ENGLISH	F	043	A	6	4
STEPHENS	DANIEL				61	IRELAND	WM	IRISH	FARMER	043	G	2	48
STEPHENS	EBENEZER				33	O	WM	FRENCH	CARPENTER	045	C	2	19
STEPHENS	FRANCIS				45	ENGLAND	CE	ENGLISH	F	043	E	2	78
STEPHENS	HENRY				72	ENGLAND	WM	ENGLISH	F	044	A	2	42
STEPHENS	JAMES				34	ENGLAND	WM	ENGLISH	F	044	A	1	16
STEPHENS	JOHN				35	ONTARIO	EM	IRISH	FARMER	043	G	2	34
STEPHENS	MELVILLE				20	O	WM	ENGLISH	CARPENTER	043	A	6	36
STEPHENS	NELSON				47	O	CE	ENGLISH	F	043	B	4	29
STEPHENS	RACHEL		1	1	21	O	QU	ENGLISH		043	A	4	24
STEPHENS	SHADRACK				72	NB	CE	WELSH	F	043	B	4	18
STEPHENS	WILLIAM				30	ONTARIO	WM	IRISH	FARMER	043	G	2	48
STEPHENS	WILLSON			M	50	O	CE	WELSH	FARMER	043	A	1	7
STEPHENSON	ARCHIBALD				49	ENGLAND	PM	SCOTCH	GARDNER	044	C	4	61
STEPHENSON	ARMSTRONG				52	IRELAND	EM	IRISH	FARMER	043	G	2	23
STEPHENSON	ATKINSON				46	ENGLAND	WM	ENGLISH	FARMER	045	D	1	24
STEPHENSON	DONALD				36	O	CP	ENGLISH	F	045	C	2	6
STEPHENSON	ELIJAH	F			25	O	NC	ENGLISH	PRINTER	043	C		27
STEPHENSON	ELIZA		1	1	21	ENGLAND	WM	ENGLISH	SERVANT	045	B	1	1
STEPHENSON	GEORGE			M	27	O	WM	ENGLAND	F	043	A	5	9
STEPHENSON	HENRY				28	O	CE	ENGLISH	BLACKSMITH	045	D	5	5
STEPHENSON	JOHN				71	ENG	CE	ENG	F	044	B	4	21
STEPHENSON	JOHN				37	O	CE	ENGLISH	BLACKSMITH	045	D	3	2
STEPHENSON	JOSEPH				33	O	WM	ENGLISH	FARMER	043	A	4	64
STEPHENSON	JOSEPH				32	ENGLAND	CE	ENGLISH	FARMER	045	D	2	33
STEPHENSON	MAJOR			M	59	ENGLAND	PM	ENGLAND	F	043	A	5	11
STEPHENSON	MARY		1	1	60	SCOTLAND	CP	SCOTCH		045	C	2	3
STEPHENSON	REBECCA		1	1	55	O	CO	GER		044	B	3	27
STEPHENSON	RUTH		1	1	26	O	WM	ENGLISH	DRESS MAKER	043	C		25
STEPHENSON	THOMAS				29	O	CP	ENGLISH	F	045	C	2	27
STEPHENSON	WILLIAM				33	O	CP	ENGLISH	F	045	C	2	34
STERENSARA	TERESA			1	74	GERMANY	RC	GERMAN		045	A	1	78
STERLAND	MARIA			1	36	O	CN	ENGLISH	F	043	E	1	46
STERLING	WM				38	ENGLAND	CE	ENGLISH	INN KEEPER	044	B	5	2
STERNE	ELISABETH		1	1	32	O	OP	IRISH		043	A	3	10
STEVENS	CHANCEY	F			54	U STATES	DI	SCOTCH	TAILOR	045	D	6	50
STEVENS	JOHN				30	ENGLAND	CE	ENGLAND	LABORER	045	D	2	28
STEVENS	JOSEPH				31	ENGLAND	CE	ENGLISH	GARDENER	045	A	1	106
STEVENS	THOMAS				48	ENGLAND	CE	ENGLISH	BLACKSMITH	045	A	1	10
STEVENSON	ANDREW				52	IRELAND	CS	IRISH	SHOEMAKER	045	D	5	23
STEVENSON	EDWARD				54	IRELAND	WM	IRISH	MERCHANT	043	C		12
STEVENSON	FRANCIS				45	IRELAND	CE	IRISH	BLACKSMITH	045	A	1	69
STEVENSON	FRANK		2		4	O				043	F		D
STEVENSON	GEO	L			50	O	WM	IRISH	SADDLER	043	C		33
STEVENSON	GEORGE				44	ENG	CE	ENG	TEAMSTER	044	B	1	14
STEVENSON	I	R	1		35	ONTARIO	CE	IRISH	MERCHANT	043	H	2	15
STEVENSON	J	R			35	O	CE	IRISH	MERCHANT	043	H	2	15
STEVENSON	JAMES		1		30	IRELAND	CP	IRISH	FARM LAB	044	C	2	37
STEVENSON	JAMES	D			40	SCOTLAND	CP	SCOTCH	PHYSICIAN	044	B	6	26
STEVENSON	JOHN				57	SCOTLAND	CP	SCOTCH	F	044	B	6	3
STEVENSON	JOHN		1		23	IRELAND	WM	IRISH	MAN	044	B	6	18
STEVENSON	JOHN				34	O	CP	ENGLISH	F	045	C	2	27
STEVENSON	MARGARET		1	1	22	O	WM	SCOTCH	SERVANT	045	B	2	2
STEVENSON	MARGARET			1	57	SCOTLAND	CP	SCOTCH		045	A	4	4
STEVENSON	NATHANIEL				22	O	CE	ENG	F	044	B	2	56
STEVENSON	RICHARD		2		52	ENGLAND	WM		LAB	043	C		D
STEVENSON	ROBERT				26	IRELAND	CP	IRISH	IRON TURNER	045	A	1	74
STEVENSON	SARAH			1	41	O	WM	ENGLISH		043	C		14
STEVENSON	WILLIAM		1		39	O	CS	ENGLISH	LAB	043	F		9
STEVENSON	WILLIAM				35	ENG	CE	ENG	CARPENTER	044	B	2	41
STEWARD	ANN			1	70	IRELAND	WM	IRISH		045	A	4	10
STEWARD	MARY			1	35	IRELAND	RC	IRISH	WASHERWOMAN	043	A	6	14
STEWARD	MARY			1	59	ENGLAND	CE	ENGLISH		045	B	2	25
STEWARD	ROSA			1	40	IRELAND	CE	ENGLISH		045	B	2	13
STEWARD	THOMAS				33	ENGLAND	CE	SCOTCH	PLASTERER	043	H	2	13
STEWARD	THOMAS				33	ENGLAND	CE	SCOTCH	PLASTERER	043	H	2	13
STEWART	ALEX				32	SCOTLAND	CS	SCOTCH	MOULDER	043	D		76
STEWART	ALEXANDER				35	SCOTLAND	CP	SCOTCH	F	045	C	3	20
STEWART	ALEXANDER				38	SCOTLAND	CP	SCOTCH	F	045	C	4	33
STEWART	CHARLES				41	O	CP	IRISH	FARMER	043	A	4	41
STEWART	DAVID				52	IRELAND	PM	IRISH	SHOEMAKER	044	A	3	25
STEWART	DAVID				30	O	WM	IRISH	CLERK	044	A	3	31

SURNAME	NAME1	NAME2	STRAY	SEX	AGE	BIRTHPL	RELIGION	ORIGIN	OCCUP	DIST	SUB_DIST	DIV	PAGE
STEWART	EDWD		1		19	0	WM	IRISH	PAINTER	044	B	5	12
STEWART	ELIZABETH			1	56	IRELAND	CE	IRISH	CHARWOMAN	045	D	5	33
STEWART	EMMA		1	1	35	ENGLAND	CE	ENGLISH		045	B	1	15
STEWART	FRANCIS		1		17	0	CE	SCOTCH	GARDENER	044	C	1	23
STEWART	GEORGE				30	0	CP	IRISH	F	043	B	1	30
STEWART	GEORGE		1		6	0	LU	GERMAN		043	D		16
STEWART	HENRY		2	M	85	SCOTLAND	UP		F	043	A	1	D
STEWART	HENRY				35	0	WM	IRISH	F	044	C	2	31
STEWART	ISABELL		1	1	18	CANADA	BA	SCOTCH		045	D	6	37
STEWART	JAMES			M	50	SCOTLAND	UP	SCOTCH	FARMER	043	A	1	15
STEWART	JAMES				47	0	FK	IRISH	F	043	A	3	22
STEWART	JAMES		2		6	0	CS			043	D		D
STEWART	JAMES				50	SCOT	PS	SCOT	BAILIFF	044	B	2	11
STEWART	JAMES				67	IRELAND	CP	IRISH	FARMER	045	A	3	33
STEWART	JAMES				34	0	WM	IRISH	F	044	C	2	31
STEWART	JANE			1	60	SCOTLAND	CP	SCOTCH		045	A	1	100
STEWART	JOHN				36	IRELAND	CP	IRISH	F	043	B	1	5
STEWART	JOHN				37	SCOTLAND	MN	SCOTCH	FARMER	045	D	2	60
STEWART	JOSEPH		2			0	TU			045	D	2	D
STEWART	LEVINIA		1	1	36	GERMANY	LU	GERMAN	SERVANT	043	D		16
STEWART	MARGARET		1	1	22	0	UP	SCOTCH		043	A	1	19
STEWART	MARY		1	F	45	IRELAND	RC	IRELAND		043	A	5	38
STEWART	MARY		1	1	19	0	PS	IRISH	SERVANT	043	A	6	58
STEWART	MARY		1	1	15	0	WM	IRISH	SERVANT	045	D	5	43
STEWART	MINNIE		1	1	8	0	CE	ENGLISH		043	D		39
STEWART	MOSSES				36	0	WM	IRISH	CARPENTER	043	E	3	58
STEWART	NEIL				58	ENGLAND	PM	ENGLISH	FARMER	043	A	4	51
STEWART	NORMAN		1		4	0	CE	ENGLISH		045	B	1	15
STEWART	PETER				24	SCOTLAND	CS	SCOTCH	SHOEMAKER	043	D		18
STEWART	ROBERT			M	31	0	PS	SCOTCH	FAR	043	A	1	65
STEWART	ROBERT				46	SCOTLAND	CP	SCOTCH	CARPENTER	043	C		6
STEWART	SAMUEL				41	0	WM	IRISH	F	044	C	2	36
STEWART	SARAH		1		55	IRELAND	CE	IRISH		044	A	2	46
STEWART	THOMAS				60	IRELAND	PS	IRISH	WEAVER	043	E	3	58
STEWART	THOMAS				35	SCOTLAND	PS	SCOTCH	F	045	C	3	44
STEWART	WILLIAM		1		28	SCOTLAND	PS	SCOTCH	SCHOOL TEACHER	045	D	2	67
STEWART	WILLIAM				39	0	WM	IRISH	F	044	C	2	31
STEWARTSON	SAMUEL		1		13	0	WM	ENGLISH		045	D	1	46
STIBBARD	JOHN				30	0	WM	ENGLISH	FARMER	045	A	2	7
STIBBARD	ROBERT				55	0	WM	ENGLISH	GARDENER	045	A	2	3
STIBBARD	THOS				42	ENG	CE	ENG	SHOEMAKER	045	C	1	34
STICKLAND	GEORGE				34	ENGLAND	CE	ENGLISH	LABORER	045	D	1	34
STICKLEY	JOSEPH				74	0	ZZ	GERMAN	FARMER	045	D	6	3
STICKNER	CATHERIN			1	51	0	PS	GER		044	B	1	62
STICKWOOD	CHAS				47	ENGLAND	CE	ENGLISH	F	043	E	2	79
STICKWOOD	ISAAC				47	ENGLAND	CE	ENGLISH	BRICKMAKER	043	D		29
STICKWOOD	WM	JOHN			24	ENGLAND	CE	ENGLISH	BRICKMAKER	043	D		29
STIKEMAN	ARTHUR		1		11	0	CE	ENGLISH		044	A	2	40
STIKEMAN	CATHARINE		1	1	5	QUE	CE	ENGLISH		044	A	2	40
STIKEMAN	FLORENCE		1	1	45	FRANCE	CE	ENGLISH		044	A	2	40
STIKEMAN	FRANCIS		1		8	0	CE	ENGLISH		044	A	2	40
STIKEMAN	LUCY		1	1	14	QUE	CE	ENGLISH		044	A	2	40
STILES	DANIEL	H	2			CANADA	NC			043	C		D
STILES	DAVID				36	0	EM	ENGLISH	BLACKSMITH	043	E	2	69
STILES	EDGAR				33	0	WM	ENGLISH	F	043	E	2	74
STILES	GEORGE				45	0	WM	ENGLISH	F	043	E	2	74
STILES	HENRY				26	0	NC	GERMAN	MERCHANT	043	C		25
STILES	HENRY				70	UNITED STATES	NC	ENGLISH	MERCHANT	043	E	2	22
STILES	JOEL				54	0	EM	ENGLISH	F	043	E	2	75
STILES	MARTIN				42	ONTARIO	WM	ENGLISH	FARMER	043	G	2	48
STILEY	WALTER		1		18	ENG	WM	ENG	SERVANT	044	B	1	54
STINOFF	PETER				54	0	WM	GERMAN	LABOURER	045	D	5	61
STINSON	JOHN				62	IRELAND	PS	IRISH	FARMER	045	A	1	5
STINSON	ROBERT				48	IRELAND	CE	IRISH	LAB	044	A	2	49
STINSON	ROBERT	E			26	0	WM	IRISH	F	044	C	2	34
STINSON	WILLIAM			M	55	IRELAND	CE	IRELAND	L	043	A	5	36
STIRLING	ALEXANDER				69	SCOTLAND	PS	SCOTCH	GENTLEMAN	045	C	3	54
STIRLING	JAMES				34	0	PS	SCOTCH	F	045	C	3	53
STITT	MINNIE		1	1	16	0	CE	IRISH		044	B	1	2
STIVER	ANN		2	1	44	0	CM			045	D	4	D
STIVER	FRANCIS				25	0	ME	GERMAN	SCHOOL TEACHER	044	B	1	14
STIVER	FRANCIS				78	US	LU	GERMAN	FARMER	045	D	4	14
STIVER	JACOB				38	0	LU	GERMAN	FARMER	045	D	4	14
STIVER	JOHN	H			77	0	LU	GERMAN	FARMER	045	D	3	45
STIVER	JOSIAH				42	0	LU	GERMAN	FARMER	045	D	3	55
STIVER	NANCY			1	81	US	CP	GERMAN		045	D	3	41
STIVER	ROBERT				54	0	LU	GERMAN	FARMER	045	D	4	27
STIVER	WILLIAM				39	0	PM	GERMAN	FARMER	045	D	3	47
STOBBART	MARY		1	1	60	ENGLAND	BA	ENGLISH		044	A	3	53
STOBBART	ROBERT				42	ENGLAND	PM	ENGLISH	F	044	A	3	12
STOBO	JOHN				59	SCOT	CS	SCOT	F	045	C	1	20
STOBO	ROBT	H			32	0	CS	SCOT	F	045	C	1	30
STOCK	EDWARDSEN				55	ENGLAND	RC	ENGLISH	F	044	A	1	41
STOCK	JAMES				34	0	RC	ENGLISH	F	044	A	1	34
STOCK	JOHN				53	ENGLAND	RC	ENGLISH	F	044	A	1	19
STOCK	WILLIAM				50	ENGLAND	CE	ENGLISH	STONE MASON	045	D	6	54
STOCKDALE	THOMAS				59	ENGLAND	WM	ENGLAND	TAILOR	045	D	2	22
STOCKING	EDWIN				34	U STATES	WM	ENGLISH	LUMBER AGENT	043	D		34
STOCKS	AND	THOS	1		5	USA	RC	DUTCH		045	C	1	8
STOCKS	JOSEPH		1		4	0	CE	IRISH		045	C	1	8
STOCKS	ROBERT				30	ENG	WM	ENG	LAB	044	B	4	18
STODDARD	HARRY		1		1	0	CE	ENG		044	B	2	46
STODDARD	HENRY	H			28	0	CE	IRE	F	044	B	2	46
STODDARD	JANE		1	1	21	SCOTLAND	WM	SCOTCH	SERVANT	043	E	3	45
STODDARD	MORRIS		1	M	30	IRELAND	PR	IRISH	LAB	043	A	1	74
STODDART	HENERY		1		18	SCOTLAND	PM	SCOTTISH	F LAB	043	B	5	8
STOGDILL	SEYMOUR	WM			56	U STATES	CS	ENGLISH	SADDLER	043	A	4	11
STOKES	ISAAC			M	41	ENGLAND	CE	ENGLISH	F	043	A	2	49
STOKES	JAMES			M	35	0	CE	ENGLISH	AGENT	043	A	1	57
STOKES	JAMES				37	ENGLAND	CE	ENGLISH	BLACKSMITH	043	E	3	39
STOKES	JOHN				47	ENGLAND	CE	ENGLISH	ARCHITECT & T CLERK	043	E	2	1
STOKES	JOSEPH				37	U STATES	QU	ENGLISH	MILLER	043	A	4	24
STOKES	SIDNEY				35	0	CE	ENGLISH	F	043	E	3	38
STOKES	THOMAS		1		20	ENGLAND	CE	ENGLISH	BRICK MAKER	045	B	1	63
STOKES	WILLIAM				65	U STATES	QU	ENGLISH	GENTLEMAN	043	C		45
STOLLARD	JOHN		1		29	ENGLAND	WM	ENGLISH	BUTCHER	043	D		14

SURNAME	NAME1	NAME2	STRAY	SEX	AGE	BIRTHPL	RELIGION	ORIGIN	OCCUP	DIST	SUB_DIST	DIV	PAGE
STOLLERY	AGNES	L	2	1	4	ENGLAND	CE			045	B	2	D
STOLLERY	WILLIAM				39	ENGLAND	CE	ENGLISH	CONTRACTOR	045	B	2	12
STONE	JOHN				61	ENGLAND	CE	ENGLISH	LAB	044	C	3	10
STONE	MATTHEW				28	O	CE	ENGLISH	LAB	045	A	1	67
STONEHOUSE	GEORGE				25	O	CP	ENGLISH	F	044	A	2	31
STONEHOUSE	JAMES				57	ENGLAND	PM	ENGLISH	F	045	C	3	21
STONEHOUSE	JAMES				31	O	PM	ENGLISH	F	045	C	4	1
STONEHOUSE	JOHN				44	ENGLAND	CE	ENGLISH	F	043	H	1	41
STONEHOUSE	JOHN				23	O	PM	ENGLISH	MERCHANT	045	C	3	16
STONEHOUSE	JOHN				58	ENGLAND	PM	ENGLISH	F	045	C	3	21
STONEHOUSE	JOSEPH				46	ENGLAND	PM	ENGLISH	F	044	B	5	79
STONEHOUSE	MARY		1	1	64	ENGLAND	PM	ENGLISH		044	A	2	30
STONEHOUSE	MARY	JANE	1	1	22	O	WM	IRISH		044	C	3	43
STONEHOUSE	ROBERT				35	ENGLAND	CE	ENGLISH	F	043	E	1	28
STONEHOUSE	ROBERT				60	ENGLAND	WM	ENGLISH	F	044	A	2	29
STONEHOUSE	ROBT				91	ENGLAND	WM	ENGLISH	F	044	A	2	28
STONEHOUSE	WILLIAM				31	O	PM	ENGLISH	F	044	A	2	29
STONEHOUSE	WILLIAM				53	ENGLAND	PM	ENGLISH	F	045	C	3	15
STONEHOUSE	WILLMAN				40	ENGLAND	PR	ENGLISH	FARMER	043	G	2	24
STONER	ABRAHAM		1		13	O	BC	ENGLISH		045	C	2	31
STONER	ALEX	G			35	O	WM	GERMAN	CARPENTER	045	C	2	32
STONER	HANNAH		1	1	13	O	WM	GERMAN		045	C	2	48
STONER	JAMES		1		18	O	WM	GERMAN	LAB	045	C	2	48
STONER	JOHN				40	O	WM	FRENCH	TEAMSTER	045	C	2	24
STONER	LYDIA		1	1	15	O	WM	GERMAN		045	C	2	48
STONER	MARY		1	1	72	O	WM	GERMAN		045	C	2	31
STONER	PETER		1		80	O	WM	GERMAN	F	045	C	2	31
STONER	PETER				37	O	CE	GERMAN	LAB	045	C	2	46
STONER	RACHEL		1	1	59	O	WM	GERMAN		045	C	2	33
STONER	SARAH		1	1	11	O	WM	GERMAN		045	C	2	48
STONER	THOMAS				33	O	WM	GERMAN	F	045	C	2	52
STONER	WILLIAM				41	O	PS	GERMAN	LAB	045	C	2	47
STONES	RICHARD		1		12	O	CE	ENGLISH		044	A	2	41
STONES	SARAH		1	1	19	O	CE	ENGLISH	COOK	044	C	3	30
STONG	DANIEL				37	O	EM	GERMAN	F	044	C	1	37
STONG	JACOB				50	O	LU	GERMAN	FARMER	044	C	1	18
STONG	JOHN				60	US	LU	GER	F	044	B	3	27
STONG	JOSEPH				43	O	EM	GER	F	044	B	3	1
STONG	MARY			1	64	U STATES	WM	GERMAN	F	044	C	1	33
STONG	WILLIAM		1		14	CANADA	MN	GERMAN		045	D	6	38
STOOK	JOEL				46	ENGLAND	CO	ENGLISH	PLASTERER	043	B	3	60
STOREY	MARGARET			1	38	SCOTLAND	WM	SCOTLAND	TAILORESS	045	D	2	21
STOREY	MARY				60	ENG	WM	ENG	SEAMSTRESS	044	B	2	17
STOREY	PETER			M	68	ENGLAND	EM	ENGLISH	F	043	A	1	48
STORK	GEORGE				43	ENGLAND	WM	ENGLISH	LAB	045	B	1	34
STORKE	JOHN		1	M	23	QUE	CE	ENGLISH	F	043	A	1	29
STORM	ADAM				37	O	LU	GER	F	044	B	2	70
STORRY	JOHN				28	ENGLAND	ME	ENGLISH	FARMER	043	B	3	7
STORY	JOHN			M	44	ENGLAND	PM	ENGLISH	F	043	A	1	45
STORY	JUNE	S	1	1	27	O	WM	ENGLISH	DRESSMAKER	043	A	6	43
STORY	WILLIAM				48	ENGLAND	WM	ENGLISH	FARMER	043	B	3	50
STORY ?	CHRISTIAN		1		9	O	CP	GERMAN		045	D	2	51
STOTT	ANN		1	1	75	ENGLAND	PM	ENGLISH		044	A	1	38
STOTTS	DEWITT				46	O	CP	ENGLISH	F	045	C	2	23
STOTTS	WILLIAM				51	O	CP	ENGLISH	F	045	C	2	36
STOTTS	WILLIAM				44	O	WM	GERMAN	FARMER	045	D	3	82
STOUFFER	ABRAHAM				41	O	MN	GERMAN	FARMER	043	B	3	65
STOUFFER	ABRAHAM				65	UNITED STATES	MN	GERMAN	FARMER	043	B	3	69
STOUFFER	SIMEON				24	O	WM	GERMAN	FARMER	043	B	3	69
STOUGHTON	GEORGE		1		18	ENGLAND	CE	ENGLISH	FARM SERVANT	045	C	3	53
STOUTENBURG	JAMES				49	O	WM	GERMAN	FARMER	045	D	2	49
STOUVER	JACOB				56	CANADA	MN	GERMAN	LABORER	045	D	6	45
STOVER	ABRAHAM		1		35	O	OM	GERMAN		045	D	3	52
STOVER	BETSEY		1	1	30	CANADA	CN	GERMAN		045	D	6	25
STOVER	ELIZABETH		2	1	86	US	MN			045	D	4	D
STOVER	FRANK		1		38	O	WM	ENGLISH	LAB	044	B	5	12
STOVER	JOHN				30	O	MN	GERMAN	FARMER	045	D	5	48
STOVER	MILTON		1		16	CANADA	MN	GERMAN		045	D	6	19
STOVER	PETER				61	O	MN	GERMAN	FARMER	045	D	4	11
STRADER	JOHN				28	USA	WM	ENGLISH	LABOURER	045	A	1	39
STRAIN	ANNIE		1	1	20	O	WM	GERMAN	SERVANT	045	D	5	72
STRAIN	ROBERT				33	IRELAND	CP	IRISH	FARMER	045	D	2	57
STRAINGER	W		1		40	USA	CP	UNKNOWN		045	C	1	8
STRAND	JOSEPH		1		27	IRELAND	CE	IRISH	SERVANT	045	A	3	29
STRANGE	FRED'K				35	ENGLAND	CE	ENGLISH	PHYSICIAN	043	C		24
STRANGE	THOMAS				29	ENGLAND	CE	ENGLISH	PAINTER	045	B	1	54
STRATHY	HENRY	C			39	SCOTLAND	CE	SCOTCH	BANK MANAGER	044	C	2	47
STREET	F	RICHARD			32	ENGLAND	CE	ENGLISH	HOTEL KEEPER	043	A	3	7
STREET	JOSEPH			M	29	O	CE	ENGLAND	F	043	A	5	29
STREET	MARY			1	61	ENGLAND	CE	ENGLISH		043	A	4	46
STREET	ROBERT				35	O	CE	ENGLISH	MASON	043	A	3	35
STREET	SAMUEL				48	O	CP	SCOTCH	LAB	043	B	1	36
STREET	WALKER				24	O	CE	ENGLISH	F	043	A	3	35
STREET	WILIAM				47	O	WM	IRISH	F	045	A	4	30
STREET	WILLIAM				24	O	WM	IRISH	F	044	C	1	28
STREIGHT	DAVID	L			27	O	WM	IRISH	CARPENTER	044	A	2	6
STRICKLAND	CHARLOTTE			1	58	ENGLAND	CE	ENGLISH		043	E	2	48
STRICKLAND	JOSIAH				24	ENGLAND	WM	ENGLISH	LAB	043	E	2	44
STRICKLER	ABRAHAM				53	U STATES	MN	GERMAN	FARMER	045	D	6	25
STRICKLER	BARBARA		2	1	90		MN			045	D	6	D
STRICKLER	DANIEL				51	U STATES	CN	GERMAN	FARMER	045	D	6	29
STRINGER	BENJAMIN		1		27	ENGLAND	WM	ENGLISH	SERVANT	043	G	2	56
STRINGER	WM		1		26	ENGLAND	PM	ENGLISH	LAB	044	B	5	36
STRONG	IDA		1	1	8	O	CE	SCOTCH		043	A	6	53
STRONG	JOHN				30	O	CE	IRISH	F	044	A	2	39
STRONG	JOHN				48	O	WM	GERMAN	F	044	C	1	6
STRONGE	WILLIAM		1		22	ENGLAND	CE	ENGLISH	SERVANT	044	C	4	79
STROWBRIDGE	HENRY			M	38	ENGLAND	CE	ENGLISH	BUTCHER	043	A	1	31
STUBBS	JAMES				68	ENGLAND	PM	ENGLISH	F	043	A	3	51
STUDRIDGE	JOHN		1		18	O	RC	ENGLISH		043	H	2	7
STUDRIDGE	JOHN		1		18	ONTARIO	RC	ENGLISH		043	H	2	7
STUDRIDGE	RICHARD		1		21	O	RC	ENGLISH	LAB	043	H	2	14
STUDRIDGE	RICHARD		1		21	ONTARIO	RC	ENGLISH	LABOURER	043	H	2	14
STUFFOLDS	CHARLES				32	O	EM	GERMAN	LAB	043	E	2	83
STUFFOLDS	DAVID				23	O	EM	GERMAN	LAB	043	E	2	83
STUFFOLDS	JOHN				59	O	PM	GERMAN	LAB	043	E	2	83

SURNAME	NAME1	NAME2	STRAY	SEX	AGE	BIRTHPL	RELIGION	ORIGIN	OCCUP	DIST	SUB_DIST	DIV	PAGE
STUMP	JACOB				75	US	TU	GER	F	044	B	4	42
STUMP	JACOB				40	0	LU	GER	SHINGLE MAKER	044	B	4	42
STUMP	JOHN				49	0	WM	GERMAN	LAB	044	B	6	8
STUNDEN	THOMAS		1		21	ENGLAND	CP	ENGLISH	FARM SERVANT	045	C	3	51
STURDY	CHARLES			M	36	ENGLAND	CE	ENGLISH	FARMER	043	A	2	52
STURDY	MARY		1	1	14	0		ENGLISH		045	A	4	32
STURDY	OLIVER			M	71	ENGLAND	CE	ENGLISH	F	043	A	2	52
STURGES	CELINA		1	1	5	0	WM	ENGLISH		045	D	3	43
SUDDABY	WILLIAM				60	ENGLAND	WM	ENGLISH	TAILOR	044	B	1	5
SUGAL	PETER			M	67	0	PR	FRENCH	F	043	A	1	41
SUGET	FRANKLIN		1		20	0	PM	ENGLISH		045	A	3	36
SUGGETT	WILLIAM				55	ENGLAND	PM	ENGLISH	LAB	045	A	2	21
SULIVAN	BENJAMIN				29	UNITED STATES	CO	GERMAN	LABOURER	043	B	3	65
SULIVAN	DAN		1		47	IRELAND	RC	IRISH	COOPER	044	B	6	58
SULIVAN	DANIEL				44	IRELAND	RC	IRISH	LAB	045	A	4	12
SULIVAN	JAMES			M	45	IRELAND	RC	IRISH	LAB	043	A	2	11
SULIVAN	JOHN				64	U STATES	MN	IRISH		045	D	6	11
SULIVAN	PATRICK			M	60	IRELAND	RC	IRISH	F	043	A	2	55
SULLIVAN	BARTHOLOMEW				50	IRELAND	RC	IRISH	ROPE MAKER	044	C	4	42
SULLIVAN	DANIEL		1		50	IRELAND	RC	IRISH	LAB	045	A	1	17
SULLIVAN	ELLEN		1	1	16	0	RC	IRISH		043	A	3	17
SULLIVAN	MARIA		1	1	18	0	CE	IRISH		044	C	4	89
SULLIVAN	MORRIS				40	IRELAND	RC	IRISH	LAB	044	C	4	34
SULLIVAN	OWEN		1		19	ONT	RC	IRISH	F	043	A	3	17
SULLIVAN	OWEN				70	IRELAND	RC	IRISH	F	043	A	6	14
SULLIVAN	OWEN				25	0	RC	IRISH	LAB	043	E	1	35
SULLIVAN	PATRICK				45	IRELAND	RC	IRISH	LAB	044	C	4	58
SULLIVAN	THOMAS				31	0	RC	IRISH	TOLE GATE KEEPER	043	E	1	20
SULLIVAN	WILLIAM		1	M	25	0	CE	IRELAND	SAWYER	043	A	5	6
SULLY			2	1		0	CE			045	D	5	D
SULLY	ROBT				44	ENGLAND	CE	ENGLISH	SHINGLE MAKER	045	D	5	39
SUMERS	JEMIMA			1	45	ENGLAND	WM	ENGLISH		044	B	5	14
SUMMERFELDT	EUPHEMIA			1	48	ONTARIO	WM	GERMAN	FARMER	045	D	3	1
SUMMERFELDT	JOHN	H			54	0	WM		FARMER	045	D	3	D
SUMMERFELDT	MARY	ELLEN	2	1	19	0	WM			045	D	3	D
SUMMERFELT	ESTER MRS			1	45	US	CE	GERMAN		045	D	4	45
SUMMERFELT	GEORGE				47	0	LU	GERMAN	FARMER	045	D	4	34
SUMMERFELT	WILLIAM				27	0	WM	GERMAN	FARMER	045	D	4	25
SUMMERFELT	WM	HENRY			51	0	PS	GERMAN	MILLER	043	E	3	49
SUMMERS	HORATIO	G			37	0	CE	GERMAN	AGENT	043	D		7
SUMMERS	JOSEPH	A			44	PRUSSIA	LU	GERMAN	SEED MERCHANT AND FL	045	A	1	33
SUMMERS	THOMAS				50	ENGLAND	WM	ENGLISH	BLACKSMITH	045	A	3	26
SUMMERVILLE	CHRISTOPHER				50	IRELAND	WM	IRISH	LAB	043	E	2	35
SUMMERVILLE	JAMES				48	IRELAND	CE	IRISH	F	043	A	6	50
SUMMERVILLE	JAMES				70	IRELAND	PS	IRISH	F	043	A	6	51
SUMMERVILLE	JANE			1	75	IRELAND	CE	IRISH		043	A	6	51
SUMMERVILLE	WILLIAM				33	0	PS	SCOTCH	CURRIER	043	B	3	51
SUNNY	WILLIAM				35	IRELAND	CE	IRISH	LAB	043	B	1	37
SUNOR	JEREMIAH		1		22	ENGLAND	WM	ENGLISH	WOOLEN FIXER	044	C	3	15
SUTER	CAROLINE	W	1	1	23	ENGLAND	CE	ENGLISH		045	B	1	54
SUTER	CHARLES	A	1		28	ENGLAND	CE	ENGLISH	PAINTER	045	B	1	54
SUTER	WALTER	J			31	ENGLAND	CE	ENGLISH	CARPENTER	045	A	1	74
SUTHERLAND	A	G			52	SCOTLAND	CP	SCOTCH	TAILOR	043	D		88
SUTHERLAND	ALEX				70	SCOTLAND	WM	SCOTCH	COOPER	043	F		8
SUTHERLAND	ALEXANDER				50	SCOTLAND	CP	SCOTCH	TAILOR	043	D		81
SUTHERLAND	DONALD			M	44	SCOTLAND	PS	SCOTCH	STONE MASON	043	A	2	6
SUTHERLAND	DONALD				55	SCOTLAND	CP	SCOTCH	MERCHANT	043	D		39
SUTHERLAND	EVA		1	1	50	MALTA	CE	ENGLISH		045	B	2	17
SUTHERLAND	JAMES		1		27	0	CE	ENGLISH	STUDENT	045	B	2	18
SUTHERLAND	JOHN				52	SCOT	CP	SCOT	SWITCHMAN	044	B	1	48
SUTHERLAND	JOHN		1		21	0	CP	SCOTLAND	SERVANT	045	D	2	4
SUTHERLAND	WILLIAM			M	40	SCOTLAND	PS	SCOTCH	STONE MASON	043	A	2	22
SUTHERLAND	WILLIAM				29	SCOTLAND	BA	SCOTCH	TINSMITH	043	G	1	42
SUTTLE	FRED K				35	ENGLAND	CE	ENGLISH	LUMBER MERCHANT	043	C		12
SUTTLEWORTH	GEORGE				63	ENGLAND	CE	ENGLISH	MERCHANT	045	A	3	17
SUTTON	CATHERINE		1	1	18	0	RC	IRISH	SERVANT	044	C	3	31
SUTTON	DAVID				46	IRELAND	RC	IRISH	LAB	044	C	3	26
SUTTON	ELIZABETH		1	1	21	0	RC	IRISH	SERVANT	044	C	3	30
SUTTON	GEORGE				66	ENGLAND	EP	ENGLISH	SHOEMAKER	043	A	3	44
SUTTON	HENRY				29	0	CE	ENGLISH	F	044	B	5	25
SUTTON	JULIUS				47	UNITED STATES	NG	ENGLISH	CLOTHIER	043	B	3	9
SUTTON	MARGRET			1	50	IRELAND	CC	IRISH		045	A	3	8
SUTTON	MATILDA		1	1	12	0	WM	ENGLISH	SERVANT	045	D	1	49
SUTTON	RALPH				31	0	WM	ENG	LAB	044	B	3	43
SUTTON	RICHARD				50	IRISH	RC	IRISH		044	C	3	35
SUTTON	WILLIAM				77	IRELAND	WM	IRISH	WEAVER	045	D	3	42
SWAILS	HANNAH		1	1	69	ENG	CE	ENG		044	B	2	54
SWAIN	JOHN				48	IRELAND	CE	IRISH	FARMER	043	G	2	46
SWAIN	JOSEPH				25	ONT	WM	ENGLISH	LAB	043	D		44
SWALES	THOMAS				35	ENGLAND	PM	ENGLISH	FARMER	045	D	6	35
SWALES	WILLIAM				65	ENGLAND	WM	ENGLISH	FARMER	043	B	3	42
SWALLOW	CHARLES				33	0	WM	ENGLISH	F	045	C	2	26
SWALLOW	F	WILLIAM			32	0	CE	ENGLISH	SCHOOL TEACHER	045	A	3	10
SWALLOW	ROBERT	J			29	0	CE	ENGLISH	HARNESS MAKER	045	A	1	7
SWAN	THOMAS				53	ENGLAND	WM	ENGLISH	LABORER	043	D		76
SWANSON	ANN	J	1	1	20	0	WM	IRISH	SERVANT	045	D	1	44
SWEANY	ELLEN		1	1	74	IRELAND	RC	IRISH		043	D		44
SWEASY	ALEX				30	0	NC	IRISH	F	043	F		21
SWEASY	GEORGE				40	IRELAND	WM	ENGLISH	F	043	F		1
SWEENEY	DENNIS				40	IRELAND	RC	IRISH	LAB	044	C	4	52
SWEET	ADA	E	1	1		ONTARIO	EM	DUTCH		043	G	1	48
SWEET	ANDREW				60	ONTARIO	EM	SCOTCH	FARMER	043	G	1	44
SWEET	ORIN				35	ONTARIO	WM	SCOTCH	FARMER	043	G	1	49
SWEET	THOMAS				52	0	CN	GERMAN	LAB	043	E	2	30
SWEET	WILLIAM				33	ONTARIO	PR	ENGLISH	LABORER	043	G	2	33
SWEETAPPLE	BENJAMIN		1		40	ENG	CE	ENG	LAB	044	B	1	63
SWEETEN	E	H	1	1	44	0	CO	SCOTCH	SEAMSTRESS	045	D	3	4
SWEEZY	WILLIAM				54	0	CE	ENGLISH	F	043	E	1	8
SWEISIE	HIRAM				22	0	CE	IRISH	F	043	A	6	58
SWEISIE	JOHN				63	0	CE	IRISH	F	043	A	6	58
SWERN	JOHN				63	ENGLAND	CE	ENGLISH	BREWER	045	B	2	21
SWIFT	JOSEPH				39	ENGLAND	CE	ENGLISH	ARTIST	045	D	4	31
SWIFT	WILLIAM				30	ENGLAND	RC	IRISH	CLERK	045	A	1	24
SWINTON	HECTOR		1		7	0	FK	SCOTCH		043	A	3	59
SWINTON	HENRY		1		11	0	FK	SCOTCH		043	A	3	59
SWINTON	MARY		1	1	9	0	FK	SCOTCH		043	A	3	59

SURNAME	NAME1	NAME2	STRAY	SEX	AGE	BIRTHPL	RELIGION	ORIGIN	OCCUP	DIST	SUB_DIST	DIV	PAGE
SWIRE	JOHN				64	ENGLAND	WM	ENGLISH	WEAVER	043	B	5	16
SWIRES	ELIZABETH			1	45	IRELAND	OP	IRISH		043	B	5	24
SWIRES	WILLIAM				31	ENGLAND	WM	ENGLISH	F	043	B	5	16
SWITZER	ANNA		1	1	17	O	CE	IRISH	SERVANT	043	A	4	12
SWITZER	CATHERINE		1	1	3	O	CP	IRISH		043	A	4	33
SWITZER	GEORGE				30	QUE	CE	IRISH	F	043	F		9
SWITZER	HENRIETTA		2	1	8	O	WM			043	H	1	D
SWITZER	ROBERT		1		24	ENGLAND	CE	ENGLISH	LAB	045	A	3	30
SWITZER	SARAH		2	1	97	IRELAND	WM			043	H	1	D
SWITZER	TOBIAS				43	IRELAND	CE	IRISH	SHOEMAKER	043	H	1	34
SWITZER	TOBIAS				43	IRELAND	CE	IRISH	SADDLER	045	B	2	8
SYER	THOMAS				38	ENGLAND	CE	ENGLISH	F	044	C	4	23
SYKES	JAMES				40	ENGLAND	CE	ENGLISH	ENGINEER	043	F		7
SYKES	SAMUEL				50	ENGLAND	CE	ENGLISH	MACHINIST	043	D		41
SYKES	SAMUEL		1		26	ENGLAND	WM	ENGLISH	LABOURER	045	D	5	58
SYLVESTER	HANNAH			1	43	O	CP	IRISH	F	045	C	4	40
SYLVESTER	HENRY				32	O	CC	IRISH	CARPENTER	045	A	3	8
SYLVESTER	JOHN				43	O	FK	IRISH	FARMER	045	A	3	31
SYLVESTER	RICHARD				52	IRE	CE	IRE	CRADLEMAKER	045	C	1	67
SYLVESTER	RICHARD				65	IRELAND	CE	IRISH		045	D	3	63
SYLVESTER	WILLIAM				29	O	BA	ENGLISH	FARMER	045	A	3	13
SYLVESTER	WILLIAM		2		74	IRELAND	PS		F	045	A	3	D
SYLVESTER	WILLIAM		1		43	ENGLAND	CE	ENGLAND	SERVANT	045	D	2	4
SYMONS	HENRY				60	ENGLAND	CE	ENGLISH		044	C	2	54
TABER	JOHN				68	ENG	CE	ENG	F	045	C	1	48
TABOR	JOHN				41	O	CE	ENGLISH	F	045	C	3	37
TACKABERRY	WILLIAM				28	IRELAND	CE	IRISH	SALES MAN	045	B	1	17
TAD	ELIZA		1	1	70	IRELAND	CE	IRISH	SEAMSTRESS	044	C	3	7
TAGATALY	MARY		1	1	12	O	EP	ENG		044	B	3	46
TAGGART	M	ISABELLA	2	1	26	ONTARIO	CS			043	A	3	D
TAGGERT	CLARK		1		24	O	WM	IRISH	COOPER	044	B	6	43
TAGGERT	JOHN		1		29	O	CS	IRISH	COOPER	044	B	6	58
TAGGERT	MARY	ELLEN	1	1	25	O	WM	IRISH		044	B	6	43
TAIT	JAMES				32	ENGLAND	CP	ENGLAND	MACHINIST	045	D	2	21
TAIT	JAMES		2		1	ENGLAND	PS			045	D	2	D
TAIT	JAMES		1		50	IRELAND	CE	IRISH		044	C	3	59
TAIT	JOHN				39	ENGLAND	CP	ENGLISH	F	043	E	1	8
TALE	WILLIAM				32	ENG	CE	ENGLISH	LAB	045	A	3	11
TALES	MATTHEW		1		22	ENGLAND	PM	ENGLISH	F LAB	044	A	3	14
TALES	THOS		1		40	ENGLAND	CE	ENGLISH	F LAB	044	A	3	52
TALES	THOS				31	ENGLAND	CE	ENGLISH	F	044	A	3	53
TALLIS	MICHAEL				50	IRELAND	RC	IRISH	TEAMSTER	044	B	6	16
TALLON	WALLIS				53	IRELAND	RC	IRISH	COOPER	044	B	5	56
TALON	DANIEL		1		22	O	RC	IRISH	COOPER	044	B	6	57
TALON	WILLIAM		1		20	O	RC	IRISH	COOPER	044	B	6	57
TANE	HENRY				49	FRANCE	CE	ENGLISH	STOREKEEPER	045	D	5	11
TANNAHILL	JAMES		1		22	QUE	WM	SCOTCH	MILLER	045	C	2	8
TANNER	ELIJAH	C	1		13	O	EM	ENGLISH		043	E	2	59
TANNER	JOHN				43	ENGLAND	CE	ENGLISH	TEAMSTER	044	B	5	21
TANNER	MARGARET		1	1	17	O	WM	ENG	SERVANT	044	B	3	48
TARELENY	JAMES		1		20	ENGLAND	CE	ENGLISH	SERVANT	044	B	6	42
TATE	JAMES				36	ENGLAND	WM	ENGLISH	FARM LABOURER	043	B	3	61
TATE	WILLIAM				40	SCOTLAND	PS	SCOTCH	BLACKSMITH	043	F		10
TATE	WM	AUSTIN	2		8	O	WM			043	B	3	D
TATON	THOMPSON		1	M	30	IRELAND	PR	IRISH	FARM LAB	043	A	1	47
TATTERSALL	EDWARD				36	ENGLAND	CE	ENGLISH	WEAVER	043	E	1	42
TATTLE	GEORGE				63	ENGLAND	CE	ENGLISH	GARDNER	044	C	4	54
TATTLE	WILLIAM	W			32	O	CE	ENGLISH	GARDINER	044	C	2	3
TATTON	JOHN		1	M	82	NB	CN	ENGLAND		043	A	5	43
TATTON	NELSON			M	40	NB	CN	ENGLAND	F	043	A	5	24
TAVENER	JOHN				52	ENGLAND	CE	ENGLISH	LAB	045	B	1	24
TAWS	JOHN			M	27	O	PS	SCOTCH	F	043	A	1	36
TAWS	JOHN			M	72	SCOTLAND	PS	SCOTCH	MINISTER	043	A	1	36
TAYLER	HENERY				30	O	QU	IRISH	F	043	B	5	5
TAYLOR	ABRAHAM				40	O	QU	IRISH	LUMBERMAN	043	B	5	27
TAYLOR	ALFRED		1		29	ENGLAND	CE	ENGLISH	LABOURER	045	A	1	60
TAYLOR	ALFRED				21	IRELAND	CE	ENGLISH	CARPENTER	045	D	3	20
TAYLOR	AMELIA		1	1	20	O	OB	IRISH		044	A	2	10
TAYLOR	ANDREW				45	O	CS	IRE	F	045	C	1	50
TAYLOR	ARCH				51	SCOT	CP	SCOT	BLACKSMITH	045	C	1	11
TAYLOR	DAVID			M	30	O	CE	ENGLAND	L	043	A	5	27
TAYLOR	DAVID				27	O	CE	ENGLISH	FARMER	045	D	1	21
TAYLOR	EDW		1		34	O	ME	IRE	LAB	045	C	1	55
TAYLOR	EDWARD				28	ENGLAND	CE	ENGLISH	LABORER	043	D		80
TAYLOR	ELIZABETH		1	1	74	ENG	CE	ENG		044	B	3	5
TAYLOR	GEO				56	ENG	PM	ENG	F	045	C	1	70
TAYLOR	GEORGE				50	IRE	CE	IRE	LAB	044	B	2	62
TAYLOR	GEORGE				57	ENGLAND	CE	ENGLISH	PAPER MANUFACTURER	045	A	1	87
TAYLOR	GEORGE				42	ENGLAND	WM	ENGLISH	MASON	044	C	3	53
TAYLOR	HARRY		1		24	O	PM	IRISH		045	B	2	14
TAYLOR	HENRY				31	IRELAND	CE	IRISH	FARMER	045	D	4	36
TAYLOR	JAMES				40	IRELAND	CE	IRISH	F	043	H	1	29
TAYLOR	JAMES				71	IRELAND	CE	IRISH	FARMER	045	A	2	9
TAYLOR	JAMES				36	SCOTLAND	CP	SCOTCH	FARMER	045	A	2	30
TAYLOR	JAMES				28	O	CE	ENGLISH	LAB	045	C	2	17
TAYLOR	JAMES				59	ENGLAND	CE	ENGLISH	GARDENER	044	C	2	23
TAYLOR	JAMES	NELSON			22	O	CE	SCOTCH	LAB	043	E	3	36
TAYLOR	JOHN				39	O	QU	IRISH	F	043	B	5	29
TAYLOR	JOHN				33	O	PS	SCOTCH	LAB	043	E	3	35
TAYLOR	JOHN				48	ENGLAND	WM	ENGLISH	FARMER	043	G	2	10
TAYLOR	JOHN				30	ON THE SEA	WM	IRISH	F	043	H	1	30
TAYLOR	JOHN				55	ENGLAND	CE	ENGLISH	GENTLEMAN	045	A	1	31
TAYLOR	JOHN				60	ENGLAND	CE	ENGLISH	PAPER MANUFACTURER	045	A	2	39
TAYLOR	JOHN				30	O	CE	ENGLISH	LAB	045	C	2	8
TAYLOR	JOHN				66	ENGLAND	CE	ENGLISH	F	045	C	2	34
TAYLOR	JOHN				27	O	CE	ENGLISH	FARM LABORER	045	D	1	20
TAYLOR	JOSEPH				63	O	QU	IRISH	F	043	B	4	32
TAYLOR	JOSEPH				45	ENGLAND	CE	ENGLISH	CABINET MAKER	043	F		17
TAYLOR	JOSEPH				33	ENGLAND	CE	ENGLISH	F	044	B	6	45
TAYLOR	LUCINDA		1	1	25	O	WM	ENGLISH		043	B	5	39
TAYLOR	MALCOLM				50	SCOTLAND	FK	SCOTCH	F	043	A	3	54
TAYLOR	MARGARET			1	60	IRELAND	RC	IRISH		043	D		25
TAYLOR	MARK				25	O	CE	ENGLISH	LAB	045	C	2	11
TAYLOR	MARTIN				44	ENGLAND	CE	ENGLISH	F	043	A	6	9
TAYLOR	MARTIN				52	ENGLAND	WM	ENGLISH	FARMER	043	G	2	12
TAYLOR	MARY		1	1	20	SCOTLAND	CP	SCOTCH	SERVANT	045	B	1	15

SURNAME	NAME1	NAME2	STRAY	SEX	AGE	BIRTHPL	RELIGION	ORIGIN	OCCUP	DIST	SUB_DIST	DIV	PAGE
TAYLOR	MARYANN		1	1	4	0	WM	IRISH		043	B	5	39
TAYLOR	NANCY		1	1	76	SCOTLAND	FK	SCOTCH		043	A	3	39
TAYLOR	PETER				25	ENGLAND	CE	IRISH	FARMER	043	G	2	11
TAYLOR	RICHARD				30	ENGLAND	WM	ENGLISH	F	044	C	3	12
TAYLOR	RICHARD				39	ENGLAND	CE	ENGLISH	F	044	C	4	30
TAYLOR	RICHARD	J			38	ENGLAND	CE	ENGLISH	CLERK	045	A	1	42
TAYLOR	ROBART				50	ENGLAND	CE	ENGLISH	BAKER	044	C	3	21
TAYLOR	ROBERT		1		16	0	CE	ENGLISH	CLERK	044	A	3	18
TAYLOR	SARAH			1	65	ENGLAND	CE	ENGLISH		044	C	4	40
TAYLOR	THOMAS				50	IRELAND	PM	IRISH	F	044	A	3	49
TAYLOR	THOMAS				58	ENGLAND	CE	ENGLISH	PAPER MANF'R	045	A	1	90
TAYLOR	THOMAS				38	0	CE	ENGLISH	F	045	C	2	33
TAYLOR	WILLIAM				41	ENGLAND	CE	ENGLISH	PAINTER	043	C		34
TAYLOR	WILLIAM				53	QUEBEC	CE	ENGLISH	F	044	B	6	6
TAYLOR	WILLIAM				34	ENGLAND	WM	ENGLISH	STORE CLERK	045	A	1	54
TAYLOR	WILLIAM				60	ENGLAND	CE	ENGLISH		045	B	1	45
TAYLOR	WILLIAM	H			28	0	CP	IRISH	PHYSICIAN	043	A	4	21
TAYLOR	WM				22	0	PM	ENG	STOREKEEPER	045	C	1	70
TEALESS	PATRICK				55	IRELAND	RC	IRELAND	FARMER	045	D	2	19
TEASDALE	GEORGE				39	0	WM	ENG	F	044	B	2	20
TEASDALL	THOMAS				37	0	WM	ENG	F	044	B	2	7
TEBO	PETER				52	0	CE	FRENCH	LAB	043	H	1	38
TECTOR	WILLIAM				39	IRELAND	CE	IRISH	LAB	045	B	1	14
TEDDER	THOMAS				27	0	WM	ENGLISH	CARPENTER	044	B	6	55
TEDDER	WILLIAM				55	ENGLAND	WM	ENGLISH	F	044	B	6	28
TEDMAN	ELI		1		21	ENGLAND	CE	ENGLISH	MACHINIST	043	A	6	62
TEEFY	MATHEW				48	IRE	RC	IRISH	POSTMASTER	044	B	2	9
TEESON	JOSEPH				41	ENGLAND	PM	ENGLISH	FARM LABOURER	045	C	3	46
TEGART	ANDERSON				43	0	NC	IRISH	BLACKSMITH	043	A	4	19
TEGART	EDMOND	A	2		17	0	NC		HARNESS MAKER	043	A	4	D
TELFER	ALEXANDER	H			38	SCOTLAND	CP	SCOTCH	POST MASTER	045	C	3	38
TELFER	THOMAS				58	SCOTLAND	CO	SCOTTISH	F	043	B	4	3
TELFER	WILLIAM				73	SCOTLAND	CP	SCOTCH	F	045	C	3	54
TELFOR	JOS				65	ENG	CE	ENG		045	C	1	18
TELLES	JAMES				60	IRELAND	RC	IRISH	LAB	044	B	6	31
TEMAN	ABRAHAM				45	CANADA	MN	GERMAN	FARMER	045	D	6	20
TEMPLETON	MARY	ANN	1	1	14	0	EM	ENGLISH		043	E	2	83
TENANT	ALEXANDER		1		49	IRELAND	CE	IRISH	LAB	045	A	1	106
TENCH	CHARLES			M	56	ENGLAND	BA	ENGLAND	F	043	A	5	29
TENNANT	DAVID		2		70	SCOTLAND	CP		STONE CUTTER	044	C	2	D
TENNENT	JAMES				25	QUE	WM	IRE	F	044	B	2	74
TERRALL	WILLIAM				47	ENGLAND	CE	ENGLISH	LAB	043	D		9
TERRIS	THOMAS				25	SCOTLAND	CS	SCOTCH	GARDENER	045	A	1	21
TERRY	BENJAMIN			M	62	US	CN	SCOTCH	F	043	A	5	2
TERRY	CHARLES				28	0	ON	ENGLISH	F	043	G	1	51
TERRY	CHARLES		1		24	ENGLAND	CE	ENGLISH	HOSLOR	044	C	3	30
TERRY	CHRISTOPHER		1		22	0	CE	IRE	LAB	044	B	2	37
TERRY	DAVID				60	0	BA	WELSH	PM	043	E	3	55
TERRY	EDWARD		1		17	0	CP	ENGLISH	FARMER	045	D	4	43
TERRY	ELIZABETH		1	1	82	UNITED STATES	ZZ	GERMAN		043	E	2	34
TERRY	ESTHER	ANN	1	1	27	ONT	CN	ENGLISH		043	D		52
TERRY	GILBERT			M	27	0	CE	IRELAND	L	043	A	5	7
TERRY	ISABELLA		1	1	15	0	PM	ENGLISH	SERVANT	043	B	2	19
TERRY	JAMES		1		19	0	CE	IRE	APPRENTICE	044	B	2	37
TERRY	JOHN		2		57	0	WM		F	043	E	2	D
TERRY	JONATHAN			M	55	U S	QU	SCOTLAND	F	043	A	5	9
TERRY	JOSEPH			M	48	0	QU	SCOTCH	F	043	A	2	55
TERRY	SARAH	A	1	1	57	0	WM	ENGLISH		043	E	2	1
TERRY	STEPHEN				44	0	CE	ENGLISH	BLACKSMITH	043	E	2	23
TERRY	STEPHEN				32	0	BA	WELSH	F	043	E	3	55
TERRY	THOMAS		1		23	0	ZZ	IRISH	LAB	043	E	2	85
TERRY	THOMAS		1		23	0	CE	ENG	APPRENTICE	044	B	2	36
TERRY	WILLIAM		1		35	0	CN	GERMAN	LAB	043	E	2	10
TERRY	WILLIAM				44	0	BA	WELSH	F	043	E	3	55
TERRY	WILLIAM	B			55	ONTARIO	CN	ENGLISH	FARMER	043	G	1	50
TESTER	WILLIAM				22	ENG	CE	ENG	FARM LAB	044	B	1	37
THAYER	GEORGE	H			40	USA	CE	IRISH	CARPENTER	043	H	2	1
THAYER	GEORGE	H			40	UNITED STATES	CE	IRISH	CARPENTER	043	H	2	1
THEAKSTON	CHARLES				40	ENGLAND	PM	ENGLISH	LAB	043	B	2	30
THEAKSTON	HARRIET		2	1		0	PM		F	043	B	2	D
THEAKSTON	WILLIAM				37	ENGLAND	PM	ENGLISH	F	043	B	2	18
THIRD	GEORGE				31	SCOTLAND	CP	SCOTCH	BLACKSMITH	045	A	1	59
THIRKETT	CHRISTOPHER				61	ENGLAND	CE	ENGLISH	BLACKSMITH	044	A	2	16
THIRSK	GEORGE				41	ENGLAND	WM	ENGLISH	CARPENTER	043	E	3	56
THIRSK	JANE			1	62	ENGLAND	CN	ENGLISH		043	E	3	56
THOM	CHARLES				30	0	FW	SCOTCH	BLACKSMITH	043	C		13
THOM	CHARLES				52	SCOTLAND	PS	SCOTCH	INN KEEPER	045	B	1	7
THOMAS	CHARLES		1		25	ENGLAND	CE	ENGLISH	SERVANT	045	B	2	21
THOMAS	ELIZABETH		2	1	26	0	PM			044	A	3	D
THOMAS	EMMA		1	1	20	ENGLAND	PM	ENGLISH		045	D	4	6
THOMAS	FLORA		1	1	40	SCOTLAND	CS	SCOTCH	SERVANT	045	A	1	77
THOMAS	GEORGE				37	ENGLAND	PM	ENGLISH	LAB	043	B	2	32
THOMAS	GEORGE				75	ENG	CE	ENG	F	044	B	2	8
THOMAS	HENRY		1	M		0	WM	GERMAN		043	A	1	18
THOMAS	HENRY				53	ENGLAND	PM	ENGLISH	F	044	A	3	38
THOMAS	JAMES				73	ENGLAND	WM	ENGLISH	FARMER	045	D	6	24
THOMAS	JAMES				24	ENGLAND	CE	ENGLISH	LABORER	045	D	1	18
THOMAS	JOHN		1		60	ENGLAND	CE	ENGLISH	F LAB	043	B	4	34
THOMAS	JOHN				45	US	PM	AFRICAN	F	044	B	2	32
THOMAS	JONATHAN				47	ENGLAND	CE	ENGLISH	F	045	C	2	52
THOMAS	NATHAN		1		14	ONTARIO	NG	ENGLISH	SERVANT	043	G	2	13
THOMAS	RICHARD				61	ENGLAND	PM	ENGLISH	F	044	A	3	51
THOMAS	VICTOR				47	QUE	RC	FRENCH	BLACKSMITH	045	A	1	29
THOMAS	WILLIAM				55	ENGLAND	BC	ENGLISH	F	043	B	5	10
THOMAS	WILLIAM		1		26	ISLE OF JERSEY	CE	ENGLISH	HARNESS MAKER	043	E	2	20
THOMAS	WILLIAM		1		15	0	WM	ENGLISH	SERVANT	043	E	3	32
THOMAS	WILLIAM				26	0	PM	ENGLISH	F	044	A	3	11
THOMAS	WILLIAM				55	ENGLAND	CP	SCOTCH	SERVANT	044	B	6	38
THOMAS	WILLIAM				48	USA	WM	AFRICAN	PLASTERER	045	A	1	24
THOMBURN	ALEX				42	ENGLAND	CE	ENGLISH	INN KEEPER	044	B	5	57
THOMLINSON	GEORGE				57	ENGLAND	EM	ENGLISH	FARMER	043	G	2	20
THOMPSON	AGNES			1	72	SCOTLAND	CS	SCOTCH		043	H	1	12
THOMPSON	ALBERT		1		13	0	CE	ENGLISH		043	C		36
THOMPSON	ALEX				70	0	CE	SCOTCH	F	044	A	1	20
THOMPSON	ALEXANDER				60	SCOTLAND	FK	SCOTCH	F	043	A	3	48
THOMPSON	ALEXANDER				25	0	EM	ENGLISH	LAB	043	E	3	13

SURNAME	NAME1	NAME2	STRAY	SEX	AGE	BIRTHPL	RELIGION	ORIGIN	OCCUP	DIST	SUB_DIST	DIV	PAGE
THOMPSON	ALIDA		2	1	10	0	WM	SCOTCH	F	043	F		D
THOMPSON	ANDW	F			26	0	CE	SCOTCH	F	044	A	1	26
THOMPSON	ARCH				39	0	PM	SCOT	F	045	C	1	47
THOMPSON	BEATRICE		2	1	1	0	NG			043	D		D
THOMPSON	BENJ				46	ENGLAND	CE	ENGLISH	BOOKKEEPER	043	D		43
THOMPSON	CHARLES				20	0	CE	ENGLISH	F	043	B	1	8
THOMPSON	CHRISTINA		1	1	15	SCOT	PS	SCOT	SERVANT	044	B	3	16
THOMPSON	DAVID				47	SCOT	PS	SCOT	F	044	B	3	19
THOMPSON	DAVID				42	SCOTLAND	PM	SCOTCH	LAB	045	B	1	41
THOMPSON	DONALD		1	M	15	US	PS	SCOTCH		043	A	1	63
THOMPSON	DOUGLAS				45	0	EM	GERMAN	F	043	E	2	63
THOMPSON	EDWARD				44	ENGLAND	WM	ENGLISH	F	045	B	1	30
THOMPSON	ELLEN		1	1	19	0	WM	IRISH	SERVANT	044	A	3	56
THOMPSON	FRANK				50	0	CP	IRE	F	045	C	1	60
THOMPSON	FREDERICK				34	ENGLAND	CE	ENGLISH	F LAB	043	A	3	60
THOMPSON	GEORGE				65	IRELAND	CE	IRISH	LAB	043	C		37
THOMPSON	GEORGE				22	0	WM	ENGLISH	LAB	043	E	2	50
THOMPSON	GEORGE				39	SCOTLAND	CP	SCOTCH	F	044	B	6	3
THOMPSON	GEORGE				36	ENGLAND	CE	ENGLISH	FARM LABOURER	045	C	4	10
THOMPSON	GEORGI				79	QUE	RC	AFRICAN	LABOURER	045	D	3	50
THOMPSON	HANNAH			1	54	IRE	WM	IRE		045	C	1	60
THOMPSON	HECTOR				45	SCOTLAND	CS	SCOTCH	FARMER	045	D	5	72
THOMPSON	HENRY				34	ENGLAND	CE	ENGLISH	F	043	A	3	54
THOMPSON	HENRY		1		8	0	CE	ENGLISH		043	C		36
THOMPSON	HENRY				36	IRELAND	CE	IRISH	SADDLER	043	D		25
THOMPSON	JACOB				52	IRELAND	CE	IRISH	F	043	E	3	31
THOMPSON	JAMES			M	23	0	CE	ENGLISH	FARMER	043	A	1	14
THOMPSON	JAMES		1	M	61	IRELAND	PS	IRISH	LAB	043	A	1	30
THOMPSON	JAMES		1	M	18	0	WM	ENGLISH	SERVANT	043	A	1	31
THOMPSON	JAMES				68	0	WM	SCOTCH		044	A	1	21
THOMPSON	JAMES				72	SCOT	PS	SCOT	F	044	B	3	21
THOMPSON	JANE		1	1	40	0	CP	SCOTCH		043	H	2	8
THOMPSON	JANE		1	1	40	ONTARIO	CS	SCOTCH		043	H	2	8
THOMPSON	JOEL				38	ONTARIO	EM	ENGLISH	FARMER	043	G	2	6
THOMPSON	JOHN			M	37	IRELAND	PS	IRISH	LAB	043	A	1	72
THOMPSON	JOHN				28	0	CE	ENGLISH	FARMER	043	A	4	45
THOMPSON	JOHN				33	ONTARIO	WM	SCOTCH	HOOP&SHINGLE MAKER	043	G	1	21
THOMPSON	JOHN				32	IRELAND	CE	IRISH	SAWYER	043	H	1	39
THOMPSON	JOHN		1		24	0	PS	IRISH	F	044	B	2	63
THOMPSON	JOHN		1		71	ENGLAND	PM	ENGLISH	SHOEMAKER	045	A	2	22
THOMPSON	JOHN				30	0	PM	IRE	LAB	045	C	1	69
THOMPSON	JOHN				30	0	WM	ENGLISH	STAGE PROPRIETOR	045	D	1	20
THOMPSON	JOHN				36	ENGLAND	WM	ENGLISH	F	044	C	3	4
THOMPSON	JOS				48	ENG	CE	ENG	F	045	C	1	15
THOMPSON	KEMP				67	ENGLAND	WM	ENGLISH	F	043	E	3	9
THOMPSON	MARGARET			F	49	SCOTLAND	PS	SCOTCH		043	A	2	4
THOMPSON	MARGARET		1	1	9	0	CP	FRENCH		043	H	1	36
THOMPSON	MARGARET		1	1	50	IRELAND	RC	IRISH	SERVANT	045	B	1	70
THOMPSON	MARGRET		1	1	46	IRELAND	RP	IRISH		044	C	3	60
THOMPSON	MARTHA		1	1	6	ONTARIO	CE	IRISH		043	G	1	17
THOMPSON	MARY		1	1	10	0	CE	ENGLISH		043	C		36
THOMPSON	MARY		1	1	55	ENGLAND	PM	ENGLISH		045	A	2	22
THOMPSON	MARY		1	1		0	CE	IRISH		045	B	1	23
THOMPSON	MARY		1	1	48	0	CE	SCOT		045	C	1	32
THOMPSON	PERMELIA	ANN	1	1	18	ONTARIO	EM	IRISH	SERVANT	043	G	2	10
THOMPSON	RICHARD				33	ONTARIO	CN	DUTCH	FARMER	043	G	1	40
THOMPSON	ROBERT			M	22	0	PM	ENGLISH	F	043	A	2	46
THOMPSON	ROBERT				51	ENGLAND	WM	ENGLISH	FARMER	043	A	4	64
THOMPSON	ROBERT				32	0	CE	ENGLISH	F	043	B	1	29
THOMPSON	ROBERT				58	IRELAND	CE	IRISH	F	043	E	2	35
THOMPSON	ROBERT				48	IRE	CS	IRE	LAB	044	B	4	5
THOMPSON	SAMUEL		1		40	ENGLAND	CE	ENGLISH	LAB	043	B	1	25
THOMPSON	SAMUEL				34	0	EM	GERMAN	F	043	E	2	64
THOMPSON	SAMUEL				59	ENG	PM	ENG	F	044	B	2	54
THOMPSON	SARAH		1	1	18	0	WM	IRISH	SERVANT	044	C	1	53
THOMPSON	SIMON				48	ENGLAND	CE	ENGLISH	F	043	E	3	29
THOMPSON	STUTELEY				43	ONTARIO	EM	IRISH	FARMER	043	G	2	55
THOMPSON	THOMAS				38	ENGLAND	CE	ENGLISH	ENGLISH COMTRAVELLER	043	F		32
THOMPSON	THOMAS		1		27	ENG	CE	ENG	BLACKSMITH	044	B	3	6
THOMPSON	THOMAS		1		15	0	CS	IRE	SERVANT	044	B	4	10
THOMPSON	THOMAS				31	ENG	WM	ENG	F	044	B	4	38
THOMPSON	THOMAS				65	ENGLAND	CE	ENGLISH	FIRE INSURANCE AGENT	045	B	2	3
THOMPSON	WILLIAM			M	36	0	CE	ENGLISH	FARMER	043	A	1	16
THOMPSON	WILLIAM		1	M	35	IRELAND	CE	IRISH	R FOREMAN	043	A	1	49
THOMPSON	WILLIAM		1		25	0	WM	IRISH	SERVANT	043	A	4	38
THOMPSON	WILLIAM				30	0	CE	ENGLISH	FARMER	043	A	4	45
THOMPSON	WILLIAM				61	ENGLAND	CE	ENGLISH	FARMER	043	A	4	45
THOMPSON	WILLIAM		2		81	ENGLAND	CE		F	043	B	1	D
THOMPSON	WILLIAM				50	0	EM	ENGLISH	F	043	E	3	12
THOMPSON	WILLIAM		1		22	SCOTLAND	CE	SCOTCH	SHOEMAKER	044	A	3	26
THOMPSON	WILLIAM		2		22	0	WM		SERVANT	044	B	4	D
THOMPSON	WILLIAM		1		20	ENGLAND	CP	ENGLISH	FARM LAB	044	C	2	38
THOMPSON	WM				26	0	WM	SCOT	F	045	C	1	60
THOMS	MARY		1	1	20	0	CE	IRISH	SERVANT	045	A	1	9
THOMSON	A	S			74	0	WM	SCOTCH		045	D	3	4
THOMSON	ADOLPHUS		1		20	0	UV	ENGLISH	CARPENTER	045	A	1	64
THOMSON	ALEXANDER		1		30	0	CS	ENGLISH	STORE CLERK	045	D	3	71
THOMSON	AMOS				46	0	CP	SCOTCH	F	045	C	4	20
THOMSON	ANDREW				76	SCOTLAND	CP	SCOTCH	F	045	C	3	46
THOMSON	ANDREW		1		13	0	CP	SCOTCH		045	C	4	33
THOMSON	ANDREW	J			44	0	CP	SCOTCH	F	045	C	3	7
THOMSON	ANNE	JANE	1	1	47	IRELAND	PB	IRISH		044	C	4	81
THOMSON	ARCHIBALD				45	0	CP	SCOTCH	F	045	C	4	18
THOMSON	ARCHIBALD				74	0	CP	SCOTCH	F	045	C	4	20
THOMSON	ARCHIBALD		1		10	0	CP	SCOTCH		045	C	4	33
THOMSON	CHRISTINE			1	34	0	CP	SCOTCH	FARM OWNER	045	C	4	34
THOMSON	CHRISTOPHER				75	SCOTLAND	CP	SCOTCH	F	045	C	4	37
THOMSON	CLARISSA		1	1	71	US	CP	SCOTCH		045	C	2	16
THOMSON	DAVID				34	SCOTLAND	CE	SCOTCH	F	044	A	1	20
THOMSON	DAVID				67	SCOTLAND	PS	SCOTCH	F	044	B	5	46
THOMSON	DAVID				37	0	CP	SCOTCH		045	C	4	20
THOMSON	DAVID				42	0	CP	SCOTCH	F	045	C	4	23
THOMSON	DAVID	A			37	0	PS	SCOTCH		045	C	3	46
THOMSON	DAVID	GEORGE			36	0	PS	SCOTCH	F	045	C	3	49
THOMSON	DAVID	J			48	0	CP	SCOTCH	CARPENTER	045	C	3	31
THOMSON	DAVID	R			49	0	CP	SCOTCH	F	045	C	4	20

SURNAME	NAME1	NAME2	STRAY	SEX	AGE	BIRTHPL	RELIGION	ORIGIN	OCCUP	DIST	SUB_DIST	DIV	PAGE
THOMSON	ELIZA		2	1	1	0	CP			045	C	4	D
THOMSON	ELIZABETH		1	1	36	0	CP	SCOTCH		045	C	4	33
THOMSON	ELLEN		1	1	15	SCOTLAND	CP	SCOTCH		045	C	4	19
THOMSON	GEORGE		1		21	0	PM	ENG	MINISTER	044	B	2	52
THOMSON	GEORGE				37	0	NG	ENGLISH	CARPENTER	045	D	3	4
THOMSON	JAMES				45	SCOT	PS	SCOT	LAB	044	B	2	54
THOMSON	JAMES				61	SCOTLAND	PS	SCOTCH	MILLER	044	B	5	38
THOMSON	JAMES				63	ENGLAND	WM	ENGLISH	LAB	044	B	5	39
THOMSON	JAMES				38	0	PS	SCOTCH	F	045	C	3	24
THOMSON	JAMES	A			69	0	PS	SCOTCH	F	045	C	3	48
THOMSON	JAMES	GEORGE			31	0	PS	SCOTCH	F	045	C	3	48
THOMSON	JANE			1	39	0	CP	IRISH	WASHER WOMAN	045	C	4	21
THOMSON	JOHN		1		47	0	PS	ENGLISH	LAB	044	B	5	40
THOMSON	JOHN				88	SCOTLAND	CP	SCOTCH	GENTLEMAN	045	A	1	57
THOMSON	JOHN				67	0	CP	SCOTCH	F	045	C	4	22
THOMSON	JOHN	R			34	0	PS	SCOTCH	F	045	C	3	37
THOMSON	JOHN	W			44	0	PS	SCOTCH	SHINGLE MAKER	045	C	3	51
THOMSON	MARGARET		2	1	1	0	WM			045	D	3	D
THOMSON	MARY			1	32	0	CE	IRISH	DRESS MAKER	045	D	3	73
THOMSON	MARYANN			1	34	0	CP	ENGLISH	F	045	C	3	28
THOMSON	MENASSAH				29	0	UP	IRE	F	044	B	2	62
THOMSON	RICHARD		2			0	CP			045	C	3	D
THOMSON	RICHARD				45	0	CP	SCOTCH	F	045	C	3	35
THOMSON	RICHARD				76	SCOTLAND	CP	SCOTCH	F	045	C	4	20
THOMSON	ROBERT				27	0	PS	SCOTCH	F	045	C	3	50
THOMSON	SELINA			1	68	0	CS	IRISH		044	C	4	7
THOMSON	SIMON				75	SCOTLAND	PS	SCOTCH	F	045	C	3	13
THOMSON	SIMON				35	0	PS	SCOTCH	FARMER	045	D	2	51
THOMSON	SINACA				32	0	CP	SCOTCH	MASON	045	C	2	16
THOMSON	SMITH				41	0	PS	SCOTCH	MERCHANT	045	C	3	12
THOMSON	THOMAS				35	SCOTLAND	CP	SCOTCH	STORE KEEPER	045	D	3	42
THOMSON	WILLIAM				48	0	CP	SCOTCH	F	045	C	4	22
THOMSON	WILLIAM				39	SCOTLAND	PS	SCOTCH		045	D	6	67
THOMSON	WILLIAM	D			69	0	PS	SCOTCH	F	045	C	3	50
THORN	ANN			1	82	ENGLAND	WM	ENGLISH		044	C	3	31
THORN	HERBERT		2			0	WM			043	A	6	D
THORN	THOMAS				39	0	CE	ENGLISH	F	043	A	6	23
THORNBACK	ANNIE			1	45	IRE	CE	IRE		045	C	1	40
THORNBECK	JOHN		1		16	0	CP	ENGLISH		045	C	2	30
THORNBER	JAMES				30	0	CE	ENGLISH	F	043	H	2	30
THORNBER	JAMES		1		30	ONTARIO	CE	ENGLISH	FARMER	043	H	2	30
THORNBER	JOHN				67	ENGLAND	CE	ENGLISH	F	043	H	2	30
THORNBER	JOHN				67	ENGLAND	CE	ENGLISH	FARMER	043	H	2	30
THORNE	B	J			33	0	CE	ENGLISH	MERCHANT	043	F		14
THORNE	THOMAS	F			61	ENGLAND	CE	ENGLISH	MASON	045	A	1	103
THORNE	WILLIAM				45	ENGLAND	CP	ENGLISH	LAB	045	C	2	4
THORNE	WILLIAM	H			39	0	CE	ENGLISH	MERCHANT	043	F		31
THORNTON	JOHN				46	IRELAND	WM	IRISH	SHOEMAKER	045	D	6	62
THORNTON	MARY		1	1	62	ENGLAND	CE	ENGLISH		043	C		7
THORNTON	WILLIAM				52	ENGLAND	EM	ENGLISH	LAB	043	E	1	6
THORP	GEORGE			M	33	ENGLAND	CE	ENGLISH	F	043	A	2	54
THORP	WILLIAM				36	ENGLAND	PM	ENGLISH	FIREMAN ON ENGINE	044	C	3	26
THRACY	PATRICK				30	IRELAND	RC	IRISH	LAB	044	C	4	42
THROWES	CHRISTOPHER				40	ENGLAND	CE	ENGLISH	F LAB	044	A	2	15
THURLOW	JOSEPH				43	ENGLAND	CE	ENGLISH	FARMER	043	B	3	19
THURSTON	LYMAN		1		22	0	BA	ENGLISH	BLACKSMITH	043	B	3	7
TIBB	RICHARD		1		15	0	CP	ENGLISH		044	B	6	41
TIBBLE	THOMAS				53	ENGLAND	CE	ENGLISH	LAB	043	H	2	52
TIBBLE	THOMAS				53	ENGLAND	CE	ENGLISH	LABOURER	043	H	2	52
TIBNON	JAS				40	IRELAND	CE	IRISH	LAB	044	B	5	31
TIBY	JOHN		1		55	IRELAND	RC	IRISH	LAB	043	A	3	26
TIBY	PATRICK				40	IRELAND	RC	IRISH	LABOURER	043	A	3	2
TIER	ROBERT	H			32	ENGLAND	CE	ENGLISH	LINEN DRAPER	044	A	2	5
TIERNEY	EDWARD	JAMES	1		2	US	RC	IRISH		043	D		3
TIERNEY	ELLEN		1	1	32	0	RC	IRISH		043	D		3
TIERNEY	ELLEN		1	1	6	0	RC	IRISH		043	D		3
TIERNEY	MICHAEL				37	IRELAND	RC	IRISH	LAB	045	A	1	100
TIFFIN	EMMA		2	1	2	0	WM			043	E	3	D
TIFFIN	GRACE		1	1	15	0	WM	ENGLISH		043	E	3	48
TIFFIN	JOHN		1		16	0	WM	ENGLISH	F	044	A	2	15
TIFFIN	JOHN				32	ENGLAND	CE	ENGLISH	FARM LAB	044	B	1	2
TIFFIN	MARY		1	1	37	0	WM	ENGLISH		043	E	3	48
TIFFIN	SARAH	ANN	1	1	18	ENGLAND	PM	ENGLISH		044	A	2	32
TIGHE	MARGARET		1	1	31	IRELAND	WM	IRISH		044	A	3	49
TILL	ROBERT				33	IRELAND	CE	SCOTCH	WAGON MAKER	043	H	2	17
TILLETT	ROBERT				36	ENGLAND	CE	ENGLISH	FARMER	043	G	1	7
TILLISON	AGNES		1	1	20	ENGLAND	CE	ENGLISH		045	C	1	54
TILLISON	JANE		1	1	7	ENGLAND	CE	ENGLISH		045	C	1	54
TILLISON	SAMUEL		1			ENGLAND	CE	ENGLISH		045	C	1	54
TILLISON	THOS		1		36	ENG	CE	ENG	LAB	045	C	1	54
TILLITT	JAMES		1		40	ENGLAND	CE	ENGLISH	LABORER	043	G	1	36
TILLITT	SAMUEL		1		28	ENGLAND	CE	ENGLISH	LABORER	043	G	1	36
TILSON	HENRY				55	IRELAND	CE	IRISH	F	044	A	1	15
TILSON	HUMPHREY		1		23	IRELAND	WM	IRISH	WHEELWRIGHT	043	A	4	17
TILSON	ROBERT			M	28	IRELAND	WM	IRELAND	BLACKSMITH	043	A	5	13
TILSON	SARAH		2	1	18	0	CE			044	A	1	D
TIMORD	HESTOR		1	1	28	ENGLAND	WM	ENGLISH	SERVANT	045	B	2	31
TIMSON	ALMEDA		1	1	30	UNITED STATES	NC	ENGLISH	SEAMSTRESS	043	E	2	38
TINDAL	THOMAS				59	ENGLAND	CE	ENGLISH	FARM SERVANT	043	G	2	55
TINDALL	CHARLES		1		24	0	WM	ENGLISH	LAB	043	B	5	39
TINDALL	FRANCES				41	ENGLAND	WM	ENGLISH	FARMER	043	G	1	36
TINDALL	JOHN		1		26	ENGLAND	CE	ENGLISH	F LAB	044	A	3	4
TINDALL	MARY		1	1	13	ONTARIO	BC	ENGLISH		043	B	5	10
TINDALL	WILLIAM				36	0	WM	ENGLISH	F	043	B	5	14
TINFOOT	ELISABETH		1	1	23	0	WM	ENGLAND	SERVANT	045	D	2	14
TINGLE	ANDREW				50	0	PS	ENGLISH	CARPENTER	045	C	3	7
TINGLE	ELLEN		1	1	20	0	PM	ENGLISH	SERVANT	044	A	3	3
TINGLE	JOHN				35	0	PS	ENG	STOREKEEPER	045	C	1	72
TINGLE	JOHN				78	ENGLAND	CP	ENGLISH	F	045	C	4	37
TINLINE	JAMES			M	44	SCOTLAND	PS	SCOTCH	MERCHANT	043	A	1	39
TINLINE	WILLIAM			M	85	SCOTLAND	PS	SCOTCH	F	043	A	2	40
TIONON	JAMES				70	IRELAND	RC	IRISH	LAB	044	B	5	32
TIPP	DANIEL				70	0	WM	GERMAN	FARMER	045	D	4	15
TIPP	JOHN				67	0	TU	GERMAN		045	D	2	54
TISDALE	JAMES				42	IRELAND	CE	IRISH	F LAB	044	C	1	3
TISDALE	WILLIAM				40	0	EM	ENGLISH	FARMER	045	D	1	41

SURNAME	NAME1	NAME2	STRAY	SEX	AGE	BIRTHPL	RELIGION	ORIGIN	OCCUP	DIST	SUB_DIST	DIV	PAGE
TISHER	SAMUEL		1		18	0	WM	ENGLISH	SERVANT	044	B	6	11
TITUS	BENJAMIN				28	0	CE	ENGLISH	LABOURER	045	D	5	43
TITUS	ELI				31	0	CE	ENGLISH	LABOURER	045	D	5	25
TITUS	WILLIAM				35	0	CE	FRENCH	LAB	045	C	2	46
TIVY	WILLIAM				60	0	CP	IRISH	SHOEMAKER	044	A	2	4
TOASE	ELIZA		1	1	20	0	WM	ENG	SERVANT	044	B	3	12
TOASE	HENRY				37	ENGLAND	WM	ENGLISH	BRICKMAKER	043	A	4	37
TODD	JAMES			M	40	IRELAND	WM	IRISH	FARMER	043	A	1	18
TODD	JAMES				64	IRELAND	CE	IRISH	GENTLEMAN	043	C		11
TODD	JANE		1		39	IRELAND	CP	IRISH	BOARDINGHOUSE KEEPER	045	D	5	10
TODD	RACHEL		1		60	IRELAND	CE	IRISH		044	C	4	28
TOLIVER	LEWIS				50	USA	PM	AFRICAN	LAB	045	A	1	93
TOM	JAMES				50	IRELAND	CE	IRISH	FARM LAB	045	A	1	53
TOM	THOMAS	H	1		32	IRELAND	QU	IRISH		043	H	2	6
TOMILSON	GORDON				27	ONT	PM	IRISH	LAB	045	A	4	2
TOMKIN	SARAH		1	1	21	0	MN	IRISH		045	D	2	39
TOMKINS	JOHN		1		14	0	TU	IRISH		045	D	4	5
TOMLINSON	ALFRED				51	0	EM	GERMAN	SAW MILLING?	045	D	5	45
TOMLINSON	BARTLET				30	ONTARIO	PR	ENGLISH	FARMER	043	G	2	27
TOMLINSON	CHAS				55	ENGLAND	CE	ENGLISH	F	044	A	1	36
TOMLINSON	CICERO				41	0	CS	GERMAN	FARMER	045	D	5	45
TOMLINSON	FRANCIS		1		15	0	CE	GERMAN		045	D	3	76
TOMLINSON	FRANCIS	B	1		26	0	WM	GERMAN	FARM LABORER	045	D	1	46
TOMLINSON	JOHN				43	ENGLAND	CE	ENGLISH	FARMER	043	G	2	35
TOMLINSON	MANUEL				55	0	WM	WELSH	FARMER	045	D	3	43
TOMLINSON	ROBERT				61	ENGLAND	CE	ENGLAND	F	043	H	2	42
TOMLINSON	ROBERT				61	ENGLAND	CE	ENGLISH	FARMER	043	H	2	42
TOMLINSON	SARAH			1	69	U STATES	EM	GERMAN		045	D	5	47
TOMLINSON	SIMEON				23	0	EM	GERMAN	FARMER	045	D	5	51
TOMLINSON	SYLVESTER				48	0	LU	GERMAN	FARMER	045	D	5	50
TOMLINSON	WILLIAM				47	ENGLAND	CE	ENGLISH	F	043	H	2	33
TOMLINSON	WILLIAM				47	ENGLAND	CE	ENGLISH	FARMER	043	H	2	33
TOMMAS	RICHARD			M	53	ENGLAND	PM	ENGLISH	FARMER	043	A	1	12
TOMPKINS	WILLIAM				65	ENGLAND	WM	ENGLISH	LAB	045	C	2	26
TOMS	WILLIAM				25	0	CE	IRISH	FARMER	045	A	1	58
TONARGE	THOMAS				35	IRELAND	RC	IRISH	LABORER	043	G	2	16
TOOL	ALFRED				26	0	QU	IRISH	F	043	B	4	43
TOOL	ALLEN				45	0	QU	IRISH	F	043	B	5	37
TOOL	AMOS				54	0	QU	WELSH	F	043	E	3	34
TOOL	ARON				51	0	QU	GERMAN	FARMER	045	D	4	39
TOOL	CATHARINE		1	1	77	0	CN	GERMAN		043	B	4	45
TOOL	ELIZABETH		1	1	20	0	PM	WELSH		043	E	3	34
TOOL	GILISE				52	IRELAND	RC	IRISH	CARPENTER	043	B	4	8
TOOL	LEWIS		1		18	0	PM	WELSH	LAB	043	E	3	34
TOOL	MAHLON				71	0	QU	IRISH	F	043	B	4	43
TOOL	MOSES				76	UNITED STATES	QU	WELSH	GENT	043	E	3	33
TOOL	SILAS				39	0	QU	IRISH	F	043	B	4	43
TOOLE	EDWARD		1		56	IRELAND	RC	IRISH	LABORER	043	G	1	35
TOOMBS	SAMUEL				47	ENGLAND	WM	ENGLISH	FARM LABOURER	045	C	4	45
TOOTH	WILLIAM		1		30	ENGLAND	CE	ENGLISH	FARM LAB	044	C	2	42
TOPHAM	JOHN		1		30	IRELAND	CE	IRISH	LABOURER	045	D	3	43
TOPHAM	WILLIAM				39	IRELAND	CE	IRISH	FARMER	045	D	3	18
TOPIN	JOHN				70	IRISH	CE	IRISH	LAB	044	B	5	58
TOPPER	FRANK				25	ENGLAND	PM	ENGLISH	LAB	044	B	5	33
TOPPER	GEO				34	ENGLAND	PM	ENGLISH	INN KEEPER	044	B	5	36
TOPPER	WILLIAM				33	ENGLAND	CE	ENGLISH	F	045	C	3	17
TOPPIN	JOHN				30	0	WM	IRISH	FARMER	045	D	1	36
TOPPIN	MARY			1	52	IRELAND	WM	IRISH		045	D	1	33
TORRANCE	JOHN				40	SCOTLAND	CP	SCOTCH	F	044	A	3	21
TORRANCE	JOHN				40	SCOT	CP	SCOT	F	045	C	1	43
TORRANCE	JOHN				81	SCOT	CS	SCOTCH		045	C	1	26
TORRENS	MARY		1	1	60	SCOTLAND	CS	SCOTCH		043	D		83
TOTTEN	JAMES				60	IRE	WM	IRE	YEOMAN	044	B	3	46
TOUL	JACOB	S		M	12	0	WM	SCOTLAND		043	A	5	17
TOULMINS	FREDERICK				39	ENGLAND	CE	ENGLISH	BAND MASTER	045	B	1	24
TOWN	THOMAS		1		26	IRELAND	CP	IRISH	LABORER	045	D	2	40
TOWNLEY	ALICE		1	1	37	ENGLAND	CE	ENGLISH		043	D		21
TOWNLEY	FANNY		1	1	18	ENGLAND	CE	ENGLISH		043	D		20
TOWNLEY	FANNY		1	1	18	ENGLAND	CE	ENGLISH		043	D		68
TOWNLEY	JAMES		1		12	0	CE	ENGLISH		043	D		21
TOWNLEY	JOHN		1		16	0	CE	ENGLISH	LAB	043	D		21
TOWNLEY	LILLY		1	1	14	0	CE	ENGLISH		043	D		21
TOWNLEY	ROBERT		1		10	0	CE	ENGLISH		043	D		21
TOWNLEY	ROSA		1	1	6	0	CE	ENGLISH		043	D		21
TOWNLEY	THOMAS		1		8	0	CE	ENGLISH		043	D		21
TOWNLEY	W	D			26	ENGLAND	CE	ENGLISH	TELEGRAPH OPERATOR	043	H	2	8
TOWNLEY	W	F	1		26	ENGLAND	CE	ENGLISH	TELEGRAPH OPERATOR	043	H	2	8
TOWNSEND	JAMES				42	WALES	CE	WELSH	HOTEL KEEPER	045	A	1	56
TOWNSEND	MARTHA		1		25	0	CE	ENGLISH		044	A	3	41
TOWNSEND	THOMAS				43	ENG	PS	ENG	FOREMAN	044	B	2	73
TOWNSLEY	GEORGE				40	ENGLAND	WM	ENGLISH	BRICKMAKER	044	C	4	21
TOWNSLEY	HANNA		1		60	ENGLAND	WM	ENGLISH		045	B	1	20
TOWNSLEY	HARIOTT				74	ENGLAND	WM	ENGLISH		045	B	1	59
TOWNSLEY	MARY		1		64	ENGLAND	PM	ENGLISH	BRICK MANUFACTURER	045	B	1	73
TOWNSLEY	WILLIAM				44	ENGLAND	WM	ENGLISH	BRICK MANUFACTUERER	045	B	1	65
TOWSE	ELIZABETH		1	1	57	ENGLAND	PM	ENGLISH		043	B	5	7
TRACEY	WILLIAM				58	IRELAND	RC	IRISH	F	044	C	1	54
TRACY	JOHN				41	IRELAND	RC	IRISH	TAILOR	043	C		28
TRACY	MARY	ANN		1	32	IRELAND	EM	IRISH		043	D		63
TRACY	THOMAS				25	IRELAND	RC	IRISH	LAB	044	C	4	50
TRAIN	FREDERICK			M	32	US	CE	ENGLAND	SAWYER	043	A	5	5
TRAIN	JOHN				39	0	CE	ENGLISH	F	044	B	6	56
TRAIN	JOHN		1		13	0	CP	SCOTCH		044	B		
TRAIN	MARIA		1	1	70	ENGLAND	WM	ENGLISH		044	B	6	9
TRAIN	RICHARD		1		17	0	CP	SCOTCH	F	044	B	1	3
TRAINOR	JANE		1	1	5	0	RC	IRISH		043	A	3	34
TRAINOR	JOHN				31	0	RC	IRISH	F	043	A	3	23
TRAINOR	MICHAEL				27	0	RC	IRISH	F	043	A	3	36
TRAINOR	PATRICK				25	0	RC	IRISH	F	043	A	3	36
TRAINOR	PATRICK				62	IRELAND	RC	IRISH	F	043	A	3	37
TRAMPLEASURE	JOHN				57	ENGLAND	WM	ENGLISH		044	A	2	34
TRAN	CLEMENDINE		1	1	17	0	CE	ENGLISH	SERVANT	045	D	5	76
TRAN	DAVID				52	ENGLAND	WM	ENGLISH	FARMER	045	D	4	9
TRAN	HENRY		1		35	ENGLAND	CE	ENGLISH	LABOURER	045	D	5	76
TRAN	JAMES				56	ENGLAND	WM	ENGLISH	FARMER	045	D	5	64
TRAN	JOSEPH		1		40	ENGLAND	CE	ENGLISH	LABOURER	045	D	5	75

SURNAME	NAME1	NAME2	STRAY	SEX	AGE	BIRTHPL	RELIGION	ORIGIN	OCCUP	DIST	SUB_DIST	DIV	PAGE
TRAN	THOMAS				45	ENGLAND	WM	ENGLISH	FARMER	045	D	4	28
TRAVIS	HYRAM				27	ONTARIO	PR	ENGLISH	LABORER	043	G	2	43
TRAVIS	NATHAN				31	ONTARIO	PR	ENGLISH	FARMER	043	G	2	28
TRAVIS	ROBERT		1	M	26	0	DI	GERMAN	SERVANT	043	A	1	35
TRAVISS	ALEXANDER		1	M	8	0	FK	SCOTLAND		043	A	5	33
TRAVISS	ALFRED				35	ONTARIO	CN	IRISH	FARMER	043	G	1	13
TRAVISS	BARNES				46	0	CE	SCOTCH	F	043	E	3	23
TRAVISS	CHARLES				49	0	CN	ENGLISH	F	043	E	3	23
TRAVISS	CHARLES				30	ONTARIO	EM	IRISH	FARMER	043	G	1	31
TRAVISS	CHAS	E			27	0	CN	ENGLISH	F	043	E	2	50
TRAVISS	EPHRAIM				38	0	CN	ENGLISH	LAB	043	E	3	20
TRAVISS	GEORGE				47	0	ZZ	GERMAN	F	043	E	3	52
TRAVISS	HENERY				24	0	CN	ENGLISH	F	043	B	5	36
TRAVISS	ISAAC				58	0	CN	ENGLISH	F	043	E	2	47
TRAVISS	JAMES	ALBERT			25	0	CN	GERMAN	F	043	E	3	25
TRAVISS	JAS	R			25	0	CE	ENGLISH	BLACKSMITH	043	E	2	18
TRAVISS	JOHN				48	0	CN	IRISH	LAB	043	E	2	77
TRAVISS	JOSEPH				63	NB	CE	WELSH	F	043	E	2	49
TRAVISS	MARY	A	2	1		ONTARIO	CN			043	G	1	D
TRAVISS	MARY	H	1	1	12	0	CN	ENGLISH		043	E	2	10
TRAVISS	ROBERT	R		M	54	0	FK	SCOTLAND	F	043	A	5	33
TRAVISS	ROSETTA		1	1	13	0	WM	SCOTTISH		043	B	5	4
TRAVISS	RUSSELL				44	0	EM	ENGLISH	F	043	E	3	14
TRAVISS	SAMUEL				50	0	CN	ENGLISH	F	043	E	2	17
TRAVISS	SEVE				36	0	PM	ENGLISH	F	043	E	3	14
TRAVISS	STEPHEN				60	0	CN	ENGLISH	F	043	E	2	50
TRAVISS	WHITNEY				78	NS	CN	ENGLISH		043	E	3	6
TRAVISS	WILLIAM		1		16	0	CN	WELSH	FARM LABOURER	043	E	2	49
TRAVISS	WILLIAM				24	ONTARIO	CN	IRISH	MASON	043	G	1	16
TRAYLING	MARY	A	1	1	30	0	CE	ENGLISH	SERVANT	044	C	2	35
TREACY	MICHAEL				36	0	RC	IRISH	HOTEL KEEPER	043	A	4	24
TREADGOLD	CHARLES		1		19	ENGLAND	PM	ENGLISH		043	B	4	14
TREADGOLD	GEORGE				38	ENGLAND	WM	ENGLISH	SCHOOL TEACHER	044	A	3	42
TREADGOLD	GEORGE	WILLIAM	2			0	PM			044	A	3	D
TREADGOLD	MANTON				29	ENGLAND	PM	ENGLISH	SCHOOL TEACHER	044	A	3	39
TREAKER	MARK				48	ENGLAND	CE	ENGLISH	LABORER	045	D	2	26
TREBLECOCK	ELIZABETH		1	1	22	ENGLAND	CE	ENGLISH		044	C	4	53
TREBLECOCK	JOSEPH		1		20	0	CP	SCOTCH		045	A	1	102
TREDWAY	WILLIAM				38	ENGLAND	WM	ENGLISH	MERCHANT	045	C	2	12
TREE	DANIEL				48	ENGLAND	CE	ENGLISH	F	045	B	2	24
TREE	WILLIAM		1		25	ENGLAND	WM	ENGLISH	SERVANT	045	B	2	37
TREE?	ELI	MARK	1		15	ENGLAND	WM	ENGLISH	SERVANT	045	B	2	37
TREJASKIS	EDWARD		1		27	ENGLAND	CE	ENGLISH		044	C	3	38
TRELOAR	HENRY				40	ENGLAND	CE	ENGLISH	BLACKSMITH	043	H	2	7
TRELOAR	HENRY				40	ENGLAND	CE	ENGLISH	BLACKSMITH	043	H	2	7
TRELSAR	SAMUEL				65	ENGLAND	CE	ENGLISH	BLACKSMITH	043	G	1	1
TREMBLE	GEORGE				32	IRELAND	CE	IRISH	LAB	045	A	4	22
TRENCH	ROBERT				28	0	WM	SCOT	BLACKSMITH	044	B	2	15
TRENCH	WILLIAM				39	SCOTLAND	WM	SCOTLAND	BLACKSMITH	045	D	2	4
TRENCH	WILLIAM				63	SCOTLAND	CP	SCOTLAND		045	D	2	11
TRENT	EARNEST		1		7	0	CO	ENGLISH		045	D	1	2
TRENT	EDWARD				41	ENGLAND	CE	ENGLISH	F	043	B	4	5
TRENT	EZRA	M	1		6	0	CE	ENGLISH		043	H	2	45
TRENT	EZRA	M	1		6	ONTARIO	CE	ENGLISH		043	H	2	45
TRENT	GEORGE	S	1		3	0	CO	ENGLISH		045	D	1	2
TRENT	HENRY				45	ENGLAND	CE	ENGLISH	F	043	A	6	6
TRENT	JAMES		1		37	ENGLAND	CE	ENGLISH		043	H	2	15
TRENT	JOSEPH		1		23	0	CE	ENGLISH		043	H	2	15
TRENT	MARY		1	1	72	ENGLAND	CE	ENGLISH		043	H	2	15
TRENT	MARY			1	72	ENGLAND	CE	ENGLISH	FARMER	043	H	2	15
TREUR	THOMAS				28	0	CP	IRISH	BLACKSMITH	044	B	1	11
TREW	ARCHIBALD				29	0	CE	ENGLISH	CLERGYMAN	045	B	2	16
TREW	GEORGE		2		2	0	PS			044	B	1	D
TREWSDALE	JOHN		1		62	IRELAND	PS	IRISH	TAILOR	045	B	1	7
TRIBLE	WILLIAM				28	ENGLISH	WM	ENGLISH	TEAMSTER	044	C	3	45
TRIMBLE	JAMES				32	IRELAND	CE	IRISH	TEAMSTER	045	B	1	50
TRIMMER	ROBERT				59	ENGLAND	WM	ENGLISH	FARMER	043	B	3	56
TRIPP	JOSHUA				40	0	CX	GERMAN	CARPENTER	045	C	2	20
TRISSEL	WILLIAM				27	NFLD	CE	IRISH	LAB	044	B	6	29
TRISTIAN	RICHARD				36	ENGLAND	PM	ENGLISH	F	043	A	6	31
TRIVETT	TIMOTHY				45	ENGLAND	CE	ENGLISH	LAB	043	E	2	45
TROTT	JOB				61	ENGLAND	WM	ENGLISH	MASON	045	D	1	8
TROTT	MARY		2	1	60	IRELAND	WM			045	D	1	D
TROYER	BARBARY		1	1	19	0	LU	GER		044	B	1	48
TROYER	CHRISTIAN				73	0	MN	GER	RETIRED	044	B	1	24
TROYER	DAVID		2		47	0	MN		SAWYER	044	B	3	D
TROYER	EVA			1	58	0	MN	GER	F	044	B	1	28
TROYER	JACOB				42	0	WM	GER	F	044	B	1	24
TROYER	SAMUEL				33	0	EM	GER	F	044	B	1	23
TROYER	WILLIAM				42	0	EM	GERMAN	BLACKSMITH	044	C	1	5
TRUDGEON	JOHN				31	0	WM	ENGLISH	FARMER	045	D	4	15
TRUDGEON	MARY	JANE	1	1	33	0	WM	ENGLISH		045	D	4	34
TRUDGEON	WILLIAM				63	ENGLAND	ME	ENGLISH	SHOEMAKER	045	A	1	46
TRUDGEON	WM		1		27	0	WM	ENGLISH	FARMER	045	D	4	34
TRUM	MATILDA			1	60	ENGLAND	CE	ENGLISH		044	B	5	59
TRUMAN	JOHN				67	ENGLAND	WM	ENGLISH		045	D	3	66
TRUMAN	MARY		1	1	15	0	WM	ENGLISH	ADOPTED DGT	043	C		19
TUCK	WILLIAM				27	ENGLAND	RC	ENGLISH	F	043	C	2	32
TUCKER	BENJAMIN				23	0	PM	ENGLISH	LAB	043	E	2	40
TUCKER	HIRAM				35	0	WM	ENGLISH	LAB	043	E	2	40
TUCKER	JOHN				30	UNITED STATES	WM	ENGLISH	FARM LABOURER	043	E	2	41
TUCKER	JOHN				22	ENGLAND	PM	ENGLISH	F	043	H	1	29
TUCKER	MICHAEL				55	0	CE	ENGLISH	F	043	H	1	23
TUCKER	MOSES				64	UNITED STATES	PS	ENGLISH	LAB	043	E	2	81
TUCKER	RUBEN				35	ENGLAND	BA	ENGLISH	MASON	045	D	4	3
TUDHOPE	JAMES		1		4	0	PM	ENGLISH		045	A	1	101
TUER	JOSEPH				27	0	BA	ENGLISH	MILLER	043	E	2	19
TUER	THOMAS				38	0	CE	ENGLISH	INNKEEPER & FARMER	044	C	4	32
TULLOH	JOHN	G			45	QUE	CE	SCOTCH	CONTRACTOR	045	D	1	6
TULLY	DENNIS		1		7	0	RC	IRISH		043	D		55
TULLY	MICHAEL				40	IRELAND	RC	IRISH	LABORER	043	D		5
TUNES	WM		1		19	0	PM	ENGLISH	LAB	044	B	5	79
TUNKEY	JOSEPH		1		33	ONTARIO	CE	FRENCH	LABORER	043	G	1	1
TUNY	PETER			M	48	IRELAND	RC	IRISH	LAB	043	A	1	43
TUPPER	FLORENCE	E	1	1	18	0	CE	ENGLISH	GOVERNESS	045	D	2	32
TURKINGTON	WILLIAM			M	36	IRELAND	DI	IRISH	TINSMITH	043	A	1	62

SURNAME	NAME1	NAME2	STRAY	SEX	AGE	BIRTHPL	RELIGION	ORIGIN	OCCUP	DIST	SUB_DIST	DIV	PAGE
TURLIN	WILLIAM				47	ENGLAND	CE	ENGLISH	F LAB	043	B	4	6
TURNBULL	MARGARET		1	1	23	O	CP	SCOTCH	SCHOOL TEACHER	045	D	2	6
TURNER	ALFRED		1		20	WALES	CE	IRISH	F	044	A	1	20
TURNER	CAMMACK				47	ENGLAND	CE	ENGLISH	LAB	045	A	3	36
TURNER	CHARLES		1		24	ENGLAND	CE	ENGLISH	TEAMSTER	044	C	3	30
TURNER	CHARLES				53	ENGLAND	WM	ENGLISH	MINISTER	044	C	4	74
TURNER	COREY		2		1	O	CE		LABORER	045	A	1	D
TURNER	DAVID	W			37	ENGLAND	WM	ENGLISH	WAGON MAKER	045	A	1	56
TURNER	GEORGE				26	ENGLAND	CE	ENGLISH	FARMER	045	A	3	17
TURNER	HENRY				44	ENGLAND	CE	ENGLISH	FARM LABOURER	045	C	3	32
TURNER	HUGH				25	O	CE	ENGLISH	CARPENTER	044	C	4	81
TURNER	JAMES				37	ENGLAND	CE	ENGLISH	LABOURER	045	A	1	70
TURNER	MARYANNE		1	1	12	O	CE	ENGLISH		044	C	4	72
TURNER	PROSER				54	ENGLAND	CE	ENGLISH	LAB	044	B	5	47
TURNER	ROBERT				55	ENGLAND	CE	ENGLISH	LAB	045	A	2	37
TURNER	ROBERT	J			75	ENGLAND	CE	ENGLISH	BARRISTER	044	C	4	73
TURNER	SAMUEL				50	ENGLAND	CE	ENGLISH	GARDNER	044	C	4	78
TURNER	SARAH			1	41	IRELAND	CE	IRISH		043	C		49
TURNER	SOLOMAN				39	ENGLAND	CE	ENGLISH	FARMER	045	A	3	16
TURNER	WALTER				41	ENG	EP	ENG	SAWYER	044	B	3	49
TURNER	WILLIAM				41	ENGLAND	NC	ENGLISH	CARPENTER	043	E	1	51
TURNER	WILLIAM				36	IRELAND	WM	IRISH	SHOEMAKER	043	F		10
TURNER	WILLIAM				46	ENGLAND	CE	ENGLISH	SHOE MAKER	045	B	1	35
TUSCAN	WILLIAM		1		22	ENG	EM	ENG	FARM LAB	044	B	1	47
TUSKIN	JOSEPH		1		8	O	RC	IRISH		045	A	1	99
TUSTIN	GEORGE				26	ENG	PM	ENG	LAB	044	B	1	28
TWADDLE	ROBT				45	IRELAND	CE	IRISH	LAB	044	B	5	68
TWEEDIE	JAMES				39	SCOTLAND	CP	SCOTCH	LAB	045	C	4	8
TYE	ANNA		1	1	40	IRELAND	RC	IRISH	SERVANT	045	B	2	31
TYLER	SILVANUS				27	ENGLAND	CE	ENGLISH	HORTICULTURIST	043	G	1	56
TYNOTT	NICHOLLES				24	O	RC	IRISH	FARMER	045	D	2	34
TYNOTT	NICHOLLS				50	IRELAND	RC	IRELAND	FARMER	045	D	2	23
TYRRELL	WILLIAM				54	IRELAND	WM	IRISH	BUILDER	044	C	3	20
TYRWHITT	RICHARD				24	O	CE	ENGLISH	FARMER	045	D	2	33
TYSON	THOS	W			59	U STATES	UV	GERMAN	MILLER	043	A	4	5
TYYRELL	THOMAS		1		18	ENGLAND	CP	ENGLAND	FARM LABORER	045	D	2	1
UMPHREY	MICHAEL				27	O	WM	GERMAN	LUMBER MERCHANT	043	H	1	28
UNDERWOOD	ARCHIBALD				26	O	PM	ENGLISH	F	045	C	3	53
UNDERWOOD	ARCHIBALD				74	ENGLAND	CE	ENGLISH	F	045	C	3	37
UNDERWOOD	FRANCIS				38	ENGLAND	CE	ENGLISH	F	045	C	3	13
UNWIN	EDWD				25	IRELAND	WM	ENGLISH	CARPENTER	044	B	5	39
URMY	ERETUS				40	O	EM	GERMAN	FARMER	045	D	6	1
URQUHART	ALEXANDER				33	O	WM	SCOTCH	CARPENTER	043	H	1	18
URQUHART	DAVID				34	SCOTLAND	EM	SCOTCH	ENGINEER	043	D		57
URQUHART	HECTOR				59	SCOTLAND	PS	SCOTCH	WHEELWRIGHT	043	B	3	64
URQUHART	JOHN		1		27	QUEBEC	CO	SCOTCH	WHEEL WRIGHT	043	B	3	54
USHER	ELIZABETH		1	1	17	O	NC	IRISH		043	A	4	49
USHER	JOHN		1		12	O	FK	IRISH		043	A	3	49
USHER	JOHN				28	ENGLAND	WM	ENGLISH	LAB	043	H	1	28
USHER	JOHN				61	ENGLAND	CE	ENGLISH	LABORER	045	D	1	28
USHER	THOMAS		1		14	O	WM	ENGLISH	F LAB	044	A	3	10
USHER	THOMAS				46	ENGLAND	WM	ENGLISH	LAB	044	A	3	48
USHER	WILLIAM		1		15	O	WM	IRISH		043	A	4	26
USHER	WILLIAM				45	ENGLAND	CE	ENGLISH	F	044	A	3	13
USHERWOOD	JOHN				46	ENGLAND	PM	ENGLISH	F	043	B	1	22
USHERWOOD	WILLIAM		1		18	O	PM	ENG	SERVANT	044	B	3	8
VACHER	FREDRICK				41	ENGLAND	CE	ENGLISH	COL BRITISH ARMY	043	E	1	11
VACY	MARIA		1	1	9	ONTARIO	CE	ENGLISH		043	G	1	9
VACY	SARAH		1	1	35	ENGLAND	CE	ENGLISH		043	G	1	9
VAGUE	THOMAS		1		51	ENGLAND	CE	ENGLISH	FARMER	045	D	4	15
VALERE	WM	HENRY			48	O	CE	IRISH	COOPER	045	A	4	8
VALES	THOMAS				28	IRELAND	RC	IRISH	LABORER	043	D		56
VALIANT	GEORGE				35	ENGLAND	CE	ENGLISH	PAINTER	044	C	4	91
VALIE	JOHN				42	O	WM	GERMAN	HOTEL KEEPER	045	D	2	4
VAN EVRY	PETER				78	O	CE	GERMAN	F	044	A	1	29
VAN NOSTRAND	JOHN		2		67	O	CE		F	045	A	3	D
VAN NOSTRAND	JOSEPH				31	O	CE	GERMANY	FARMER	045	A	3	6
VAN NOSTRAND	MARY			1	67	O	CE	GERMANY	FARMER	045	A	3	6
VAN SOUTHARD	WILLIAM				59	U STATES	CN	SCOTCH	CARPENTER	043	D		23
VAN ZANDT	GARRETT				31	O	CO	GERMAN SCOTCH	TINSMITH	045	D	5	21
VANALLEN	JAMES				45	U STATES	QU	DUTCH	F S MILLER	043	A	6	36
VANDEBURGH	JOHN				40	O	PS	DUTCH	CARPENTER	043	A	6	63
VANDER BURG	PHOEBE			1	60	O	CP	ENGLISH	FARMER	045	D	2	2
VANDERBURG	ELIZA		1	1	72	IRELAND	RC	IRISH		043	A	2	54
VANDERBURG	ISAAC				53	ONTARIO	WM	DUTCH	SHINGLE MAKER	043	G	2	49
VANDERBURGH	PETER				52	O	PS	GER	F	044	B	2	58
VANDERBURGH	STEPHEN			M	47	O	PS	DUTCH	F	043	A	2	57
VANDERS'T	CLEMENT				23	US	WM	FRENCH	HATTER	043	A	3	3
VANDERWATERS	SAMUEL				40	O	WM	GERMAN	F	043	E	3	9
VANHORN	FREDRICK				69	O	EM	GERMAN	GENTLEMAN	045	D	1	36
VANHORN	GEORGE				41	O	EM	GERMAN	FARMER	045	D	1	36
VANHORN	ISAAC			M	62	US	NR	GERMANY	F	043	A	5	44
VANHORN	JOHN				29	O	WM	GERMAN	LAB	043	E	3	59
VANHORN	ROBERT				36	O	EM	ENGLISH	MAIL CARRIER	045	D	1	11
VANHORN	WILLIAM				24	O	WM	GERMAN	FARMER	045	D	1	37
VANNORMAN	DAVID				54	ONTARIO	CN	DUTCH	FARMER	043	G	1	27
VANNORMAN	RICHARD				26	O	CN	DUTCH	MERCHANT	043	E	1	52
VANOSTRAND	CORNELIUS				74	US	CE	GERMAN	F RETIRED	043	B	2	44
VANOSTSRAND	JOHN				47	O	CE	GERMAN	F	043	B	2	44
VANSANT	ALMER				57	CANADA	WM	GERMAN	FARMER	045	D	6	61
VANSANT	LUDWICK				28	CANADA	WM	GERMAN	FARMER	045	D	6	61
VANSANT	MARY		1	1	32	O	EM	GERMAN		045	D	1	36
VANSICKLE	ISAAC		1		15	O	WM	GERMAN	SERVANT	044	B	6	14
VANSLYKE	JAMES		1		22	ONTARIO	WM	GERMAN	LABORER	043	G	1	31
VANZANT	ALBEY				37	O	DI	GERMAN	CARPENTER	043	B	3	73
VARDON	MARY		1	1	31	O	WM	ENGLISH		045	D	3	26
VARDON	WILLIAM		1		9	O	WM	ENGLISH		045	D	3	27
VAREANT	VALENTINE		1		56	GER	LU	GER	LAB	044	B	3	33
VARY	RICHARD				81	ENGLAND	WM	ENGLISH	LABOURER	045	D	5	19
VAUGHAN	THOMAS				56	ENGLAND	CE	ENGLISH	GARDNER	044	C	4	80
VEITCH	JOHN				19	O	CE	SCOTCH	LAB	045	A	3	26
VELIE	ANNIE		1	1	62	US	WM			044	B	2	15
VERNON	CHARLES		1		23	ENGLAND	WM	ENGLISH	BLACKSMITH	045	D	5	10
VERNON	HANNAH		1	1	31	SCOTLAND	WM	ENGLISH	HOUSEKEEPER	044	C	2	31
VERNON	LOUISA		1	1	01	ONT	WM	ENGLISH		044	C	2	31
VERNON	MARGARET		1	1	30	IRELAND	WM	IRISH		045	D	5	10

SURNAME	NAME1	NAME2	STRAY	SEX	AGE	BIRTHPL	RELIGION	ORIGIN	OCCUP	DIST	SUB_DIST	DIV	PAGE
VERNON	MOSES				48	0	QU	ENGLISH	F	043	B	4	36
VERNON	NATHANIEL				80	NS	QU	ENGLISH	F	043	B	4	36
VICARS	JOHNSTONE				60	SCOTLAND	CE	SCOTCH	CLERGYMAN	043	G	1	8
VICKERMAN	DAN				32	ENGLAND	CE	ENGLISH	CARDER	044	C	3	9
VICKERS	WILLIAM		1		63	ENGLAND	WM	ENGLISH		045	D	3	46
VILLIER	WILLIAM				22	0	PS	FRENCH	LAB	044	B	2	71
VINCENT	ANN		1		45	0	PM	GERMAN		043	B	3	12
VINCENT	GEORGE	M			39	ENGLAND	RC	ENGLISH	GARDENER	045	A	1	42
VINE	GEORGE	SEN			50	ENGLAND	ME	ENGLISH	F	045	A	4	23
VINE	WILLIAM				53	ENGLAND	CE	ENGLISH	BUTCHER	045	A	1	75
VIRGO	JAMES				60	ENGLAND	CE	ENGLISH	GARDENER	045	A	1	44
VONER	HARRY				40	IRELAND	RC	IRISH		045	B	2	13
VOULLS	EDWARD				35	ENGLAND	CE	ENGLISH	LABORER	045	D	2	48
VRANDENBURGH	ICHABOD				55	USA	CP	GERMAN	F	045	C	4	31
WACH	WILLIAM				30	0	NC	IRISH	LAB	043	C		49
WADE	FANNY		1	1	17	0	WM	SCOTTISH	SERVANT	044	C	1	36
WADE	JOHN			M	40	ENGLAND	PS	ENGLISH	LAB	043	A	2	10
WADSWORTH	T	PAGE			32	0	CE	ENGLISH	MILLER	044	A	3	24
WADSWORTH	TOM				36	0	CE	ENGLISH	GENTLEMAN	044	C	3	46
WADSWORTH	WILLIAM	R			68	ENGLAND	CE	ENGLISH	MILLER	044	A	3	56
WADWORTH	JAMES				34	IRELAND	CE	IRISH	LAB	045	B	2	4
WAGG	JOHN				55	ENGLAND	PM	ENGLISH	F	043	E	3	36
WAGG	WILLIAM				54	ENGLAND	CE	ENGLISH	FARMER	045	D	5	71
WAGGONER	FRANCIS		1		23	0	MN	FRENCH	LABOURER	045	D	6	4
WAGGONER	WILLIAM				25	IRELAND	CE	IRISH	F	043	H	1	10
WAGGOT	ELIZA		1	F	60	IRELAND	PS	IRISH		043	A	2	13
WAGNER	ELIZABETH		1	1	22	CANADIAN	MN	GERMAN		045	D	6	23
WAGNER	MICHAEL			M	43	0	EM	GERMAN	LAB	043	A	1	60
WAGSTAFF	ROBERT		1		24	ENGLAND	CE	ENGLISH	BRICKMAKER	045	A	1	101
WAGSTAFF	WILLIAM				30	0	WM	ENGLISH	BRICKMAKER	045	A	1	27
WAITS	ALFRED				26	ENGLAND	CE	ENGLISH	LABORER	045	D	2	53
WAITS	GLINTON				30	ENGLAND	CE	ENGLISH	LABORER	045	D	2	53
WAITS	ROBERT				37	ENGLAND	CE	ENGLISH	F LAB	044	A	1	5
WAKEFIELD	BROOKS				78	UNITED STATES	CN	ENGLISH	F	043	E	1	7
WAKEFIELD	JOHN				42	ENG	PS	ENG	F	045	C	1	72
WAKEFIELD	WILLIAM		2			0	CP			045	C	1	D
WALACE	NORMAN				36	0	EM	GERMAN	LAB	043	H	2	4
WALDEN	JOSEPH				40	GERMANY	PM	GERMAN	LABORER	045	D	2	65
WALDON	JOSHUA				36	ENGLAND	CE	ENGLISH	F	043	E	1	13
WALES	HENRY				47	ENGLAND	CO	ENGLISH	CARRIAGE MAKER	045	D	5	3
WALES	JAMES				21	0	CO	ENGLISH	CARRIAGE PAINTER	045	D	5	3
WALES	JOHN		2	M	60	ENGLAND	CE		F	043	A	1	D
WALES	JOSEPH				34	0	NR	ENGLISH	CARRIAGE MAKER	045	D	5	4
WALKER	ANDREW				43	0	CP	SCOTCH	CARPENTER	045	C	3	10
WALKER	DAVID				34	0	CP	IRISH	LAB	045	A	3	4
WALKER	ELLEN		1	1	71	0	WM	ENGLISH		044	B	6	53
WALKER	ELLEN			1	41	0	CP	SCOTCH		045	C	3	10
WALKER	ESTHAR		1	1	65	ENGLAND	WM	ENGLISH		045	B	1	17
WALKER	FRANCIS				51	ENGLAND	WM	ENGLISH	BLACKSMITH	045	D	4	35
WALKER	GEORGE				44	ENGLAND	PM	ENGLISH	F	043	B	4	4
WALKER	GEORGE				50	ENGLAND	WM	ENGLISH	F	043	E	3	26
WALKER	GEORGIE				30	SCOTLAND	RP	SCOTCH	LAB	044	C	3	15
WALKER	HENRY				34	WEST INDIES	CE	IRISH	FARMER	045	D	1	23
WALKER	HUGH				45	ENGLAND	WM	ENGLISH	F	043	B	2	37
WALKER	JAMES		1		25	SCOTLAND	CS	SCOTCH	F LAB	044	A	1	8
WALKER	JAMES				29	ENGLAND	PM	ENGLISH	PAPER MAKER	045	A	1	63
WALKER	JAMES				37	SCOTLAND	CP	SCOTCH	F	045	C	3	55
WALKER	JAMES				51	IRELAND	CP	IRISH	FARMER	045	D	2	42
WALKER	JAMES	F	1		29	0	CE	ENGLISH	COM TRAVELLER	044	C	4	7
WALKER	JAMES	W	2			0	CE			044	C	4	D
WALKER	JANE		1	1	22	0	WM	IRISH	MILINER & DRESS MAKE	045	B	1	34
WALKER	JOHN		1		21	0	CE	ENGLISH	LAB	043	E	2	36
WALKER	JOHN				32	ENGLAND	CE	ENGLISH	TANNER	043	F		10
WALKER	JOHN				52	IRELAND	WM	IRISH	F	044	B	6	48
WALKER	JOHN				31	0	PM	ENGLISH	WAGGON MAKER	045	B	2	23
WALKER	JOSEPH				51	0	BA	SCOTCH	FARMER	043	B	3	14
WALKER	JOSEPH				50	IRE	CS	IRE	STONEMASON	044	B	4	5
WALKER	MARGERY		1	1	30	IRELAND	CE	IRISH	SERVANT	045	A	1	6
WALKER	MARY	E	1	1	25	0	CE	ENGLISH		044	C	4	7
WALKER	MARY	W	1	1	2	0	CE	ENGLISH		044	C	4	7
WALKER	MATILDA		1	1	18	0	WM	IRISH		045	B	1	34
WALKER	RICHARD				29	ENGLAND	CE	ENGLISH	F LAB	044	A	2	1
WALKER	ROBERT				36	0	WM	ENGLISH	BLACKSMITH	045	B	2	35
WALKER	ROBERT		2		2	0	PS			045	D	6	D
WALKER	SAMUEL				43	0	CE	IRISH	FARMER	043	A	3	4
WALKER	SAMUEL				31	SCOTLAND	PS	SCOTCH	LABOURER	045	D	6	15
WALKER	SARAH	MARIA	2		6	0	WM			045	B	1	D
WALKER	STEWART				47	0	WM	IRISH	F	043	B	4	3
WALKER	THOMAS				27	0	CN	ENGLISH	FARM LABOURER	043	B	3	15
WALKER	THOMAS				40	0	CP	SCOTCH	F	045	C	3	17
WALKER	THOMAS				37	0	WM	SCOTCH	FARMER	045	D	3	35
WALKER	THOMAS				27	0	CN	SCOTCH	LABOURER	045	D	4	47
WALKER	WALTER				33	0	WM	ENGLISH	CARPENTER	045	B	1	62
WALKER	WALTER	F	2		1	0	WM			045	B	1	D
WALKER	WILLIAM				60	IRELAND	CP	IRISH	LABOURER	045	D	4	52
WALKER	WILLIAM		1		32	0	CE	ENGLISH	BLACKSMITH	045	D	5	20
WALKER	WILLIAM		1		21	ENGLAND	NG	ENGLISH		045	D	6	64
WALKER	WILLIAM		2			0	PS			045	D	6	D
WALKER	WM		1		50	ENGLAND	PM	ENGLISH	LAB	044	B	5	36
WALKINGTON	JOHN			M	50	ENGLAND	WM	ENGLISH	F	043	A	2	43
WALKINSHAW	RICHARD				34	SCOTLAND	UP	SCOTCH	TEAMSTER	045	D	1	26
WALL	JAMES				50	IRELAND	WM	IRISH	LABOURER	044	C	3	65
WALL	LEWIS		1		50	GERMANY	RC	GERMAN	FARMER	045	A	1	78
WALL	TERESA		1	1	48	GERMANY	RC	GERMAN		045	A	1	78
WALLACE	ALEX				40	SCOTLAND	PS	SCOTTISH	F	044	C	1	24
WALLACE	ALEX	R			67	IRELAND	WM	IRISH	GENTLEMAN	043	C		1
WALLACE	CHARLES				54	IRELAND	WM	IRISH	F	044	B	5	53
WALLACE	CLARKE				26	0	CE	IRISH	MERCHT	044	B	5	47
WALLACE	ELIZABETH			1	37	SCOTLAND	CP	SCOTCH	SEAMSTRESS	045	C	3	1
WALLACE	ELLEN		1	1	50	IRELAND	RC	IRISH		043	B	5	1
WALLACE	GEO				62	IRELAND	WM	IRISH	F	044	B	5	60
WALLACE	GEORGE		1		38	ENGLAND	CE	ENGLISH	CLERK	043	D		69
WALLACE	GEORGE				31	ONTARIO	PS	SCOTCH	FARMER	043	G	2	15
WALLACE	IRWIN				64	IRELAND	CE	SCOTCH	LAB	045	A	1	6
WALLACE	JAMES				41	ENGLAND	PM	ENGLISH	SAWYER	043	H	1	19
WALLACE	JAMES				38	0	ZZ	IRISH	CARPENTER	045	A	1	18

SURNAME	NAME1	NAME2	STRAY	SEX	AGE	BIRTHPL	RELIGION	ORIGIN	OCCUP	DIST	SUB_DIST	DIV	PAGE
WALLACE	JANE		1	1	35	SCOTLAND	CP	SCOTCH	SEAMSTRESS	045	C	3	1
WALLACE	JESSIE		1	1	33	SCOTLAND	CP	SCOTCH	SEAMSTRESS	045	C	3	1
WALLACE	JOHN				36	IRELAND	RC	IRISH	TEAMSTER	043	B	5	18
WALLACE	JOHN				68	SCOTLAND	WM	SCOTCH	SHOEMAKER	043	E	1	49
WALLACE	JONATHON				27	0	WM	IRISH	F	043	B	4	21
WALLACE	MARY			1	74	SCOT	CS	SCOT		044	B	4	31
WALLACE	NATHL				60	IRELAND	CE	IRISH	INN KEEPER	044	B	5	30
WALLACE	NORMAN				36	ONTARIO	EM	GERMAN	LABOURER	043	H	2	4
WALLACE	ROBERT		1		37	SCOTLAND	CP	SCOTCH	LAB	045	C	2	39
WALLACE	ROBT	JOHN	1		13	0	CS	SCOTCH	SERVANT	045	D	5	61
WALLACE	STEPHEN				52	IRELAND	WM	IRISH	F	043	B	1	39
WALLACE	SYLVESTER		1		25	UNITED STATES	PM	SCOTCH	LAB	043	B	2	24
WALLACE	THOMAS			M	25	ENGLAND	WM	ENGLISH	FARMER	043	A	1	8
WALLACE	WM		1		22	IRELAND	CE	IRISH	PAINTER	044	B	5	30
WALLACE	WM				40	SCOTLAND	PS	SCOTTISH	FARMER	044	C	1	21
WALLACE	WM	H			23	0	WM	SCOTCH	F	044	A	1	19
WALLIS	JAMES				64	ENGLAND	WM	ENGLISH	BLACKSMITH	045	B	2	3
WALLIS	JOS	WILLIAM			25	0	CO	ENGLISH	F	044	A	3	21
WALLIS	JOSEPH	T W			50	0	CO	ENGLISH	F	044	A	3	20
WALLIS	PATRICK				37	IRELAND	RC	IRELAND	TEAMSTER	043	D		74
WALLIS	RICHARD	JUN			58	SCOTLAND	CP	SCOTCH	F	045	A	4	25
WALLIS	ROBERT				68	ENGLAND	WM	ENGLISH	LAB	043	D		26
WALLIS	WILLIAM				59	ENGLAND	RC	ENGLISH	SADDLER & TANNER	043	D		19
WALLIS	WILLIAM	A			46	0	CO	ENGLISH	F	044	A	3	36
WALLISS	ESTER			1	53	0	CN	ENGLISH		043	B	4	29
WALLS	CHRISTIANA			1	52	SCOTLAND	CP	SCOTCH		045	C	2	49
WALLS	DANIEL	V			42	ENGLAND	WM	ENGLISH	LAB	045	A	4	29
WALLS	JOHN				21	0	CP	SCOTCH	LAB	045	C	2	49
WALLS	JOSEPH				46	ENG	EM	ENG	CARPENTER	044	B	4	21
WALLS	THOMAS		1		16	0	CS	SCOTCH	F LAB	043	A	3	26
WALMSLEY	JAMES				41	0	PM	ENGLISH	FARMER	045	A	2	14
WALPOOL	JOHN				55	IRELAND	RC	IRISH	LABOURER	045	A	1	47
WALSH	BRIDGET			1	60	IRELAND	RC	IRISH		044	C	2	23
WALSH	ELIZA			1	32	0	CE	IRISH		043	C		56
WALSH	HONORA		1	1	52	IRELAND	RC	IRISH		043	D		47
WALSH	JAMES				60	IRELAND	RC	IRISH	LAB	044	B	5	32
WALSH	JOHN				51	IRELAND	RC	IRISH	SHOEMAKER	045	C	2	11
WALSH	MICHAEL				60	IRELAND	RC	IRISH	LABOURER	045	A	1	100
WALSH	PATRICK				39	IRELAND	RC	IRISH	DEALER	044	C	4	19
WALSH	ROBERT				62	IRELAND	RC	IRISH	P L SURVEYOR	043	A	4	1
WALSH	SOUSIN		2	1	26	0	RC		DRESSMAKER	043	A	4	D
WALSH	WALTER				58	IRELAND	RC	IRISH	LAB	044	C	4	53
WALTON	ADAM				52	ENG	PM	ENG	F	045	C	1	69
WALTON	ADAM		2		27	0	PM		LAB	045	C	3	D
WALTON	ELIZABETH		1	1	20	0	PM	IRISH		045	C	3	39
WALTON	GEORGE		2			0	PM			045	C	4	D
WALTON	GUY		2		47	0	PM		F	045	C	1	D
WALTON	GUY				30	0	PS	ENGLISH	F	045	C	3	50
WALTON	ISABELLA		1	1	26	0	PM	ENGLISH	SERVANT	045	C	4	22
WALTON	J	M			25	0	WM	ENGLISH	CARRIAGE BUILDER	045	C	4	46
WALTON	JACOB			M	45	0	CN	WELSH	MERCHANT	043	A	5	13
WALTON	JOHN				33	0	PM	ENGLISH	F	045	C	3	7
WALTON	JOHN				35	0	PM	ENGLISH	F	045	C	4	22
WALTON	JOHN	SENIOR			72	ENG	WM	IRE	F	045	C	1	60
WALTON	JOSEPH				67	ENG	WM	ENG	F	045	C	1	41
WALTON	MARY		1	1	23	IRELAND	RC	IRISH	TAILORESS	045	A	1	100
WALTON	MARY			1	46	0	PM	ENG		045	C	1	30
WALTON	MARY	ANN	1	1	30	IRELAND	RC	IRISH	SERVANT	044	A	2	45
WALTON	MARY	JANE	1	1	6	0	CP	IRISH		045	C	3	39
WALTON	MATHEW				57	ENG	PM	ENG	F	045	C	1	50
WALTON	THOMAS				43	0	PM	ENGLISH	F	045	C	4	39
WALTON	WALLACE				23	0	PM	ENG	F	045	C	1	42
WALTON	WILLIAM	M			39	0	QU	SCOTCH	BAKER	043	A	4	20
WALTON	WM	W			36	0	PM	ENG	F	045	C	1	73
WALZ	JOSEPH				36	GER	RC	GER	TANNER	044	B	2	47
WAMSLEY	JOSEPH				58	ENGLAND	WM	ENGLISH	POTTER	045	A	3	22
WANZER	FRANCIS				40	US	WM	AFRICAN	GARDNER	044	C	4	92
WARD	ALEXANDER		1		63	IRELAND	WM	IRISH		044	C	2	8
WARD	ANDREW		1		68	IRELAND	WM	IRISH	F	044	A	1	12
WARD	EDWARD				24	ENGLAND	PM	ENGLISH	TEACHER	043	B	4	14
WARD	GEORGE				43	0	WM	IRISH	F	044	C	2	8
WARD	HENRY				49	ENGLAND	WM	ENGLISH	F LAB	043	B	4	29
WARD	HENRY		1		26	ENG	EM	ENG	SCHOOL TEACHER	044	B	1	22
WARD	JAMES				54	IRELAND	WM	IRISH	TAVERN KEEPER	043	C		46
WARD	JAMES				37	SCOTLAND	EM	SCOTCH	F	044	A	1	8
WARD	JANE		1	1	70	ENGLAND	CP	ENGLISH		045	D	6	6
WARD	JOHN				41	ENGLAND	CE	ENGLISH	CARPENTER	043	G	1	10
WARD	JOHN				36	0	WM	IRISH	F	044	A	2	18
WARD	MARTHA		1	1	65	ENGLAND	WM	ENGLISH		044	A	1	12
WARD	THOMAS				37	0	CE	ENGLISH	SHOEMAKER	044	A	3	39
WARD	WILLIAM				71	SCOTLAND	RC	IRISH	F	044	A	3	46
WARD	WILLIAM	JR			21	0	RC	IRISH	F	044	A	3	47
WARDEL	THOMAS				43	ONTARIO	PR	ENGLISH	FARMER	043	G	2	3
WARDELL	SUSAN			1	60	0	PM	ENGLISH		043	E	1	23
WARDLAW	PETER				48	SCOTLAND	CP	SCOTCH	F	044	A	3	2
WARDLE	PAUL			M	38	0	CE	ENGLAND	F	043	A	5	16
WARDLOW	ALEXANDER				40	SCOTCH	RP	SCOTCH	FARMER	044	C	3	55
WARDLOW	JAMES				54	SCOTLAND	WM	SCOTCH	FARMER	044	C	3	69
WARE	CHARLES				46	ENGLAND	CE	ENGLISH	MERCHANT	044	A	2	46
WAREN	HENRY				29	ENGLAND	CE	ENGLISH	DYER	045	D	4	41
WARNER	HENRY				36	ENGLAND	CO	ENGLISH	CABINET MAKER	043	D		62
WARNER	JOHN				37	ENGLAND	CO	ENGLISH	CABINET MAKER	043	D		65
WARNER	THOMAS				77	ENGLAND	CO	ENGLISH	CABINET MAKER	043	D		23
WARNER	TUTTLE				51	0	PS	GERMAN	SAWER	043	E	3	39
WARREN	STEPHEN				24	0	CE	ENGLISH	LAB	043	F		5
WARREN	WILLIAM			M	39	U STATES	PM	ENGLISH	COOPER	043	A	2	24
WARREN	WILLIAM				55	0	WM	ENGLISH	FARMER	045	D	2	6
WARRINER	JOHN				32	ONTARIO	EM	SCOTCH	CARPENTER	043	G	1	56
WARRINER	WILLIAM				64	UNITED STATES	CN	SCOTCH	FARMER	043	G	1	53
WARTFIELD	MATHEW				33	ENGLAND	WM	ENGLISH	ENGINE DRIVER	044	C	3	26
WARTFIELD	WILLIAM				69	ENGLAND	CE	ENGLISH	GENTLEMAN	044	C	3	33
WASHINGTON	GEORGE		1		57	US	CE	ENGLISH	TEAMSTER	045	A	1	3
WASHINGTON	JOHN				33	US	WM	AFRICAN	LABORER	045	D	2	39
WASHINGTON	WILLIAM		2		2	0	WM			045	D	2	D
WASHINGTON	WILLIAM				44	ENGLAND	CE	ENGLISH	F	044	C	4	17
WASLEY	HENRY				27	0	QU	ENGLISH	F	043	B	4	35

SURNAME	NAME1	NAME2	STRAY	SEX	AGE	BIRTHPL	RELIGION	ORIGIN	OCCUP	DIST	SUB_DIST	DIV	PAGE
WASLEY	JOHN				50	0	QU	ENGLISH	THRASHER AND LAB	043	B	4	32
WASLEY	JOSEPH				31	0	CP	ENGLISH	F	043	B	4	35
WASLEY	MICHAEL				35	0	PS	ENGLISH	F	043	E	1	45
WASS	JOHN				25	ENGLAND	WM	ENGLISH	FARMER	043	G	2	44
WASS	NOAH				49	ENGLAND	WM	ENGLISH	FARMER	043	G	2	47
WATERFIELD	JOHN			M	32	ENGLAND	BA	ENGLISH	SCHOOL TEACHER	043	A	2	46
WATERHOUSE	GEORGE		1		20	ENGLAND	CP	ENGLISH	POTTER	044	C	2	19
WATERS	GEORGE				40	ENGLAND	CE	ENGLISH	SHOEMAKER	043	E	1	2
WATES	WILLSON			M	30	ENGLAND	CE	ENGLISH	FARMER	043	A	1	11
WATKINS	CHAS				78	ENG	CE	ENG	LAB	045	C	1	34
WATKINS	JAS		1		16	0	PM	IRISH		044	B	5	68
WATMAN	ROBERT		1		24	ENGLAND	CE	ENGLISH	LAB	044	B	6	6
WATSON	ANDREW	RIDDELL			29	ENGLAND	CE	ENGLISH	WATCH MAKER	043	D		14
WATSON	ANN		1	1	40	ENGLAND	CE	ENGLISH		043	H	2	45
WATSON	ANN		1	1	40	ENGLAND	CE	ENGLISH		043	H	2	45
WATSON	ANN		1		48	ENGLAND	PB	ENGLISH		045	B	1	47
WATSON	ARTHUR				49	IRELAND	CE	IRISH	COOPER	044	A	3	20
WATSON	CHARLES				30	0	CE	ENGLISH	FARMER	045	A	3	39
WATSON	CHARLES				55	ENGLAND	CE	ENGLISH	F	044	C	1	56
WATSON	CHAS				38	ENGLAND	CE	ENGLISH	COOPER	043	E	2	25
WATSON	CLARISSA		1	F	52	0	QU	ENGLAND		043	A	5	46
WATSON	DANIEL				30	0	CP	SCOT	THRESHER	044	B	1	64
WATSON	DAVID				30	ENGLAND	CE	ENGLISH	MILLER	043	H	2	1
WATSON	ELIZABETH			F	58	US	WM	IRELAND		043	A	5	15
WATSON	ELIZABETH		1	1	21	ENGLAND	CE	ENGLISH		044	C	2	21
WATSON	EMILY		1	1	21	0	ME	IRE		044	B	2	37
WATSON	F	DAVID			30	ENGLAND	CE	ENGLISH	MILLER	043	H	2	1
WATSON	FANNY		1	1	12	0	WM	ENGLISH		045	D	2	68
WATSON	FRANCIS				53	IRELAND	CP	IRISH	F	044	C	2	15
WATSON	GEORGE			M	35	ENGLAND	NC	ENGLAND	F	043	A	5	37
WATSON	GEORGE				42	ENGLAND	EM	ENGLISH	BRICKMAKER	043	E	2	51
WATSON	GEORGE		1		18	CANADA	MN	GERMAN		045	D	6	55
WATSON	HARVEY		1		3	0	CN	ENGLISH		043	A	6	45
WATSON	HENRY		1		70	ENGLAND	CE	ENGLISH	F	044	B	6	35
WATSON	HERBERT				40	ENGLAND	PM	ENGLISH	F	043	A	3	14
WATSON	HUGH				51	IRE	EM	IRISH	SHOEMAKER	044	B	1	25
WATSON	INFANT		2			0	NG		LAB	044	B	4	D
WATSON	JAMES				59	ENGLAND	CE	IRISH	LAB	043	C		53
WATSON	JAMES				42	SCOT	PS	SCOT	F	044	B	2	74
WATSON	JAMES		1		25	0	VM	ENG	LAB	044	B	3	25
WATSON	JAMES				65	IRE	CP	IR	F	044	B	4	51
WATSON	JAMES				45	SCOTLAND	BA	SCOTCH	DRUGGIST	045	B	2	33
WATSON	JAMES				58	IRELAND	CP	IRISH	STORE KEEPER	044	C	2	15
WATSON	JANE			1	65	SCOTLAND	CP	SCOTCH		044	B	6	41
WATSON	JOHN				50	SCOTLAND	CP	SCOTCH	F	043	A	3	52
WATSON	JOHN				35	ENGLAND	PM	ENGLISH	F	043	A	3	60
WATSON	JOHN				29	0	QU	ENGLISH	F	043	B	4	47
WATSON	JOHN				57	ENGLAND	CE	ENGLISH	MILLER	043	H	1	22
WATSON	JOHN				31	0	WM	ENG	F	044	B	2	73
WATSON	JOHN				40	SCOT	PS	SCOT	F	044	B	3	14
WATSON	JOHN				30	0	VM	ENG	F	044	B	3	26
WATSON	JOHN		2		69	SCOTLAND	CS			044	B	6	D
WATSON	JOHN				60	ENGLAND	CE	ENGLISH	FARMER	045	A	3	27
WATSON	JOHN				48	0	WM	ENGLISH	F	044	C	1	44
WATSON	JOHN				56	SCOTLAND	CE	SCOTCH	GARDNER	044	C	4	85
WATSON	JOHN	H			34	0	WM	ENGLISH	FARMER	044	C	3	57
WATSON	JOHN	MARSHAL	2		19	ENGLAND	WM			044	C	3	D
WATSON	JOHN	PENN			52	ENGLAND	WM	ENGLISH	FARMER	044	C	3	17
WATSON	JOSEPH			M	35	0	PM	ENGLISH	BLACKSMITH	043	A	2	28
WATSON	JOSEPH				31	0	PM	ENGLISH	F	043	A	3	60
WATSON	JOSEPH				47	0	WM	ENGLISH	F	044	C	2	17
WATSON	LEVI		1		71	U STATES	CN	ENGLISH		043	A	6	45
WATSON	LEVI		1		6	0	CN	ENGLISH		043	A	6	45
WATSON	MARIA		1	1	19	0	WM	AFRICAN		044	C	4	62
WATSON	MARK				35	ENGLAND	CE	ENGLISH	FARMER	045	A	3	31
WATSON	MARY			1	62	U STATES	XC	IRISH		043	A	4	33
WATSON	MARY		1	1	81	ENGLAND	QU	ENGLISH		043	A	6	5
WATSON	MARY		1	1	22	IRELAND	CE	ENGLISH		044	C	2	17
WATSON	MARY	JANE	1	1	34	0	CE	IRISH		044	C	3	68
WATSON	RACHAEL		1	1	5	0	QU	ENGLISH		043	C		45
WATSON	RICHARD		1		24	0	WM	IRISH	FARM LAB	044	C	2	33
WATSON	ROBERT		1		19	0	CO	ENG	LAB	044	B	3	44
WATSON	ROBT				44	ENGLAND	WM	ENGLISH	MILL WRIGHT	044	B	5	26
WATSON	SAMUEL		2	M	25	IRELAND	CE		SCHOOL TEACHER	043	A	1	D
WATSON	SAMUEL				36	ENGLAND	CE	ENGLISH	FARMER	043	G	2	42
WATSON	SAMUEL				42	SCOTLAND	CP	SCOTCH	TINSMITH	045	D	3	20
WATSON	SARAH			1	66	ENG	WM	ENG		044	B	3	33
WATSON	THOMAS				62	ENG	CE	ENG	F	044	B	4	15
WATSON	THOMAS				34	0	CE	ENG	CARPENTER	044	B	4	27
WATSON	THOMAS				34	IRELAND	CP	IRISH	F	045	C	2	30
WATSON	THOMAS				50	ENGLAND	CE	ENGLISH	F	044	C	1	11
WATSON	WILLIAM			M	45	IRELAND	PS	IRISH	CARPENTER	043	A	2	30
WATSON	WILLIAM		1		28	0	CN	ENGLISH	F	043	A	6	45
WATSON	WILLIAM				60	ENG	CE	ENG	LAB	044	B	3	35
WATSON	WILLIAM		1		70	ENGLAND	CE	ENGLISH		045	D	1	2
WATSON	WILLIAM				52	ENGLAND	WM	ENGLISH	SUPT OF SCHOOLS	044	C	3	27
WATSON	WM				56	IRELAND	CE	IRISH	WATCHMAKER	044	B	1	2
WATSON	WM				48	ENGLAND	PM	ENGLISH	F	044	B	5	78
WATSON	WM				40	SCOT	CP	SCOT	F	045	C	1	53
WATT	ALLAN		1		17	SCOTLAND	WM	SCOTTISH	LABOURER	044	C	1	28
WATT	CHAS				42	ENGLAND	CE	ENGLISH	SHOEMAKER	044	B	5	2
WATT	DAVID				44	SCOTLAND	PS	SCOTTISH	F	044	C	1	46
WATT	JOHN				50	SCOTLAND	PS	SCOTCH	BLACKSMITH	044	A	3	25
WATT	JOHN				44	SCOT	PS	SCOT	LAB	044	B	2	3
WATT	JOHN				38	SCOTLAND	CP	SCOTCH	F	044	C	4	22
WATT	LYDIA			1	72	IRELAND	CE	IRISH		044	B	5	34
WATT	ROBERT				39	SCOTLAND	PS	SCOTCH	LAB	045	A	1	65
WATTAM	WILLIAM				40	ENGLAND	CE	ENGLISH	LABOURER	044	C	3	61
WATTERHOUSE	JOHN				48	ENG	CS	ENG	MERCHANT	044	B	4	2
WATTERS	ELLEN			1	58	SCOTLAND	RP	SCOTCH		044	C	3	43
WATTONBERG	PETER				63	0	WM	GERMAN		045	D	3	5
WATTS	CHARLES		1		19	ENGLAND	CE	ENGLISH	LABOURER	045	D	3	67
WATTS	HENRY		1		17	ENGLAND	CE	ENGLISH	LABOURER	045	D	3	67
WATTS	SAMUEL				34	ENGLAND	CE	ENGLISH	F LAB	044	A	2	13
WATTS	SAMUEL		2			0	CE			044	A	2	D
WAUGH	JOHN			M	79	IRELAND	PS	IRISH	F	043	A	1	28

SURNAME	NAME1	NAME2	STRAY	SEX	AGE	BIRTHPL	RELIGION	ORIGIN	OCCUP	DIST	SUB_DIST	DIV	PAGE
WAWE	JOHN		1		29	ENGLAND	CE	ENGLISH	LABOURER	045	D	3	75
WAY	JOHN	JR			26	0	CE	ENGLISH	F	043	H	1	1
WAYLING	HARRIETT			1	44	0	CE	GERMAN		043	E	2	37
WAYLING	JAMES				28	0	CE	ENGLISH	F	043	E	1	44
WAYLING	JAMES				40	IRELAND	RC	IRISH	LAB	043	H	1	1
WAYLING	RICHARD				31	0	NC	ENGLISH	F	043	E	2	14
WAYMOUTH	ANN		1	1	55	IRELAND	CE	IRISH		045	A	1	13
WAYMOUTH	ELLEN		1	1	23	0	CE	IRISH		045	A	1	13
WAYMOUTH	EMMA		1	1	22	0	CE	IRISH		045	A	1	13
WAYMOUTH	MARY		1	1	19	0	CE	IRISH		045	A	1	13
WAYS	THOMAS				50	IRELAND	CE	IRISH	LAB	043	F		20
WEADOW	WILLIAM				34	ENGLAND	CE	ENGLISH	DROVER	043	C		24
WEATHERHEAD	MARY		1	1	20	0	WM	IRISH	SERVANT	045	B	2	12
WEATHERILL	JOHN		1		24	0	PM	ENGLISH	F LAB	044	A	3	54
WEATHERILL	JOSEPH				38	ENGLAND	CE	ENGLISH	F	044	A	3	33
WEATHERILL	WILLIAM				39	ENGLAND	WM	ENGLISH	BLACKSMITH	045	D	3	8
WEATHERSPOON	PETER				63	SCOT	CO	SCOT	F	044	B	4	43
WEAVER	SAMUEL				35	UNITED STATES	PS	GERMAN	LAB	043	E	2	51
WEAVER	WILLIAM			M	51	ENGLAND	CE	ENGLISH	F	043	A	1	65
WEB	WALTER		1		33	ENGLAND	CE	ENGLISH	LABORER	045	D	6	55
WEBB	ABRATHAR				50	0	WM	WELSH	FARMER	043	A	4	36
WEBB	CHARLES				50	ENGLAND	WM	ENGLISH	LABORER	045	D	5	23
WEBB	CLAYTON				72	UNITED STATES	QU	ENGLISH	F	043	B	4	7
WEBB	DANIEL		1		17	0	QU	ENGLISH	MILLER	043	A	4	24
WEBB	GEO		1		32	ENG	CE	ENG	LAB	045	C	1	32
WEBB	HENRY				30	ENGLAND	PM	ENGLISH	BRICK MAKER	045	B	1	65
WEBB	HENRY				28	0	CO	ENGLISH	F	044	C	2	37
WEBB	JOB		1	M	22	0	PR	IRELAND	SAWYER	043	A	5	6
WEBB	JOHN			M	73	US	QU	ENGLAND	F	043	A	5	16
WEBB	JOHN				43	ENGLAND	CE	ENGLISH	MASON	043	A	C	21
WEBB	MARY			F	76	US	WM	ENGLAND		043	A	5	44
WEBB	MARY	R		1	42	0	QU	ENGLISH		043	A	6	38
WEBB	THOMAS				70	ENGLAND	CE	ENGLISH		045	A	1	56
WEBB	THOMAS	L		M	49	0	QU	ENGLAND	FARMER	043	A	5	16
WEBB	WALTER		1		33	ENGLAND	BA	ENGLISH	BUTCHER	045	C	3	12
WEBBER	JAMES				35	ENGLAND	CE	ENGLISH	LAB	044	C	2	1
WEBBER	SAMUEL		1		31	ENGLAND	CE	ENGLAND	FARM LABORER	045	D	2	1
WEBER	JOHN				43	ENGLAND	CE	ENGLISH	HOTEL KEEPER	045	D	3	40
WEBSTER	ALEXANDER				35	SCOT	CP	SCOTCH	F	044	B	1	24
WEBSTER	CATHERINE		1	1	18	0	EM	SCOT	SERVANT	044	B	1	31
WEBSTER	CHARLES				38	ENGLAND	CE	ENGLISH	FARMER	045	D	1	7
WEBSTER	DAVID				33	SCOTLAND	CP	SCOTCH	LABOURER	045	D	5	43
WEBSTER	FREDERICK				36	ENGLAND	CN	ENGLISH	F	043	A	6	50
WEBSTER	JOHN				39	ENG	CP	ENG	F	044	B	1	18
WEBSTER	ROBERT				78	SCOT	PS	SCOT	F	044	B	3	16
WEBSTER	THOMAS				43	ENGLAND	CN	ENGLISH	F	043	A	6	48
WEBSTER	THOS				37	0	WM	ENGLISH	F	044	B	5	77
WEBSTER	WILLIAM				69	ENGLAND	WM	ENGLISH	F	043	A	6	48
WEBSTER	WILLIAM		2		95	SCOTLAND	CS		SERVANT	043	A	6	D
WEBSTER	WILLIAM				41	ENGLAND	CE	ENGLISH	FARMER	045	D	4	40
WEDDEL	CALVIN				53	0	CN	ENGLISH	F	043	E	2	2
WEDDEL	JOHN		1		3	0	CN	ENGLISH		043	E	2	40
WEDDEL	JOHN				34	0	CN	ENGLISH	F	043	E	2	67
WEDDEL	ROBERT				63	0	CN	ENGLISH	F	043	E	1	46
WEDDEL	WM	HERBERT	2		1	0	WM			043	E	2	D
WEDDLE	ANN			1	54	0	WM	ENGLISH	SEAMSTRESS	043	E	3	40
WEDDLE	JACOB				28	0	WM	ENGLISH	F	043	E	3	37
WEIGHT	HENRY		1		12	0	WM	IRISH	LABOURER	045	D	4	28
WEIGHT	MARY		1	1	34	QUEBEC	WM	IRISH	HOUSEKEEPER	045	D	4	28
WEIGHTMAN	ELIZABETH			1	62	ENGLAND	CE	ENGLISH		043	E	2	29
WEIR	ELIZABETH		1	1	45	IRELAND	CS	IRISH		043	H	1	6
WEIR	GEO				69	SCOT	CP	SCOT	F	045	C	1	18
WEIR	GEORGE				50	IRELAND	CE	IRISH	FARMER	043	A	4	70
WEIR	JAMES				35	IRELAND	WM	IRISH	BOOT & SHOE MAKER	045	B	1	1
WEIR	JAMES				57	SCOTLAND	PS	SCOTCH	F	045	C	3	22
WEIR	JANE		1	1	72	SCOT	CS	SCOT		045	C	1	61
WEIR	JOHN		2		48	IRELAND	CE		LAB	043	E	3	D
WEIR	JOHN				64	SCOTLAND	CP	SCOTCH	F	045	C	3	2
WEIR	JOHN	JAMES			38	IRELAND	CS	IRISH	F	043	H	1	6
WEIR	JOHN	JR			29	0	CP	SCOTCH	F	045	C	3	2
WEIR	THOMAS				42	IRELAND	CE	IRISH	F	043	H	1	5
WELBON	THOMAS				61	ENGLAND	PM	ENGLISH	F	043	A	6	40
WELBOURN	ANN		1	1	45	ENGLAND	CS	ENGLISH		043	H	2	20
WELBOURN	ROBERT		1		45	ENGLAND	CS	ENGLISH	LAB	043	H	2	20
WELBOURN	ROBERT				45	ENGLAND	CS	ENGLISH	LABOURER	043	H	2	20
WELBOURNE	JOHN				40	ENGLAND	WM	ENGLISH	F	043	B	5	3
WELBY	OLIVER		1		32	ENGLAND	WM	ENGLISH	WOOLEN MANUFACT	044	C	3	15
WELCH	ABRAHAM				62	IRELAND	CE	IRISH		044	C	3	63
WELCH	GEORGE	A	2			0	CN			043	B	3	D
WELCH	JOSEPH				30	0	CN	ENGLISH	FARMER	043	B	3	27
WELDON	WILLIAM		1		40	ENG	CO	ENG		044	B	3	30
WELDRICK	GEORGE				45	ENG	ME	ENG	F	044	B	1	16
WELLAR	JAMES				37	ENGLAND	WM	ENGLISH	F	044	A	1	2
WELLAR	JOHN				30	0	CE	IRISH	MAIL CARRIER	043	A	3	11
WELLAR	NELSON				35	0	CE	IRISH	FARMER	043	A	3	11
WELLER	CHARLES		1		22	ENGLAND	CE	ENGLAND	LABORER	045	D	2	4
WELLER	LORENZO				44	0	WM	IRISH	LAB	044	B	6	44
WELLINGTON	GEORGE				28	0	CE	IRISH	CARPENTER	045	A	1	64
WELLINGTON	MARY		1	1	32	ENGLAND	WM	ENGLISH	SERVANT	044	C	2	52
WELLS	DAVID			M	29	0	PS	ENGLISH	F	043	A	2	32
WELLS	ELIZA		1	1	20	0	EM	ENG	SERVANT	044	B	4	30
WELLS	ELIZABETH				39	ENGLAND	CE	ENGLISH		044	C	4	57
WELLS	GABRIEL			M	51	0	DI	ENGLISH	F	043	A	1	63
WELLS	HENRY				49	ENG	PM	ENG	LAB	044	B	4	35
WELLS	JACOB				73	ENGLAND	UP	ENGLISH	F	043	C		22
WELLS	JAMES			M	40	0	PS	ENGLISH	F	043	A	1	36
WELLS	JAMES	P		M	49	0	DI	ENGLISH	FARMER	043	A	1	34
WELLS	JOB			M	58	0	PR	ENGLISH	F	043	A	1	38
WELLS	JOHN			M	80	ENGLAND	PS	ENGLISH	YEOMAN	043	A	1	35
WELLS	JOHN				41	0	UP	ENGLISH	DENTIST	043	C		22
WELLS	JOHN		1		17	0	EM	ENG	F	044	B	1	36
WELLS	JOSEPH			M	72	ENGLAND	PS	ENGLISH	F	043	A	1	38
WELLS	LAMBERT		1	M	16	0	WM	ENGLAND	F	043	A	5	15
WELLS	LYDIA			1	42	0	WM	IRISH		043	B	4	25
WELLS	MARY	ANN	1	1	30	0	CS	ENGLISH	SCHOOL MISTRESS	043	E	2	63
WELLS	RICHARD				32	0	NG	ENGLISH	F	043	C		41

SURNAME	NAME1	NAME2	STRAY	SEX	AGE	BIRTHPL	RELIGION	ORIGIN	OCCUP	DIST	SUB_DIST	DIV	PAGE
WELLS	SEN			M	76	ENGLAND	EM	ENGLISH	F	043	A	2	45
WELLS	SUSANNAH		2			0	EM				044	B	1	D
WELLS	WILLIAM			M	54	0	CP	ENGLISH	F	043	A	2	34
WELLS	WILLIAM				31	0	EM	ENG	F	044	B	1	29
WELMAN	DAVID		1		7	0	NG	ENGLISH		045	D	2	23
WELSH	EDWARD				62	IRELAND	CE	IRISH	LAB	045	A	2	9
WELSH	HANNAH		1	1	72	IRELAND	RC	IRISH		045	A	1	17
WELSH	HENERY				25	0	CE	IRISH	FARMER	044	C	3	63
WELSH	HENRY				40	0	WP	GER	SAWYER	044	B	4	25
WELSH	JAMES				56	IRELAND	CE	IRISH	FARMER	044	C	3	63
WELSH	JOHN		1		25	0	PS	SCOTCH	SCHOOL TEACHER	043	E	3	6
WELSH	JOHN				57	SCOTLAND	UP	SCOTCH	FARMER	045	D	1	30
WELSH	MIKEL				35	CANADA	CE	GERMAN	FARMER	045	D	6	65
WELSH	ROBERT				45	CANADA	PS	IRISH	FARMER	045	D	6	70
WELSH	THOMAS				51	IRELAND	RC	IRISH	F	044	A	3	17
WERNHAM	WILLIAM		1		20	ENGLAND	CE	ENGLISH	SERVANT	043	C		42
WESLEY	ELIZABETH			1	37	ENGLAND	CE	ENGLISH	DRESS MAKER	043	C		26
WEST	ANDREW				34	0	CN	ENGLISH	LAB	043	E	1	9
WEST	ANTHONY			M	29	0	CN	ENGLAND	SAWYER	043	A	5	5
WEST	ELIZABETH		1	1	17	0	CE	ENG	SERVANT	044	B	1	20
WEST	GEORGE				32	0	CN	ENGLISH	F	043	A	6	54
WEST	GEORGE	W			20	0	CN	ENGLISH	LAB	043	F		18
WEST	HIRAM				38	0	CE	ENGLISH	SAWYER	043	F		26
WEST	JAMES		1		52	0	WM	ENGLISH	HOSTLER	043	F		19
WEST	JAMES				62	ENGLAND	WM	ENGLISH	DROVER	045	A	2	37
WEST	JOHN				44	ENGLAND	WM	ENGLISH	F	043	H	2	31
WEST	JOHN				44	ENGLAND	WM	ENGLISH	FARMER	043	H	2	31
WEST	JOHN				33	IRELAND	CE	IRISH	LAB	045	A	2	26
WEST	JOHN				39	ENG	CE	ENG	LAB	045	C	1	17
WEST	JOHN	A			46	UNITED STATES	BA	ENGLISH	FARMER & HUNTER	043	E	1	54
WEST	LUCY			1	65	ENG	WM	ENG		044	B	2	20
WEST	PHEBE		1	1	80	IRELAND	PS	SCOTCH		045	C	3	45
WEST	ROBERT	A			53	ENG	WM	ENG	SHOP KEEPER	044	B	1	8
WEST	THOMAS		1		14	0	EM	ENG	FARM SERVANT	044	B	1	29
WEST	THOMAS	G			46	ENGLAND	WM	ENGLISH	BRICK LAYER	045	B	1	2
WEST	THOS				44	ENG	CE	ENG	F	045	C	1	34
WEST	W	D			46	IRELAND	RC	IRISH	GARDENER	045	A	1	24
WEST	WILLIAM			M	42	ENGLAND	WM	ENGLISH	LABOURER	043	A	1	16
WEST	WILLIAM		1		30	ENGLAND	WM	ENGLISH	BAKER	045	A	1	2
WEST	WILLIAM		1		20	0	WM	IRISH	LAB	044	C	1	48
WEST	WILLIAM		1		31	ENGLAND	CE	ENGLISH	LABOURER	044	C	3	44
WESTBROOK	MOSES		1		42	ENGLAND	BA	ENGLISH	LABORER	043	G	1	15
WESTCOTT	GEORGINA		1	1	14	0	CP	ENGLISH	SERVANT	045	D	5	54
WESTLAKE	HENRY		1		23	ENGLAND	WM	ENGLISH	F LAB	043	A	3	43
WESTLAKE	JOHN				28	ENGLAND	WM	ENGLISH	F	043	A	3	45
WESTLAKE	THOMAS				30	ENGLAND	WM	ENGLISH	F LAB	043	A	3	43
WESTLAKE	THOS				39	ENG	WM	ENG	F	045	C	1	56
WESTNEY	WILLIAM				57	ENGLAND	CE	ENGLISH	F	045	C	2	34
WESTON	JOHN				24	ENGLAND	BA	ENGLISH	UPHOLSTERER	045	B	2	6
WESWICK	W	J			30	ENGLAND	CE	ENGLISH	BLACKSMITH	044	C	1	39
WETHERALD	JOSEPH				60	ENGLAND	QU	ENGLISH		045	B	1	55
WETHERALL	JOHN		1		15	0	WM	ENGLISH	LAWYER CLK	044	C	1	24
WETHERALL	RACHEL			1	68	ENGLAND	WM	ENGLISH		044	C	1	26
WETHERD	WILLIAM				24	ENGLAND	NC	ENGLISH	LAB	043	C		53
WETHEREL	WILLIAM				46	0	WM	ENGLISH	MACHINIST	043	C		18
WETHERELL	JAMES	S			50	0	EM	ENGLISH	BLACKSMITH	043	D		11
WETHERSTON	ADAM				55	ENGLAND	CE	ENGLISH	TAYLOR	045	A	2	36
WHALEN	BOSETT		1	1	36	IRELAND	RC	IRISH		043	H	2	39
WHALEN	DANIEL				50	IRE	RC	IRE	LAB	044	B	2	24
WHALEN	MARY		2	1	42	IRE	RC			044	B	2	D
WHALES	JOSIAH				40	ENGLAND	CO	ENGLISH	FARMER	045	D	3	72
WHALEY	ALEXANDER				43	0	CS	IRISH	FARMER	045	D	5	46
WHALEY	DAVID				62	IRELAND	CE	IRISH	FARMER	045	D	5	46
WHALEY	ELIZA			1	60	IRELAND	CS	IRISH		045	D	5	41
WHALEY	MARGARET				58	IRELAND	CS	IRISH		045	D	5	41
WHALEY	THOMAS				21	0	WM	IRISH	FARMER	045	D	5	55
WHALIN	PATRICK				44	IRELAND	RC	IRISH	LAB	045	A	4	18
WHALIN	ROSETT		1	1	36	IRELAND	RC	IRISH		043	H	2	39
WHARFF	ANDREW				32	0	CE	ENG	F	045	C	1	35
WHARFF	JESSE				26	0	CE	ENG	F	045	C	1	35
WHEELER	BIRON				36	US	CE	GERMAN	CARPENTER	044	C	3	72
WHEELER	EPHRIAM		1	M	21	0	PR	SCOTCH	SERVANT	043	A	1	30
WHEELER	EPHRIAM			M	59	0	CE	ENGLISH	F	043	A	1	45
WHEELER	MARIA		1	1	43	ONTARIO	CE	ENGLISH		043	G	1	7
WHELAN	JAMES				33	IRELAND	RC	IRISH	F	045	C	3	14
WHELER	EDWARD				57	ENGLAND	CO	ENGLISH	MILLER	043	B	3	53
WHELER	J	P			61	ENG	WM	ENG	F	045	C	1	16
WHIPPLE	SUSANNA			1	68	CANADA	CN	GERMAN		045	D	6	29
WHITAKER	RICHARD				32	ENGLAND	CE	ENGLISH	LABOURER	045	A	1	63
WHITCHELD	JAMES				36	ENG	BA	ENG	WHEELWRIGHT	044	B	1	62
WHITE	ALEX	M			38	ENGLAND	CE	ENGLISH	MILLER	044	A	3	10
WHITE	ALLAN				47	SCOTLAND	PS	SCOTCH	BLACKSMITH	045	C	3	16
WHITE	BENJAMIN	F			41	0	UT	ENGLAND	MILLER	045	D	5	75
WHITE	CHARLES				50	ENGLAND	CP	ENGLISH	CARPENTER	045	C	2	19
WHITE	DAVID		1		20	IRE	PS	IRISH	MAIL CARRIER	044	B	2	73
WHITE	DAVID				47	IRE	PM	IRE	F	044	B	4	9
WHITE	EDWARD				53	ENGLAND	ZZ	ENGLISH	MERCHANT TAILOR	043	B	3	55
WHITE	ELLEN		1		63	IRELAND	CP	IRELAND		045	D	2	21
WHITE	EMILY		1	1	18	0	EM	ENGLISH		045	A	3	20
WHITE	F	E	1		44	US	RP	SCOTCH	TEAMSTER	045	D	3	4
WHITE	FRANCIS				45	IRELAND	RC	IRISH	LAB	044	A	2	3
WHITE	GEORGE				56	IRELAND	CE	IRISH	F	044	A	1	22
WHITE	GEORGE		2		2	0	PS			044	B	3	D
WHITE	GEORGE				52	ENGLAND	CE	ENGLISH	GARDNER	045	B	2	19
WHITE	GEORGE	H			62	IRELAND	WM	IRISH	BUILDER	045	B	1	39
WHITE	HANNAH			F	52	ENGLAND	CE	ENGLAND	F	043	A	5	22
WHITE	HENRY				52	0	CE	ENGLISH	F	043	A	6	42
WHITE	HENRY				45	0	CE	ENGLISH	F	044	B	1	1
WHITE	HENRY				40	0	WM	GERMAN	FARMER	045	D	2	67
WHITE	HIRAM				44	0	CE	ENG	F	044	B	1	28
WHITE	ISAAC				46	0	EM	ENG	BLACK SMITH	044	B	1	28
WHITE	ISABELLA		1	1	45	SCOTLAND	CS	SCOTCH	SERVANT	043	E	2	24
WHITE	JAMES			M	47	ENGLAND	RC	ENGLISH	LABOURER	043	A	1	7
WHITE	JAMES				33	0	CE	ENGLISH	F	044	B	1	1
WHITE	JAMES				35	ENGLAND	CE	ENGLISH	FARMER	045	A	3	26
WHITE	JAMEY				23	ENGLAND	CE	ENGLISH	BLACKSMITH	044	B	5	37

SURNAME	NAME1	NAME2	STRAY	SEX	AGE	BIRTHPL	RELIGION	ORIGIN	OCCUP	DIST	SUB_DIST	DIV	PAGE
WHITE	JOHN		1		30	SCOTLAND	CP	SCOTCH	F LAB	044	A	1	28
WHITE	JOHN		1		32	IRE	PS	IRE	SERVANT	044	B	3	11
WHITE	JOHN				50	IRE	CP	IR	F	044	B	4	51
WHITE	JOSEPH				60	QUEBEC	RC	FRENCH	FARM SERVANT	045	C	3	47
WHITE	MARY		1	1	56	ENGLAND	CE	IRISH		045	B	2	33
WHITE	MOSES				33	0	WM	GERMAN	FARMER	045	D	2	43
WHITE	ROBERT				32	0	OP	IRISH	CARPENTER	043	A	3	9
WHITE	ROBERT		1		26	IRELAND	CE	IRISH	FARMER	043	A	4	34
WHITE	ROBERT				35	IRELAND	CS	IRISH	COOPER	044	B	6	10
WHITE	SARAH		1	1	22	IRELAND	CE	IRISH		043	A	4	34
WHITE	SARAH		1	1	20	0	EM	GER		044	B	1	46
WHITE	THOMAS			M	23	IRELAND	PS	IRELAND	L	043	A	5	7
WHITE	THOMAS		1		28	0	PS	IRE	F	044	B	3	35
WHITE	THOMAS				59	IRELAND	CS	IRISH	MERCHANT	044	B	6	56
WHITE	THOMAS				59	ENGLAND	WM	ENGLISH	BLACKSMITH	045	D	5	76
WHITE	W	L			42	IRELAND	WM	SCOTCH	SHOEMAKER	043	B	3	11
WHITE	WALTER				33	ENGLAND	CE	ENGLISH	DROVER	044	A	1	21
WHITE	WILLIAM			M	37	ENGLAND	WM	ENGLISH	LABOURER	043	A	2	35
WHITE	WILLIAM				27	0	OP	IRISH	FARM LAB	043	A	3	5
WHITE	WILLIAM		1		20	0	CE	IRISH	LAB	043	C		49
WHITE	WILLIAM		1		21	0	WM	IRE	SADDLER	044	B	3	9
WHITE	WILLIAM		1		22	ENGLAND	CE	ENGLISH	FARM LABOURER	045	C	4	14
WHITE	WILLIAM				40	ENGLAND	CE	ENGLISH	FARM LABOURER	045	C	4	37
WHITE	WILLIAM				49	ENGLAND	CE	ENGLISH	LAB	044	C	2	26
WHITEHEAD	HENRY		1		63	ENGLAND	CE	ENGLISH	LAB	044	C	4	2
WHITEHEAD	WILLIAM				44	ENGLAND	CE	ENGLISH	FARM LAB	044	A	2	26
WHITEHEAD	WILLIAM		2			0	CE			044	A	2	D
WHITEHEAD	WILLIAM		1		22	QUEBEC	CE	ENGLISH	MILLER	044	B	6	41
WHITELY	SAMUEL				32	ENGLAND	CE	ENGLISH	F	045	B	2	2
WHITEMAN	JAS		1		60	IRELAND	CE	IRISH		045	C	1	32
WHITEOAK	WILLIAM				62	ENGLAND	CE	ENGLISH	FARMER	045	D	3	37
WHITEOAK	WILLIAM				34	0	CE	ENGLISH	FARMER	045	D	3	67
WHITESIDE	DANIEL		1		51	IRELAND	PS	ENGLISH	TRAVELLING AGENT	045	C	3	57
WHITESIDE	JOHN				38	0	CP	IRISH	F	045	C	4	28
WHITESIDE	PHINEAS				52	IRELAND	CP	IRISH	LAB	043	A	6	20
WHITESIDE	SARAH		2	1	81	IRELAND	CP			045	C	4	D
WHITESIDE	THOMAS				44	0	CP	IRISH	F	045	C	4	29
WHITESIDE	THOMAS		2		88	IRELAND	CP		F	045	C	4	D
WHITESIDE	THOMAS	J G	1		3	SAN FRANSISCO	PS	ENGLISH		045	C	3	57
WHITESIDES	ARTHUR				30	0	CE	IRISH	BRICKMAKER	045	A	1	37
WHITFIELD	WILLIAM		1		23	ENGLAND	CE	ENGLISH	LAB	044	C	4	68
WHITIT	DAVID		1		30	SCOTLAND	PS	SCOTCH	SERVANT	044	C	4	67
WHITLAM	HENRY				26	0	WM	ENGLISH	F	044	A	1	27
WHITLAM	MARY		1	1	41	QUEBEC	CP	IRISH	HOUSE KEEPER	043	B	1	42
WHITLAN	THOMAS		1		17	0	CP	ENGLISH	LAB	043	B	1	42
WHITLOCK	ISAAC		1		23	0	WM	ENGLISH	MILLER	044	A	3	24
WHITMAN	WM				31	0	EM	IRISH	F	044	C	1	41
WHITMARSH	GEORGE		1		25	ENG	EP	ENG	LAB	044	B	3	3
WHITMORE	CATHRINE			1	51	0	LU	IRISH		044	B	3	23
WHITMORE	EPHRIAM				23	0	VM	GER	F	044	B	3	20
WHITMORE	HENRY		1		15	0	VM	ENG		044	B	3	25
WHITMORE	JOHN				44	0	WM	ENGLISH	LABOURER	044	C	1	33
WHITMORE	LAFEAT				31	0	LU	GER	F	044	B	3	22
WHITMORE	SAM				47	0	CO	ENGLISH	F	044	C	1	50
WHITNEY	ALEXANDER				40	0	CE	IRISH	FARMER	045	A	3	21
WHITNEY	MARGARET		1	1	13	0	CE	ENGLISH		044	C	2	47
WHITNEY	MARY		1	1	77	0	EM	SCOTCH		045	D	5	5
WHITNEY	THOMAS			M	62	0	CE	ENGLISH	LABOURER	043	A	1	4
WHITTAKER	ALEXANDER		1		30	IRELAND	CE	IRISH	LABOURER	044	C	3	63
WHITTAKER	ROBERT				32	ENGLAND	CE	ENGLISH	GROOM	044	C	2	45
WHITTICAR	HENRY		1		13	ONTARIO	CE	ENGLISH		043	G	1	18
WHITTIER	ALLFRETTA		1	1	16	0	WM	ENGLISH		044	C	4	75
WHITTINGTON	JAS				33	ENG	CE	ENG	F	045	C	1	48
WHITTINGTON	JEMIMA		2	1	1	CE				045	C	1	D
WHITTOCK	FREDERICK				49	ENG	WM	ENG	LAB	044	B	2	14
WHITTON	JOHN				38	SCOTLAND	CP	SCOTCH	F	044	C	2	33
WHITTY	THOMAS				50	ENG	PM	ENG	F	044	B	3	33
WHITTY	THOMAS				29	ENG	CO	ENG	F	044	B	3	44
WICE	MARY			1	72	0	EM	GERMAN		045	D	1	40
WICKS	FRANK				50	ENGLAND	CE	ENGLISH	SADLER	045	D	6	44
WICKS	JAMES		1		40	ENGLAND	CE	ENGLISH	F	045	B	1	9
WICKSON	HENRY				27	0	CO	ENGLISH	BUTCHER	045	B	1	61
WICKSON	JANE			1	80	ENGLAND	CO	ENGLISH		045	B	1	38
WICKSON	THOMAS		1		22	ENGLAND	CE	ENGLISH	LAB	044	A	1	34
WIDDIFIELD	CHARLES				57	0	QU	ENGLISH	F	043	B	4	34
WIDDIFIELD	J	HENRY			25	ONT	CE	ENGLISH	PHYSICIAN	043	D		51
WIDDIFIELD	JONATHAN				53	0	QU	ENGLISH	F	043	B	5	39
WIDDIFIELD	LEVI				25	0	NG	IRISH	F	043	B	5	31
WIDDIFIELD	OBED				42	US	QU	ENGLISH	F	043	B	5	41
WIDDIFIELD	WILLIAM				33	0	QU	ENGLISH	F	043	B	5	5
WIDDIS	JAMES				33	0	CE	IRISH	MOULDER	043	D		85
WIDEMAN	ABRAHAM				26	0	MN	GERMAN	F	043	B	2	2
WIDEMAN	ABRHM				47	0	MN	GERMAN	MAIL CARRIER	043	B	2	29
WIDEMAN	ANDREW				21	CANADA	MN	GERMAN	FARMER	045	D	6	26
WIDEMAN	CASPER				49	0	MN	GERMAN	F	043	B	2	28
WIDEMAN	CHRISTIAN				61	0	MN	GER	F	044	B	2	69
WIDEMAN	CHRISTOPHER				45	0	MN	GERMAN	FARMER	045	D	4	19
WIDEMAN	CRISTOPHER				28	CANADA	MN	GERMAN	FARMER	045	D	6	75
WIDEMAN	ELIZABETH		1	1	33	0	CN	GERMAN	SERVANT	043	B	3	71
WIDEMAN	ELIZABETH		2	1	72	US	MN			045	D	4	D
WIDEMAN	ELIZABETH		2	1	53	US	MN			045	D	4	D
WIDEMAN	ESTHER		1	1	10	0	MN	GERMAN		043	B	3	69
WIDEMAN	HENEREY				60	CANADA	MN	GERMAN	FARMER	045	D	6	37
WIDEMAN	HENERY				69	U STATES	MN	GERMAN	FARMER	045	D	6	16
WIDEMAN	JACOB				42	0	MN	GERMAN	FARMER	045	D	4	20
WIDEMAN	JOHN				52	0	MN	GERMAN	FARMER	045	D	4	20
WIDEMAN	JOSEPH				35	CANADA	MN	GERMAN	POTTER	045	D	6	26
WIDEMAN	MARY		1	1	89	U STATES	MN	GERMAN		045	D	6	19
WIDEMAN	PHILLIP				49	0	CP	GERMAN	FARMER	045	D	6	8
WIDEMAN	SAMUEL				50	CANADA	MN	GERMAN	FARMER	045	D	6	19
WIDEMAN	TRUEMAN		1		22	CANADA	CE	IRISH		045	D	6	51
WIDEMAN	WILLIAM				46	0	WM	GERMAN	FARMER	043	SUB DIST	3	30
WIESMORE	CHARLES	H			26	UNITED STATES	RC	FRENCH	PAINTER	044	A	3	40
WIGGINS	ELLEN		2	1	67	IRELAND	CE			045	A	1	D
WIGGINS	JOHN				38	IRELAND	CE	IRISH	SHOEMAKER	043	A	4	18
WIGGINS	JOHN				73	IRELAND	CE	IRISH	YEOMAN	045	A	1	34

SURNAME	NAME1	NAME2	STRAY	SEX	AGE	BIRTHPL	RELIGION	ORIGIN	OCCUP	DIST	SUB_DIST	DIV	PAGE
WIGHT	ANNE		1	1	7	O	WM	ENG		044	B	3	9
WIGHT	GEORGE				56	SCOTLAND	CP	SCOTCH	FARMER	043	G	2	46
WIGHT	JAMES				46	ENGLAND	PS	ENGLISH	FARMER	043	G	2	13
WIGHT	WILLIAM				45	ENGLAND	PS	ENGLISH	FARMER	043	G	2	13
WIGHTON	ISABELLA			F	82	SCOTLAND	CP	SCOTCH		043	A	1	67
WIGHTON	JOHN			M	44	SCOTLAND	CP	SCOTCH	FAR	043	A	1	67
WILCOCK	MELNA	A	1	1	9	O	EM	GERMAN		043	E	2	64
WILCOX	MARY			1	43	O	CE	ENG		044	B	2	76
WILDER	THOMAS				41	O	BA	ENGLISH	F	043	H	2	54
WILDER	THOMAS				41	ONTARIO	BA	ENGLISH	FARMER	043	H	2	54
WILDMAN	MOSES				32	ENGLAND	WM	ENGLISH	F	043	B	2	25
WILDS	THOMAS				57	IRELAND	RC	IRISH	GARDENER	045	A	1	19
WILES	LAWDON			M	42	O	CE	ENGLISH	F	043	A	2	19
WILES	PARKINS				50	ENGLAND	WM	ENGLISH	GARDNER	045	B	1	66
WILES	ROBERT				54	ENG	WM	ENG	F	044	B	4	32
WILES	ROBERT				73	ENGLAND	CE	ENGLISH	GENTLEMAN	045	D	1	13
WILES	WILLIAM		1		17	O	CE	ONT	SHOEMAKER	045	D	1	13
WILES	WILLIAM				50	ENGLAND	PS	ENGLISH	F	044	C	1	8
WILEY	CHARLES				30	US	UV	GERMAN	MILL MAN	045	D	3	41
WILEY	FRANCIS				41	O	WM	IRE	CARPENTER	044	B	2	14
WILEY	REBECCA			1	73	ENGLAND	PM	ENGLISH		044	A	3	40
WILFORD	ERNEST				65	IRE	CE	IRISH	LAB	044	B	1	38
WILKENSON	ELIZABETH		1	F	23	O	PM	ENGLISH		043	A	1	46
WILKES	ROBERT				39	IRELAND	NC	IRISH	MERCHANT	045	B	2	26
WILKES	WILLIAM		1		61	ENGLAND	QU	ENGLISH	SERVANT	043	D		40
WILKIE	ANGUS			M	39	SCOTLAND	PS	SCOTCH	F	043	A	2	44
WILKIE	ANGUS				41	O	FK	SCOTCH	F	043	A	3	38
WILKIE	DUNCAN			M	78	SCOTLAND	PS	SCOTCH	F	043	A	2	44
WILKIE	JOHN				38	O	OP	SCOTCH	FARMER	043	A	3	9
WILKIE	NEIL			M	65	SCOTLAND	PS	SCOTCH	F	043	A	2	44
WILKIE	SARAH		1	1	20	SCOTLAND	CP	SCOTCH	SERVANT	044	A	1	20
WILKIN	ROBERT				31	ENGLAND	CE	ENGLISH	LAB	045	B	2	13
WILKINS	JOHN				56	O	QU	ENGLISH	F	043	B	4	32
WILKINS	MARY	ANN	1	1	48	O	CE	WELSH		043	B	4	22
WILKINSON	GEO				43	ENGLAND	CE	ENGLISH	CARPENTER	044	B	5	28
WILKINSON	GEORGE				30	O	WM	ENGLISH	BLACKSMITH	043	B	1	20
WILKINSON	HANNAH			1	34	O	WM	ENGLISH		043	B	1	21
WILKINSON	HENRY				56	U STATES	NC	SCOTCH	MINISTER	043	A	4	18
WILKINSON	HOSEA	G			44	ENGLAND	CS	ENGLISH	BLACKSMITH	045	D	5	17
WILKINSON	JAMES		2	M	30	LC	BA		F	043	A	1	D
WILKINSON	JAMES		1	M	40	IRELAND	PS	IRISH	LAB	043	A	2	9
WILKINSON	JEREMIAH				50	ENGLAND	CE	ENGLISH	F	043	E	2	5
WILKINSON	JONATHAN				34	O	WM	ENGLISH	PHYSICIAN	044	A	3	28
WILKINSON	JOSEPH				48	ENGLAND	CE	ENGLISH	F	043	E	2	6
WILKINSON	RICHARD			M	30	O	WM	ENGLAND	L	043	A	5	15
WILKINSON	RICHARD				54	ENGLAND	CE	ENGLISH	F	043	B	2	11
WILKINSON	THOMAS				32	SCOT	PS	SCOT	F	044	B	2	52
WILKINSON	THOMAS				38	ENGLAND	CE	ENGLISH	F	045	A	4	5
WILKS	THOMAS				78	ENGLAND	WM	ENGLISH	LAB	044	A	3	35
WILLARD	HENRY				49	ENGLAND	CE	ENGLISH	LAB	045	B	1	19
WILLAS	CHARLOTTE		1	1	12	ENGLAND	QU	ENGLISH		043	E	2	3
WILLCOCK	ROBERT				25	O	WM	ENGLISH	F	044	A	2	27
WILLCOCK	STEPHEN				23	O	WM	ENGLISH	F	044	A	2	27
WILLCOX	HIRAM		1		20	O	CP	SCOTCH	SERVANT	044	B	6	35
WILLCOX	JAMES			M	38	O	PS	IRISH	CARPENTER	043	A	1	6
WILLER	ALONZO		1	M	45	O	NG	IRISH	LAB	043	A	2	3
WILLET	PETER	A			73	QUEBEC	CN	FRENCH	COOPER	045	D	4	46
WILLIAMES	THOMAS	B			33	ENGLAND	CE	ENGLISH	CARPENTER	045	A	4	8
WILLIAMS	A	D			23	ENGLAND	CO	ENGLISH	PHYSICIAN	044	B	5	28
WILLIAMS	ADDISON				36	O	CN	ENGLISH	BLACKSMITH	043	E	2	11
WILLIAMS	ALEXANDER				34	SCOTLAND	CS	SCOTCH	TANNER	043	F		29
WILLIAMS	ANNIE		1	1	17	ENGLAND	CE	IRISH	SERVANT	044	C	2	39
WILLIAMS	ARON				63	UNITED STATES	CN	ENGLISH	F	043	E	2	9
WILLIAMS	CHAS				44	ENGLAND	CE	ENGLISH	LAB	044	B	5	56
WILLIAMS	COLIN				29	O	CN	ENGLISH	F	043	E	2	17
WILLIAMS	DAVID				19	O	WM	ENGLISH	F	045	A	4	19
WILLIAMS	ELIJAJAH				36	O	WM	ENGLISH	LABOURER	043	B	3	57
WILLIAMS	EMILY		1	1	34	UNITED STATES	CE	AFRICAN		044	C	2	48
WILLIAMS	EV		1	1	6	O	CN	ENGLISH		043	B	3	45
WILLIAMS	FANNY			1	38	O	TU	GERMAN	FARMER	045	D	2	54
WILLIAMS	FREDERICK		1	M	44	O	WM	GERMAN		043	A	2	10
WILLIAMS	FREDERICK				38	ENGLAND	CE	ENGLISH	COACHMAN	045	A	1	6
WILLIAMS	GEORGE				36	ENGLAND	PM	ENGLISH	FARMER	043	D		31
WILLIAMS	GEORGE		1		63	ENGLAND	WM	ENGLISH	SAILOR	043	G	1	35
WILLIAMS	GEORGE				40	USA	WM	AFRICAN	BRICKMAKER	045	A	1	20
WILLIAMS	GEORGE				40	ENGLAND	WM	ENGLISH	FARMER	045	D	2	46
WILLIAMS	HENRY				42	UNITED STATES	CN	ENGLISH	FARMER	043	B	3	16
WILLIAMS	ISABELLA		1		4	O	LU	ENG		044	B	3	7
WILLIAMS	ISIAC			M	60	O	WM	ENGLISH	MANUFACTURER	043	A	2	25
WILLIAMS	JOHN				36	IRELAND	CE	IRISH	LAB	043	B	1	24
WILLIAMS	JOHN				72	UNITED STATES	CN	ENGLISH	F	043	B	4	30
WILLIAMS	JOHN				75	US	WM	ENGLISH		043	B	5	2
WILLIAMS	JOHN				23	O	CN	ENGLISH	F	043	E	2	16
WILLIAMS	JOHN				87	IRELAND	CE	IRISH	FARMER	043	G	1	30
WILLIAMS	JOHN				46	US	CE	AFRICAN	COOPER	044	A	2	46
WILLIAMS	JOHN				79	ENGLAND	CE	ENGLISH	YEOMAN	044	B	5	27
WILLIAMS	JOHN				49	ENGLAND	WM	ENGLISH	COOPER	045	B	2	21
WILLIAMS	JOHN				31	O	CE	IRISH	LABORER	045	D	2	36
WILLIAMS	JOHN		1		18	O	CE	ENGLISH	SERVANT	044	C	3	9
WILLIAMS	JOHN				50	IRELAND	WM	IRISH	CLERK	044	C	3	37
WILLIAMS	JOHN				37	O	CE	IRISH	BRICK MAKER	044	C	3	58
WILLIAMS	JOHN				35	US	WM	IRISH	LABOURER	044	C	3	71
WILLIAMS	JOSEPH				31	O	WM	ENGLAND	LAB	043	B	5	22
WILLIAMS	JOSEPH				35	IRELAND	CE	ENGLISH	F	044	B	6	16
WILLIAMS	JOSEPH				45	ENGLAND	CE	ENGLISH	SAILOR	045	A	1	5
WILLIAMS	MARY		1	1	17	O	CE	ENGLISH		044	C	3	46
WILLIAMS	MARY	ANN	1	1	67	UNITED STATES	CN			043	G	2	34
WILLIAMS	MARY	ANN	2	1	32	O	WM			045	D	1	D
WILLIAMS	MICHAEL				35	ENGLAND	WM	ENGLISH	BUTCHER	045	D	1	3
WILLIAMS	ROBERT				21	O	WM	ENGLISH	F	043	B	5	2
WILLIAMS	ROBERT				38	WALES	WM	WALES	STORE KEEPER	045	D	6	46
WILLIAMS	ROBT		1		19	O	CO	ENGLISH	CARPENTER	044	B	5	12
WILLIAMS	SAMUEL				50	U STATES	WM	AFRICAN	LAB	045	A	2	13
WILLIAMS	SARAH		1	1	30	O	CE	ENGLISH		045	A	3	17
WILLIAMS	STEPHEN		1		8	O	CN	ENGLISH		043	B	3	44
WILLIAMS	STEPHEN				66	ENG	CE	ENG	LAB	044	B	2	19

SURNAME	NAME1	NAME2	STRAY	SEX	AGE	BIRTHPL	RELIGION	ORIGIN	OCCUP	DIST	SUB_DIST	DIV	PAGE
WILLIAMS	THOMAS				37	ENGLAND	PM	ENGLISH	FARMER	045	A	2	17
WILLIAMS	WILLIAM				51	ENGLAND	CE	ENGLISH	SHOE MAKER	045	D	3	73
WILLIAMS	WILLIAM		1		16	O	CE	ENGLISH	LABOURER	045	D	6	1
WILLIAMS	WILLIAM		1		27	ENGLAND	CE	ENGLISH	GARDNER	044	C	4	54
WILLIAMSON	ANNE		1	1	28	O	EM	ENG	SEAMSTRESS	044	B	2	9
WILLIAMSON	BETTY		1	1	39	O	CP	SCOTCH		045	A	3	19
WILLIAMSON	DAVID		1		21	O	CP	IRISH	PAINTER	043	A	4	23
WILLIAMSON	DAVID		1		5	O	PM	ENGLISH		045	D	4	10
WILLIAMSON	GEORGE				54	SCOTLAND	CP	SCOTCH	TINSMITH	043	A	4	13
WILLIAMSON	ISAC		1		25	O	WM	ENGLISH	F	045	A	4	7
WILLIAMSON	JOHN				32	O	WM	ENGLISH	F	043	B	2	35
WILLIAMSON	JOHN				65	ENGLAND	CE	ENGLISH	FARMER	045	D	6	4
WILLIAMSON	JOHN				36	ENGLAND	CE	ENGLISH	FARMER	045	D	6	5
WILLIAMSON	JOSEPH				26	CANADA	FW	ENGLISH	CURRIER	045	D	6	26
WILLIAMSON	JOSEPH				41	ENGLAND	WM	ENGLISH	STOREKEEPER	045	A	4	16
WILLIAMSON	LYDIA		1	1	21	O	WM	ENGLISH		045	A	4	7
WILLIAMSON	MATHEW		1		58	ENGLAND	PM	ENGLISH	F	045	A	4	7
WILLIAMSON	MATTHEW				40	O	WM	ENGLISH	F	043	B	1	34
WILLIAMSON	ROBERT				54	ENG	CE	ENG	SHOE MAKER	044	B	2	33
WILLIAMSON	THOMAS		1		20	CANADA	LU	GERMAN		045	D	6	78
WILLIAMSON	WILLIAM				78	ENGLAND	WM	ENGLISH	F RETIRED	043	B	2	37
WILLIAMSON	WILLIAM		1		28	SCOTLAND	CP	SCOTCH		045	B	1	16
WILLIAMSON	WILLIAM	R	1		0	O	WM	ENGLISH		045	A	4	7
WILLIE	ELIZA		1	1	18	IRELAND	CE	IRISH		044	C	3	63
WILLIE	JAMES				60	ENGLAND	CE	ENGLISH	LABOURER	044	C	1	32
WILLIS	ALBERT		1		8	ENGLAND	QU	ENGLISH		043	B	4	44
WILLIS	ARCHELAUS				32	US	CE	ENGLISH	INSURANCE AGENT	045	D	3	76
WILLIS	BENJAMIN				51	O	NC	ENGLISH	F	043	B	1	2
WILLIS	CORNELIUS				63	O	QU	WELSH	F	043	E	1	21
WILLIS	EDWARD		1		20	ENGLAND	CE	ENGLISH	FARM SERVANT	043	E	1	19
WILLIS	FREDERICK			M	58	O	CP	WELSH	F	043	A	2	22
WILLIS	GEORGE				24	ENGLAND	CE	ENGLISH	F	043	E	3	10
WILLIS	GEORGE	A			31	IRELAND	BA	IRISH	STOREKEEPER	043	G	1	3
WILLIS	HENRY		1		14	ENGLAND	QU	ENGLISH		043	B	4	44
WILLIS	JAMES				58	IRELAND	CP	IRISH	FARMER	045	D	2	43
WILLIS	JOHN			M	27	O	NG	WELSH	F	043	A	2	23
WILLIS	JOSHUA				35	UNITED STATES	CE	ENGLISH	LAB	044	C	2	6
WILLIS	LEONARD				40	ENGLAND	WM	ENGLISH	BAKER	045	B	1	25
WILLIS	MARTIN				39	IRELAND	CE	IRISH	F	045	C	3	6
WILLIS	PHEBE		1	1	21	O	QU	ENGLISH		043	B	4	35
WILLIS	RICHARD		1		23	ENGLAND	CE	ENGLISH	F LAB	043	B	4	31
WILLIS	SILAS				26	O	UP	ENGLISH	F	043	A	6	57
WILLIS	WILLIAM		1		20	ENGLAND	QU	ENGLISH	F	043	B	4	44
WILLIS	WILLIAM				48	ENGLAND	CE	ENGLISH	SADDLER	043	C		11
WILLIS	WILLIAM		1		19	IRELAND	CE	IRISH	F LAB	044	A	1	27
WILLIS	WILLIAM		1		28	ENG	WM	ENG	LAB	044	B	3	28
WILLISON	WILLIAM				70	ENGLAND	WM	ENGLISH	F	044	B	6	48
WILLISS	JAMES		1		16	ENGLAND	QU	ENGLISH		043	E	2	3
WILLMOT	EDWARD				53	ENGLAND	CE	ENGLISH	BUTCHER	045	B	1	1
WILLOBY	ANNE			1	69	ENGLAND	CE	ENGLISH		045	B	1	21
WILLOUGHBY	BENJAMIN				57	ONTARIO	EM	SCOTCH	FARMER	043	G	2	18
WILLOUGHBY	DANIEL				35	ONTARIO	CE	SCOTCH	FARMER	043	G	1	38
WILLOUGHBY	DAVID				44	ONTARIO	CE	SCOTCH	FARMER	043	G	1	52
WILLOUGHBY	GEORGE				31	ONTARIO	EM	SCOTCH	LABORER	043	G	2	24
WILLOUGHBY	JOHN				29	ONTARIO	WM	IRISH	FARMER	043	G	1	7
WILLOUGHBY	JOSHUAH				32	ONTARIO	CE	IRISH	FARMER	043	G	1	5
WILLOUGHBY	JOSIAH				42	ONTARIO	CN	SCOTCH	CARPENTER	043	G	1	53
WILLOUGHBY	LINDA		2	1	61	ONTARIO	CN			043	G	1	D
WILLOUGHBY	PETER		1		12	ONTARIO	PR	ENGLISH		043	G	2	51
WILLOUGHBY	SALINA		1	1	46	ENGLAND	PR	ENGLISH		043	G	2	51
WILLOUGHBY	WILLIAM				25	ONTARIO	CN	SCOTCH	CARPENTER	043	G	1	41
WILLOWS	JAMES				45	ENGLAND	CE	ENGLISH	F	043	E	2	13
WILLSON	A	L			32	O	WM	ENGLISH	LAWYER	044	C	1	24
WILLSON	AMOS				36	O	ZZ	IRISH	F	043	E	1	42
WILLSON	CAROLINE		1	1	18	O	WM	IRISH	SERVANT	043	E	3	55
WILLSON	DAVID	T			54	ONTARIO	CN	IRISH	FARMER	043	G	1	49
WILLSON	EGERTON				29	O	WM	ENGLISH	FARMER	044	C	1	25
WILLSON	ELIZA		1	1	60	O	WM	ENGLISH		043	C		48
WILLSON	ELIZABETH			1	44	ENGLAND	WM	ENGLISH	MERCHANT	043	E	3	42
WILLSON	GEORGE		1	M	35	ENGLAND	CE	ENGLISH	LAB	043	A	1	49
WILLSON	GEORGE				42	ENG	WM	ENG	MERCHANT	044	B	4	19
WILLSON	GEORGE				80	ENGLAND	CE	ENGLISH	F	044	C	1	43
WILLSON	HARRIETT			1	51	ONTARIO	CN	ENGLISH	WEAVER	043	G	1	43
WILLSON	HENRY				68	IRELAND	CE	IRISH	SCHOOL TEACHER	043	B	3	16
WILLSON	HUGH				55	IRELAND	CE	IRISH	FARMER	045	A	2	31
WILLSON	HUGH	H			67	ONTARIO	CE	IRISH	MINISTER	043	G	1	57
WILLSON	ISRAEL				71	UNITED STATES	QU	IRISH	F	043	E	1	53
WILLSON	JACOB				65	IRELAND	WM	IRISH	TAILOR	043	H	1	23
WILLSON	JAMES				65	IRELAND	CE	IRISH	TAILOR	043	E	3	19
WILLSON	JAMES	H			54	U STATES	EM	IRISH	TAILOR	043	D		7
WILLSON	JANE		1	1	4	O	WM	IRE		044	B	4	6
WILLSON	JOHN				67	NB	QU	ENGLISH	F	043	B	4	28
WILLSON	JOHN				46	IRELAND	RC	IRISH	SHOEMAKER	043	D		47
WILLSON	JOHN				30	O	BA	IRISH	F	043	E	2	1
WILLSON	JOHN				25	ONTARIO	PR	IRISH	FARMER	043	G	2	24
WILLSON	JOHN	A			26	O	CN	IRISH	F	043	E	2	10
WILLSON	JOHN	D			73	UNITED STATES	ZZ	IRISH	F	043	E	1	45
WILLSON	JOHN	N	2		1	US	WM			044	B	4	D
WILLSON	JOSEPH				43	SCOTLAND	UP	SCOTCH	PAINTER	043	C		25
WILLSON	JOSEPH				25	ENG	PM	ENG	FARM SERVANT	044	B	4	19
WILLSON	JOSEPH				65	ENGLAND	WM	ENGLISH	FARMER	044	B	6	17
WILLSON	JULIA		1	1	13	ENGLAND	BA	ENGLISH		045	B	2	21
WILLSON	MARY	J	1	1	31	O	WM	ENGLISH		043	D		64
WILLSON	MARY	J	1	1	10	ENGLAND	BA	ENGLISH		045	B	2	21
WILLSON	MOSES				64	NEW BRUNSWICK	CN	ENGLISH	GENTLEMAN	043	E	2	3
WILLSON	PATRICK		1		19	IRELAND	RC	IRISH	LABORER	043	D		85
WILLSON	REUBEN				34	O	CN	IRISH	CARPENTER	043	E	1	42
WILLSON	ROBERT				29	O	WM	ENG	F	044	B	4	27
WILLSON	RODNEY				37	O	NC	IRISH	F	043	E	2	43
WILLSON	SARAH			1	74	IRELAND	CE	IRISH		045	A	2	31
WILLSON	SILUS				31	ONTARIO	CP	IRISH	FARMER	043	G	2	25
WILLSON	STEPHEN				28	O	CN	IRISH	F	043	E	2	10
WILLSON	THOMAS				45	O	BA	ENGLISH	LAB	043	E	3	32
WILLSON	WILLIAM				42	O	NC	IRISH	SAWMILLER	043	E	2	83
WILLSON	WILLIAM				41	SCOTLAND	CP	SCOTCH	F	043	H	1	31
WILLSON	WILLIAM				44	ENG	CS	ENG	F	044	B	4	39

SURNAME	NAME1	NAME2	STRAY	SEX	AGE	BIRTHPL	RELIGION	ORIGIN	OCCUP	DIST	SUB_DIST	DIV	PAGE
WILLSON	WILLIAM	H	1		67	UNITED STATES	ZZ	IRISH	GENT	043	E	2	39
WILLY	CHARLES		1		84	ENGLAND	CE	ENGLISH		043	C		35
WILMER	JAMES		1		45	ENGLAND	CE	ENGLISH		045	D	5	71
WILMOT	JOSEPH				30	0	WM	ENGLISH	FARMER	045	D	1	49
WILMOT	LYDIA	ANN	2	1	36	0	EM			045	D	2	D
WILMOT	PETER				67	0	WM	ENGLISH	FARMER	045	D	2	43
WILMOT	PETER				26	0	WM	ENGLISH	FARMER	045	D	2	67
WILMOT	WILLIAM				36	0	WM	GERMAN	FARMER	045	D	3	47
WILSON	ABRAHAM	H			42	0	WM	IRISH	F	044	C	2	14
WILSON	ALBERT				30	0	CE	IRISH	SCHOOL TEACHER	044	B	5	3
WILSON	ALEXANDER				46	SCOTLAND	CP	SCOTCH	FARMER	043	A	4	61
WILSON	ANN		1	1	53	ENGLAND	CP	SCOTCH	INMATE	045	B	1	72
WILSON	ASA	B			29	0	WM	IRISH	CARPENTER	044	B	2	12
WILSON	C	E			44	0	QU	IRISH	LAB	043	F		17
WILSON	CHARLES				29	0	QU	ENGLISH	F	043	B	4	41
WILSON	CHARLOTTE		1	1	73	ENGLAND	WM	ENGLISH		045	D	5	21
WILSON	DANIEL				47	ENGLAND	WM	ENGLISH	TEAMSTER	044	C	4	64
WILSON	DAVID				28	0	CE	SCOTCH	STORE KEEPER	045	B	1	14
WILSON	DAVID				22	0	PM	SCOT		045	C	1	49
WILSON	DAVID				68	ENGLAND	CE	ENGLISH	FARMER	045	D	6	39
WILSON	EDWARD				27	0	QU	ENGLISH	F	043	B	4	38
WILSON	ELIZA		1	1	36	QUEBEC	PM	IRISH		045	C	3	15
WILSON	ELIZA			1	40	IRELAND	CP	IRISH		045	D	6	9
WILSON	ELLEN		1	F	18	0	RC	IRELAND		043	A	5	8
WILSON	F	W			37	ENGLAND	CE	ENGLISH	F	044	C	1	26
WILSON	FRANCES	P	1	1	30	0	CE	IRISH		044	A	2	53
WILSON	FRANK		1		40	ENG	CE	ENG	SERVANT	044	B	3	5
WILSON	GEORGE			M	30	US	CN	IRELAND	CARPENTER	043	A	5	22
WILSON	GEORGE				56	IRELAND	CE	IRISH	PEDLAR	045	C	3	57
WILSON	GEORGE		2		72	ENGLAND	CE		BRICKLAYER	045	D	5	D
WILSON	GEORGE		1		10	0	WM	IRISH		044	C	4	28
WILSON	HENRY				57	0	QU	ENGLISH	F	043	B	4	40
WILSON	HENRY				34	0	WM	ENGLISH	STORE KEEPER	045	D	3	80
WILSON	HUGH				60	SCOTLAND	CS	SCOTCH	FARMER	043	A	4	43
WILSON	JAMES			M	39	US	NR	IRELAND	L	043	A	5	19
WILSON	JAMES		1		11	QUE	PS	IRISH		044	B	3	9
WILSON	JAMES		1		10	0	PM	IRISH		045	C	3	28
WILSON	JAMES				63	IRELAND	UP	IRISH	FARMER	045	D	1	31
WILSON	JANE		1	1	47	US	BA	ENGLISH		043	B	5	6
WILSON	JANET		1	1	26	0	PM	SCOTCH		044	A	1	2
WILSON	JANET			1	47	SCOT	WM	SCOT		045	C	1	18
WILSON	JOB				50	0	CE	IRISH	SHOEMAKER	045	A	1	8
WILSON	JOHN		1	M	16	0	EM	ENGLISH		043	A	2	44
WILSON	JOHN				57	IRE	CE	IRE	MECHANIC	045	C	1	11
WILSON	JOHN				67	ENGLAND	CE	ENGLISH	F	045	C	2	2
WILSON	JOHN				26	0	WM	ENGLISH	F	045	C	2	14
WILSON	JOHN				48	ENGLAND	WM	ENGLISH	MASON	045	D	3	71
WILSON	JOHN				57	ENGLAND	CE	ENGLISH	WEAVER	045	D	2	49
WILSON	JOSEPH				61	0	QU	ENGLISH	F	043	B	4	41
WILSON	JOSEPH				52	IRELAND	CE	IRISH	FARMER	045	A	2	31
WILSON	JOSHUA				39	0	QU	ENGLISH	F	043	B	4	42
WILSON	JOSHUA				76	NB	QU	ENGLISH	F	043	B	4	29
WILSON	KATHERINE			1	77	IRE	CE	IRISH		044	B	1	7
WILSON	MARTHA		1	1	30	0	WM	ENGLISH	SERVANT	044	A	3	4
WILSON	MARY		1	1	14	0	ZZ	IRISH		043	B	4	12
WILSON	MARY		1		77	UNITED STATES	QU	IRISH		043	B	4	40
WILSON	MARY			1	36	IRELAND	RC	IRISH		044	A	1	30
WILSON	MARY		1	1	77	ENGLAND	WM	ENGLISH		045	A	2	2
WILSON	R	T	1		78	UNITED STATES	NG	IRISH	AGENT	043	F		16
WILSON	ROBERT		1		34	0	CP	IRISH	HOTEL KEEPER	044	A	2	53
WILSON	ROBERT				55	IRELAND	CO	IRISH	DROVER	044	A	3	27
WILSON	ROBERT				75	IRELAND	WM	IRISH	GENTLEMAN	044	B	1	5
WILSON	ROBERT				28	0	WM	GER	BLACKSMITH	044	B	2	44
WILSON	ROBERT				33	IRE	PS	IRE	LAB	044	B	2	77
WILSON	ROBERT				50	ENGLAND	CO	ENGLISH	MASON	045	D	3	70
WILSON	ROBT				36	0	EM	IRISH	TEAMSTER	043	B	3	58
WILSON	SAMUEL				60	0	CE	IRISH	SHOEMAKER	045	D	5	19
WILSON	SAMUEL				40	0	WM	IRISH	FARMER	045	D	1	32
WILSON	SARAH			1	64	0	QU	ENGLISH		043	B	4	41
WILSON	STEPHEN				43	0	PS	DUTCH	F	043	A	6	32
WILSON	STEWART		1		20	0	CE	IRISH	WAGGON MAKER	045	D	5	6
WILSON	THOMAS				53	IRE	WM	IRISH	CARPENTER	044	B	2	11
WILSON	THOMAS				24	IRELAND	CE	IRISH	LAB	045	B	1	47
WILSON	THOMAS				46	SCOTLAND	CP	SCOTCH	FARM LABOURER	045	D	3	7
WILSON	THOMAS				43	ENGLAND	CE	ENGLISH	BRICKLAYER	045	D	5	7
WILSON	WALTER				33	ENGLAND	CE	ENGLISH	F	044	A	1	35
WILSON	WILLIAM				50	ENGLAND	PM	ENGLISH	FARMER	043	A	4	50
WILSON	WILLIAM				64	IRELAND	CP	IRISH	F	044	A	1	24
WILSON	WILLIAM		1		24	0	CP	IRISH	HARNESS MAKER	045	D	5	12
WILSON	WILLIAM		1		33	0	CE	ENGLISH	CARPENTER	045	D	5	21
WILSON	WILLIAM		1		26	0	WM	ENGLISH	SCHOOL TEACHER	045	D	1	27
WILSON	WM				37	0	WM	ENG	F BUTCHER	045	C	1	17
WILTON	SAMUEL				56	ENGLAND	CE	ENGLISH	F	043	B	1	31
WIMBATH	JANE		1	1	39	ENGLAND	CE	ENGLISH		045	B	2	30
WIMNER	JANE		1	1	60	SCOTLAND	PS	SCOTCH	SERVANT	045	B	2	34
WINCH	HENRY				40	ONTARIO	PR	ENGLISH	FARMER	043	G	2	31
WINCH	JOHN				72	UNITED STATES	CN	ENGLISH	FARMER	043	G	1	28
WINCH	THOMAS				65	ENGLAND	CE	ENGLISH	SAILOR	043	F		19
WINDER	WALTER		1		11	0	BA	AFRICAN		045	A	1	40
WINDER	WILLIAM		1		15	0	BA	AFRICAN		045	A	1	40
WINDMAR	CHARLES				30	0	WM	ENGLISH	BUCHER	044	C	4	81
WINDRISS	MOSES				68	ENG	CE	ENG	TOLLGATE KEEPER	044	B	2	60
WINDROSS	GEORGE				48	ENGLAND	WM	ENGLISH	F	043	E	3	26
WINDROSS	JOHN				23	ENGLAND	WM	ENGLISH	BLACKSMITH	043	E	3	24
WINDSOR	HENRY		1		37	ENGLAND	CE	ENGLISH	LABOURER	045	A	1	54
WINDSOR	ROBERT				37	0	CE	ENGLISH	LABOURER	045	D	6	9
WINDSOR	SILAS				31	0	KB	ENGLISH	SHOEMAKER	045	D	5	68
WINFIELD	GEORGE				45	ENGLAND	BC	ENGLISH	F	043	H	2	51
WINFIELD	GEORGE				45	ENGLAND	BC	ENGLISH	FARMER	043	H	2	51
WINFIELD	JAMES				50	ENGLAND	CE	ENGLISH	F	043	H	1	10
WINFIELD	JOHN				20	0	CE	ENGLISH	F	043	H	2	40
WINFIELD	JOHN				20	ONTARIO	CE	ENGLISH	FARMER	043	H	2	40
WINFIELD	JOHN		1		81	ENGLAND	CE	ENGLISH	LAB	043	H	2	1
WINFIELD	JOHN		1		81	ENGLAND	CE	ENGLISH	LABOURER	043	H	2	1
WINFIELD	MARY			1	39	0	WM	ENGLISH		043	H	2	49
WINFIELD	MARY			1	39	ONTARIO	WM	ENGLISH		043	H	2	49

SURNAME	NAME1	NAME2	STRAY	SEX	AGE	BIRTHPL	RELIGION	ORIGIN	OCCUP	DIST	SUB_DIST	DIV	PAGE
WINN	FREDERICK		1		19	ENGLAND	CE	ENGLISH	LAB	045	C	4	5
WINN	GEORGE				58	ENGLAND	WM	ENGLISH	FARMER	043	A	4	65
WINNING	MARGARET			1	53	IRELAND	RC	IRISH		045	D	5	28
WINSTANLY	WILLIAM				54	ENGLAND	CE	ENGLISH	GENTLEMAN	043	D		80
WINSTONE	DANIEL				66	ENGLAND	CE	ENGLISH	LAB	044	C	3	8
WINTER	CHARLES	R			40	ENGLAND	CE	ENGLISH	AGENT	045	B	1	56
WINTER	JOHN				25	O	WM	ENGLISH	FARMER	043	A	4	45
WINTER	JOHN				49	ENGLAND	WM	ENGLISH	F	043	E	1	26
WINTER	MICHAEL			M	38	ENGLAND	EM	ENGLISH	F	043	A	1	75
WINTER	ROBERT				35	ENGLAND	CE	ENGLISH	FARMER	043	A	4	45
WINTER	THOMAS				68	ENGLAND	NC	ENGLISH	RETIRED	043	A	4	17
WINTER	WILLIAM				34	O	WM	ENGLISH	FARMER	043	A	4	55
WINTERS	CHARLES				32	ENGLAND	CE	ENGLISH	F	044	C	2	23
WINTERS	CHARLOTTE			1	45	O	WM	GERMAN	INNKEEPER	044	B	6	6
WINTERS	EMMA		1	1	17	ENGLAND	CE	ENGLISH		045	A	2	11
WINTERS	FRANCIS				28	IRELAND	CP	IRISH	FARM LABORER	045	D	1	10
WINTERS	FREDERICK		1		23	ENGLAND	CE	ENGLISH	BAKER	043	A	4	21
WINTERS	HIRAM				56	O	WM	ENGLISH	F	044	A	3	22
WINTERS	JANE		1	1	60	IRELAND	WM	IRISH		045	B	1	43
WINTERS	MOSES				60	O	EM	GER	LAB	044	B	3	35
WINTERS	SARAH		2	1	5	O	ME			044	B	3	D
WINTERSTEIN	HENRY				49	O	CN	GERMAN	F	043	B	2	42
WISE			2			O	PR			045	A	1	D
WISE	ALEXANDER		1		24	ENG	WM	ENG	LAB	044	B	3	41
WISE	ALEXANDER				61	ENGLAND	WM	ENGLISH	LAB	044	C	3	2
WISE	BETTY		1	1	65	U STATES	WM	ENGLAND	SERVANT	043	A	6	2
WISE	GEORGE				38	O	EM	ENG	SHINGLE MAKER	044	B	1	34
WISE	GEORGE	D			41	ENGLAND	CE	ENGLISH	FARMER	045	A	1	24
WISE	HENRY				47	O	EM	GERMAN	FARMER	045	D	2	55
WISE	IRVINE		2			O	NG			044	B	1	D
WISE	WILLIAM				28	ENG	VM	ENG	LAB	044	B	3	23
WISEMAN	ALFRED		1		40	ENGLAND	CE	ENGLISH	BRICK MAKER	045	B	1	63
WISEMAN	JNO				54	ENGLAND	CE	ENGLISH	BLACKSMITH	043	C		18
WISMER	BARBARA		2	1	77	U S	MN			045	D	3	D
WISMER	DAVID				51	ONTARIO	CN	GERMAN	LABOURER	043	G	1	18
WISMER	DAVID				63	CANADIAN	CN	GERMAN	FARMER	045	D	6	28
WISMER	DAVID	L			48	O	CN	GERMAN	FARMER	045	D	3	68
WISMER	ELI				39	CANADA	LU	GERMAN	SADLER	045	D	6	40
WISMER	HENRY				70	US	MN	GERMAN	FARMER	045	D	3	10
WISMER	HENRY				41	O	CN	GERMAN	FARMER	045	D	3	66
WISMER	JACOB				94	US	CE	GERMAN	FARMER	045	D	3	64
WISMER	LEVY				42	CANADA	CN	GERMAN	CARPENTER	045	D	6	25
WISMER	MARSHEL		1		21	O	CN	GERMAN	SCHOOLTEACHER	043	E	3	56
WISMER	SAMUEL				60	U STATES	EM	GERMAN	FARMER	045	D	6	1
WISMORE	EUNICE		1	1	70	UNITED STATES	CN	ENGLISH	WEAVER	043	G	1	23
WISNER	ZEPHANIAH			M	52	O	WM	GERMANY	F	043	A	5	38
WISTENFELT	JOHN				24	GERMANY	LU	GERMANY	LABORER	045	D	2	64
WITHARS	ROBERT				42	IRELAND	CE	IRISH	F	044	C	2	36
WITHERS	CHARLOTTE		2	1	43?	IRELAND	PS			043	B	3	D
WITHERS	ROBERT				17	O	PS	SCOTLAND	WEAVER	043	B	3	65
WITHERS	WILLIAM		2		45	SCOTLAND	PS		WEAVER	043	B	3	D
WITHERSPOON	DAVID				60	SCOT	CO	SCOT	F	044	B	3	47
WITHERSPOON	GEO				38	SCOTLAND	UP	SCOTCH	F	044	B	5	78
WITHERSPOON	JOSEPH				25	O	CO	SCOT	F	044	B	3	47
WITHERSPOON	WM				70	SCOTLAND	PS	SCOTCH	TOLL KEEPER	044	B	5	2
WITTERS	WM		1		30	O	WM		CLOTH DRESSER	044	B	5	20
WITTMORE	HENRY				38	O	WM	ENGLISH	LABOURER	044	C	1	34
WITTY	CHARLES				80	O	WM	ENGLISH	CARPENTER	044	A	3	24
WIX	JOHN				60	NOV SCOTIA	NG	ENGLISH	LAB	043	A	6	49
WOCHNER	JOHN				42	GERMANY	RC	GERMAN	BUTCHER	045	A	1	61
WOLFF	CHARLES				69	GERMANY	PM	GERMAN	CABINET MAKER	044	A	3	38
WOLLIS	WILLIAM				45	ENGLAND	CE	ENGLISH	LABOURER	043	B	3	68
WOLMEN	JAMES		1		30	ENGLAND	WM	ENGLISH	F LAB	043	A	6	56
WONCH	GEORGE	E			30	O	WM	GERMAN	FARMER	045	D	3	11
WONCH	WILLIAM	H			55	US	WM	GERMAN	FARMER	045	D	3	11
WOOD	AMELIA		2	1	29	O	CE			045	C	1	D
WOOD	ANN			1	50	ENGLAND	CE	ENGLISH		043	D		57
WOOD	BENJAMIN		1		25	ONTARIO	PR	ENGLISH		043	G	2	54
WOOD	BROCK				67	ENGLAND	WM	ENGLISH	WESLYAN MINISTER	044	C	4	74
WOOD	CATHN		1	1	15	O	UP	SCOTCH		044	B	5	71
WOOD	ELIAS				40	ENGLAND	CE	ENGLISH	F	045	C	4	14
WOOD	ELIZA		1	1	7	O	CP	ENGLISH		044	C	2	15
WOOD	FREDERICK				28	ENGLAND	CE	ENGLISH	LAB	045	B	1	54
WOOD	GEO	CLARK			52	ENGLAND	CO	ENGLISH	F	044	A	3	41
WOOD	GEORGE			M	45	ENGLAND	PM	ENGLISH	MINISTER	043	A	2	29
WOOD	GEORGE				31	O	CP	ENGLISH	F	044	B	6	38
WOOD	GEORGE					ENGLAND	WM	ENGLISH	F	044	C	4	29
WOOD	HENRICK		1		15	O	PM	ENGLISH		043	E	2	55
WOOD	HENRY				20	O	CE	ENGLISH	PAINTER	043	D		59
WOOD	JAMES	W	1		23	O	WM	ENGLISH	MERCHANT	043	A	4	16
WOOD	JAS		1		26	O	CP	SCOTCH	F	044	B	5	61
WOOD	JEAN			F	66	SCOTLAND	CP	SCOTCH	RETIRED	043	A	1	31
WOOD	JOHN				30	ENGLAND	IM	ENGLISH	F	043	B	4	23
WOOD	JOHN				55	ENGLAND	AD	ENGLISH	CARPENTER	045	A	1	89
WOOD	JOHN	M	1		25	O	WM	ENGLISH	WHEELWRIGHT	043	A	4	17
WOOD	JOSEPH			M	54	ENGLAND	WM	ENGLISH	F	043	A	2	27
WOOD	JOSEPH		2		49	ENGLISH	CE		PAINTER	043	D		D
WOOD	MARGARET			1	21	IRELAND	CE	IRISH		043	B	3	60
WOOD	MARY		2	1	58	IRELAND	WM			043	B	3	D
WOOD	PHELIX				70	U STATES	NG	AFRICAN	LAB	043	A	3	20
WOOD	ROBERT				77	ENGLAND	CE	ENGLISH		043	B	1	17
WOOD	ROBERT				56	ENGLAND	CE	ENGLISH	HOTEL KEEPER	045	B	2	5
WOOD	ROBERT				25	ENGLAND	CE	ENGLISH	LAB	045	B	1	35
WOOD	ROBERT		1		17	IRELAND	RP	SCOTCH	SERVANT	044	C	3	73
WOOD	SAMUEL				62	ENGLAND	CE	ENGLISH	F	044	A	2	22
WOOD	THOMAS				60	ENGLAND	WM	ENGLISH	F	043	E	1	1
WOOD	THOMAS				33	O	CE	ENG	LAB	045	C	1	17
WOOD	TRYPHONA			1	48	ENGLAND	CE	ENGLISH	F	045	C	3	39
WOOD	WM				60	ENGLAND	PM	ENGLISH	F	044	A	3	35
WOOD	WM				29	ENGLAND	CE	ENGLISH	WEAVER	044	B	5	21
WOODALE	JONATHAN				23	ENGLAND	CE	ENGLISH	FARM SERVANT	043	E	1	38
WOODALL	WILLIAM	H			55	O	WM	ENGLISH	CABINET MAKER	045	D	3	60
WOODARD	AARON				41	ONTARIO	WM	ENGLISH	LABORER	043	G	1	7
WOODARD	ELIZABETH		1	1	5	O	PM	GERMAN		043	B	2	30
WOODARD	FRANKLIN				30	ONTARIO	CN	ENGLISH	FARMER	043	G	1	33
WOODARD	JAMES		1		16	O	BA	GERMAN	FARM LABOURER	045	D	4	44

SURNAME	NAME1	NAME2	STRAY	SEX	AGE	BIRTHPL	RELIGION	ORIGIN	OCCUP	DIST	SUB_DIST	DIV	PAGE
WOODARD	JOSHUA		1		42	0	WM	ENG	LAB	044	B	2	63
WOODARD	MARY		1	1	7	0	PM	GERMAN		043	B	2	30
WOODARD	SUSAN		1	1	61	0	CN	GERMAN	HOUSE KEEPER	045	D	4	46
WOODARD	SYLVANUS			M	45	0	DI	ENGLISH	F	043	A	1	43
WOODBURN	CHRISTOPHER				36	ENG	CE	ENG	CARPENTER	044	B	4	1
WOODCOCK	JACOB				62	0	PM	GERMAN	F	043	E	3	21
WOODCOCK	JAMES				23	0	CE	ENGLISH	SAWYER	043	E	3	32
WOODCOCK	JOEL				33	0	WM	GERMAN	SAWER	043	E	3	32
WOODCOCK	JOHN	JACOB	2				CE			043	E	3	D
WOODCOCK	SYLVESTER				36	QUE	WM	GERMAN	SAWYER	043	E	3	20
WOODEN	MARK				45	ENGLAND	CE	ENGLISH	ENGINEER	043	G	1	33
WOODEN	WILLIAM		1		15	ONTARIO	NG			043	G	2	28
WOODFIELD	SARAH		1	1	46	SCOTLAND	CP	SCOTCH		044	A	1	36
WOODGATE	HENERY				34	ENGLAND	PM	ENGLISH	F	043	B	5	15
WOODGATE	HENRY				42	ENGLAND	CE	ENGLISH	LABOURER	043	G	1	10
WOODHOUSE	JOSEPH				27	ENG	WM	ENG	TAILOR	044	B	3	8
WOODHOUSE	WILLIAM				65	ENGLAND	CE	ENGLISH	LAB	045	B	1	23
WOODLEY	JOHN				70	ENGLAND	CE	ENGLISH	WEAVER	044	B	5	57
WOODMAN	JOHN		1		22	ENG	CE	ENG	FARM LAB	044	B	1	32
WOODMAN	THOMAS		1		16	ENGLAND	WM	ENGLISH	F LAB	044	C	1	35
WOODROW	JOHN		1	M	35	0	BA	ENGLAND	F	043	A	5	33
WOODROW	JOSEPH			M	29	0	BA	ENGLAND	F	043	A	5	32
WOODROW	WILLIAM			M	71	US	BA	ENGLAND	F	043	A	5	32
WOODRUFF	LARANCE				31	0	WM	ENG	F	045	C	1	2
WOODS	ARTHUR				56	IRELAND	CE	ENGLISH	F	044	C	2	11
WOODS	BENJAMIN				25	QUE	WM	ENGLISH	F LAB	043	A	3	20
WOODS	ELIZABETH		1	1	14	0	RP	SCOTCH	SERVANT	044	C	3	45
WOODS	ELVIRA			1	39	ENGLAND	WM	ENGLISH		044	C	1	15
WOODS	EMANUEL				51	ENGLAND	WM	ENGLISH	F	043	A	3	21
WOODS	FRANK				67	IRELAND	RC	IRISH	LAB	044	C	4	55
WOODS	GEORGE				37	SCOTLAND	RP	SCOTCH	TINSMITH	044	C	3	23
WOODS	JAMES					IRELAND	RC	IRISH	F	044	A	1	40
WOODS	JAMES				52	IRE	PS	IRE	BLACKSMITH	044	B	2	73
WOODS	JOHN				58	IRE	CE	IRE	LAB	044	B	2	43
WOODS	JOHN				65	IRELAND	CE	IRISH	F	044	B	6	48
WOODS	JOHN				52	ENGLAND	CE	ENGLISH	MASON	044	C	1	13
WOODS	JOHN	C			50	US	WM	AMERICAN	AGENT	045	D	1	4
WOODS	MICHAEL		1		23	IRELAND	RC	IRISH	BUCHER	044	C	4	48
WOODS	SARAH		1	1	51	IRELAND	CE	IRISH		043	C		55
WOODS	THOMAS				40	IRELAND	WM	IRISH	LAB	045	B	2	6
WOODS	THOS				40	ENGLAND	UP	ENGLISH	LAB	044	B	5	71
WOODS	WILLIAM				49	ENGLAND	CE	ENGLISH	FARMER	043	G	1	36
WOODS	WILLIAM				22	ONTARIO	WM	ENGLISH	FARMER	043	G	1	37
WOODS	WM				33	0	WM	ENGLISH	F	044	B	5	70
WOODSON	THOMPSON			M	31	ST HELENA	PR	FRENCH	LAB	043	A	1	70
WOODSWORTH	ELIZABETH		1	1	22	0	CE	ENGLISH		044	A	3	39
WOODSWORTH	JOHN				66	ENGLAND	WM	ENGLISH	F	043	A	3	56
WOODWARD	JOHN				72	ENGLAND	PM	ENGLISH	TAYLOR	045	D	4	7
WOODWARD	JOSHUA				45	UNITED STATES	WM	GERMAN	F	043	E	3	59
WOOF	JANE		1	1	21	0	RC	IRISH		043	H	2	13
WOOF	JOSEPH				49	ENGLAND	CE	ENGLISH	LAB	043	H	2	2
WOOF	JOSEPH				49	ENGLAND	CE	ENGLISH	LABOURER	043	H	2	1
WOOF	THOMAS		1		21	ENGLAND	CE	ENGLISH	LAB	043	H	2	13
WOOF	THOMAS				21	ENGLAND	CE	ENGLISH	LABOURER	043	H	2	13
WOOLEY	A	W			51	US	BA	ENGLISH	AGENT	043	F		31
WOOLEY	IDA		2	1	1	0	BA			043	F		D
WOOLEY	JEMIMA			1	89	ENGLAND		ENGLISH		045	B	2	31
WOOTEN	ALICE		1	1	20	0	WM	ENGLISH		045	D	3	80
WOOTEN	DAVID				55	ENGLAND	CE	ENGLISH	HOTELKEEPER	045	D	5	20
WOOTEN	ISRAEL				65	ENGLAND	NC	ENGLISH	CARPENTER	043	C		53
WOOTEN	THOMAS				30	0	CN	ENGLISH	SHOEMAKER	045	D	5	22
WORKMAN	WILLIAM		1		74	ENGLAND	WM	ENGLISH		045	D	3	72
WORM	ROBERT				49	ENGLAND	WM	ENGLISH	GARDNER	044	C	4	46
WORNHAM	CHARLES				57	ENGLAND	CE	ENGLISH	F	043	F		7
WORSNOP	CLARA		2	1	2	0				043	F		D
WORSNOP	SAM'L				60	ENGLAND	CE	ENGLISH	WATCHMAN	043	F		11
WORSNOP	THOMAS				35	ENGLAND	CE	ENGLISH	TANNER	043	F		10
WORTH	DAVID		1		37	ENGLAND	CE	ENGLISH	LABORER	043	D		70
WORTH	EDWARD					ENGLAND	WM	ENGLISH	LAB	044	C	4	87
WORTHY	JOHN				28	0	CE	ENGLISH	LAB	045	B	1	20
WORTHY	JOSEPH				31	0	CE	ENGLISH	LAB	045	B	1	53
WORTHY	MARY			1	70	ENGLAND	CE	ENGLISH		044	C	3	18
WORTHY	THOMAS	P			59	ENGLAND	CE	ENGLISH	GARDNER	045	B	1	56
WORTS	MARY		1	1	48	0	LU	FRENCH		045	C	2	8
WRAGGET	GEORGE				45	ENGLAND	WM	ENGLISH	FARM LABOURER	045	C	3	25
WRAY	CATHERINE				47	0	EM	SCOTTISH	F	044	C	1	40
WRAY	JOHN				43	ENGLAND	PM	ENGLAND	F	044	B	5	64
WRAY	SETH				24	0	WM	ENGLISH	F	043	A	6	55
WREGGET	THOMAS				56	ENG	NG	ENG	LAB	044	B	4	20
WREGGETT	RICHARD				48	ENGLAND	CE	ENGLISH	F	044	B	6	30
WREGGIT	JAMES				36	ENGLAND	WM	ENGLISH	CARPENTER	043	A	4	8
WREGGIT	SETH		1		35	ENGLAND	WM	ENGLISH	LABOURER	043	A	4	12
WREGGITT	WILLIAM			M	50	ENGLAND	PR	ENGLISH	F	043	A	1	57
WREN	CHARLES	J			26	ENGLAND	CE	ENGLISH	SHOEMAKER	045	D	5	29
WREN	CHARLES	J	1		4	ENGLAND	CE	ENGLISH		045	D	5	30
WREN	THOMAS	J	1		1	0	CE	ENGLISH		045	D	5	30
WRENCH	DAVID		1		53	ENGLAND	WM	ENGLISH	LAB	043	C		11
WRIGGET	JAMES				35	ENGLAND	CE	ENGLISH	F	043	E	2	15
WRIGGET	JANE		1	1	11	0	CE	ENGLISH		043	E	2	5
WRIGGET	RACHAEL		1	1	8	0	CE	ENGLISH		043	E	2	5
WRIGGET	ROBERT		1		13	0	CE	ENGLISH		043	E	2	5
WRIGGETT	WM				77	ENGLAND	CE	ENGLISH	F	044	C	1	5
WRIGHT	ABRAHAM				38	ENGLAND	PM	ENGLISH	FARMER	043	B	3	48
WRIGHT	ARCHIBALD				42	0	WM	SCOTCH	CARRIAGE & WAGGON MA	045	C	4	8
WRIGHT	CATHRINE			1	44	ENGLAND	PM	ENGLISH		043	B	2	14
WRIGHT	CHARLOTTE		1	1	64	0	WM	US	HOUSEKEEPER	045	D	1	18
WRIGHT	DANIEL				33	ENGLAND	CE	ENGLISH	F	043	B	2	37
WRIGHT	DAVID		1		21	0	CP	IRISH	STORE KEEPER	044	C	2	15
WRIGHT	ELIZABETH			F	35	ENGLAND	WM	ENGLAND		043	A	5	42
WRIGHT	EMILY		1	1	18	0	PM	ENG		044	B	3	20
WRIGHT	FREDERICK				45	ENGLAND	CE	ENGLISH	SOLICITOR	045	B	1	38
WRIGHT	GEORGE			M	71	0	CE	IRELAND	F	043	A	5	3
WRIGHT	GEORGE				43	0	NC	ENGLISH	CARRIAGE MAKER	043	E	2	20
WRIGHT	GEORGE		1		26	0	PM	ENGLISH	CARPENTER	045	B	2	14
WRIGHT	HENRY		1		15	0	PM	ENGLISH	F LAB	044	A	3	14
WRIGHT	HULET				74	N BRUNSWICK	WM	SCOTCH	F	045	C	4	5

SURNAME	NAME1	NAME2	STRAY	SEX	AGE	BIRTHPL	RELIGION	ORIGIN	OCCUP	DIST	SUB_DIST	DIV	PAGE
WRIGHT	JAMES		1		28	US	NG	DUTCH	HOTEL KEEPER	043	B	1	1
WRIGHT	JAMES		1		17	O	CE	ENGLISH		043	C		28
WRIGHT	JAMES				44	ENGLAND	WM	ENGLISH	BLACKSMITH	044	B	5	20
WRIGHT	JAMES				44	ENGLAND	WM	ENGLISH	GARDNER	045	B	1	40
WRIGHT	JANE			1	46	ENG	CE	ENG		044	B	1	16
WRIGHT	JOHN				39	ENGLAND	WM	ENGLISH	F	043	B	4	39
WRIGHT	JOHN				43	IRELAND	CP	IRISH	CARPENTER	043	C		1
WRIGHT	JOHN				62	ENGLAND	WM	ENGLISH	F	043	E	1	24
WRIGHT	JOHN				53	ENGLAND	CE	ENGLISH	LAB	044	A	3	53
WRIGHT	JOHN				46	IRELAND	CE	IRISH	LAB	044	B	5	54
WRIGHT	JOHN				46	IRELAND	CE	IRISH	LAB	044	B	6	5
WRIGHT	JOHN				46	ENGLAND	CE	ENGLISH	LABOURER	045	A	1	61
WRIGHT	JOHN				52	ENG	CE	ENG	F	045	C	1	1
WRIGHT	JOHN	JNR			46	ENGLAND	CE	ENGLISH	CARPENTER	043	A	4	8
WRIGHT	MARGARET		1	1	30	IRELAND	CE	IRISH	SERVANT	045	B	2	20
WRIGHT	MARY		1	1	19	O	BA	ENGLISH		043	E	1	22
WRIGHT	MARY		1	1	43	O	CE	SCOTCH		045	A	3	19
WRIGHT	MATHEW		1		15	O	NC	ENGLISH		043	E	1	22
WRIGHT	NORMAN		1		64	ENGLAND	WM	ENGLISH	SHOE MAKER	044	B	5	9
WRIGHT	PETER				44	ENGLAND	WM	ENGLISH	F	043	B	4	39
WRIGHT	ROBERT				61	IRELAND	CN	IRISH	REVEREND	043	B	3	5
WRIGHT	SILAS				55	ENGLAND	CE	ENGLISH	F	043	E	1	11
WRIGHT	TABETHA		1		26	O	CE	ENGLISH	LAB	044	B	6	12
WRIGHT	THOMAS				62	O	QU	ENGLISH	F	043	H	1	33
WRIGHT	THOS		1		21	UNITED STATES	EM	IRISH	LAB	043	E	2	24
WRIGHT	WATSON				26	O	WM	ENGLISH	F	043	E	2	50
WRIGHT	WILLIAM				28	O	WM	ENGLISH	F	043	E	1	8
WRIGHT	WILLIAM		1		10	O	NC	ENGLISH		043	E	1	22
WRIGHT	WILLIAM				45	ENGLAND	CE	ENGLISH	LAB	044	A	3	23
WRIGHT	WILLIAM				25	O	PM	ENGLISH	F MANAGER	044	A	3	52
WRIGHT	WILLIAM				58	ENGLAND	WM	IRISH	TOLL KEEPER	044	B	6	44
WRIGHT	WILLIAM				55	O	WM		FARMER	045	D	2	14
WRIGHTLEY	FREDERICK				49	ENGLAND	CE	ENGLAND	FARMER	045	D	2	27
WRIGLEY	JOHN				48	ENGLAND	CE	ENGLISH	MECHANIC	044	C	3	4
WURTZ	SUSANNA		1	1	14	O	WM	GERMAN	SERVANT	045	D	5	61
WYATT	CORDELIA		1	1	21	O	CE	ENGLISH		044	C	4	57
WYATT	ELIZA		1	1	21	ENGLAND	WM	IRISH		045	B	1	27
WYATT	WILLIAM		1		28	ENGLAND	CE	ENGLISH	FARM LAB	044	C	2	39
WYER	JOHN			M	36	ENGLAND	CE	ENGLISH	FARMER	043	A	1	21
WYLIE	DAVID				22	SCOTLAND	CP	SCOTCH	FARM LABOURER	045	D	3	22
WYLIE	ELIZA	S	1	1	26	SCOTLAND	CP	SCOTCH		045	D	3	22
WYLIE	GERARD				38	O	WM	IRE	CARPENTER	044	B	2	35
WYLIE	ROBERT		1		18	SCOT	WM	SCOT	PRINTER	044	B	1	66
WYLIE	ROBERT	C	1		17	SCOTLAND	CP	SCOTCH	CARPENTER	045	D	3	22
WYNDHAM	ALFRED				34	ENGLAND	CE	ENGLISH	GENTLEMAN	043	G	1	55
WYPER	JOSEPH				54	SCOTLAND	CP	SCOTCH	SADDLER	045	C	3	31
WYTHE	W	A			34	O	WM	IRISH	BLACKSMITH	043	D		67
YAKE	ABRAHAM				28	O	NG	GERMAN	TAVERN KEEPER	043	B	3	63
YAKE	CALVIN				27	CANADA	WM	GERMAN	HOTEL KEEPER	045	D	6	48
YAKE	JACOB				68	O	BA	GERMAN	F	043	B	5	32
YAKE	JOHN				28	O	NG	GERMAN	LAB	043	B	5	29
YAKE	LEWIS				32	CANADA	DI	GERMAN	FARMER	045	D	6	59
YAKE	WILLIAM				41	CANADA	DI	GERMAN	FARMER	045	D	6	58
YAKES	APINS				31	O	WM	GERMAN	LAB	043	B	5	40
YAKLE	JACOB				60	GERMANY	CN	GERMANY	SHOEMAKER	043	B	3	29
YAKLEY	ANDREW				31	GERMANY	MN	GERMAN	F	043	B	2	19
YARDON	JOSEPH				41	NEW BRUNSWICK	BA	ENGLISH	CARPENTER	045	B	2	10
YATES	JOHN				35	O	CE	IRISH	BLACKSMITH	043	H	2	47
YATES	JOHN				35	ONTARIO	CE	IRISH	BLACKSMITH	043	H	2	47
YATES	JONATHAN				42	QUEBEC	CN	IRISH	FARMER	043	G	1	53
YEKE	ADAM				30	CANADA	DI	GERMAN	FARMER	045	D	6	74
YEO	JAMES				40	ENGLAND	CE	ENGLISH	R R INSPECTOR	043	C		50
YEO	WILLIAM		2		81	ENGLAND	CE		SHOEMAKER	043	G	1	D
YEOMANS	CATHERINE			1	54	USA	CE	ENGLISH	F	045	C	4	14
YORK	ALBERT				29	ONTARIO	CN	ENGLISH	FARMER	043	G	2	34
YORK	CHAS	H			43	ENGLAND	WM	ENGLISH	CARPENTER	043	C		39
YORK	DANIEL				25	O	EM	ENGLISH	F	043	H	2	49
YORK	DANIEL				25	ONTARIO	EM	ENGLISH	FARMER	043	H	2	49
YORK	FREDERICK				56	ONTARIO	PR	ENGLISH	SHINGLE MAKER	043	G	2	17
YORK	GORDON				76	USA	EM	ENGLISH	F	043	H	2	48
YORK	GORDON				76	UNITED STATES	EM	ENGLISH	FARMER	043	H	2	48
YORK	JOHN				57	ONTARIO	CN	ENGLISH	FARMER	043	G	2	33
YORK	SQUIRE				22	ONTARIO	CN	ENGLISH	FARMER	043	G	1	51
YOUMAS	WILLIAM				60	O	CE	SCOTCH	LAB	043	A	6	16
YOUNG	ALEXANDER				53	SCOTLAND	CP	SCOTCH	FARMER	045	D	3	46
YOUNG	ALFRED		1		17	ENGLAND	CE	ENGLISH		045	B	2	18
YOUNG	ANDREW				51	ONTARIO	CP	SCOTCH	FARMER	043	G	1	47
YOUNG	ANDREW				50	SCOTLAND	CP	SCOTCH	F	045	C	4	33
YOUNG	ANDREW	W			46	IRELAND	CE	IRISH	MILKMAN	045	A	1	3
YOUNG	GODFREY				44	IRELAND	CE	IRISH	F	045	C	3	4
YOUNG	IRA	L			46	ONTARIO	CN	SCOTCH	FARMER	043	G	1	46
YOUNG	JAMES				39	IRELAND	CE	IRISH	F	044	A	1	37
YOUNG	JAMES				47	SCOTLAND	CP	SCOTCH	INNKEEPER	045	A	1	89
YOUNG	JAMES				26	O	CP	SCOT	F	045	C	1	29
YOUNG	JAMES		1		25	ENGLAND	WM	ENGLISH	LABOURER	045	D	5	72
YOUNG	JAMES				58	SCOTLAND	CP	SCOTCH	F	044	C	2	40
YOUNG	JANE		1	1	67	ENGLAND	CE	ENGLISH		045	B	2	13
YOUNG	JOHN		1	M	18	O	PS	SCOTCH	BLACKSMITH	043	A	2	34
YOUNG	JOHN				44	UNITED STATES	EM	SCOTCH	LABORER	043	G	1	11
YOUNG	JOHN				51	GER	LU	GER	LAB	044	B	1	63
YOUNG	JOHN	R	2		1	O	PB			045	A	1	D
YOUNG	JONATHAN				47	ENGLAND	WM	ENGLISH	FARMER	045	D	6	1
YOUNG	JOSEPH				28	O	PM	IRISH	F	043	B	1	37
YOUNG	MARY			1	56	O	WM	SCOTCH		043	H	2	2
YOUNG	MARY			1	56	ONTARIO	WM	SCOTCH		043	H	2	2
YOUNG	MARY	CHRISTINE	1	1	8	O	WM	ENGLISH		045	C	1	17
YOUNG	PHEBY		1	1	61	ENGLAND	CE	ENGLISH		045	B	2	18
YOUNG	SARAH		1	1	84	UNITED STATES	EM	ENGLISH		043	G	1	21
YOUNG	SERAH		2	1	45	ENGLAND	WM			045	D	6	D
YOUNG	THOMAS		1		45	ENGLAND	CE	ENGLISH	HOSTLER	044	A	2	53
YOUNG	THOMAS				40	SCOT	CP	ENG	F	045	C	1	5
YOUNG	WALTER				30	ENGLAND	CE	ENGLISH	LABOURER	045	A	1	39
YOUNG	WILLIAM			M	27	SCOTLAND	PS	SCOTCH	F	043	A	2	53
YOUNG	WILLIAM				49	ONTARIO	CN	SCOTCH	CARPENTER	043	G	1	12
YOUNG	WILLIAM				28	ENGLAND	CE	ENGLISH	WOOD CARVER	045	B	1	34
YOUNG	WILLIAM				62	SCOT	CP	SCOT	CARPENTER	045	C	1	10

SURNAME	NAME1	NAME2	STRAY	SEX	AGE	BIRTHPL	RELIGION	ORIGIN	OCCUP	DIST	SUB_DIST	DIV	PAGE
YOUNG	WILLIAM				54	SCOTLAND	CP	SCOTCH	FARMER	045	D	3	15
YOUNG	WILLIAM				26	SCOTLAND	CP	SCOTCH	FARMER	045	D	3	45
YOUNG	WM				28	ENGLAND	CE	ENGLISH	LABOURER	043	G	1	9
YOUNGS	FREDINCA		1	1	37	0	EM	ENGLISH		043	E	2	25
YOUNGS	WILLIAM				45	IRELAND	RC	IRISH	F	043	B	2	9
YULE	ANDREW				31	SCOTLAND	CN	SCOTCH	SCHOOL TEACHER	043	F		12
YULE	GEORGE		1		18	SCOTLAND	CP	SCOTCH		045	D	6	67
YULE	JOHN			M	61	SCOTLAND	CP	SCOTCH	F	043	A	1	44
ZEAGMAN	JOHN				56	GERMANY	RC	GERMAN	STOREKEEPER	044	C	2	12
ZEAGMAN	JOHN	JR			28	0	RC	GERMAN	DROVER	044	C	2	9
ZELLE	CHRISTIAN				53	GERMANY	LU	GERMAN	SHOE MAKER	044	B	5	31
ZENAS	BLACK				27	0	NG	IRISH	F	043	A	6	49
ZIMMERMAN	PETER				49	0	WM	GER	CARPENTER	044	B	2	37
ZINK	AUGUSTUS				65	PRUSSIA	LU	PRUSSIAN	LABOURER	045	A	1	45
ZIPP	PETER				35	PRUSSIA	LU	PRUSSIAN	TANNER & CURRIER	045	D	5	27
ZONPHER	ELIZABETH		1	1	25	0	CN	SCOTCH		043	B	3	2
ZURKEY	JOHN				30	0	CP	GERMAN	SADDLER	043	H	2	16
ZWICKEY	JOHN				30	ONTARIO	CS	GERMAN	SADDLER	043	H	2	16